SMITHSONIAN INSTITUTION
UNITED STATES NATIONAL MUSEUM
BULLETIN 50

THE BIRDS OF
NORTH AND MIDDLE AMERICA

A DESCRIPTIVE CATALOG

OF THE

HIGHER GROUPS, GENERA, SPECIES, AND SUBSPECIES OF BIRDS
KNOWN TO OCCUR IN NORTH AMERICA, FROM THE ARCTIC
LANDS TO THE ISTHMUS OF PANAMA, THE WEST INDIES
AND OTHER ISLANDS OF THE CARIBBEAN SEA,
AND THE GALÁPAGOS ARCHIPELAGO

commenced by the late

ROBERT RIDGWAY

continued by

HERBERT FRIEDMANN

PART X

Family Cracidae—The Curassows, Guans, and Chachalacas
Family Tetraonidae—The Grouse, Ptarmigan, etc.
Family Phasianidae—The American Quails, Partridges, and Pheasants
Family Numididae—The Guineafowls
Family Meleagrididae—The Turkeys

UNITED STATES
GOVERNMENT PRINTING OFFICE
WASHINGTON : 1946

For sale by the Superintendent of Documents, U. S. Government Printing Office
Washington 25, D. C. - Price $1.25

Washington 25, D. C. - - - - - Price $1.25

PREFACE

The families of birds included in the present and preceding volumes of this work are as follows:

Part I, issued October 24, 1901, included the Fringillidae (finches) alone.

Part II, issued October 16, 1902, included the Tanagridae (tanagers), Icteridae (troupials), Coerebidae (honeycreepers), and Mniotiltidae (wood warblers).

Part III, issued December 31, 1904, included the Motacillidae (wagtails and pipits), Hirundinidae (swallows), Ampelidae (waxwings), Ptilogonatidae (silky flycatchers), Dulidae (palm chats), Vireonidae (vireos), Laniidae (shrikes), Corvidae (crows and jays), Paridae (titmice), Sittidae (nuthatches), Certhiidae (creepers), Troglodytidae (wrens), Cinclidae (dippers), Chamaeidae (wrentits), and Sylviidae (warblers).

Part IV, issued July 1, 1907, contained the remaining groups of Oscines, namely, the Turdidae (thrushes), Zeledoniidae (wren-thrushes), Mimidae (mockingbirds), Sturnidae (starlings), Ploceidae (weaverbirds), and Alaudidae (larks), together with the haploophone or oligomyodian Mesomyodi, comprising Oxyruncidae (sharpbills), Tyrannidae (tyrant flycatchers), Pipridae (manakins), and Cotingidae (chatterers).

Part V, issued November 29, 1911, included the tracheophone Mesomyodi, represented by the Pteroptochidae (tapaculos), Formicariidae (antbirds), Furnariidae (ovenbirds), and Dendrocolaptidae (woodhewers); the Macrochires, containing the Trochilidae (hummingbirds) and Micropodidae (swifts); and the Heterodactylae, represented only by the Trogonidae (trogons).

Part VI, issued April 8, 1914, contained the Picariae, comprising the families Picidae (woodpeckers), Capitonidae (barbets), Ramphastidae (toucans), Bucconidae (puffbirds), and Galbulidae (jacamars); the Anisodactylae, with the families Alcedinidae (kingfishers), Todidae (todies), and Momotidae (motmots); the Nycticoraciae, with the families Caprimulgidae (goatsuckers) and Nyctibiidae (potoos); and the Striges, consisting of the families Tytonidae (barn owls) and Bubonidae (eared owls).

Part VII, issued May 5, 1916, contained the Coccygiformes (cuckoolike birds), Psittaciformes (parrots), and Columbiformes (pigeons).

Part VIII, issued June 26, 1919, contained the Charadriiformes (ploverlike birds) with the families Jacanidae (jaçanas), Oedicnemidae (thickknees), Haematopodidae (oystercatchers), Arenariidae (turnstones), Aphrizidae (surfbirds), Charadriidae (plovers), Scolopacidae (snipes, sandpipers, etc.), Phalaropodidae (phalaropes), Recurvirostridae (avocets and stilts), Rynchopidae (skimmers), Sternidae (terns), Laridae (gulls), Stercorariidae (skuas and jaegers), and Alcidae (auks).

Part IX, issued October 2, 1941, contained the Gruiformes with the families Gruidae (cranes), Rallidae (rails, gallinules, and coots), Heliornithidae (sun-grebes), and Eurypygidae (sun-bitterns).

Part X (the present part) contains the Galliformes, with the families Cracidae (curassows, guans, and chachalacas), Tetraonidae (grouse and ptarmigan), Phasianidae (American quails, partridges, and pheasants), Numididae (guineafowl), and Meleagrididae (turkeys).

Part XI, now ready for press, will contain the Falconiformes, with the families Cathartidae (New World vultures), Accipitridae (hawks, kites, buzzards, eagles, and harriers), Pandionidae (ospreys), and Falconidae (falcons, caracaras, and laughing falcons).

Part XII, now in course of preparation, will contain the Anseriformes (ducks, geese, and swans); the Ciconiiformes, with the families Ardeidae (herons, bitterns, etc.), Cochleariidae (boatbills), Ciconiidae (storks and wood ibises), Threskiornithidae (ibises and spoonbills), and Phoenicopteridae (flamingoes); the Pelecaniformes, with the families Phaethontidae (tropicbirds), Pelecanidae (pelicans), Sulidae (boobies and gannets), Phalacrocoracidae (cormorants), and Fregatidae (man-o-warbirds); the Procellariiformes, with the families Diomedeidae (albatrosses), Procellariidae (shearwaters and petrels), and Hydrobatidae (stormy petrels); the Colymbiformes (grebes); the Gaviiformes (loons); the Sphenisciformes (penguins); and the Tinamiformes (tinamous).

In the ten volumes thus far published there have been treated in detail (that is, with full descriptions and synonymies), besides the families above mentioned and higher groups to which they belong, 695 genera and 2,756 species and subspecies, besides 237 extralimital genera and 638 extralimital species and subspecies whose principal characters are given in the keys and whose principal synonymy is given in footnotes.

For the privilege of examining, or for the loan of, specimens needed in the preparation of the present volume acknowledgments are due to the authorities of the Academy of Natural Sciences of Philadelphia; the American Museum of Natural History, New York; Carnegie Museum, Pittsburgh; Chicago Natural History Museum; Museum of Comparative Zoology, Cambridge; National Museum of Canada, Ottawa; Royal Ontario Museum of Zoology, Toronto; Museum of Vertebrate Zoology, Berkeley; University of Michigan Museum, Ann Arbor; Cornell University Museum, Ithaca; California Academy of Sciences, San Francisco; California Institute of Technology, Pasadena; Princeton University Museum; U. S. Fish and Wildlife Service, Washington, D. C.; Museum of Birds and Mammals, University of Kansas, Lawrence; British Museum (Natural History), London; Muséum d'Histoire Naturelle, Paris; Naturhistorisches Museum, Vienna; Natural History Museum, Leyden;

Robert T. Moore, Pasadena, and the late J. H. Fleming, Toronto. The total number of specimens thereby made available for study in the present connection is hard to estimate but runs into many thousands.

As in Part IX, the author has made extensive use of the manuscript notes left by the late Robert Ridgway. His notes covered the diagnoses of genera and higher groups and partial synonymies for many of the species and subspecies. Wherever possible his manuscript has been included with the minimum of change (other than addition to synonymies) permitted by more recent data. In fact, it has been, and still is, the present author's feeling that this work should be as largely Ridgway's as possible; thus, for instance, he has kept and included Ridgway's diagnoses of certain genera now relegated to the position of subgenera, and where Ridgway's manuscript gave extensive synonymies for extralimital forms, he has retained them without attempting to supply equally detailed accounts for other extralimital forms. However, all such manuscript material has been thoroughly studied with the specimens and the literature; nothing has been accepted merely because it was written. From the start, the author has felt himself responsible for the entire contents of this volume and has not considered himself as an editor of an unpublished work.

Measurements of specimens for use in the preparation were made by the author and by A. L. O'Leary, Dr. E. M. Hasbrouck, and J. S. Webb under the author's supervision. Maj. Allan Brooks contributed (before the present author began this work) a series of notes on the colors of the unfeathered parts of many of the species discussed herein. The outline drawings of generic details, except those previously published, were made partly by E. R. Kalmbach, and partly, under the author's supervision, by Mrs. Aime Awl, of the United States National Museum staff.

HERBERT FRIEDMANN.

CONTENTS

Order GALLIFORMES: Fowllike birds—Continued.
  Superfamily PHASIANOIDEA: Grouse, pheasants, turkeys—Continued.
    Family Phasianidae: American quail, partridges, and pheasants—Continued.

TEXT FIGURES ILLUSTRATING GENERIC DETAILS

THE BIRDS OF
NORTH AND MIDDLE AMERICA

Commenced by the late ROBERT RIDGWAY; continued by HERBERT FRIEDMANN

PART X

Order GALLIFORMES: Fowllike Birds

Gallinae FORSTER, Enchiridion, 1788, 36.
⹀Gallinae BAIRD, Rep. Pacific R. R. Surv., ix, 1858, 594, 609.
<Gallinæ SCLATER and SALVIN, Nom. Av. Neotr., 1873, 135.—ELLIOT, Stand. Nat.
   Hist., iv, 1885, 197.—AMERICAN ORNITHOLOGISTS' UNION, Check-list, 1886,
   167; ed. 3, 1910, 134.—RIDGWAY, Man. North Amer. Birds, 1887, 184.—
   OGILVIE-GRANT, Cat. Birds Brit. Mus., xxii, 1893, xi, 33.—SALVIN and GOD-
   MAN, Biol. Centr.-Amer., Aves, iii, 1902, 270.
><Gallinacei VIEILLOT, Analyse, 1816, 49 (Alectorides+Cracidæ+Crypturi+
   Pterocles).
><[Gallinacei] Nupidedes VIEILLOT, Analyse, 1816, 50 (excludes Tetraonidae; in-
   cludes Crypturi).
   Giratores ou Gallinacées BLAINVILLE, Journ. Phys., lxxxiii, 1816, 252 (sub-
   order I. Brevicaudes; II. Longicaudes).
   Gradatores ou Gallinacés BLAINVILLE, Bull. Soc. Phil., 1816, 110 (I. Longicaudes; II. Brevicaudes).
⹀Phasianidæ BONAPARTE, Saggio Distr. Anim. Vertebr., 1831, 54.
>Alectoromorphæ HUXLEY, Proc. Zool. Soc. London, 1867, 459 (includes Hemi-
   podii and Pterocletes).
>Rasores CARUS, Handb. Zool., i, 1868-75, 317 (includes Pterocletes, Hemipodii,
   and Opisthocomi).
⹀Rasores REICHENOW, Vög. Zool. Gart., 1882; Die Vögel, i, 1913, 270.
>Galliformes GADOW, Classif. Vertebr., 1898, 33 (includes Mesoenatidae, Hemi-
   podii).—KNOWLTON, Birds of the World, 1909, 49, 263 (includes Mesoena-
   tidae and Hemipodii).
⹀Gallidae FÜRBRINGER, Bijd. Dierkunde, ii, 1888 (Unters. Morph. Syst. Vög.),
   1567.
⹀Galliformes FÜRBRINGER, Bijd. Dierkunde, ii, 1888 (Unters. Morph. Syst. Vög.),
   1567.—SHARPE, Rev. Rec. Att. Classif. Birds, 1891, 68; Hand-list, i, 1899, x,
   12.—WETMORE, Proc. U. S. Nat. Mus., lxxvi, art. 24, 1930, 3; Smiths. Misc.
   Coll., lxxxix, No. 13, 1934, 6; xcix, No. 7, 1940, 5.—AMERICAN ORNITHOLO-
   GISTS' UNION, Check-list, ed. 4, 1931, 78.—PETERS, Check-list Birds of World,
   ii, 1934, 3.—HELLMAYER and CONOVER, Cat. Birds Amer., i, No. 1, 1942, 114.
>Kolobathrornithes BOETTICHER, Verh. Orn. Ges. Bay., xvii, 1927, 190 (includes
   rails, cranes, bustards, gallinaceous birds, shorebirds, pratincoles, gulls, and
   terns).

1

Schizognathous, holorhinal, terrestrial, or arboreal rasorial birds with sternum usually deeply 4-notched or cleft (2-notched in Opisthocomi); 16–19 cervical vertebrae (19 in Opisthocomi, 16 in all the rest); coracoids without a subclavicular process and with basal ends overlapping or crossed; quadrate bone double; intestinal convolutions of type V (plagiocoelous); bill relatively short, with maxilla vaulted, its tip overhanging that of the mandible, vaulted, not compressed, and with hallux always present.

Nares holorhinal, impervious; palatines without internal lamina; maxillopalatines not coalesced with one another or with the vomer[1]; quadrate bone double; basipterygoid processes absent but represented by sessile facets on anterior part of sphenoidal rostrum; rhamphotheca simple; angle of mandible produced and recurved. Cervical vertebrae, 16; ankylosed sacral vertebrae preceded by a free vertebra, this by four ankylosed dorsal vertebrae, the latter heterocoelous; coracoids with or without (Opisthocomi) a subclavicular process and with basal ends overlapping or crossed; furcula with median process (hypocleidium) much developed. Metasternum with four deep notches or clefts (Galli), or two notches (Opisthocomi), in the former case the median xiphoid process very long and narrow, the internal processes much shorter, the external processes shorter still and bent outward over posterior ribs, their extremities expanded; spina communis sterni and processus obliquus present, large; episternal process perforated to receive a process from base of coracoids; muscle formula usually ABXY+(the femorocaudal muscle absent in *Pavo* and *Meleagris,* very slender in Cracidae); expansor secundariorum present, but in *Tetrao, Francolinus* (except *F. clappertoni*), *Rollulus, Euplocomus, Gallus, Ceriornis,* and *Pavo,* instead of being inserted into the scapulosternal fibrous head, after blending more or less with the axillary margin of the teres, it ceases by becoming fixed to a fibrous intersection about one-third way down the coracobrachialis brevis muscle; biceps slip usually present (absent in *Ortalis araucuan, Crax, Mitua, Talegallus,* and *Numida,* but present in *Megapodius* and *Megacephalon*); tensor patagii brevis with a thin, wide, diffused tendon (as in Crypturi); ectepicondyloulnaris muscle present (as in Crypturi); anconeus with humeral head not always present; gluteus primus present, large; gluteus V present (tendinous in *Chrysolophus pictus*); intrinsic syringeal muscles absent; deep plantar tendons of type I (if reaching the hallux proceeding from flexor longus hallucis, not from flexor perforans digitorum). Intestinal convolutions of type V (plagiocoelous); crop present, globular; stomach usually a gizzard (*Centrocercus* the only known exception); gall bladder present; caeca large; oil gland usually tufted (nude in Megapodii, absent

---

[1] In some Cracidae, however, the maxillopalatines are said to be united medially into an ossified septum.

in *Argus*). Aftershafts present; neck without lateral apteria; adult downs on pterylae only; wing eutaxic (quintocubital) in Galli and Cracidae, diastataxic (aquintocubital) in Megapodii; primaries, 10; rectrices, 10 or, usually, more. Nest usually on the ground; eggs numerous (except in Cracidae), variable in form and coloration. Young ptilopaedic and nidifugous (those of the Megapodii highly so, being able to fly and care for themselves soon after hatching).

The following additional external characters may be mentioned:

Bill short (usually much shorter than head), generally rather stout, the culmen regularly and rather strongly decurved, the maxilla depressed rather than compressed (except in some Cracidae), its obtuse vaulted tip overhanging the tip of the mandible; maxillary tomium never dentate or serrate, the mandibular tomium dentate only in Odontophorinae; nasal fossae naked (except in Tetraonidae and some Cracidae), the horizontal or longitudinal nostril overhung by a corneous operculum. Frontal feathers (if present) parted by the backward extension of the culmen. Tibiae always feathered, frequently the tarsi also (at least in part); sometimes (in genus *Lagopus*) the toes also; the tarsi, if unfeathered, usually transversely scutellate in front, frequently provided with one or more spurs behind; hallux always present, but varying in relative size and position; anterior toes usually webbed between the basal phalanges; claws obtuse, slightly curved. Wing strong but relatively short, much rounded, and very concave beneath. Tail excessively variable in shape and development, the rectrices varying from 8 to 32 in number.

The Galliformes are nearly cosmopolitan in their distribution, only Polynesia, New Zealand, and the Antarctic regions being without representatives of the order.[2] They are much more numerous in the Northern Hemisphere, to which the typical suborder, Galli, is mostly confined, these being far better represented in the Old World than in America, the large and varied family Phasianidae having its focus in temperate and subtropical Asia. The aberrant superfamily Cracoidea is chiefly confined to the Southern Hemisphere, the Megapodidae to the Australian Region, the Cracidae to the Neotropical Region. One family of Phasianoidea is peculiar to America, this being the Meleagrididae. One phasianoid family (Numididae) is restricted to Africa, another (Tetraonidae) is common to the Palearctic and Nearctic Regions, while the remaining and much more numerous and varied one (Phasianidae) has the widest range of all, every portion of Europe and Asia (except the far Arctic parts), besides portions of the Indo-Malayan and Nearctic Regions, possessing representatives (represented in America not by true pheasants, but only by quail).

---

[2] They are, however, also lacking in certain areas within regions the greater part of which is inhabited by them; for example, the greater part of the West Indies, and the Revillagigedo and Galápagos island groups. New Zealand formerly possessed a species of *Coturnix* (*C. novae-zealandiae*), but this has become extinct.

The species of Galliformes are very numerous. Peters's Check-list of Birds of the World (vol. ii, 1934, pp. 3-141) enumerates no fewer than 94 genera, a considerable number of which contain many forms each.

KEY TO THE SUBORDERS AND SUPERFAMILIES OF GALLIFORMES

a. Sternum 4-notched, narrower posteriorly than anteriorly...suborder **Galli** (p. 4)
  b. Sternum with inner notches very deep, extending for more than half length of sternum, outer division of long and narrow posterior lateral process slightly expanded only on outer side, costal process elongated and nearly parallel to long axis of sternum; hallux relatively small, attached above level of anterior toes, its basal phalanx much shorter than that of toe.
                                     superfamily **Cracoidea** (p. 4)
  bb. Sternum with inner notches relatively short, extending for less than half length of sternum, the outer division of the short and broad posterior lateral process widely expanded terminally on both sides, the costal process short with anterior edge at right angle with long axis of sternum; hallux relatively large, attached at same level as anterior toes, its basal phalanx as long as that of the third toe..................superfamily **Phasianoidea** (p. 62)
aa. Sternum 2-notched, wider posteriorly than anteriorly.
                                   suborder **Opisthocomi** (extralimital)[3]

Suborder GALLI: Megapodes, Curassows, Grouse, Pheasants

Galli GADOW, Classif. Vertebr., 1898, 34.—BEDDARD, Struct. and Classif. Birds, 1898, 290.—KNOWLTON, Birds of the World, 1909, 49, 267.—WETMORE, Proc. U. S. Nat. Mus., lxxvi, art. 24, 1930, 3; Smiths. Misc. Coll., lxxxix, No. 13, 1934, 6; xcix, No. 7, 1940, 5.—PETERS, Checklist Birds of World, ii, 1934, 3.

Superfamily CRACOIDEA: Pigeon-footed Galli

=Peristeropodes HUXLEY, Proc. Zool. Soc. London, 1868, 296.—OGILVIE-GRANT, Cat. Birds Brit. Mus., xxii, 1893, xv, 33, 445.—SALVIN and GODMAN, Biol Centr.-Amer., Aves, iii, 1902, 271.—KNOWLTON, Birds of the World, 1909, 267, in text.
=Gallinæ Peristeropodes SCLATER and SALVIN, Nom. Av. Neotr., 1873, vii, 135.
=Gallinæ-Peristeropodes ELLIOT, Stand. Nat. Hist., iv, 1885, 229.
>Pullastrae COPE, Amer. Nat., xxiii, 1889, 871, 873 (includes also Pterocletes and Columbae!).
<Megapodii SHARPE, Rev. Rec. Att. Classif. Birds, 1891, 68 (Megapodidae only); Hand-list, i, 1899, x, 12.
<Megapodes MILLER, Bull. Amer. Mus. Nat. Hist., xxxiv, 1915, 33 (Megapodidae only).
<Craces SHARPE, Rev. Rec. Att. Classif. Birds, 1891, 68; Hand-list, i, 1899 x, 14 (Cracidae only).
<Penelopes AMERICAN ORNITHOLOGISTS' UNION, Check-list, 1886, 178 (Cracidae only); ed. 3, 1910, 146.

---

[3] Opisthocomi Forbes, Ibis, 1884, 119.—Sclater, Ibis, 1880, 407.—Ogilvie-Grant, Cat. Birds Brit. Mus., xxii, 1893, 523.—Stejneger, Stand. Nat. Hist., iv, Birds, 1885, 196.—Beddard, Struct. and Classif. Birds, 1898, 285.—Wetmore, Proc. U. S. Nat. Mus., lxxvi, art. 24, 1930, 3; Smiths. Misc. Coll., lxxxix, No. 13, 1934, 6; xcix, No. 7, 1940, 6.—Peters, Check-list Birds of World, ii, 1934, 141.

=Cracoidea WETMORE, Smiths. Misc. Coll., lxxxix, No. 13, 1934, 6; xcix, No. 7, 1940, 5.—AMERICAN ORNITHOLOGISTS' UNION, Check-list, ed. 4, 1931, 78.— PETERS, Check-list Birds of World, ii, 1934, 3.
=Cracides WETMORE and MILLER, Auk, xliii, 1926, 342.—WETMORE, Proc. U. S. Nat. Mus., lxxvi, art. 24, 1930, 3.

Galliform birds with the hallux incumbent (inserted at same level as anterior toes), its basal phalanx as long as that of third toe; sternum with inner notches relatively short, extending for less than half the length of the sternum, the outer division of the short and broad lateral process widely expanded terminally on both sides, the costal process short, with anterior edge at right angles with long axis of sternum, the episternal process perforated to receive the feet of the coracoids.

KEY TO THE FAMILIES OF CRACOIDEA

a. Sternum less than twice as long as its inner notch; trachea generally coiled; both carotids present; biceps slip never present; oil gland feathered; hallux relatively shorter, toes all much shorter and smaller; wing eutaxic (quintocubital); arboreal; nidification normal..................**Cracidae** (p. 5)
aa. Sternum more than twice as long as its inner notch; trachea always straight; only one carotid (the left) present; biceps slip sometimes present; oil gland nude; hallux relatively longer, all the toes much longer and stouter; wing diasataxic (aquintocubital); terrestrial; nidification highly peculiar.
Megapodidae (extralimital)[4]

Family CRACIDAE: Curassows, Guans, and Chachalacas

=Alectrides VIEILLOT, Analyse, 1816, 49 (includes actually only genus *Penelope* but by implication entire family).

---

[4] =Megapodidæ Lilljeborg, Proc. Zool. Soc. London, 1866, 15.—Elliot, Stand. Nat. Hist., iv, 1885, 229, in text.—Grant, Cat. Birds Brit. Mus., xxii, 1893, 33, 445.— Knowlton, Birds of the World, 1909, 49, 268. =Megapodiidae Carus, Handb. Zool., i, 1868-75, 324.—Gadow, Classif. Vertebr., 1898, 34. =Megapodiidæ Sharpe, Hand-list, i, 1899, x, 12. >Struthiones alis volantibus Wagler, Nat. Syst. Av., 1830, 6, 127 (includes Crypturi). >Crypturidae Nitzsch, Syst. Pterylog., 1840, 117 (includes Crypturi and Hemipodii). >Megapodinae Gray, Gen. Birds, iii, 1849, 490. <Megapodiinae Carus, Handb. Zool., i, 1868-75, 325. <Talegalinae Gray, Gen. Birds, iii, 1849, 488. <Talegallinae Carus, Handb. Zool., i, 1868-75, 325. The Megapodidae or moundfowls are a group of plainly colored terrestrial gallinaceous birds of most remarkable habits. They are unique among birds (as far as known) in their nidification; for, instead of building a nest and incubating their eggs, several individuals of the same species together scrape up, with their powerful feet, dead leaves and other rubbish of the forest floor into an immense heap, sometimes as much as 30 feet in diameter, in which their eggs are deposited, then covered with the same material, and left to be hatched by the heat generated by the decomposing mass. The young are hatched with wings sufficiently developed for immediate flight, and after emerging they shift for themselves without any help or protection from their parents. One monotypic genus, *Megacephalon,* represented by the Males, or Mallee-fowl, of Celebes and Sanghir (*M. males*), buries its eggs in the warm sand along the seashore. The group is essentially confined to the Australian Region, one species only occurring in Borneo and the Philippines.

>Penelopidæ BONAPARTE, Saggio Distr. Anim. Vertebr., 1831, 54 (includes Menuridae, Megapodidae, and Opisthocomidae!).

=Penelopidae NITZSCH, Syst. Pterylog., 1840, 167.—BAIRD, Rep. Pacific R. R. Surv., ix, 1858, 609, 610.

<Penelopinae CARUS, Handb. Zool., i, 1868–75, 325 (genera *Penelope* and *Oreophasis*).

<Penelopinæ SCLATER and SALVIN, Nom. Av. Neotr., 1873, 135 (*Stegnolaema, Penelope, Penelopina, Pipile, Aburria, Chamaepetes,* and *Ortalis*).—BAIRD, BREWER, and RIDGWAY, Hist. North Amer. Birds, iii, 1874, 397.—ELLIOT, Stand. Nat. Hist., iv, 1885, 233, in text.—COUES, Key North Amer. Birds, ed. 2, 1884, 573.—AMERICAN ORNITHOLOGISTS' UNION, Check-list, 1886, 178; ed. 3, 1910, 146.—OGILVIE-GRANT, Cat. Birds Brit. Mus., xxii, 1893, 473.—SALVIN and GODMAN, Biol. Centr.-Amer., Aves, iii, 1902, 275.

>Cracidae CARUS, Handb. Zool., i, 1868–75, 325 (includes Meleagridae!).

=Cracidae GADOW, Classif. Vertebr., 1898, 34.—WETMORE, Proc. U. S. Nat. Mus., lxxvi, art. 24, 1930, 3; Smiths. Misc. Coll., lxxxix, No. 13, 1934, 6; xcix, No. 7, 1940, 5.—AMERICAN ORNITHOLOGISTS' UNION, Check-list, ed. 4, 1931, 78.—PETERS, Check-list Birds of World, ii, 1934, 9.—HELLMAYR and CONOVER, Cat. Birds Amer., i, No. 1, 1942, 141.

=Cracidae SCLATER and SALVIN, Nom. Av. Neotr., 1873, vii, 135.—BAIRD, BREWER, and RIDGWAY, Hist. North Amer. Birds, iii, 1874, 397.—COUES, Key North Amer. Birds, ed. 2, 1884, 572.—ELLIOT, Stand. Nat. Hist., iv, 1885, 229, 232, in text.—AMERICAN ORNITHOLOGISTS' UNION, Check-list, 1886, 178; ed. 3, 1910, 146.—OGILVIE-GRANT, Cat. Birds Brit. Mus., xxii, 1893, 33, 473.—SHARPE, Hand-list, i, 1899, x, 14.—SALVIN and GODMAN, Biol. Centr.-Amer., Aves, iii, 1902, 271.—KNOWLTON, Birds of the World, 1909, 49, 271.

<Cracinae CARUS, Handb. Zool., i, 1868–75, 325.

>Cracinæ SCLATER and SALVIN, Nom. Av. Neotr., 1873, 135.—BAIRD, BREWER, and RIDGWAY, Hist. North Amer. Birds, iii, 1874, 397.—ELLIOT, Stand. Nat. Hist., iv, 1885, 233, in text.—OGILVIE-GRANT, Cat. Birds Brit. Mus., xxii, 1893, 473.—SALVIN and GODMAN, Biol. Centr.-Amer., Aves, iii, 1902, 271.

><Cracinæ RIDGWAY, Man. North Amer. Birds, 1887, 207 (includes all genera except *Oreophasis*).

<Oreophasinæ SCLATER and SALVIN, Nom. Av. Neotr., 1873, 137 (*Oreophasis* only).—BAIRD, BREWER, and RIDGWAY, Hist. North Amer. Birds, iii, 1874, 397.—ELLIOT, Stand. Nat. Hist., iv, 1885, 232, in text.—RIDGWAY, Man. North Amer. Birds, 1887, 208.—GRANT, Cat. Birds Brit. Mus., xxii, 1893, 473.—SALVIN and GODMAN, Biol. Centr.-Amer., Aves, iii, 1902, 274.

=Duodecempennatae SUNDEVALL, öfv. Svensk. Vet.-Akad. Förh., 1873, 118.

Gallinaceous birds with hallux incumbent and more than half as long as lateral toes, its basal phalanx as long as that of the third (middle) toe; with tufted oil gland; sternum less than twice as long as its inner notch; both carotids present; trachea usually coiled; biceps slip never present; wing eutaxic (quintocubital), habits arboreal, nidification normal.

Bill variable, usually relatively small, with culmen longer than mesorhinium and broadly rounded (not ridged), the tomia never denticulate; sometimes much higher than broad basally, with the mesorhinium high and more or less arched, sometimes produced into a swollen knob or bony tubercle. Nostril more or less longitudinal, the cere entirely nude (except in *Oreophasis*). Wing moderately large, relatively very broad, the large and broad secondaries nearly as long as longest primaries, sometimes a little longer; undersurface of wings strongly concave, the outer primaries strongly bowed or incurved distally, sometimes with terminal portion abruptly attenuate or falcate; primaries, 10, the outermost much the shortest. Tail nearly as long as to slightly longer than wing, more or less rounded, flat (not vaulted), the rectrices relatively broad, with broadly rounded tips. Tarsus less than one-fourth to about one-third as long as wing, the acrotarsium with a single row of large transverse scutella, the planta tarsi usually with a single row of smaller scutella along outer side and smaller, irregular scutella on inner side; middle toe about two-thirds to three-fourths as long as tarsus, the lateral toe reaching to or slightly beyond penultimate articulation of middle toe (the outer usually slightly longer than the inner); hallux about as long as combined length of first two phalanges of outer toe; claws moderately to rather strongly curved (that of hallux most strongly so), moderately large, compressed; a well-developed web between basal phalanges of anterior toes. Plumage in general rather compact, the feathers rather broad and with rounded tips except on anal region and rump, where soft and downy, those of neck sometimes sublanceolate, those of pileum sometimes elongated, forming a bushy erectile crest, more rarely (in *Crax*) rigid, erect, and recurved terminally; loral region wholly nude, orbital region more or less (sometimes extensively) nude, the throat also sometimes nude, the naked skin sometimes developed into a wattle or dewlap.

Nidification normal, the nest placed in trees; eggs (said to be only two in number) relatively large, with rough, granular surface, immaculate whitish.

Range.—The whole of continental tropical America.

The Cracidae are arboreal gallinaceous birds that differ from all other Gallinae except the Megapodidae (of the Australian Region) in having the hallux large and on the same level with the anterior toes, and from the Megapodidae in having the legs and feet conspicuously less stout, all the toes shorter; in having the trachea usually coiled instead of straight; the presence of two carotid arteries and tufted oil gland, absence of biceps slip, and normal nidification; although, unlike the Tetraonidae, Phasianidae, and other alectoropode Gallinae, the nest is usually built in a tree, and the eggs, said to be only two in number, are very large in proportion to the size of the bird, plain dull white, and very different in shape and texture of the shell, which is roughly granulated.

The members of the Cracidae are never of brilliant plumage, though many of them are very handsome birds. They dwell in forests and spend much of their time among the branches of the higher trees, where they build their nests. Easily domesticated, they become excessively tame, gentle, and affectionate.

The true curassows (subfamily Cracinae), of the genera *Crax, Nothocrax, Mitu,* and *Pauxi,* are the largest and finest birds of the family, being nearly equal in size, though inferior in bulk, to the turkeys. The plumage of the males is usually of a glossy black, the underparts of most species chiefly white; the recurved crest and bright color (yellow or orange) of the cere and (if present) frontal protuberance adding to their fine appearance. They are known to the natives of the countries they inhabit as *pavo* or *pavo del monte* (peacock or mountain peacock). Their flesh is held in great esteem, being much like that of the turkey, but richer.

KEY TO THE GENERA OF CRACIDAE

a. Planta tarsi wholly covered by a continuous series (single row) of large, quadrate scutella on each side; bill compressed, relatively large and heavy, deep at base, the mesorhinium ascending and arched proximally or surmounted by a swollen knob or egg-shaped bony tubercle; postacetabular area of pelvis narrow; sexes usually (except in *Mitu* only) more or less different in coloration. (CRACINAE.)
  b. Pileum with an erectile crest; forehead without an egg-shaped protuberance.
    c. Feathers of crest semierect, narrow, rigid, and recurved or curled forward at tips ....**Crax** (p. 9)
    cc. Feathers of crest decumbent, broad, soft, and blended.
      d. Loral region nude; sexes very different in coloration.
             Nothocrax (extralimital)[5]
      dd. Loral region densely feathered; sexes alike in coloration.
             Mitu (extralimital)[6]
  bb. Pileum not crested; forehead with a large, egg-shaped, naked, bony tubercle or protuberance.....................................**Pauxi** (extralimital)[7]
aa. Planta tarsi with a continuous series (single row) of quadrate scutella only on outer side, these conspicuously smaller than scutella of acrotarsium, or with none on either side; bill depressed, relatively small, not deeper than broad at base, the mesorhinium not distinctly ascending nor arched, and never surmounted by a knob or tubercle; postacetabular area of pelvis broad; sexes usually alike in coloration (different only in *Penelopina*).
  b. Entire base of bill, including cere and mesorhinium, together with forehead, densely covered with short, erect, plushlike feathers, quite concealing nostrils; crown nude, with an elongated nude bony protuberance; loral and orbital regions covered with short feathers; mandibular rami and chin densely covered with plushlike feathers; feathers of hindneck sublanceolate. (OREOPHASINAE.)
               Oreophasis (p. 58)

---

[5] *Nothocrax* Burmeister, Syst. Übers. Th. Bras., iii, 1856, 347 (type, by monotypy, *Crax urumutum* Spix). British Guiana to upper Amazon Valley. (Monotypic.)
[6] *Mitu* Lesson, Traité d'Orn., 1831, 485 (type, by tautology, *Crax galeata* Latham =*Crax mitu* Linnaeus).—*Mitua* (emendation) Strickland, Ann. Mag. Nat. Hist., vii, 1841, 36. Guiana to upper Amazon Valley. (Three species.)
[7] *Pauxi* Temminck, Pig. et Gallin., ii, 1813, 456, 468 (type, by tautonymy, "*Crax pauxi*" Latham et Gmelin = *Crax Pauxi* Linnaeus).—*Ourax* Cuvier, Règne Anim., i, 1817, 440 (type, by monotypy, *Crax pauxi* Linnaeus).—*Lephocercus* Swainson, Classif. Birds, ii, 1837, 353 (type, by monotypy *Crax pauxi* Linnaeus). Colombia to Venezuela and Peru. (Monotypic.).—*Urax* (emendation) Reichenbach, Av. Syst. Nat. Vög., 1852, xxvi.—*Pauxis* (emendation) Sclater, Trans. Zool. Soc. London, ix, 1875, 285.

bb. Entire base of bill, including cere and mesorhinum, nude, the forehead (together with rest of pileum) covered with relatively large, distinctly outlined, more or less elongated feathers, forming when erected a bushy crest; crown without a bony protuberance; loral and orbital regions nude (the former sometimes partly feathered) ; feathers of hindneck not sublanceolate, but rounded or, sometimes, blended. (PENELOPINAE.)

 c. Outer primaries with inner webs not distinctly, if at all, incised distally, never with attenuated tips.

  d. Throat without a median feathered area.

   e. Chin (sometimes more or less of upper throat also) feathered; lower throat with wattle or dewlap less developed, sometimes not evident; sexes alike in color, the plumage never uniform black.

Penelope (p. 20)

   ee. Chin, as well as whole throat, nude; lower throat with wattle or dewlap conspicuously developed; pileum less distinctly crested; sexes very different in color, adult males uniform black.......**Penelopina** (p. 50)

  dd. Throat with a median feathered strip, completely nude laterally only.

Ortalis (p. 28)

 cc. Outer primaries with inner webs deeply incised distally, their terminal portion narrowly falcate.

  d. Foreneck more or less naked and wattled or caruncled.

   e. Foreneck mostly naked, with a median wattle or dewlap.

Pipile (extralimital)[8]

   ee. Foreneck mostly feathered and with a long fusiform tubercle.

Aburria (extralimital)[9]

  dd. Foreneck entirely feathered and without wattle or caruncle.

Chamaepetes (p. 55)

Genus CRAX Linnaeus

Crax LINNAEUS, Syst. Nat., ed. 10, i, 1758, 157. (Type, by subsequent designation, *Crax rubra* Linnaeus (Ridgway, Man. North Amer. Birds, ed. 2, 1896, 207).)

Craxa (emendation) BILLBERG, Synop. Faunae Scand., i, pt. 2, 1828, table A.

Alector MERREM, Av. Rar. Icon. et Descr., fasc. 2, 1786, 40. (Type, by tautonymy, *Crax alector* Linnaeus.)

Crossolaryngus REICHENBACH, Handb. Orn., Columb., 1861, 136. (Type, as designated by Sclater and Salvin, 1870, *Crax globulosa* Spix.)

Mituporanga REICHENBACH, Handb. Orn., Columb., 1861, 136. (Type, as designated by Sclater and Salvin, 1870, *Crax globicera* Linnaeus.)

Sphaerolyngus REICHENBACH, Handb. Orn., Columb., 1861, 136. (Type, by monotypy, *Crax alberti* Fraser.)

Very large Cracidae (length about 762–916 mm.), with bill deep and compressed, the culmen mesorhinium long and more or less arched, the

---

[8] *Pipile* Bonaparte, Compt. Rend., xlii, 1856, 877 (type, by tautonymy, *Penelope leucolophos* Merrem = *Crax pipile* Jacquin).—*Cumana* Coues, Auk, xvii, 1900, 65 (new name for *Pipile* Bonaparte, alleged to be preoccupied by *Pipilo* Vieillot, 1816). Colombia to Guiana, upper Amazon Valley, and southeastern Brazil. (Three species.)

[9] *Aburria* Reichenbach, Av. Syst. Nat. Vög., 1852, xxvi (type, by original designation and monotypy, *Penelope carunculata* Temminck = *aburri* Lesson).—*Opetioptila* Sundevall, Tentamen, 1873, 118 (new name for *Aburria* Reichenbach, on grounds of purism; 'οπητλον, subula, Sundevall). Colombia and Ecuador. (Monotypic.)

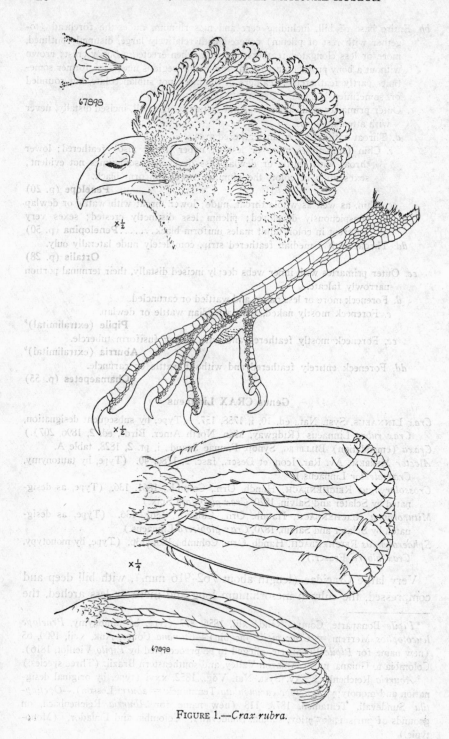

FIGURE 1.—*Crax rubra*.

cere and anterior half (more or less) of mandibular rami wholly nude; pileum with a more compressed erectile crest of elongated, rigid terminally recurved feathers, and forehead with an egg-shaped tubercle or protuberance.

Bill deep at base, compressed, its greatest basal width equal to less than three-fourths (sometimes barely two-thirds) its height; culmen strongly decurved, not ridged, much shorter than length of mesorhinium, the latter more or less arched proximally, sometimes much compressed (almost ridged), sometimes broad and flattened basally; cere and anterior half (more or less) of mandibular rami, sometimes loral and at least part of orbital region also, wholly nude; nostril more or less comma-shaped, rounded anteriorly, acute or subacute posteriorly, in anterior middle portion of cere sometimes touching base of rhinotheca, overhung, at least for proximal half, by a convex membranous operculum. Wing relatively large and broad, the very large and broad secondaries extending beyond tips of primaries; primaries rigid, strongly rounded, composed of 12 rather rigid, broad, roundish-tipped rectrices, then decidedly incurved terminally and slightly but distinctly bent vertically, the tail thus convex above and concave beneath. Tarsus long and stout, less than one-fourth to nearly one-third as long as wing, entirely nude, the acrotarsium and planta tarsi both with a continuous series of large and broad transverse scutella; middle toe nearly to about two-thirds as long as tarsus, the inner toe reaching about to its penultimate articulation, the outer toe slightly longer; hallux incumbent, longer than first two phalanges of outer toe; claws rather large, strongly curved (especially that of hallux), moderately compressed.

Plumage and coloration.—Plumage in general rather soft, but feathers distinctly outlined, except on sides and under portion of head and on upper neck, where short and velvety, and abdomen, flanks, and under tail coverts, where very soft and full; pileum with an erectile compressed crest of elongated, rigid feathers, recurved at tips. Adult males plain black, more or less glossed, especially on upper parts, with greenish, bluish, or purplish, the abdomen, flanks, and under tail coverts—sometimes also tips of rectrices—white. Adult female with plumage more or less barred, sometimes with rufescent and ochreous hues predominating; in one species differing from adult male only in having the feathers of the crest barred with white.

Range.—Southern Mexico to Brazil. (Seven species with several additional subspecies. Only a single species, with two races, in the regions covered by this work.)

KEY TO THE NORTH AND MIDDLE AMERICAN FORMS OF THE GENUS CRAX[10]

a. Crest uniform black (male).

    b. A wattle present on each side of his chin........**Crax alberti** (extralimital)[11]

    bb. No wattles at base of lower mandible.

        c. Plumage of upperparts with a purplish gloss....**Crax nigra** (extralimital)[12]

        cc. Plumage of upperparts glossed with dull greenish.

            d. Smaller, wings averaging 340 mm.........**Crax rubra griscomi** (p. 19)

            dd. Larger, wings averaging 385 mm.............**Crax rubra rubra** (p. 13)

aa. Some white bars in crest (females).

    b. Secondaries uniform black......................**Crax nigra** (extralimital)

    bb. Secondaries not uniform black.

        c. Secondaries black with narrow white bars......**Crax alberti** (extralimital)

        cc. Secondaries chestnut, or, if blackish, then widely barred with whitish.

            d. Size smaller, wings averaging 330 mm......**Crax rubra griscomi** (p. 19)

            dd. Size larger, wings averaging 370 mm........**Crax rubra rubra** (p. 13)

---

[10] Included in the key are two South American species, whose ranges extend near enough to Panama to make them worth considering as potential additions in time to come.

[11] *Crax alberti* Fraser.—*Crax alberti* Fraser, Proc. Zool. Soc. London, 1850, 246, pls. 27, 28 (locality unknown; coll. Knowsley Menagerie) ; Gray, List Birds Brit. Mus., pt. 5, Gallinae, 1867, 15; Sclater and Salvin, Proc. Zool. Soc. London, 1870, 517 (monogr.; Colombia) ; Sclater, Trans. Zool. Soc. London, ix, 1875, 280, pl. 48; Ogilvie-Grant, Cat. Birds Brit. Mus., xxii, 1893, 483 (vicinity of Bogotá, Colombia) ; Bangs, Proc. Biol. Soc. Washington, xii, 1898, 132 (Santa Marta, Colombia) ; Allen, Bull. Amer. Mus. Nat. Hist., xiii, 1900, 127 (Bonda, Naranjo, and Santa Marta, Colombia) ; Chapman, Bull. Amer. Mus. Nat. Hist., xxxvi, 1917, 194 (west of Honda, Colombia, 2,000 feet) ; Todd and Carriker, Ann. Carnegie Mus., xiv, 1922, 176 (Don Diego and San Lorenzo, Santa Marta, Colombia).—HELLMAYR and CONOVER, Cat. Birds Amer., i, No. 1, 1942, 127.—*C*[*rax*] *alberti* Reichenbach, Voll. Nat. Tauben, 1861, 136.—[*Crax*] *alberti* Gray, Hand-list, ii, 1870, 253, No. 9527; Sclater and Salvin, Nom. Av. Neotr., 1873, 135; Sharpe, Hand-list, i, 1899, 15.—*Crax alberti alberti* Peters, Check-list Birds of World, ii, 1934, 11.—(?) *Crax mikani*, part, Pelzeln, Orn. Bras., 1870, 343 (female).—*Crax viridirostris* Sclater, Trans. Zool. Soc. London, ix, 1875, 282 ("South America"; type now in coll. Brit. Mus.) ; x, 1879, 544, pl. 92; Proc. Zool. Soc. London, 1876, 463 (Cartagena, Colombia).—*Crax annulata* Todd, Proc. Biol. Soc. Washington, xxviii, 1915, 170 (Don Diego, Santa Marta, Colombia).

[12] *Crax nigra* Linnaeus, Syst. Nat., ed. 10, i, 1758, 157 (South America) ; Peters, Check-list Birds of World, ii, 1934, 10 (distr.; syn.).—[*Crax*] *alector* Linnaeus, Syst. Nat., ed. 12, i, 1766, 269 ("America Calidiore"; based on *Crax guianensis* Brisson, Orn., i, 1725, 298, pl. 29).—*Gallus indicus* Sloane, Jam., ii, 1725, 302, pl. 260; Gmelin, Syst. Nat., i, pt. 2, 1788, 735; Latham, Index Orn., ii, 1790, 622; Gray, Hand-list, ii, 1870, 253, No. 9523; Sclater and Salvin, Nom. Av. Neotr., 1873, 135; Sharpe, Hand-list, i, 1899, 14.—*Crax alector* Bonnaterre, Tabl. Encycl. Méth., i, 1791, 173, pl. 85, fig. 4; Temminck, Pig. et Gallin., iii, 1815, 27, 689; Vieillot, Nouv. Dict. Hist. Nat., xiv, 1817, 584; Gal. Ois., ii, 1825, 6; Lesson, Traité d'Orn., 1831, 484; Bennett, Gard. and Menag., ii, 1831, 9; Reichenbach, Synop. Av., Columb., ii, 1837, pl. 173, fig. 1515; Gray, List Birds Brit. Mus., pt. 3, Gallinae, 1844, 20, pt. 5, Gallinae, 1867, 14; Voll. Nat. Tauben, 1861, 148 (crit.) ; Burmeister, Syst. Übers, Th. Bras., iii, 1856, 344; Pelzeln, Orn. Bras., 1870, 286 (Rio Negro, Rio Vaupé,

CRAX RUBRA RUBRA Linnaeus

CENTRAL AMERICAN CURASSOW

Adult male.—Entire feathering of head, neck, wings, tail, and body black with a very dark greenish gloss, except for the middle and posterior part of the abdomen, the flanks, and the under tail coverts, which are white; in some cases the rectrices are slightly margined with white; the feathers of the lower back and rump are short and often reveal their dark brownish bases, causing this area to appear somewhat mixed black and dull sepia, iris red; cere with swollen wattle pale yellow to bright yellow, tip of bill somewhat duskier; tarsi and toes grayish "horn color."

Adult female.—Extremely variable, the plumages falling into at least three phases, which, as far as present data indicate, are all equally adult:

1. *Dark phase:* Feathers of head and neck and upper two-thirds of throat blackish broadly crossed subterminally with white, causing a barred or sometimes a scalloped appearance, the white areas much smaller on the sides of the head than on the chin, throat, and sides and back of the neck, making the lores, circumorbital area, cheeks, and auriculars definitely blacker in appearance; crest feathers black with a broad white band and sometimes a narrow basal one; posterior part of neck, lower throat, upper breast, scapulars, and interscapulars dark slate black with a slight greenish gloss, the scapulars and interscapulars more or less washed or edged with dark warm sepia to mars brown; back and rump rich dark chestnut-brown somewhat mottled or tinged with blackish; upper wing coverts bright chestnut with a slight suffusion of orange-rufous, the feathers with dusky shafts and irregularly mottled with dusky fuscous to blackish; primaries and outer secondaries bright chestnut mottled with black and with the shaft edged with blackish on the inner web; in some specimens the outer webs unmottled, in others both webs are heavily sprinkled with black markings; inner secondaries generally darker, much more heavily mottled with blackish, and with narrow whitish transverse irregular marks on the outer webs; in some specimens the inner secondaries are more blackish than chestnut and blend easily

and Rio Brancho, n. Brazil); Sclater and Salvin, Proc. Zool. Soc. London, 1870, 514 (monogr.); Sclater, Trans. Zool. Soc. London, ix, 1875, 277, pl. 43 (monogr.); Brown, Canoe and Camp Life in Brit. Guiana, 1876, 345; Ogilvie-Grant, Cat. Birds Brit. Mus., xxii, 1893, 475 (int. Colombia; San Gabriel, upper Rio Negro; Barra do Rio Negro; Camacusa and Demerara, Brit. Guiana; Surinam); Chapman, Bull. Amer. Mus. Nat. Hist., xxxvi, 1917, 194 (Buena Vista, e. Colombia).—*C[rax] alector* Cabanis, *in* Schomburgk, Reis. Brit. Guiana, iii, 1848, 746; Reichenbach, Voll. Nat. Tauben, 1861, 130.—*Crax globicera* (not of Linnaeus) Temminck, Cat. Syst., 1807, 151 (Surinam).—*Crax mitu* (not of Linnaeus) Vieillot, Nouv. Dict. Hist. Nat., xiv, 1817, 583; Gal. Ois., ii, 1825, pl. 199.—*Crax erythrognatha* Sclater and Salvin, Proc. Zool. Soc. London, 1877, 22 (interior of Colombia; coll. Salvin and Godman, now in coll. Brit. Mus.); Sclater, Trans. Zool. Soc. London., x, 1879, 543, pl. 90.

into the dark interscapulars; upper tail coverts blackish washed or edged with dark warm sepia and with a faint greenish gloss; rectrices variable, in some specimens all are uniform blackish with a greenish gloss; in others the median pair are heavily vermiculated with dull orange-chestnut; in still others the outer webs of all the tail feathers have incomplete, narrow, irregular, white bars and whitish tips; lower breast and sides tawny-russet paling into light ochraceous-tawny to light ochraceous-buff on the adbomen, flanks, thighs, and under tail coverts; under wing coverts chestnut vermiculated with blackish; bill yellowish, darker and somewhat olive-brown basally; tarsi and toes dull "pinkish gray."

2. *Red phase:* Similar to the dark phase but with the lower throat, entire breast, the scapulars, interscapulars, entire back, rump, upper wing coverts, and remiges bright orange-chestnut to Sanford's brown, the inner secondaries obscurely and incompletely barred with blackish, and the rectrices broadly barred black chestnut and cinnamon-buff, the chestnut usually confined to the median two pairs and edged with black, not coming directly into contact with the buff bars, of which there are seven or eight, including the terminal one.

3. *Barred-backed phase:* Feathers of head and neck white with small black tips, the whole area definitely much whiter than in the two phases described above; the crest mostly white instead of black barred with white; the black tips practically absent in the feathers of the chin and upper throat; lower throat, upper breast, posterior part of hindneck, and interscapulars broadly barred with black and white, the bars about equal in width (8 mm.) in one specimen, the black ones wider than the white ones in several others; scapulars, upper wing coverts, and secondaries very conspicuously banded with broad bars of pinkish buff to cinnamon-buff, the dark (wider) bars dull deep chestnut edged with black or, in some birds, and especially on the interscapulars, almost solid black; primaries pinkish buff to cinnamon-buff, terminally suffused with pinkish cinnamon and banded with orange-cinnamon to mikado brown, these dark bands more widely spaced (narrower than the pale interspaces) and more developed on the inner than the outer webs; on the innermost primaries the dark bands have some blackish margins; back and rump pale cinnamon-buff barred with black-edged chestnut bands; upper tail coverts and median rectrices like the scapulars and secondaries, the outer rectrices becoming blacker and the pale bars narrower, sometimes almost disappearing in the outermost pair; underparts of body paler than in the other phases—the lower breast and sides pale ochraceous-buff, abdomen, flanks, thighs, and under tail coverts as in other phases; under wing coverts ochraceous-buff speckled with dull chestnut.[13]

---

[13] This plumage is very different from anything else seen in this species; the only character elsewhere exhibited that approaches it is in the tail of the rufous phase. I

Subadult male.—Similar to the adult but without the swollen wattle on the cere.

Juvenal male.—Similar to the adult female dark phase but with the entire breast and upper abdomen blackish, the abdominal feathers basally pale chestnut, which color shows through the black; thighs with dusky edges and tips to each of the feathers producing a scalloped appearance; and entire back and scapulars blackish like the interscapulars; primaries darker—very dark chestnut on the outer webs, dark sepia on the inner ones.

Juvenal female.[14]—Three phases, as follows:

1. *Dark phase:* Similar to the adult of the same phase but with the secondaries and the long scapulars mottled with white, the irregular elongated whitish marks surrounded with black; the central pair of rectrices vermiculated with black and chestnut and similarly mottled with white; the next pair with a few white marks on the outer webs; upper tail coverts dark chestnut vermiculated with black like the median rectrices but with no white, breast very dark chestnut, not black, the lower breast, upper abdomen, and sides barred more or less with dusky fuscous and ochraceous-buff; occasional feathers have the buff replaced by white; thighs similarly barred with fuscous; crest with several white bars.

2. *Red phase:* Similar to the corresponding adult but with the lower breast, abdomen, and thighs barred with fuscous, and the remiges crossed by numerous rather fine wavy blackish bars; crest with several white bars.

3. *Barred-backed phase:* Similar to the corresponding adult but the crest feathers with several white bars instead of one very broad one; upper abdomen and sides and flanks barred with fuscous-black.

Natal down.—Down of head, upperparts generally, breast, sides, flanks, and thighs grayish warm buff, abdomen white; the chin also whitish; tip and sides of head with blackish spots which tend to become connected into longitudinal stripes on the hindneck and back (where there are one median and two lateral stripes separated by slightly more grayish, less buffy, down than that of the upperparts generally; bill dusky yellowish, tending toward lead grayish on the maxillary tomium; tarsi and toes pale ochraceous-salmon. (descr. ex col. fig. in Heinroth, Journ. für Orn., lxxix, 1931, pl. xvii, facing p. 282).

---

have seen four examples of the barred-backed form "*chapmani* Nelson," all females. As far as I have been able to discover, all the known specimens of this type come from Campeche and Yucatán; the plumage is not represented from other parts of the range of *rubra* and is not known to occur in the Cozumel Island subspecies *griscomi*. It is impossible to decide the status of *chapmani* definitely; it may be a color phase of *rubra* as here treated, and as considered by several recent authors, or it may be a distinct species. A similar case in South America is to be found in *Crax grayi* Ogilvie-Grant and in *Crax pinima* Pelzeln.

[14] There seems to be no subadult stage that may be told from skins.

Adult male.—Wing 365–445 (388); tail 305–362 (331.3); culmen from cere 27–33.5 (31.5); culmen including cere 46–58 (53.2); tarsus 113–127 (117.8); middle toe without claw 70–86 (76.8 mm.).[15]

Adult female.—Wing 355–410 (372.4); tail 315–345 (322); culmen from cere 24–30 (27.2); culmen including cere 43.5–50 (48.3); tarsus 108–117 (112.4); middle toe without claw 70–80 (73.5 mm.).[16]

Range.—Resident in forested areas in the tropical zone from southeastern Mexico—southern Tamaulipas (Guiaves; Sierra Madre above Ciudad Victoria); Veracruz (Misantla); Oaxaca (Tapana; Chimalapa); Campeche (La Tuxpena; Champotón); Yucatán (eastern Quintana Roo; Puerto Morelos; La Vega); British Honduras (Belize; Cayo District); Honduras (Lake Yojoa; Tigre Island; Comayagua; San Pedro; Lancetilla); Guatemala (local on the Pacific slope; Chilomó; Lake Petén; Los Amates; Naranjo; Pozo del Río Grande; Panzos; Rexché; Santo Tomás; Savanna Grande; Sepacuite; Vera Paz); Nicaragua (Río Escondido; Los Sábalos); Costa Rica (Guacimo; La Palma de Nicoya; Naranjo; Río Frío; San Carlos; San José; Sarapiquí; Talamanca; Valza; Volcán de Irazú; Volcán de Miravalles); and Panama (Almirante; Boquete; Canal Zone; Cerro Bruja; Jesusito, Darién; Lion Hill; Obaldia; Permé); south through western Colombia (Choco; Bando; Bagado); to western Ecuador (Chongon Hills; Paramba; Bunlún).

Type locality.—No locality given; designated as western Ecuador by Hellmayr and Conover (Cat. Birds Amer., i, No. 1, 1942, 130).

[*Crax*] *rubra* LINNAEUS, Syst. Nat., ed. 10, i, 1758, 157 ("America"; based on *Gallina peruviana rubra* Albin, Av., iii, 37, pl. 40); ed. 12, i, 1766, 270.—GMELIN, Syst. Nat., i, pt. 2, 1788, 736.—REICHENBACH, Synop. Av., Columb., ii, 1837, pl. 175, figs. 1523, 1524.

Crax rubra TEMMINCK, Pig. et Gallin., iii, 1815, 21, 687.—VIEILLOT, Nouv. Dict. Hist. Nat., xiv, 1817, 582.—STEPHENS, *in* Shaw, Gen. Zool., xi, pt. i, 1819, 168, pl. 9.—BENNETT, Gard. and Menag., ii, 1831, 225.—LESSON, Traité d'Orn., 1831, 484.—REICHENBACH, Voll. Nat. Tauben, 1861, 139 (crit.).—SUTTON and BURLEIGH, Occ. Pap. Mus. Zool. Louisiana State Univ. No. 3, 1939, 27 (Tamaulipas). —SUTTON and PETTINGILL, Auk, lix, 1942, 10 (Tamaulipas; habits; nest and eggs).

C[*rax*] *rubra* REICHENBACH, Voll. Nat. Tauben, 1861, 133, part (Mexico).

C[*ras*] *rubra* CUBAS, Cuadro Geogr., Estadístico, Descr. e Hist. de los Estados Unidos Mexicanos, 1884, 169 (Mexico; common names).

Crax rubra ? LAWRENCE, Ann. Lyc. Nat. Hist. New York, vii, 1861, 301 (Panama).

Crax rubra rubra PETERS, Check-list Birds of World, ii, 1934, 12 (distr.).—GRISCOM, Bull. Mus. Comp. Zool., lxxviii, 1935, 303 (Panama).—VAN TYNE, Misc. Publ. Mus. Zool. Univ. Michigan, No. 27, 1935, 10 (Uaxactún, Petén, Guatemala).— ALDRICH, Sci. Publ. Cleveland Mus. Nat. Hist., vii, 1937, 51 (Cerro Viejo, Azuero Peninsula, Panama; plum.; crit.).—SASSI, Temminckia, iii, 1938, 304 (Costa Rica; Bebedero; spec.).—HELLMAYR and CONOVER, Cat. Birds Amer.,

[15] Eleven specimens from Mexico, Guatemala, Costa Rica, and Panama.
[16] Seven specimens from Mexico.

i, No. 1, 1942, 129 (syn.; distr.).—Brodkorb, Misc. Publ. Mus. Zool. Univ.
Michigan, No. 56, 1943, 30 (Mexico; Chiapas, Palenque; spec.).
[*Crax*] *globicera* Linnaeus, Syst. Nat., ed. 12, i, 1766, 270 ("Brasilia; Curacao";
based on *Crax curassous* Brisson, Orn., 300; *Gallus indicus alius* Aldrovandi,
Orn., ii, 332; *Gallina indica* Aldrovandi, Orn., ii, 333; Ray, Av., 31, 32; Edwards,
Av., 2, pl. 295, fig. 1).—Gmelin, Syst. Nat., i, pt. 2, 1788, 736.—Latham, Index
Orn., ii, 1790, 624 ("Guiana").—Reichenbach, Synop. Av., Columb., ii, 1837,
pl. 174, figs. 1517, 1518.—Sclater and Salvin, Nom. Av. Neotr., 1873, 135.—
Sharpe, Hand-list, i, 1899, 14 (Mexico to Honduras).
Crax globicera Bonnaterre, Tabl. Encycl. Méth., i, 1791, 175.—Vieillot, Nouv.
Dict. Hist. Nat., xiv, 1817, 582.—Lesson, Traité d'Orn., 1831, 484.—Sclater,
Proc. Zool. Soc. London, 1860, 253 (Veracruz) ; Trans. Zool. Soc. London,
ix, 1875, 274, pl. 40 (fig. ♂, ♀ ; monogr.) ; x, 1879, 543, pl. 89 (Panama; Costa
Rica).—Taylor, Ibis, 1860, 311 (Tigre Island and between Pacific coast and
Comayagua, and Lake Yojoa, Honduras).—Salvin, Ibis, 1861, 143 in text
(Vera Paz, Guatemala).—Sallé and Parzudaki, Cat. Oiseaux Mexique, 1862
6 (Mexico).—Lawrence, Ann. Lyc. Nat. Hist. New York, viii, 1863, 12, 490
(Panama) ; ix, 1868, 139 (San José, Costa Rica) ; U. S. Nat. Mus. Bull. 4,
1876, 44 (Tapana, Oaxaca).—Huxley, Proc. Zool. Soc. London, 1868, 297, 298
figs. of sternum and pelvis).—Frantzius, Journ. für Orn., 1869, 373 (Río
Sarapiquí; Costa Rica).—Sumichrast, Mem. Boston Soc. Nat. Hist., i, 1869,
560 (hot region of Veracruz) ; La Naturaleza, ii, 1871, 37 (Veracruz, Mexico).
—Sclater and Salvin, Proc. Zool. Soc. London, 1870, 513, 543 (monogr.) ; 838
(Honduras).—Boucard, Proc. Zool. Soc. London, 1878, 42 (San Carlos, Volcán
de Irazú, and Naranjo, Costa Rica) ; 1883, 459 (Yucatán; habits).—Nutting,
Proc. U. S. Nat. Mus., v, 1882, 408 (La Palma de Nicoya, Costa Rica) ; vi,
1884, 408 (Los Sábalos, Nicaragua; habits; fresh colors unfeathered parts).—
Ferrari-Perez, Proc. U. S. Nat. Mus., ix, 1886, 175 (Veracruz).—Rovirosa,
La Naturaleza, vii, 1887, 380 (Tabasco; Río Macuspana).—Zeledón, Anal.
Mus. Nac. Costa Rica, i, 1887, 128 (Costa Rica).—Ogilvie-Grant, Cat. Birds
Brit. Mus., xxii, 1893, 478, part (Sierra Madre above Ciudad Victoria, Tamau-
lipas; Misantla, Veracruz; Chimalapa, Oaxaca; n. Yucatán; Sabana Grande,
Guatemala) ; Handb. Game Birds, ii, 1897, 203, part (monogr., excl. of Cozumel
Island).—Richmond, Proc. U. S. Nat. Mus., xvi, 1893, 524 (Río Escondido,
Nicaragua; Río Frío, Costa Rica; habits).—Beristain and Laurencio, Mem.
y Rev. Soc. Cient. "Antonio Alzate," vii, 1894, 220 (Mexico; forests of both
coasts).—Underwood, Ibis, 1896, 448 (Volcán de Miravalles, Costa Rica;
habits).—Lantz, Trans. Kansas Acad. Sci. for 1896-7 (1899), 219 (Naranjo
and Santo Tomás, Guatemala).—Salvin and Godman, Biol. Centr.-Amer.,
Aves, iii, 1902, 271, part (Sierra Madre above Ciudad Victoria, Tamaulipas;
Misantla, Veracruz; Chimalapa and Tapana, Oaxaca; n. Yucatán; Lake Petén,
Chilomo, Sabana Grande, Rexché, and Vera Paz, Guatemala; Lake Yojoa and
San Pedro, Honduras).—Dearborn, Publ. Field Mus. Nat. Hist., No. 125,
1907, 77 (Los Amates, Guatemala).—Phillips, Auk, xxviii, 1911, 74 (Guiaves,
Tamaulipas).—Miller and Griscom, Amer. Mus. Nov., No. 25, 1921, 7, 8
(crit.).—Bangs and Barbour, Bull. Mus. Comp. Zool., lxv, 1922, 195 (Jesusito,
Darién; crit.).—Griscom, Amer. Mus. Nov., No. 235, 1926, 7 (eastern Quin-
tana Roo, Yucatán) ; Bull. Mus. Comp. Zool., lxxii, 1932, 318 (Permé, Obaldia,
Panama; crit.).—Chapman, Bull. Amer. Mus. Nat. Hist., lv, 1926, 151 (distr.
in Ecuador; spec. Chongon Hills).—Sturgis, Field Book Birds Panama Canal
Zone, 1928, 26 (descr.; habits; Panama Canal).—Heinroth, Journ. für Orn.,
lxxix, 1931, 278, pl. 17-19 (development; habits).—Caum, Occ. Pap. Bishop
Mus., x, No. 9, 1933, ii (Hawaii; introduced in 1928; uncertain status in 1933).—

ALDRICH, Sci. Publ. Cleveland Mus. Nat. Hist., vii, 1937, 51, in text.—GROEBBELS, Der Vögel, ii, 1937, 165 (data on breeding biology).

C[rax] globicera REICHENBACH, Voll. Nat. Tauben, 1861, 133.—REICHENOW, Die Vögel, i, 1913, 280.

Cras globicera CUBAS, Cuadro Geogr., Estadístico, Descr. e Hist. de los Estados Unidos Mexicanos, 1884, 169 (Mexico; common names).

Crax globicera globicera AUSTIN, Bull. Mus. Comp. Zool., lxix, 1929, 369 (distr.; Cayo District, British Honduras).—PETERS, Bull. Mus. Comp. Zool., lxix, 1929, 403 (hills e. of Lancetilla, Honduras; type loc. fixed) ; lxxi, 1931, 297 (Almirante, Panama).—GRISCOM, Bull. Amer. Mus. Nat. Hist., lxiv, 1932, 99 (distr. in Guatemala; abundant between Sepacuite and Panzos).—STONE, Proc. Acad. Nat. Sci. Philadelphia, lxxxiv, 1932, 301 (Honduras).—DICKEY and VAN ROSSEM, Birds El Salvador, 1938, 147 (Puerto del Triunfo, El Salvador).—DEL CAMPO, Anal. Inst. Biol., xiii, No. 2, 1942, 700 (Chiapas; Catarinas; spec.).

[Crax] alector (not of Linnaeus), part, LATHAM, Index Orn., ii, 1790, 623 (female).

Crax alector STEPHENS, in Shaw, Gen. Zool., xi, pt. i, 1819, 163, part (Mexico).— SCLATER and SALVIN, Ibis, 1859, 223 (Guatemala; Belize, British Honduras; habits).

Crax alector ? MOORE, Proc. Zool. Soc. London, 1859, 61 (Petén and Chilomó, Guatemala).

Crax alberti FRAZER, Proc. Zool. Soc. London, 1850, 246, part, pls. 27, 28 (female).

(?) Crax blumenbachii SPIX, Av. Bras., ii, 1825, 50 pl. 64 ("Rio de Janeiro," but locality said to be erroneous).—GRAY, List Birds Brit. Mus., pt. 5, Gallinae, 1867, 15.

[Crax] blumenbachii GRAY, Hand-list, ii, 1870, 253, No. 9525.

(?) Crax albini LESSON, Traité d'Orn., 1931, 484 (based on "Albin, t. ii, pl. 32; Hoazin Hernandez ?").—REICHENBACH, Voll. Nat. Tauben, 1862, 155.

Crax temminckii TSCHUDI, Archiv für Naturg., x, 1844, 308 (based on "The Red Peruvian Hen" of Abin and Crax rubra Temminck) ; Fauna Peruana, Aves, 1844-46, 287 (w. Mexico).—BURMEISTER, Syst. Übers. Th. Bras., iii, 1856, 347.

Crax edwardsii REICHENBACH, Voll. Nat. Tauben, 1862, 134 (based on "The Curasso-Bird" Edwards, Glean. Nat. Hist., ii, 181, pl. 295, fig. 1: Aviary bird without locality).

C[rax] pseudalector REICHENBACH, Voll. Nat. Tauben, 1862, 131, pl. 174, fig. 1516 (Yucatán; cites "t. 237, i.e. 1516 'Crax' syst. nat. t. xxiv").

Crax sp. SCLATER and SALVIN, Proc. Zool. Soc. London, 1864, 371 (Panama).

Crax panamensis OGILVIE-GRANT, Cat. Birds Brit. Mus., xxii, 1893, 479 ("Southern Nicaragua and Costa Rica to the United States of Colombia"; Valza, Costa Rica; Lion Hill, Panama; type locality not specified) ; Handb. Game Birds, ii, 1897, 205 (monogr.).—SALVADORI and FESTA, Boll. Mus. Zool. Torino, xiv, 1899, 9, Río Lara, Darién, Panama).—FESTA, Boll. Mus. Zool. Torino, xv, 1899, 1 (breeding in captivity).—BANGS, Proc. New England Zool. Club, iii, 1902, 21 (Boquete, w. Panama) ; Auk, xxiv, 1907, 290 (Pozo del Río Grande, Costa Rica).—SALVIN and GODMAN, Biol. Centr.-Amer., Aves, iii, 1902, 278 (Los Sábalos and Río Escondido, Nicaragua; San José, Valza, Sarapiquí, San Carlos, Volcán de Irazú, Naranjo, La Palma de Nicoya, Río Frío, and Miravalles, Costa Rica; Lion Hill, Panama).—HARTERT, Nov. Zool., ix, 1902, 601 (Paramba, 3,500 feet, and Bulún, nw. Ecuador; crit.).—CARRIKER, Ann. Carnegie Mus., vi, 1910, 382 (Guacimo, Costa Rica; crit.; habits).—CHAPMAN, Bull. Amer. Mus. Nat. Hist., xxxvi, 1917, 194 (Chocó, Bando, and Bagado, nw. Colombia).—STONE, Proc. Acad. Nat. Sci. Philadelphia, 1918, 242 (Canal Zone, Panama).—RENDAHL, Ark. Zool., xii, No. 8, 1919, 10 (Siquirres, Costa Rica, and

Zapatera, Nicaragua).—MILLER and GRISCOM, Amer. Mus. Nov., No. 25, 1921, 7 (crit.).—GROEBBELS, Der Vögel, ii, 1937, 166 (breeding data).

C[rax] panamensis REICHENOW, Die Vögel, i, 1913, 280.

[Crax] panamensis SHARPE, Hand-list, i, 1899, 14.—BRABOURNE and CHUBB, Birds South Amer., i, 1912, 8 (Colombia; nw. Ecuador).

Crax hecki REICHENOW, Journ für Orn., 1894, 231, pl. 2 (aviary bird; ♀).— GROEBBELS, Der Vögel, ii, 1937, 166 (data on breeding biology).

Crax chapmani NELSON, Proc. Biol. Soc. Washington, xiv, Sept. 25, 1901, 170 (Puerto Morelos, e. Yucatán; coll. U. S. Nat. Mus.).—SALVIN and GODMAN, Biol. Centr.-Amer., Aves, iii, 1902, 273.

Crax sclateri BERISTAIN and LAURENCIO, Mem. y Rev. Soc. Cient. "Antonio Alzate," vii, 1894, 220 (Mexico).

CRAX RUBRA GRISCOMI Nelson

COZUMEL CURASSOW

Adult male.—Similar to that of the nominate form but smaller.

Adult female.—Similar to the dark phase adult female of the typical race but smaller, the median white band on the crest slightly broader; the inner primaries and the secondaries with slightly wider whitish transverse markings, and the scapulars, greater upper wing coverts, and upper surface of secondaries generally more irregularly marked with dusky mottlings.

Subadult male.—Similar to the adult but without the swollen wattle on the cere.

Juvenal male.—None seen.

Juvenal female.—Similar to the adult but with the lower breast, upper abdomen, and sides barred with narrow wavy blackish bands, some of the feathers with whitish tips.

Natal down.—Apparently not known.

Adult male.—Wing 325–355 (339.5); tail 300–310 (306.8); culmen from cere 26.5–29 (27.8); culmen including cere 44–52 (48); tarsus 98–109.5 (104.5); middle toe without claw 62.5–71.5 (67 mm.).[17]

Adult female.—Wing 320–330 (328.3); tail 273–305 (289.3); culmen from cere 22.5–26 (24.5); culmen including cere 42–45 (43); tarsus 97–98 (97.5); middle toe without claw 60.5–63 (62.1 mm.).[17]

Confined to the type locality, Cozumel Island, off the coast of Yucatán.

Crax globicera (not of Linnaeus, 1766) SALVIN, Ibis, 1889, 378; 1890, 89 (Cozumel Island; crit.).—OGILVIE-GRANT, Cat. Birds Brit. Mus., xxii, 1893, 478, part (Cozumel Island); Handb. Game Birds, ii, 1897, 203, part (Cozumel Island).— SALVIN and GODMAN, Biol. Centr.-Amer., Aves, iii, 1902, 271, part (Cozumel Island).

Crax globicera ? RIDGWAY, Proc. U. S. Nat. Mus., viii, 1885, 581 (Cozumel Island; crit.).

Crax globicera griscomi NELSON, Proc. Biol. Soc. Washington, xxxix, 1926, 106

---

[17] Three specimens of each sex.

(orig. descr.; Cozumel Island).—HELLMAYR and CONOVER, Cat. Birds Amer., i, No. 1, 1942, 132 (syn.; distr.).

Crax rubra griscomi PETERS, Check-list Birds of World, ii, 1934, 12.

Genus PENELOPE Merrem

Penelope MERREM, Av. Rar. Icones et Descr., fasc. 2, 1786, 39. (Type, as designated by Sclater and Salvin, 1870, *P. jacupema* Merrem = *P. marail* Gmelin?[18].)

Penelophe (emendation) BILLBERG, Synop. Faunae Scand., i, pt. 2, 1828, table A.

Ponolope (emendation) JAROCKI, Zoologiia, ii, 1821, 186.

Salpiza WAGLER, Isis, 1832, 1226. (Type, as designated by Gray, 1840, *Penelope marail* Gmelin.)

Salpizusa (emendation) HEINE and REICHENOW, Nom. Mus. Hein. Orn., 1890, 301.

Gouan LACEPÈDE, Tabl. Ois., 1799, 12. (Type, by tautonymy, The *Quan* or *Guan* Edwards = *Penelope cristata* Gmelin = *Penelope purpurascens aequatorialis* Salvadori and Festa.)

Guan (emendation) FISCHER DE WALDHEIM, Nat. Mus. Naturg. Paris, ii, 1803, 183.

Guanus (emendation) FISCHER DE WALDHEIM, Zoognesia, i, ed. 3, 1813, 34, 51.

Ganix RAFINESQUE, Analyse, 1815, 69. (New name for *Gouan* Lacepède.)

Stegnolæma SCLATER and SALVIN, Proc. Zool. Soc. London, 1870, 521. (Type, by monotypy, *Ortalida montagnii* Bonaparte.)

Steganolæma (emendation) WATERHOUSE, Index Gen. Avium, 1889, 211.

Large Cracidae (length about 558–890 mm. but less bulky and more slender than *Crax*), with bill relatively small and not compressed, loral, orbital, and gular regions nude, the last with a median wattle or dewlap (sometimes not evident in dried skins), pileum with decumbent but erectile crest of broad, flattened soft feathers, tail as long as or longer than wing, and coloration mostly brownish or olivaceous, without bars, usually without any solid black, and sometimes with whitish streaks on underparts.

Bill relatively small (only about half as long as head), its depth at base about equal to its width at same point; culmen about as long as nude portion of mesorhinium, gradually decurved, broadly rounded on top, the rhinotheca slightly to decidedly broader than deep at base; mesorhinium straight or very slightly convex toward base, gently ascending proximally; nostril relatively rather large, narrowly elliptical or slit-like to comma-shaped (broadly rounded anteriorly, acute or subacute posteriorly), its posterior half or more overhung by a convex membrane, its anterior end touching base of rhinotheca, or nearly so. Wing large and broad, the longer primaries and secondaries about equal in length

---

[18] Merrem had two species, *P. leucolophos* (p. 43), which = *Crax cumanensis* Jacquin (a *Pipile*), and *P. jacupema* (p. 39), which is doubtfully referred to *P. marail* Gmelin; Sclater and Salvin, P.Z.S. 1870, 523, say it 'must always remain doubtful' what species was intended by Merrem under this name." (Richmond, MS.)

In 1816 Vieillot (Analyse, p. 49) gave only *Marail* Buffon (= *Penelope marail* Gmelin) under the generic term *Penelope;* while in 1832 Wagler (Isis, p. 1226) included *P. pipile* (= *Pipile jacuntinga*), *P. cumanensis* (= *Pipile cumanensis*), and *P. aburri* (= *Aburria aburri*).

or (in *P. montagnii*) the former decidedly longer; outer primaries strongly bowed, especially the outermost, of which the narrow tip is strongly incurved; sixth to eighth primaries longest; none of primaries with inner

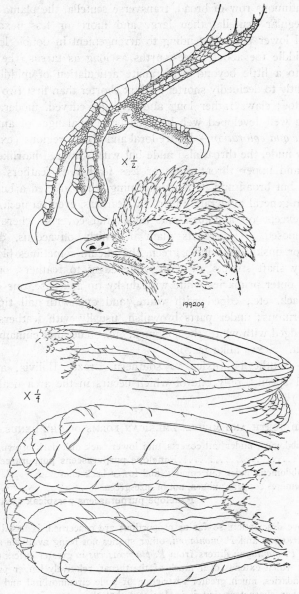

FIGURE 2.—*Penelope purpurascens.*

web incised; secondaries strong and relatively broad, with rounded tips. Tail about as long as wing or a little shorter, distinctly rounded, the rectrices (12) very broad, the lateral ones slightly or moderately bowed, all faintly but distinctly bent downward terminally (the upper surface slightly convex, the under side slightly concave). Tarsus moderately long and stout (about one-fourth as long as wing), the acrotarsium with a single continuous row of broad, transverse scutella, the planta tarsi with small irregular scutella, then large and more or less hexagonal, on upper and lower portion, tending to arrangement in double longitudinal series; middle toe about three-fourths as long as tarsus, the outer toe reaching to a little beyond penultimate articulation of middle toe, the inner slightly to decidedly shorter; hallux shorter than first two phalanges of outer toe; claws rather long and strongly curved, moderately compressed; a well-developed web between basal phalanges of anterior toe.

Plumage and coloration.—Entire loral and orbital regions (extensively) completely nude, the throat also nude but with scattered hairlike feathers, the chin and upper throat more or less feathered; feathers of pileum elongated, but broad and flattened, forming when erected a bushy crest; plumage in general moderately firm, the feathers, even on neck, distinctly outlined, except on abdomen and under tail coverts, where soft and semidecomposed. Upperparts plain brownish, olivaceous, dull olive-greenish, or dusky dull bluish green, the pileum sometimes black, white with dusky shaft streaks, or with white edges to feathers, one species with eight outer primaries white with dusky tip and base, one with wing coverts, back, etc., edged with white, and one with tail tipped with cinnamon-rufous; under parts brownish, usually with feathers of chest or breast edged with white, the abdomen, etc., sometimes cinnamon-rufous or chestnut. Sexes alike in color.

Range.—Southern Mexico to southern Brazil, Bolivia, and Peru. (About 11 species, only one of which occurs in the area dealt with in this work.)[19]

KEY TO THE NORTH AND MIDDLE AMERICAN FORMS OF THE GENUS PENELOPE

a. Lower abdomen, under tail coverts, and lower back dull dark brown, not chestnut..........................**Penelope purpurascens purpurascens** (p. 23)
aa. Lower abdomen, under tail coverts, and lower back chestnut.
  b. Inner remiges coppery auburn, not bronze-green.
                Penelope purpurascens perspicax (extralimital)[20]

---

[19] The above description, so far as proportions are concerned, is based essentially on *P. purpurascens* and *P. montagnii,* other species not being available at the time of writing. *P. montagnii* differs from *P. purpurascens* in greater extent of feathering of chin, which extends over much of the throat, relatively longer primaries or shorter secondaries, much greater restriction of nude circumorbital and loral area, and some other characters, but it is doubtful that the genus *Stegnolaema* Sclater and Salvin, of which it is the type, should be granted recognition.

[20] *Penelope purpurascens perspicax* Bangs.—*Penelope perspicax* Bangs, Proc. Biol. Soc. Washington, xxiv, 1911, 187 (San Luis, Bitaco Valley, w. Colombia; crit.; E. A. and O. Bangs coll., now in Mus. Comp. Zool.).—Chapman, Bull. Amer. Mus. Nat. Hist., xxxvi, 1917, 195 (San Antonio, Miraflores, Salento, Colombia).—Bangs,

bb. Inner remiges bronze-green, not coppery auburn.
  c. Crown and upper back greenish. **Penelope purpurascens aequatorialis** (p. 25)
  cc. Crown and upper back dull metal bronze, not greenish.
              Penelope purpurascens brunnescens (extralimital)[21]

PENELOPE PURPURASCENS PURPURASCENS Wagler
NORTHERN CRESTED GUAN

Adult (sexes alike).—Forehead, crown, occiput, and hindneck dark fuscous with a very slight purplish to greenish bronzy sheen; scapulars, interscapulars, upper wing coverts, and remiges similar but sheen more greenish, the outer primaries less greenish, more fuscous-black, the interscapulars, scapulars, and upper wing coverts with narrow lateral, but not terminal, white edges; back and rump dull dusky sepia to mummy brown; upper tail coverts and rectrices like the inner remiges but the tail feathers with a little brighter sheen and averaging slightly more olive, less bronzy; lores bare except for some sparse black bristlelike feathers; circumocular area bare; chin and upper throat also bare except for a very few black hairlike feathers, a malar band of feathers from the posterior end of the mandibular ramus, broadening over the auriculars to extend dorsad to the feathers of the occiput and caudally to the sides of the upper throat, dark fuscous; rest of sides of neck, lower throat, and breast dark fuscous with a faint bronzy brownish gloss, each feather laterally narrowly edged with white; abdomen, sides, flanks, thighs, and under tail coverts like the back and rump; under wing coverts dark fuscous; iris carmine-red; circumorbital skin and lores violaceous-black; bill black; upper part of gular skin violaceous-black, the lower part carmine-red; tarsus carmine-red to magenta.

Immature (sexes alike).—Similar to the adult but with the white marks on the interscapulars, scapulars, and upper wing coverts much less developed; inner remiges and median rectrices with a little more purplish sheen.

Juvenal (only one male and one unsexed bird seen).—Much paler than adult or immature birds, the fuscous of the latter replaced by dusky earth brown to dull sepia; no white marks on the upperparts and very faintly present on the breast; scapulars, upper wing coverts, inner secondaries, upper tail coverts, and rectrices sepia abundantly flecked and

Bull. Mus. Comp. Zool., lxx, 1930, 154 (type spec.; crit.).—*P[enelope] purpurascens perspicax* Hellmayr and Conover, Auk, xlix, 1932, 332 (crit.; distr.).—*Penelope purpurascens perspicax* Peters, Check-list Birds World, ii, 1934, 13.—HELLMAYR and CONOVER, Cat. Birds Amer., i, No. 1, 1942, 137.

[21] *Penelope purpurascens brunnescens* Hellmayr and Conover.—*P[enelope] purpurascens brunnescens* Hellmayr and Conover, Auk, xlix, 1932, 333 (Río Cogollo, Perijá, Zulia, Venezuela; coll. of H. B. Conover; crit.).—*Penelope purpurascens brunnescens* Peters, Check-list Birds World, ii, 1934, 13.—HELLMAYR and CONOVER, Cat. Birds Amer., i, No. 1, 1942, 137.

vermiculated with mikado brown; no crest on top of head; chin and upper throat clothed in warm-buff down.

Natal down.—Forehead and supraorbital bands grayish light ochraceous-salmon, center of crown and occiput deep bright chestnut bordered laterally by a broad line of black, laterad of which is a band of pale olive-gray, which in turn is bordered on the outside (laterally) by a narrow line of chestnut next to the ochraceous-salmon supraorbitals; hindneck like the occiput; back with a spinal band of deep chestnut bordered with black, otherwise pinkish buff; chin and upper throat pale pinkish buff, lower throat and breast between cinnamon-buff and clay color; abdomen white with a very faint ivory-yellow tinge; flanks and thighs cinnamon-buff splotched with dusky.[22]

Adult male.—Wing 370–415 (390.6); tail 350–408 (384); culmen from base 32–44 (36.1); tarsus 81–90 (85.1); middle toe without claw 63–72 (67.2 mm.).[23]

Adult female.—Wing 362–390 (380); tail 372–408 (385.5); culmen from base 32–44 (36.1); tarsus 81–90 (85.1); middle toe without claw 65–70 (67.1 mm.).[24]

Range.—Resident in tropical forests from Sinaloa (Mazatlán, Escuinapa) and southern Tamaulipas (Sierra Madre above Ciudad Victoria, Guiaves) south through Veracruz (Jalapa, Santa Ana); Jalisco (Tonila); Guerrero (Omilteme); Oaxaca (Chimalapa, Río Grande, Santa Efigenia, Villa Alta); Puebla (Hacienda Atlixco); Yucatán (Yualahau, Yak-Jonat); Chiapas (Tonalá); and Campeche (La Tuxpena) to Guatemala (Naranjo, Vera Paz, Retalhuleu, Santo Tomás, Sabana Grande, Volcán de Fuego, Medio Monte, Raxché, Los Amates, Finca Sepacuite, and Sacchich, Petén), and Honduras (Lancetilla Valley).

Type locality.—Mexico.

Penelope cristata (not *Meleagris cristata* Linnaeus) BONNATERRE, Tabl. Encycl. Méth., i, 1791, 171, pl. 84, fig. 2.—LANTZ, Trans. Kansas Acad. Sci. for 1896–7 (1899), 219 (Naranjo and Santo Tomás, Guatemala).

P[enelope] purpurascens WAGLER, Isis, 1830, 1110 (Mexico; coll. Monaco Mus.).— GRAY, Proc. Zool. Soc. London, 1860, 269 (Mexico; monogr.).—REICHENBACH, Voll. Nat. Tauben, 1861, 149.—REICHENOW, Die Vögel, i, 1913, 276.

Penelope purpurascens MOORE, Proc. Zool. Soc. London, 1859, 61 (Honduras).— SCLATER and SALVIN, Ibis, 1859, 223 (Guatemala); Proc. Zool. Soc. London, 1870, 522, 543 (monogr.).—SCLATER, Proc. Zool. Soc. London, 1859, 368 (Jalapa, Veracruz), 391 (Río Grande, Oaxaca, s. Mexico).—SALLÉ and PARZUDAKI, Cat. Oiseaux Mexique, 1862, 6 (Mexico).—GRAY, List Birds Brit. Mus., pt. 5, Gallinae, 1867, 6 (Guatemala).—SUMICHRAST, Mem. Boston Soc. Nat. Hist., i, 1869, 560 (tierra caliente of Veracruz).—LAWRENCE, Mem. Boston Soc. Nat. Hist., ii, 1874, 306 (Mazatlán, Sinaloa; Tonila, Jalisco); U. S. Nat. Mus. Bull.

[22] Taken from a specimen in an early stage of the postnatal molt; rest of down already replaced.

[23] Eight specimens from Mexico.

[24] Six specimens from Mexico.

4, 1876, 45 (Santa Efigenia, Oaxaca; fresh colors of nude parts).—Boucard, Proc. Zool. Soc. London, 1883, 459 (Yak-Jonat, Yucatán; habits).—Ferrari-Perez, Proc. U. S. Nat. Mus., ix, 1886, 175 (Jalapa, Veracruz).—Ogilvie-Grant, Cat. Birds Brit. Mus., xxii, 1893, 496 (Sierra Madre above Ciudad Victoria, Tamaulipas; Santa Ana near Jalapa, Veracruz; Hacienda Atlixco, Puebla; Villa Alta and Chimalapa, Oaxaca; Yalahan, n. Yucatán; Vera Paz, Retalhuleu, Sabana Grande, Volcán de Fuego, and Medio Monte, Guatemala).— Beristain and Laurencio, Mem. y Rev. Soc. Cient. "Antonio Alzate," vii, 1894, 220 (Mexico; along both coasts).—Salvin and Godman, Biol. Centr.-Amer., Aves, iii, 1902, 276 (Mazatlán, Sinaloa; Sierra Madre, Tamaulipas; Jalapa and Santa Ana, Veracruz, Hacienda Atlixco, Puebla; Río Grande, Villa Alta, Chimalapa, and Santa Efigenia, Oaxaca; Tonalá, Chiapas; Yak-Jonat, n. Yucatán; Retalhuleu, Raxché, Vera Paz, Sabana Grande, Volcán de Fuego, and Medio Monte, Guatemala; Honduras).—Miller, Bull. Amer. Mus. Nat. Hist., xxi, 1905, 343 (Escuinapa, etc., s. Sinaloa; fresh colors of nude parts).—Dearborn, Publ. Field Mus. Nat. Hist., No. 125, 1907, 77 (Los Amates, Guatemala).— Phillips, Auk, xxviii, 1911, 74 (Guiaves, Tamaulipas).—Peters, Bull. Mus. Comp. Zool., lxix, 1929, 403 (eastern border, Lancetilla Valley, Honduras).— Stone, Proc. Acad. Nat. Sci. Philadelphia, lxxxiv, 1932, 301 (Honduras; Lancetilla).

[Penelope] purpurascens Gray, Hand-list, ii, 1870, 250, No. 9474.—Sclater and Salvin, Nom. Av. Neotr., 1873, 136.—Sharpe, Hand-list, i, 1899, 16.

Penelope purpurasceus Cubas, Cuadro Geogr., Estadístico, Descr. e Hist. de los Estados Unidos Mexicanos, 1884, 168 (Mexico; common names).

Penelope purpurascens purpurascens Griscom, Bull. Amer. Mus. Nat. Hist., lxiv, 1932, 100 (distr. in Guatemala; tropical forests on both slopes; spec. Finca Sepacuite).—Peters, Check-list Birds of World, ii, 1934, 12.—van Tyne, Misc. Publ. Mus. Zool. Univ. Michigan No. 27, 1935, 10 (Uaxactún and Sacchich, Petén, Guatemala; spec.; downy young).—Griscom, Auk, liv, 1937, 192 (Omilteme, Guerrero; spec.).—Sutton and Burleigh, Occ. Pap. Mus. Zool. Louisiana State Univ., No. 3, 1939, 28 (northeastern Mexico; Gómez Farias, Tamaulipas; spec.).—Traylor, Publ. Field Mus. Nat. Hist., zool. ser., xxiv, 1941, 204 (Matamoros and Pacaitun, Yucatán).—Hellmayr and Conover, Cat. Birds Amer., i, No. 1, 1942, 134 (syn.; distr.).—del Campo, Anal. Inst. Biol., xiii, No. 2, 1942, 700 (Chiapas; Paval, Catarinas; spec.).—Brodkorb, Misc. Publ. Mus. Zool. Univ. Michigan, No. 56, 1943, 30 (Mexico; Tabasco and Chiapas; plum.; crit.).

P[enelope] purpurascens purpurascens Hellmayr and Conover, Auk, xliv, 1932, 331 (crit.; range).

S[alpiza] purpurascens Wagler, Isis, 1832, 1226.

PENELOPE PURPURASCENS AEQUATORIALIS Salvadori and Festa

Southern Crested Guan

Adult (sexes alike).—Similar to the adult of the nominate form but with the abdomen, thighs, flanks, under tail coverts, back, rump, and upper tail coverts more reddish-tawny russet to dark hazel; the median pair of rectrices more coppery auburn; and the scapulars, interscapulars, and upper wing coverts with no, or only few, white lateral edges; "iris carmine; naked skin of throat dull carmine; scutellae of tarsus and feet coral red." (Ex Richmond, Proc. U. S. Nat. Mus., xvi, 1893, 523.)

Juvenal (sexes alike).—Similar to the adult but with the rectrices, remiges, and upper wing coverts washed with rufescent and mottled with dusky, especially on the edges of the webs in the rectrices and remiges.

Natal down.—Apparently unknown.

Adult male.—Wing 349–380 (363.9) ; tail 341–375 (360.6) ; culmen from base 31–37 (34.5) ; tarsus 85–95 (90.4) ; middle toe without claw 62–69 (65.1 mm.).[25]

Adult female.—Wing 338–378 (353.4) ; tail 346–384 (357.1) ; culmen from base 30–36 (32.6) ; tarsus 84–88 (86.6) ; middle toe without claw 58–65 (61.8 mm.).[26]

Range.—Resident in tropical forests from Nicaragua (Los Sábalos, Río Escondido, Río San Juan, San Carlos) ; Costa Rica (Bonilla, Barranca, La Palma de Nicoya, Volcán de Miravalles, Volcán de Irazú, Jiménez, Naranjo de Cartago, La Palma de San José, Angostura, Pozo Azul de Pirrís, El Pozo de Terraba) ; and Panama (Lion Hill, Davilla, Boquete, Chiriquí, Jesusito, Barro Colorado, Guabo, Ranchon) to western Colombia (Remedios, Antioquia, "Bogotá," La Canela, Río Frío, and Santa Marta; Bonda, Las Tinajao, Don Diego, Minca) ; and western Ecuador (Chimbo, Gualea, Naranjo, Balzar Mountains, Foreste del Río Peripa, Paramba, below Mindo, above Bucay, El Chiral).

Type locality.—Foreste del Río Peripa, western Ecuador.

[*Meleagris*] *cristata* LINNAEUS, Syst. Nat., ed. 10, i, 1758, 157, part ("America australi"; based on *The Quan* or *Guan* Edwards, Nat. Hist. Birds, i, 13, pl. 13; *Jacupema* Marcgrave, Bras., 198; *Coxolitli* Hernández, Mex. . . . ; *Phasianus brasiliensis* Ray, Av., 56) ; ed. 12, i, 1766, 269.

Meleagris cristata MÜLLER, Syst. Nat. Suppl., 1776, 122.

[*Penelope*] *cristata* GMELIN, Syst. Nat., i, pt. 2, 1788, 733.—LATHAM, Index Orn., ii, 1790, 619 ("Brazil"; "Guiana").—REICHENBACH, Synop. Av., Columb., ii, 1837, pl. 171, figs. 1501, 1502.—SCLATER and SALVIN, Proc. Zool. Soc. London, 1870, 543; Nom. Av. Neotr., 1873, 136.—SHARPE, Hand-list, i, 1899, 16 (Nicaragua and Ecuador).

Penelope cristata TEMMINCK, Pig. et Gallin., iii, 1815, 46, 691.—STEPHENS, *in* Shaw, Gen. Zool., xi, pt. i, 1819, 178 ("Brazil").—VIEILLOT, Nouv. Dict. Hist. Nat., xxxvi, 1819, 337.—BENNETT, Gard. and Menag., ii, 1831, 131.—LESSON, Traité d'Orn., 1831, 481.—JARDINE, Contr. Orn., 1848, 27, pl. (anatomy, etc.).—BURMEISTER, Syst. Übers. Th. Bras., iii, 1856, 339.—GRAY, Proc. Zool. Soc. London, 1860, 269 ("West Indies?"; monogr.).—HUXLEY, Proc. Zool. Soc. London, 1868, 298, fig. of pelvis (osteology).—SCLATER and SALVIN, Proc. Zool. Soc. London, 1870, 525 (monogr.) ; 1879, 544 (Remedios, Antioquia, Colombia).—NUTTING, Proc. U. S. Nat. Mus., v, 1882, 409 (La Palma de Nicoya, Costa Rica; habits) ; vi, 1884, 408 (Los Sábalos, Nicaragua; fresh colors of unfeathered parts).—BERLEPSCH and TACZANOWSKI, Proc. Zool. Soc. London, 1883, 576 (Chimbo, w. Ecuador; fresh color of nude parts).—ZELEDÓN, Anal. Mus. Nac. Costa Rica, i, 1887, 128 (Jiménez and Naranjo de Cartago, Costa Rica).—OGILVIE-GRANT, Cat. Birds Brit. Mus., xxii, 1893, 498 (Valza and La

---

[25] Ten specimens from Costa Rica and Panama.

[26] Eight specimens from Costa Rica and Panama.

Palma de San José, Costa Rica; Lion Hill, Panama; Bogotá, Colombia; Balzar Mountains, w. Ecuador) ; Handb. Game Birds, ii, 1897, 226, part (Nicaragua to Panama and Ecuador).—RICHMOND, Proc. U. S. Nat. Mus., xvi, 1893, 523 (Río Escondido, Nicaragua; fresh colors of nude parts).—UNDERWOOD, Ibis, 1896, 448 (Volcán de Miravalles, Costa Rica; food).—HARTERT, Nov. Zool., v, 1898, 504 (Paramba, nw. Ecuador, 3,500 feet.; crit.).—SALVADORI and FESTA, Boll. Mus. Zool. Torino, xiv, No. 399, 1899, 10 (Laguna della Pita, Río Lara, and Río Cianati, Darién, Panama).—ALLEN, Bull. Amer. Mus. Nat. Hist., xiii, 1900, 126 (Bonda, Santa Marta, Colombia).—BANGS, Auk, xviii, 1901, 356 (Divalá, Chiriquí, Panama) ; Proc. New England Zool. Club, iii, 1902, 21 (Boquete, etc., Chiriquí, w. Panama, 4,000–7,000 feet) ; Auk, xxiv, 1907, 291 (El Pozo de Térraba, Costa Rica).—SALVIN and GODMAN, Biol. Centr.-Amer., Aves, iii, 1902, 277 (Los Sábalos, Río San Juan, Río Escondido, and San Carlos, Nicaragua; Valza, Barranca, Angostura, La Palma de San José, La Palma de Nicoya, Jiménez, Naranjo de Cartago, Volcán de Irazú, and Volcán de Miravalles, Costa Rica; Divalá and Lion Hill, Panama; Colombia; Ecuador).— CARRIKER, Ann. Carnegie Mus., vi, 1910, 382 (Bonilla, Pozo Azul de Pirrís, Río Síesola, Miravalles, and El Pozo de Térraba, Costa Rica; crit.; habits).— CHAPMAN, Bull. Amer. Mus. Nat. Hist., xxxvi, 1917, 195 (Chocó and La Canela, nw. Colombia; Gualea and Naranjo, Ecuador; Chiriquí and Panama Railway, Panama; crit.).—STONE, Proc. Acad. Nat. Sci. Philadelphia, 1918, 242 (Panama Canal Zone).—RENDAHL, Ark. Zool., xii, 1919, 10 (Volcán Ometepe, Nicaragua).—BANGS and BARBOUR, Bull. Mus. Comp. Zool., lxv, 1922, 195 (Jesusito, Darién).

P[enelope] cristata WAGLER, Isis, 1830, 1110 ("Guiana"; "Brasilia").—(?) TSCHUDI, Archiv für Naturg., x, pt. i, 1844, 308 (Peru).—REICHENBACH, Voll. Nat. Tauben, 1861, 148.—REICHENOW, Die Vögel, i, 1913, 276.

Penelope cristata cristata STURGIS, Field Book Birds Panama Canal Zone, 1928, 27 (Canal Zone).—KENNARD and PETERS, Proc. Boston Soc. Nat. Hist., xxxviii, 1928, 446 (Boquete Trail, Panama; spec.).—HEATH, Ibis, 1931, 468 (Barro Colorado Island, Panama).—PETERS, Bull. Mus. Comp. Zool., lxxi, 1931, 297 (Guabo, Panama).—CAUM, Occ. Pap. Bishop Mus., x, No. 9, 1933, 12 (Hawaii; introduced in 1928; not known to breed).

S[alpiza] cristata WAGLER, Isis, 1932, 1226.

Salpiza cristata GRAY, List Birds Brit. Mus., pt. 3, Gallinae, 1844, 19.

Penelope brasiliensis BONAPARTE, Compt. Rend., xlii, 1856, 877.

Penelope jacucaca (not of Spix) SCLATER, Proc. Zool. Soc. London, 1860, 72 (Pallatanga, Ecuador).

Penelope jacuaca (not P. jacuacu Spix) GRAY, List Birds Brit. Mus., pt. 5, Gallinae, 1867, 6.—SALVIN, Ibis, 1869, 317 (Costa Rica; Panama).

Penelope purpurascens (not of Wagler, 1832) LAWRENCE, Ann. Lyc. Nat. Hist. New York, viii, 1863, 12 (Panama) ; ix, 1868, 139 (Barranca, Angostura, and La Palma de San José, Costa Rica).—SALVIN, Ibis, 1869, 317 (Costa Rica and Panama; crit.)—FRANTZIUS, Journ. für Orn., 1869, 372 (Costa Rica).— BOUCARD, Proc. Zool. Soc. London, 1878, 42 (Volcán de Irazú and San Carlos, Costa Rica).

Penelope aequatorialis SALVADORI and FESTA, Boll. Mus. Zool. Torino, xv, No. 368, Feb. 19, 1900, 38 (Foreste del Río Peripa, w. Ecuador; coll. Turin Mus.).— TODD and CARRIKER, Ann. Carnegie Mus., xiv, 1922, 174 (Las Tinajao, Bonda, Don Diego, and Minca, Santa Marta, Colombia; crit.).—DARLINGTON, Bull. Mus. Comp. Zool., lxxi, 1931, 371 (Río Frío foothills, Magdalena, Colombia; habits).

Penelope æquatorialis CHUBB, Ibis, 1919, 16, part (Colombia; Ecuador; crit.).—
LONNBERG and RENDAHL, Ark. Zool., xiv, 1922, 15 (Gualea and Nanegal,
Ecuador).—CHAPMAN, Bull. Amer. Mus. Nat. Hist., lv, 1926, 153 (trop. zone
w. Ecuador; Gualea; below Mindo; above Bucay; El Chiral).

[*Penelope*] *aequatorialis* BRABOURNE and CHUBB, Birds South Amer., i, 1912, 10
(Colombia; Ecuador).

Penelope purpurascens aequatorialis GRISCOM, Bull. Mus. Comp. Zool., lxxii, 1932,
318 (Ranchon, Panama) ; lxxviii, 1935, 303 (Costa Rica to western Ecuador).—
PETERS, Check-list Birds of World, ii, 1934, 13.—ALDRICH, Sci. Publ. Cleveland Mus. Nat. Hist., vii, 1937, 53 (Azuero Peninsula, Panama; spec.).—
SASSI, Temminckia, iii, 1938, 304 (Bebedero, Costa Rica; spec.).—HELLMAYR
and CONOVER, Cat. Birds Amer., i, No. 1, 1942, 135 (syn.; distr.).

P[enelope] purpurascens aequatorialis HELLMAYR and CONOVER, Auk, xlix, 1932,
331 (crit.; distr.).

P[enelope] p[urpurascens] aequatorialis VAN TYNE, Misc. Publ. Mus. Zool. Univ.
Michigan, No. 27, 1935, 10, in text (Panama; Canal Zone).

Genus ORTALIS Merrem

Ortalis MERREM, Av. Rar. Icon. et Descr., fasc. 2, 1786, 40. (Type, as designated
by Lesson, 1829, *Phasianus motmot* Linnaeus.)

Ortalida "Merr[em]" WAGLER, Isis, 1832, 1226.

Ortalidia (emendation) FLEMING, Philos.-Zool., ii, 1822, 230.

Penelops "Plin." REICHENBACH, Av. Syst. Nat. Vög., 1853, xxvi. (Type, by
monotypy, *Penelope albiventris* "Gould" = Lesson = *P. leucogastra* Gould.)

Penelopsis (emendation) BONAPARTE, Compt. Rend., xlii, May 1856, 877.

Penelopides VAN ROSSEM, Condor, xliv, 1942, 77. (Type, by original designation,
Ortalida wagleri (Gray).)

Small, plainly colored Cracidae (length about 412–649 mm.), with sides
of gular area nude, divided longitudinally by a narrow feathered area on
median strip.

Bill relatively small (from frontal feathers less than half as long as
head), broader than deep at base of exposed culmen; culmen rather
strongly decurved terminally, not ridged; nostril longitudinal, narrowly
elliptical to rather broadly fusiform, anteriorly nearly in contact with base
of rhinotheca, a membranous or cartilaginous piece showing within the
basal portion; cere straight, slightly ascending basally, and, together with
greater part of loral and orbital regions and sides of gular region, nude.
Wing rather large, very broad and rounded, the longer primaries with
tips extending decidedly beyond those of longest secondaries (except in
O. wagleri) ; fourth to sixth primaries longest, the first (outermost)
about one-half (in *O. v. leucogastra*) to nearly three-fifths (in *O. wagleri*)
as long as the longest and strongly bowed or incurved. Tail longer than
wing (very slightly as in *O. v. leucogastra*), strongly rounded, the rectrices (12) relatively broad to very broad, with rounded tips. Tarsus
relatively long and stout, less than one-third as long as wing, the acrotarsium with a single series of large transverse scutella, the planta tarsi
with a series of smaller transverse scutella along each side (these less
distinct, especially on inner side, in *O. v. leucogastra*) ; middle toe nearly

to quite three-fourths as long as tarsus, the lateral toes reaching about to penultimate articulation of middle toe, the outer usually a little longer than the inner; hallux about as long as combined length of first two phalanges of outer toe; claws moderately large to rather small, moderately curved (that of hallux more strongly curved) compressed.

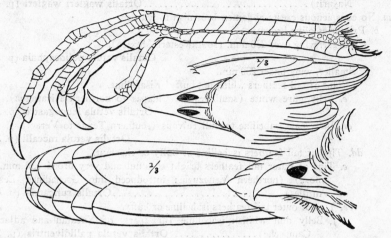

FIGURE 3.—*Ortalis vetula.*

Plumage and coloration.—Frontal feathers erect or suberect, more or less elongated (very much so in *O. wagleri*), rigid and lanceolate or sub-lanceolate, those of crown and occiput more or less elongated (very much so in *O. wagleri;* very slightly so in *O. v. leucogastra*) but broader and with rounded tips; feathers of neck variable, in *O. wagleri* rather long and blended on hindneck, rigid and acuminate-lanceolate on foreneck, malar region, and median line of throat, on *O. v. leucogastra* short and rounded, even on foreneck; plumage in general soft, the feathers distinctly outlined, with broadly rounded tips (more blended on underparts) that of anal region soft and downy; loral and orbital regions mostly nude, the sides of chin and throat also nude, separated by a narrow strip of feathers, these small and bristlelike in *O. v. leucogastra,* much broader and lanceolate in *O. wagleri.* Coloration plain brownish above, paler beneath, the abdomen, thighs, and under tail coverts sometimes whitish, sometimes deep cinnamon-rufous or chestnut; rectrices usually tipped with pale brown, whitish or chestnut, sometimes mostly chestnut, and outer primaries sometimes chestnut.

Range.—Southern Texas (Rio Grande Valley) to Paraguay, Argentina, and Peru. (About 13 species and 30 subspecies.)

KEY TO THE NORTH AND MIDDLE AMERICAN FORMS
OF THE GENUS ORTALIS

a. With a conspicuous crest on head; abdomen chestnut-rufous.
  b. Top of head pale slate-gray (southern Chihuahua to northern Sinaloa).
                       Ortalis wagleri griseiceps (p. 49)
  bb. Top of head dark slate (central and eastern Sinaloa to Durango, Jalisco, and
     Nayarit)..............................**Ortalis wagleri wagleri** (p. 47)
aa. No conspicuous crest; abdomen brownish to whitish.
  b. Primaries olive-brown.
    c. Larger, wing over 230 mm. (southwestern Mexico).
                       Ortalis vetula poliocephala (p. 35)
    cc. Smaller, wing under 230 mm.
      d. Tips of tail feathers white, not buffy or isabelline.
        e. Belly pure white (southwestern Chiapas to northern Nicaragua).
                   Ortalis vetula leucogastra (p. 37)
        ee. Belly pale isabelline to dull fulvous (southern Texas to Veracruz).
                   Ortalis vetula mccalli (p. 31)
      dd. Tips of tail feathers isabelline or buffy or chestnut.
        e. Tips of outer tail feathers bright chestnut and very broad (30 mm. or
          more) (northern Venezuela; introduced into Grenadines, Lesser
          Antilles) ....**Ortalis ruficauda** (p. 46)
        ee. Tips of outer tail feathers isabelline or buffy.
          f. Belly dull whitish isabelline (dry parts of Yucatán and adjacent
          Campeche)................**Ortalis vetula pallidiventris** (p. 38)
         ff. Belly darker—isabelline to dull fulvous.
          g. Tips of tail feathers dull buffy brown.
            h. Tips of tail feathers noticeably bicolored, distinctly rufescent
           proximally (humid coastal forests from southern British
           Honduras to eastern Guatemala and northwestern Honduras).
                   Ortalis vetula plumbiceps (p. 40)
           hh. Tips of tail feathers not noticeably bicolored.
             i. Feathers of upper throat decidedly blackish (Utila Island,
             Honduras).............**Ortalis vetula deschauenseei** (p. 42)
             ii. Feathers of upper throat not decidedly blackish (southeastern
             Mexico)......................**Ortalis vetula vetula** (p. 34)
         gg. Tips of tail feathers light grayish isabelline.
          h. Larger; wing averaging 210 mm. (male), 195 mm. (female)
          (Grand Valley of Interior of Chiapas).
                    Ortalis vetula vallicola (p. 40)
        hh. Smaller; wing averaging 193 (male); 185 mm. (female)
         (Quintana Roo and Petén)..**Ortalis vetula intermedia** (p. 39)
  bb. Primaries chestnut.
    c. Head and neck rusty brownish....**Ortalis garrula garrula** (extralimital)[27]

---

[27] **Ortalis garrula garrula** (Humboldt).—*Phasianus garrulus* Humboldt, Obs. de
Zool., i, 1811, 4 (Río Magdalena, Colombia; Caracas, Venezuela).—*P*[*enelope*]
garrula Wagler, Isis, 1830, 1111 (Cartagena, "Mexico", i.e., Colombia).—*O*[*rtalida*]
garrula Wagler, Isis, 1832, 1227; Reichenbach, Voll. Nat. Tauben, 1861, 144.—
Ortalida garrula Gray, List Birds Brit. Mus., iii, Gallinae, 1844, 20; ed. 1867, 12;
Sclater and Salvin, Proc. Zool. Soc. London, 1870, 539 (monogr.).—[*Ortalida*]
garrula Reichenbach, Synop. Av., Columb., ii, 1847, pl. 169, fig. 1491; Gray, Hand-
list, ii, 1870, 252, No. 9506; Sclater and Salvin, Nom. Av. Neotr., 1873, 137.—
Ortalis garrula Ogilvie-Grant, Cat. Birds Brit. Mus., xxii, 1893, 515 (Cartagena

    cc. Head and neck slate-gray.
        d. Abdomen white, the under tail coverts pale brownish gray (Caribbean
            slope of Darién) ....**Ortalis garrula mira** (p. 45)
        dd. Abdomen pale fulvescent.
           e. Tail shorter, usually under 230 mm. (eastern Nicaragua to Panama).
                              Ortalis garrula cinereiceps (p. 42)
           ee. Tail longer, over 230 mm. (Montijo Bay, Veraguas).
                              Ortalis garrula olivacea (p. 45)

ORTALIS VETULA MCCALLI (Baird)

NORTHERN CHACHALACA

Adult (sexes alike).—Forehead, crown, and occiput dull brownish chaetura black, the individual feathers somewhat paler, more grayish, medially; hindneck, scapulars, interscapulars, upper wing coverts, secondaries, back, rump, and upper tail coverts deep olive to dark greenish olive, the hindneck and interscapulars averaging slightly more brownish olive; primaries olive-brown, externally edged with deep olive; rectrices dark greenish olive with an oil-green sheen, the median pair indistinctly tipped with pale, ashy buffy brown, the other pairs with white tips about 15–20 mm. wide, the white tips joined to the greenish part of the feather by a narrow, grayish-brown band; lores and sides of head largely nude but lower cheeks with some black hairlike feathers; auriculars and sides of upper throat, center and sides of lower throat, and the upper breast deep olive, each feather with an indistinctly defined median streak of dark olive-buff; a wide band of black hairlike feathers extending from chin along the middle of the upper throat; sides of upper throat bare; lower breast paler and washed with fulvescent; abdomen, sides, and flanks pale fulvous, palest on the middle abdomen; the thighs, lower abdomen, and under tail coverts darker—isabelline buffy brown; bare areas on upper throat grayish flesh color, alike in both sexes except in spring when the male has these patches red; iris light brown; bill, tarsi, and toes light horn bluish.

Juvenal (sexes alike).—In a general way similar to the adult but the hindneck, scapulars, interscapulars, upper wing coverts, secondaries, back, rump, and upper tail coverts Saccardo's umber instead of deep olive, the center of the back and rump indistinctly barred with ashy buckthorn brown[28]; remiges also Saccardo's umber, faintly tipped and mottled

---

and Santa Marta, Colombia); Todd and Carriker, Ann. Carnegie Mus., xiv, 1922, 171 (Donjaca, Mamatoco, Fundación, and Trojas de Cataca, Santa Marta, Colombia; crit.).—*Ortalis garrula garrula* Peters, Check-list Birds World, ii, 1934, 20; Hellmayr and Conover, Cat. Birds Amer., i, No. 1, 1942, 178.

[28] According to Bent, U. S. Nat. Mus. Bull. 162, 1932, 350, the upper wing coverts are barred with cinnamon-buff in this plumage. This appears to be a variable character, as I have not found it in all the juvenal birds examined in the present connection.

on the outer edge with cinnamon-buff; rectrices as in adult but all tipped with ashy buffy brown and pointed in shape; auriculars, sides and lower parts of the neck, and the breast dark isabelline buffy brown; rest of under-parts as in adult but more washed with cinnamon-buff.

Downy young.—Forehead, crown, cheeks, and auriculars pale pinkish buff barred narrowly with dull sepia, the light interspaces much wider than the bars, the crown, cheeks, and auriculars tinged with light buffy cinnamon, and the coronal bars more or less confluent along the median line forming a dark irregular spot; occiput and hindneck fuscous washed with sepia, the sides of neck and posterior part of hindneck cinnamon-buff irregularly and incompletely barred with fuscous to dark sepia; back, wings, rump, and upper tail coverts sepia mottled, chiefly transversely, with cinnamon-buff, the wings sepia edged with tawny cinnamon-buff; chin and middle upper throat and all of abdomen, sides, and flanks white; the breast forming a broad band of cinnamon-buff between these white areas; thighs and vent washed with pale cinnamon-buff transversely narrowly mottled with sepia.

In some specimens the pinkish buff of the top and sides of the head is replaced by pallid neutral gray, and all the brownish parts are slightly washed with ashy.

Adult male.—Wing 197–219 (208.2); tail 222–255 (239); exposed culmen 22–27 (25); tarsus 55–63 (60); middle toe without claw 44–51 (47.4 mm.).[29]

Adult female.—Wing 185–212 (196.6); tail 205–264 (225); exposed culmen 19–26 (22.6); tarsus 49–63 (56.7); middle toe without claw 42–49 (44.4 mm.).[30]

Range.—Resident in the chaparral areas from Lower Rio Grande Valley in Texas (Ringgold Barracks, Lomita Ranch, Hidalgo, Brownsville, and Rio Grande City); south through Tamaulipas (Sierre Madre above Ciudad Victoria, Aldama, Matamoros, Jiménez, Xicoténcatl, and Río Pilon) to extreme northern Veracruz; and west to Nuevo León (Boquilla); and southeastern San Luis Potosí (Valles).

Type locality.—Boquilla, Nuevo León, Mexico.

(?) [*Penelope*] *vociferans* GMELIN, Syst. Nat., i, pt. 2, 1788, 735 (Mexico; based on Chacamel of Buffon and Crying Curassow of Latham).

(?) [*Crax*] *vociferans* LATHAM, Index Orn., ii, 1790, 625.

(?) *Crax vociferans* VIEILLOT, Nouv. Dict. Hist. Nat., vi, 1816, 3.

(?) *Penelope vociferans* BONNATERRE, Tabl. Encycl. Méth., 1791, 172.

(?) *Phasianus chacamel* MÜLLER, Syst. Nat. Suppl., 1776, 125 (new name for *Penelope vociferans* Gmelin).

Ortalida vetula LAWRENCE, Ann. Lyc. Nat. Hist. New York, v, 1851, 116 (Texas).— BAIRD, Rep. Stansbury's Expl. Great Salt Lake, 1852, 334 (Rio Grande, Tex.).—

---

[29] Seven specimens from Texas and Tamaulipas, Nuevo León, and northern Veracruz, Mexico.

[30] Ten specimens from Texas and Tamaulipas, Mexico.

McCown, Ann. Lyc. Nat. Hist. New York, vi, 1853, 10 (Rio Grande Valley up to Ringgold Barracks; etc.; habits).—Sallé and Parzudaki, Cat. Oiseaux Mexique, 1862, 6 (Mexico).—Sclater and Salvin, Proc. Zool. Soc. London, 1869, 364, part (crit.); 1870, 538, part (monogr.).—Coues, Check List North Amer. Birds, 1874, No. 378.—Beristain and Laurencio, Mem. y Rev. Soc. Cient. "Antonio Alzati," vii, 1894, 220 (Mexico; distr.).

O[rtalida] vetula Reichenbach, Voll. Nat. Tauben, 1861, 144, part.—Baird, Brewer, and Ridgway, Hist. North Amer. Birds, iii, 1874, 398, footnote, part.

[Ortalida] vetula Gray, Hand-list, ii, 1870, 252, No. 9502, part.

Ortalis vetula Sennett, U. S. Geol. and Geogr. Surv. Terr., Bull. 4, No. 1, 1878, 50 (Hidalgo, Texas; habits); 5, No. 3, 1879, 426 (Lomita Ranch, Tex.; habits; descr. nest and eggs).—Ogilvie-Grant, Cat. Birds Brit. Mus., xxii, 1893, 512, part (Brownsville, Tex.; Sierra Madre above Ciudad Victoria, Aldoma, and Tampico, Tamaulipas; Valles, San Luis Potosí).—Salvin and Godman, Biol. Centr.-Amer., Aves, iii, 1902, 280, part (s. Texas; Matamoros, Sierra Madre, and Tampico, Tamaulipas; Vallés, San Luis Potosí).

O[rtalis] vetula Mendizabal, Rev. Soc. Mex. Hist. Nat., i, No. 3, 1940, 180, in text (Mexico).

[Ortalis] vetula Sharpe, Hand-list, i, 1899, 17, part.

Ortalis vetula vetula American Ornithologists' Union, Check List North Amer. Birds, ed. 3, 1910, 146; ed. 4, 1931, 78.—Oberholser, Auk, xxxix, 1922, 247.— Bent, U. S. Nat. Mus. Bull. 162, 1932, 345 (life hist., descr., distr.).—Peters, Check-list Birds of World, ii, 1934, 19.—Cottam and Knappen, Auk, lvi, 1939, 152 (food).—Sutton and Burleigh, Occ. Pap. Mus. Zool. Louisiana State Univ., No. 3, 1939, 28 (Tamaulipas—Gómez Farias and Guemes); Wils. Bull., liii, 1940, 223 (Tamazunchale, San Luis Potosí); Condor, xlii, 1940, 259 (Vallés, San Luis Potosí).—Sutton and Pettingill, Auk, lix, 1942, 12 (Gómez Farias region, sw. Tamaulipas; abundance; habits).

Ortalis v[etula] vetula Groebbels, Der Vögel, ii, 1937, 165 (breeding biology).

Ortalida mccalli Baird, Rep. Pacific R.R. Surv., ix, 1858, 611 (Boquilla, Nuevo León, ne. Mexico; coll. U. S. Nat. Mus.); Rep. U. S. and Mex. Bound. Surv., ii, pt. 2, 1859, 1922 (Boquilla, Nuevo León; Rio Grande Valley up to Ringgold Barracks, Texas; habits); Cat. North Amer. Birds, 1859, No. 456.

O[rtalida] mccalli Reichenbach, Voll. Nat. Tauben, 1861, 145 (crit.).

Ortalida mc-calli Cubas, Cuadro Geogr., Estadístico, Descr. e Hist. de los Estados Unidos Mexicanos, 1884, 169 (common names, Mexico).

Ortalida maccalli Dresser, Ibis, 1866, 24 (s. Texas).—Baird, Brewer and Ridgway, Hist. North Amer. Birds, iii, 1874, pl. 37, fig. 1.

O[rtalida] maccalli Sclater and Salvin, Proc. Zool. Soc. London, 1870, 538, 539 (crit.).

Ortalida maccaulii Boucard, Cat. Avium, 1876, 13, No. 326 ("New Mexico").

Ortalida vetula, var. maccalli Baird, Brewer, and Ridgway, Hist. North Amer. Birds, iii, 1874, 398.—Merrill, Proc. U. S. Nat. Mus., i, 1878, 159 (Fort Brown, Tex.; habits; descr. nest and eggs).

Ortalida vetula maccalli Goode, U. S. Nat. Mus. Bull. 20, 1883, 332.

Ortalis vetula maccalli Ridgway, Proc. U. S. Nat. Mus., iii, 1880, 9, 195; Nom. North Amer. Birds, 1881, No. 469.—Coues, Check List North Amer. Birds, ed. 2, 1882, No. 552.—American Ornithologists' Union, Check-list, No. 311, 1886; ed. 2, 1895, No. 311.—Cooke, Bird Migr. Mississippi Valley, 1888, 108 (ne. Mexico; lower Rio Grande Valley).—Bendire, Life Hist. North Amer. Birds, i, 1892, 119, pl. 3, fig. 16.—Dury, Journ. Cincinnati Soc. Nat. Hist., xviii, 1896, 201, figs. (habits in captivity; structure of trachea).—Bailey, Handb. Birds Western United States, 1902, 137 (descr.; distr.).—Bent, Wils. Bull., xxxvi,

1924, 12 (Brownsville, Tex.).—GRISCOM and CROSBY, Auk, xlii, 1925, 533 (Brownsville, Tex.).—FRIEDMANN, Auk, xlii, 1925, 543 (Lower Rio Grande Valley, Tex.).

O[*rtalis*] *vetula maccalli* COUES, Key North Amer. Birds, ed. 2, 1884, 573.—RIDGWAY, Man. North Amer. Birds, 1887, 209.

Ortalis vetula mccalli AMERICAN ORNITHOLOGISTS' UNION, Check-list, ed. 3, 1910, 146.—PEARSON, Auk, xxxviii, 1921, 518 (near Brownsville, Tex.; coll. notes; habits).—HELLMAYR and CONOVER, Cat. Birds Amer., i, No. 1, 1942, 169 (syn.; distr.).

Ortalis mccalli PETRIDES, Trans. 7th North Amer. Wildlife Conf., 1942, 310, footnote (age indicators—plumage; Brownsville, Tex.).

[*Ortalis*] *maccalli* SHARPE, Hand-list, i, 1899, 17.

Penelope poliocephala (not of Wagler) BAIRD, Rep. Stansbury's Expl. Great Salt Lake, 1852, 334 (Matamoros, Tamaulipas; Rio Grande, Tex.).

Ortalida poliocephala CASSIN, Illustr. Birds California, Texas, etc., 1855, 267, pl. 44 (Texas).

ORTALIS VETULA VETULA (Wagler)

OAXACA CHACHALACA

Adult (sexes alike).—Similar to *Ortalis vetula mccalli* but smaller, the tips of the tail feathers not white, but isabelline buffy, the throat slightly more fulvous, less olive, the upperparts, in worn specimens, more brownish, less olive-green than in *mccalli*.

Juvenal.—None seen.

Downy young.—Similar to the corresponding buffy (not grayish) stage of *mccalli*, but much more rufescent, the brownish parts replaced by chestnut to buffy chestnut.

Adult male.—Wing 177–202 (192.8); tail 197–225 (214.3); exposed culmen 24–28 (25.9); tarsus 58–65 (62); middle toe without claw 42–51 (47.5 mm.).[31]

Adult female.—Wing 181–195 (186.6); tail 208–227 (215.6); exposed culmen 22–25 (23.4); tarsus 54–60 (56.6); middle toe without claw 43–47 (45.2 mm.).[32]

Range.—Resident from southeastern Mexico, excluding Yucatán Peninsula (central Veracruz—Jalapa, Acayucan, Playa Vicente, Cueste de Misantla, Plan del Río, Vega de Casadero, and La Antigua; eastern Oaxaca —Chimalapa, Guichicovi, Tolosa, and Tuxtepec; Puebla—Haciende de los Atlixcos and San José Acetano; southern Campeche; Tabasco—Montecristo; western and southern Chiapas (Tecpatan, Mapastepec); to British Honduras (Cayo District) and the Caribbean slope, but not the coastal belt itself, of Guatemala (Sepacuita, Secanquim, and Finca Chama).

Type locality.—Veracruz, Veracruz, Mexico.

P[*enelope*] *vetula* WAGLER, Isis, 1830, 1112 (Mexico; coll. Monaco Mus.).

Penelope vetula VAN ROSSEM, Trans. San Diego Soc. Nat. Hist., vii, 1934, 349 (type spec.; crit.).

---

[31] Eight specimens from Oaxaca, Tabasco, and southern Veracruz.
[32] Five specimens from Oaxaca and Campeche.

Ortalida vetula GRAY, List Birds Brit. Mus., pt. 3, Gallinae, 1844, 20 (Mexico);
ed. 2, 1867, ii (Mexico).—SCLATER, Proc. Zool. Soc. London, 1859, 391 (ne.
Oaxaca); 1869, 391 (Playa Vicente, Veracruz; crit.).—SUMICHRAST, Mem.
Boston Soc. Nat. Hist., i, 1869, 560 (hot region of Veracruz); La Naturaleza,
ser. 1, v, 1882, 229, part (Chimalapa, Oaxaca).—SCLATER and SALVIN, Proc.
Zool. Soc. London, 1869, 364, part (crit.); 1870, 538, part (monogr.).—LAW-
RENCE, U. S. Nat. Mus. Bull. 4, 1876, 45 (Guichicovi, Oaxaca).
O[*rtalida*] *vetula* WAGLER, Isis, 1832, 1227 (*O. betula* in Willughby Society re-
print).—REICHENBACH, Voll. Nat. Tauben, 1861, 144, part.—BAIRD, BREWER,
and RIDGWAY, Hist. North Amer. Birds, iii, 1874, 398, footnote, part.
[*Ortalida*] *vetula* GRAY, Hand-list, ii, 1870, 252, No. 9502, part.—SCLATER and SALVIN,
Proc. Zool. Soc. London, 1870, 543, part; Nom. Av. Neotr., 1873, 137, part.
Ortalis vetula OGILVIE-GRANT, Cat. Birds Brit. Mus., xxii, 1893, 512, part (Veracruz,
Cuesta de Misantla, Plan del Río, Vega de Casadero, and La Antigua, Veracruz;
Hacienda de los Atlixcos, Puebla); Handb. Game Birds, ii, 1897, 245, part.—
SALVIN and GODMAN, Biol. Centr.-Amer., Aves, iii, 1902, 280, part (Guichicovi,
Oaxaca; San José Acateno, Vega de Casadero, and La Antigua, Playa Vicente,
Córdoba, and Uvero, Veracruz; Hacienda de los Atlixcos, Puebla).
O[*rtalis*] *vetula* REICHENOW, Die Vögel, i, 1913, 277.
Ortalis vetula vetula MILLER and GRISCOM, Auk, xxxviii, 1921, 46 (type locality
designated, erroneously, as Tampico, Tamaulipas; crit.).—GRISCOM, Ibis, 1935,
810 (Sierra de las Minas, eastern Guatemala; spec.).—HELLMAYR and CONOVER,
Cat Birds Amer., i, No. 1, 1942, 170 (syn.; distr.).
Ortalis v[*etula*] *vetula* MILLER and GRISCOM, Auk, xxxviii, 1921, 455 (corr. type
loc., Veracruz).
Ortalis vetula jalapensis MILLER and GRISCOM, Auk, xxxviii, 1921, 46 (Jalapa, Veracruz, e. Mexico; coll. Amer. Mus. N. H.).—AUSTIN, Bull. Mus. Comp. Zool.,
lxix, 1929, 370 (Cayo District, Mountain Cow Water Hole, British Honduras).—
GRISCOM, Bull. Amer. Mus. Nat. Hist., lxiv, 1932, 101 (distr. in Guatemala;
spec. from Sepacuite, Secanquim, and Finca Chama, all in the Caribbean forest,
50 to 60 miles east of Cobán, 1,800 to 3,500 feet altitude).—PETERS, Check-list
Birds of World, ii, 1934, 19.—DEL CAMPO, Anal. Inst. Biol., xiii, No. 2, 1942,
700 (Chiapas; Tecpatan and Mapastepec; spec.).—BRODKORB, Misc. Publ. Mus.
Zool. Univ. Michigan, No. 56, 1943, 30 (Veracruz; Tabasco; spec.).
Ortalis vetula fulvicauda MILLER and GRISCOM, Auk, xxxviii, 1921, 47 (Tolosa,
Oaxaca; coll. Amer. Mus. N. H.).
Ortalis vetula maccalli (not of Baird) FERRARI-PEREZ, Proc. U. S. Nat. Mus., ix,
1886, 176 (San José Acetano, Puebla).—CHAPMAN, Bull. Amer. Mus. Nat.
Hist., x, 1898, 36 (Jalapa, Veracruz).
Ortalida mc-calli ROVIROSA, La Naturaleza, vii, 1887, 380 (Tabasco; Río Macuspana).
Ortalida poliocephala SCLATER, Proc. Zool. Soc. London, 1856, 310 (Córdoba, Vera-
cruz).
[*Ortalis*] [*vetula*] *jalapensis* VAN TYNE, Misc. Publ. Mus. Zool. Univ. Michigan,
No. 27, 1935, ii (Guatemala).

ORTALIS VETULA POLIOCEPHALA (Wagler)

GRAY-HEADED CHACHALACA

Adult (sexes alike).—Similar to *Ortalis vetula vetula* but larger, the
abdomen and underparts generally much lighter—the abdomen whitish,
washed to a varying degree with light ochraceous-buff, the sides, flanks,
thighs, and under tail coverts more heavily so tinged—varying from light

ochraceous-buff to dark ochraceous-buff with a trace of ochraceous-
salmon; breast less olive, more grayish—ashy grayish olive; upperparts
of body more brownish—light brownish olive; rectrices slightly more
ashy and the pale tips light to dark ochraceous-buff, not white, and much
broader than in the nominate form (45–60 mm.); iris hazel-brown; bare
orbital and gular skin carmine; bill light plumbeous; tarsi and toes ashy.

Juvenal (sexes alike).—Similar to the corresponding stage of *Ortalis
vetula vetula* but the abdomen whitish as in the adult (above), the breast
less tawny, more grayish, the sides, flanks, thighs, and under tail coverts
light ochraceous-buff; the upperparts of the body slightly paler—light
brownish olive; rectrices slightly more ashy, tipped with fulvescent and
pointed in shape.

Downy young (male only seen).—Similar to the buffy (not the grayish) type of the similar plumage in the nominate form, but all of the rufes-
cent-brownish areas paler, more buffy; the breast more grayish—drab
mottled with buffy avellaneous.

Adult male.—Wing 235–282 (248.4); tail 263–310 (283.2); exposed
culmen 26–33 (29.8); tarsus 68–77 (71.5); middle toe without claw
52–62 (55.5 mm.).[33]

Adult female.—Wing 229–263 (244); tail 247–304 (276); exposed
culmen 25–28 (27.3); tarsus 66–72 (70.1); middle toe without claw
52–57 (55 mm.).[34]

Range.—Resident in southwestern Mexico from Colima (Mazanillo and
Río de la Armeria); Michoacán (La Salada and Tupila River); Morelos
(Tetela del Volcán); western Puebla (Chachapa); and Valley of Mexico
(City of Mexico and Real Aribe); to Guerrero (Tlalixtaquilla, Papayo,
Camarón, Ometepec, Sepuatenejo, and Mexcala); to western Oaxaca
(Chivela, Pluma, Huilotepec, Llano Grande, Chicapa, Tapana, Barrio,
Tehuantepec City, Salina Cruz, Río Grande, Santa Efigenia, Torullo, and
Tapantapec); and western Chiapas (Tonalá).

Type locality.—Mexico. I restrict it to La Salada, Michoacán.

P[enelope] *poliocephala* WAGLER, Isis, 1830, 1112 (Mexico; coll. Berlin Mus.).
O[rtalida] *poliocephala* WAGLER, Isis, 1832, 1227.—REICHENBACH, Voll. Nat.
    Tauben, 1861, 145.—BAIRD, BREWER, and RIDGWAY, Hist. North Amer. Birds,
    iii, 1874, 398, footnote.
[Ortalida] *poliocephala* REICHENBACH, Synop. Av., Columb., ii, 1847, pl. 169, fig.
    1490.—SALLÉ and PARZUDAKI, Cat. Oiseaux Mexique, 1862, 6 (Mexico).—
    GRAY, Hand-list, ii, 1870, 252, No. 9512.—SCLATER and SALVIN, Proc. Zool. Soc.
    London, 1870, 543; Nom. Av. Neotr., 1873, 137.
Ortalida poliocephala SCLATER and SALVIN, Proc. Zool. Soc. London, 1869, 364 (near
    City of Mexico; crit.); 1870, 537 (monogr.).—LAWRENCE, Mem. Boston Soc.
    Nat. Hist., ii, 1874, 306 (Río Tupila, Colima); U. S. Nat. Mus. Bull. 4, 1876,
    45 (Tapana, Barrio, and Tehuantepec City, Oaxaca; fresh colors of nude

---

[33] Fifteen specimens from Michoacán, Morelos, western Oaxaca, and Guerrero.
[34] Six specimens from Michoacán, Colima, western Oaxaca, and Guerrero.

parts).—Beristain and Laurencio, Mem. y Rev. Soc. Cient. "Antonio Alzate," vii, 1894, 220 (Tehuantepec, Mexico).
Ortalis poliocephala Ferrari-Perez, Proc. U. S. Nat. Mus., ix, 1886, 175 (Chachapa, Puebla).—Ogilvie-Grant, Cat. Birds Brit. Mus., xxii, 1893, 511 (Tehuantepec and Salina Cruz, Oaxaca).—Salvin and Godman, Biol. Centr.-Amer., Aves, iii, 1902, 279 (Real Arriba, Mexico; Río de la Armeria and Río Tupila, Colima; Chachapa, Puebla; Río Grande, Tapana, Santa Efigenia, Barrio, Torullo, Tapantapec, and Salina Cruz, Oaxaca; Tonalá, Chiapas).—Bangs and Peters, Bull. Mus. Comp. Zool., lxviii, 1928, 386 (Chivelas, Oaxaca, Mexico).—Mendizabal, Rev. Soc. Mex. Hist. Nat., i, No. 3, 1940, 180, in text (Mexico).—Petrides, Trans. 7th North Amer. Wildlife Conf., 1942, 311, in text (age indicators in plumage).
O[rtalis] poliocephala Ridgway, Man. North Amer. Birds, 1887, 209.—Reichenow, Die Vögel, i, 1913, 277.
[Ortalis] poliocephala Sharpe, Hand-list, i, 1899, 17.
Ortalis vetula poliocephala Peters, Check-list Birds of World, ii, 1934, 19.—Hellmayr and Conover, Cat. Birds Amer. i, No. 1, 1942, 168 (syn.; distr.).—Blake and Hanson, Publ. Field Mus. Nat. Hist., zool. ser., xxii, 1942, 527 (Michoacán; Cerro de Tancitaro; spec.).
Ortalida leucogastra (not *Penelope leucogastra* Gould) Sclater, Proc. Zool. Soc. London, 1859, 391 (Río Grande, Oaxaca; crit.).
Ortalis poliocephala subsp. *longicauda* Lampe, Jahrb. Nassau Ver. Natur., lix, 1906, 232 ("Mexico"; type in Wiesbaden Mus.).
Ortalida plumbeiceps (not *plumbiceps* Gray) Beristain and Laurencio, Mem. y Rev. Soc. Cient. "Antonio Alzate," vii, 1894, 220 (Tehuantepec, Mexico).

ORTALIS VETULA LEUCOGASTRA (Gould)

White-bellied Chachalaca

Adult (sexes alike).—Similar to the corresponding stage of *Ortalis vetula poliocephala* in the whiteness of the abdomen and posterior underparts, but with less ochraceous wash on the under tail coverts, flanks, thighs, and sides, and almost none on the abdomen; very much smaller in all dimensions; upper parts of body darker—Dresden brown to sepia, and the crown washed with mummy brown; rectrices as in *Ortalis vetula vetula*, with a well-developed greenish sheen and white tips.

Juvenal.—None seen.

Downy young.—None seen.

Adult male.—Wing 207–220 (215.6); tail 197–212 (202.6); exposed culmen 27 (27); tarsus 52–55 (53.6); middle toe without claw 45–46 (45.6 mm.).[35]

Adult female.—Wing 200–203; tail 195–197; exposed culmen 24–25; tarsus 50–54; middle toe without claw 43 (43 mm.).[36]

Range.—Resident from southwestern Chiapas (Huehuetán); Pacific lowlands of western Guatemala (Naranjo, Escuintla, Retalhuleu, Costa Grande, San José, Hacienda California, Finca Cipres, and Espina); the

---

[35] Three specimens from Chiapas.
[36] Two specimens from Chiapas.

Pacific coast of Honduras; El Salvador (La Libertad); and northern Nicaragua (Realejo and Momotombo).

Type locality.—None given; Realejo, Nicaragua.[37]

Penelope albiventer (not *P. albiventris* Wagler) LESSON, Rev. Zool., v, 1842, 174 (Realejo, Nicaragua).—GOULD, Voy. *Sulphur*, Zool., 1844, 48, pl. 31.

Penelopsis albiventer BONAPARTE, Compt. Rend., xlii, 1856, 877.

Penelope leucogastra GOULD, Proc. Zool. Soc. London, 1843, 105 (locality unknown; new name for *P. albiventer* Lesson from Realejo, Nicaragua).

Ortalida leucogastra GRAY, List Birds Brit. Mus., pt. 3, Gallinae, 1944, 20.—SCLATER and SALVIN, Ibis, 1859, 224 (Pacific coast Guatemala; habits; descr. nest and eggs); Proc. Zool. Soc. London, 1870, 539 (monogr.).—TAYLOR, Ibis, 1860, 311 (Pacific coast Honduras).—BERISTAIN and LAURENCIO, Mem. y Rev. Soc. Cient. "Antonio Alzate," vii, 1894, 220 (Chiapas and Tabasco).—LANTZ, Trans. Kansas Acad. Sci. for 1896-7 (1899), 219 (Naranjo, Guatemala).

O[rtalida] leucogastra BAIRD, BREWER, and RIDGWAY, Hist. North Amer. Birds, iii, 1874, 399, footnote.

[Ortalida] leucogastra SALLÉ and PARZUDAKI, Cat. Oiseaux Mexique, 1862, 6 (Mexico).—SCLATER and SALVIN, Proc. Zool. Soc. London, 1870, 543; Nom. Av. Neotr., 1873, 137.

Ortalida leucogaster GRAY, List Birds, Brit. Mus., pt. 5, Gallinae, 1867, 13.

[Ortalida] leucogaster GRAY, Hand-list, ii, 1870, 252, No. 9517.

Chamaepetes leucogastra REICHENBACH, Voll. Nat. Tauben, 1862, 142.

[Penelopsis] leucogastra HEINE and REICHENOW, Nom. Mus. Hein. Orn., 1890, 301 (Escuintla, Guatemala).

O[rtalis] leucogastra RIDGWAY, Man. North Amer. Birds, 1887, 208.

Ortalis leucogastra OGILVIE-GRANT, Cat. Birds Brit. Mus., xxii, 1893, 514 (Retalhuleu and Costa Grande, Guatemala; La Libertad, El Salvador; Momotombo, Nicaragua); Handb. Game Birds, ii, 1897, 247 (monogr.).—SALVIN and GODMAN, Biol. Centr.-Amer., Aves, iii, 1903, 281 (Retalhuleu and Costa Grande, Guatemala; La Libertad, El Salvador; Momotombo and Realejo, Nicaragua).—DEARBORN, Publ. Field Mus. Nat. Hist., No. 125, 1907, 78 (San José, Guatemala; habits).

[Ortalis] leucagastra SHARPE, Hand-list, i, 1899, 17.

Ortalis vetula leucogastra GRISCOM, Bull. Amer. Mus. Nat. Hist., lxiv, 1932, 103 (Pacific lowlands of western Guatemala to northwestern Nicaragua; spec. from Hacienda California, Finca Cipres, and Espina, Guatemala).—PETERS, Check-list Birds of World, ii, 1934, 19.—HELLMAYR and CONOVER, Cat. Birds Amer., i, No. 1, 1942, 173 (syn.; distr.).

ORTALIS VETULA PALLIDIVENTRIS Ridgway

YUCATÁN CHACHALACA

Adult (sexes alike).—Similar to the adult of *Ortalis vetula vetula* but paler below, the abdomen dull whitish isabelline, darkening on the sides, flanks, thighs, and under tail coverts to isabelline; the breast less olive-brown, more ashy olive; and the tips of the rectrices not pure white but washed with isabelline to pale buffy.

---

[37] This designation appears to be proper, inasmuch as the name *leucogastra* was originally proposed as a new name for *Penelope albiventer* Lesson from Realejo, Nicaragua (Proc. Zool. Soc. London, 1843, 105).

Juvenal (sexes alike).—Like the corresponding stage of *Ortalis vetula vetula* but with the pale underparts as in the adult.

Downy young.—None seen.

Adult male.—Wing 173–204 (188.5); tail 201–226 (214); exposed culmen 24–28 (25.5); tarsus 56–66 (61.3); middle toe without claw 42–50 (45.5 mm.).[38]

Adult female.—Wing 174–203 (189); tail 197–228 (211.5); exposed culmen 24–26 (24.8); tarsus 55–62 (59); middle toe without claw 42–45 (44.4 mm.).[39]

Range.—Resident in the drier parts of the Yucatán Peninsula (Chichen Itzá and Mérida, and Meco, Holbox, Mujeres, and Cozumel Islands), and adjacent parts of Campeche (La Tuxpena and Apazote).

Type locality.—Yucatán.

Ortalida maccalli (not *O. mccalli* Baird) LAWRENCE, Ann. Lyc. Nat. Hist. New York, ix, 1869, 209 (Mérida, Yucatán; crit.).

Ortalida vetula (not *Penelope vetula* Wagler) SCLATER and SALVIN, Proc. Zool. Soc. London, 1870, 538, part (monogr.).

[*Ortalida*] *vetula* GRAY, Hand-list, ii, 1870, 252, No. 9502, part.—SCLATER and SALVIN, Proc. Zool. Soc. London, 1870, 543, part; Nom. Av. Neotr., 1873, 137, part.

O[*rtalida*] *vetula* BAIRD, BREWER, and RIDGWAY, Hist. North Amer. Birds, iii, 1874, 398, footnote, part.

Ortalis vetula BOUCARD, Proc. Zool. Soc. London, 1883, 460, Yucatán; habits).—SALVIN, Ibis, 1889, 378 (Meco and Holbox Islands, Yucatán, crit.).—OGILVIE-GRANT, Cat. Birds Brit. Mus., xxii, 1893, 512, part (Holbox, Mujeres, Meco, and Cozumel Islands, Yucatán); Handb. Game Birds, ii, 1897, 245, part.—SALVIN and GODMAN, Biol. Centr.-Amer., Aves, iii, 1902, 280, part (Meco, Holbox, Cozumel, and Mujeres Islands and Mérida, Yucatán).

O[*rtalis*] *vetula pallidiventris* RIDGWAY, Man. North Amer. Birds, 1887, 209 (Yucatán; coll. U. S. Nat. Mus.).

Ortalis vetula pallidiventris RIDGWAY, Man. North Amer. Birds, 1887, 591.—CHAPMAN, Bull. Amer. Mus. Nat. Hist., viii, 1896, 288 (Chichen Itzá, Yucatán; habits; notes).—COLE, Bull. Mus. Comp. Zool., 1, 1906, 115 (Chichen Itzá).—MILLER and GRISCOM, Auk, xxxviii, 1921, 48 (crit.).—PETERS, Check-list Birds of World, ii, 1934, 19.—TRAYLOR, Publ. Field Mus. Nat. Hist., zool. ser., xxiv, 1941, 204 (Chichen Itzá, Yucatán; spec.).—HELLMAYR and CONOVER, Cat. Birds Amer., i, No. 1, 1942, 172 (syn.; distr.).

[*Ortalis*] *pallidiventris* SHARPE, Hand-list, i, 1899, 17.

ORTALIS VETULA INTERMEDIA Peters

PETÉN CHACHALACA

Adult (sexes alike).—Very similar to the adult of *Ortalis vetula pallidiventris* but slightly darker above, more brownish, less grayish olive; abdomen pale isabelline, the breast slightly duskier than in *pallidiventris;* all but the median pair of rectrices tipped with light grayish isabelline.

Juvenal.—None seen.

---

[38] Eight specimens from Yucatán and Campeche.
[39] Five specimens from Yucatán and Campeche.

Downy young.—None seen.

Adult male.—Wing 181–190 (186.6) ; tail 225–258 (237) ; exposed culmen 23.5–27 (25) ; tarsus 58–65 (61.8) ; middle toe without claw 42–43 (42.5 mm.).[40]

Adult female.—Wing 172–183 ; tail 215–235 ; exposed culmen 22–24.5 ; tarsus 62.5–64 ; middle toe without claw 41 mm.[41]

Range.—Resident in southern Quintana Roo (Camp Mengel) and the Petén district of Guatemala (Uaxactún and Chuntuqui). Doubtfully distinct from *pallidiventris.*

Type locality.—Camp Mengel, Quintana Roo, Mexico.

Ortalis vetula intermedia PETERS, Auk, xxx, 1913, 371 (Camp Mengel, Quintana Roo, se. Mexico; coll. Mus. Comp. Zool.).—MILLER and GRISCOM, Auk, xxxviii, 1921, 48 (crit.).—GRISCOM, Amer. Mus. Nov. No. 235, 1926, 7 (e. Quintana Roo, Yucatán).—BANGS, Bull. Mus. Comp. Zool., lxx, 1930, 154 (type spec. in Mus. Comp. Zool.; crit.).—PETERS, Check-list Birds of World, ii, 1934, 19.— VAN TYNE, Misc. Publ. Univ. Michigan Mus. Zool., No. 27, 1935, 11 (Petén, Guatemala, Uaxactún, Chuntuqui; crit.).—TRAYLOR, Publ. Field Mus. Nat. Hist., zool. ser., xxiv, 1941, 198, 204 (Campeche; Matamoros—spec.).—HELLMAYR and CONOVER, Cat. Birds Amer., i, No. 1, 1942, 171, part (syn.; distr.).

O[rtalis] v[etula] intermedia MILLER and GRISCOM, Auk, xxxviii, 1921, 50 (diagnosis).

ORTALIS VETULA VALLICOLA Brodkorb

BRODKORB'S CHACHALACA

Adult (sexes alike).—Very "similar to *O. v. intermedia,* but larger ; breast somewhat paler and grayer ; flanks, crissum, and thighs on average more brownish olive, less rufescent. . . . Resembles *O. v. vetula* in size but is paler throughout, including the tips of the rectrices" (*ex* original description as are also the measurements).

Adult male.—Wing 207–214 (210.3) ; tail 234–252 (245.3 mm.).

Adult female.—Wing 192–199 ; tail 216–239 mm.

Range.—Known only from the dry upper part of the Grand Valley of the interior of Chiapas.

Type locality.—Malpaso, Chiapas.

Ortalis vetula intermedia HELLMAYR and CONOVER, Cat. Birds. Amer., i, No. 1, 1942, 171, part (Malpaso, Chicomuselo).

Ortalis vetula vallicola BRODKORB, Proc. Biol. Soc. Washington, lv, 1942, 182 (Malpaso, Chiapas; meas.; distr.; crit.).

ORTALIS VETULA PLUMBICEPS (Gray)

PLUMBEOUS-CAPPED CHACHALACA

Adult (sexes alike).—Similar to *Ortalis vetula jalapensis* but slightly more olivaceous above, especially in fresh plumage, and the tips of the

---

[40] Three specimens from Quintana Roo and Petén.
[41] Two specimens from Quintana Roo and Petén.

rectrices bicolored, the basal part of the tip being ochraceous-tawny, the distal part grayish fulvescent.

Other plumages.—None seen.

Adult male.—Wing 189; tail 238; exposed culmen 25; tarsus 66; middle toe without claw 48 mm. (1 specimen).

Adult female.—Wing 180–194; tail 230–241; exposed culmen 23.5–24; tarsus 63–65; middle toe without claw 47 mm.[42]

Range.—Resident in the humid coastal forest areas of the southern half of British Honduras (Belize); Tabasco (Teapa); eastern Guatemala (Quirigua, Gualan, Cobán, Vera Paz, Los Amates, and Virginia Plantations near Puerto Barrios); to northwestern Honduras (Omoa, Chamelecon, San Pedro, Progreso, Lancetilla).

Type locality.—Omoa, Honduras.

Penelope vetula (not of Wagler) BONAPARTE, Proc. Zool. Soc. London, 1837, 119 (Guatemala; descr.; crit.).
Ortalida vetula MOORE, Proc. Zool. Soc. London, 1859, 62 (Omoa, Honduras; habits). —SCLATER and SALVIN, Ibis, 1859, 224 (Guatemala; habits); Proc. Zool. Soc. London, 1870, 538, part (monogr.), 838 (San Pedro, Honduras).—TAYLOR, Ibis, 1860, 311 (Atlantic slope of Honduras; habits).
[*Ortalida*] *vetula* SCLATER and SALVIN, Nom. Av. Neotr., 1873, 137, part.
Ortalis vetula OGILVIE-GRANT, Cat. Birds Brit. Mus., xxii, 1893, 512, part (Teapa, Tabasco; vicinity of Belize, British Honduras; Cobán, Vera Paz, Guatemala); Handb. Game Birds, ii, 1897, 245, part.—SALVIN and GODMAN, Biol. Centr.-Amer., Aves, iii, 1902, 280, part (Teapa, Tabasco; Belize, British Honduras; Omoa and San Pedro, Honduras; Cobán, Guatemala).
[*Ortalis*] *vetula* SHARPE, Hand-list, i, 1899, 17, part.
Ortalida plumbiceps GRAY, List Birds Brit. Mus., pt. 5, Gallinae, 1867, 11 (British Honduras; Guatemala; coll. Brit. Mus.).
[*Ortalida*] *plumbiceps* GRAY, Hand-list, ii, 1870, 252, No. 9504.
O[*rtalida*] *plumbeiceps* SCLATER and SALVIN, Proc. Zool. Soc. London, 1870, 538 (crit.).
O[*rtalis*] *vetula plumbeiceps* RIDGWAY, Man. North Amer. Birds, 1887, 209.
Ortalis vetula plumbeiceps STONE, Proc. Acad. Nat. Sci. Philadelphia, lxxxiv, 1932, 301 (Honduras; Omoa, Chiloma, Lancetilla, and Progreso).—DEIGNAN, Auk, liii, 1936, 188 (Honduras; La Ceiba; spec.; colors of soft parts).
Ortalis vetula plumbiceps DEARBORN, Publ. Field Mus. Nat. Hist., No. 125, 1907, 78 (Gualan and Los Amates, Guatemala; notes, etc.).—MILLER and GRISCOM, Auk, xxxviii, 1921, 47 (Guatemala; Honduras; highlands of Pacific slope in Nicaragua; crit.; meas.).—PETERS, Bull. Mus. Comp. Zool., lxix, 1929, 403 (Progreso, Lancetilla, Honduras; habits); Check-list Birds of World, ii, 1934, 19.— GRISCOM, Bull. Amer. Mus. Nat. Hist., lxiv, 1932, 101 (humid coastal forest areas of eastern Guatemala; spec. Virginia Plantation near Puerto Barrios).— CARRIKER and DE SCHAUENSEE, Proc. Acad. Nat. Sci. Philadelphia, lxxxvii, 1935, 413 (Guatemala; Gualan and Quirigua).—HELLMAYR and CONOVER, Cat. Birds Amer., i, No. 1, 1942, 172 (syn.; distr.).
O[*rtalis*] *v*[*etula*] *plumbiceps* MILLER and GRISCOM, Auk, xxxviii, 1921, 50 (diagnosis).

---

[42] Two specimens from Guatemala and Honduras.

ORTALIS VETULA DESCHAUENSEEI Bond

UTILA CHACHALACA

Adult male (unique specimen).—Similar to *Ortalis vetula vetula* but larger; the tips of the outer rectrices ochraceous-drab instead of white; the feathers of the upper throat decidedly blacker; the lower throat grayer; hindneck grayish merging imperceptibly with the dark gray of the crown and occiput; wing 208; tail 225; exposed culmen 25.5; tarsus 58; middle toe without claw 45 mm.

Known only from the type locality—Utila Island, Spanish Honduras.[43]

Ortalis vetula deschauenseei BOND, Proc. Acad. Nat. Sci. Philadelphia, lxxxviii, 1936, 356 (Utila Island, Spanish Honduras; descr.; meas.; crit.).—HELLMAYR and CONOVER, Cat. Birds Amer., i, No. 1, 1942, 173 (syn.; distr.).

ORTALIS GARRULA CINEREICEPS (Gray)

DUSKY-HEADED CHACHALACA

Adult (sexes alike).—Forehead, crown, occiput, nape, hindneck, feathered parts of sides of head, chin, and upper throat deep mouse gray to dark mouse gray; interscapulars, scapulars, back, rump, upper wing and tail coverts, and inner secondaries raw umber with a slight olivaceous wash (in fresh plumage almost medal bronze); primaries hazel, the inner ones vaguely washed with olive-brown at the tips; outer secondaries olivaceous raw umber with a fairly broad median shaft line of hazel (except terminally) widening across the inner webs for their basal two-thirds; the upper surface of the wings with a faint oily green sheen not present on the back or interscapulars; rectrices olivaceous-black with a strong dark-green sheen, the middle pair paling to grayish medal bronze terminally, the other pairs broadly tipped (20–35 mm.) with pale grayish fulvescent, fading to almost white at the tips; lower throat and breast light brownish olive with a varying degree of isabelline wash; abdomen pale fulvescent, washed with isabelline anteriorly and on thighs, sides, and flanks, the thighs with a grayish tone; under tail coverts grayish buffy brown; under wing coverts hazel; iris burnt umber to sepia; bill pale bluish horn, darker and more plumbeous on basal half, including cere; bare skin of face and throat reddish; naked lores and orbits dull slate color; tarsi and toes slate color, claws horn color.

Juvenal (only one chick in early postnatal molt seen).—Upper wing coverts and remiges dull bister to dark sepia edged and tipped with bright ochraceous-buff. (Rest of specimen still in downy plumage.)

Downy young.—Forehead, crown, occiput, cheeks, auriculars, and malar area fuscous-black, a little dark chestnut mixed with the black on the middle of the crown; hindneck and middle of back posterior to the

---

[43] Additional material of this form is much to be desired, but the unique type is remarkably distinct from its mainland neighbor *O. v. plumbiceps* and, as indicated above, from the nominate race as well.

tail fuscous-black, the feathers of the hindneck barred with ochraceous-tawny, the dark middorsal band laterally bordered with a line of light orange-buff, laterad of which is another blackish area; wings fuscous-blackish barred with ochraceous-tawny; chin and upper throat white very slightly suffused with cartridge buff; lower throat and breast bright cinnamon-brown, paling on lower breast and upper abdomen to light ochraceous-buff; middle of abdomen like the chin; sides, flanks, thighs, and vent ochraceous-buff mottled with dusky.

Adult male.—Wing 194–216 (204.5); tail 201–236 (218.9); exposed culmen 24–27 (25.3); tarsus 59–67 (65); middle toe without claw 47–53 (50.2 mm.).[44]

Adult female.—Wing 184–208 (193.7); tail 190–232 (206.3); exposed culmen 22–26 (23.6); tarsus 54–61 (60); middle toe without claw 42–46 (44.1 mm.).[45]

Range.—Resident from eastern Nicaragua (Chontales; Río Grande; Muy Muy; Las Cañas; Los Sábalos; and Río Escondido); south through Costa Rica (Atlanta; Buenos Aires; Cariblanco de Sarapiquí; Cartago; Cuabre; Guacimo; Guapiles; Guayabo; Jiménez; Juan Viñas; La Palma de San José; Pozo Azul de Pirris; San José; Sibueno; Talamanca; Turrialba; Volcán de Irazú; and Volcán de Miravalles); to Panama, except the coastal strip of Veraguas, and stopping short of the Caribbean slope of Darién (Boquerón, Chiriquí; Canal Zone; Castillo; Chapignana; Cricamola; Cordillera de Tole; Divalá; Gatún; Guabo; Lion Hill; Paraiso; Pearl Islands—San Miguel, San Pedro, and Pedro González Islands in the Bay of Panama; and Santiago).

Type locality.—"North-west coast of America" error=Pearl Islands? Designated by Aldrich, Sci. Publ. Cleveland Mus. Nat. Hist., vii, 1937, 55, as San Miguel, Pearl Islands, Bay of Panama.

Ortalida poliocephala (not *Penelope poliocephala* Wagler) LAWRENCE, Ann. Lyc. Nat. Hist. New York, vii, 1861, 333 (Lion Hill, Panama); ix, 1868, 139 (San José, Turrialba, and La Palma de San José, Costa Rica).—SCLATER and SALVIN, Proc. Zool. Soc. London, 1864, 371 (Panama; crit.).—SALVIN, Proc. Zool. Soc. London, 1867, 161 (Santiago and Cordillera de Tole, Veraguas, w. Panama; crit.); Ibis, 1869, 318 (Costa Rica; crit.).—FRANTZIUS, Journ. für Orn., 1869, 372 (Costa Rica).

Ortalida cinereiceps GRAY, List Birds Brit. Mus., pt. 5, Gallinae, 1867, 12 ("northwest coast of America" = Panama; coll. Brit. Mus.).—SALVIN, Ibis, 1869, 318 (Panama); Proc. Zool. Soc. London, 1870, 217 (Castillo, Veraguas, w. Panama).—SCLATER and SALVIN, Proc. Zool. Soc. London, 1870, 540 (localities in Panama; Costa Rica; monogr.), 543.—NUTTING, Proc. U. S. Nat. Mus., vi, 1884, 408 (Los Sábalos, Nicaragua).

[*Ortalida*] *cinereiceps* GRAY, Hand-list, ii, 1870, 252, No. 9507 (Costa Rica; Panama).—SCLATER and SALVIN, Nom. Av. Neotr., 1873, 137 (Costa Rica; Panama).

---

[44] Fourteen specimens from Panama, Costa Rica, and Nicaragua.
[45] Seven specimens from Panama, Costa Rica, and Nicaragua.

Ortalis cinereiceps ZELEDÓN, Proc. U. S. Nat. Mus., viii, 1885, 112 (Costa Rica);
Anal. Mus. Nac. Costa Rica, i, 1888, 128 (Jiménez and Cartago, Costa Rica).—
CHERRIE, Expl. Zool. Merid. Costa Rica, 1893, 54 (Buenos Aires, sw. Costa
Rica).—RICHMOND, Proc. U. S. Nat. Mus., xvi, 1893, 523 (Río Escondido,
Nicaragua; habits).—OGILVIE-GRANT, Cat. Birds Brit. Mus., xxii, 1893, 515
(San José, Costa Rica; Cordillera de Tole, Castillo, and Paraiso, Panama);
Handb. Game Birds, ii, 1897, 249, part.—UNDERWOOD, Ibis, 1896, 448 (Volcán
de Miravalles, Costa Rica; habits).—SALVADORI and FESTA, Boll. Mus. Zool.
Torino, xiv, No. 339, 1899, 10 (Laguna della Pita, Darién).—BANGS, Proc. New
England Zool. Club, ii, 1900, 14 (Loma del León, Panama); Auk, xviii, 1901,
25, 356 (Pearl Islands, and Divalá, Chiriquí); Auk, xxiv, 1907, 291 (Boruca,
Terraba, Costa Rica).—SALVIN and GODMAN, Biol. Centr.-Amer., Aves, iii,
1903, 382 (Los Sábalos and Río Escondido, Nicaragua; Turrialba, San José,
La Palma de San José, Jiménez, Cartago, Volcán de Irazú, and Volcán de
Miravalles, Costa Rica; Divalá, Santiago de Veraguas, Cordillera de Tole,
Castillo, and Paraiso, Panama).—THAYER and BANGS, Bull. Mus. Comp. Zool.,
xlvi, 1905, 145 (San Miguel Island, Bay of Panama; crit.), 214 (Savana de
Panama).—CARRIKER, Ann. Carnegie Mus., vi, 1910, 383 (Costa Rica—Pozo
Azul, Cuabre, Guayabo, Miravalles, Juan Viñas, etc.).—FERRY, Publ. Field Mus.
Nat. Hist., orn. ser., i, No. 6, 1910, 260 (Guayabo, Costa Rica; habits; crit.).—
CARRIKER, Ann. Carnegie Mus., vi, 1910, 383 (Guayabo, Miravalles, Cariblanco
de Sarapiquí, Pozo Azul de Pirris, Juan Viñas, and Cuabre, Costa Rica; crit.;
habits; descr. nest and eggs).—STONE, Proc. Acad. Nat. Sci. Philadelphia,
1918, 242 (Panama Canal Zone).—RENDAHL, Ark. Zool., xiii, No. 4, 1920, 22
(San Miguel Island).

O[*rtalis*] *cinereiceps* RIDGWAY, Man. North Amer. Birds, 1887, 209.

[*Ortalis*] *cinereiceps* SHARPE, Hand-list, i, 1899, 17.

Ortalis cinereiceps cinereiceps MILLER and GRISCOM, Amer. Mus. Nov., No. 25, 1921,
1, in text (Boquerón, Chiriquí; Canal Zone, Chapigana, e. Panama).—STURGIS,
Field Book Birds Panama Canal Zone, 1928, 28 (descr.; Panama Canal).—
KENNARD and PETERS, Proc. Boston Soc. Nat. Hist., xxxviii, 1928, 446 (Boquete
Trail, Panama; spec.; colors of soft parts).—PETERS, Bull. Mus. Comp. Zool.
lxxi, 1931, 297 (Guabo, Cricamola, Panama; crit.).—CAUM, Occ. Pap. Bishop
Mus., x, No. 9, 1933, 12 (Hawaii; introduced in 1928; not known to breed).

Ortalis struthopus BANGS, Proc. New England Zool. Club, ii, 1901, 61 (San Miguel
Island, Bay of Panama; coll. E. A. and O. Bangs, now in coll. Mus. Comp.
Zool.); Bull. Mus. Comp. Zool., lxx, 1930, 154 (type spec. in Mus. Comp.
Zool. = *Ortalis cinereiceps cinereiceps*).—SALVIN and GODMAN, Biol. Centr.-
Amer., Aves, iii, 1903, 283 (San Pedro and Pedro González Islands, Bay of
Panama).

Ortalis garrula cinereiceps GRISCOM, Bull. Mus. Comp. Zool., lxxviii, 1935, 303
(Panama—common almost throughout).—ALDRICH, Sci. Publ. Cleveland Mus.
Nat. Hist., vii, 1937, 53, 54, 55, in text (crit.).—HELLMAYR and CONOVER, Cat.
Birds Amer., i, No. 1, 1942, 176 (syn.; distr.).

Ortalis cinereiceps frantzii HUBER, Proc. Acad. Nat. Sci. Philadelphia, lxxxiv, 1932,
206 (northeastern Nicaragua; spec.; nest; eggs).

Ortalida frantzii CABANIS, Journ. für Orn., 1869, 211 (Costa Rica; coll. Berlin
Mus.).—FRANTZIUS, Journ. für Orn., 1869, 373 (Costa Rica).

[*Ortalida*] *frantzii* GRAY, Hand-list, ii, 1870, 252, No. 9515.

Ortalis garrula frantzii PETERS, Check-list Birds of World, ii, 1934, 20.—ALDRICH,
Sci. Publ. Cleveland Mus. Nat. Hist., vii, 1937, 53, 55, in text (crit).—
HELLMAYR and CONOVER, Cat. Birds Amer., i, No. 1, 1942, 175 (syn.; distr.).

Ortalis cinereiceps saturatus MILLER and GRISCOM, Amer. Mus. Nov., No. 25, 1921,
1 (near Matagalpa, Nicaragua; coll. Amer. Mus. N. H.).

Ortalis garrula saturata ALDRICH, Sci. Publ. Cleveland Mus. Nat. Hist., vii, 1937, 55 in text.

ORTALIS GARRULA MIRA Griscom

DARIÉN CHACHALACA

Adult (sexes alike).—Similar to *Ortalis garrula cinereiceps* but with the lower middle abdomen white and the under tail coverts pale brownish gray; tail longer; iris gray-brown; bill blue-gray; tarsi and toes slate gray; throat skin red.

Other plumages unknown.

Adult male.—Wing 214–228 (219.7), tail 237–265 (249.5); exposed culmen 23–28 (26.6); tarsus 65–72 (70.1); middle toe without claw 47–53 (50.6 mm.).[46]

Adult female.—Wing 204–208 (205.7); tail 232–235 (233.5); exposed culmen 25–26 (25.2), tarsus 67–71 (68.5); middle toe without claw 45–52 (48 mm.). (4 specimens.)

Range.—Resident in the Caribbean slope of eastern Darién, Panama (Ranchon, Port Obaldia, Río Tuicuisa).

Type locality.—Ranchon, Caribbean slope of eastern Panama.

Ortalis garrula mira GRISCOM, Bull. Mus. Comp. Zool., lxxii, 1932, 318 (Ranchon, Caribbean slope of e. Panama); Bull. Mus. Comp. Zool., lxxviii, 1935, 303 Panama; known chiefly from the caribbean slope, eastern Darién).—PETERS, Check-list Birds of World, ii, 1934, 20.—ALDRICH, Sci. Publ. Cleveland Mus. Nat. Hist., vii, 1937, 56, in text (Caribbean coast of e. Panama).—HELLMAYR and CONOVER, Cat. Birds Amer., i, No. 1, 1942, 178 (syn.; distr.).

ORTALIS GARRULA OLIVACEA Aldrich

AZUERO CHACHALACA

Adult (sexes alike).—Similar to *Ortalis garrula cinereiceps* but with wing and tail longer.[47]

Other plumages unknown.

Adult male.—Wing 213–223 (219.3); tail 245–256 (249.7); exposed culmen 25–25.5 (25.1); tarsus 69–74 (71); middle toe without claw 49–50 (49.5 mm.).[48]

Adult female.—Wing 203; tail 239; exposed culmen 25; tarsus 67; middle toe without claw 44 mm. (1 specimen).

Range.—Known only from the type locality; possibly other western Veraguas records (listed under *O. g. cinereiceps* in this work) may be of this form.

---

[46] Five specimens from Darién.

[47] The color characters given by Aldrich (Sci. Publ. Cleveland Mus. Nat. Hist., vii, 1937, 53) do not serve to differentiate this form from a good series of *cinereiceps* (which includes *frantzii*).

[48] Three specimens, all from the type locality.

Type locality.—Paracoté, 50 feet, eastern shore of Montijo Bay, 1 mile south of the mouth of the Angulo River, Veraguas, Panama.

Ortalis garrula olivacea ALDRICH, Sci. Publ. Cleveland Mus. Nat. Hist., vii, 1937, 53 (Paracoté, Veraguas, Panama; crit.).—HELLMAYR and CONOVER, Cat. Birds Amer., i, No. 1, 1942, 177 (syn.; distr.).

ORTALIS RUFICAUDA (Jardine)

RUFOUS-TAILED CHACHALACA

Adult (sexes alike).—Forehead, crown, occiput, nape, suboculars, cheeks, and auriculars dark slate gray, the forehead and crown with a dull brownish wash, the posterior part of the auriculars, the nape, and the throat just posterior to the bare upper throat paling to slate gray; hindneck, sides of neck, interscapulars, scapulars, back, rump, upper wing and tail coverts dark citrine to brownish olive; the greater upper wing coverts with a blue-green sheen on their outer webs; primaries brownish olive; outer secondaries brownish olive tinged on the outer web with a blue-green sheen, inner secondaries like the back but with faint transverse striations; rectrices greenish black with blue-green sheen, the median pair uniformly of this color, the next pair narrowly, the others broadly, tipped with bright chestnut; lower throat and upper breast grayish dark olive-buff paling on the lower breast, abdomen, sides, flanks, and thighs to grayish buff, tinged on the breast, sides, flanks, and thighs with ochraceous-buff; under tail coverts russet; under wing coverts russet; bare skin around eye dark blue; bare sides of throat red; bill, tarsi, and toes dark blue.

Juvenal (one unsexed seen, but the sexes probably alike).—Similar to the adult but the feathering of the head and neck browner—dark drab to hair brown with an olivaceous wash; posterior hindneck and interscapulars with a dull cinnamon-brown wash; upperparts blackish olive, the feathers narrowly tipped with dull light buffy olive; the lower back, rump, and upper tail coverts mixed with brownish olive; remiges as in adult; rectrices as in adult but without the chestnut tips (the only specimen seen was in very abraded plumage, however); underparts as in adult.

Downy young.—None seen.

Adult male.—Wing 222–236 (228); tail 264–274 (269.6); exposed culmen 24–27.5 (25.9); tarsus 64–71.5 (69.1); middle toe without claw 48–54 (52.2 mm.).[49]

Adult female.—Wing 208–229 (219.3); tail 253–267 (261.6); exposed culmen 24–25 (24.3); tarsus 64.5–71 (68.8); middle toe without claw 47–50 (49 mm.).[50]

---

[49] Five specimens from Tobago and Venezuela.

[50] Three specimens from Tobago and Venezuela.

Range.—Resident in northern Venezuela (Margarita Island, San Julián, La Guaira, and Orinoco Valley) ; and the island of Tobago. Introduced and established in Bequia and Union Islands, Grenadines, Lesser Antilles.

Type locality.—Tobago.

Ortalida ruficauda JARDINE, Ann. Mag. Nat. Hist., xx, 1847, 374 (Tobago) ; Contr. Orn., 1848, 16, pl. 4.—SCLATER and SALVIN, Proc. Zool. Soc. London, 1870, 534 (monogr.).—SCLATER, Proc. Zool. Soc. London, 1870, 796 (Tobago).—CORY, List Birds West Indies, rev. ed., 1886, App. (Union Island, Grenadines, introduced) ; Cat. West Indian Birds, 1892, 138 (Union Island, Grenadines).

O[rtalida] ruficauda REICHENBACH, Voll. Nat. Tauben, 1861, 144.

[Ortalida] ruficauda GRAY, Hand-list, ii, 1870, 252, No. 9510.—SCLATER and SALVIN, Nom. Av. Neotr., 1873, 136.

Ortalis ruficauda BERLEPSCH, Ibis, 1884, 440 (Río Apure, Venezuela ; crit.).—CORY, Cat. West Indian Birds, 1892, 96 (Union Island, Grenadines) ; Auk, x, 1893, 220 (Tobago) ; Publ. Field Mus. Nat. Hist., No. 137, 1909, 239 (Margarita Island, Venezuela ; crit.).—OGILVIE-GRANT, Cat. Birds Brit. Mus., xxii, 1893, 507 (Venezuela ; Tobago ; Bequia Island, Grenadines) ; Handb. Game Birds, ii, 1897, 237 (monogr.).—ROBINSON and RICHMOND, Proc. U. S. Nat. Mus., xxiv, 1901, 165 (La Guaira and San Julián, Venezuela ; habits).—CLARK, Auk, xix, 1902, 261 (Margarita Island) ; Proc. Boston Soc. Nat. Hist., xxxii, 1905, 245 (Bequia and Union Islands, Grenadines).—LOWE, Ibis, 1909, 322 (Cariaco Peninsula, Venezuela).—CORY, Publ. Field Mus. Nat. Hist., orn. ser., i, 1909, 239 (Margarita Island).—BRABOURNE and CHUBB, Birds South Amer., i, 1912, 11 (Venezuela ; Trinidad).—CHERRIE, Bull. Brooklyn Inst. Sci., ii, 1916, 356 (Orinoco Valley, Venezuela).—CHERRIE and REICHENBERGER, Amer. Mus. Nov., No. 27, 1921, 3, in text (Venezuela ; Cristóbal Colón, Paria Peninsula, and Tucacas, Falcon).—DELACOUR, Ibis, 1923, 138 (San Fernando de Apure, Venezuela).—PETERS, Checklist Birds of World, ii, 1934, 20.— BELCHER and SMOOKER, Ibis, 1935, 279 (Tobago ; eggs).—BOND, Birds West Indies, 1936, 402 (introduced in Bequia and Union Islands, Grenadines) ; Check List Birds West Indies, 1940, 163.—HELLMAYR and CONOVER, Cat. Birds Amer., i, No. 1, 1942, 180.

O[rtalis] ruficauda REICHENOW, Die Vögel, i, 1913, 276.

[Ortalis] ruficauda SHARPE, Hand-list, i, 1899, 17.

? *Ortalis ruficauda* ROBINSON, Proc. U. S. Nat. Mus., xviii, 1896, 658 (Margarita Island).

Ortalis rufficauda CORY, Cat. West Indian Birds, 1892, 96 (Union and Grenadine Islands).

Ortalida bronzina GRAY, List Birds Brit. Mus., pt. 5, Gallinae, 1867, 11 (Venezuela).

[Ortalida] bronzina GRAY, Hand-list, ii, 1870, 252, No. 9503.

Phasianus garrulus HUMBOLDT, Obs. Zool. Anat. Comp., i, livr. 1, 1805, 4, part ("prov. de Caracas et Nouvelle Andalousie") ; Beob. Zool., i, 1806, 7, part (Prov. Caracas, Cumaná, and New Barcelona, Venezuela).

ORTALIS WAGLERI WAGLERI (Gray)

WAGLER'S RUFOUS-BELLIED CHACHALACA

Adult (sexes alike).—Forehead, crown, occiput, and hindneck dark slate with a brownish tinge; malar band, cheeks, auriculars, middle of chin and upper throat, and band across lower throat similar, but each feather with a broad median area of light neutral gray; lower hindneck, sides of lower neck, scapulars, interscapulars, upper wing coverts, back, rump, upper tail coverts, and breast light brownish olive to deep olive; primaries olive-brown, externally washed with deep olive; outer secondaries dark olive internally, deep olive with a very faint oily green sheen externally, the inner secondaries deep olive with an almost imperceptible oily green sheen; rectrices deep olivaceous-black with a dark blue-green sheen, the middle pair uniformly of this color, the next pair narrowly tipped with chestnut, the lateral pairs very broadly (35–50 mm.) tipped with chestnut; abdomen, sides, flanks, thighs, and under tail coverts deep hazel to russet; iris reddish hazel; bill "med(ium?) horn" (Batty); tarsi and toes brownish lead; bare skin around eye reddish blue, nude throat areas red.

Juvenal (female only seen, but sexes probably alike).—Similar to the adult but the upperparts of the body and wings browner, less olive— deep Saccardo's umber to sepia; rectrices pointed and not tipped with bright chestnut but merely very faintly freckled with tawny terminally; remiges clove brown externally edged with sepia.

Downy young.—None seen.

Adult male.—Wing 250–289 (262.7); tail 269–307 (287.1); exposed culmen 25–28 (26); tarsus 69–80 (74); middle toe without claw 53–60 (56.9 mm.).[51]

Adult female.—Wing 238–260 (252.1); tail 269–294 (281.6); exposed culmen 23–27 (24.5); tarsus 69–79 (73.6); middle toe without claw 49–60 (54.8).[52]

Range.—Resident from central and southern Sinaloa (Escuinapa, Mazatlán, Labrados, and Limoncito) to Durango (Chacala and Sayapa), Jalisco (Bahía de Banderas), and Nayarit (San Blas, Rancho San Pablo, and Santiago, Tepic).

Type locality.—"Western Mexico"; restricted to San Blas, Nayarit (van Rossem, Bull. Mus. Comp. Zool., lxxvii, 1934, 431).

Ortalida wagleri GRAY, List Birds Brit. Mus., pt. 5, Gallinae, 1867, 12 (w. Mexico; coll. Brit. Mus.).—SCLATER and SALVIN, Proc. Zool. Soc. London, 1870, 534 (monogr.).—LAWRENCE, Mem. Boston Soc. Nat. Hist., ii, 1874, 306, part (Mazatlán, Sinaloa; fresh colors of nude parts; geogr. range).—BERISTAIN and LAURENCIO, Mem. y Rev. Soc. Cient. "Antonio Alzata," vii, 1894, 220 (Sinaloa).
[Ortalida] wagleri GRAY, Hand-list, ii, 1870, 282, No. 9505.—SCLATER and SALVIN, Proc. Zool. Soc. London, 1870, 543; Nom. Av. Neotr., 1873, 136.
O[rtalida] waglerii CUBAS, Cuadro Geogr., Estadístico, Descr. e Hist. de los Estados Unidos Mexicanos, 1884, 169 (Mexico; common names).
Ortalis wagleri OGILVIE-GRANT, Cat. Birds Brit. Mus., xxii, 1893, 507 (Presidio de Mazatlán, Sinaloa; San Blas and Santiago, Tepic); Handb. Game Birds, ii, 1897, 237, pl. 39 (monogr.).—LANTZ, Trans. Kansas Acad. Sci. for 1896-7

---

[51] Eight specimens from Durango, Sinaloa, and Tepic.
[52] Seven specimens from Durango, Sinaloa, and Jalisco.

(1899), 219 (Limoncito, Sinaloa).—SALVIN and GODMAN, Biol. Centr.-Amer., Aves, iii, 1903, 279, pl. 72 (Mazatlán and Presidio de Mazatlán, Sinaloa; San Blas and Santiago, Tepic).—MILLER, Bull Amer. Mus. Nat. Hist., xxi, 1905, 343 (Escuinapa, etc., s. Sinaloa; habits) ; xxii, 1906, 163 (Sayapa, Durango, 2,500 feet).—MCLELLAN, Proc. California Acad. Sci., ser. 4, xvi, 1927, 6 (Labrados, Sinaloa).—PETERS, Check-list Birds of World, ii, 1934, 18, part (Sinaloa to Jalisco).—BAILEY and CONOVER, Auk, lii, 1935, 424, in text (Durango, Mexico).— VAN ROSSEM, Condor, xliv, 1942, 77 in text (tax.; fig. of head).
O[rtalis] wagleri RIDGWAY, Man. North Amer. Birds, 1887, 208.—MENDIZABAL, Rev. Soc. Mex. Hist. Nat., i, No. 3, 1940, 180, in text (Mexico).
[Ortalis] wagleri SHARPE, Hand-list, i, 1899, 17.
Ortalis wagleri wagleri HELLMAYR and CONOVER, Cat. Birds Amer., i, No. 1, 1942, 168 (syn.; distr.).
Ortalis vetula maccalli (not Ortalida mccalli Baird) BAILEY, Auk, xxiii, 1906, 385 (San Blas, Tepic).

ORTALIS WAGLERI GRISEICEPS van Rossem

NORTHERN RUFOUS-BELLIED CHACHALACA

Adult (sexes alike).—Similar to that of *Ortalis wagleri wagleri* but with the head and upper hindneck paler—ashy neutral gray to pale slate gray and with less brownish wash; upperparts slightly grayer, especially in worn plumage; breast and lower throat more grayish, less greenish— ashy deep grayish olive; abdomen, sides, flanks, thighs, and under tail coverts averaging slightly paler than in the nominate race, averaging more hazel than russet.

Juvenal.—None seen.

Downy young.—None seen.

Adult male.—Wing 256–272; tail 277–279; exposed culmen 26–27; tarsus 67, 67; middle toe without claw 54–60 mm.[53]

Adult female.—Wing 248–258 (253) ; tail 265–288 (275) ; exposed culmen 24–26 (24.8) ; tarsus 67–70 (68.5) ; middle toe without claw 52–58 (56 mm.).[54]

Range.—Resident from southern Chihuahua (Hacienda de San Rafael) and southern Sonora (Alamos) south into northern Sinaloa for an undetermined distance.

Type locality.—Alamos, Sonora, Mexico.

Ortalida wagleri (not of Gray, 1867) LAWRENCE, Mem. Boston Soc. Nat. Hist., ii, 1874, 306 part (Sonora).—PETERS, Check-list Birds of World, ii, 1934, 18 part (Chihuahua and Sonora).
Ortalis wagleri (not of Gray, 1867) VAN ROSSEM, Trans. San Diego Soc. Nat. Hist., vi, No. 19, 1931, 244 (Sonora, Mexico).—PETERS, Check-list Birds of World, ii, 1934, 18, part.
Ortalis wagleri griseiceps VAN ROSSEM, Bull. Mus. Comp. Zool., lxxvii, 1934, 431 (Alamos, Sonora, Mexico; crit.).—HELLMAYR and CONOVER, Cat. Birds Amer., i, No. 1, 1942, 167 (syn.; distr.).

---

[53] Two specimens from Sonora.
[54] Four specimens from Sonora and Chihuahua.

Genus PENELOPINA Reichenbach

Penelopina Reichenbach, Handb. Orn., Columb., 1861, 152. (Type, by monotypy, *Penelope niger* Fraser.)
Penelope Reichenow, Die Vögel, i, 1913, 275, part.

Medium-sized Cracidae (length about 534–635 mm.) with entire chin as well as throat nude, the lower throat with a conspicuous compressed lobe or dewlap, the adult male with plumage entirely black.

Bill relatively rather small (from laterofrontal antiae about as long as distance from same point to middle of eye), rather compressed, its

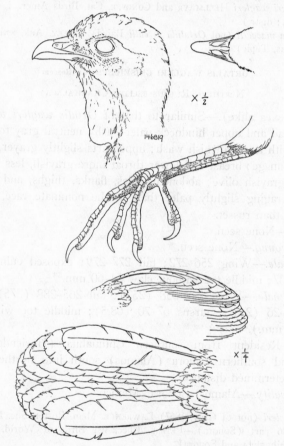

FIGURE 4.—*Penelopina nigra.*

depth at base about equal to its height at same point; culmen rather strongly decurved, broadly rounded, decidedly longer than distance from its base to laterofrontal antiae; mesorhinium rather narrow anteriorly, much broader basally, where flattened, its upper outline straight, gradually but slightly ascending toward base; nostrils fusiform, longitudinal, their anterior ends in contact with rhinotheca, the nasal fossae posterior to and underneath posterior half or more of nostril occupied by naked membrane. Wing rather large, the longest primaries shorter than longest secondaries; eighth to eleventh primaries longest, the first (outermost) about two-thirds as long as the longest; the three outermost rather strongly bowed, or incurved terminally. Tail decidedly longer than wing, much rounded, the rectrices (12) broad, firm, with broadly rounded tips. Tarsus rather long and slender, about one-third as long as wing to tips of longest secondaries; acrotarsium with a single series of large, broad scutella on upper portion and outer side and an additional series on the lower half (approximately) of inner side; planta tarsi with two series of much smaller scutella, which on lower portion become more or less indistinct or obsolete; middle toe about two-thirds as long as tarsus, the lateral toes about equal in length and extending to about penultimate articulation of middle toe; hallux about as long as basal phalanx of middle toe; claws relatively rather small, not strongly curved, except that of the hallux.

Plumage and coloration.—Feathers of pileum moderately elongated (much less so than in *Penelope*), forming, when erected, a short bushy crest; loral region mostly covered by short feathers, and orbital region nude for a narrow space beneath and behind eyes; entire chin and throat nude, the former, however, with sparse, hairlike feathers, the throat with a conspicuous median compressed wattle or dewlap; feathers in general distinctly outlined, broad, with rounded tips, except on rump, abdomen, and anal region, where soft, downy, and blended. Adult male uniform glossy blue-black, the rump, abdomen, and anal region plain sooty; adult female and immature male with plumage variously barred and otherwise variegated with black, rufous, and ochraceous.

Range.—Highlands of Chiapas, Guatemala, El Salvador, Honduras, and Nicaragua. (Monotypic.)

KEY TO THE RACES OF PENELOPINA NIGRA (FRASER)

a. Plumage black (males).
 b. Plumage with more of a greenish than a bluish hue above; seminude ocular area purplish in life (Chiapas, Guatemala, sw. El Salvador).
          Penelopina nigra nigra (p. 52)
 bb. Plumage with more of a bluish than a greenish hue above; seminude ocular area dull reddish brown in life.
  (interior of El Salvador and adjacent parts of Honduras).
       Penelopina nigra dickeyi (p. 54)
  (mountains of Nicaragua)........**Penelopina nigra rufescens** (p. 54)
aa. Plumage brown (females).
 b. General tone of plumage sandy brown.
  c. Ocular area dusky; lower eyelid pink in life (interior of El Salvador and adjacent parts of Honduras)..........**Penelopina nigra dickeyi** (p. 54)
  cc. Ocular area not dusky; lower eyelid apparently dusky in life (Chiapas, Guatemala, sw. El Salvador)............**Penelopina nigra nigra** (p. 52)
 bb. General tone of plumage pale rufescent-brown (mountains of Nicaragua).
       Penelopina nigra rufescens (p. 54)

PENELOPINA NIGRA NIGRA (Fraser)

GUATEMALAN BLACK CHACHALACA

Adult male.—Forehead, crown, occiput, cheeks, auriculars, nape, sides of neck, entire upperparts, wings and tail, and lower throat and upper breast black with a dark bluish to greenish gloss,[55] darkest on the head, becoming somewhat greenish on the scapulars, wings, back, and tail; lower breast, abdomen, sides, flanks, and under tail coverts dark fuscous-black, the sides and under tail coverts with a blue-green sheen; under wing coverts like the upper ones; chin and upper throat bare and red in color; circumocular area purplish; iris dark brown; bill and feet red.

Adult female.—Forehead, crown, occiput, and nape dark fuscous, each feather narrowly edged with Brussels brown to Argus brown; sides of head, auriculars, sides of neck, lower throat, and upper breast fuscous indistinctly barred with Brussels brown; interscapulars, inner, lesser, and median upper wing coverts banded narrowly with fuscous-black and Argus brown, the two colors present in about equal widths; back, lower back, and rump similar but paler and duller—pale, rather olive-brown and Brussels brown; scapulars, remiges, and outer and greater upper wing coverts dark fuscous-black with an oily greenish gloss and crossed with numerous narrow Brussels-brown bands, these bands narrower than the darker interspaces and restricted to the outer webs of all the remiges except the innermost secondaries and much reduced even on the outer web toward the tips of the feathers, the under surface of the wing being uniform fuscous-black; upper tail coverts olive-brown with irregular, fairly broad cross bars of blackish and Argus brown; central pair of rectrices bright Argus brown barred with fuscous-black, the bars not quite so wide as the interspaces, there being about 20–25 dark bars on the median rectrices, these bars tending to break up laterally toward the tip of the feather; the other rectrices similar but with an increasing restriction of the Argus brown to the outer webs, and with a narrowing of the same (widening of the fuscous-black areas) toward the tip; lower breast, abdomen, sides, flanks, and under tail coverts grayish buffy brown, darkening posteriorly to Saccardo's umber on the thighs and under tail coverts, and the feathers more or less marked with irregular, wavy pale bars of pale buffy to buffy whitish, these bars edged narrowly with dusky.[56]

Juvenal male.—Above similar to adult female but with the rectrices different, not Argus brown barred with black, but blackish with two pairs of longitudinal, wavy, interrupted, narrow streaks of brownish, one pair next to the shaft (one on each side) and one pair slightly nearer the outer than the inner edge of each web, this pair confluent about

---

[55] There may be some seasonal variation in the bluish or greenish sheen.
[56] In older birds the ventral barring is restricted to thighs, flanks, and under tail coverts; in younger birds more of the underparts generally are affected.

15 mm. from the tip, which terminal area is crossed by three narrow bars of brownish; the rectrices also very narrowly edged with pale brown; chin and throat with buffy down; lower throat like the underparts of the body, darker and more barred with fuscous than in the adult female.

Juvenal female.—None seen.

Adult male.—Wing 223–266 (247); tail 265–300 (282); exposed culmen 24.5–26.4 (25.6); tarsus 72–81 (77.7); middle toe without claw 48–54.5 (51.8 mm.).[57]

Adult female.—Wing 226–254 (240.1); tail 274–312 (289); exposed culmen 22.5–26.5 (24.8); tarsus 67–79 (76.3); middle toe without claw 48.7–51 (50 mm.).[58]

Range.—Resident in the humid subtropical zone of the mountainous areas of Chiapas (Finca Juárez, Mount Ovando, Tumbala, Santa Rita), through Guatemala (near Antigua, Barrillos, Nebaj, Sepacuite, La Primavera, Cobán, Vera Paz, Volcán de Agua, Volcán de Fuego, El Rincón, San Marcos) to the extreme southwestern part of El Salvador (Cerro del Aquila, Volcán de Santa Ana; possibly more widely ranging formerly in El Salvador and since killed off).

Type locality.—Guatemala (*ex* van Rossem, Trans. San Diego Soc. Nat. Hist., vii, 1934, 364).

Penelope niger FRASER, Proc. Zool. Soc. London, 1850, 246, pl. 29 (locality unknown; type in coll. Derby Mus.).
P[enelope] niger SALVIN, Ibis, 1860, 194 (Cobán, Guatemala).
Penelope nigra SCLATER and SALVIN, Ibis, 1859, 224 (Guatemala).—GRAY, Proc. Zool. Soc. London, 1860, 272 (Guatemala; monogr.).—SALVIN, Proc. Zool. Soc. London, 1867, 160 (Volcán de Agua, Guatemala).
P[enelope] nigra REICHENOW, Die Vögel, i, 1913, 276.
[Penelope] nigra GRAY, Hand-list, ii, 1870, 251, No. 9495 (Guatemala).
P[enelopina] nigra REICHENBACH, Handb. Orn., Columb., 1861, 152.
Penelopina nigra SCLATER and SALVIN, Proc. Zool. Soc. London, 1870, 528, 543 (monogr.; Guatemala—Vera Paz, Volcán de Agua, and Volcán de Fuego).—OGILVIE-GRANT, Cat. Birds Brit. Mus., xxii, 1893, 503 (Vera Paz, Cobán, El Rincón in San Marcos, and Volcán de Agua, Guatemala); Handb. Game Birds, ii, 1897, 233 (monogr.).—NELSON, Auk, xv, 1898, 156 (Tumbala e. Chiapas).—SALVIN and GODMAN, Biol. Centr.-Amer., Aves, iii, 1902, 277, part (Santa Rita, Chiapas, Cobán, Volcán de Agua, Volcán de Fuego, and El Rincón in San Marcos, Guatemala).—GRISCOM, Bull. Amer. Mus. Nat. Hist., lxiv, 1932, 100 part (distr. in Guatemala).—PETERS, Check-list Birds World, ii, 1934, 21, part (Chiapas and Guatemala).—BERLIOZ, Bull. Mus. Hist. Nat. Paris, ser. 2, xi, 1939, 361 (Santa Rosa, Chiapas; spec.).—DEL CAMPO, Anal. Inst. Biol., xiii, No. 2, 1942, 700 (Cerro Brujo, Ocozocoautla, and Triunfo, Chiapas; spec.).
[Penelopina] nigra SCLATER and SALVIN, Nom. Av. Neotr., 1873, 136 (Guatemala).—SHARPE, Hand-list, i, 1899, 16, part (highlands of Guatemala).
Penelopina nigra nigra VAN ROSSEM, Trans. San Diego Soc. Nat. Hist., vii, No. 31, May 31, 1914, 364 (chars., range).—DICKEY and VAN ROSSEM, Birds El Salvador,

---

[57] Five specimens from Chiapas, Guatemala, and El Salvador.
[58] Eight specimens from Chiapas and Guatemala.

1938, 143 (Cerro del Aquila, El Salvador, spec., seen on Cerro de Los Naranjo and main cone of Volcán de Santa Ana; possibly also on Volcán de San Miguel).—HELLMAYR and CONOVER, Cat. Birds Amer., i, No. 1, 1942, 183 (syn.; distr.).

PENELOPINA NIGRA DICKEYI van Rossem

SALVADOREAN BLACK CHACHALACA

Adult male.—Similar to that of the nominate race but with the bare area around the eye dull brownish red instead of purplish, the lower eyelid paler and more orange, "iris dark, maroon-red; bill, gular patch with wattle, tarsi, and feet, between orange-red and coral-red; ocular space, dull brownish red, lower eyelid paler; claws reddish-brown."[59]

Adult female.—Similar to that of the nominate race, but area about eye "dusky" and lower eyelid dull pink in life. "Iris, reddish-brown; tarsi and feet dull, brownish red; bill dull brown; ocular space, dusky; lower eyelid dusky pink; gular skin, salmon pink; claws dull, brownish red, slightly darker than toes."[59]

Juvenal male.—Like that of the nominate race.

Adult male.—Wing 230–260 (245.8); tail 273–292 (282.6); exposed culmen 24.2–26.5 (24.8); tarsus 72–82 (77.6); middle toe without claw 49–53.5 (50.9 mm.).[60]

Adult female.—Wing 241–245 (242.7); tail 260–310 (280); exposed culmen 19.5–25 (23.1); tarsus 71.5–80 (75.7); middle toe without claw 49–51 (50 mm.).[61]

Range.—Inhabits the cloud forest of the humid Upper Tropical Zone in the interior cordillera of El Salvador (Los Esesmiles) and the adjacent part of Honduras (Cantoral and Montaña El Chorro).

Type locality.—Los Esesmiles, Chalatenango, El Salvador.

Penelopina nigra dickeyi VAN ROSSEM, Trans. San Diego Soc. Nat. Hist., vii, 1934, 364-365 (orig. descr.; Los Esesmiles, El Salvador).—DICKEY and VAN ROSSEM, Birds of El Salvador, 1938, 144 (habits; nest; El Salvador).—HELLMAYR and CONOVER, Cat. Birds Amer., i, No. 1, 1942, 184 (syn.; distr.).

PENELOPINA NIGRA RUFESCENS van Rossem

NICARAGUAN BLACK CHACHALACA

Adult male.—Similar to that of the nominate race.

Adult female—Like that of *P. n. nigra* but paler and less sandy, more rufescent, especially on the upperparts, wings, and tail, the dark bars narrower and the pale interspaces relatively wider.

Juvenal.—None seen.

[59] *Ex* Dickey and van Rossem, Birds El Salvador, 1938, 146.
[60] Eight specimens including the type from El Salvador and Honduras.
[61] Three specimens from Honduras.

Adult male.—Wing 235–245 (239.5); tail 281–289 (286.2); exposed culmen 23–25 (24.1); tarsus 75–79 (77.0); middle toe without claw 49.2–54 (52.1 mm.).[62]

Range.—Occurs in the humid forests of the Upper Tropical Zone in Nicaragua (Ocotal and San Rafael del Norte).

Type locality.—Ocotal, Nicaragua.

Penelopina nigra SALVIN and GODMAN, Ibis, 1892, 328 (Matagalpa, Nicaragua);
 Biol. Centr.-Amer., Aves, iii, 1902, 277, part (Matagalpa, n. Nicaragua).—
 GRISCOM, Bull. Amer. Mus. Nat. Hist., lxiv, 1932, 100, part (northern Nica-
 ragua).—PETERS, Check-list Birds of World, ii, 1934, 21, part (Nicaragua).
Penelopina nigra rufescens VAN ROSSEM, Trans. San Diego Soc. Nat. Hist., vii,
 No. 31, 1934, 365 (Ocotal, Nicaragua; descr.; meas.).—HELLMAYR and CON-
 OVER, Cat. Birds Amer., i, No. 1, 1942, 184 (syn.; distr.).

Genus CHAMAEPETES Wagler

Chamaepetes WAGLER, Isis, 1832, 1227. (Type, by monotypy, *Ortalida goudotii* Lesson.)
Chamapetes (emendation) GRAY, List Gen. Birds, 1840, 59.
Penelopsis (not of Bonaparte, 1856) REICHENBACH, Voll. Nat. Tauben, 1861, 147. (Type, *Penelope rufiventris* Tschudi.)

Medium-sized Cracidae (length about 520–638 mm.) with gular region completely feathered and three outer primaries with terminal portion abruptly attenuated.

Bill relatively small but rather elongated (more than half as long as head, the culmen decidedly longer than the mesorhinium), rather depressed, its width at base of culmen equal to or greater than its depth at same point; culmen broadly rounded (not ridged); nostril relatively rather large, longitudinal, elliptical or fusiform, anteriorly nearly in contact with the rhinotheca, a cartilaginous lobe or tubercle distinctly visible within the posterior half (more or less). Entire loral and orbital regions, sides of forehead, and anterior half of malar region nude, but with scant, minute bristles, at least on malar region and sides of frontal region, but entire throat completely feathered. Wing moderately large, relatively very broad, the longest primaries extending but slightly beyond tips of longest secondaries; sixth to eighth primaries longest, the first (outermost) nearly three-fourths as long as the longest, the three outer primaries strongly bowed or incurved, and with terminal portion abruptly and conspicuously attenuated. Tail decidedly shorter than wing (about five-sixths as long), decidedly to rather strongly rounded, the rectrices (12) broad, with broadly rounded tips. Tarsus moderately long (about one-fourth to nearly one-third as long as wing), relatively rather slender, the acrotarsium with a single series of large, transverse scutella, the planta tarsi with a more or less continuous series of transverse or hexagonal

---

[62] Four specimens from Nicaragua. This race is only doubtfully distinct.

scutella on outer side (then sometimes large and regularly obliquely transverse and bending around posterior side, almost meeting those of acrotarsium); middle toe two-thirds (*C. g. rufiventris*) to three-fourths (*C. unicolor*) as long as tarsus, the lateral toes reaching to about penultimate articulation of middle toe (on the outer somewhat beyond), the hallux as long as or slightly longer than combined length of first two

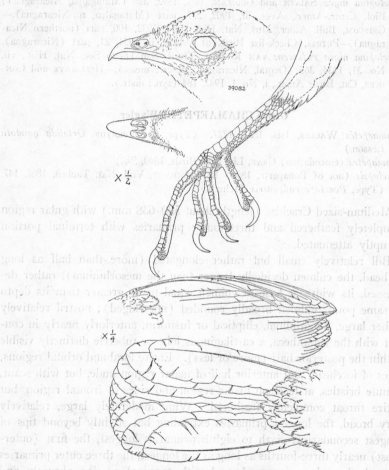

FIGURE 5.—*Chamaepetes unicolor.*

phalanges of outer toe; claws moderate in size, rather strongly curved (that of hallux especially), compressed.

Plumage and coloration.—Gular region completely feathered except anterior point and narrow lateral margins of chin; entire loral and orbital regions nude, the sides of forehead and anterior half of malar region also nude but with sparse short bristles; feathers of pileum but slightly if at all elongated; plumage in general with feathers moderately broad, rounded, distinctly outlined, except on rump and anal region, where soft, downy, and blended. Coloration plain blackish or sooty above, more or less glossed with greenish, dusky or sooty below, in one species with under parts of body cinnamon-rufous; sexes alike.

Range.—Costa Rica to Peru. (Two species, only one in the area covered by this work.)

CHAMAEPETES UNICOLOR Salvin

BLACK GUAN

Adult (sexes alike).—Entire feathered areas of head, neck, upperparts, wings, and tail black with a strong, dark greenish blue sheen, the primaries with little if any sheen, and washed with fuscous; upper breast, thighs, and flanks like the upperparts but less glossy, mixed with grayish; lower breast, abdomen, and under tail coverts chaetura drab to fuscous washed to a varying degree with dark grayish olive to olivaceous-black, the olivaceous feathers with a slight oily gloss; the feathers of the lower midabdomen more downy in texture and without any olivaceous wash—fuscous to clove brown; under wing coverts like the upperparts; "bare skin of nasal (cere) and frontal areas azure blue shading to ultramarine near the eyes; skin of basal region of lower mandible azure blue shading to ultramarine farther back; iris wine purple; tarsus burnt carmine "(W. W. Brown on label of M.C.Z. No. 118923)."

Immature.—No specimen or description seen, but Carriker (Ann. Carnegie Mus., iv, 1908, 385) writes that several young birds taken on Volcán Turrialba, Costa Rica, and not saved, had the feathers of the lower parts edged with rufous, which "even persists after the upperparts have assumed the adult plumage." Apparently no one has published anything on any but the adult plumage.

Adult male.—Wing 285–298 (290); tail 295–303 (293.6); culmen from base of cere 30.5–33 (31.9); tarsus 63.7–76.5 (71.7); middle toe without claw 5156.5 (54.4 mm.).[63]

Adult female.—Wing 264; tail 287; culmen from base of cere 33.2; tarsus 69.6; middle toe without claw 52.1 mm. (1 specimen, Costa Rica).

Range.—Resident in the subtropical zone in the mountains of Costa Rica (La Palma de San José, Rancho Redondo, Volcán de Irazú, Volcán de Turrialba, Varra Blanca de Sarapiquí, and Ujurras de Terraba) and western Panama (Calovevora, Veraguas; Cordillera de Tole; and Boquete, Chiriquí, 5,600–5,800 feet).

Type locality.—Veraguas, Panama.

Chamœpetes unicolor SALVIN, Proc. Zool. Soc. London, 1867, 159, 160 (Calovevora, Veraguas, w. Panama; coll. Salvin and Godman, now in coll. Brit. Mus.) ; 1870, 217 (Calovevora, Veraguas).—LAWRENCE, Ann. Lyc. Nat. Hist. New York, ix,

[63] Five specimens from Panama and Costa Rica.

1868, 139 (La Palma de San José and Rancho Redondo, Costa Rica).—Sclater and Salvin, Proc. Zool. Soc. London, 1870, 531 (monogr.).—Boucard, Proc. Zool. Soc. London, 1878, 42 (Volcán de Irazú, Costa Rica).—Zeledón, Cat. Aves Costa Rica, 1882, 28; Anal. Mus. Nac. Costa Rica, i, 1887, 128 (Rancho Redondo, Costa Rica).—Ogilvie-Grant, Cat. Birds Brit. Mus., xxii, 1893, 522 (San José and Volcán de Irazú, Costa Rica; Calovevora and Cordillera de Tole, w. Panama) ; Handb. Game Birds, ii, 1897, 257 (monogr.).—Bangs, Proc. New England Zool. Club, iii, 1902, 22 (Boquete, 5,600-5,800 feet, Chiriquí, w. Panama).—Salvin and Godman, Biol. Centr.-Amer., Aves, iii, 1902, 278, pl. 71 (Volcán de Irazú, San José, La Palma de San José, and Rancho Redondo, Costa Rica; Calovevora and Cordillera de Tole, w. Panama).—Ferry, Publ. Field Mus. Nat. Hist., No. 146, 1910, 260 (Volcán de Turrialba, Costa Rica; habits).—Carriker, Ann. Carnegie Mus., vi, 1910, 384 (Varra Blanca de Sarapiquí, Volcán de Turrialba at 8,000-9,000 feet, and Ujurras de Terraba, Costa Rica, crit.; habits).

Ch[amaepetes] unicolor Reichenow, Die Vögel, i, 1913, 277.

[Chamæpetes] unicolor Sclater and Salvin, Proc. Zool. Soc. London, 1870, 543; Nom. Av. Neotr., 1873, 136.—Sharpe, Hand-list, i, 1899, 18.

Chamaepetes unicolor Frantzius, Journ. für Orn., 1869, 372 (Costa Rica).—Kennard and Peters, Proc. Boston Soc. Nat. Hist., xxxviii, 1928, 446 (Boquete Trail, Panama; spec.; common; plum.).—Peters, Check-list Birds of World, ii, 1934, 22.—Griscom, Bull. Mus. Comp. Zool., lxxviii, 1935, 303 (subtropical. zone, mountains of Costa Rica and w. Panama).—Hellmayr and Conover, Cat. Birds Amer., i, No. 1, 1942, 184 (syn.; distr.).

[Ortalida] unicolor Gray, Hand-list, ii, 1870, 253, No. 9521 (Veraguas).

Genus OREOPHASIS Gray

Oreophasis Gray, Gen. Birds, iii, 1844, 485. (Type, by monotypy, *O. derbianus* Gray.)

Oreophasianus (emendation) Schlegel, Handl. Dierk., i, 1857, 387.

Rather large Cracidae (length about 812–915 mm.) with an upright, nearly cylindrical, nude bony tubercle or casque springing from center of the nude vertex; cere, mesorhinium, forehead, chin, and malar region densely covered with velvety or plushlike feathers, those on mesorhinium longer and erect, especially anteriorly; orbital region and posterior portion of lores more or less covered by short feathers; vertex nude, with a conspicuous erect bony, nearly cylindrical, nude tubercle or casque, inclined backward at a decided angle; feathers of occiput, hindneck, and sides of neck distinctly outlined, sublanceolate, but with obtuse or rounded tips. Wing rather large, very broad, the longest primaries extending slightly but decidedly beyond tips of longest secondaries; fifth primary longest, the first (outermost) a little less than two-thirds as long and distinctly bowed or bent inward. Tail a little shorter than wing, strongly rounded, the rectrices (12) broad and firm, with subrounded tips. Tarsus about one-fourth as long as wing, stout; acrotarsium with a single series of about 12 large, transverse scutella, the three uppermost covered by the rather elongated feathers of thigh; planta tarsi covered on both sides by rather small, irregular, mostly roundish or hexagonal scales; middle toe about three-fourths as long as tarsus, the lateral toes reaching to or very slightly beyond its penultimate articulation; hallux shorter than combined length of first three phalanges of outer toe; claws rather long, rather strongly curved, compressed.

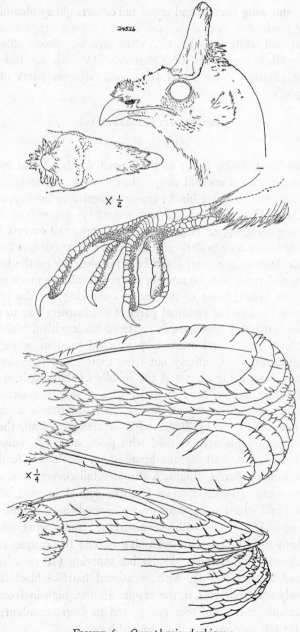

× ½

× ¼

FIGURE 6.—*Oreophasis derbianus.*

Plumage and coloration.—Feathers of upperparts distinctly outlined, rather broad, with rounded tips; those of underparts more blended (except anteriorly, where narrower) and with thickened and rigid shafts, except on thighs, where soft but broad and rounded, and on abdomen and under tail coverts very soft and downy. Adults with neck, back, scapulars, and wing coverts and upper tail coverts glossy blue-black, rump dull sooty black, abdomen, under tail coverts plain sooty, foreneck, chest, and breast dull white with blackish shaft streaks. Sexes alike in color.

Range.—High mountains of Guatemala (Volcán de Fuego, Cerro Zunil, etc., mostly above 7,000 feet) and adjacent parts of Chiapas. (Monotypic.)

OREOPHASIS DERBIANUS Gray

HORNED GUAN

Adult male.—Culmen as far as the nostril, forehead, and crown anterior to the cylindrical coronal casque, lores, cheeks, auriculars, chin, and upper throat glossy velvety black; crown posterior to the casque, occiput, hindneck, and sides of neck black with a dark ivy-greenish sheen; scapulars, interscapulars, upper wing coverts, and upper tail coverts black with a pronounced dark blue to dark greenish-blue sheen; remiges black with a faint bluish sheen on the outer and a faint purplish one on the inner webs; lower back and rump like the interscapulars but with so much of the dark sepia to clove-brown bases of the feathers showing (or the bluish-black areas so restricted to the terminal parts of the feathers) as to give these areas a much-mottled appearance; rectrices black with a bluish to dark purplish-bluish sheen, and crossed by a broad band of white (40 mm. wide) a little less than halfway out from their bases (the distal border of the white band being almost at the middle of the length of the tail); middle of throat almost entirely nude, with a very few small blackish feathers, extreme lower throat, breast, and anterior abdomen white, each feather with a dusky shaft stripe of chaetura drab, the posterolateral feathers of this area washed with pale Saccardo's umber to pale Dresden brown, the shaft streaks broadest on the lateral feathers; rest of abdomen, sides, flanks, thighs, and under tail coverts mummy brown to fuscous, some of the abdominal feathers with desiccated whitish tips and washed and edged with buffy brown around the vent, the sides and flanks more or less glossy with greenish blue; under wing coverts dark mummy brown with some greenish-blue sheen; the casque is straight, slopes backward, and is fairly slender but tapering (18 mm. in diameter at base and 5 mm. at tip), with occasional hairlike blackish feathers very sparsely scattered over it, the casque 55 mm. high in front, 37 mm. in back; casque, tarsi, and toes orange-red to deep vermilion; bare eye ring purple; bill pale straw color; iris white.

Adult female.—Similar to the male but smaller, with the lower back and rump somewhat less mottled with greenish blue, more sepia; casque shorter (less than 45 mm. long in front).

Young (juvenal?).—Similar to the adult but with no or very little casque on the crown, the area involved sprinkled with hairlike blackish feathers; the lower back and rump with practically no greenish-blue sheen; the outer primaries fuscous with very little bluish sheen externally.

Natal down.—Unknown.

Adult male.—Wing 394; tail 350; exposed culmen 21; tarsus 83; middle toe without claw 71 mm.[64]

Adult female.—Wing 332–378 (362); tail 300–368 (329.1); exposed culmen 19–23 (21.1); tarsus 80–92 (85.1); middle toe without claw 63–71 (67.5 mm.).[65]

Range.—Resident in the temperate zone forests above 7,500 feet in the high mountains of western Guatemala (above Huehuetenango, Chicaman, Cerro Zunil, Volcán de Fuego, Volcán San Lucas, Volcán de Santa María, near Quezaltenango, probably also the Guatemala slope of Tacana, Tajumulco), and adjacent highlands of Chiapas (near Pinabete, and Volcán de Tacana).

Type locality.—Guatemala.

Oreophasis derbianus GRAY, Gen. Birds, iii, 1844, 485, pl. 121; List Birds Brit. Mus., pt. 5, Gallinae, 1867, 14.—SCLATER and SALVIN, Ibis, 1859, 224 (Volcán de Fuego, Guatemala; 7,000-11,000 feet; habits, etc.); Proc. Zool. Soc. London, 1870, 541, 543 (monogr.).—SCLATER, Proc. Zool. Soc. London, 1860, 184 (Volcán de Fuego).—SALVIN, Ibis, 1860, 43, 248 (Volcán de Fuego; habits); 1873, 429; 1874, 188 (Chicaman, Guatemala).—OGILVIE-GRANT, Cat. Birds Brit. Mus., xxii, 1893, 489; Handb. Game Birds, ii, 1897, 218 (Volcán de Fuego).—NELSON, Auk, xv, 1898, 156 (Volcán de Santa María, Guatemala; near Pinabete, Chiapas). —SALVIN and GODMAN, Biol. Centr.-Amer., Aves, iii, 1902, 274 (Volcán de Fuego, Chicaman, and Cerro Zunil, Guatemala).—GRISCOM, Bull. Amer. Mus. Nat. Hist., lxiv, 1932, 99 (Volcán San Lucas, Guatemala spec.).—PETERS, Checklist Birds World, ii, 1934, 24.—CARRIKER and DE SCHAUENSEE, Proc. Acad. Nat. Sci. Philadelphia, lxxxvii, 1935, 413 (Guatemala; Chichoy, 10,000 feet).— HELLMAYR and CONOVER, Cat. Birds Amer., i, No. 1, 1942, 196 (syn.; distr.).
O[reophasis] derbianus REICHENOW, Die Vögel, i, 1913, 278.
[Oreophasis] derbianus GRAY, Hand-list, ii, 1870, 253, No. 9522.—SHARPE, Hand-list, i, 1899, 15.
Orephasis derbyanus REICHENBACH, Synop. Av., Columb., ii, 1837, pl. 172, fig. 1508.
O[reophasis] derbyanus REICHENBACH, Voll. Nat. Tauben, 1861, 155, pl. 270.
[Oreophasis] derbyanus SCLATER and SALVIN, Nom. Av. Neotr., 1873, 137.
Penelope fronticornis VAN DER HOEVEN, Handb. Zool., ii, 1852-56, 435; Handb. Dierkunde, ii, 1855, 664.

---

[64] One specimen, unsexed, but undoubtedly a male.

[65] Six specimens from Guatemala.

Superfamily PHASIANOIDEA: Grouse, Pheasants, Turkeys

>Gallinaceae NITZSCH, *in* Meckel, Deutsch. Arch. Phys., 1820, 258 (includes Otididae!).

=Alectoropodes OGILVIE-GRANT, Cat. Birds Brit. Mus., xxii, 1893, xi, 33.—SALVIN and GODMAN, Biol. Centr.-Amer. Aves, iii, 1902, 283.—KNOWLTON, Birds of the World, 1909, 267, in text.

>Alectoromorphae HUXLEY, Proc. Zool. Soc. London, 1867, 459 (includes Turnicidae, Pteroclidae, Megapodidae, Cracidae, and Phasianidae).

=Gallinæ Alectoropodes SCLATER and SALVIN, Nom. Av. Neotr., 1873, vii, 137.— ELLIOT, Stand. Nat. Hist., iv, 1885, 198, in text.

=Gallinae COPE, Amer. Nat., xxiii, 1889, 871, 873.

=Phasiani AMERICAN ORNITHOLOGISTS' UNION, Check-list, 1886, 167; ed. 3, 1910, 134.—SHARPE, Rev. Rec. Att. Classif. Birds, 1891, 68; Hand-list, i, 1899, x, 18.

<Phasianidæ ELLIOT, Stand. Nat. Hist., iv, 1885, 213, in text (excludes Tetraonidae, Odontophorinae, and Old World partridges and quails).—GRANT, Cat. Birds Brit. Mus., xxii, 1893, xi, 33, 94 (excludes Tetraonidae).

<Phasianinæ OGILVIE-GRANT, Cat. Birds Brit. Mus., xxii, 1893, 95 (excludes Tetraonidae, Odontophorinae, and Old World partridges and quails).

=Phasianidæ KNOWLTON, Birds of the World, 1909, 49, 276.

=Gallidae GADOW, Classif. Vertebr., 1898, 34.

=Phasianides WETMORE, Proc. U. S. Nat. Mus., lxxvi, art. 24, 1930, 3.

=Phasianoida AMERICAN ORNITHOLOGISTS' UNION, Check-list, ed. 4, 1931, 78.— WETMORE, Smiths. Misc. Coll., lxxxix, No. 13, 1934, 6; xcix, No. 7, 1940, 6.— PETERS, Check-list Birds of World, ii, 1934, 24.

Galliform birds with the hallux elevated and relatively small, with basal phalanx shorter than that of third toe; inner notch of sternum very deep, more than half as long as sternum; outer division of the long and narrow posterior lateral process of sternum slightly expanded on outer side only, and costal process elongated, nearly parallel to long axis of sternum.

Palate schizognathous; nares holorhinal; basipterygoid processes articulating with pterygoids as far as possible from quadrate; episternal process perforated to receive feet of coracoids; oil gland tufted.

KEY TO THE AMERICAN (NATIVE AND NATURALIZED) FAMILIES AND SUBFAMILIES OF PHASIANOIDEA

a. Head and at least upper neck naked, the former usually with a bony, erect, vertical helmet or bristly or curly crest, or with an occipital feathered patch or band; tail relatively small, drooping (decumbent), not erectile (?), mostly hidden by coverts, the very full plumage of rump presenting a strongly arched outline; second metacarpal without backward process; costal processes outwardly inclined ....**Numididae** (p. 430)

aa. Head and neck not naked (except in Meleagrididae), without a bony vertical helmet or (except very rarely) a bristly or curly crest or occipital patch or band; tail extremely variable but never (?) decumbent, always erectile, usually very distinct from coverts, the plumage of rump not presenting a strongly arched outline; second metacarpal with backward processes; costal processes not outwardly inclined.

  b. Head and upper neck naked and more or less wattled or wrinkled, forehead with a fleshy tubercle or cylindrical appendage, capable of great enlargement in males; contour feathers truncate; postacetabulum longer than preacetabu-

lum and longer than broad; furcula weak and (viewed laterally) straight,
with rodlike hypocleideum........................**Meleagrididae** (p. 436)
  bb. Head and upper neck feathered or mostly so; contour feathers not truncate;
postacetabulum shorter than (in Tetraonidae, part, equal to) preacetabulum,
and broader than long; furcula strong and (viewed laterally) curved, with
expanded hypocleideum.
    c. Tarsus never feathered (except, very rarely, extreme upper portion); toes
never pectinated nor feathered; nasal fossae wholly unfeathered (except,
sometimes, a narrow strip along lower posterior portion); neck never
with inflatable air sacs; postacetabular region only moderately broad;
hypocleideum oval in contour; tarsometatarsus more than half as long
as tibia ....**Phasianidae** (p. 230)
      d. Mandibular tomium without serrations; maxilla relatively broader and
more depressed, with tip more produced; planta tarsi frequently
spurred ....**Phasianinae** (p. 232)
      dd. Mandibular tomium serrated subterminally; maxilla relatively narrower
and higher, with tip less produced; planta tarsi never spurred.
                                      Odontophorinae (p. 234)
  cc. Tarsus more or less (sometimes wholly) feathered; toes with lateral pectinations or else densely feathered; nasal fossae densely feathered; neck
usually with lateral inflatable air sacs; postacetabular region very broad;
hypocleideum triangular; tarsometatarsus less than as long as tibia.
                                          Tetraonidae (p. 63)

Family TETRAONIDAE: Grouse; Ptarmigan; etc.

=Tetraoninæ GRAY, List Gen. Birds, 1840, 62.—COUES, Key North Amer. Birds,
1872, 232; ed. 2, 1884, 557.—ELLIOT, Stand. Nat. Hist., iv, 1885, 198, 207, in
text.—AMERICAN ORNITHOLOGISTS' UNION, Check-list, 1886, 170.—KNOWLTON,
Birds of the World, 1909, 280, in text.
=Tetraoninae CARUS, Handb. Zool., i, 1868-75, 321.
>Tetraoninae GADOW, *in* Bronn, Thier-Reich, Vög., ii, 1891, 172 (includes Odon-
tophorinae and genera *Perdix, Caccabis, Francolinus,* and *Coturnix!*).
>Tetraonidae COUES, Key North Amer. Birds, 1872, 232; ed. 2, 1884, 576 (includes
Odontophorinae).—SCLATER and SALVIN, Nom. Av. Neotr., 1873, vii, 137 (in-
cludes Odontophorinae).—CARUS, Handb. Zool., i, 1868-75, 321 (includes
Odontophorinae and Old World partridges).—ELLIOT, Stand. Nat. Hist., iv,
1885, 198, in text (includes Odontophorinae and Old World partridges).—AMERI-
CAN ORNITHOLOGISTS' UNION, Check-list, 1886, 167 (includes Odontophorinae).
=Tetraonidae BAIRD, Rep. Pacific R. R. Surv., ix, 1858, 619.—WETMORE, Proc. U. S.
Nat. Mus., lxxvi, art. 24, 1930, 3; Smiths. Misc. Coll., lxxxix, No. 13, 1934, 6;
xcix, No. 7, 1940, 6.—AMERICAN ORNITHOLOGISTS' UNION, Check-list, ed. 4,
1931, 78.—PETERS, Check-list Birds of World, ii, 1934, 24.
=Tetraonidæ BAIRD, BREWER, and RIDGWAY, Hist. North Amer. Birds, iii, 1874,
414.—SHARPE, Rev. Rec. Att. Classif. Birds, 1891, 68; Hand-list, i, 1899, x, 18.—
OGILVIE-GRANT, Cat. Birds Brit. Mus., xxii, 1893, xi, 33, 34.—AMERICAN
ORNITHOLOGISTS' UNION, Check-list, ed. 3, 1910, 137.
>Perdicidae ELLIOT, Stand. Nat. Hist., iv, 1885, 207, in text (includes Odonto-
phorinae and Old World partridges and quails).

Galliform birds with nasal fossae completely and densely feathered; at
least upper half of tarsus (usually whole tarsus) feathered, and toes with
lateral pectinations or else densely feathered; neck usually with lateral

inflatable air sacs; postacetabular region of pelvis very broad; hypocleid-eum triangular; tarsometatarsus less than half as long as tibia.

Bill relatively small, the culmen rounded (not ridged), the tomia smooth; cere completely and densely feathered. Wing moderate, very concave beneath, the longest primaries much longer than longest seconda-ries; third or fourth primaries longest (fifth and third sometimes equal), the first (outermost) intermediate between sixth and seventh, seventh and eighth, or equal to eighth; primaries rigid, the outer ones much bowed or incurved distally. Tail variable in form, usually decidedly shorter than wing, the rectrices 16-20. Tarsus shorter than middle toe with claw (except in *Centrocercus*), with at least the upper half densely feathered (wholly feathered except in *Bonasa* and *Tetrastes,* the toes also feathered in winter specimens of *Lagopus*), never spurred; middle toe, without claw, shorter than tarsus; lateral toes about equal, reaching to or slightly beyond penultimate articulation of middle toe; hallux shorter (sometimes much shorter) than basal phalanx of middle toe; claws relatively small, slightly curved, rather blunt; toes usually with more or less distinct lateral horny pectinations or comblike or fringelike processes (deciduous, however, in summer); anterior toes connected at base by a web between first phalanges. Head completely feathered except, sometimes, a naked superciliary space.

Of the characters that distinguish the Tetraonidae from other Galli-formes some are variable in their development in different genera. The naked superciliary space, for example, is inconspicuous in the campestrian genera *Tympanuchus, Pedioecetes,* and *Centrocercus* but is conspicuously developed in *Lagopus, Dendragapus,* and *Canachites,* especially the first, and is brightly colored (red, orange, or yellow) during the breeding season. Many genera possess, in the male, an inflatable air sac on the side of the neck, this reaching its greatest development in *Tympanuchus,* in which the sac when inflated is of nearly the size and color of a small orange. The males of some genera also possess an ornamental erectile tuft of feathers on each side of the neck, *Tympanuchus* having elongated, rigid, narrow feathers inserted immediately above the air sacs, while *Bonasa* has, in nearly the same position (the air sacs, however, being absent) very broad, soft, nearly truncated feathers. The tail is extremely variable in form and development. It is short and rounded in *Lagopus* and *Tympanuchus;* much longer and more or less fan-shaped in *Bonasa, Dendragapus,* and *Canachites;* very short and graduated, with the middle rectrices projecting considerably beyond the others, in *Pedioecetes;* and considerably elongated, excessively graduated, with narrowly acuminate rectrices in *Centrocercus;* while in the Palearctic genus *Tetrao* the tail is forked, with the lateral rectrices curved or curled outward in the males. The feathering of the tarsus extends nearly, if not quite, to the base of the toes, except in *Bonasa* and *Tetrastes,* in which only about the upper half is feathered. The extent and development of this feathering vary greatly with the season, being denser and longer in winter, when, in *Lagopus,* the toes themselves are densely clothed with long feathers, while in the northern forms of *Pedioecetes* the feathers on the lower portion of the tarsus are so long as to almost conceal the toes. The "purpose" of this dense feathering of the feet seems to be to enable the birds to walk more easily upon soft snow, the fringelike processes along the sides of the toes in some genera possibly serving the same purpose, for in summer, when there is no need of "snowshoes," the toes of *Lagopus* become quite nude. At the same time the claws, which during winter are large, broad, and concave beneath, like inverted spoons, are also shed.[66]

The geographic range of the Tetraonidae embraces practically the entire North Temperate Zone. North America possesses six peculiar genera (*Bonasa, Canachites, Dendragapus, Tympanuchus, Pedioecetes,* and *Centrocercus*), while the Palearctic Region has only four genera (*Tetrao, Urogallus, Falcipennis,* and *Tetrastes*). One genus (*Lagopus*) is circumpolar. Two of the Old World species (*Tetrao lyrurus* and *Urogallus urogallus*) have been introduced into North America but seem not to have become established.

KEY TO THE GENERA OF TETRAONIDAE

a. Tail decidedly shorter than wing, not graduated (or else middle rectrices abruptly longer than rest and with rounded tips), rectrices rounded (sometimes nearly truncate) at tips; tarsus shorter than middle toe without claw; feathers of neck without spiny shafts; portion of culmen between feathered nasal fossae less than half as long as apical portion; stomach a muscular gizzard.
  b. Tarsus with lower half (approximately) naked, scutellate; tail more than two-thirds as long as wing.
    c. Rectrices 18–20; sides of neck with a conspicuous erectile tuft of broad, soft, decumbent feathers, capable of being expended into a ruff; sexes alike in coloration..Bonasa (p. 153)
    cc. Rectrices 16; sides of neck without tufts or with these rudimentary; sexes different in coloration.......................Tetrastes (extralimital)[67]
  bb. Tarsus densely feathered to or nearly to base of toes.
    c. Tail more or less forked (deeply emarginate to lyre-shaped).
                                                        Lyrurus (extralimital)[68]

---

[66] See Stejneger, On the shedding of the claws in ptarmigans and allied birds. Amer. Nat., xviii, 1884, 774–776.

[67] **Bonasia** (not of Bonaparte, 1827) Kaup, Skizz. Entw.-Gesch. Eur. Thierw., 1829, 193 (type, by monotypy and tautonymy, *Tetrao bonasia* Linnaeus).—*Tetrastes* Keyserling and Blasius, Wirbelth. Eur., lxix, 1840, 109, 200 (type, by monotypy, *Tetrao bonasia* Linnaeus).—Hartert, Vög. Pal. Fauna, iii, 1921, 1887.—Peters, Checklist Birds of World, ii, 1934, 37. Palearctic Region (Europe to Kamchatka, Japan, etc.). Two species with 10 subspecies.

[68] **Tetrao** Linnaeus, Syst. Nat., ed. 10, i, 1758, 159 (type, by subsequent designation, *Tetrao urogallus* Linnaeus) (type, by tautonymy, according to Opinion 16 Internatl. Nomencl. Comm., 1910, is *Tetrao tetrix* Linnaeus, but this is not accepted).—

  cc. Tail not at all forked (rounded, truncate, or even graduated).
    d. Tail rounded or truncate, with middle pair of rectrices not projecting beyond next pair.
      e. Larger (wing 275 mm. or more) ; adult males with feathers of throat elongated and plumage partly metallic.......**Tetrao** (extralimital)[69]
      ee. Smaller (wing less than 255 mm.) ; adult male with feathers of throat not elongated and plumage without any metallic colors.
        f. Tail more than half as long as wing; no elongated feathers on sides of neck and air sac, if present (usually absent or not obvious), relatively small.
          g. Tail more than three-fifths as long as wing with longer coverts falling far short of its tip; toes never feathered and plumage never wholly or mostly white.
            h. Rectrices 20; males with a distinct cervical air sac; larger (wing more—usually much more—than 218 mm.).
                      Dendragapus (p. 67)
            hh. Rectrices 16; males without a cervical air sac; smaller (wing less than 190 mm.).
              i. Outermost primaries of normal form......**Canachites** p. 136)
              ii. Outer primaries falcate............**Falcipennis** (extralimital)[70]
          gg. Tail less than three-fifths as long as wing, with longer coverts reaching to its tip; toes densely feathered in winter; plumage entirely or for much the greater part white in winter.
                      Lagopus (p. 90)

Tetrao (emendation) Ledru, Vog. Teneriffe, i, 1810, 184.—*Tetroa* (lapsus or typog. error) Richardson, Parry's Journ. Second Voy., Appendix, 1825 (1827), 347.— *Lyrurus* Swainson and Richardson, Fauna Bor.-Amer., ii, 1831 (1832), 342, 497 (type, by monotypy, *Tetrao tetrix* Linnaeus) ; Hartert, Vög. pal. Fauna, iii, 1921, 1872; Peters, Check-list Birds of World, ii, 1934, 26.—*Lyurus* (lapsus?) Gould, Proc. Zool. Soc. London, 1837 (1838), 132.—*Lyura* (emendation) Giebel, Thes. Orn., ii, 1875, 512.—*Tetrix* Morris, *in* W. Woods' Naturalist, ii, No. 9, June 1837, 126 (type, by tautonymy, *Tetrao tetrix* Linnaeus).—*Lagopotetrix* Malm, Vet-Akad. Förh., 1880, No. 7, 7, 30 (type, by monotypy, *L. dicksoni* Malm=hybrid of *Tetrao tetrix* and *Lagopus scoticus*). Palearctic Region (western Europe to western Siberia). Two species.

  The type species, the black cock or black game, of Europe (*L. tetrix*), has been introduced into North America but seems not to have become established.

  [69] **Tetrao** Linnaeus, Syst. Nat., ed. 10, i, 1758, 159 (type by subsequent designation, *Tetrao urogallus* Linnaeus, Gray, List Gen. Birds, 1840, 62).—*Urogallus* Scopoli, Introd. Nat. Hist., 1777, 478 (type, by tautonymy, *Tetrao urogallus* Linnaeus).—*Capricalea* "Niles[son]" S.D.W., Analyst, iii, No. 14, Jan. 1836, 206 (type, by tautonymy, *C. arborea* S.D.W.=*Tetrao urogallus* Linnaeus). Palearctic Region. Two species.

  The type species of this genus also, the capercaille, wood grouse, or cock-of-the-woods (*Tetrao urogallus*), has been liberated in North America but seems not to have become established. It is the largest of the grouse, the adult male nearly if not quite equaling a hen turkey in bulk and weight.

  [70] **Falcipennis** Elliot, Proc. Acad. Nat. Sci. Philadelphia, 1864, 23 (type, by monotypy, *F. hartlaubii* Elliot=*Tetrao falcipennis* Hartlaub).

  This monotypic genus of northeastern Asia is the Palearctic representative of *Canachites,* from which it seems to differ chiefly in its falcate outer primaries.

ff. Tail less than half as long as wing; males with a conspicuous tuft of elongated feathers and a large inflatable air sac on each side of neck..................................**Tympanuchus** (p. 206)
  dd. Tail strongly graduated, with middle pair of rectrices projecting conspicuously beyond the next pair..................**Pedioecetes** (p. 187)
aa. Tail nearly, to quite, as long as wing, strongly graduated, rectrices (20) narrow, acuminate, and rigid; tarsus longer than middle toe with claw; feathers of chest very rigid, with spiny shafts; portion of culmen between nasal fossae much longer than terminal portion; stomach membranous.
Centrocercus (p. 223)

Genus DENDRAGAPUS Elliot

Dendragapus ELLIOT, Proc. Acad. Nat. Sci. Philadelphia, 1864, 23. (Type, as designated by Baird, Brewer, and Ridgway, 1874, *Tetrao obscurus* Say.)
Dendrogapus (emendation) GIEBEL, Thesaurus Orn., ii, 1874, 33.
Tympanuchus REICHENOW, Die Vögel, i, 1913, 320, part.

Medium-size or rather large wood grouse (length about 432–584 mm.) with tarsi feathered to or beyond base of toes; tail more than two-thirds as long as wing, rounded to truncate, of 20 rectrices; side of neck with an inflatable air sac but without tufts; the adult males with underparts mostly plain grayish.

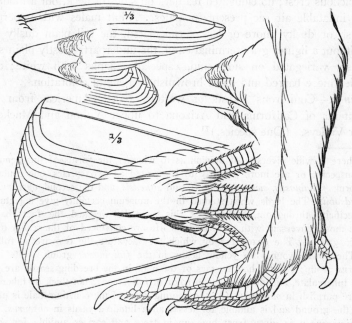

FIGURE 7.—*Dendragapus obscurus.*

Bill relatively small, its length from nostril about one-fourth the length of head, about as deep as wide at frontal antiae; the culmen rounded (not distinctly ridged), the rhamphotheca completely smooth, the maxillary tomium moderately concave, slightly inflexed. Wing moderately large, with longest primaries exceeding longest secondaries by nearly one-third the length of wing; fourth primary longest, but third and fifth nearly as long, the first (outermost) intermediate between seventh and eighth. Tail about two-thirds as long as wing or slightly more, moderately rounded to truncate, the rectrices (20) broad, with broadly rounded to truncate tips. Tarsus about one-fifth as long as wing, completely clothed (except on heel) with dense, soft, hairlike feathers, these extending over greater part of basal phalanx of middle toe on each side; middle toe decidedly shorter than tarsus, the inner toe reaching to penultimate articulation of middle toe, the outer toe very slightly longer; hallux slightly shorter than basal phalanx of inner toe; upper surface of toes with a continuous single series of very distinct transverse scutella, on each side of which is a single series of rather small, subquadrate scutella, edged with short, more or less indistinct, marginal pectinations (these sometimes obsolete); claws relatively short, slightly curved, and blunt.

Plumage and coloration.—Plumage in general compact, the feathers distinctly outlined, except on anal region, where soft, downy, and blended; feathers of crown but slightly elongated, forming, when erected, an inconspicuous crest; no elongated feathers on sides of neck, but a moderate sized inflatable air sac present in males. Adult males with upperparts grayish or dusky, more or less vermiculated, the tail plain dusky with or without a lighter gray terminal band, the underparts mostly plain sooty grayish, variegated on sides and, especially, flanks with white; adult females more barred and more brownish in general coloration.

Range.—Coniferous forests of western North America, from high mountains of California and Arizona to upper Yukon and Mackenzie River Valleys. (One species.)[71]

---

[71] There is wide diversity of opinion as to whether the forms of this genus are all conspecific or are more properly to be treated as two species, one containing the forms *fuliginosus, sierrae, howardi,* and *sitkensis,* and the second, *obscurus* and *richardsonii.* The birds when studied in the museum certainly give a picture of conspecificity throughout, but against this must be weighed the fact that the people most conversant with these birds in life are convinced of the reality of two specific groups. The characters by which they separate the two are as follows: (1) The downy young are yellow below in the *fuliginosus* group, white in the *obscurus* group; (2) the hooting sacs of the male in the breeding season are thick, large, tuberculate, and deep yellow in color in *fuliginosus;* not thick or tuberculate and are purplish in *obscurus;* (3) the hooting noise of the courting male is uttered from the ground and is audible for less than a hundred yards in *obscurus,* while in *fuliginosus* it is given from high up in trees and carries audibly for several miles; (4) in *fuliginosus* the tail of the adult male is rounded, the feathers also rounded at the tip; while in *obscurus* the tail of the adult male is nearly square, the feathers terminally truncate.

KEY TO THE FORMS (ADULTS) OF DENDRAGAPUS OBSCURUS (SAY)

a. Top of head, nape, and interscapulars uniform, unbarred (males).
   b. Rectrices usually with no grayish terminal band (or terminal band very dark, not conspicuously different from rest of rectrices).
      c. Under tail coverts blackish tipped with white (s. Yukon to Idaho and nw. Wyoming) ....**Dendragapus obscurus richardsonii** (p. 82)
     cc. Under tail coverts grayish chaetura drab tipped with white (mountains of e. Washington, ne. Oregon, se. to c. Nevada).
                             Dendragapus obscurus pallidus (p. 88)
  bb. Rectrices with a distinct grayish terminal band.
      c. Terminal gray band on tail broader (20–35 mm. broad).
         d. Tail longer (average 189 mm.) (coniferous forests Kern to Calaveras Counties, Calif.) ....**Dendragapus obscurus howardi** (p. 80)
        dd. Tail shorter (average 170 mm.).
            e. Terminal band much speckled with black (sc. Washington to ne. California and w. Nevada) ......**Dendragapus obscurus sierrae** (p. 77)
           ee. Terminal band not or only slightly speckled with black (Rocky Mountains from s. Montana to n. Arizona and wc. New Mexico).
                             Dendragapus obscurus obscurus (p. 85)
     cc. Terminal gray band on tail averaging narrower (15–22 mm. broad) (mountains of extreme w. North America from sw. Yukon to nw. California).
                             Dendragapus obscurus fuliginosus (p. 74)
        (islands and coast of se. Alaska to Queen Charlotte Islands).
                             Dendragapus obscurus sitkensis (p. 70)
aa. Top of head, nape, and interscapulars barred (females).
   b. Rectrices with no distinct grayish terminal band.
      c. Under tail coverts dark fuscous tipped with white (s. Yukon to Idaho and nw. Wyoming) ....**Dendragapus obscurus richardsonii** (p. 82)
     cc. Under tail coverts grayish banded with chaetura drab and tipped with white. (mountains of e. Washington, ne. Oregon, se. to c. Nevada).
                             Dendragapus obscurus pallidus (p. 88)
  bb. Rectrices with a distinct grayish terminal band.
      c. Terminal gray band on tail broader (20–35 mm.).
         d. Tail longer (average 153 mm.) (coniferous forests Kern to Calaveras Counties, Calif.) ....**Dendragapus obscurus howardi** (p. 80)
        dd. Tail shorter (average 144 mm. or less).
            e. Sides and flanks with conspicuous white marks (Rocky Mountains from s. Montana to n. Arizona and wc. New Mexico).
                             Dendragapus obscurus obscurus (p. 85)
           ee. Sides and flanks with no or little white (sc. Washington to ne. California and w. Nevada) ....**Dendragapus obscurus sierrae** (p. 77)
     cc. Terminal gray band on tail narrower (10–20 mm. broad).
         d. Upperparts with a distinct rufescent tone (islands and coast of se. Alaska to Queen Charlotte Islands).
                             Dendragapus obscurus sitkensis (p. 70)
        dd. Upperparts not distinctly rufescent, but grayish (mountains of extreme w. North America from sw. Yukon to nw. California).
                             Dendragapus obscurus fuliginosus (p. 74)

DENDRAGAPUS OBSCURUS SITKENSIS Swarth

SITKAN DUSKY GROUSE

Adult male.—Forehead and anterior part of crown very dark, rich chestnut-brown merging gradually into fuscous or grayish fuscous on the posterior crown, occiput, nape, and anterior interscapulars; interscapulars and upper back dark bister to dark clove brown, the feathers vermiculated to a varying degree with Saccardo's umber to sepia (sometimes entirely without vermiculations but usually with vermiculations on the more posterior feathers at least); lesser upper wing coverts very variable, sometimes Dresden brown to Prout's brown abundantly vermiculated with blackish, in other birds much more grayish except at their extreme bases—hair brown, likewise vermiculated with blackish; median upper wing coverts sepia to very dark clove brown, greater upper wing coverts and remiges similarly dark clove brown, but the greater coverts narrowly edged and tipped with dusky mouse gray to dark drab, and the innermost secondaries with their inner webs terminally broadly gray or drab vermiculated with dark bister or clove brown; some of the remiges with flecks of drab on their outer webs; feathers of the rump and upper tail coverts sepia to clove brown becoming deep mouse gray terminally vermiculated with blackish, and proximally to the grayish areas they are much washed with snuff brown to Saccardo's umber, also vermiculated with blackish; rectrices fuscous to clove brown, tipped with mouse gray to light quaker drab, this terminal band 15–22 mm. broad on median pair of rectrices; the tail only slightly rounded; all the rectrices broad and fairly blunt at their tips; lores, cheeks, and auriculars fuscous to dark clove brown paling on the chin and throat to clove brown in some birds and to very dusky wood brown with clove-brown edges to the feathers in other specimens; upper throat with a varying amount of the white bases of the feathers showing; lower throat often slightly darker than upper throat; breast and abdomen dusty drab gray to deep quaker drab, with a general tinge of drab to wood brown, due largely to the amount of the basal and median portions of the feathers exposed, as the more grayish color is largely a matter of broad edges and tips; side and flanks like the abdomen but the feathers with white tips and the more lateral of the side feathers (i.e., more up away from the under surface of the body) are sepia to clove brown vermiculated with blackish and with white shafts terminally broadening into wedge-shaped white marks; thighs like abdomen but some of the feathers tipped with white; lower abdomen and vent like abdomen but feathers broadly tipped with white; under tail coverts similar but darker and broadly tipped with white, subterminally crossed by two narrow grayish bands margined with blackish; under wing coverts like the lesser upper coverts; axillars largely white with some of the feathers with grayish centers. In the breeding season, the

males have a distensible sac on either side of the neck, the feathers sur-
rounding which are largely white broadly tipped with dark sepia; the
sacs deep yellow, carunculated, iris Vandyke brown; orbital skin dull
yellow, supraorbital "comb" deep orange-yellow; bill blackish, feet light
brownish gray; claws blackish brown.[72]

Adult female.—Very different from the male: Forehead and crown
fuscous-black tipped and basally banded with tawny to amber brown, the
brown color more noticeable than the black, occiput and nape similar
but with the brown tips paler and lighter—pale tawny-olive and with the
black areas reduced to narrow bands, each feather having three brown
bands, giving somewhat the appearance of dusky vermiculations on the
pale brown ground; interscapulars and upper back barred black and cinnamon, each feather with four cinnamon bands (including the terminal
one); the feathers of the lower back with the bands reduced in number
and restricted to the terminal third or less, only two black bands and
these doubly concave distally and the terminal area much washed with
grayish, especially posteriorly (in the feathers of the posterior part of
the lower back these gray areas are almost pure gray with a fine subterminal wavy black line); lesser and median upper wing coverts cinnamon to tawny mottled and subbasally broadly marked with black, and
with the tips of the shafts white broadening into whitish wedges, which
spread laterally to form in some cases a narrow terminal band on either
side; greater upper coverts clove brown narrowly edged and distally
mottled with cinnamon; remiges (except inner secondaries) clove brown
tipped with pale tawny, the outer webs of the primaries mottled with pale
cinnamon; the inner secondaries tipped with white, this area proximally
narrowly edged with black, the rest of the feathers black both broadly
and narrowly crossed by tawny areas, upper tail coverts like the lower
back; median rectrices cinnamon to tawny crossed by broad blackish
blotches and by irregular fine black lines, the tips grayer, banded irregularly with fine black lines; the rest of the rectrices deep clove brown to
fuscous tipped with dusky neutral gray, this area on the pair next to the
brown median rectrices breaking up proximally into a series of irregular
flecks which become brownish basally; tail slightly rounded as in the
male; lores white flecked with blackish; feathers of malar area, cheeks,
auriculars, and gular area white basally, tawny to amber brown distally,
edged and tipped with black; chin lightly washed with tawny and the
feathers edged with black; upper throat white, each feather with a V-
shaped terminal blackish band, these edgings becoming broader posterolaterally, where the white centers tend to disappear; breast and upper
abdomen clove brown to fuscous, banded with pale cinnamon, tipped with
grayish pale cinnamon, and with the white shafts enlarging terminally to

---

[72] Colors of soft parts from manuscript note by Allan Brooks.

form white wedges; center of abdomen as in the male; sides, flanks, vent, thighs, and under tail coverts as in the male but with the white tips far more developed and (on the sides and flanks) with the brown and black markings much coarser, less like vermiculations, and the brown pale tawny, not sepia; under wing coverts like the lesser upper ones but with much more white; supraorbital "comb" dull orange-yellow; iris brown, bill blackish; feet varying from pale brownish gray to pale greenish gray, soles and back of tarsi yellowish; claws pale horn gray.

Immature male.—Similar to the adult but with the rectrices narrower and more pointed at the tip; body plumage often retaining some of the juvenal plumage, especially the innermost secondaries and in the head and neck regions which are the last to molt, except for the innermost secondaries (tertials).

Immature female.—Similar to the adult but differing from it in the same way that the immature and adult males differ.

Juvenal (sexes alike).—Similar to that of the adult female but with the feathers of the upperparts, wing, and tail with conspicuous shaft streaks of white (more or less tinged with tawny); the rectrices brown to the tips (no terminal gray band); the chin and upper throat more extensively whitish; the breast and abdomen paler—buffy whitish to pale tawny whitish, the dark sepia to clove brown markings broken so as to appear more like spots than bars; no median abdominal gray area as in adult; iris pale sepia; bill grayish brown; feet light olive-green, claws pale brown to horn color.

Downy young (sexes alike).—Above between buckthorn brown and ochraceous-tawny, paler and more yellowish on the forehead and inter-scapular area; the forehead, crown, and sides of head with fuscous to dark sepia elongated blotches, and with smaller, less conspicuous dark marks on the lower back; lores, chin, throat, and abdomen amber yellow, the breast, sides, and flanks similar but with an ochraceous wash; iris pale gray-brown; bill brownish, tipped flesh color; feet yellow, claws horn color.

Adult male.—Wing 208–224 (217.1); tail 131–160 (151.7); exposed culmen 19.2–22 (20.1); tarsus 43.1–47 (45.1); middle toe without claw 42.3–49.5 (45.9 mm.).[73]

Adult female.—Wing 178–205 (194.7); tail 116–131 (121.1); exposed culmen 16.6–22.8 (19.4); tarsus 39.8–42.9 (41.1); middle toe without claw 37.2–42.8 (39.8 mm.).[74]

Range.—Resident in the islands of southeastern Alaska except Prince of Wales Island (Admiralty, Baranof, Chichagof, Coronation, Douglas, Etolin, Kupreanof, Mitkof, Wrangell Islands) and immediately adjacent

---

[73] Six specimens from Queen Charlotte Islands and Alaska.

[74] Nine specimens from Alaska.

mainland (Glacier Bay, Juneau); south to Porcher Island and the Queen Charlotte Islands, British Columbia.

Type locality.—Kupreanof Island, southeastern Alaska.

Tetrao obscurus (not of Say) DALL and BANNISTER, Trans. Chicago Acad. Sci., i, 1869, 287 (Sitka, Alaska).—FINSCH, Abh. Nat. Ver. Bremen, iii, 1872, 61 (Sitka, Alaska).—COUES, Check List North American Birds, 1873, No. 381, part.—SCHALOW, Journ. für Orn., 1891, 258 (Kittlitz specimen from Alaska).

[*Tetrao*] *obscurus* COUES, Key North Amer. Birds, 1872, 233, part.

Canace obscura, var. *fuliginosa* RIDGWAY, Bull. Essex Inst., v, 1873, 199, part (Sitka).

Canace obscura fuliginosa RIDGWAY, Proc. U. S. Nat. Mus., iii, 1880, 196, part; Nom. North Amer. Birds, 1881, No. 471a, part.—COUES, Check List North Amer. Birds, ed. 2, 1882, No. 559, part.

Canace obscurus, var. *fuliginosus* BAIRD, BREWER, and RIDGWAY, Hist. North Amer. Birds, iii, 1874, 425, part (Sitka).

C[*anace*] *o*[*bscura*] *fuliginosa* COUES, Key North Amer. Birds, ed. 2, 1884, 580, part.

Tetrao obscurus . . . var. *fuliginosa* COUES, Check List North Amer. Birds, 1874, App., 133, No. 381b (Sitka only).

Tetrao obscurus fuliginosus HARTLAUB, Journ. für Orn., 1883, 275 (Portage Bay, Alaska).—SCHALOW, Journ. für Orn., 1891, 258 in text.

Dendragapus obscurus fuliginosus RIDGWAY, Proc. U. S. Nat. Mus., viii, 1885, 355, part.—AMERICAN ORNITHOLOGISTS' UNION, Check-list, 1886, No. 297a, part; ed. 2, 1895, No. 297a, part; ed. 3, 1910, 138, part.—BENDIRE, Auk, vi, 1889, 32, part (Sitka); Life Hist. North Amer. Birds, i, 1892, 43, part (Sitka).—BISHOP, North Amer. Fauna, No. 19, 1900, 71, part (above Glacier, Alaska).—MACOUN, Cat. Can. Birds, 1900, 198, part (Sitka).—OSGOOD, North Amer. Fauna, No. 21, 1901, 42 (Cumshewa Inlet and adjacent mountains up to 3,000 feet; Queen Charlotte Islands, British Columbia).—BAILEY, Handb. Birds Western United States, 1902, 125, part.—MACOUN and MACOUN, Cat. Can. Birds, ed. 2, 1909, 216, part (Sitka).—GRINNELL, Univ. California Publ. Zool., v, 1909, 203 (Admiralty, Baranof, and Chichagof Islands and Glacier Bay, se. Alaska; crit.; habits; descr. nest and eggs).—SWARTH, Univ. California Publ. Zool., vii, 1911, 56 (Kuiu, Kupreanof, Mitkof, Coronation, and Etolin Islands, Boca de Quadra, and Thomas Bay, se. Alaska; absent from island s. south of Sumner Strait and west of Clarence Strait; habits).—BROOKS, Bull. Mus. Comp. Zool., lix, 1915, 366 (Point Gustavus, Glacier Bay, se. Alaska).

D[*endragapus*] *obscurus fuliginosus* RIDGWAY, Man. North Amer. Birds, 1887, 196, part (Sitka).

D[*endragapus*] *o*[*bscurus*] *fuliginosus* CHAPMAN, Bull. Amer. Mus. Nat. Hist., xx, 1904, 160, part (Sitka, Alaska).

Dendragapus fuliginosus OGILVIE-GRANT, Cat. Birds Brit. Mus., xxii, 1893, 75, part (Sitka).

[*Dendragapus*] *fuliginosus* SHARPE, Hand-list, i, 1899, 20, part (Sitka).

[*Dendragapus obscurus*] subsp. α. *Dendragapus fuliginosus* OGILVIE-GRANT, Cat. Birds Brit. Mus., xxii, 1893, 75, part (Sitka).

Dendragapus obscurus sitkensis SWARTH, Condor, xxiii, 1921, 59 (Kupreanof Island, 25 miles south of Kaka Village, se. Alaska; coll. Mus. Vert. Zool.); Univ. California Publ. Zool., xxiv, 1922, 205 (Mitkof Island, se. Alaska).—OBER-HOLSER, Auk, xxxix, 1922, 246 (se. Alaska).—BROOKS, Auk, xl, 1923, 220 (Porcha Island, British Columbia; crit.).—BAILEY, Auk, xliv, 1927, 197 (se. Alaska—Kupreanof Island; Douglas Island; near Juneau; Oliver Inlet; Wrangell; Point Couverton; Berg Bay; Mount Robert; McGinnis Creek; Salmon Creek; Seymour Canal; Point Retreat; habits).—CUMMING, Murrelet, xii, 1931, 16 (British Columbia; Queen Charlotte Islands).—Peters, Check-list Birds of World, ii, 1934, 28 (range).

Dendragapus fuliginosus sitkensis Swarth, Univ. California Publ. Zool., xxx, 1926, 81, in text (fig. of tail feathers), 84 in text.—Brooks, Auk, xlvi, 1929, 113 (rev., crit.).—American Ornithologists' Union, Check-list, ed. 4, 1931, 79 (distr.).—Bent, U. S. Nat. Mus. Bull. 162, 1932, 119 (habits; plumage; etc.).—Taverner, Birds Canada, 1934, 153 in text (Queen Charlotte Islands and islands of south Alaska).—Moffitt, Auk, lv, 1938, 589, pl. 19, fig. 5 (downy young; col. fig.; descr.).—Hellmayr and Conover, Cat. Birds Amer., i, No. 1, 1942, 199 (syn.; distr.).

D[endragapus] fuliginosus sitkensis Swarth, Univ. California Publ. Zool., xxx, 1926, 74 in text (map; distr.).

Dendragapus obscurus munroi Griscom, Amer. Mus. Nov., No. 71, 1923, 1 (Queen Charlotte Islands, British Columbia; coll. L. L. Sanford).—Oberholser, Auk, xli, 1924, 593, 594 (syn.).

DENDRAGAPUS OBSCURUS FULIGINOSUS (Ridgway)

Sooty Grouse

Adult male.—Not distinguishable from that of *Dendragapus obscurus sitkensis.*

Adult female.—Similar to that of *Dendragapus obscurus sitkensis* but less reddish in general coloration, the upperparts being duller brown with a great deal of black showing through and with the brownish areas everywhere speckled with blackish or grayish. This grayish color is predominant on the hindneck, upper tail coverts, rectrices, breast, and sides, and to a lesser extent the flanks. The brown on the forehead varies from Saccardo's umber to sepia (tawny to amber brown in *sitkensis*), and the brownish bars and markings on the occiput, interscapulars, and back, besides being much more reduced than in *sitkensis,* are paler—avellaneous to light pinkish cinnamon; in the tail feathers only the central pair has any appreciable cinnamon-buff mottling, the other rectrices having their mottlings grayish to light drab; the feathers of the flanks, lower abdomen, and under tail coverts have the white tips smaller than in *sitkensis,* and have the upper and central abdomen slightly darker and very slightly more brownish than in *sitkensis.*

Immature male.—Similar to the adult but with the rectrices narrower and more pointed terminally and with the body plumage often retaining some of the juvenal tertials and some of the coronal and occipital feathers. Practically indistinguishable from the corresponding stage of *Dendragapus obscurus sitkensis,* except by such juvenal feathers as may be present.

Immature female.—Similar to the adult female but differing from it in the narrower rectrices and the retention (in some cases) of juvenal tertials and head feathers.

Juvenal (sexes alike).—Similar to the corresponding plumage of *Dendragapus obscurus sitkensis* but less rufescent generally (sepia to Saccardo's umber); similar to the adult female of the present subspecies but with the feathers of the interscapulars, scapulars, upper back, lower throat, breast, upper abdomen, and sides with white shaft streaks; chin and upper throat more whitish, less heavily marked with brown and the brown feather tips paler; breast and abdomen paler—buffy whitish to pale tawny white, the breast, sides of abdomen, and flanks spotted with dusky and pale buff; rectrices narrower and more pointed, mottled like the feathers of the back and with no gray terminal band; remiges barred, and with no gray terminal band; remiges barred, mottled, or flecked with pale grayish buff on the outer webs.[75]

Downy young (sexes presumably alike).—Forehead, cheeks, chin, throat, and the underpart of body vary from ivory yellow to straw yellow, the crown mottled with fuscous-black and strongly washed with pale ochraceous-tawny; auriculars sparsely blotched with fuscous-black; the back is pale ochraceous-tawny mottled with fuscous and ochraceous-buff; iris brown; bill flesh color with duskier culmen; feet yellow with dusky claws.

Adult male.—Wing 214–238 (221.1); tail 131–171 (149.1); exposed culmen 18.1–21.3 (19.1); tarsus 42.6–46.3 (44.1); middle toe without claw 40.8–45.4 (43.2 mm.).[76]

Adult female.—Wing 188–226 (204.4); tail 111–140 (127.4); exposed culmen 16.4–21.8 (19.4); tarsus 38.7–42.7 (40.2); middle toe without claw 36.2–42 (38.9 mm.).[77]

Range.—Resident in the coastal mountains of the North American mainland from the border between southwestern Yukon, Canada, and Alaska (Skagway; White Pass), south through southeastern Alaska, through coastal British Columbia and Vancouver Island (Alta Lake Region; Beecher Bay, Chilliwak, Coldstream, Klippan River Valley, Lund), western Washington (Fort Steilacoom, Puget Sount, Mount Rainier, Mount Stewart, Tacoma, Hannegan Pass, Cat Creek, Beaver

---

[75] "The juvenal remiges are molted during July and August; the molt begins as soon as the last of these feathers are fully grown, or even before that; and the body molt into the first winter plumage (= immature plumage in this book) is continuous from August to October. The postjuvenal molt is complete, except that the outer pairs of primaries are retained for a full year" (ex Bent, U. S. Nat. Mus. Bull. 162, 1932, 108). This accounts for the paucity of true juvenal specimens in collections, as this plumage is begun to be shed before it is hardly complete.

Van Rossem has demonstrated that the juvenal rectrices are shed at a very early age beginning with the outermost pair and progressing medially. These feathers are shed when the chicks are scarcely more than two or three weeks old, and then the slow-growing immature tail feathers begin to appear beyond the tips of the coverts. The immature tail is more rounded (owing to the lesser relative length of the lateral rectrices) than the adult tail. Most of these rectrices are replaced during the following winter, spring, and summer in a gradual molt, but often the outermost pair are retained until the following autumn.

[76] Eleven specimens from British Columbia, Washington, and Oregon.

[77] Twenty-one specimens from Alaska, British Columbia, Washington, and Oregon.

Creek, etc.) ; western Oregon (Coast Ranges, Willamette Valley, Cascade Mountains, and intervening ranges to Siskiyou) ; south to the semihumid northwestern corner of California (Hayfork and Kuntz, Trinity County, and Seaview, Sonoma County).

Type locality.—Cascade Mountains at foot of Mount Hood, Oreg., and Chiloweyuck Depot, Wash. (=Mount Hood).

Tetrao obscurus (not of Say) NEWBERRY, Rep. Pacific R.R. Surv., vi, pt. 4, 1857, 90, part (Cascade Moutains).—BAIRD, Rep. Pacific R.R. Surv., ix, 1858, 620, part (Cascade Moutains; Fort Dalles; Clikatet; Fort Steilacoom; St. Marys Pass ?) ; Cat. North Amer. Birds, 1859, No. 459, part *in* Cooper, Orn. California, Land Birds, 1870, 526, part (Oregon; Coast Range south nearly to San Francisco Bay).—SCLATER, Proc. Zool. Soc. London, 1859, 236 (Vancouver Island; crit.).—HEERMANN, Rep. Pacific R.R. Surv., x, pt. 4, No. 2, 1859, 61, part ("pine regions" of Oregon).—COOPER and SUCKLEY, Rep. Pacific R.R. Surv., xii, book 2, pt. 3, 1860, 219, part (Cascade Mountains, Oreg., and Washington).— LORD, Proc. Roy. Artil. Inst. Woolwich, iv, 1864, 122 (British Columbia).— BROWN, Ibis, 1868, 423 (Vancouver Island).—COUES, Check List North Amer. Birds, 1873, No. 381, part.

[*Tetrao*] *obscurus* COUES, Key North Amer. Birds, 1872, 233, part.

Canace obscura HENSHAW, Rep. Orn. Spec. Wheeler's Surv., 1876, 266, part (Coast Range, n. California).

Dendragapus obscurus MACOUN, Cat. Can. Birds, 1900, 198, part (sw. Brit. Colombia).—BAILEY, Handb. Birds Western United States, 1902, 124 part.—MACOUN and MACOUN, Cat. Can. Birds, ed. 2, 1909, 216 (British Columbia).

Canace obscura, var. *fuliginosa* RIDGWAY, Bull. Essex. Inst., v, 1873, 199 (Cascade Mountains, Oreg.; coll. U. S. Nat. Mus.).

Canace obscurus, var. *fuliginosus* BAIRD, BREWER, and RIDGWAY, Hist. North Amer. Birds, iii, 1874, 425, part (Cascade Mountains, Oreg.; Chiloweyuck Depot, Wash.).

Canace obscura fuliginosa RIDGWAY, Proc. U. S. Nat. Mus., iii, 1880, 196, part; Nom. North Amer. Birds, 1881, No. 471c, part.—COUES, Check List North Amer. Birds, ed. 2, 1882, No. 559, part.

C[*anace*] *o*[*bscura*] *fuliginosa* COUES, Key North Amer. Birds, ed. 2, 1884, 580, part.

Dendragapus obscurus fuliginosus RIDGWAY, Proc. U. S. Nat. Mus., viii, 1885, 355, part.—AMERICAN ORNITHOLOGISTS' UNION, Check-list, 1886, No. 297a, part; ed. 2, 1895, No. 297a, part; ed. 3, 1910, 138, part.—BENDIRE, Auk, vi, 1889, 32, part (Cascade Range; habits, etc.) ; Life Hist. North Amer. Birds, i, 1892, 43, part.— CHAPMAN, Bull. Amer. Mus. Nat. Hist., iii, 1890, 133 (Vancouver Island; habits).— RHOADS, Proc. Acad. Nat. Sci. Philadelphia, 1893, 38 (British Columbia w. of Cascade Range).—DAWSON, Wils. Bull., iii, 1896, 1 (Okanogan, Wash.; habits) ; Auk, xiv, 1897, 172 (Okanogan, Wash.; up to 7,000 feet) ; Birds California (stud. ed.), iii, 1923, 1589 (genl.; California).—BISHOP, North Amer. Fauna, No. 19, 1900, 71 (heights above Skagway, se. Alaska).—MACOUN, Cat. Can. Birds, 1900, 198, part (Brit. Columbia, west of coast range).—GRINNELL, Pacific Coast Avif., No. 3, 1902, 30 (California; common east of humid coast belt) ; No. 8, 1912, 10 (California) ; No. 11, 1915, 60 (Hayfork and Kuntz, Trinity County, in semihumid nw. corner of California).—WOODCOCK, Oregon Agr. Exp. Stat. Bull. 68, 1902, 26 (Oregon; range).—BOWLES, Auk, xxiii, 1906, 442 (Tacoma, Wash.).—MACOUN and MACOUN, Cat. Can. Birds, ed. 2, 1909, 216, part (Vancouver; coastal British Columbia).—DAWSON and BOWLES, Birds Washington, ii, 1909, 571 (Washington; habits; distr.).—SWARTH, Rep. Birds

and Mammals Vancouver Island, 1912, 19 (Vancouver Island; habits, etc.);
Condor, xxiii, 1921, 59 in text (syn.; crit.).—BROOKS, Auk, xxxiv, 1917, 37
(Chilliwack, British Columbia).—SHELTON, Univ. Oregon Bull., new ser., xiv,
No. 4, 1917, 20, 26 (west-central Oregon; breeds).—GRINNELL, BRYANT, and
STORER, Game Birds California, 1918, 552 (distr. in California; descr.; habits).—
RACEY, Auk, xliii, 1926, 321 (Alta Lake region, British Columbia).—ALFORD,
Ibis, 1928, 197 (Vancouver Island, British Columbia).—BURLEIGH, Auk, xlvi,
1929, 509 (Kirkland, Tacoma, Wash.; breed.).—JEWETT, Condor, xxxiv, 1932,
191 (hybrid between this form and ring-necked pheasant).—PETERS, Check-list
Birds of World, ii, 1934, 28 (range).—HARTHILL, Murrelet, xvi, 1935, 40 (Wash-
ington; Clallam County; habits).

D[endragapus] obscurus fuliginosus RIDGWAY, Man. North Amer. Birds, 1887,
196, part.

D[endragapus] o[bscurus] fuliginosus BAILEY, Handb. Birds Western United States,
1902, 125, part.

Dendragopus obscurus fuliginosus ANTHONY, Auk, iii, 1886, 164 (Washington
County, Oreg.; habits).—TAVERNER, Birds Western Canada, 1926, 164 in text
(w. of Cascade and Coast Range Divide; descr.)

[Dendragapus obscurus] subsp. α Dendragapus fuliginosus OGILVIE-GRANT, Cat.
Birds Brit. Mus., xxii, 1893, 75, part (Vancouver Island; Deschutes River,
Oreg.; Round Valley, Mendocino County, Calif.).

[Dendragapus] fuliginosus SHARPE, Hand-list, i, 1899, 20, part.

Dendragapus fuliginosus OGILVIE-GRANT, Cat. Birds Brit. Mus., xxii, 1893, 75,
part (coastal British Columbia).—GROEBBELS, Der Vögel, ii, 1937, 239 in text
(number of eggs); 241 in text (eggs in mixed sets).

Dendragopus fuliginosus TAVERNER, Birds Canada, 1934, 153 in text (distr.); Can.
Water Birds, 1939, 165.

Dendragapus fuliginosus fuliginosus SWARTH, Univ. California Publ. Zool., xxx,
1926, 83 in text (fig. of tail feathers), 84 in text.—BROOKS, Auk, xlvi, 1929,
112 in text (crit.; rev.).—AMERICAN ORNITHOLOGISTS' UNION, Check-list, ed.
4, 1931, 79 (distr.).—BENT, U. S. Nat. Mus. Bull. 162, 1932, 103 (habits;
distr.).—CUMMING, Murrelet, xiii, 1932, 7 (Vancouver, British Columbia).—
ALCORN, Murrelet, xiii, 1932, 94, in text (Mount Rainier).—HALL, Murrelet,
xiv, 1933, 33, 35 in text (Puget Sound); 64, 69 (hist.); xv, 1934, 10 in text
(Washington; dist.).—MILLER, Murrelet, xvi, 1935, 57 (Washington, San Juan
Islands).—GRIFFEE and RAPRAEGER, Murrelet, xviii, 1937, 16 (Portland, Oreg.;
nesting habits).—MOFFITT, Auk, lv, 1938, 589, pl. 19, fig. 6 (downy young; col.
fig.).—GABRIELSON and JEWETT, Birds Oregon, 1940, 208 (Oregon; descr.;
distr.; habits; photo).—HELLMAYR and CONOVER, Cat. Birds Amer., i, No. 1,
1942, 199 (syn.; distr.).

Dendragopus fuliginosus fuliginosus TAVERNER, Birds Canada, 1934, 153 in text.

Dendragapus f[uliginosus] fuliginosus JOHNSON, Auk, xlvi, 1929, 291 in text (habits;
photos; Mount Rainier).—GROEBBELS, Der Vögel, ii, 1937, 166 (data on breeding
biology).—KITCHIN, Murrelet, xx, 1939, 29 (Mount Rainier; common).

D[endragapus] f[uliginosus] fuliginosus SWARTH, Univ. California Publ. Zool.,
xxx, 1926, 74 in text (map; distr.).

DENDRAGAPUS OBSCURUS SIERRAE Chapman

SIERRA DUSKY GROUSE

Adult male.—Similar to that of Dendragapus obscurus fuliginosus but
averaging paler above, the feathers being more noticeably vermiculated
(owing to the slightly paler ground color), with the terminal gray tail

band usually broader (20–30 mm.) and speckled with blackish; underparts averaging slightly paler than in *fuliginosus,* chin and upper throat
averaging slightly more whitish than in the latter; "naked skin above and
below eye light orange; iris hazel brown; bill dusky . . . feet light
gray or olive drab . . . nails dusky" (*ex* Grinnell, Bryant, and Storer);
hooting sacs said to be orange, large, and carunculated during the breeding season.

Adult female.—Similar to the corresponding state of *Dendragapus
obscurus fuliginosus* but more grayish, less brownish above and below,
much paler on the abdomen, the gray terminal tail band averaging broader.

Immature male.—Similar to the adult male but differs in having narrower rectrices, and often some juvenal inner secondaries and head
feathers.

Immature female.—Differs from the adult of its sex in the same way
as the immature male differs from the adult.

Juvenal (sexes alike).—Very similar to that of *Dendragapus obscurus
fuliginosus,* but the feathers of the upperparts more tipped with grayish,
and the light brown areas of these feathers paler and slightly grayer—
grayish avellaneous to grayish light buffy brown.

Downy young.—Similar to that of *D. o. fuliginosus* but paler, especially
on the sides of the head, chin, throat, and underparts of the body, which
are between ivory yellow and Marguerite yellow.[78]

Adult male.—Wing 196–248 (226.5); tail 136–181 (160.5); exposed
culmen 18.8–23 (20.7); tarsus 40.2–45 (42.5); middle toe without claw
39.7–46.6 (43.3 mm.).[79]

Adult female.—Wing 199–234 (209.4); tail 118–143 (127.5); exposed
culmen 17.4–22.9 (19.8); tarsus 36.6–41.4 (38.9); middle toe without
claw 34.5–41.8 (38.2 mm.).[80]

Range.—Resident in Canadian and Upper Transition Zone evergreen
forests from central-southern Washington (Husum), and the southern
Cascade Mountains and the Warner Mountains, Lake and Klamath
Counties, Oreg., to northern California from Modoc County, Lassen
County, Shasta County, and Trinity County to Eldorado County, Cala-
veras County, and Madera County, and to adjacent western Nevada
(Washoe County, Ormsby County, Esmeralda County; Sierra Nevada
and White Mountains).

Type locality—Echo, El Dorado County, Calif.

Tetrao obscurus (not of Say) NEWBERRY, Rep. Pacific R. R. Surv., vi, 1857, 90,
    part (Sierra Nevada).—BRIDGES, Proc. Zool. Soc. London, 1858, 1 (Sierra
    Nevada 4,000-6,000 feet; Trinity Mountains; Yosemite Valley, near headwaters
    of Merced River).—SCLATER, Proc. Zool. Soc. London, 1858, 1 (Trinity Moun-

---

[78] None seen in the present study; this description based on Moffitt's excellent colored plate (Auk, lv, 1938, pl. 19, opp. p. 589).

[79] Three specimens from Oregon and California.

[80] Fourteen specimens from southern Washington, Oregon, and California.

tains, n. California).—HEERMANN, Rep. Pacific R. R. Surv., ix, pt. vi, 1859, 61,
part ("pine regions of California").—BAIRD, in Cooper, Orn. California, Land
Birds, 1870, 526, part (Sierra Nevada south to about lat. 38°).—COUES, Check
List North Amer. Birds, 1873, No. 381, part.—BAIRD, BREWER, and RIDGWAY,
Hist. North Amer. Birds, iii, 1874, 522, part (Cisco, 6,000 feet, Emigrant Gap,
5,800 feet, etc., and up to 9,000 feet, Sierra Nevada).

[*Tetrao*] *obscurus* COUES, Key North Amer. Birds, 1872, 283, part.

Canace obscura RIDGWAY, Bull. Essex Inst., vi, 1874, 174 (e. slope Sierra Nevada,
near Carson, Nev.) ; Orn. 40th Parallel, 1877, 598, part (e. slope Sierra Nevada,
near Carson, Nev.) ; Proc. U. S. Nat. Mus., iii, 1880, 196, part; Nom. North
Amer. Birds, 1881, No. 471, part.—MEARNS, Bull. Nuttall Orn. Club, iv, 1879,
197 (Fort Klamath, se. Oregon).—BELDING, Proc. U. S. Nat. Mus., i, 1879, 438
(summit of Sierra Nevada, lat. 39° ; Big Trees of Calaveras County, Calif., etc. ;
habits).—COUES, Check List North Amer. Birds, ed. 2, 1882, No. 557, part.

C[*anace*] *obscura* COUES, Key North Amer. Birds, ed. 2, 1884, No. 579, part.

Canace obscurus BENDIRE, Proc. Boston Soc. Nat. Hist., 1877, 137, part (Camp
Harney, se. Oregon ; habits, etc. ; descr. nest and eggs).

Canace fuliginosus BENDIRE, Proc. Boston Soc. Nat. Hist., xviii, 1875, 163 (Camp
Harney, Oreg.).

Dendragapus obscurus fuliginosus (not *Canace obscura,* var. *fuliginosa* Ridgway)
AMERICAN ORNITHOLOGISTS' UNION, Check-list, 1886, No. 297a, part; ed. 2,
1895, No. 297a, part.—TOWNSEND, Proc. U. S. Nat. Mus., x, 1887, 200 (Mount
Shasta; Mount Lassen).—MERRILL, Auk, v, 1888, 145 (Fort Klamath, se.
Oregon).—BENDIRE, Auk, vi, 1889, 32, part (range, breeding habits, etc.) ; Life
Hist. North Amer. Birds, i, 1892, 43, part, pl. 1, figs. 16–19).—RAY, Auk,
xx, 1903, 182 (Lake Valley, centr. Sierra Nevada, 6,500 feet).—STONE, Proc.
Acad. Nat. Sci. Philadelphia, 1904, 580 (Mount Sanhedrin, Mendocino County,
Calif.).—FERRY, Condor, x, 1908, 40 (Yolla-Bolly Mountains, n. California).—
KELLOGG, Univ. California Publ. Zool., xii, 1916, 380 (Hay Ford, n. California).

D[*endragapus*] *obscurus fuliginosus* RIDGWAY, Man. North Amer. Birds, 1887,
196, part.

[*Dendragapus obscurus*] subsp. a. *Dendragapus fuliginosus* OGILVIE-GRANT, Cat.
Birds Brit. Mus., xxii, 1893, 75, part (Fort Klamath, Oreg.; North Honey
Lake, Calif.).

Dendragapus fuliginosus OGILVIE-GRANT, Cat. Birds Brit. Mus., xxii, 1893, 75,
part.

[*Dendragapus*] *fuliginosus* SHARPE, Hand-list, i, 1899, 20, part.

Dendragapus obscurus sierræ CHAPMAN, Bull. Amer. Mus. Nat. Hist., xx, 1904,
159 (Echo, El Dorado County, Calif.; coll. Amer. Mus. Nat. Hist.).—AMERICAN
ORNITHOLOGISTS' UNION, Auk, xxi, 1904, 412; Check-list, ed. 3, 1910, 138.—
RAY, Auk, xxii, 1905, 365 in text, 366 (centr. Sierra Nevada at 7,500 feet).—
WILLETT, Pacific Coast Avif., No. 7, 1912, 43, part (Sierra Nevada, Calif.).—
WYMAN and BURNELL, Field Book Birds Southwestern United States, 1925,
88 (descr.).—GRINNELL, Univ. California Publ. Zool., xxxviii, 1932, 268 (type
loc.; crit.).

Dendragapus obscurus sierrae WILLETT, Pacific Coast Avif., No. 7, 1912, 43 (sw.
California).—GRINNELL, Pacific Coast Avif., No. 8, 1912, 10 (California) ; No.
11, 1915, 60, part (Coast Range from Mount Shasta to Mount Sanhedrin, and
Sierra Nevada; Warner Moutains, Modoc County, Calif.).—KELLOGG, Univ.
California Publ. Zool., xii, 1916, 380 (Callahan, North Fork Coffee Creek, Sum-
merville, head of Rush Creek, head of Bear Creek, etc., n. California; crit.).—
GRINNELL, BRYANT, and STORER, Game Birds California, 1918, 544, part (descr.;
habits, distr. in California; col. plate).—DICKEY and VAN ROSSEM, Condor, xxv,
1923, 168 (crit.).—DAWSON, Birds California (stud. ed.), iii, 1923, 1590 (genl.;

California).—GRINNELL and STORER, Animal Life in Yosemite, 1924, 272 (descr.;
    distr.; habits; Yosemite).—RICHARDS, Condor, xxvi, 1924, 99 (Grass Valley
    district, California).—MICHAEL, Condor, xxvii, 1925, 110 (Yosemite).—MAIL-
    LIARD, Proc. California Acad. Sci., ser. 4, xvi, No. 10, 1927, 295 (Modoc County,
    Calif.).—GRINNELL, DIXON, and LINSDALE, Univ. of California Publ. Zool.,
    xxxv, 1930, 200 (distr.; Lassen Peak region, n. California).—GABRIELSON, Con-
    dor, xxxiii, 1931, 112 (Grants Pass, Winona, Evans Creek, and Gold Hill,
    Oreg.).—PETERS, Check-list Birds of World, ii, 1934, 29 (range).
Dendragapus fuliginosus sierrae SWARTH, Univ. California Publ. Zool., xxx, 1926,
    82 in text (figs. of tail feathers), 84 in text.—BROOKS, Auk, xlvi, 1929, 113
    (rev.; crit.).—AMERICAN ORNITHOLOGISTS' UNION, Check-list, ed. 4, 1931, 79
    (range).—BENT, U. S. Nat. Mus. Bull. 162, 1932, 114 (habits, etc.).—DEGROOT,
    Condor, xxxvi, 1934, 6 (abundant at Echo Lake, Calif.).—LINSDALE, Pacific
    Coast Avif., No. 23, 1936, 47 (w. Nevada; resident in Sierra Nevada and White
    Mountains).—MOFFITT, Auk, lv, 1938, 589, pl. 19, fig. 4 (downy young; col.
    fig.; descr.).—GABRIELSON and JEWETT, Birds Oregon, 1940, 212 (Oregon;
    descr.; distr.; habits).—HELLMAYR and CONOVER, Cat. Birds Amer., i, No. 1,
    1942, 200 (syn.; distr.).—DIXON, Condor, xlv, 1943, 208 (Kings Canyon Na-
    tional Park, Calif.).
D[endragapus] f[uliginosus] sierrae SWARTH, Univ. California Publ. Zool., xxx,
    1926, 74 in text (map; distr.).
Canace richardsoni BENDIRE, Proc. Boston Soc. Nat. Hist., xviii, 1875, 163 (Camp
    Harney, Oreg.).
Tetrao California (not Shaw and Nodder) MAY, California Game "Marked Down"
    (Southern Pacific Co.), 1896, 41, fig. (Lake Tahoe region on the Sierra Nevada,
    El Dorado County, Calif.).—GRINNELL, Univ. California Publ. Zool., xxxviii,
    1932, 268 (type loc.; crit.).

DENDRAGAPUS OBSCURUS HOWARDI Dickey and Van Rossem

MOUNT PIÑOS DUSKY GROUSE

Adult male.—Very similar to that of *Dendragapus obscurus sierrae* but
with the vermiculations on the feathers of the upperparts heavier and
more conspicuous, the ground color of these feathers very slightly paler,
more grayish, than in *sierrae;* tail decidedly longer and much more graduated, with the gray terminal band averaging broader.

Adult female.—Similar to that of *D. o. sierrae* but with the tail longer
and more graduated and with the gray terminal band averaging broader.

Immature.—None seen, but undoubtedly the immature birds of either
sex differ from their respective adult plumages in having narrower rectrices and usually some juvenal feathers on the head and inner part of
the wing.

Juvenal (sexes alike).—Very close to that of *sierrae* from which it
cannot be separated with certainty but apparently averaging slightly more
sandy in general color above.

Downy young (sexes alike).—Like that of *D. o. sierrae* but slightly
paler, sandier above and on the wings.[81]

---

[81] None seen; description based on Moffitt's plate, Auk, lv, 1938, pl. 18, fig. 3.

Adult male.—Wing 230–240 (234.7); tail 172–201 (187.7); exposed culmen 21.1–24.5 (22.8); tarsus 42.7–45.9 (43.7); middle toe without claw 44.5–46.8 (45.6 mm.).[82]

Adult female.—Wing 209–222 (216); tail 147–159 (153); tarsus 38–41.3 (39.9); middle toe without claw 37.3–41.4 (39.4 mm.).[83]

Range.—Resident in the coniferous forests[84] from Mount Piños, Kern County, Calif., east through the Tehachapi Range north in the main Sierra Nevada to about 36° N., and to Bloods, Calaveras County, Calif.

Type locality.—Mount Piños, Kern County, Calif.; altitude 7,500 feet.

Tetrao obscurus (not of Say) BAIRD, *in* COOPER, Orn. California, Land Birds, 1870, 526, part (s. Sierra Nevada).

Canace obscura RIDGWAY, Bull. Essex Inst., vi, No. 10, 1874, 174 (e. slopes Sierra Nevada, California).—HENSHAW, Rep. Orn. Spec. Wheeler's Surv., 1876, 276, part (s. Sierra Nevada, including Mount Whitney).

Dendragapus obscurus fuliginosus (not *Canace obscura,* var. *fuliginosa* RIDGWAY) FISHER, North Amer. Fauna, No. 7, 1893, 30 (White Mountains, Nev.; Menache Meadows, Independence Creed, and Bishop Creek, e. slope s. Sierra Nevada; head of Owens Valley, Sequoia National Park, Kings River Canyon, etc., w. slope s. Sierra Nevada).—WILLETT, Pacific Coast Avif., No. 21, 1933, 48 (in syn.).

Dendragapus obscurus sierræ (not of Chapman) GRINNELL, Auk, xxii, 1905, 382 (Mount Piños, Ventura County, Calif.; habits).—WILLETT, Pacific Coast Avif., No. 7, 1912, 43, part (Mount Piños, Ventura County).

Dendragapus obscurus sierrae GRINNELL, Pacific Coast Avif., No. 11, 1915, 10, part (Puite Mountains, and Mount Piños, Kern County; White Mountains, Mono County, Calif.).—GRINNELL, BRYANT, and STORER, Game Birds California, 1918, 544, part (descr.; distr.; and habits, California).—WILLETT, Pacific Coast Avif., No. 21, 1933, 48 (in syn.).

Dendragapus obscurus howardi DICKEY and VAN ROSSEM, Condor, No. 5, 1923, 168 (Mount Piños, Kern County, Calif., 7,500 feet; coll. D. M. Dickey); xxvi, 1924, 36 (range; corr.).—OBERHOLSER, Auk, xli, 1924, 592 (add. A.O.U. Check-list).—GRINNELL, Condor, xxvii, 1925, 76 (added to California list); Univ. California Publ. Zool., xxxviii, 1932, 268 (type loc.; crit.).—BROOKS, Auk, xlvi, 1929, 113 (rev. crit.).—WILLETT, Pacific Coast Avif., No. 21, 1933, 48 (in syn.).—PETERS, Check-list Birds of World, ii, 1934, 29 (range).—HELLMAYR and CONOVER, Cat. Birds Amer., i, No. 1, 1942, 201 (syn.; distr.).

Dendragapus obscurus . . . howardi PEMBERTON, Condor, xxx, 1928, 347 in text (nesting, Kern County, Calif.).

Dendragapus o[bscurus] howardi PALMER, Condor, xxx, 1928, 283 in text (patronymics).

Dendragapus fuliginosus howardi SWARTH, Univ. California Publ. Zool., xxx, 1926, 84 in text.—AMERICAN ORNITHOLOGISTS' UNION, Check-list, ed. 4, 1931, 79 (distr.).—BENT, U. S. Nat. Mus. Bull. 162, 1932, 117 (habits, etc.).—

[82] Four specimens from Mount Whitney, Tehachapi Peak, Sierra Nevada, and Bloods, Calaveras County, Calif.

[83] All measurements for females *ex* Dickey and van Rossem, Condor, xxv, 1923, 168, as no fully adult material of this sex was available to me in the present connection. These authors give the following data on culmen length for this series, measured, however, from the base, and therefore not comparable: 27–30.8 (28.8 mm).

[84] Silver-fir association, according to Dickey and van Rossem.

WILLETT, Pacific Coast Avif., No. 21, 1933, 48 (sw. California; nest and eggs, Mount Piños).—MOFFITT, Auk, lv, 1938, 589, pl. 19, fig. 3 (downy, young, descr.; col. fig.).

D[endragapus] f[uliginosus] howardi SWARTH, Univ. California Publ. Zool., xxx, 1926, 74 in text (map, distr.), 82 in text (fig. of tail feathers).

DENDRAGAPUS OBSCURUS RICHARDSONII (Douglas)

RICHARDSON'S GROUSE

Adult male.—Similar to that of *Dendragapus obscurus sitkensis* but lacking the gray terminal band on the tail feathers (or, at most, with this band so dark as to be hardly distinct from the rest of the feathers), the rectrices more truncate terminally, the tail outline squarer, and with more whitish on the chin and throat; the cervical air sacs, or hooting sacs, are smaller and deep purplish, instead of yellow as in the coastal forms, and its skin is not thickened and carunculated in the present form; iris bister; "comb" deep yellow; eyelid dull greenish yellow; bill blackish; feet brownish gray.

Adult female.—Similar to that of *D. o. sierrae* but much darker above, the broad dark bars and bands being dark fuscous to fuscous-black (as against dark sepia to clove brown in *sierrae*), with no gray terminal band on the tail, and the breast and abdomen slightly duskier; iris hazel brown; "comb" deep dull yellow; bill grayish black; the lower mandible yellowish flesh color basally; feet horn gray, claws brown.

Immature male.—Like the adult but with narrower rectrices, the tail less squarish, more graduated; and with occasional juvenal feathers on the head and nape and inner edge of wing.

Immature female.—Differs from its adult in the same way that the immature male does from its corresponding adult state.

Juvenal (sexes alike).—Similar to that of *D. o. sierrae* but much darker, less tawny; the general dorsal coloration Saccardo's umber to cinnamon-brown (instead of ochraceous-tawny as in *sierrae*) and the dusky vermiculations and black bars more conspicuous.

Downy young.—Similar to that of *D. o. sierrae,* but with the forehead, superciliaries, and breast and abdomen whitish instead of buffy; chin and upper throat washed with pale buffy.

Adult male.—Wing 201–241 (224.5); tail 134–176 (158.2); exposed culmen 18.3–22.6 (20.9); tarsus 41–47.8 (44.7); middle toe without claw 39.1–45.1 (41.8 mm.).[85]

Adult female.—Wing 193–224 (207.9); tail 121–147 (133.7); exposed culmen 17.4–21.9 (19.4); tarsus 38.2–44 (40.9); middle toe without claw 36–43.3 (38.4 mm.).[86]

---

[85] Twenty-seven specimens from Mackenzie, British Columbia, Alberta, Idaho, Montana, and Wyoming.

[86] Thirty-five specimens from Mackenzie, British Columbia, Alberta, Idaho, Montana, and Wyoming.

Range.—Resident in coniferous forests from southern Yukon (Lake Teslin), the Stikine region of Alaska, southwestern Mackenzie, south through British Columbia (east of the range of *D. o. fuliginosus,* south to the Okanagan Valley) and Alberta (east as far as Liard River, Fort Simpson, Henry House, Jasper House, Moose Pass, etc.) to all of Idaho,[87] the western half or so of Montana (Belt Mountains; Judith Mountains; west side of Rocky Mountains; Gallatin County); and to northwestern Wyoming (Yellowstone Park, Teton Pass, Jackson, Big Horn Mountains, Salt River Mountains, Kendall, etc.).

Type locality.—" . . . subalpine regions of the Rocky Mountains, in lat. 52° N., long. 115° W. . . . the mountainous districts of the Columbia in lat. 48° N., long. 118° W."; restricted to vicinity of Kettle Falls, Stevens County, Washington, by Hall, Murrelet, xv, January 1934, 9.

T[etrao] *richardsonii* DOUGLAS, Trans. Linn. Soc. London, xvi, 1829, 141 ("subalpine regions of the rocky Mountains in lat. 52° N., long. 115° W." . . . "mountainous districts of the river Columbia in lat. 48° N., long. 118° W."; ex Sabine, manuscript; crit.).

Tetrao richardsonii WILSON, Illustr. Zool., 1831, pls. 30, 31.—LORD, Proc. Roy. Artil. Inst. Woolwich, i, 1863, 122.—GRAY, List Birds Brit. Mus., pt. 5, Gallinæ, 1867, 86 (Fort Halkett; Fort Simpson).—BAIRD, *in* Cooper, Orn. California, Land Birds, 1870, 528 (crit.), part.—MERRIAM, 6th Ann. Rep. U. S. Geol. Surv., 1873, 711 (Teton Canyon, Idaho; breeding).

[Tetrao] *richardsonii* GRAY, Hand-list, ii, 1870, 276, No. 9824.

Tetrao richardsoni LESSON, Traité d'Orn., 1831, 502.

[Tetrao] *richardsoni* BAIRD, Ibis, 1867, 271.

Dendragapus richardsoni ELLIOT, Proc. Acad. Nat. Sci. Philadelphia, 1864, 23; Monogr. Tetraonidae, 1865, pl. 8, and text.—OGILVIE-GRANT, Cat. Birds Brit. Mus., xxii, 1893, 76 (Fort Halkett; Fort Simpson; Fort Dufferin; Teton Canyon, and Chief Mountain Lake, Mont.).—BROOKS (A.), Auk, xxix, 1912, 252 (Selkirk Range and Rocky Mountains, British Columbia; crit.).—PALMER, Condor, xxx, 1928, 227, in text.

[Dendragapus] *richardsoni* SHARPE, Hand-list, i, 1899, 20, part.

Dendragapus richardsonii JEWETT, Auk, xxvi, 1909, 5 (Baker County, Oreg.; abundant; nests in April and May).

Dendragapus obscurus richardsoni RIDGWAY, Proc. U. S. Nat. Mus., viii, 1885, 355.—PREBLE, North Amer. Fauna, No. 27, 1908, 336 (Mount Thu-on-thu, near mouth of Nahami River; foothills west of Fort Simpson; mountains along Liard River; Fort Halkett; Fort Simpson; Jasper House, Alberta; Henry House; Fort Providence).—AMERICAN ORNITHOLOGISTS' UNION, Check-list, ed. 3, 1910, 138, part; ed. 4, 1931, 79, part (distr.).—DICE, Auk, xxvii, 1910, 217 (Snake River, Wash.; not uncommon).—RILEY, Can. Alpine Journ., 1912, 55 (Moose Pass, British Columbia; plum.; food).—GRAVE and WALKER, Birds Wyoming, 1913, 89 (Wyoming).—MUNRO, Auk, xxxvi, 1919, 65 Okanagan Valley, British Columbia; abundant resident; habits, etc.).—BURLEIGH, Auk, xxxviii, 1921, 553 (Warland, Mont.; scarce).—SAUNDERS, Pacific Coast Avif., No. 14, 1921, 55 (Montana; in the mountains).—BROOKS, Auk, xliii, 1926, 281 in text, pls. x–xi (courtship habits); Auk, xlvi, 1929, 112 in text (tax., crit.).—

---

[87] In western Idaho the birds are somewhat intermediate between this form and *pallidus,* the females tending toward *pallidus* and the males being closer to *richardsoni.*

KELSO, Ibis, 1926, 701 (Arrow Lakes, British Columbia; resident).—SKINNER, Wils. Bull., xxxix, 1927, 208 in text (Yellowstone Park).—KEMSIES, Wils. Bull., xlii, 1930, 203 (Yellowstone Park, Wyo.).—BENT, U. S. Nat. Mus. Bull. 162, 1932, 96 (habits, distr., etc.).—RANSOM, Murrelet, xiii, 1932, 51, in text (Idaho; Harrison; flight).—HALL, Murrelet, xv, 1934, 9, 14 (Washington; Kettle Falls, Stevens County; spec.).—ULKE, Can. Alpine Journ., 1934-35 (1936), 79 (Yoho Park, Canada; summer, fairly common).—MOFFITT, Auk, lv, 1938, 589, pl. 19, fig. 2 (downy young; descr.; col. fig.).—COWAN, Occ. Papers British Columbia Prov. Mus., No. 1, 1939, 26 (Peace River district, British Columbia).

Dendragopus obscurus richardsoni TAVERNER, Birds Western Canada, 1926, 164 in text (distr. in Canada; habits) ; Birds Canada, 1934, 152 in text.

Dendragapus o[bscurus] richardsoni STENHOUSE, Scottish Nat., 1930, 81 (spec. ex Franklin's Exped.).

Dendragapus obscurus richardsonii AMERICAN ORNITHOLOGISTS' UNION, Check-list, No. 297b, part, 1886; ed. 2, 1895, No. 297b, part.—CHAPMAN, Bull. Amer. Mus. Nat. Hist., iii, 1890, 133 (interior British Columbia; habits).—MERRIAM, North Amer. Fauna, No. 5, 1891, 93 (Sawtooth, Pashimeroi, and Salmon River Mountains and upper part of Henry's Fork of Snake River, Idaho).—BENDIRE, Life Hist. North Amer. Birds, i, 1892, 50, part.—RHOADS, Proc. Acad. Nat. Sci. Philadelphia, 1893, 38 (British Columbia, east of Cascade Range).—MERRILL, Auk, xiv, 1897, 352 (Fort Sherman, Idaho).—MACOUN, Cat. Can. Birds, 1900, 199 (range).—BROOKS, Auk, xx, 1903, 281 (Cariboo district, Brit. Columbia).— MACOUN and MACOUN, Cat. Can. Birds, ed. 2, 1909, 217 (range; nest and eggs at Revelstoke, Brit. Col.).—SWARTH, Univ. California Publ. Zool., xxx, 1926, 77 in text (fig. of tail feathers), 84 in text.—SKINNER, Condor, xxx, 1928, 237 (Yellowstone Park, winter).—FULLER and BOLE, Sci. Publ. Cleveland Mus. Nat. Hist., i, 1930, 51 (observ.; Wyo.).—PETERS, Check-list Birds of World, ii, 1934, 29 (distr.).—HELLMAYR and CONOVER, Cat. Birds Amer., i, No. 1, 1942, 198 (syn.; distr.).

Dendragapus o[bscurus] richardsonii BROOKS, Auk, xxiv, 1907, 167, in text (hybrid chick; Osoyoos, British Columbia).

D[endragapus] obscurus richardsonii RIDGWAY, Man. North Amer. Birds, 1887, 196, part.

D[endragapus] o[bscurus] richardsonii BAILEY, Handb. Birds Western U. S., 1902, 126.—SWARTH, Univ. California Publ. Zool., xxx, 1926, 74 in text (map: distr.).

[*Tetrao obscurus*] Var. *richardsonii* COUES, Key North Amer. Birds, 1872, 233, part.

Tetrao obscurus . . . var. *richardsonii* COUES, Check List North Amer. Birds, 1874, No. 381a, part.

Tetrao obscurus, var. *richardsonii* MERRIAM, 6th Ann. Rep. U. S. Geol. Surv., 1873, 698 (Teton Canyon at North Fork, Idaho).

Tetrao obscurus richardsoni COUES, U. S. Geol. Surv. Terr., Bull. 4, 1878, 639 (Rocky Mountains of Montana, lat. 48°).—WILLIAMS, Bull. Nuttall Orn. Club, vii, 1882, 63 (Belt Mountains, Mont.; habits).

Tetrao obscurus var. *richardsoni* COUES, Birds Northwest, 1874, 400 (west side of Rocky Moutains [in Montana] ; Yellowstone River; Teton Canyon and North Fork of Snake River, Idaho; crit.).

[*Canace obscura*] var. *richardsoni* RIDGWAY, Bull. Essex Inst., v, 1873, 199 in text.

Canace obscurus, var. *richardsoni* BAIRD, BREWER, and RIDGWAY, Hist. North Amer. Birds, iii, 1874, 427, part.

Canace obscura richardsonii RIDGWAY, Proc. U. S. Nat. Mus., iii, 1880, 196, part.

Canace obscura richardsoni RIDGWAY, Nom. North Amer. Birds, 1881, No. 471b, part.—COUES, Check-list North Amer. Birds, ed. 2, 1882, No. 558, part.

C[anace] o[bscura] richardsoni Coues, Key North Amer. Birds, ed. 2, 1884, 579, part.

Canace richardsoni Baird, Brewer, and Ridgway, Hist. North Amer. Birds, iii, 1874, pl. 59, fig. 4, part.—Bendire, Proc. Boston Soc. Nat. Hist., xviii, 1875, 163 (Camp Harney, Oreg.).

Tetrao obscurus (not of Say) Swainson and Richardson, Fauna Bor.-Amer., ii, 1831 (1832), 344, pls. 59, 60.—Audubon, Orn. Biogr., iv, 1838, 446, pl. 361, part; Synopsis, 1839, 203, part; Birds Amer., 8vo ed., v, 1842, 89, pl. 295, part.—Baird, Rep. Pacific R. R. Surv., ix, 1858, 620, part (spec. No. 2859); Cat. North Amer. Birds, 1859, No. 459, part.—Blakiston, Ibis, 1862, 8 (east base Rocky Mountains near Belly River); 1863, 121 (Rocky Mountains, nw. Canada).—Grinnell, *in* Ludlow, Rep. Recon., 1876, 84 (Judith Mountains to Yellowstone Park, Mont.; habits).

(?) *Canace obscurus* Bendire, Proc. Boston Soc. Nat. Hist., xix, 1877, 137, part? (Camp Harney, south-central Oregon; crit.).

Dendragapus obscurus Hand, Condor, xliii, 1941, 225 (St. Joe National Forest, Idaho).

Dendragapus obscurus obscurus Saunders, Auk, xxviii, 1911, 35, part? (Gallatin County, Mont.; crit.).—Hellmayr and Conover, Cat. Birds Amer., i, No. 1, 1942, 198 (syn.; distr., part).

Dendragapus obscurus fuliginosus Bendire, Auk, vi, 1889, 32, part (Bitterroot Mountains, Mont.; near Fort Lapwai, Idaho).—Saunders, Pacific Coast Avif., No. 14, 1921, 55 (Montana).

Dendragapus o[bscurus] fuliginosus Merriam, North Amer. Fauna, No. 5, 1891, 93 in text (Idaho—Boise Mountains, foothills of Wiser Valley Mountains, and mountains near Fort Lapwai).

Canace fuliginosus Bendire, Proc. Boston Soc. Nat. Hist., xviii, 1875, 163 (Camp Harney, Oreg.).

Dendragapus obscurus flemingi Taverner, Auk, xxxi, 1914, 385, (near Teslin Lake, s. Yukon; coll. Mus. Geol. Surv., Dept. Mines, Canada); Can. Dept. Mines Mus. Bull. 7 (biol. ser.), 1914, 2.—Swarth, Univ. California Publ. Zool., xxiv, 1922, 203 (Doch-da-on Creek and Kirk's Mountain, Stikine region, south Alaska; crit.); xxx, 1926, 73 (crit.; rev.; plum.; distr.), 84 in text; Condor, xxix, 1927, 169 in text (corr.).—American Ornithologists' Union, Auk, xi, 1923, 517 (east Yukon and southwest Mackenzie to north British Columbia; Check-list, No. 297d); Check-list, ed. 4, 1931, 79 (distr.).—Brooks, Condor, xxix, 1927, 113 (crit.); Auk, xlvi, 1929, 112 in text (crit.; tax.).—Bent, U. S. Nat. Mus. Bull. 162, 1932, 102 (habits, plumage; etc.).—Hellmayr and Conover, Cat. Birds Amer., i, No. 1, 1942, 197 (syn.; distr.).

D[endragapus] obscurus flemingi Swarth, Univ. California Publ. Zool., xxx, 1926, 74 in text (map; distr.), 75 in text (fig. of tail feathers).

Dendragopus obscurus flemingi Taverner, Birds Western Canada, 1926, 165 in text (north interior of Canada); Birds Canada, 1934, 152 in text.

T[ympanuchus] richardsoni Reichenow, Die Vögel, i, 1913, 320.

DENDRAGAPUS OBSCURUS OBSCURUS (Say)

Dusky Grouse

Adult male.—Similar to that of *Dendragapus obscurus sierrae* but with a much broader and clearer, unmarked, gray terminal band on the tail; somewhat paler above and clearer gray, less brownish, below; more white on the chin and throat, and with the under tail coverts gray banded with chaetura drab and tipped with white (sometimes the dark bands are wanting) ; cervical sac in breeding season purplish and only slightly carunculated.

Adult female.—Similar to that of *D. o. sierrae,* but the sides and flanks are very much more marked with white (tips, bars, and shafts of the feathers) and with a much broader and clearer gray terminal band on the rectrices.

Immature male.—Like the adult but with narrower retrices, more graduated tail, and often with some juvenal feathers running on the head, nape, and wings.

Immature female.—Like the adult but with narrower rectrices, more graduated tail, and often with some juvenal feathers remaining on the head, nape, and wings.

Juvenal (sexes alike).—Similar to that of *D. o. pallidus,* from which it is not certainly distinguishable.

Downy young (sexes alike).—Like that of *D. o. richardsonii* but slightly more ochraceous-tawny above.[88]

Adult male.—Wing 221–243 (232.5) ; tail 148–192 (168.7) ; exposed culmen 18.3–23.1 (21.2) ; tarsus 41.1–46.8 (43.1) ; middle toe without claw 38.4–46.5 (44.8 mm.).[89]

Adult female.—Wing 197–229 (212.1) ; tail 123–153 (142.3) ; exposed culmen 16–23.8 (18.9) ; tarsus 36.6–41.5 (39.9) ; middle toe without claw 36–41 (38.8 mm.).[90]

Range.—Resident in the Rocky Mountan region from southern Montana, central Wyoming, western South Dakota and northern Colorado south through northeastern Nevada, and Utah to northern Arizona and west-central New Mexico.

Type locality.—"Defile Creek," about 20 miles north of Colorado Springs, Colo.

Tetrao obscurus SAY, *in* Long's Exped. Rocky Mountains, ii, 1823, 14 (near "Defile Creek," about 20 miles north of Colorado Springs, Colo.).—BONAPARTE, Ann. Lyc. Nat. Hist. New York, ii, pt. 1, 1826, 127; ii, 1828, 442; Contr. Maclurian Lyc., i, 1827, 23; Amer. Orn., iii, 1828, 27, pl. 18; Geogr. and Comp. List, 1838, 43.—LESSON, Traité d'Orn., 1831, 503.—NUTTALL, Man. Orn. United States and Canada, Land Birds, 1832, 666; ed. 2, 1840, 809.—WOODHOUSE, Rep. Sitgreaves Expl. Zuñi and Colorado R., 1853, 96 (mountain near Santa Fe, N. Mex.).—BAIRD, Rep. Pacific R. R. Surv., ix, 1858, 620, part (Black Hills and Laramie Peak, Wyo.) ; Cat. North Amer. Birds, 1859, No. 459, part.—GRAY, List Birds Brit. Mus., pt. 5, Gallinae, 1867, 86, part.—ALLEN, Bull. Mus. Comp. Zool., iii, 1872, 164 (Mount Lincoln, Colo.), 170 (Wahsatch Mountains, Utah, near Ogden), 181, part (mountains of Colorado and Utah).—

---

[88] See col. fig., Moffitt, Auk, lv, 1938, pl. 19, fig. 1.

[89] Sixteen specimens from Wyoming, Utah, Colorado, Nebraska, New Mexico, and Arizona.

[90] Ten specimens from Montana, Colorado, Utah, New Mexico, and Arizona.

Coues, Check-list North Amer. Birds, 1873, No. 381, part); Birds Northwest, 1874, 395, part (Deer Creek, Bitter Cottonwood Creek, and Laramie Peak, Wyo.).—Henshaw, Ann. Lyc. Nat. Hist. New York, xi, 1874, 10 (Utah).—Nelson, Proc. Boston Soc. Nat. Hist., xvii, 1875, 347 (Salt Lake City, Utah).—Drew, Bull. Nuttall Orn. Club, vi, 1881, 142 (San Juan County, Colo.).

[*Tetrao*] *obscurus* Reichenbach, Synop. Av., iii, Gallinaceae, 1848, pl. 215, figs. 1887–1889.—Gray, Hand-list, ii, 1870, 276, No. 9823, part.—Coues, Key North Amer. Birds, 1872, 233, part.

Canace obscura Bonaparte, Compt. Rend., xlv, 1857, 428.—Ridgway, Bull. Essex Inst., v, 1873, 186 (Colorado; pine region); vii, 1875, 22 (e. slope E. Humboldt Mountains), 34 (Parleys Peak, Wahsatch Mountains), 39 (Nevada); Orn. 40th Paral., 1877, 598, part (Wahsatch and Uintah Mountains, Utah); Proc. U. S. Nat. Mus., iii, 1880, 196, part; Nom. North Amer. Birds, 1881, No. 471, part.—Coues, Check-list North Amer. Birds, ed. 2, 1882, No. 557, part.—Henshaw, Auk, iii, 1886, 80 (upper Pecos River, N. Mex.).

C[*anace*] *obscura* Coues, Key North Amer. Birds, ed. 2, 1884, 579, part.

Canace obscurus Baird, Brewer, and Ridgway, Hist. North Amer. Birds, iii, 1874, pl. 59, figs. 1, 2.—Bendire, Proc. Boston Soc. Nat. Hist., xix, 1877, 137 (se. Oregon; common; habits; eggs).

Canace obscurus, var. *obscurus* Baird, Brewer, and Ridgway, Hist. North Amer. Birds, iii, 1874, 422, part (except from Sierra Nevada).

Canace obscura obscura Goode, U. S. Nat. Mus. Bull. 20, 1883, 310.

Dendragapus obscurus Elliot, Proc. Acad. Nat. Sci. Philadelphia, 1864, 23; Monogr. Tetraon., 1865, pl. 7 and text.—American Ornithologists' Union, Check-list, No. 297, part, 1886; ed. 2, 1895, No. 297, part.—Cooke, Bird Migr. Mississippi Valley, 1888, 103 (Black Hills); Colorado State Agr. Coll. Bull. 37, 1897, 70 (Colorado); Bull. 56, 1900, 202 (Colorado; breeds; Breckenridge).—Mearns, Auk, vii, 1890, 52 (White Mountains, east-central Arizona).—Bendire, Life Hist. North Amer. Birds, i, 1892, 41, part.—Ogilvie-Grant, Cat. Birds Brit. Mus., xxii, 1893, 74, part (excl. synonymy, part, and specimens, part).—Mitchell, Auk, xv, 1898, 307 (San Miguel County, N. Mex., breeding at 10,000 feet).—Macoun, Cat. Can. Birds, 1900, 198 (Montana and Idaho).—Cary, Auk, xviii, 1901, 232 (Black Hills, Wyo.).—Bailey, Handb. Birds Western United States, 1902, 124, part; Auk, xxi, 1904, 351 (upper Pecos River, N. Mex.; food, etc.).—Judd, U. S. Biol. Surv. Bull. 24, 1905, 41–44, part.—Gilman, Condor, ix, 1907, 153 (n. slope La Plata Mountains, sw. Colo.).—Henderson, Univ. Colorado Stud. Zool., vi, 1909, 228 (Boulder County, Colo., in mountains).—Visher, Auk, xxvi, 1909, 145 (hills, w. South Dakota; fairly common).—Sclater, Hist. Birds of Colorado, 1912, 145 (Colorado; resident).—Tanner, Condor, xxix, 1927, 197 (Pine Valley Mountains, Utah).—Palmer, Condor, xxx, 1928, 295 in text.—Lee, Condor, xxxviii, 1936, 122 in text (female with 5 chicks, near Paradise, Utah; July).—Monson, Condor, xli, 1939, 117 (Lukachukai Mountains, N. Mex., Oct. 26, 1937; pair seen; rare).

Dendragopus obscurus Taverner, Birds Western Canada, 1926, 164, pl. 21 B (fig.; descr.; distr. w. Can.); Birds Canada, 1934, 152 in text (distr.); Can. Water Birds, 1939, 164.—Petrides, Trans. 7th North Amer. Wildlife Conf., 1942, 313 in text (age indicators in plumage).

D[*endragapus*] *obscurus* Ridgway, Man. North Amer. Birds, 1887, 195, part.

[*Dendragapus*] *obscurus* Sharpe, Hand-list, i, 1899, 20, part.

Dendragapus obscurus obscurus American Ornithologists' Union, Check-list, ed. 3, 1910, 138, ed. 4, 1931, 78 (distr.).—(?) Saunders, Auk, xxviii, 1911, 35 (Gallatin County, Mont.; crit.).—Betts, Univ. Colorado Stud. Zool., x, 1913, 191 (Boulder County, Colo.).—Grave and Walker, Birds Wyoming,

1913, 39 (Wyoming; common in south).—ROCKWELL and WETMORE, Auk, xxxi, 1914, 314 (Lookout Mountain, Colo.).—SWARTH, Pacific Coast Avif., No. 10, 1914, 22 (Arizona; White Mountains, San Francisco Mountains).—OVER and THOMS, Birds South Dakota, 1921, 75 (Black Hills).—JENSEN, Auk, xi, 1923, 454 (n. Santa Fe County, N. Mex., 9,000 feet to timberline).—WYMAN and BURNELL, Field Book Birds Southwestern United States, 1925, 88 (descr.).— SWARTH, Univ. California Publ. Zool., xxx, 1926, 79 in text (fig. of tail feathers), 84 in text.—NEILSON, Condor, xxviii, 1926, 99 (Wheatland, Wyo.).— BAILEY, Birds New Mexico, 1928, 196 (genl., New Mexico).—BROOKS, Auk, xlvi, 1929, 111 (crit., tax., syn.).—HAYWARD, Proc. Utah Acad. Sci., viii, 1931, 151 (Uintah Mountains, Utah).—BENT, U. S. Nat. Mus. Bull. 162, 1932, 91 (habits, distr., etc.).—PETERS, Check-list Birds of World, ii, 1934, 29 (distr.).—McCREARY and MICKEY, Wils. Bull., xlvii, 1935, 129 in text (se. Wyoming, res.).—LINSDALE, Pacific Coast Avif., No. 23, 1936, 23, 47 (Nevada; res. on several mountain ranges in ne. part of State).—HUEY, Wils. Bull., xlviii, 1936, 122 (White Mountains, Ariz.; nest.; not uncommon).—ALEXANDER, Univ. Colorado Studies, Zool., xxiv, 1937, 91 (Boulder County, Colo.; spec.).—PHILLIPS, Auk, liv, 1937, 203 in text (8 miles se. Lukachukai, Apache Country, Ariz.; 8,800 feet; pair seen).—MOFFITT, Auk, lv, 1938, 589, pl. 17, fig. 1 (downy young; col. fig.).—NIEDRACH and ROCKWELL, Birds Denver and Mountain Park, 1939, 59 (Denver area, Colo.).—BOND, Condor, xlii, 1940, 220 (Lincoln County, Nev.; Wilson Peak, 8,000–8,500 feet; also Geyser Ranch, 8,000–9,000 feet).—HELLMAYR and CONOVER, Cat. Birds Amer., i, No. 1, 1942, 198 (syn.; distr.).—BEHLE, Bull. Univ. Utah, xxxiv, No. 2, 1943, 24, 37 (Pine Valley Mountain Region, Washington County, Utah) ; Condor, xlvi, 1944, 71 (Utah).

Dendragapus o[bscurus] obscurus LINCOLN, Auk, xxxvii, 1920, 65 (Clear Creek district, Colorado; late summer and full).—STANFORD, Proc. Utah Acad. Sci., ix, 1932, 73 (n. Utah; Mill Hollow).—GROEBBELS, Der Vögel, ii, 1937, 166 (data on breeding biology).

D[endragapus] o[bscurus] obscurus SWARTH, Univ. California Bubl. Zool., xxx, 1926, 74 in text (map; distr.).

T[ympanuchus] obscurus REICHENOW, Die Vögel, i, 1913, 320.

DENDRAGAPUS OBSCURUS PALLIDUS Swarth

SWARTH'S DUSKY GROUSE

Adult male.—Very similar to that of *Dendragapus obscurus richardsonii* but averaging slightly paler above and below and with the under tail coverts averaging paler—chaetura drab (instead of fuscous-black)— and with broader white tips.

Adult female.—Very similar to that of *D. o. richardsonii* but with paler under tail coverts—grayish banded with chaetura drab (instead of solid fuscous-black)—and with broader white tips.

Immature male.—Like the adult male but with narrower rectrices, more graduated tail, and often some juvenal feathers remaining on head and wings.

Immature female.—Like the adult female but with narrower rectrices, more graduated tail, and often some juvenile feathers remaining on head and wings.

Juvenal (sexes alike).—Like that of *D. o. richardsonii;* possibly averaging paler but not certainly distinguishable from it.

Downy young.—None seen; probably like that of *D. o. richardsonii.*

Adult male.—Wing 212–244 (233.8); tail 142–180 (166.4); exposed culmen 18.6–23.8 (20.7); tarsus 41.2–48.3 (44.5); middle toe without claw 40–47.5 (42.9 mm.).[91]

Adult female.—Wing 196–221 (208.7); tail 125–139 (131.8); exposed culmen 18–20.5 (19.5); tarsus 38.6–43.8 (40.9); middle toe without claw 35.6–42 (39.1 mm.).[92]

Range.—Resident in the mountains of eastern Washington (Mazama, Winthrop, Twisp, Bly, Loomis, Walla Walla, Fort Benton, Tunk Mountain, etc.), and south to the northeastern quarter of Oregon (Wallowa, Baker, Union Counties; northern Malheur and Harney Counties; eastern Crook, Grant, and Wheeler Counties; southern Morrow County, and southern and eastern Unatilla County),[93] southeast to central Nevada (Toyabe, Toquima, and Monitor Mountains).

Type locality.—Cornucopia, Baker County, Oreg.

Tetrao richardsonii (not Douglas) BAIRD, *in* Cooper, Orn. California, Land Birds, 1870, 528 (crit.), part.
Dendragapus obscurus richardsonii AMERICAN ORNITHOLOGISTS' UNION, Check-list, 1886, No. 297b; ed. 2, 1895, No. 297b, part.—BENDIRE, Life Hist. North Amer. Birds, i, 1892, 50, part.—WOODCOCK, Oregon Agr. Exp. Stat. Bull. 68, 1902, 26 (Camp Harney and Sparta, Oreg.).
D[endragapus] obscurus richardsonii RIDGWAY, Man. North Amer. Birds, 1887, 196, part.
[Dendragapus] richardsoni SHARPE, Hand-list, i, 1899, 20, part.
Dendragapus obscurus richardsoni AMERICAN ORNITHOLOGISTS' UNION, Check-list, ed. 3, 1910, 138, part; ed. 4, 1931, 79, part.—DICE, Auk, xxxv, 1918, 44 (Blue Mountains, Butte Creek, and near Twin Buttes Ranger Station, se. Washington).—GABRIELSON, Auk, xli, 1924, 555 (near Memaloose Ranger Station, Wallowa County, Oreg.).—GABRIELSON and JEWETT, Birds Oregon, 1940, 207 (Oregon; descr.; distr.; habits).
[Tetrao obscurus] var. *richardsonii* COUES, Key North Amer. Birds, 1872, 233, part.
Tetrao obscurus . . . var. *richardsonii* COUES, Check List North Amer. Birds, 1874, No. 381a, part.
Canace obscurus, var. *richardsoni* BAIRD, BREWER, and RIDGWAY, Hist. North Amer. Birds, iii, 1874, 427, part.
Canace obscura richardsonii RIDGWAY, Proc. U. S. Nat. Mus., iii, 1880, 196, part.
Canace obscura richardsoni RIDGWAY, Nom. North Amer. Birds, 1881, No. 471b, part.—COUES, Check List North Amer. Birds, ed. 2, 1882, No. 558, part.
C[anace] o[bscura] richardsoni COUES, Key North Amer. Birds, ed. 2, 1884, 579, part.
Canace richardsoni BAIRD, BREWER, and RIDGWAY, Hist. North Amer. Birds, iii, 1874, pl. 59, fig. 4, part.

---

[91] Sixteen specimens from Washington and Oregon.

[92] Thirteen specimens from Washington and Oregon.

[93] Birds from northeastern Washington are intermediate between *D. o. richardsonii* and *D. o. pallidus.*

Tetrao obscurus (not of Say) Audubon, Orn. Biogr., iv, 1838, 446, pl. 361, part; Synopsis, 1839, 203, part; Birds Amer., 8vo. ed., v, 1842, 89, pl. 295, part.—Baird, Rep. Pacific R.R. Surv., ix, 1858, 620, part (e. Oregon and Washington); Cat. North Amer. Birds, 1859, No. 459, part.

Dendragapus obscurus pallidus Swarth, Proc. California Acad. Sci., ser. 4, xx, 1931, 4 (descr.; crit.; range).—Peters, Check-list Birds of World, ii, 1934, 29 (range).—Linsdale, Pacific Coast Avif., No. 23, 1936, 23, 47 (Nevada; res.; Toyabe, Toquima, and Monitor Mountains); Amer. Midl. Nat., xix, 1938, 51 (Toyabe Mountains, Nev.; res.; habits; weight; color of soft parts).—Hellmayr and Conover, Cat. Birds Amer., i, No. 1, 1942, 199 (syn.; distr.).

Dendragapus obscurus pallidus Taverner, Birds Canada, 1934, 152 in text.

[*Dendragapus obscurus*] *pallidus* Moffitt, Auk, lv, 1938, 590 in text (mountains of eastern Oregon and possibly Washington; not in British Columbia).

Genus LAGOPUS Brisson

Lagopus Brisson, Orn., i, 1760, 26, 181. (Type, by tautonymy, *Lagopus* Brisson= *Tetrao lagopus* Linnaeus.)

Lagophus (emendation) Bonaparte, Atti Congr. Scienz. Ital. [Napoli], i, 1844, Zool., 8.

Oreias Kaup, Skizz. Entw.-Gesch. Eur. Thierw., 1829, 177, 193. (Type, by monotypy, *Tetrao scoticus* Latham.)

Oreas (emendation) Agassiz, Index Zool., 1846, 263.

Attagen Kaup, Skizz. Entw.-Gesch. Eur. Thierw., 1829, 170, 193. (Type, by original designation, "*Tetrao montanus* and *islandicus*.")

Acetinornis Bonaparte, Compt. Rend., xlii, May, 1856, 880. (Type, by monotypy, *Lagopus persicus* Gray=*Tetrao persicus* Latham.)

Keron "Montin" Gray, Hand-list, ii, 1870, 278. (Type, as designated by Ogilvie-Grant, *Tetrao mutus* Montin [*Keron* Montin, Physiogr. Sälsk. Handl., i, 1776, 155, is not a systematic but a vernacular name.])

Medium-sized to small Tetraonidae (length about 305–430 mm.) with toes, as well as tarsi, densely feathered in winter (more sparsely in summer); tail more than half but less than three-fifths as long as wing, very slightly rounded or nearly truncate, the rectrices (16) moderately broad, rounded at tips; neck without air sacs or elongated feathers; all the American and most of the Palearctic species white in winter, the remiges white in summer.

Bill varying from stout to rather slender but always much shorter (from frontal antiae) than distance from base to anterior angle of eye, its depth at frontal antiae sometimes slightly less, sometimes much greater than its width at same point; culmen rounded or very indistinctly ridged; maxillary tomium more or less strongly concave or arched, slightly inflected; rhamphotheca smooth. Wing moderate, strongly concave beneath, the longest primaries exceeding longest secondaries by between one-fourth and one-third the length of wing; third and fourth primaries longest, the first (outermost) equal to seventh or intermediate between sixth and seventh; outer primaries only moderately bowed or incurved, four or five outer ones with inner webs distinctly sinuated. Tail between one-half and three-fifths as long as wing, very slightly rounded to nearly truncate, the rectrices (16) not wider distally than tips, more or less rounded. Tarsus slightly less than one-sixth to a little more than one-fifth as long as wing, completely and densely clothed with long, hair-like feathers, in winter plumage, with much shorter feathers, the planta tarsi nude, in summer; middle toe decidedly shorter than tarsus, completely feathered (the feathering even sometimes concealing claws) in winter, in summer nude except basally, their upper surface without distinct transverse scutella except on terminal phalanx, being elsewhere covered with small, rounded, rather indistinct scales; claws relatively broad, very concave beneath, long in winter, much shorter in summer.

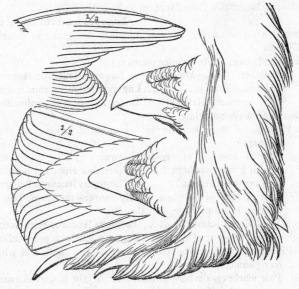

FIGURE 8.—*Lagopus lagopus.*

Plumage and coloration.—A more or less extensive nude superciliary space, brightly colored (red) and fringed in summer; neck with neither air sacs nor elongated feathers; plumage in general rather soft (except remiges and rectrices), the feathers relatively broad, rounded, and distinctly outlined, except on lower abdomen, anal region, and legs, where soft, hairlike, and blended. In winter plumage entirely white except tail (in part) and, sometimes, a black stripe on side of head—the tail also entirely white in one species.[94] In summer the plumage, more or less extensively mottled or barred or spotted with black, brown, dusky, gray, or ochraceous; the remiges, however, always remaining white (except in *L. scoticus*).

---

[94] In *L. scoticus* the plumage is entirely blackish and brown or rarely mottled, even in winter, even the primaries being wholly dusky.

Range.—Arctic and cold-temperate portions of Northern Hemisphere; in North America south to northern border of United States and along higher part of western mountain ranges to Colorado and to northern New Mexico. (Four species with many races).

KEY TO THE NORTH AMERICAN FORMS (ADULTS) OF THE GENUS LAGOPUS

a. Tail feathers white (*Lagopus leucurus*).
  b. Bill longer and more decurved, the exposed culmen over 16 mm. in length (chord) (Vancouver Island)..........**Lagopus leucurus saxatilis** (p. 132)
  bb. Bill shorter and less decurved, the exposed culmen under 15 mm. in length (chord).
    c. Wing longer, averaging, in males, over 185 mm.; in females, over 180 mm. (Rocky Mountains from Montana to New Mexico).
                            Lagopus leucurus altipetens (p. 134)
    cc. Wing shorter, averaging, in male, not over 181 mm.; in female, not over 170 mm.
      d. Entire plumage white (winter plumage) :
         (northern Rocky Mountains)...**Lagopus leucurus leucurus** (p. 127)
         (Mount Rainier)...........**Lagopus leucurus rainierensis** (p. 133)
         (south-central Alaska)......**Lagopus leucurus peninsularis** (p. 131)
      dd. Entire plumage not white.
        e. Plumage of upperparts finely vermiculated brown and gray (autumn plumage).
          f. General tone of upperparts browner—usually tawny-olive mottled with gray (northern Rocky Mountains from northern Washington to northern Alaska)..........**Lagopus leucurus leucurus** (p. 127)
          ff. General tone of plumage usually grayer—the tawny-buff being definitely less noticeable than the gray :
            (Mount Rainier).......**Lagopus leucurus rainierensis** (p. 133)
            (south-central Alaska)..**Lagopus leucurus peninsularis** (p. 131)
      ee. Plumage of upperparts coarsely barred black, buff, and whitish (summer plumage).
        f. Pale markings darker—pinkish buff to light pinkish cinnamon (northern Rocky Mountains from northern Washington to Alaska).
                            Lagopus leucurus leucurus (p. 127)
        ff. Pale markings paler—whitish to pale pinkish buff; only the broader ones slightly darker—pinkish buff.
          g. The dark areas deep pure black (Mount Rainier district).
                          Lagopus leucurus rainierensis (p. 133)
          gg. The dark areas black with a slight brownish tinge (south-central Alaska)...............**Lagopus leucurus peninsularis** (p. 131)
aa. Tail feathers black.
  b. Bill heavier, broader, and higher, its height at angle of gonys usually over 9.5 mm.; in winter (white) plumage with no black loreal mark (*Lagopus lagopus*).
    c. Shafts of primaries broadly dusky, often widening terminally; basal half of shafts of secondaries usually dusky (Newfoundland).
                            Lagopus lagopus alleni (p. 108)
    cc. Shafts of primaries whitish or narrowly dusky, dark color becoming narrower terminally; basal half of shafts of secondaries usually white.
      d. Shafts of primaries usually white or nearly so (Arctic islands from Baffin Island northward).......**Lagopus lagopus leucopterus** (p. 107)

dd. Shafts of primaries usually dusky.

    e. Bill slenderer, width at gape averaging about 12 mm. (nw. Mackenzie to Quebec)......................**Lagopus lagopus albus** (p. 100)

    ee. Bill broader, width at gape averaging 13 mm. or more.

        f. Bill very broad, the width at gape averaging 14.3 mm. in males, 13.6 mm. in females.

            g. Wings longer, averaging 199.2 mm. in males, 194 mm. in females.

                Lagopus lagopus koreni (extralimital)[95]

            gg. Wings shorter, averaging 193 mm. in males, 184 mm. in females.

                h. Bill longer, from nostril to tip averaging 11.8 mm. in males, 10.7 mm. in females (northern Quebec and Labrador).

                    Lagopus lagopus ungavus (p. 106)

                hh. Bill shorter, from nostril to tip averaging 10.9 mm. in males, 10.1 mm. in females (northern Alaska to the Kenai Peninsula).

                    Lagopus lagopus alascensis (p. 97)

    ff. Bill not so broad.

        g. Plumage entirely white except for tail.

            Lagopus lagopus lagopus, winter (extralimital)[96]

    Lagopus lagopus alexandrae, winter (southeastern Alaska) (p. 104)

---

[95] **Lagopus lagopus koreni.**—*Tetrao lagopus* (not of Linnaeus) Pallas, Zoogr. Rosso-Asiat., ii, 1826, 56, part.—*Lagopus lagopus* Stejneger, U. S. Nat. Mus. Bull. 29, 1885, 194 (Kamchatka; e. Asiatic references) ; Ogilvie-Grant, Cat. Birds Brit. Mus., xxii, 1893, 40, part (Tobolsk and Omsk, Siberia) ; Allen, Bull. Amer. Mus. Nat. Hist., xxi, 1905, 242 (Gichiga, etc., ne. Siberia; habits).—*Lagopus lagopus lagopus* Peters, Check-list Birds of World, ii, 1934, 30, part.—*Lagopus albus* Middendorff, Sibir. Reise, ii, 1883, 190; Schrenck, Reise Amurland, i, 1860, 395 ; Radde, Reisen Süd. Ost. Sibir., 1863, 294; (not *Tetrao albus* Gmelin) Taczanowski, Journ. für Orn., 1873, 98 (e. Siberia) ; Bull. Soc. Zool. France, 1876, 242; Orn. Fauna Vost. Sibir., 1877, 47; Seebohm, Ibis, 1879, 148 (Siberia; habits; crit.) ; Bogdanow, Consp. Av. Ross., i, 1884, 32.—*Tetrao albus* Seebohm, Ibis, 1888, 347 (Great Liakoff Island, Siberia; descr. eggs and young).—*Lagopus lagopus albus* Riley, Proc. Biol. Soc. Washington, xxiv, 1911, 233, part (e. Siberia).—*Lagopus alpinus* (not *Tetrao alpinus* Nilsson) Nelson, Cruise *Corwin* in 1881 (1883), 82 (n. coast Siberia).— *Lagopus lagopus koreni* Thayer and Bangs, Proc. New England Zool. Club, v, 1914, 4 (Nijni Kalymsk, Kolyma, e. Siberia; coll. Mus. Comp. Zool.) ; Riley, Proc. U. S. Nat. Mus., liv, 1918, 606 (Little Annuj River, Nijni Kolymsk, Kolyma Delta, ne. Siberia; measurements).—(?) *Lagopus lagopus okadai* Momiyama, Annot. Orn. Orient, i, 1928, 236 (Nairo, Nairo-mura, Sisuka-gun, Sisuka Prefect.-district, s. Sakhalin).—*Lagopus lagopus kamtschatkensis* Momiyama, Annot. Orn. Orient., i, 1928, 238 (Koshegofschenski, w. coast of Kamchatka) ; Bergman, Kenntn. Nordostasiat. Vög., 1935, 153 (Kamchatka; habits).

[96] **Lagopus lagopus lagopus.**—[*Tetrao*] *lagopus* Linnaeus, Syst. Nat., ed. 10, i, 1758, 159 (Lapland; cites Fauna Suecica, 169; etc.) ; ed. 12, 1766, 274; Brünnich, Orn. Bor., 1764, 59; Latham, Synopsis Birds, Suppl., i, 1787, 290; Index Orn., ii, 1790, 639, part (Europe; Siberia) ; Gmelin, Syst. Nat., i, pt. 2, 1788, 749.— *Tetrao lagopus* Temminck, Cat. Syst., 1807, 154; Pallas, Zoogr. Rosso-Asiat., ii, 1826, 63, part; Lesson, Traité d'Orn., 1831, 501; Yarrell, Hist. Brit. Birds, ii, 1843, 322.—*Lagopus lagopus* Hartert, Ibis, 1892, 511 (Dingken, Germany) ; Ogilvie-Grant, Cat. Birds Brit. Mus., xxii, 1893, 40, part.—[*Lagopus*] *lagopus* Sharpe, Hand-list, i, 1899, 18, part (n. Europe).—*Lagopus lagopus lagopus* Clark, Proc. U. S. Nat. Mus., xxxviii, 1910, 52, in text (Norway; crit.) ; American Ornithologists' Union, Check-list, ed. 3, 1910, 140, part; Riley, Proc. Biol. Soc. Washington,

gg. Plumage not white.
   h. Upperparts dark reddish brown narrowly marked with whitish
      and buff.
      i. Lower back, rump, and upper tail coverts more reddish—Prout's
         brown to argus brown (southeastern Alaska).
            Lagopus lagopus alexandrae, male, summer (p. 104)
      ii. Lower back, rump, and upper tail coverts less reddish—Dres-
         den brown abundantly cross-barred with blackish.
            Lagopus lagopus lagopus, male, summer (extralimital)
   hh. Upperparts not dark reddish brown, but narrowly barred buffy
      brown and black, many of the feathers with white tips (south-
      eastern Alaska).
            Lagopus lagopus alexandrae, female, summer (p. 104)
            Lagopus lagopus lagopus, female, summer (extralimital)

---

xxiv, 1911, 233, in text (Europe); Hartert, Vög. pal. Fauna, iii, 1921, 1859
(monogr.); Ramsay, Guide to Birds Europe and N. Africa, 1923, 323 (descr.;
distr.); Bianchi, Journ. für Orn., 1926, 456 (n. Russia); Groebbels, Der Vögel,
i, 1932, 618, 619 (data on body weight); Peters, Check-list Birds of World, ii,
1934, 30, part.—*Lagopus l[agopus] lagopus* Hortling and Baker, Ibis, 1932, 127
(Lapland); Kratzig, Journ. für Orn., 1940, 139 (young).—*[Tetrao] albus* (not of
Gmelin) Latham, Index Orn., ii, 1790, 639, part (Lapland).—*Tetrao albus* Naumann,
Nat. Vög. Deutschl., vi, 1833, 381, pl. 159.—*L[agopus] albus* Keyserling and Blasius,
Wirbelth. Eur., 1840, lxiii, 199.—*[Lagopus] albus* Reichenbach, Synop. Av., Gallinaceae, iii, 1848, pl. 213b, figs. 1858-1862.—*Lagopus albus* Brandt, *in* Hofmann,
N. Ural Exped., ii, App. 1856, 68; Elliot, Monogr. Tetraonidae, 1865, text & pls.
17, 18, part; Degland and Gerbe, Orn. Eur., ii, 1867, 37; Fritsch, Nat. Vög. Eur.,
1870, 278, pl. 20, figs. 1, 4; Collett, Forh. Vid. Selsk. Christiania, 1868, 159; 1872, 237
(n. Norway); Pearson and Bidwell, Ibis, 1872, 233 (n. Norway, breeding); Alston
and Brown, Ibis, 1873, 66 (Archangel, n. Russia); Dresser, Birds Eur., v, 1874,
183, pls. 483, 484, part; Palmén, Journ. für Orn., 1876, 42 (Finland); Seebohm and
Brown, Ibis, 1876, 220 (lower Petchova River, Russia; habits); Taczanowski, Bull.
Soc. Zool. France, ii, 1877, 153 (Poland); Seebohm, Ibis, 1879, 148 (Yenesei River,
Siberia); 1882, 379 (Archangel, n. Russia); Brandt, Journ. für Orn., 1880, 240
(St. Petersburg; Helsingfors); Bogdanow, Consp. Av. Ross., i, 1884, 32; Pearson,
Ibis, 1896, 216 (Kolguez, Russia; descr. egg).—*[Tetrao] lapponicus* Gmelin, Syst.
Nat., i, pt. 2, 1788, 751 (Lapland); Latham, Index Orn., ii, 1790, 640.—*Tetrao lap-
ponicus* Vieillot, Nouv. Dict. Hist. Nat., xxxiii, 1819, 455.—*Lagopus lapponicus*
Stephens, *in* Shaw Gen. Zool., xi, pt. 2, 1819, 296.—*Tetrao rehusak* Bonnaterre, Tabl.
Encycl. Méth., i, 1791, 204 (*ex* Montin and Pennant).—*Tetrao cachinnans* Retzius,
Fauna Suecica, 1800, 210 (Sweden, Lappland).—*Tetrao saliceti* Temminck, Pig. et
Gallin., iii, 1815, 207, 709, part; Man. d'Orn., ii, 1820, 471; Schinz, Nat. Abbild.
Vög., 1833, pl. 105; Godman, Ibis, 1861, 85 (Bodö); Bree, Birds Eur., iii, 1867, 212,
pl.—*Lagopus saliceti* Gould, Birds Eur., iv, 1837, pl. 255 and text; Cabanis, Journ.
für Orn., 1886, 348 (Germany).—*Tetrao sub-alpinus* Nilsson, Orn. Suec., i, 1817,
307 (n. Scandinavia and Finland).—*Lagopus subalpinus* Brehm, Handb. Vög.
Deutschl., 1831, 517; Nilsson, Skand. Fauna, Fögl., ii, 1858, 93; Olphe-Galliard,
Faun. Orn. Eur. Occ., fasc. 37-40, 1886, 55.—*Lagopus subalpina* Nilsson, Ill. Skand.
Faun., i, 1832, pls. 6, 7; Sundevall, Öfv. Svensk. Vet.-Akad. Forh. Fugl., 1856, pl. 35,
figs. 5, 6; Collin, Skand. Fugle, 1877, 421, Suppl. pl. 5.—*Lagopus brachydactylus*
Gould, Birds Eur., iv, 1837, pl. 256 and text; Olphe-Galliard, Faun. Orn. Eur. Occ.,
fasc. 37-40, 1886, 61.—*Tetrao brachydactylus* Temminck, Man. d'Orn., 1840 ed., iv,
328.—(?) *Lagopus lagopus kapustini* Sserebrowsky, Journ. für Orn., 1926, 512
(Lapland).

bb. Bill smaller, shorter, and narrower, its height at angle of gonys usually under
8.5 mm.; in winter (white) plumage with a black loreal band in males,
none in famales (*Lagopus mutus*).
  c. Plumage entirely white except for black tail and black loreal stripe.
                             Lagopus mutus, all races[97]
  cc. Plumage not entirely white.
    d. Upperparts and throat and breast coarsely banded with blackish (sum-
mer females).
      e. General color of paler areas decidedly more grayish than brownish.
        f. Lower back and rump barred with pale bars about as noticeable as
dark ones (Newfoundland).
           Lagopus mutus welchi, summer, female (p. 126)
        ff. Lower back and rump with the paler bars much reduced, much less
noticeable than the dark areas (northern Canada).
           Lagopus mutus rupestris, summer, female (p. 122)
      ee. General color of paler areas decidedly more brownish than grayish.
        f. Blackish bars on breast heavier, usually 4-5 mm. in width:
          (Attu Island) **Lagopus mutus evermanni,** summer, female (p. 109)
          (Alaska)......**Lagopus mutus nelsoni,** summer, female (p. 117)
          (se. Alaska).....**Lagopus mutus dixoni,** summer, female (p. 120)
          (Amchitka) **Lagopus mutus gabrielsoni,** summer, female (p. 116)
        ff. Blackish bars on breast narrower, usually under 3 mm. in width:
          (Tanaga)......**Lagopus mutus sanfordi,** summer, female (p. 113)
          (Kiska).....**Lagopus mutus townsendi,** summer, female (p. 111)
          (Atka Island)**Lagopus mutus atkhensis,** summer, female (p. 115)
          (Adak Island)
           Lagopus mutus chamberlaini, summer, female (p. 114)
    dd. Upperparts and throat and breast finely barred or vermiculated, some-
times almost solidly colored (males).
      e. General tone of upperparts dark, sepia or darker, and not noticeably
rufescent.
        f. Upperparts very dark, the upper back largely black.
          g. Feathers of the back abundantly mottled or barred with dark fer-
ruginous.
          Lagopus mutus ridgwayi, summer, male (extralimital)[98]

---

[97] The subspecies are not distinguishable in this plumage (no winter specimens of
L. m. evermanni appear to have been collected or described).
[98] **Lagopus mutus ridgwayi.**—*Tetrao lagopus* (not of Linnaeus) Pallas, Zoogr.
Rosso-Asiat., ii, 1826, 63, part.—*Lagopus albus* (not *Tetrao albus* Gmelin) Stejneger,
Proc. U. S. Nat. Mus., vi, 1883, 72 (Bering Island).—*Lagopus alpinus* (not of Midden-
dorff) Dybowski, Bull. Soc. Zool. France, 1883, 368.—*Lagopus ridgwayi* Stejneger,
Proc. Biol. Soc. Washington, i, 1884, 98 (Bering Island, Commander Group, Kam-
chatka; coll. U. S. Nat. Mus.); Zeitschr. ges. Orn., i, 1884, 89, pl. 5; Amer. Nat.,
xviii, 1884, 774; Ibis, 1885, 50; U. S. Nat. Mus. Bull. 29, 1885, 194; Palmén, Vega-
Exped., 1887, 301 (Bering Island); Clark, Proc. U. S. Nat. Mus., xxxviii, 1910, 56
(Commander Islands); Brooks, Bull. Mus. Comp. Zool., lix, 1915, 365 (Copper
Island).—[*Lagopus*] *ridgwayi* Sharpe, Hand-list, i, 1899, 18.—*Lagopus rupestris*
subsp. *insularis* Bogdanow, Consp. Av. Ross., 1884, 34 (Bering Island).—*Lagopus
mutus ridgwayi* Hartert, Vögel pal. Fauna, iii, 1921, 1871 (Bering and Copper
Island); Peters, Check-list Birds World, ii, 1934, 33 (Commander Islands).—
L[*agopus*] m[*utus*] *ridgwayi* Steinbacher, Ergänzungsband to Hartert, Vögel pal.
Fauna, Heft 6-7, 1938, 516 in text.

    gg. Feathers of the back not abundantly mottled or barred with dark
      ferruginous, but more solidly blackish (Attu Island).
            Lagopus mutus evermanni, summer, female (p. 109)
  ff. Upperparts not so dark, upper back not largely blackish. Upperparts
    fairly dark—general color sepia or darker, with or without a gray-
    ish tone.
    g. Brownish markings bright ochraceous-tawny (mainland of Alaska).
          Lagopus mutus nelsoni, summer, male (p. 117)
    gg. Brownish markings pale and much reduced in size and number (se.
      Alaska) . . . .**Lagopus mutus dixoni,** summer, male (p. 120)
  ee. General tone of upperparts paler—not darker than bright sayal brown
    or tawny-olive, often with a pronounced mixture of pale ashy gray.
    f. Upperparts very pale and ashy.
    g. General ground color of upperparts browner—lower back and rump
      pale tawny-olive (Atka Island).
          Lagopus mutus atkhensis, summer, male (p. 115)
    gg. General ground color of upperparts more grayish—lower back and
      rump isabella color.
      h. Lower throat and breast slightly paler—brownish feathers cin-
        namon-buff to pale tawny-olive (Tanaga Island).
          Lagopus mutus sanfordi, summer, male (p. 113)
      hh. Lower throat and breast slightly darker—brownish feathers cin-
        namon-buff to very pale tawny-olive (Adak Island).
       Lagopus mutus chamberlaini, summer, male (p. 114)[99]
  ff. Upperparts not so pale and not noticeably ashy.
    g. General tone of upperparts grayish—no bright tawny markings,
      brownish markings dull and mixed with grayish.
      h. Upperparts with many blackish blotches and with heavy blackish
        vermiculations.
        i. With considerable brownish in the upperparts (northern
          Canada) . .**Lagopus mutus rupestris,** summer, male (p. 122)
        ii. With little or almost no brownish in the upperparts (Newfound-
          land) . . . .**Lagopus mutus welchi,** summer, male (p. 126)
      hh. Upperparts with very few blackish blotches and finely vermicu-
        lated with blackish (northern Canada).
          Lagopus mutus rupestris, autumn, male (p. 122)
    gg. General tone of upperparts brownish—with bright tawny markings.
      h. General tone of upperparts bright rufescent.
        i. Throat and breast with few blackish bars or vermiculations
          (Tanaga Island).
          Lagopus mutus sanfordi, autumn, male (p. 113)
        ii. Throat and breast with many blackish bars or vermiculations.
          j. Upper back with many broad black bars (Amchitka).
          Lagopus mutus gabrielsoni, autumn, male (p. 116)
          jj. Upper back with few broad black bars (Kiska and Little
            Kiska Islands).
          Lagopus mutus townsendi, autumn, male (p. 111·)
      hh. General tone of upperparts not bright rufescent.
        i. Broadly barred with blackish above and on breast and upper
          tail coverts (Amchitka).
          Lagopus mutus gabrielsoni, summer, male (p. 116)

---

[99] The differences between *chamberlaini* and *sanfordi,* being very small, are almost
impossible to express in a key.

ii. Narrowly barred with blackish above and on breast, upper tail coverts merely vermiculated (Kiska and Little Kiska Islands)..**Lagopus mutus townsendi**, summer, male (p. 111)

LAGOPUS LAGOPUS ALASCENSIS Swarth

ALASKA WILLOW PTARMIGAN

Adult male, summer plumage.—Feathers around nostrils to base of maxilla and of mandible and chin white or black (!) with more or less chestnut; eye ring white; forehead, crown, occiput, and nape bright hazel to chestnut, each feather with an incomplete subterminal broad black cross bar; nape, interscapulars, scapulars, and upper back slightly darker, dark chestnut narrowly banded with fuscous-black to blackish and narrowly tipped with buffy white; back, rump, and inner upper wing coverts similar but with a white feather here and there; upper tail coverts similar but brown areas paler—hazel to pale hazel; a line of anterior scapulars, the outer upper wing coverts and the remiges white, the shafts of the primaries dusky becoming white terminally; rectrices dark fuscous tipped with white (the white tips broadest on the inner feathers), except the median pair which are like the upper coverts but with finer bars and vermiculations; sides of head, throat, and upper breast bright hazel to chestnut becoming darker on the lower breast where the feathers are barred with fuscous-black; rest of underparts white with an occasional chestnut feather on the sides; "comb" scarlet; bill bluish black; claws brownish basally becoming white on the distal half or so.

Adult male, autumn plumage.—Forehead, crown, and occiput russet to hazel, each feather subterminally blackish and with a terminal median spot of pale hazel; nape, scapulars, interscapulars, back, rump, and upper tail coverts russet to hazel, each feather crossed by several wavy blackish to fuscous-blackish bars, the next to the subterminal one usually the heaviest, followed by a paler, much buffier pale area which is distally narrowly edged with fuscous to fuscous-brown; tips of feathers white, the tips wearing off quickly, however; outer upper wing coverts and remiges white, the primaries with partly dusky brownish shafts (some with white shafts) innermost upper wing coverts like the back; rectrices dark fuscous except the median pair which are hazel to russet mottled and irregularly barred with dark fuscous to fuscous-black; lores and sides of head, chin, and upper throat hazel, eye ring white; lower throat and breast slightly darker hazel; upper abdomen, sides, flanks, and under tail coverts hazel irregularly and incompletely barred with fuscous to fuscous-black and tipped with white; center of abdomen to vent, thighs, and feathers of feet white; under wing coverts white; "comb" less prominent, more shriveled than in summer plumage.

Adult male, winter plumage.—Entire plumage pure white except for all but the median pair of rectrices, which are dark fuscous to fuscous-black, and for the shafts of the primaries, which are dusky except at the tip; the crown feathers are blackish in their concealed basal portions; feathers of toes longer and denser than in summer.

Adult female, summer plumage.—Forehead, crown, occiput, nape, inter scapulars, scapulars, inner upper wing coverts, back, rump, and upper tail coverts ochraceous-tawny to tawny-olive, each feather barred (and in the case of the interscapulars, scapulars, and upper back often broadly blotched) with fuscous-black, and tipped with pale tawny to pale olive-buff, and occasionally to almost white; rest of upper wing coverts and the remiges white, the primaries with dusky brown shafts, which are white terminally; rectrices dark fuscous tipped with white; lores and sides of head cinnamon-buff to light ochraceous-buff, the feathers with small fuscous transverse spots; chin and upper throat similar but often with no or almost no dusky markings; lower throat, breast, upper abdomen, sides, flanks, and under tail coverts ochraceous-buff to light ochraceous-tawny heavily barred with wavy bands of clove brown to fuscous; middle of abdomen to vent, and thighs slightly paler and without dark bands; under wing coverts white; "comb" pale vermilion; bill dull blackish, dull flesh color below at extreme base of lower mandible; claws dark brown, whitish on terminal third.

Adult female, autumn plumage.—Similar to that of the male but slightly more grayish on the back, rump, and upper tail coverts, the tips of the feathers being more ashy and the other brownish bars slightly less rufescent; the throat and breast paler—bright tawny, and the extent of this color on the sides much reduced compared with the male; the white of the abdomen correspondingly more extensive. In this plumage there usually is a sprinkling of feathers left over from the summer plumage, especially on the lower breast and sides.

Adult female, winter plumage.—Like the corresponding plumage of the male, but the bases of the feathers of the crown are more grayish.

First winter plumage (sexes alike).—Indistinguishable from the adult female winter plumage. (Females are therefore not separable, but first-winter males have the bases of the crown feathers more grayish, less blackish than in adults.)

First autumn plumage (sexes alike).—Similar to the summer plumage of the adult female but with the brownish bars, edges, and tips of the feathers of the upperparts paler and yellower—cinnamon-buff to honey yellow, the dark marks on the throat and breast and upper abdomen smaller, usually some of the rectrices retained from the juvenal plumage —narrow, pointed, tipped with white, otherwise fuscous-black barred and edged with cinnamon-buff to honey yellow, and with the outermost two remiges also retained from the juvenal plumage; lower abdomen and thighs grayish white.

Juvenal (sexes alike).—Similar to the first autumn plumage but with all but the outermost two remiges chaetura drab to clove brown, bordered narrowly and barred incompletely on the outer web with pale pinkish buff; all the upper wing coverts like the back; the general tone of the dorsal feather bars and edges richer, more orange—raw sienna to antique brown, and the abdomen more buffy; thighs buffy also.

Downy young (sexes alike).—Forehead, sides of crown and occiput, sides of head chamois to cream buff; with a black loreal spot and a median frontal line, and a postauricular wavy line of chaetura black; the median frontal line bifurcating to enclose most of the crown and occiput which are deep auburn to deep chestnut bordered by blackish, the lateral borders uniting again posteriorly to form a broad but much interrupted spinal stripe, which bifurcates on the lower back and the branches of which meet again at the base of the tail; wings and middle of back cinnamon-buff to clay color; sides of back (lateral to the blackish lines) and underparts straw yellow, washed on the breast with pale orange-yellow.

Adult male.—Wing 186–205 (195.6); tail 114–135 (122.9); bill from anterior end of nostril to tip 9.7–11.7 (10.9); width of bill at gape 13–14.3 (13.7); height of bill at angle of gonys 10.2–11.5 (10.8 mm).[1]

Adult female.—Wing 174–192 (185); tail 103–125 (112.6); bill from anterior end of nostril to tip 8.8–10.8 (10.1); width of bill at gape 11.7–14.4 (13.1); height of bill at angle of gonys 9.4–11.1 (10.2 mm.).[2]

Range.—Breeds from northern Alaska (Point Barrow, Cape Lisbourne, Wainwright, Smith Bay, Demarcation Point, Humphrey Point, Camden Bay, etc.) south throughout most of Alaska to Nushagak on the west coast and to the Kenai Peninsula and Mount McKinley, farther to the east.

Winters throughout its breeding range north as far as Nunivak Island, Nulato, Kutuk River, Miller Creek, Kotzebue Sound.

Type locality.—Kowak River Delta, Alaska.

Lagopus lagopus STEJNEGER, Proc. U. S. Nat. Mus., viii, 1885, 20, part.—AMERICAN ORNITHOLOGISTS' UNION, Check-list, No. 301, part, 1886; ed. 2, 1895, No. 301, part.—TURNER, Contr. Nat. Hist. Alaska, 1886, 152 (St. Michael, etc., Alaska; habits).—NELSON, Rep. Nat. Hist. Coll. Alaska, 1887, 131, pl. 5, fig. 3 (habits).—BENDIRE, Life Hist. North Amer. Birds, i, 1892, 69, part.—OGILVIE-GRANT, Cat. Birds Brit. Mus., xxii, 1893, 40, part (Point Barrow, Kotzebue Sound, St. Michael, Kegiktouik, and Nushagak, Alaska); Handb. Game Birds, i, 1896, 36, part.—GRINNELL, Pacific Coast Avif., No. 1, 1900, 32, 75 (Kowak River, Kotzebue Sound area; common; habits; plum.; nests and eggs).—MACOUN, Cat. Can. Birds, 1900, 205, part (Alaska).—CHAPMAN, Bull. Amer. Mus. Nat. Hist., xvi, 1902, 235, part (Homer and Kenai Mountains, Alaska; habits).—OSGOOD, North Amer. Fauna, No. 24, 1904, 65 (Alaska Peninsula; habits).—JUDD, U. S. Biol. Surv. Bull. 24, 1905, 44-46, part (range, food, etc.).—MACOUN and MACOUN, Cat. Can. Birds, ed. 2, 1909, 223, part (Alaska).—ANDERSON, Rep. Dept. Mines Canada for 1914 (1915), 165 (Alaska, Collinson Point and Endicott Mountains; spec.).—HILL, Condor, xxiv, 1922, 105, in text (habits; breeding,

[1] Twenty-one specimens from northern and north-central Alaska.
[2] Twenty specimens from northern Alaska.

etc., near Nome, Alaska).—LAING and TAVERNER, Ann. Rep. Nat. Mus. Canada
for 1927 (1929), 75 (Chitina River region, Alaska).—SHORTT, Contr. Roy.
Ontario Mus. Zool., No. 17, 1939, 12 (Yakutat Bay, Alaska; spec.; downy
young).

L[agopus] lagopus RIDGWAY, Man. North Amer. Birds, 1887, 199, part.

[Lagopus] lagopus SHARPE, Hand-list, i, 1899, 18, part.

Lagopus lagopus lagopus AMERICAN ORNITHOLOGISTS' UNION, Check-list, ed. 3,
1910, 140, part.—HERSEY, Smiths. Misc. Coll., lxvi, No. 2, 1916, 26 (n. to Cape
Espenberg, Alaska).—DICE, Condor, xxii, 1920, 179 (Tanana, Cosna River, and
North Fork Kuskokwim River, Alaska; habits; food).—CONOVER, Auk, xliii,
1926, 316 (Hooper Bay, Alaska; habits).—PETERS, Check-list Birds of World,
ii, 1934, 30, part.—HELLMAYR and CONOVER, Cat. Birds Amer., i, No. 1, 1942,
201, part.

Lagopus albus ELLIOT, Monogr. Tetraonidae, 1865, pls. 17, 18, text part.—DALL and
BANNISTER, Trans. Chicago Acad. Sci., i, 1869, 287, part (Fort Yukon, Alaska,
to Bering Sea; habits; molts).—BAIRD, BREWER, and RIDGWAY, Hist. North
Amer. Birds, iii, 1874, 457, part (habits; distr.; descr.).—McLENEGAN, Cruise
Corwin, 1884, 119 (Kowak River, Hotham Inlet, and Kotzebue Sound, nw.
Alaska); Cruise Corwin, 1885 (1887), 78 (Noatak River, Alaska).—HELLMAYR
and CONOVER, Cat. Birds Amer., i, No. 1, 1942, 201, part (syn.; distr.).

L[agopus] albus COUES, Key North Amer. Birds, ed. 2, 1884, 586, part.

[Lagopus] albus COUES, Key North Amer. Birds, 1872, 235, part.

Lagopus lagopus albus CLARK, Proc. U. S. Nat. Mus., xxxviii, 1910, 53 in text,
part (n. Alaska, Point Barrow, Kotzebue Sound, Cape Lisbourne, Kowak River;
crit.).—RILEY, Proc. Biol. Soc. Washington, xxiv, 1911, 233, part (n. Alaska).—
BROOKS, Bull. Mus. Comp. Zool., lix, 1915, 363 (Camden Bay, Humphrey Point,
and Demarcation Point, n. Alaska; habits).—OBERHOLSER, Auk, xxxiv, 1917,
200, part (Alaska).—BAILEY, Condor, xxviii, 1926, 121 (nw. Alaska; distr.;
habits).

Lagopus lagopus alascensis SWARTH, Univ. California Publ. Zool., xxx, No. 4,
1926, 87 (Kowak River Delta, Alaska; descr.; crit.); Pacific Coast Avif., No.
22, 1934, 25 (Nunivak Island, Alaska; spec.; crit.).—DIXON, Condor, xxix,
1927, 213 (life hist.; photos).—AMERICAN ORNITHOLOGISTS' UNION, Check-list,
ed. 4, 1931, 82 (distr.).—BENT, U. S. Nat. Mus. Bull. 162, 1932, 200 (habits).—
HURLEY, Murrelet, xiii, 1932, 38 (Bristol Bay, Alaska; eggs).—BAILEY, BROWER,
and BISHOP, Progr. Activ. Chicago Acad. Sci., iv, No. 2, 1933, 24 (Point
Barrow, Alaska).—FRIEDMANN, Journ. Washington Acad. Sci., xxiv, 1934, 237
(Cape Denbeigh, Norton Sound); xxxi, 1941, 407 (Cape Prince of Wales,
Alaska).—GROEBBELS, Der Vögel, ii, 1937, 166 (data on breed. biol.).—DIXON.
Condor, xlv, 1943, 54 (Arctic Alaska; Humphrey Point; abundant; nests).

L[agopus] l[agopus] alascensis AUSTIN, Mem. Nuttall Orn. Club, No. 7, 1932, 74,
in text (crit.).

Tetrao saliceti (not of Temminck) ADAMS, Ibis, 1878, 436 (St. Michael, Alaska;
habits, etc.).

LAGOPUS LAGOPUS ALBUS (Gmelin)

KEEWATIN WILLOW PTARMIGAN

Adult male, summer plumage.—Similar to that of *Lagopus lagopus
alascensis* but generally slightly darker above and on the throat and
breast, less brightly rufescent, and the bill slenderer, the width at the
gape averaging about 12 mm.

Adult male, autumn plumage.—Similar to that of *L. l. alascensis* but slightly grayer above, the terminal band of the feathers being ashy to wood brown and the bill slenderer.

Adult male, winter plumage.—Similar to that of *L. l. alascensis* but the bill slenderer.

Adult female, summer plumage.—Similar to that of *L. l. alascensis* but with less rufescent tone, the black areas larger and the brown markings somewhat duller, the feather edgings more grayish and the bill slenderer.

Adult female, autumn plumage.—Similar to that of *L. l. alascensis* but darker, more grayish above, and the bill slenderer.

Adult female, winter plumage.—Similar to the corresponding plumage of *L. l. alascensis* but the bill slenderer.

First winter plumage (sexes alike).—Similar to that of *L. l. alascensis* but the bill slenderer.

Juvenal plumage (sexes alike).—Like that of *L. l. alascensis* but very slightly less brightly orange-brown, slightly more grayish, and with the dark markings on the underside more broken into spots, not forming fairly complete bars.

Downy young.—Indistinguishable from that of *L. l. alascensis*.

Adult male.—Wing 178–201 (190.9); tail 112–126 (120); bill from anterior end of nostril to tip 9–11.5 (10.4); width of bill at gape 10.5–13 (12.2); height of bill at angle of gonys 9–11.2 (9.8 mm.).[3]

Adult female.—Wing 168–203 (180); tail 94–121 (106.8); bill from anterior end of nostril to tip 8.5–11.2 (9.7); width of bill at gape 10.6–13.5 (12); height of bill at angle of gonys 8.3–10.1 (9.5 mm.).[4]

Range.—Breeds from northwestern and central Mackenzie (Franklin, Great Bear and Great Slave Lakes, Fort Resolution, Fort Simpson, Fort Anderson) and Yukon (head of Coal Creek) to northeastern Manitoba (Churchill), northern Ontario and south-central Quebec to Anticosti Island, south through northern and central British Columbia (intergrading in northwestern British Columbia with *Lagopus lagopus alexandrae*), central Alberta, central Saskatchewan, and central Ontario.

Winters throughout most of its breeding range and south to Cumberland House and Fort Carleton, Saskatchewan; Norway House and Grand Rapids, central Manitoba; Cochrane and Martin Falls, central Ontario; Lake St. John, Maniwaki, and Bonne Esperance, Quebec.

Casual in Montana (Midvale, Glacier National Park); North Dakota (Killdeer Mountains, Dunn County); Minnesota (Sandy Island, Lake of the Woods); Wisconsin (Racine); ? Michigan (Keweenaw Point); New

---

[3] Twenty-two specimens from Yukon, Mackenzie, British Columbia, Alberta, and Hudson Bay.

[4] Twenty-three specimens from Mackenzie, British Columbia, Alberta, and Hudson Bay.

York (Watson, Lewis County) ; Nova Scotia; and Maine (Kenduskeag).
Type locality.—Western side of Hudson Bay.

Tetrao . . . *lagopus* (not of Linnaeus) FORSTER, Philos. Trans., lxii, 1772, 390.
Tetrao lagopus NUTTALL, Man. Orn. United States and Canada, Land Birds, 1832,
   671; ed. 2, 1840, 813 (Melville Island; Churchill River).
T[*etrao*] *lagopus* DOUGLAS, Trans. Linn. Soc. London, xvi, 3, 1829, 146 (Rocky
   Mountains, lat. 54° and northward; "on the northwest coast . . . as low as
   45°7′, the position of Mount Hood").
Lagopus lagopus STEJNEGER, Proc. U. S. Nat. Mus., viii, 1885, 20, part.—AMERICAN
   ORNITHOLOGISTS' UNION, Check-list, No. 301, part, 1886; ed. 2, 1895, No. 301,
   part.—SETON, Auk, iii, 1886, 153 (e. shore Lake Winnipeg; Norway House).—
   MACFARLANE, Proc. U. S. Nat. Mus., xiv, 1891, 430 (Fort Anderson, lower Anderson River, etc., Mackenzie; habits; descr. nest and eggs).—THOMPSON, Proc.
   U. S. Nat. Mus., xiii, 1891, 514 (Manitoba).—HATCH, Notes Birds Minnesota,
   1892, 162, 457 (rare; distr.; spec.).—BENDIRE, Life Hist. North Amer. Birds, i,
   1892, 69, part.—MERRILL, Auk, ix, 1892, 300 (Kenduskeag, Maine, 1892).—
   OGILVIE-GRANT, Cat. Birds Brit. Mus., xxii, 1893, 40, part (North American
   localities, except Alaska and Fort Chimo, Ungava) ; Handb. Game Birds, i,
   1896, 36, part.—CLARK, Auk, xi, 1894, 177 (spec. from Nova Scotia with rose-
   tinted plumage).—AMES, Auk, xiv, 1897, 411 (Whitby, Ontario, May 15, 1897).
   —NASH, Check List Birds Ontario, 1900, 26 (winter visitor in Ontario).—
   MACOUN, Cat. Can. Birds, 1900, 205, part (Hudson Bay westward).—PREBLE,
   North Amer. Fauna, No. 22, 1902, 103 (50 miles n. of York Factory northward;
   localities in Keewatin).—KUMLIEN and HOLLISTER, Bull. Wisconsin Nat. Hist.
   Soc., iii, 1903, 57 (rare straggler to Wisconsin).—JUDD, U. S. Biol. Surv. Bull.
   24, 1905, 44-46, part (distr.; food; etc.).—[NASH], Check List Vert. Ontario:
   Birds, 1905, 35 (Ontario; winter; spec.).—TOWNSEND, Mem. Nuttall Orn. Club
   No. 3, 1905, 202, 203 in text (Essex County, Massachusetts; accid.).—FLEMING,
   Auk, xxiv, 1907, 71 (Whitby, Ontario, May 15, 1897).—KNIGHT, Birds Maine,
   1908, 205 (Kenduskeag, Maine, April 23, 1892).—MACOUN and MACOUN, Cat.
   Can. Birds, 1909, 223, part (Hudson Bay westward).—CORY, Publ. Field Mus.
   Nat. Hist. No. 131, 1909, 438 (Racine, Wis., 2 spec., Dec. 1840; formerly
   winter visitant to extreme ne. Illinois ?).—EATON, Birds New York, i, 1910,
   375 (Watson, Lewis County, N. Y., 1 spec.).—DEXTER, Auk, xxxix, 1922, 269
   Green Lake, Saskatchewan, 4 spec., Dec. 1920).—TAVERNER, Birds Western Canada, 1926, 168 (fig.; descr.; habits; distr.; w. Canada).—TAVERNER and SUTTON,
   Ann. Carnegie Mus., xxiii, 1934, 30 (Churchill, Manitoba; breeds abundantly;
   habits).—BAILLIE and HARRINGTON, Contr. Roy. Ontario Mus. Zool., No. 8, pt. 1,
   1936, 29 (Ontario, only along extreme northern edge; prob. fairly common in
   summer; two breeding records).—ULKE, Can. Alpine Journ., 1934-35 (1936),
   79 (Yoho Park, Canada; summer; very rare).—? BRASSARD and BERNARD, Auk,
   liv, 1937, 514 in text (n. Quebec; food; captivity studies).—SHORTT and WALLER,
   Contr. Roy. Ontario Mus. Zool., No. 10, 1937, 18 (Lake St. Martin region,
   Manitoba; common; winter; spec.).—RICKER and CLARKE, Contr. Roy. Ontario
   Mus. Zool., No. 16, 1939, 8 (Lake Nipissing, Ontario).—CLARKE, Nat. Mus.
   Canada Bull. 96, 1940, 48 (Thelon Game Sanctuary, nw. Canada).—HAWKSLEY,
   Auk, lix, 1942, 436 (Churchill, Manitoba).
L[*agopus*] *lagopus* RIDGWAY, Man. North Amer. Birds, 1887, 199, part.—REICHENOW,
   Die Vögel, i, 1913, 323, part.—TAVERNER, Nat. Mus. Canada Bull. 50, 1928, 92
   (near Belvedere, Alberta).
[*Lagopus*] *lagopus* SHARPE, Hand-list, i, 1899, 18, part.

Lagopus lagopus lagopus American Ornithologists' Union, Check-list, ed. 2, 1895, 113; ed. 3, 1910, 140, part.—Barrows, Michigan Bird Life, 1912, 228.— Stanford, Auk, xxxi, 1914, 399 (near Midvale, Mont., in New Glacier Park).— Townsend, Mem. Nuttall Orn. Club, No. 5, 1920, 97 (Essex County, Mass.).— Saunders, Pacific Coast Avif., No. 14, 1921, 58 (Montana; Glacier National Park; spec.).—Wood, Misc. Publ. Univ. Michigan Mus. Zool., No. 10, 1923, 35 (Killdeer Mountains, Dunn County, N. Dak., Oct., 1909).—Mitchell, Can. Field Nat., xxxviii, 1924, 108 (Saskatchewan; not common winter visitant; spec.).—Racey, Auk, xliii, 1926, 321 (near Red Mountains, Alta Lake region, British Columbia).—Taverner, Birds Western Canada, 1926, 167, in text (distr.).—Forbush, Birds Massachusetts and Other New England States, ii, 1927, 37 (descr., habits, New England).—? Lewis, Auk, xliv, 1927, 64 (nesting; 8 miles e. of Romaine, Labrador Peninsula).—Sutton, Condor, xxxiii, 1931, 157 (w. coast Hudson Bay).—Peters, Check-list Birds of World, ii, 1934, 30, part.— Hellmayr and Conover, Cat. Birds Amer., i, No. 1, 1942, 201, part (syn.; distr.).

[*Tetrao*] *albus* Gmelin, Syst. Nat., i, pt. 2, 1788, 750 (Hudson Bay; based on *Lagopede de la Baye Hudson* Buffon, Ois., ii, 276, pl. 9; *White Partridge* Ellis, Huds., i, pl. 1; Edwards, Av. pl. 72; *White Grous* Pennant, Arctic Zool., ii, 308).—Latham, Index Orn., ii, 1790, 639, part (Hudson Straits).

Tetrao albus Lesson, Traité d'Orn., 1831, 501.—Vigors, Zool. Voy. *Blossom*, 1839, 26 nomencl.).—Nuttall, Man. Orn. United States and Canada, Land Birds, ed. 2, 1840, 816.

Lagopus albus Vieillot, Nouv. Dict. Hist. Nat., xvii, 1817, 203.—Stephens, *in* Shaw, Gen. Zool., xi, pt. 2, 1819, 292, pl. 20.—Bonaparte, Geogr. and Comp. List, 1838, 44, part.—Audubon, Synopsis, 1839, 207; Birds America, 8vo ed., v, 1842, 114, pl. 299.—Baird, Rep. Pacific R.R. Surv., ix, 1858, 633, part (Red River; Nelson River; Hudson Bay); Cat. North Amer. Birds, 1859, No. 467, part.—Coues, Proc. Acad. Nat. Sci. Philadelphia, 1861, 227 (Labrador); Proc. Essex Inst., v, 1868, 41 (Maine—rare in winter; Essex County, Mass.; spec. (supposed to have been brought from Labrador?)); Check List North Amer. Birds, 1874, No. 386, part; ed. 2, 1882, No. 568, part; Bull. Nuttall Orn. Club, iii, 1878, 41 (Lewis County, N. Y., 1 spec., May 22, 1876).—Verrill, Proc. Essex Inst., iii, 1862, 157 (n. Maine in winter).—Elliot, Monogr. Tetraonidae, 1865, pls. 17, 18, and text, part.—Baird, Brewer, and Ridgway, Hist. North Amer. Birds, iii, 1874, 457, part, pl. 61, fig. 8, pl. 62, figs. 1-3.—Brewer, Proc. Boston Soc. Nat. Hist., xvii, 1875, 12 (New England; accid.).—Gibbs, U. S. Geol. and Geogr. Surv. Terr. Bull. 5, 1879, 491 (Upper Peninsula, Mich.).— Merriam, Bull. Nuttall Orn. Club, vi, 1881, 233 (Lewis County, N. Y.; in winter); vii, 1882, 238 (Point de Monts, Quebec).—Brewster, Proc. Boston Soc. Nat. Hist., xxii, 1883, 383 (Anticosti Island, breeding).—Groebbels, Der Vögel, ii, 1937, 240, in text (eggs in mixed sets), 383, in text (runt eggs).

L[*agopus*] *albus* Ridgway, Ann. Lyc. Nat. Hist. New York, x, 1874, 382 (Cook County, ne. Illinois, formerly in winter).—Hatch, Bull. Minnesota Acad. Nat. Sci., 1874, 62 (Minnesota; rare).—Nelson, Bull. Essex Inst., viii, 1876, 122 (no longer occurring in ne. Illinois).—Coues, Key North Amer. Birds, ed. 2, 1884, 586, part.

[*Lagopus*] *albus* Coues, Key North Amer. Birds, 1872, 235, part.

Lagopus lagopus albus Clark, Proc. U. S. Nat. Mus., xxxviii, 1910, 53 in text, part.—Riley, Proc. Biol. Soc. Washington, xxiv, 1911, 233, part (w. side Hudson Bay); Can. Alpine Journ., 1912, 58 (Moose Pass branch of Smoky River, Alberta; crit.; habits).—Oberholser, Auk, xxxiv, 1917, 200, part.— Hartert, Vög. pal. Fauna, iii, 1921, 1862 (monogr.).—Swarth, Univ. California Publ. Zool., xxx, No. 4, 1926, 86 (Atlin region, British Columbia; crit.).—

American Ornithologists' Union, Check-list, ed. 4, 1931, 82 (distr.).—Bent,
U. S. Nat. Mus. Bull. 162, 1932, 178 (habits; distr.).—Roberts, Birds Minne-
sota, i, 1932, 384 (distr.; habits, Minn.).—Taverner, Birds Canada, 1934, 158,
in text.—Groebbels, Der Vögel, ii, 1937, 166 (data on breeding biology) ; 318,
in text (egg color—postmortem changes).—MacLulich, Contr. Roy. Ontario
Mus. Zool., No. 13, 1938, 2 (Algonquin Prov. Park, Ontario; rare in winter).
L[agopus] lagopus albus Baillie and Harrington, Contr. Roy. Ontario Mus. Zool.,
No. 8, pt. 1, 1936, 29 in text (Ontario).
L[agopus] l[agopus] albus Austin, Mem. Nuttall Orn. Club, No. 7, 1932, 74, in
text (crit.).
Tetroa saliceti (not Tetrao saliceti Temminck) Richardson, in Appendix to Parry's
Journ. Second Voy., 1825 (1827), 347.
T[etrao] saliceti Douglas, Trans. Linn. Soc. London, xvi, 1829, 147 ("Rocky Mts.").
Tetrao saliceti Nuttall, Man. Orn. United States and Canada, Land Birds, 1832,
674, part.—Audubon, Orn. Biogr., ii, 1834, 528, pl. 191.
Tetrao (Lagopus) saliceti Swainson in Swainson and Richardson, Fauna Bor.-
Amer., ii, 1831 (1832), 351.

LAGOPUS LAGOPUS ALEXANDRAE J. Grinnell

ALEXANDER'S PTARMIGAN

Adult male, summer plumage.—Like that of *Lagopus lagopus alascensis*
but with slenderer bill and the brown areas, especially on the upperparts,
averaging darker.[5]

Adult male, autumn plumage.—Similar to that of *L. l. alascensis* but
with slenderer bill and more uniformly dark brown dorsally, less rufescent; the throat and breast dark cinnamon to dark cinnamon-tawny.

Adults in winter plumage.—Similar to the corresponding sex in the
same plumage of *L. l. alascensis* but with slenderer bill.

Adult female, summer plumage.—Similar to that of *L. l. alascensis*
but slenderer bill.

Adult female, autumn plumage.—Similar to that of *L. l. alascensis* but
with slenderer bill.

Juvenal (sexes alike).—Like that of *L. l. alascensis*.

Downy young (sexes alike).—Like that of *L. l. alascensis*.

Adult male.—Wing 185–205 (192.8); tail 112–127 (117.7); bill from
anterior end of nostril to tip 9.4–12.2 (10.5); width of bill at gape 12.4–
14.5 (13.8); height of bill at angle of gonys 9.7–10.8 (10.1 mm.).[6]

Adult female.—Wing 171–191 (181); tail 96–112 (106.1); bill from
anterior end of nostril to tip 9.2–10.4 (9.9); width of bill at gape 12.6–13.6
(13.1); height of bill at angle of gonys 9.3–10.3 (9.8 mm.).[7]

---

[5] In some specimens of both sexes the shafts of the primaries, secondaries, and
greater upper coverts are almost as dusky as in the Newfoundland race, *L. l. alleni*,
but not in the majority.

[6] Twenty-two specimens from Shumagin Islands, Kodiak Island, and south to
Prince William Sound, Alaska.

[7] Twenty specimens from southeast Alaska from the Shumagin Islands and the
base of the Alaska Peninsula and Kodiak Island.

Range.—Inhabits the islands off the coasts and the adjacent mainland of southern and southeastern Alaska from the Shumagin Islands, Unalaska, Unimak, Atka and adjacent islands of the Aleutian Chain, Kodiak, and the base of the Aleutian Peninsula, south to the Prince of Wales Archipelago, and to Porcher Island, British Columbia; intergrading with *Lagopus lagopus albus* in the Skeena River area of northwestern British Columbia and with *Lagopus lagopus alascensis* just north of the base of the Aleutian Chain (Nushagak, etc.).

Type locality.—Mountain at Bear Bay, Baranof Island, Alaska.

Lagopus albus (not *Tetrao albus* Gmelin) ELLIOT, Monogr. Tetraonidae, 1865, pls. 17, 18, and text, part.—DALL and BANNISTER, Trans. Chicago Acad. Sci., i, 1869, 287, part (Sitka and Kodiak, Alaska; habits; molts).—DALL, Proc. California Acad. Sci., advance reprint 1873, 4, part; v, pt. 1, 1873, 38, part; v, 1874, 273 (Shumagin Islands to Unalaska, Alaska).—BEAN, Proc. U. S. Nat. Mus., v, 1882, 163 (Unga Island, Shumagin group; crit.).—HARTLAUB, Journ. für Orn., 1883, 276 (Chilcoot, Alaska).

L[*agopus*] *albus* COUES, Key North Amer. Birds, ed. 2, 1884, 586, part.

[*Lagopus*] *albus* COUES, Key North Amer. Birds, 1872, 235, part.

Tetrao lagopus (not of Linnaeus) SCHALOW, Journ. für Orn., 1891, 258 (Aleutian Islands).

Lagopus lagopus CHAPMAN, Bull. Amer. Mus. Nat. Hist., xvi, 1902, 235, part (Popof Island, Alaska; habits).

Lagopus alexandrae GRINNELL (J.), Univ. California Publ. Zool., v, No. 2, 1909, 204 (mountain at Bear Bay, Baranof Island, se. Alaska; coll. Univ. California, Mus. Vert. Zool.).—BAILEY, Auk, xliv, 1927, 198 (Glacier Bay; Beardslee Islands; Sandy Cove; etc.; se. Alaska; habits).

Lagopus lagopus alexandræ AMERICAN ORNITHOLOGISTS' UNION, Auk, xxvi, No. 3, 1909, 275 (Check-list No. 301b); Check-list, ed. 3, 1910, 141.—CLARK, Proc. U. S. Nat. Mus., xxxviii, 1910, 51-54, part (mountains of se. Alaska to Kodiak; crit.).—RILEY, Proc. Biol. Soc. Washington, xxiv, 1911, 233 (sw. coast Alaska).—BROOKS (W.S.), Bull. Mus. Comp. Zool., lix, 1915, 364 (Portage Bay, Alaska Peninsula).—BROOKS (A.), Auk, xl, 1923, 221 (Porcher Island, British Columbia).

Lagopus lagopus alexandrae WILLETT, Auk, xxxviii, 1921, 128 (Kalu, Prince of Wales, Decatur, Selemez, San Juan, Dall, and Long Islands, se. Alaska).—HARTERT, Vög. pal. Fauna, iii, 1921, 1863 (crit.).—TAVERNER, Birds Western Canada, 1926, 169 in text; Birds Canada 1934, 158, in text.—AMERICAN ORNITHOLOGISTS' UNION, Check-list, ed. 4, 1931, 83 (distr.).—BENT, U. S. Nat. Mus. Bull. 162, 1932, 194 (habits).—PETERS, Check-list Birds of World, ii, 1934, 31 (distr.).—FRIEDMANN, Bull. Chicago Acad. Sci., v, No. 3, 1935, 31 (Kodiak Island; spec.).—HELLMAYR and CONOVER, Cat. Birds Amer., i, No. 1, 1942, 203 (syn.; distr.).—CLARK, Smiths. War Background Stud. No. 21, 1945, 78 (list birds Aleutians).

Lagopus l[*agopus*] *alexandrae* PALMER, Condor, xxx, 1928, 264, in text (patronymics).—SWARTH, Pacific Coast Avif., No. 22, 1934, 25, in text (Unalaska; Atka; spec.).

L[*agopus*] l[*agopus*] *alexandrae* AUSTIN, Mem. Nuttall Orn. Club, No. 7, 1932, 74, in text (crit.).

LAGOPUS LAGOPUS UNGAVUS Riley

UNGAVA PTARMIGAN

Adults, all plumages.—Similar to the corresponding plumage of *Lagopus lagopus alascensis* but with the bill heavier—its outline, when viewed from above, more swollen.

Juvenal (sexes alike).—Similar to that of *L. l. alascensis* but bill wider at gape.

Downy young (sexes alike).—Similar to that of *L. l. alascensis* but with the blackish markings reduced in width and the general body color slightly tinged with pale orange-buff.

Adult male.—Wing 182–203 (193); tail 110–130 (121.4); bill from anterior end of nostril to tip 10.9–13 (11.8); width of bill at gape 13–15.8 (14.3); height of bill at angle of gonys 10.8–12.2 (11.6 mm.).[8]

Adult female.—Wing 176–191 (184); tail 101–119 (106.7); bill from anterior end of nostril to tip 10.1–11.6 (10.7); width of bill at gape 12.2–14.1 (13.3); height of bill at angle of gonys 10.1–11.1 (10.6 mm.).[9]

Range.—Inhabits northern Quebec (Fort Chimo) and Labrador (Okkak); southern limits not known.

Type locality.—Fort Chimo, Ungava.

Lagopus albus (not *Tetrao albus* Gmelin) BAIRD, Rep. Pacific R.R. Surv., ix, 1858, 633, part (Labrador); Cat. North Amer. Birds, 1859, No. 467, part.—COUES, Proc. Acad. Nat. Sci. Philadelphia, 1861, 227 (Labrador) Check List North Amer. Birds, 1874, No. 386, part; ed. 2, 1882, No. 568, part.—ELLIOT, Monogr. Tetraonidae, 1865, pls. 17, 18, and text, part.—BAIRD, BREWER, and RIDGWAY, Hist. North Amer. Birds, iii, 1874, 457, part (habits; descr.; distr.).—TURNER, Proc. U. S. Nat. Mus., viii, 1885, 245 (Fort Chimo, Ungava; breeding).—STEARNS, Bird Life in Labrador, n. d. *ca.* 1890, 48 (Labrador; habits).—HANTSZCH, Can. Field Nat., xlii, 1928, 12, 13 (Cumberland Sound, Labrador).

L[agopus] albus COUES, Key North Amer. Birds, ed. 2, 1884, 586, part.

[Lagopus] albus COUES, Key North Amer. Birds, 1872, 235, part.

Lagopus lagopus (not *Tetrao lagopus* Linnaeus) OGILVIE-GRANT, Cat. Birds Brit. Mus., xxii, 1893, 40, part (Fort Chimo); Handb. Game Birds, i, 1896, 36, part.—MACOUN, Cat. Can. Birds, 1900, 205, part (Labrador).—MACOUN and MACOUN, Cat. Can. Birds, 1909, 223, part (Labrador).

Lagopus lagopus lagopus HANTZSCH, Journ. für Orn., 1908, 365 (ne. Labrador).—AMERICAN ORNITHOLOGISTS' UNION, Check-list, ed. 3, 1910, 140, part.—CLARK, Proc. U. S. Nat. Mus., xxxviii, 1910, 53 in text, part (n. Labrador).—? LEWIS, Auk, xlv, 1928, 228 (breeding near Bluff Harbor, Labrador).—? AUSTIN, Mem. Nuttall Orn. Club, No. 7, 1932, 74 (habits, descr.; Newfoundland, Labrador).—PETERS, Check-list Birds of World, ii, 1934, 30, part.—HELLMAYR and CONOVER, Cat. Birds Amer., i, No. 1, 1942, 201, part.

Lagopus lagopus ungavus RILEY, Proc. Biol. Soc. Washington, xxiv, 1911, 233 (Fort Chimo, Ungava; coll. U. S. Nat. Mus.).—AMERICAN ORNITHOLOGISTS' UNION, Auk, xxix, 1912, 381; Check-list, ed. 4, 1931, 82 (distr.).—BENT, U. S. Nat. Mus. Bull. 162, 1932, 197 (habits).

---

[8] Thirteen specimens from northern Ungava.

[9] Ten specimens from northern Ungava.

? *Lapogus lapogus ungavus* HARTERT, Vög. pal. Fauna, iii, 1921, 1863 (crit.).
L[agopus] l[agopus] ungavus AUSTIN, Mem. Nuttall Orn. Club, No. 7, 1932, 74, in text (crit.).

LAGOPUS LAGOPUS LEUCOPTERUS Taverner

BAFFIN ISLAND PTARMIGAN

Adults.—Similar to the corresponding sex and plumage of *Lagopus lagopus alascensis,* but with the shafts of the primaries and secondaries almost always white; only occasionally is one partly dusky.

Juvenal.—None seen; apparently unknown.

Downy young.—None seen; apparently unknown.

Adult male.—Wing 197–216 (206.1); tail 116–125 (121.3); length of bill from anterior end of nostril to tip 9.9–12.5 (11.5); width of bill at gape 13.6–14.9 (14.3); height of bill at angle of gonys 9.6–10.7 (10.4 mm.).[10]

Adult female.—Wing 188–214 (196.4); tail 107–139 (116.7); bill from anterior end of nostril to tip 9–12.3 (10.9); width of bill at gape 12.1–12.8 (12.6); height of bill at angle of gonys 9.1–10 (9.6 mm.).[11]

Range.—Inhabits the Arctic islands of America from southern Banks Island and the mainland adjacent to Dolphin and Union Straits to Southampton and southern Baffin Islands; indefinitely northward. One record for Point Barrow, Alaska.

Type locality.—Camp Kungovik, western coast of Baffin Island, lat. 65° 35′ N.

Lagopus lagopus TAVERNER, Canada's Eastern Arctic, 1934, 119, text (Lancaster Sound; Melville Island); Birds Canada, 1934, 157, in text, part.
Lagopus lagopus lagopus SOPER, Nat. Mus. Canada, Bull. 53, 1928, 104 (s. Baffin Island).
Lagopus lagopus leucopterus TAVERNER, Ann. Rep. Nat. Mus. Canada for 1930 (1932), 87 (Camp Kungovik, w. coast of Baffin Island, lat. 65°35′ n.).— SUTTON, Mem. Carnegie Mus., xii, 1932, 88 (Southampton Island; spec.; meas.; habits).—TAVERNER, Birds Canada, 1934, 158 in text.—PETERS, Check-list Birds of World, ii, 1934, 31 (distr.).—HELLMAYR and CONOVER, Cat. Birds Amer., i, No. 1, 1942, 202 (syn.; distr.).—BRAY, Auk, lx, 1943, 516 (Southampton Island; Baffin Island; Melville Peninsula).
L[agopus] l[agopus] leucopterus AUSTIN, Mem. Nuttall Orn. Club, No. 7, 1932, 74 in text (crit.).—TAVERNER, Canada's Eastern Arctic, 1934, 119, in text (distr.; chars.).—SALOMONSEN, Moults and Sequence of Plumage in Rock Ptarmigan, 1939, 265, in text (molt).

---

[10] Fourteen specimens from Baffin Island, Victoria Land, and Southampton Island.
[11] Eleven specimens from Banks Island, Baffin Island, Southampton Island, and Victoria Land.

LAGOPUS LAGOPUS ALLENI Stejneger

ALLEN'S PTARMIGAN

All adult plumages.—Similar to the corresponding ones of *Lagopus lagopus albus* but with the shafts of the primaries usually chaetura drab to fuscous, broadening terminally, and the distal portion of the remiges often mottled with the same; the shafts of the secondaries and of the greater upper coverts also frequently similarly dark.[12]

Juvenal and downy young.—Similar to those of *L. l. albus.*

Adult male.—Wing 187–205 (199.2); tail 108–127 (119.3); bill from anterior end of nostril to tip 10.2–11 (10.7); width of bill at gape 13–13.3 (13.1); height of bill at angle of gonys 10–10.2 (10.1 mm.).[13]

Adult female.—Wing 183–193 (189); tail 98–119 (109); bill from anterior end of nostril to tip 10.2–11.8 (11); width of bill at gape 12–12.8 (12.4); height of bill at angle of gonys 10–10.2 (10.1 mm.).[14]

Range.—Resident in Newfoundland.

Type locality.—Newfoundland.

Lagopus albus (not *Tetrao albus* Gmelin) BAIRD, Rep. Pacific R.R. Surv., ix, 1858, 633, part (St. John's, Newfoundland); Cat. North Amer. Birds, 1859, No. 467, part.—MAYNARD, Birds North Amer., 1881, 348, part (Newfoundland).— [SCLATER], Ibis, 1889, 261 (Newfoundland).

Lagopus alba alleni STEJNEGER, Auk, i, 1884, 369 (Newfoundland; coll. U. S. Nat. Mus.).

Lagopus lagopus MACOUN and MACOUN, Cat. Can. Birds, ed. 2, 1909, 223, part (Newfoundland).

Lagopus lagopus alleni STEJNEGER, Proc. U. S. Nat. Mus., viii, 1885, 20.—AMERICAN ORNITHOLOGISTS' UNION, Check-list, No. 301a, 1886; ed. 2, 1895, No. 301a; ed. 3, 1910, 141; ed. 4, 1931, 82.—BENDIRE, Life Hist. North Amer. Birds, i, 1892, 75.—MACOUN, Cat. Can. Birds, 1900, 206 (Newfoundland).—MACOUN and MACOUN, Cat. Can. Birds, ed. 2, 1909, 225 (Newfoundland).—CLARK, Proc. U. S. Nat. Mus., xxxviii, 1910, 52 in text (crit.).—HENNINGER, Wils. Bull., xxii, 1910, 119 (descr. eggs).—HARTERT, Vög. pal. Fauna, iii, 1921, 1863 (monogr.).—GRISCOM, Ibis, 1926, 672 (w. Newfoundland).—BENT, U. S. Nat. Mus. Bull. 162, 1932, 191 (habits; distr.; etc.).—TAVERNER, Birds Canada, 1934, 158, in text.—ROOKE, Ibis, 1936, 865 (Newfoundland).—BROOKS, Auk, liii, 1936, 343 (Avalon Peninsula, Newfoundland).—GROEBBELS, Der Vögel, ii, 1937, 166 (data on breeding biology).—ALDRICH and NUTT, Sci. Publ. Cleveland Mus. Nat. Hist., iv, 1939, 19 (e. Newfoundland).—HELLMAYR and CONOVER, Cat. Birds Amer., i, No. 1, 1942, 203 (syn.; distr.).

L[agopus] lagopus alleni RIDGWAY, Man. North Amer. Birds, 1887, 199.

L[agopus] l[agopus] alleni COUES, Key North Amer. Birds, ed. 5, ii, 1903, 745.— TOWNSEND, Mem. Nutt. Orn. Club, No. 3, 1905, 203, in text.—AUSTIN, Mem. Nuttall Orn. Club, No. 7, 1932, 74, in text (crit.).—SALOMONSEN, Moults and

---

[12] Freshly killed October and November birds are said to have a faint pinkish flush on the white feathers, but this quickly fades and is not to be seen in the dried skins in the National Museum.

[13] Six specimens from Newfoundland.

[14] Seven specimens from Newfoundland.

Sequence of Plumage in Rock Ptarmigan, 1939, 263 in text (Newfoundland; molts and plumages).

L[agopus] l[agopus] alleni TAVERNER, Birds Eastern Canada, 1919, 110 in text (Newfoundland).

[Lagopus lagopus] subsp. a. Lagopus alleni OGILVIE-GRANT, Cat. Birds Brit. Mus. xxii, 1893, 44, 557 (spec. Newfoundland).

Lagopus alleni OGILVIE-GRANT, Handb. Game Birds, i, 1896, 38, in text (Newfoundland; crit.).

[Lagopus] alleni SHARPE, Hand-list, i, 1899, 18.

LAGOPUS MUTUS EVERMANNI Elliot

EVERMANN'S PTARMIGAN

Adult male, summer.—Anterior forehead white with a faint buffy wash; rest of forehead and the short supraorbital marks white; crown, occiput, nape, and upper interscapulars fuscous-black finely barred with tawny-olive to Saccardo's umber; rest of interscapulars deep chaetura black narrowly tipped with tawny-olive; the back, rump, upper tail coverts, inner secondaries, and some of the inner lesser and median upper wing coverts fuscous-black faintly vermiculated with tawny-olive to Saccardo's umber; some of these dorsal feathers darker—deep chaetura drab—and without any tawny; outer upper wing coverts and some of the inner ones as well, the primaries and all but the innermost secondaries pure white, the primaries (except the outermost one) with dusky shafts; rectrices plain fuscous-black to chaetura black; loreal band blackish; auriculars and cheeks fuscous-black, the feathers tipped with white and faintly banded with tawny-olive; chin, throat, and lower sides of head white; upper breast deep chaetura black narrowly tipped with white; sides similar but with some white feathers mixed in lower breast, abdomen, flanks, thighs, under tail coverts, under wing coverts, and feathering of feet white; bill and claws black; comb bright scarlet.

Adult female, summer.—Feathers covering nostrils white with a faint buffy wash; forehead, crown, occiput, nape, scapulars, interscapulars, back, rump, upper tail coverts, inner secondaries, and some of the inner upper wing coverts deep chaetura black, each feather with wavy bars of ochraceous-buff, and tipped with white or buffy white; rest of upper wing coverts, primaries, outer secondaries, and under wing coverts white, the primaries, except the outermost one with pale brownish shafts; sides of head, chin, and throat pale ochraceous-buff, each feather with a fuscous-black to blackish median streak, these streaks widening terminally in the feathers of the lower throat; feathers of breast, sides, flanks, and under tail coverts, chaetura black broadly tipped and banded with ochraceous-buff; abdomen similar but with a great many white feathers mixed in; thighs and feathering of feet white; bill and claws black.

Adult male, winter.—Pure white except for black tail and loreal stripe.[15]

Other plumages.—Unknown. It may however, be assumed that the female also has a white winter plumage, because summer birds have an irregular sprinkling of white feathers on the wings and underparts. Incomplete and inconclusive evidence also seems to indicate that the male in autumn is more vermiculated with tawny-olive above than in the summer plumage. This is in keeping with the known tendency of the plumage sequence in this group. Similarly, an undated, unsexed specimen examined appears to be a female in autumn plumage. It differs from the summer female in having the ochraceous marks on the scapulars, back, rump, upper tail coverts, breast, and sides narrower and darker—ochraceous-tawny instead of ochraceous-buff. However, at present it cannot be proved that this is an autumn bird rather than an aberrant summer specimen, although it has a scattering of *new* white feathers in the colored areas suggesting the start of the molt into the winter plumage.

Adult male.—Wing 182–193 (187.8); tail 103–113 (108–1); culmen from anterior end of nostrils 9.5–10.8 (9.9); width of bill at gape 12–13.1 (12.5); height of bill at angle of gonys 7.1–8.6 (7.8 mm.).[15]

Adult female.—Wing 166–185 (176.3); tail 96–99 (97.3); culmen from anterior tip of nostril 9.5–9.7 (9.6); width of bill at gape 11.6–12 (11.7); height of bill at angle of gonys 6.7–7.5 (7.1 mm.).[16]

Range.—Known only from Attu Island, the westernmost of the Aleutian Islands.

Type locality.—Attu Island.

Lagopus albus (not *Tetrao albus* Gmelin) DALL, Proc. California Acad. Sci., v, 1874, 274, part (Attu Island, Aleutian Chain).

Lagopus rupestris, var. TURNER, Auk, ii, 1885, 157 (Attu Island).

Lagopus rupestris atkhensis TURNER, Contr. Nat. Hist. Alaska, 1886, 155-156 (Attu Island; plentiful).—NELSON, Rep. Nat. Hist. Coll. Alaska, 1887, 139, part (Attu Island, ex Dall).—MACOUN, Cat. Can. Birds, 1900, 208, part (Attu Island).—MACOUN and MACOUN, Cat. Can. Birds, ed. 2, 1909, 227, part (Attu Island).

Lagopus evermanni ELLIOT, Auk, xiii, 1896, 25, pl. 3 (Attu Island, Aleutian Chain, Alaska; coll. U. S. Nat. Mus.).—AMERICAN ORNITHOLOGISTS' UNION, Auk, xiv, 1897, 119 (Check-list No. 302.1); Check-list, ed. 3, 1910, 142.—MACOUN, Cat. Can. Birds, 1900, 208 (Attu Island).—MACOUN and MACOUN, Cat. Canadian Birds, ed. 2, 1909, 228 (Attu Island).—CLARK, Proc. U. S. Nat. Mus., xxxviii, 1910, 55 (Attu Island).—LAING, Victoria Mem. Mus. Bull. 40, 1925, 30 (Attu Island; spec.; plum.).

L[*agopus*] *evermanni* COUES, Key North Amer. Birds, ed. 5, 1903, ii, 749 (Attu Island.; descr.).

[*Lagopus*] *evermanni* SHARPE, Hand-list, i, 1899, 19.

---

[15] This plumage is worn until late in April, according to Laing, who collected two specimens on April 21, just beginning the prenuptial molt (Victoria Mem. Mus. Bull. 40, 1925, 30).

[15] Seven specimens including the type.

[16] Three specimens.

Lagopus mutus evermanni OBERHOLSER, Auk, xxxix, 1922, 247.—PETERS, Check-list
   Birds of World, ii, 1934, 33 (Attu Island).—SALOMONSEN, Moults and Sequence
   of Plumage in Rock Ptarmigan, 1939, 10 (spec.).—HELLMAYR and CONOVER,
   Cat. Birds Amer., i, No. 1, 1942, 208 (syn.; descr.).—CLARK, Smiths. War Background Stud. No. 21, 1945, 78 (list birds Aleutians).
Lagopus rupestris evermanni AMERICAN ORNITHOLOGISTS' UNION, Check-list, ed. 4,
   1931, 84.—BENT, U. S. Nat. Mus. Bull. 162, 1932, 230 (habits, range).

LAGOPUS MUTUS TOWNSENDI Elliot

TOWNSEND'S PTARMIGAN

Adult male, summer plumage.—Forehead buffy white speckled and
mottled with fuscous-black; crown, occiput, nape, scapulars, and interscapulars between cinnamon-buff and clay color, each feather heavily
barred with wavy marks of black and narrowly tipped with whitish; the
feathers of the crown with the subterminal black area so wide it almost
hides the clay-colored parts; back, rump, upper tail coverts, inner secondaries, and inner upper wing coverts tawny-olive (brightest on the
rump) finely banded (sometimes some of the feathers blotched) and
vermiculated with black and narrowly tipped with white, many of the
feathers of the back with a light grayish-olive tone instead of the more
frequent tawny-olive, giving a somewhat ashy sprinkling to the upperparts; outer upper wing coverts, all the primaries, and all but the inner
secondaries pure white, the primaries with dusky shafts; rectrices dark
clove brown, narrowly white basally and narrowly tipped with buffy white;
lores blackish spotted with white (the tips of the feathers being white);
auricles and upper cheeks cinnamon-buff to clay color narrowly banded
with black and tipped with white; chin and upper throat white; lower
throat cinnamon-buff to clay color banded with black, the buffy interspaces wider than the black marks; breast tawny-olive more narrowly
banded with black, the bands and the interspaces nearly equal in width;
sides and flanks similar but with the dark marks finer becoming mere
vermiculations; abdomen, thighs, feathering of tarsi and toes, and under
wing coverts white; under tail coverts tawny-olive barred with black;
bill and claws black; comb scarlet.

Adult female, summer plumage.—Forehead and lores light ochraceous-
buff somewhat speckled with black; crown, occiput, nape, scapulars, interscapulars, back, rump, upper tail coverts, and all but the outer upper
wing coverts bright ochraceous-buff barred with black and the feathers
narrowly tipped with white or buffy white, the black marks being very
broad on the interscapulars and back and on the crown, much narrower
on the occiput, nape, upper wing and tail coverts, and rump; the nape
is often somewhat tinged with pale ashy gray; outermost upper wing
coverts, primaries, and all but the innermost secondaries white, the primaries with dusky shafts; rectrices clove brown narrowly tipped with
whitish, and vermiculated with tawny-olive on the basal two-thirds or so

of the outer web, the very base itself white; cheeks and auriculars light ochraceous-buff sparsely flecked with dusky fuscous; chin whitish mixed with light ochraceous-buff, which color without the white extends over the throat as well, the throat feathers with narrow terminal dusky shaft streaks; breast, sides, flanks, thighs, under tail coverts, and all but the median part of the abdomen bright ochraceous-buff barred with clove brown to fuscous, the dark bars narrower than the paler interspaces and becoming more widely spaced posteriorly; middle of abdomen, some of the under tail coverts, and the feathering of the tarsi and toes white; bill and claws black.

Adult male, autumn plumage.—Above like the summer plumage but much more ochraceous, the back without any ashy feathers and with the black markings deeper and broader especially on the rump and upper tail coverts and also the upper wing coverts; below quite different from the summer plumage; chin, throat, and sides of head and of neck ochraceous-buff, the feathers crossed by narrow bars of fuscous, the dark bars much narrower than the buffy interspaces; lower throat, breast, upper abdomen, sides, flanks, and under tail coverts somewhat darker, between clay color and dark ochraceous-buff finely banded and vermiculated with clove brown to fuscous, the dark bars becoming broader on the sides, flanks, and under tail coverts; middle of abdomen and thighs white, feathering of feet much sparser than in summer plumage.

Female, autumn plumage.—Like the corresponding plumage of the male but paler and slightly buffier, less rufescent.

Adult male, winter plumage.—Completely white except for a black loreal stripe which continues for a short distance behind the eye; and for the tail feathers, which are dark clove brown narrowly tipped with white; feathering of the tarsi and toes much denser and longer than in summer plumage.

Adult female, winter plumage.—Like that of the male but without the black loreal stripe.

Other plumages apparently unknown.

Adult male.—Wing 181–196 (188); tail 98–113 (104); culmen from anterior end of nostril 9–10.5 (9.8); width of bill at gape 12.1–13.5 (12.7); height of bill at angle of gonys 7.3–8.2 (7.7 mm.).[17]

Adult female.—Wing 169–180 (175.3); tail 93–98 (95.5); culmen from anterior end of nostril 8.4–9.4 (8.9); width of bill at gape 11–12.4 (11.6); height of bill at angle of gonys 7–7.6 (7.3 mm.).[18]

Range.—Inhabits Kiska and Little Kiska Islands in the Aleutians, Alaska.

Type locality.—Kiska Island.

---

[17] Sixteen specimens from Kiska and Little Kiska Islands.
[18] Four specimens from Kiska and Little Kiska Islands.

Lagopus albus (not *Tetrao albus* Gmelin) DALL, Proc. California Acad. Sci., v, 1874, 274, part (Kiska Island, Aleutian Chain).

Lagopus rupestris townsendi ELLIOT, Auk, xiii, No. 1, 1896, 26, part (type from Kiska Island, Aleutian Chain, Alaska; coll. U. S. Nat. Mus.).—AMERICAN ORNITHOLOGISTS' UNION, Auk, xiv, 1897, 119, part (Check-list North Amer. Birds, No. 302d, part) ; Check-list, ed. 3, 1910, 142; ed. 4, 1931, 84.—MACOUN, Cat. Can. Birds, 1900, 208 (Kiska and Adak Islands).—MACOUN and MACOUN, Cat. Can. Birds, ed. 2, 1909, 227 (Kiska and Adak Islands).—BENT, U. S. Nat. Mus. Bull. 162, 1932, 220 (distr.; habits).

Lagopus rupestris townsendi ? LAING, Victoria Mem. Mus. Bull. 40, 1925, 30 Kiska Island).

[*Lagopus*] *townsendi* SHARPE, Hand-list, i, 1899, 19, part (Kiska Island).

Lagopus rupestris atkhensis NELSON, Birds Alaska, 1887, 139, part (Kiska Island).

Lagopus mutus townsendi PETERS, Check-list Birds of World, ii, 1934, 33 (distr.).—HELLMAYR and CONOVER, Cat. Birds Amer., i, No. 1, 1942, 208 (syn.; distr.).—CLARK, Smiths. War Background Stud., No. 21, 1945, 78 (list birds Aleutians).

LAGOPUS MUTUS SANFORDI Bent

SANFORD'S PTARMIGAN

Adult male, summer plumage.—Like the corresponding plumage of *L. m. chamberlaini* but paler, the brownish feathers cinnamon-buff to pale tawny and with more ashy grayish feathers on the upperparts.

Adult female, summer plumage.—Like that of *L. m. chamberlaini* but averaging very slightly paler; not certainly distinguishable.

Adult male, autumn plumage.—Like that of *L. m. townsendi* but much more rufescent, the general tone being bright ochraceous-tawny and the dark bars greatly reduced; the upper tail coverts buckthorn brown with fine dusky vermiculations.

Adult female, autumn plumage.—Like that of the male but with the dark bars much broader and blacker and with some of the feathers with blackish blotches; the central pair of upper tail coverts pale ochraceous-buff abundantly marked with broad fuscous oblique bars, the other upper tail coverts more narrowly and more transversely (less obliquely) barred with blackish.

Other plumages unknown.

Adult male.—Wing 190–199 (195.2) ; tail 101–121 (110.1) ; bill from anterior end of nostrils 9.7–11.7 (10.5) ; width of bill at gape 12.1–13.2 (12.8) ; height of bill at angle of gonys 7.8–8.5 (8.1 mm.).[19]

Adult female.—Wing 181–195 (188.1) ; tail 101–111 (105.6) ; bill from anterior end of nostril 8.5–10.8 (9.5) ; width of bill at gape 10.6–12.3 (11.6) ; height of bill at angle of gonys 7.4–8 (7.8 mm.).[20]

Range.—Resident on Tanaga and Kanaga Islands, in the Aleutian Islands, Alaska.

Type locality.—Tanaga Island.

---

[19] Ten specimens from Tanaga Island.

[20] Ten specimens from Tanaga Island.

Lagopus rupestris sanfordi BENT, Smiths. Misc. Coll., lvi, No. 30, 1912, 1 (Tanaga Island, Aleutian Chain, Alaska; coll. U. S. Nat. Mus.) ; U. S. Nat. Mus. Bull. 162, 1932, 225 (habits).—[EDITOR] Rev. Franç. d'Orn., ii, 1912, 346, in text; 409, in text.—AMERICAN ORNITHOLOGISTS' UNION, Auk, xl, 1923, 517 (Check-list, No. 302g) ; Check-list, ed. 4, 1931, 84.

Lagopus mutus sanfordi OBERHOLSER, Auk. xxxix, No. 2, 1922, 247.—PETERS, Check-list Birds of World, ii, 1934, 33 (Tanaga Island).—SALOMONSEN, Moults and Sequence of Plumages in the Rock Ptarmigan, 1939, 10 (spec.).—HELLMAYR and CONOVER, Cat. Birds Amer., i, No. 1, 1942, 208 (syn.; distr.).—CLARK, Smiths. War Background Stud. No. 21, 1945, 78 (list birds Aleutians).

LAGOPUS MUTUS CHAMBERLAINI A. H. Clark

CHAMBERLAIN'S PTARMIGAN

Adult male, summer plumage.—Similar to that of *Lagopus mutus townsendi* but the brownish areas paler, more grayish, the lower back and rump isabella color to ashy wood brown, the dark vermiculations averaging slightly finer; the feathers of the lower throat and breast cinnamon-buff to very pale tawny-olive.

Adult female, summer plumage.—Not certainly separable from that of *Lagopus mutus townsendi,* but usually with more pronounced grayish edges to the dorsal feathers.

Adults in winter.—Like those of *L. m. townsendi,* judged by birds partly in this plumage.

Other plumages unknown.

Adult male.—Wing 185–202 (193.5) ; tail 97–112 (104.6) ; bill from anterior end of nostril 10.1–11.7 (10.9) ; width of bill at gape 12–13 (12.5) ; height of bill at angle of gonys 7.5–8.6 (8 mm.).[21]

Adult female.—Wing 183–189 (185.4) ; tail 95–102 (98.3) ; bill from anterior end of nostril 9.1–10.3 (9.8) ; width of bill at gape 11.1–11.8 (11.5) ; height of bill at angle of gonys 7.1–7.2 (7.1 mm.).[22]

Range.—Resident in Adak Island, Aleutian Islands, Alaska.

Type locality.—Adak Island.

Lagopus rupestris townsendi ELLIOT, Auk, xiii, 1896, 26, part (Attu Island).—AMERICAN ORNITHOLOGISTS' UNION, Auk, xiv, 1897, 119, part (Adak Island). L[*agopus*] r[*upestris*] *townsendi* COUES, Key North Amer. Birds, ed. 5, 1903, ii, 748 (Adak Island).

[*Lagopus*] *townsendi* SHARPE, Hand-list, i, 1899, 247, part (Adak Island).

Lagopus rupestris chamberlaini CLARK (A. H.), Proc. U. S. Nat. Mus., xxxii, 1907, 479 (Adak Island, Aleutian Chain, Alaska; coll. U. S. Nat. Mus.).—AMERICAN ORNITHOLOGISTS' UNION, Auk, xxvi, 1909, 295 (Check-list No. 302e) ; Check-list, ed. 3, 1910, 142; ed. 4, 1931, 84.—LAING, Victoria Mem. Mus. Bull. 40, 1925, 29 (Adak Island; spec.; plum.).—BENT, U. S. Nat. Mus. Bull. 162, 1932, 221 (distr., habits).

Lagopus mutus chamberlaini OBERHOLSER, Auk, xxxix, 1922, 247.—PETERS, Check-list Birds of World, ii, 1934, 33 (Adak Island).—SALOMONSEN, Moults and

---

[21] Twenty-three specimens from Adak Island.
[22] Nine specimens from Adak Island.

Sequence of Plumage in Rock Ptarmigan, 1939, 10 (spec.).—HELLMAYR and CONOVER, Cat. Birds Amer., i, No. 1, 1942, 207 (syn., distr.)—CLARK, Smiths. War Background Stud. No. 21, 1945, 78 (list birds Aleutians).

LAGOPUS MUTUS ATKHENSIS Turner

TURNER'S PTARMIGAN

Adult male, summer plumage.—There seem to be two fairly distinct color phases of this plumage in this race, as follows:

1. Reddish phase: Similar to the summer male of *L. m. sanfordi* but the brownish areas with less of the ashy tinge and with the general ground color darker brown, the lower back and rump pale ochraceous tawny olive; differs from *L. m. townsendi* in having more ashy and in being somewhat paler and more tawny.

2. Olive-brown phase: Similar to the reddish phase but with the ground color Saccardo's umber to pale olive-brown extensively tinged with ashy.

Adult female, summer plumage.—Like that of *L. m. townsendi.* This is perhaps the most variable plumage of any of the island races of this species. Probably some of the differences, especially in the longer upper tail coverts, may eventually be found to be a matter of age; but in our present state of knowledge, this is mere conjecture.

Autumn adults.—Not yet known.

Adult male, winter plumage.—All white except for the black loreal stripe which continues behind the eye for a short distance, and for the dark clove brown rectrices narrowly tipped with white.

Adult female, winter plumage.—Like that of the male but without the black loreal stripe.

Juvenal.—Unknown.

Downy young, male.—Marguerite yellow, slightly washed with pale ochraceous on the breast and abdomen, and marked above with blackish and russet as follows: Narrow median line of black runs from the base of the culmen to the crown where it divides to encircle a large russet coronal patch, and meets again in a broader dorsal band on the nape and upper back; it divides on the lower back to form two parallel bands which come almost together at the tail end, enclosing a spinal tract of Marguerite yellow much suffused with pale russet; in addition to these marks there is a blackish femoral band on each side, as well as two wavy ones on each wing and a very narrow line from the bill through the eyes to the hind end of the auriculars.

Adult male.—Wing 185–197 (191.2); tail 98–112 (109.6); bill from anterior end of nostril to tip 9.7–11.3 (9.3); width of bill at gape 12–13.1 (12.7); height of bill at angle of gonys 7.3–8.5 (8 mm.).[23]

---

[23] Twenty-six specimens.

Adult female.—Wing 175–188 (181.6); tail 91–101 (96.6); bill from anterior end of nostril to tip 9.7–10.7 (10.2); width of bill at gape 11.1–12.3 (11.6); height of bill at angle of gonys 7.3–8.2 (7.8 mm.).[24]

Range.—Resident in Atka Island, Aleutian Islands, Alaska.

Type locality.—Atka Island.

Lagopus mutus atkhensis TURNER, Proc. U. S. Nat. Mus., v, 1882, 230, 231 (Atka Island, Aleutian Chain, Alaska; coll. U. S. Nat. Mus.).—RIDGWAY, Bull. Nuttall Orn. Club, vii, 1882, 258.—REICHENOW and SCHALOW, Journ. für Orn., 1883, 409 (reprint of orig. descr.).—HARTERT, Vög. pal. Fauna, iii, 1921, 1871.—OBER-HOLSER, Auk, xxxix, 1922, 247.—PETERS, Check-list Birds of World, ii, 1934, 34 (Atka Island).—SALOMONSEN, Moults and Sequence of Plumage in Rock Ptarmigan, 1939, 10 (spec.).—HELLMAYR and CONOVER, Cat. Birds Amer., i, No. 1, 1942, 207 (syn.; distr.).—CLARK, Smiths. War Background Stud. No. 21, 1945, 78 (list birds Aleutians).

[*Lagopus*] m[*utus*] *atkhensis* SALOMONSEN, Medd. Grønland, cxviii, No. 2, 1936, 31 in text (Atka Island).

Lagopus rupestris atkhensis STEJNEGER, Zeitschr. Ges. Orn., i, 1884, 92.—AMERICAN ORNITHOLOGISTS' UNION, Check-list, No. 302c, 1886; ed. 2, 1895, No. 302c; ed. 3, 1910, 141; ed. 4, 1931, 83.—TURNER, Contr. Nat. Hist. Alaska, 1886, 155, pls. 3, 4.—NELSON, Rep. Nat. Hist. Coll. Alaska, 1887, 139.—BENDIRE, Life Hist. North Amer. Birds, i, 1892, 81.—MACOUN, Cat. Can. Birds, 1900, 208, part (Atka Island).—MACOUN and MACOUN, Cat. Can. Birds, ed. 2, 1909, 227, part (Atka Island).—CLARK, Proc. U. S. Nat. Mus., xxxviii, 1910, 55 (habits).—LAING, Victoria Mem. Mus. Bull. 40, 1925, 28 (Atka Island; spec.; habits; plum.).—BENT, U. S. Nat. Mus. Bull. 162, 1932, 218 (Atka Island; habits).—EYERDAM, Murrelet, xvii, 1936, 50 (Atka Island; abundant).

L[*agopus*] *rupestris atkhensis* RIDGWAY, Man. North Amer. Birds, 1887, 201.

L[*agopus*] *r*[*upestris*] *atkhensis* COUES, Key North Amer. Birds, ed. 5, ii, 1903, 747 (Atka Island).

[*Lagopus*] *atkensis* SHARPE, Hand-list, i, 1899, 19.

Lagopus rupestris occidentalis (not *Lagopus rupestris,* var. *occidentalis* Sundevall) NELSON, Cruise of *Corwin* in 1881 (1883), 82 (Atka Island, Aleutian Chain, Alaska; coll. U. S. Nat. Mus.).

Lagopus rupestris (not *Tetrao rupestris* Gmelin) OGILVIE-GRANT, Cat. Birds Brit. Mus., xxii, 1893, 527, part.

LAGOPUS MUTUS GABRIELSONI Murie

AMCHITKA PTARMIGAN

Adult male, summer plumage.—Like that of *L. m. townsendi* but the upperparts with the blackish barring heavier and darker, and the brownish ground color slightly less tawny.

Adult female, summer plumage.—Like that of *L. m. nelsoni.*

Adult male, autumn plumage.—Similar to that of *L. m. townsendi* but darker, the general tone of the brownish parts being dark buckthorn brown with an ochraceous tinge, and with many more blackish bars,

---

[24] Fourteen specimens.

agreeing in its abundance of bars with the corresponding plumage of
L. m. sanfordi.

Juvenal, unsexed.—Similar above to the adult male in autumn plumage
but paler, more ochraceous-tawny, the blackish bars on the interscapulars,
scapulars, and upper back and on the upper wing and upper tail coverts
broader, below much paler, the chin and throat light pinkish cinnamon
darkening to pinkish cinnamon on the breast and upper abdomen and
sides; the breast, upper abdomen, and sides barred fairly broadly with
black; rest of abdomen pale pinkish buff, flanks, thighs, and under tail
coverts light pinkish cinnamon irregularly barred with fuscous.

Other plumages unkown.

Adult male.—Wing 182–189 (186.3); tail 100–110 (105.3); bill from
anterior end of nostril 7.9–9.8 (9); width of bill at gape 11.4–12.2
(11.7); height of bill at angle of gonys 7.2–8.2 (7.7 mm.).[25]

Adult female.—Wing 171–179 (174.3); tail 85–93 (88.3); bill from
anterior end of nostril 9.4; width of bill at gape 9.8–11.4 (10.8); height
of bill at angle of gonys 6.7–7.2 (7 mm.).[26]

Range.—Known only from the type locality, Amchitka Island, Aleutian
Islands, Alaska.

Lagopus rupestris atkhensis TURNER, Contr. Nat. Hist. Alaska, 1886, 155–156, part
(Amchitka, plentiful).—MACOUN, Cat. Can. Birds, 1900, 208, part (Amchitka).
—MACOUN and MACOUN, Cat. Can. Birds, ed. 2, 1909, 227, part (Amchitka).
Lagopus mutus gabrielsoni MURIE, Condor, xlvi, 1944, 121 (Amchitka Island, Aleu-
tion Islands; descr.; crit.).—CLARK, Smiths. War Background Stud. No. 21,
1945, 78 (list birds Aleutians).

LAGOPUS MUTUS NELSONI Stejneger
NELSON'S PTARMIGAN

Adult male, summer plumage.—Similar to that of *L. m. townsendi*
but the brownish areas much darker and without any grayish-dark Saccardo's umber crossed by fine bars and vermiculations of clove brown
to dark fuscous, the central elongated upper tail coverts almost as dark
as the rectrices.

Adult female, summer plumage.—Indistinguishable from that of *L. m.
evermanni.*

Adult male, autumn plumage.—Similar to the summer plumage but
very slightly paler, the feathers of the upper parts with narrow whitish
tips; below like the autumn male of *L. m. townsendi.*

Adult female, autumn plumage.—Similar to the summer female but
with the ochraceous-tawny much more extensive below, extending over
the throat, chin, and a large part of the abdomen; above, the feathers
more finely barred and vermiculated, not so broadly barred with blackish.

---

[25] Three specimens.
[26] Three specimens.

Adult male, winter plumage.—Entirely white except for the black loreal stripe through the eye and the dark clove brown tail; feathers of tarsi and toes longer and denser than in summer.

Adult female, winter plumage.—Like the winter male but without the black loreal stripe.

First autumn plumage (unsexed).—Like the autumn plumage of the adult but paler and buffier with some of the back feathers with concentric longitudinal dusky marks; the outer primaries more pointed and often more mottled than dusky.

Juvenal (sexes alike).—Like the adult female in summer plumage but with the light brownish areas brighter and slightly more rufescent; the primaries are not white, however, but dark brown mottled with tawny. Females seem to have slightly more black above than males, but this may be individual and not definitely sexual, as only a few specimens have been seen.

Downy young.—Like that of *L. m. atkhensis* but the pale areas above darker, washed with pale tawny-olive; below less yellowish, faintly tinged with cinnamon-buff.

Adult male.—Wing 179–197 (189.5); tail 101–121 (108); bill from anterior end of nostril to tip 8.5–10.6 (9.6); width of bill at gape 11.1–13.2 (12.1); height of bill at angle of gonys 6.1–9.6 (7.6 mm.).[27]

Adult female.—Wing 171–190 (181.7); tail 89–107 (98.2); bill from anterior end of nostril to tip 8–10 (9); width of bill at gape 10.5–12.2 (11.4); height of bill at angle of gonys 6.6–9.4 (7.4 mm.).[28]

Range.—Breeds in the eastern end of the Aleutian Chain (Unalaska, Amaknak, Unimak, Kagamil, Chuginadak, and Umnak Islands, and the mainland of Alaska south to the base of the Alaskan Peninsula and Kodiak Island, Hinchinbrook Island, Dolgoi Island, and Ushagat in the Barren Islands, north to Point Barrow and the Arctic Ocean; intergrades with *L. m. rupestris* in the interior of Alaska and northern Northwest Territory. On Kodiak Island it approaches *L. m. dixoni* in its characters. It is said to be the form of the Jamal Peninsula and the adjacent tundra of northeastern Siberia, but no specimens from there have been seen.

Winters throughout, but chiefly in the southern part of, its breeding range and possibly beyond.

Type locality.—Unalaska Island.

Tetrao lagopus (not of Linnaeus) KITTLITZ, Denkwünd, i, 1858, 289 (Amaknak Island, near Unalaska).

---

[27] Forty-six specimens from Unalaska, Amaknak, Unimak, Kagamil, Chuginadak, and Umnak Islands in the Aleutian Chain, and on the mainland of Alaska south to the Alaska Peninsula and Kodiak Island, north to the Arctic Ocean.

[28] Thirty-one specimens from Unalaska and Amaknak Islands, Aleutian Chain, Kodiak Island, and the Alaska mainland north to Point Barrow.

Lagopus rupestris DALL and BANNISTER, Trans. Chicago Acad. Sci., i, 1869, 289
(Gens de Large Mountains and Fort Yukon, Alaska).—NELSON. Bull. Nutall
Orn. Club, iii, 1878, 38, part (Unalaska Island, Akutan Island, and St. Michael,
Alaska) ; Cruise *Corwin* in 1881 (1883), 81 (Unalaska) ; Rept. Nat. Hist. Coll.
Alaska, 1887, 136, part (Alaska mainland).—McLENEGAN, Cruise *Corwin*, 1884,
119 (Kowak River, nw. Alaska).—MURDOCH, Auk, ii, 1885, 63 (Point Barrow,
Alaska) ; Rep. Int. Polar Exped. Point Barrow, 1885, 108.—TURNER, Contr. Nat.
Hist. Alaska, 1886, 154, part (Unalaska and Alaska mainland).—OGILVIE-GRANT,
Cat. Birds Brit. Mus., xxii, 1893, 48, part (Golsova River, Kegitowik, Nulata,
and Kotzebue Sound, Alaska).—GRINNELL, Pacific Coast Avif., No. 1, 1900, 35,
75 (Kotzebue Sound region and Kowak Valley Alaska; habits; plum.; breed.).
—BISHOP, North Amer. Fauna, No. 19, 1900, 72 (summit of White Pass,
Alaska; breed.; Kuskokwim River).—OSGOOD, North Amer. Fauna, No. 21,
1901, 75 (mountains on n. side Bear Creek, Cook Inlet, Alaska) ; No. 30, 1909,
37 (mountains at head of Seward Creek, east-central Alaska) ; 60 (Ogilvie
Range, Yukon Territory) ; 87 (Russell Mountains, Macmillan River region,
Yukon; habits).—JUDD, Biol. Surv. Bull., No. 24, 1905, 46, part (food, range,
etc.)—PREBLE, North Amer. Fauna, No. 27, 1908, 347, part (localities in Alaska).
—ANDERSON, Rep. Dept. Mines Canada for 1914 (1915), 195 (Collinson Point,
Alaska; spec.), for 1916 (1917), (?) 379 (Arctic coast of Northwest Territory;
spec.).—LAING and TAVERNER, Ann. Rep. Nat. Mus. Canada for 1927 (1929),
76 (Chitina River, Alaska).—FRIEDMANN, Journ. Washington Acad. Sci., xxxi,
1941, 407 (Cape Prince of Wales, Alaska; bones).
L[agopus] rupestris FRIEDMANN, Journ. Washington Acad. Sci., xxvii, 1937, 436
(Unalaska).
Lagopus rupestris nelsoni STEJNEGER, Auk, i, 1884, 226 (Unalaska Island, Aleutian
Chain, Alaska; coll. U. S. Nat. Mus.) ; Zeitschr. Ges. Orn., i, 1884, 91.—
AMERICAN ORNITHOLOGISTS' UNION, Check-list, No. 302b, 1886; ed. 2, 1895,
No. 302b; ed. 3, 1910; ed. 4, 1931, 83, 141.—TOWNSEND, Cruise *Corwin* in 1885
(1887), 100 (Unalaska).—NELSON, Rep. Nat. Hist. Coll. Alaska, 1887, 131,
138, pl. 10.—BENDIRE, Life Hist. North Amer. Birds, i, 1892, 80.—MACOUN,
Cat. Can. Birds, 1900, 208 (Unalaska eastward).—OSGOOD, North Amer. Fauna,
No. 24, 1904, 66 (Portage Mountain, between head of Chulitna River and Swan
Lake; mountains of Kanatak Portage and about Cold Bay; food; crit.).—
McGREGOR, Condor, viii, 1906, 119 (Unalaska).—MACOUN and MACOUN, Cat.
Can. Birds, ed. 2, 1909, 227 (Unalaska eastward).—CLARK, Proc. U. S. Nat.
Mus., xxxviii, 1910, 55 (Unalaska).—BENT, U. S. Nat. Mus. Bull. 162, 1932,
215 (habits, etc.).—SWARTH, Pacific Coast Avif., No. 22, 1934, 26 (Alaska;
Akutan and Unalaska Islands; spec.).—EYERDAM, Murrelet, xvii, 1936, 50
(distr.; spec.).
L[agopus] rupestris nelsoni RIDGWAY, Man. North Amer. Birds, 1887, 201.
L[agopus] r[upestris] nelsoni COUES, Key North Amer. Birds, ed. 5, ii, 1903, 747
(Unalaska).—HANTZSCH, Journ. für Orn., 1908, 367, in text; Can. Field Nat.,
xlii, 1928, 14.
Lagopus rupestris subsp. FRIEDMANN, Journ. Washington Acad. Sci., xxiv, 1934,
237 (Cape Danbeigh, Norton Sound; Alaska; bones).
[Lagopus] nelsoni SHARPE, Hand-list, i, 1899, 18.
Lagopus mutus nelsoni HARTERT, Vög. pal. Fauna, iii, 1921, 1871.—OBERHOLSER,
Auk, xxxix, 1822, 247.—PETERS, Check-list Birds of World, ii, 1934, 34 (Unimak,
Unalaska, and Amaknak Islands).—SALOMONSEN, Moults and Sequence of
Plumages in the Rock Ptarmigan, 1939, 10 (spec.).—CLARK, Smiths. War Back-
ground Stud. No. 21, 1945, 78 (list birds Aleutians).

Lagopus rupestris kelloggae GRINNELL, Univ. California Publ. Zool., v, 1910, 383 (Kaikoff Bay, Montague Island, Prince William Sound, Alaska, 1,600 feet altitude; coll. Univ. California Mus. Vert. Zool.).—OBERHOLSER, Auk, xxxiv, 1917, 200.—AMERICAN ORNITHOLOGISTS' UNION, Check-list, ed. 4, 1931, 84 (distr.).—BENT, U. S. Nat. Mus. Bull. 162, 1932, 227 (habits, etc.).—BAILEY, BROWER, and BISHOP, Progr. Activ. Chicago Acad. Sci., iv, 1933, 24 (Point Barrow, Alaska).—SWARTH, Pacific Coast Avif., No. 22, 1934, 26 (Nunivak Island, Alaska; spec.).—TAVERNER, Birds Canada, 1934, 159 in text.—FRIEDMANN, Journ. Washington Acad. Sci., xxiv, 1934, 235 (Kodiak Island; bones); Bull. Chicago Acad. Sci., v, 1935, No. 3, 31 (Kodiak Island); Journ. Washington Acad. Sci., xxvii, 1937, 433 (Kodiak Island; bones).—BRAY, Auk, lx, 1943, 516 (Southampton Island; Baffin Island; Melville Peninsula).—DIXON, Condor, xlv, 1943, 55 (Arctic Alaska; Camden Bay; Demarcation Point).

L[agopus] r[upestris] kelloggae TAVERNER, Canada's Eastern Arctic, 1934, 119, in text (Arctic islands and coast regions of nw. mainland of Canada).

Lagopus mutus kelloggae OBERHOLSER, Auk, xxxix, 1922, 247.—PETERS, Check-list Birds of World, ii, 1934, 34 (nw. North America from Alaska east along Arctic coast and adjoining islands to ca. 100° W., south to Alaskan Peninsula, and s. Alaska to ca. 60° N.).—SALOMONSEN, Medd. Grønland, cxviii, No. 2, 1936, 34 (syn.; diag.; distr.).—STEINBACHER, Ergänzungsband to Hartert's Vög. pal. Fauna, 1938, 515, part (Alaska and North Amer. at least to Bathurst Inlet).—SALOMONSEN, Moults and Sequence of Plumage in Rock Ptarmigan, 1939, 10 (spec.).

L[agopus] m[utus] kelloggae SALOMONSEN, Medd. Grønland, cxviii, 1936, 4 in text, 22 in text (Alaska and Northwest Territory east to Coronation Gulf and to Bathurst Inlet).

Lagopus mutus rupestris (not of Gmelin) GROTE, Falco, Sonderheft, 1925, 201 (Jenissei region, Siberia).—BAILEY, Condor, xxviii, 1926, 122 (nw. Alaska; distr.; habits.—SSEREBROWSKY, Journ. für Orn., 1926, 694 in text (spec.; Alaska).

Lagopus mutus americanus HELLMAYR and CONOVER, Cat. Birds Amer., i, No. 1, 1942, 205, part (syn.; distr.).

LAGOPUS MUTUS DIXONI J. Grinnell

DIXON'S PTARMIGAN

Adult male, summer plumage.—Like that of *L. m. nelsoni* but with the brownish markings less ochraceous-tawny, duller and much reduced in size and number, making the bird much darker, approaching in this character *L. m. evermanni,* but with more tawny to hazel vermiculations on the breast and back. Above, general color of all but the white areas, sooty bister; whole crown and occiput sooty, minutely and rather sparsely barred with tawny-olive to hazel; breast barred with tawny, the bars becoming narrower posteriorly and practically disappearing on the lower breast.

Adult female, summer plumage.—Like the corresponding plumage of *L. m. evermanni.*

Adult male, autumn plumage.—Like the male in summer plumage but paler, more grayish above—dark hair brown with a grayish "bloom," the blackish areas greatly reduced.

Adult female, autumn plumage.—Like the autumn male with the black bars and vermiculations more pronounced and without the grayish "bloom."

Female, first autumn plumage.—Like the adult female in autumn, but outer primaries more pointed and the pale bars decidedly more ochraceous-tawny and broader, above and on the breast.[29]

Juvenal (unsexed).—Like the females in first autumn plumage but with the remiges dull hair brown externally mottled with buffy; entire underparts barred like the breast, the dark bars somewhat paler on the abdomen.

Downy young.—Apparently unknown.

Adult male.—Wing 172–195 (181.7); tail 101–120 (107.8); bill from anterior end of nostril to tip 9–10.2 (9.6); width of bill at gape 11.2–12 (11.6); height of bill at angle of gonys 6.8–7.4 (7.2 mm.).[30]

Adult female.—Wing 163–179 (172); tail 91–107 (97.7); bill from anterior end of nostril to tip 8.8–9.8 (9.3); width of bill at gape 10.7–11.8 (11.2); height of bill at angle of gonys 6.3–7.2 (6.9 mm.).[31]

Range.—Resident in the islands and coastal mainland of the Glacier Bay region of Alaska, south to Baranof Island, and inland for an undetermined distance, intergrading with *L. m. rupestris* in central northern British Columbia (Ingenika, Chapa-atan, and Sheslay Rivers).

In winter the birds wander southward from the northern parts of the range but do not seem to go south beyond the limits of the breeding range. It is possible that in winter some of the birds in the northern mainland part of the range of this race actually belong to the forms *nelsoni* or *rupestris,* but there is no way to tell them apart in winter plumage, other than size (which is only an average character).

Type locality.—Near Port Frederick, 2,700 feet, Chichagof Island, Alaska.

Lagopus dixoni GRINNELL (J.), Univ. California Publ. Zool., v, 1909, 207 (mountains near Port Frederick, Chichagof Island, s. Alaska, 2,700 feet alt.; coll. Univ. California Mus. Vert. Zool.).

Lagopus rupestris dixoni AMERICAN ORNITHOLOGISTS' UNION, Auk, xxvi, No. 3, 1909, 296 (Check-list No. 302f); Check-list, ed. 3, 1910, 142; ed. 4, 1931, 84.— SWARTH, Univ. California Publ. Zool., vii, 1911, 59 (Port Snettisham, s. Alaska; crit.).—BROOKS, Bull. Mus. Comp. Zool., lix, 1915, 365 (Muir Inlet, Glacier Bay, Alaska).—BAILEY, Auk, xliv, 1927, 200 (near Juneau, se. Alaska; habits).— BENT, U. S. Nat. Mus. Bull. 162, 1932, 223 (habits, etc.).

Lagopus mutus dixoni OBERHOLSER, Auk, xxxix, 1922, 247.—PETERS, Check-list Birds of World, ii, 1934, 34 (islands and adjacent mainland of the Glacier Bay region, Alaska, s. to Baranof Island).—SALOMONSEN, Moults and Sequence of Plumage in the Rock Ptarmigan, 1939, 10 (spec.).

---

[29] No first autumn males seen.

[30] Nine specimens from Juneau and near Sitka, Alaska.

[31] Six specimens from Juneau, Sitka, and Kruzof Island, Alaska.

L[agopus] m[utus] dixoni SALOMONSEN, Medd. Grønland, cxviii, No. 2, 1936, 4 in text.

Lagopus mutus americanus HELLMAYR and CONOVER, Cat. Birds Amer., i, No. 1, 1942, 205, part (syn.; distr.).

Lagopus rupestris SHORTT, Contr. Roy. Ontario Mus. Zool., No. 17, 1939, 12 (Alaska; Yakutat Bay region).

LAGOPUS MUTUS RUPESTRIS (Gmelin)

ROCK PTARMIGAN

Adult male, summer plumage.—Like that of *L. m. dixoni,* but paler and grayer, the brown markings hair brown to dull grayish olive-brown.

Adult female, summer plumage.—Similar to that of *L. m. dixoni* but upperparts more grayish, the general appearance being more grayish than brownish and with the black blotches much larger. In worn plumage some of these birds are almost black above. Breast, sides, and upper abdomen whitish or only very pale ochraceous-buff barred with heavy black bars. Occasional specimens are found, especially in the far northern part of the range, that are not to be distinguished from *L. m. nelsoni,* having more of the brownish color, but most of these brown specimens are first-year birds.

Adult male, autumn plumage.—Similar to the summer male but slightly browner, the vermiculations averaging finer, giving an appearance of greater uniformity to the upperparts and breast.

Adult female, autumn plumage.—More hair brown, less marked with black than summer females; many of the dorsal feathers only vermiculated with blackish. Apparently this plumage is never (?) fully present, as by the time many of the black summer feathers have been replaced by the vermiculated hair brown ones, the white feathers of the winter plumage begin to appear as well.

Adult male, winter plumage.—Entirely white except for the blackish loreal stripe extending through and behind the eye, and the rectrices, which are dark clove brown; feathering of tarsi and toes longer and denser than in summer plumage.

Adult female, winter plumage.—Similar to the winter male but without the black loreal stripe.

Female, first autumn plumage.—Browner and more narrowly barred with blackish above and on the breast than the adult female in autumn; outer primaries more pointed and often with one or more of the juvenal remiges retained.

Juvenal (unsexed).—Differs from the female in first autumn plumage in having the upperparts with bright ochraceous edges and bars on the otherwise blackish feathers; breast, sides, and flanks ochraceous-buff, brightest on the breast, barred with fuscous; remiges dark hair brown to grayish clove brown externally mottled with pale buffy.

Downy young (unsexed).—Similar to that of *L. m. atkhensis* but back and rump generally russet with the black bifurcated spinal stripe wanting or reduced to dark brownish, disconnected markings, and the yellowish areas slightly darker and more ochraceous.

Adult male.—Wing 183–200 (191.5); tail 102–115 (109.5); bill from anterior end of nostril to tip 8.7–10 (9.4; width of bill at gape 10.8–11.9 (11.3); height of bill at angle of gonys 7.1–7.9 (7.6 mm.).[32]

Adult female.—Wing 175–198 (182.9); tail 90–115 (100.4); bill from anterior end of nostril to tip 6–10.4 (8.4); width of bill at gape 10.5–12.8 (11.5); height of bill at angle of gonys 6.3–9.6 (7.3 mm.).[33]

Range.—Breeds in northern North America from east-central Alaska and central Northwest Territories (where it intergrades with *L. m. nelsoni*) eastward, including Melville, Victoria, Ellesmere and Baffin Islands, to Labrador and northwestern Greenland, north of latitude 66°, south to the mountains of Vancouver and of central northern British Columbia (Ingenika, Chapa-atan, and Sheslay Rivers, where it intergrades with *L. m. dixoni*), Great Slave Lake, Great Whale River, and the Straits of Belle Isle.

Winters throughout but probably mostly in the southern part of its breeding range and possibly (rarely) farther south.

Type locality.—Hudson Bay.

Tetrao lagopus (not of Linnaeus) FABRICIUS, Fauna Groenlandica, 1780, 114.— SABINE, Trans. Linn. Soc. London, xii, 1818, 530 (Hare Island) ; Suppl. Parry's First Voy., 1824, 197 (s. of Barrow Straits).

Lagopus mutus (not *Tetrao mutus* Montin) STEPHENS, *in* Shaw, Gen. Zool., xi, pt. 2, 1819, 287, part (Greenland).—KNEELAND, Proc. Boston Soc. Nat. Hist., vi, 1857, 237 (Kewcenaw Point, Lake Superior).

[*Tetrao*] *rupestris* GMELIN, Syst. Nat., i, pt. 2, 1788, 751 (Hudson Bay; based on Rock Grouse, Pennant, Arctic Zool., ii, 312).—LATHAM, Index Orn., ii, 1790, 640.

Tetrao rupestris SABINE, Suppl. Parry's First Voyage, 1824, 195.—RICHARDSON, App. Parry's Second Voy., 1824, 348.—NUTTALL, Man. Orn. United States and Canada, Land Birds, 1832, 610; ed. 2, 1840, 818.—AUDUBON, Orn. Biogr., iv, 1838, 483, pl. 368.—VIGORS, Zool. Voyage *Blossom,* 1839, 26.

Tetrao (Lagopus) rupestris SWAINSON and RICHARDSON, Fauna Bor.-Amer., ii, 1831 (1832), 354.

Lagopus rupestris LEACH, Zool. Misc., ii, 1817, 290.—STEPHENS, *in* Shaw, Gen. Zool., xi, pt. 2, 1819, 290 (Hudson Bay).—SWAINSON and RICHARDSON, Fauna Bor.-Amer., ii, 1831 (1832), pl. 64.—BONAPARTE, Geogr. and Comp. List, 1838, 44.—AUDUBON, Synopsis, 1839, 208; Birds Amer., 8vo. ed., v, 1842, 122, pl. 301.— BAIRD, Rep. Pacific R.R. Survey, ix, 1858, 635; Cat. North Amer. Birds, 1859, No. 468.—COUES, Proc. Acad. Nat. Sci. Philadelphia, 1861, 229 (coast Labrador) ; Check List North Amer. Birds, 1874, No. 387; ed. 2, 1882, No. 569.— BLAKISTON, Ibis, 1863, 127 (Mackenzie River).—ELLIOT, Monogr. Tetraonidae, 1865, pl. 23 and text.—GRAY, List Birds Brit. Mus., pt. 5, Gallinae, 1867, 92.— HARTING, Proc. Zool. Soc. London, 1871, 111, 117 (Melville Island; w. coast

---

[33] Fourteen specimens from Ungava, Ellesmereland, and Northwest Territories.

Greenland).—DRESSER, Birds Europe, vii, pt. 28, 1874, 175, pls. 477 (fig. 2), 480, 481.—BAIRD, BREWER, and RIDGWAY, Hist. North Amer. Birds, iii, 1874, pl. 62, figs. 4, 5 (Labrador).—FEILDEN, Ibis, 1877, 405 (Feilden Peninsula; Smith Sound; n. to lat. 83°6' Greenland) ; Proc. Zool. Soc. London, 1877, 29–31 (Dobbin Bay; North Polar Basin to lat. 82°46'N.—STEJNEGER, Zeitschr. Ges. Orn., i, 1884, 90 (crit.).— TURNER, Proc. U. S. Nat. Mus., viii, 1885, 245 (Ungava).— BREWSTER, Auk, ii, 1885, 221 (Anticosti Island).—AMERICAN ORNITHOLOGISTS' UNION, Check-list, 1886; No. 302, part ed. 2, 1895, No. 302, part.—STEARNS, Bird Life in Labrador, n.d. ca. 1890, 50 (Labrador).—CLARKE, Auk, vii, 1890, 321 (Fort Churchill, Keewatin).—MACFARLANE, Proc. U. S. Nat. Mus., xiv, 1891, 431 (Barren Grounds from Horton River to Franklin Bay; habits; descr. nest and eggs).—RHOADS, Proc. Acad. Nat. Sci. Philadelphia, 1893, 38 (Clinton, Lake La Hache, high Cascades, Field, Hector, and Ottertail, high Rocky Mountains, British Columbia, descending to 4,000 ft. in winter).—OGILVIE-GRANT, Cat. Birds Brit. Mus., xxii, 1893, 48, part (Hudson Bay; Fort Resolution; Lichtenfels, Musk Ox Bay, Hare Ravine, Ritenbank, and Discovery Bay, and lat. 82°31', Greenland; Northumberland Sound, Port Bowen, Cockburn Island), 557, part (Feilden Peninsula, Grinnell Land, May.)—BIGELOW, Auk, xix, 1902, 29 (coast ne. Labrador, n. of Hamilton Inlet).—PREBLE, North Amer. Fauna, No. 22, 1902, 104 (Fort Churchill, Keewatin, in winter only) ; No. 27, 1908, 347, part (localities in Mackenzie).—JUDD, U. S. Biol. Surv. Bull. 24, 1905, 46, part (food, range, etc.).—EIFRIG, Auk, xxii, 1905, 239.—KERMODE, [Visitors' Guide] Provincial Mus., 1909, 41 (Atlin, British Columbia, common).—TAVERNER, Birds Western Canada, 1926, 169, part (fig.; descr.; habits; distr.; w. Canada; Canada's Eastern Arctic, 1934, 119 in text (north Ellesmere Island s. to mainland to east and west) ; Birds of Canada, 1934, 158 in text part (distr.; characters), Can. Water Birds, 1939, 170 (Canada; genl.).—BROOKS, Condor, xxix, 1927, 113 (crit.).—HANTZSCH, Can. Field Nat., xlii, 1928, 13, 14 (Baffin Island).—TAVERNER and SUTTON, Ann. Carnegie Mus., xxiii, 1934, 31 (Churchill, Manitoba; winter visitor; irregularly common).—DALGETY, Ibis, 1936, 590 (Baffin Land to Greenland).—CLARKE, Nat. Mus. Canada Bull. 96, 1940, 48 (Thelon Game Sanctuary, northwestern Canada).

L[agopus] rupestris COUES, Key North Amer. Birds, ed. 2, 1884, 587; ed. 5, 1903, ii, 745.—RIDGWAY, Man. North Amer. Birds, 1887, 200.—REICHENOW, Die Vögel, i, 1913, 323.

[Lagopus] rupestris REICHENBACH, Synop. Av., iii, Gallinaceae, 1848, pl. 213b, figs. 1876–1878.—COUES, Key North Amer. Birds, 1872, 236.—SHARPE, Hand-list, i, 1899, 18 (Arctic America; n. Asia west to Ural Mountains ?).

Attagen rupestris REICHENBACH, Av. Syst. Nat., Vög. 1851, xxix.

Lagopus rupestris rupestris HANTZSCH, Journ. für Orn., 1908, 366 (ne. Labrador; crit.).—GRINNELL, Univ. California Publ. Zool., v, 1910, 383, 384, in text.—AMERICAN ORNITHOLOGISTS' UNION, Check-list, ed. 2, 1895, 113; ed. 3, 1910, 141; ed. 4, 1931, 83.—BROOKS, Bull. Mus. Comp. Zool., lix, 1915, 364 (Camden Bay, Alaska, to Mackenzie River delta; near Herschel Island; Humphrey Point; Demarcation Point; East Cape, Siberia ?; habits).—HERSEY, Smiths. Misc. Coll., lxvi, No. 2, 1916, 27 (Cape Lisburne and near Nome, Alaska).—GIANINI, Auk, xxxiv, 1917, 399 (mountains near Stepovak Bay, Alaska Peninsula).—DICE, Condor, xxii, 1920, 180 (Tanana, head of North Fork of Kuskokwim River, Mount Sischu, etc., Alaska).—CONOVER, Auk, xliii, 1926, 317 (habits; breeding; Hooper Bay, Alaska).—TAVERNER, Birds Western Canada, 1926, 170, in text; Birds Canada, 1934, 159, in text).—DeMILLE, Auk, xliii, 1926, 516 (Bonaventure Island).— SWARTH, Univ. California Publ. Zool., xxx, No. 4, 1926, 94 (Atlin region,

British Columbia; distr.; crit.; habits; plum.).—SOPER, Nat. Mus. Canada Bull. 53, 1928, 104 (southern Baffin Island; breeding).—HANTZSCH, Can. Field Nat., xlii, 1928, 13, 14 (northeastern Labrador).—SUTTON, Condor, xxxiii, 1931, 157 (Chesterfield, Hudson Bay); Mem. Carnegie Mus., xii, 1932, 94 (Southampton Island; habits).—BENT, U. S. Nat. Mus. Bull. 162, 1932, 202 (habits; distr.).— GROSS, Auk, liv, 1937, 22 (Button Islands, Labrador, Cape Chidley, and Eclipse Harbor; common; breeding; food habits; meas.), 41 (parasites).—(?) CUM-MING, Murrelet, xvi, 1935, 39 (Vancouver, British Columbia; spec.; food).

Lagopus r[upestris] rupestris GROEBBELS, Der Vögel, ii, 1937, 166 (data on breeding biology).

L[agopus] r[upestris] rupestris TAVERNER, Canada's Eastern Arctic, 1934, 119 in text (interior of Northwest Territories and Ungava, north to south Baffin Island).

Tetrao (Lagopus) mutus (not *Tetrao mutus* Montin) SWAINSON and RICHARDSON, Fauna Bor.-Amer., ii, 1831 (1832), 350.—Ross, Arct. Exp., 1835, 28.

Tetrao mutus AUDUBON, Orn. Biog., v, 1839, 196, pl. 418, fig. 1.

Lagopus mutus, var. *rupestris* BAIRD, BREWER, and RIDGWAY, Hist. North Amer. Birds, iii, 1874, 462.

Lagopus mutus rupestris TURNER, Proc. U. S. Nat. Mus., v, 1882, 228, part (Barren Grounds; Fort Yukon; Gens de Large Mountains, and Arctic coast east of Port Anderson).—HARTERT, Vög. pal. Fauna, iii, No. 1, 1921, 1871 (monogr.).— OBERHOLSER, Auk, xxxix, 1922, 247.—AUSTIN, Mem. Nuttall Orn. Club, No. 7, 1932, 77 (distr.; habits; Newfoundland, Labrador).—GROEBBELS, Der Vögel, i, 1932, 619 (body weight).—PETERS, Check-list Birds of World, ii, 1934, 34 (nw. North Amer. [except area occupied by *kelloggae*], including Melville, Victoria, Ellesmere and Baffin Islands, south to mountains of British Columbia, Great Slave Lake, Great Whale River, and Belle Isle Straits; nw. Greenland north of 66°N.).—SALOMONSEN, Medd. Grønland, cxviii, No. 2, 1936, 32 (syn.; meas.; descr.; distr.); Moults and Sequence of Plumage in Rock Ptarmigan, 1939, 11 (spec.).—STEINBACHER, Ergänzungsband to Hartert, Vög. pal. Fauna, 1938, 516 (British Columbia and Yukon to Baffin Island and Labrador, west and south Greenland).—HELLMAYR and CONOVER, Cat. Birds Amer., i, No. 1, 1942, 206 (syn.; distr.).

L[agopus] m[utus] rupestris SALOMONSEN, Medd. Grønland, cxviii, No. 2, 1936, 4, in text, 16, 17 in tables (wing lengths), 22 in text (Canadian islands and the mainland from British Columbia to Hudson Bay and Labrador).

Lagopus rupestris reinhardtii HANTZSCH, Journ. für Orn., 1908, 367, in text (Greenland; crit.).

Lagopus rupestris, var. *occidentalis* SUNDEVALL, Öfv. Svensk. Vet.-Akad. Forh., No. 3, 1874, 20 (Groenlandia et America maxime boreali).

Lagopus mutus reinhardti TURNER, Proc. U. S. Nat. Mus., v, 1882, 229 (w. Greenland; Niantalik, Cumberland Gulf).—RIDGWAY, Bull. Nuttall Orn. Club, vii, 1882, 258.—OBERHOLSER, Auk, xxxix, 1922, 247.

Lagopus groenlandicus BREHM, Naumannia, 1855, 287; Vögelf, 1855, 264, footnote (w. Greenland).

[Lagopus] (rupestris) kelloggae PETERS, Check-list Birds of World, ii, 1934, 34, footnote (Anticosti Island).—GROSS, Auk, liv, 1937, 22 in text (Button Islands, Labrador).

Lagopus alpinus (not *Tetrao alpinus* Nilsson) FINSCH, Zweite Deutsche Nord-Polfahrt, ii, 1874, 195, part (synonymy, part).

Lagopus Reinhardi macruros SCHIØLER, Dansk. Orn. Tidskr., xix, 1925, 114 (nw. coast of Greenland, ex label on 2 skins in Brehm Coll.).

Tetrao ruesptris (typog. error or lapsus) Ross, in Parry's Journ. Third Voy., 1826, Appendix, 99.

Lagopus dispar Ross, Voy. *Discovery*, ed. 2, ii, 1819, 168 (Disko, Greenland).

Lagopus americanus Audubon, Synopsis, 1839, 207 (Melville Island; Churchill River, Keewatin); Birds Amer., 8vo. ed., v, 1842, 119, pl. 300 (Churchill River).—Baird, Rep. Pacific R. R. Surv., ix, 1858, 637 (Baffin's Bay); Cat. North Amer. Birds, 1859, No. 470.

Lagopus mutus americanus Hellmayr and Conover, Cat. Birds Amer., i, No. 1, 1942, 205 (syn.; distr.) part.

Lagopus rupestris, var. *occidentalis* Sundevall, Öfv. Svensk. Vet.-Akad. Forh., 1874, No. 3, 19, part.

Lagopus rupestris reinhardi American Ornithologists' Union, Check-list, ed. 2, 1895, No. 302a; ed. 3, 1910, 141.

Tetrao reinhardti Walker, Ibis, 1860, 166 (Godhavn, Greenland).

Tetrao reinhardtii Reinhardt, Journ. für Orn., 1854, 440, part (Greenland).

Lagopus reinhardti Brehm, Naumannia, 1855, 287 (Greenland).—Reinhardt, Ibis, 1861, 9 (Greenland; crit.).

[*Lagopus*] *reinhardti* Sharpe, Hand-list, i, 1899, 18 (Greenland; "Labrador").

Lagopus rupestris reinhardti American Ornithologists' Union, Check-list, 1886, No. 302a.—Bendire, Life Hist. North Amer. Birds, i, 1892, 78.—Schalow, Journ. für Orn., 1895, 471 (Ikerasak, nw. Greenland; crit.; descr. eggs).— Chapman, Bull. Amer. Mus. Nat. Hist., xii, 1899, 241 (Disko Island, Nuwatak, and Bowdoin Range, Greenland).—Gibson, Auk, xxxix, 1922, 361 (Inglefield Gulf, near Cape Cleveland, and Five Glacier Valley, n. Greenland, April).

L[*agopus*] *rupestris reinhardti* Ridgway, Man. North Amer. Birds, 1887, 200.

L[*agopus*] r[*upestris*] *reinhardti* Coues, Key North Amer. Birds, ed. 5, ii, 1903, 747 (Ungava).

LAGOPUS MUTUS WELCHI Brewster

Welch's Ptarmigan

Adult male, summer plumage.—Very similar to that of *L. m. rupestris* but averaging less brownish, the brownish areas of the latter being largely grayish in the present subspecies. Above dark brownish gray, vermiculated and coarsely spotted with black, many of the feathers tipped with white; breast and sides similar but without the black central blotches to the feathers; head and neck more coarsely barred with black, grayish white, and pale grayish buff, the lores almost entirely blackish; throat, remiges, except the innermost secondaries, abdomen, and thighs white; under tail coverts dusky grayish tipped with white.

Adult female, summer plumage.—Similar to that of *L. m. rupestris* but with still less brownish, being largely black and grayish white above, slightly suffused with buffy below.

Adult male, autumn plumage.—Slightly more brownish and less blotched with black than the summer male.

Adult female, autumn plumage.—Like the adult female in summer but slightly buffier, the pale bars above finer; below more strongly tinged with buffy.

Adult male, winter plumage.—Like that of *L. m. rupestris.*

Adult female, winter plumage.—Like that of *L. m. rupestris.*
Other plumages apparently unknown.

Adult male.—Wing 173–196 (186.3); tail 97–125 (115.8); bill from anterior end of nostril to tip 9.6–10.4 (9.9); width of bill at gape 10.6–11.4 (11.1); height of bill at angle of gonys 7.9–7.9 (7.9 mm.).[34]

Adult female.—Wing 174–182; tail 96–98; bill from anterior end of nostril to tip 8–8.9; width of bill at gape 10.4–11.5; height of bill at angle of gonys 7.8–7.9 mm.[35]

Range.—Resident in the highest diorite and syenite rock barrens of the alpine summits of Newfoundland.

Type locality.—Newfoundland.

Lagopus welchi BREWSTER, Auk, ii, 1885, 194 (Newfoundland; coll. W. Brewster).—
AMERICAN ORNITHOLOGISTS' UNION, Check-list, No. 303, 1886, ed. 2, 1895, No.
303; ed. 3, 1910, 142.—PALMER, Proc. U. S. Nat. Mus., xiii, 1890, 261 (Cloud
Hills, Canada Bay, Newfoundland).—BENDIRE, Life Hist. North Amer. Birds,
i, 1892, 82.—MACOUN, Cat. Can. Birds, 1900, 209 (Newfoundland).—MACOUN
and MACOUN, Cat. Can. Birds, ed. 2, 1909, 228 (Newfoundland).—GRISCOM,
Ibis, 1926, 672 (Newfoundland).—HENNINGER, Wils. Bull., xxii, 1910, 119
(descr. eggs).—ARNOLD, Auk, xxix, 1912, 76.—BANGS, Bull. Mus. Comp. Zool.,
lxx, No. 4, 1930, 155 (type in Mus. Comp. Zool.).
L[agopus] welchi RIDGWAY, Man. North Amer. Birds, 1887, 201.—COUES, Key North
Amer. Birds, ed. 5, 1903, ii, 748.
[Lagopus] welchi SHARPE, Hand-list, i, 1899, 19.
Lagopus rupestris welchi ELLIOT, Gallin. Game Birds North Amer., 1897, 157,
207.—AMERICAN ORNITHOLOGISTS' UNION, Check-list, ed. 4, 1931, 83.—TAVERNER,
Birds Canada, 1934, 159 in text.—BROOKS, Auk, liii, 1936, 343 (Avalon Penin-
sula, Newfoundland).—ALDRICH and NUTT, Sci. Publ. Cleveland Mus. Nat.
Hist., iv, 1939, 19 (e. Newfoundland).
L[agopus] r[upestris] welchi HANTZSCH, Journ. für Orn., 1908, 367, in text; Can.
Field Nat., xlii, 1928, 14 (Newfoundland).
Lagopus mutus welchi OBERHOLSER, Auk, xxxix, 1922, No. 2, 247.—PETERS, Check-
list Birds of World, ii, 1934, 34 (Alpine summits of Newfoundland).—SALO-
MONSEN, Moults and Sequence of Plumages in Rock Ptarmigan, 1939, 10 (spec.).
Lagopus rupestris (not *Tetrao rupestris* Gmelin) [SCLATER], Ibis, 1889, 261 (New-
foundland).—OGILVIE-GRANT, Cat. Birds Brit. Mus., xxii, 1893, 48, 247, part
(Newfoundland).
Lagopus rupestris rupestris TAVERNER, Ann. Rep. Nat. Mus. Canada for 1928
(1929), 37, 38, part (Newfoundland).
Lagopus mutus rupestris HELLMAYR and CONOVER, Cat. Birds Amer., i, No. 1,
1942, 206, part (Newfoundland; syn.).

LAGOPUS LEUCURUS LEUCURUS (Swainson)

WHITE-TAILED PTARMIGAN

Adult male, summer plumage.—Forehead, crown, nape, occiput, interscapulars, inner upper wing coverts and scapulars, back, rump, upper

---

[34] Four specimens.
[35] Two specimens.

tail coverts, and central pair of rectrices black to dark fuscous-black coarsely vermiculated, barred, and irregularly mottled with cream buff, dull grayish buff and whitish (the white largely restricted to the narrow tips of the feathers), the buffy tones richest and darkest on the lower back, rump, and upper tail coverts; remiges and all but the inner upper wing coverts white; all but the median pair of rectrices white; entire underparts whiter than the dorsum; the feathers of the throat and sides of head, the breast, upper abdomen, sides, flanks, and under tail coverts pale cream buff to cream buff heavily barred with dark fuscous-black and tipped with white; center of abdomen, thighs, and a varying amount of the flanks unbarred white; under wing coverts white; feathers of tarsi and toes white more or less tinged with pale buffy; iris dark brown; bill black; supraorbital "comb" vermilion; toes and claws brownish gray.

Adult female, summer plumage.—Similar to that of the male but with, on the average, a richer, more ochraceous-buffy tone in the buffy areas.

Adult male, autumn plumage.—Remiges, all but the innermost upper wing coverts, the under wing coverts, all but the median pair of rectrices, abdomen (except for narrow sides and to some extent flanks) and under tail coverts pure white; head, nape, interscapulars, scapulars, and innermost upper wing coverts, back, rump, and upper tail coverts with a ground color of pale tawny to fulvous-buff (in one very dark specimen, Dresden brown) mixed with grayish, finely vermiculated and freckled with fuscous-black, these dark markings heavier and forming more regular bars on the head and nape, and becoming smaller and scarcer (i.e., leaving more of the tawny fulvous-buff exposed) on the scapulars, rump, and upper tail coverts; sides of head, chin, and throat white narrowly barred with dull sepia to clove brown; breast similar but with the brown areas broader; sides and upper flanks tawny-buff coarsely mottled and speckled with dull sepia; feathers of tarsi and toes white more or less tinged with buffy.

Adult female, autumn or tutelar plumage.—Similar to that of the male, but upperparts and throat and breast much more ochraceous—the general appearance being isabelline to cinnamon-buff only sparingly mixed with gray, and with the blackish vermiculations somewhat heavier and more widely spaced than in the males; some of the remiges occasionally with dusky shafts.

Adult male, winter plumage.—Entirely white, the feathering of the tarsi and toes much longer and denser than in the summer or autumn plumages; supraorbital "comb" reduced or absent.

Adult female, winter plumage.—Similar to the male.

First autumn plumage (sexes alike).—Similar to the adult female in autumn plumage, but slightly less isabelline, more grayish; the tail and wings very different; in the tail the median two pairs being isabelline narrowly barred with dark clove brown, the next pair with the inner web the same, but the outer web largely white, and the remaining pairs white narrowly and rather faintly edged with brownish mottlings; in the wing only the two outer primaries are white, the remainder dark hair brown, the secondaries edged with dusky isabelline vermiculations.

Juvenal plumage (sexes alike).—Similar to the first autumn plumage but with the top of the head mottled and barred with buff, white, and black, and a number of feathers on the back and rump having large blackish and whitish blotches; chin and upper throat unspotted white; iris dark horn; bill black; toes brownish gray, soles greenish; claws gray, tips pale brownish.

Downy young.—Center of crown and occiput cinnamon-brown bordered with black, forehead and lores white with black spots; sides of head white with a black line through the eye and a somewhat broken blackish malar stripe; center of hind neck, posteriorly widening to include the interscapular region, sepia; broad middle of back and rump to tail pale cinnamon brown barred and laterally margined with blackish brown; scapulars and wings cinnamon-buff barred and mottled with dark sepia; rest of upperparts dirty pale buffy white to grayish white; underparts pale grayish white, washed with buffy on the breast and faintly so on the abdomen; sides and flanks mottled with sepia and cinnamon-brown.

Adult male.—Wing 164–188 (174.2); tail 86–104 (96); exposed culmen 10.4–14.1 (12.4); tarsus 30.5–33.4 (31.6); middle toe without claw 23.8–25.4 (24.6 mm.).[36]

Adult female.—Wing 155–179 (168); tail 84–92 (88.4); exposed culmen 10.7–14.4 (12.3); tarsus 29.8–32.6 (31.5); middle toe without claw 23.6–26.3 (24.9 mm.).[37]

Range.—Resident above timber line (Alpine–Arctic Zone) of the Rocky Mountain area from northwestern Mackenzie and adjacent Yukon (head of Coal Creek, Ogilvie Mountains, La Pierre House; Nahanni Mountains), all of mainland British Columbia and central Alberta south to the northern border of the United States (nw. Washington—Skagit, Puget Sound). In British Columbia it has not been recorded from the coast ranges nearest the coast, but is known from the Cascades; absent in the Queen Charlotte Islands; replaced by an allied race in Vancouver Island. In northern British Columbia it probably descends into the lowlands occasionally in winter.[38]

Type locality.—Rocky Mountains, latitude 54° N.

Tetrao (*Lagopus*) *leucurus* SWAINSON, *in* Swainson and Richardson, Fauna Bor.-Amer., ii, 1831 (1832), 356, pl. 63 (Rocky Mountains, lat. 54° N.).—NUTTALL, Man. Orn. United States and Canada, Land Birds, 1832, 612; ed. 2, 1840, 820, part ("lofty ridges of the Rocky Mountains").

---

[36] Twelve specimens from Alberta and British Columbia.

[37] Twenty-four specimens from Alberta and British Columbia.

[38] According to Brooks and Swarth.

Tetrao leucurus AUDUBON, Orn. Biogr., v, 1839, 200, pl. 418, fig. 2.

Lagopus leucurus SWAINSON, *in* Swainson and Richardson, Fauna Bor.-Amer., ii, 1831ᐧ (1832), pl. 63, part.—BONAPARTE, Geogr. and Comp. List, 1838, 44 part.— AUDUBON, Synopsis, 1839, 208, part; Birds Amer., 8vo ed., v, 1842, 125, part, pl. 302.—BAIRD, Cat. North Amer. Birds, 1859, No. 469, part; ? *in* Cooper, Orn. California, Land Birds, 1870, 542, part (British Columbia).—BLAKISTON, Ibis, 1863, 128, part (Rocky Mountains north to Arctic Circle).—ELLIOT, Monogr. Tetraonidae, 1865, pl. 25 and text, part.—COUES, Check List North Amer. Birds, 1874, No. 388, part; ed. 2, 1882, No. 570, part; Birds Northwest, 1874, 425, part (Rocky Mountains from Arctic Ocean; British Columbia?).—BAIRD, BREWER, and RIDGWAY, Hist. North Amer. Birds, iii, 1874, 464, part, pl. 62, fig. 6.—AMERICAN ORNITHOLOGISTS' UNION, Check-list, 1886, No. 304, rev. ed., 1889, No. 304, part (Liard River; British Columbia) ; ed. 2, 1895, No. 304.— BENDIRE, Life Hist. North Amer. Birds, i, 1892, 83, part.—RHOADS, Proc. Acad. Nat. Sci. Philadelphia, 1893, 38, part (Kicking Horse Pass, Hector, and near Clinton, British Columbia).—OGILVIE-GRANT, Cat. Birds Brit. Mus., xxii, 1893, 52, part (British Columbia; Fort Halkett).—MACOUN, Cat. Birds, pt. 1, 1900, 209, part (Mackenzie River to La Pierre House; summits of most mountains in mainland of British Columbia).—BAILEY, Handb. Birds Western United States, 1902, 129, part (descr.; distr.).—JUDD, U. S. Biol. Surv. Bull. 24, 1905, 47, 48, part (geogr. range, food, etc).—PREBLE, North Amer. Fauna, No. 27, 1908, 348 (Liard River; Fort Simpson; Fort Halkett; La Pierre House; etc.).— MACOUN and MACOUN, Cat. Can. Birds, ed. 2, 1909, 228, part.—RACEY, Auk, xliii, 1926, 321 (between Red Mountain and Mount Whistler, British Columbia).—TAVERNER, Birds Western Canada, 1926, 170 (fig.; descr.; habits; distr.; w. Canada) ; Birds Canada, 1934, 159 in text (distr.; char.) ; Water Birds, 1939, 170, part.—LAING and TAVERNER, Ann. Rep. Nat. Mus. Canada for 1927 (1929), 76 (Chitina River region, Alaska).—STENHOUSE, Scottish Nat., 1930, 81 (type spec.; Roy. Scottish Mus.).

L[agopus] leucurus COUES, Key North Amer. Birds, ed. 2, 1884, 588, part.—RIDGWAY, Man. North Amer. Birds, 1887, 202, part.—REICHENOW, Die Vögel, i, 1913, 323.

[Lagopus] leucurus REICHENBACH, Synop. Aves, iii, Gallinaceae, 1848, pl. 213b, fig. 1879.—COUES, Key North Amer. Birds, 1872, 236, part.—SHARPE, Handlist, i, 1899, 19, part.

Lagopus leucura STEJNEGER, Zeitschr. ges. Orn., i, 1884, 92, part.

Lagopus leucurus leucurus AMERICAN ORNITHOLOGISTS' UNION, Check-list, ed. 3, 1910, 142, part; ed. 4, 1931, 85, part.—RILEY, Can. Alpine Journ., 1912, 59 (Henry House, at Moose Pass branch of Smoky River, Alberta; habits; crit.).—WHEELER, Auk, xxix, 1912, 202 (w. of Conghia Ti, n. of Great Slave Lake, Mackenzie, June 4).—BROOKS, Auk, xxxiv, 1917, 37 (Chilliwack, British Columbia, on higher Eastern Cascade range).—SWARTH, Univ. California Publ. Zool., xxiv, 1922, 208 (mountains above Doch-da-on Creek, Stikine River, s. Alaska; food; etc.) ; Univ. California Publ. Zool., xxx, 1926, 103 (Atlin region, British Columbia, plum.).—TAVERNER, Birds, Western Canada, 1926, 171, in text (distr. in w. Canada) ; Birds Canada, 1934, 160, in text part.—BENT, U. S. Nat. Mus. Bull., 162, 1932, 232 (habits; distr.).—PETERS, Check-list Birds of World, ii, 1934, 35, part (range, except Vancouver Island).—COWAN, Condor, xli, 1939, 82 in text (crit.).—HELLMAYR and CONOVER, Cat. Birds Amer., i, No. 1, 1942, 209 (syn.; distr.).

Lagopus l[eucurus] leucurus GROEBBELS, Der Vögel, i, 1932, 184 (alt. distr.) ; 739 in text (limiting distr. factors).

Lagopus leucurus peninsularis Osgood, North Amer. Fauna, No. 30, 1909, 60
   Ogilvie Range, Yukon; crit.; voice).

LAGOPUS LEUCURUS PENINSULARIS Chapman

KENAI WHITE-TAILED PTARMIGAN

Adults in summer plumage.—Similar to the corresponding plumage of
the nominate form but with the blackish areas more extensive, the buff
areas paler—whitish to pale pinkish buff, only the broader marks slightly
darker—pinkish buff.

Adults in autumn plumage.—Similar to the corresponding plumage of
the nominate form but with the general tone of the plumage usually
grayer, the buff being definitely less noticeable than the gray (exceptions
do occur, however).

Adults in winter plumage.—Like that of the nominate form.

First autumn plumage.—Similar to that of the nominate race but
averaging grayer.

Juvenal plumage.—Like that of the typical race.

Downy young.—Like that of the typical race.

Adult male.—Wing 168–180 (174); tail 92–103 (95); exposed culmen
12–14.5 (13.4); tarsus 32.4–34 (33.3); middle toe without claw
24.4–27 (25.6 mm.). [39]

Adult female.—Wing 164–171 (167.8); tail 85–93 (90); exposed culmen 13.4–13.9 (13.7); tarsus 32.5–33.6 (33); middle toe without claw
24.1–27.3 (25.2 mm.). [40]

Range.—Resident in the alpine summits from south-central Alaska
(Mount McKinley) south to the Kenai Peninsula (Bear Creek, Lake
Clark, Cook Inlet, White Pass, Glacier Bay, Seward, Kenai Mountains).

Type locality.—Kenai Mountains, Alaska.

(?) *Lagopus leucurus* Hartlaub, Journ. für Orn., 1883, 277 (Alaska; crit.).
Lagopus leucurus (*Tetrao leucurus* Swainson) Bishop, North Amer. Fauna, No.
   19, 1900, 72 (summits of cliffs above Glacier, Alaska; breeding).—Osgood,
   North Amer. Fauna, No. 21, 1901, 75 (head of Bear Creek, Cook Inlet, breeding); No. 24, 1904, 67 mountains on nw. side Lake Clark, Alaska Peninsula).—
   Bailey, Handb. Birds Western United States, 1902, 129, part.
L[*agopus*] *leucurus* Coues, Key North Amer. Birds, ed. 5, 1903, ii, 749, part
   (Alaska).
Lagopus leucurus leucurus Brooks, Bull. Mus. Comp. Zool., lix, 1915, 366 (Muir
   Inlet, Glacier Bay, Alaska).—Bailey, Auk, xliv, 1927, 201 (valley of Granite
   Creek Basin, se. Alaska).
Lagopus leucurus peninsularis Chapman, Bull. Amer. Mus. Nat. Hist., xvi, 1902,
   236 (Kenai Mountains, Alaska; coll. Amer. Mus. Nat. Hist.); Ibis, 1903, 267,
   in text (crit.).—American Ornithologists' Union, Auk, xxv, 1908, 346; Checklist, ed. 3, 1910, 143; ed. 4, 1931, 84.—Macoun and Macoun, Cat. Can. Birds ed. 2,

[39] Five specimens from Kenai area, Alaska.
[40] Six specimens from the Kenai area, Alaska.

1909, 229 (Kenai Mountains, Bear Creek, Cook Inlet, Alaska).—RILEY, Can. Alpine Journ., 1912, 60, in text (crit.).—BENT, U. S. Nat. Mus. Bull. 162, 1932, 234 (habits, etc.).—PETERS, Check-list Birds of World, ii, 1934, 35.—HELL-MAYER and CONOVER, Cat. Birds Amer., i, No. 1, 1942, 209 (syn.; distr.).

LAGOPUS LEUCURUS SAXATILIS Cowan

VANCOUVER PTARMIGAN

Adults in summer plumage.—Said to be like those of the typical race but larger, with longer tail and larger, more decurved bill; head and neck black and white without or almost without, buffy wash, shafts of primaries black. [41]

Adult male in autumn plumage.—Like that of the nominate race but larger, with longer bill and tail, buffy areas of back and flanks less grayish, more brownish, and with little or no buffy on head and neck.

Adult female in autumn plumage.—Like that of the nominate race but with the ground color of the upperparts and sides of the breast more brownish, less grayish.

Juvenal.—Differs from that of the typical race in having the head and neck barred black and white, and in the longer more decurved bills.

Downy young.—Apparently not known.

Adult male.—Wing 178–187 (181); tail 100–106 (104); exposed culmen 16–18 (17.4); nostril to tip 10.5–11 (10.9); depth of bill 8–9 (8.7 mm.). [42]

Adult female.—Wing 172, exposed culmen 18, nostril to tip 11.2; depth of bill 7.6 mm.[43]

Range.—Resident in the alpine peaks of Vancouver Island (Mount Arrowsmith, Crown Mountain, Upper Campbell Lake, Cowichan Lake, mountains south of Alberni; mountains north of Great Central Lake.

Type locality.—Mount Arrowsmith, Vancouver Island, 6,000 feet.

Lagopus leucurus MACOUN, Cat. Can. Birds, 1900, 209, part (breeding, Mount Arrowsmith, Vancouver).—MACOUN and MACOUN, Cat. Can. Birds, ed. 2, 1909, 228, part (breeding, 6,000 feet, Mount Arrowsmith, Vancouver).

Lagopus leucurus leucurus SWARTH, Univ. California Publ. Zool., x, 1912, 23 (Vancouver Island: all the higher peaks).—BROOKS and SWARTH, Pacific Coast Avif., No. 17, 1925, 52 part (Vancouver Island, Mount Arrowsmith; mountains south of Alberni, and mountains north of Great Central Lake).—AMERICAN ORNITHOLOGISTS' UNION, Check-list, ed. 4, 1931, 85, part.—BENT, U. S. Nat. Mus. Bull. 162, 1932, 232 (habits; distr.; Mount Arrowsmith).—TAVERNER, Birds Canada, 1934, 160, in text, part.—PETERS, Check-list Birds of World, ii, 1934, 35, part.

Lagopus leucurus saxatilis COWAN, Condor, xli, 1939, 82 (Mount Arrowsmith, Vancouver; descr.; distr.; crit.).—HELLMAYR and CONOVER, Cat. Birds Amer., i, No. 1, 1942, 210 (syn.; distr.).

---

[41] All descriptions *ex* Cowan, Condor, xli, 1939, 82.

[42] Five specimens, all measurements ex Cowan.

[43] One specimen, ex Cowan.

LAGOPUS LEUCURUS RAINIERENSIS Taylor

MOUNT RAINIER PTARMIGAN

Adults in summer plumage.—Very similar to the corresponding plumage of *Lagopus leucurus peninsularis,* but with the dark areas deep black without a slight brownish tinge found in the Kenai form.

Other adult plumages identical with the Kenai subspecies, but with longer wings on the average; the young plumages not distinguishable from those of *Lagopus leucurus peninsularis.*

Adult male.—Wing 177–187 (180.3); tail 85–106 (98.2); exposed culmen 13.1–14.9 (14.1); tarsus 33.8–35.0 (34.3); middle toe without claw 26.8–28.5 (27.7 mm.).[44]

Adult female.—Wing 171–183 (174.6); tail 87–92 (87.5); exposed culmen 12.2–14.2 (13.4); tarsus 34.4–34.7 (34.6); middle toe without claw 27.2–28.3 (26.3 mm.).[45]

Range.—Resident on the alpine summits of Washington from Barron (6,000 feet, near Windy Pass, Whatcom County) to Mount Rainier south to Mount St. Helens.[46]

Type locality.—Pinnacle Peak, 6,200 feet, Mount Rainier, Wash.

Tetrao (*Lagopus*) *leucurus* (not of Swainson) NUTTALL, Man. Orn. United States and Canada, Land Birds, ed. 2, 1840, 820, part ("snowy peaks of the Columbia River").
Lagopus leucurus BAIRD, *in* Cooper, Orn. California, Land Birds, 1870, 542, part ("highest peaks of Washington Territory").—BAIRD, BREWER, and RIDGWAY, Hist. North Amer. Birds, iii, 1874, 464, part (Cascade Mountains, Washington and Oregon).—COUES, Check List North Amer. Birds, ed. 2, 1882, No. 570.—AMERICAN ORNITHOLOGISTS' UNION, Check-list, No. 304, 1886; ed. 2, 1895, No. 304, part (mountains of Washington and Oregon).—RHOADS, Proc. Acad. Nat. Sci. Philadelphia, 1893, 38, part (Mount Tacoma, Wash.).—OGILVIE-GRANT, Cat. Birds British Mus., xxii, 1893, 52, part (Oregon, Washington).—DAWSON, Wils. Bull., iii, 1896, 3 (Okanogan County, Wash., 9,000 feet); Auk, xiv, 1897, 173 (same).—BAILEY, Handb. Birds Western United States, 1902, 129, part.—WOODCOCK, Oregon Agr. Exp. Stat. Bull. 68, 1902, 27 (Oregon range).—JUDD, U. S. Biol. Surv. Bull. 24, 1905, 47, 48, part (range, food, etc.).—DAWSON and BOWLES, Birds Washington, ii, 1909, 590 (descr., habits, etc., Washington).
L[*agopus*] *leucurus* COUES, Key North Amer. Birds, ed. 2, 1884, 588, part.—RIDGWAY, Man. North Amer. Birds, 1887, 202, part (high mountains of Oregon and Washington).
[*Lagopus*] *leucurus* SHARPE, Hand-list, i, 1899, 19, part.
Lagopus leucurus leucurus AMERICAN ORNITHOLOGISTS' UNION, Check-list, ed. 3, 1910, 142, part (Washington; nw. Montana ?).—GABRIELSON and JEWETT, Birds Oregon, 1940, 602 (no definite Oregon records).

---

[44] Six specimens from Washington.
[45] Five specimens from Washington.
[46] In Whatcom and Skagit Counties, northwestern Washington, this form and the nominate race meet, and the individual specimens may resemble either race.

Lagopus leucurus rainierensis TAYLOR, Condor, xxii, 1920, 146 (Pinnacle Peak, Mount Rainier, Wash., at 6,200 feet; coll. U. S. Nat. Mus.).—OBERHOLSER, Auk, xxxviii, 1921, 266.—AMERICAN ORNITHOLOGISTS' UNION, Check-list, ed. 4, 1931, 85.—BENT, U. S. Nat. Mus. Bull. 162, 1932, 240 (habits).—PETERS, Check-list Birds World, ii, 1934, 35.—COWAN, Condor, xli, 1939, 82, 83 in text (crit.).—KITCHIN, Murrelet, xx, 1939, 30 (Mount Rainier National Park; resident; spec.).—HELLMAYR and CONOVER, Cat. Birds Amer., i, No. 1, 1942, 209 (syn.; distr.).

LAGOPUS LEUCURUS ALTIPETENS Osgood

SOUTHERN WHITE-TAILED PTARMIGAN

Adults in summer plumage.—Like the corresponding plumage of *Lagopus leucurus leucurus,* but with longer wings and tail.

Adults in autumn plumage.—Similar to the corresponding plumage of the nominate race but with longer wings and the general color above paler, in some specimens more brownish buff—tawny-olive to sayal brown and in others with very little buff and that little pale and ashy.

Adults in winter plumage.—Distinguished from those of the nominate race only by the longer wings of the present subspecies.

First autumn plumage.—Like that of the typical race but averaging more tawny-buff.

Juvenal.—Similar to that of the typical race.

Downy young.—Similar to that of the typical race.

Adult male.—Wing 178–194 (187.5); tail 98–109 (104); exposed culmen 11.7–14.9 (13.8); tarsus 30.2–33.7 (31.8); middle toe without claw 23.3–26.3 (25.1 mm.).[47]

Adult female.—Wing 173–192 (181.6); tail 93–98 (95.6); exposed culmen 12.5–14.3 (13.6); tarsus 31.3–33.4 (32.1); middle toe without claw 24.1–26.1 (25.1 mm.).[48]

Range.—Resident in the alpine summits of the Rocky Mountains from Montana (Lewis and Clark, Teton, and Carbon Counties) through Wyoming and Colorado to northern New Mexico (Sangre de Cristo Mountains, Taos Mountains, Truchas Peaks, Culebra Mountains, Wheeler Peak, Costilla Peaks).

Type locality.—Mount Blaine, Colo.

Tetrao (Lagopus) leucurus NUTTALL, Man. Orn. United States and Canada, Land Birds, 1832, 612, part; ed. 2, 1840, 820, part ("lofty ridge of the Rocky Mountains," part).

Lagopus leucurus SWAINSON, *in* Swainson and Richardson, Fauna Bor.-Amer., ii, 1831 (1832), pl. 63, part.—BONAPARTE, Geogr. and Comp. List, 1838, 44, part.—AUDUBON, Synopsis, 1839, 208, part; Birds Amer., 8vo ed., v, 1842, 125, part.—BAIRD, Rep. Pacific R. R. Surv., ix, 1858, 636 (west side of Rocky Mountains, near Cochetopa Pass, lat. 39°); Cat. North Amer. Birds, 1859, No. 469,

---

[47] Eleven specimens from Wyoming, Colorado, and New Mexico.

[48] Five specimens from Wyoming and Colorado.

part.—BLAKISTON, Ibis, 1863, 128, part (Rocky Mountains south to lat. 39°).—
ELLIOT, Monogr. Tetraonidae, 1865, pl. 25 and text, part.—COUES, Proc. Acad.
Nat. Sci. Philadelphia, 1866, 94 (Cantonment Burgwyn, N. Mex.); Check
List North Amer. Birds, 1874, No. 388, part; ed. 2, 1882, No. 570, part;
Birds Northwest, 1874, 425, part (Rocky Mountains south to lat. 37°); U. S.
Geol. and Geogr. Surv. Terr. Bull. 5, ser. 2, 1879, 263–266 (breeding habits;
descr. nest and eggs; Colorado).—RIDGWAY, Bull. Essex Inst., v, 1873, 186
(Colorado; alpine summits).—BAIRD, BREWER, and RIDGWAY, Hist. North Amer.
Birds, iii, 1874, 464, part, pl. 62, fig. 6.—DREW, Auk, i, 1884, 392 (shedding
of claws; plumage note).—AMERICAN ORNITHOLOGISTS' UNION, Check-list, 1886,
No. 304, part; ed. 2, 1889, No. 304, part (New Mexico, etc.).—BENDIRE, Life Hist.
North Amer. Birds, i, 1892, 83, part.—OGILVIE-GRANT, Cat. Birds British Mus.,
xxii, 1893, 52, part (New Mexico, Colorado; spec.).—COOKE, Colorado State
Agr. Coll. Bull. 37, 1897, 70 (Colorado); ibid., Bull. 56, app., 1900, 202 (breeds at
Breckenridge, Colo.).—JUDD, U. S. Biol. Surv. Bull. 24, 1905, 47, 48, part (geogr.
range; food; etc.).—HENDERSON, Univ. Colorado Stud. Zool., vi, 1909, 228
(Boulder, Colo., above 8,500 feet).—SCLATER, Hist. Birds Colorado, 1912, 145
(Colorado; resident).

L[agopus] leucurus COUES, Key North Amer. Birds, ed. 2, 1884, 588, part; ed. 5,
1903, ii, 749, part.—RIDGWAY, Man. North Amer. Birds, 1887, 202, part.

[Lagopus] leucurus COUES, Key North Amer. Birds, 1872, 236, part.—SHARPE,
Hand-list, i, 1899, 19, part.

Lagopus leucura STEJNEGER, Zeitschr. ges. Orn., i, 1884, 92, part.

Lagopus leucurus leucurus AMERICAN ORNITHOLOGISTS' UNION, Check-list, ed. 3,
1910, 142, part.—GRAVE and WALKER, Birds Wyoming, 1913, 39 (Wyoming;
alpine areas).—BETTS, Univ. Colorado Stud. Zool., x, 1913, 192 (Boulder
County, Colo., above 9,000 feet).—SAUNDERS, Pacific Coast Avif., No. 14,
1921, 58 (Montana; Bitterroot Mountains; St. Marys Lake; Glacier National
Park; Teton, Lewis and Clark, and Carbon Counties).—JENSEN, Auk, xl,
1923, 454 (Sangre de Cristo Mountains, N. Mex.).

Lagopus leucurus altipetens OSGOOD, Auk, xviii, 1901, 189 ("Mount Blaine," i.e.,
Summit Peak, s. Colorado; coll. U. S. Nat. Mus.).—BAILEY, Auk, xxi, 1904,
351 (upper Pecos River, N. Mex., 9,300–13,300 feet); xxii, 1905, 316 (Taos
Mountains, New Mexico, above timberline).—HENSHAW, Auk, xxii, 1905, 315,
in text (correction of type locality).—WARREN, Condor, x, 1908, 20 (Boreas
Pass, Colo.).—AMERICAN ORNITHOLOGISTS' UNION, Auk, xl, 1923, 517 (Check-
list No. 304b); Check-list, ed. 4, 1931, 85.—TAVERNER, Birds Western Canada,
1926, 171, in text (distr.); Birds Canada, 1934, 160, in text.—BAILEY,
Birds New Mexico, 1928, 202 (genl.; New Mexico).—BENT, U. S. Nat. Mus.
Bull. 162, 1932, 234 (habits; distr.; etc.).—PETERS, Check-list Birds of World,
ii, 1934, 35.—McCREARY and MICKEY, Wils. Bull., xlvii, 1935, 129 in text (se.
Wyoming; resident).—ULKE, Can. Alpine Journ., 1934–35 (1936), 79 (Yoho
Park, Canada; summer; common).—ALEXANDER, Univ. Colorado Stud., xxiv,
1937, 91 (Boulder County, Colo., moderately common, above timberline in sum-
mer, down to 9,000 feet in winter; spec.).—NIEDRACH and ROCKWELL, Birds
Denver and Mountain Parks, 1939, 61 (not common resident; habits; Colorado).
—HELLMAYR and CONOVER, Cat. Birds Amer., i, No. 1, 1942, 210, (syn; distr.).—
BEHLE, Condor, xlvi, 1944, 72 (Utah).

[Lagopus] leucurus altipetens GROEBBELS, Der Vögel, ii, 1937, 238 in text (care of
eggs).

L[agopus] l[eucurus] altipetens BAILEY, Handb. Birds Western United States, 1902,
129 (Colorado).

Genus CANACHITES Stejneger

Canace (not of Curtis, 1838) REICHENBACH, Av. Syst. Nat. Vög., 1853, xxix.
(Type, by monotypy, *Tetrao canace* Linnaeus, which here = *T. canadensis*
Linnaeus.)

Canachites STEJNEGER, Proc. U. S. Nat. Mus., viii, 1885, 410. (Type, by original
designation, *Tetrao canadensis* Linnaeus.)

Tympanuchus REICHENOW, Die Vögel, i, 1913, 320, part.

Small wood grouse (length about 165–187 mm.) with a general resemblance in form to *Dendragapus* but with only 16 (instead of usual 20)
rectrices, and adult males without an inflatable air sac on sides of neck;
coloration very different.

Bill relatively small, its length from frontal antiae about one-fourth
the length of head, its depth at same point about equal to its width;
culmen very indistinctly ridged; rhamphotheca smooth throughout; maxil-

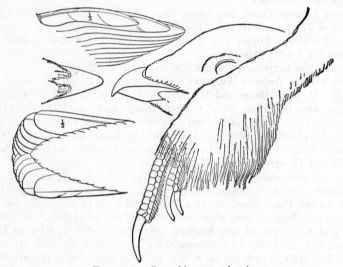

FIGURE 9.—*Canachites canadensis.*

lary tomium distinctly but not strongly concave or arched. Wing moderate or rather small, with longest primaries projecting beyond tips of
longest secondaries between one-fourth and one-third the length of wing;
third and fourth primaries longest (the fifth nearly as long), the first
(outermost) intermediate between seventh and eighth; inner webs of
three outer primaries slightly emarginate or sinuate. Tail about two-
thirds as long as wing, more or less rounded, the rectrices (16) broad,
with tips broadly rounded (*C. canadensis*) or nearly truncate (*C.
franklinii*). Tarsus less than one-fourth as long as wing, completely and
densely clothed with soft, hairlike feathers, except on heel, the basal
phalanx of middle toe also feathered along each side (except in summer); middle toe very slightly shorter than tarsus; lateral toes about

equal, extending to slightly beyond penultimate articulation of middle toe; hallux slightly shorter than second phalanx of middle toe; upper surface of toes with a continuous series of transverse scutella, margined along each side by a row of rather small more or less quadrate scales; edges of toes distinctly fringed or pectinated in winter, but not in summer.

Plumage and coloration.—Feathers of crown slightly elongated, forming a moderate crest when erected; a nude superciliary space, larger and brightly colored in adult males in summer; no tufts nor air sac on side of neck; plumage in general rather compact, with feathers distinctly outlined, except on anal region, where soft, downy, and blended. Adult males barred with black and grayish above, the tail plain blackish, sometimes tipped with cinnamon-rufous; throat, cheek, breast, etc., black, the former margined with white spotting, the feathers along sides, etc., and under tail coverts (sometimes upper tail coverts also) broadly tipped with white. Adult females barred above with blackish and rusty or buffy, beneath everywhere barred and spotted with blackish, buffy, and white.

Range.—Northern coniferous forests of North America (Hudsonian and Canadian Zones). (Two species.)

KEY TO THE FORMS (ADULTS) OF THE GENUS CANACHITES[49]

a. Throat and breast black (males).
  b. Rectrices not broadly tipped with pale brownish; upper tail coverts with broad white tips (se. Alaska to c. Alberta and nw. Wyoming).
      Canachites franklinii (p. 138)
  bb. Rectrices broadly tipped with pale brownish; upper tail coverts with no white tips.
    c. Grayish edges of feathers of lower back, rump, and upper tail coverts usually lightly tinged with olivaceous (coast of s. Alaska).
      Canachites canadensis atratus (p. 150)
    cc. Grayish edges of feathers of lower back, rump, and upper tail coverts clear grayish, not tinged with olivaceous (n. North America from c. Alaska to Labrador).......Canachites canadensis canadensis (p. 143)
      (s. Canada from Manitoba s. to Wisconsin and n. New England).
      Canachites canadensis canace (p. 147)
      (Gaspé, Nova Scotia, New Brunswick).
      Canachites canadensis torridus (p. 151)
aa. Throat and breast tawny to whitish barred with dark brown (females).
  b. Upper tail coverts tipped with white (se. Alaska to c. Alberta and nw. Wyoming) ....Canachites franklinii (p. 138)
  bb. Upper tail coverts not tipped with white.
    c. Above predominantly fuscous and gray, brownish bars pale and largely restricted to hindneck and upper back. (n. North America from c. Alaska to Labrador)........Canachites canadensis canadensis (p. 143)

[49] The races *atratus, canace,* and *torridus* are quite poorly defined. Inasmuch as it has been found possible to see their characters in series, they have been maintained, but no great loss would result if they were all united under *canadensis.*

    cc. Above decidedly brownish or brownish gray barred with dark.
        d. Pale tips of dorsal feathers suffused with pale olive-brown (coast of
           s. Alaska) ....**Canachites canadensis atratus** (p. 150)
        dd. Pale tips of dorsal feathers clear grayish.
           e. Brownish areas more extensive and brighter in color—ochraceous-buff
             to ochraceous-salmon (Gaspé, Nova Scotia, New Brunswick).
                                    Canachites canadensis torridus (p. 151)
        ee. Brownish areas less extensive and paler in color—light ochraceous-buff
           (s. Canada from Manitoba s. to Wisconsin and n. New England).
                                  Canachites canadensis canace (p. 147)

CANACHITES FRANKLINII (Douglas)

FRANKLIN'S GROUSE

    Adult male.—Supranarial feathers black posteriorly bordered with white (interrupted medially); feathers of forehead, crown, occiput, nape, and interscapulars, dark olive-brown to ashy mummy brown narrowly barred with fuscous-black, the tips becoming slightly paler on the nape and interscapulars, even whitish on a few posterolateral interscapulars, the dark subterminal band becoming much broader on the interscapulars, which are much more blackish than olive-brown; back, lower back, and rump like the interscapulars but with the dark areas narrower, the paler interspaces more numerous; lesser upper wing coverts like the back but paler, the dark areas less intense and, except for the subterminal band, the markings more crescentic and the brown areas mottled with dusky; median and greater upper wing coverts dark olive-brown, indistinctly mottled and submarginally irregularly marked with paler—snuff brown to light olive-brown; secondaries like the greater upper coverts but with the paler color restricted to the outer margins and the tips of the feathers; the innermost few pairs with the pale tips extending backward along the shaft in a proximally pointed, distally expanded white wedge-shaped mark; primaries dark olive-brown to fuscous, the outer webs of the second, third, fourth, and fifth pairs (from the outside) largely whitish; short upper tail coverts like the rump but with grayer tips; long upper tail coverts fuscous, laterally mottled and vermiculated with pale olive-brown, and broadly tipped with white, the feathers graduated, increasing in length centripetally, so that in the closed tail the white tips form a longitudinal series of white blotches; rectrices deep fuscous, the median pair very narrowly tipped with white, the others either without pale tips or very faintly tipped with snuff brown; chin, upper throat, cheeks, and lower auriculars black, the whole area bounded by a narrow white line beginning below the eyes, forming a circle open only in front of the eyes (and, in many specimens, this is continued to the bill by a narrow white subloreal line); sides of neck and lower throat like the nape but the feathers of the midventral line blacker, and with whitish terminal edges; breast and an area extending dorsally to a point over and in front of the bend of the wing, blackish with a faint bluish sheen, the brownish basal areas often showing also; this blackish area extending caudally along the midline of the upper abdomen, giving this area a posteriorly convex outline; the extreme dorsal-lateral feathers of the black area narrowly tipped with bright snuff brown to pale tawny, the lateral ones with broad white tips; lower abdomen blackish but with the white tips much broader and with some white bars and subterminal shaft spots making the area as much white as blackish; sides and flanks grayish Sayal brown to Saccardo's umber with a series of concentric irregular bands of dark olive-brown and with a medioterminal white wedge-shaped mark, the dark olive-brown bands becoming transverse bars on the flank feathers, which also have the white wedges reduced and flattened into terminal bands; thighs narrowly barred dusky olive-brown and pale grayish snuff brown; under tail coverts black, very broadly tipped with white, the feathers graduated so that in the closed tail the white tips appear almost like a broad longitudinal band, while in the open tail they form a circle incomplete only at the base; under wing coverts dark olive-brown to fuscous, some with whitish tips and narrow white outer edges; those near the bend of the wing with pale snuff-brown edges; iris Vandyke brown; bill black; "comb" scarlet-vermilion; feet gray, soles tinged yellow.

Adult female, gray phase.—Forehead, crown, and occiput barred black, smoke gray, and ochraceous-buff; nape similar but with the gray predominant at the expense of the ochraceous-buff; interscapulars, upper back, and scapulars black conspicuously barred with ochraceous-buff and inconspicuously tipped with grayish; feathers of the back, lower back, and rump blackish tipped with smoke gray and with a usually concealed pale ochraceous-buff bar about two-thirds of the way from the base to the tip, these bars occasionally showing; wings as in male but less brownish, the feather edgings hair brown with a faint tawny wash, the dark areas fuscous; the light outer edges of primaries 2 to 5, inclusive, somewhat mottled with dusky, and all the remiges very narrowly tipped with whitish, this being least noticeable on the outer primaries; upper tail coverts black tipped with white (the white tips less than half as wide as in the males) and banded with pale grayish ochraceous-buff; rectrices blackish narrowly tipped with white and abundantly but irregularly crossed and mottled with cinnamon-buff to tawny-olive, these markings largely restricted to the outer edges of the outer webs of the lateral feathers and extending across both webs in the more median ones; lores, postocular stripe, chin, and upper throat white speckled or barred with dark fuscous; auriculars tawny-olive spotted with dark fuscous; lower throat and breast pale ochraceous-buff heavily banded with fuscous-black, the feathers of the breast more extensively black than ochraceous-buff, the latter color brighter there than on the lower throat; abdomen sharply distinct, white, instead of ochraceous-buff and the dark fuscous-black bands more continuous, less broken than on the breast feathers; sides, flanks, and thighs as in the male—but more ochraceous; under tail coverts as in the male but with more white bars (not only the terminal one as in the males); iris Vandyke brown; "comb" vermilion; bill blackish; feet pale brownish gray, claws blackish.

Adult female, rufous phase.—Similar to the gray phase but with the ochraceous-buff extending over the whole underparts from the chin to as far as the middle of the abdomen, and brighter, slightly more ochraceous-tawny as well; above the ochraceous color more pronounced on the head, nape, interscapulars, lower back, rump, and upper tail coverts; the pale markings on the wings more buffy—pale grayish clay color; rectrices often with narrow buffy tips or subterminal blotches.

Immature male.—Like the adult but with the juvenal outer primaries (narrowly marked with buff on the outer webs instead of whitish as in adults) and with the rectrices more often tipped very narrowly with whitish.

Immature female.—Like the adult of the corresponding phase but with the juvenal outer primaries; not readily distinguishable in many cases.

Juvenal (sexes alike).—Above similar to the adult female, rufous phase, but with the scapulars and inner secondaries with white terminal shaft streaks and these feathers abundantly marked with concentric longitudinal as well as transverse ochraceous-buff irregular bands; the interscapulars and upper wing coverts with small medioterminal white marks; the chin and upper throat largely devoid of buffy-white speckled with blackish; and the lower abdomen, flanks, and thighs dirty smoke gray indistinctly barred with dusky; iris Vandyke brown; "comb" pale vermilion; lower mandible yellowish beneath at base, brownish elsewhere.

Downy young (sexes alike).—Forehead, sides of head, and entire underparts mustard yellow to Naples yellow; a black line from the bill through the eye to the sides and back of the nape; another black spot on the middle of the forehead, and another fuscous-black line bordering the crown and occiput, which are amber brown to Sanford's brown; wings, back, lower back, and rump like the crown and occiput, from which they are separated in color by an intrusion of the yellow of the sides of the head across the interscapulars; an irregular blackish line from the flanks around the lower back to the tail.

Adult male.—Wing 172–192 (182.3); tail 118–144 (129.3); exposed culmen 14–20.7 (16.9); tarsus 31.8–37.2 (34.9); middle toe without claw 32.3–40.2 (35.4 mm.). [50]

---

[50] Forty-six specimens from Alberta, British Columbia, Saskatchewan, Washington, Idaho, and Montana.

Adult female.—Wing 171–190 (179.2) ; tail 94–119 (107.9) ; exposed culmen 12.7–19.7 (15.8) ; tarsus 32–35.8 (34.2) ; middle toe without claw 32.5–36.8 (34.2 mm.). [51]

Range.—Resident in spruce forests and swamps of northwestern United States and southwestern Canada, from southeastern Alaska (Prince of Wales Island, Warren Island, Zarembo Island, and Kasaan Bay) ; north-central British Columbia (Yellowhead Pass; Hudson's Hope on the Peace River; 40 miles north of Hazelton; Ingenika River, Thudade, and Kluetantan Lake; etc) ; and central Alberta (Athabasca River; Edmonton; Banff; Henry House, Jasper House, Siffleur and Pipestone Rivers) ; south through the interior of Washington (Yakima Pass, Nachess Pass, Pasayten River, Hidden Lakes, Cascade Mountains) to northeastern Oregon (Wallowa County and extreme northern Baker County) ; central Idaho (Baker Creek, Sawtooth City, Resort, Fort Lapwai, Fort Sherman, Blue Mountains) ; western Montana (St. Marys Lake, Belton, Poala, Mount McDonald, Belt Mountains, Bitterroot Mountains, Belly River, Rock Creek) ; and to northwestern Wyoming (Yellowstone Park).

Accidental in Colorado (Palmer House).

Type locality.—Rocky Mountains from latitude 50°–54°, near the source of the Columbia River, restricted to Athabasca Pass region, British Columbia, by Hall, Murrelet, xv, January 1944, 11.

Tetrao canadensis, var. BONAPARTE, Amer. Orn., iii, 1828, 47, pl. 10.

Tetrao canadensis (not of Linnaeus) SWAINSON and RICHARDSON, Fauna Bor.-Amer., ii, 1831 (1832), 346.

Tetrao canadensis "*T. franklinii* Doug. ♂" SWAINSON and RICHARDSON, Fauna Bor.-Amer., ii, 1831 (1832), pl. 61.

Tetrao canadensis "*T. franklinii* Doug. ♀" SWAINSON and RICHARDSON, Fauna Bor.-Amer., ii, 1831, pl. 62.

T[*etrao*] *franklinii* DOUGLAS, Trans. Linn. Soc. London, xvi, 1829, 139 ("Valleys of the Rocky Mountains, from latitude 50° to 54°, near the sources of the Columbia River").[52]

Tetrao franklinii SWAINSON and RICHARDSON, Fauna Bor.-Amer. ii, 1831 (1832), pl. 61.—BAIRD, Rep. Pacific R. R. Surv., ix, 1858, 623 (St. Marys "Rocky Mts.," i.e. Montana ?) ; Cat. North Amer. Birds, 1859, No. 461; *in* Cooper, Orn. California, Land Birds, 1870, 529 (crit.).—COOPER and SUCKLEY, Rep. Pacific R. R. Surv., xii, book 2, pt. 3, 1860, 221 (Rocky and Bitterroot Mountains, Mont.; near Yakima Pass, Cascade Mountain, Wash.).

Tetrao franklini LESSON, Traité d'Orn., 1831, 502.—BLAKISTON, Ibis, 1862, 8 (w. side Rocky Mountains, lat. 49°) ; 1863, 122 (Kootenay Pass to valley of Flathead River).—LORD, Proc. Roy. Artil. Inst. Woolwich, ix, 1864, 123 (British Columbia).

---

[51] Thirty-nine specimens from Alaska, British Columbia, Alberta, Washington, and Montana.

[52] "Sparingly seen . . . on the high mountains which form the base or platform of the snowy peaks 'Mount Hood,' 'Mount St. Helena,' and 'Mount Baker.' "

Canace franklinii ELLIOT, Proc. Acad. Nat. Sci. Philadelphia, 1864, 23; Monogr. Tetraonidae, 1865, pl. 10 and text.

Canace franklini BAIRD, BREWER, and RIDGWAY, Hist. North Amer. Birds, iii, 1874, pl. 59, fig. 3.

[*Tetrao canadensis*] var. *franklini* REICHENBACH, Synop. Av., iii, Gallinaceae, 1848, pl. 215, fig. 1886.

Tetrao canadensis . . . var. *franklini* COUES, Check List North Amer. Birds, 1874, No. 380a.

Tetrao canadensis var. *franklini* COUES, Birds Northwest, 1874, 394 (synonymy under "b. *franklini*").

Tetrao canadensis franklini COUES, U. S. Geol. and Geogr. Surv. Terr. Bull. 4, 1878, 628 (Rocky Mountains, Mont., lat. 49°).—WILLIAMS, Bull. Nuttall Orn. Club, vii, 1882, 61 (Belt Mountains, Mont.).

[*Tetrao canadensis.*] Var. *franklinii* COUES, Key North Amer. Birds, 1872, 233.

Canace canadensis, var. *franklini* BAIRD, BREWER, and RIDGWAY, Hist. North Amer. Birds, iii, 1874, 419.—BENDIRE, Proc. Boston Soc. Nat. Hist., xix, 1877, 140 (Blue Mountains, near Fort Lapwai, Idaho).

? *Canace canadensis* var. *franklini* NELSON, Proc. Boston Soc. Nat. Hist., xvii, 1875, 364 (Nevada City, Calif.).

Canace canadensis franklini RIDGWAY, Proc. U. S. Nat. Mus., iii, 1880, 196; Nom. North Amer. Birds, 1881, No. 472a.—COUES, Check List North Amer. Birds, ed. 2, 1882, No. 579.

C[*anace*] c[*anadensis*] *franklini* COUES, Key North Amer. Birds, ed. 2, 1884, 579.

Dendragapus franklini RIDGWAY, Proc. U. S. Nat. Mus., viii, 1885, 355.—MERRIAM, North Amer. Fauna, No. 5, 1891, 93 (Sawtooth Mountains, Idaho).—ALLEN, Auk, x, 1893, 126.

Dendragapus franklinii AMERICAN ORNITHOLOGISTS' UNION, Check-list, No. 299, 1886; ed. 2, 1895, No. 299.—RHOADS, Auk, x, 1893, 17 (Washington); Proc. Acad. Nat. Sci. Philadelphia, 1893, 38 (Cascade and Rocky Mountains, British Columbia, s. to Nachess Pass, Wash.).—DAWSON, Wils. Bull., iii, 1896, 3 (Okanogan County, Wash.; descr. nest; measurements of eggs); Auk, xiv, 1897, 173 (Okanogan County, Wash.).—MERRILL, Auk, xiv, 1897, 352 (Fort Sherman, Idaho).

Dendrophagus franklini HALL, Murrelet, xv, 1934, 12 in text (in synonymy).

[*Canachites*] *franklini* SHARPE, Hand-list, i, 1899, 19.

Canachites franklini OGILVIE-GRANT, Cat. Bird Brit. Mus., xxii, 893, 71 (descr.; range).—JUDD, U. S. Biol. Surv. Bull. 24, 1905, 40 (range, food, etc.).—PREBLE, North Amer. Fauna, No. 27, 1908, 339 (about headwaters of the Athabasca River; Banff, Alberta, Henry House; Jasper House).—AMERICAN ORNITHOLOGISTS' UNION, Check-list, ed. 3, 1910, 139; ed. 4, 1931, 80.—SWARTH, Univ. California Publ. Zool., vii, 1911, 58 (Prince of Wales, Warren, and Zarembo Islands, se. Alaska).—RILEY, Can. Alpine Journ., 1912, 55, pls. 1, 2 (Moose River, East Fork Moose River, and 3 miles e. of Moose Lake, British Columbia; crit.; habits).—GRAVE and WALKER, Birds Wyoming, 1913, 89 (Wyoming; one record).—BERGTOLD, Auk, xxxi, 1914, 246 (Palmer Lake, Colo., 1896).—SAUNDERS, Pacific Coast Avif., No. 14, 1921, 57 (Montana; common; habits).— BURLEIGH, Auk, xl, 1923, 656 (Clarks Ford, Idaho; habits).—GABRIELSON, Auk, xli, 1924, 555 (Lick Creek Ranger Station; Memaloose Ranger Station, Wallowa County, Oreg.).—KELSO, Ibis, 1926, 701 (Arrow Lakes, British Columbia; resident).—PALMER, Condor, xxx, 1928, 277.—KEMSIES, Wils. Bull., xlii, 1930, 203 (Yellowstone Park, Wyo.).—BENT, U. S. Nat. Mus. Bull. 162, 1932, 136 (habits; plum.; distr.; etc.).—HALL, Murrelet, xiv, 1933, 69 (Idaho; mountains); xv, 1934, 11 (Athabasca Pass, British Columbia).—TAVERNER, Birds

Canada, 1934, 154, in text (distr.; descr.); Canad. Water Birds, 1939, 166 (field chars.).—ULKE, Can. Alpine Journ., 1934-35 (1936), 79 (Yoho Park, Canada; common).—GABRIELSON and JEWETT, Birds Oregon, 1940, 213 (Oregon; distr.; descr.; habits).

C[anachites] franklini PETRIDES, Trans. 7th North Amer. Wildlife Conf., 1942, 315, in text (age indicators in plumage).

[Canachites] franklini AUSTIN, Mem. Nuttall Orn. Club, No. 7, 1932, 71, in text (distr.).

Canachites franklinii AMERICAN ORTHOLOGISTS' UNION, Auk, xvi, 1899, 107.—GRINNELL, Pacific Coast Avif., No. 1, 1900, 31, in text.—MACOUN, Cat. Can. Birds, 1900, 201 (distr.).—BAILEY, Handb. Birds Western United States, 1902, 126 (descr.; habits; distr.).—BROOKS, Auk, xx, 1903, 281 (Cariboo District, British Columbia; abundant).—EDSON, Auk, xxv, 1908, 438 (Bellingham Bay Region, Wash.; hypothetical).—DAWSON and BOWLES, Birds Washington, ii, 1909, 578 (distr., habits; Washington).—MACOUN and MACOUN, Cat. Can. Birds, ed. 2, 1909, 219 (distr.).—RACEY, Auk, xliii, 1926, 321 (Nita and Alpha Lakes, British Columbia).—PETERS, Check-list Birds of World, ii, 1934, 36 (distr.).—HAND, Condor, xliii, 1941, 225 (St. Joe National Forest, Idaho).—HELLMAYR and CONOVER, Cat. Birds Amer., i, No. 1, 1942, 213 (syn.; distr.).

(?) Tetrao fusca ORD, in Guthrie's Geogr., 2d Amer. ed., ii, 1815, 317 (based on Small Brown Pheasant, Lewis and Clark, ii, 182).

T[ympanuchus] franklini REICHENOW, Die Vögel, i, 1913, 320.

CANACHITES CANADENSIS CANADENSIS (Linnaeus)

HUDSONIAN SPRUCE PARTRIDGE

Adult male.—Similar to that of *Canachites franklinii* but rectrices with broad ochraceous-tawny tips and upper tail coverts without broad white tips (tips usually not more than 4 mm. wide, as opposed to 10 mm.) in *franklinii*, and usually gray, not white, and when white very seldom without a grayish tinge); general color of upper parts variable, terminal margins of the feathers varying from gull gray to grayish drab; the margins of the upper wing coverts from buffy hair brown to Saccardo's umber; sides and flanks likewise varying from buffy hair brown to Saccardo's umber[53]; bill dark gray or blackish; feet dusky; iris brown.

Adult female.—Like that of the same phase of *Canachites franklinii* but without tips to the longer upper tail coverts and with the rectrices tipped with ochraceous-buff.

Immature male.—Similar to the adult but with the juvenal outer primaries.

Immature female.—Similar to the adult of the corresponding phase but with the juvenal outer primaries.

Juvenal (sexes alike).—Like the adult female of the rufous phase but still more rufescent, the crown varying from cinnamon-rufous to

---

[53] The palest bird seen is from Fort Simpson, Mackenzie; the darkest ones are from British Columbia and Labrador. A careful study of these variations, however, bears out Uttal's contention that there is not enough constant geographic variation to warrant the recognition of the supposedly paler Yukon-Mackenzie race named *osgoodi* by Bishop in 1900.

hazel marked with black; the back and upper wing coverts vary from ochraceous-tawny to bright tawny with black bars or blotches, and with wide buffy shaft stripes expanding into whitish wedge-shaped tips; remiges sepia, the primaries narrowly marked with buff; the innermost secondaries and the scapulars irregularly barred and speckled with ochraceous-tawny; rectrices more pointed than in adults and fuscous barred, speckled, and irregularly vermiculated with ochraceous-tawny; abdomen grayish white indistinctly barred or spotted with dusky and sometimes with a faint yellowish wash; chin and throat white with a buffy yellowish wash.

Downy young.—Very similar to that of *Canachites franklinii* but with the upper back more extensively cream buff, the rest of the back between amber brown and antique brown, more or less diluted with buffy.

Adult male.—Wing 165–194 (180.4); tail 108–142 (121.9); exposed culmen 12.3–19 (15.2); tarsus 32.5–38.8 (35.8); middle toe without claw 33–40.1 (36.2 mm.).[54]

Adult female.—Wing 164–191 (177.1); tail 97–116 (106.7); exposed culmen 12.8–18.9 (15.4); tarsus 31.7–37.4 (34.5); middle toe without claw 30.6–36.5 (33.9 mm.).[55]

Range.—Resident chiefly in spruce forests, from the Yukon, Kowak River, and Mount McKinley areas of Alaska (McKinley Park, Nulato River, Kowak River, Happy River, Tanana, Circle, etc.) to Yukon (60° 40′ N); Mackenzie (Mackenzie River, Gros Cape, Fort Simpson, etc.); northern Saskatchewan and Alberta (Smith Landing, Athabasca, etc.); northern Manitoba (Fort Churchill, York Factory); northern Ontario (Fort Severn); northern Quebec (Fort Chimo, Ungava, etc.); and Labrador (Okkak, Paradise River); south to central and to southeastern British Columbia (Atlin, Telegraph Creek, Bennett, Fort Hudson's Hope; Laurier Pass, Cypress Creek, Goat Mountain); central Alberta (Simpson Pass, Blueberry Hills, etc.); northern Ontario; northern Quebec; Ungava; and Labrador to Newfoundland Labrador.

Type locality.—Hudson Bay.

[*Tetrao*] *canadensis* LINNAEUS, Syst. Nat., ed. 10, i, 1758, 159 (Canada; based on *Urogallus maculatus canadensis* Edwards, Av., 118, pl. 118; and *Urogallus minor americanus* Edwards, Av., 71, pl. 71); ed. 12, i, 1766, 274.—GMELIN, Syst. Nat., i, pt. 2, 1788, 749.—LATHAM, Index Orn., ii, 1790, 637.—GRAY, Hand-list, ii, 1870, 276, No. 9825, part.—COUES, Key North Amer. Birds, 1872, 233, part.

Tetrao . . . canadensis FORSTER, Philos. Trans., lxii, 1772, 389 (Severn River).

Tetrao canadensis STEPHENS, *in* Shaw, Gen. Zool., xi, pt. 2, 1819, 275.—VIEILLOT, Nouv. Dict. Hist. Nat., xxxiii, 1819, 457 (cites Pl. Enl., 131, 132).—BONAPARTE, Ann. Lyc. Nat. Hist. New York, ii, pt. i, 1826, 127, part; ii, 1828, 442, part; Contr. Maclurian Lyc., i, 1827, 23; Geogr. and Comp. List, 1838, 44, part.—

---

[54] Seventy-five specimens from Alaska, Mackenzie, British Columbia, Yukon, Alberta, Saskatchewan, Ungava, and Labrador.

[55] Fifty-five specimens from Alaska, Yukon, Mackenzie, British Columbia, Alberta, Saskatchewan, Ungava, and Labrador.

SWAINSON and RICHARDSON, Fauna Bor.-Amer., ii, 1831 (1832), 346, part.—
LESSON, Traité d'Orn., 1831, 501, part.—NUTTALL, Man. Orn. United States
and Canada, Land Birds, 1832, 664, part; ed. 2, 1840, 811, part.—JARDINE, Nat.
Libr., Orn., iv, 1834, 125, part, pl. 15.—AUDUBON, Orn. Biogr., ii, 1834, 437, part,
pl. 176; v, 1839, 563, part; Synopsis, 1839, 203, part; Birds Amer., 8vo ed., v,
1842, part, pl. 294.—REICHENBACH, Synop. Av., iii, Gallinaceae, 1848, pl. 225,
figs. 1883-1885.—BAIRD, Rep. Pacif. R. R. Surv., ix, 1858, 622, part; Cat. North
Amer. Birds, 1859, No. 460, part.—COUES, Proc. Acad. Nat. Sci. Philadelphia,
1861, 226 (Labrador) ; Check List North Amer. Birds, 1874, No. 380, part.—
BLAKISTON, Ibis, 1863, 122 (Fort Carleton; Saskatchewan River; Mackenzie
River).—DALL and BANNISTER, Trans. Chicago Acad. Sci., i, 1869, 287 (Nulato,
Alaska).—STENHOUSE, Scottish Nat., 1930, 77, in text (spec. ex Franklin's
First Exped.).
T[etrao] canadensis DOUGLAS, Trans. Linn. Soc. London, xvi, 1829, 147 (e. base of
Rocky Mountains near source of Athabasca River, lat. 55° ; Lesser Slave Lake;
wood of the Saskatchewan, and streams flowing into Hudson Bay).
Canace canadensis REICHENBACH, Av. Syst. Nat. Vög., 1851, xxix.—ELLIOT, Monogr.
Tetraonidae, 1865, pl. 9 and text, part.—RIDGWAY, Proc. U. S. Nat. Mus., iii,
1880, 9, part, 196, part; Nom. North Amer. Birds, 1881, No. 472, part.—COUES,
Check List North Amer. Birds, ed. 2, 1882, No. 555, part.—McLENEGAN, Cruise
Corwin, 1884, 118 (Kowak River, nw. Alaska).—STEARNS, Bird Life in Labra-
dor, n. d., ca. 1890, 46 (Labrador; habits; distr.).
C[anace] canadensis COUES, Key North Amer. Birds, ed. 2, 1884, 578, part.
Canace canadensis, var. *canadensis* BAIRD, BREWER, and RIDGWAY, Hist. North Amer.
Birds, iii, 1874, 416, part.
Canace canadensis canadensis GOODE, U. S. Nat. Mus. Bull. 20, 1883, 310, part.
Dendragapus canadensis TURNER, Proc. U. S. Nat. Mus., viii, 1885, 245 (Fort
Chimo, Ungava) ; Contr. Nat. Hist. Alaska, 1886, 152 (Yukon Valley).—RIDG-
WAY, Proc. U. S. Nat. Mus., viii, 1885, 355, part.—AMERICAN ORNITHOLOGISTS'
UNION, Check-list, No. 298, part, 1886; ed. 2, 1895, No. 298, part.—TOWNSEND,
Auk, iv, 1887, 12 (Kowak River, nw. Alaska, breeding) ; Cruise *Corwin* in 1885
(1887), 92 (middle Kowak River).—CLARKE, Auk, vii, 1890, 321 (Fort Churchill,
Keewatin).—MACFARLANE, Proc. U. S. Nat. Mus., xiv, 1891, 430 (wooded region
s. of Fort Anderson).—BENDIRE, Life Hist. North Amer. Birds, i, 1892, 51,
part, pl. 1, figs. 20-23.
D[endragapus] canadensis RIDGWAY, Man. North Amer. Birds, 1887, 196, part.
Canachites canadensis OGILVIE-GRANT, Cat. Birds Brit. Mus., xxii, 1893, 69, part
(Nulato and Fort Reliance, Alaska; Mackenzie; Fort Simpson; Jasper House;
Repulse Bay; Fort Chimo and Ungava Forks, Ungava).—AMERICAN ORNI-
THOLOGISTS' UNION, Auk, xvi, 1899, 107, part.—MACOUN, Cat. Can. Birds, 1900,
200, part (distr.).—NORTON, Proc. Portland Soc. Nat. Hist., ii, 1901, 151 (Eskimo
Island and Cul de Sac, Labrador; crit.—PREBLE, North Amer. Fauna, No. 22,
1902, 102 (Mackenzie and Alberta; Oxford House; Hayes River; Hill River;
Echimamish; Severn River; Trout Lake; York Factory; Fort Churchill; Moose
Factory).—JUDD, U. S. Biol. Surv. Bull. 24, 1905, 38-40, part (range, food,
etc.).—MACOUN and MACOUN, Cat. Can. Birds, 2 ed., 1909, 218 (distr.).—
TAVERNER, Birds Western Canada, 1926, 165, pl. 22 A (col. fig.; descr.; distr.;
habits; w. Canada) ; Nat. Mus. Canada, Bull. 50, 1928, 91 (Alberta) ; Birds
Canada, 1934, 153 in text, pl. 18 A (col. fig.; descr.; distr.) ; Canada's Eastern
Arctic, 1934, 120, in text (Hudson Bay, Ungava).—LAING and TAVERNER, Ann.
Rep. Nat. Mus. Canada, for 1927, 1929, 75 (Chitna River, Alaska; spec.).—
TAVERNER and SUTTON, Ann. Carnegie Mus., xxiii, 1934, 30 (Churchill, Mani-
toba; very rare).—BAILLIE and HARRINGTON, Contr. Roy. Ontario Mus. Zool.,

No. 8, 1936, 27, part (extreme northern Ontario).—GROEBBELS, Der Vögel, ii,
1937, 139 in text (courtship), 402 in text (parental care).—LACK, Condor, xlii,
1940, 270 in text, 273 in text (pairing habit).—CLARKE, Nat. Mus. Canada Bull.
96, 1940, 48 (Thelon Game Sanctuary, northwestern Canada).

[*Canachites*] *canadensis* SHARPE, Hand-list, i, 1899, 19, part.

Canachites canadensis canadensis BANGS, Proc. New England Zool. Club., i, 1899,
48.—AMERICAN ORNITHOLOGISTS' UNION, Check-list, ed. 3, 1910, 139, part; ed.
4, 1931, 80 (distr.).—RILEY, Can. Alpine Journ., 1912, 55, pl. 1, fig. 2 (Brulé
Lake and Henry House, Alberta).—FLEMING, Ibis, 1920, 401 (Lake Île-à-la-
Crosse and Cochrane River, Saskatchewan, Manitoba).—TAVERNER, Birds West-
ern Canada, 1926, 165 in text (distr.) ; Birds Canada, 1934, 154 in text (distr.;
Labrador w. to base of Rocky Mountains near Jasper Park).—BENT, U. S.
Nat. Mus. Bull. 162, 1932, 120 (habits; distr.).—AUSTIN, Mem. Nuttall Orn.
Club, No. 7, 1932, 71 (distr.; habits; Newfoundland, Labrador).—PETERS,
Check-list Birds of World, ii, 1934, 36.—GROSS, Auk, liv, 1937, 22 (Labrador,
Assisez Island; Nain, Anaktalak Bay).—COWAN, Occ. Pap. British Columbia
Prov. Mus., No. 1, 1939, 26 (Peace River Distr., Brit. Columbia; habits; young;
food; spec.).—UTTAL, Auk, lvi, 1939, 460 (syn.; range; descr.; spec.; crit.).
—HELLMAYR and CONOVER, Cat. Birds Amer., i, 1942, 211.

Canachites c[*anadensis*] *canadensis* STENHOUSE, Scottish Nat., 1930, 81 (spec. Fort
Franklin, Nov. 1825, in Roy. Scot. Mus.).—GROEBBELS, Der Vögel, ii, 1937, 166
(data on breeding biology).

[*Canachites*] *canadensis canadensis* BAILLIE and HARRINGTON, Contr. Roy. Ontario
Mus. Zool., No. 8, 1936, 27 in text (Ontario; breeds in northern part).

[*Canachites canadensis*] *canadensis* AUSTIN, Mem. Nuttall Orn. Club, No. 7, 1932,
71 in text (distr.).

Canachites canadensis labradorius BANGS, Proc. New England Zool. Club, i, 1899,
47 (Rigoulette, Hamilton Inlet, Labrador; coll. E. A. and O. Bangs. See
Norton, Proc. Portland Soc. Nat. Hist., ii, 1901, 151).—MACOUN, Cat. Can.
Birds, 1900, 200 (Rigoulette, Hamilton Inlet, Labrador).—GRINNELL, Pacific
Coast Avif. No. 1, 1900, 30, 75 (Kowak Valley, Alaska; habits).—HANTZSCH,
Journ. für Orn., 1908, 364 (ne. Labrador) ; Can. Field Nat., xlii, 1928, 12 (ne.
Labrador).—BANGS, Bull. Mus. Comp. Zool., lxx, 1930, 155 (type in Mus.
Comp. Zool.; not a valid race).—UTTAL, Auk, lvi, 1939, 461 in text (crit.).

Canachites canadensis osgoodi BISHOP, Auk, xvii, 1900, 114 (Lake Marsh, Yukon
Territory; coll. L. B. Bishop) ; North Amer. Fauna, No. 19, 1900, 71 part (Lake
Marsh, Lake Labarge, Rampart City, Tatchun River, Kuskokwim River, Thirty
Mile River).—MACOUN and MACOUN, Cat. Can. Birds, ed. 2, 1909, 218 (Yukon,
Alaska; localities).—OSGOOD, North Amer. Fauna, No. 30, 1909, 36 (Mission
Creek, 10 miles w. of Circle, Alaska) ; 86 (Macmillan River, Yukon).—AMERI-
CAN ORNITHOLOGISTS' UNION, Check-list, ed. 3, 1910, 139; ed. 4, 1931, 80.—GRIN-
NELL, Univ. California Publ. Zool., v, 1910, 380, in text.—DICE, Condor, xxii,
1920, 178 (Fairbanks, Tanana, Takotna, Akiak, etc., Alaska; resident).—
SWARTH, Univ. California Publ. Zool., xxiv, 1922, 205 (Glenora, Stikine region,
s. Alaska; crit.) ; xxx, 1926, 84 (Atlin region, British Columbia; crit.).—BAILEY,
Condor, xxviii, 1926, 121 (Kotzebue, Kobuk, and Noatak Rivers, Alaska).—
TAVERNER, Birds Western Canada, 1926, 165 in text (distr.) ; Birds Canada,
1934, 154 in text (central Alaska, the Yukon, northern British Columbia, and
Mackenzie Valley).—BENT, U. S. Nat. Mus. Bull. 162, 1932, 129 (habits; etc.).—
PETERS, Check-list Birds of World, ii, 1934, 36.—HELLMAYR and CONOVER, Cat.
Birds Amer., i, No. 1, 1942, 212, part (syn.; distr.).

C[*anachites*] c[*anadensis*] *osgoodi* UTTAL, Auk, lvi, 1939, 461 in text (crit.; not
valid form).

[*Canachites canadensis*] *osgoodi* AUSTIN, Mem. Nuttall Orn. Club, No. 7, 1932, 72 in text (distr.).

T[*ympanuchus*] *canadensis* REICHENOW, Die Vögel, i, 1913, 320.

CANACHITES CANADENSIS CANACE (Linnaeus)

CANADIAN SPRUCE PARTRIDGE

Adult male.—Indistinguishable from that of the nominate race.

Adult female (gray phase).—Like that of the nominate race but more brownish, the dorsal brown markings light ochraceous-buff, as are also those of the breast, sides, and flanks; upper wing coverts darker, with their edges more tawny-buff, less hair brown.

Adult female (rufous phase).—Not distinguishable with certainty from that of the nominate race, but usually with the light markings on the upper wing coverts and inner remiges brighter—antique brown to tawny (as against pale grayish clay color in the nominate race).

Immature male.—Indistinguishable from that of the nominate race.

Immature female.—Not distinguishable with certainty from that of the nominate form.

Juvenal.—Not certainly distinguishable from that of the typical race.

Downy young.—Like that of the typical race.

Adult male.—Wing 166–183 (174.1); tail 107–130 (120.7); exposed culmen 13.6–18.4 (15.7); tarsus 33.7–37.2 (35.2); middle toe without claw 35.7–39.4 (37 mm.).[56]

Adult female.—Wing 163–176 (172.1); tail 96–111 (103); exposed culmen 14.2–18.6 (15.5); tarsus 33–34.2 (33.9); middle toe without claw 32.8–36 (34.6 mm.).[57]

Range.—Resident from southern Manitoba; northwestern Minnesota; southern Ontario (Port Arthur); southern Quebec (Charlevoix, Kamarooska, Saguenay, and western Gaspé Counties); south locally in Minnesota (from eastern Marshall County to Lake Superior; formerly to Wadena and Mille Lacs Counties); northern Wisconsin (where only casual); Michigan (south to Ogemaw County); northern New York (Adirondacks, now largely extirpated); northern New Hampshire (northern Coos County; White Mountains, south to Mount Passaconaway); extreme northern Vermont and northern Maine, except the extreme eastern part adjacent to New Brunswick.

Accidental in Massachusetts (Gloucester and Roxbury).

Type locality.—Canada; restricted to City of Quebec (Uttal, Auk, lvi, 1939, 462).

[*Tetrao*] *canace* LINNAEUS, Syst. Nat., ed. 12, i, 1766, 275 (Canada; based on *Bonasia canadensis* Brisson, Orn., i, 203, pl. 20, figs. 1, 2).—GMELIN, Syst. Nat., i, pt. 2, 1788, 749).

---

[56] Thirteen specimens from Michigan, Quebec, and Maine.

[57] Eleven specimens from Michigan and Quebec.

Canachites canadensis canace NORTON, Proc. Portland Soc. Nat. Hist., ii, 1901, 151, 152, in text.—ALLEN, Proc. Manchester Inst. Sci. and Arts, iv, 1902, 92 (New Hampshire, resident in Canadian Zone).—KUMLIEN and HOLLISTER, Bull. Wisconsin Nat. Hist. Soc., iii, 1903, 56 (Wisconsin; habits).—TOWNSEND, Mem. Nuttall Orn. Club, No. 3, 1905, 201 (Essex County, Mass.; accidental).—HALL, Wils. Bull., xviii, 1906, 124 (w. Adirondacks, New York).—KNIGHT, Birds Maine, 1908, 198 (n. and e. Maine).—MACOUN and MACOUN, Cat. Can. Birds, ed. 2, 1909, 219, part (n. Minnesota, n. New England).—CORY, Publ. Field Mus. Nat. Hist., No. 131, 1909, 435 (Wisconsin).—AMERICAN ORNITHOLOGISTS' UNION, Check-list, ed. 3, 1910, 139, part; ed. 4, 1931, 80, part (distr.).—EATON, Birds New York, i, 1910, 365, pl. 41 (Adirondacks).—BARROWS, Michigan Bird Life, 1912, 221.—FORBUSH, Game Birds, Wild-fowl, and Shore Birds, 1912, 375 (history).—MOUSLEY, Auk, xxxiii, 1916, 66 (Hatley, Quebec; rare).—WOOD, Occ. Pap. Mus. Zool. Univ. Michigan, No. 50, 1918, 6 (Alger County, Mich., rare).—TOWNSEND, Mem. Nuttall Orn. Club, No. 5, 1920, 96 (Essex County, Mass.).—JOHNSON, Auk, xxxvii, 1920, 544 (Lake County, Minn., breeding).—JACKSON, Auk, xl, 1923, 481 (Mamie Lake, etc., n. Wisconsin).—SOPER, Auk, xi, 1923, 497 (Wellington and Waterloo Counties, Ontario).—CHRISTY, Wils. Bull., xxxvii, 1925, 210 (Huron Mountain, Mich., hypothetical).—TAVERNER, Birds Western Canada, 1926, 165 in text (distr.) ; Birds Canada, 1934, 154, part (Manitoba n. to head of big lakes, s. Ontario, etc.).—FORBUSH, Birds Massachusetts and Other New England States, ii, 1927, 23, pl. 34 (fig.; descr.; habits; distr. in New England).—CAHN, Wils. Bull., xxxix, 1927, 27 (summer, Vilas County, Wisconsin).—SNYDER, Trans. Roy. Can. Inst., xvi, 1928, 258 (Lake Nipigon region, Ontario).—BENT, U. S. Nat. Mus. Bull. 162, 1932, 131, part (habits; distr.; etc.).—ROBERTS, Birds Minnesota, i, 1932, 367, pl. 20, 24, part (col. fig.; descr.; distr.; habits in Minnesota).—PETERS, Check-list Birds of World, ii, 1934, 36.—OLSEN, Auk, lii, 1935, 100 (Michigan, 5 seen Superior State Forest, Luce County, Aug. 31, 1934).—GROEBBELS, Der Vögel, ii, 1937, 137 in text (display of male).—BEEBE, Wils. Bull., xlix, 1937, 34 (Upper Peninsula of Michigan; formerly common).—VAN TYNE, Occ. Pap. Mus. Zool. Univ. Michigan, No. 379, 1938, 11 (Michigan; local; breeds).—UTTAL, Auk, lvi, 1939, 462 (crit.; distr.; descr.; type loc. designated as Quebec).—DEAR, Trans. Roy. Can. Inst., xxiii, 1940, 126 (Thunder Bay, Lake Superior, Ontario; very local permanent resident; never plentiful).—HELLMAYR and CONOVER, Cat. Birds Amer., i, No. 1, 1942, 211 (syn.; distr.).

[*Canachites*] *canadensis canace* BAILLIE and HARRINGTON, Contr. Roy. Ontario Mus. Zool., No. 8, 1936, 27, in text (Ontario; breeds in southern and central parts).

C[*anachites*] c[*anadensis*] *canace* UTTAL, Auk, lvi, 1939, 461 in text (crit.) ; lix, 1942, 432, in text (Somerset County, Maine).

[*Canachites canadensis*] *canace* AUSTIN, Mem. Nuttall Orn. Club, No. 7, 1932, 71 in text (distr.).

Tetrao canadensis (not of Linnaeus) BONAPARTE, Ann. Lyc. Nat. Hist. New York, ii, pt. 1, 1826, 127, part; ii, 1828, 442, part; Geogr. and Comp. List, 1838, 44, part.—LESSON, Traité d'Orn., 1831, 501, part.—NUTTALL, Man. Orn. United States and Canada, Land Birds, 1832, 667, part; ed. 2, 1840, 811, part.—AUDUBON, Orn. Biogr., ii, 1834, 437, part, pl. 176; v, 1839, 563, part; Synopsis, 1839, 203, part; Birds Amer., 8vo ed., v, 1842, 83, part, pl. 294.—BARRY, Proc. Boston Soc. Nat. Hist., vol. 5, 1854, 9 (Wisconsin; extreme northern part).—PUTNAM, Proc. Essex Inst., i, 1856, 224 (Gloucester, Mass.).—KNEELAND, Proc. Boston Soc. Nat. Hist., vi, 1857, 237 (Keweenaw Point, Lake Superior).—BAIRD, Rep. Pacif. R. R. Surv., ix, 1858, 622, part (n. United States; Selkirk Settlement, Manitoba) ; Cat. North Amer. Birds, 1859, No. 460, part.—VERRILL, Proc. Essex

Inst., iii, 1862, 152 (Maine; Oxford County; rare; near Lake Umbagog, common).—Coues, Proc. Essex Inst., v, 1868, 39 (n. New England; spec.) ; Check List North Amer. Birds, 1874, No. 380, part.—Maynard, Proc. Boston Soc. Nat. Hist., xiv, 1872, 383 (White Mountains, New Hampshire).—Merriam, Bull. Nuttall Orn. Club, iii, 1878, 53 (Adirondack Mountains, N. Y., breeding).—Allen, Bull. Essex Inst., x, 1878, 22 (Massachusetts; accidental).—Brewster, Bull. Nuttall Orn. Club, iv, 1879, 43 (descr. young and chick).—Gibbs, U. S. Geol. and Geogr. Surv. Terr., Bull. 5, 1879, 491 (Michigan; common near Mackinaw).

T[etrao] canadensis Trippe, Comm. Essex Inst., vi, 1871, 118 (Minnesota; abundant; breeds).

[Tetrao] canadensis Gray, Hand-list, ii, 1870, 276, No. 9825, part.—Coues, Key North Amer. Birds, 1872, 233, part.

Canace canadensis Elliot, Monogr. Tetraonidae, 1869, pl. 9 and text, part.—Baird, Brewer, and Ridgway, Hist. North Amer. Birds, iii, 1874, pl. 61, fig. 5 (Maine).—Brewer, Proc. Boston Soc. Nat. Hist., xvii, 1875, 12 (New England).—Ridgway, Proc. U. S. Nat. Mus., iii, 1880, 9, 196, part; Nom. North Amer. Birds, 1881, No. 472, part.—Merriam, Bull. Nuttall Orn. Club, vi, 1881, 233 (Lewis County, N. Y., resident).—Coues, Check List North Amer. Birds, ed. 2, 1882, No. 555, part.

C[anace] canadensis Coues, Key North Amer. Birds, ed. 2, 1884, 578, part.

Canace canadensis, var. canadensis Baird, Brewer, and Ridgway, Hist. North Amer. Birds, iii, 1874, 416, part.

Dendragapus canadensis Ridgway, Proc. U. S. Nat. Mus., viii, 1885, 355, part.—American Ornithologists' Union, Check-list, No. 298, part, 1886; ed. 2, 1895, No. 298, part.—Ralph and Bagg, Trans. Oneida Hist. Soc., iii, 1886, 116 (Greig, Lewis County, N. Y.).—Chadbourne, Auk, iv, 1887, 103 (White Mountains, N. H., at 3,500 feet).—Cooke, Bird Migr. Mississippi Valley, 1888, 103 (Minnesota, from Minneapolis north, and at White Earth; Racine, Wis.).—Thompson, Proc. U. S. Nat. Mus., xiii, 1891, 507 (n. and e. Manitoba, resident).—Hatch, Notes Birds Minnesota, 1892, 158, 455 (Minnesota; distr.; habits).—Nutting, Bull. Iowa State Lab. Nat. Hist., ii, 1893, 265 (Lower Saskatchewan River; spec.; plum.).—Roberts, in Wilcox, Hist. Becker County, Minn., 1907, 170 (coniferous forests).

Dendragopus canadensis Seton, Auk, iii, 1886, 153 (n. of Fort Pelly and about Lake Winnipeg, Manitoba, abundant).

D[endragapus] canadensis Ridgway, Man. North Amer. Birds, 1887, 196, part.

Canachites canadensis Ogilvie-Grant, Cat. Birds Brit. Mus., xxii, 1893, 69, part (St. Croix River and Lake Sebowis, Maine; Lake Terror and Watson, N. Y.).—American Ornithologists' Union, Auk, xvi, 1899, 107, part.—Nash, Check List Birds Ontario, 1900, 26 (Ontario; common) ; Check List Vert. Ontario, Birds, 1905, 35 (Ontario).—Judd, U. S. Biol. Surv. Bull. 24, 1905, 38–40, part (range, food, etc.).—Wood (W.C.), Wils. Bull., xix, 1907, 27 (mainland off Marquette Island, Mich.).—Mitchell, Can. Field Nat., xxxviii, 1924, 108 (Saskatchewan; common).—Taverner, Birds Canada, 1934, 153 in text, pl. 18a, part (col. fig.; descr.; distr.) ; Can. Water Birds, 1939, 167.—Baillie and Harrington, Contr. Roy. Ontario Mus. Zool., No. 8, 1936, 27, part (central and southern Ontario; breeds).—Shortt and Waller, Contr. Roy. Ontario Mus. Zool., No. 10, 1937, 17 (Lake St. Martin region, Manitoba; not uncommon; spec.).—Snyder, Trans. Roy. Can. Inst., xxii, 1938, 185 (Western Rainy River Distr., Ontario).—Ricker and Clarke, Contr. Roy. Ontario Mus. Zool. No. 16, 1939, 8 (Lake Nipissing, Ontario).—Petrides,

Trans. 7th North Amer. Wildlife Conf., 1942, 315, in text (age indicators in plum.).

[*Canachites*] *canadensis* SHARPE, Hand-list, i, 1899, 19, part.

Canachites canadensis subsp. ? MACLULICH, Contr. Roy. Ontario Mus. Zool., No. 13, 1938, 11 (Algonquin Prov. Park, Ontario; permanent resident; breeds in small numbers; records; spec.).

CANACHITES CANADENSIS ATRATUS J. Grinnell

VALDEZ SPRUCE PARTRIDGE

Adult male.—Very similar to that of the nominate race, but with the edges of the feathers of the lower back, rump, and upper tail coverts usually lightly tinged with olivaceous.

Adult female.—Like that of the nominate race, but with the pale tips of the dorsal feathers suffused with pale olive-brown, giving the upper parts generally a brownish-gray appearance (barred with fuscous-black) as compared with the predominantly grayish and blackish of the typical form.

Immature male.—Indistinguishable from that of the nominate race.

Immature female.—Indistinguishable from that of the nominate race.

Juvenal (sexes alike).—Indistinguishable from that of the nominate race.

Downy young.—None seen; probably indistinguishable from that of the nominate race.

Adult male.—Wing 176–189 (181.4); tail 111–125 (120.4); exposed culmen 14.1–19.1 (16.1); tarsus 33.7–38.8 (36.7); middle toe without claw 36.4–40.1 (37.7 mm.).[58]

Adult female.—Wing 173–184 (178.6); tail 102–111 (106); exposed culmen 14.3–17.1 (15.8); tarsus 33.7–36.6 (35.1); middle toe without claw 32.8–36.8 (35.5 mm.).[59]

Range.—Resident in the coast region of southern Alaska from Bristol Bay to Cook Inlet, Kodiak Island, and Prince William Sound.

Type locality.—Cedar Bay, Hawkins Island, Prince William Sound, Alaska.

Tetrao canadensis LESSON, Traité d'Orn., 1831, 501, part.—SWAINSON and RICHARDSON, Fauna Bor.-Amer., ii, 1831 (1832), 346, part.—NUTTALL, Man. Orn. United States and Canada, Land Birds, 1832, 664, part; ed. 2, 1840, 811, part.—AUDUBON, Orn. Biogr., ii, 1834, 437, part; v, 1839, 563, part; Synopsis, 1839, 203, part; Birds Amer., 8vo. ed., v, 1842, 83, part.—BAIRD, Cat. North Amer. Birds, 1859, No. 460, part.

[*Tetrao*] *canadensis* GRAY, Hand-list, ii, 1870, 276, No. 9825, part.—COUES, Key North Amer. Birds, 1872, 233, part.

(?) *Tetrao canadensis* (not of Linnaeus) HARTLAUB, Journ. für Orn., 1883, 276, Portage Bay and Chilkat, Alaska).

---

[58] Twelve specimens from Alaska.

[59] Eight specimens from Alaska.

Canace canadensis ELLIOT, Monogr. Tetraonidae, 1865, pl. 9 and text, part.—RIDG-
WAY, Proc. U. S. Nat. Mus., iii, 1880, 9, part, 196, part; Nom. North Amer.
Birds, 1881, No. 472, part.—COUES, Check List North Amer. Birds, ed. 2, 1882,
No. 555, part.

C[anace] canadensis COUES, Key North Amer. Birds, ed. 2, 1884, 578, part.

Canace canadensis var. *canadensis* BAIRD, BREWER, and RIDGWAY, Hist. North Amer.
Birds, iii, 1874, 416, part.

Canace canadensis canadensis GOODE, U. S. Nat. Mus. Bull. 20, 1883, 310, part.

Dendragapus canadensis RIDGWAY, Proc. U. S. Nat. Mus., viii, 1885, 355, part.—
AMERICAN ORNITHOLOGISTS' UNION, Check-list, 1886, No. 298, part; ed. 2,
1895, No. 298, part.—BENDIRE, Life Hist. North Amer. Birds, i, 1892, 51, part.

D[endragapus] canadensis RIDGWAY, Man. North Amer. Birds, 1887, 196, part.

Canachites canadensis OGILVIE-GRANT, Cat. Birds Brit. Mus., xxii, 1893, 69, part.—
AMERICAN ORNITHOLOGISTS' UNION, Auk, xvi, 1899, 107, part.—JUDD, U. S.
Biol. Surv. Bull. 24, 1905, 38–40, part (range, food, etc.).

[Canachites] canadensis SHARPE, Hand-list, i, 1899, 19, part.

Canachites canadensis canadensis AMERICAN ORNITHOLOGISTS' UNION, Check-list
North Amer. Birds, ed. 3, 1910, 139, part (Alaska from Bristol Bay to Cook
Inlet and Prince William Sound).

Canachites canadensis osgoodi BISHOP, North Amer. Fauna, No. 19, 1900, 71,
part (Bennett City, Caribou Crossing (?)).—CHAPMAN, Bull. Amer. Mus.
Nat. Hist., xvi, 1902, 238 (Homer, Sheep Creek, and Kenai Mountains, Alaska;
habits) ; xx, 1904, 401 (Seldovia, Bird Island, Sheep Creek, and Barbovi, Kenai
Peninsula).—OSGOOD, North Amer. Fauna, No. 24, 1904, 64 (near Iliamna
Village, etc., Alaska Peninsula; habits; range).—HELLMAYR and CONOVER, Cat.
Birds Amer., i, No. 1, 1942, 212, part.

Canachites canadensis atratus GRINNELL (J.), Univ. California Stud. Zool., v, No.
12, 1910, 380 (Hawkins Island, Prince William Sound, Alaska; coll. Mus.
California Acad. Sci.).—AMERICAN ORNITHOLOGISTS' UNION, Auk, xxix, 1912,
385.—SWARTH, Univ. California Publ. Zool., xxiv, 1922, 205 (Flood Glacier,
Stikine region, s. Alaska; crit.).—OBERHOLSER, Auk, xl, 1923, 679.—AMERICAN
ORNITHOLOGISTS' UNION, Check-list, ed. 4, 1931, 80 (distr.).—BENT, U. S. Nat.
Mus. Bull. 162, 1932, 135 (habits, distr., etc.).—PETERS, Check-list Birds World,
ii, 1934, 36.—FRIEDMANN, Bull. Chicago Acad. Sci., v, 1935, 31 (Kodiak
Island).—UTTAL, Auk, lvi, 1939, 461 (crit.; range; descr.).

[Canachites canadensis] atratus AUSTIN, Mem. Nuttall Orn. Club, No. 7, 1932, 72
in text (distr.).

CANACHITES CANADENSIS TORRIDUS Uttal

NOVA SCOTIAN SPRUCE PARTRIDGE

Adult male.—Very similar to that of the nominate race but said to
have the plumage more suffused with brown, especially the upper wing
coverts, upper dorsals, scapulars, and flank feathers.[60]

Adult female.—Similar to that of *Canachites canadensis canace,* but
the brown markings more intense, the rufous phase much more reddish
tawny than in *canace,* the gray phase only slightly more so than in the
corresponding stage of *canace.*

---

[60] The material examined in the present work does not bear this out. Birds from
the Bay of Fundy and Kejimkujik, Nova Scotia, are not separable from typical
canadensis or *canace.*

Immature male.—Like the adult but with juvenal outer primaries.

Immature female.—Like the adult but with juvenal outer primaries.

Juvenal (sexes alike).—Not certainly distinguishable from that of the nominate race.

Downy young.—Like that of the nominate race but slightly duller, more grayish below, and with the sides of the head faintly washed with ochraceous-buff.

Adult male.—Wing 161–166; tail 116–120; exposed culmen 14–16; tarsus 34.2–37.3; middle toe without claw 36.7–37.8.[61]

Adult female.—Wing 159–165 (162.3); tail 97–103 (100.7); exposed culmen 13.8–17 (15.8); tarsus 34.8–35.9 (35.3); middle toe without claw 34–36.5 (35.5 mm.).[62]

Range.—Resident in spruce forests in the Gaspé Peninsula, New Brunswick, Nova Scotia, and northeastern Maine (Calais, Washington County, St. Croix River).

Type locality.—Kejimkujik Lake, on the boundary between Annapolis and Queens Counties, Nova Scotia.

Tetrao canadensis (not of Linnaeus) BONAPARTE, Ann. Lyc. Nat. Hist. New York, ii, pt. 1, 1826, 127, part; ii, 1828, 442, part; Geogr. and Comp. List, 1838, 44, part.—LESSON, Traité d'Orn., 1831, 501, part.—NUTTALL, Man. Orn. United States and Canada, Land Birds, 1832, 667, part; ed. 2, 1840, 811, part.— AUDUBON, Orn. Biogr., ii, 1834, 437, part; v, 1839, 563, part; Synopsis, 1839, 203, part; Birds Amer., 8vo ed., v, 1842, 83, part.—BAIRD, Rep. Pacif. R. R. Surv., ix, 1858, 622, part (Nova Scotia); Cat. North Amer. Birds, 1859, No. 460, part.—COUES, Check List North Amer. Birds, 1874, No. 380, part.

[*Tetrao*] *canadensis* GRAY, Hand-list, ii, 1870, 276, No. 9825, part.—COUES, Key North Amer. Birds, 1872, 233, part.

Canace canadensis ELLIOT, Monogr. Tetraonidae, 1869, pl. 9 and text, part.— BAIRD, BREWER, and RIDGWAY, Hist. North Amer. Birds, iii, 1874, pl. 59, figs. 5, 6 (Nova Scotia).—RIDGWAY, Proc. U. S. Nat. Mus., iii, 1880, 196, part; Nom. North Amer. Birds, 1881, No. 472, part.—COUES, Check List North Amer. Birds, ed. 2, 1882, No. 555, part.

C[anace] canadensis COUES, Key North Amer. Birds, ed. 2, 1884, 578, part.

Canace canadensis var. *canadensis* BAIRD, BREWER, and RIDGWAY, Hist. North Amer. Birds, iii, 1874, 416, part.

Dendragapus canadensis RIDGWAY, Proc. U. S. Nat. Mus., viii, 1885, 355, part.— AMERICAN ORNITHOLOGISTS' UNION, Check-list, No. 298, part, 1886; ed. 2, 1895, No. 298, part.

D[endragapus] canadensis RIDGWAY, Man. North Amer. Birds, 1887, 196, part.

Canachites canadensis OGILVIE-GRANT, Cat. Birds Brit. Mus., xxii, 1893, 69, part (Musquash, New Brunswick; Bay of Fundy, Nova Scotia).—AMERICAN ORNITHOLOGISTS' UNION, Auk, xvi, 1899, 107, part.—MACOUN, Cat. Can. Birds, 1900, 200, part (Nova Scotia; New Brunswick).—JUDD, U. S. Biol. Surv. Bull. 24, 1905, 38–40, part (range, food, etc.).—MACOUN and MACOUN, Cat. Can. Birds, ed. 2, 1909, 218 part (Nova Scotia; New Brunswick).—TAVERNER, Birds Canada, 1934, 153 in text, part.

---

[61] Two specimens from Nova Scotia and New Brunswick.

[62] Three specimens from Nova Scotia and New Brunswick.

[*Canachites*] *canadensis* SHARPE, Hand-list, i, 1899, 19, part.

Canachites canadensis canace MACOUN and MACOUN, Cat. Can. Birds, ed. 2, 1909, 219, part (New Brunswick).—AMERICAN ORNITHOLOGISTS' UNION, Check-list, ed. 3, 1910, 139, part; ed. 4, 1931, 80, part.—PHILIPP and BOWDISH, Auk, xxxvi, 1919, 34 (Northumberland County, New Brunswick).—DE MILLE, Auk, xliii, 1926, 516 (near Mont Luis Lake, Gaspé County, Quebec).—FORBUSH, Birds Massachusetts and Other New England States, ii, 1927, 23, part.—BENT, U. S. Nat. Mus. Bull. 162, 1932, 131, part.—ROBERTS, Birds Minnesota, i, 1932, 367, part (Nova Scotia; New Brunswick).—TAVERNER, Birds Canada, 1934, 154, part.—PETERS, Check-list Birds of World, ii, 1934, 36, part (New Brunswick; Nova Scotia).—HELLMAYR and CONOVER, Cat. Birds Amer., i, No. 1, 1942, 211, part (Nova Scotia; New Brunswick).

[*Canachites canadensis*] *canace* TOWNSEND, Auk, xl, 1923, 87, footnote (Gaspé Peninsula).

Canachites canadensis torridus UTTAL, Auk, lvi, 1939, 462 (Kejimkujik Lake, Nova Scotia; descr.; distr.; crit.).; lix, 1942, 432, in text (Penobscot County, Maine).

Genus BONASA Stephens

Bonasa STEPHENS, *in* Shaw, Gen. Zool., xi, pt. 2, 1819, 298. (Type, as designated by Gray, List Genera Birds, 1840, 62, *Tetrao umbellus* Linnaeus.)

Bonasia BONAPARTE, Ann. Lyc. Nat. Hist. New York, ii, 1826, 126. (Type, by monotypy, *Tetrao umbellus* Linnaeus.)

Hylobrontes STONE, Auk, xxiv, 1907, 198. (Type, by original designation and monotypy, *Tetrao umbellus* Linnaeus.) (New name to replace *Bonasa* Stephens, thought to be transferable to *Tetrao cupido* Linnaeus under the "first species" rule.)

Medium-sized wood grouse (length about 394–482 mm.) with lower half (more or less) of tarsus nude and scutellate; tail nearly if not quite as long as wing, fan-shaped, with 18–20 rectrices, three relatively broad, with broadly rounded or subtruncate tips; sides of neck without inflatable air sacs, but with a conspicuous erectile tuft of large, broad, slightly rounded or nearly truncate soft, decumbent feathers (less developed in females).

Bill relatively small, its length from nostril about one-third the length of head, its depth at frontal antiae about equal to its width at same point, the culmen slightly ridged, the rhamphotheca smooth throughout, the maxillary tomium regularly and rather deeply concave. Wing moderate in size, deeply concave beneath, the longest primaries exceeding longest secondaries by about one-third the length of wing; third or third and fourth primaries longest, the first (outermost) intermediate between seventh and eighth. Tail nearly as long as wing, slightly to distinctly rounded, the rectrices (18–20) becoming gradually broader distally, their tips broadly rounded or subtruncate. Tarsus less than one-fourth as long as wing, its upper half (more or less) densely clothed with rather long, hairlike but soft feathers (much shorter in summer), the lower portion nude and scutellate, the acrotarsium with two rows of rather large scutella, the planta tarsi with small hexagonal scales; middle toe decidedly shorter than tarsus, the inner toe reaching to penultimate articulation of middle

toe, the outer toe slightly longer, hallux about as long as basal phalanx
of lateral toe or very slightly shorter; top of toes with a continuous row
of rather large transverse scutella, with a row of much smaller subquadrate scutella along each side, outside of which are horny pectinations or
fringelike processes (these less distinct in summer); claws moderate
in size and curvature, rather blunt, that of hallux smaller.

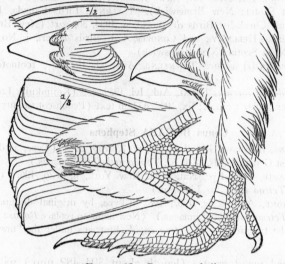

FIGURE 10.—*Bonasa umbellus.*

Plumage and coloration.—Plumage in general soft, the remiges, especially the primaries, firm, almost rigid; feathers rather distinctly outlined, except on lower abdomen, anal region, and thighs, where soft,
downy, and blended, those of sides and flanks large and very broad; a
naked space immediately above eye (most developed as brightly colored—
orange or red—in males during summer); feathers of crown distinctly
elongated, forming, when erected, a rather conspicuous crest; on each
side of neck a conspicuous erectile tuft of large, very broad, soft, nearly
truncate, decumbent feathers. Upperparts variegated with black, buff
and different tones of brown and rusty or gray, the tail, scapulars, and
wing coverts streaked with buff or whitish, the rump with rather small
cordate or ovate spots of pale grayish or dull buffy; tail gray or rusty,
with numerous irregular or zigzag narrow bars of blackish and with a
broad subterminal band of blackish or dark brown; neck tufts black, dark
brown, or chestnut, each feather with a glossy or semimetallic terminal
margin or bar; throat buffy or ochraceous, sometimes with dusky markings; rest of underparts buff or whitish, more or less broken by broad
bars of brownish, these much broader and darker on flanks.

Range.—Wooded portions of North America, except in Lower Austral
Life Zone. (Monotypic.)

KEY TO THE FORMS OF BONASA UMBELLUS (LINNAEUS)

a. General coloration more brownish than grayish.
  b. Dark-brown ventral barring pronounced.
    c. General coloration very dark (chestnut to dark auburn).
      d. General coloration distinctly brownish with little or no grayish cast.
        e. Very reddish, back bright argus brown to dark chestnut, tail auburn
          to bay (Olympic Peninsula).....**Bonasa umbellus castanea** (p. 169)
        ee. Duller and less reddish, back between Prout's brown and Dresden
          brown; tail dull ochraceous-umber (brown phase) (Vancouver Island).
          Bonasa umbellus brunnescens (p. 170)
      dd. General coloration with more grayish or dusky appearance; tail argus
        brown to cinnamon-brown (w. slopes of Rocky Mountains, Idaho, to
        ne. Washington).....**Bonasa umbellus phaia** (brown phase) (p. 178)
    cc. General coloration lighter (sayal brown to argus brown).
      d. Distinctly brownish with little or no grayish cast.
        e. Ventral barring darker—cinnamon-brown to dark mummy brown (sw.
          British Columbia to nw. California) **Bonasa umbellus sabini** (p. 166)
        ee. Ventral barring lighter—dusky isabelline to buckthorn brown (Appala-
          chian Mountains from ne. Pennsylvania to Georgia).
          Bonasa umbellus monticola (p. 163)
      dd. Browns mixed with some gray.
        e. Blackish areas of upperparts more pronounced; brown parts darker and
          less rufescent—cinnamon-brown to dark Prout's brown (n. New
          England, Nova Scotia, w. to s. Ontario).
          Bonasa umbellus togata (p. 171)
        ee. Blackish areas of upperparts less well developed, brown areas paler
          and more rufescent—Mikado brown to snuff brown (nc. British
          Columbia s. to ne. Oregon).
          Bonasa umbellus affinis (brown phase) (p. 175)
  bb. Light brown, barring less pronounced.
    c. General coloration darker, head and neck with little if any grayish suf-
      fusion, tail (brown phase) nearly hazel (s. New England, e. New York,
      s. to District of Columbia).........**Bonasa umbellus umbellus** (p. 156)
    cc. General coloration paler, head and neck with pale grayish suffusion, tail
      (brown phase) nearly ochraceous-tawny (sw. Michigan s. to c. Arkansas).
      Bonasa umbellus mediana (p. 161)
aa. General coloration more grayish than brownish.
  b. Definitely gray, with little or no brownish wash.
    c. Very pale (smoke gray to pale neutral gray).
      d. Tarsus unfeathered[63] for one-quarter its length or less; more white in
        upperparts (w. Alaska to n. Alberta).
        Bonasa umbellus yukonensis (p. 182)
      dd. Tarsus unfeathered[63] for not less than half its length; less white in
        upperparts (c. Utah, se. Idaho, to ne. North Dakota).
        Bonasa umbellus incana (p. 179)
    cc. Darker (mouse gray to light grayish olive) (w. slope of Rocky Mountains,
      Idaho, to ne. Washington)..**Bonasa umbellus phaia** (gray phase) (p. 178)
  bb. Gray mixed with considerable brown.
    c. Tarsus unfeathered for more than half its length (nc. British Columbia
      to ne. Oregon)..........**Bonasa umbellus affinis** (gray phase) (p. 175)

---

[63] Point of insertion of feathers on outside of tarsus to junction of tarsus with
middle toe is measurement for unfeathered tarsus.

cc. Tarsus unfeathered for less than half its length (nw. British Columbia e. across Canada to s. Hudson Bay and Gulf of St. Lawrence).

Bonasa umbellus umbelloides (p. 184)

BONASA UMBELLUS UMBELLUS (Linnaeus)

EASTERN RUFFED GROUSE

Adult male (brown phase).—Feathers of the forehead, crown, and occiput sayal brown to cinnamon-brown, barred with blackish, and tipped with smoke gray to pale smoke gray; the elongated crest feathers with the blackish extended toward the base on the outer edges of both webs, leaving the brown as a broad basal shaft stripe with lateral branches, the blackish marks very narrowly edged on their distal margins with cinnamon-brown; nape sayal brown to cinnamon-brown tipped with smoke gray; interscapulars similarly brownish, but with the smoke gray confined to the distal portion of the shaft and a large terminal shaft spot, the remaining part of the feathers irregularly crossed by blackish marks which fail to connect toward the shaft; the outermost of these marks often very broad (8–10 mm.); neck ruffs either deep black with a slight bluish purplish sheen, dark fuscous-black with blue-black tips to the feathers, or bright auburn with narrow fuscous tips to the feathers; upper back, lower back, and rump cinnamon-brown to dark Brussels brown, the feathers of the upper back with cordate terminal shaft spots of tilleul buff to vinaceous-buff narrowly edged with black and occasionally sparsely flecked with blackish; the feathers of the lower back and rump with these spots broader, more oval and with a distally converging V of blackish within the light area, and the spots separated from the tips of the feathers by 3 to 8 mm. of dark smoke gray; the rump feathers have the brown areas faintly and sparsely vermiculated with blackish on their concealed basal portions; upper tail coverts cinnamon-brown, very broadly tipped with smoke gray (about 15 mm. wide) and crossed by five or six narrow, equally spaced, wavy, fuscous-black bands, each of which (except for the most distal one, which borders on the proximal edge of the gray terminal area) is distally followed by a narrow band (but which is wider than the black band) of cinnamon-buff to pale tawny-olive, which in turn is followed by a broken line of fine blackish dots; the gray tips are finely speckled or vermiculated with black and have a large blotch of dark fuscous-black edged with auburn in their middle portion; lesser and median upper wing coverts sayal brown to cinnamon-brown, very narrowly and incompletely edged with blackish and with mesial streaks of pale buffy white narrowly edged with dusky; greater upper secondary coverts similar but with the brown areas faintly vermiculated with blackish; greater upper primary coverts fuscous, externally narrowly edged with cinnamon-brown, the edging widest basally; primaries fuscous on the inner webs and terminally on the outer ones, most of the outer webs cartridge buffy to buffy white, with five to seven dusky fuscescent triangular bars, each of which has its base against the shaft and its apex at the outer edge of the vane, causing the whitish areas to appear like reversed triangles, these dusky marks becoming small and faint or disappearing entirely on the distal third of the feathers; secondaries fuscous externally broadly edged with sayal brown coarsely vermiculated with fuscous, and tipped with drab; the innermost secondaries have their inner webs also margined with vermiculated sayal brown with a wash of drab; the scapulars like the greater secondary coverts but with the light mesial streaks much wider and the adjacent part of the inner web extensively blackish; rectrices cinnamon to clay color tipped broadly with smoke gray with fine black vermiculations subterminally broadly banded with fuscous-black to bister, this band sometimes breaking down to a series of vermiculations in the median pair of rectrices (possibly in younger adult birds); the subterminal dark band edged basally with another smoke-gray band similar to the terminal one, and the remainder of the feathers crossed by seven to nine narrow, wavy, fuscous-black bands, each of which is followed distally by a band of cinnamon-buff, which in turn is edged distally by a broken series of blackish vermiculations, which extend, in reduced size, into the brown interspaces; loreal stripe pale pinkish buff narrowly edged with blackish spots; lower eyelid a line of pinkish-buff and black spots; feather of cheeks and auriculars elongated, sayal brown, with blackish edges and pale ashy-brown shaft streaks; chin whitish washed with buffy or pale ochraceous-buff and the feathers sometimes tipped narrowly with black; throat light ochraceous-buff, becoming whitish laterally on the upper throat, the feathers forming the lateral and posterior portions of the gular area tipped with fuscous-black, producing a somewhat scalloped pattern; upper breast cinnamon-brown to light auburn, each feather broadly tipped with smoke gray, so that in fresh plumage the brown is largely obscured; the brown areas of the feathers basally largely light pinkish cinnamon, with the darker cinnamon-brown forming incomplete bands, especially subterminally; lower breast and upper and lateral parts of the abdomen grayish white to pale smoke gray subterminally crossed by broad bands of wood brown to buffy brown narrowly edged on both sides with darker, and the feathers washed with buffy basally; the brownish subterminal bands usually largely hidden by the grayish-white tips of the feathers, especially on the abdomen, these bands darker and more exposed on the lateral feathers middle of abdomen with no brown, pure grayish white; feathers of the sides sayal brown to Saccardo's umber slightly vermiculated with blackish and with white shaft streaks that expand distally into broad terminal spots, flanks similar but the brown areas ashier and more vermiculated, the vermiculations forming narrow bands, the shaft streaks washed with grayish and not expanding into terminal spots; thighs drab to whitish washed with pale vinaceous-buff; under tail coverts clay color to cinnamon-buff, broadly tipped with white, the white sometimes extending back in a narrow streak along the shaft, the brown parts frequently with a few blackish spots; under wing coverts sayal brown to Saccardo's umber with whitish mesial streaks; axillars white banded broadly with sayal brown; iris hazel; bill dark brown; feet dark grayish olive with a brownish wash.

Adult male (gray phase).—Similar to the red phase except that the interscapulars, back, lower back, rump feathers, and upper wing coverts have the brown areas vermiculated and irregularly banded with smoke gray, the feathers completely margined with the same; the upper tail coverts and the rectrices have the rufescent replaced by smoke gray, which is generally somewhat more abundantly flecked and vermiculated with black than in the red phase; the subterminal band is usually fuscous to fuscous-black, but occasionally it is dark argus brown (in which examples the ruffs are usually auburn with blackish tips); the outer margin of the greater upper primary coverts paler—wood brown; the sides, flanks, and thighs ashier, and the brown on the under tail coverts reduced largely to narrow, incomplete cross bars.[64]

Adult female (both phases).—Similar to the corresponding males but averaging smaller with shorter ruffs, the gray phase females less pure gray on the tail, more mixed or washed with rufescent than in gray males, and the pectoral area in both phases more extensively tawny or hazel; the cordate spots on the feathers of the back and rump smaller than in the males and also more washed with avellaneous to wood brown.

Immature (both sexes).—Similar to the adults of the corresponding sex and phase, but the ruffs slightly duller and slightly smaller; birds in this stage may be told, however, chiefly by the fact that they have the two outer primaries of the juvenal plumage, which differ from the adult feathers in that their outer webs are not cartridge buff or whitish marked with sayal brown but pale fuscous mottled and stippled with pinkish buff to pale cinnamon-buff.[65]

Juvenal (sexes alike).—Similar to the adult female but browner above, more abundantly marked with sayal brown to Saccardo's umber on the underparts, but these marks more irregularly disposed, not so clearly forming bars, but something between bars and heavy transverse mottling;

---

[64] In winter, grouse (both sexes) differ from summer birds in the presence of "snowshoes" caused by the growth of the lateral scales on the toes, and also in more extensive grayish tips and margins to the feathers which wear off by spring.

[65] In literature one finds statements to the effect that the juvenal primaries, such as are retained in the immature plumage, are "light vinaceous cinnamon unmarked except for a very fine sprinkling of a slightly darker shade . . .," but the only difference between them and adult primaries is confined to their outer webs as given above.

tail feathers lacking the heavy black subterminal band and having the smoke-gray tips poorly developed; the narrow blackish rectricial bands (about as in the adults in number) each followed distally by a band of pale sayal brown or cinnamon, lighter than the rest of the feather, or by a band of pale smoke gray (possibly birds that would become gray-phased later on?); head quite different from adult—forehead, crown, and occiput snuff brown to Saccardo's umber spotted with fuscous-black, a buffy-whitish line from the loreal antiae to the eye, both eyelids, and continuing back of the eye to the sides of the occiput; cheeks and auriculars snuff brown to Saccardo's umber, the former spotted with dusky sepia to fuscous-black; chin and most of upper throat whitish unmarked; the feathers of the back and rump and upper tail coverts different from the adult—ashy sayal brown narrowly barred with sepia to fuscous; iris hazel brown; bill "brown and slate," feet bluish white.

Downy young.—Forehead, crown, occiput, and nape pale ochraceous-tawny, darkening medially and posteriorly to tawny and paling laterally to light ochraceous-buff on the sides of the crown and occiput and on the lores, cheeks, and auriculars, the middorsal area from the nape to the tail bright russet, this area widening very considerably on the lower back, the body down on each side of this ochraceous-buff becoming lighter ventrally, entire underparts ivory yellow to light cream buff, a fuscous-black line extending from the hind end of the eye to the posterolateral angle of the occiput; upper surface of wings pale russet, under surface cream buff.

Adult male.—Wing 174–190 (183.6); tail 144–174 (159.0); culmen from base 25.8–29 (27.0); tarsus 41.9–47.0 (43.9); middle toe without claw 32.4–39.0 (36.7); unfeathered part of tarsus 21.7–31.1 (26.3 mm.).[66]

Adult female.—Wing 170–188 (176.4); tail 123–141 (132.6); culmen from base 23.8–28.1 (26.3); tarsus 39.6–43.6 (41.2); middle toe without claw 32.7–36.9 (34.2); unfeathered part of tarsus 20.2–30.0 (24.9 mm.).[67]

Range.—Climax and subclimax deciduous woodland of the Atlantic coastal oak-pine subclimax and the northeastern portion of the mixed mesophytic association in the eastern deciduous forest biome (Upper Austral and Lower Transition Life Zones) north to central eastern and central Massachusetts, east-central and central New York, west to central New York and east-central Pennsylvania, south, formerly, along the coastal plain to Washington, D. C.

Type locality.—Eastern Pennsylvania; restricted to "vicinity of Philadelphia."

Tetrao umbellus LINNAEUS, Syst. Nat., ed. 12, i, 1776, 275 (Pennsylvania; based on *Urogallus collari extenso pensylvanicus* Edwards, Gleanings, 79, pl. 248;

[66] Twenty specimens from Massachusetts, Rhode Island, eastern Pennsylvania, and New York.
[67] Sixteen specimens from Massachusetts, New York, and District of Columbia.

Attagen pensylvaniæ Brisson, Orn., i, 214).—GMELIN, Syst. Nat., i, pt. 2, 1788, 752.—LATHAM, Index Orn., ii, 1790, 638.—WILSON, Amer. Orn., vi, 1812, 45, pl. 49, part (eastern States, Pennsylvania).—BONAPARTE, Obs. Wilson's Orn., 1826, 182; Genera North Amer. Birds, 1828, 126 ("found in temperate regions") ; Amer. Philos. Trans., iii, 1830, 389.—DOUGHTY, Cab. Nat. Hist., i, 1830, 13, pl. 2.—AUDUBON, Orn. Biogr., i, 1831, 211 part (New York, Pennsylvania) ; v, 1836, 560, part; Birds Amer., 8vo ed., v, 1842, 72, part (New York; Pennsylvania) ; Synopsis, 1839, 202, part (Maryland northward).—WILSON and BONAPARTE, Amer. Orn., ii, 1832 (printed by Whittaker, Treacher, and Arnot), 249, part; ii, 1832 (?) (printed by Cassell, Petter, and Galpin), 251, part.—NUTTALL, Man. Orn. United States and Canada, Land Birds, i, 1832, 657, part; ed. 2, 1840, 794, part.—JARDINE, Nat. Libr., Orn., iv, Gallinaceous Birds, pt. 2, Game-birds, 1834, 149, pl. 14, part (Pennsylvania).—WILSON, Amer. Orn., ed. by Brewer, 1840, 430, part.—GIRAUD, Birds Long Island, 1844, 191 (Long Island, New York).

T[etrao] umbellus WILSON and BONAPARTE, Amer. Orn., ii, 1871, 265, part.

Tetrao (Bonasia) umbellus BONAPARTE, Syn., 1828, 126; Trans. Amer. Philos. Soc., iii, 1830, 389.

Tetrao tympanus BARTRAM, Trav. in Florida, etc., 1792, 288 (Pennsylvania).

Tetrao tympanistes SMITH, Wonders of Nature and Art, rev. ed., 1807, xiv, 67.

Bonasia umbellus BONAPARTE, Geogr. and Comp. List, 1838, 43.

Bonasa umbellus STEPHENS, *in* Shaw, Gen. Zool., xi, 1819, 300, part.—BAIRD, Rep. Pacific R. R. Surv., ix, 1858, 630, part.—BAIRD, CASSIN, and LAWRENCE, Birds North America, 1860, 629, 630, part.—ELLIOT, Monogr. Tetraonidae, 1865, pl. 1 and text, part.—LAWRENCE, Ann. Lyc. Nat. Hist. New York, viii, 1866, 291 (Long Island, Staten Island, N. Y.).—MAYNARD, Proc. Boston Soc. Nat. Hist., xiv, 1872, 383 part.—BREWER, Proc. Boston Soc. Nat. Hist., xvii, 1875, 12 (New England).—MERRIAM, Trans. Connecticut Acad. Sci., iv, 1877, 100 (Connecticut; common).—RATHBUN, Revised List Birds Central New York, 1879, 29 (central New York; common).—GREGG, Revised Cat. Birds Chemung County, N. Y., 1880, 19 (common).—AMERICAN ORNITHOLOGISTS' UNION, Check-list, 1886, 172, No. 300, part.—RICHMOND, Auk, v, 1888, 20 (District of Columbia; rare).—BENDIRE, Life Hist. North Amer. Birds, i, 1892, 59, part (s. Massachusetts, New York, Pennsylvania).—OGILVIE-GRANT, Cat. Birds Brit. Mus., xxii, 1893, 85, part; Handbook Game Birds, i, 1896, 71, part.—STONE, Auk, xi, 1894, 136 (New Jersey; Pine Barrens) ; Birds New Jersey, 1908, 150 (New Jersey; distr.; nest, habits).—DWIGHT, Auk, xxii, 1900, 145 (molts and plumage).—RHOADS and PENNOCK, Auk, xxii, 1905, 199 (Delaware; formerly not uncommon).—WEBER, Auk, xxiii, 1906, 459 in text (food; crop contents).—PENNOCK, Auk, xxv, 1908, 286 (Delaware; Ashland, Mount Cuba, Brandywine and Red Clay Creeks).—GRISCOM, Birds New York City Region, 1923, 176 (status, New York City region).—(?) WETMORE, Auk, xliv, 1927, 561 in text (Pleistocene of Maryland).—KNAPPEN, Auk, xlv, 1928, 513 (bibliogr. relating to food habits).—GROEBBELS, Der Vögel, i, 1932, 272 in text (food habits) ; ii, 1937, 137 in text (drumming of male), 139 in text courtship), 241 in text (eggs in mixed sets).—ALLEN, Auk, li, 1934, 180 (sex behavior).—CORNELL and DOREMUS, Auk, liv, 1937, 321 in text (endoparasites).—BAGG and ELLIOT, Birds Connecticut Valley; Massachusetts, 1937, 170 (habits; status).—TODD, Birds Western Pennsylvania, 1940, 131 in text (remains found in goshawk stomachs).—UTTAL, Auk, lviii, 1941, 74, 76 in text (tarsal feathering) ; lx, 1943, 266, in text (Long Island, N. Y., plum.).—PETRIDES, Trans. 7th North Amer. Wildlife Conference, 1942, 316, in text (age indicators in plumage).

Bonasa umbella Coues, Proc. Essex Inst., v, 1868, 39 part (New England; common) ;
Check List North Amer. Birds, ed. 2, 1882, No. 565, part; Key North Amer.
Birds, ed. 2, 1884, 585, part.
B[onasa] umbellus Ridgway, Man. North Amer. Birds, 1887, 197, part.—Coues,
Key North Amer. Birds, ed. 5, 1903, ii, 741, part.—Reichenow, Die Vögel, i,
1913, 319.
[Bonasa] umbellus Coues, Key North Amer. Birds, 1872, 235, part.
Bonasa umbellus var. *umbellus* Baird, Brewer, and Ridgway, Hist. North Amer.
Birds, iii, 1874, 448, part.
Bonasa umbellus a. *umbellus* Coues, Birds Northwest, 1874, 420, part.
Bonasa umbellus umbellus American Ornithologists' Union, Check-list, ed. 2,
1895, 112; ed. 3, 1910, 140 part; ed. 4, 1931, 81 part.—Eaton, Birds New York,
i. 1909, 366 (New York).—Harlow, Auk, xxix, 1912, 469 (Chester County,
Pa.; abundant) ; xxxv, 1918, 23 (Pennsylvania and New Jersey; egg dates).—
Burns, Orn. Chester County, Pa., 1919, 48 (Chester County, Pa., rare; eggs).—
Smith, Auk, xxxviii, 1921, 466 (Meriden, Conn.; nest with 23 eggs all hatched).
—Daley, Auk, xxxix, 1922, 178 (Slide Mountain, Catskill Mountains, N. Y.),
180 (Frost Valley, Catskill Mountains, N. Y.).—Burleigh, Wils. Bull., xxxvi,
1924, 69 (Centre County, Pa.).—Beck, Auk, xli, 1924, 292 in text (Pennsylvania—
German common names).—Clay, Wils. Bull., xxxvii, 1925, 43 in text (behavior
of a stunned bird).—Sutton, Wils. Bull., xxxix, 1927, 171 in text (killed by
screech owl) ; Birds Pennsylvania, 1928, 53, part (e. Pennsylvania; habits; etc.).
—Forbush, Birds Massachusetts and Other New England States, ii, 1927, 26,
pl. 35 (col. fig.; descr.; habits, New England).—Cooke, Proc. Biol. Soc. Washington, xlii, 1929, 33 (Washington, D. C.).—Burleigh, Wils. Bull., xliii, 1931,
38 (State College, Centre County, Pa.).—Bent, U. S. Nat. Mus. Bull. 162,
1932, 141 (habits; plum.; distr.).—Griscom, Trans. Linn. Soc. New York, iii,
1933, 96 (Dutchess County, N. Y.; fairly common).—Towers, Auk, li, 1934,
516 in text (feather structure).—Peters, Check-list Birds of World, ii, 1934,
40.—Fisher, Proc. Biol. Soc. Washington, xlviii, 1935, 161 (Plummers
Island, Md.).—Stone, Bird Studies Cap May, i, 1937, 319 (Cape May, N. J.;
status; habits).—Wetmore, Proc. U. S. Nat. Mus., lxxxiv, 1937, 406 (distr.;
tax.).—Todd, Auk, lvii, 1940, 396 (crit.; characters).—Hellmayr and Conover,
Cat. Birds Amer., i, No. 1, 1942, 215, part.—Cruickshank, Birds New York
City, 1942, 150 (status; habits).—Aldrich and Friedmann, Condor, xlv, 1943,
90 (tax.; descr.; distr.).
Bonasa u[mbellus] umbellus Urner, Abstr. Linn. Soc. New York, Nos. 39, 40, 1930,
71 (Union County, N. J.).—Groebbels, Der Vögel, ii, 1937, 166 in text (data on
breeding biology).—Poole, Auk, lv, 1938, 516 in table (weight; wing area).—
Stabler, Auk, lviii, 1941, 561 (parasite experiment).
B[onasa] umbellus umbellus Uttal, Auk, lviii, 1941, 74 (tarsal feathering).
B[onasa] u[mbellus] umbellus Uttal, Auk, lviii, 1941, 75, 77 in text (tarsal feathering).
Bonasa jobsii Jaycox, Cornell Era, Dec. 8, 1871 (Ithaca, N. Y.); iv, No. 14, Jan. 13,
1872 (crit.).—Anon., Ibis, 1872, 191, 439 in text.
Bonasa umbellus helmei Bailey, Bailey Mus. and Libr. Nat. Hist. Bull. 14, January
5, 1941, 1st page (Miller Place, Long Island, N. Y.).

BONASA UMBELLUS MEDIANA Todd

Midwestern Ruffed Grouse

Adults.—Very similar to the corresponding sex and phase of *B. u.*
umbellus but very slightly paler, the top and sides of the head and neck

with a pale grayish suffusion, the breast averaging less extensively washed with brownish, the abdomen averaging more albescent, and, in the brown phase, the tail paler, nearly ochraceous-tawny (in the brown phase of *umbellus* it is nearly hazel). On the whole this race is more often gray-tailed than brown-tailed, while the reverse is true of the nominate form.[68]

Juvenal and downy young apparently unknown.

Adult male.—Wing 174–185 (178.9); tail 140–163 (150.6); culmen from base 25.2–30.6 (27.8); tarsus 41.8–45.8 (43.5); middle toe without claw 34.5–39.5 (36.8); unfeathered part of tarsus 18.4–30.2 (23.8 mm.).[69]

Adult female.—Wing 174–183 (176.6); tail 127–159 (141.3); culmen from base 26.0–28.2 (27.3); tarsus 40.8–44.8 (42.7); middle toe without claw 34.5–37.4 (35.4); unfeathered part of tarsus 21.6–30.0 (25.4 mm.).[70]

Range.—Climax and subclimax deciduous woodland of the oak-hickory association in the eastern deciduous forest biome (Upper Austral Life Zone); from southwestern Michigan, southern Wisconsin, and east central Minnesota (Elk River); south, east of the Great Plains grassland, to central Arkansas (Hot Springs). To the east *Bonasa umbellus mediana* intergrades with *Bonasa umbellus monticola*, over a broad area in southern Michigan, eastern Indiana, and western Ohio, and probably formerly in western Kentucky and Tennessee.

Type locality.—Excelsior, Minn.

Tetrao umbellus WILSON, Amer. Orn., vi, 1812, 45, part (w. Kentucky; Indiana).— AUDUBON, Orn. Biogr., i, 1831, 211, part; Birds Amer., 8vo ed., v, 1842, 72, part (Illinois, Indiana, Kentucky).—WILSON and BONAPARTE, Amer. Orn., ii, 1832 (printed by Whittaker, Treacher, and Arnot), 249, part; (printed by Cassell, Petter, and Galpin) 251, part (Indiana Terr.).—NUTTALL, Man. Orn. United States and Canada, Land Birds, 1832, 657, part; ed. 2, 1840, 764, part.—JARDINE, Nat. Libr., Orn., iv, Gallinaceous Birds, pt. ii, Game Birds, 1834, 149, part (Indiana Terr.).—WILSON, Amer. Orn., ed. by Brewer, 1840, 430, part.— TRIPPE, Comm. Essex Inst., vi, 1871, 118 (Minnesota, abundant; plum.).
T[*etrao*] *umbellus* WILSON and BONAPARTE, Amer. Orn., ii, 1871, 265, part (Indiana).
tetrao umbellus BRACKENRIDGE, Views of Louisiana, 1817, 119.
Bonasa umbellus BARRY, Proc. Boston Soc. Nat. Hist., v, 1854, 9 (Racine, Wis.; abundant).—ALLEN, Mem. Boston Soc. Nat. Hist., i, 1868, 501 (w. Iowa; common), 526 (Richmond, Ind.).—SNOW, Cat. Birds Kansas, ed. 2, 1872, 12 (Kansas, extremely rare); ed. 2, reprint, 1873, 9 (e. Kansas); ed. 3, 1875, 11 (e. Kansas); ed. 5, 1903, 15 (Kansas; very rare).—TRIPPE, Proc. Boston Soc. Nat. Hist., xv, 1872, 240 (s. Iowa; abundant).—NELSON, Bull. Essex Inst., ix, 1877, 44 (Wabash County, Ill.).—GIBBS, U. S. Geol. and Geogr. Surv. Terr., Bull. 5, v, 1879, 491 part (Michigan).—AMERICAN ORNITHOLOGISTS' UNION, Check-list, 1886, 172, No. 300, part.—EVERMANN, Auk, v, 1888, 349 (Carroll County,

---

[68] If this race were not separated geographically from *B. u. umbellus* by *B. u. monticola,* its recognition might be questioned. There is less difference between *mediana* and *umbellus* than between any other two subspecies of the ruffed grouse.

[69] Nineteen specimens from Minnesota, Wisconsin, southwestern Michigan, and Iowa.

[70] Three specimens from Minnesota and Illinois.

Ind.; rare).—Goss, Hist. Birds Kansas, 1891, 223 (Kansas, formerly; descr.,
eggs).—HATCH, Notes Birds Minnesota, 1892, 160, 452 (Minnesota; habits,
etc.).—BENDIRE, Life Hist. North Amer. Birds, i, 1892, 59 part (Minnesota;
Arkansas).—OGILVIE-GRANT, Cat. Birds Brit. Mus., xxii, 1893, 85 part (Indiana,
Illinois).—LANTZ, Trans. Kansas Acad. Sci. for 1896–97 (1899) ; 254 (Kansas;
rare resident in e. Kansas).—WOODRUFF, Auk, xxv, 1908, 198 (Current River,
Shannon County, Mo.).
B[onasa] umbellus RIDGWAY, Ann. Lyc. Nat. Hist., New York, x, 1874, 382
(Illinois) ; Man. North Amer. Birds, 1887, 197, part (Arkansas).—HATCH,
Bull. Minnesota Acad. Nat. Sci., 1874, 62 (Minnesota; abundant).—BOIES, Cat.
Birds Southern Michigan, 1875, No. 147, part (s. Michigan; resident).—NELSON,
Bull. Essex Inst., viii, 1876, 121, part (ne. Illinois; common) ; ix, 1877, 43 (s.
Illinois; not common).—COUES, Key North Amer. Birds, ed. 5, 1903, ii, 741
part.
Bonasa umbellus, var. umbellus BAIRD, BREWER, and RIDGWAY, Hist. North Amer.
Birds, iii, 1874, 448, part.—LANGDON, Journ. Cincinnati Soc. Nat. Hist., 1879,
15 (Cincinnati, Ohio; resident; spec. from Brookville, Ind.).
Bonasa umbellus umbellus AMERICAN ORNITHOLOGISTS' UNION, Check-list, ed. 2,
1895, 112; ed. 3, 1910, 140, part; ed. 4, 1931, 81, part.—HOWELL, Auk, xxviii,
1911, 232 (Crooked Lake region, Minn.; common).—BETTS, Auk, xxxii, 1915,
238 in text (Ashland County, Wis.) ; xxxiii, 1916, 438 (Wisconsin; food
habits).—EIFRIG, Auk, xxxvi, 1919, 517 (Chicago, Ill.).—JOHNSON, Auk, xxxvii,
1920, 544 (Lake County, Minn.; breeds).—PINDAR, Wils. Bull., xxxvi, 1924,
204 (e. Arkansas).—WHEELER, Birds Arkansas, 1925, 39, xiv (very scarce;
last record in 1883).—SCHORGER, Auk, xlii, 1925, 65 (summer; Lake Owen,
Wis.; habits).—PIERCE, Wils. Bull., xlii, 1930, 266 (Buchanan County, Iowa).—
BAERG, Univ. Arkansas Agr. Exp. Stat. Bull. 258, 1931, 53 (Arkansas; genl.).—
BENT, U. S. Nat. Mus. Bull. 162, 1932, 141, part (life hist.).—ROBERTS, Birds
Minnesota, i, 1932, 376 (distr.; habits; Minnesota).—BENNITT, Univ. Missouri
Studies, vii, No. 3, 1932, 25 (eastern Missouri; rare).—DU MONT, Wils. Bull.,
xliv, 1932, 237 (Iowa; spec.).—PETERS, Check-list Birds of World, ii, 1934, 40,
part.—BRECKENRIDGE, Condor, xxxvii, 1935, 269 (Minnesota).—LONG, Trans.
Kansas Acad. Sci., xliii, 1940, 440 (Kansas; formerly common, now extinct).—
PIERCE, Proc. Iowa Acad. Sci., xlvii, 1941, 376 (northeastern Iowa; resident).—
POLDERBOER, Iowa Bird Life, xii, 1942, 50 in text (cover requirements in ne.
Iowa).—HELLMAYR and CONOVER, Cat. Birds Amer., i, No. 1, 1942, 215, part.
Bonasa umbellus togata CURRIER, Auk, xxi, 1904, 34 (Leach Lake, Minn.; common).
—ROBERTS, Birds Minnesota, i, 1932, 376 part (distr.; habits, etc., Minnesota).—
HELLMAYR and CONOVER, Cat. Birds Amer., i, No. 1, 1942, 214, part.
B[onasa] u[mbellus] togata CONOVER, Condor, xxxvii, 1935, 206 part (Minnesota).
Bonasa umbellus medianus TODD, Auk, ivii, 1940, 394 (Excelsior, Minn.; descr.;
distr.; crit.), 396 (distr.).—HELLMAYER and CONOVER, Cat. Birds Amer., i,
No. 1, 1942, 214, footnote.—ALDRICH and FRIEDMANN, Condor, xlv, 1943, 92
(tax.; descr.; distr.).
B[onasa] u[mbellus] medianus UTTAL, Auk, lviii, 1941, 74 in text (tarsal feathering).

BONASA UMBELLUS MONTICOLA Todd

APPALACHIAN RUFFED GROUSE

Adult (brown phase).—Similar to that of *Bonasa umbellus umbellus,*
but the general coloration darker, the underparts more regularly and
more heavily barred and more strongly suffused with buffy; the upperparts more brownish, less rufescent—Prout's brown (instead of cinnamon-

brown as in *umbellus*); the ventral bars becoming dark (dark sepia to clove brown) on the flanks.

Adult (gray phase).—Similar to that of *B. u. umbellus,* but the upper and lower back darker, more brownish, with little or no grayish mixture, the tail apparently never so pure gray but always with a faint buffy tinge; ventral bars darker, as in the brown phase, but the underparts less washed.

Juvenal.—There seem to be two phases in this plumage, both (as far as available material goes) with brown tails, but one considerably grayer than the other (which is difficult to interpret as the great majority of the adults are brown-phased in this race): in the browner of the two phases juvenals are like those of *B. u. umbellus* but darker, browner, less rufescent above, the blackish marks on the upperparts larger, and the ventral barrings darker as in the adults; in the grayer of the two phases, the areas of the nape, interscapulars, upper wing coverts, back, rump, and upper tail coverts that are Dresden brown to Saccardo's umber in the brown phase are wood brown; the pale areas of the interscapulars are pinkish buff (as opposed to cinnamon-buff to pale clay color in the browner phase), and the ventral barrings are darker and less rufescent— buffy brown to sepia.

Downy young.—Indistinguishable from that of the nominate race.

Adult male.—Wing 172–196 (186.8); tail 139–181 (160); culmen from base 24.4–31 (27.4); tarsus 40–48.2 (44.5); middle toe without claw 32.8–40 (36.5); unfeathered part of tarsus 21.4–34.5 (28.5 mm.).[71]

Adult female.—Wing 166–190 (178.6); tail 121–156 (134.8); culmen from base 23.8–29.3 (26.6); tarsus 37.4–45 (41.1); middle toe without claw 32.2–39.6 (35.1); unfeathered part of tarsus of 19.4–33.6 (27.2 mm.).[72]

Range.—Climax and subclimax deciduous forest communities of the mixed mesophitic association in the eastern deciduous forest biome (Upper Austral Life Zone) in the eastern United States and the ecotone between this biome and the Canadian Zone coniferous forest of the Appalachian Mountains (pine-maple-beech-hemlock association); north to northeastern Pennsylvania, northeastern Ohio, and southeastern Michigan, east to northeastern and south-central Pennsylvania, central Maryland, northeastern, central, and southwestern Virginia, southwestern North Carolina, and northern Georgia; south to northern Georgia and northeastern Alabama. The western limit of the range of this race is ill defined because of the fact that the species has been extirpated over much of the Mississippi Valley region where it formerly occurred. *Bonasa umbellus monticola* intergrades with *mediana* in central southern Michigan, eastern

---

[71] Thirty-nine specimens from Virginia, West Virginia, North Carolina, Georgia, Maryland, Western Pennsylvania, Tennessee, and southeastern Michigan.

[72] Thirty-five specimens from Virginia, West Virginia, North Carolina, Georgia, Tennessee, western Pennsylvania, Maryland, Ohio, and southeastern Michigan.

Indiana, and western Ohio, and probably also formerly in western Kentucky and Tennessee.

Type locality.—Two and one-half miles east of Cheat Bridge, Randolph County, W. Va. (4,000 feet elevation).

Tetrao umbellus Wilson, Amer. Orn., vi, 1812, 45, part (upper parts of Georgia).—Audubon, Orn. Biogr., i, 1831, 211, part; v, 1839, 560, part; Birds Amer., 8vo ed., v, 1842, 42, part.—Wilson and Bonaparte, Amer. Orn., ii, 1832 (Whittaker, Treacher, and Arnot), 249, part; ii, 1832 (Cassell, Petter, and Galpin), 251, part (Carolina, Georgia, Florida).—Nuttall, Man. Orn. United States and Canada, Land Birds, 1832, 657, part; ed. 2, 1840, 794, part.—Wilson, Amer. Orn., ed. by Brewer, 1840, 430, part.

T[etrao] umbellus Wilson and Bonaparte, Amer. Orn., ii, 1871, 265, part (Georgia).

Bonasa umbellus Baird, Rep. Pacific R. R. Surv., ix, 1858, 630, part (Georgia).—Baird, Cassin, and Lawrence, Rep. Pacific R. R. Surv., 1860, 629 in table, part, 630 in table, part (Georgia).—Scott, Proc. Boston Soc. Nat. Hist., xv, 1872, 227 (West Virginia, Kenawha County).—Gibbs, U. S. Geol. and Geogr. Surv. Terr. Bull. 5, 1879, 491, part (Michigan).—Wheaton, Rep. Birds Ohio, 1882, 447, 579 (Ohio; descr.; syn.).—Beckham, Journ. Cincinnati Soc. Nat. Hist., vi, 1883, 145 (Kentucky).—Brewster, Auk, iii, 1886, 102 (w. North Carolina).—Fox, Auk, iii, 1886, 319 (e. Tennessee).—Loomis, Auk, iii, 1886, 483 (nw. South Carolina); vii, 1890, 36 (Pickens County, S. C.; common); viii, 1891, 326 (Caesars Head, S. C.; young seen).—American Ornithologists' Union, Check-list, 1886, 172, No. 300, part (Georgia; North Carolina).—Langdon, Auk, iv, 1887, 129 (Chilhowee Mountains, Tenn., Mount Nebo).—Rives, Auk, vi, 1889, 52 in text (White Top Mountain, Va.).—Bendire, Life Hist. North Amer. Birds, i, 1892, 59, part (n. South Carolina, Georgia, Tennessee).—Dwight, Auk, ix, 1892, 134 (North Mountain, Pennsylvania Alleghenies).—Todd, Auk, x, 1893, 38 (Yellow Creek bottom, w. Pennsylvania), 44 (Indiana County, Pa.).—Ogilvie-Grant, Cat. Birds Brit. Mus., xxii, 1893, 85, part; Handb. Game Birds, i, 1896, 71, part (mountains n. Alabama).—Young, Auk, xiii, 1896, 281 (Nescopeck, Pa.).—Bailey, Auk, xiii, 1896, 292 (n. Elk County, Pa.).—Rives, Auk, xv, 1898, 134 (Blackwater River, W. Va.).—Jones, Birds Ohio, Revised Cat., 1903, 84 (Ohio).—Dawson, Birds Ohio, 1903, 433, 652, pl. 51 (Ohio; habits; fig.).—Eifrig, Auk, xxi, 1904, 237 (w. Maryland; common).—Brown, Auk, xxiii, 1906, 336 in text (near Camden, S. C.).—Howell, Auk, xxvi, 1909, 132 (Brasstown Bald, s. Georgia; breeds); xxvii, 1910, 301 (Walden Ridge and Cross Mountain, Tenn.).—Johnston, Birds West Virginia, 1923, 10 (West Virginia).—Shelter, Wils. Bull., xlix, 1937, 49 in text (Michigan; speed of flight).—Trautman, Bills, and Wickliff, Wils. Bull., li, 1939, 102, in text (winter mortality in Ohio).—Stewart, Auk, lx, 1943, 390 (Shenandoah Mountains; breeds).

Bonassa umbellus Johnston, Birds West Virginia, 1923, 88 (West Virginia).

B[onasa] umbellus Ridgway, Man. North Amer. Birds, 1887, 197, part (Georgia, Tennessee).—Coues, Key North Amer. Birds, ed. 5, 1903, ii, 741, part.

B[onsa] umbellus Boies, Cat. Birds Southern Michigan, 1875, No. 147, part (s. Michigan; resident).

[Bonasa] umbellus Coues, Key North Amer. Birds, 1872, 235, part.

Bonasa umbellus subsp. Mengel, Auk, lvii, 1940, 424 (e. Kentucky).

Bonasa umbellus umbellus American Ornithologists' Union, Check-list, ed. 2, 1895, 112; ed. 3, 1910, 140, part; ed. 4, 1931, 81, part.—Bailey, Auk, xxix, 1912, 80 (mountains of Virginia).—Bruner and Field, Auk, xxix, 1912, 371 (mountains of North Carolina—Grandfather Mountains and Mount Mitchell at 6,500

feet), 375 (Canadian and Transition Zone, 2,000 to 5,000 feet and above).—
SMYTH, Auk, xxix, 1912, 514 (Montgomery County, Va.).—BAILEY, Birds
Virginia, 1913, 88 (Virginia; habits, etc.).—BROOKS, Auk, xxxi, 1914, 544 (Rich
Mountains, W. Va.) ; Wils. Bull. xlii, 1930, 246 (Cranberry Glades, W. Va.).—
PEARSON, BRIMLEY, and BRIMLEY, Birds North Carolina, 1919, 153 (North
Carolina; distr.; habits).—HOWELL, Birds Alabama, 1924, 119; ed.
2, 1928,
119 (Alabama; habits).—BLINCOE, Auk, xlii, 1925, 408 (Bardstown, Ky.).—
SUTTON, Birds Pennsylvania, 1928, 53 part (w. Pennsylvania).—PICKENS, Wils.
Bull., xl, 1928, 189 (upper South Carolina).—BENT, U. S. Nat. Mus. Bull. 162,
1932, 141 part (life hist.).—PETERS, Check-list Birds of World, ii, 1934, 40, part.
—HUDSON and SHERMAN, Auk, liii, 1936, 311 (South Carolina; still present
but reduced in numbers in Pickens and Oconee Counties).—VAN TYNE, Occ.
Pap. Mus. Zool. Univ. Michigan, No. 379, 1938, 11 (Michigan; south of range
B. u. togata).—CAMPBELL, Bull. Toledo Mus. Sci., i, 1940, 61 (Lucas County,
Ohio; now extirpated; last record is 1905).—TRAUTMAN, Misc. Publ. Mus.
Zool. Univ. Michigan Mus. Zool., No. 44, 1940, 223 (Buckeye Lake, Ohio;
formerly common, now extirpated).—TODD, Birds Western Pennsylvania, 1940,
168 (w. Pennsylvania; descr., habits, syn.) ; Auk, lvii, 1940, 390 in text (spec.,
w. Pennsylvania; crit.), 396 (distr.).—GOODPASTER, Journ. Cincinnati Soc. Nat.
Hist., xxii, 1941, 13 (sw. Ohio—only one known record—Clermont County,
October 1878).—BURLEIGH, Auk, lviii, 1941, 337 (Mount Mitchell, N. C.;
young).—HELLMAYR and CONOVER, Cat. Birds Amer., i, No. 1, 1942, 215, part.
Bonasa umbellus var. *umbellus* BAIRD, BREWER, and RIDGWAY, Hist. North Amer.
Birds, iii, 1874, 448, part.
B[onasa] *u[mbellus]* *umbellus* HICKS, Wils. Bull., xlv, 1933, 179 (Ashtabula
County, Ohio).
[Bonasa] *[umbellus]* *umbellus* WHEATON, Rep. Birds Ohio, 1882, 447.
Bonasa umbellus togata WETMORE, Proc. U. S. Nat. Mus., xxxiv, 1937, 406, 407
(West Virginia; many records; crit.; ranges s. to the mountains of n. Georgia) ;
lxxxvi, 1939, 183 (Tennessee; spec. from Shady Valley, Roan Mountain, and
Mount Guyot; sev. sight records) ; lxxxviii, 1940, 535 (Kentucky; near Mount
Vernon).—PEARSON, BRIMLEY, and BRIMLEY, Birds North Carolina, 1942, 107
(North Carolina; descr.; habits).
Bonasa umbellus monticola TODD, Auk, lvii, 1940, 392 (Cheat Bridge, W. Va.;
descr., range, crit.), 396 (distr.).—ALDRICH and FRIEDMANN, Condor, xlv, 1943,
94 (tax.; descr.; distr.).
B[onasa] *u[mbellus]* *monticola* UTTAL, Auk, lviii, 1941, 74 in text (tarsal feathering).

BONASA UMBELLUS SABINI (Douglas)

PACIFIC RUFFED GROUSE

Adult (brown phase).—Similar to that of *Bonasa umbellus umbellus* but
much more darkly and richly colored (darker and richer than *B. u.
monticola* also) ; the black markings above more extensive and conspicuous, the areas which are sayal brown to cinnamon-brown in *umbellus* being orange-cinnamon, cinnamon-rufous, or hazel, those that are cinnamon-
brown to dark Brussels brown in *umbellus* are bright dark amber brown
to rufescent argus brown; rectrices bright amber brown; ventral barrings
darker—dark Dresden brown narrowly edged with fuscous, the lateral
bars (on sides and flanks darker still)—mummy brown to clove brown;
thighs darker—wood brown to avellaneous tinged with cinnamon-buff.

There are two varieties of this phase agreeing in all respects except the color of the breast; in one variety this area is blackish, the feathers narrowly tipped with whitish or tawny, while in the other there is no black but the feathers are bright tawny, becoming mummy brown only basally.

Adult (gray phase).—Similar to the brown phase but with the feathers of the crown, occiput, and nape tipped with smoke gray; those of the upper and lower back, rump, and upper tail coverts terminally edged with pale neutral gray vermiculated with blackish; rectrices as in the gray phase of *B. u. umbellus* but darker, more washed with wood brown.

Juvenal.—None seen.

Downy young.—Indistinguishable from that of *B. u. umbellus.*

Adult male.—Wing 177–187 (182); tail 142–159 (151.7); culmen from base 25.8–28.1 (26.5); tarsus 43.0–45.1 (44.1); middle toe without claw 39.0–41.9 (40.1); unfeathered part of tarsus 16–28.6 (22.8 mm.).[73]

Adult female.—Wing 170–181 (174.3); tail 124–137 (130.2); culmen from base 24.9–28.4 (26.4); tarsus 41.2–44.2 (43.0); middle toe without claw 33–39 (36.5); unfeathered part of tarsus 17.8–28.0 (22.3 mm.).[74]

Range.—Subclimax deciduous woodlands of the cedar-hemlock-association in the moist coniferous forest biome of the Canadian Life Zone, from southwestern British Columbia (exclusive of Vancouver Island and the immediate vicinity of the coast) southward west of the Cascade Range, through Washington and Oregon (exclusive of the Olympic Peninsula and the immediate vicinity of Puget Sound) to northwestern California (Humboldt Bay and Salmon River.)

Type locality.—Vicinity of Fort Vancouver, Clark County, Wash.

Tetrao umbellus WILSON and BONAPARTE, Amer. Orn., ii, 1832 (printed by Whittaker, Treacher, and Arnot), 249, part; ii, 1832 (?) (printed by Cassell, Petter, and Galpin), 251 part.—AUDUBON, Synopsis, 1839, 202 part (Columbia River); Orn. Biogr., v, 1839, 560 part; Birds Amer., 8vo ed., v, 1842, 72 part (Columbia River).—NUTTALL, Man. Orn. United States and Canada, Land Birds, ed. 2, 1840, 794, part (Columbia River to the Pacific).—WILSON, Amer. Orn., ed. by Brewer, 1840, 430, part.—NEWBERRY, Pacific R. R. Rept., vi, 1857, 94 (Cascade Mountains and Willamette Valley, Oreg.).

Bonasa umbellus OGILVIE-GRANT, Cat. Birds Brit. Mus., xxii, 1893, 85, part; Handb. Game Birds, i, 1896, 71, part.

T[etrao] sabini DOUGLAS, Trans. Linn. Soc. London, xvi, 1829, 137, part (Pacific coast "from Cape Mendocino to Straits of Juan de Fuca, Quadra").—SWAINSON and RICHARDSON, Fauna Bor.-Amer., ii, 1831 (1832), 343, footnote.

Tetrao sabini HALL, Murrelet, xv, 1934, 5 in text (Washington; Columbia River; hist; rec. 1826).

Bonasa sabini PALMER, Condor, xxx, 1928, 277 in text, 294 in text (patronymics).

Bonasa sabinii BAIRD, Rep. Pacific R. R. Surv., ix, 1858, 631, part.—COOPER and SUCKLEY, Rep. Pacific R. R. Surv., xii, book 2, pt. 3, 1860, 224 (Washington, w. side of Cascades).—BAIRD, CASSIN, and LAWRENCE, Rep. Pacific R. R. Surv., 1860, 361.—LORD, Proc. Roy. Artil. Inst. Woolwich, iv, 1864, 123 (Brit. Colum-

---

[73] Six specimens from Washington and Oregon.

[74] Six specimens from Washington, Oregon, and California.

bia).—GRAY, List Birds Brit. Mus., pt. 5, Gallinae, 1867, 89.—BAIRD, *in* Cooper, Orn. Calif., 1870, 540.—COUES, Key North Amer. Birds, ed. 2, 1884, 585, part.—TOWNSEND, Auk, iii, 1886, 491 (Humboldt Bay, Calif.).

B[onasa] sabinii COUES, Key North Amer. Birds, rev. ed., 1896, 585.

Bonasa sabinei ELLIOT, Monogr. Tetraonidae, 1865, pl. 3 and text, part.

[Bonasa] sabinei GRAY, Hand List, ii, 1870, 277, No. 9834.

B[onasa] sabinei REICHENOW, Die Vögel, i, 1913, 319.

[Bonasa umbellus] var. *sabinei* COUES, Key North Amer. Birds, 1872, 235, part.

Bonasa umbellus var. *sabini* BAIRD, BREWER, and RIDGWAY, Hist. North Amer. Birds, iii, 1874, 454, part.

[Bonasa umbellus] c. var. *sabinii* COUES, Birds Northwest, 1874, 421, part.

Bonasa umbellus sabini ANTHONY, Auk, iii, 1886, 164 (Washington County, Oreg.).—AMERICAN ORNITHOLOGISTS' UNION, Check-list, 1886, No. 300c; ed. 2, 1895, 112; ed. 3, 1910, 140 part; ed. 4, 1931, 82, part.—RIDGWAY, Man. North Amer. Birds, 1887, 198, part.—TOWNSEND, Proc. U. S. Nat. Mus., x, 1887, 200, 235 (Humboldt Bay, Calif.).—BENDIRE, Life Hist. North Amer Birds, i, 1892, 68, part.—FANNIN, Check List British Columbia Birds, 1898, 32, part.—DWIGHT, Auk, xvii, 1900, 145 (plum. and molt).—BOWLES, Condor, iii, 1901, 47 in text (nests destroyed by mice).—KERMODE, Cat. British Columbia Birds, 1904, 26, part (British Columbia w. of Cascades).—MACOUN and MACOUN, Cat. Can. Birds, ed. 2, 1909, 223, part.—DAWSON and BOWLES, Birds Washington, ii, 1909, 587, part (Washington; habits; distr.).—GRINNELL, Pacific Coast Avif. No. 8, 1912, 10 (California); No. 11, 1915, 61 (California; distr.).—JEWETT, Condor, xviii, 1916, 75 (Tillamook County, Oreg.; not uncommon).—BRYANT, Condor, xix, 1917, 168 in text (food habits; Requa, Del Norte County, Calif.).—GRINNELL, BRYANT, and STORER, Game Birds California, 1918, 552 (descr.; habits; distr.; California).—DAWSON, Birds California (stud. ed.), iii, 1923, 1596 (genl.; California).—BROOKS and SWARTH, Pacific Coast Avif. No. 17, 1925, 50, part.—TAVERNER, Birds Western Canada, 1926, 167 in text, part; Birds Canada, 1934, 155 in text.—JEWETT and GABRIELSON, Pacific Coast Avif., No. 19, 1929, 19 (Portland, Oreg.; photo of nest and eggs).—GABRIELSON, Condor, xxxiii, 1931, 112 (Jackson County, Oreg.).—BENT, U. S. Nat. Mus. Bull. 162, 1932, 174, part (habits).—HALL, Murrelet, xiv, 1933, 70 (Washington; Columbia River; history); xv, 1934, 10, 14 (type loc. restricted to vicinity of Fort Vancouver, Clark County, Wash.; hist.).—PETERS, Check-list Birds of World, ii, 1934, 39, part.—GROEBBELS, Der Vögel, ii, 1934, 241 in text (eggs in mixed nests).—CONOVER, Condor, xxxvii, 1935, 204 in text (crit., distr., type loc.), 206 (spec. Oregon, Washington, British Columbia).—GRIFFEE and RAPRAEGER, Murrelet, xviii, 1937, 16 (Portland, Oreg., nesting).—GABRIELSON and JEWETT, Birds Oregon, 1940, 215 part (Oregon, distr.; descr.; habits).—TODD, Auk, lvii, 1940, 393 in text (charts) 396 part (distr.).—HELLMAYR and CONOVER, Cat. Birds Amer., i, No. 1, 1942, 218, part.—ALDRICH and FRIEDMANN, Condor, xlv, 1943, 94 (tax.; descr.; distr.).

Bonasa umbellus sabinei COUES, Hist. Exped. Lewis and Clark, iii, 1893, 872 in text (syn.).—FISHER, Condor, iii, 1901, 91 in text; iv, 1902, 114 in text, 132 (nw. California; heavy redwood forest north of Mad River, Humboldt Bay).—GRINNELL, Pacific Coast Avif., No. 3, 1902, 30 (California; fairly common resident of the humid coast from Cape Mendocino northward).

Bonasa u[mbellus] sabini ALLEN, Auk, x, 1893, 126.

B[onasa] u[mbellus] sabini BAILEY, Handb. Birds Western United States, 1902, 128, part (descr.; distr.).—UTTAL, Auk, lviii, 1941, 75, 77 in text (tarsal feathering).

[*Bonasa umbellus*] *sabini* UTTAL, Auk, lviii, 1941, 76 in text (tarsal feathering).
(?) *Tetrao fusca* ORD, *in* Guthrie's Geogr., 2d Amer. ed., 1815, 317 (based on Small Brown Pheasant, Lewis and Clark's Exp., ii, 182).
Bonasa umbellus fusca AMERICAN ORNITHOLOGISTS' UNION, Auk, xii, 1895, 169 (nomencl.).
B[*onasa*] *umbella fusca* COUES, Key North Amer. Birds, ed. 5, ii, 1903, 743 in text.
Bonasa umbellus fuscus COUES, Hist. Exped. Lewis and Clark, iii, 1893, 872 in text ("Oregon").

BONASA UMBELLUS CASTANEA Aldrich and Friedmann

OLYMPIC RUFFED GROUSE

Adult.—The darkest and most richly colored of all the predominantly brown races of the species; the brown of the upperparts deep chestnut to dark auburn with no grayish mixture, the ventral barrings Dresden brown to raw umber, darkening to mummy brown on the sides and flanks, the chin, throat, breast and upper abdomen, sides, flanks, and under tail coverts heavily washed with ochraceous-buff. No gray-phase birds have been seen; the brown birds have either black or rufescent ruffs, the black being the commoner of the two.

Juvenal.—None seen.

Downy young.—Indistinguishable from that of *B. u. umbellus*.

Adult male.—Wing 176–187 (182.8); tail 145–168 (153.9); culmen from base 25.6–29.9 (27.8); tarsus 43.6–48 (45.3); middle toe without claw 38.9–42.2 (40.7); unfeathered part of tarsus 16.0–29.4 (23.5 mm.).[75]

Adult female.—Wing 170–178 (174.9); tail 130–139 (131.8); culmen from base 23.6–28.0 (26.5); tarsus 41.2–45.5 (44.0); middle toe without claw 37.0–39.7 (38.6); unfeathered part of tarsus 20.8–29 (24.6 mm.).[76]

Range.—Subclimax woodland of the very wet portion (spruce-cedar association) of the Pacific coastal moist coniferous forest biome of the Transition Life Zone; on the Olympic Peninsula and in the immediate vicinity of the shore of Puget Sound in western Washington, south to Fort Steilacoom, Cedarville, and Shoalwater Bay, possibly also farther south along the "fog forest" belt in Oregon, although no specimens have been seen from the coast south of the Columbia River to establish this as a fact.

Type locality.—Soleduck River, Olympic Mountains, Wash.

Bonasa sabini BAIRD, CASSIN, and LAWRENCE, Rep. Pacific R. R. Surv., 1860, 629 in table (Puget Sound).
Bonasa umbellus sabini LAWRENCE, Auk, ix, 1892, 43 (Grays Harbor, Wash.).—
AMERICAN ORNITHOLOGISTS' UNION, Check-list, ed. 2, 1895, 112; ed. 3, 1910,
140, part.—KOBLE, Auk, xvii, 1900, 351 (Cape Disappointment, Wash.; not abundant).—RATHBUN, Auk, xix, 1902, 133 (Seattle, Wash.; breeds; common).—
BOWLES, Auk, xxiii, 1906, 142 (Tacoma, Wash.; breeds; common).—EDSON,

---

[75] Eleven specimens from the Olympic Peninsula.
[76] Nine specimens from the Olympic Peninsula.

Auk, xxv, 1908, 432 (Bellingham Bay region, Wash.; common except on higher mountains).—DAWSON and BOWLES, Birds Washington, ii, 1909, 587, part (habits; distr.).—(?) WILLETT, Condor, xvi, 1914, 89 (doubtful record for Sitka, Alaska; apparently=Westminster, British Columbia).—BURLEIGH, Auk, xlvi, 1929, 510 (Tacoma, Wash.; breeding habits).—AMERICAN ORNITHOLOGISTS' UNION, Check-list, ed. 4, 1931, 82, part.—MILLER, LUMLEY, and HALL, Murrelet, xvi, 1935, 57 (San Juan Islands, Wash.).—KITCHIN, Murrelet, xx, 1939, 30 (Mount Ranier National Park).—HELLMAYR and CONOVER, Cat. Birds Amer., i, No. 1, 1942, 218 part.

Bonasa sabinei ELLIOT, Monogr. Tetraonidae, 1865, pl. 3 and text, part.

Bonasa umbellus togata EDSON, Auk, xxv, 1908, 432 (Bellingham Bay region, Wash.; in the mountains).

Bonasa umbellus castaneus ALDRICH and FRIEDMANN, Condor, xlv, 1943, 95 (Soleduck River, Olympic Mountains, Washington; tax.; crit.; descr.; distr.).

BONASA UMBELLUS BRUNNESCENS Conover

VANCOUVER ISLAND RUFFED GROUSE

Adult (brown phase).—Similar to that of *Bonasa umbellus umbellus* but darker, more brownish, less rufescent (darker, more brownish than *sabini* also); general color of the upperparts between Prout's brown and Dresden brown, tail dull ochraceous-umber; underparts heavily barred with grayish ochraceous-umber and washed extensively with tawny-buff.

Adult (gray phase).—Similar to the brown phase, but the top of head, neck, back, rump, and upper tail coverts mixed and vermiculated with dark smoke gray; rectrices dark smoke gray barred and vermiculated with black and without any brownish tinge (the heavy black wavy bars are single in this race in both phases, while in *sabini* and *castanea* they are double with a pale ochraceous band in between them); underparts as in the brown phase but much less washed with buffy.

Juvenal.—Similar to that of *B. u. umbellus* but darker brown (darker than juvenal *monticola* also); above, cinnamon-brown to Prout's brown (as opposed to sayal brown in the nominate form); below, the ventral barrings darker—dusky Dresden brown.

Downy young.—None seen.

Adult male.—Wing 179–189 (183.7); tail 144–157 (148.6); culmen from base 26.6–28.3 (27.6); tarsus 44.0–46.8 (45.6); middle toe without claw 40–41 (40.3); unfeathered part of tarsus 24.7–29 (26.7 mm.).[77]

Adult female.—Wing 173–181 (176.3); tail 124–134 (128.4); culmen from base 24.4–27.4 (26); tarsus 41.8–45.2 (43.0); middle toe without claw 37–39.9 (38.4); unfeathered part of tarsus 20.5–28 (25.3 mm.).[78]

Range.—Subclimax woodland of the cedar-hemlock association in the moist coniferous forest biome (Transition Life Zone); on Vancouver Island, British Columbia, and the adjoining mainland from the vicinity

---

[77] Six specimens including the type.

[78] Six specimens.

of the city of Vancouver north at least to Lund. There are no records for the ruffed grouse on the coast of British Columbia between this locality and Port (Fort) Simpson near the Alaska line, and so it is doubtful if *brunnescens* ranges much farther north than the immediate vicinity of Vancouver Island.

T[etrao] Sabini Douglas, Trans. Linn. Soc. London, xvi, 1829, 137 part (Vancouver Island).

Bonasa sabinii Sclater, Proc. Zool. Soc. London, 1859, 236 (Vancouver Island).

Bonasa sabinei Elliot, Monogr. Tetraonidae, 1865, pl. 3 and text, part (Vancouver Island).

Bonasia sabinii Brown, Ibis, 1868, 424 (Vancouver Island).

Bonasa umbellus var. *sabini* Bendire, Proc. Boston Soc. Nat. Hist., xix, 1877, 140, part (Vancouver Island).

Bonasa umbellus sabini Bendire, Life Hist. North Amer. Birds, i, 1892, 68, part (Vancouver Island).—American Ornithologists' Union, Check-list, ed. 2, 1895, 112; ed. 3, 1910, 140, part.—Fannin, Check List British Columbia Birds, 1898, 32, part.—Dwight, Auk, xvii, 1900, 145, part (molt).—Macoun, Cat. Can. Birds, 1900, 204 part (coastal British Columbia including Vancouver Island).—Kermode, Cat. British Columbia Birds, 1904, 26, part (Vancouver Island).—Macoun and Macoun, Cat. Can. Birds, 1909, ed. 2, 1909, 223 part.—Swarth, Condor, xiv, 1912, 21 (Nootka Sound, Vancouver Island).—Brooks and Swarth, Pacific Coast Avif., No. 17, 1925, 50, part (Vancouver Island).—Taverner, Birds Western Canada, 1926, 167 in text, part.—Alford, Ibis, 1928, 197 (Vancouver Island).—American Ornithologists' Union, Check-list, ed. 4, 1931, 82, part.—Cumming, Murrelet, xiii, 1932, 7 (Vancouver Island).—Bent, U. S. Nat. Mus. Bull. 162, 1932, 174 part (life history).—Peters, Check-list Birds of World, ii, 1934, 39, part.

Bonasa umbellus Ogilvie-Grant, Cat. Birds Brit. Mus., xxii, 1893, 85, part (Vancouver Island).—Taverner, Condor, xx, 1918, 185 (Alert Bay, Vancouver Island).

Bonasa umbellus brunnescens Conover, Condor, xxxvii, 1935, 204 (Comox, Vancouver Island, orig. descr.; distr.; crit.), 206 (spec.; Vancouver and Saturna Islands). —Todd, Auk, lvii, 1940, 393, in text.—Hellmayr and Conover, Cat. Birds Amer., i, No. 1, 1942, 217 (distr.; syn.).—Aldrich and Friedmann, Condor, xlv, 1943, 96 (distr.; descr.).

B[onasa] u[mbellus] brunnescens Uttal, Auk, lviii, 1941, 75, 76, 77 in text (tarsal feathering).

BONASA UMBELLUS TOGATA (Linnaeus)

St. Lawrence Ruffed Grouse

Adult (brown phase).—Similar to that of *Bonasa umbellus umbellus* but darker brown, less rufescent, above, the areas that are sayal brown to cinnamon-brown in *umbellus* being Dresden brown to Prout's brown in *togata*, the parts that are Brussels brown in the nominate race being similar but washed with raw umber in the present form, and the upperparts generally with a little more mixture of grayish and with the blackish marks more extensive, the underparts similar but more heavily barred than in *umbellus*. In *B. u. umbellus* the brown phase is more frequent than the gray; in *B. u. togata* the opposite is true.

172   BULLETIN 50, UNITED STATES NATIONAL MUSEUM

Adult (gray phase).—Similar to that of *B. u. umbellus* but darker both in the browns and the grays of the upperparts, the brown as in the brown phase of *togata*—Dresden brown to Prout's brown, the blackish markings more extensive, the gray areas including the tail smoke gray much more finely and abundantly vermiculated with blackish than in *umbellus*; underparts more heavily and abundantly barred than in *umbellus*.

Juvenal.—Indistinguishable from that of *B. u. umbellus.*

Downy young.—Indistinguishable from that of *B. u. umbellus.*

Adult male.—Wing 173–192 (181.5); tail 142–174 (156.9); culmen from base 22.8–29.2 (26.1); tarsus 40.3–46.0 (42.7); middle toe without claw 33.0–39.9 (35.9); unfeathered part of tarsus 20.0–30.9 (25.2 mm.).[79]

Adult female.—Wing 168–184 (176.0); tail 119–144 (130.6); culmen from base 21.0–29.3 (25.2); tarsus 36.8–44.0 (41.4); middle toe without claw 31.3–36.7 (34.6); unfeathered part of tarsus 20.0–28.0 (23.8 mm.).[80]

Range.—Subclimax deciduous woodland (birch and aspen communities) of the pine-maple-beech-hemlock association, in the ecotone between the northern coniferous and the eastern deciduous forest biomes (Canadian and Upper Transition Life Zones); from northern New England and Nova Scotia, probably north to Cape Breton Island, and the Gaspé Peninsula, westward across southern Quebec and southern Ontario (including the north shore of Lake Superior) to northwestern Minnesota, south to northeastern Massachusetts (Manchester), east-central New York (Piseco), southeastern Ontario (Toronto), midway down the Lower Peninsula of Michigan (Midland County) and northern Wisconsin (Ashland County).

Type locality.—City of Quebec.

Tetrao togatus LINNAEUS, Syst. Nat., ed. 12, i, 1766, 275 (Canada; based on *Lagopus Bonasia canadensis* Brisson, Orn., i, 207, pl. 21, fig. 1).—FORSTER, Philos. Trans., lxii, 1772, 393 (Albany Fort, James Bay).—GMELIN, Syst. Nat., i, pt. 2, 1788, 752.

Tetrao umbellus NUTTALL, Man. Orn. U. S. and Canada, Land Birds, 1832, 657, part; ed. 2, 1840, 794, part.—AUDUBON, Orn. Biogr., 1839, 560, Birds Amer., 8vo ed., 1842, 72, part (Massachusetts, Maine, New Brunswick, Nova Scotia).

T[etrao] umbellus McILWRAITH, Birds Hamilton, Can. Journ., July 1860, 7 (common; Hamilton, Ontario).

Bonasa umbellus STEPHENS, *in* Shaw, Genl. Zool., xi, 1819, 300, part (Nova Scotia, and syn., part).—KNEELAND, Proc. Boston Soc. Nat. Hist., vi, 1857, 237 (Keweenaw Point, Lake Superior).—BAIRD, Rep. Pacific R.R. Surv., ix, 1858, 630, part.—ELLIOT, Monogr. Tetraonidae 1865, pl. 1 and text, part.—McILWRAITH, Proc. Essex Inst., v, 1866, 91 (Ontario).—MAYNARD, Proc. Boston Soc. Nat. Hist., xiv, 1872, 383, part.—HERRICK, Bull. Essex Inst., v, 1873, 11

[79] Thirty-two specimens from Ontario, Nova Scotia, New Brunswick, Maine, New Hampshire, Massachusetts, northern New York, northern Michigan, northern Wisconsin, and northeastern Minnesota.

[80] Twenty-one specimens from Ontario, Quebec, Nova Scotia, New Brunswick, Maine, New Hampshire, northern New York, northern Michigan, and northern Wisconsin.

(Grand Manan, New Brunswick; 1 seen).—GIBBS, U. S. Geol. and Geogr. Surv. Terr. Bull. 5, 1879, 491, part (Michigan).—CHADBOURNE, Auk, iv, 1887, 143 (White Mountains, N. H.; hen and chicks seen).—FAXON and ALLEN, Auk, v, 1888, 149 (Squam Lake, N. H.), 151 (Franconia, N. H.), 153 (Franconia and Bethlehem, N. H.).—BREWSTER, Auk, v, 1888, 389 (Winchendon, Mass.) ; Mem. Nuttall Orn. Club, No. 14, 1906, 171 (Cambridge, Mass.; habits, eggs).—FAXON, Auk, vi, 1889, 44, 99 (Berkshire County, Mass.).—ALLEN, Auk, vi, 1889, 76 (Bridgewater, N. H.).—OGILVIE-GRANT, Cat. Birds Brit. Mus., xxii, 1893, 85, part (Calais, Maine; Massachusetts) ; Handb. Game Birds, i, 1896, 71, part.— WARREN, Auk, xii, 1895, 191 in text (Upper Peninsula, Mich.; eaten by gos- hawk).—NASH, Check List Birds Ontario, 1900, 26 (Ontario).—[NASH], Check List Vert. Ontario: Birds, 1905, 35 (Ontario; common).—WIDMANN, Auk, xix, 1902, 233 (Wequetonsing, Emmet County, Mich.).—WOOD and FROTHINGHAM, Auk, xxii, 1905, 46 (Au Sable Valley, Mich.; spec.).—TOWNSEND, Mem. Nuttall Orn. Club, No. 3, 1905, 202 (Essex County, Mass.).—BLACKWELDER, Auk, xxvi, 1909, 366 (Iron County, Mich.; common).—CHANEY, Auk, xxvii, 1910, 273 (Hamlin Lake region, Mason County, Mich.).—JOHNSON, Auk, xliv, 1927, 319, in text (n. New York; winter; habits).—CHRISTY, Auk, xlviii, 1931, 394 (change of status; Sandusky Bay, Lake Erie).—TAVERNER, Birds Canada, 1934, 154 in text, pl. 18b (distr.; descr.) ; Can. Water Birds, 1939, 168 (field chars.).— CLARKE, Univ. Toronto Studies, biol. ser., No. 41, 1936, 1 (fluctuations in number; Ontario).—BAILLIE and HARRINGTON, Contr. Roy. Ontario Mus. Zool., No. 8, pt. 1, 1936, 28 (Ontario; common and widely distributed; breeds).— SNYDER, Trans. Roy. Can. Inst., xxii, 1938, 185 (w. Rainy River district, Ontario; spec.; sight record; drumming).—PETTINGILL, Proc. Nova Scotian Inst. Sci., xix, 1937-38 (1939), 333 (Grand Manan; common; habits).—RICKER and CLARKE, Contr. Roy. Ontario Mus. Zool., No. 16, 1939, 8 (Lake Nipissing, Ontario).—ALLIN, Trans. Roy. Can. Inst., xxiii, pt. 1, 1940, 96 (Darlington Township, Ontario; common).—SNYDER ET AL., Contr. Roy. Ontario Mus. Zool., No. 19, 1941, 46 (Prince Edward County, Ontario; irregular; color phases).—LEWIS, Wils. Bull., liii, 1942, 77 (Anticosti Island, Quebec; introd.).

B[onasa] umbellus NELSON, Bull. Essex Inst., viii, 1876, 121, part (n. Michigan).— COUES, Key North Amer. Birds, ed. 5, ii, 1903, 741, part.

Bonasa umbella COUES, Proc. Essex Inst., v, 1868, 39, part (New England; common) ; Key North Amer. Birds, 1884, 585, part.—MERRIAM, Bull. Nuttall Orn. Club, vii, 1882, 238 (Point de Monts, Canada).

Bonasa umbellus subsp. WHITE, Auk, x, 1893, 230 (Mackinac Island, Mich.).— ALLEN, Auk, xxv, 1908, 59 (s. Vermont).

Bonasa umbellus var. umbellus BAIRD, BREWER, and RIDGWAY, Hist. North Amer. Birds, iii, 1874, 448, part.

Bonasa umbellus umbellus TOWNSEND, Mem. Nuttall Orn. Club, No. 5, 1920, 96 (Essex County, Mass.; common).—CAHN, Wils. Bull., xxxix, 1927, 27 (summer, Vilas County, Wis.).—STONER, Roosevelt Wild Life Ann., ii, Nos. 3, 4, 1932, 433 (habits, Oneida Lake, N. Y.).—ELIOT, Auk, xlix, 1932, 101 (West Chester- field, Mass.).—HELLMAYR and CONOVER, Cat. Birds Amer., i, No. 1, 1942, 215, part (s. Ontario; Massachusetts, part).

B[onasa] umbellus umbellus TOWNSEND, Mem. Nuttall Orn. Club, No. 3, 1905, 202, in text (Essex County, Mass.).

[Bonasa umbellus] umbellus TOWNSEND, Mem. Nutt. Orn. Club, No. 3, 1905, 202 in text (Essex County, Mass.).—SNYDER and LOGIER, Trans. Roy. Can. Inst., xviii, pt. 1, 1931, 177 in text (intermediate spec.).

Bonasa umbellus togata RIDGWAY, Proc. U. S. Nat. Mus., viii, 1885, 355 (nomencl.).—
AMERICAN ORNITHOLOGISTS' UNION, Check-list, 1886, 172, No. 300a.; ed. 2, 1895,
111; ed. 3, 1910, 140, part; ed. 4, 1931, 81, part.—RIDGWAY, Man. North Amer.
Birds, 1887, 198, part.—DWIGHT, Auk, iv, 1887, 16 (Cape Breton Island, Nova
Scotia) ; xvii, 1900, 145 (plum. and molt).—BRITTAIN and Cox, Auk, vi, 1889,
117 (Restigouche Valley, New Brunswick).—CAULFIELD, Can. Rec. Sci., July
1890, 145 (Montreal; rare).—ALLEN, Auk, viii, 1891, 165 (Bras D'Or, Cape
Breton Island, Nova Scotia) ; Auk, x, 1893, 126.—BENDIRE, Life Hist. North
Amer. Birds, i, 1892, 64, part.—DWIGHT, Auk, x, 1893, 8 (Prince Edward
Island, few seen).—HOFFMAN, Auk, xii, 1895, 88 (Graylock Mountain, Mass.).
—MORRELL, Auk, xvi, 1899, 251 (Nova Scotia; Cumberland County, abundant).
—MACOUN, Cat. Can. Birds, 1900, 202 (abundant in Nova Scotia, New
Brunswick, Prince Edward Island, Quebec, and Ontario).—HOWELL, Auk, xviii,
1901, 340 (Mount Mansfield, Vt.; numerous).—BAILEY, Handb. Birds Western
United States, 1902, 127 part (descr., distr.).—TOWNSEND, Mem. Nuttall Orn.
Club, No. 3, 1905, 202 in text (Essex County, Mass.) ; Auk, xxix, 1912, 19
(Glenwood and Upper Greenwich, New Brunswick).—FLEMING, Auk, xxiv,
1907, 71 (Toronto, north to Lake Nipissing).—MACOUN and MACOUN, Cat.
Can. Birds, ed. 2, 1909, 220, part.—WRIGHT, Auk, xxix, 1912, 324 in text
(White Mountains, N. H.; drumming).—MACNAMARA, Ottawa Nat., xxvi, 1912,
101, text, part.—BANGS, Auk, xxix, 1912, 378, in text (crit.).—MOUSLEY, Auk,
xxxiii, 1916, 66 (Hatley, Quebec; common; eggs).—JACKSON, Auk, xl, 1923, 481
(Mamie Lake, Wis.).—SOPER, Auk, xl, 1923, 497 (Wellington and Waterloo
Counties, Ontario).—CHRISTY, Wils. Bull., xxxvii, 1925, 210 (status in summer;
Huron Mountain, Mich.).—TAVERNER, Birds Western Canada, 1926, 167, in
text, part; Birds Canada, 1934, 155 in text, part.—GRANGE, Wils. Bull., xlviii,
1936, 104 (Wisconsin, population studies).—DE MILLE, Auk, xliii, 1926, 516
(Mont Luis Lake, Gaspé County, Quebec).—FORBUSH, Birds Massachusetts and
Other New England States, ii, 1927, 36 (fig., descr.; habits; New England).—
SNYDER, Trans. Roy. Can. Inst., xvi, pt. 2, 1928, 258 (Lake Nipigon region,
Ontario; summer) ; xvii, pt. 2, 1930, 186 (King Township, Ontario; summer).—
SNYDER and LOGIER, Trans. Roy. Can. Inst., xviii, pt. 1, 1931, 177 (Long Point
area, Norfolk County, Ontario; extirpated or nearly so; sight record in 1924;
nest and eggs 1931).—BENT, U. S. Nat. Mus. Bull. 162, 1932, 166, part (life
hist.; range).—PETERS, Check-list Birds World, ii, 1934, 39.—BEEBE, Wils.
Bull., xlix, 1937, 34 (Upper Peninsula Michigan; as abundant now as in past).—
GROEBBELS, Der Vögel, ii, 1937, 166 (data on breeding biology).—MACLULICH,
Contr. Roy. Ontario Mus. Zool., No. 13, 1938, 11 (Algonquin Prov. Park,
Ontario; common; habitat; spec.).—VAN TYNE, Occ. Pap. Mus. Zool. Univ.
Michigan, No. 379, 1938, 11 (Michigan, south to Midland and Oceana Counties;
breeds).—TODD, Auk, lvii, 1940, 396 (distr.).—DEAR, Trans. Roy. Can. Inst.,
xxiii, pt. 1, 1940, 126 (Thunder Bay, Lake Superior, Ontario; varies from
uncommon to plentiful; breeding records).—HELLMAYR and CONOVER, Cat. Birds
Amer., i, No. 1, 1942, 214 part.—ALDRICH and FRIEDMANN, Condor, xlv, 1943, 96
(tax; descr.; distr.).

B[onasa] umbellus togata RIDGWAY, Man. North Amer. Birds, 1887, 198, part.—
UTTAL, Auk, lviii, 1941, 74, figure (tarsal feathering).

B[onasa] u[mbellus] togata AUSTIN, Mem. Nuttall Orn. Club, No. 7, 1932, 73 in
text (centr. and e. Canada).—CONOVER, Condor, xxxvii, 1935, 204 in text (crit.),
206, part (spec.; Maine, Michigan, Quebec, and Ontario).—PETTINGILL, Proc.
Nova Scotian Inst. Sci., xix, 1937-38 (1939), 333 (Grand Manan, New Brunswick; mentioned).—SNYDER ET AL., Contr. Roy. Ontario Mus. Zool., No. 19,

1941, 46, in text (Prince Edward County, Ontario; gray phase).—UTTAL, Auk, lviii, 1941, 75, 77, and 78 in text (tarsal feathering).

[*Bonasa*] *umbellus togata* BAILLIE and HARRINGTON, Contr. Roy. Ontario Mus. Zool., No. 8, pt. 1, 1936, 28 in text (Ontario; resident in greater part of province).

[*Bonasa*] [*umbellus*] *togata* TOWNSEND, Mem. Nuttall Orn. Club, No. 3, 1905, 202 in text (Essex County, Mass.).—SNYDER and LOGIER, Trans. Roy. Can. Inst., xviii, pt. 1, 1931, 177 in text.—TODD, Auk, lvii, 1940, 391 in text (crit.).—UTTAL, Auk, lviii, 1941, 76 and 77 in text (tarsal feathering).

Bonasa umbellus thayeri BANGS, Auk, xxix, 1912, 378 (orig. descr., Digby, Nova Scotia; meas.; crit.).—[STONE], Auk, xxxiii, 1916, 426 (Digby, Nova Scotia). —AMERICAN ORNITHOLOGISTS' UNION, Auk, xl, 1923, 517 (Nova Scotia); Check-list, ed. 4, 1931, 81.—BANGS, Bull. Mus. Comp. Zool., lxx, No. 4, 1930, 156 (type spec. in Mus. Comp. Zool., crit.).—BENT, U. S. Nat. Mus. Bull. 162, 1932, 177 (habits, etc.).—TAVERNER, Birds Canada, 1934, 155 in text.—PETERS, Check-list Birds of World, ii, 1934, 40 (Nova Scotian Peninsula, possibly also eastern New Brunswick).—TODD, Auk, lvii, 1940, 391 in text (crit.).—HELLMAYR and CONOVER, Cat. Birds Amer., i, No. 1, 1942, 215.

B[*onasa*] *u*[*mbellus*] *thayeri* AUSTIN, Mem. Nuttall Orn. Club, No. 7, 1932, 73 in text (Nova Scotia).—CONOVER, Condor, xxxvii, 1935, 205 in text (crit.), 206 (spec.).—PETTINGILL, Proc. Nova Scotian Inst. Sci., xix, 1937-38 (1939), 333 (Grand Manan; mentioned).—UTTAL, Auk, lviii, 1941, 75 and 77 in text (tarsal feathering).

BONASA UMBELLUS AFFINIS Aldrich and Friedmann

COLUMBIAN RUFFED GROUSE

Adult (gray phase).—Similar to the corresponding phase of *Bonasa umbellus umbellus* but darker, more brownish above, more heavily barred below (in its general appearance intermediate between the gray phase of *umbellus* and that of *sabini*); feathers of top of head more solidly blackish edged with smoke gray, and basally pale ochraceous-tawny on their hidden portions; interscapulars and inner upper wing coverts cinnamon-brown with large blotches and some vermiculations of fuscous to black, and with pale shaft streaks of tilleul buff to pale smoke gray; feathers of upper back similar but with less blackish and more mottled with smoke gray on their terminal portions; feathers of lower back, rump, and upper tail coverts Prout's brown, sparingly vermiculated with black, with broad, tear-shaped, whitish shaft spots, which are longitudinally streaked and edged narrowly with black, the feathers edged with smoke gray, the extent of the terminal gray increasing on the upper tail coverts; rectrices darker gray than in *umbellus*—smoke gray to light grayish olive with a faint ochraceous tinge especially along the shaft and on the proximal edge of each of the black wavy bands; and slightly more heavily vermiculated with black; below more heavily barred, the bars dusky isabelline to tawny-olive, darkening on the sides and flanks to sepia and mummy brown; the lower throat and upper breast more strongly washed with ochraceous-tawny than in *umbellus* of the same phase. The gray phase is commoner than the brown one.

Adult (brown phase).—Similar to the gray phase but the tail sayal brown with a cinnamon wash, instead of smoke gray, the upperparts of the head and body and the upper wing coverts browner, less grayish, more rufescent, but not so rufescent as the brown phase of *sabini*—the pale shaft streaks of the interscapulars pale ochraceous-tawny, the upper back and the lateral brown areas of the interscapulars Dresden brown to mikado brown vermiculated with blackish, lower back and rump dark mikado brown to rufescent Prout's brown; ventral barrings darker than in the gray phase—Dresden brown darkening on the sides and flanks to mummy brown. This phase is like the brown phase of *togata,* but has the black markings less extensive.

Juvenal.—Similar to that of *B. u. umbellus* but very slightly more rufescent (more than in *monticola* also) above and with the ventral bars darker—sepia to mummy brown; the rectrices and the outer webs of the secondaries bright ochraceous-tawny.

Downy young.—None seen.

Adult male.—Wing 171–191 (181.7); tail 130–170 (152.4); culmen from base 23.4–28.8 (26.3); tarsus 40.4–45.5 (42.9); middle toe without claw 34.2–41.0 (37.6); unfeathered part of tarsus 14.5–29.2 (21.6 mm.).[81]

Adult female.—Wing 170–185 (176.2); tail 123–157 (132.4); culmen from base 23.9–28.4 (26.2); tarsus 36.0–42.2 (40.6); middle toe without claw 32.5–39.3 (35.2); unfeathered part of tarsus 14.0–25.0 (19.4 mm.).[82]

This race is intermediate between *sabini* on the one hand and *umbelloides* and *phaia* on the other.

Range.—Subclimax deciduous woodlands (aspen, poplar, and willow communities) of the montane and subalpine forests (Transition and Canadian Life Zones); from Fort Klamath and Harney, Oreg., northward, east of the Cascades, excluding the mountains of northeastern Oregon, southeastern and northeastern Washington, through the interior of British Columbia, to Hazelton, and to Canyon Island, Taku River, near Juneau, southeastern Alaska. Specimens from Bear Lake in north-central British Columbia and from Telegraph Creek farther to the northwest in the same province are intermediate between *affinis* and *umbelloides;* birds from southeastern Alaska are darker than typical *affinis.*

The range of *Bonasa umbellus affinis,* as here delineated, includes populations of much paler and more grayish birds from the more arid interior regions of Washington and Oregon. The extreme examples of this type are found among specimens from Tunk Mountain, Aeneas, Twisp, Mazama, Molson, and Oroville, in Okanogan County, and Swan

---

[81] Forty-two specimens from British Columbia, Washington, and Oregon.

[82] Sixteen specimens from British Columbia, Washington, Oregon, and Idaho.

Lake and Curlew in Ferry County, Wash. Apparently there is here represented a well-marked "ecological race" which shows a greater resemblance to *incana* than anything else and yet completely cut off from that form by *affinis* and *phaia*. This may be a case of morphological and ecological parallelism, since in central northern Washington the prairie grassland merges with the montane forest in much the same way that it does in Utah and Wyoming, where typical *incana* occurs. Since the variation seems not to have a geographical range distinct from *affinis,* it is not here given a subspecific name. A more thorough study of the problem in the field, however, might show such recognition to be desirable on the basis of ecological segregation of the type mentioned by Miller (Amer. Midl. Nat., lxxvi, 1942, 34) in certain species of the San Francisco Bay region.

Type locality.—Fort Klamath, Oreg.

Bonasa umbellus var. *umbelloides* BENDIRE, Proc. Boston Soc. Nat. Hist., xix, 1877, 140 (se. Oregon; rare).

Bonasa umbellus umbelloides MEARNS, Bull. Nuttall Orn. Club, iv, 1879, 197, (Fort Klamath, e. Oregon).—AMERICAN ORNITHOLOGISTS' UNION, Check-list, ed. 2, 1895, 112; ed. 3, 1910, 140, part; ed. 4, 1931, 81, part.—JEWETT, Auk, xxvi, 1909, 6 (Baker County, Oreg.; common).—GABRIELSON, Auk, xli, 1924, 555 (common in Wallowa County, Oreg.).—TAVERNER, Birds Western Canada, 1926, 167, in text (interior of British Columbia; plum.). Birds Canada, 1934, 155 in text, part.—KELSO, Ibis, 1926, 701 (Arrow Lakes, British Columbia; crit.; habits).—EDSON, Murrelet, xiii, 1932, 42 (Yakima River, Wash.).—PETERS, Check-list Birds World, ii, 1934, 39, part.—HELLMAYR and CONOVER, Cat. Birds Amer., i, No. 1, 1942, 216, part.

Bonasa sabinii BAIRD, Rep. Pacific R.R. Surv., ix, 1858, 631, part.—DALL and BANNISTER, Trans. Chicago Acad. Sci.; i, 1869, 287 (Alaska; Sitka; and British Columbia).

Bonasa sabini BENDIRE, Proc. Boston Soc. Nat. Hist., xviii, 1875, 164 (Camp Harney, Oreg.).

Bonasa umbellus var. *sabini* BAIRD, BREWER, and RIDGWAY, Hist. North Amer. Birds, iii, 1874, 454, part.—BENDIRE, Proc. Boston Soc. Nat. Hist., 1877, 140, part (John Day River, Oreg.; and Fort Colville, Wash.).

Bonasa umbellus sabinii BREWSTER, Bull. Nuttall Orn. Club, vii, 1882, 227, 232 (Walla Walla, Wash.).

Bonasa umbellus sabini MERRILL, Auk, v, 1888, 145 (Fort Klamath, Oreg.; common in aspen groves).—MACOUN and MACOUN, Cat. Can. Birds, ed. 2, 1909, 223, part. —RATHBUN, Auk, xxxiii, 1916, 364 (Crescent Lake, Wash.; not common).— SHELTON, Univ. Oregon Bull., new ser., xiv, No. 4, 1917, 20, 26 (west-central Oregon).—TAVERNER, Birds Western Canada, 1926, 167 in text, part.—RACEY, Auk, xliii, 1926, 521 (swamp between Alta and Green Lakes, British Columbia). —MILLER and CURTIS, Murrelet, xxi, 1940, 42 (n. of University of Washington campus).—GABRIELSON and JEWETT, Birds Oregon, 1940, 215 part (e. slope of Cascades, Oreg.).

Bonasa umbellus togata AMERICAN ORNITHOLOGISTS' UNION, Check-list, 1886, 172, No. 300a, part.—BENDIRE, Life Hist. North Amer. Birds, i, 1892, 64, part (British Columbia, Washington, Oregon).—DAWSON, Auk, xiv, 1897, 173 (Okanogan County, Wash.).—FANNIN, Check List British Columbia Birds.

1898, 32 (British Columbia, e. of and including Cascade Mountains).—MACOUN, Cat. Can. Birds, 1900, 202, part.—BAILEY, Handb. Birds Western United States, 1902, 127, part.—KERMODE, Cat. British Columbia Birds, 1904, 26 (e. of and including Cascade Mountains).—JOHNSON, Condor, viii, 1906, 26 (Cheney, Wash.).—DAWSON and BOWLES, Birds Washington, ii, 1909, 583, part (e. Washington, habits; distr.).

B[onasa] umbellus togata RIDGWAY, Man. North Amer. Birds, 1887, 198, part (e. Oregon, and Washington Territory).

Bonasa umbellus OGILVIE-GRANT, Cat. Birds Brit. Mus., xxiii, 1893, 85 part (Fort Klamath, Oreg.).

Bonasa umbellus affinis ALDRICH and FRIEDMANN, Condor, xlv, 1943, 97 (Fort Klamath, Oreg.; tax.; crit.; descr.; distr.).

BONASA UMBELLUS PHAIA Aldrich and Friedmann

IDAHO RUFFED GROUSE

Adult (gray phase).—Similar to that of Bonasa umbellus umbellus but less brownish, more grayish, and much darker, the smoke gray of the upperparts of the latter being replaced by mouse gray to light grayish olive, abundantly and heavily vermiculated with black; the general dorsal coloration being more grayish than brownish, only the interscapulars and upper surface of the wings being brownish—Saccardo's umber to dusky olive-brown to dull sepia (and even the interscapulars are largely grayish terminally); lower back and rump feathers basally and laterally sepia, but this color less extensive than the vermiculated gray parts of the feathers; below more heavily barred than umbellus (more like affinis and togata), the bars pale Saccardo's umber to mummy brown, the throat and breast strongly tinged with pale ochraceous-tawny.

Adult (brown phase).—Similar to that of B. u. umbellus but much darker, less rufescent, more brownish (more like the corresponding phase of brunnescens, but with more grayish or dusky); the tail Dresden brown tinged, especialy laterally, with ochraceous-tawny, the brown of the upper parts of head, body and wings dark, dull Saccardo's umber to dark Dresden brown, vermiculated with black, the feathers of the upper and lower back with a dark grayish mixture; the feathers of the rump darkening to Prout's brown medially tipped with dark smoke gray to pale grayish olive; below similar to the gray phase but slightly less buffy on the breast.

Juvenal (male only seen).—Above much grayer than that of B. u. umbellus, even grayer than the gray-phase juvenal of B. u. monticola, the general coloration of the upper parts of head, body, wings, and tail being drab to ashy hair brown, the interscapulars, scapulars, and a few of the feathers of the back having ashy tilleul-buff shaft stripes and cross bars with incomplete broad clove brown to blackish interspaces; outer margin of secondaries buffy avellaneous, lesser upper wing coverts with a light brownish-olive tinge; crown and occiput dark mouse gray, the feathers with broad black terminal areas, margined and narrowly tipped with dark mouse gray; hind neck, sides of neck, and breast washed with ochraceous-tawny; ventral barring mummy brown.

Downy young.—None seen.

Adult male.—Wing 175–193 (182.7); tail 141–171 (157.7); culmen from base 24.8–28.6 (26.6); tarsus 39.8–46.0 (42.7); middle toe without claw 34.8–39.7 (37.6); unfeathered part of tarsus 15.7–28.8 (23.2 mm.).[83]

Adult female.—Wing 173–182 (178.6); tail 124–134 (130.2); culmen from base 23.5–27.0 (25.2); tarsus 39.6–43.4 (41.1); middle toe without claw 34.4–37.5 (36.2); unfeathered part of tarsus 20.9–27.0 (23.8 mm.).[84]

Range.—Subclimax deciduous woodlands of the Idahoan montane forest (larch-pine association) of the Transition Zone, on the west slopes of the Rocky Mountains in Idaho, west to northeastern Oregon in the Blue Mountains, southeastern and northeastern Washington. Possibly it extends farther into southeastern British Columbia, but no specimens have been seen to establish this fact.

Type locality.—Priest River, Idaho.

Bonasa umbellus var. *sabini* BENDIRE, Proc. Boston Soc. Nat. Hist., xix, 1877, 140 (Fort Lapwai, Idaho).

Bonasa umbellus togata AMERICAN ORNITHOLOGISTS' UNION, Check-list, 1886, 172, No. 300a, part.—MERRIAM, North Amer. Fauna, No. 5, 1891, 93 (Salmon River Mountains, south-central Idaho).—BENDIRE, Life Hist. North Amer. Birds, i, 1892, 64, part (Idaho).—MERRILL, Auk, xiv, 1897, 352 (Fort Sherman, Idaho; very abundant).—SNYDER, Auk, xvii, 1900, 243 (Diamond Lake and Mount Carleton, n. Washington).—DAWSON and BOWLES, Birds Washington, ii, 1909, 583, part (e. Washington).—RUST, Condor, xvii, 1915, 123 (Kootenai County, Idaho).—(?) DICE, Auk, xxxv, 1918, 44 (Prescott, se. Washington; rare).

Bonasa umbellus var. *umbelloides* BAIRD, BREWER, and RIDGWAY, Hist. North Amer. Birds, iii, 1874, 453, part.

Bonasa umbellus umbelloides AMERICAN ORNITHOLOGISTS' UNION, Check-list, ed. 4, 1931, 81, part.—BENT, U. S. Nat. Mus. Bull. 162, 1932, 171, part (life hist.).—PETERS, Check-list Birds World, ii, 1934, 37, part.—GABRIELSON and JEWETT, Birds Oregon, 1940, 214 part (Blue Mountains, Oreg.; descr.; habits).—HELLMAYR and CONOVER, Cat. Birds Amer., i, No. 1, 1942, 216, part.

B[onasa] u[mbellus] umbelloides BAILEY, Handb. Birds Western United States, 1902, 128, part.—COUES, Key North Amer. Birds, ed. 5, ii, 1903, 742, part.

B[onasa] u[mbella] umbelloides COUES, Key North Amer. Birds, rev. ed., 1896, 585, part.

Bonasa umbellus HAND, Condor, xliii, 1941, 225 (St. Joe National Forest, Idaho).

Bonasa umbellus phaios ALDRICH and FRIEDMANN, Condor, xlv, 1943, 98 (Priest River, Idaho; crit.; tax.; descr.; distr.).

BONASA UMBELLUS INCANA Aldrich and Friedmann

HOARY RUFFED GROUSE

Adult (brown phase).—A very ashy bird, similar not to the brown but to the gray phase of *Bonasa umbellus umbellus*, but paler and, except

---

[83] Thirty-four specimens from Washington, Oregon, and Idaho.

[84] Ten specimens from Washington and Idaho.

for the tail, less brownish, more like that of *B. u. umbelloides* but paler, and less brownish on the interscapulars, back, and upper surface of wings; the general color of the forehead, crown, occiput, nape, upper back, and upper wing coverts, light neutral gray tinged or mixed with from pale light brownish olive to pale tawny-olive, the head and nape with very little of this brownish wash; interscapulars with large fuscous to black blotches on the feathers which are otherwise ashy tilleul buff, basally washed with pale ochraceous-tawny; feathers of lower back, rump, and upper tail coverts snuff brown, tipped, edged, and vermiculated with ashy light neutral gray and with subterminal large tear-shaped tilleul buff to whitish shaft spots laterally narrowly edged with black and sparingly speckled with the same, rectrices cinnamon-buff to pale clay color, the lateral feathers the palest, the terminal inch pale smoke gray traversed by a broad band of dark dull sepia and sparingly speckled with fuscous, the broad dark band occupying more than half the width of the gray area, and breaking up into a mass of frecklings on the median pair of rectrices; below as in *B. u. umbellus* but the barrings more numerous, especially on the abdomen, and averaging paler—pale ashy buffy drab, and the tarsus more fully feathered.

Adult (gray phase).—Similar to the brown phase but with the tail feathers smoke gray with no buffy tone; ventral barrings duskier—light brownish olive darkening to sepia on the sides and flanks.

Juvenal.—None seen.

Downy young.—None seen.

Adult male.—Wing 172–191 (181); tail 138–164 (151.8); culmen from base 25.3–28.8 (27.0); tarsus 40.3–44.9 (42.6); middle toe without claw 35.0–39.9 (37.4); unfeathered part of tarsus 12.0–22.5 (17.4 mm.).[85]

Adult female.—Wing 165–178 (171.5); tail 120–147 (133.2); culmen from base 25.0–27.8 (26.3); tarsus 36.9–44.7 (39.8); middle toe without claw 33.2–38.8 (35.0); unfeathered part of tarsus 13.8–21.7 (17.3 mm.).[86]

Range.—Subclimax deciduous woodland and thickets (cottonwood and willow communities) chiefly of the Rocky Mountain montane forest (western yellow-pine consociation) of the Transition Zone, but to some extent also in similar subclimax deciduous communities in the upper fringe of the grassland biome of the Upper Austral Zone, east of the Rocky Mountains; from west-central and central-northern Utah, southeastern Idaho, and central-western Wyoming northeastward across Wyoming and the Dakotas to northeastern North Dakota (Walhalla). *Bonasa umbellus incana* intergrades with *umbelloides* in northwestern Wyoming, and probably also in the intervening areas wherever the species occurs, and in southern Manitoba in the aspen parklands and along

[85] Twenty specimens from Wyoming, Utah, North Dakota, and southeastern Idaho.
[86] Eight specimens from Utah, North Dakota, and southeastern Idaho.

cottonwood-bordered streams. This race probably extends to the southern limits of the species' range in the Rocky Mountains and Great Plains region in southwestern and north-central Colorado (Nucla and Estes Park); southeastern and central southern South Dakota (Custer State Park and Rosebud). No specimens have been seen to definitely establish this, however.

Type locality.—Barclay, 15 miles east of Salt Lake, Utah.

Bonasa umbellus var. *umbelloides* BAIRD, Rep. Pacific R. R. Surv. ix, 1858, 925 (Fort Bridger, Wyo.).—RIDGWAY, Bull. Essex Inst., v, 1873, 188 (Colorado); vii, 1875, 39 (Nevada).—BAIRD, BREWER, and RIDGWAY, Hist. North Amer. Birds, iii, 1874, 453, part.

Bonasa umbellus umbelloides RIDGWAY, Bull. Essex Inst., vi, 1875, 34 (Parleys Park, Wahsatch Mountains, Utah).—BENDIRE, Life Hist. North Amer. Birds, i, 1892, 67 part (North Dakota, Wyoming, Utah, Colorado).—COOKE, Colorado State Agr. Coll. Bull. No. 37, 1897, 70 (Colorado; rare); No. 44, 1898, 159 (Colorado; Denver); No. 56, 1900, 202 (Colorado; Estes Park).—VISHER, Auk, xxvi, 1909, 147 (w. South Dakota, brood seen); xxviii, 1911, 10 (Harding County, S. Dak.).—MACOUN and MACOUN, Cat. Can. Birds, ed. 2, 1909, 222, part.—SCLATER, Hist. Birds Colorado, 1912, 147 (Colorado; very rare resident at lower elevations in the mountains).—OVER and THOMS, Birds South Dakota, 1921, 76 (South Dakota; abundant in Black Hills).—WOOD, Misc. Publ. Mus. Zool. Univ. Michigan, No. 10, 1923, 35 (North Dakota; common; specs.).—WILLIAMS, Wils. Bull., xxxviii, 1926, 29 (Red River Valley, ne. North Dakota). —FULLER and BOLE, Sci. Publ. Cleveland Mus. Nat. Hist., i, 1930, 50 (Wyoming).—AMERICAN ORNITHOLOGISTS' UNION, Check-list, ed. 4, 1931, 81, part.— BENT, U. S. Nat. Mus. Bull. 162, 1932, 171, part (life hist.).—STANFORD, Proc. Utah Acad. Sci., ix, 1932, 73 (Logan Canyon, Utah; spec.).—PETERS, Check-list Birds of World, ii, 1934, 39 part.—MILLER, Wils. Bull., xlvi, 1934, 159 (near Experiment Station, s. Utah).—ALEXANDER, Univ. Colorado Stud., xxiv, 1937, 87 (Boulder County, Colo.; hypothetical).—NIEDRACH and ROCKWELL, Birds Denver and Mountain Parks, 1939, 61 (probably now extinct, last record 1898). —Fox, Auk, lvii, 1940, 109 in text (North Dakota; feeding habits).—HELLMAYR and CONOVER, Cat. Birds Amer., i, No. 1, 1942, 216 part (syn.; distr.).

Bonasa umbellus β *umbelloides* RIDGWAY, Orn. 40th Parallel, 1877, 319 (Wahsatch Mountains, Utah).

B[onasa] u[mbellus] umbelloides BAILEY, Handb. Birds Western United States, 1902, 128, part.—COUES, Key North Amer. Birds, ed. 5, 1903, ii, 742, part.— CONOVER, Condor, xxxvii, 1935, 204 in text (crit.), 206 part (spec.; North Dakota, Utah, Manitoba).

Bonasa umbella umbelloides DREW, Auk, ii, 1885, 17 (Colorado).

B[onasa] u[mbella] umbelloides COUES, Key North Amer. Birds, rev. ed., 1896, 585, part.

Bonasa umbellus ALLEN, Bull. Mus. Comp. Zool., iii, 1872, 131 (mountains of Colorado, Wyoming, and Utah).—BENDIRE, Life Hist. North Amer. Birds, i, 1892, 59, part (North and South Dakota, se. Nebraska).—OGILVIE-GRANT, Cat. Birds Brit. Mus., xxii, 1893, 85, part (Deadwood, Dakota); Handb. Game Birds, i, 1896, 71, part (Utah, Colorado).—REAGAN, Auk, xxv, 1908, 464 (Rosebud Reservation, S. Dak.; rare).—Fox, Auk, lvii, 1940, 109 in text (food habits, North Dakota).

Bonasa umbellus togata GRAVE and WALKER, Birds Wyoming, 1913, 39 (Wyoming).— AMERICAN ORNITHOLOGISTS' UNION Check-list, ed. 4, 1931, 81, part.

Bonasa umbellus incanus ALDRICH and FRIEDMANN, Condor, xlv, 1943, 99 (Barclay, 15 miles e. of Salt Lake City, Utah; distr.; descr.; tax.).—BEHLE, Condor, xlvi, 1944, 72 (Utah).

BONASA UMBELLUS YUKONENSIS Grinnell
YUKON RUFFED GROUSE

Adult (gray phase).—Similar to that of *Bonasa umbellus umbellus* but much paler, the palest of all the races of the species, the whitish areas above more extensive and purer white, less washed with buffy; nearest to the gray phase of *incana* but paler, with more white, and with the most extensive tarsal feathering of all the subspecies; the gray areas of the upperparts of head, body, wings, and tail pale neutral gray to smoke gray, the brown, restricted to the top of the head, the interscapulars, wings, and middle of the back, is pale tawny-olive to pale Saccardo's umber; below as in *umbellus* but more abundantly barred with buffy drab.

Adult (brown phase).—Similar to the gray phase but with the tail between sayal brown and Saccardo's umber distally vermiculated and washed with smoke gray, with the feathers of the interscapulars, back, and rump with very broad transverse subterminal bands of mummy brown (these bands present but concealed in the gray phase), and with the ventral barrings darker—Dresden brown to mummy brown.

Juvenal (female only seen).—Above much grayer than any seen of *B. u. umbellus*, nearest to that of *B. u. phaia*, the general coloration of the upper side of the head, body, and wings being drab to hair brown, the interscapulars, scapulars, crown, and upper back being broadly transversely blotched with fuscous to black, and with pale tilleul-buff shaft streaks and narrow cross bars of slightly darker tilleul buff; rectrices as in *phaios* but slightly more washed with drab.

Downy young.—None seen.

Adult male.—Wing 174–190 (182); tail 129–168 (148.5); culmen from base 24.9–29.1 (26.8); tarsus 38.3–45.0 (42.4); middle toe without claw 34–38.5 (36.7); unfeathered part of tarsus 8.8–15.7 (11.2 mm.).[87]

Adult female.—Wing 170–182 (177.6); tail 127–137 (130.8); culmen from base 24–27.9 (26.6); tarsus 38.8–43.5 (41.2); middle toe without claw 33–37 (34.9); unfeathered part of tarsus 7.3–14.9 (11.0 mm.).[88]

Range.—Subclimax deciduous woodlands (aspen, poplar, and willow communities) chiefly in the white-spruce, pine, and larch association, in the ecotone, between the northern coniferous and tundra biomes (Hudsonian Life Zone); from western Alaska (Akiak and Nulato) eastward across Alaska, chiefly in the valleys of the Yukon and Kuskokwim Rivers,

---

[87] Thirty-four specimens from Alaska, Mackenzie, and northern Alberta.

[88] Ten specimens Alaska, Mackenzie, and northern Alberta.

across Yukon from Selkirk and the Lewes River Valley, north to La Pierre House, east at least to Great Slave Lake and Lake Athabaska, and southward along the Liard River, at least to Fort Liard, Mackenzie, and along the Athabaska River to Fort McMurray, Alberta. There are records of ruffed grouse from farther east in the Hudsonian Zone of northern Manitoba (Brochet and York Factory) which may also belong to this race, but specimens have not been seen to substantiate this. Although primarily a Hudsonian Zone form, *yukonensis* apparently includes within its range a sizable area characterized by pure coniferous forest climax (Canadian Zone) in southwestern Mackenzie and northern Alberta.

Type locality.—Forty-mile, Yukon, on Yukon River, near Alaska boundary.

Tetrao umbellus (not of Linnaeus, 1766) SABINE, Append. Franklin's Journ., 1823, 697, part.—SWAINSON and RICHARDSON, Fauna Bor.-Amer., ii, 1831 (1932), 342, part.
Bonasa umbellus DALL and BANNISTER, Trans. Chicago Acad. Sci., i, 1869, 287 (Nulato, Alaska).—OGILVIE-GRANT, Cat. Birds Brit. Mus., xxii, 1893, 85, part (Nulato, Fort Simpson) ; Handb. Game Birds, i, 1896, 71, part (Alaska).
B[onasa] umbellus COUES, Key North Amer. Birds, ed. 5, 1903, ii, 741, part.
T[etrao] umbelloides DOUGLAS, Trans. Linn. Soc. London, xvi, 1829, 148 in text, part.
B[onasa] umbelloides REICHENOW, Die Vögel, i, 1913, 319 (Alaska).
Bonasa umbellus var. *umbelloides* BAIRD, BREWER, and RIDGWAY, Hist. North Amer. Birds, iii, 1874, 453, part.
Bonasa umbellus umbelloides NELSON, Cruise *Corwin* in 1881 (1883), 80 (Bering Sea coast of Alaska—Bristol Bay).—AMERICAN ORNITHOLOGISTS' UNION, Check-list, 1886, 172, No. 300b, part.—TURNER, Contr. Nat. Hist. Alaska, 1886, 152 (Yukon Valley).—NELSON, Rep. Nat. Hist. Coll. Alaska, 1887, 131 (lower Yukon Valley; Koviak Peninsula).—BENDIRE, Life Hist. North Amer. Birds, i, 1892, 67, part (Yukon River).—MACOUN, Cat. Can. Birds, 1900, 203, part (Alaska). —GRINNELL, Pacific Coast Avif., No. 1, 1900, 75 (Kotzebue Sound region; a few; Kowak River).—MACOUN and MACOUN, Cat. Can. Birds, ed. 2, 1909, 222, part.—GRINNELL, Condor, xi, 1909, 204 (Forty Mile, Yukon Territory; spec.) ; xii, 1910, 42 (Russian Mission, lower Yukon; Fort Yukon; spec.).— PREBLE, North Amer. Fauna, No. 27, 1909, 340, part (n. Mackenzie to lat. 63° N.).
B[onasa] umbellus umbelloides RIDGWAY, Man. North Amer. Birds, 1887, 198, part (Yukon valley).
Bonasa umbellus sabini MACOUN and MACOUN, Cat. Can. Birds, ed. 2, 1909, 223, part.
Bonasa umbellus yukonensis GRINNELL, Condor, xviii, 1916, 166 (orig. descr., Forty-mile, Yukon Territory; crit.; meas.; distr.).—[STONE], Auk, xxxiii, 1916, 426 (Yukon Territory).—AMERICAN ORNITHOLOGISTS' UNION, Auk, xl, 1923, 517 (interior of Yukon Territory and Alaska) ; Check-list, ed. 4, 1931, 81 (distr.).— TAVERNER, Birds Western Canada, 1926, 167, in text.—BENT, U. S. Nat. Mus. Bull. 162, 1932, 177 (habits).—PETERS, Check-list Birds of World, ii, 1934, 39.— TAVERNER, Birds Canada, 1934, 155 in text.—TODD, Auk, lvii, 1940, 396 (distr.).— HELLMAYR and CONOVER, Cat. Birds Amer., i, No. 1, 1942, 217 (distr.; syn.).— ALDRICH and FRIEDMANN, Condor, xlv, 1943, 100 (tax.; distr.; descr.).

B[onasa] u[mbellus] yukonensis CONOVER, Condor, xxxvii, 1935, 204 in text (crit.), 206 (spec., Yukon Territory).—UTTAL, Auk, lviii, 1941, 75, 76 in text (tarsal feathering).

[Bonasa] [umbellus] yukonensis TODD, Auk, lvii, 1940, 394 in text.—UTTAL, Auk, lviii, 1941, 76, 77, 78 in text (tarsal feathering).

BONASA UMBELLUS UMBELLOIDES (Douglas)

GRAY RUFFED GROUSE

Adult (gray phase).—Similar to the corresponding phase of *Bonasa umbellus umbellus* but much less brownish, more grayish and darker, being closest in appearance to the gray phase of *phaia* from which it differs in being paler gray (and the brown areas paler also) above, less heavily barred below, and with a longer part of the tarsus feathered. The gray of the feathers of the nape, back, rump, upper tail coverts, and the tail smoke gray lightly vermiculated with fuscous to blackish; the brown areas of the interscapulars cinnamon-brown to russet heavily blotched with black; the brown of the upper surface of the wings dull Saccardo's umber speckled and washed with grayish; below more heavily banded than *umbellus*, less so than *phaia*, the brown bands averaging slightly darker than in *umbellus*—pale tawny-olive darkening on the sides and flanks to sepia; tarsus feathered for more than half its length.

Adult (brown phase).—Similar to the gray phase but with the tail tawny-olive instead of gray and interscapulars and upper surface of the wings slightly more extensively brownish, and the breast and upper abdomen averaging more washed with tawny-buff.

Juvenal (brown phase).—Similar to the corresponding plumage of *B. u. umbellus* but less rufescent, more grayish, the general color of the upperparts of the head, body, and wings being buffy brown to grayish olive-brown, the rectrices between wood brown and drab; ventral barring darker—grayish buffy brown.

Juvenal (gray phase).—Like the brown phase but gray—the ground color of the upperparts of the body and wings and tail being grayish drab to ashy hair brown; ventral barrings darker—mummy brown, the underparts less washed with buffy.

Downy young.—Not distinguishable from that of the nominate race.

Adult male.—Wing 171–195 (182.6); tail 144–174 (157.7); culmen from base 24.4–29.4 (26.3); tarsus 39–45.5 (42.5); middle toe without claw 35.0–40.6 (37.5); unfeathered part of tarsus 10.9–24.0 (17.7) mm.).[89]

Adult female.—Wing 169–180 (174.6); tail 125–134 (130.4); culmen from base 23.6–27.6 (25.6); tarsus 37.5–43.2 (41.0); middle toe without claw 33.8–36.3 (34.9); unfeathered part of tarsus 10.9–17.8 (15.3 mm.).[90]

[89] Forty-three specimens from Alberta, northern British Columbia, and Montana.
[90] Eleven specimens from Alberta, British Columbia, Montana, and northwestern Wyoming.

Range.—Subclimax deciduous woodland (aspen, poplar, and willow communities) of the Rocky Mountain subalpine forest (Engelmann spruce–alpine fir association) and the northern coniferous forest (white spruce–balsam fir association) in the Canadian Life Zone; from northwestern British Columbia (Atlin) southward along the east slopes of the Rocky Mountains to central eastern Idaho and northwestern Wyoming; eastward through the aspen parkland and spruce-fir forest of the prairie provinces of Canada, north to middle Manitoba (Oxford House) and south to southwestern Ontario (Lake of the Woods), across Ontario between Lake Superior and James Bay and across Quebec to the north shore of the Gulf of St. Lawrence.[91]

Type locality.—Henry House, Alberta.

Tetrao umbellus (not of Linnaeus) WILSON, Amer. Orn., vi, 1812, 45, part (Moose Fort, Hudson Bay; also the mountains that divide the waters of the Columbia and the Missouri Rivers).—SABINE, Append. Franklin's Journ., 1823, 697, part.— SWAINSON and RICHARDSON, Fauna Bor.-Amer., ii, 1831 (1832), 342, part.— WILSON and BONAPARTE, Amer. Orn., ii, 1832 (printed by Whittaker, Treacher, and Arnot) 249, part; ii, 1832 (?) (printed by Cassell, Petter, and Galpin) 251, part (Moose Fort, Hudson Bay).—JARDINE, Nat. Libr., Orn., iv, Gallinaceous Birds, pt. ii, Game birds, 1834, 149, part (banks of the Saskatchewan).— AUDUBON, Synopsis, 1839, 202, part (Saskatchewan to Labrador); Orn. Biogr., v, 1839, 560, part; Birds Amer., 8vo ed., v, 1842, 72, part (banks of Saskatchewan).—WILSON, Amer. Orn., ed. by Brewer, 1840, 430, part.

T[etrao] umbellus WILSON and BONAPARTE, Amer. Orn., ii, 1871, 265, part (Moose Fort, Hudson Bay).

Bonasa umbellus BAIRD, Rep. Pacific R. R. Surv., ix, 1858, 630, part (Hudson Bay Territory).—BAIRD, CASSIN, and LAWRENCE, Rep. Pacific R. R. Surv., 1860, 630 in table, part (Red River, Hudson Bay Territory).—BLAKISTON, Ibis, 1863, 127 (forks of Saskatchewan to Hudson Bay).—TURNER, Proc. U. S. Nat. Mus., viii, 1885, 245 (Labrador).—OGILVIE-GRANT, Cat. Birds Brit. Mus., xxii, 1893, 85, part (Hudson Bay); Handb. Game Birds, i, 1896, 71, part.—NUTTING, Bull. Lab. Nat. Hist. State Univ. Iowa, ii, 1893, 266 (Lower Saskatchewan River).— COUBEAUX, Ottawa Nat., 1909, 27 (s. Saskatchewan).—TAVERNER, Auk, xxxvi, 1919, 13 (Red Deer River, Alberta) 264 in text (Miquelon Lake, near Camrose, Alberta); Nat. Mus. Canada Bull. 50, 1928, 92 (near Belvedere, Alberta).— SHORTT and WALLER, Contr. Roy. Ontario Mus. Zool., No. 10, 1937, 17 (Lake

---

[91] Although specimens from northern Ontario and middle Quebec average slightly darker and have a greater proportion of the tarsus unfeathered than typical *umbelloides* from the east slopes of the Canadian Rockies, the difference seems to be too slight to recognize as a distinct subspecies. These characters merely indicate the trend toward intergradation between *umbelloides* and *togata*. Therefore, *canescens* Todd becomes a synonym of *umbelloides*. Ruffed grouse recorded farther east in Quebec (Anticosti Island, Natashquan, and Wolf Bay) and in southeastern Labrador (Hamilton Inlet and Sandwich Bay) may belong to this race also, but no specimens from these regions have been examined in the present study.

Specimens from southern Manitoba (Shoal Lake and Carberry) are intermediate between *umbelloides, incana,* and *mediana,* but on average characters, particularly relatively short unfeathered tarsus, they seem a little closer to *umbelloides.*

St. Martin region, Manitoba).—CLARKE, Nat. Mus. Canada Bull. 96, 1940, 48 (Thelon Game Sanctuary, northwestern Canada).

B[onasa] umbellus COUES, Key North Amer. Birds, ed. 5, ii, 1903, 741, part.

Bonasa umbellus subsp. RICHMOND and KNOWLTON, Auk, xi, 1894, 302 (Taylors Fork, Mont.).—BETTS, Condor, xviii, 1916, 162 (Flathead River, Mont.).— AUSTIN, Mem. Nuttall Orn. Club, No. 7, 1932, 73 (Newfoundland Labrador).

Bonasa umbellus var. umbellus BAIRD, BREWER, and RIDGWAY, Hist. North Amer. Birds, iii, 1874, 448, 453, part.

T[etrao] umbelloides DOUGLAS, Trans. Linn. Soc. London, xvi, 1829, 148, in text, part ("valleys of the Rocky Mountains, 54° North latitude . . .").

Bonasa umbelloides ELLIOT, Proc. Acad. Nat. Sci. Philadelphia, 1864, 23, part; Monogr. Tetraonidae, 1865, pl. 2 and text, part.

Bonasa umbellus var. umbelloides MERRIAM, 6th Ann. Rep. U. S. Geol. Surv. Terr., 1873, 699 (e. Idaho and w. Wyoming).—COUES, Birds Northwest, 1874, 425, part.—BAIRD, BREWER, and RIDGWAY, Hist. North Amer. Birds, iii, 1874, 448, part, pl. 61, fig. 10.

[Bonasa umbellus] var. umbelloides, COUES, Key North Amer. Birds, 1872, 235, part.

[Bonasa umbellus] b. var. umbelloides COUES, Birds Northwest, 1874, 421 part.

Bonasa umbellus umbelloides RIDGWAY, Man. North Amer. Birds, 1887, 198, part.— AMERICAN ORNITHOLOGISTS' UNION, Check-list, 1886, 172, No. 300b; ed. 2, 1895, 112; ed. 3, 1910, 140, part; ed. 4, 1931, 81, part.—THOMPSON, Proc. U. S. Nat. Mus., xiii, 1891, 509 (w. Manitoba).—BENDIRE, Life Hist. North Amer. Birds, i, 1892, 67, part.—FANNIN, Check List British Columbia Birds, 1898, 32 (British Columbia; Rocky Mountain district).—DWIGHT, Auk, xvii, 1900, 145 (plum. and molt).—MACOUN, Cat. Can. Birds, 1900, 203 (Manitoba and Alberta.)—BROOKS, Auk, xx, 1903, 281 (Cariboo District, British Columbia).—KERMODE, Cat. British Columbia Birds, 1904, 26 (British Columbia; Rocky Mountains).—PREBLE, North Amer. Fauna, No. 27, 1908, 340, part (Alberta).—COUBEAUX, Ottawa Nat., 1909, 27 (s. Saskatchewan).—STANSELL, Auk, xxvi, 1909, 393 (nw. Edmonton, Alberta; very common).—MACOUN and MACOUN, Cat. Can. Birds, ed. 2, 1909, 222, part.—FERRY, Auk, xxvii, 1910, 198 (Prince Albert, Saskatchewan; common), 204 (Quill Lake, Saskatchewan).—DuBOIS, Auk, xxviii, 1911, 468 (e. Alberta). —RILEY, Can. Alpine Journ., 1912, 57 (Henry House, Alberta).—GRAVE and WALKER, Birds Wyoming, 1913, 39 (fairly common; nw. Wyoming).—SAUNDERS, Condor, xvi, 1914, 131 (n. Montana, 4,500-6,000 feet); Pacific Coast Avif., No. 14, 1921, 57 (Montana; habits; distr.).—GRINNELL, Condor, xviii, 1916, 166 in text (crit.).—SWARTH, Univ. California Publ. Zool., xxx, 1926, 85 (Atlin region, British Columbia).—SKINNER, Condor, xxx, 1928, 237 (Yellowstone Park).—KEMSIES, Wils. Bull., xlii, 1930, 204 (Yellowstone Park, Wyo.).— BENT, U. S. Nat. Mus. Bull. 162, 1932, 171, part (habits, etc.).—PETERS, Checklist Birds World, ii, 1934, 39, part.—TAVERNER, Birds Canada, 1934, 155 in text, part.—COWAN, Occ. Pap. British Columbia Prov. Mus., No. 1, 1939, 27 (Peace River district, British Columbia; abundant; eggs; young; spec.)—TODD, Auk, lvii, 1940, 394, in text (crit.), 396 (distr.).—UTTAL, Auk, lviii, 1941, 74, figure (tarsal feathering).—HELLMAYR and CONOVER, Cat. Birds Amer., i, No. 1, 1942, 216, part.—ALDRICH and FRIEDMANN, Condor, xlv, 1943, 99 (tax.; descr.; distr.).

Bonasa umbella umbelloides COUES, Check List North Amer. Birds, ed. 2, 1882, No. 566, part; Key North Amer. Birds, ed. 2, 1884, 585, part.

Bonasa u[mbellus] umbelloides ALLEN, Auk, x, 1893, 126.

B[onasa] umbellus umbelloides RIDGWAY, Man. North Amer. Birds, 1887, 198, part.

B[onasa] u[mbellus] umbelloides.—BAILEY, Handb. Birds Western United States, 1902, 128, part (distr.; descr.).—COUES, Key North Amer. Birds, ed. 5, ii, 1903,

742, part.—SAUNDERS, Condor, xiv, 1912, 25 in text (sw. Montana, at lower elevations).—CONOVER, Condor, xxxvii, 1935, 204 in text, 206, part (spec.; Alberta; British Columbia; Manitoba, Saskatchewan).—UTTAL, Auk, lviii, 1941, 75, 76 in text (tarsal feathering).

B[onasa] u[mbella] umbelloides COUES, Key North Amer. Birds, rev. ed., 1896, 585, part.

[Bonasa umbellus] umbelloides UTTAL, Auk, lviii, 1941, 75, 76, 77, 78 in text (tarsal feathering).

Bonasa umbellus togata BENDIRE, Life Hist. North Amer. Birds, i, 1892, 64, part.— NUTTING, Bull. Lab. Nat. Hist. State Univ. Iowa, ii, 1893, 266 (lower Saskatchewan River).—AMERICAN ORNITHOLOGISTS' UNION, Check-list, ed. 2, 1895, 111; ed. 3, 1910, 140, part; ed. 4, 1931, 81, part.—MACOUN, Cat. Can. Birds, 1900, 202, part.—FLEMING, Auk, xviii, 1901, 37 (Parry Sound and Muskoka, Ontario; plentiful).—BAILEY, Handbook Birds Western United States, 1902, 127, part.— BROOKS, Auk, xx, 1903, 281 (Cariboo District, British Columbia).—SETON, Auk, xxv, 1908, 71 (Fort Resolution; not seen or heard east of Great Slave Delta).— STANSELL, Auk, xxvi, 1909, 393 (nw. Edmonton, Alberta; very common).— MACOUN and MACOUN, Cat. Can. Birds, ed. 2, 1909, 220, part (Cariboo District, British Columbia).—TOWNSEND and BENT, Auk, xxvii, 1910, 13 (Natashquan and Betchewun, Labrador).—SAUNDERS, Auk, xxviii, 1911, 35 (Gallatin County, Mont.; abundant); Condor, xiv, 1912, 25 (sw. Montana; common); xviii, 1916, 86 in text (Flathead Lake, Montana); Pacific Coast Avif., No. 14, 1921, 57 (Montana; common; distr.; habits).—MACNAMARA, Ottawa Nat., xxvi, 1912, 101, in text, part.—TOWNSEND, Auk, xxx, 1913, 6 (Labrador, Natashquan River). —RUST, Condor, xix, 1917, 32 (Freemont County, Idaho—Little Dry Creek Canyon, and near Rea Post Office).—BURLEIGH, Auk, xxxviii, 1921, 553 (Warland, Lincoln County, Mont.; common in the valleys).—ROWAN, Auk, xxxix, 1922, 227 (Indian Bay, Lake of the Woods, Manitoba).—MITCHELL, Can. Field Nat., xxxviii, 1924, 108 (Saskatchewan; common resident).—TAVERNER, Birds Western Canada, 1926, 167 in text, part; Birds Canada, 1934, 155 in text, part.— BENT, U. S. Nat. Mus. Bull. 162, 1932, 166, part (Manitoba).—HELLMAYR and CONOVER, Cat. Birds Amer., i, No. 1, 1942, 214, part (n. Quebec, n. Ontario).

B[onasa] umbellus togata RIDGWAY, Man. North Amer. Birds, 1887, 198, part (Moose Factory).

B[onasa] u[mbellus] togata SAUNDERS, Condor, xvi, 1914, 131 in text (s. Montana).— TAVERNER, Nat. Mus. Canada Bull. 50, 1928, 92 (near Belvedere, Alberta; spec.).

Bonasa umbellus canescens TODD (not "Bonasa canescens Sparrm." Menzbier, Vög. Russl., i, 1895, 480), Auk, lvii, 1940, 395 (Abitibi River, n. Ontario; descr.; distr.; crit.), 396 (distr.).

B[onasa] u[mbellus] canescens UTTAL, Auk, lviii, 1941, 74 in text (tarsal feathering).

Genus PEDIOECETES Baird

Pedioecetes BAIRD, Rep. Pacific R. R. Surv., ix, 1858, xxi, xliv. (Type, by monotypy, Tetrao phasianellus Linnaeus.)

Pediocœtes (emendation) BAIRD, Rep. Pacific R. R. Surv., ix, 1858, 625.

Pediaecaetes (emendation) ELLIOT, Proc. Acad. Nat. Sci. Philadelphia, 1864, 23.

Pediecœtes (emendation) ELLIOT, Monogr. Tetraonidae, 1865, Introd., 5.

Pediocœtus (emendation) SUNDEVALL, Tentamen, 1873, 114.

Pediocoetus (emendation) SUNDEVALL, Tentamen, 1873, 176.

Pediœcetes (emendation) SCLATER, Ibis, 1863, 109, footnote.

Medium-sized terrestrial grouse (length about 381–483 mm.) with neither elongated feathers nor air sacs on sides of neck and with the tail (not including elongated middle rectrices) much less than half as long as wing, strongly graduated, the middle pair of rectrices projecting much beyond the next, narrow, with parallel edges and subtruncate tips.

Bill relatively small (from frontal antiae about one-fourth as long as rest of head), its depth at frontal antiae about equal to or slightly exceeding its width at same point; culmen rounded (not ridged); maxillary tomium distinctly and regularly concave or arched; rhamphotheca wholly smooth. Wing moderate, strongly concave beneath, the longest primaries exceeding longest secondaries by about one-fourth the length of wing; third and fourth primaries longest, the first (outermost) intermediate between sixth and seventh; outer primaries distinctly bowed or incurved, the inner web of four or five outer ones distinctly emarginate. Tail much less than half as long as wing (not including elongated middle

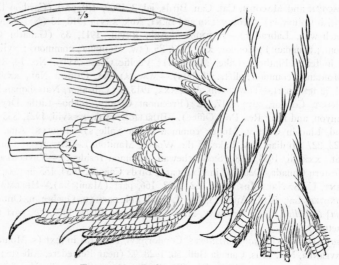

FIGURE 11.—*Pedioecetes phasianellus.*

rectrices), strongly graduated almost wholly concealed by coverts, the middle pair of rectrices projecting much beyond the next pair, rather narrow, with parallel edges and subtruncate tips; rectrices (18) rather soft. Tarsus between one-fourth and one-fifth as long as wing, completely clothed with long, soft, hair-like feathers, these, in winter plumage, concealing basal half or more of toes; middle toe slightly shorter than tarsus[92]; lateral toes extending to or a little beyond penultimate articulation of middle toe; hallux about as long as second phalanx of middle toe; upper side of toes with a continuous series of transverse scutella, with

---

[92] Owing to the extensive and dense feathering, it is very difficult to make accurate measurements of length of tarsus and middle toe.

a row of rather long scutella along each side, outside of which are long
fringelike processes or pectinations (at least in winter) ; claws relatively
long and slender, slightly curved.

Plumage and coloration.—Feathers of crown distinctly elongated, decurved, forming, when erected, a rather conspicuous crest; no elongated
feathers on sides of neck, and no obvious cervical air sacs; plumage
in general rather soft, the feathers of upperparts distinctly outlined,
rounded, the plumage of lower abdomen, anal region, etc., soft, hairlike,
and blended. Upperparts variegated with tawny-brown and blackish,
the scapulars and wings spotted with white or buffy; rectrices (except
two middle pairs) mostly white distally; underparts white, the breast
and sides with V-shaped markings of dusky, the chin, throat, and fore
neck mostly buff.

Range.—Open districts of northwestern and central North America,
from prairies of upper Mississippi Valley, north side of Lake Superior,
northwestern Ontario, and western Ungava to central Alberta, northwestern British Columbia, northeastern California, Utah, and Colorado.
(Monotypic.)

KEY TO THE FORMS OF PEDIOECETES PHASIANELLUS (LINNAEUS)

a. Darker above, the black or dark fuscous areas predominating, giving an appearance of a dark bird barred with buffy brown and spotted with white.
  b. Upperparts very dark, the brownish barrings and edges and tips of feathers
    of mantle and upper back much reduced, marks in inner portions of vanes
    very narrow or absent; feathers of breast dark buffy brown with only narrow
    white shaft stripes (central and northern Mackenzie).
                                      Pedioecetes phasianellus kennicottii (p. 193)
  bb. Upperparts less dark, the brownish barrings and edges and tips of feathers well
    developed.
    c. White spots on upperparts much reduced; feathers of breast pale buffy brown
      with fairly broad white shaft stripes (Hudson's Bay region).
                                      Pedioecetes phasianellus phasianellus (p. 194)
    cc. White spots on the upperparts large and prominent; feathers of breast white,
      merely edged with dark olive-brown (Alaska, the Yukon district to ex-
      treme northern British Colombia).
                                      Pedioecetes phasianellus caurus (p. 190)
aa. Paler above, the brown areas larger, the blackish ones more hidden, giving the
  appearance of a brownish bird mottled with blackish.
  b. Brown of upperparts more rufescent—ochraceous-tawny to almost hazel (Illi-
    nois, Wisconsin, Minnesota, and southern Manitoba).
                                      Pedioecetes phasianellus campestris (p. 203)
  bb. Brown of upperparts less rufescent—buckthorn brown to tawny-olive.
    c. Smaller and paler; tail averaging less than 110 mm., height of bill at base
      averaging 12 mm., brown of upperparts pale, grayish tawny-olive (from
      north-central British Columbia to northern California (Modoc region),
      Nevada, Utah, and southwestern Colorado).
                                      Pedioecetes phasianellus columbianus (p. 200)

cc. Larger and darker brown of upperparts buckthorn brown; tail averaging over 115 mm., height of bill at base averaging 13 mm. (Great Plains area from north-central Alberta, central Saskatchewan, to (all but extreme western) Montana, the Dakotas, Wyoming, western Nebraska, and north-eastern Colorado)............**Pedioecetes phasianellus jamesi** (p. 196)

PEDIOECETES PHASIANELLUS CAURUS Friedmann
ALASKAN SHARP-TAILED GROUSE

Adult male (autumn).—Forehead fuscous to fuscous-black, the feathers tipped with dark snuff brown; feathers of the crown and occiput similar but crossed with widely spaced whitish bars and tipped with cinnamon-buff; the pale bars more abundant, less widely spaced on the lateral coronal feathers, and blending into a fairly definite whitish or buffy whitish superciliary stripe on each side; nape like the sides of the crown but washed with pale ochraceous-buff; "mantle," i. e., interscapulars, fuscous-black broadly barred with white, the more distal bars, especially on the more posterior feathers, washed with pale ochraceous-buff; feathers of sides of neck and of breast similar to anterior interscapulars; back, rump, and upper tail coverts fuscous-black, broadly but incompletely barred with cinnamon-buff to tawny-olive, the latter color often sparsely vermiculated with fuscous-black, and broadly tipped with pale cinnamon-buff to pinkish buff, darkest on the back and becoming paler on the rump and upper tail coverts; scapulars and inner median and greater upper wing coverts like the upper back but with the brownish areas more extensive (at the expense of the blackish parts) and each feather with a large terminal white wedge-shaped spot; rest of the upper wing coverts and the secondaries grayish olive-brown externally incompletely and sparsely barred with white, the coverts with terminal white spots on their outer webs, the secondaries completely edged with white on the tips of both webs; primaries grayish olive-brown with white spots on the outer webs; median rectrices pinkish buff longitudinally and trans-versely marbled with fuscous-black; the next pair largely fuscous-black tipped with white and with their outer webs mixed with white; lateral rectrices white with dusky smudges along the shafts; circumocular region fuscous-black; lores, subocular stripe, cheeks, and auriculars pale ochra-ceous-buff dappled with dusky; the dusky markings concentrating on either side to form a fairly distinct malar stripe; the auriculars tipped with fuscous-black; chin and upper throat whitish suffused with pale ochraceous-buff and with many small pale clove-brown spots; lower throat white, the feathers narrowly edged with dark olive-brown; breast feathers white with heavy margins of dark olive-brown; feathers of sides and flanks white barred with dark olive-brown, the more posterior of these feathers with considerable tawny-olive on their outer webs and with the dark bars darker—clove brown to almost fuscous; upper abdomen and sides of lower abdomen white with a few small dark olive-brown subterminal **V**-shaped marks; center of abdomen and under tail coverts white, sometimes tinged with pale ashy buff; thighs pale light cinnamon-drab, the distal tarsal plumes paler, more whitish and very long, covering all but the claw of the middle toe.

Adult male (spring).—Similar to the fresh autumn plumage but generally darker, the pale tips and margins of the feathers reduced by wear; the tarsal plumes shorter (also because of wear).

Adult female.—Very similar to the plumage of the male in comparable degree of freshness or abrasion, but with the median rectrices more strictly transversely barred, less longitudinally marbled.

Juvenal[93].—Crown and occiput hazel with a median, longitudinal, posteriorly broadening black stripe; interscapulars, scapulars, greater and median upper wing coverts, and inner secondaries irregularly barred and blotched with fuscous-black and cinnamon-buff to tawny-olive as in the adults but with prominent white shaft stripes and without white bars or spots; the upper wing coverts with the brownish areas duller than the interscapulars; primaries and outer secondaries similar to the adult but terminally more pointed; back, lower back, rump, and upper tail coverts generally similar to the adult; rectrices as in the adult but the median ones shorter, and all, especially the lateral ones, less whitish, more buffy, and more mottled and speckled with dusky brownish; the median two pairs with a broad buffy whitish median stripe; chin, throat, and sides of head cream buff to colonial buff; lower throat, breast, and upper abdomen dirty white spotted with clove brown and sepia, the feathers of the sides of the neck similar but with white shaft stripes; sides and flanks similar but with the spots paler drab to somewhat tawny-drab; abdomen dirty white almost unspotted; thighs tinged strongly with colonial buff.

Downy young.—Forehead, crown, occiput, and nape mustard yellow, tinged on the occiput and nape with pale ochraceous-buff; a black median line, beginning as a spot on the base of the culmen extending back to the crown where it bifurcates forming a loop on the occiput, the two branches reuniting on the nape; a few small black spots lateral to this on the anterior part of the occiput and on the nape; rest of upperparts straw yellow tinged strongly on the middorsal line with ochraceous-tawny, and blotched and streaked broadly with black, these markings more or less confining the ochraceous spinal areas and also forming semi-transverse humeral lines; sides of head bright light mustard yellow, with a black spot on the auriculars; underparts bright straw yellow, tinged with mustard yellow on the chin, throat, and side.

Adult male.—Wing 196–212 (203.2); tail 113–125 (118.7); culmen, from anterior end of nostril, 10.3–11.8 (10.9); tarsus 40.4–44.3 (42.3);

---

[93] Female only seen, but sexes undoubtedly alike.

middle toe without claw 36–39.2 (38.1) ; height of bill at base 10.3–12.4 (11.5 mm.).[94]

Adult female.—Wing 190–202 (196.3) ; tail 107–119 (111.9) ; culmen from anterior end of nostril 9.9–11.9 (10.8) ; tarsus 39.2–42.8 (41.2) ; middle toe without claw 35.7–39.3 (37.5) ; height of bill at base 10.9–12.5 (11.8 mm.).[95]

Range.—Resident from north-central Alaska (Circle, Fairbanks, Tanana, Tanana Crossing, north fork of Kuskokwim River, Delta and Taklat Rivers) to southern Yukon (Tagish Lake on the Yukon River—British Columbia border) and to extreme northeastern Alberta (Fort Chippewyan, Smith Landing, Fort Smith, and Peace Point).

Type locality.—Fairbanks, Alaska.

Pedioecetes phasianellus DALL and BANNISTER, Trans. Chicago Acad. Sci., i, 1869, 287 (Nulato to Fort Yukon).
Pediocætes phasianellus AMERICAN ORNITHOLOGISTS' UNION, Check-list, 1886, No. 308, part.—NELSON, Birds Alaska, 1887, 139 part (Alaska; nesting).
Pediocaetes phasianellus BENDIRE, Life Hist. North Amer. Birds, i, 1892, 97, part 1.
Pediæcetes phasianellus OSGOOD, North Amer. Fauna, No. 30, 1907, 87 (Yukon Territory; Macmillan River; Thirtymile River, Seltark, and Pelly region).
Pediæcetes phasianellus phasianellus AMERICAN ORNITHOLOGISTS' UNION, Check-list, ed. 3, 1910, 144 part (central Alaska).—BROOKS and SWARTH, Pacific Coast Avif., No. 17, 1925, 52 (extreme northwestern British Columbia; Tagish Lake, and Hudson's Hope, upper Peace River).
Pedioecetes phasianellus phasianellus TAVERNER, Birds Western Canada, 1926, 172 in text, part; Birds Canada, 1934, 161, in text, part.—AMERICAN ORNITHOLOGISTS' UNION, Check-list, ed. 4, 1931, 86, part (central Alaska).—PETERS, Check-list Birds of World, ii, 1934, 40 part.
[*Tetrao*] *columbianus* GRAY, Hand-list, ii, 1870, 276, No. 9830 part (?).
P[*ediocætes*] *phasianellus columbianus* RIDGWAY, Man. North Amer. Birds, 1887, 204, part (Fort Yukon, Alaska).
Pedioceteo phasianellus columbianus BAILEY, Handb. Birds Western United States, 1902, 132, part (Alaska).
Pediocætes phasianellus columbianus AMERICAN ORNITHOLOGISTS' UNION, Check-list, ed. 2, 1895, 116 part (central Alaska).
Pedioecetes phasianellus kennicottii SNYDER, Univ. Toronto Studies, biol. serv., No. 40, 1935, 4, 48, part (monogr., crit.) ; Occ. Pap. Roy. Ontario Mus. Zool., No. 2, 1935, 2, part (monogr.).—HELLMAYR AND CONOVER, Cat. Birds Amer., i, No. 1, 1942, 221 part (syn., distr.).
P[*edioecetes*] p[*hasianellus*] *kennicottii* SNYDER, Auk, lvi, 1939, 184, part (distr.).
P[*ediocetes*] p[*hasianellus*] *kennicotti* COWAN, Occ. Papers, British Columbia Prov. Mus., No. 1, 1939, 27 (Peace River district, British Columbia).
Pedioecetes phasianellus caurus FRIEDMANN, Journ. Washington Acad. Sci., xxxiii, 1943, 190 (Fairbanks, Alaska; descr.; distr.; crit.).

---

[94] Thirteen specimens from Alaska, Yukon, and extreme northern Alberta.
[95] Thirty-three specimens from Alaska.

PEDIOECETES PHASIANELLUS KENNICOTTII Suckley

MACKENZIE SHARP-TAILED GROUSE

Adult male.—Much darker and less barred and spotted than *P. p. caurus;* forehead, crown, occiput, and nape mummy brown to dark sepia; a narrow whitish loreal-superciliary stripe on each side running posteriorly in a somewhat broken line to the sides of the nape, the feathers of the forehead, sides of crown, the occiput, and nape narrowly edged and narrowly barred with Saccardo's umber; interscapulars dark sepia with hidden, small, incomplete and very sparse whitish shaft marks and with a few tawny-buffy subterminal spots, the feathers narrowly tipped with tawny-olive; scapulars similar to the interscapulars but much more extensively banded and vermiculated with tawny-olive to buckthorn brown and each feather with a conspicuous, large, median, terminal, white elongated spot; innermost secondaries like the scapulars; primaries and outer secondaries and upper wing coverts as in *P. p. caurus;* back, lower back, rump, and upper tail coverts as in *P. p. caurus* but the dark mummy brown to fuscous areas more extensive and more noticeable, the transverse spots and the tips of cinnamon-buff (a few almost whitish) to tawny-olive narrower; rectrices as in *P. p. caurus,* sides of head, chin, and upper throat as in *P. p. caurus* but with the dusky markings larger and more abundant; feathers of the breast dark buffy brown with only narrow white shaft stripes, and fringed with whitish; rest of underparts as in *P. p. caurus.* The darkening, by abrasion of the pale tips, of the plumage from fresh autumn to worn spring and early summer birds is comparable to that in *P. p. caurus.*

Adult female.—Similar to the male but with the median rectrices less marbled longitudinally, more barred transversely.

Juvenal.—Similar to that of *P. p. caurus* but with the dark spots on the breast slightly paler.

Downy young.—Indistinguishable from that of *P. p. caurus.*

Adult male.—Wing 198–211 (207); tail 118–135 (124.2); culmen from anterior end of nostril 10.8–12.4 (11.5); tarsus 41.1–43.7 (42.2); middle toe without claw 38.6–40.9 (39.5); height of bill at base 12.1–13.5 (12.8 mm.).[96]

Adult female.—Wing 193–198 (195.7); tail 108–114 (111.7); culmen from anterior end of nostril 10.8–11.5 (11.2); tarsus 39.9–40.5 (40.3); middle toe without claw 37.9–39.6 (38.7); height of bill at base 11.7–12.0 (11.8 mm.).[97]

Range.—Northern Mackenzie (Fort Rae, Big Island, Great Slave Lake; to Fort Simpson).

Type locality.—Fort Rae and Big Island, near Great Slave Lake.

---

[96] Five specimens from Fort Rae and Fort Simpson, Mackenzie.

[97] Three specimens from Fort Simpson, Mackenzie.

Tetrao urogallus β LINNAEUS, Syst. Nat., ed. 12, i, 1766, 273 (Fort Rae and Big Island, Great Slave Lake).

Tetrao phasianellus SABINE, Append. Franklin's Journ., 1823, 681, part.—AUDUBON, Orn., Biogr., iv, 1838, 539 part; Synopsis, 1839, 205, part (Slave Lake); Birds Amer., 8vo ed., 1842, v, 110, pl. 298, part.

Tetrao (Centrocercus) phasianellus SWAINSON and RICHARDSON, Fauna Bor.-Amer., ii, 1831 (1832), 361, part.

Centrocercus phasianellus GRAY, List Birds Brit. Mus., pt. 3, Gallinae, 1844, 46; pt. 5, Gallinae, 1867, 87, part (Fort Simpson).

Pediocaetes phasianellus ELLIOT, Proc. Acad. Nat. Sci., Philadelphia, 1862, 403, part.— BENDIRE, Life Hist. North Amer. Birds, i, 1892, 97, part (life hist.).—OGILVIE-GRANT, Cat. Birds Brit. Mus, xxii, 1893, 82 part (Fort Simpson).

Pediocœtes phasianellus AMERICAN ORNITHOLOGISTS' UNION, Check-list, 1886, No. 308 part; ed. 2, 1895, 116, part (Fort Simpson).—NELSON, Birds Alaska, 1887, 139, part (along Mackenzie River).

Pediœcetes phasianellus PREBLE, North Amer. Fauna, No. 27, 1908, 348 (Fort Chippewyan; Great Slave Lake, habits).

Pedioecetes phasianellus phasianellus TAVERNER, Birds Western Canada, 1926, 172 in text, part.—AMERICAN ORNITHOLOGISTS' UNION, Check-list ed. 4, 1931, 86, part.—TAVERNER, Birds Canada, 1934, 161, in text, part.—PETERS, Check-list Birds of World, ii, 1934, 40, part.

Pediocœtes kennicottii SUCKLEY, Proc. Acad. Nat. Sci. Philadelphia, 1861, 361 (Fort Rae and Big Island, Great Slave Lake; descr.).

Pedioecetes phasianellus kennicottii DuMONT, Auk, l, 1933, 432 (Fort Rae, Great Slave Lake, Mackenzie; crit.).—SNYDER, Univ. Toronto Studies, biol. ser., No. 40, 1935, 4, 48, part (monogr.); Occ. Papers Roy. Ontario Mus. Zool., No. 2, 1935, 2, part (monogr.).—HELLMAYR AND CONOVER, Cat. Birds Amer., i, No. 1, 1942, 221, part (syn.; distr.).—FRIEDMANN, Journ. Washington Acad. Sci., xxxiii, 1943, 191 (crit.).

P[edioecetes] p[hasianellus] kennicotti SNYDER, Auk, lvi, 1939, 184, part (distr.).

P[ediocœtes] phasianellus columbianus RIDGWAY, Man. North Amer. Birds, 1887, 204, part.

[*Tetrao*] *columbianus* GRAY, Hand-list, ii, 1870, 276, No. 9830 part.

PEDIOECETES PHASIANELLUS PHASIANELLUS (Linnaeus)

NORTHERN SHARP-TAILED GROUSE

Adult.—Similar to the corresponding sex (and season) of *P. p. caurus* but with less white above, the white bars and spots much reduced, and the tips of the dorsal feathers generally darker, more rufescent—pale tawny-olive, often with a pale cinnamon wash (instead of pale cinnamon-buff to pinkish buff tips as in *caurus*); feathers of the breast intermediate in character between *caurus* and *kennicottii*—pale buffy brown with fairly broad white shaft streaks; thighs slightly darker cinnamon-drab than in *caurus*.

Juvenal.—Not certainly distinguishable from that of *P. p. caurus.*

Downy young.—Not distinguishable from that of *P. p. caurus.*

Adult male.—Wing 205–212 (209.5); tail 110–124 (120.4); culmen from anterior end of nostril 10.5–12.7 (11.6); tarsus 43.0–45.5 (43.9);

middle toe without claw 37.5–41.8 (39.8) ; height of bill at base 12.5–13.0 (12.7 mm.).[98]

Adult female.—Wing 195–208 (201.2) ; tail 113–126 (117.3) ; culmen from anterior end of nostril 10.1–11.9 (11.3) ; tarsus 40.0–44.4 (42.8) ; middle toe without claw 36.3–40.5 (38.3) ; height of bill at base 12.2–13.1 (12.4 mm.).[99]

Range.—Resident in the Hudson and James Bay watersheds of northeastern Manitoba (Norway House) northern Ontario and Quebec.

Type locality.—Canada=Hudson Bay.

Tetrao phasianellus LINNAEUS, Syst. Nat., ed. 10, i, 1758, 160 (based on *Urogallus minor foemina cauda longiore, Canadensis,* Long-tailed grouse from Hudson's Bay, Edwards, Nat. Hist., iii, pl. 117) ; ed. 12, i, 1766, 273.—FORSTER, Philos. Trans., lxii, 1772, 394, 425 (Hudson Bay).—GMELIN, Syst. Nat., i, pt. 2, 1788, 747, part.—LATHAM, Index Ornith., in 1790, 635, part.—ORD, *in* Guthrie's Geogr., 2d Amer. ed., ii, 1815, 317.—SABINE, Append. Franklin's Journ., 1823, 681, part. —BONAPARTE, Syn., 1828, 127, part ; Amer. Orn., ii, 1828, 37, part.—WILSON and BONAPARTE, Amer. Orn., iii, 1832, 303, pl. 19.—NUTTALL, Man. Orn. United States and Canada, Land Birds, 1832, 669, part.—AUDUBON, Orn. Biogr., iv, 1838, 539, pl. 382, part ; Birds Amer., 8vo ed., v, 1842, 110, pl. 298, part.—MURRAY, Proc. Phys. Soc. Edinb., ii, 1859, 49 (Troutlake Station).

Tetrao [Centrocercus] phasianellus SWAINSON and RICHARDSON, Fauna Bor.-Amer., ii, 1831 (1832), 361, part.

Centrocercus phasianellus GRAY, List Birds Brit. Mus., pt. 3, Gallinae, 1844, 46 ; pt. 5, Gallinae, 1867, 87, part.—BONAPARTE, Compt. Rend., xlv, 1857, 428.

Pediocaetes phasianellus ELLIOT, Proc. Acad. Nat. Sci. Philadelphia, 1862, 403, part ; Monogr. Tetraonidae, 1865, pl. 15, part.—AMERICAN ORNITHOLOGISTS' UNION, Check-list, 1886, No. 308, part ; ed. 2, 1895, 116, part.—BENDIRE, Life Hist. North Amer. Birds, i, 1892, 97, part.—MACOUN, Cat. Can. Birds, 1900, 210 part.

P[ediocaetes] phasianelleus REICHENOW, Die Vögel, i, 1913, 322.

Pedioecetes phasianellus COUES, Key North Amer. Birds, 1872, 234, part ; ed. 2, 1884, 581, part.—GILL, Auk, xvi, 1899, 23 (nomencl.).—[NASH], Check List Vert. Ontario: Birds, 1905, 35 (Ontario, scarce).—BAILLIE and HARRINGTON, Contr. Roy. Ontario Mus. Zool., No. 8, pt. 1, 1936, 29, part (Ontario, more or less common summer resident in extreme northern part).—SNYDER, Trans. Roy. Can. Inst. xxii, 1938, 186 (w. Rainy River District, Ontario, formerly common; eggs ; 3 juv. spec.).

Pediœcetes phasianellus DWIGHT, Auk, xvii, 1900, 164 (molt).—FLEMING, Auk, xviii, 1901, 37 (Parry Sound and Muskoka, n. Ontario).—PREBLE, North Amer. Fauna, No. 22, 1902, 104 (Norway House, Oxford House, Playgreen Lake, Hudson Bay Region).—EIFRIG, Auk, xxiii, 1906, 313 in text (Great Whale River, east coast of Hudson Bay, 55° 30′ N.).—MACOUN and MACOUN, Cat. Can. Birds, 1909, 230, part.

Pediaecaetes phasianellus ELLIOT, Monogr. Tetraonidae, 1865, text opposite pl. 15 part.

Pediecœtes phasianellus ELLIOT, Monogr. Tetraonidae, 1865, introd. 5, part.

Pedioecetes phasianellus var. *phasianellus* BAIRD, BREWER, and RIDGWAY, Hist. North Amer. Birds, iii, 1874, 434 part, pt. 69, fig. 3 (part, life hist., descr., distr.).

---

[98] Seven specimens from Norway House, James Bay, and Churchill.

[99] Eleven specimens from James Bay and Churchill.

Pediocetes phasianellus phasianellus McLuLICH, Contr. Roy. Ontario Mus. Zool., No. 13, 1938, 12 (Algonquin Prov. Park, Ontario, hypothetical).

Pedioecetes phasianellus phasianellus TAVERNER, Birds Western Canada, 1926, 172 in text, part; Birds Canada, 1934, 161 in text, part.—AMERICAN ORNITHOLOGISTS' UNION, Check-list, ed. 4, 1931, 86, part (n. Manitoba, n. Ungava).—BENT, U. S. Nat. Mus. Bull. 162, 1932, 285 (habits; descr.; monogr.).—PETERS, Check-list Birds of World, ii, 1934, 40, part.—SNYDER, Univ. Toronto Studies, biol. ser., No. 40, 1935, 3, 4, 7, 40 in text (monogr.) ; Occ. Pap. Roy. Ontario Mus. Zool., No. 2, 1935, 3 (monogr.; crit.).—CAMPBELL, Bull. Toledo Mus. Sci., i, 1940, 62 (Lucas County, Ohio, introduced in 1939).—HELLMAYR and CONOVER, Cat. Birds Amer., i, No. 1, 1942, 219 (syn., distr.).—FRIEDMANN, Journ. Washington Acad. Sci., xxxiii, 1943, 191 (crit.).

Pediœcetes phasianellus phasianellus AMERICAN ORNITHOLOGISTS' UNION, Check-list, ed. 3, 1910, 144, part.

Pedioecetes p[hasianellus] phasianellus DERY, Quebec Zool. Soc., Bull. 1', 1933, 3 (migr. in Quebec).

P[edioecetes] p[hasianellus] phasianellus SNYDER, Auk, lvi, 1939, 184 (distr.).

[*Pedioecetes*] *phasianellus phasianellus* BAILLIE and HARRINGTON, Contr. Roy. Ontario Mus. Zool., No. 8, pt. 1, 1936, 29 in text (Ontario; breeds in extreme northern part).

[*Pedioecetes phasianellus*] *phasianellus* DEAR, Trans. Roy. Can. Inst., xxiii, pt. 1, 1940, 127 in text.

Pediocœtes phasianellus Subsp. a. *Pediocaetes columbianus* OGILVIE-GRANT, Cat. Birds Brit. Mus., xxii, 1893, 83, part (Hudson's Bay).

Pediocœtes p[hasianellus] phasianellus STENHOUSE, Scottish Nat., 1930, 76 in text (2 spec. ex Franklin's First Exp.; from York Factory and from Cumberland House, now in Roy. Scottish Mus.).

PEDIOECETES PHASIANELLUS JAMESI Lincoln

GREAT PLAINS SHARP-TAILED GROUSE

Adult.—Similar to the corresponding sex (and season) of *P. p. caurus* but paler above the brownish black areas reduced and more hidden, the buffy-brown areas larger, paler—buckthorn brown, giving the bird the appearance of a brown bird mottled with blackish, rather than a predominantly blackish bird mottled with brownish; the brown margins of the breast feathers paler—tawny drab, the tarsal plumes relatively shorter, and the chin and upper throat usually without dusky spots. Very worn late spring and early summer birds are very much more grayish above, the buckthorn brown fading to smoke gray with an ochraceous wash.

Juvenal.—Similar to that of *P. p. caurus* but with the brownish areas above paler and more grayish—very pale Saccardo's umber, and the top of the head less rufescent—deep ochraceous-tawny (instead of hazel).

Downy young.—Similar to that of *P. p. caurus* but slightly more extensively tinged with ochraceous-buff above.

Adult male.—Wing 199–223 (210.3) ; tail 111–135 (119.7) ; culmen from anterior end of nostril 10.9–13.1 (12.1) ; tarsus 41.1–46 (43.8) ;

middle toe without claw 36.3–42.8 (39.1) ; height of bill at base 12.4–15.0 (13.4 mm.).[1]

Adult female.—Wing 195–221 (205.9) ; tail 103–130 (114.8) ; culmen from anterior end of culmen 10.4–13.0 (12.0) ; tarsus 40.0–46.2 (43.2) ; middle toe without claw 35.6–41.8 (38.5) ; height of bill at base 11.4–14.3 (12.7 mm.).[2]

Range.—Resident in the Great Plains from north-central Alberta (Lac La Biche, Sturgeon River, Saskatchewan River, Athabaska Lake, Edmonton, etc.) ; north-central Saskatchewan (Cumberland House; St. Louis) and the southwestern part of Manitoba (Carberry) ; south through Montana (except the extreme western part) and the Dakotas, Wyoming to western Nebraska and east-central Colorado, and, formerly to western Kansas and the "Panhandle" of northwestern Oklahoma.

Type locality.—Castle Rock, Douglas County, Colo.

Tetrao phasianellus SABINE, Append. Franklin's Journ., 1823, 681, part.—BONAPARTE, Syn., 1828, 127, part.—AUDUBON, Orn. Biogr., iv, 1838, 569, part, pl. 382; Synopsis, 1839, 205, part; Birds Amer., 8vo ed., 1842, v, 110, pl. 298, part.—MAXIMILIAN, Journ. für Orn., 1858, 435 (Missouri River).

[*Tetrao*] *columbianus* GRAY, Hand-list, ii, 1870, 276, no. 9830, part.

Pedioecetes phasianellus SNOW, Cat. Birds Kansas, 1873, ed. 2, reprint, 9 (central and western Kansas).—YOUNGSWORTH, Wils. Bull., xlvii, 1935, 217 (Fort Sisseton, S. Dak.; present in small numbers).—CLARKE, Nat. Mus. Canada, Bull. 96, 1940, 49 (Thelon Game Sanctuary, northwestern Canada).

Pediœcetes phasianellus BLAKISTON, Ibis, 1862, 8 (Forks of the Saskatchewan).— MACOUN and MACOUN, Cat. Can. Birds, 1909, 230, part.—STANSELL, Auk, xxvi, 1909, 393, (central Alberta).—TAVERNER, Auk, xxxvi, 1919, 13 (Red Deer River, Alberta).

Pediocaetes phasianellus BAIRD, Rep. Pacific R. R. Surv., ix, 1858, 626, part.—BAIRD, CASSIN, and LAWRENCE, Rep. Pacific R. R. Surv., 1860, 626, part.—ELLIOT, Proc. Acad. Nat. Sci. Philadelphia, 1862, 403, part.—SNOW, Cat. Birds Kansas, ed. 2, 1872, 12 (Kansas; common).—TRIPPE, Proc. Boston Soc. Nat. Hist., xv, 1872, 240 in text (Iowa; Nebraska).—BENDIRE, Life Hist. North Amer. Birds, i, 1892, 97, part.—OGILVIE-GRANT, Cat. Birds Brit. Mus., xxii, 1893, 82, part.

Pediocœtes phasianellus AMERICAN ORNITHOLOGISTS' UNION, Check-list, 1886, No. 308, part; ed. 2, 1895, 116, part.—NUTTING, Bull. Lab. Nat. Hist., State Univ. Iowa, ii, 1893, 267 (Lower Saskatchewan River; abundant; plum. of young).— MACOUN, Cat. Can. Birds, 1900, 210, part.

Pediœcetes phasianellus phasianellus AMERICAN ORNITHOLOGISTS' UNION, Check-list, ed. 3, 1910, 144, part.

Pedioecetes phasianellus phasianellus TAVERNER, Birds Western Canada, 1926, 172 in text, part; Birds Canada, 1934, 161 in text, part.

? *Pediœcetes urophasianellus* BLAKISTON, Ibis, 1863, 127.

Pediocetes phasianellus campestris COOKE, Colorado State Agr. Coll. Bull. 56, 1900, 203 (Colorado; Middle Park; breeds; distr.).—COWAN, Occ. Pap. British Co-

---

[1] Thirty-four specimens from Alberta, Saskatchewan, Manitoba, Montana, the Dakotas, and Nebraska.

[2] Fifty-two specimens from Alberta, Saskatchewan, Manitoba, Montana, Wyoming, and the Dakotas.

lumbia Prov. Mus. No. 1, 1939, 27 (Peace River District, British Columbia; spec.; young).

Pediocaetes phasianellus campestris Cooke, Colorado State Agr. Coll. Bull. 37, 1897, 71 (Colorado; not common); Bull. 44, 1898, 159 (Colorado; not uncommon in northwestern part of the state).

Pediocætes phasianellus campestris American Ornithologists' Union, Check-list, 1886, No. 308b, part; ed. 2, 1895, 117, part; ed. 3, 1910, 144, part.—Ridgway, Man. North Amer. Birds, 1887, 204, part.—Cooke, Bird Migr. Mississippi Valley, 1888, 106, part.—Bendire, Auk, vi, 1889, 301 in text (Fort Custer, Mont.); Life Hist. North Amer. Birds, i, 1892, 101, part.—Thorne, Auk, xii, 1895, 213 (Fort Keogh, Mont.).—Macoun, Cat. Can. Birds, 1900, 213, part (plains of U. S. and northward).—Sclater, Hist. Birds Colorado, 1912, 152, part (Colorado; not common, chiefly east of the mountains).

Pediocætes phasianellus campestris? Richmond and Knowlton, Auk, xi, 1894, 302 (Montana).

P[ediocætes] phasianellus campestris Ridgway, Man. North Amer. Birds, 1887, 204, part.

Pediocaetes phasianellus campestris Goss, Hist. Birds Kansas, 1891, 228 (Kansas; habits; descr.).

Pedioecetes phasianellus campestris Zimmer, Proc. Nebraska Orn. Union, v, pt. 2, 1911, 21 (Nebraska; Dawes County Forest Reserve; young).—Grave and Walker, Birds Wyoming, 1913, 40 (Wyoming; common in eastern and northwestern parts).—Saunders, Pacific Coast Avif. No. 14, 1921, 59 (Montana; intergrades with *columbianus* in western part of state).—Over and Thoms, Birds South Dakota, 1921, 77 (South Dakota).—Wood, Misc. Publ. Mus. Zool. Univ. Michigan, No. 10, 1923, 36 (North Dakota; common).—Mitchell, Can. Field Nat., xxxviii, 1924, 108 (Saskatchewan; common resident).—Gabrielson and Jewett, Auk, xli, 1924, 297 (in badlands and brakes of Missouri River, N. Dak.).—Nice and Nice, Birds Oklahoma, 1924, 37 (Oklahoma Panhandle; former resident, now nearly extirpated).—Lincoln, Auk, xlii, 1925, 60 (Turtle and Devils Lakes, N. Dak.; food).—Williams, Wils. Bull., xxxviii, 1926, 30 (Red River Valley, ne. N. Dak.).—Taverner, Birds Western Canada, 1926, 172 in text, part; Birds Canada, 1934, 161 in text, part.—Larson, Wils. Bull., xl, 1928, 46 (e. McKenzie County, N. Dak.).—American Ornithologists' Union, Check-list, ed. 4, 1931, 86, part.—Nice, Birds Oklahoma, rev. ed., 1931, 81 (Oklahoma Panhandle, former resident, now nearly extirpated).—Harrold, Wils. Bull., xlv, 1933, 19 (Lake Johnston, Saskatchewan).—Peters, Check-list Birds of World, ii, 1934, 41, part.—Johnson, Wils. Bull., xlvi, 1934, 8 (nw. Manitoba; habits; migr.).—McCreary and Mickey, Wils. Bull., xlvii, 1935, 129 in text (se. Wyo.; resident).—Snyder, Univ. Toronto Studies, biol. ser., No. 40, 1935, 4, 7, 40 in text, 55 (crit.; monogr.); Occ. Papers Roy. Ontario Mus. Zool., No. 2, 1935, 5 (monogr.).—Weydemeyer and Marsh, Condor, xxxviii, 1936, 194 (Lake Bowdoin, Mont.).—Fox, Auk, liv, 1937, 534 in text (North Dakota; feeding on wild plum).—Alexander, Univ. Colorado Studies Zool., xxiv, 1937, 91 (Boulder County, Colo.; correction; no recent records).—Long, Trans. Kansas Acad. Sci., xliii, 1940, 440 (Kansas; common formerly, now probably extirpated).—Hellmayr and Conover, Cat. Birds Amer., 1, No. 1, 1942, 219 part (syn.; distr.).—Wright and Hiatt, Auk, lx, 1943, 265 in text (age indicators in plum.; Montana).

Pediæcetes phasianellus campestris Lantz, Trans. Kansas Acad. Sci., for 1896-1897 (1899), 254 (Kansas; common in western part).—Cary, Auk, xviii, 1901, 232 (Black Hills, S. Dak.).—Snow, Cat. Birds Kansas, ed. 5, 1903, 15 (w. Kansas; common).—Bent, Auk, xxiv, 1907, 428 (sw. Saskatchewan; nests and eggs).—

CAMERON, Auk, xxiv, 1907, 256, pl. ix, fig. 1 (Custer and Davenport Counties, Mont.; habits; nesting; photo); xxv, 1908, 260, in text (Montana; common).—REAGAN, Auk, xxv, 1908, 464 (Rosebud Reservation, S. Dak.).—VISHER, Auk, xxvi, 1909, 147 (w. South Dakota; abundant); xxviii, 1911, 10 (Harding County, S. Dak.).—COOKE, Auk, xxvi, 1909, 411 (ne. Colorado).—MACOUN AND MACOUN, Cat. Can. Birds, 1909, 232 (abundant from Manitoba westward, but not high up in the mountains).—FERRY, Auk, xxvii, 1910, 198 (Saskatchewan).—SAUNDERS, Auk, xxviii, 1911, 35 (Galatin County, Mont.).—BROOKS AND COBB, Auk, xxviii, 1911, 468 (e. Alberta).—VISHER, Auk, xxx, 1913, 567 (Sanborn County, S. Dak.).

P[edioecetes] p[hasianellus] phasianellus BAILEY, Handb. Birds Western U. S., 1902, 132, part.—DUMONT, Auk, l, 1933, 432 in text (spec.; Nebraska and South Dakota; Elbert County, Colo.).—SNYDER, Auk, lvi, 1939, 184, part (Montana; c. Alberta; Saskatchewan).

Pediocaetes columbianus ELLIOT, Proc. Acad. Nat. Sci. Philadelphia, 1862, 403, part.—HOLDEN and AIKEN, Proc. Boston Soc. Nat. Hist., xv, 1872, 208 (e. Wyoming and Colorado).

Pediocætes phasianellus columbianus AMERICAN ORNITHOLOGISTS' UNION, Check-list, ed. 2, 1895, 116, part; ed. 3, 1910, 144, part.

P[ediocætes] phasianellus columbianus RIDGWAY, Man. North Amer. Birds, 1887, 204, part.

Pediocætes phasianellus Subsp. a Pediocætes columbianus, OGILVIE-GRANT, Cat. Birds Brit. Mus., xxii, 1893, 83, part (Atkinson, Nebr.).

Pediecætes columbianus ELLIOT, Monogr. Tetraonidae, 1865, introd., 5, part.

Pediaecaetes columbianus ELLIOT, Monogr. Tetraonidae, 1865, text opp. pl. 14, part.

Pedioecetes columbianus RIDGWAY, Field and Forest, 1877, 209 (Colorado).

Pediocaetes phasianellus var. columbianus RIDGWAY, Bull. Essex Inst., v, 1873, 186 (Colorado).

Pedioecetes phasianellus var. columbianus ALLEN, Bull. Mus. Comp. Zool., iii, 1872, 181, part (Colorado; Wyoming).—BAIRD, BREWER, and RIDGWAY, Hist. North Amer. Birds, iii, 1874, 436, part.

Pediæcetes phasianellus var. columbianus COUES, Birds Northwest, 1874, 407, part.—ALLEN, Proc. Boston Soc. Nat. Hist., xvii, 1874, 36 (Missouri River to the Musselshell River; occas.).

[Pediæcetes phasianellus] var. columbianus COUES, Key North Amer. Birds, 1872, 234, part; Check-list North Amer. Birds, 1874, No. 383a, part.

Pedioecetes phasianellus columbianus GRAVE and WALKER, Birds Wyoming, 1913, 39 (Wyoming; rather uncommon but reported by most observers in northern part of State).—WILLIAMS, Wils. Bull., xxxviii, 1926, 30 (Red River Valley, ne. North Dakota).—KEMSIES, Wils. Bull., xlii, 1930, 204 (Yellowstone Park).—NIEDRACH and ROCKWELL, Birds Denver and Mountain Parks, 1939, 62 (Denver; Colorado; uncommon).

Pediæcetes phasianellus columbianus RIDGWAY, Proc. U. S. Nat. Mus., iii, 1880, 196, part; Nom. North Amer. Birds, 1881, No. 478a, part.—DREW, Auk, ii, 1885, 17 (Colorado; 7,000 feet).—AGERSBORG, Auk, ii, 1885, 285 (se. Dakota).—SETON, Auk, iii, 1886, 153 (w. Manitoba; very abundant resident; in open prairies in the summer and in woods in the winter).—CAMERON, Auk, xxii, 1905, 161 in text (Montana).—PREBLE, North Amer. Fauna, No. 27, 1908, 350 (n. central Alberta).

P[edioecetes] p[hasianellus] columbianus COUES, Check-list North Amer. Birds, ed. 2, 1882, No. 562, part; Key North Amer. Birds, ed. 2, 1884, 581, part.—DUMONT, Auk, l, 1933, 432 in text, part (Pincher Creek, Alberta).

Pedioecetes phasianellus jamesi Lincoln, Proc. Biol. Soc. Washington, xxx, 1917, 84 (Castle Rock, Douglas County, Colo.; descr.; crit.).—Peters, Check-list Birds of World, ii, 1934, 40 (c. and e. Colorado).—Snyder, Univ. Toronto Studies, biol. ser., No. 40, 1935, 4, 40 in text, 56 (crit.; monogr.); Occ. Papers Roy. Ontario Mus. Zool., No. 2, 1935, 6 (crit.; monogr.).—Friedmann, Journ. Washington Acad. Sci., xxxiii, 1943, 191 (crit.).

Pediœcetes phasianellus jamesi Oberholser, Auk, xxxv, 1918, 206 (foothills of Rocky Mountains from Colorado to Wyoming).

P[edioecetes] p[hasianellus] jamesi Snyder, Auk, lvi, 1939, 185 (distr.).—Niedrach and Rockwell, Birds Denver and Mountain Parks, 1939, 64, in text.

PEDIOECETES PHASIANELLUS COLUMBIANUS (Ord)

Columbian Sharp-tailed Grouse

Adult.—Similar to the corresponding sex of *P. p. jamesi* but usually duller, the brown areas above pale, grayish tawny-olive instead of buckthorn brown, the bill smaller and the tail shorter; iris hazel inclining to olive; "comb" medium cadmium; maxilla dusky brownish; mandible with basal half buffy; toes brownish gray; claws dusky brown.

Juvenal.—Indistinguishable from that of *P. p. jamesi.*

Downy young.—Indistinguishable from that of *P. p. jamesi.*

Adult male.—Wing 194–210 (202.4); tail 103–117 (109.2); culmen from anterior end of nostril 10.5–12.1 (11.3); tarsus 40.8–44.0 (42.0); middle toe and claw 37.1–40.2 (38.3); height of bill at base 11.5–12.8 (12.1 mm.).[3]

Adult female.—Wing 186–201 (194.5); tail 92–113 (104.2); culmen from anterior end of nostril 10.0–13.0 (11.1); tarsus 38.5–42.0 (40.5); middle toe without claw 35.3–38.8 (37.0); height of bill at base 11.3–12.8 (12.0 mm.).[4]

Range.—Resident from British Columbia (except extreme northern edge; from Cariboo District to the Okanagan region, Kamloops, etc., in the lowlands of the interior between the Cascades and the Rocky Mountains), south through extreme western Montana, Idaho (Blue Springs Hills; Fort Lapwai), Washington and Oregon east of the Cascades, to northeastern California (Modoc County—formerly); northeastern Nevada (Elko County; Bull Run Mountains; Upper Humboldt Valley; Trout Creek, Clover Mountains); western and the southern half or so of Utah (Wasatch Mountains, Salt Lake City, etc.) to western to south-central Colorado (Routt County south to Garfield, San Miguel, Dolores, Montezuma, and Archuleta Counties), to New Mexico.

Introduced into Lucas County, Ohio.

Type locality.—Great Plains of the Columbia River.

---

[3] Fifteen specimens from Washington, Oregon, Idaho; western Montana; Colorado; and California.

[4] Twelve specimens from Washington, Oregon, Idaho, and western Montana.

Tetrao phasianellus (not of Linnaeus) ORD, Guthrie's Geogr., 2d Amer. ed., ii, 1815, 317.—BONAPARTE, Amer. Orn., iii, 1828, pl. 19, part.—NUTTALL, Man. Orn. United States and Canada, Land Birds, 1832, 669, part (Oregon; Rocky Mountains).— AUDUBON, Orn. Biogr., iv, 1838, 569 part, pl. 382; Synopsis, 1839, 205, part; Birds Amer., 8vo ed., 1842, v, 110, pl. 298, part.—NEWBERRY, Rep. Pacific R. R. Surv., vi, 1857, 94.

Tetrao urophasianellus HALL, Murrelet, xv, 1934, 13, in text (ex Douglas Journ.; Washington; Columbia River).

T[etrao] urophasianellus DOUGLAS, Trans. Linn. Soc., London, xvi, 1829, 136 (Plains of the Columbia and interior of northern California); Douglas's Journal, 1914, 62.—HALL, Murrelet, xv, 1934, 7, 8 in text (Washington; Columbia River; hist.).

Centrocercus phasianellus JARDINE, Nat. Libr., Orn., iv, 1834, 136, pl. 16, part.

Centrocercus columbianus GRAY, List Birds Brit. Mus., pt. 5, Gallinæ, 1867, 88 (west side of Rocky Mountains).

Phasianus columbianus ORD, Guthrie's Geogr., 2d Amer. ed., ii, 1815, 317 (based on *Columbian Pheasant* LEWIS and CLARK, ii, 180).—HALL, Murrelet, xiv, 1933, 66 (hist.).

Pedioecetes columbianus BAIRD, *in* Cooper, Orn. California, 1870, 532.

[Tetrao] columbianus GRAY, Hand-list, ii, 1870, 276, No. 9830, part.

Pediaecaetes columbianus ELLIOT, Monogr. Tetraonidae, 1865, text opp. pl. 14, part.

Pediecætes columbianus ELLIOT, Monogr. Tetraonidae, 1865, introd., 5, part.

Pediocætes columbianus ELLIOT, Proc. Acad. Nat. Sci. Philadelphia, 1862, 403, part; Monogr. Tetraonidae, 1865, pl. 14.

Pediocetes phasianellus var. *columbianus* NELSON, Proc. Boston Soc. Nat. Hist., xvii, 1875, 347 (Salt Lake City).

Pediocætes phasianellus var. *columbianus* RIDGWAY, Bull. Essex Inst. v, 1873, 186 (Colorado; rye grass meadows).

Pediocætes phasianellus columbianus RIDGWAY, Bull. Essex Inst., vii, 1875, 22 (Upper Humboldt Valley); vii, 1875, 31 (Salt Lake Valley), 34 (Parley's Peak, Wasatch Mountains, Utah).—AMERICAN ORNITHOLOGISTS' UNION, Check-list, 1886, No. 308a, part; ed. 2, 1895, 116, part; ed. 3, 1910, 144, part.—MERRILL, Auk, v, 1888, 145 (Fort Klamath, Oreg.); xiv, 1897, 352 (Fort Sherman, Idaho; common).—MERRIAM, North Amer. Fauna, No. 5, 1891, 93 (Idaho; Lemhi Indian Agency; Fort Hall, Portaeuf River, Snake River, Fort Lapwai).—DAWSON, Auk, xiv, 1897, 173 (Okanogan County, Wash.; common).—MACOUN, Cat. Can. Birds, 1900, 212, part (east of Coast Range, w. Canada).—SCLATER, Hist. Birds Colorado, 1912, 151 (Colorado, Hahn's Park; n. Routt County; San Miguel, Dolores, Montezuma, and Archuleta Counties).

Pediocaetes phas[ianellus] columbianus ALLEN, Auk, x, 1893, 134.

P[ediocætes] phasianellus columbianus RIDGWAY, Man. North Amer. Birds, 1887, 204, part (New Mexico).

Pedioecetes columbianus BENDIRE, Proc. Boston Soc. Nat. Hist., xix, 1877, 139 (Camp Harney, Oreg.; fairly common; also at Fort Lapwai, Idaho).

[Pedioecetes phasianellus var. *columbianus]* b. *columbianus* COUES, Birds Northwest, 1874, 407, part.

Pedioecetes phasianellus β *columbianus* RIDGWAY, Orn. 40th Parallel, 1877, 599 (upper Humboldt Valley, Nevada; Wasatch District, Utah).

[Pediocætes phasianellus] Subsp. a. *Pediocaetes columbianus* OGILVIE-GRANT, Cat. Birds Brit. Mus., xxii, 1893, 83 (part).

Pedioecetes phasianellus var. *columbianus* BAIRD, BREWER, and RIDGWAY, Hist. North Amer. Birds, iii, 1874, 436, part.

Pediæcetes phasianellus var. *columbianus* COUES, Birds Northwest, 1874, 407, part (life hist.).—RIDGWAY, Bull. Essex Inst., vii, 1875, 39 (Nevada).

[*Pediœcetes phasianellus*] var. *columbianus* Coues, Key North Amer. Birds, 1872,
234, part; Check List North Amer. Birds, 1874, No. 383a, part.
Pedioecetes phasianellus columbianus Mearns, Bull. Nuttall Orn. Club, iv, 1879, 197
(Fort Klamath, Oreg.).—Brewster, Bull. Nuttall Orn. Club, vii, 1882, 227, 233
(Walla Walla, Wash.; crit.).—Bailey, Handb., Birds Western United States,
1902, 132, part; Birds New Mexico, 1928, 209 (New Mexico).—Dawson and
Bowles, Birds Washington, ii, 1909, 596 (Washington; habits; distr.).—Grinnell, Pacific Coast Avif., No. 8, 1912, 10 (California) ; No. 11, 1915, 61 (California; distr.).—Grinnell, Bryant, and Storer, Game Birds California, 1918,
558 (descr.; habits; distr.; California).—Saunders, Pacific Coast Avif., No. 14,
1921, 58 (Montana; fairly common in western part; intergrades with *campestris*
(= *jamesi*) in central part).—Dawson, Birds California (stud. ed.), iii, 1923,
1599 (California).—Gabrielson, Auk, xli, 1924, 555 (Wallowa County, Oreg.).
—Taverner, Birds Western Canada, 1926, 172 in text (southern British Columbia).—Mailliard, Proc. California Acad. Sci., ser. 4, xvi, 1927, 295 (Modoc
County, Calif.).—Fuller and Bole, Sci. Publ. Cleveland Mus. Nat. Hist., 1,
1930, 50 (Wyoming).—American Ornithologists' Union, Check-list, ed. 4,
1931, 86, part (distr.).—Bent, U. S. Nat. Mus. Bull. 162, 1932, 288 (life hist.).—
Peters, Check-list Birds of World, ii, 1934, 40.—Snyder, Univ. Toronto Studies,
biol. ser., No. 40, 1935, 4, 7, 40 in text, 53 (crit.; monogr.) ; Occ. Papers Roy.
Ontario Mus. Zool., No. 2, 1935, 2 (crit.; monogr.).—McCreary and Mickey,
Wils. Bull., xlvii, 1935, 129, in text (se. Wyoming).—Linsdale, Pacific Coast
Avif., No. 23, 1936, 48 (Nevada; Elko County; Bull Run Mountains; Upper
Humboldt Valley; Trout Creek; Clover Mountains).—Groebbels, Der Vögel,
ii, 1937, 166 (breeding biology).—Campbell, Bull. Toledo Mus. Sci., i, 1940, 62
(Lucas County, Ohio; introduced 1939).—Dalquest, Murrelet, xxi, 1940, 10, in
text (Washington; Okanogan County).—Gabrielson and Jewett, Birds
Oregon, 1940, 216 (Oregon; distr.; descr.; habits).—Hellmayr and Conover,
Cat. Birds Amer., i, No. 1, 1942, 221 (syn.; distr.).—Friedmann, Journ. Wash-
ington Acad. Sci., xxxiii, 1943, 191 (crit.).—Behle, Condor, xlvi, 1944, 72
(Utah).
Pediœcetes phasianellus columbianus Ridgway, Bull. Essex Inst., vii, 1875, 22
(Upper Humboldt Valley, Nev.), 31 (Salt Lake Valley, Utah), 34 (Parley's
Park, Utah) ; Proc. U. S. Nat. Mus., iii, 1880, 196, part; Nom. North Amer.
Birds, 1881, No. 478a., part; Man. North Amer. Birds, 1887, 204, part.—Ameri-
can Ornithologists' Union, Check-list, 1886, No. 308a, part.—Townsend,
Proc. U. S. Nat. Mus., x, 1887, 200, 235 (ne. California).—Bendire, Life Hist.
North Amer. Birds, i, 1892, 98, part.—Gill, Auk, xvi, 1899, 23 (nomencl.).—
Snodgrass, Auk, xxi, 1904, 227 (abundant—Touchet Creek, Walla Walla
County, Wash.).—Cary, Auk, xxvi, 1909, 181 (w. Colorado).—Cooke, Auk,
xxvi, 1909, 411 (w. and sw. Colorado).—Macoun and Macoun, Cat. Can.
Birds, ed. 2, 1909, 232 (abundant east of Coast Range, British Columbia: Mid-
way, Meyers Creek, Similkameen River, Spence Bridge, Kamloops, Quesnel,
150-Mile House).—Dice, Auk, xxxv, 1918, 44 (se. Washington).—Brooks and
Swarth, Pacific Coast Avif., No. 17, 1925, 52 (British Columbia; common
locally from southern part n. to Cariboo District).—Taverner, Birds Canada,
1934, 161, in text (distr.).
Pediœcetes phasainellus columbianus Grinnell, Pacific Coast Avif., No. 3, 1902,
30 (California; fairly common in northeastern part of state).
Pediœcetes phasianellus columbianus Brooks, Auk, xx, 1903, 281 (Cariboo Distr.,
British Columbia).
P[*edioecetes*] *p*[*hasianellus*] *phasianellus* Coues, Check List North Amer. Birds,
ed. 2, 1882, No. 562, part; Key North Amer. Birds, ed. 2, 1884, 581, part.—

Cooke, Colorado State Agr. Coll. Bull. 37, 1897, 71 (Colorado; Routt County).
—Cowan, Occ. Pap. British Columbia Prov. Mus., No. 1, 1939, 27 (mentioned).
—Snyder, Auk, lvi, 1939, 184 (distr.).

Pediœcetes p[hasianellus] columbianus Brooks, Auk, xxiv, 1907, 167, pl. 4 (hybrid).

[*Pediœcetes phasianellus*] *columbianus* Dwight, Auk, xvii, 1900, 164 (molt).

Pediocaetes phasianellus (not of Linnaeus) Baird, Rep. Pacific R. R. Surv., ix,
1858, 626, part.—Baird, Cassin, and Lawrence, Rep. Pacific R. R. Surv., 1860,
626, part.—Cooper and Suckley, Rep. Pacific R. R. Surv., xii, book 2, pt. 3,
1860, 223 (plains of the Columbia River, Wash.).

Pediœcetes phasianellus Munro, Condor, xlii, 1940, 168 (young eaten by sharp-
shinned hawk; Brit. Columbia).—Hand, Condor, xliii, 1941, 225 (St. Joe
Natl. Forest, Idaho).

Pediocaetes phasianellus campestris American Ornithologists' Union, Check-list
1886, No. 308b, part.—Ridgway, Man. North Amer. Birds, 1887, 204, part.—
Bendire, Life Hist. North Amer. Birds, i, 1892, 101, part.—Sclater, Hist.
Birds Colorado, 1912, 152, part (sw. Colorado).

PEDIOECETES PHASIANELLUS CAMPESTRIS Ridgway

Prairie Sharp-tailed Grouse

Adult.—The most rufescent of all the races of the species; similar to
the corresponding sex (and season) of *P. p. jamesi* but much more rufescent above, the buckthorn brown of the latter form being replaced
by ochraceous-tawny to hazel in the present race, and with the white
marks and spots greatly reduced.

Juvenal.—Similar to that of *P. p. jamesi* but the upperparts somewhat
more rufescent—ochraceous-tawny.

Downy young.—None seen.

Adult male.—Wing 194–216 (206.2); tail 109–112 (110.5); culmen
from anterior end of nostril 11.1–12.8 (12.0); tarsus 45.1–48.6 (46.6);
middle toe without claw 39.5–42.7 (41.3); height of bill at base 12.2–
13.5 (12.8 mm.).[5]

Adult female.—Wing 199–210 (202.5); tail 116–116 (116); culmen
from anterior end of nostril 11.6–12.3 (11.9); tarsus 44.5–45.0 (44.7);
middle toe without claw 38.7–40.2 (39.4); height of bill at base 11.9–13.0
(12.5 mm.).[6]

Range.—Resident from southeastern Manitoba, southern and western
Ontario, east to the Upper Peninsula of Michigan and south throughout
Minnesota (now chiefly in the northern half of the State) and north-
western Wisconsin (Pitcher Lake, Marston), and (formerly) to northern
Illinois. In winter to northwestern Iowa (Polk, Tama, Bremer, Butler,
Franklin, Webster, Kossuth, and O'Brien Counties). One record for
Indiana (Tremont).

Type locality.—Illinois, and Rosebud Creek, Montana=Illinois.

---

[5] Fourteen specimens from Wisconsin and Minnesota.

[6] Four specimens from Wisconsin and Illinois.

Tetrao phasianellus (not of Linnaeus) NUTTALL, Man. Orn. United States and Canada, Land Birds, 1832, 669, part (Lake Superior).—AUDUBON, Orn. Biogr., iv, 1838, 569, pl. 382, part; Synopsis, 1839, 205, part (Illinois) ; Birds Amer., 8vo ed., 1842, v, 110, pl. 298, part.—TRIPPE, Comm. Essex Inst., vi, 1871, 118 (Minnesota).

T[etrao] phasianellus BARRY, Proc. Boston Soc. Nat. Hist., v, 1854, 9 (Wisconsin; occasional).—TRIPPE, Comm. Essex Inst., vi, 1871, 118 (Minnesota; very common).

Pediocaetes phasianellus BAIRD, Rep. Pacific R. R. Surv., ix, 1858, 626, part.—BAIRD, CASSIN, and LAWRENCE, Rep. Pacific R. R. Surv., 1860, 626, part.

Pediocætes phasianellus MACOUN, Cat. Can. Birds, 1900, 210, part.

P[ediocætes] phasianellus HATCH, Bull. Minnesota Acad. Nat. Sci., 1874, 62 (Minnesota; common locally).

Pedioecetes phasianellus BAILLIE and HARRINGTON, Contr. Roy. Ontario Mus. Zool., No. 8, pt. 1, 1936, 29, part (Ontario; extreme western part).—SHORTT and WALLER, Contr. Roy. Ont. Mus. Zool., No. 10, 1937, 18 (Lake St. Martin region, Manitoba; not common).—RICKER and CLARKE, Contr. Roy. Ont. Mus. Zool., No. 16, 1939, 8 (Lake Nipissing, Ontario; migr.).

Pediæcetes phasianellus GIBBS, Bull. U. S. Geol. and Geogr. Surv. Terr., Bull. 5, 1879, 496 (n. Illinois).—NASH, Check List Birds Ontario, 1900, 27, part.— MACOUN and MACOUN, Cat. Can. Birds, ed. 2, 1909, 230, part.

Pediæcetes phasianellus (?) WOOD, Auk, xxii, 1905, 177 (Isle Royale, Mich.).

Pediocaetes phasianellus campestris HATCH, Notes Birds Minnesota, 1892, 168, 460 (Minnesota; distr.; descr.; abundant).

Pediocætes phasianellus campestris AMERICAN ORNITHOLOGISTS' UNION, Check-list, 1886, No. 308b, part; ed. 2, 1895, 117, part; ed. 3, 1910, 144, part.—RIDGWAY, Man. North Amer. Birds, 1887, 204, part.—COOKE, Bird Migr. Mississippi Valley, 1888, 106 (Mississippi Valley, records and range).—BENDIRE, Life Hist. North Amer. Birds, i, 1892, 101, part.—MACOUN, Cat. Can. Birds, 1900, 213, part (prairie n. to Manitoba).

P[ediocætes] phasianellus campestris RIDGWAY, Man. North Amer. Birds, 1887, 204, part.

Pediocætes phas[ianellus] campestris ALLEN, Auk, x, 1893, 134.

Pediocætes p[hasianellus] campestris SHUFELDT, Auk, x, 1893, 281, 283 in text (meas.).

Pediæcetes phasianellus campestris RIDGWAY, Proc. Biol. Soc. Washington, ii, 1884, 93 (Illinois and Rosebud Creek, Mont.; descr.; crit.; spec.).

[Pediæcetes phasianellus] campestris DWIGHT, Auk, xvii, 1900, 164 (molt).

Pedioecetes phasianellus campestris GILL, Auk, xvi, 1899, 23 (nomencl.).—SCHORGER, Auk, xlii, 1925, 65 (between Pitcher Lake and Marston, Wis.; habits).— TAVERNER, Birds Western Canada, 1926, 172 in text, part; Birds Canada, 1934, 161 in text, part.—AMERICAN ORNITHOLOGISTS' UNION, Check-list, ed. 4, 1931, 86, part.—BENT, U. S. Nat. Mus. Bull. 162, 1932, 291 (habits).— (?) BENNITT, Univ. Missouri Studies, vii, No. 3, 1932, 25, footnote (New Boston, Linn County, Mo. (?).—ROBERTS, Birds Minnesota, i, 1932, 395 (habits, etc., Minnesota; col. fig.).—PETERS, Check-list Birds of World, ii, 1934, 41, part.—DUMONT, Birds Iowa, 1934, 57 (rare winter migrant in northwestern part of Iowa).—SCHMIDT, Wils. Bull., xlviii, 1936, 187 (winter food in Wisconsin).—BAGG and ELIOT, Birds of Connecticut Valley in Massachusetts, 1937, 172 (status; habits; food). —GROEBBELS, Der Vögel, ii, 1937, 166 (data on breeding biology).—VAN TYNE, Occ. Pap. Mus. Zool. Univ. Michigan, No. 379, 1938, 11 (Michigan; breeds).— HAMERSTROM, Wils. Bull., li, 1939, 105 in text (Wisconsin; life hist.).—

DEAR, Trans. Roy. Can. Inst., xxiii, pt. 1, 1940, 126 (Thunder Bay, Lake Superior, Ontario; very local).—HELLMAYR and CONOVER, Cat. Birds Amer., i, No. 1, 1942, 219, part (syn.; distr.).—FRIEDMANN, Journ. Washington Acad. Sci., xxxiii, 1943, 191 (crit.).

Pediœcetes p[hasianellus] campestris BRENNAN, Auk, xxxv, 1918, 75 (Tremont, Ind.).

P[edioecetes phasianellus] campestris BAILEY, Handb. Birds Western United States, 1902, 132, part.—SNYDER, Auk, lvi, 1939, 184, part (Upper Peninsula; Michigan, formerly s. to nw. Illinois).

[*Pedioecetes phasianellus*] *campestris* DEAR, Trans. Roy. Can. Inst., xxiii, pt. 1, 1940, 127 in test.

[*Pedioecetes*] *phasianellus campestris* BAILLIE and HARRINGTON, Contr. Roy. Ontario Mus. Zool., No. 8, pt. 1, 1936, 29 in text (extreme western Ontario).

Pediocœtes phasianellus Subsp. a. *Pediocœtes columbianus* OGILVIE-GRANT, Cat. Birds Brit. Mus., xxii, 1893, 83, part (Minnesota).

Pediocaetes phasianellus var. *columbianus* NELSON, Bull. Essex Inst., viii, 1876, 121, 153 (n. Illinois).

P[ediocaetes] phasianellus var. *columbianus* RIDGWAY, Ann. Lyc. Nat. Hist. New York, x, 1874, 382 (Illinois).

Pedioecetes phasianellus var. *columbianus* BAIRD, BREWER, and RIDGWAY, Hist. North Amer. Birds, iii, 1874, 436, part.

Pediœcetes phasianellus var. *columbianus* COUES, Birds Northwest, 1874, 407, part.

P[ediœcetes] phasianellus var. *columbianus* NELSON, Bull. Essex Inst., viii, 1876, 121 (ne. Illinois; extremely rare).

[*Pediœcetes phasianellus*] var. *columbianus* COUES, Key North Amer. Birds, 1872, 234, part; Check List North Amer. Birds, 1874, No. 383a; part.

? *Pediocœtes phasianellus columbianus* MACOUN, Cat. Can. Birds, 1900, 212, part (Manitoba).

Pediœcetes phasianellus columbianus ROBERTS and BENNER, Bull. Nuttall Orn. Club, v, 1880, 17 (Minnesota).—RIDGWAY, Proc. U. S. Nat. Mus., iii, 1880, 196, part; Nomencl. North Amer. Birds, 1881, No. 478a, part.—COALE, Auk, xxix, 1912, 238 (Oconto County, Wash.).

P[edioecetes] p[hasianellus] columbianus COUES, Check List North Amer. Birds, ed. 2, 1882, No. 562, part; Key North Amer. Birds, ed. 2, 1884, 581, part.

Pediocetes columbianus ELLIOT, Proc. Acad. Nat. Sci. Philadelphia, 1862, 403, part.

Pediecœtes columbianus ELLIOT, Monogr. Tetraonidae, 1865, introd., 5, part.

Pediocaetes columbianus ELLIOT, Monogr. Tetraonidae, 1865, pl. 14.

Pediaecaetes columbianus ELLIOT, Monogr. Tetraonidae, 1865, text opp. pl. 14.

Pediœcetes columbianus COUES, Proc. Essex Inst., v, 1868, 40 (spec.; probably Illinois).

Pediocetes phasianellus phasianellus BEEBE, Wils. Bull., xlv, 1933, 121 (Isle Royal, Lake Superior).

Pediœcetes phasianellus HONEYWILL, Auk, xxxi, 1914, 85 (Ox Meadow; Minnesota).

Pedioecetes phasianellus phasianellus AMERICAN ORNITHOLOGISTS' UNION, Check-list, ed. 4, 1931, 86, part.—PETERS, Check-list Birds of World, ii, 1934, 40, part (s. Ontario).

P[edioecetes] p[hasianellus] phasianellus DU MONT, Auk, 1, 1933, 432 in text (spec.; Grand Rapids, Lake Winnipeg; and Virginia, St. Louis County, Minn.; plum.; crit.).

Pedioecetes phasianellus campisylvicola SNYDER, Occ. Pap. Roy. Ontario Mus. Zool., No. 2, 1935, 4 (St. Charles, Manitoba; descr.; crit.; distr.).

[*Pedioecetes*] *phasianellus campisylvicola* BAILLIE and HARRINGTON, Contr. Roy. Ontario Mus. Zool., No. 8, pt. 1, 1936, 29 in text.—SNYDER, Trans. Roy. Can. Inst., xxii, 1938, 186, in text (w. Rainy River district, Ontario).

P[*edioecetes*] *p*[*hasianellus*] *campisylvicola* SNYDER, Auk, lvi, 1939, 184, in text (crit.).

Genus TYMPANUCHUS Gloger

Tympanuchus GLOGER, Hand- und Hilfsbuch, 1842 (1841), 396. (Type, by monotypy, *Tetrao cupido* Linnaeus.)

Cupidonia REICHENBACH, Av. Syst. Nat. Vög., 1853, xxix. (Type, by monotypy, *Tetrao cupido* Linnaeus.)

Cupidinea (emendation) COUES, Check List North Amer. Birds, ed. 2, 1882, 94.

Bonasa STONE, Auk, xxiv, April 1907, 198 (thought to be transferable to *Tetrao cupido* Linnaeus under the "first species" rule).

Medium-sized terrestrial grouse (length about 381–483 mm.), with tail decidedly less than half as long as wing, rounded, the rectrices (18) broad, rigid, and with broadly rounded tips, the longer under tail coverts reaching to or slightly beyond its tip; sides of neck with an inflatable air sac (much less developed in females), overhung in adult males by a tuft of long, rather narrow, rigid feathers with tips obtusely pointed or narrowly rounded.

Bill relatively small (less than one-third as long as rest of head), its depth at frontal antiae about equal to its width at same point; culmen rounded to indistinctly ridged; rhamphotheca completely smooth; maxillary tomium moderately concave or arched, smooth. Wing moderate, strongly concave beneath, the longest primaries exceeding longest secondaries by more than one-fourth to nearly if not quite one-third the length of wing; third to fifth primaries longest, the first (outermost) nearly equal to, sometimes longer than, seventh; outer primary moderately bowed or incurved, the four or five outer ones distinctly emarginate or sinuate basally. Tail decidedly less than half as long as wing, rounded, the rather broad and rigid rectrices (18) with broadly rounded or subtruncate tips. Tarsus one-fifth to considerably more than one-fifth as long as wing, completely clothed in winter with soft hairlike feathers except on heel and part of planta tarsi, in summer with short feathers only on acrotarsium, the planta tarsi covered with small and rather indistinct roundish and hexagonal scales; middle toe slightly shorter to about as long as tarsus; lateral toes about equal, reaching to about penultimate articulation of middle toe; hallux about as long as second phalanx of middle toe; upper surface of toes with a continuous series of transverse scutella, bordered along each side by a row of smaller subquadrate scutella, edged (in winter) with a fringe of horny pectinations; claws moderate in size, rather slightly curved, moderately acute or slightly blunt.

Plumage and coloration.—Feathers of crown elongated, decurved, forming, when erected, a conspicuous crest (less distinct in females); a very narrow nude superciliary space; sides of neck with an inflatable air sac (less developed in females, large in males, and bright orange-colored in breeding season), males having also on each side of neck, immediately above the air sac, a conspicuous erectile tuft of much elongated, rather rigid narrow feathers with obtusely pointed or narrowly rounded tips;

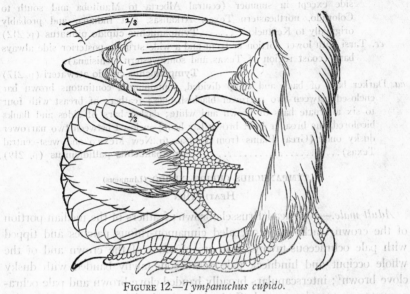

FIGURE 12.—*Tympanuchus cupido.*

plumage in general compact, the feathers broad and rounded, except on lower abdomen, anal region, etc., where soft, hairlike, and blended. Upperparts barred with tawny-brown, buffy, and blackish, the tail plain grayish brown (darker distally) narrowly tipped with whitish or buffy (narrowly barred with buffy in females); underparts pale buffy or whitish, barred, more or less broadly, with grayish brown; the under side of head buffy with a cluster of grayish brown spots or bars on posterior portion of malar region.

Range.—Open districts of eastern North America, from western portion of the Great Plains to the Atlantic coast (locally) and from Texas and southwestern Louisiana (formerly also Virginia?) northward to coast of Massachusetts, southwestern Ontario, southern Manitoba, and southwestern Saskatchewan. (Two species.)

KEY TO THE FORMS (ADULTS) OF THE GENUS TYMPANUCHUS

a. Darker bars of back and rump very broad, solid blackish brown; feathers of breast brown with tips and subterminal band whitish; brown bars on sides and flanks unicolored.

b. Scapulars with large and very conspicuous terminal spots of buffy whitish; neck tufts or pinnae of adult male composed of not more than 10 lanceolate,

pointed feathers; dark buffy brown bars on underparts broad averaging about 5 mm. (coastal plain from New England and Long Island to Potomac River; now extinct) .... **Tympanuchus cupido cupido** (p. 208)
 bb. Scapulars without conspicuous buffy whitish terminal spots; pinnae of male composed of more than 10 elongate feathers with nearly truncated tips; dark bars on underparts narrower—averaging about 2.5 mm.
  c. Tarsi feathered to base of toes, without an exposed bare strip on posterior side except in summer (central Alberta to Manitoba and south to Colorado, northeastern Texas, Arkansas, and Indiana, and probably originally to Kentucky) .... **Tympanuchus cupido pinnatus** (p. 212)
  cc. Tarsi with lower portion in front and a wide strip on posterior side always bare (coast region of Texas and southwestern Louisiana).

Tympanuchus cupido attwateri (p. 217)
 aa. Darker bars of back and rump divided, containing a continuous brown bar enclosed between two narrower blackish ones; feathers of breast with four to six alternate bars of brown and white; darker bars of sides and flanks bicolored, the broader light brown bar being enclosed between two narrower dusky ones (Great Plains from Kansas to New Mexico and west-central Texas) .... **Tympanuchus pallidicintus** (p. 219)

TYMPANUCHUS CUPIDO CUPIDO (Linnaeus)

HEATH HEN

Adult male.—Forehead Brussels brown; feathers of the median portion of the crown black with concealed cinnamon-rufous patches and tipped with pale ochraceous-tawny; feathers of sides of the crown and of the whole occiput and hindneck pale ochraceous-tawny banded with dusky clove brown[7]; interscapulars broadly banded clove brown and pale ochraceous-tawny to ochraceous-buff; back, lower back, rump, and upper tail coverts similar but with the pale terminal bands more yellowish—pale tawny-olive to yellow-ocher; scapulars and inner secondaries like the interscapulars but with large terminal spots of buffy white; upper wing coverts and outer secondaries olive-brown to pale clove brown banded and tipped with buffy white, the pale bands more widely spaced on the outer coverts than on the inner ones; primaries olive-brown to pale clove brown with buffy-white spots on the outer webs only; rectrices olive-brown to pale clove brown narrowly tipped with whitish, the median ones with some irregular pale cinnamomeous markings; lores, upper throat, and lower cheeks light warm buff; feathers of sides of neck and lower throat cinnamon-rufous incompletely crossed by blackish lines and with elongated terminal shaft streaks or spots of light warm buff; elongated pinnae with five or six wholly black feathers and four or five that have broad pale warm-buff stripes occupying most of the inner, dorsal web, the inner webs of these feathers narrowly edged with cinnamon and sometimes irregularly toothed with blackish-brown diagonal marks; malar stripe and

---

[7] In no specimen examined have I seen anything comparable to the description taken from living birds by Gross (Mem. Boston Soc. Nat. Hist., vi, 1928, 563), who found the tips of these feathers to be white.

auriculars cinnamon-brown mottled with blackish; feathers of the breast, sides, flanks, and abdomen buffy brown to dark buffy brown, washed with cinnamomeous anteriorly and broadly banded with white; these white bands somewhat tinged with ochraceous-tawny or cinnamon on the sides and flanks; thighs and tarsi pale, buffy brown to pale drab with a grayish tinge and indistinctly barred with darker; under tail coverts white with broad, largely concealed, basal areas of olive-brown more or less tinged or mottled with ochraceous-tawny; under wing coverts barred white and buffy brown on the outer ones, the inner ones and the axillars almost wholly white; iris Verona brown; bill light to dark olive-gray, paler at the tip; toes ochraceous-buff to ochraceous-orange; superciliary comb orange, very brilliant in the breeding season; vocal sacs ochraceous orange when deflated but approaching pure orange when inflated; the edges of the sacs with a narrow margin of scarlet.[8]

Adult female.—Similar to the adult male but slightly smaller, the pinnae shorter and without the stiff feathers, the vocal sacs not developed, the superciliary comb lacking.[9]

First-winter plumage.—Like that of the adult of corresponding sex but with the upperparts somewhat more rufescent and with the throat cinnamon-buff instead of warm buff and without the stiffened elongated pinnae.

Juvenal.—Apparently unknown.[10]

Downy young[11].—Underparts cream buff, the throat and middle of abdomen approaching colonial buff; sides of head marguerite yellow with three small black spots back of the eye; upperparts tawny-olive to Isabella color, turning to snuff brown and russet on the rump, and variously marked with black, the markings most prominent on the nape and the middle of the back; a conspicuous black mark on the forehead.

Adult male.—Wing 215–225 (222.2); tail 115–128 (121.7); culmen from the base 24–26 (25.2); tarsus 41.50 (44.1); pinna 66–72 (69.3 mm.).[12]

Adult female.—Wing 201–219 (209.2); tail 100–115 (107.5); culmen from the base 21–24 (22.7); tarsus 41–49 (45.1); pinna 27–32 (29.9 mm.).[13]

Range.—Formerly resident in suitable areas, chiefly brushy plains, from southern Maine, Massachusetts, southern New England, and Long

---

[8] Colors of soft parts *ex* Gross, *cit. supra,* p. 564.

[9] Adults in worn, spring plumage tend to be less rufescent, more grayish than autumn fresh plumaged birds.

[10] Not only were no specimens in this stage available in the present study, but Gross was unable to find any when writing his monograph on this bird.

[11] Taken from Gross, *cit. supra,* p. 568.

[12] Ten specimens, *ex* Gross, p. 567.

[13] Ten specimens, *ex* Gross, p. 567.

Island south along the Atlantic seaboard through New Jersey and eastern Pennsylvania to the Potomac River (Washington, D. C.) and possibly into Virginia and the Carolinas[14]; since 1830 confined to the island of Marthas Vineyard, reduced to a single bird in 1932; now extinct.

Type locality.—"Virginia" (*ex* Catesby).

[*Tetrao*] *cupido* LINNAEUS, Syst. Nat., ed. 10, i, 1758, 160 ("Virginia," i.e., Pennsylvania or New York? based on *Urogallus minor, muscus*, etc., Catesby, Nat. Hist. Carolina, iii, 1, pl. 1; Brisson, Orn., i, 212); ed. 12, i, 1766, 274.—GMELIN, Syst. Nat., i, pt. 2, 1788, 751.—LATHAM, Index Orn., ii, 1790, 638.—REICHENBACH, Synop. Av., iii, Gallinacae, 1848, pl. 217, fig. 1896-1898.

Tetrao cupido WILSON, Amer. Orn., iii, 1811, 104, part, pl. 27, fig. 1.—TEMMINCK, Pig. et Gallin., iii, 1815, 161, 703, part.—VIEILLOT, Nouv. Dict. Hist. Nat., xxxiii, 1819, 448, part (Long Island; New Jersey; Pennsylvania).—VIEILLOT and OUDART, Gal. Ois., ii, 1825, 55, pl. 219.—EMMONS, Cat. Birds Massachusetts, 1825, 4.—BONAPARTE, Ann. Lyc. Nat. Hist. N. Y., ii, pt. i, 1826, 126, part; ii, 1828, 442, part; Contr. Maclurean Lyc., i, 1827, 23; Amer. Philos. Trans., iii, 1830, 302, part; Geogr. and Comp. List, 1838, 44, part.—LESSON, Traité d'Orn., 1831, 500.—NUTTALL, Man. Orn. United States and Canada, Land Birds, 1832, 662, part; ed. 2, 1840, 799, part.—AUDUBON, Orn. Biogr., ii, 1834, 490, part; v, 1839, 559, part; Synopsis, 1839, 204 part; Birds Amer., 8vo ed., v, 1842, 93, part.—PEABODY, Rep. Orn. Massachusetts, 1839, 355.—LINDSLEY, Amer. Journ. Sci. and Arts, 1843, 264 (Connecticut).—DEKAY, Zool. New York, 1844, 205.—GIRAUD, Birds Long Island, 1844, 195 (Long Island, N. Y.; nearly extinct; habits).—CABOT, Proc. Boston Soc. Nat. Hist., v, 1855, 154 (Long Island).—PUTNAM, Proc. Essex Inst., i, 1856, 229 (Massachusetts).

Tetra cupido BLADGEN, *in* Farley, Auk, xl, 1933, 322 in text (Long Island, N. Y., in letter of 1758).

T[*etrao*] *cupido* BONAPARTE, Journ. Acad. Nat. Sci. Philadelphia, iv, pt. 2, 1825, 267, part; Obs. Wilson's Orn., 1826, [126], part.

Bonasa cupido STEPHENS, *in* Shaw, Gen. Zool., xi, pt. 2, 1819, 299 ("Carolina"; New Jersey; Long Island).

Cupidonia cupido BAIRD, Rep. Pacific R. R. Surv., ix, 1858, 628, part (Pocono Mountains, Pa.; Long Island; "Eastern Coast"); Cat. North Amer. Birds, 1859, No. 464, part.—LAWRENCE, Ann. Lyc. Nat. Hist. New York, vii, 1861, 291 (Long Island).—SAMUELS, App. Sec. Rep. Orn. Massachusetts, 1864, 11 (Marthas Vineyard and Naushon Islands).—ALLEN, Proc. Essex Inst., iv, 1864, 85 (Massachusetts); Bull. Nuttall Orn. Club, i, 1876, 53 in text (Massachusetts; becoming scarce); Bull. Essex Inst., x, 1878, 22 (Massachusetts; extirpated except on Marthas Vineyard).—COUES, Proc. Essex Inst., v, 1868, 39 part (New England; soon to become extinct); 287 (Massachusetts); Check List North Amer. Birds, 1873, No. 384, part; Birds Northwest, 1874, 419, part (in synonymy).—TURNBULL, Birds Eastern Pennsylvania and New Jersey, 1869, 27 (Monroe and Northampton Counties, Pennsylvania; New Jersey plains).—MAYNARD, Naturalists' Guide, 1870, 138 (Marthas Vineyard at Naushon island,

---

[14] Doubt has been cast on the southern records for this bird, but in all fairness it should be pointed out that no actual specimens exist from any part of its range other than Marthas Vineyard, Nashawena Island, and from Burlington County, N. J. It is only an assumption that the records from the mainland of New England were of this form and not of the inland prairie chicken, but an assumption that has been generally accepted.

Mass.).—Brewer, Proc. Boston Soc. Nat. Hist., xvii, 1875, 12 (New England).
—Brewster, Auk, ii, 1885, 82 (crit.; descr.; Marthas Vineyard).—Smith, Auk,
iii, 1886, 139 in text (District of Columbia).

[*Cupidonia*] *cupido* Coues, Key North Amer. Birds, 1872, 234, part ("New York,
New Jersey, Pennsylvania, Long Island, Nantucket and Marthas Vineyard,
etc.").

C[*upidonia*] *cupido* Coues, Key North Amer. Birds, ed. 2, 1884, 583, part.

Cupidonia cupido, var. *cupido* Baird, Brewer, and Ridgway, Hist. North Amer.
Birds, iii, 1874, 440, part.

Cupidonia cupido cupido Goode, U. S. Nat. Mus. Bull. 20, 1883, 316.

Tympanuchus cupido Ridgway, Proc. U. S. Nat. Mus., viii, 1885, 355.—American
Ornithologists' Union, Check-list, 1886, No. 306; ed. 2, 1895, No. 306; ed. 3,
1910, p. 143.—Chapman, Auk, v, 1888, 402 (nomencl.).—Bendire, Life Hist.
North Amer. Birds, i, 1892, 93.—Marshall, Auk, ix, 1892, 203, in text
(Marthas Vineyard; spec.).—Ogilvie-Grant, Cat. Birds Brit. Mus., xxii, 1893,
77.—Allen, Auk, x, 1893, 133.—Dutcher, Auk, x, 1893, 272 (plains near Comac
Hills, Long Island, in 1836; "not plentiful").—Judd, U. S. Biol. Surv. Bull. 24,
1905, 18, 19 (range, food, etc.).—Townsend, Mem. Nuttall Orn. Club No. 3,
1905, 64, in text, 203 in text (Essex County, Mass.; hist.) ; Mem. Nuttall Orn.
Club, No. 5, 1920, 97 (Essex County, Mass.; extinct).—Brewster, Mem. Nuttall Orn. Club, No. 4, 1906, 172 (Cambridge region, Mass.).—Stone, Birds
New Jersey, 1908, 151 (New Jersey; hist.).—Eaton, Birds New York, i, 1910,
376.—Forbush, Game Birds, Wild-fowl, and Shore Birds, 1912, 385 (history,
etc.) ; Amer. Mus. Journ., xviii, No. 4, 1918, [279–285], 6 text cuts from
photographs (history, habits, etc.) ; Birds Massachusetts and Other New
England States, ii, 1927, 39, pl. 35 (fig.; descr.; habits; New England).—
Swales, Proc. Biol. Soc. Washington, xxxii, 1919, 198 (Washington, D. C.,
April 10, 1846).—Burns, Orn. Chester County, Pa., 1919, 48 (Chester County,
Pa.; hist.).—Phillips, Verh. 6th Internat. Orn. Kongr., 1929, 507 (Marthas
Vineyard; on verge of extinction).—Cooke, Proc. Biol. Soc. Washington, xlii,
1929, 34 (Washington, D. C.).

T[*ympanuchus*] *cupido* Ridgway, Man. North Amer. Birds, 1887, 203.—Goss, Hist.
Birds Kansas, 1891, 225 (Marthas Vineyard).—Reichenow, Die Vögel, i,
1913, 320.

[*Tympanuchus*] *cupido* Sharpe, Hand-list, i, 1899, 20.

Cupidonia cupido brewsteri Coues, Key North Amer. Birds, ed. 3, 1887, 884; ed. 4,
1890, 884 (Marthas Vineyard, Mass.).

Tympanuchus cupido cupido Gross, Mem. Boston Soc. Nat Hist, vi, 1928, 491 in
text (syn., monogr.; col. pl.; etc.).—American Ornithologists' Union, Check-
list, ed. 4, 1931, 85.—Bent, U. S. Nat. Mus. Bull. 162, 1932, 264 (life hist.).—
Burns, Wils. Bull., xliv, 1932, 28 (spec. ex Peale coll.).—Peters, Check-list
Birds of World, ii, 1934, 41 (extinct).—Taverner, Birds Canada, 1934, 160 in
text (extinct).—Stone, Bird Studies Cape May, i, 1937, 320 (New Jersey;
former status and hunting recollections).—Bagg and Eliot, Birds Connecticut
Valley in Massachusetts, 1937, 171 (habits; status; extinct).—Huber, Auk, lv,
1938, 527 in text (2 spec.; Burlington County, N. J.).—Hellmayr and Conover, Cat. Birds Amer., i, No. 1, 1942, 222 (syn.; distr.).—Cruickshank, Birds
New York City, 1942, 151 (extinct; New York City area).

Tympanuchus c[*upido*] *cupido* Groebbels, Der Vögel, ii, 1937, 137 in text (dancing
of males), 139 in text (courtship), 166 (data on breeding) ; 238 in text (care
of eggs).

TYMPANUCHUS CUPIDO PINNATUS (Brewster)

GREATER PRAIRIE HEN

Adults.—Similar to that of the corresponding sex of the nominate race but differing in having no conspicuous buffy-whitish terminal spots on the scapulars; the pinnae or neck tufts are composed of more than 10 feathers and the feathers are less pointed more abruptly truncate in shape; the general tone of the upper parts averages less rufescent, the broad tips of the feathers of the back, rump, and upper tail coverts especially are less rufescent than in *T. c. cupido,* being pinkish buff (instead of pale tawny-olive), and the dark bars on the underparts are generally narrower, and the thighs paler, the whole underparts seeming more whitish[15] iris raw umber; "comb" deep cadmium; gular sacs dark Indian yellow tinged brownish and slightly veined with red; toes dark brownish ocher, back of tarsi and lower surface of toes bright ocher-yellow; claws blackish tipped with whitish on the outer claw only.

First-winter plumage.—Not certainly separable from the same stage of the nominate race.

Juvenal.—Forehead, sides of crown, and occiput between russet and Sudan brown; center of crown fuscous-blackish (formed by blackish tips of the otherwise russet feathers, occiput speckled with blackish; hindneck pinkish buff to pale pinkish buff, the feathers edged with fuscous, giving a streaked appearance to the area, the more lateral feathers with the buff more whitish; scapulars and interscapulars as in the adult but the pale bars paler—pinkish buff to cinnamon-buff and the feathers with prominent white shaft streaks; upper wing coverts and primaries as in the adult, the latter feathers somewhat more pointed; secondaries with the pale bars restricted to their outer webs except on the innermost feathers, the brown areas broader than in the adults and somewhat freckled and vermiculated with blackish; back, lower back, rump, and upper tail coverts as in adult but more rufescent, the pale tips cinnamon-buff; rectrices unlike the adult, fuscous to fuscous-black, crossed by seven or eight narrow buffy-whitish to pale pinkish-buff bars and narrowly tipped with the same, these bars largely restricted to the outer webs of the lateral rectrices, the dark interspaces mottled with clay color the size of the patches increasing distally[16]; lores, supraorbital, and supraauricular band pale pinkish buff to whitish; malar stripe extending below the eye to, and including, the auriculars, like the top of the head, mixed with fuscous-black posterior to the front end of the eye; lower cheeks, chin,

[15] Occasionally erythristic specimens occur, but these do not constitute a "normal" plumage.
[16] The rectricial pattern is the easiest character by which young *Tympanuchus* may be told from young *Pedioecetes.* In the latter, the median rectrices have longitudinal pale median stripes.

and throat less ochraceous than in adult—pale pinkish buff to whitish; feathers of breast whitish tinged with pale ochraceous-buff and transversely spotted (the bars broken into spots) with Prout's brown to clove brown, the spots tending to coalesce into bars on the more posterior breast feathers; sides and flanks pale ochraceous-buff heavily barred with dark buffy brown to sepia; abdomen and thighs whitish barred with buffy brown to pale buffy brown, the bars faint and small on the middle of the abdomen; under tail coverts white with transverse spots of dark buffy brown.

Downy young.—Similar to that of the nominate race but richer yellow below—straw yellow, the breast washed with yellow ocher; the top of head ochraceous-tawny (Isabella color in *T. c. cupido*), and lower back and rump ochraceous-buff to ochraceous-tawny; the dark markings as in the nominate race.

Adult male.—Wing 217–241 (226); tail 90–103 (96.2); exposed culmen 16–21 (18.7); tarsus 46.5–51.5 (49.7); middle toe without claw 43–47 (45); height of bill at base 9.5–13.5 (11.4 mm.).[17]

Adult female.—Wing 208–220 (219); tail 87.5–93.5 (90.3); exposed culmen 17–19.5 (18.6); tarsus 46–52 (49.1); middle toe without claw 41–44.6 (43); height of bill at base 10–12 (11.3 mm.).[18]

Range.—Resident in the prairie districts of the Mississippi Valley from central Alberta (Edmonton; casually as far north as Lac la Biche), southern Saskatchewan, and southern Manitoba south through the Dakotas, Minnesota, Wisconsin, and Michigan and southern Ontario (Wallaceburg) to southeastern Michigan, western and southern Indiana, northwestern Ohio, and (probably, formerly) western Kentucky in the east,[19] and through Nebraska and central Kansas to eastern Colorado (Barton and Barr), southeastern Wyoming (Chugwater), and to Oklahoma (where now largely gone) and to extreme northern Texas (Gainesville, Cooke County, and Tascosa).

Occasional in Montana (1 record—near Huntley); in winter to Arkansas. While this form does migrate to some extent, the limits of its winter range are largely contained within the breeding range; it occurs casually in winter in northern Louisiana.

Type locality.—Vermillion, S. Dak.

Tetrao cupido (not of Linnaeus) WILSON, Am. Orn., iii, 1811, 104, part, pl. 27, fig. 1.—VIEILLOT, Nouv. Dict. Hist. Nat., xxxiii, 1819, 448, part (Kentucky; "plains of the Columbia River").—BONAPARTE, Ann. Lyc. Nat. Hist. New York, ii, pt. 1, 1826, 126, part; ii, 1828, 442, part; Geogr. and Comp. List, 1838, 44, part.

---

[17] Seventeen specimens from Michigan, Minnesota, North Dakota, and northern Texas.

[18] Eleven specimens from Michigan, North Dakota, Nebraska, and northern Texas.

[19] The subspecific status of the Kentucky birds is uncertain; the species is extinct there and no local specimens appear to have been preserved.

—Nuttall, Man. Orn. United States and Canada, Land Birds, 1832, 662, part; ed. 2, 1840, 799, part.—Audubon, Orn. Biogr., ii, 1834, 490, part, pl. 186; v, 1839, 559, part; Synopsis, 1839, 204, part; Birds Amer., 8vo ed., v, 1842, part, pl. 296. —Reichenbach, Synop. Av., Gallinaceae, 1848, pl. 217, figs. 1896-1898.—Wood-house, Rep. Sitgreaves Expl. Zuñi and Colorado R., 1853, 96, part (Arkansas).

T[etrao] cupido Bonaparte, Journ. Acad. Nat. Sci. Philadelphia, iv, pt. ii, 1825, 267, part; Obs. Wilson's Orn., 1826, [126].—Douglas, Trans. Linn. Soc. London, xvi, 1829, 148 (between Red River and Pembina, lat. 49° N.).—Barry, Proc. Boston Soc. Nat. Hist., 1854, 9 (Wisconsin; common).—Maximilian, Journ. für Orn., 1858, 439 (upper Missouri River).

Cupidonia cupido Baird, Rep. Pacific R. R. Surv., ix, 1858, 628, part (Missouri; Tremont, Illinois; mouth of Running Water River; Big Sioux River); Cat. North Amer. Birds, 1859, No. 464, part.—Wheaton, Ohio Agr. Rep., 1860, No. 178 (nw. Ohio); Bull. Nuttall Orn. Club, iv, 1879, 62 (near Columbus, Ohio, Nov. 16, 1898); Rep. Birds Ohio, 1882, 445, 579 (Ohio; syn.; descr.; distr.; spec.).—Hayden, Trans. Amer. Philos. Soc., xii, 1862, 172 (upper Missouri to the Niobrara River).—Elliot, Monogr. Tetraonidae, 1865, pl. 16, and text, part.—Coues, Proc. Essex Inst., v, 1868, 39 part (spec.; Illinois); Check List North Amer. Birds, 1873, No. 384, part; ed. 2, 1882, No. 563, part; Birds Northwest, 1874, 419, part.—Allen, Mem. Boston Soc. Nat. Hist., i, 1868, 500 (w. Iowa); Bull. Mus. Comp. Zool., iii, 1872, 130 (Leavenworth, Kans.), 141 (Fort Hays, w. Kansas), 144 (Coyote, nw. Kansas), 181 (e. and middle Kansas).—Trippe, Proc. Boston Soc. Nat. Hist., xv, 1872, 240 (Iowa). —Snow, Cat. Birds Kansas, ed. 2, reprint, 1873, 9.—Ridgway, Proc. Boston Soc. Nat. Hist., xvi, 1874, 23 (lower Wabash Valley).—Ridgway, Proc. U. S. Nat. Mus., iii, 1880, 196, part; Nom. North Amer. Birds, 1881, No. 477, part; Forest and Stream, xxiv, No. 11, 1885, 204 (District of Columbia, 1 spec., introduced or offspring of introduced parents).—Baird, Brewer, and Ridgway, Hist. North Amer. Birds, iii, 1874, pl. 61, figs. 1, 7.—Hoffman, Proc. Boston Soc. Nat. Hist., xviii, 1875, 174 (Grand River Agency, Dakota Territory; abundant).—Brewster, Bull. Nuttall Orn. Club, ii, 1877, 66 in text (hybrid); 1882, 59 in text (spec., ex market, from Iowa; plum.).—Nelson, Bull. Essex Inst., ix, 1877, 65 (s. Illinois).—Gibbs, Bull. U. S. Geol. and Geogr. Surv. Terr. Bull. 5, 1879, 491 (Michigan; common).—Langdon, Journ. Cincinnati Soc. Nat. Hist., 1879, 15 (Cincinnati, Ohio; formerly; few still in nw. Ohio).—Roberts and Benner, Bull. Nuttall Orn. Club, v, 1880, 18 (Grant County, Minn.).— Cooke, Auk, i, 1884, 247 (Minnesota; Chippewa Indian name).—Drew, Auk, ii, 1885, 17 (vertical range in Colorado).—Agersborg, Auk, ii, 1885, 285 (se. South Dakota, abundant).

C[upidonia] cupido Ridgway, Ann. Lyc. Nat. Hist. New York, x, 1874, 382 (Illinois). —Hatch, Bull. Minnesota Acad. Nat. Sci., 1874, 62 (Minnesota; abundant).— Deane, Bull. Nuttall Orn. Club, i, 1876, 22 in text (albinism).—Nelson, Bull. Essex Inst., viii, 1876, 121 (ne. Illinois, formerly abundant).—Coues, Key North Amer. Birds, ed. 2, 1884, No. 583, part.

C[apidonia] cupido Boies, Cat. Birds Southern Michigan, 1875, No. 146 (s. Michigan).

[Cupidonia cupido] var. cupido Ridgway, Bull. Essex Inst., v, 1873, 199, in text.

Cupidonia cupido, var. cupido Baird, Brewer, and Ridgway, Hist. North Amer. Birds, iii, 1874, 440, part.

Cupidonia cupido cupido Goode, U. S. Nat. Mus. Bull. 20, 1883, 316, part.

Bonasa cupido Gray, List Birds Brit. Mus., pt. 5, Gallinae, 1867, 88 (North America).

[*Bonasa*] *cupido* GRAY, Hand-list, ii, 1870, 277, No. 9831.

Tympanuchus cupido TAVERNER, Can. Water Birds, 1939, 172 (field chars.; Canada). —SHETTER, Wils. Bull., li, 1939, 46, in text (Michigan; speed of flight).— PETRIDES, Trans. 7th North Amer. Wildlife Conf., 1942, 318 in text (age indicators in plumage).

Cupidonia americana BONAPARTE, Compt. Rend., xiv, 1857, 428.

Tympanuchus cupido americanus AMERICAN ORNITHOLOGISTS' UNION, Check-list, ed. 4, 1931, 85.—BAERG, Univ. Arkansas Agr. Exp. Stat. Bull. 258, 1931, 53 (Arkansas; distr.; descr.).—NICE, Birds Oklahoma, rev. ed., 1931, 79 (Oklahoma).—BENT, U. S. Nat. Mus. Bull. 162, 1932, 242 (life hist.; distr.).— ROBERTS, Birds Minnesota, i, 1932, 385 (Minnesota; habits; distr.).—DuMONT, Wils. Bull., xliv, 1932, 237 (Iowa; spec.).—HARROLD, Wils. Bull., xlv, 1933, 19 (Lake Johnston, Saskatchewan).—YOUNGSWORTH, Auk, l, 1933, 124 (Sioux City, Iowa; numerous in autumn; breeds).—ESTEN, Auk, l, 1933, 356 in text (Indiana; 150 birds seen at Jasper-Pulaski Game Reserve).—JOHNSON, Wils. Bull., xlvi, 1934, 3 (habits, nw. Minnesota).—MONSON, Wils. Bull., xlvi, 1934, 43 (Cass County, N. Dak.; common).—TAVERNER, Birds Canada, 1934, 160, in text, pl. 19a (col. fig.; distr.; characters).—BRECKENRIDGE, Condor, xxxvii, 1935, 269 (Minnesota).—McCREARY and MICKEY, Wils. Bull., xlvii, 1935, 130 in text (se. Wyoming; rare).—YOUNGWORTH, Wils. Bull., xlvii, 1935, 217 (nests, Fort Sisseton, S. Dak.).—LONG, Bull. Univ. Kansas Sci., xxxvi, 1935, 232 (w. Kansas, November).—TRAUTMAN, Auk, lii, 1935, 321 (Ohio).—SCHMIDT, Wils. Bull., xlviii, 1936, 196 (Wisconsin; winter food).—ALEXANDER, Univ. Colorado Stud. Zool., xxiv, 1937, 87 (Boulder County, Colo.; hypothetical).—BEEBE, Wils. Bull., xlix, 1937, 35 (Upper Peninsula Michigan, recently spread).—GROEBBELS, Der Vögel, ii, 1937, 137 in text (courtship dance), 166 (data on breeding), 239 in text (number of eggs), 397 in text (time of day of hatching).—BAGG and ELIOT, Birds of Connecticut Valley in Massachusetts, 1937, 172 (introduced unsuccessfully).—SUTTON, Ann. Carnegie Mus., xxvii, 1938, 178 (Tarrant County, Tex.; probably breeds).—OBERHOLSER, Bird Life Louisiana, 1938, 190 (Louisiana; casual winter visitor).—TODD, Auk, lv, 1938, 274 in text (old w. Pennsylvania record erroneous; should be Kentucky).—BENNETT, Blue-winged Teal, 1938, 38 in text (market hunting).—NIEDRACH and ROCKWELL, Birds of Denver and Mountain Parks, 1939, 61 (c. Colorado; rare; food habits; spec.).— HAMMERSTROM, Wils. Bull., li, 1939, 105 in text (Wisconsin; life hist.).— CAMPBELL, Bull. Toledo Mus. Sci., i, 1940, 61 (Lucas County, Ohio; extirpated by 1880).—LONG, Trans. Kansas Acad. Sci., xliii, 1940, 440 (Kansas; formerly abundant; now rare in east, and uncommon in western part).—GOODPASTER, Journ. Cincinnati Soc. Nat. Hist., xxii, 1941, 13 (sw. Ohio; almost extirpated). —HAMERSTROM, HOPKINS, and RINZEL, Wils. Bull., liii, 1941, 185, footnote (winter food).

[*Tympanuchus*] *cupido americanus* GROEBBELS, Der Vögel, ii, 1937, 139 in text (courtship), 238 in text (covers eggs).

Tympanuchus cupido americus BENNITT, Univ. Missouri Studies, vii, No. 3, 1932, 25 (Missouri; uncommon resident).

Tympanuchus americanus RIDGWAY, Auk, iii, 1886, 133 (nomencl.).—AMERICAN ORNITHOLOGISTS' UNION, Check List, 1886, No. 305, part; ed. 2, 1895, No. 305, part.—SETON, Auk, iii, 1886, 153 (Winnipeg and Portage la Prairie, Manitoba), 329 (Westbourne, w. Manitoba).—EVERMANN, Auk, v, 1888, 349 (Carroll County, Indiana; rare).—THOMPSON, Proc. U. S. Nat. Mus., xiii, 1891, 514 (Winnipeg and Portage la Prairie, Manitoba; claimed to be of recent occurrence and increasing).—GOSS, Hist. Birds Kansas, 1891, 225 (Kansas; common;

habits; descr.).—HATCH, Notes Birds Minnesota, 1892, 167, 463 (Minnesota; hist.; descr.).—NUTTING, Bull. Lab. Nat. Hist. State Univ. Iowa, ii, 1893, 267 (Lower Saskatchewan River).—OGILVIE-GRANT, Cat. Birds Brit. Mus., xxii, 1893, 78, part (Rockford and Richland Counties, Ill.; Iowa; Moody County, S. Dak.).—BREWSTER, Auk, xii, 1895, 99, pl. 2 (descr. and colored pl. of rufescent color variety; 4 spec. of unknown locality); Mem. Nuttall Orn. Club, No. 4, 1906, 171 (Cambridge, Mass.; liberated in 1885).—JONES, Auk, xii, 1895, 236 in table (Ohio; migr.); Birds Ohio, Rev. Cat., 1903, 221 (Ohio, extinct).— ULREY and WALLACE, Proc. Indiana Acad. Sci., 1895, 151 (Wabash, Ind.).— COOKE, Colorado State Agr. Coll. Bull. 44, 1898, 159 (e. Colorado; rare and local summer visitant); Bull. 56, 1900, 202 (Wyoming, resident breeding).— BUTLER, Rep. State Geol. Indiana for 1897 (1898), 755 (Indiana; reported as occurring "within recent years in Newton, Stark, Carroll, Steuben, Boone, Knox, Clinton, Wabash, Lake, Laporte, Benton, Allen, De Kalb, and Noble counties").—LANTZ, Trans. Kansas Acad. Sci., 1896-97 (1899), 254 (Kansas; common; formerly abundant).—NASH, Check List Birds Ontario, 1900, 26 (Ontario; now extinct).—DWIGHT, Auk, xvii, 1900, 163 (molt).—MACOUN, Cat. Can. Birds, 1900, 210 (Ontario and Manitoba).—BAILEY, Handb. Birds Western United States, 1902, 130 (descr.; distr.).—WOODCOCK, Oregon Agr. Exp. Stat. Bull. 68, 1902, 27 (Dayton, Oreg., Oct., 1892).—KUMLIEN and HOLLISTER, Bull. Wisconsin Nat. Hist. Soc., iii, 1903, 57 (Wisconsin; habits).—DAWSON, Birds Ohio, 1903, 435, pl. 52, 652 (Ohio; descr.; extinct).—SNOW, Cat. Birds Kansas, ed. 5, 1903, 15 (Kansas; common; formerly abundant).—[NASH], Check List Vert. Ontario: Birds, 1905, 35 (Ontario; extinct).—JUDD, U. S. Biol. Surv. Bull. 24, 1905, 10-18 (range, food, economic value, etc.).—WILSON, Wils. Bull., xviii, 1906, 3 (Scott County, Iowa, common resident).—FLEMING, Auk, xxiv, 1907, 87 (Toronto; doubtful).—WIDMANN, Birds Missouri, 1907, 81 (once common, now rare).—WOODRUFF, Chicago Acad. Sci. Bull., vi, 1907, 84 (vicinity of Chicago, formerly abundant, now rare).—ROBERTS, in Wilcox, Hist. Becker County, Minn., 1907, 170 (nearly all parts of Minnesota).—ANDERSON, Proc. Davenport Acad. Sci., xi, 1907, 233 (Iowa; habits).—BEYER, ALLISON, and KOPMAN, Auk, xxv, 1908, 439, in text (w. Louisiana).—REAGAN, Auk, xxv, 1908, 464 (Rosebud Reservation, S. Dak.).—MACOUN and MACOUN, Cat. Can. Birds, ed. 2, 1909, 229 (Hamilton Beach, Ontario; Manitoba).—VISHER, Auk, xxvi, 1909, 147 (w. South Dakota; west to Kadoka); xxviii, 1911, 10 (Harding County, S. Dak., fairly abundant).—COOKE, Auk, xxvi, 1909, 411 (e. Colorado; breeds west to Yuma, Wray County; also near Barr).—CORY, Publ. Field Mus. Nat. Hist., i, 131, 1909, 439 (Illinois; Wisconsin).—HESS, Auk, xxvii, 1910, 22 (c. Illinois; eggs).—WOOD and TINKER, Auk, xxvii, 1910, 131 (Michigan; formerly common near Ann Arbor; Fourmile Lake).—FERRY, Auk, xxvii, 1910, 198 (Quill Lake, Saskatchewan; breeds).—HOWELL (A.H.), U. S. Biol. Surv. Bull. 38, 1911, 34 (now mostly extirpated in Arkansas).—LANO, Auk, xxix, 1912, 239, in text (Minnesota; eaten by gyrfalcon); xxxviii, 1921, 112 (8 miles w. of Fayetteville, Ark., 1 spec. Nov. 15, 1919).—SCLATER, Hist. Birds Colorado, 1912, 150 (Colorado; uncommon in ne. part).—ISELY, Auk, xxix, 1912, 28 (Sedgwick County, Kans.; formerly abundant but "not been seen for many years").—ZIMMER, Proc. Nebraska Orn. Union, v, pt. 5, 1913, 70 (Nebraska; Thomas County; nests and young).—JENSEN, Auk, xxxv, 1918, 344 (Wahpeton, N. Dak., breeding).—HORSBAUGH, Ibis, 1918, 483 (Buffalo Lake, Alberta, 1 spec., Dec. 26, 1914).—TAVERNER, Auk, xxxvi, 1919, 13 (near Red Deer, Alberta, Dec. 26, 1914); Ottawa Nat., xxxii, 1919, 161 (Shoal Lake, Manitoba; first nests found in 1899; increasing); Birds W. Canada, 1926, 171, pl. 23A, (descr.; habits; distr.; Canada).—LARSON, Wils. Bull., xl, 1928, 46 (e. McKenzie County, N. Dak.).—HICKS, Wils. Bull. xli, 1929, 43 (Bay Point, Ohio).—CAUM, Occ. Pap. Bishop Mus., x, No. 9, 1933, 16 (Hawaii; introduced unsuccessfully). —GROEBBELS, Der Vögel, ii, 1937, 384 in text (infertile eggs).

[*Tympanuchus*] *americanus* RIDGWAY, Man. North Amer. Birds, 1887, 203, part.— REICHENOW, Die Vögel, i, 1913, 320.

[*Tympanuchus*] *americanus* SHARPE, Hand-list, i, 1899, 20.

Tympanuchus americanus americanus AMERICAN ORNITHOLOGISTS' UNION, Check List, ed. 3, 1910, 143.—BARROWS, Michigan Bird Life, 1912, 229 (s. Michigan).— BUNKER, Univ. Kansas Sci. Bull., vii, 1913, 146 (w. Kansas, mostly).—VISHER, Auk, xxx, 1913, 567 (Sanborn County, S. Dak., resident).—TINKER, Auk, xxxi, 1914, 77 (Clay and Palo Alto Counties, Iowa; nearly exterminated).—HONEY-WILL, Auk, xxxi, 1914, 85 (Minnesota; Cass and Crow Wing Counties).— COOKE, Auk, xxxi, 1914, 478 (Oklahoma; near Caddo; common).—HORSBAUGH, Ibis, 1916, 682 (Alix and Buffalo Lake district, Alberta, fairly numerous).— HARRIS, Trans. Acad. Sci. St. Louis, 1919, 257 (extirpated in Jackson County, Missouri).—SAUNDERS, Pacific Coast Avif. No. 14, 1921, 58 (Montana; Hervey Beach; spec.).—OVER and THOMS, Birds South Dakota, 1921, 76.—WOOD, Misc. Publ. Univ. Michigan Mus. Zool., No. 10, 1923, 35 (Red River Valley, Medora, etc., N. Dak.).—KOELZ, Wils. Bull., xxxv, 1923, 38 (Jackson County, Michigan; common).—MITCHELL, Canad. Field Nat., xxxviii, 1924, 108 (Saskatchewan; resident).—NICE and NICE, Birds Oklahoma, 1924, 36 (Oklahoma).—PINDAR, Wils. Bull., xxxvi, 1924, 204 (e. Arkansas).—GABRIELSON and JEWETT, Auk, xli, 1924, 297 (Fort Clark, N. Dak.).—WHEELER, Birds Arkansas, 1925, 39, xiv, xx (descr.; nest; eggs; Arkansas).—LARSON, Wils. Bull., xxxvii, 1925, 28 (Sioux Falls, S. Dak.).—ROWAN, Auk, xliii, 1926, 333, pl. xvi (hybrid; Alberta). —WILLIAMS, Wils. Bull., xxxviii, 1926, 29 (Red River Valley, N. Dak.).— TAVERNER, Birds Western Canada, 1926, 172, in text.—LINSDALE, Auk, xliv, 1927, 52 (Kansas; between Shields and Gove).—LINSDALE and HALL, Wils. Bull., xxxix, 1927, 96 (s. of Lawrence, Kans.).—CAHN, Wils. Bull., xxxix, 1927, 27 (summer, Vilas County, Wisconsin).—GARDNER, Condor, xxx, 1928, 128 in text (eaten by horned owls).—PIERCE, Wils. Bull., xlii, 1930, 266 (Buchanan County, Iowa, status).

Tympanuchus a[*mericanus*] *americanus* LINCOLN, Proc. Colorado Mus. Nat. Hist., 1915, 6 (Yuma County, Colo., resident).—STODDARD, Wils. Bull., xxxiv, 1922, 72 (Sauk Prairie, s. Wisconsin; habits).

Cupidonia pinnata BREWSTER, Auk, ii, 1885, 82 (Vermillion, South Dakota; coll. William Brewster).—BANGS, Bull. Mus. Comp. Zool., lxx, 1930, 155 (type spec. in Mus. Comp. Zool.).

Tympanuchus pinnatus RIDGWAY, Proc. U. S. Nat. Mus., viii, 1885, 355.

Tympanuchus cupido pinnatus PETERS, Check-list Birds of World, ii, 1934, 41.— VAN TYNE, Occ. Pap. Mus. Zool. Univ. Michigan, No. 379, 1938, 11 (Michigan; resident in Lower Peninsula and west in Upper Peninsula to Sidnaw; breeding records).—HELLMAYR and CONOVER, Cat. Birds Amer., i, No. 1, 1942, 223 (syn.; distr.).

TYMPANUCHUS CUPIDO ATTWATERI Bendire

LOUISIANA PRAIRIE HEN

Adult.—Similar to that of the corresponding sex and wear of *T. c. pinnatus* but smaller, darker in general coloration, tawnier above, usually with more pronounced cinnamon-rufous on the neck; light-colored spots on the upper wing coverts smaller and tawnier; tarsi longer and much more scantily feathered; the feathers much shorter and never extending down to the base of the toes, even in front, the posterior side of the tarsus always (even in winter) with a broad exposed naked strip (much the greater part of the tarsus naked in summer). From the nominate form this race differs in lacking the conspicuous pale terminal spots on the scapulars, in having the pinnae composed of more than 10 feathers which are abruptly truncated and not pointed, and in having the ventral bars somewhat narrower (but nearer to *T. c. cupido* than to *T. c. pinnatus* in this respect) and considerably paler—drab to pale buffy brown, and in having the upper breast washed with cinnamon to cinnamon-rufous.

Juvenal.—None seen.

Downy young.—Not certainly distinguishable from that of *T. c. pinnatus* but apparently very slightly darker in its general tone above.

Adult male.—Wing 202–213 (209); tail 84–90 (87.5); exposed culmen 18–21 (19.5); tarsus 50–52 (51); middle toe without claw 44–46 (44.7); height of bill at base 11–12.5 (12.0 mm.).[20]

Adult female.—Wing 195–206 (202); tail 78–83 (80.8); exposed culmen 17–20 (18.2); tarsus 47–50 (49); middle toe without claw 42–46 (43.4); height of bill at base 11–11.5 (11.2 mm.).[21]

Range.—Resident in the coastal prairies of southwestern Louisiana (a small area in the western parts of Cameron and Calcasieu Parishes; formerly east of Bayou Teche, Opelousas, and Abbeville) and in coastal Texas (north to Austin, where now scarce; Refugio, Aransas, and Jefferson Counties; to within 30 miles of the Rio Grande—Miradores Ranch).

Type locality.—Refugio County, Tex.

Tetrao cupido (not of Linnaeus) WOODHOUSE, Rep. Sitgreaves Expl. Zuñi and Colorado R., 1853, 96, part (e. Texas).

Cupidonia cupido BAIRD, Rep. Pacific R. R. Surv., ix, 1858, 629, part (Calcasieu Pass, La.); Cat. North Amer. Birds, 1859, No. 464, part.—NEHRLING, Bull. Nuttall Orn. Club, vii, 1882, 175 (se. Texas).

Cupidonia cupido, var. *cupido* BAIRD, BREWER, and RIDGWAY, Hist. North Amer. Birds, iii, 1874, 440, part.

Cupidonia cupido, var. *pallidicincta* (not of Ridgway, 1873) MERRILL, Proc. U. S. Nat. Mus., i, 1878, 159 (prairies near coast 30 miles n. of Fort Brown, Tex.).

Tympanuchus attwateri BENDIRE, Forest and Stream, xl, No. 20, 1893, 425 (Refugio County, Tex.; coll. U. S. Nat. Mus.).—ELLIOT, Gallin. Game Birds North Amer., 1897, 122.

[*Tympanuchus*] *attwateri* SHARPE, Hand-list, i, 1899, 20.

Tympanuchus americanus attwateri AMERICAN ORNITHOLOGISTS' UNION, Auk, xi, 1894, 46; Check-list, ed. 2, 1895, No. 305a (ex Bendire, manuscript); ed. 3, 1910, p. 143.—BENDIRE, Auk, xi, 1894, 130–132 (diagnosis, measurements, etc.; Calcasieu, La.; Orange, Refugio, Aransas, and Jefferson Counties, Tex.).—RIDGWAY, Man. North Amer. Birds, ed. 2, 1896, 589.—CARROLL, Auk, xvii, 1900, 341 (Re-

---

[20] Five specimens including the type.

[21] Five specimens.

fugio County, Tex.).—SIMMONS, Auk, xxxii, 1915, 322 (Harris County, Tex.;
Aldine; adults and young seen); Birds Austin Region, 1925, 82 (Austin, Tex.;
habits; descr.).—CAHN, Wils. Bull., xxxiii, 1921, 171 (near Marshall, ne. Texas;
nearly extirpated).—FIGGINS, Auk, xl, 1923, 674 (Black Bayou, La.; rare;
winter and spring).—GRISCOM and CROSBY, Auk, xliii, 1926, 34 (Brownsville,
Tex.).—BAILEY and WRIGHT, Wils. Bull., xliii, 1931, 201 (Cameron Parish,
La.).—ARTHUR, Birds Louisiana, 1931, 214 (descr., status, Louisiana).
T[ympanuchus] americanus attwateri BEYER, ALLISON, and KOPMAN, Auk, xxv, 1908,
439, in text (w. Louisiana).
T[ympanuchus] a[mericanus] attwateri BAILEY, Handb. Birds Western United
States, 1902, 131 (descr.; habits).
[Tympanuchus americanus] attwateri DWIGHT, Auk, xvii, 1900, 163 (molt).
Tympanuchus cupido attwateri AMERICAN ORNITHOLOGISTS' UNION, Check-list North
Amer. Birds, ed. 4, 1931, 86 (distr.).—BENT, U. S. Nat. Mus. Bull. 162, 1932, 263
(life hist.; distr.).—PETERS, Check-list Birds of World, ii, 1934, 41.—OBER-
HOLSER, Bird Life Louisiana, 1938, 190 (Louisiana, common on coastal prairies
formerly; now rare).—HELLMAYR and CONOVER, Cat. Birds Amer., i, No. 1, 1942,
223 (syn.; distr.).—McILHENNY, Auk, lx, 1943, 544 (s. Louisiana).
T[ympanuchus] c[upido] attwateri HAMERSTROM, Wils. Bull., li, 1939, 115, in text
(nesting habits).
Tympanuchus cupido americanus LOWERY, Bull. Louisiana Polytech. Inst., xxix, 1931,
22 (spec.; ne. of Ruston, La.; December 20, 1925).
Tympanuchus americanus (not Cupidonia americana Reichenbach) BEYER, Proc.
Louisiana Soc. Nat. for 1897–99 (1900), 98 (sw. Louisiana).

TYMPANUCHUS PALLIDICINCTUS (Ridgway)

LESSER PRAIRIE HEN

Adult male.—Similar to *Tympanuchus cupido* but differs in having the
darker bars of the back and rump divided, containing a continuous brown
bar enclosed between two narrower blackish ones; the feathers of the
breast with four to six alternate bars of brown and white; the darker bars
of the sides and flanks bicolored—the broader light brown bar being
enclosed between two narrower dusky ones; forehead and anterior part
of crown pale cartridge buff, the feathers mummy brown on their concealed basal portions; rest of crown feathers dark mummy brown broadly
tipped with cartridge buff to light ochraceous-buff and subterminally
banded with light ochraceous-salmon and still more basally spotted with
the same; occiput and nape similar but with the dark mummy brown areas
reduced to narrow bars, the tips more strongly ochraceous; interscapulars,
back, lower back, rump, and upper tail coverts buffy brown to pale olive-
brown narrowly banded with pinkish buff to cinnamon-buff and with
dark clove brown to fuscous-black, the subterminal fuscous-black bars
divided lengthwise to include a continuous pale olive-brown to pale
cinnamon-buffy band bordered by narrower fuscous-black ones; the tips
of these feathers becoming somewhat more grayish on the lower rump
and upper tail coverts; scapulars, lesser upper wing coverts, and secondaries tawny-olive to olive-brown barred with pinkish buff to whitish,

these pale bars edged with fuscous on the scapulars and secondaries and with clove brown on the upper coverts; the scapulars and secondaries broadly tipped with pale pinkish buff; median and greater upper wing coverts and primaries buffy brown, the coverts banded with buffy white, the primaries spotted transversely on their outer webs with pale pinkish buff; rectrices clove brown paling on the lateral feathers to dark olive-brown, and all narrowly tipped with pale pinkish buff; lores, chin, upper throat, and sides of head cartridge buff, tinged especially on the sides of the head with pale chamois; a dark subocular band Saccardo's umber, the feathers tipped with clove brown; the lower cheeks with a mass of closely packed dark clove-brown spots; feathers of the sides of neck and the lower throat ochraceous-tawny (chiefly on the concealed parts of the feathers) broadly tipped with white and edged with fuscous-black, the ochraceous-tawny showing much more on the lower throat than on the sides of the neck; pinnae composed mostly of black, abruptly truncated feathers, a few of the lateral ones with various widths of buffy-white shaft stripes, these pale areas edged with ochraceous-buffy and these feathers with considerable ochraceous-tawny basally, their upper coverts, largely ochraceous-tawny and buffy white; breast, upper abdomen, sides, and flanks, whitish, each feather crossed by several fairly narrow bars of buffy brown to olive-brown, these bars becoming broader and darker on the sides and flanks, where they are bicolored, paler in the middle and darker on the margins; middle and lower abdomen with the dark bars greatly reduced in breadth and darkness or wanting; under tail coverts clove brown very broadly tipped with ochraceous-tawny on their inner webs; under wing coverts whitish, the outer ones terminally spotted with drab to pale buffy brown, bill dark brown; iris brown, gular sacs, yellow in the breeding season; toes yellowish, claws brownish black.[22]

Adult female.—Similar to the adult male, but averaging smaller.

First-winter plumage.—Like the adult but with the outer two primaries more pointed than the others (juvenal feathers that are retained in the postjuvenal molt, all the juvenal primaries being rather pointed).

Juvenal.—Much more rufescent than the adult, more rufescent than the juvenal of *T. cupido;* forehead, crown, and occiput bright ochraceous-tawny, with some of the largely concealed basal blackish showing through as spots, especially on the midcrown; interscapulars and scapulars bright tawny-olive with no white shaft stripes and with less (narrower and rowly edged with blackish, all these feathers with conspicuous white shaft stripes; feathers of back, lower back, rump, and upper tail coverts bright tawny-olive with not white shaft stripes and with less (narrower and

---

[22] As in the other members of its genus, in worn plumage the tips of the dorsal feathers seem to become bleached as well as abraded and are more grayish than in freshly plumaged specimens.

paler) blackish barring and less difference between the paler bars (which
are cinnamon-buff to pale cinnamon-buff) and the interspaces of tawny-
olive, the tips paler and grayer; upper wing coverts dull olive-brown to
clove brown banded with pale pinkish buff; secondaries pale clove brown,
their outer webs olive-brown barred with pale pinkish buff, these pale
bars margined with dark clove brown; primaries pale clove brown, their
outer webs spotted transversely with pale pinkish buff; rectrices bright
tawny-olive with terminal tear-shaped whitish shaft streaks, and barred
with pale cinnamon-buff each buffy bar distally edged narrowly, and
proximally much more broadly, with blackish; lores, chin, and upper
throat whitish; a pale cinnamon-buffy superciliary stripe from the lores
to the posterolateral angle of the occiput; cheeks ochraceous-buffy, the
auriculars tawny-olive; feathers of breast and sides light tawny-olive incompletely barred with clove brown and with white shaft stripes; feathers
of sides and flanks similar but the dark bars complete; abdomen whitish
barred with pale olive-brown to drab; thighs whitish tinged with drab;
under tail coverts white, basally spotted and splotched with olive-brown.

Downy young.—Apparently unknown.

Adult male.—Wing 207–220 (212.0); tail 88–95 (92.4); exposed
culmen 16.5–18 (17.1); tarsus 43–47 (44.4); middle toe without claw
36.5–40 (39.0); height of bill at base 9.5–11 (10.5 mm.).[23]

Adult female.—Wing 195–201 (198); tail 81–87 (84.2); exposed culmen 42–43 (42.3); middle toe without claw 36–40 (38.4); height of bill
at base 9.5–10.5 (10.0 mm.).[24]

Range.—Breeds from southeastern Colorado (Gaumes Ranch, Baca
County, and Holly, Powers County, north to the Arkansas River),
Nebraska (formerly), and southwestern Kansas (Cimarron, Neosho
Falls), south through southwestern Oklahoma (near Arnett, Fort Cobb,
Ivanhoe Lake, Fort Reno) to northern Texas (Mobeetie, Alanreed)
and to east-central New Mexico (Portales and Staked Plains).[25]

Winters chiefly in central Texas, from Colorado City, Monahans, and
Midland, north to Bandera, Fort Clark, Concho and Tom Green Counties,
and the Davis Mountains.

Casual in southern and southwestern Missouri (Pierce County and
Lawrence County), central Kansas (Oakley and Garnett).

Recorded in fossil state from Oregon (Pleistocene).

Type locality.—Prairies of Texas (near lat. 32° N.).

---

[23] Five specimens from New Mexico, Texas, and Oklahoma.
[24] Four specimens from Nebraska and Oklahoma.
[25] Bent, U. S. Nat. Mus. Bull. 162, 1932, 285, writes that while this species has been
reported from Nebraska there are no specimens to substantiate this claim. In the
U. S. National Museum are three birds obtained in the Fulton Market, New York,
said to have been killed in Nebraska.

Tetrao cupido (not of Linnaeus) McCall, Proc. Acad. Nat. Sci. Philadelphia, 1851, 222 (between Lavaca, Victoria, and Goliad, Tex.).

(?) *Cupidonia cupido* Baird, Rep. Pacific R. R. Surv., ix, 1858, 628, part (Texas); Cat. North Amer. Birds, 1859, No. 464, part.

Cupidonia cupido, var. *pallidicincta* Ridgway, Bull. Essex Inst., v, 1873, 199 ("Southwestern prairies—Staked plains?" Coll., U. S. Nat. Mus.).

Cupidonia cupido . . , var. *pallidicincta* Coues, Check List North Amer. Birds, 1874, 133, No. 384a.

C[upidonia] c[upido] pallidicincta Coues, Check List North Amer. Birds, ed. 2, 1882, 584.

Cupidonia cupido, var. *pallidicinctus* Baird, Brewer, and Ridgway, Hist. North Amer. Birds, iii, 1874, 446.—Lawrence, Bull. Nuttall Orn. Club, ii, 1877, 52 (Pierce City, sw. Missouri; weight).

[*Cupidonia cupido*] b? *pallidicinctus* Coues, Birds Northwest, 1874, 420.

Cupidonia cupido pallidicincta Ridgway, Proc. U. S. Nat. Mus., iii, 1880, 196; Nom. North Amer. Birds, 1881, No. 477a.—Coues, Check List North Amer. Birds, ed. 2, 1882, No. 564.

Cupidonia cupido pallidicinctus Goode, U. S. Nat. Mus. Bull. 20, 1883, 316.

[*Cupidonia cupido*] *pallidicinctus* Wheaton, Rep. Birds Ohio, 1882, 446 (distr.).

Tympanuchus pallidicinctus Ridgway, Proc. U. S. Nat. Mus., viii, 1885, 355.— American Ornithologists' Union, Check-list, 1886, No. 307; ed. 2, 1895, No. 307; ed. 3, 1910, p. 144; ed. 4, 1931, 86 (distr.).—Lloyd, Auk, iv, 1887, 187 (Concho County, Middle Concho in Tom Green County, and Colorado City, Mitchell County, w. Tex.).—Cooke, Bird Migr. Mississippi Valley, 1888, 106 (geogr. range).—Goss, Hist. Birds Kansas, 1891, 227 (Kansas; rare; descr.).—Shufeldt, Auk, viii, 1891, 367, in text (fossil bones).—Bendire, Life Hist. North Amer. Birds, i, 1892, 96.—Allen, Auk, x, 1893, 344, in text (fossil, Oregon).— Ogilvie-Grant, Cat. Birds Brit. Mus., xxii, 1893, 80 (Kansas).—Lantz, Trans. Kansas Acad. Sci. for 1896–97 (1899), 254 (Neosho Falls, Kans.).—Bailey, Handb. Birds Western United States, 1902, 131 (descr.; distr.).—Snow, Cat. Birds Kansas, ed. 5, 1903, 15 (sw. Kansas; rare).—Judd, U. S. Biol. Surv. Bull. 24, 1905, 19, 20 (range, food, etc.).—Widmann, Birds Missouri, 1907, 82 (s. and sw. Missouri; no recent records).—Cooke, Auk, xxvi, 1909, 411 (sw. Baca County, Colorado).—Lacey, Auk, xxviii, 1911, 206 (Kerrville, Tex.; none seen since 1886).—Bunker, Kansas Univ. Sci. Bull. vii, 1913, 146 (sw. Kansas, rare resident).—Lincoln, Auk, xxxv, 1918, 236 (Baca County, Colo., May, Sept. near Holly, Prowers County, Colo.; Arkansas River is northern boundary of the range of the species).—Nice and Nice, Birds Oklahoma, 1924, 36 (Oklahoma).— Rothschild, Bull. Brit. Orn. Club, xlvii, 1927, 141 (spec.; melanistic mutant).— Bailey, Birds New Mexico, 1928, 207 (New Mexico).—Nice, Birds Oklahoma, rev. ed., 1931, 80 (Oklahoma).—Bent, U. S. Nat. Mus. Bull 162, 1932, 280 (life hist.; distr.).—Wetmore, Condor, xxxiv, 1932, 142 (remains; cave deposits n. of Carlsbad, New Mexico).—Bennitt, Univ. Missouri Studies, vii, No. 3, 1932, 25 (southwestern Missouri; formerly uncommon; now probably extinct).— Howard and Miller, Condor, xxxv, 1933, 16 (bones; New Mexico cave deposits).—Sutton, Ann. Carnegie Mus., xxiv, 1934, 11 (w. Panhandle of Oklahoma; near Arnett; molt).—Peters, Check-list Birds of World, ii, 1934, 41.— Long, Bull. Univ. Kans. Sci., xxxvi, 1935, 232 (w. Kansas; November).—Long, Trans. Kansas Acad. Sci., xliii, 1940, 440 (Kansas; formerly common resident in south and west; now rare).—Imler, Trans. Kansas Acad. Sci., xxxix, 1936, 301 (Rooks County, Kansas; occasional).—Tiemeier, Auk, lviii, 1941, 359 in text (healing of bone injuries).—Hellmayr and Conover, Cat. Birds Amer., i, No. 1, 1942, 224 (syn.; distr.).

T[*ympanuchus*] *pallidicinctus* RIDGWAY, Man. North Amer. Birds, 1887, 203.—
   PETRIDES, Trans. 7th North Amer. Wildlife Conf., 1942, 318 in text (age indicators in plumage).
[*Tympanuchus*] *pallidicinctus* SHARPE, Handlist, i, 1899, 20.—DWIGHT, Auk, xvii,
   1900, 163 (molt).
(?) *Tympanuchus americanus* LACEY, Auk, xxviii, 1911, 206 (Kerrville, Tex., 1885,
   1886).

Genus CENTROCERCUS Swainson

Centrocercus SWAINSON, *in* Swainson and Richardson, Fauna Bor.-Amer., ii, 1831
   (1832), 358, 496. (Type, by monotypy, *Tetrao urophasianus* Bonaparte.)
Centrocircus (emendation) SWAINSON, Classif. Birds, i, 1836, 110.

Large terrestrial Tetraonidae (wing about 266–331 mm.) with tarsus
longer than middle toe with claw; internasal portion of culmen longer
than apical portion, and tail about as long as wing, strongly graduated,
consisting of 18 narrow, attenuated, rigid rectrices; adult males with
an inflatable air sac on sides of neck and with feathers of lower neck,

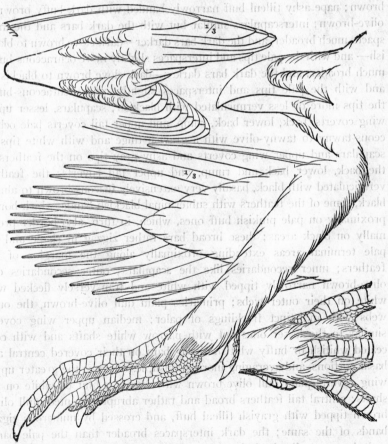

FIGURE 13.—*Centrocercus urophasianus.*

laterally and in front, short, very rigid, and with spinous tips, as if much abraded, some of the feathers with filamentous tips; stomach membranous.

Coloration.—Upperparts irregularly variegated with grayish brown, buffy, and black; the tertials with whitish terminal margins and wing coverts with white medial streaks; under parts mostly whitish, broken by a large black abdominal area.

Range.—Sagebrush plains of western North America, from northwestern North Dakota and Nebraska to middle eastern California, and from northwestern New Mexico to southern Saskatchewan and southern British Columbia. (Monotypic.)

CENTROCERCUS UROPHASIANUS (Bonaparte)

SAGE GROUSE

Adult male.—Narial tufts pale raw umber; feathers of the forehead, crown, and occiput light drab to light wood brown, the feathers crossed by narrow bars of dark clove brown to black, and basally dark olive-brown; nape ashy tilleul buff narrowly banded with dark buffy brown to olive-brown; interscapulars similar but with the dark bars and the interspaces much broader, and the dark bars darker—dark clove brown to blackish— and with the pale tips and interspaces slightly more ochraceous-buffy, much broader, and the dark bars darker—dark clove brown to blackish— and with the pale tips and interspaces slightly more ochraceous-buffy, the tips more or less vermiculated with blackish; scapulars, lesser upper wing coverts, back, lower back, rump, and upper tail coverts pale ochraceous-tawny to tawny-olive with a grayish tinge and with white tips on scapulars and upper wing coverts and ashy gray tips on the feathers of the back, lower back and rump, and upper tail coverts; the feathers vermiculated with black, basally very extensively fuscous-brown to almost black, some of the feathers with subterminal blackish bands, which border proximally on pale pinkish buff ones, which, in turn, also border proximally on black areas; these broad bars rather zigzag in shape and the pale terminal areas extending proximally along the margins of the feathers; inner secondaries like the scapulars; outer secondaries dull olive-brown narrowly tipped with white and transversely flecked with white on their outer webs; primaries plain dull olive-brown, the outer webs with indistinct frecklings of paler; median upper wing coverts similar to the lesser ones but with narrow white shafts and with concealed whitish or buffy whitish zigzag bars on their covered central and basal portions, and averaging more grayish, less tawny; the greater upper wing coverts plain dull olive-brown with merely a hint of white on the shafts; central tail feathers broad and rather abruptly pointed, dull olive-brown tipped with grayish tilleul buff, and crossed by numerous zigzag bands of the same; the dark interspaces broader than the pale bands and the more distal of these interspaces darkening to fuscous and to fuscous-black; other tail feathers with long attenuated narrowly pointed tips extending far beyond (75 mm. or more) the central rectrices, dark dull olive-brown in color, with lengthwise irregular and incomplete wavy markings of tilleul buff on the outer webs and close to the shafts on the inner webs, these pale markings reduced or almost absent on the protruding narrow terminal portions of the feathers; lores, circumocular area, and auriculars mummy brown; a discontinuous white line from the gape to the front and below the eye; lower eyelid largely whitish; cheeks whitish splotched and speckled with mummy brown; chin and upper throat white thickly speckled with dark buffy brown, the more lateral of these markings darker—approaching mummy brown; following this a white V-shaped band across the throat to the auriculars; lower throat forming a broad band of pinkish buff, the feathers crossed by narrow bars of fuscous; immediately posterior to this band the feathers are white tipped with dark buffy brown to dark olive-brown; two large bare gular sacs on lower throat completely surrounded with white feathers with narrow mummy brown tips; posterior to these feathers on each side, but not on the midventral area, are patches of very stiff, short, white feathers with strong yellowish-white shafts and reduced white vanes; on each side of neck is a patch of fluffy, soft, long, white feathers, and at the anterior end of this are a number of long black hairlike feathers, the shortest about 75 mm. and the longest twice that length (by July these are worn down to mere stubs, but in fresh nuptial plumage they are very striking); breast feathers long, white, tipped with fuscous-black and with narrow blackish shafts, some of which protrude beyond the vanes giving a hair-like appearance, the more anterior of these feathers with the blackish "tips" actually terminally edged with white and very small in size, the more posterior ones with no such white edges and with the dark spots large; sides with the upper (dorsal) vane of the feathers similar to those of the back but with a coarser pattern, the lower (more ventral) vane solid fuscous-black broadly tipped with white; flanks like the lower back; abdomen solid fuscous to fuscous-black; under tail coverts similar but broadly tipped with white; thighs drab obscurely barred and speckled with dusky buffy brown; under wing coverts white; iris light brown, the pupils bluish black; bill black; gular sacs olive-green; toes and claws black.

Adult female.—Similar to the adult male but smaller and without the four long stiff black feathers on each side of the neck, without gular sacs and the patches of short stiff white feathers on each side; the chin and upper throat without dusky brown specklings, the lower throat and breast light pinkish buff crossed with narrow bars of blackish, the posterior pectoral and anterior abdominal feathers white tipped with black but with white shafts (black in male), and lower abdomen and vent drab barred with dark buffy brown to olive-brown like the thighs; lores, suboculars, and auriculars paler than in male—pale pinkish buff barred narrowly with buffy brown.

Immature (sexes alike).—Similar to the adult female but paler, the blackish marks on the upper parts smaller, the browns less ochraceous, ashier, very pale buffy brown, the scapulars and the inner lesser and median upper wing coverts with conspicuous white shaft stripes; rectrices pale buffy brown crossed by eight or more wavy white bars each of which is margined narrowly by fuscous, the broad brown interspaces sparsely freckled and vermiculated with fuscous, the shafts dusky; breast as in adult female but the dark tips of the feathers paler, buffy brown; abdomen paler—dark hair brown to chaetura drab and fuscous; under tail coverts drab to dusky hair brown broadly tipped with whitish buffy, the whitish areas banded sparingly with hair brown.

Juvenal.—Similar to the immature but with the ground color of the breast less buffy, more whitish; the abdominal feathers tipped with white, basally broadly dusky hair brown; the white shaft stripes of the feathers of the upperparts more pronounced; the forehead, sides of head, and superciliary area much paler—tilleul buff; the tail very different—the shafts white terminally, bordered on each side with blackish, the edges of the feathers broadly pale tawny olive freckled with blackish; the white shaft stripes spreading out into narrow terminal white fringes.

Natal down.—"Crown, back, and rump are mottled and marbled with black, dull browns, pale buff, and dull white; the sides of the head and neck are boldly spotted and striped with black; there are two large spots of sayal brown bordered with black on the foreneck or chest; underparts grayish white, suffused with buff on the chest."[26]

Adult male.—Wing 286–323 (303.9); tail 297–332 (315.3); culmen from base 38.3–41.6 (40.1); tarsus 53.1–59.0 (56.3); middle toe without claw 45.5–51.4 (48.0 mm.).[27]

Adult female.—Wing 251–273 (260.6); tail 188–213 (198.9); culmen from base 33.0–37.5 (35.0); tarsus 44.0–49.6 (47.2); middle toe without claw 36.6–41.9 (40.3 mm.).[28]

Range.—Originally resident in the prairie areas where the sagebrush (*Artemisia tridentata*) grows; now extirpated or greatly reduced in parts of its range: Extreme western Kansas (formerly), extreme northwestern Nebraska (formerly), Colorado (formerly nearly everywhere except high in the mountains, now found chiefly in Rio Blanco, Moffat, Routt, and Jackson Counties), South Dakota (in western part), North Dakota (still found in Billings County, south of Sentinel Butte); Wyo-

---

[26] Ex Bent, U. S. Nat. Mus. Bull. 162, 1932, 304.

[27] Seventeen specimens from Nebraska, Montana, Wyoming, Nevada, Oregon, and Idaho.

[28] Ten specimens from Montana, Oregon, Nevada, and Wyoming.

ming (all except eastern part, where rare); Utah (whole northwestern half of State); New Mexico (Tierra Amarillas; Tres Piedras; no recent records); Nevada (the northern two-thirds of the State); California (extreme eastern and northeastern parts only); Oregon (formerly over all of eastern part with the possible exception of Wallowa County, now restricted to the southeastern part of the State); Washington (a narrow belt east of the Cascades in central part north to the Canadian border); Idaho (southern half only, to 20 miles north of Boise) and Montana (east of Rocky Mountains), north to British Columbia (known only from 2 records at Osoyoos Lake), and Saskatchewan (from Rocky Creek west to Farewell Creek in the Cypress Hills).

Type locality.—Northwestern countries beyond the Mississippi, especially on the Missouri=North Dakota.

Tetrao urophasianus BONAPARTE, Zool. Journ., iii, 1828, 214 ("Northwestern countries beyond the Mississippi, especially on the Missouri"); Ann. Lyc. Nat. Hist. New York, ii, 1828, 442 (extensive plains near the source of the Missouri); Amer. Orn., iii, 1830, 212, pl. 21; Geogr. and Comp. List, 1838, 44.—WILSON, Illustr. Zool., 1831, pls. 26, 27.—NUTTALL, Man. Orn. United States and Canada, Land Birds, 1832, 666; ed. 2, 1840, 803.—AUDUBON, Orn. Biogr., iv, 1838, 503, pl. 371; Synopsis, 1839, 205; Birds Amer., 8vo ed., v, 1842, 106, pl. 297.—BAIRD, Rep. Stansbury's Expl. Great Salt Lake, 1852, 310 (Salt Lake Valley, Utah; Columbia River).—NEWBERRY, Rep. Pacific R. R. Surv., vi, pt. 4, 1857, 95 (Pitt River, se. Oregon, etc.; habits).—HALL, Murrelet, xv, 1934, 7 in text (Washington; Columbia River; history).

Γ[etrao] urophasianus DOUGLAS, Trans. Linn. Soc. London, xvi, 1829, 133 (arid plains of Columbia River; interior n. California; crit.).—MAXIMILIAN, Journ. für Orn., 1858, 439 (upper Missouri River).

[Tetrao] urophasianus REICHENBACH, Synop. Av., iii, 1848, pl. 216, figs. 1890–1892.—GRAY, Hand-list, ii, 1870, 276, No. 9828.

Tetrao (Centrocercus) urophasianus SWAINSON, in Swainson and Richardson, Fauna Bor.-Amer., ii, 1831 (1832), 358.—NUTTALL, Man. Orn. United States and Canada, Water Birds, 1832, 613.

Centrocercus urophasianus SWAINSON, in Swainson and Richardson, Fauna Bor.-Amer., ii, 1831 (1832), 342, footnote (crit.), pl. 58.—JARDINE, Nat. Libr., Orn. iv, 1834, 140, pl. 17.—BAIRD, Rep. Pacific R. R. Surv., ix, 1858, 624; x, pt. 2, 1859, 14 (Cochetops Pass); Cat. North Amer. Birds, 1859, No. 462; in Cooper, Orn. Calif., Land Birds, 1870, 536.—COOPER and SUCKLEY, Rep. Pacific R. R. Surv., xii, book 2, pt. 3, 1860, 222 (Washington and Oregon, e. of Cascade Mountain; habits).—ELLIOT, Monogr. Tetraonidae, 1865, pl. 13 and text.—COUES, Proc. Acad. Nat. Sci. Philadelphia, 1866, 94 (Mojave River, se. Calif.); Ibis, 1866, 265 (Soda Lake, se. Calif.); Proc. Essex Inst., v, 1868, 40 (Colorado Mountains, w. of Denver; spec.); Check List North Amer. Birds, 1874, No. 382; ed. 2, 1882, No. 560; Birds Northwest, 1874, 400.—HOLDEN and AIKEN, Proc. Boston Soc. Nat. Hist., xv, 1872, 209 (Wyoming; Colorado).—SNOW, Cat. Birds Kansas, ed. 2, 1872, No. 164 (w. Kansas).—RIDGWAY, Bull. Essex Inst., v, 1873, 186 (Colorado; on the Artemisia plains); vii, 1875, 11 (Carson Valley, Nev.), 16 (West Humboldt Mountains; common), 21 (e. slope Ruby Mountains; summer), 24 (City of Rocks; s. Idaho), 31 (Salt Lake Valley), 34 (Parleys Peak, Wahsatch Mountains), 39 (Nevada); Amer. Nat., viii, 1874, 240 (peculiar structure of stomach) ; Orn. 40th Parallel, 1877, 600 (locality in Nevada and Utah; habits, measurements, etc.) ; Proc. U. S. Nat. Mus., iii, 1880, 196; Nom. North Amer. Birds, 1881, No. 479.—ALLEN, Proc. Boston Soc. Nat. Hist., xvii, 1874, 35 (Montana and Dakota; fairly common on Yellowstone and Musselshell Rivers; none seen east of the Little Missouri).—HENSHAW, Ann. Lyc. Nat. Hist. New York, xi, 1874, 10 (Utah, up to 7,000 feet).—BAIRD, BREWER, and RIDGWAY, Hist. North Amer. Birds, iii, 1874, 429, pl. 59, figs. 2, 4; pl. 61, fig. 6.—BENDIRE, Proc. Boston Soc. Nat. Hist., xviii, 1875, 164 (Camp Harney, Oreg.; numerous) ; xix, 1877, 139 (e. Oregon; habits, etc.; descr. nest and eggs) ; Auk, v, 1888, 367 in text (Camp Harney, Oreg.) ; vi, 1889, 33 in text; Life Hist. North Amer. Birds, i, 1892, 106, pl. 3, figs, 11–13.—HOFFMAN, Proc. Boston Soc. Nat. Hist., xviii, 1875, 174, (Grand River Agency, Dakota Territory; not frequent).— NELSON, Proc. Boston Soc. Nat. Hist., xvii, 1875, 342 (Fort Bridger, Utah; abundant), 347 (Salt Lake City), 351 (Elko, Mont.), 355 (25 miles north of Elko, Nev.).—BREWER, Bull. Nuttall Orn. Club, iv, 1879, 96 (Twin Lakes, Colo.). —MEARNS, Bull. Nuttall Orn. Club, iv, 1879, 197 (Fort Klamath, Oreg.; near Linterville).—DREW, Auk, ii, 1885 (Colorado; vertical distr.).—AMERICAN OR- NITHOLOGISTS' UNION, Check-list, 1886, No. 309; ed. 2, 1895, No. 309; ed. 3, 1910, p. 145; ed. 4, 1931, 87.—COOKE, Bird Migr. Mississippi Valley, 1888, 107 (w. Mississippi Valley records) ; Colorado State Agr. Coll. Bull. 37, 1897, 71 (Colo- rado; common; distr.) ; 56, 1900, 203 (breeding up to 9,000 feet, migrating up to 14,000 feet, Colorado).—MERRIAM, North Amer. Fauna, No. 5, 1891, 93 (sage- brush plains and valley of Idaho).—FISHER, North Amer. Fauna, No. 7, 1893, 31 (Mt. Magruder, head of Owens River, White Mountains, etc., sw. Nevada).— OGILVIE-GRANT, Cat. Birds Brit. Mus., xxii, 1893, 81 (Fort Dufferin; Middle Fort Snake River, Idaho; Laramie River, Wyoming; Clear Fork, Nebr.).— RICHMOND and KNOWLTON, Auk, xi, 1894, 302 (Montana; abundant).—THORNE, Auk, xii, 1895, 214 (Fort Keogh, Mont.).—DAWSON, Auk, xiv, 1897, 181 (Oka- nogan County, Wash.; formerly) ; Birds California (stud. ed.), iii, 1923, 1602 (California; habits).—DWIGHT, Auk, xvii, 1900, 165 (molt; Wyoming).—BOND, Auk, xvii, 1900, 325 in text, pl. 12 (nuptial display); Condor, xlii, 1940, 220 (Lincoln County, Nev.; Table Mountain, 8,500 feet).—MACOUN, Cat. Can. Birds, 1900, 213 (Saskatchewan).—BAILEY, Handb. Birds Western United States, 1902, 133 (descr.; distr.).—GRINNELL, Pacific Coast Avif., No. 3, 1902, 30 (Cali- fornia; arid Great Basin region east of Sierras; common); No. 8, 1912, 10 California; No. 11, 1915, 61 (arid parts of California from Modoc County w. to Rhett Lake, s. along e. base of Sierra Nevada, through Lassen, Sierra, and Alpine Counties to head of Owens River and White Mountains, Mono County; Fort Mojave?).—WOODCOCK, Oreg. Agr. Exp. Stat. Bull. 68, 1902, 28 (Oregon range).—SNODGRASS, Auk, xx, 1903, 204 (Grand Coulee, etc., c. Washington) ; xxi, 1904, 227 (Douglas County, Wash.).—JUDD, U. S. Biol. Surv. Bull. 24, 1905, 23–25, pl. 2 (range, food, etc.).—CAMERON, Auk, xxiv, 1907, 258 (Custer and Davenport Counties, Mont.; habits; breeds).—BENT, Auk, xxiv, 1907, 428 (sw. Saskatchewan; Skull Creek; White Mud River) ; U. S. Nat. Mus. Bull. 162, 1932, 300 (habits; plum.; distr.).—DAWSON and BOWLES, Birds Washington, ii, 1909, 599 (Washington; habits; distr.).—MACOUN and MACOUN, Cat. Can. Birds, ed. 2, 1909, 233 (Saskatchewan; Frenchman River Valley; south of Wood Moun- tain; Oroyoos Lake; Skull Creek).—VISHER, Auk, xxvi, 1909, 147 (w. South Dakota) ; xxviii, 1911, 10 (Harding County, S. Dak.) ; Wils. Bull., 1913, 90, 91 (habits, etc.).—KERMODE, (Visitors' Guide) Publ. Provinc. Mus., 1909, 42 (Osoyoos Lake, British Columbia).—SAUNDERS, Auk, xxviii, 1911, 35 (Gallatin County, Mont.) ; Pacific Coast Avif., No. 14, 1921, 59 (Montana; distr.; nests and eggs).—TAYLOR, Univ. Calif. Publ. Zool., vii, 1912, 362 (Humboldt County, Nev.; habits; etc.).—SCLATER, Hist. Birds Colorado, 1912, 153 (Colorado; distr.).— WARREN, Auk, xxxiii, 1916, 300 (Elk Mountain; Colorado).—HOWELL, Condor, xix, 1917, 187 (Big Pine, Mono County, Calif.).—GRINNELL, BRYANT, and STORER, Game Birds California; 1918, 564 (descr.; distr.; habits; California).— DICE, Auk, xxxv, 1918, 44 (se. Washington).—WILLETT, Condor, xxi, 1919, 202 (Clear Lake, Malheur Lake, etc., se. Oregon and ne. California).—OVER and THOMS, Birds South Dakota, 1921, 77 (formerly w. half of state, now limited to Fall River, Butte, and Harding Counties).—WOOD, Misc. Publ. Mus. Zool. Univ. Michigan, No. 10, 1923, 36 (30 miles s. of Medora; near Marmarth, Slope County, and 30 mi. s. of Sentinel Butte, Butte County, N. Dak.).— POTTER, Condor, xxv, 1923, 103 in text (sw. Saskatchewan; increasing.— MITCHELL, Can. Field Nat., xxxviii, 1924, 108 (Saskatchewan; resident).— GABRIELSON and JEWETT, Auk, xli, 1924, 298 (North Dakota; Sentinel Butte); Birds Oregon, 1940, 217 (Oregon; distr.; descr.; habits).—GRINNELL and STORER, Animal Life in Yosemite, 1924, 275 (descr.; distr.; habits; Yosemite).— NICE and NICE, Birds Oklahoma, 1924, 37 (Oklahoma).—JEWETT, Condor, xxvii, 1925, 115 (nesting; Siskiyou County, Calif.) ; Murrelet, xvii, 1936, 43 (Oregon; Harney County).—BAILEY, Condor, xxvii, 1925, 172 in text (segregation of sexes).—TAVERNER, Birds Western Canada, 1926, 173 (fig.; descr.; distr.; w. Canada) ; Birds Canada, 1934, 162 in text (descr.; distr.; habits) ; Can. Water Birds, 1939, 174 (Canada; field marks).—TANNER, Condor, xxix, 1927, 198 (Pine Valley Mountains; Utah).—MAILLAIRD, Proc. California Acad. Sci., ser. 4, xvi, 1927, 296 (Modoc County, Calif.; numbers).—BAILEY, Birds New Mexico, 1928, 211 (New Mexico).—HENDEE, Condor, xxvi, 1929, 25 (Moffat County, Colo.).— PHILLIPS, Verh. 6th Internat. Orn. Kongr., 1929, 508 (range in detail).—BROOKS, Condor, xxxii, 1930, 205 (specialized feathers).—GRINNELL, DIXON, and LINS- DALE, Univ. Calif. Publ. Zool., xxxv, 1930, 201 (Lassen Peak Region, n. Califor- nia).—KEMSIES, Wils. Bull., xlii, 1930, 204 (Yellowstone Park, Wyoming).—FUL- LER and BOLE, Sci. Publ. Cleveland Mus. Nat. Hist., i, 1930, 49 (Wyoming).— NICE, Birds Oklahoma, rev. ed., 1931, 81 (Oklahoma).—HOWARD and MILLER, Condor, xxxv, 1933, 16 (bones ex New Mexican cave deposits).—HALL, Murrelet, xiv, 1933, 57 footnote, 70 (Washington; Columbia River) ; xv, 1934, 12, 14 (Wash- ington; Columbia River).—MILLER, Wils. Bull., xlvi, 1934, 160 (s. Utah; Fish Lake).—DAVIS, Murrelet, xv, 1934, 71 (Idaho; Owyhee County; young).— McCREARY and MICKEY, Wils. Bull., xlvii, 1935, 129 in text (se. Wyoming; resident).—LINSDALE, Pacific Coast Avif., No. 23, 1936, 23, 48 (Nevada; resident in northern part; formerly commoner than now) ; Amer. Midl. Nat., xix, 1938, 53 (Joyabe Mountains, Nev.; nesting; many records).—HANNA, Condor, xxxviii, 1936, 38 (breeding at Fort Bidwell, Modoc County, Calif.).—WEYDEMEYER and MARSH, Condor, xxxviii, 1936, 194 (Lake Bowdoin, Montana).—GIRARD, Univ. Wyoming Publ., iii, 2, 1937 1–56 (life hist.; food, etc.).—GROEBBELS, Der Vögel, ii, 1937, 106 in text (polygyny), 113 in text (dancing grounds), 137 in text (dancing of male), 139 in text (courtship), 167 data on breeding).—HUEY, Auk, lvi, 1939, 321 (Arizona, near Nixon Spring, Mount Trumbull region, July 29). —BORELL, Condor, xli, 1939, 85 in text (Utah; killed by flying against telephone covers).—ROWLEY, Condor, xli, 1939, 248 (Mono County, Calif.; near Virginia Lakes; pair with young).—LACK, Condor, xlii, 1940, 269 in text (pairing habits). —SIMON, Auk, lvii, 1940, 467 in text (mating performance; Kemmerer, Wyo- ming; photos).—MOOS, Auk, lvii, 1941, 255 (Montana; Winnett; food).—SCOTT, Auk, lix, 1942, 477, in text (mating behavior).—PETRIDES, Trans. 7th North Amer. Wildlife Conf., 1942, 318, in text (age indicators in plumage).—BEHLE,

Bull. Univ. Utah, xxxiv, 1943, 24, 37 (Pine Valley Mountain Region, Utah);
Condor, xlvi, 1944, 72 (Utah).

[*Centrocercus*] *urophasianus* COUES, Key North Amer. Birds, 1872, 233.—SHARP,
Hand-list, i, 1899, 20.

C[*entrocercus*] *urophasianus* COUES, Key North Amer. Birds, ed. 2, 1884, 580.—
RIDGWAY, Man. North Amer. Birds, 1887, 205.—REICHENOW, Die Vögel, i, 1913,
322.

Centrocercus phasianus KNOWLTON and HARMSTON, Auk, lx, 1943, 589 (Utah; food).

Family PHASIANIDAE: American Quails, Partridges, and Pheasants

><Phasianidae BAIRD, Rep. Pacific R. R. Surv., ix, 1858, 609, 613 (includes Mele-
agrididae, and Numididae).—CARUS, Handb. Zool., i, 1868–75, 323 (includes
Numididae).

<Phasianidae WETMORE, Proc. U. S. Nat. Mus., lxxvi, art. 24, 1930, 3 (excludes
Odontophorinae).

<Phasianidæ SHARPE, Rev. Recent. Att. Classif. Birds, 1891, 68; Hand-list, i, 1899,
x, 21 (Phasianinae only).—BEDDARD, Struct. and Classif. Birds, 1898, 303, in
text (= Phasianinae).

=Phasianidae WETMORE, Smiths. Misc. Coll., lxxxvix, No. 13, 1934, 6; xcix, No.
7, 1940, 6.—PETERS, Check-list Birds of World, ii, 1934, 42.

><Phasianidae NITZSCH, Syst. Pterylog., 1840 (includes *Meleagris* and *Numida*).—
AMERICAN ORNITHOLOGISTS' UNION, Check-list, 1886, 177 (includes Meleagrididae).

=Phasianidæ SALVIN and GODMAN, Biol. Centr.-Amer., Aves, iii, 1902, 286.

<Phasianinæ ELLIOT, Stand. Nat. Hist., iv, 1885, 216, in text (genera *Ithaginis*,
Euplocomus, *Lobiophasis*, *Thaumalea*, and *Phasianus*).—GADOW, in Bronn,
Thier-Reich, Vög., ii, 1891, 172.—KNOWLTON, Birds of the World, 1909, 304
(excludes Old World partridges and quails).

<Phasianinae CARUS, Handb. Zool., i, 1868–75, 323 (genera *Lophophorus*, *Phasi-
anus*, *Gallophasis*, and *Gallus*).

<Perdicinae CARUS, Handb. Zool., i, 1868–75, 322 (genera *Caccabis*, *Tetraogallus*,
Cryptonyx, *Francolinus*, *Perdix*, and *Coturnix*).

<Perdicinæ, BONAPARTE, Geogr. and Comp. List, 1838, 42 (genera *Lophortyx*,
Ortyx, *Francolinus*, *Perdix*, *Starna*, *Bonasia*, *Tetrao*, and *Lagopus*).—COUES,
Key North Amer. Birds, ed. 2, 1884, 594 (genera *Perdix*, *Coturnix*, etc.).—
ELLIOT, Stand, Nat. Hist., iv, 1885, 198, in text (genera *Coturnix*, *Synoicus*,
Perdicula, *Ophrysia*, *Microperdix*, *Excalfactoria*, *Rollulus*, *Hæmatortyx*, *Per-
dix*, *Ammoperdix*, *Oreoperdix*, *Caccabis*, *Tetraogallus*, *Lerwa*, *Bambusicola*,
Caloperdix, *Francolinus*, *Pternistes*, *Ortygornis*, *Rhizothera*, and *Galloperdix*).
—OGILVIE-GRANT, Cat. Birds Brit. Mus., xxii, 1893, 94, in text (genera *Lerwa*,
Tetraogallus, *Tetraophasis*, *Perdix*, *Caccabis*, *Francolinus*, *Pternistes*, *Arbo-
ricola*, *Caloperdix*, *Rollulus*, *Melanoperdix*, *Hæmatortyx*, *Rhizothera*, *Micro-
perdix*, *Perdicula*, *Ammoperdix*, *Margaroperdix*, *Coturnix*, *Synoicus*, and *Ex-
calfactoria*).—KNOWLTON, Birds of the World, 1909, 299 (genera *Bambusicola*,
Galloperdix, *Ptilopachys*, *Perdix*, *Lerwa*, *Tetraophasis*, *Tetraogallus*, *Caccabis*,
Francolinus, *Perdicula*, *Arboricola*, and *Coturnix*).

><Perdicidae BAIRD, Rep. Pacific R. R. Surv., ix, 1858, 638 (includes Odonto-
phorinae and Turnicidae).

>Perdicidæ, BAIRD, BREWER, and RIDGWAY, Hist. North Amer. Birds, iii, 1874,
466 (includes Odontophorinae).

>Perdicidae WETMORE, Proc. U. S. Nat. Mus., lxxvi, art. 24, 1930, 3.

<Lophophorinæ, Elliot, Stand. Nat. Hist., iv, 1885, 223, in text (genera *Lophophorus, Ceriornis,* and *Pucrasia*).

<Pavoninae Carus, Handb. Zool., i, 1868–75, 324 (genera *Pavo, Polyplectron, Argusianus*).

<Pavoninae Gray, List Gen. Birds, 1840, 59 (genera *Polyplectron, Crossoptilon,* and *Pavo*).

<Gallinæ Elliot, Stand. Nat. Hist., iv, 1885, 215 in text (*Gallus* only).—Gadow, *in* Bronn, Thier-Reich, Vög., ii, 1891, 172 (=Phasianinae).

<Caccabininæ, Gray, Cat. Gen. and Subgen. Birds, 1855, 107 (genera *Caccabis, Alectoris, Ammoperdix, Tetraogallus,* and *Lerwa*).

<Odontophorinæ Gray, Cat. Gen. and Subgen. Birds, 1855, 107; Hand-list, ii, 1870, 271.—Coues, Key North Amer. Birds, 1872, 236; ed. 2, 1884, 588.— Sclater and Salvin, Nom. Av. Neotr., 1873, 137.—Elliot, Stand. Nat. Hist., iv, 1885, 198, 205, in text.—Ogilvie-Grant, Cat. Birds Brit. Mus., xxii, 1893, 99.—Ridgway, Orn. Illinois, ii, 1895, 14.—Salvin and Godman, Biol. Centr.-Amer., Aves, iii 1902, 287.—Knowlton, Birds of the World, 1909, 293.

<Odontophoridæ Sharpe, Hand-list, i, 1899, xi, 43.—American Ornithologists' Union Committee, Check-list, ed. 3, 1910, 134.—Dubois, Rev. Franç. d'Orn. Nos. 49, 50, 1913 (3).

<Ortyginæ Baird, Rep. Pacific R. R. Surv., ix, 1858, 638.—Baird, Brewer, and Ridgway, Hist. North Amer. Birds, iii, 1874, 466.

<Odontophorinae Carus, Handb. Zool., i, 1868-75, 321.

><Perdicidae Baird, Rep. Pacific R. R. Surv., ix, 1858, 638 (includes Old World partridges and quails and Turnicidæ).

<Perdicidæ Baird, Brewer, and Ridgway, Hist. North Amer. Birds, iii, 1874, 466 (includes Old World partridges and quails).—Sharpe, Rev. Rec. Att. Classif. Birds, 1891, 68 (includes Old World partridges and quails).

Alectoropode galline birds with postacetabular region only moderately broad; hypocleideum oval in contour; tarsometatarsus more than half as long as tibia; tarsus never wholly feathered (rarely with upperpart feathered), the planta tarsi frequently spurred (spurs 1–5); toes never pectinated or feathered; nasal fossae wholly unfeathered (except, sometimes, a narrow strip along lower posterior margin); neck never with inflatable air sacs and mandibular tomium not serrated or toothed (except in subfamily Odontophorinae).

The Phasianidae comprise so many types of such diverse form that it is difficult to frame a more detailed diagnosis of the group than that given above. The group comprises over 50 genera and between 250 and 300 species and subspecies, ranging in size from the peacocks, the males of which are 6 to nearly 7 feet long (including the long "train"), to the diminutive quails, some of which are less than 6 inches in total length. Some, as the true pheasants, the monals or Impeyan pheasants, and the peacocks, are among the most magnificent of birds, the brilliant and varied coloration of the males rivaling even that of the humming-birds and birds-of-paradise; while many other groups are composed of species as plainly colored as it is possible for birds to be.

With so great a number of excessively diverse forms, it is exceedingly difficult to classify the genera satisfactorily into trenchant subfamily and other groups. No attempt will be made here, since so few of the genera have any relation to the scope of the present work. It may, however, be of interest to define, roughly, the major groups into which the family may, for convenience, be divided, although some of these, at least, may be purely artificial groups:

(1) *Phasianinae* (the true pheasants). These exquisite game birds are characterized by a vaulted[27] and greatly elongated and graduated tail, the adult males being brilliant, more or less metallic colors, softened and relieved by other hues in elegant pattern. The typical genus is *Phasianus* (whence the English name pheasant and French faisan), of which the so-called English pheasant (*P. colchicus*) is a more or less familiar example; but the group includes besides several other genera, as *Chrysolophus*, including the golden pheasant (*C. pictus*) and Lady Amherst pheasant (*C. amherstiae*); *Gennaeus,* represented by the silver pheasant (*G. nycthemerus*) and more than half a dozen other species. The subfamily Phasianinae may be divided into several subgroups:

(a) GALLINAE (the junglefowls). This group is composed of several species of the genus *Gallus,* from one or more of which, but chiefly from one (*G. ferrugineus*), have been derived, by artificial selection, all the varieties or "breeds" of our domestic fowls. They differ from the pheasants in having the tail more arched (or sickle-shaped) and in the possession of a fleshy "comb" and wattles. The common or Bankiva junglefowl (*G. ferrugineus*) is very similar to the ordinary red gamecock and is undoubtedly the wild stock from which the latter and related domestic breeds have been derived. It is a native of parts of India, Burma, Assam, and the Malay countries, though to what extent its original range has been extended by artificial means cannot now be ascertained.

(b) LOPHOPHOREAE (the Impeyan pheasants, or monals, and the tragopans, or horned pheasants). This group comprises the genera *Pucrasia* (Pucrus or Koklass pheasants), *Ceriornis* (tragopans), and *Lophophorus* (Impeyan pheasants, or monals). They are heavy-bodied birds, with comparatively short, rounded or slightly cuneate tails, all the feathers of which lie in the same plane, like those of the various kinds of grouse and most other birds, instead of being vaulted as in the true pheasants and junglefowl. The tragopans have fleshy wattles, hornlike protuberances, or other appendages about the head, and their plumage is characterized by variety and beauty of pattern, rather than brilliancy of colors. There are about five species, found in the mountainous parts of India and China. The monals, or Impeyan pheasants, are birds of about the same size and general form as the tragopans (the males weighing about 4¼ to 5 pounds). They have no wattles or other fleshy appendages about

---

[27] ᴧ-shaped in transverse section.

the head, which, however, is ornamented in males of at least two species by a hawthorn crest, and the plumage is brilliant almost beyond comparison. "It is difficult by means of a written description to give any idea of the magnificent appearance of these brilliant birds to anyone who has not seen them. Their metallic hues of fiery red, green, purple, and gold vie in beauty and in their iridescent quality with the brightest of those seen among the hummingbirds, and if one could imagine one of these small flying gems increased to the size of a fowl, something of the appearance of these monauls might be conveyed to the mind."

These birds inhabit the Himalayan Mountains, always near the snow-line, and in summer ascend to elevations of 14,000 to 16,000 feet above sea level. Being thus inured to great cold, it is probable that these splendid birds would thrive and increase if liberated on our higher western mountains.

(c) POLYPLECTRONEAE (the peacock-pheasants). This group includes a single genus (*Polyplectron*) comprising six or seven species, inhabiting India, Burma, Cochin China, the Malay Peninsula, etc. They are rather small size and are characterized by the presence of two or more spurs on each leg and a broad, fan-shaped tail ornamented by large eye-like spots of metallic green, blue, or purple, the upper tail coverts and wing coverts having similar markings. Some of the species are crested.

(d) PAVONEAE (the peacocks). This group also includes a single genus (*Pavo*), but with only two, possibly three, species. The common peacock (*P. cristatus*), being domesticated, is too well known to require description. It is a native of India and Ceylon. The Javan peacock (*P. muticus*) is similar in size and form and, to a certain degree, in coloration, but has the neck and underparts green instead of blue and the crest quite different, the feathers composing it being fully webbed. It inhabits Burma, Ceylon, and some of the Malay countries as well as Java.

(e) ARGUSIANAE (the argus pheasants). This group contains two remarkable genera, one of only two or three species, the other monotypic. The well-known argus pheasant (*Argusianus argus*), the adult male of which is 6 feet long (including the greatly elongated middle rectrices), is distinguished by the enormous development, both in length and breadth, of the secondary remiges, which are ornamented by exquisitely shaded eyelike spots or ocelli, while the middle rectrices are also enormously developed. The colors are not brilliant, consisting wholly of various hues and tones of brown and gray, with minor markings of black, but the exquisite shadings and pencilings, especially those on the secondaries, produce an effect that is the envy of every artist. This remarkable bird is a native of the Malay Peninsula, and Sumatra, while the closely related *A. grayi* inhabits Borneo. A third species, whose native country is as yet a mystery, is known only from a single primary quill feather.

A second genus of the group, *Rheinardia,* contains a single species (*R. ocellata*). This, which inhabits the interior of Tonkin, is much like *Argusianus* in form, having equally elongated middle rectrices (the adult male measuring about seven feet in total length), but the secondaries are much less developed, being but little if any longer than the primaries, and the coloration quite different.

(2) *Perdicinae* (the Old World quails). This group contains relatively plain-colored birds of small to medium size, with the bill relatively shorter and stouter, the maxilla deeper and narrower (transversely) and its tip less produced, than in most true pheasants.

(3) *Odontophorinae* (New World quails). Galliform birds of small to medium size (wing 95–165 mm.) with the mandibular tomia serrated or toothed subterminally. This group agrees in other characters with the other members of the family, especially the Perdicinae, which it represents in the Western Hemisphere. Besides the presence of the serrations of the cutting edge of the mandible, possessed by all its members and by none of the other groups of the family, the Odontophorinae have the bill still stouter and shorter. None of them have spurs, though many of the Perdicinae also do not. Additional characters are as follows: Tail less than half as long as to slightly longer than wings, the rectrices (10–14) never acuminate; tarsus less than one-fourth to more than one-third as long as wing, the acrotarsium with a single row of broad, transverse scutella, the planta tarsi with two or (usually) more definite rows of moderately long scutella but partly covered with small scales.

The remaining members of the Phasianidae, comprising about 26 genera and more than 175 species and subspecies, are not so easily classified. Some of them are more or less nearly allied to one or another of the groups described above; but much the greater number are very different, including the various partridges, francolins, and spurfowl, for the most part rather plainly colored birds of small to very small size. These may well be dismissed, in this connection, without further mention, since the present work has to do directly only with the few forms introduced into North America with the view to their naturalization.

The Phasiani are peculiar to Asia, including the outlying islands of the Malay Archipelago, Japan, and Formosa. One species at present occurs in Europe but is generally supposed, on the evidence of "what passes for history,"[28] to have been introduced from western Asia into continental Europe by the Argonauts, and into the British Islands by the Romans. This, the so-called English pheasant (*Phasianus colchicus*), has been introduced into the United States and is already naturalized locally, while several other very beautiful species have been introduced into Oregon, Washington, and other parts of the Far West, with more

---

[28] Alfred Newton, Dictionary of Birds, 1894, 713.

or less success. Several of the smaller and less ornamental species have
also been introduced but, for the most part at least, with unsatisfactory
results.

The following "key" to the genera includes only those that are native
to our region or that have been introduced into North America. One
of the genera is known only in a domesticated state as far as our region
is concerned and therefore will not be further noticed in this work.

KEY TO THE NORTH AND MIDDLE AMERICAN GENERA OF PHASIANIDAE[29]

a. Mandibular tomium serrated or toothed (ODONTOPHORINAE).

  b. Rectrices 12-14; tarsus little if any longer (usually shorter) than middle toe
    with claw; claws medium-sized to large, the longest as long as or longer
    than second phalanx of middle toe; chord of culmen much shorter than
    combined length of first and second phalanges of middle toe; planta tarsi
    with more than 2 definite rows of scutella, or else if only 2 definite rows
    the remaining scutella of planta tarsal area much smaller.

    c. Tips of lateral claws extending little if any beyond base of middle claw,
      the claws not noticeably elongated (that of middle toe usually much
      less than one-third as long as tarsus) ; tail moderately long to very long,
      always more than half as long as wing, its tip reaching to or beyond
      extremities of outstretched feet.

      d. Tarsus decidedly less than one-third as long as wing; outermost primary
        not longer than ninth (from outside), usually longer than eighth.

        e. Tail less than three-fifths as long as wing.

          f. Scapulars, tertials, and rump spotted; flanks spotted or striped, not
            banded; chest never plain slate-gray; crest (if obvious) always
            shorter than head; sexes more or less different in color (coloration
            of head always different); smaller (wing less than 110 mm.).

                                Colinus (p. 305)

          ff. Scapulars, tertials, and rump unspotted; flanks banded with chestnut,
            white, and black; chest plain slate-gray; a conspicuous crest of
            2 slender much-elongated plumes; sexes alike in color; larger
            (wing 130–140 mm.)........................**Oreortyx** (p. 253)

        ee. Tail more than three-fifths as long as wing.

          f. Tail less than two-thirds as long as wing; scapulars and tertials
            spotted; sides and flanks banded with black and white.

                            Philortyx (p. 272)

          ff. Tail more than two-thirds as long as wing; scapulars and tertials
            unspotted; sides and flanks not barred.

            g. Tail three-fourths as long as wing, or more, of 12 rectrices; crest
              longer, club-shaped, its plumes narrower basally, more rigid,
              their webs conduplicate; chest not squamated; sexes conspicu-
              ously different in color.....................**Lophortyx** (p. 275)

            gg. Tail less than three-fourths as long as wing, with 14 rectrices;
              crest shorter, bushy, its plumes broad, softer and blended, their
              webs not conduplicate; chest conspicuously squamated; sexes
              alike in color............................**Callipepla** (p. 264)

---

[29] Including introduced genera.

　　　dd. Tarsus very nearly one-third as long as wing or longer; outermost
　　　　　primary shorted than ninth (from outside).
　　　　　　e. Tail less than one-half as long as wing........**Odontophorus** (p. 364)
　　　　　ee. Tail about two-thirds as long as wing or longer....**Dendrortyx** (p. 239)
　　cc. Tips of lateral claws extending far beyond base of middle claw, claws
　　　　elongated (that of middle toe more than one-third as long as tarsus);
　　　　tail very short (decidedly less than half as long as wing), its tip falling
　　　　far short of extremities of outstretched feet.
　　　　　d. Tarsus less than one-fourth as long as wing; rectrices soft, narrower
　　　　　　terminally, hardly distinguishable from coverts; crest occipital and
　　　　　　nuchal, very full or bushy, feathers blended; sides and flanks spotted
　　　　　　or barred; sexes wholly unlike in color............**Cyrtonyx** (p. 390)
　　　　　dd. Tarsus more than one-fourth as long as wing; rectrices firm, broad and
　　　　　　rounded terminally, very distinct from coverts; crest coronal (vertical),
　　　　　　moderately developed, the feathers distinctly outlined; sexes not con-
　　　　　　spicuously different in color....................**Dactylortyx** (p. 379)
　bb. Rectrices 10; tarsus much longer than middle toe with claw; claws very small,
　　　the longest much shorter than second phalanx of middle toe; chord of
　　　culmen nearly equal to combined length of first two phalanges of middle
　　　toe; planta tarsi with 2 definite rows (one on each side) of rather large,
　　　oblique quadrate, transverse scutella...............**Rhynchortyx** (p. 403)
aa. Mandibular tomium not serrated or toothed (PHASIANINAE).
　　b. Larger (wing not less than 177 mm.); tail at least three-fifths as long as
　　　wing, more or less graduated (in adult males much longer than wing,
　　　excessively graduated, the rectrices tapering toward their narrow tips);
　　　sexes very different in coloration, adult males bright colored, the colors in
　　　part metallic.
　　　　c. Plumage bright colored. (Males.)
　　　　　d. Throat feathered; no "comb" on forehead; middle rectrices not strongly
　　　　　　falcate; feathers of rump broad and rounded or at least not linear or
　　　　　　lanceolate (PHASIANI).
　　　　　　e. Loral and orbital regions partly feathered, the malar region completely
　　　　　　　feathered; tail flat or moderately compressed; rectrices 18.
　　　　　　　f. Tail flat; pileum not crested; no nuchal "cape"....**Phasianus** (p. 417)
　　　　　　ff. Tail distinctly vaulted or compressed (ʌ-shaped in cross section);
　　　　　　　　pileum crested; a conspicuous nuchal "cape" of very large, broad,
　　　　　　　　subtruncate feathers..**Chrysolophus** (introduced unsuccessfully).[30]

---

[30] **Chrysolophus** Gray, Illustr. Indian Zool., ii, 1833-34, pl. 41, fig. 2 (type, by
monotypy, *Phasianus pictus* Linnaeus).—*Thaumalea* (not of Ruthe, 1831) Wagler,
Isis, 1832, 1227 (type, as designated by Gray, 1840, *Phasianus pictus* Linnaeus).—
Thaumelia (emendation) Eyton, Osteol. Avium, 1867, 168, 172.—*Epomia* Hodgson,
in Gray, Zool. Misc., No. 3, 1844, 85 (type, as designated by Elliot, 1872, *Phasianus
pictus* Linnaeus).—*Epoima* (emendation) Gray, Cat. Mamm. and Birds Nepal and
Thibet, 1846, 124.—*Epomis* (emendation) Gray, Gen. Birds, iii, 1845, 497.

Two species of this genus, *Chrysolophus pictus* (Linnaeus) and *Chrysolophus
amherstiae* (Leadbeater), have occasionally either escaped from aviaries or been
liberated, but neither has ever succeeded in becoming established in the wild in
North America.

    ee. Loral, orbital, and malar region completely nude, the skin finely papillose or granulated, developed on upper and lower edges into a conspicuous free lobe; tail excessively compressed; rectrices 16.

Gennaeus (introduced unsuccessfully)[31]

   dd. Throat nude and wattled; a median fleshy "comb" on forehead; middle rectrices strongly falcate; feathers of rump elongated and linear, or lanceolate ....Gallus (extralimital)[32]

  cc. Plumage dull-colored (brownish, more or less mottled or barred). (Females.)

   d. Tail more than four-fifths as long as wing, usually much longer than wing, excessively graduated (PHASIANI).

    e. Orbital region mostly feathered; rectrices narrower, distinctly tapering toward their acuminate or subacuminate tips; rectrices 18.

     f. Tail flat, with middle pair of rectrices not conspicuously longer than next pair....................................Phasianus (p. 417)

     ff. Tail distinctly compressed (∧-shaped in cross section), with middle pair of rectrices conspicuously longer than next pair.

Chrysolophus (unsuccessfully introduced)

    ee. Orbital region extensively nude; rectrices much broader, only slightly tapering to their rounded tips; rectrices 16.

Gennaeus (unsuccessfully introduced)

   dd. Tail less than two-thirds as long as wing, slightly graduated, or rounded.

Gallus (extralimital)

  bb. Smaller (wing usually much less than 177 mm.)[33]; tail less than three-fifths as long as wing, flat, slightly rounded; adult males not brightly colored or at least without metallic colors, the sexes alike or essentially alike in coloration.

---

[31] **Gennaeus** Wagler, Isis, 1832, 1228 (type, as designated by Gray, 1840, *Phasianus nycthemerus* Linnaeus).—*Gennæeus* (emendation) Engel, Rev. Franç. d'Orn., iv, 1915, 73.—*Nycthemerus* Swainson, in Murray, Encycl. Geogr., 1834, 264; Amer. ed. of 1837, i, 271, fig. 80 (type, by monotypy and tautonymy, *N. argentatus* Swainson = *Phasianus nycthemerus* Linnaeus).—*Alectrophasis* Gray, List Gen. Birds, ed. 2, 1841, 78 (type, as designated by Gray, 1845, *Lophophorus cuvieri* Temminck).—*Alectorophasis* (emendation) Agassiz, Index Zool., 1846, 13, 14.—*Grammatoptilus* Reichenbach, Av. Syst. Nat. Vög., 1853, xxx (type, by monotypy, *Phasianus lineatus* Vigors).—*Grammatoptilos* (emendation) Elliot, Monogr. Phasianidae, ii, 1870, text to pl. 21.

One species, *Gennaeus nycthemerus* (Linnaeus), has occasionally escaped from aviaries or been liberated in North America but has never succeeded in becoming established in the wild.

[32] **Gallus** Brisson, Orn., i, 1760, 26, 166 (type, by tautonymy, *"Gallus"* = *Phasianus varius* Linnaeus).—*Alector* Klein, Hist. Av. Prodr. 1750, 111 (not of Merrem).—*Alector* Schrank, Fauna Boica, i, 1798, 135.—*Alector* Gloger, Hand- und Hilfsbuch, i, 1842, 384.—*Creagrius* Gloger, ibid., 387.

Indo-Malayan Region, Cochin China, Hainan, Philippine Islands, Palawan, Sumatra, Java, Timor, Lombock, and Celebes. (Three established species and four forms of doubtful status.) The type of this genus, *Gallus gallus,* the wild junglefowl of India and the Malay countries, is the original stock of most if not all of our domestic breeds of "chickens." It resembles very closely the domesticated "red game" variety. Although introduced by the earliest colonists into America, it seems not to have become "wild" or feral in any area.

[33] These characters apply to the genera that have been introduced into the United States, but not to many others of the group.

  c. Rectrices 14-18, firm, broad, with broadly rounded tips, the tail at least
   half as long as wing, moderately rounded, and projecting considerably
   beyond coverts; longer primaries exceeding longest (proximal) secondaries by much less than length of tarsus; nearly straight (not distinctly if at all bowed); outermost primary not longer (usually shorter)
   than sixth (from outside), the third to fifth longest; bill relatively
   much larger and thicker; the culmen broad and rounded, the basal
   portion (mesorhinium) broad, short, obtuse or rounded at posterior
   end; legs and feet much stouter; size larger (wing 150 mm. or more)
   (PERDICINAE).
    d. Rectrices 14 or more.
     e. Rectrices 14.
      f. Tail half or more than half as long as wing.
       g. Tail less than three-fourths as long as wing.
            Alectoris (introduced; status uncertain)[34]
       gg. Tail more than three-fourths the length of the wing.
          Bambusicola (introduced unsuccessfully)[35]
    ee. Rectrices 16-18; outermost primary shorter than seventh (from outside);
     bill relatively longer, smaller, and slenderer, the distance from anterior
     margin of nasal fossa to tip of maxilla equal to or slightly more
     than distance from former point to anterior angle of eye; tarsus
     longer than middle toe with claw, without trace of rudimentary spur;
     upper parts conspicuously variegated.................**Perdix** (p. 409)
  cc. Rectrices less than 14.
   d. Rectrices 8...................**Excalfactoria** (introduced unsuccessfully)[36]

---

[34] **Alectoris** Kaup, Naturl. Syst., 1829, 180 (type, by monotypy, *Perdix petrosa*
auct., not of Gmelin = *Perdix barbara* Bonnaterre).—*Caccabis* Kaup, Naturl.
Syst., 1829, 183 (type, by monotypy, *Perdix saxatilis* Wolf and Meyer).—*Chacura*
Hodgson, *in* Gray, Zool. Misc., 1844, 85 (type by monotypy, *Perdix chukar* Gray).
—*Pyctes* Hodgson, *in* Gray, Zool. Misc., 1844, 85 (type by monotypy, *Perdix chukar*
Gray).
  Two species, *Alectoris graeca* (Meisner) and *A. rufa* (Linnaeus) have been
introduced in North America, but whether successfully or not remains to be deter-
mined. At least three subspecies of the first species are involved in these introductions, probably hopelessly mixed.
  [35] **Bambusicola** Gould, Proc. Zool. Soc. London, 1862 (1863), 285 (type, by
subsequent designation, *Perdix thoracica* Temminck); Hartert, Vög. pal. Fauna,
iii, 1921, 1943-44; Stuart Baker, Fauna Brit. India, ed. 2, Birds, v, 1928, 365-367;
Peters, Check-list Birds of World, ii, 1934, 105-106.
  Introduced unsuccessfully in Stevens, Spokane, Yakima, and Garfield Counties,
Wash.
  [36] **Excalfactoria** Bonaparte, Compt. Rend., xlii, 1856, 881 (type, by tautonymy,
Tetrao chinensis Linnaeus [*Coturnix excalfactoria* Temminck in synonymy]).—
Compsortyx Heine, Nom. Mus. Hein. Ornith., 1890, 292 (new name for *Excalfactoria*
Bonaparte on grounds of purism).—*Excalfatoria* (emendation) Gould, Handb. Birds
Australia, ii, 1865, 197.—*Excalphatoria* (emendation) A. Newton, Dict. Birds, 1894,
756.
  A few specimens of the Australian form, *Excalfactoria chinensis australis* Gould,
were liberated near Alvarado, Calif., but apparently disappeared.

dd. Rectrices 10-12, soft, narrow, with narrowly rounded tips, the tail only one-third as long as wing, graduated, and hidden by coverts; longer primaries exceeding longest (proximal) secondaries by more than length of tarsus, strongly bowed; outermost primary as long as second and third or else very little shorter, the second and third (from outside), or first to third, longest; bill relatively much smaller and weaker, the culmen narrow and somewhat rigid, especially the basal portion (mesorhinium), which is very narrow, distinctly ridged, and extended much farther between the laterofrontal antiae, its posterior end acute, or cuneate; legs and feet much slenderer; size much smaller (wings not more than 117 mm.)............**Coturnix** (unsuccessfully introduced)[37]

Genus DENDRORTYX Gould

Dendrortyx GOULD, Monogr. Odontoph., pt. 1, 1844, pl. 20 and text; pt. iii, 1850, introd., p. 20. (Type by monotypy, *Ortyx macroura* Jardine and Selby.)

Very large, long-tailed Odontophoridae (wing about 150–165 mm., the tail about two-thirds to quite as long) with outermost primary shorter than tenth (from outside), the fourth to eighth (from outside), longest, the tail graduated for half the length of tarsus to more than the tarsal length, and either with a continuous row of large transverse scutella on outer side of planta tarsi, or with the planta tarsi largely covered by small hexagonal scales with a continuous series of rather small transverse scutella on upper portion of outer side only (*D. barbatus*).

Bill relatively large and stout, the chord of culmen (from extreme base) equal to decidedly more than one-third to nearly one-half the length of tarsus; depth of bill at base equal to much more than distance from anterior end of nasal fossa to tip of maxilla, and equal to or greater than width of bill at rictus; culmen strongly convex, sometimes arched basally, broadly rounded though more narrow basally; gonys very broad, distinctly to slightly convex, its basal angle prominent. Outermost primary shorter than ninth or tenth (from outside), shorter than distal secondaries, the fifth to eighth or fourth, fifth and sixth longest. Tail two-thirds to quite as long as wing, graduated for from half length of tarsus to the length of the tarsus, the rectrices (12) broad, with broadly rounded tips. Tarsus

---

[37] **Coturnix** (ex Moehring) Bonnaterre, Tabl. Encycl. Méth., i, 1791, lxxxvii, 216 (type, by tautonymy, *C. communis* Bonnaterre = *Tetrao coturnix* Linnaeus).— *Ortygion* Keyserling and Blasius, Wirbelth. Eur., 1840, lxvi, 112, 202 (type, by monotypy, *Tetrao coturnix* Linnaeus).—*Perdortyx* Montessus, Mém. Soc. Saóne, vi, 1886, 36 (type, by monotypy, *P. lodoisiæ* Montessus = *Tetrao coturnix* Linnaeus). —*Coturnyx* (emendation) Marno, Zool. Garten, ix, 1868, 83.—*Ortygium* (emendation; not *Ortygia* Boie, 1828) Agassiz, Index Zool., 1846, 265.—*Ortyx* (emendation; —not of Stephens, 1819) Des Murs, *in* Chenu, Encycl. Hist. Nat. Ois., vi, 1854, 154.— *Mauroturnix* Mathews, Austral Avian Rec., ii, No. 5, Sept. 24, 1914, 112 (type, by original designation and monotypy, *Coturnix pectoralis* Gould).

One species, *Coturnix coturnix* (Linnaeus), was introduced in large numbers in New England, eastern Canada, Ohio, and Virginia, but after migrating south in the autumn the birds were never heard of again.

nearly one-third as long as wing, equal to or slightly shorter or longer than middle toe with claw, both sides of the planta tarsi either with a posterior continuous row of large, transverse scutella, or mostly covered with rather small hexagonal scales but with larger obliquely transverse scutella on the upper posterior part of outer side.

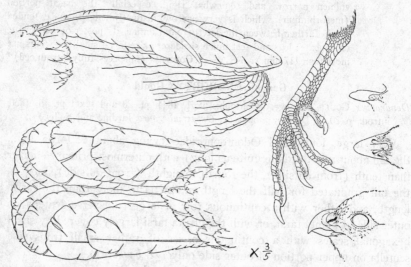

FIGURE 14.—*Dendrortyx macroura.*

Plumage and coloration.—Feathers of pileum more or less elongated, forming, when erected, a bushy crest of rather narrow to moderately broad soft and decumbent, or decurved feathers, with plane surface and rounded tips; orbital region and lores more or less extensively naked, especially postocular portion of the former. Coloration rather dull, olive and rufescent hues predominantly on upperparts, hindneck striped with chestnut, underparts dull olive-grayish more or less streaked with chestnut or dusky, the throat uniform black, gray, white, or buffy white. Sexes alike in coloration.

Range.—Southern Mexico to highlands of Costa Rica. (Three species with eight races.)

KEY TO THE ADULTS OF THE FORMS OF DENDRORTYX

a. Chin and throat gray, breast uniform chestnut (mountain forest of Veracruz).
                                                        D. barbatus (p. 241)
aa. Chin and throat white or black, breast gray streaked with blackish or brownish.
   b. Chin and throat white.
      c. Streaks on breast almost blackish or at least tipped and edged with blackish (highlands of Costa Rica).......**D. leucophrys hypospodius** (p. 252)
      cc. Streaks on breast chestnut to auburn (highlands of Guatemala, El Salvador, Honduras, and northwestern Nicaragua).
         d. Auriculars brown; ground color of underparts buffy brown; gray of breast pale (Vera Paz, Guatemala).**D. leucophrys leucophrys** (p. 249)

    dd. Auriculars sooty gray; ground color of underparts gray; gray of breast fairly dark (western Guatemala, El Salvador, Honduras, and northwestern Nicaragua)..............**D. leucophrys nicaraguae** (p. 250)
  bb. Chin and throat black.
    c. With prominent white superciliary and malar stripes.
      d. Chestnut median stripes on breast feathers small and faint, these stripes absent on breast feathers.
        e. Lower back and rump barred with black; thighs and flanks grayish brown (Morelos)..............**D. macroura griseipectus** (p. 245)
        ee. Lower back and rump with no or little black; thighs and flanks olive-brown (northwest Jalisco)...........**D. macroura diversus** (p. 246)
      dd. Chestnut median stripes on breast feathers large and prominent.
        e. General color of back and rump decidedly olive-brown with little or no whitish transverse flecking (Michoacán and Guerrero highlands).
                           D. macroura striatus (p. 247)
        ee. General color of back and rump not decidedly olive-brown but gray-brown with a slightly olive tinge, and abundantly cross-flecked with whitish ....**D. macroura macroura** (p. 243)
    cc. Superciliary and malar stripes not white and conspicuous but heavily suffused with brownish.......................**D. macroura oaxacae** (p. 248)

DENDRORTYX BARBATUS Gould

BEARDED WOOD PARTRIDGE

Adult (sexes alike in color).—Forehead and anterior part of crown buffy brown, darkening to buffy brown and pale sepia on the hindcrown and occiput, the feathers of the forehead with pale buffy shafts which, being largely uncovered, show noticeably; feathers of hindneck mouse gray to dark mouse gray with terminally broadening shaft streaks of russet to chestnut, these streaks subterminally obscurely blotched with dusky chaetura drab; anterior interscapulars similar but with the chestnut areas broader, the gray restricted to the margins of the feathers and these margins subterminally crossed by black spots; posterior interscapulars similar but with the terminal part of the edges, distal to the black marks, white, and the more proximal, grayish part much suffused with chestnut; scapulars, all but the outermost upper wing coverts, and the feathers of upper back buffy brown to olive-brown heavily blotched with fuscous-black and barred irregularly with the same and with light pinkish cinnamon to pinkish buff and marginally with white, the feathers of the upper back with a chestnut wash along the shafts; outermost upper wing coverts with no white and little blackish; the secondaries russet, externally edged and tipped with pinkish buff to cinnamon-buff, these areas minutely speckled with blackish, and the feathers crossed by 8 to 10 flatly V-shaped bars of chaetura drab, the russet immediately distal to each bar paler than elsewhere; primaries and alula cinnamon-russet, their outer webs barred with pale chaetura drab, their inner webs extensively mottled and washed with the same; back, lower back, rump, and upper tail coverts buffy brown to olive-brown, tipped and subterminally banded with pale buffy to almost white and with blackish blotches between the tips and the subterminal bands; median rectrices with a fairly narrow chestnut shaft streak paling laterally into buffy dark vermiculated and speckled with chaetura drab, and crossed by six to eight wavy whitish bars, each of which is broadly edged proximally and narrowly edged distally with blackish; the width of the chestnut median area increases laterally on each pair of rectrices, with consequent reduction of the drab and blackish areas, until on the outermost ones the entire feathers are chestnut, incompletely banded with chaetura drab; lores like the forehead; upper cheeks and auriculars similar also; sides of neck like the hindneck; chin and throat mouse gray with a slate tinge; breast and upper abdomen amber brown to bright cinnamon, paling posteriorly to cinnamon-buff; feathers of sides cinnamon edged with grayish drab, splotched with black and white; flanks and under tail coverts buffy brown to olive-brown edged with buffy to cinnamon and with large subterminal blotches of black and with blackish freckling on the more basal brownish parts; thighs olive-brown; under wing coverts dark olive-brown freckled with russet; bare skin around eye, bill, tarsi, and toes red.

Juvenal.—Similar to the adult, but the upper abdomen pale buffy whitish narrowly barred with drab; middle of breast pale cinnamon narrowly barred with drab; secondaries as in adult but with much less external buffy mottling, the edges more cinnamomeous, darker and duller.

Downy young.—Forehead and superciliaries broadly antimony yellow becoming suffused posteriorly with buckthorn brown; middle of crown and occiput dark auburn; scapular area cinnamon-buffy to pinkish cinnamon; spinal tract very broadly auburn, fading laterally to pale Mikado brown and pinkish cinnamon; wings and thighs auburn obscurely mottled with dusky; chin, throat, breast, abdomen, and sides between cream color and Naples yellow, washed on the breast with pale ochraceous; cheeks pale buckthorn brown.

Adult male.—Wing 147–166 (154.8); tail 117–121 (118.9); culmen from the base 20.4–22.5 (21.6); tarsus 49.1–54 (51.8); middle toe without claw 42.0–45.6 (43.2 mm.).[38]

Adult female.—Wing 148–152 (150); tail 110–119 (114); culmen from base 20.0–21.7 (20.6); tarsus 44.5–47.4 (46.6); middle toe without claw 37.4–41 (38.8 mm.).[39]

Range.—Resident in the mountain forests of the State of Veracruz, Mexico (Jalapa, Orizaba, Jico).

Type locality.—Jalapa, Veracruz.

---

[38] Seven specimens from Jico, Veracruz.

[39] Four specimens from Jico, Orizaba, and Jalapa, Veracruz.

Dendrortyx barbatus GOULD, Monogr. Odontoph., pt. 2, 1846, pl. 22 and text (Jalapa, Veracruz, Mexico; coll. Berlin Museum).—SCLATER, Proc. Zool. Soc. London, 1859, 369 (Jalapa, Mexico; spec.).—GRAY, List Birds Brit. Mus., pt. 5, Gallinae, 1867, 74.—SUMICHRAST, Proc. Boston Soc. Nat. Hist, xii, 1868, 225 (alpine region, Veracruz); Mem. Boston Soc. Nat. Hist., i, 1869, 562 (alpine region of Veracruz); La Naturaleza, ser. 1, v, 1882, 229 (alpine region of Orizaba).— OGILVIE-GRANT, Cat. Birds Brit. Mus., xxii, 1893, 393 (Jalapa); Handb. Game Birds, ii, 1897, 113 (monogr.).—BERISTAIN and LAURENCIO, Mem. y Revista Soc. Cient. "Antonio Alzate," vii, 1894, 219 (Orizaba).—SALVIN and GODMAN, Biol. Centr.-Amer., Aves, iii, 1903, 289 (Jalapa and Orizaba, Veracruz).— PETERS, Check-list Birds of World, ii, 1934, 42.—HELLMAYR and CONOVER, Cat. Birds Amer., i, No. 1, 1942, 225 (syn.; distr.).

[*Dendrortyx*] *barbatus* GRAY, Hand-list, ii, 1870, 272, No. 9773.—SCLATER and SALVIN, Nom. Av. Neotr., 1873, 138.—SHARPE, Hand-list, i, 1899, 44.

D[*endrortyx*] *barbatus* REICHENOW, Die Vögel, i, 1913, 315.

Dendrortyx barbata SCLATER, Proc. Zool. Soc. London, 1857, 206 (Jalapa).—BAIRD, List Described Birds Mexico, Central America, and West Indies not in Coll. Smithsonian Inst., 1863, 6.

DENDRORTYX MACROURA MACROURA (Jardine and Selby)

EASTERN LONG-TAILED PARTRIDGE

Adult (sexes alike in color).—Broad forehead, supraorbital line, chin, and upper throat black; feathers of crown and occiput black broadly tipped with distally widening tear-shaped spots of dull, rather pale, russet to Mikado brown; a broad white superciliary stripe on each side, the feathers composing which are black basally and the posteriormost of which have narrow terminal shaft marks of dull russet; feathers of hind neck dark bright hazel to dark Sanford's brown edged termino-laterally with white, and blackish basally, the more posterior feathers with the white edges darkening to light mouse gray; interscapulars dark bright hazel to dark Sanford's brown broadly edged with neutral gray, the gray areas, especially of the more posterior feathers, mottled with buffy brown and blackish and with small white lateral flecks; scapulars grayish buffy brown, tipped and crossed by three to five more or less complete white bars, each of which is proximally broadly bordered with dark fuscous to black, the subterminal black area bent basally on the two sides enclosing a median area of dull dark hazel, the grayish-brown areas of the feathers finely speckled with black dots; inner secondaries like the scapulars but with the hazel reduced or wanting; outer secondaries with the pale and the black marking restricted to the outer edge of the outer webs, the rest of the feathers being dark dull olive-brown only faintly mottled with paler; primaries dark dull olive-brown, their outer webs faintly flecked with light pinkish cinnamon; lesser upper wing coverts pale buffy brown vermiculated sparingly with blackish; median upper wing coverts similar but with faint hazel shaft lines and tipped with pale buffy brown to almost white, the tip basally edged with blackish; greater upper wing coverts like the scapulars but with less whitish; alula dark dull olive-brown, the outer webs with a dull hazel streak next to the shaft; upper back, lower back, and rump, light brownish olive tipped with smoke gray to almost white, these tips basally bordered with black; upper tail coverts slightly darker and coarsely but sparingly vermiculated with black and with two small lateral white flecks on each; median rectrices olive-brown crossed by 10 distally pointed broad V-shaped bands of pale buffy brown to pale olive-buff, each of these bordered proximally by an irregular blackish band, the broad interspaces flecked and stippled with blackish, the median portion of the feathers suffused with dull hazel; lateral rectrices with their inner webs darker and more uniform clove brown, the outer webs flecked and incompletely banded as in the median ones but in decreasing amounts centrifugally, the median area of all the rectrices somewhat suffused with hazel, which color also replaces in the lateral ones the olive-brown found in the median pair; circumocular space bare, subocular area and auriculars blackish, the feathers of the latter sometimes tinged with hazel; a white malar stripe beginning narrowly under the anterior end of the eye broadens posteriorly on the sides of the neck, where it sometimes appears faintly speckled with hazel due to narrow dusky tips of the color on its posterior feathers; lower throat, breast, and sides of neck pale neutral gray to deep gull gray, each feather with a broad shaft stripe of hazel, the hazel paling slightly all along the margin of the shaft stripe forming halationlike edge, all these feathers hair brown on their concealed basal portion; feathers of the sides similar but with the hazel stripes narrower and paler, the gray portions becoming buffy brown to buffy drab vermiculated and flecked with dark drab, and spotted with dirty white; middle of abdomen pale drab gray to very pale light drab, each feather medially suffused and mottled with grayish drab; flanks, thighs, and lower abdomen olive-drab indistinctly mottled with hair brown and tipped with grayish buffy white; under tail coverts dark chaetura drab to black narrowly tipped with white and crossed by a narrow but irregular white band slightly distal to the middle of their length, under wing coverts like the lesser upper coverts but somewhat darker, iris, circumocular bare skin, bill, tarsi, and toes coral red; claws buffy.

Other plumages unknown.

Adult male.—Wing 163–166 (164.7); tail 157–169 (163); culmen from the base 19.7–21.4 (20.5); tarsus 47.1–52.8 (50.7); middle toe without claw 37.1–41.2 (39.2 mm.).[40]

Adult female.—Wing 155–158 (157); tail 147–151 (149.3); culmen from base 18.9–19.5 (19.3); tarsus 49.2–53.3 (51.4); middle toe without claw 37.4–41.8 (39.6 mm.).[41]

---

[40] Four specimens.
[41] Three specimens.

Range.—Resident in the mountain forests of the Valley of Mexico and the highlands of Veracruz.

Type locality.—Mexico = mountains about the Valley of Mexico.

Ortyx macroura JARDINE and SELBY, Illustr. Orn., i, pt. 3, 1828, pls. 38, 49 and text (Mexico).—JARDINE, Nat. Libr., Orn., iv, 1834, 128, pl. 12.

Dendrortyx macrurus GOULD, Monogr. Odontoph., pt. 1, 1844, pl. 20 and text.—SCLATER, Proc. Zool. Soc. London, 1864, 178 (near City of Mexico).—GRAY, List Birds Brit. Mus., Gallinae, 1867, 73.—BERISTAIN and LAURENCIO, Mem. y Rev. Soc. Cient. "Antonio Alzate," vii, 1894, 219 (Orizaba).—OGILVIE-GRANT, Ibis, 1902, 237.—SALVIN and GODMAN, Biol. Centr.-Amer., Aves, iii, 1903, 287, part (alpine region of Orizaba, Veracruz).

[*Dendrortyx*] *macrurus* GRAY, Hand-list, ii, 1870, 272, No. 9771.—SCLATER and SALVIN, Nom. Av. Neotr., 1873, 138, part.—SHARPE, Hand-list, i, 1899, 43, part.

Dendrortyx macrourus OGILVIE-GRANT, Cat. Birds Brit. Mus., xxii, 1893, 392, part (in synonymy; descr.?).—NELSON, Auk, xiv, 1897, 44, in text (crit.).

D[*endrortyx*] *macrourus* REICHENOW, Die Vögel, i, 1913, 315.

Dendrortyx macrorus OGILVIE-GRANT, Handb. Game Birds, ii, 1897, 112 part (s. Mexico; highlands of Oaxaca).

[*Odontophorus*] *macrourus* REICHENBACH, Synop. Av., iii, 1848, pl. 194, figs. 1692, 1693.

Dendrortyx macroura macroura PETERS, Check-list Birds of World, ii, 1934, 42.—HELLMAYR and CONOVER, Cat. Birds Amer., i, No. 1, 1942, 225 (syn.; distr.).

[*Dendrortyx macroura*] *macroura* GRISCOM, Auk, liv, 1937, 192, in text (crit.).

Tetrao marmoratus LA LLAVE, Registro Trimestro, i, 1832, 144 (mountains near City of Mexico); La Naturaleza, vii, 1884, App., p. 65.

DENDRORTYX MACROURA GRISEIPECTUS Nelson

GRAY-BREASTED LONG-TAILED PARTRIDGE

Adult.—Similar to that of the nominate race but with the hazel shaft stripes of the breast feathers confined to the basal two-thirds or less of the feathers, and almost hidden by the overlapping of these feathers, giving the breast a nearly uniform deep gull gray; the hazel stripes of the feathers of the sides also greatly reduced; back and rump slightly more olivaceous.

Other plumages unknown.

Adult.—Wing 167; tail 145; culmen from base 19.5; tarsus 54; middle toe without claw 42 mm. (type).

Adult female.—Wing 157; tail 131; culmen from base 20; tarsus 54; middle toe without claw 40 mm. (1 specimen).

Range.—Known only from the heavy oak forest on the Pacific slope of the Cordillera, in the State of Morelos (and possibly in the State of Mexico as well).

Type locality.—Huitzilac, Morelos, Mexico.

Dendrortyx macrurus (not *Ortyx macroura* Jardine and Selby) SALVIN and GODMAN, Biol. Centr.-Amer., Aves, iii, 1903, 287, part (Morelos).

Dendrortyx macrourus griseipectus NELSON, Auk, xiv, 1897, 44 (Huitzilac, Pacific slope of Morelos, c. Mexico; coll. U. S. Nat. Mus.).—OGILVIE-GRANT, Ibis, 1902, 237.

D[*endrortyx*] *macrourus griseipectus* NELSON, Auk, xix, 1902, 388 (crit.).—SALVIN and GODMAN, Biol. Centr.-Amer., Aves., iii, 1903, 288, in text (crit.).

Dendrortyx macroura griseipectus PETERS, Check-list Birds of World, ii, 1934, 42.— HELLMAYR and CONOVER, Cat. Birds Amer., i, No. 1, 1942, 225.—FRIEDMANN, Journ. Washington Acad. Sci., xxxiii, 1943, 272 in text (crit.).

[*Dendrortyx macroura*] *griseipectus* GRISCOM, Auk, liv, 1937, 192 in text, part— FRIEDMANN, Journ. Washington Acad. Sci., xxxiii, 1943, 272 in text, 273 in text (crit.; distr.).

[*Dendrortyx*] *griseipectus* SHARPE, Hand-list, i, 1899, 43.

DENDRORTYX MACROURA DIVERSUS Friedmann

JALISCO LONG-TAILED PARTRIDGE

Adult.—Similar to that of *D. m. griseipectus* but differing from it in having the lower back, rump, and upper tail coverts more olive-brown and with no or little black barring, in having the flanks and thighs more olive-brown, less barred, and in having the under tail coverts more brownish, less blackish, with less contrast between the dark areas and the whitish tips.

Juvenal.—Similar to the adult but with the subocular line and the auriculars hazel instead of black, the lateral portions of the feathers of the mantle olive buffy-brown instead of gray; the hazel shaft stripes on the underparts small and largely concealed, and the black feathers of the chin and upper throat with whitish bases and narrow shaft streaks.

Adult male.—Wing 153–161 (156); tail 138–149 (144.5); culmen from the base 20.6–20.8 (20.65); tarsus 50–53 (51.1); middle toe without claw 39.7–41.1 (40.2 mm.).[42]

Adult female.—Wing 141–151 (146); tail 119–141 (128.7); culmen from the base 19.5–20.8 (20.3); tarsus 47–47.5 (47.2); middle toe without claw 38–38.9 (38.3 mm.).[43]

Range.—Resident in the highland forests of northwestern Jalisco (Mascota and San Sebastián).

Type locality.—San Sebastián, Jalisco, Mexico.

Dendrortyx macroura griseipectus (not of Nelson, 1897) HELLMAYR and CONOVER, Cat. Birds Amer., i, No. 1, 1942, 225, part (San Sebastián, northwest of Mascota, Jalisco, Mexico).

[*Dendrortyx macroura*] *griseipectus* GRISCOM, Auk, liv, 1937, 192 in text.

Dendrortyx macroura diversus FRIEDMANN, Journ. Washington Acad. Sci., xxxiii, 1943, 273 (San Sebastián, Jalisco, Mexico; crit.; descr.; meas.).

---

[42] Four specimens, including the type.

[43] Three specimens.

DENDRORTYX MACROURA STRIATUS Nelson

GUERRERO LONG-TAILED PARTRIDGE

Adult.—Similar to that of the nominate race but with the crest feathers more extensively black, only narrowly tipped with hazel, the back and rump more olive brownish, less gray-brown, and with little or no transverse whitish and blackish flecking; the hazel shaft stripes longer and more pronounced on the feathers of the sides and extending posteriorly to include the feathers of flanks. This is the most variable of all the forms of the species (possibly it only seems so because of the far more extensive material of it available); thus two males from the same place and date present the two extremes. In one the sides and flanks and lower abdomen are pale buffy brown, in the other dark olive-brown; in the former the middle of the abdomen is very pale light drab, in the latter hair brown to pale olive-brown; in the former the lateral portions of the breast feathers are very pale light drab with a grayish tinge, in the latter light mouse gray; "bill and feet bright yellowish scarlet" (Goodknight).

Natal down.—Broad forehead and superciliaries chamois darkening to honey yellow over the eyes; middle of crown, occiput and nape auburn; entire upperparts of body and wings Brussels brown, obscurely banded on the dorsolateral portions of the body with dusky clove brown; chin, throat, and underpart of the body cream buff, brightest on the chin and throat and becoming tinged with tawny-olive on the sides and flanks which merge into the Brussels brown of the back; thighs pale Brussels brown; bill and feet yellowish (in dried skins).

Adult male.—Wing 143–167 (154.7); tail 132–175 (147.1); culmen from base 18.7–22.4 (20.8); tarsus 45.3–52 (49.5); middle toe without claw 37.4–43 (40.1 mm.).[44]

Adult female.—Wing 147–159 (151.6); tail 131–146 (138.3); culmen from the base 19.5–21.7 (20.8); tarsus 46.3–50 (48.5); middle toe without claw 37.6–39.5 (38.4 mm.).[45]

Range.—Resident in the highland forests of the southern part of the State of Jalisco (Sierra Nevada de Colima, Talpa, Los Masos) to Michoacán (Sierra Madre, Mount Tancitaro, Pátzcuaro, Patamban) and the Cordillera of Guerrero above 8,000 feet (Omilteme, Chilpancingo).

Type locality.—Chilpancingo, Guerrero, Mexico.

Dendrortyx macrourus (not *Ortyx macroura* Jardine and Selby) OGILVIE-GRANT, Cat. Birds Brit. Mus., xxii, 1893, 392, part (Guerrero).

Dendrortyx macrorus OGILVIE-GRANT, Handb. Game Birds, ii, 1897, 112, part (highlands of Guerrero).

---

[44] Twenty-one specimens from Guerrero and Michoacán.

[45] Twelve specimens from Guerrero and Michoacán.

Dendrortyx macrurus SALVIN and GODMAN, Biol. Centr.-Amer., Aves, iii, 1903, 287, part (Guerrero; Michoacán).

Dendrortyx macrourus striatus NELSON, Auk, xiv, 1897, 44 (Chilpancingo, Guerrero, sw. Mexico, coll. U. S. Nat. Mus.).—OGILVIE-GRANT, Ibis, 1902, 237.—GRISCOM, Bull. Mus. Comp. Zool., lxxv, 1934, 422 (Guerrero).

D[endrortyx] macrourus striatus NELSON, Auk, xix, 1902, 388.—SALVIN and GODMAN, Biol. Centr.-Amer., Aves, iii, 1903, 288, in text (crit.).

Dendrortyx macroura striatus PETERS, Check-list Birds of World, ii, 1934, 42.— GRISCOM, Auk, liv, 1937, 192, (Omilteme, Guerrero, spec.; crit.).—HELLMAYR and CONOVER, Cat. Birds. Amer., i, No. 1, 1942, 226 (syn.; distr.).

D[endrortyx] m[acroura] striatus FRIEDMANN, Journ. Washington Acad. Sci., xxxiii, 1943, 272 in text, 273 in text (crit.).

[Dendrortyx] striatus SHARPE, Hand-list, i, 1899, 43.

Dendrortyx macrourus dilutus NELSON, Auk, xvii, 1900, 254 (Pátzcuaro, Michoacán, sw. Mexico; coll. U. S. Nat. Mus.).—OGILVIE-GRANT, Ibis, 1902, 237.

D[endrortyx] macrourus dilutus NELSON, Auk, xix, 1902, 388.

Dendrortyx macroura dilutus PETERS, Check-list Birds of World, ii, 1934, 42.

DENDRORTYX MACROURA OAXACAE Nelson

OAXACA LONG-TAILED PARTRIDGE

Adult.—Similar to that of the nominate race but with the superciliary and malar stripes not white and conspicuous but heavily suffused with brownish, reducing markedly the contrast between them and the adjacent hazel areas, and with the broad brown shaft stripes on the breast and hindneck and interscapulars darker—bright argus brown to almost chestnut, and with the back, rump, and upper tail coverts less barred with blackish, more like *D. m. diversus* in these parts.

Other plumages unknown.

Adult male.—Wing 156; tail 140; culmen from the base 19.5; tarsus 49; middle toe without claw 38 mm. (1 specimen, the type).

Adult female.—Wing 152; tail 122; culmen from the base 19.7; tarsus 50; middle toe without claw 37 mm. (1 specimen).

Range.—Resident in the mountain forests of eastern Oaxaca from the Cerro San Felipe, near Oaxaca City, to Mount Zempoaltepec.

Type locality.—Totontepec, Oaxaca, Mexico.

Dendrortyx oaxacae NELSON, Auk, xiv, 1897, 43 (Totontepec, Oaxaca; coll. U. S. Nat. Mus.); xix, 1902, 388 (crit.).—OGILVIE-GRANT, Ibis, 1902, 237.

D[endrortyx] oaxacae SALVIN and GODMAN, Biol. Centr.-Amer., Aves, iii, 1903, 288, in text (crit.).

[Dendrortyx] oaxacae SHARPE, Hand-list, i, 1899, 43.

Dendrortyx macrourus OGILVIE-GRANT, Cat. Birds Brit. Mus., xxii, 1893, 392, part (Tonaguia, Oaxaca).

Dendrortyx macrurus SALVIN and GODMAN, Biol. Centr.-Amer., Aves, iii, 1903, 287, part (e. Oaxaca).

Dendrortyx macroura oaxacae PETERS, Check-list Birds of World, ii, 1934, 43.— HELLMAYR and CONOVER, Cat. Birds Amer. i, No. 1, 1942, 226 (syn.; distr.).

[Dendrortyx macroura] oaxacae GRISCOM, Auk, liv, 1937, 192 in text.

DENDRORTYX LEUCOPHRYS LEUCOPHRYS (Gould)

GUATEMALAN LONG-TAILED PARTRIDGE

Adult (sexes alike in coloration).—Forehead, anterior part of crown, and superciliaries light ivory yellow to pale pinkish buff; rest of crown and occiput dull sepia tinged, especially terminally and posteriorly, with russet; feathers of nape and the interscapulars bright russet to bay prominently edged with white, the longest, most posterior interscapulars with the white replaced by neutral gray and these edgings broader; median and lesser upper wing coverts between bright buffy brown and isabella color, very slightly darker and more rufescent along the shafts; greater upper wing coverts more rufescent, washed with orange-cinnamon, and with numerous transverse irregular markings of pale isabella color, each of these markings bordered proximally with clove brown; scapulars buffy brown paling laterally to brownish olive-gray and darkening medially to Saccardo's umber tinged with russet; secondaries pale cinnamon-brown mottled and flecked with Prout's brown to mummy brown, these mottlings most strongly developed on the inner secondaries; primaries externally bright tawny with a slight orange tinge, their inner webs duller and indistinctly mottled with Prout's brown, the darker color increasing toward the inner edge of the feathers; upper back like the interscapulars but with the bright bay of their median part replaced by tawny-russet transversely flecked with blackish, and with the gray lateral parts tinged with buffy brown and indistinctly barred with dusky clove brown; rest of back, rump, and upper tail coverts buffy brown, indistinctly crossed by fine dusky bars, the lower rump and upper tail coverts with whitish transverse markings proximally and distally edged with blackish; lateral rectrices bright russet, the median ones with this color largely restricted to a broad indistinct shaft stripe the rest of the feathers abundantly crossed by transverse zigzag markings of light ochraceous-buff, each of which markings is broadly edged on both sides by clove brown; suboculars and auriculars dull sepia; chin and upper throat white; sides of throat and lower throat bright russet to tawny-russet, each feather edged with light neutral gray; breast feathers similar but with the edges broader and darker—neutral gray—and the centers paler—tawny-russet to tawny; upper and lateral parts of abdomen and sides pale grayish buffy brown, most grayish on the upper abdomen, and with tawny to ochraceous-tawny shaft stripes; lower middle of abdomen, flanks, and under tail coverts darkening, especially posteriorly, to dusky olive-brown; under wing coverts dull cinnamon-brown; bare skin around eye, tarsi, and toes orange-red; bill black, lower mandible orange below; iris grayish olive.

Other plumages unknown.

Adult male.—Wing 146.3; tail 128; culmen from the base 18.1; tarsus 53.3; middle toe without claw 49.1 mm. (1 specimen).

Adult female.—Wing 139; tail 123.7; culmen from the base 18.5; tarsus 49; middle toe without claw 36.7 mm. (1 specimen).

Range.—Resident in the highlands of northern Guatemala above 3,000 feet, in states of Alta Vera Paz (Cobán, Finca Sepacuite), Huetuetenango (Barrillos), and El Quiché (Nebaj).

Type locality.—Cobán, Guatemala.

Ortyx leucophrys GOULD, Proc. Zool. Soc. London, 1843 (1844), 132 (Cobán, Vera Paz, Guatemala; coll. Derby Mus., now Liverpool Mus.).

Dendrortyx leucophrys GOULD, Mon. Odontoph., pt. 2, 1846, pl. 21 and text.—SCLATER and SALVIN, Ibis, 1859, 226 (Cobán, Guatemala).—GRAY, List Birds Brit. Mus., pt. 5, Gallinae, 1867, 73.—OGILVIE-GRANT, Cat. Birds Brit. Mus., xxii, 1893, 394, part (Dueñas, Guatemala); Handb. Game Birds, 1897, ii, 114, part.—SALVIN and GODMAN, Biol. Centr.-Amer., Aves, iii, 1903, 289 part (Cobán, Dueñas).

D[endrortyx] leucophrys REICHENOW, Die Vögel, i, 1913, 315.

[Dendrortyx] leucophrys GRAY, Hand-list, ii, 1870, 272, No. 9772.—SCLATER and SALVIN, Nom. Av. Neotr., 1873, 138.—SHARPE, Hand-list, i, 1899, 44, part.

Dendrortyx leucophrys leucophrys GRISCOM, Bull. Amer. Mus. Nat. Hist., lxiv, 1932, 105 (Sepacuite, Guatemala; habits; distr.).—PETERS, Check-list Birds of World, ii, 1934, 43.—HELLMAYR and CONOVER, Cat. Birds Amer., i, No. 1, 1942, 227, part (syn.; distr.; Guatemala).

Dendrortyx l[eucophrys] leucophrys MILLER and GRISCOM, Amer. Mus. Nov. No. 183, 1925, 2 (Guatemala).

D[endrortyx] l[eucophrys] leucophrys DICKEY and VAN ROSSEM, Birds El Salvador, 1938, 156, in text (El Salvador; possibly Volcán de Santa Ana; Guatemala).

[Dendrortyx leucophrys] leucophrys WETMORE, Proc. U. S. Nat. Mus., lxxxix, 1941, 535, in text (crit.).

DENDRORTYX LEUCOPHRYS NICARAGUAE Miller and Griscom

NICARAGUAN LONG-TAILED PARTRIDGE

Adult.—Similar to that of the nominate race but with the abdomen, sides, and flanks less buffy brown, more grayish; the gray of the margins of the feathers of the breast somewhat darker pale gray to dark gull gray; the russet to bay centers of the feathers of the lower throat, breast, and the paler ochraceous-tawny ones of the abdomen, sides, and flanks, reduced in size and duller in color, those of the lower throat and breast occasionally tinged and edged with blackish; ground color of the back, rump, and upper tail coverts darker, less greenish olive, more brownish; and auriculars dark sooty gray, occasionally tinged with brownish; "iris, grayish olive or yellowish hazel; bill, black; bare skin of ocular area, bright red, lower eyelid, flesh color; tarsi and feet, dull, brownish red or dark orange-red; feet slightly darker. These slight differences do not seem to be correlated with sex or season."[46]

First "winter" plumage.—Very similar to that of the adult but with the upper throat streaked with sooty and the dark dull sepia of the crown extending forward over the eyes and to the base of the culmen leaving only a large loreal and supraloreal buffy whitish area on each side; the

---

[46] *Ex* Dickey and van Rossem, Birds of El Salvador, 1938, 158.

auriculars brownish; rectrices with their marking more definitely arranged in bars; remiges more pointed.

Juvenal.—Forehead, broad superciliaries, and lores pale cream buff; center of crown dusky sepia anteriorly becoming bister to snuff brown posteriorly and on the occiput; interscapulars bright tawny-olive to Sayal brown with narrow whitish shaft streaks which broaden out terminally into triangular spots, the whitish shafts edged laterally with clove brown, which extends out laterally as incomplete bars of the same; upper wing coverts similar but with dusky clove brown shafts, the greater coverts tipped with buffy white, edged with blackish proximally; scapulars and secondaries bright tawny-olive to bright dark ochraceous-tawny heavily mottled with clove brown and irregularly and incompletely barred with pale cinnamon-buff; primaries as in adults but more pointed terminally; back, lower back, rump, and upper tail coverts as in adult but indistinctly but abundantly barred with Saccardo's umber; all the rectrices snuff brown barred with cinnamon, each of the cinnamon bars broadly edged on both sides with blackish; chin and upper throat pale cream buff but the feathers with dusky shaft streaks; lower throat, breast, abdomen, sides, and flanks dark hair brown to pale sepia, the feathers with distally spreading triangular terminal spots of white or cinnamon-buff, terminally edged with blackish.

Natal down.—Apparently unknown.

Adult male.—Wing 138–155 (146.2); tail 113–149 (131.6); culmen from base 18.7–20.8 (19.7); tarsus 48.8–54 (51.7); middle toe without claw 36.2–50 (40.5 mm.).[47]

Adult female.—Wing 129.9–142.6 (134.8); tail 107.8–124.1 (118.6); culmen from base 17.6–19.2 (18.4); tarsus 49.0–55.5 (50.9); middle toe without claw 35–47.7 (40.0 mm.).[48]

Range.—Resident in second growth and brushy places from the upper limits of the Arid Lower Tropical Zone to over 9,000 feet in the Humid Upper Tropical Zone, from the Pacific Cordillera of Guatemala (Sierra Santa Elena, Panajachel, and Sololá), the higher mountains throughout El Salvador (Volcán de San Miguel, Volcán de Santa Ana, Mount Cacaguatique, Los Esesmiles, San José del Sacare), and Honduras (Tegucigalpa; Alto Contoral; Cerro Contoral; Santa Bárbara; Yaro, Santa Marta; Rancho Quemada, La Libertad Copan) to northern Nicaragua (Jalapa).[49]

---

[47] Twenty specimens from Honduras, Nicaragua, and the Pacific slopes of Guatemala.

[48] Twelve specimens from Honduras, Nicaragua, and El Salvador.

[49] Birds from the Pacific Cordillera of Guatemala and from El Salvador are intermediate between this form and the nominate race. I have seen specimens from the former area that are clearly *nicaraguae* and others from El Salvador that are just as clearly *leucophrys*. Inasmuch as the bulk are nearer to *nicaraguae* I put them all in this form.

Type locality.—Jalapa, Nicaragua.

Dendrortyx leucophrys (not of Gould) SALVIN and GODMAN, Biol. Centr.-Amer., Aves, iii, 1903, 289, part (Panajachel, Sololá, Pacific Cordillera of Guatemala).

Dendrortyx leucophrys leucophrys HELLMAYR and CONOVER, Cat. Birds Amer., i, No. 1, 1942, 227 part (syn.; distr.; Honduras, Nicaragua).

Dendrortyx leucophrys nicaraguae PETERS, Check-list Birds of World, ii, 1934, 43.—
  DICKEY and VAN ROSSEM, Birds El Salvador, 1938, 156 (El Salvador—Volcán de San Miguel, Mount Cacaguatique, and Los Esesmiles; spec.; habits; colors of soft parts; crit.).—WETMORE, Proc. U. S. Nat. Mus., lxxxix, 1941, 534 (Sierra Santa Elena, west-central Guatemala; spec.; crit.).—HELLMAYR and CONOVER, Cat. Birds Amer., i, No. 1, 1942, 227 (syn.; distr.).

Dendrortyx leucophrys nicaraguæ MILLER and GRISCOM, Amer. Mus. Nov. No. 183, 1925, 1 (Jalapa, Nicaragua, alt. 4,000 feet; type in Amer. Mus. Nat. Hist.).—
  GRISCOM, Ibis, 1935, 549 (Panajachel, Sololá, Pacific Cordillera of Guatemala; crit.).

Dendrortyx l[eucophrys] nicaraguæ MILLER and GRISCOM, Amer. Mus. Nov., No. 183, 1925, 2 (Jalapa).

DENDRORTYX LEUCOPHRYS HYPOSPODIUS Salvin

COSTA RICAN LONG-TAILED PARTRIDGE

Adult.—Similar to that of *D. leucophrys nicaraguae* but with the median streaks on the feathers of the lower throat and breast much darker—dark bay edged broadly with black; the streaks thinning out to narrow blackish shaft lines on the feathers of the abdomen, only the feathers of the sides and flanks with tawny to ochraceous-tawny shaft streaks; and the gray tone of the underparts generally darker—neutral gray to deep neutral gray.

First winter plumage.—Similar to that of *D. leucophrys nicaraguae* but generally darker and without the tawny shaft stripes on the feathers of the sides and abdomen, the median stripes on the breast feathers narrower and darker—dark bay narrowly edged with black.

Other plumages apparently unknown.

Adult male.—Wing 149.9–160 (152.4); tail 132.4–145 (137.8); culmen from the base 19.1–20.3 (19.9); tarsus 51.7–55 (53); middle toe without claw 41.1–41.5 (41.2 mm.).[50]

Adult female.—Wing 143–153 (147.1); tail 116–157 (132.5); culmen from base 19.9–20.9 (20.4); tarsus 50.3–51.8 (50.9); middle toe without claw 39.9–40.4 (40.1 mm.).[51]

Range.—Resident in the higher mountains of Costa Rica (Alajuela, Azahár de Cartago, Dota, Estrella de Cartago, La Palma de San José, Las Cruces de Candelaria, Poás, Volcán de Irazú, Agua Caliente, Pacaca, Navarro).

Type locality.—Azahár de Cartago, Costa Rica.

---

[50] Six specimens.
[51] Five specimens.

Dendrortyx leucophrys (not of Gould) LAWRENCE, Ann. Lyc. Nat. Hist. New York,
 ix, 1868, 140 (Dota and Las Cruces de Candelaria, Costa Rica).—FRANTZIUS,
 Journ. für. Orn., xvii, 1869, 373 (Costa Rica).—BOUCARD, Proc. Zool. Soc.
 London, 1878, 42 (Volcán de Irazú, Costa Rica, 7,000 feet).—ZELEDÓN, Anal.
 Mus. Nac. Costa Rica, i, 1888, 128 (La Palma de San José, Costa Rica).—
 OGILVIE-GRANT, Cat. Birds Brit. Mus., xxii, 1893, 394, part (Costa Rica);
 Handb. Game Birds, ii, 1897, 114, part (Costa Rica).—SALVIN and GODMAN,
 Biol. Centr.-Amer., Aves, iii, 1903, 289, part (Las Cruces de Candelaria, La
 Palma de José, Dota Mountains, Poás, and Volcán de Irazú, Costa Rica).
Dendrortyx hypospodius SALVIN, Bull. Brit. Orn. Club, vi, 1896, v ("Azalia," *i.e.*
 Azahár de Cartago, Costa Rica; coll. Salvin and Godman); Ibis, 1897, 112
 (reprint of descr.).—SALVIN and GODMAN, Biol. Centr.-Amer., Aves, iii, 1903,
 289, part (Azahár de Cartago, Estrella de Cartago, Alajuela, and La Palma de
 San José, Costa Rica).—CARRIKER, Ann. Carnegie Mus., vi, 1910, 385 (Volcán
 de Irazú, Costa Rica).—PETERS, Check-list Birds of World, ii, 1934, 42.
[*Dendrortyx*] *hypospodius* SHARPE, Hand-list, i, 1899, 44.
Dendrortyx leucophrys hypospodius HELLMAYR and CONOVER, Cat. Birds Amer., i,
 No. 1, 1942, 228 (syn.; distr.).
[*Dendrortyx leucophrys*] *hypospodius* WETMORE, Proc. U. S. Nat. Mus., lxxxix,
 1941, 535 in text (Costa Rica; crit.).

Genus OREORTYX Baird

Oreortyx BAIRD, Rep. Pacific R. R. Surv., ix, 1858, xlv, 642. (Type, by original
 designation, *Ortyx picta* Douglas.)
Oreoortyx (emendation) SCLATER, Proc. Zool. Soc. London, 1859, 236.
Orortyx (emendation) COUES, Check List North Amer. Birds, ed. 2, 1882, 98.
Callipepla REICHENOW, Die Vögel, i, 1913, 317, part.

Rather large Odontophorinae (wing about 130–140 mm.) with tarsus
less than one-third as long as wing, tail less than three-fifths as long as
wing, scapulars, tertials, and rump unspotted, flanks broadly banded with
chestnut, white, and black, chest plain slate-gray, and crown with a long,
slender crest of two plumes.

Bill relatively small, the chord of culmen (from extreme base) much
less than half as long as tarsus (but slightly exceeding length of basal
phalanx of middle toe; depth of bill at base slightly exceeding distance
from anterior end of nasal fossa to tip of maxilla, slightly exceeding its
width at rictus; culmen moderately convex, not distinctly ridged (the
ridge rather broad and rounded). Outermost primary intermediate in
length between seventh and eighth (from outside), the fourth and fifth
longest. Tail scarcely more than half as long as wing, moderately rounded,
the rectrices (12) firm, broad, and rounded at tips. Tarsus decidedly
less than one-third as long as wing, shorter than middle toe with claw,
the planta tarsi mostly covered on outer side by a posterior continuous
series of rather large transverse scutella, the inner side covered by smaller,
more hexagonal scales.

Plumage and coloration.—A conspicuous crest of two elongated, slender,
nearly straight plumes springing from center of vertex, their webs con-

duplicate, the upper and longer plume slightly recurved distally and enclosing the lower and shorter one. Upperparts plain olive, the inner webs of tertials edged with buff; malar and suborbital regions, throat, and foreneck chestnut, margined posteriorly by a white stripe; rest of

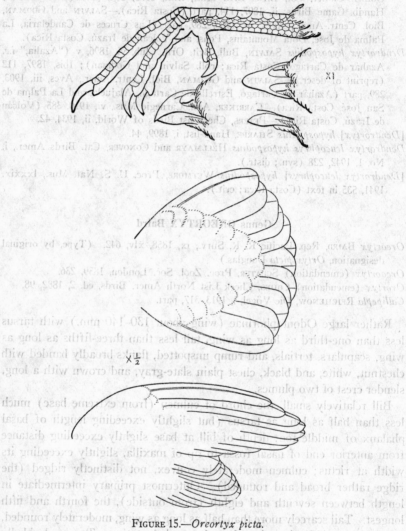

FIGURE 15.—*Oreortyx picta.*

head and neck, and breast, plain slate-gray, the crest black; sides and flanks broadly banded with chestnut, black, and white. Sexes alike in color.

Range.—Mountains near Pacific coast of North America, from southern Washington to northern Baja California. (Monotypic.)

KEY TO THE FORMS (ADULTS IN FRESH PLUMAGE) OF OREORTYX PICTA (DOUGLAS)

a. Brown of the back darker, between dark olive-brown and sepia, and extending anteriorly over the mantle and nape to the base of the occipital crest (southwestern Washington, western Oregon, and western California, south to San Luis Obispo County)....................**Oreortyx picta palmeri** (p. 255)

aa. Brown of the back paler, seldom darker than dark buffy brown, and grayer, and usually not extending anteriorly beyond the interscapulars, the mantle usually slate-gray but occasionally washed with buffy brown.

    b. Brown of the black more olivaceous than grayish; the mantle washed with buffy brown (southern Washington east of Cascades to Nevada).

                                         Oreortyx picta picta (p. 258)

    bb. Brown of the back more grayish than olivaceous, the mantle almost always pure slate-gray.

        c. Breast paler, between light neutral gray and deep gull gray (southern and west-central California)..........**Oreortyx picta eremophila** (p. 262)[52]

        cc. Breast darker, between neutral gray and dark gull gray (Baja California).

                                  Oreortyx picta confinis (p. 261)

OREORTYX PICTA PALMERI Oberholser

NORTHWESTERN MOUNTAIN QUAIL

Adult male.—Forehead narrowly white or pale buffy white; crown slate-gray to slate color; occipital crest of long narrow black feathers; rest of occiput, nape, and anterior interscapulars similar but heavily washed with dark olive-brown (sometimes to the virtual exclusion of the slate color); rest of interscapulars, back, lower back, rump, upper tail coverts, and upper wing coverts dark olive-brown; innermost secondaries and their greater upper coverts similar but internally edged with white to pale ochraceous-white and very narrowly tipped with the same; outer secondaries and the primaries fuscous washed with olive-brown on their outer webs; rectrices fuscous very finely speckled and vermiculated with olive-brown; lores and narrow superciliary stripe white; chin white; throat and cheeks dark bright chestnut becoming blackish under the eye, posterior to the lores, and on the posterior edge of the cheeks and throat, a broad white line from the eye runs posteroventrally to the lateroposterior corner of the throat separating the chestnut area from the slate-gray to slate-color sides of the neck and of the breast; posterior breast feathers slate-gray to slate color very broadly tipped with dark bright chestnut; sides of lower breast and upper and lateral parts of abdomen dark bright chestnut broadly barred with white, the white bars often proximally edged with blackish brown; flanks tawny-russet with concealed, subterminal blackish bands; thighs pale tawny-buff; middle of lower abdomen

---

[52] Doubtfully distinct. This race is an intermediate group combining characters of *picta* and of *confinis*. In series it can be made out as a faintly marked aggregate.

whitish, more or less tinged with pale tawny-buffy, the feathers grayish basally; under tail black with dark russet shafts; under wing coverts slate color washed with brownish; bill black, slightly brownish terminally; iris Vandyke brown; tarsi and toes pale sepia.

Adult female.—Similar to the male but smaller and with a shorter crest.

Juvenal (sexes alike).—Top of head, nape, interscapulars, and back between dark drab and hair brown, the feathers minutely speckled with buffy drab, many with a terminal triangular white shaft spot; long occipital crest feathers dull fuscous banded on their terminal third with tawny-drab; lower back, rump, and upper tail coverts similar but more rufescent—pale Saccardo's umber vermiculated and transversely mottled with black; upper wing coverts pale Saccardo's umber transversely vermiculated with black and each feather with a terminal shaft spot of white; innermost secondaries similar but with large black blotches; rest of secondaries and all the primaries dull fuscous, their outer webs heavily mottled and washed with pale Saccardo's umber; rectrices dusky grayish Saccardo's umber barred with black, the black wavy bars distally edged with pale grayish; a pale grayish line from the bill across the lores, through the eye to the posterodorsal angle of the auriculars; cheeks and auriculars and sides of neck like the upper back but slightly more grayish, less brownish; the cheeks also averaging paler; chin grayish white; throat, breast, and upper abdomen dusky hair brown with a slight slate tinge on the most posterior parts, and each feather with a small white median terminal spot; middle of abdomen grayish, the feathers edged and tipped with white; sides similar but with traces of dull chestnut; flanks, thighs, and under tail coverts pale cinnamon-brown.

Natal down.—Forehead, lores, broad supraorbital bands, sides of crown and occiput, sides of nape pale buffy or tawny-buff; center of crown, occiput, nape, and upperparts posteriorly to the tail deep chestnut-brown, this color narrowly bordered with black; on either side of this on the body is a whitish line followed, on the caudal half or so of the body, by a second blackish one, lateral to which the bird is pale Saccardo's umber transversely vermiculated with blackish and with whitish; wings pale Saccardo's umber the upper coverts and remiges, just sprouting, broadly tipped with pale buffy; a patch of deep chestnut brown on the band of the wing; chin, throat, and underparts of body whitish with a faint buffy tinge; sides, flanks, and thighs pale Saccardo's umber; bill and legs pale dull brown.

Adult male.—Wing 129–136 (131.2); tail 71–82 (76.5); culmen from base 15.7–17.9 (16.9); tarsus 35.0–37 (36.3); middle toe without claw 29.1–32.9 (31.4 mm.).[53]

---

[53] Eleven specimens from western Washington, Oregon, and California.

Adult female.—Wing 125–134 (130.2); tail 69–79 (74.4); culmen from base 15.3–16.5 (16.0); tarsus 33.6–36.4 (35.1); middle toe without claw 27.2–32.3 (29.9 mm.).[54]

Range.—Resident in the humid coastal area from southwestern Washington (Cedarville, Columbia River, San Juan Island, Tacoma, Puget Sound) south through western Oregon (coastal counties, and in the Willamette Valley, including the west slope of the Cascades at least as far south as Eugene) to western California as far as San Luis Obispo County.

Introduced into Vancouver Island; erroneously (?) reported from Kalama, British Columbia.

Type locality.—Yaquina, Oreg.

Oreortyx pictus (not *Ortyx picta* Douglas) BAIRD, Rep. Pacific R. R. Surv., ix, 1858, 642, part; Cat. North Amer. Birds, 1859, No. 473, part; *in* Cooper, Orn. California, Land Birds, 1870, 546, part.—COOPER and SUCKLEY, Rep. Pacific R. R. Surv., xii, book ii, pt. 3, 1860, 225 (Vancouver, Washington, Willamette Valley, Oreg.).—COUES, Check List North Amer. Birds, 1874, No. 390, part.—BAIRD, BREWER, and RIDGWAY, Hist. North Amer. Birds iii, 1874, 475, part.—AMERICAN ORNITHOLOGISTS' UNION, Check-list, 1886, No. 292, part.—ANTHONY, Auk, iii, 1886, 164 (Washington County, Oreg.).—CHAPMAN, Bull. Amer. Mus. Nat. Hist., iii, 1890, 133 (Kalama, British Columbia, flock of about 20).—RHOADS, Proc. Acad. Nat. Sci. Philadelphia, 1893, 37 (Nisqually, British Columbia, introduced; Tacoma, Wash., indigenous).—OGILVIE-GRANT, Cat. Birds Brit. Mus., xxii, 1893, 397, part (Portland, Oreg.; Cloverdale and San Francisco, Calif.).—MACOUN, Cat. Can. Birds, 1900, 197 (Vancouver Island; introduced).—McGREGOR, Pacific Coast Avif., No. 2, 1901, 5 (California; Santa Cruz Mountains; rare; breeds).—BAILEY, Handb. Birds Western United States, 1902, 117, part (descr.; distr.).—JUDD, U. S. Biol. Surv. Bull., 1905, 58, part (range; habits; food).—BOWLES, Auk, xxiii, 1906, 142 (Tacoma, Wash., resident; introduced?). —KERMODE, [Visitors' Guide] Publ. Provinc. Mus., 1909, 40 (Vancouver Island; introduced).—DAWSON and BOWLES, Birds of Washington, ii, 1909, 564 (Washington; habits; distr.).—MACOUN and MACOUN, Cat. Can. Birds, ed. 2, 1909, 215 (Vancouver Island; introd.; common).

[*Oreortyx*] *pictus* COUES, Key North Amer. Birds, 1872, 237 part.—SHARPE, Handlist, i, 1899, 44, part.

O[reortyx] pictus RIDGWAY, Man. North Amer. Birds, 1887, 191, part; Auk, xi, 1894, 195 part (crit.; range).

Oreortyx picta RIDGWAY, Proc. U. S. Nat. Mus., iii, 1880, 196, part; Nom. North Amer. Birds, 1881, No. 481, part.—TAVERNER, Birds Western Canada, 1926, 161 (Vancouver Island; introd.); Birds Canada, 1934, 165, in text (introd.); Can. Water Birds, 1939, 176 (Vancouver Island; introd.).—ALFORD, Ibis, 1928, 196 (Vancouver Island).—CLARK, Condor, xxxii, 1930, 51 (Mount St. Helena, Napa County, Calif.).

Oreoortyx pictus SCLATER, Proc. Zool. Soc. London, 1859, 236 (Vancouver Island).

Orortyx pictus COUES, Check List, ed. 2, 1882, No. 574, part.

O[rortyx] pictus COUES, Key North Amer. Birds, ed. 2, 1884, 591, part.

[*Oreortyx pictus*] Var. *pictus* BAIRD, BREWER, and RIDGWAY, Hist. North Amer. Birds, iii, 1874, 476, part.

---

[54] Eight specimens from western Washington, Oregon, and California.

Oreortyx pictus pictus, GRINNELL, Pacific Coast Avif., No. 3, 1902, 29 (California; common; distr.).

Oreortyx p[ictus] pictus JENKINS, Condor, viii, 1906, 125 (Monterey County, Calif., above 2,000 feet; habits).

Oreortyx picta picta AMERICAN ORNITHOLOGISTS' UNION, Check-list, ed. 3, 1910, 135, part.—BOWLES, Auk, xxviii, 1911, 172 (Tacoma, Wash., and most of Puget Sound district, resident).—GRINNELL, Pacific Coast Avif., No. 8, 1912, 10 (California; listed); No. 11, 1915, 58 (humid coast belt from Humboldt County to Sonoma County in Santa Cruz Mountains).—KELLOGG, Univ. California Publ. Zool., xii, 1916, 379 (Helena, Bear Creek, Castle Lake, and n. fork of Copper Creek, n. California; crit.).—KIMBALL, Condor, xxiv, 1922, 96 (near Adams, Lake County, Calif.).—DAWSON, Birds California (stud. ed.), iii, 1923, 1570 (California; habits).—OBERHOLSER, Auk, xli, 1924, 592 (syn.).—TAVERNER, Birds Western Canada, 1926, 162 in text (introduced); Birds Canada, 1934, 165, in text.—HALL, Murrelet, xiv, 1933, 64, footnote, 70 (history of discovery; spec. Multnomah County, Oreg., 1805, *ex* Lewis and Clark Exped.).—GRIFFEE and RAPRAEGER, Murrelet, xviii, 1937, 16 (Portland, Oreg.; nesting dates).

Callipepla picta NEWBERRY, Rep. Pacific R. R. Surv., vi, pt. 4, 1857, 93, part (hills bordering Willamette Valley, Oreg.; habits).

Lophortyx plumifera NUTTALL, Man. Orn. United States and Canada, Land Birds, ed. 2, 1840, 791 (Willamette Valley).

Oreortyx pictus plumiferus AMERICAN ORNITHOLOGISTS' UNION, Check-list, 1886, No. 292a, part.—WOODCOCK, Oregon Agr. Exp. Stat. Bull. 68, 1902, 25 (w. slope Cascade Mountains, Oreg.).—ANDERSON and GRINNELL, Proc. Acad. Nat. Sci. Philadelphia, 1903, 6 (Siskiyou Mountains, n. Calif.).—RAY, Auk, xx, 1903, 182 (Lake Valley, centr. Sierra Nevada, 6,500 ft.).—STONE, Proc. Acad. Nat. Sci. Philadelphia, 1904, 580 (Mount Sanhedrin, e. Mendocino County, Calif.).

O[reortyx] pictus plumiferus RIDGWAY, Man. North Amer. Birds, 1887, 191.

[Oreortyx] plumiferus SHARPE, Hand-list, i, 1899, 44.

Oreortyx picta palmeri OBERHOLSER, Auk, xl, 1923, 84 (Yaquina, Oreg.; coll. U. S. Nat. Mus.); Auk, xli, 1924, 592 (syn.).—PALMER, Condor, xxx, 1928, 291, in text (patronymics).—AMERICAN ORNITHOLOGISTS' UNION, Check-list, ed. 4, 1931, 90. —BENT, U. S. Nat. Mus. Bull. 162, 1932, 40 (life hist., distr.).—CAUM, Occ. Pap. Bishop Mus., x, No. 9, 1933, 14 (Hawaii; introduced; not known to have become established).—PETERS, Check-list Birds of World, ii, 1934, 43.—MILLER, LUMLEY, and HALL, Murrelet, xvi, 1935, 57 (Washington, San Juan Islands; introduced). —VAN ROSSEM, Condor, xxxix, 1937, 21 (crit.; distr.).—GABRIELSON and JEWETT, Birds of Oregon, 1940, 223 (Oregon; distr.; descr.; habits; photo of nest and eggs).—HELLMAYR and CONOVER, Cat. Birds Amer., i, No. 1, 1942, 227 (syn.; distr.).

OREORTYX PICTA PICTA (Douglas)

PLUMED MOUNTAIN QUAIL

Adult.—Similar to that of the corresponding sex of *O. picta palmeri,* but with the brown of the upper surface of the body and wings paler, buffy brown to dark buffy brown with an olivaceous tinge; the nape and mantle slate-gray, occasionally washed with buffy brown, but never solidly so as in *palmeri;* the forehead averaging paler, often whitish, the inner edges of the innermost secondaries and the scapulars paler light buff to buffy whitish.

Juvenal.—Similar to that of *O. picta palmeri* but generally somewhat more grayish above.

Natal down.—Not distinguishable from that of *O. picta palmeri.*

Adult male.—Wing 125–140 (131.8); tail 73–84 (81.7); culmen from base 15–17.6 (16.5); tarsus 33.1–38.2 (35.7); middle toe without claw 28.6–33.8 (30.5 mm.).[55]

Adult female.—Wing 126–135 (129.2); tail 71–79 (75.6), culmen from base 13.4–17.9 (16.1); tarsus 32–36.8 (34.8); middle toe without claw 27.3–32.9 (29.8 mm.).[55a]

Range.—Resident in the Transition Zone from southwestern Washington (where, however, introduced) south through Oregon east of the Cascades, and in the Rogue River Valley west of the Cascades (Jackson and Josephine Counties), and east to southwestern Idaho (Indian Creek, Boise Bottom, and Owyhee foothills), south through the Modoc region and the Sierra Nevada of California to about latitude 37°30′N. and to extreme western Nevada (east as far as Landon County); known from Esmeralda, Humboldt, Lander, Mineral, Ormsby, and Washoe Counties.

Formerly to New Mexico, whence its bones have been found in prehistoric, but recent, sites from north of Carlsbad.

Type locality.—Interior of New California=headquarters of the Umpqua River near the Calapooia Mountains, Oreg.; *fide* Oberholser, Auk, xl, 1923, 82.

Ortyx picta DOUGLAS, Philos. Mag., v, Jan. 1, 1829, 74 (headwaters of Umpqua River, near the Calapooia Mountains; see Oberholser, Auk, xl, 1923, 82).—LESSON, Traité d'Orn., 1831, 507.—BAILEY, Handb. Birds Western United States, 1902, 117, part.—PALMER, Condor, xxx, 1928, 277 in text.—WETMORE, Condor, xxxiv, 1932, 141 (bones in cave deposits, north of Carlsbad, N. Mex.).—HOWARD and MILLER, Condor, xxxv, 1933, 16 (bones, Organ Mountains, N. Mex.).—HALL, Murrelet, xiv, 1933, 69 in text, 64, footnote (history).—GROEBBELS, Der Vögel, ii, 1937, 238 in text (care of eggs), 402 in text (parental care).

O[rtyx] picta DOUGLAS, Trans. Linn. Soc. London, xvi, 1829, 143 ("interior of California, and . . . extending as far northward as 45° north latitude . . . within a few miles of the Columbia Valley"; habits).

Callipepla picta GOULD, Monogr. Odontoph., pt. 3, 1850, pl. 15.—BAIRD, Rep. Stansbury's Expl. Great Salt Lake, 1852, 334 (California).—NEWBERRY, Rep. Pacific R. R. Surv., vi, pt. 4, 1857, 93, part (Lassen Butte, Siskiyou, Calapoosa, and Trinity Mountains, n. California; habits).—BLAAUW, Ardea, xiv, 1925, 96, in text (California).

C[allipepla] picta REICHENOW, Die Vögel, i, 1913, 317.

Oreortyx pictus BAIRD, Cat. North Amer. Birds, 1859, No. 473, part; *in* Cooper, Orn. California, Land Birds, 1870, 546, part.—COUES, Check List North Amer. Birds, 1874, No. 390, part.—BAIRD, BREWER, and RIDGWAY, Hist. North Amer. Birds, iii, 1874, 475, part, pl. 63, fig. 5, 523, part (Sierra Nevada, 6,000 to 8,000 ft.).—NELSON, Proc. Boston Soc. Nat. Hist., xvii, 1875, 364 (Nevada City, Calif.).—

---

[55] Twenty-six specimens from Oregon, California, and Nevada.

[55a] Sixteen specimens from Oregon, California, and Nevada.

OGILVIE-GRANT, Cat. Birds Brit. Mus., xxii, 1893, 397, part (Bear Valley, Michigan Bluffs, Lake "Begles" = Bigler, i.e. Tahoe, Calaveras County, Sierra Nevada, and Walker's Basin, Calif.; Carson, Nev.).—AMERICAN ORNITHOLOGISTS' UNION, Check-list, ed. 2, 1895, 107; ed. 3, 1910, 135.—DWIGHT, Auk, xvii, 1900, 46 (molt, etc.).—WOODCOCK, Oregon Agr. Exp. Stat. Bull. 68, 1902, 25 (Oregon range).—JUDD, U. S. Biol. Surv. Bull. 21, 1905, 58, part (range; habits; food).—SETH-SMITH, L'Oiseau, x, 1929, 760 (care in captivity).

[*Oreortyx*] *pictus* COUES, Key North Amer. Birds, 1872, 237 part.

Oreortyx picta BELDING, Proc. U. S. Nat. Mus., i, 1879, 438 (Sierra Nevada, California, 4,000 to 8,000 ft.; habits, etc.).—HERMAN, JANKIEWICZ, and SAARNI, Condor, xliv, 1942, 169 in text (coccidiosis).—AMADON, Auk, lx, 1943, 226 (body weight and egg weight).

Oreortyx picta picta SHELTON, Univ. Oregon Bull., new ser., xiv, No. 4, 1917, 20, 26 (west central Oregon; breeds).—OBERHOLSER, Auk, xl, 1923, 84, part (range).— GRINNELL, DIXON, and LINSDALE, Univ. California Publ. Zool., xxxv, 1930, 210 (distr.; Lassen Peak region, n. California).—AMERICAN ORNITHOLOGISTS' UNION, Check-list, ed. 4, 1931, 91, part.—GABRIELSON, Condor, xxxiii, 1931, 112 (common, Cascades; nests, Butte Creek, Oreg.).—BENT, U. S. Nat. Mus., Bull. 162, 1932, 43 (habits; distr.).—PETERS, Check-list Birds of World, ii, 1934, 43, part.—LINSDALE, Pacific Coast Avif., No. 23, 1936, 23, 49 (Nevada; resident in mountains of western part).—VAN ROSSEM, Condor, xxxix, 1937, 22 (crit.; tax.; distr.; char.).—LINSDALE, Amer. Midl. Nat., xix, 1938, 54 (Toyabe Mountains, Nev.; nest; not common).—GABRIELSON and JEWETT, Birds Oregon, 1940, 225 (Oregon; distr.; descr.; habits).—VOGT, Condor, xliii, 1941, 162 (Lassen Volcanic National Park).—HELLMAYR and CONOVER, Cat. Birds Amer., i, No. 1, 1942, 228, part (syn.; distr.).—DIXON, Condor, xlv, 1943, 208 (Kings Canyon National Park, Calif.).

Oreortyx p[*icta*] *picta* GROEBBELS, Der Vögel, ii, 1937, 167 (data on breeding biology).

Orortyx picta COUES, Check-list, North Amer. Birds, ed. 2, 1882, No. 574, part.

O[*rortyx*] *picta* COUES, Key North Amer. Birds, ed. 2, 1884, 571, part.

Ortyx plumifera GOULD, Proc. Zool. Soc. London, 1837 (1838), 42 ("California"; coll. David Douglas).—AUDUBON, Synopsis, 1839, 200.

Ortix plumifera AUDUBON, Birds Amer., 8vo. ed., v, 1842, 69, pl. 291.

Perdix plumifera AUDUBON, Orn. Biogr., v, 1839, 226, pl. 423, figs. 1, 2 (Columbia River).

Ortyx plumifera OBERHOLSER, Auk, xl, 1923, 83 in text.

Oreortyx pictus plumifera RIDGWAY, Bull. Essex Inst., vii, 1875, 10 (w. Nevada).— FISHER, North Amer. Fauna, No. 7, 1893, 26 (Cajon Pass, Panamint Mountains, Argus Range, Coso Mountains, near Owens Lake, Sierra Liebre, Sequoia National Park, etc., Calif.; Mt. Magruder, Nev.).—AMERICAN ORNITHOLOGISTS' UNION, Check-list, ed. 2, 1895, 107; ed. 3, 1910, 135.—DAWSON and BOWLES, Birds of Washington, ii, 1909, 567 (Washington; habits; distr.).—TAYLOR, Univ. Calif. Publ. Zool., vii, 1912, 361 (mountains of Humboldt County, Nev., above 5,000 ft.).

Oreortyx pictus plumiferus RIDGWAY, Bull. Essex Inst., vii, 1875, 10 (e. of Sierra Nevada, Calif.); 13 (Carson City, Nev.).

[*Oreortyx pictus*] Var. *plumiferus* BAIRD, BREWER, and RIDGWAY, Hist. North Amer. Birds, iii, 1874, 476.

Oreortyx pictus . . . var. *plumifera* RIDGWAY, Bull. Essex Inst., vii, 1875, 39 (Nevada).

Oreortyx pictus β plumiferus RIDGWAY, Orn. 40th Parallel, 1877, 601 (Virginia Mountains, near Pyramid Lake, and near Carson, Nev.).

O[*reortyx*] *p*[*ictus*] *plumiferus* BAILEY, Handb. Birds Western United States, 1902, 117.

Oreortyx picta plumiferus GRINNELL, Pacific Coast Avif., No. 3, 1902, 29 (California; abundant resident of arid Transition Zone).

Oreortyx picta plumifera RIDGWAY, Proc. U. S. Nat. Mus., iii, 1880, 197; Nom. North Amer. Birds, 1881, No. 481a.—AMERICAN ORNITHOLOGISTS' UNION, Check-list, ed. 3, 1910, 135.—GRINNELL, Pacific Coast Avif., No. 8, 1912, 10 (California; listed); No. 11, 1915, 58 (California).—TYLER, Pacific Coast Avif., No. 9, 1913, 32 (Fresno, Calif.; resident in higher Sierras).—WILLETT, Condor, xxi, 1919, 202 (mountains w. of Warner Valley, se. Oregon).—OBERHOLSER, Auk, xl, 1923, 81, 82, 83, in text (crit.), 84 (distr.).—GRINNELL and STORER, Animal Life in Yosemite, 1924, 267 (descr.; distr.; habits; Yosemite).—GABRIELSON, Auk, xli, 1924, 555 (Imnaha Canyon, Wallowa County, Oreg.).—OBERHOLSER, Auk, xli, 1924, 592 (syn.).—RICHARDS, Condor, xxvi, 1924, 99 (Grass Valley distr., California).—WYMAN and BURNELL, Field Book Birds Southwestern United States, 1925, 84 (descr., distr.).—TAVERNER, Birds Western Canada, 1926, 162, in text.—WYTHE, Condor, xxix, 1927, 65 (ecol., distr.).—MAILLIARD, Proc. California Acad. Sci., ser. 4, xvi, 1927, 294 (Modoc County, Calif.; common).—GROEBBELS, Der Vögel, ii, 1937, 135, in text (one brood a year in higher altitudes, two a year in lower areas), 167 (data on breeding biology).

Oreortyx p[icta] plumifera HANNA, Condor, xxvi, 1924, 147, in text (egg weight).

[*Oreortyx picta*] *plumifera* WYMAN, Auk, xxix, 1912, 539, in text (Indian Creek, Boise bottom, Owyhee foothills, etc., w. Idaho).

OREORTYX PICTA CONFINIS Anthony

SOUTHERN MOUNTAIN QUAIL

Adult.—Similar to that of corresponding sex of *O. picta picta* but with the upperparts of the body and wings more grayish, less olivaceous, the mantle almost always pure grayish, not tinged with brownish; from *O. picta eremophila* it differs in having the breast darker, between neutral gray and dark gull gray; the posterior underparts are dark claret brown as in *eremophila*.

Juvenal.—Similar to that of *O. picta picta*.

Natal down.—Similar to that of *O. picta picta*.

Adult male.—Wing 132–139 (135.1); tail 79–92 (84.9); culmen from base 16.0–17.4 (16.9); tarsus 32.3–37.4 (35.7); middle toe without claw 25.0–30.8 (28.4 mm.).[56]

Adult female.—Wing 129–137 (132.8); tail 76–86 (79.4); culmen from base 15.9–17.0 (16.4); tarsus 32.7–36.0 (34.8); middle toe without claw 27.9–29.9 (28.7 mm.).[57]

Range.—Resident in the mountains of Baja California in the Sierra Juárez and Sierra San Pedro Mártir, north to the California boundary.

Type locality.—San Pedro Mártir Range, alt. 8,500 feet, Baja California.

Oreortyx picta plumifera (not *Ortyx plumifera* Gould) RIDGWAY, Proc. U. S. Nat. Mus., v, 1883, 533, footnote (Cape San Lucas, Baja California, April).—GRINNELL, Pacific Coast Avif., No. 11, 1915, 58, part.

---

[56] Ten specimens.
[57] Seven specimens.

Oreortyx picta confinis ANTHONY, Proc. California Acad. Sci., ser. 2, ii, 1889, 74
(San Pedro Mártir Mountains, at 8,500 feet, n. Baja California; coll. A. W.
Anthony).—AMERICAN ORNITHOLOGISTS' UNION, Check List, ed. 3, 1910, 135,
part; ed. 4, 1931, 91 (distr.).—OBERHOLSER, Auk, xi, 1923, 84, part (San Bernardino and San Gabriel Mountains, Calif.).—DAWSON, Birds California (stud.
ed.), iii, 1923, 1571 (genl.; California; part).—TODD, Ann. Carnegie Mus., xviii,
1928, 336 (type spec. in Carnegie Museum).—GRINNELL, Univ. California Publ.
Zool., xxxii, 1928, 100 (distr.; Baja California).—BENT, U. S. Nat. Mus., Bull.
162, 1932, 51 (habits; distr.).—PETERS, Check-list Birds of World, ii, 1934, 43.—
ROWLEY, Condor, xxxvii, 1935, 163 (nest and eggs; near La Paz, Lower California).—VAN ROSSEM, Condor, xxxix, 1937, 22 (crit.; distr.; chars.).—HELL-
MAYR and CONOVER, Cat. Birds Amer., i, No. 1, 1942, 230 (syn.; distr.).

O[reortyx] p[icta] confinis WILLETT, Pacific Coast Avif., No. 7, 1912, 43, in text
(does not occur in California).

Oreortyx pictus confinis BRYANT, Proc. California Acad. Sci., ser. 2, ii, 1889, 276
(San Pedro Mártir Mountains; nesting at from 2,500 to 9,000 feet, in winter
down to 1,000 feet).—ANTHONY, Zoë, i, 1890, 5 (descr. nest and eggs; etc.);
iv, 1893, 232 (San Pedro Mártir Mountains, crit.).—AMERICAN ORNITHOLOGISTS'
UNION, Auk, vii, 1890, 61 (Check-list No. 292b, part); ed. 2, 1895, 108; ed. 3,
1910, 135, part.—BENDIRE, Life Hist. North Amer. Birds, i, 1892, 17, part.—
RIDGWAY, Man. North Amer. Birds, ed. 2, 1896, 588, part.

[Oreortyx] confinis SHARPE, Hand-list, i, 1899, 44.

OREORTYX PICTA EREMOPHILA van Rossem

DESERT MOUNTAIN QUAIL

Adult.—Similar to that of the corresponding sex of *O. picta picta* but
averaging slightly paler on the upperparts and breast and darker brown
—claret brown—on the posterior underparts. This race, which is only
doubtfully valid, combines characters of *O. picta picta* and *O. picta confinis,* and numerous individuals occur that cannot be told from one or the
other of these two; only in a series can the average characters of *eremophila* be appreciated.

Juvenal.—Similar to that of *O. picta picta.*

Natal down.—Not distinguishable from that of *O. picta picta* or *O. picta
palmeri.*

Adult male.—Wing 127–140 (134.9); tail 74–89 (82.2); culmen from
base 15.7–17.9 (16.7); tarsus 35.5–37.7 (36.4); middle toe without claw
28.4–33.6 (30.3 mm.).[58]

Adult female.—Wing 128–138 (131.6); tail 72–86 (79.4); culmen from
base 15.4–17.2 (16.1); tarsus 34.9–36.3 (35.5); middle toe without claw
28.4–29.9 (29.3 mm.).[59]

Range.—Resident in the mountains of southern and west-central California from about latitude 37°30′N. in the Sierra Nevada south to the
Baja California boundary; also in extreme southwestern Nevada.

[58] Sixteen specimens.
[59] Eight specimens.

Type locality.—Lang Spring, Mountain Spring Canyon, Argus Mountains, Inyo County, Calif.

Oreortyx pictus (not *Ortyx picta* Douglas) BAIRD, Rep. Pacific R. R. Surv., ix, 1858, 642, part (Fort Tejon, Calif.) ; Cat. North Amer. Birds, 1859, No. 473, Part; *in* Cooper, Orn. California, Land Birds, 1870, 546, part.—XANTUS, Proc. Acad. Nat. Sci. Philadelphia, 1859, 192, (Fort Tejon).—COUES, Ibis, 1866, 266 (Cajon Pass, San Bernardino Mountains, s. California) ; Check List, North Amer. Birds, 1874, No. 390, part.—BAIRD, BREWER, and RIDGWAY, Hist. North Amer. Birds, iii, 1874, 475, part.—AMERICAN ORNITHOLOGISTS' UNION, Check-list, 1886, No. 292, part.—OGILVIE-GRANT, Cat. Birds Brit. Mus., xxii, 1893, 397, part (San Bernardino Mountains, and Ballena, Nigger Canyon, and Cuyamaca Mountains, San Diego County, Calif.).

O[reortyx] pictus RIDGWAY, Man. North Amer. Birds, 1887, 191, part; Auk, xi, 1894, 195, part (crit.; distr.).

[Oreortyx] pictus COUES, Key North Amer. Birds, 1872, 237, part.—SHARPE, Hand-list, i, 1899, 44, part.

Oreortyx picta RIDGWAY, Proc. U. S. Nat. Mus., iii, 1880, 196, part; Nomencl. North Amer. Birds, 1881, No. 481, part.—BAILEY, Handb. Birds Western United States, 1902, 117, part.

Orortyx pictus COUES, Check List, North Amer. Birds, ed. 2, 1882, No. 574, part.

O[rortyx] pictus COUES, Key North Amer. Birds, ed. 2, 1884, 591, part.

Oreortyx picta picta AMERICAN ORNITHOLOGISTS' UNION, Check-list, ed. 3, 1910, 135, part; ed. 4, 1931, 91, part.—OBERHOLSER, Auk, xl, 1923, 84, part.—WILLETT, Pacific Coast Avif., No. 21, 1933, 50 (sw. California; common Upper Sonoran zone of foothills up through Transition Zone in the higher mountains).—PETERS, Check-list Birds of World, ii, 1934, 43, part.—HELLMAYR and CONOVER, Cat. Birds Amer., i, No. 1, 1942, 228, part (syn.; distr.).

Callipepla picta HEERMANN, Rep. Pacific R. R. Surv., x, pt. 4, No. 2, 1859, 61 (near Tejon Valley, Calif.; habits).

Oreortyx picta plumifera (not *Ortyx plumifera* Gould) WILLETT, Pacific Coast Avif., No. 7, 1912, 42 (Pasadena, Calif.; San Gabriel Mountains; breeding in San Antonio Canyon; crit.).—GRINNELL, Univ. California Publ. Zool., x, 1913, 228 (San Jacinto Mountains, s. California; habits; crit.) ; Pacific Coast Avif., No. 11, 1915, 58, part (mountains of California except Pacific coastal belt).

Oreortyx pictus plumiferus GRINNELL, Pasadena Acad. Sci., Publ. 2, 1898, 19 (Los Angeles County, Calif.; resident) ; Auk, xxii, 1905, 381 (Mount Piños, Calif.) ; Birds San Bernardino Mountains, 1908, 56 (Breeding).

Oreortyx picta confinis AMERICAN ORNITHOLOGISTS' UNION, Check-list North Amer. Birds, ed. 3, 1910, 135, part.—WILLETT, Pacific Coast Avif., No. 7, 1912, 43, in text (distr.).—OBERHOLSER, Auk, xl, 1923, 84, part (San Bernardino and San Gabriel Mountains, s. Calif.).—DAWSON, Birds California (stud. ed.), iii, 1923, 1571, part.—GRINNELL, Condor, xxvii, 1925, 76 (San Bernardino and San Gabriel Mountains).

Oreortyx pictus confinis AMERICAN ORNITHOLOGISTS' UNION, Auk, vii, 1890, 61 (Check-list No. 292b, part) ; Check-list, ed. 2, 1895, 108, part.—BENDIRE, Life Hist. North Amer. Birds, i, 1892, 17, part.—RIDGWAY, Man. North Amer. Birds, ed. 2, 1895, 588, part.

Oreortyx picta eremophila VAN ROSSEM, Condor, xxxix, 1937, 22 (Lang Spring, Mountain Spring Canyon, Argus Mountains, Inyo County, Calif.; descr.; distr.; crit.).

Genus CALLIPEPLA Wagler

Callipepla WAGLER, Isis, 1832, 277. (Type, by monotypy, *C. strenua* Wagler = *Ortyx squamatus* Vigors.)
Calipepla (emendation) HARTLAUB, Arch. für Naturg., 1853, ii, 40.

Medium-sized Odontophorinae (wing about 112–127 mm.) with 14 rectrices, tail more than two-thirds (but less than three-fourths) as long as wing, crest rather short and bushy with its feathers not conduplicate, neck, chest, and breast conspicuously squamated, and sexes alike in coloration.

Bill relatively small, the chord of culmen (from extreme base) much less than half the length of tarsus, its depth at base not greater than dis-

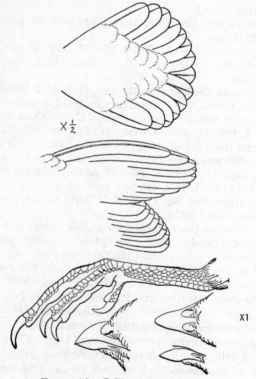

FIGURE 16.—*Callipepla squamata.*

tance from anterior end of nasal fossa to tip of maxilla and slightly less than its width at rictus; culmen not very strongly convex, broadly rounded. Outermost primary equal to eighth or very slightly shorter, the third, fourth, and fifth longest. Tail a little more than two-thirds (decidedly less than three-fourths) as long as wing, graduated (the graduation about equal to length of first two phalanges of middle toe), the rectrices (14) firm, slightly tapering terminally, but with rounded tips. Tarsus much less than one-third as long as wing, slightly shorter than middle toe with claw, the planta tarsi covered with hexagonal or rhomboidal scales, of which the more posterior (on both sides) are larger, more transverse, and form a more or less continuous row.

Plumage and coloration.—Crest bushy, occupying whole of pileum, but its central feathers longest, these rather soft, broad with rounded tips, their webs not conduplicate; contour feathers with very sharply defined regularly convex outlines, especially on neck, chest, and breast. Head light grayish brown, the crest tipped with dull white; neck and chest light bluish gray, the feathers (those of breast also) sharply margined with black, producing a conspicuous squamated effect; upperparts plain light brownish gray or drab, the inner webs of tertials edged with buff or buffy whitish. Sexes alike in coloration.

Range.—Mexican plateau and contiguous portion of United States, from southern Texas to Arizona. (Monotypic.)

KEY TO THE FORMS OF CALLIPEPLA SQUAMATA (VIGORS)

a. Scapulars and upper surface of wings deep grayish brown; posterior lower parts deep buffy to ochraceous; the abdomen with an extensive patch of rusty chestnut in the male and usually with an indication of it in the female (south-central Texas to northeastern Mexico)..**Callipepla squamata castanogastris** (p. 269)

aa. Scapulars and upper surface of wings pale grayish brown or brownish gray; abdomen pale buffy or whitish; usually without trace of chestnut in either sex.

   b. Breast and upper back plumbeous-gray, lower back and rump dusky olive-brown abdomen, especially in the male, strongly suffused with yellowish brown (Valley of Mexico from southern Coahuila south to near City of Mexico)......................**Callipepla squamata squamata** (p. 270)

   bb. Breast and upper back pale dull gray; lower back and rump dull, pale olive-brown; abdomen cream-buff to buff, not suffused, in either sex, with yellowish brown (Arizona, New Mexico, and western Texas, south to northwestern Mexico)..........................**Callipepla squamata pallida** (p. 265)

CALLIPEPLA SQUAMATA PALLIDA Brewster

ARIZONA SCALED PARTRIDGE

Adult (sexes alike in coloration).—Forehead and crown between light buff and pale ochraceous-buff, often with a grayish wash; center of crown with a short, bushy crest, the anterior feathers of which are wood brown to buffy brown, the posterior ones paler, all broadly tipped with white; feathers of occiput and posterior sides of neck pale grayish with a buffy tinge, barred with narrow bands of dark wood brown; nape and interscapulars gull gray, each feather narrowly tipped with fuscous to chaetura drab; upper wing coverts, upper back, and scapulars pale olive-brown washed with gull gray and tipped with slightly darker olive-brown; back, rump, and upper tail coverts similar but with a grayish wash; secondaries drab, their inner webs edged with buffy white and narrowly tipped with the same; primaries uniformly drab; upper tail coverts pale drab washed with gull gray; rectrices between mouse gray and light mouse gray; chin and upper throat light buff; lores, cheeks, and sides of throat pale ochraceous-buff with a grayish wash; auriculars tinged with wood brown; lower throat with a grayish wash; feathers of breast and sides of breast gull gray, each feather narrowly tipped with fuscous and with a lanceolate shaft marking of wood brown, ending in a point some distance short of the terminal border of fuscous; feathers of abdomen white, more or less tinged with pinkish buff on the middle of the abdomen, and each feather sharply banded and tipped with narrow, but widely spaced, bands of mummy brown to fuscous; feathers of sides and flanks between drab and hair brown with long terminal tear-shaped shaft markings of white; thighs white, more or less tinged with buffy; under tail coverts similar but with pale buffy brown centers and terminally converging V-shaped marks of the same; under wing coverts grayish white with hair-brown centers; iris brown; bill blackish; feet ashy gray.

Juvenal (sexes alike).—Forehead, lores, sides of head light buff; center of crown and occiput wood brown, the crest averaging paler—avellaneous; the feathers sometimes with white terminal shaft stripes; nape and interscapulars drab with white shaft streaks; scapulars, upper wing coverts, and upper back pinkish cinnamon to pale tawny-olive, each feather with a shaft streak of white and crossed by four or five fuscous bands, the bands about as broad as the interspaces; lower back, rump, and upper tail coverts grayish drab mottled obscurely with darker, and many of the feathers with small white medioterminal spots; secondaries like the scapulars but with their inner webs largely dusky hair brown; primaries dusky hair brown, their outer webs mottled with pale tawny-olive to buffy; median rectrices drab to hair brown with many cross bars of chaetura drab and with some whitish in the interspaces; lateral rectrices similar but with their inner webs more uniformly hair brown, less barred; chin and upper throat white; breast pale wood brown to pale tawny-olive with white shaft streaks; lower breast feathers with the dark areas paler; abdomen, sides, flanks, thighs, and under tail coverts similar but still paler, the dark bars almost disappearing, and without the white shaft streak.

Natal down.—Forehead, front half of crown, in front of a little gray topknot, and the sides of the head cinnamon-buff to pinkish buff; a broad band of chestnut from the middle of the crown, back of the topknot, down to the hindneck, bordered narrowly with black and with broad stripes of buffy white; auricular spots dark chestnut; chin and throat buffy white; rest of underparts pale grayish buff; back mottled with pale buff and russet.[60]

Adult male.—Wing 116–121 (118.8); tail 80–90 (83.7); culmen from base 16.1–17.7 (16.7); tarsus 31–35 (33); middle toe without claw 27–28 (27.4 mm.).[61]

---

[60] None seen; description *ex* Bent, U. S. Nat. Mus. Bull. 162, 1932, 54.
[61] Ten specimens from Texas.

Adult female.—Wing 113–119 (116.2) ; tail 76–86 (81) ; culmen from base 15–17.2 (16.3) ; tarsus 30.5–34 (32.4) ; middle toe without claw 26–28 (26.9 mm.).[62]

Range.—Resident in arid open country from southern Arizona (Ask Peak, Bisbee, Camp Grant, Clifton, Dos Cabesos, Fort Huachuca, Pima and Pinal Counties, Picacho, Oracle, Rice, Santa Rita Mountains, San Bernardino Ranch, Tucson, Wilcox), northern New Mexico (Haynes and the Taos Mountains), east-central Colorado (Matteson and Holly), extreme southwestern Oklahoma (western Cimarron County) and adjacent parts of southwestern Kansas, and Texas east almost to longitude 100° W. (to Lipscomb in the north to Del Rio in the south) and to northwestern and central-northern Mexico (Sonora—San José Mountains; northern Chihuahua—Casas Grandes and Whitewater).

Introduced, but unsuccessfully, in Louisiana, Florida, Georgia, and Washington; more successfully in Colorado.

Type locality.—Rio San Pedro and Fort Bowie, Ariz.=Rio San Pedro.

Ortyx squamatus (not of Wagler) Abert, Proc. Acad. Nat. Sci. Philadelphia, iii, 1847, 221 (New Mexico).

Ortyx squamata Lesson, Illustr. Zool., 1832, text to pl. 52.

Callipepla squamata Gambel, Journ. Acad. Nat. Sci. Philadelphia, i, 1847, 219 (New Mexico and "adjoining parts of California").—McCall, Proc. Acad. Nat. Sci. Philadelphia, 1851, 222, part (Santa Fe, N. Mex.).—Baird, *in* Stansbury's Rep. Great Salt Lake, 1853, 326, 334 (New Mexico) ; Rep. Pacific R. R. Surv., ix, 1858, 646, part (Organ Mountains, Pecos, etc., N. Mex.) ; Cat. North Amer. Birds, 1859, No. 476, part; Rep. U. S. and Mex. Bound. Surv., ii, pt. 2, 1859, 23, part (San Bernardino, Sonora); *in* Cooper, Orn. California, Land Birds, 1870, 556, part.—Cassin, Illustr. Birds California, Texas, etc., 1854, 129, pl. 19.—Heermann, Rep. Pacific R. R. Surv., x, No. 1, 1859, 19, part (San Pedro River, Ariz.; Fort Clark, Tex.; habits).—Coues, Proc. Acad. Nat. Sci. Philadelphia, 1866, 95 (valleys of Gila and Colorado Rivers, Ariz.) ; Check List North Amer. Birds, 1874, No. 393, pt.; ed. 2, 1882, No. 577, part; Birds Northwest, 1874, 487, part.—Baird, Brewer, and Ridgway, Hist. North Amer. Birds, iii, 1874, 487, part, pl. 63, fig. 6.—Brewster, Bull. Nuttall Orn. Club, vi, 1881, 72 (San Pedro River, Ariz.; crit.) ; viii, 1883, 33 (w. to Picacho Station, Ariz.; crit.).—American Ornithologists' Union, Check-list, 1886, No. 293; ed. 2, 1895, No. 293, part; and ed. 3, 1910, 136, part.—Scott, Auk, iii, 1886, 387 (San Pedro slope of Santa Catalina Mountains, Ariz., up to 3,500 feet; etc.; habits).—Allen, Auk, iii, 1886, 388 (Arizona; crit.).—(?) Lloyd, Auk, iv, 1887, 187 (Tom Green and Concho Counties, w. Tex.).—Thurber, Auk, vii, 1890, 89 (Point of Rocks, Colfax County, N. Mex.).—Bendire, Life Hist. North Amer. Birds, i, 1892, 18, part (chiefly).—Ogilvie-Grant, Cat. Birds Brit. Mus., xxii, 1893, 395, part (Pinal County, Ariz.; Engle, N. Mex.; Chupadero and San Diego, Chihuahua; Presidio County, w. Tex.) ; Handb. Game Birds, ii, 1897, 115, part.—Lowe, Auk, xii, 1895, 298 (e. foothills of Wet Mountains, Pueblo County, Colo., at 6,000 ft., June 10, 1895) ; xxxiv, 1917, 453 (Pueblo and Huerfano Counties, Colo.).—Anthony, Auk, xii, 1895, 388 (Platte River s. of Denver, Colo.).—Cooke, Colorado State Agr. Coll. Bull. 37, 1897, 69 (e. foothills Wet Mountains, 1 spec., June 1895) ;

---

[62] Eleven specimens from Texas, Arizona, and New Mexico.

Platte River e. of Denver, winter of 1892–3); Bull. 56, 1900, 202 (near Rocky Ford, Colo., common resident).—DWIGHT, Auk, xvii, 1900, 47, part (molt, etc.).—BAILEY, Handb. Birds Western United States, 1902, 118, part.—SALVIN and GODMAN, Biol. Centr.-Amer., Aves, iii, 1903, 290, part (w. Texas; New Mexico; Arizona; San Pedro and Bisbee, Sonora; Chupadera and San Diego, Chihuahua).—SWARTH, Pacific Coast Avif., No. 4, 1904, 4 (Huachuca Mountains, Ariz.; seldom; common along San Pedro River).—(?) MONTGOMERY, Auk, xxii, 1905, 13 (Brewster County, w. Tex.).—JUDD, U. S. Biol. Surv. Bull. 21, 1905, 61, part (range; habits; food).—ANDERSON, Proc. Davenport Acad. Sci., xi, 1907, 232 (Tabor, Iowa, 1 spec., May 2, 1889; probably introduced).—SCLATER, Hist. Birds Colorado, 1912, 141 (Colorado; abundant in cedar country, now spreading north and east, even to sw. Kansas).—GARDNER, Proc. U. S. Nat. Mus., lxvii, art. 19, 1925, pl. 2 (structure of tongue).—LAW, Condor, xxxi, 1929, 219 (Altar Valley and Tucson, Ariz.).—ABBOTT, Wils. Bull., xli, 1929, 44 (common; Uvalde, Tex.).—HOWARD and MILLER, Condor, xxxv, 1933, 16 (bones, Organ Mountains, N. Mex.).—DEL CAMPO, Anal. Inst. Biol., viii, Nos. 1, 2, 1937, 268 (Hidalgo; Valle del Mezquital; spec.).

[Callipepla] squamata COUES, Key North Amer. Birds, 1872, 238, part.—SCLATER and SALVIN, Nom. Av. Neotr., 1873, 138, part.—SHARPE, Hand-list; i, 1899, 44, part.

C[allipepla] squamata COUES, Key North Amer. Birds, ed. 2, 1884, 573, part.

Callipepla squamata squamata AMERICAN ORNITHOLOGISTS' UNION, Check-list, ed. 3, 1910, 136, part.—SWARTH, Pacific Coast Avif., No. 10, 1914, 21 (Arizona; common resident in Lower Sonoran Valleys of se. Arizona, north to Fort Grant and Clifton).—JENSEN, Auk, xxxviii, 1923, 454; xlii, 1925, 129 (near Santa Fe, N. Mex.).—AMERICAN ORNITHOLOGISTS' UNION, Auk, xl, 1923, 517 (nomencl.; crit.).—WYMAN and BURNELL, Field Book Birds Southwestern United States, 1925, 84 (descr.; chars.).

[Callipepla squamata] pallida BREWSTER, Bull. Nuttall Orn. Club, vi, 1881, 72 (San Pedro River, Ariz.; coll. William Brewster).

Callipepla squamata pallida BANGS, Proc. New England Zool. Club, iv, 1914, 100 (crit.; diagnosis; Arizona to w. Texas, n. to s. Colorado, s. to n. Sonora, Chihuahua, and Coahuila).—AMERICAN ORNITHOLOGISTS' UNION, Auk, xl, 1923, 517 (nomencl.; crit.); Check-list, ed. 4, 1931, 89 (distr.).—NICE and NICE, Birds Oklahoma, 1924, 36 (Oklahoma).—SIMMONS, Birds Austin Region, 1925, 81 (Austin, Tex.; habits; nests; eggs; descr.).—BURT, Auk, xliv, 1927, 262 (spec.; near Elkhart, Kans.; new to State list).—BAILEY, Birds New Mexico, 1928, 215 (N. Mex.); Auk, xlv, 1928, 216 (hybridizing).—SWARTH, Proc. California Acad. Sci., ser. 4, xviii, 1929, 288 (southern Arizona; distr.; breeds).—BANGS, Bull. Mus. Comp. Zool., lxx, 1930, 158 (type spec. in Mus. Comp. Zool.).—NICE, Birds Oklahoma, rev. ed., 1931, 82 (Oklahoma).—BIRD and BIRD, Wils. Bull., xliii, 1931, 293 in text (food in winter; Oklahoma).—BENT, U. S. Nat. Mus. Bull. 162, 1932, 51 (habits; distr.).—BENNITT, Univ. Missouri Studies, vii, No. 3, 1932, 26 in footnote (Tabor, Iowa; probably an escaped cage bird).—PHILLIPS, Condor, xxxv, 1933, 228 (Baboquivari Mountains, Arizona).—PETERS, Check-list Birds of World, ii, 1934, 44 (distr.).—SUTTON, Ann. Carnegie Mus., xxiv, 1934, 13 (Kenton, Okla.; common on mesa slopes).—LONG, Bull. Univ. Kansas Sci., xxxvi, 1935, 233 (Hamilton County, w. Kans.; 2 spec.; Nov. 18).—VAN ROSSEM, Trans. San Diego Soc. Nat. Hist. viii, 1936, 127, 128 (photo; south-central Arizona; abundance; distr.).—KELSO, U. S. Dept. Agr. Wildlife Research and Management Leaflet BS–84, 1937, 2, in text (distr.; food).—GROEBBELS, Der Vögel, ii, 1937, 167 (data on breeding biology).—VAN TYNE and SUTTON, Misc. Publ. Mus. Zool. Univ. Michigan, No. 37, 1937, 26 (Brewster County, Tex.; common).—NIEDRACH and ROCKWELL, Birds Denver and Mountain Parks, 1939,

64 (rare straggler).—BURLEIGH and LOWERY, Occ. Pap. Mus. Zool., Louisiana State Univ., No. 8, 1940, 98 (w. Texas; Guadalupe Mountains; abundant in open desert).—LONG, Trans. Kansas Acad. Sci., xliii, 1940, 441 (Kansas; fairly common resident in southwestern part of State).—HELLMAYR and CONOVER, Cat. Birds Amer., i, No. 1, 1942, 231 (syn.; distri.).—AMADON, Auk, lx, 1943, 22 (body weight and egg weight).

CALLIPEPLA SQUAMATA CASTANOGASTRIS Brewster

CHESTNUT-BELLIED SCALED PARTRIDGE

Adult male.—Similar to that of *Callipepla squamata pallida* but with the posterior lower parts more and deeper buffy to ochraceous and the abdomen with an extensive median patch of dark rusty chestnut; the scapulars and upper wing coverts somewhat darker grayish brown; interscapulars and breast darker—light neutral gray to neutral gray; head darker and more brownish.

Adult female.—Like the male but with little or none of the dark rusty chestnut on the midabdomen.

Juvenal.—Like that of *C. s. pallida.*

Natal down.—Like that of *C. s. pallida.*

Adult male.—Wing 109–117.5 (115.2); tail 77–86 (82); culmen from base 16.1–17.2 (16.8); tarsus 31–34.5 (32.8); middle toe without claw 25–28.5 (26.3 mm.).[63]

Adult female.—Wing 109.5–117.5 (113.7); tail 75.5–83.5 (79.7); culmen from base 15.2–16.8 (16.1); tarsus 28–33 (31); middle toe without claw 24–27 (25.3 mm.).[64]

Range.—Resident from southeastern Texas, in the lower Rio Grande valley, west to Kinney, Dimmit, and Maverick Counties, east to Laredo and to Cameron County, and to northern Tamaulipas (Nuevo Laredo; Reynosa), northern Nuevo León (Camargo, China, Rodríguez, Mier), and northern Coahuila (Sabinas).

Type locality.—Rio Grande City, Texas.

Callipepla squamata (not *Ortyx squamatus* Vigors) McCALL, Proc. Acad. Nat. Sci. Philadelphia, 1851, 222, part (Camargo, Nuevo León).—(?) McCOWN, Ann. Lyc. Nat. Hist. New York, vi, 1853, 9 (Texas; habits).—CASSIN, Illustr. Birds California, Texas, 1854, 129, part, pl. 19.—BAIRD, Rep. Pacific R. R. Surv., ix, 1858, 646, part (Nuevo León); Cat. North Amer. Birds, 1859, No. 476, part; Rep. U. S. and Mex. Bound. Surv., ii, pt. 2, 1859, 23, part (Nuevo León); *in* Cooper, Orn. California, Land Birds, 1870, 556, part.—HEERMANN, Rep. Pacific R. R. Surv., x, No. 1, 1859, 19, part (San Antonio, Tex.; habits).—DRESSER, Ibis, 1866, 28 (s. Texas).—BUTCHER, Proc. Acad. Nat. Sci. Philadelphia, 1868, 150 (Laredo, Tex.).—BAIRD, BREWER, and RIDGWAY, Hist. North Amer. Birds, iii, 1874, 487, part.—COUES, Check List North Amer. Birds, 1874, No. 393, part; ed. 2, 1882, No. 577, part; Birds Northwest, 1874, 441, part.—MERRILL, Proc. U. S. Nat. Mus., i, 1878, 160 (Ringgold Barracks and Hidalgo, s. Texas).—

---

[63] Ten specimens from Texas and from Tamaulipas and Nuevo León, Mexico.
[64] Eight specimens from Texas and from Tamaulipas and Nuevo León, Mexico.

SENNETT, U. S. Geol. and Geogr. Surv. Terr., Bull. 5, No. 3, 1879, 429 (Lomita Ranch, Tex.; habits; descr. nest and eggs).—SALVIN and GODMAN, Biol. Centr.-Amer., Aves, iii, 1903, 290, part (Lower Rio Grande Valley; Nuevo León).— JUDD, U. S. Biol. Surv. Bull. 21, 1905, 61, part (range; habits; food).—LACEY, Auk, xxviii, 1911, 206 (Kerrville, Tex.).

C[allipepla] squamata COUES, Key North Amer. Birds, ed. 2, 1884, 593, part.

[Callipepla] squamata COUES, Key North Amer. Birds, 1872, 238, part.—SCLATER and SALVIN, Nom. Av. Neotr., 1873, 138, part.

Callipepla squammata McCALL, Proc. Acad. Nat. Sci. Philadelphia, v, 1851, 222.

Callipepla squamata castanogastris BREWSTER, Bull. Nuttall Orn. Club, viii, 1883, 34 (Rio Grande City, s. Tex.; coll. W. Brewster).—AMERICAN ORNITHOLOGISTS' UNION, Check-list, 1886, No. 293a; ed. 2, 1895, No. 293a; ed. 3, 1910, p. 136; ed. 4, 1931, 89.—SENNETT, Auk, iv, 1887, 25 (descr. first plumage).—BECKHAM, Proc. U. S. Nat. Mus., x, 1888, 656 (16 miles nw. of Beeville, Tex.).—BENDIRE, Life Hist. North Amer. Birds, i, 1892, 22.—DWIGHT, Auk, xvii, 1900, 47 (molt). —PHILLIPS, Auk, xxviii, 1911, 74 (San Fernando and Aguas Calientes, Tamaulipas).—BANGS, Proc. New England Zool. Club, iv, 1914, 100 (range; diagnosis; lower Rio Grande Valley, s. to n. Tamaulipas, Nuevo León, and Coahuila); Bull. Mus. Comp. Zool., lxx, 1930, 159 (type spec. in Mus. Comp. Zool.).—GRISCOM and CROSBY, Auk, xliii, 1925, 532 (Brownsville, Tex.).—BENT, U. S. Nat. Mus. Bull. 162, 1932, 58 (distr.; life hist.).—PETERS, Check-list Birds of World, ii, 1934, 44.—HELLMAYR and CONOVER, Cat. Birds Amer., i, No. 1, 1942, 230 (syn.; distr.).

C[allipepla] s[quamata] castanogastris BAILEY, Handb. Birds Western U. S., 1902, 119 (distr., descr.).—KELSO, U. S. Dept. Agr. Wildlife Research and Management Leaflet BS-84, 1937, 2 in text (distr.; food).

[Callipepla] [squamata] castanogastris BURLEIGH and LOWERY, Occ. Pap. Mus. Zool. Louisiana State Univ., No. 12, 1942, 189, in text (distr.).

[Callipepla] castanogastris SHARPE, Hand-list, i, 1899, 44.

Callipepla squamata castaneogastris REICHENOW and SCHALOW, Journ. für Orn., 1885, 456 (reprint of orig. descr.).—ATTWATER, Auk, ix, 1892, 233 (near San Antonio, Tex.).

Subsp. a. Callipepla castaneiventer OGILVIE-GRANT, Cat. Birds Brit. Mus., xxii, 1893, 396 (ne. Mexico and lower Rio Grande Valley, Tex.); Handbook Game Birds, ii, 1897, 117 (monogr.).

C[allipepla] castaneiventer SALVIN and GODMAN, Biol. Centr.-Amer., Aves, iii, 1903, 291, in text (crit.).

[Callipepla squamata] Subsp. a. Callipepla castaneiventer OGILVIE-GRANT, Cat. Birds Brit. Mus., xxii, 1893, 396 (Rio Grande City, Fort Duncan, Eagle Pass, Benavides in Duval County, and Laredo, Tex.; Nuevo Laredo, Tamaulipas).

CALLIPEPLA SQUAMATA SQUAMATA (Vigors)

SCALED PARTRIDGE

Adult.—Similar to the corresponding sex of Callipepla squamata pallida, but darker, the forehead and crown washed with wood brown to buffy brown, less distinct from the crest; the interscapulars, nape, sides of breast, and breast somewhat darker—between dark gull gray and light neutral gray; lower back, rump, and upper tail coverts averaging slightly duskier; middle of abdomen, in the male especially, more strongly suffused with pale tawny or pale ochraceous-tawny.

Juvenal.—Very similar to that of *C. s. pallida* but the brownish tones slightly more mixed with grayish (only 1 specimen seen).

Natal down.—Apparently unknown.

Adult male.—Wing 113–121 (116.9) ; tail 75–90 (84.9) ; culmen from base 15.5–17.5 (16.4) ; tarsus 30.7–32.5 (31.8) ; middle toe without claw 24.6–26.9 (25.8 mm.).[65]

Adult female.—Wing 111–120 (115.4) ; tail 75–88 (81.7) ; culmen from the base 15.4–16.6 (15.9) ; tarsus 27.6–32.0 (29.6) ; middle toe without claw 23.9–26.0 (24.8 mm.).[66]

Range.—Resident in Mexico from southern Coahuila, southern Chihuahua, and southern Sonora, south to Guanajuato, Jalisco, Hidalgo, and Mexico (District Federal).

Type locality.—Mexico.

Ortyx squamatus VIGORS, Zool. Journ., v, 1830, 275 (dry interior of Mexico).
Ortyx squamata LESSON, Illustr. Zool., 1832, pl. 52 and text.
C[*allipepla*] *squamata* GRAY, List Gen. Birds, 1840, 61; Gen. Birds, iii, 1846, 514.—
    REICHENOW, Die Vögel, i, 1913, 317.
Callipepla squamata GOULD, Monogr. Odontoph., pt. i, 1844, pl. 19 and text.—
    GRAY, List Birds Brit. Mus., pt. 5, Gallinae, 1867, 78.—LAWRENCE, Mem. Boston
    Soc. Nat. Hist., ii, 1874, 307 (Durango).—AMERICAN ORNITHOLOGISTS' UNION,
    Check-list, 1886, No. 293, part; ed. 2, 1895, 108, part; ed. 3, 1910, 136, part.—
    BERISTAIN and LAURENCIO, Mem. y Rev. Soc. Cient. "Antonio Alzate," vii,
    1894, 219 (Mexico; Valle de Mexico; San Luis Potosí and Tamaulipas).—
    BENDIRE, Life Hist. North Amer. Birds, i, 1892, 18, part.—OGILVIE-GRANT, Cat.
    Birds Brit. Mus., xxii, 1893, 395, part (San Luis Potosí; near City of Mexico) ;
    Handb. Game Birds, ii, 1897, 115, part.—JOUY, Proc. U. S. Nat. Mus., xvi, 1894,
    790 (Ahualulco, San Luis Potosí; Guadalajara, Jalisco).—DWIGHT, Auk, xvii,
    1900, 47 (molt).—BAILEY, Handb. Birds Western United States, 1902, 118, part.
    —SALVIN and GODMAN, Biol. Centr.-Amer., Aves, iii, 1903, 290, part (Durango;
    Ahualulco and plain of San Luis Potosí; Guanajuato; Guadalajara, Jalisco;
    near City of Mexico).—SETH-SMITH, L'Oiseau, x, 1929, 760 (care in captivity).
    —DEL CAMPO, Anales Inst. Biol., viii, 1937, 268 (Hidalgo; Valle del Mezquital).—
    STEVENSON, Condor, xliv, 1942, 110 (central Panhandle of Texas).
[*Callipepla*] *squamata* REICHENBACH, Synop. Av., iii, Gallinaceae 1848, pl. 199, figs.
    1918, 1919.—GRAY, Hand-list, ii, 1870, 273, No. 9794.—SCLATER and SALVIN, Nom.
    Av. Neotr., 1873, 138, part.
Callipepla squammata CUBAS, Cuadro Geogr., Estadístico, Descr., e. Hist. de los
    Estados Unidos Mexicanos, 1884, 168 (common names; Mexico).
Callipepla squamata squamata MILLER, Bull. Amer. Mus. Nat. Hist., xxii, 1906, 162
    (Rancho Baillou, nw. Durango).—AMERICAN ORNITHOLOGISTS' UNION, Check
    List, ed. 3, 1910, 136, part.—BANGS, Proc. New England, Zool. Club, iv, 1914, 99
    (diagnosis; Valley of Mexico; San Luis Potosí; n., probably, to s. Chihuahua
    and s. Sonora).—PETERS, Check-list Birds of World, ii, 1934, 44.—BURLEIGH and
    LOWERY, Occ. Pap. Mus. Zool. Louisiana State Univ., No. 12, 1942, 188 (se.

---

[65] Ten specimens from Chihuahua, Coahuila, Durango, San Luis Potosí, Hidalgo, and Tamaulipas.

[66] Eleven specimens from Chihuahua, Nuevo León, Tamaulipas, Durango, and Hidalgo.

Coahuila; spec.).—HELLMAYR and CONOVER, Cat. Birds Amer., i, No. 1, 1942, 231 (syn.; distr.).

[*Callipepla*] [*squamata*] *squamata* BURLEIGH and LOWERY, Occ. Pap. Mus. Zool., Louisiana State Univ., No. 12, 1942, 189, in text (se. Coahuila).

Tetrao cristata (not *T. cristatus* Linnaeus) LA LLAVE, Registro Trimestro, i, 1832, 144 (Mexico); La Naturaleza, vii, 1884, app., p. 65.

Callipepla strenua WAGLER, Isis, 1832, 278, 1229 (Mexico; coll. Würtemberg Mus.).

Callipepla squamulata SALLE and PARZUDAKÍ, Cat. Oiseaux Mexique, 1862, 6 (Mexico).

Genus PHILORTYX Gould

Philortyx GOULD, Monogr. Odontoph., pt. 2, 1846, pl. 14 and text, and Introd. 1850, p. 17. (Type, by monotypy, *Ortyx fasciatus* Gould.)

Small Odontophoridae (wing about 95–100 mm.) with tail nearly two-thirds as long as wing, scapulars and tertials spotted with black, and with sides and flanks broadly banded with brownish black and white.

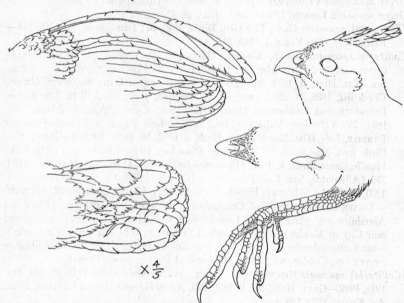

$\times \frac{4}{5}$

FIGURE 17.—*Philortyx fasciatus.*

Bill relatively rather small, the chord of culmen (from extreme base) less than half as long as tarsus; depth of bill at base slightly exceeding distance from anterior end of nasal fossa to tip of maxilla and decidedly greater than width at rictus. Outermost primary nearly as long as sixth (from outside), the third and fourth longest. Tail nearly two-thirds as long as wing, strongly rounded, its graduation equal to about half the length of tarsus, the rectrices (12) firm, rather broad, obliquely rounded or subtruncate at tips. Tarsus less than one-third as long as wing, shorter than middle toe with claw, the outer side of planta tarsi mostly covered by a continuous series of obliquely transverse scutella, the inner side with similar but less oblique scutella—both with smaller scutella of longitudinal tendency next to margins of acrotarsium.

Plumage and coloration.—A distinct elongated crest of several rather narrow parallel-edged nearly straight flat plumes springing from center of vertex. Scapulars and tertials spotted with black and tipped with buff; sides and flanks banded with white and brownish black, the breast and chest more narrowly banded or barred. Sexes alike in color.

Range.—Highlands of Mexico. (Monotypic.)

PHILORTYX FASCIATUS (Gould)

BANDED QUAIL

Adult male.—Forehead, crown, and occiput light Saccardo's umber, tinged with bright tawny-olive on the crown; from the middle of the crown arises a crest of fairly long, truncated, fuscous-black feathers tipped with bright tawny-olive; feathers of hindneck and lower sides of neck, and the anterior interscapulars, mouse gray, tipped with tawny-olive, the tips broader on the neck than on the interscapulars, and, in the former area, largely hiding the gray areas in the overlapping feathers; posterior interscapulars, back, and rump feathers dark mouse gray narrowly tipped with pale tawny-white, many of them, especially in the upper back, subterminally blotched with fuscous-black; scapulars, upper wing coverts, and innermost secondaries grayish Saccardo's umber, tipped and crossed by fine tawny-white to white bars and heavily blotched with fuscous-black subterminally on both webs (in some feathers the blotches on the two webs are coalesced; in others they are separate); secondaries between grayish Saccardo's umber and olive-brown crossed by incomplete marginal fine bars of tawny-white to white; primaries dull olive-brown, some of the outer webs with faint indications of marginal spots of paler; upper tail coverts like the rump but finely speckled and vermiculated with dull tawny-olive tinged with gray, the longer ones crossed sparingly by indistinct fine whitish bars, and slightly blotched with fuscous-black subterminally; rectrices dusky grayish Saccardo's umber tipped and crossed by six or more wavy whitish bands each of which is proximally bordered by a slightly broader one of blackish, the umber interspaces finely speckled with dusky; lores, cheeks, auriculars, and sides of throat dusky Saccardo's umber; chin and throat whitish; upper breast feathers light mouse gray broadly tipped with tawny-olive, the more posterior ones similar but blotched with fuscous-blackish succeeded by a white subterminal band separating the blackish from the brownish tips; feathers of upper abdomen, sides, and flanks white banded heavily with fuscous to fuscous-black, the width of the blackish bands and tips increasing posteriorly; middle of abdomen, and vent white, more or less tinged with buffy; thighs similar but tawnier; under tail coverts buffy white, each with a large median, subterminal blotch of fuscous-black; under wing coverts dull wood brown to hair brown, margined with slightly paler.

Adult female.—Like the male but with the coronal crest shorter.

Juvenal.—Similar to the adult but with the forehead, lores, chin, throat, and cheeks black, the blackish coronal crest banded with bright hazel, the black of the forehead extending back over the eyes, and the whole crown hazel irregularly transversely mottled with black; the feathers of sides and back of neck, interscapulars, upper back, upper wing coverts, and secondaries with narrow white or buffy-white shaft streaks and with the rest of the feathers tawnier, the pale cross bars pale tawny-olive and pale antique brown, the interspaces bright tawny-olive; rump, upper tail coverts, and rectrices slightly paler and more olivaceous, less dusky than in adult; primaries more pointed and with their outer webs more distinctly notched with pale pinkish buffy; bill light reddish brown; tarsi and toes horn brown.

Adult male.—Wing 95–102.5 (99); tail 58.3–66 (61.8); culmen from base 14.3–15.9 (14.9); tarsus 26.7–29.7 (28.2); middle toe without claw 24–27.6 (25.7 mm.).[67]

Adult female.—Wing 94–104 (98.7); tail 59–68 (62.3); culmen from base 14.9–15.5 (15.2); tarsus 26.7–29.7 (28.5); middle toe without claw 24–27.9 (25.4 mm.).[68]

Range.—Resident in open bushy places in southwestern Mexico; in the states of Colima, Guerrero, Michoacán, Morelos, and Puebla.

Type locality.—California = Mexico.

Ortyx fasciatus GOULD, Proc. Zool. Soc. London, 1843 (1844), 133 ("California"; coll. Mus. Prince Massena, now in coll. Acad. Nat. Sci. Philadelphia; ex Natterer, manuscript).—COOPER, Bull. Nuttall Orn. Club, ii, 1877, 95 (not known north of Colima, Mexico).

Philortyx fasciatus GOULD, Monogr. Odontoph., pt. 2, 1846, 17, pl. 14 and text.—SCLATER, Proc. Zool. Soc. London, 1864, 178 (near City of Mexico).—LAWRENCE, Mem. Boston Soc. Nat. Hist., ii, 1874, 307 (plains of Colima, sw. Mexico).—RIDGWAY, Proc. U. S. Nat. Mus., ix, 1886, 177, in text (Colima).—OGILVIE-GRANT, Cat. Birds Brit. Mus., xxii, 1893, 406 (plains of Colima; Sierra Madre del Sur and Dos Arroyos, Guerrero); Handb. Game Birds, ii, 1897, 127 (monogr.).—SALVIN and GODMAN, Biol. Centr.-Amer., Aves, iii, 1903, 294 (Colima; Sierra Madre del Sur; Dos Arroyos; Chietta, Puebla).—TODD, Auk, xxxvii, 1920, 217, in text (syn.).—GRISCOM, Bull. Mus. Comp. Zool., lxxv, 1934, 422 (Guerrero).—PETERS, Check-list Birds of World, ii, 1934, 46 (distr.).—HELLMAYR and CONOVER, Cat. Birds Amer., i, No. 1, 1942, 238 (syn.; distr.).—BLAKE and HANSON, Publ. Field Mus. Nat. Hist., Zool. Ser., xxii, No. 9, 1942, 527 (Michoacán; Apatzingan; spec.).

[*Philortyx*] *fasciatus* SHARPE, Hand-list, i, 1899, 45.

Phylortix fasciatus CUBAS, Cuadro Geogr., Estadístico, Descr. e Hist. de los Estados Mexicanos, 1884, 168 (common names; Mexico).

---

[67] Ten specimens from Michoacán, Guerrero, and Morelos.
[68] Six specimens from Michoacán, Guerrero, Colima, and Morelos.

Ptilortyx fasciatus Seth-Smith, L'Oiseau, x, 1929, 761 (care in captivity).
[*Eupsychortyx*] *fasciatus* Sclater and Salvin, Nom. Av. Neotr., 1873, 138.
Eupsychortyx fasciatus Beristain and Laurencio, Mem. y Rev. Soc. Cient. "Antonio Alzate," vii, 1894, 219 (Colima, Mexico).
C[*allipepla*] *fasciata* Ridgway, Man. North Amer. Birds, 1887, 193.
Callipepla fasciata del Campo, Anal. Inst. Biol., viii, 1937, 336 (Morelos, Tecuman; Las Estacas; spec.).
Ortyx perrotiana Des Murs, Rev. Zool., 1845, 207 (Mexico).
Philortyx personatus Ridgway, Auk, iii, No. 3, July, 1886, 333 (Chietta, Pueblo, Mexico; coll. Com. Expl. Geog. de Mexico); Proc. U. S. Nat. Mus., ix, 1886, 176 (Chietta).—Beristain and Laurencio, Mem. y Rev. Soc. Cient. "Antonio Alzate," vii, No. 7–8, 1894, 218 (Puebla, Mexico).
C[*allipepla*] *personata* Ridgway, Man. North Amer. Birds, 1887, 193.

Genus LOPHORTYX Bonaparte

Lophortyx Bonaparte, Geogr. and Comp. List, 1838, 42. (Type, as designated by Gray, 1840, *Tetrao californicus* Shaw.)
Lophortix (emendation) Bonaparte, Compt. Rend., xxxviii, 1854, 663.
Callipepla Reichenow, Die Vögel, i, 1913, 317, part.

Medium-sized Odontophorinae (wing about 108–120 mm.) with tail more than three-fourths as long as wing, 12 rectrices, crest long, club-shaped, consisting of several plumes with webs convolute, the uppermost plume thus enclosing those beneath; chest plain grayish (not squamated), and sexes conspicuously different in coloration.

Bill relatively small, the chord of culmen (from extreme base) less than half as long as tarsus, its depth at base not greater than distance from anterior end of nasal fossa to tip of maxilla, and about equal to its width at rictus. Outermost primary shorter than eighth (shorter than ninth in *L. douglasii*), the fourth, fifth, and sixth or fourth (in *L. douglasii*) longest. Tail three-fourths as long as wing or more, graduated, the graduation equal to two-thirds the length of tarsus or more; rectrices (12) rather broad, slightly tapering terminally (except in *L. douglasii*), with rounded tips. Tarsus decidedly less than one-third as long as wing (about one-fourth as long in *L. douglasii*), shorter than middle toe with claw, the planta tarsi covered mostly with rather small hexagonal scutella but those near posterior edge of outer side larger, more transverse, and tending to form a continuous linear series.

Plumage and coloration.—Feathers of forehead narrow, erectile, somewhat bristlelike; springing from center of crown a conspicuous elongated club-shaped crest comprised of several plumes with conduplicate webs narrower basally, broader terminally (in *L. californica* and *L. gambelii*) or in middle portion (in *L. douglasii*), the uppermost plume folding over or enclosing anteriorly and laterally the other plumes. Scapulars, tertials, rump, etc., unspotted, but inner webs of tertials edged with buff or white; chest plain gray. Sexes conspicuously different in coloration.

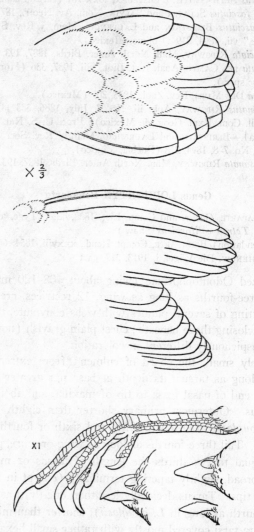

$\times \frac{2}{3}$

$\times 1$

FIGURE 18.—*Lophortyx californica.*

Range.—Pacific coast district of United States, Baja California, Arizona, New Mexico, extreme western Texas, and southward over western and central Mexico. (Three species.)[69]

---

[69] *Lophortyx leucoprosopon* Reichenow (Orn. Monatsb., iii, 1895, 11, fig. opp. p. 97) is omitted from this account as it is almost certainly a hybrid between *L. gambelii* and *L. douglasii,* and has no locality, being based on two captive birds in a German aviary.

KEY TO THE FORMS (ADULTS) OF THE GENUS LOPHORTYX

a. Breast feathers with a scalloped pattern like those of abdomen.
  b. Crest usually uniform dark sepia to fuscous (Sonora).
                  Lophortyx douglasii bensoni, ♀ (p. 302)
  bb. Crest usually spotted or incompletely barred with dull tawny.
    c. Brown of underparts darker—dark olive-brown.
      d. With a wing tip (the primaries extending beyond the secondaries in the folded wing) of 15–20 mm. (Nayarit).
                  Lophortyx douglasii impedita, ♀ (p. 304)
      dd. With little or no wing tip (northwestern Jalisco).
                  Lophortyx douglasii teres, ♀ (p. 303)
    cc. Brown of underparts paler—olive-brown to pale olive-brown (Sinaloa).
                  Lophortyx douglasii douglasii, ♀ (p. 299)
aa. Breast feathers uniform gray or brownish gray.
  b. Flanks dark chestnut.
    c. Throat solid black rimmed with white.
      d. Upper back gray with little or no olive wash.
        e. Anterior upperparts between neutral gray and light neutral gray (Tiburón Island, Gulf of California).
                  Lophortyx gambelii pembertoni, ♂ (p. 297)
        ee. Anterior upperparts between neutural gray and light mouse gray (western Colorado)..............**Lophortyx gambelii sana,** ♂ (p. 297)
      dd. Upper back gray with a distinct olive wash.
        e. Abdomen deep buffy in fresh plumage (southern Sonora).
                  Lophortyx gambelii fulvipectus, ♂ (p. 296)
        ee. Abdomen pale buffy in fresh plumage.
          f. Paler, the elongated feathers of sides and flanks between Sanford's brown and chestnut (western Texas, extreme southeastern New Mexico)............**Lophortyx gambelii ignoscens,** ♂ (p. 298)
         ff. Darker, the elongated feathers of sides and flanks between chestnut and bay (Utah, southern Nevada, New Mexico, southern California; south to northeast Baja California, north-central Sonora, and extreme northwestern Chihuahua).
                  Lophortyx gambelii gambelii, ♂ (p. 291)
    cc. Throat buffy or grayish lightly streaked with dusky gray.
      d. Crown sepia (western Colorado)..**Lophortyx gambelii sana,** ♀ (p. 297)
      dd. Crown cinnamon-drab.
        e. Anterior upperparts with little or no oblivaceous wash (Tiburón Island).
                  Lophortyx gambelii pembertoni, ♀ (p. 297)
        ee. Anterior upperparts with an olivaceous wash.
          f. Abdomen pale buffy in fresh plumage.
            g. Paler, elongated feathers of sides and flanks between Sanford's brown and chestnut (western Texas, extreme southeastern New Mexico)..........**Lophortyx gambelii ignoscens,** ♀ (p. 298)
            gg. Darker, elongated feathers of sides and flanks between chestnut and bay (southern Utah, southern Nevada, southern California, most of New Mexico, Arizona, southern to central Sonora, northeastern Baja California, and northwestern Chihuahua).
                  Lophortyx gambelii gambelii, ♀ (p. 291)
         ff. Abdomen deep buffy in fresh plumage (southern Sonora).
                  Lophortyx gambelii fulvipectus, ♀ (p. 296)

bb. Flanks gray or olive-brown.
  c. Throat solid black rimmed with white.
    d. Back averaging more brown than gray in fresh plumage.
      e. Back very dark, averaging more olive-brown than grayish brown
        (coastal belt from southwestern Oregon to Santa Cruz County,
        Calif.)............**Lophortyx californica brunnescens**, ♂ (p. 284)
      ee. Back lighter, averaging more grayish brown than olive-brown.
        f. Larger, wings averaging 116 mm. (Catalina Island).
                Lophortyx californica catalinensis, ♂ (p. 286)
        ff. Smaller, wings averaging 110 mm. (coastal belt from San Francisco
          south to San Diego, and interior valleys west of the Sierra Nevada.)
                Lophortyx californica californica, ♂ (p. 279)
    dd. Back averaging more gray than brown in fresh plumage.
      e. Back with considerable olive-brownish suffusion.
        f. Darker, the breast deep neutral gray (southern Baja California).
                Lophortyx californica achrustera, ♂ (p. 289)
        ff. Paler, the breast neutral gray (Owens Valley, east-central California).
                Lophortyx californica canfieldae, ♂ (p. 290)
      ee. Back with little or no olive-brownish suffusion.
        f. Darker, the breast neutral gray (northwestern Baja California).
                Lophortyx californica plumbea, ♂ (p. 287)
        ff. Paler, the breast light neutral gray (Warner Valley, Oreg.).
                Lophortyx californica orecta, ♂ (p. 290)
  cc. Throat not solid black rimmed with white.
    d. Throat black barred with white.
      e. Breast very pale—smoke gray with a faint bluish tinge (Sonora).
                Lophortyx douglasii bensoni, ♂ (p. 302)
      ee. Breast darker—light neutral gray or darker.
        f. Breast feathers mostly with indistinct pale rufescent terminal spots
          (Chihuahua).........**Lophortyx douglasii languens**, ♂ (p. 305)
        ff. Breast feathers mostly with no such spots.
          g. With a wing tip of 15–20 mm.
            h. General coloration averaging darker, gray of breast and abdomen
               neutral gray, white abdominal spots more or less ringed with
               blackish (Nayarit).**Lophortyx douglasii impedita**, ♂ (p. 304)
           hh. General coloration averaging paler, gray of breast and abdomen
               light neutral gray, white abdominal spots with no blackish rings
               (Sinaloa)........**Lophortyx douglasii douglasii**, ♂ (p. 299)
        gg. With little or no wing tip (Jalisco).
                Lophortyx douglasii teres, ♂ (p. 303)
    dd. Throat not black barred with white, but grayish or grayish buffy streaked
      with dusky.
      e. Back decidedly brownish.
        f. Upperparts dark olive-brown; breast brownish (coastal belt from
          southwestern Oregon to Santa Cruz County, Calif.).
                Lophortyx californica brunnescens, ♀ (p. 284)
        ff. Upperparts grayish brown; breast grayish.
          g. Larger, wings averaging 116 mm. (Catalina Island).
                Lophortyx californica catalinensis, ♀ (p. 286)
         gg. Smaller, wings averaging 108 mm. (coastal belt from San Francisco
          Bay south to San Diego and inland west of Sierra Nevada).
                Lophortyx californica californica, ♀ (p. 279)

ee. Back decidedly grayish.

   f. Darker, the breast mouse gray (northwestern Baja California).

Lophortyx californica plumbea, ♀ (p. 287)

   ff. Paler, the breast grayish drab to light grayish drab.

     g. Back suffused with olive-brownish (southern Baja California).

Lophortyx californica achrustera, ♀ (p. 289)

     gg. Back with little or no brownish suffusion.

       h. Paler, the sides and flanks buffy brown (Owens Valley, east-central California).Lophortyx californica canfieldae, ♀ (p. 290)

       hh. Darker, the sides and flanks olive-brown (Warner Valley, Oreg.).

Lophortyx californica orecta, ♀ (p. 290)

LOPHORTYX CALIFORNICA CALIFORNICA (Shaw)

Valley Quail

Adult male.—Forehead and anterior part of crown back to middle of the eyes pale olive-buff, the feathers with fine dusky shafts and the more posterior ones tipped with white, forming a white line of demarcation across the crown; this followed by a broader blackish one which turns posteriorly at the sides to form the lateral margins of the hindcrown and occiput, which are raw umber; coronal crest of six forward-drooping, terminally expanded black feathers; feathers of hindneck and posterior sides of neck dark brownish gray margined with fuscous to black and subterminally spotted finely with white, giving a finely speckled appearance; anterior interscapulars slate-gray with margins, tips, and shaft streaks of fuscous to chaetura drab, the gray often paler subterminally, giving a diluted reflection of the nape pattern; posterior interscapulars, back, lower back, and rump brownish olive; scapulars and upper wing coverts between buffy brown and olive-brown in fresh plumage (fading to more slate-gray in spring), the longer scapulars internally edged with light ochraceous-buff; secondaries dark olive-brown narrowly edged toward their ends with light ochraceous-buff; primaries dark olive-brown; upper tail coverts like the rump but with a slate-gray tinge; rectrices between slate-gray and deep mouse gray; lores, chin, and throat jet-black, the throat bordered posteriorly by a broad white band beginning at the lower hind end of the eye and continuing between the cheeks and the auriculars to the sides of the throat and across the throat; another white band begins just above it at the hind end of the eye and borders the blackish rim of the crown and occiput; auriculars and a posterolateral border of the white throat border black; breast solid deep neutral gray with a slate wash; middle of upper abdomen warm buff, sides of upper abdomen white, all the feathers heavily margined with black terminally; a large patch in the center of the abdomen bright hazel, the feathers margined with black; lower middle of abdomen pale buffy whitish barred with dark olive-brown, the dark bars becoming fainter posteriorly; feathers of sides deep olive-brown with terminal lanceolate white shaft streaks, some of the most anterior ones, actually on the lower sides of the breast with the brown replaced by deep neutral gray on all but their exposed areas, and the most posterior ones, bordering on the flanks, with broad margins of pale ochraceous-buff on both webs; flanks, vent, and under tail coverts pale ochraceous-buff with broad median streaks of olive-brown, these streaks darkening to chaetura drab on the longer under tail coverts; under wing coverts dull grayish brown margined with paler; iris dark brown; bill black; tarsi and toes blackish.

Adult female.—Forehead, lores, and anterior part of crown pale buffy brown, the feathers with fine black shafts; posterior half of crown and the occiput sepia, the coronal crest smaller and less recurved than in male, dark fuscous; nape and lower sides of neck as in male but the grays replaced by light, dull buffy brown which color also tinges the pale subterminal spots on these feathers; rest of upperparts of body as in the male but averaging darker and more brownish, less olive; wings and tail as in male; chin and throat grayish white, the feathers with dull olive-brown shaft streaks, cheeks similar but with the streaks finer and blacker; breast grayish buffy brown in fresh plumage (becoming more grayish less buffy brown with wear) ; upper and lateral parts of abdomen white the feathers heavily bordered with blackish; middle lower abdomen, vent, sides, flanks, and under tail coverts as in the male.

Juvenal (sexes alike).—Forehead and anterior part of crown as in adult female but the feathers with indistinct pale grayish terminal spots; rest of crown and the occiput as in adult female except that the lateral, loreal-supraorbital area is paler, more washed with pale ochraceous-buff, and the coronal crest shorter and lighter—sepia; lower sides of neck and hindneck between dusky buffy brown and hair brown with no dusky edges or pale spots; interscapulars and upper back hair brown with narrow white shafts, which spread out laterally at the tip and with fuscous blotches on each web just before this whitish tip; interscapulars and upper wing coverts similar but with the hair brown washed and mottled with dull tawny-olive; secondaries with their outer webs chiefly dull tawny-olive barred with blackish, each bar distally broadly bordered with pale warm buff, the tawny-olive interspaces finely dotted with black; their inner webs dull clove brown sparsely flecked, chiefly terminally, with tawny-olive; primaries similar but without the tawny-olive, their inner webs uniform dusky clove brown, their outer ones largely pale pinkish buff with incomplete, indistinct transverse dusky brownish bars; back, lower back, rump, and upper tail coverts dark hair brown with faint cross bars of grayish buffy and faint shafts of the same; median rectrices dark hair brown with incomplete marginal cross bars of fuscous distally bordered by dirty white on both webs; the ground color of the rectrices becoming more slate-gray on the lateral ones and the marginal bars becoming shorter; chin and throat grayish white; cheeks, auriculars, and sides of neck buffy hair brown; breast feathers hair brown with narrow whitish shafts terminally broadening into round spots and subterminally crossed by fuscous transverse spots; feathers of sides similar; rest of underparts white with a faint grayish buffy tinge, barred with faint dull olive-brown; the posterior underparts more heavily washed with buffy than the more anterior areas.

Natal down.—General color above light buff tinged with pale cinnamon-buff; a lengthwise patch of pale snuff brown on the middle of the fore-head; center of crown and occiput snuff brown bordered by blackish; a spot of pale snuff brown on the auriculars; a longitudinal fuscous line on each side of the spinal tract, paralleled by a similar pair on the sides of the back, the spinal tract itself becoming more and more tinged with pale hazel posteriorly; a semitransverse humeral line of blackish brown and two incomplete transverse bands of the same on each wing; below dull white, tinged with pale buff on the breast, flanks, thighs, and vent.

Adult male.—Wing 106–117 (110.6); tail 83.8–99.5 (89.2); culmen from base 14.8–16.0 (15.1); tarsus 31.5–34.5 (32.9); middle toe without claw 25–30 (27.4 mm.).[70]

Adult female.—Wing 105–111.5 (107.8); tail 79–88.5 (83.8); culmen from base 14–16 (14.8); tarsus 28.5–32.5 (30.4); middle toe without claw 24–28 (26 mm.).[71]

Range.—Resident in the semiarid interior of California from the Oregon line south to central San Diego County; in the coastal belt from just south of San Francisco Bay to San Diego, and east to extreme western Nevada. Oregon occurrences are apparently due to introductions. Introduced into Hawaii, Utah, Arizona (native?), and New Mexico (Santa Fe County).

Type locality.—Monterey, Calif.

Tetrao californicus SHAW, Nat. Misc., ix, 1798, pl. 345 (California; San Francisco or Monterey ?).

Callipepla californica NEWBERRY, Rep. Pacific R. R. Surv., vi, pt. 4, 1857, 92 part (Sacramento Valley; Willamette Valley).—HEERMANN, Rep. Pacific R. R. Surv., x, pt. 4, No. 2, 1859, 60, part (chiefly; s. to Vallecito; habits).—AMERICAN ORNITHOLOGISTS' UNION, Check-list, ed. 2, 1895, 109, part.

C[allipepla] californica REICHENOW, Die Vögel, i, 1913, 318.

Lophortyx californica NUTTALL, Man. Orn. United States and Canada, Land Birds, ed. 2, 1840, 789, part.—COOPER and SUCKLEY, Rep. Pacific R. R. Surv., xii, book 2, pt. 3, 1860, 225, part.—BELDING, Proc. U. S. Nat. Mus., i, 1879, 439 (valleys and foothills, and w. slope of Sierra Nevada; habits).—RIDGWAY, Proc. U. S. Nat. Mus., iii, 1830, 197; Nom. North Amer. Birds, 1881, No. 482, part.—COUES, Check List North Amer. Birds, ed. 2, 1882, No. 575, part.—GABRIELSON, Auk, xli, 1924, 505 (Wallowa Valley, Oregon; common); (?) Condor, xxxiii, 1931, 112 (abundant in Rogue River Valley, Oreg.).—(?) MILLER, *in* Chaney, Miller, and

---

[70] Thirty-five specimens.
[71] Thirteen specimens.

Dice, Carnegie Inst. Washington Publ. 349, 1925, 79 (bones; Rancho La Brea).
—(?) MILLER, Condor, xxxii, 1930, 118 (San Pedro Pleistocene); (?) Condor,
xxxvii, 1935, 78 (bones, McKittrick Pleistocene deposits).—PRICE, Condor,
xxxiii, 1931, 1 (flocking habits); xl, 1938, 87 in text (male incubating).—
COMPTON, Condor, xxxiii, 1931, 249 (young); xxxiv, 1932, 48 (hybrid between
this form and Texas bobwhite).—WYTHE, Condor, xxxv, 1933, 34 (attached by
snake).—SUMNER, California Fish and Game, xxi, 1935, 200-221 (behavior).—
GRINNELL and LINSDALE, Vert. Anim. Point Lobos Reserve, 1936, 39, 59 (Point
Lobos, Calif.; nesting; food).—GROEBBELS, Der Vögel, ii, 1937, 115 (territory),
145 in text (mating behavior), 237 in text (egg laying), 239 in text (no. of eggs),
280 (white eggs), 323 in text (107 eggs laid in 115 days by one bird), 397 in text
(time of day of hatching), 415 in text (eggs eaten by snakes).—EMLEN, Journ.
Wildlife Manag., iii, 1939, 118-130 (behavior).—JEWETT, Condor, xli, 1939, 30,
in text (Tule Lake, Calif.; killed by snake).—HERMAN, JANKIEWICZ, and
SAARNI, Condor, xliv, 1942, 169, in text (coccidiosis).—DE MAY, Condor, xliv,
1942, 229 (Buena Vista Lake, Calif.; bones).—MILLER, Condor, xlv, 1943, 105,
in text (bone meas.).—BEHLE, Condor, xlvi, 1944, 72 (Utah, introduced).
L[ophortyx] californica COUES, Key North Amer. Birds, ed. 2, 1884, 592, part.
Lophortyx californicus BAIRD, Rep. Pacific R. R. Surv., ix, 1858, 644, part (Tulare
Valley, Tejon Valley, Fort Tejon, San Diego, and Mohave River, Calif.; Wil-
lamette Valley, Oreg. ?); Rep. U. S. and Mex. Bound Surv., ii, pt. 2, 1859, 22
(near San Diego); Cat. North Amer. Birds, 1859, No. 474, part; in Cooper, Orn.
California, Land Birds, 1870, 549, part.—XANTUS, Proc. Acad. Nat. Sci. Philadelphia, 1859, 192 (Fort Tejon).—COUES, Proc. Essex Inst., v, 1868, 40 (Bridgeport,
Conn., escaped cage bird); Check List North Amer. Birds, 1874, No. 391, part.—
BAIRD, BREWER, and RIDGWAY, Hist. North Amer. Birds, iii, 1874, 479, part, pl.
61, fig. 4, pl. 64, figs. 1, 2.—RIDGWAY, Bull. Essex Inst., vi, 1874, 172 (Nevada;
western foothills of Sierra Nevada, 1867); Orn. 40th Parallel, 1877, 602, part
(w. foothills of Sierra Nevada).—NELSON, Bull. Boston Soc. Nat. Hist., xvii,
1875, 364 (Nevada City, Calif.; abundant).—BREWSTER, Bull. Nuttall Orn. Club,
viii, 1883, 32, in text (San Gorgonio Pass, Ariz.; most eastern locality).—
OGILVIE-GRANT, Cat. Birds Brit. Mus., xxii, 1893, 400 part (Kernville, Fort
Tejon, Jolon, San Bernardino County, Coahuila Valley, Colton, San Diego
County, Colorado Desert, etc., Calif.; Carson, w. Nevada).—JUDD, U. S. Biol.
Surv. Bull. 21, 1905, 47, part (range; habits; food).—PORTIELJE, Ardea, xvi,
1927, 20, in text (psychology).—SETH-SMITH, L'Oiseau, x, 1929, 760 (captivity).
—GROEBBELS, Der Vögel, i, 1932, 185 (alt. distr.), 619 (body weight), 664 (body
temperature).—GRINNELL, Univ. California Publ. Zool., xxxviii, 1932, 268 (type
loc.; crit.).
[Lophortyx] californicus COUES, Key North Amer. Birds, 1872, 238, part.
Callipepla californica vallicola RIDGWAY, Proc. U. S. Nat. Mus., viii, 1885, 355
("interior valleys of California; type from Baird, Shasta County, in coll. U. S.
Nat. Mus.).—AMERICAN ORNITHOLOGISTS' UNION, Check-list, 1886, No. 294a; ed.
2, 1895, No. 294 a; ed. 3, 1910, 136.—FISHER, North Amer. Fauna, No. 7, 1893,
28 (Cajon Pass, Lone Willow Spring, Panamint Mountains, Argus Range, Coso
Mountains, Owens Lake, Walker Pass, Kern River, etc., Calif.).—HOLZNER,
Auk, xiii, 1896, 81, part (San Diego County; habits).—GRINNELL, Pasadena
Acad. Sci., Publ. 1, 1897, 12 (San Clemente Island; introduced).—WOODCOCK,
Oregon Agr. Exp. Stat. Bull. 68, 1902, 25 (interior valleys, etc., of w. Oregon).
C[allipepla] california vallicola RIDGWAY, Man. North Amer. Birds, 1887, 192.
Lophortyx californicus vallicola ELLIOT, Gallin. Game Birds North America, 1897,
60.—AMERICAN ORNITHOLOGISTS' UNION, Auk, xvi, 1899, 106.—STONE, Proc.
Acad. Nat. Sci. Philadelphia, 1904, 580 (Mount Sanhedrin, Mendocino County,

n. California).—GOLDMAN, Condor, x, 1908, 203 (w. side Tulare Lake and Buena Vista Lake, s. California).—DAWSON and BOWLES, Birds of Washington, ii, 1909, 570 (Washington; habits; distr.; introduced).—KESSEL, Condor, xxiii, 1921, 167 in text (flocking habits).—BENNITT, Univ. Missouri Studies, vii, No. 3, 1932, 26 footnote (Missouri; introduced; established in Newton and McDonald Counties).—CAUM, Occ. Pap. Bishop Mus., x, No. 9, 1933, 13 (Hawaii; introduced; established).—EMLEN and LORENZ, Auk, lix, 1942, 369 in text (pairing response to sex hormone pellet implants).

L[ophortyx] c[alifornicus] vallicola BAILEY, Handb. Birds Western United States, 1902, 120.

Lophortyx californica vallicola AMERICAN ORNITHOLOGISTS' UNION, Check-list, ed. 3, 1910, 136; ed. 4, 1931, 89, part.—GRINNELL, Pacific Coast Avif., No. 8, 1912, 10 (California); No. 11, 1915, 59, part (Sonoran zones of California e. of humid coast belt and w. of Mojave and Colorado Deserts); Univ. California Publ. Zool., x, 1913, 230 (San Jacinto Mountains, s. California; habits, etc.); xxxviii, 1932, 269 (type loc.; crit.); Condor, xxviii, 1926, 128 in text (crit.).—WILLETT, Pacific Coast Avif., No. 7, 1912, 43, part (Pacific slope of s. California); Condor, xxi, 1919, 202 (Clear Lake to Diamond Valley, ne. California).—TYLER, Pacific Coast Avif., No. 9, 1913, 32 (Fresno district, Calif.; very common; economic status).—KELLOGG, Univ. California Publ. Zool., xii, 1916, 379 (Helena, Scott River, and Tower House, n. Calif.).—HOWELL, Pacific Coast Avif., No. 12, 1917, 52, part (introduced on San Clemente and Santa Cruz Islands; crit.).—DAWSON, Birds California (stud. ed.), iii, 1923, 1576, part (California; habits; distr.).—RICHARDS, Condor, xxvi, 1924, 99 (Grass Valley district, Calif.).—GRINNELL and STORER, Animal Life in Yosemite, 1924, 270 (Yosemite; habits; descr.; distr.).—WYMAN and BURNELL, Field Book Birds Southwestern United States, 1925, 86 (descr.; chars.).—MAILLIARD, Proc. California Acad. Sci., ser. 4, xvi, 1927, 294 (Modoc County, Calif.; nesting season).—GRINNELL, DIXON, and LINSDALE, Univ. California Publ. Zool., xxxv, 1930, 208 (Lassen Peak region, n. California).—CLARK, Condor, xxxii, 1930, 51 (Mount St. Helena, Napa County, Calif.).—COOKMAN, Wils. Bull., xlii, 1930, 65 (Santa Cruz, Idaho, Calif.).—BENT, U. S. Nat. Mus. Bull. 162, 1932, 62 (habits; distr.).—COMPTON, Condor, xxxv, 1933, 71 (eggs eaten by snake).—LINSDALE, Pacific Coast Avif., No. 23, 1936, 23, 48 (Nevada; resident in w. part of State).—ARNOLD, Condor, xxxix, 1937, 32 (Coalinga area, Fresno, Calif., abundant).—GROEBBELS, Der Vögel, ii, 1937, 167 (breeding biology).—EMLEN, Condor, xl, 1938, 41 in text (near Madera, Calif.; nests robbed by squirrels).—GABRIELSON and JEWETT, Birds Oregon, 1940, 221 (Oregon; distr.; habits).—EINARSEN, Murrelet, xxii, 1941, 9, 11, in text (management).—ERRINGTON, Wils. Bull., liii, 1941, 91.

Lophortyx californicus vallicolus GRINNELL, Pacific Coast Avif., No. 3, 1902, 30 (California; abundant resident arid Upper Sonoran Zone); Auk, xxii, 1905, 381 (Mount Pinos, Calif.).

Lophortyx c[alifornica] vallicola HANNA, Condor, xxvi, 1924, 147, in text (egg weight).

[Lophortyx] vallicola SHARPE, Hand-list, i, 1899, 44, part.

Lophortyx californica californica JENSEN, Auk, xl, 1923, 454 (n. Santa Fe County, N. Mex., nesting).—WILLETT, Pacific Coast Avif., No. 21, 1933, 49 (common resident in lowlands and foothills of sw. California).—PETERS, Check-list Birds of World, ii, 1934, 44.—GLADING, Condor, xl, 1938, 261 in text (male incubating).—EMLEN, Condor, xl, 1938, 85 in text (chicks attacked by ants).—VAN ROSSEM, Auk, lvi, 1939, 68, in text (crit.).—MILLER and CURTIS, Murrelet, xxi, 1940, 42

(Washington).—HELLMAYR and CONOVER, Cat. Birds Amer., i, No. 1, 1942, 232 (syn.; distr.).

Lophortyx c[alifornica] DUNLAVY, Auk, lii, 1935, 428 (ecol., distr.).—GROEBBELS, Der Vögel, ii, 1937, 167 (data on breeding biology).

Lophortyx c[alifornica] californica MARSHALL and LEATHAM, Auk, lix, 1942, 44 (Great Salt Lake Islands, Utah).—AMADON, Auk, lx, 1943, 226 (body weight and egg weight).

LOPHORTYX CALIFORNICA BRUNNESCENS Ridgway
CALIFORNIA QUAIL

Adult.—Similar to the corresponding sex of the nominate race but darker, the upperparts much browner, the back and upper surface of the wings olive-brown to almost Dresden brown in fresh plumage; the breast in the male slightly deeper and more slate colored; in the female the breast is more olive-brownish, less grayish than in the typical form.

Juvenal.—Similar to that of the nominate race but with the upperparts more suffused with tawny-olive, the lower parts with an ochraceous wash, and the dark markings averaging greater in size both above and below.

Natal down.—Similar to that of the typical form.

Adult male.—Wing 108–119 (113.6); tail 85–94 (88.9); culmen from base 14.8–16.5 (15.7); tarsus 30–34 (32.4); middle toe without claw 26.5–30.5 (27.9 mm.).[72]

Adult female.—Wing 106–113 (110); tail 79.5–88 (83.5); culmen from base 14.5–16 (15.2); tarsus 29–34.5 (31.4); middle toe without claw 26–29.5 (27.4 mm.).[73]

Range.—Resident in the humid coastal area of California from the northern border south to Santa Cruz County. Often recorded in literature as extending north to southwestern Oregon, but no specimens of this form have ever been taken there.[74]

Introduced into Hawaii, New Zealand, Chile, and locally in western United States (Washington, Colorado, etc.) and Vancouver Island, Canada.

Type locality.—San Francisco, Calif.[75]

P[erdix] californica LATHAM, Index Orn. Suppl., 1801, p. lxii.

Perdix californica VIEILLOT, Nouv. Dict. Hist. Nat., xxv, 1817, 259.—BONAPARTE, Ann. Lyc. Nat. Hist. New York, ii, pt. 1, 1826, 125; Contr. Maclurian Lyc., i, 1827, 22.—LESSON, Traité d'Orn., 1831, 507.—NUTTALL, Man. Orn. United States and Canada, Land Birds, 1832, 655, part.—AUDUBON, Orn. Biogr., v, 1839, 152, pl. 413.

---

[72] Twenty-five specimens.

[73] Eleven specimens.

[74] Gabrielson and Jewett, Birds of Oregon, 1940, 222.

[75] Specimens from the east side of San Francisco Bay are typical *L. c. californica*, and so the type locality must be on the western side of the Bay.

Lophortyx californica BONAPARTE, Geogr. and Comp. List, 1838, 42.—NUTTALL, Man. Orn. United States and Canada, Land Birds, ed. 2, 1840, 789, part (Oregon; Monterey).—NEWBERRY, Rep. Pacific R. R. Surv., vi, pt. 4, 1857, 92, part (habits).—COOPER and SUCKLEY, Rep. Pacific R. R. Surv., xii, book 2, pt. 3, 1860, 225, part (introduced, from San Francisco and liberated near Olympia, Washington; introduced into Puget Sound region in spring of 1857).—RIDGWAY, Proc. U. S. Nat. Mus., iii, 1880, 197; Nom. North Amer. Birds, 1881, No. 482, part.—COUES, Check List North Amer. Birds, ed. 2, 1882, No. 575, part.— HENSHAW, Bull. Nuttall Orn. Club, viii, 1883, 184 (story of a semidomesticated bird).—BRYAN, Occ. Pap. Bishop Mus., 1908, 56 [146] (Molokai, Hawaii; introduced).—BARROS, Rev. Chil. Hist. Nat., xxiii, 1919, Nos. 1-2, p. 15.—DABBENE, El Hornero, ii, 1920, 56 (introduced into Chile).—HOUSSE, Rev. Chil. Hist. Nat., xxix, 1925, 148 (San Bernardino, Chile; introduced).—TAVERNER, Birds Western Canada, 1926, 162 (fig.; descr.; habits; distr.; w. Canada).—SWARTH, Condor, xxix, 1927, 164, in text (imported from Chile).—ALFORD, Ibis, 1928, 196 (Vancouver Island).—BROWN, Murrelet, xi, 1930, 18, in text (Seattle, Wash.).— TAVERNER, Birds Canada, 1934, 164, in text (introduced in Canada); Can. Water Birds, 1939, 176 (Canada; introduced).—HAND, Condor, xliii, 1941, 225 (St. Joe National Forest, Idaho, introduced).

L[*ophortyx*] *californica* COUES, Key North Amer. Birds, ed. 2, 1884, 592, part.— BRYAN, Key to the Birds Hawaiian Group, 1901, 30 (Hawaiian Islands; introduced).

Lophortyx californicus BAIRD, Rep. Pacific R. R. Surv., ix, 1858, 644, part (Bodega, Petaluma, San Francisco, and San José, Calif.); Cat. North Amer. Birds, 1859, No. 474, part; *in* Cooper, Orn. California, Land Birds, 1870, 549, part.—ALLEN, Mem. Mus. Comp. Zool., iii, 1872, 171 (Ogden, Utah; introduced), 181 (Salt Lake Valley, Utah, introduced).—BAIRD, BREWER and RIDGWAY, Hist. North Amer. Birds, iii, 1874, 479, part.—COUES, Check List North Amer. Birds, 1874, No. 391, part.—RIDGWAY, Orn. 40th Parallel, 1877, 602, part (near San Francisco).—OGILVIE-GRANT, Cat. Birds Brit. Mus., xxii, 1893, 400, part (Whidley, Wash.; Redwood, Big Trees of Santa Cruz County, and Monterey, Calif.).— AMERICAN ORNITHOLOGISTS' UNION, Auk, xvi, 1899, 106.—VAN DENBURGH, Proc. Amer. Philos. Soc., xxxviii, 1899, 157 (Santa Clara County, Calif.; habits, etc.).—MACOUN, Cat. Can. Birds, 1900, 197 (Vancouver Island; introduced).— COOKE, Colorado State Agr. Coll. Bull. 56, 1900, 202 (Colorado; Grand Junction; introduced).—McGREGOR, Pacific Coast Avif., No. 2, 1901, 5 (California; Santa Cruz County; common).—HENSHAW, Birds Hawaiian Is., 1902, 134 (introduced on Hawaii and other islands).—BAILEY, Handb. Birds Western United States, 1902, 120, part.—JUDD, U. S. Biol. Surv. Bull. 21, 1905, 47, part (range; food; habits).—BOWLES, Auk, xxiii, 1906, 142 (Tacoma, Washington; introduced).— ROCKWELL, Condor, x, 1908, 160 (Mesa County, Colo.; introduced; abundant).— KERMODE, [Visitors' Guide] Publ. Provinc. Mus., 1909, 40 (Vancouver Island; introduced).—DAWSON and BOWLES, Birds Washington, ii, 1909, 568 (Washington; habits; distr.).—MACOUN and MACOUN, Cat. Can. Birds, ed. 2, 1909, 216 (Vancouver Island; introduced).—SCLATER, Hist. Birds Colorado, 1912, 143 (Colorado; introduced; now abundant).—REED, Av. Prov. Mendoza, 1921, 206 (Mendoza, Argentina; introduced).—POLL, Verh. Orn. Ges. Bay., xvii, 1927, 410 (lower Bavaria; escaped cage bird?).—DABBENE, Rev. Diosa Cazadora, No. 85, 1934, 125 (descr.; distr.).

[*Lophortyx*] *californicus* COUES, Key North Amer. Birds, 1872, 238, part.—SHARPE, Hand-list, i, 1899, 44.

Lophortyx californianus Henshaw, Ann. Lyc. Nat. Hist. New York, xi, 1874, 10 introduced near Ogden, Utah).—Lonnberg, Nat. Hist. Juan Fernández Is., pt. i, 1920, 2, 17 (Juan Fernández Islands, introduced; Masatierra, Masafuera).

Callipepla californica Gould, Monogr. Odontoph., pt. 1, 1844, pl. 16 and text.— Newberry, Rep. Pacific R. R. Surv., vi, pt. 4, 1857, 92, part.—Heermann, Rep. Pacific R. R. Surv., x, pt. iv, No. 2, 1859, 60, part?.—Sclater, Proc. Zool. Soc. London, 1859, 206 (length of incubation).—American Ornithologists' Union, Check-list, 1886, No. 294; 1895, 2 ed., No. 294.—Fisher, North Amer. Fauna, No. 7, 1893, 27 (coast of California, from Monterey to Boulder Creek).— Rhoads, Proc. Acad. Nat. Sci. Philadelphia, 1893, 37 (Nisqually and Vancouver Island, British Columbia; introduced).—Cooke, Colorado State Agr. Coll. Bull. 37, 1897, 69 (Colorado; introduced).—Dwight, Auk, xvii, 1900, 48 (molt, etc.).—Woodcock, Oregon Agr. Exp. Stat. Bull. 68, 1902, 25 (coast region of Oregon).—von Burg, *in* Fatio and Studer, Ois. Suisse, xv, 1926, 3154 (Switzerland; introduced).—Gaedechens, Orn. Monatsb., xli, 1933, 60, in text (Schleswig-Holstein; escaped introduced birds).

C[allipepla] californica Ridgway, Man. North Amer. Birds, 1887, 192.

[Callipepla] californica Reichenbach, Synop. Av., iii, Gallinaceae 1848, pl. 199, figs. 1914-1916.

Ortyx californica Stephens, *in* Shaw, Gen. Zool., xi, pt. 2, 1819, 384.—Lesson, Cent. Zool., 1830, 188, pl. 60.—Vigors, Zool. Voy. *Blossom*, Birds, 1839, 27.— Audubon, Synopsis, 1839, 199; Birds Amer., 8vo ed., v, 1842, 67, pl. 290.— Jardine, Nat. Libr. Orn., 1834 iv, pl. 11.

Lophortyx californica californica American Ornithologists' Union, Check-list, ed. 3, 1910, 136; ed. 4, 1931, 89.—Grinnell, Pacific Coast Avif., No. 8, 1912, 10 (California); No. 11, 1915, 59 (humid coast belt s. to Monterey).—Shelton, Univ. Oregon Bull., new ser. xiv, No. 4, 1917, 20, 26 (w. central Oregon; introduced).—Jensen, Auk, xl, 1923, 454 (n. Sante Fe County, N. Mex.).

Lophortyx californicus californicus Grinnell, Pacific Coast Avif., No. 3, 1902, 29 (California; humid coast belt s. to Monterey).—Ray, Auk, xxi, 1904, 439 (Farallon Islands, present for 7 years).—Low, Bull. Brit. Orn. Club, li, 1930, 15, in text (near Victoria, Vancouver Island).

Lophortyx c[alifornicus] californicus Jenkins, Condor, viii, 1906, 126 (Monterey County, Calif.).

Lophortyx californicus brunnescens Ridgway, Proc. Biol. Soc. Washington, ii, 1885 (pub. Apr. 10, 1884), 94 (Santa Barbara, Calif.; coll. U. S. Nat. Mus.).

Lophortyx californica brunnescens Grinnell, Condor, xxxiii, 1931, 38 (crit.); Univ. California Publ. Zool., xxxviii, 1932, 269 (type loc.; crit.).—Hellmayr, Publ. Field Mus. Nat. Hist., zool. ser., xix, 1932, 423 (Chile and Juan Fernández Islands; introduced).—Peters, Check-list Birds of World, ii, 1934, 44.— Anonymous, El Hornero, vi, 1935, 196 (introduced into Argentina and Chile— Coquimbo, Talea, Juan Fernández Islands).—Steullet and Deautier, Obra Cincuentenario Mus. Plata, i, pt. 3, 1939, 502 (introduced into Chile and Argentina). —Hellmayr and Conover, Cat. Birds Amer., i, No. 1, 1942, 233 (syn.; distr.).— Jewett, Condor, xliv, 1942, 36 (Coos County, Oreg.).—Amadon, Auk, lx, 1943, 226 (body weight and egg weight).

LOPHORTYX CALIFORNICA CATALINENSIS Grinnell

Santa Catalina Quail

Adult.—Similar to that of the corresponding sex of the nominate race but larger throughout and averaging darker.

Adult male.—Wing 116–119 (117.7); tail 89.5–90 (89.7); culmen from base 14.5–16 (15); tarsus 33–35 (34.1); middle toe without claw 27.5–29 (28.3 mm.).[76]

Adult female.—Wing 113.5–117 (115.7); tail 87.5–88 (87.8); culmen from base 14.5–16 (14.8); tarsus 32–33 (32.3); middle toe without claw 27–28 (27.6 mm.).[76]

Range.—Resident on Santa Catalina Island, Calif.

Type locality.—Avalon, Santa Catalina Island, Calif.

Lophortyx californicus (not *Tetrao californicus* Shaw) BAIRD, *in* Cooper, Orn. California, Land Birds, 1870, 549, part (Santa Catalina Island).

Callipepla californica vallicola (not of Ridgway) GRINNELL, Auk, xv, 1898, 234 (Santa Catalina Island).—HOWELL, Pacific Coast Avif., No. 12, 1917, 52, part (Santa Catalina Island; crit.).

Lophortyx catalinensis GRINNELL, Auk, xxiii, 1906, 262 (Avalon, Santa Catalina Island, Santa Barbara group, Calif.; coll. J. Grinnell); Condor, x, 1908, 94 (crit.).—CHILDS, Warbler, iii, 1907, 1, col. pl. (eggs; descr. nest and eggs).—RICHARDSON, Condor, x, 1908, 66 (Santa Catalina Island).—OBERHOLSER, Auk, xxxiv, 1917, 194 (crit.).—GRINNELL, Univ. California Publ. Zool., xxxviii, No. 3, 1932, 270 (type loc.; crit.).

Lophortyx californica catalinensis GRINNELL, Pacific Coast Avif., No. 8, 1912, 10 (California; listed); No. 11, 1915, 59 (Santa Catalina Island); Condor, xxxiii, 1931, 38 (crit.).—OBERHOLSER, Auk, xxxiv, 1917, 194 (crit.); xxxv, 1918, 206.—GRINNELL, BRYANT, and STORER, Game Birds California, 1918, 537 (distr.).—DAWSON, Birds California (stud. ed.), iii, 1923, 1578 (California; habits; distr.).—AMERICAN ORNITHOLOGISTS' UNION, Check-list, ed. 4, 1931, 89 (distr.).—BENT, U. S. Nat. Mus. Bull. 162, 1932, 70 (habits; distr.).—WILLETT, Pacific Coast Avif. No. 21, 1933, 49 (abundant; Catalina Island; considers this race only doubtfully distinct).—PETERS, Check-list Birds of World, ii, 1934, 45.—HELLMAYR and CONOVER, Cat. Birds Amer., i, No. 1, 1942, 234 (syn.; distr.).

Lophortyx [californica] catalinensis DICKEY and VAN ROSSEM, Condor, xxiv, 1922, 34, in text (crit.; maintains its validity).

LOPHORTYX CALIFORNICA PLUMBEA Grinnell

SAN QUINTÍN VALLEY QUAIL

Adult male.—Similar to that of the nominate race but with the back more grayish in fresh plumage, having little or no brownish suffusion; the breast is neutral gray, by which darker tone it may be distinguished from *L. c. orecta* (in which the breast is light neutral gray).

Adult female.—Similar to that of the nominate race but much more grayish, less brownish above; the breast is mouse gray (as opposed to grayish drab to light grayish drab in the races *achrustera, canfieldae,* and *orecta.*

Adult male.—Wing 102–115 (107.3); tail 77–88.5 (83); culmen from base 13.8–15.5 (14.5); tarsus 28–33 (30.9); middle toe without claw 24–27.5 (25.8 mm.).[77]

---

[76] Three specimens of each sex.

[77] Eighteen specimens.

Adult female.—Wing 101–110 (105.3) ; tail 78–85 (82.2) ; culmen from base 14–15 (14.5) ; tarsus 28.5–32 (29.8) ; middle toe without claw 24–27 (25 mm.).[78]

Range.—Resident in open chaparral country from southwestern San Diego County, Calif. (Dulzura, Campo, and Mountain Spring), through northwestern Baja California, roughly south to latitude 30° N.—the so-called San Quintín subfaunal district; east in canyons to the east base of the Sierra San Pedro Mártir, and to San Felipe on the Gulf of California, also on Los Coronados Islands.

Type locality.—San José, alt. 2,500 feet, 45 miles northeast of San Quintín, Baja California.

Lophortyx californica NUTTALL, Man. Orn. United States and Canada, Land Birds, ed. 2, 1840, 789, part.—SALLÉ and PARZUDAKI, Cat. Oiseaux Mexique, 1862, 6 (Mexico).—COUES, Check List North Amer. Birds, ed. 2, 1882, No. 575, part.—BERISTAIN and LAURENCIO, Mem. y Rev. Soc. Cient. "Antonio Alzate," vii, 1894, 219 part.

Lophortyx californicus BAIRD, Rep. Pacific R. R. Surv., ix, 1858, 644, part; Cat. North Amer. Birds, 1859, No. 474, part.—OGILVIE-GRANT, Cat. Birds Brit. Mus., xxii, 1893, 400, part (s. San Diego County, Calif.).—JUDD, U. S. Biol. Surv. Bull. 21, 1905, 47, part.

Callipepla californica vallicola BRYANT, Proc. California Acad. Sci., ser. 2, ii, 1889, 276, part (San Quintín, etc., Baja California; descrip. of nest and eggs).—HOLZNER, Auk, xii, 1896, 81, part (s. San Diego County, Calif.).

Lophortyx californica vallicola WILLETT, Pacific Coast Avif., No. 7, 1912, 43, part (extreme sw. California).—GRINNELL, Pacific Coast Avif., No. 11, 1915, 59, part (w. of Colorado Desert, part) ; Univ. California Publ. Zool., xxxii, 1928, 101 (extreme n. Baja California).—HOWELL, Pacific Coast Avif., No. 12, 1917, 52, part (Los Coronados Ids., Baja California).—DAWSON, Birds California (stud. ed.), iii, 1923, 1576, part (habits; etc.).—ANTHONY, Proc. California Acad. Sci., ser. 4, xiv, 1925, 294 (e. of San Quintín, Baja California).—AMERICAN ORNITHOLOGISTS' UNION, Check-list North Amer. Birds, ed. 4, 1931, 89, part (extreme n. Baja California).

Lophortyx californicus vallicola THAYER and BANGS, Condor, ix, 1907, 136 (Rosario, San Javier, San Andreas, and Rosarito, Baja California).—WRIGHT, Condor, xi, 1909, 100 (Los Coronados Islands, Baja California).

Lophortyx californica BELDING, Proc. U. S. Nat. Mus., v, 1883, 528 (San Quintín Bay, Baja California).

[*Lophortyx*] *vallicola* SHARPE, Hand-list, i, 1899, 44, part.

Lophortyx californica plumbea GRINNELL, Condor, xxviii, 1926, 128 (orig. descr.; San José, 45 miles northeast of San Quintín, Baja California; crit.) ; Univ. California Publ. Zool., xxxii, 1928, 101 (distr.).—AMERICAN ORNITHOLOGISTS' UNION, Check-list, ed. 4, 1931, 90 (distr.).—BENT, U. S. Nat. Mus. Bull. 162, 1932, 71 (life hist.).—ROWLEY, Condor, xxxvii, 1935, 163 (nesting; San Telmo to San Fernando, Baja California).

Lophortyx californica californica PETERS, Check-list Birds of World, ii, 1934, 44, part (n. Baja California s. to lat. 30° N.).—HELLMAYR and CONOVER, Cat. Birds Amer., i, No. 1, 1942, 232, part (n. Baja California, s. to lat. 30° N.).

---

[78] Twelve specimens.

LOPHORTYX CALIFORNICA ACHRUSTERA Peters

SAN LUCAS QUAIL

Adult male.—Similar to that of the nominate race but back darker, averaging more gray than brown in fresh plumage (the opposite is true in typical *californica*); the breast deep neutral gray (darker than the race *plumbea* of northern Baja California).

Adult female.—Similar to that of the nominate race but the back decidedly grayish rather than brownish, the breast grayish drab to light grayish drab. From the races *canfieldae* and *orecta* this form differs in being slightly less grayish above.

Other plumage like the corresponding ones of the nominate race.

Adult male.—Wing 107–114 (110); tail 86–100 (91); culmen from base 14–17 (15.4); tarsus 28.5–33 (31.2); middle toe without claw 24–27 (25.8 mm.).[79]

Adult female.—Wing 105–108 (106); tail 81–88 (84.9); culmen from base 14.5–15.5 (15); tarsus 29–31 (30.2); middle toe without claw 24–25.5 (24.8 mm.). [80]

Range.—Resident in the southern half or more of Baja California from Cape San Lucas north to about latitude 30° N.

Type locality.—La Paz, Baja California.

Lophortyx californicus BAIRD, Proc. Acad. Nat. Sci. Philadelphia, 1859, 305 (Cape San Lucas); Cat. North Amer. Birds, 1859, No. 474, part.—OGILVIE-GRANT, Cat. Birds Brit. Mus., xxii, 1893, 400 part (Cape San Lucas).

Lophortyx californica BELDING, Proc. U. S. Nat. Mus., v, 1883, 544 (Cape San Lucas). —BERISTAIN and LAURENCIO, Mem. y Rev. Soc. Cient. "Antonio Alzate," vii, 1894, 219 part (Baja California; part).

Lophortyx californica vallicola BRYANT, Proc. California Acad. Sci., ser. 2, ii, 1889, 276, part (Cape San Lucas region).—TOWNSEND, Bull. Amer. Mus. Nat. Hist., xlviii, 1923, 13 (Gulf Coast of Baja California from Cape San Lucas to Agua Verde Bay).—MAILLIARD, Proc. California Acad. Sci., ser. 4, xiii, 1923, 454 (San Francisquito Bay, Point Santa Antonita, and Agua Verde Bay, Baja California, May).

Callipepla californica vallicola TOWNSEND, Proc. U. S. Nat. Mus., xiii, 1890, 136 (Cape San Lucas).—ANTHONY, Zoë, iv, 1893, 232 (Baja California; habits); Auk, xii, 1895, 136 (San Fernando, Baja California).

Lophortyx californicus vallicola BREWSTER, Bull. Mus. Comp. Zool., xli, 1902 (Triunfo, San José del Rancho, La Paz, and Sierra de la Laguna, s. Baja California; crit.).

[*Lophortyx*] *vallicola* SHARPE, Hand-list, i, 1899, 44, part.

Lophortyx californica achrustera PETERS, Proc. New England Zool. Club, viii, 1923, 79 (La Paz, Baja California; orig. descr.; crit.).—OBERHOLSER, Auk, xli, 1924, 592 (addition to North Amer. Check-list).—GRINNELL, Condor, xxviii, 1926, 128, in text (crit.); Univ. California Publ. Zool., xxxii, 1928, 103 (distr. in Baja California).—BANGS, Bull. Mus. Comp. Zool., lxx, 1930, 159 (type spec. in

---

[79] Twenty specimens.
[80] Five specimens.

Mus. Comp. Zool.).—BANCROFT, Condor, xxii, 1930, 25 (José María Cañon; breeding; San Ignacio, Baja California).—AMERICAN ORNITHOLOGISTS' UNION, Check-list, ed. 4, 1931, 90 (distr.).—BENT, U. S. Nat. Mus., Bull. 162, 1932, 72 (life hist.).—PETERS, Check-list Birds of World, ii, 1934, 45.—ROWLEY, Condor, xxxvii, 1935, 163, in text (nesting; Miraflores, Baja California).—VAN ROSSEM, Auk, lvi, 1939, 68, in text (crit.).—HELLMAYR and CONOVER, Cat. Birds Amer., i, No. 1, 1942, 234 (syn.; distr.).

LOPHORTYX CALIFORNICA CANFIELDAE van Rossem

OLATHE QUAIL

Adult male.—Similar to that of *L. c. achrustera* but paler, the breast neutral gray (as opposed to deep neutral gray in the San Lucas quail).

Adult female.—Similar to that of *L. c. achrustera* but paler, the back with little or none of the olive brownish suffusion found in that form; paler than *L. c. orecta,* the sides and flanks buffy brown (as opposed to olive brown in *L. c. orecta*).

Range.—Resident in Owens Valley, east-central California.[81]

Type locality.—Lone Pine, Inyo County, Calif.

Callipepla californica vallicola FISHER, North Amer. Fauna, No. 7, 1893, 28, part (Owens Valley; young just able to fly, Lone Pine, June 4 to 15).—GRINNELL, BRYANT, and STORER, Game Birds California, 1918, 514, part (Lone Pine, Inyo County).

Lophortyx californica canfieldae VAN ROSSEM, Auk, lvi, 1939, 68 (Lone Pine, Inyo County, Calif.; orig. descr.; crit.).—HELLMAYR and CONOVER, Cat. Birds Amer., i, No. 1, 1942, 234 (syn.; crit.; distr.).

LOPHORTYX CALIFORNICA ORECTA Oberholser

WARNER VALLEY QUAIL

Adult male.—Similar to that of the nominate race but with the back much more grayish in fresh plumage, having little or no olive-brownish suffusion; very pale generally, the breast light neutral gray.

Adult female.—Similar to that of the nominate race, but with the back much grayer, with little or no brownish suffusion; nearest in color to *L. c. canfieldae,* but differs in having the sides and flanks darker— olive-brown (as opposed to buffy brown in *canfieldae*).

Adult male.—Wing 109.5–118.5 (113.1); tail 87–96.5 (91); culmen from base 13.5–15.5 (14.6); tarsus 28.5–32.5 (31.1); middle toe without claw 25–28.5 (26.5 mm.).[82]

Adult female.—Wing 110–113 (111.1); tail 84–92 (86.8); culmen from base 14–15.5 (15); tarsus 28–32.5 (30.3); middle toe without claw 25–28.5 (26.5 mm.).[83]

---

[81] Birds from the Sacramento Valley, while nearer to the typical race show some variation in the direction of *canfieldae.*

[82] Seventeen specimens.

[83] Six specimens.

Range.—Resident in the Warner Valley, southeastern Oregon. Birds from Malheur County to the west show some variation toward *orecta*. The race is only faintly characterized, but in fresh material it is recognizable.

Type locality.—Mouth of Twenty Mile Creek, Warner Valley, 9 miles south of Adel, Oreg.

Lophortyx californica orecta OBERHOLSER, Sci. Publ. Cleveland Mus. Nat. Hist., iv, 1932, 2 (mouth of Twenty Mile Creek, Warner Valley, 9 miles south of Adel, Oreg.; orig. descr.; crit.).—VAN ROSSEM, Auk, lvi, 1939, 69, in text (crit.).— —MILLER, Condor, xliii, 1941, 259 (crit.).

Lophortyx californica californica PETERS, Check-list Birds of World, ii, 1934, 44, part.—HELLMAYR and CONOVER, Cat. Birds Amer., i, No. 1, 1942, 232, part.

LOPHORTYX GAMBELII GAMBELII Gambel

GAMBEL'S QUAIL

Adult male.—Forehead, lores, and anterior part of crown black finely streaked with pale buffy, the pale streaks ending just anterior to the posterior limit of the coronal black, producing a narrow black posterior border to this area, which, in turn, is bounded posteriorly by a transverse white band between the eyes which turns back on each side to continue over the eyes and auriculars to the sides of the neck, this white band narrowly rimmed with black; the black posterior rim broadest on the crown; top and back of head between cinnamon-rufous and Sudan brown; crest of six terminally broadening, spatulate black feathers beginning at midposterior point of the coronal white band; nape and sides of neck and anterior interscapulars between neutral gray and light neutral gray, each feather with a Dresden brown narrow shaft streak; posterior interscapulars, back, rump, and upper tail coverts neutral gray, all but the posterior interscapulars washed more or less with mouse gray; upper wing coverts and scapulars mouse gray washed with drab; the scapulars and innermost secondaries with whitish or buffy whitish margins on their inner webs, the secondaries with narrower similar edges on their outer webs; primaries between buffy brown and olive-brown, grayish on their outer webs; rectrices between neutral gray and deep neutral gray; chin and throat and cheeks solid black, the area bordered by a white band running across the lower throat and turning forward on the sides of the head to separate the cheeks from the auriculars, and ending at the posterior angle of the eye, this white band narrowly rimmed posteriorly with black; auriculars between Dresden brown and sepia; breast uniform neutral gray; sides and anterior flanks with elongated feathers of bright, dark chestnut, each with a terminally widening, narrowly spatulate white shaft stripe; abdomen pale buffy white with a large patch on the midposterior part; the posterior flank feathers pale buffy white with fairly broad hazel shaft stripes; under tail coverts similar but with the shaft stripes clove brown to chaetura drab; under wing coverts dusky hair brown; iris dark brown; bill black; tarsi and toes dull greenish gray, claws black.

Adult female.—Very different from the male: forehead, lores, and anterior part of crown posterior to the hind end of the eyes pale hair brown finely streaked with buffy white; crest smaller than in male and dark clove brown to fuscous; posterior part of crown, occiput, and auriculars between wood brown and sayal brown, the auriculars with fine dusky streaks; nape and sides of neck and anterior interscapulars as in the male but washed with brownish gray and the shaft streaks less rufescent, more dusky; rest of upperparts of the body, the wings, and tail as in the male but averaging slightly more brownish; chin and throat white faintly washed with buffy and the feathers with shaft streaks of pale buffy brown; cheeks similar but with the streaks much darker— dingy sepia; breast like the back but slightly paler; abdomen light buffy whitish without the large central black patch found in the male, and the feathers with narrow, incomplete shaft streaks of dark brown, these streaks disappearing on the lower abdomen; elongated feathers of the sides and upper flanks as in the male but averaging paler chestnut; lower flanks, thighs, and under tail coverts as in the male.

Juvenal (sexes alike).—Lores, forehead, crown, and occiput Saccardo's umber, bordered on each side by very broad supraorbital bands of very pale cinnamon-buff; entire upperparts of body pale tawny-olive finely speckled with dusky; interscapulars, scapulars, innermost secondaries and inner upper wing coverts with broad white shaft streaks, which spread out at the tips of the feathers, the feathers heavily blotched with dark mummy brown subterminally; innermost secondaries with the white shaft stripes greatly reduced, the feathers crossed by heavy transverse blotches of dusky mummy brown, and their inner webs extensively suffused with the same; remaining secondaries and the primaries dull clove brown, their outer webs mottled with dull pale tawny-olive; rectrices dusky bister transversely mottled and tipped with pale dull olive-buff; chin and throat whitish somewhat tinged with pale buffy; breast, sides, flanks, thighs, and under tail coverts dingy buffy white transversely mottled and barred with hair brown to dusky hair brown; middle of abdomen uniformly dingy buffy white.

Natal down.—Forehead, lores, and anterior half of crown and the sides of the head vary from clay color to pinkish buff; a broad band of russet, rimmed with black from the point of origin of the crest to hindneck; auriculars dark brownish; remainder of upperparts light pinkish buff, broadly striped and blotched with warm sepia; underparts pale grayish buff.

Adult male.—Wing 108–122 (112.1); tail 91–107 (96.3); culmen from base 13.9–16.4 (15.4); tarsus 27.6–32.5 (30.5); middle toe without claw 24.1–29.4 (26.9 mm.).[84]

Adult female.—Wing 105–118 (112.1); tail 83–102 (94.2); culmen from base 14.3–16.2 (15.1); tarsus 27.9–31.9 (30.0); middle toe without claw 24.1–28.4 (26.0 mm.).[85]

Range.—Resident from southwestern Utah (St. George, Uinta, Toquerville) and southern Nevada (Ash Meadows, Pahrump Valley) south to southwestern New Mexico (Fort Bayard, Frisco, Joseph, Silver City, Grafton); Arizona, to extreme northwestern Chihuahua (Cajón, Bonito Creek), and through southern California (Death Valley, Needles, Calipatria, San Diego County, etc.) to central Sonora (south to Guaymas and Tecoripa) and to extreme northeastern Baja California (Cocopah Mountains; Volcano Lake, Seven Wells, etc.). Introduced in many places—Hawaii, Massachusetts, Missouri, etc., mostly without success.

Type locality.—"Some distance west [i. e., east] of California"=southern Nevada.

Lophortyx gambelii GAMBEL, Proc. Acad. Nat. Sci. Philadelphia, 1843, 260 ("some distance west [i.e., east] of California" = s. Nevada; ex Nuttall, manuscript); Journ. Acad. Nat. Sci. Philadelphia, i, 1847, 219.—BAIRD, Rep. Pacific R. R. Surv., ix, 1858, 645, part (Gila River, Ariz.; Colorado River, Calif.); Rep. U. S. and Mex. Bound. Surv., ii, pt. 2, 1859, 23 (s. to Presidio del Norte, Tex.; w. to San Bernardino, n. Sonora); Cat. North Amer. Birds, 1859, No. 475; *in* Cooper, Orn. California, Land Birds, 1870, 553 (Fort Mojave, etc.).—HEERMANN, Rep. Pacific R. R. Surv., x, Parke's Route, 1859, 19 part (Fort Yuma, Ariz.).—KENNERLY, Rep. Pacific R. R. Surv., x, No. 3, 1859, 33, part (Colorado River; habits). —COUES, Proc. Acad. Nat. Sci. Philadelphia, 1866, 94 (Fort Whipple, etc., Arizona; habits; descr. young in various stages).—HENSHAW, Ann. Lyc. Nat. Hist. New York, xi, 1874, 10 (s. Utah).—AMERICAN ORNITHOLOGISTS' UNION, Auk, xvi, 1899, 106.—BAILEY, Handb. Birds Western United States, 1902, 121 (descr.; distr.).—BRUNER, Condor, xxviii, 1926, 232 (Baboquivari Mountains, Ariz.).— MILLER, TAYLOR, and SWARTH, Condor, xxxi, 1929, 77 in text (winter at Tucson, Ariz.).—MILLER, Condor, xxxiv, 1932, 139 (bones *ex* Indian dwellings, Arizona). —GORSUCH, Condor, xxviii, 1936, 126 in text (banding records, Tucson, Ariz.). —CARTER, Condor, xxxix, 1937, 212 (Twentynine Palms, Calif.).—NEFF, Condor, xliii, 1941, 117 in text (arboreal nests in Arizona).

Callipepla gambelii GOULD, Monogr. Odontoph., 1850, pl. 17, text (unpaged).—AMERICAN ORNITHOLOGISTS' UNION, Check-list, ed. 2, 1895, 109, part.

Lophortyx gambelii gambelii GRINNELL, Proc. California Acad. Sci., ser. 4, xiii, 1923, 60 (Furnace Creek Ranch, Death Valley, Calif.; food); Distr. Summ. Orn. Baja California, Univ. California Publ. Zool., xxxii, 1928, 103 (Baja California; distr.).—ABBOTT, Condor, xxx, 1928, 163 (Borego Valley, Calif.).—SWARTH,

---

[84] Fifty-six specimens from Nevada, California, Texas, New Mexico, Arizona, Utah, and Mexico (Sonora, Chihuahua, and Baja California).

[85] Forty-one specimens from Texas, New Mexico, Arizona, Utah, California, and Mexico (Sonora, Chihuahua, and Baja California).

Proc. California Acad. Sci., ser. 4, xviii, 1929, 289 (e. of Patagonia, Ariz.;
young; distr.; plum.).—VAN ROSSEM, Trans. San Diego Soc. Nat. Hist., vi,
1931, 245 (Sonora, Mexico—El Doctor, Pesquira, Tecoripa, Saric, Guaymas, 12
miles w. of Magdalena, 15 miles sw. of Nogales, Sasabe Valley; spec.); vii, 1932,
132, in text (colors of soft parts); viii, 1936, 128, photo (south-central Arizona);
Bull. Mus. Comp. Zool., lxxvii, 1934, 431 (Mexico—Bacoachi, San Pedro, Opo-
sura, Granados; spec.); Pacific Coast Avif., No. 24, 1936, 21 (Charleston Mountains, Nev.; common resident Lower Sonoran Zone).—MILLER, Condor, xxxiv,
1932, 96 (Grand Canyon, Collums Ranch, Ariz.).—WILLETT, Pacific Coast Avif.,
No. 21, 1933, 49 (San Gorgonio Pass and near Banning, sw. California).—
PETERS, Check-list Birds of World, ii, 1934, 46.—LINSDALE, Pacific Coast Avif.,
No. 23, 1936, 23, 49 (Nevada; resident, common in southern part of State north
to Quinn Canyon Mountains).—BOND, Condor, xlii, 1940, 221 (Lincoln County,
Nev.; common in desert brush near water or wet meadows).—HELLMAYR and
CONOVER, Cat. Birds Amer., i, No. 1, 1942, 235, part (syn.; distr.).—BEHLE, Bull.
Univ. Utah, xxxiv, 1943, 24, 37 (Washington County, Utah); Condor, xlvi, 1944,
72 (Utah).

Lophortyx g[*ambelii*] *gambelii* LAW, Condor, xxxi, 1929, 219 (range in s. Arizona).
[*Lophortyx*] [*gambelii*] *gambelii* VAN ROSSEM, Trans. San Diego Soc. Nat. Hist., vii,
1932, 132, in text (distr.); viii, 1936, 128 (Sonora).

Lophortyx gambeli COUES, Ibis, 1866, 45–55 (Arizona; habits, etc.); Check List
North Amer. Birds, 1874, No. 392, ed. 2, 1882, No. 576; Birds Northwest, 1874,
432 (synonymy; habits).—BAIRD, BREWER, and RIDGWAY, Hist. North Amer.
Birds, iii, 1874, 482 pl. 64, figs. 4, 5, p. 523 (Tucson, Ariz.; descr. nest and eggs).
—BREWSTER, Bull. Nuttall Orn. Club, viii, 1883, 32 (Tucson, etc., up to 5,000
feet).—OGILVIE-GRANT, Cat. Birds Brit. Mus., xxii, 1893, 403, part (Toquerville
and Washington, s. Utah; New Mexico; Camp Grant, Gila River, and Yuma,
Arizona; Agua Caliente and Colorado Desert, Calif.).—GRINNELL, Pacific Coast
Avif., No. 3, 1902, 30 (California; common resident of Lower Sonoran Zone se.
of Sierras); No. 8, 1912, 10 (California); Univ. California Publ. Zool., x, 1913,
231 (arid eastern base of San Jacinto Mountains).—SALVIN and GODMAN, Biol.
Centr.-Amer., Aves, iii, 1903, 292, part (New Mexico; Arizona; s. Utah; s.
Nevada; Colorado Valley, se. California).—JUDD, U. S. Biol. Surv. Bull. 21,
1905, 56, part, pl. 2 (range; habits; food).—BROWN, Condor, ix, 1907, 109, in
text (valley between Cocopah and Coast ranges, w. Baja California, for 70
miles s. of boundary; w. side of Salton Sea to Calexico, on New River).—
GILMAN, Condor, ix, 1907, 148 (California range); x, 1908, 147 (Aztec, N. Mex.).
—AMERICAN ORNITHOLOGISTS' UNION, Check-list, ed. 3, 1910, 137, part.—WIL-
LETT, Pacific Coast Avif., No. 7, 1912, 43 (near Los Angeles, Calif., Sept. 16,
1896; near San Bernardino, Jan. 15, 1890).—SWARTH, Pacific Coast Avif., No.
10, 1914, 22 (Arizona; abundant in lowlands in s. and sw. parts of State).—
GRINNELL, BRYANT, and STORER, Game Birds of California, 1918, 538 (California;
habits; distr.).—WILLARD, Condor, xxv, 1923, 122, fig. 43 (near Tucson, Ari-
zona; eggs in nest of *Toxostoma palmeri*).—DAWSON, Birds of California (stud.
ed.), iii, 1923, 1586 (general; California).—BANCROFT, Condor, xxvi, 1924, 229,
in text (San Diego, Calif.).—BLINCOE, Auk, xlii, 1925, 419 (near Bardstown,
Ky.; introduced).—TANNER, Condor, xxix, 1927, 197 (Virgin River Valley,
Utah).—PALMER, Condor, xxx, 1928, 278, in text (patronymics).—CAUM, Occ.
Pap. Bishop Mus., x, No. 9, 1933, 13 (Hawaii, introduced).—GROEBBELS, Der
Vögel, ii, 1937, 232, in text (lays eggs in nests of thrasher and wren), 237 in
text (number of eggs), 383, in text (runt eggs), 402, in text (parental care).—
BAGG and ELIOT, Birds Connecticut Valley in Massachusetts, 1937, 174 (intro-
duced unsuccessfully).

L[*ophortyx*] *gambeli* SETH-SMITH, L'Oiseau, x, 1929, 761 (care in captivity).

Lophortyx gambelli BERISTAIN and LAURENCIO, Mem. y Rev. Soc. Cient. "Antonio Alzate," vii, 1894, 219 (Sonora and Chihuahua).

Lophortis gambelli CUBAS, Cuadro Geogr., Estadístico, Descr., e Hist. de los Estados Unidos Mexicanos, 1884, 168 (common names, Mexico).

L[*ophortyx*] *gambeli* COUES, Key North Amer. Birds, ed. 2, 1884, 593, part.

[*Lophortyx*] *gambeli* SHARPE, Hand-list, i, 1899, 44, part.

Callipepla gambeli GAMBEL, Journ. Acad. Nat. Sci. Philadelphia, n. s., i, 1847, 219.
—BAIRD, Rep. Stansbury's Expl. Great Salt Lake, 1852, 326 (New Mexico), 334 (New Mexico; California).—CASSIN, Illustr. Birds California, Texas, etc., 1854, 45.—GRAY, List Birds Brit. Mus., Gallinæ, pt. 5, 1867, 79, part.—BRYANT, Proc. California Acad. Sci., ser. 2, ii, 1889, 277 (e. side Baja California, lat. 30°N.).—JOHNSON, Auk, vi, 1889, 280 (Palm Springs, s. California).—BENDIRE, Life Hist. North Amer. Birds, i, 1892, 29.—WALL, Auk, x, 1893, 204 (San Bernardino, Calif.).—FISHER, North Amer. Fauna, No. 7, 1893, 29 (Death Valley, Amargosa Valley, and Resting Springs, Calif.; Ash Meadows, Pahrump Valley, Charleston Mountains, Upper Cottonwood Springs, and Great Bend of Colorado River, s. Nevada; Beaverdam Creek, nw. Arizona; Beaverdam Mountains, Santa Clara Valley, and s. end of Escalante Desert, s. Utah).—DWIGHT, Auk, xvii, 1900, 49 (molt, etc.).

C[*allipepla*] *gambeli* REICHENOW, Die Vögel, i, 1913, 317.

[*Callipepla*] *gambelii* GRAY, Hand-list, ii, 1870, 274, No. 9799.

Gallipepla gambeli CASSIN, Illustr. Birds California, Texas, etc., 1854, pl. 9.

Callipepla gambelii HEERMANN, Rep. Pacific R. R. Surv., x, pt. iv, No. 2, 1859, 60 (Mojave Desert and Big Lagoon of New River, Calif.; Fort Yuma, Ariz.; habits).—GRINNELL, Pasadena Acad. Sci., Publ. 2, 1898, 19 (near Los Angeles, Calif., Aug. 1, Sept. 16, 1896; common 50 miles n. and e.).

Lophortyx gambeli gambeli GRINNELL, Pacific Coast Avif., No. 11, 1915, 60 (abundant locally on Colorado and Mojave Deserts, n. to Amargosa and Death Valleys; w. to Hesperia and n. flank of Santa Rosa Mountains, and through Gorgonio Pass to Banning; casual in Los Angeles and San Bernardino Counties).—WYMAN and BURNELL, Field Book Birds Southwestern United States, 1925, 86 (descr.; chars.).—BAILEY, Birds New Mexico, 1928, 218, part (genl.; New Mexico).—PEMBERTON, Condor, xxxiii, 1931, 219 (San Clemente Island).—AMERICAN ORNITHOLOGISTS' UNION, Check-list, ed. 4, 1931, 90, part (distr.). —HUEY, Condor, xxxiv, 1932, 46 (introduced on San Clemente Island in 1912).— BENT, U. S. Nat. Mus. Bull. 162, 1932, 73, part (life hist., distr.; descr.).— BENNITT, Univ. Missouri Studies, vii, No. 3, 1932, 26, in footnote (Missouri; introduced; not yet with success).—GORSUCH, Bull. Univ. Arizona, v, 1935, i (Arizona; life hist.).—HUEY, Auk, lii, 1935, 252 (Punta Pinascosa, Sonora); Trans. San Diego Soc. Nat. Hist., ix, 1942, 364 (Organ Pipe Cactus National Monument, Ariz.; common; spec.).

Lophortyx g[*ambeli*] *gambeli* GROEBBELS, Der Vögel, ii, 1937, 167 (data on breeding biology).

Callipepla venusta GOULD, Proc. Zool. Soc. London, 1846 (pub. Oct. 1846), 70 (California?; coll. Mus. Neufchâtel).

Lophortyx californicus (not *Tetrao californicus* Shaw) KENNERLY, Rep. Pacific R. R. Surv., x, No. 3, 1859, 33 (Mojave River, se. California).—COUES, Ibis, 1865, 165, in text (Fort Whipple, Ariz.).

Callipepla gambeli deserticola STEPHENS, Auk, xii, 1895, 371 (Palm Springs, San Diego County, Calif.; coll. F. Stephens).—GRINNELL, Univ. California Publ. Zool., xxxviii, 1932, 270 (type loc.; crit.).

LOPHORTYX GAMBELII FULVIPECTUS (Nelson)

FULVOUS-BREASTED QUAIL

Adult male.—Similar to that of the nominate race, but with the abdomen more deeply colored—light warm buff; the pale edging of the scapulars and inner secondaries also buffier and the back slightly more washed with olive-brown.[86]

Adult female.—Similar to that of the nominate race, but with the abdomen more deeply colored—light warm buff; the pale edgings of the inner remiges also buffier; and the upperparts more extensively tinged with buffy brown. In the majority of specimens (but not in all) there is a faint but noticeable white line beginning behind the eye and posteriorly limiting the cheeks and sides of the throat, and another along the antero-lateral edge of the crown on each side. The crown and occiput average more rufescent in this race than in any of the others.

Adult male.—Wing 106–115 (112); tail 88–101 (95.6); culmen from base 14.8–16.2 (15.4); tarsus 30.5–33.0 (31.1); middle toe without claw 27.1–28.3 (27.7 mm.).[87]

Adult female.—Wing 105–118 (110.6); tail 85–98 (89.4); culmen from base 14.9–16.7 (15.7); tarsus 29.0–31.3 (30.1); middle toe without claw 26.3–26.9 (26.6 mm.).[88]

Range.—Resident in north-central to southwestern Sonora (Camoa, Obregón, Opodepe, Tesia, Tobari Bay, Agiabampo; 25 miles southeast of Guaymas), intergrading with *gambelii* near Guaymas.

Type locality.—Camoa, Río Mayo, Sonora.

Lophortyx gambelii (not of Gambel) LAWRENCE, Mem. Boston Soc. Nat. Hist., ii, 1874, 307 (Sonora).

Lophortyx gambeli BELDING, Proc. U. S. Nat. Mus., vi, 1884, 344 (Guaymas).— SALVIN and GODMAN, Biol. Centr.-Amer., Aves, iii, 1903, 292, part (Santa Bárbara, Hermosillo, Guaymas, and Río Mayo, Sonora).

Callipepla gambeli COOKE, Bird Migr. Mississippi Valley, 1888, 103, part (nw. Mexico).—ALLEN, Bull. Amer. Mus. Nat. Hist., v, 1893, 33 (Santa Bárbara, Sonora).—JOUY, Proc. U. S. Nat. Mus., xvi, 1894, 790 (Guadalajara, Jalisco).

Callipepla gambeli fulvipectus NELSON, Auk, xvi, 1899, 26 (Camoa, Río Mayo, sw. Sonora; coll. U. S. Nat. Mus.); xix, 1902, 388 (crit.).—THAYER and BANGS, Proc. Biol. Soc. Washington, xix, 1906, 18 (Opodepe, north-central Sonora).

[*Lophortyx*] *fulvipectus* SHARPE, Hand-list, i, 1899, 44.

Lophortyx gambelii fulvipectus VAN ROSSEM, Trans. San Diego Soc. Nat. Hist., vi, 1931, 245 (Sonora—Obregón, Tesia, Tobari Bay, Agiabampo); vii, 1932, 132 in text (Sonora; colors of soft parts).—PETERS, Check-list Birds World, ii, 1934, 46.

Lophortyx gambelii gambelii HELLMAYR and CONOVER, Cat. Birds Amer., i, No. 1, 1942, 235, part (Camoa, Sonora).

---

[86] These differences hold only in freshly plumaged birds. The buffy tones appear to fade away fairly rapidly so that by winter specimens of *fulvipectus* are indistinguishable from *gambelii*. This is also true of the females.

[87] Seven specimens from Sonora.

[88] Eleven specimens from Sonora.

LOPHORTYX GAMBELII PEMBERTONI van Rossem

TIBURÓN ISLAND QUAIL

Adult male.—Similar to that of the nominate race, but paler, purer gray, above with little or no olive wash, the gray of the anterior upper-parts between neutral gray and light neutral gray.

Adult female.—Similar to that of the nominate race but paler, the upperparts gray with little or no olive wash, the elongated feathers of the sides and flanks paler, as in the Texan race, *ignoscens.*

Adult male.—Wing 119; tail 97; culmen from base 13, tarsus 31, middle toe without claw 28.5 mm. (1 specimen).

Adult female.—Wing 113–115; tail 88–93; culmen from base 12–13; tarsus 30.5–31; middle toe without claw 27–28 mm. (2 specimens).

Range.—Confined to Tiburón Island, Gulf of California.

Type locality.—Petrel Bay, just south of Narragansett Point, east side of Tiburón Island, Sonora, Mexico.

Lophortyx gambelii pembertoni VAN ROSSEM, Trans. San Diego Soc. Nat. Hist., vii, 1932, 132 (Petrel Bay, Just south of Narragansett Point, east side of Tiburón Island, Sonora, Mexico; descr.; crit.).—PETERS, Check-list Birds World, ii, 1934, 46.—HELLMAYR and CONOVER, Cat. Birds Amer., i, No. 1, 1942, 236 (syn.; distr.).

LOPHORTYX GAMBELII SANA Mearns

COLORADO GAMBEL'S QUAIL

Adult male.—Similar to that of the nominate race but darker, the upper back gray with little or no olive wash, the general tone being between neutral gray and light mouse gray (being nearest to *L. g. pembertoni* in this regard, but darker).

Adult female.—Similar to that of the nominate race, but differing from it in the same way that the males of the two forms do.

Adult male.—Wing 117, tail 84; culmen from the base 14; tarsus 32; middle toe without claw 29 mm. (1 specimen).

Adult female.—Wing 115–117; tail 85–86; culmen from base 14–15; tarsus 26–29; middle toe without claw 27–28 mm. (2 specimens).

Range.—Resident in western Colorado in the drainage areas of the Uncompahgre and Gunnison Rivers and the portion of the Rio Grande Valley lying in Colorado.

Type locality.—Olathe, Montrose County, Colo.

Callipepla gambeli (not *Lophortyx gambelii* Gambel) COOKE, Colorado State Agr. Coll. Bull. 37, 1897, 70 (sw. Colorado, 40 miles sw. of Fort Lewis).
Lophortyx gambeli SCLATER, Hist. Birds Colorado, 1912, 144 (Colorado; doubtful).
—FIGGINS, Auk, xxxi, 1914, 62, 64, 68, in text (Colorado; meas.; crit.).
Lophortyx gambelii COOKE, Colorado State Agr. Coll. Bull. 56, 1900, 202 (cited; syn.).
Lophortyx gambelii sanus MEARNS, Proc. Biol. Soc. Washington, xxvii, 1914, 113 (Olathe, Montrose County, sw. Colorado; coll. U. S. Nat. Mus.).—AMERICAN ORNITHOLOGISTS' UNION, Auk, xl, 1923, 517 (sw. Colorado; Check-list No. 295a).—PETERS, Check-list Birds World, ii, 1934, 45.

Lophortyx gambeli sanus AMERICAN ORNITHOLOGISTS' UNION, Check-list, ed. 4, 1931,
90 (distr.).—BENT, U. S. Nat. Mus. Bull. 162, 1932, 84 (life histr.; distr.).
Lophortyx gambelii sana HELLMAYR and CONOVER, Cat. Birds Amer., i, No. 1, 1942,
234 (syn.; distr.).

LOPHORTYX GAMBELII IGNOSCENS Friedmann

TEXAS GAMBEL'S QUAIL

Adult.—Similar to the corresponding sex of the nominate race, but
with the long feathers of the sides and upper flanks lighter in color—
between Sanford's brown and chestnut, while in typical *gambelii* they
are between chestnut and bay; and somewhat paler generally, especially
so on the crown, breast, and back.[89]

Adult male.—Wing 111–121 (116); tail 92–100 (96.2); culmen from
base 14.5–15.6 (15.1); tarsus 29–31.5 (30.2); middle toe without claw
24.1–27.7 (26.1 mm.).[90]

Adult female.—Wing 105–118 (112.3); tail 84–92 (87); culmen from
base 13–14.9 (14.1); tarsus 29.9–31 (30.3); middle toe without claw
24.1–28 (26 mm.).[91]

Range.—Inhabits the extremely dry desert region, sometimes called
the "eastern succulent desert," from Fort Fillmore, N. Mex., east to
extreme western Texas—El Paso, Belen, San Elizario, and Fort Han-
cock, east to Presidio del Norte and to the Limpia River, Jeff Davis
County. It does not extend farther eastward into Brewster County, and
apparently does not go southward into adjacent areas of Mexico, but
is limited to the area of low rainfall (under 10 inches a year).

Type locality—San Elizario, Tex.

Lophortyx gambelii (not of Gambel, 1843) McCALL, Proc. Acad. Nat. Sci. Phila-
delphia, 1851, 221 (Limpia River, w. Texas, and westward; habits).—BAIRD,
Rep. Pacific R. R. Surv., ix, 1858, 645, part (San Elizario, Tex.; Fort Fillmore,
N. Mex.).—HEERMANN, Rep. Pacific R. R. Surv., x, Parke's Route, 1859, 19, part
Eagle Springs, Tex.).—KENNERLY, Rep. Pacific R. R. Surv., x, No. 3, 1859, 33,
part (Upper Rio Grande).
Callipepla gambelii AMERICAN ORNITHOLOGISTS' UNION, Check-list, ed. 2, 1895, 109,
part.
Lophortyx gambeli DRESSER, Ibis, 1866, 28 (near Fort Clark, Tex.).—SALVIN and
GODMAN, Biol. Centr.-Amer., Aves., iii, 1903, 292, part (w. Texas; New Mexico,
part).—JUDD, U. S. Biol. Surv. Bull. 21, 1905, 56, part, pl. 2 (range; habits;
food).—AMERICAN ORNITHOLOGISTS' UNION, Check-list, ed. 3, 1910, 137, part.
L[ophortyx] gambeli COUES, Key North Amer. Birds, ed. 2, 1884, 593, part (Pecos
and San Elizario, Tex.).
[Lophortyx] gambeli SHARPE, Hand-list, i, 1899, 44, part (w. Texas).
Callipepla gambeli GRAY, List Birds Brit. Mus., pt. 5, Gallinae, 1867, 79, part.—
COOKE, Bird Migr. Mississippi Valley, 1888, 103, part (w. Texas).

[89] The characters of this race are more pronounced in the males than the females.
[90] Five specimens including the type.
[91] Three specimens.

Lophortyx gambeli gambeli BAILEY, Birds New Mexico, 1928, 218, part (New Mexico).—AMERICAN ORNITHOLOGISTS' UNION, Check-list, ed. 4, 1931, 90, part.—BENT, U. S. Nat. Mus. Bull. 162, 1932, 73, part (life hist.; distr.; descr.).

Lophortyx californicus DRESSER, Ibis, 1866, 27 (Devils River, Tex.).

Callipepla elegans (not *Ortyx elegans* Lesson) WOODHOUSE, in Rep. Sitgreaves Expl. Zuñi and Colorado R., 1853, 95 (Rio Grande near El Paso, Tex.).

Lophortyx gambelii ignoscens FRIEDMANN, Journ. Washington Acad. Sci., xxxiii, 1943, 371 (San Elizario, Tex.; descr.; distr.; crit.; type in U. S. Nat. Mus.).

LOPHORTYX DOUGLASII DOUGLASII (Vigors)

ELEGANT QUAIL

Adult male.—Forehead, anterior and lateral parts of crown, sides of occiput, cheeks, and auriculars white narrowly streaked with black, the anterior edge of the forehead and the lores more or less suffused with olive-brown, and the immediate supra- and postocular area tinged with tawny; crest coming from hindcenter of crown ochraceous-salmon to bright orange-cinnamon; feathers of the middle of the occiput from immediately behind the base of the crest to the nape, grayish white with wedge-shaped terminal shaft spots of argus brown to Brussels brown, the more proximal (hidden) parts of the shafts blackish; hindneck and lower sides of neck between neutral gray and pale neutral gray, the feathers with tear-shaped terminal shaft spots of Brussels brown; interscapulars neutral gray somewhat tinged with buffy brown; scapulars and innermost secondaries bright to dark Sanford's brown laterally edged with white, a narrow dusky line separating the Sanford's brown from the white edges, these feathers basally dusky buffy brown; upper wing coverts buffy brown or slightly darker, the innermost ones with reduced broad medial streaks of Sanford's brown; secondaries, other than the innermost ones, olive-brown, their external edges finely dappled with buffy or whitish forming indistinct margins of paler; primaries dark olive-brown; feathers of the upper back neutral gray tinged with buffy brown and with terminally broadening shaft streaks of Sanford's brown; back, lower back, rump, and upper tail coverts light brownish olive much tinged with deep grayish; rectrices deep neutral gray tipped and edged with buffy brownish; chin and upper throat barred black and white, the chin more blackish than white; lower throat and breast between pale neutral gray and light mouse gray; upper and middle abdomen similar but spotted with fairly large oval white spots, some of the posterolateral feathers with a strong tinge of dull orange-cinnamon on the gray portions; feathers of sides and flanks with broad median areas orange-cinnamon to Sanford's brown, the gray lateral areas broken by narrow, elongate oval white spots corresponding to those on the abdomen; lower abdomen and under tail coverts pale pinkish buff to buffy white, each feather with a broad shaft stripe of dull hazel to Vandyke brown; thighs pale avellaneous to wood brown; under wing coverts pale smoky wood brown, edged with grayish white; iris hazel; bill brownish black; feet described by collectors as "bluish black," "pale olive brown," "dirty greenish white," etc.! (see Miller, Bull. Amer. Mus. Nat. Hist., xxi, 1905, 342).

Adult female.—Very different from the male: forehead, lores, crown, and sides of occiput light wood brown with shaft streaks of blackish; crest averaging shorter than in male and dark olive-brown usually inconspicuously spotted or incompletely barred with dull tawny; center of occiput from immediately behind the base of the crest to the hindneck like the sides of occiput but with broader dark shaft streaks; interscapulars dark hair brown with a grayish suffusion and vermiculated with buffy brown; back, lower back, and rump similar but with less grayish and more buffy brown; scapulars and innermost secondaries and the inner upper secondary coverts edged on both webs with cartridge buff to light pinkish cinnamon, the median portion of the feathers Saccardo's umber heavily blotched with mummy brown distally and speckled and vermiculated with the same in the more proximal parts; outer upper wing coverts buffy brown edged with light ochraceous-buff; outer secondaries dusky olive-brown with small light buffy brown frecklings on the outer part of the outer webs, these paler markings forming indistinct edgings and tips to the feathers; primaries dusky olive-brown, the longest primaries, in the folded wing, exceeding the longest secondaries by 15–20 mm.; upper tail coverts like the rump but slightly darker, less olivaceous; rectrices between neutral gray and deep neutral gray, laterally and terminally mottled with pale hair brown to pale buffy, the sides and tips of the feathers often with a buffy wash over the grayish; chin, throat, and sides of head whitish the chin and throat with small specks of hair brown the sides of the head with these specks elongated into streaks and darker; auriculars much washed with olive-brown, forming a dark area surrounded by lighter; lower throat, breast, and lower sides of neck washed with pale buffy brown, the feathers with dark olive-brown tips; feathers of abdomen dusky olive-brown, the feathers very broadly tipped and barred with whitish, these tips and bars interrupted by a dark olive-brown shaft streak causing the segments of the bars to appear like large rounded spots; sides similar but the shaft streaks broader and suffused with cinnamon-brown to Verona brown; lower abdomen, flanks, thighs, and under tail coverts similar to the upper abdomen but with the pale spots narrowed and connected longitudinally to form pale edgings to the feathers, the brown shaft streaks correspondingly increased in width; under wing coverts buffy brown edged with grayish white.

Immature (sexes alike).—Similar to the adult female but darker; more rufescent on the top of the head, wings, and upper back, and tail;

the feathers of the breast and abdomen buffy white barred with olive-brown, not with round white spots.

Natal down.—Forehead, lores, sides of head light ochraceous-buff; center of crown and occiput mummy brown, edged laterally with buffy white; this dark area extending caudally in an unbroken spinal tract to the tail, bordered from the neck back to the tail with white, almost devoid of any buffy tinge; similar but narrow stripes of mummy brown to fuscous in the following places—from behind the eye to the posterior margin of the side of the neck, two on each femoral tract, two short ones on each wing, and an incomplete, interrupted one on each side from the hind end of the postocular stripe to the wing; underparts whitish faintly tinged with buffy; bill and feet (in dried skin) light yellow.

Adult male.—Wing 109–114 (111.7); tail 70–78 (74.6); culmen from base 13–14.3 (13.7); tarsus 30–33 (31.3); middle toe without claw 27–30.4 (28.1 mm.).[92]

Adult female.—Wing 105.4–113 (108.8); tail 66–68 (67); culmen from base 13.3–14.8 (14.1); tarsus 31–33 (32); middle toe without claw 26.5–27.5 (27.1 mm.).[93]

Range.—Resident from extreme southern Sonora (Tesia, Chenobampo, Guirocoba) south throughout Sinaloa, and to northwestern Durango (Casa Blanca).

Type locality.—Mazatlán, Sinaloa.

O[*rtyx*] *douglasii* DOUGLAS, Trans. Linn. Soc. London, xvi, 1829, 145 [California]; "never higher than 42° north latitude"; ex Vigors, manuscript).

Ortyx douglasii VIGORS, Zool. Journ., iv, 1829, 353; Zool. Voy. *Blossom*, Birds, 1839, 27, pl. 11 ("Monterey, California").—JARDINE and SELBY, Illustr. Orn., ii, 1830, pl. 107.—LESSON, Traité d'Orn., 1831, 508 ("California").

[*Ortyx*] *douglassii* REICHENBACH, Synop. Av., iii, 1848, Gallinaceae [2], pl. 193, fig. 1677.

Ortyx douglassii COOPER, Proc. California Acad. Sci., vol. 6, 1875, 202 (crit.).

Callipepla douglassii GAMBEL, Journ. Acad. Nat. Sci. Philadelphia, i, 1847, 218, part ("Common about the Gulf [of California], particularly at Mazatlan").—BAIRD, Rep. Stansbury's Expl. Great Salt Lake, 1852, 334 ("Monterey, California").

Callipepla douglasii GRAY, List Birds Brit. Mus., pt. 5, Gallinæ, 1867, 78.

C[*allipepla*] *douglasi* REICHENOW, Die Vögel, i, 1943, 317.

[*Callipepla*] *douglasii* GRAY, Hand-list, ii, 1870, 273, No. 9796 (Monterey).

Lophortyx douglasi BONAPARTE, Geogr. and Comp. List, 1838, 43.—NUTTALL, Man. Orn. United States and Canada, Land Birds, ed. 2, 1840, 793.—OGILVIE-GRANT, Cat. Birds Brit. Mus., xxii, 1893, 404, part, (Mazatlán and Presidio de Mazatlán, Sinaloa); Handb. Game Birds, ii, 1897, 126, part (Sinaloa).—SALVIN and GODMAN, Biol. Centr.-Amer., Aves, iii, 1903. 293. part (Mazatlán; Presidio de Mazatlán).—GRINNELL, Pacific Coast Avif., No. 11, 1915, 180 (California; hypothetical).—PALMER, Condor, xxx, 1928, 277, in text (patronymics).

L[*ophortyx*] *douglasi* SETH-SMITH, L'Oiseau, x, 1929, 761 (care in captivity).

[*Lophortyx*] *douglasi* SHARPE, Hand-list, i, 1899, 44 (w. Mexico).

---

[92] Eight specimens, all from Sinaloa.

[93] Four specimens from Sinaloa and Durango.

Lophortyx douglasii douglasii McLellan, Proc. California Acad. Sci., ser. 4, xvi, 1927, 7 (near Labrados, Mexico; plum.).—van Rossem, Trans. San Diego Soc. Nat. Hist., vi, 1931, 245 (Sonora; Tesia, Chenobampo, Guirocoba; spec.). Peters, Check-list Birds World, ii, 1934, 46, part.—Hellmayr and Conover, Cat. Birds Amer., 1, No. 1, 1942, 237, part (syn.; distr.).

[*Lophortyx douglasii*] *douglasii* Friedmann, Journ. Washington Acad. Sci., xxxiii, 1943, 370 (crit.).

Lophortyx douglasi douglasi Miller, Bull. Amer. Mus. Nat. Hist., xxi, 1905, 342 (Escuinapa, etc., s. Sinaloa; crit.); xxii, 1906, 162 (Casa Blanca, nw. Durango, 1,000 ft.).

Ortyx elegans Lesson, Traité d'Orn., 1831, 508 ("California"); Cent. Zool., 1832, 189, pl. 61 ("California").

[*Callipepla*] *elegans* Reichenbach, Synop. Av., iii, Gallinaceae, Feb. 1848, pl. 199, fig. 1917.—Gray, Hand-list, ii, 1870, 273, No. 9795.—Sclater and Salvin, Nom. Av. Neotr., 1873, 138.

Callipepla elegans Gould, Monogr. Odontoph., pt. 3, 1850, pl. 18 and text.—Baird, Rep. Stansbury's Expl. Great Salt Lake, 1852, 334 ("California").—Gray, List Birds Brit. Mus., pt. 5, Gallinae, 1867, 78.—Finsch, Abh. Nat. Verh. Bremen, 1870, 357 (Mazatlán).—Lawrence, Mem. Boston Soc. Nat. Hist., ii, 1874, 306 (Mazatlán).—Beristain and Laurencio, Mem. Rev. Soc. Cient. "Antonio Alzate," vii, 1894, 219, part (Sinaloa).

C[*allipepla*] *elegans* Cubas, Cuadro Geograph., Estadístico, Descr. e Hist. de los Estados Unidos Mexicanos, 1884, 168 (common names; Mexico).—Ridgway, Man. North Amer. Birds, 1887, 585; 2d ed., 1895, 588.

Lophortyx elegans Nuttall, Man. Orn. United States and Canada, Land Birds, ed. 2, 1840, 792 ("Upper California").—Gray, List Birds Brit. Mus., pt. 3, Gallinae, 1844, 45.

Callipepla elegans bensoni Lantz, Trans. Kansas Acad. Sci. for 1896-7 (1899), 219 (Culiacán and Limoncito, Sinaloa).

Ortyx spilogaster Vigors, Proc. Zool. Soc. London, pt. 2, 1832, 4 (Mexico or Chile; coll. Ft. Cuming).

LOPHORTYX DOUGLASII BENSONI (Ridgway)

Benson's Quail

Adult male.—Similar to that of *Lophortyx douglasii douglasii* but the black color of the throat decidedly predominating over the white, the rusty markings of the hindneck, scapulars, inner secondaries, and flanks averaging less rufescent; the gray of the breast paler—smoke gray with a faint brownish tinge, and the crest averaging paler.

Adult female.—Similar to that of *Lophortyx douglasii douglasii* but with the crest usually uniformly dark sepia to fuscous (not barred and spotted with tawny); the upper throat more broadly and heavily streaked with dusky; whitish spots on the abdomen larger.

Juvenal female.—Similar to the adult but somewhat darker in general tone; the scapulars and inner secondaries with more extensive olive-buff; the crest feathers transversely spotted with olive-tawny; the outer webs of the primaries mottled with pale buffy hair brown and the remiges more pointedly distally.

Adult male.—Wing 107–115 (111.3); tail 77–94 (83.8); culmen from base 15–16.1 (15.6); tarsus 28.6–31 (29.7); middle toe without claw 25.6–29.4 (27.6 mm.).[94]

Adult female.—Wing 108–115 (112.2); tail 80–87 (83.8); culmen from base 14.9–15.4 (15.1); tarsus 28.9–29.3 (29.0); middle toe without claw 25.3–27.1 (26.1 mm.).[95]

Range.—Resident in Sonora from close to the northern boundary to Guaymas and San Javier; in extreme southern Sonora it is replaced by the nominate form.

Type locality.—Campos = 18 miles north of Cumpas, Sonora.

(?) *Callipepla douglassii* Gambel, Journ. Acad. Nat. Sci. Philadelphia, i, 1847, 218, part ("common about the Gulf" [of California]).
Lophortyx douglasi Ogilvie-Grant, Cat. Birds Brit. Mus., xxii, 1893, 404, part (Ysleta, Guadalupe, Quiriego, and Sierra de Alamos, Sonora).—Salvin and Godman, Biol. Centr.-Amer., Aves, iii, 1903, 293 (Ysleta, Campos, Guadalupe, Quiriego, Sierra de Alamos, and Nacori, Sonora).
Callipepla elegans bensoni Ridgway, Forest and Stream, xxviii, No. 6, 1887, 106; Proc. U. S. Nat. Mus., x, 1887, 148 (Campos, Sonora; coll. U. S. Nat. Mus.).
C[allipepla] elegans bensoni Ridgway, Man. North Amer. Birds, 1887, 585; ed. 2, 1896, 587.
[*Lophortyx*] *bensoni* Sharpe, Hand-List, i, 1899, 44.
Lophortyx bensoni Nelson, Auk, xix, 1902, 239 (crit.).
Lophortyx douglasi bensoni Thayer and Bangs, Proc. Biol. Soc. Washington, xix, 1906, 18 (Opodepe, north-central Sonora).
Lophortyx douglasii bensoni van Rossem, Trans. San Diego Soc. Nat. Hist., vi, 1931, 246 (Sonora; Pesqueira, Tecoripa, San Javier, Guaymas; spec.).—Peters, Check-list Birds World, ii, 1934, 46.—Hellmayr and Conover, Cat. Birds Amer., i, No. 1, 1942, 236 (syn.; distr.).
[*Lophortyx douglasii*] *bensoni* Friedmann, Journ. Washington Acad. Sci., xxxiii, 1943, 370 (crit.).
Callipepla elegans (not *Ortyx elegans* Lesson) Allen, Bull. Amer. Mus. Nat. Hist., v, 1893, 33 (Nacori, Sonora).

LOPHORTYX DOUGLASII TERES Friedmann

JALISCO CRESTED QUAIL

Adult male.—Like that of *Lophortyx douglasii douglasii* but with shorter wing, 101–104 (as opposed to 109–114); with the longest secondaries reaching the tips of the primaries (in *douglasii* the primaries extend 15–20 mm. beyond the secondaries) in the closed wing; and with the general coloration darker, the reddish brown on the wings chestnut instead of Sanford's brown (as in *douglasii*), the lower back and rump more brownish; the gray of the breast darker—neutral gray (pale neutral gray in *douglasii*) and the white spots on the abdomen with blackish ringlike edges.

[94] Ten specimens.
[95] Five specimens.

Adult female.—Similar to that of the nominate race but with shorter wing, 98–102 (as opposed to 101–104) ; with the longest secondaries reaching the tips of the primaries (in *douglasii* the primaries extend 15–20 mm. beyond the secondaries) in the closed wing; and generally darker in color, the brown on the underparts noticeably darker—dark olive-brown.

Adult male.—Wing 101–104 (102.6) ; tail 66–72 (68.6) ; culmen from base 14–14.5 (14.1) ; tarsus 25–29 (27.8) ; middle toe without claw 27–29 (28 mm.).[96]

Adult female.—Wing 98–102 (99.7) ; tail 65–67 (66.1) ; culmen from base 13.8–14.3 (14) ; tarsus 27.5–29 (28.3) ; middle toe without claw 26–27 (26.3 mm.).[97]

Range.—Northwestern Jalisco (Las Palmas; Las Peñas), possibly to Colima. However, no specimens appear to have been taken yet in Colima. This State is included in current accounts of the range of the species on the sole basis of Grayson's statement that he "also found it in the State of Jalisco and Colima, but not as far south as Tehuantepec" (in Lawrence's paper, Mem. Boston Soc. Nat. Hist., ii, 1874, 306).

Type locality.—Las Palmas, northwestern Jalisco.

Callipepla elegans BERISTAIN and LAURENCIO, Mem. y Rev. Soc. Cient. "Antonio Alzate," vii, 1894, 219, part (Colima).
Lophortyx douglasi OGILVIE-GRANT, Handb. Game Birds, ii, 1897, 126, part (Jalisco).—SALVIN and GODMAN, Biol. Centr.-Amer., Aves, iii, 1903, 293, part (Jalisco, Colima).
Lophortyx douglasii douglasii PETERS, Check-list Birds of World, ii, 1934, 46, part.— HELLMAYR and CONOVER, Cat. Birds Amer., i, No. 1, 1942, 237, part.
Lophortyx douglasii teres FRIEDMANN, Journ. Washington Acad. Sci., xxxiii, 1943, 369 (Las Palmas, nw. Jalisco; descr.; distr.; crit.; type in U. S. Nat. Mus.).

LOPHORTYX DOUGLASII IMPEDITA Friedmann
NAYARIT CRESTED QUAIL

Adult.—Similar to the adult of the same sex of typical *douglasii* and of *teres,* combining the darker coloration of the latter with the wing tip of the former; in other words—a dark Douglas's quail with a noticeable wing tip.

Adult male.—Wing 105.4–110 (107.7) ; tail 70–77 (73.7) ; culmen from base 14–15 (14.6) ; tarsus 29.5–34.7 (32.4) ; middle toe without claw 27–30 (28.8 mm.).[98]

Adult female.—Wing 100.5; tail 68; culmen from the base 13.5; tarsus 33; middle toe without claw 28 mm. (1 specimen).

Range.—Known only from Nayarit.

Type locality.—San Blas, Tepic, Nayarit.

---

[96] Five specimens including the type.
[97] Three specimens.
[98] Six specimens, including the type.

Lophortyx douglasi OGILVIE-GRANT, Cat. Birds Brit. Mus., xxii, 1893, 404, part (San Blas, Tepic).—SALVIN and GODMAN, Biol. Centr.-Amer., Aves, iii, 1903, 293, part (San Blas).—BAILEY, Auk, xxiii, 1906, 384 (San Blas, Tepic).

Lophortyx douglasii douglasii PETERS, Check-list Birds of World, ii, 1934, 46, part.— HELLMAYR and CONOVER, Cat. Birds Amer., i, No. 1, 1942, 237, part.

Lophortyx douglasii impedita FRIEDMANN, Journ. Washington Acad. Sci., xxxiii, 1943, 369 (San Blas, Tepic, Nayarit; descr.; distr.; crit.; type in U. S. Nat. Mus.).

LOPHORTYX DOUGLASII LANGUENS Friedmann

CHIHUAHUA CRESTED QUAIL

Adult male.—Like that of the nominate race but with the gray of the breast less pure gray, lightly washed with brownish, most of the feathers with indistinct pure rufescent medioterminal spots; the pale spots on the abdomen slightly buffier, and the pale buffy area on the lower median part of the abdomen more extensive; wing 110–111; tail 77.5–79; culmen from the base 15.5–15.8; tarsus 29–30; middle toe without claw 28.5–29.5 mm. (2 specimens, including the type).

Other plumages apparently unknown.

Range.—Known only from the type locality—Trompa, or La Trompa, western Chihuahua.

Lophortyx douglasii languens FRIEDMANN, Journ. Washington Acad. Sci., xxxiii, 1943, 370 (Trompa, Chihuahua; descr.; distr.; crit., type in Mus. Comp. Zool.).

Genus COLINUS Goldfuss

Ortyx (not of Oken, 1816) STEPHENS, *in* Shaw, Gen. Zool., xi, pt. 2, 1819, 376. (Type, as designated by Gray, 1840, *Perdix borealis* Temminck = *Tetrao virginianus* Linnaeus.)

Ortix (emendation) D'ORBIGNY, *in* La Sagra, Hist. Fis. Pol. y Nat. Cuba, iii, Aves, 1839, 10.

Ortygia (not *Ortygis* Illiger, 1811) BOIE, Isis, 1826, 978. (Type, by monotypy, "*Perdix virginiana* Lath. Wils., pl. 47, fig. 2 u.s.w.").

Colinus GOLDFUSS, Handb. Zool., ii, 1820, 220. (Type, by monotypy, *Tetrao mexicanus* Linnaeus [= *T. virginianus* Linnaeus ?].)

Colinia (emendation ?) NUTTALL, Man. Orn. United States and Canada, Land Birds, 1832, 646. (New name for *Ortyx* Stephens.)

Colina (emendation) WOOD, Orn. Guide [1837], 217.

Gnathodon STREUBEL, *in* Ersch and Gruber, Allg. Encycl., sect. 3, xvi, 1842, 283, 290. (Type, by original designation, *Perdix marilandica* Latham = *Tetrao virginianus* Linnaeus.)

Philortix (not *Philortyx* Gould, 1845) DES MURS, *in* Chenu, Encycl. Hist. Nat. Ois., vi, 1854, 147.

Eupsychortyx GOULD, Monogr. Odontoph., pt. i, 1844, pl. 10. (Type, as fixed by Reichenbach, 1850, *Tetrao cristatus* Linnaeus.)

Eupsychortix (emendation) BONAPARTE, Compt. Rend., xxxviii, 1854, 663.

Eupsichortyx (emendation) BONAPARTE, Compt. Rend., xlii, 1856, 954.

Eupsycortyx (emendation) SCLATER, Guide to Gardens Zool. Soc. London, ed. 23, 1870, 7.

Callipepla REICHENOW, Die Vögel, i, 1913, 317, part (includes *Colinus cristata* and *Colinas nigrogularis* as well as *Callipepla*, *Oreortyx*, and *Lophortyx*).

Medium-sized to rather small Odontophorinae (wing about 96–120 mm.) with tail less than three-fifths as long as wing, scapulars, tertials, and rump spotted or blotched with blackish, and with crest indistinct (obvious only when erected) or distinct (subgenus *Eupsychortyx*).

Bill moderate in size, the culmen (chord, from extreme base) less than half to half as long as tarsus, its depth at base greater than distance from anterior end of nasal fossa to tip of maxilla, its width at rictus equal to or greater than its depth at same point; culmen strongly convex, more or less distinctly ridged, especially toward base. Outermost primary usually longer than eighth (from outside) (shorter than eighth in subgenus *Eupsychortyx*), the third, fourth, and fifth (from outside) longest, the second and sixth but little shorter. Tail between one-half and three-fifths as long as wing, distinctly rounded, the rec-

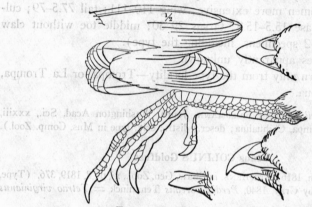

FIGURE 19.—*Colinus virginianus.*

trices (12) firm, broad, and rounded at tips. Tarsus a little less than one-third as long as wing, shorter than middle toe with claw; planta tarsi covered with small hexagonal scutella, those along posterior edge of outer side larger (more or less) and forming a nearly to quite continuous row.

Plumage and coloration.—Feathers of crown somewhat, to distinctly, elongated either forming or not a distinct crest when not erected. Upperparts mixed gray and cinnamon-rufous, vermiculated with darker, the posterior scapulars, tertials, and rump (especially upper portion) blotched or irregularly spotted with black, the upper tail coverts and median rectrices with shaft streaks of the same, the inner webs of tertials broadly edged with buff; underparts largely white variously marked with black and cinnamon-rufous, sometimes plain cinnamon-rufous; head striped with black and white, but sometimes mostly black, in males, buff replacing white in females.

Range.—Transition Life Zone of eastern North America southward to Cuba and through Central America to northern South America (northern Brazil, the Guianas, Venezuela, Colombia). (Four species with many races.)

KEY TO THE NORTH AND MIDDLE AMERICAN FORMS OF COLINUS

a. Chin and upper throat pure white, not washed with buff.
  b. White of chin and upper throat completely surrounded by a black band laterally and posteriorly.
    c. Abdomen rufescent or chestnut, unbarred.
      d. Abdomen uniform, unmarked, chestnut.
        e. Black breast band very narrow, less than 15 mm. broad in midventral line (southern tableland of Mexico from northern Jalisco and western San Luis Potosí to Valley of Mexico).
            Colinus virginianus graysoni, ad. ♂ (p. 333)
        ee. Black breast band broader, more than 30 mm. wide in midventral line.
          f. Abdomen paler—vinaceous-cinnamon to cinnamon (southern Puebla).
            Colinus virginianus nigripectus, ad. ♂ (p. 334)
          ff. Abdomen darker; sayal brown.
            g. Black feathers of pectoral band with concealed white shaft spots (eastern base of Cordillera in Veracruz from Jalapa to Isthmus of Tehuantepec) **Colinus virginianus pectoralis**, ad. ♂ (p. 335)
            gg. Black feathers of pectoral band with no, or few and small, concealed white shaft spots (Isthmus of Tehuantepec, eastern Oaxaca)...........**Colinus virginianus thayeri**, ad. ♂ (p. 343)
      dd. Abdomen not uniform chestnut, but abundantly streaked with black.
        e. Black confined to breast and upper abdomen (Cuba and Isle of Pines).
            Colinus virginianus cubanensis, ad. ♂ (p. 329)
        ee. Black marks continuing down midventrally to lower portion of abdomen.
          f. Breast and middle of abdomen nearly to vent almost solid black, chestnut largely confined to sides (lowlands of southern Veracruz).
            Colinus virginianus godmani, ad. ♂ (p. 336)
          ff. Breast and upper abdomen chestnut, the feathers edged with blackish, separating black collar from black midabdominal area (northeastern Chiapas and adjacent Tabasco).
            Colinus virginianus minor, ad. ♂ (p. 337)
    cc. Abdomen not chestnut, but whitish, more or less barred with black.
      d. Scapulars, tertials, and lower back usually without conspicuous blackish blotches.
        e. Underparts extensively reddish laterally (central and southwestern Tamaulipas to central-eastern San Luis Potosí).
            Colinus virginianus aridus, ad. ♂ (p. 332)
        ee. Underparts not extensively reddish laterally (central and southern Texas, northern and central Tamaulipas).
            Colinus virginianus texanus, ad. ♂ (p. 323)
      dd. Scapulars, tertials, and lower back with conspicuous blackish blotches.
        e. A broad conspicuous cinnamomeous area just below black pectoral band (the area may be streaked with black or plain).
          f. Reddish color of underparts richer—chestnut (Florida Peninsula; introduced in Bahamas).

  g. Smaller, wing 97 mm. (Key West; extinct; doubtfully distinct from
        the next race)....**Colinus virginianus insulanus**, ad. ♂ (p. 328)
  gg. Larger, wing over 100 mm. (Florida Peninsula; introduced in
        Bahamas).......**Colinus virginianus floridanus**, ad. ♂ (p. 326)
  ff. Reddish color of upperparts paler—hazel or paler.
    g. Black areas of upperparts well developed and extensive (arid
          tropical zone from central Tamaulipas to eastern San Luis
          Potosí).........**Colinus virginianus maculatus**, ad. ♂ (p. 331)
    gg. Black areas of upperparts reduced and grayish (between Tropical
          and Lower Sonoran Zones from central Tamaulipas to south-
          eastern San Luis Potosí).
                        Colinus virginianus aridus, ad. ♂ (p. 332)
  ee. No broad conspicuous cinnamomeous area below black pectoral band,
        sometimes washed with cinnamon, but not conspicuously enough to
        form a definite band (southeastern Canada, eastern and central
        United States; introduced in West Indies and western United States).
                        Colinus virginianus virginianus, ad. ♂ (p. 312)
  bb. White of chin and throat not completely bordered with black.
    c. Breast and most of abdomen white.
      d. Slightly paler, the scapulars and upper wing coverts only slightly suffused
            with rufescent (western Guatemala).
                        Colinus leucopogon incanus, ad. ♂ (p. 359)
      dd. Slightly darker, the scapulars and upper wing coverts richly suffused
            with rufescent (El Salvador west of Lempa River).
                        Colinus leucopogon hypoleucus, ad. ♂ (p. 358)
    cc. Breast and most of abdomen not white.
      d. With a well-developed occipital crest.
        e. Auriculars pale buffy to whitish; crest pale wood brown to buffy
              (Pacific lowlands of western Panama).
                        Colinus cristatus panamensis, ad. ♂ (p. 363)
        ee. Auriculars dusky brown; crest dark brown (chiefly extralimital—the
              Guianas, Brazil, and Venezuela; introduced in Grenadines and Virgin
              Islands)..................**Colinus cristatus sonnini**, ad. ♂ (p. 360)
      dd. With no well-developed occipital crest (El Salvador, east of Lempa
            (River)..............**Colinus leucopogon leucopogon**, ad. ♂ (p. 357)
aa. Chin and upper throat not pure white.
  b. Chin and upper throat blackish or blackish brown, uniform or spotted with
        white.
    c. Abdomen uniform hazel brown.
      d. A distinct white superciliary or postocular stripe.
        e. Sides of head and neck partly chestnut (southern Arizona and Sonora).
                        Colinus virginianus ridgwayi, ad. ♂ (p. 344)
        ee. Sides of head and neck plain black (eastern Chiapas and western
              Guatemala)...........**Colinus virginianus insignis**, ad. ♂ (p. 338)
      dd. Superciliary region entirely black, but sometimes with an indication of
            a white postocular stripe.
        e. Upper breast solid black.
          f. Lower breast and belly solid chestnut; rufous above fairly extensive
                (western Oaxaca)....**Colinus virginianus atriceps**, ad. ♂ (p. 344)
          ff. Lower breast and belly solid chestnut; usually marked with black;
                rufous above much restricted (San Benito and Tapachula,
                Chiapas)..............**Colinus virginianus salvini**, ad. ♂ (p. 341)
        ee. Upper breast mainly rufous, with black streaks or squamations.

    f. Feathers of center of crown with broad brown edges; crissum heavily marked (Tehuantepec, Oaxaca, to Tonalá, Chiapas).

Colinus virginianus coyolcos, ad. ♂ (p. 339)

    ff. Feathers of whole head and neck usually black, crissum scarcely marked (Chicomuselo, Chiapas).

Colinus virginianus nelsoni, ad. ♂ (p. 342)

  cc. Abdomen not uniform hazel brown.

    d. Breast wood brown finely vermiculated with black.

      e. A distinct, broad whitish malar stripe present; feathers of chin and throat brownish basally.

        f. Malar and postorbital stripes heavily washed with buffy (western Nicaragua)..........**Colinus leucopogon sclateri,** ad. ♂ (p. 355)

        ff. Malar and postorbital stripes white or only slightly tinged with buffy (western Honduras).

Colinus leucopogon leylandi, ad. ♂ (p. 353)

      ee. White malar stripe broken and indefinite; feathers of chin and throat white basally (plateau and western slope of Costa Rica).

Colinus leucopogon dickeyi, ad. ♂ (p. 356)

    dd. Breast not wood brown, but white, the feathers edged with black.

      e. Tail largely unspeckled (Yucatán exclusive of the Progreso region).

Colinus nigrogularis caboti, ad. ♂ (p. 347)

      ee. Tail largely speckled.

        f. Brown of hindneck and interscapulars paler—pale argus brown (arid region about Progreso, Yucatán).

Colinus nigrogularis persiccus, ad. ♂ (p. 350)

        ff. Brown of hindneck and scapulars darker—rich chestnut (Guatemala, Honduras)......**Colinus nigrogularis nigrogularis,** ad. ♂ (p. 350)

  bb. Chin and upper throat buffy.

    c. Abdomen more or less barred, not spotted, the middle of the abdomen only lightly or not at all barred.

      d. Breast with a distinct cinnamomeous wash.

        e. Upperparts (crown, nape, back, and wings) decidedly more grayish than reddish brownish.

          f. General coloration richer and darker, the ventral V-shaped bars deep black (Mexican tableland from northern Jalisco and southern San Luis Potosí to the Valley of Mexico).

Colinus virginianus graysoni, ad. ♀ (p. 333)

          ff. General coloration paler; the ventral V-shaped bars fuscous.

            g. Pinkish cinnamon pectoral band well developed.

              h. Dorsal dark markings darker—fuscous-black (Arid Tropical Zone from central Tamaulipas to eastern San Luis Potosí).

Colinus virginianus maculatus, ad. ♀ (p. 331)

              hh. Dorsal dark markings paler—marbled with sayal brown.

                i. Pale edges of dorsal feathers white (southern Arizona and northern Sonora).

Colinus virginianus ridgwayi, ad. ♀ (p. 344)

                ii. Pale edges of dorsal feathers grayish (central southern Texas to northern and central Tamaulipas).

Colinus virginianus texanus, ad. ♀ (p. 323)

            gg. Pinkish cinnamon pectoral band very faint (between Tropical Arid and Lower Sonora Zones from central and southwestern Tamaulipas to central eastern San Luis Potosí).

Colinus virginianus aridus, ad. ♀ (p. 332)

    ee. Upperparts (crown, nape, back, and wings) more reddish brown than grayish.

        f. Pale edges of feathers of crown more grayish than brownish (Palenque area, Chiapas).

                Colinus virginianus minor, ad. ♀ (p. 337)

        ff. Pale edges of feathers of crown more brownish than grayish.

           g. Size smaller; wing under 110 mm. (Florida Peninsula; introduced in the Bahamas).

                Colinus virginianus floridanus, ad. ♀ (p. 326)

           gg. Size larger; wing over 110 mm. (eastern and central United States; southeastern Canada; introduced in West Indies and western United States).

                Colinus virginianus virginianus, ad. ♀ (p. 312)

  dd. Breast without a distinct cinnamomeous wash.

    e. Size larger; wing over 106 mm. (southern Puebla).

                Colinus virginianus nigripectus, ad. ♀ (p. 334)

    ee. Size smaller; wing under 106 mm.

        f. Pale edges of feathers of crown more grayish than brownish.

           g. Smaller, wing under 95 mm.

              h. Breast washed with tawny-buff (Palenque area, Chiapas).

                Colinus virginianus minor, ad. ♀ (p. 337)

              hh. Breast not washed with tawny-buff (Honduras and Guatemala).

                Colinus nigrogularis nigrogularis, ad. ♀ (p. 350)

           gg. Larger, wing over 95 mm.

              h. Upperparts slightly darker, more brownish, less grayish[99] (Yucatán, except Progreso region).

                Colinus nigrogularis caboti, ad. ♀ (p. 347)

              hh. Upperparts slightly paler, less brownish, more grayish (Progreso region, Yucatán).

                Colinus nigrogularis persiccus, ad. ♀ (p. 350)

        ff. Pale edges of feathers of crown more brownish than grayish.

           g. Dorsal coloration grayer; interscapulars and upper brown more grayish than rufescent.

              h. Buff confined to chin and upper throat (Cuba and Isle of Pines).

                Colinus virginianus cubanensis, ad. ♀ (p. 329)

              hh. Entire throat and upper breast buffy (Putla area, western Oaxaca)........**Colinus virginianus atriceps,** ad. ♀ (p. 344)

           gg. Dorsal coloration more rufescent; interscapulars and upper back with little grayish; dark brown and rufescent-brown.

              h. Shaft streaks of interscapulars broader and darker—Mikado brown (eastern Chiapas and adjacent western Guatemala).

                Colinus virginianus insignis, ad. ♀ (p. 338)

              hh. Shaft streaks of interscapulars narrower and paler—cinnamon-rufous...........**Colinus virginianus thayeri,** ad. ♀ (p. 343)

                Colinus virginianus coyolcos, ad. ♀ (p. 339)[1]

---

  [99] The females of *C. n. caboti* and *C. n. persiccus* are impossible to "key out" except by such comparative adjectives, which are, admittedly, useless when the reader has but one of the two forms available. In such cases, geography must be used as a guide.

  [1] These two races cannot be distinguished in this sex. The range of *C. v. thayeri* is the Isthmus of Tehuantepec, eastern Oaxaca; that of *C. v. coyolcos* is the Pacific slope of Oaxaca and Chiapas, from Tehuantepec City to Tonalá.

cc. Abdomen spotted rather than barred (spots sometimes broadened so as to approximate barrings).[2]

 d. Entire chin and upper throat streaked or heavily spotted with blackish brown.

  e. Upperparts dark grayish black, not brownish (coastal plains of southern Chiapas)................**Colinus virginianus salvini**, ad. ♀ (p. 341)

  ee. Upperparts definitely brownish.

   f. Feathers of upper back tawny to dark brown with numerous black blotches as well as vermiculations.

    g. General tone of upperparts rufescent-tawny (Pacific lowlands of western Panama).

     Colinus cristatus panamensis, ad. ♀ (p. 363)

    gg. General tone of upperparts bister (largely extralimital—the Guianas, Brazil, and Venezuela; introduced in the Grenadines and Virgin Islands).......**Colinus cristatus sonnini**, ad. ♀ (p. 360)

   ff. Feathers of upper back grayish brown, with no black blotches but only vermiculations.

    g. Pale spots on abdomen definitely buffy (El Salvador, east of Lempa River).

     Colinus leucopogon leucopogon, ad. ♀ (p. 357)

    gg. Pale spots on abdomen white, only slightly tinged with buffy.

     h. Chin, throat, and superciliaries darker—ochraceous-buff to honey yellow (western Nicaragua).

      Colinus leucopogon sclateri, ad. ♀ (p. 355)

     hh. Chin, throat, and superciliaries paler—light pinkish buff to pale ochraceous-buff (western Honduras).

      Colinus leucopogon leylandi, ad. ♀ (p. 353)

 dd. Entire chin and upper throat immaculate or only faintly spotted with blackish brown.

  e. Chin and upper throat with some blackish spots.

   f. Chin and upper throat bordered laterally and posteriorly with a band of tawny spotted with blackish.

    g. Paler, general color of upperparts pale buckthorn brown with a grayish tinge (western Guatemala).

     Colinus leucopogon incanus, ad. ♀ (p. 359)

    gg. Darker, general color of upperparts snuff brown with a grayish tinge (El Salvador west of Lempa River).

     Colinus leucopogon hypoleucus, ad. ♀ (p. 358)

   ff. Chin and upper throat without a tawny, black-spotted border (plateau and western slope of Costa Rica).

     Colinus leucopogon dickeyi, ad. ♀ (p. 356)

  ee. Chin and upper throat immaculate.

   f. Breast feathers avellaneous to wood brown, finely vermiculated with blackish, forming a distinct pectoral band.

    g. Throat generally pale, slightly washed with buffy; middle of abdomen also slightly tinged with buffy (western Honduras).

     Colinus leucopogon leylandi, ad. ♀ (p. 353)

    gg. Throat generally darker, heavily suffused with ochraceous-buff; middle of abdomen definitely buffy (western Nicaragua).

     Colinus leucopogon sclateri, ad. ♀ (p. 355)

---

[2] As in some specimens of *Colinus leucopogon hypoleucus.*

ff. Breast feathers not avellaneous to wood brown, not vermiculated, but
broadly tipped with white to buff, subterminally barred with fuscous.

g. Upperparts with much hazel to pale chestnut, especially on the
back; the upper tail coverts decidedly brownish (lowlands of
southern Veracruz).

Colinus virginianus godmani, ad. ♀ (p. 336)

gg. Upperparts with little or no hazel or pale chestnut but decidedly
grayish wood brown; upper tail coverts grayish (eastern base of
the Cordillera in Veracruz from Jalapa to the Isthmus of
Tehuantepec)......**Colinus virginianus pectoralis**, ad. ♀ (335)

COLINUS VIRGINIANUS VIRGINIANUS (Linnaeus)

EASTERN BOBWHITE

Adult male (normal phase).—Forehead and broad superciliary stripe
extending back to the sides of the nape white, the forehead usually very
narrowly interrupted at the base of the culmen by the black of the anterior part of the crown which extends posteriorly as a narrow black
upper margin to the superciliaries; rest of crown and occiput hazel to
dark russet, many of the coronal feathers blackish on the basal two-
thirds, this color often showing through as spots, and many of the
occipital feathers laterally, but not terminally, edged with pale buffy
which also often shows through as streaks; feathers of nape bicolored,
their median portion russet to chestnut, separated by a blackish line
on each web from the broad lateral white edgings, the more lateral nape
feathers tending to have broader white marks on their outer than on
their inner webs; interscapulars and upper back Mikado brown to Verona brown edged and clouded with light drab to smoke gray, and laterally incompletely barred with blackish, the more posterior feathers frequently completely crossed by these bars; scapulars dark hazel to amber
brown very heavily blotched, and basally irregularly barred with black;
and broadly edged, especially on their inner webs with pale warm buff;
upper wing coverts orange-cinnamon to cinnamomeous Mikado brown,
the lesser coverts often with largely grayish median portions, and the
feathers incompletely, narrowly barred with dusky along their edges;
secondaries between pale clove brown and hair brown, the innermost
ones suffused with hazel terminally and crossed by narrow, but widely
spaced grayish white wavy bars each of which is narrowly bordered
with blackish, the intervening dark area sparingly vermiculated with
dusky, and the feathers edged on both webs, and narrowly tipped, with
pinkish buff to pale pinkish buff; remaining secondaries similar but with
the pale bars restricted to the outer half of the outer web, which alone
is edged with pinkish buff (in some specimens the edging and the incomplete external bars are heavily washed with pale russet); primaries
uniform, between pale clove brown and hair brown; feathers of middle
of upper back dark amber brown to almost chestnut, subterminally very

heavily blotched with fuscous-black, and very narrowly tipped and edged with pale warm buff; lateral feathers of upper back, and feathers of lower back, and rump paler—pale slightly grayish buckthorn brown to antique brown, narrowly barred with dusky and crossed by numerous dusky-bordered, pale warm buffy bands; upper tail coverts similar but more rufescent and with black shaft streaks, the streaks sometimes broken into a series of connected blotches; rectrices neutral gray to deep neutral gray, the median pair freckled with pale vinaceous-buff becoming slightly rufescent terminally, the more lateral ones either uniform or only slightly freckled terminally; lores white in their upper part, black in their lower part; circumocular ring blackish; cheeks and auriculars hazen to dark russet bordered above and below by a narrow line of black; chin and upper throat white; a fairly broad blackish band across the lower throat, followed posteriorly by a broader one of cinnamon to sayal brown; this band is fairly uniform in some birds while in others it is broken to the extent of being little more than a series of brownish lateral segments of white centered feathers; the posterior feathers comprising this band are narrowly tipped with black and are subterminally white; upper abdomen white washed with pale warm buff, the feathers crossed by 4 or 5 narrow black bars; lower abdomen without the buffy wash and with the blackish bars fewer or absent; feathers of sides and flanks like those of the abdomen but longer and with broad median stripes of bright ochraceous-tawny; thighs like the abdomen but slightly washed in spots with pale ochraceous-tawny; under tail coverts pale ochraceous-tawny, the longer ones with incomplete blackish shaft stripes; inner under wing coverts hair brown broadly edged with white; outer under wing coverts similar but with narrow whitish margins; bill blackish; iris dark brown; tarsi and toes grayish flesh color, claws horn color.

Adult male (erythristic phase).—Entire bird rich auburn to chestnut; the blackish or fuscous markings of the normal plumage (on head, scapulars, upper back, etc.) also present in this plumage but less distinct as there is less contrast in tone in these dark birds; chin and throat blackish; a white transverse patch on the breast in some and not in other specimens; dusky ventral barrings smaller, finer, and more restricted to the margins of the feathers than in normal plumaged birds.

Adult female (normal phase)—Similar to the adult male except for the coloration of the head, which is as follows: Lores, broad superciliary stripe, chin, and throat between ochraceous-buff and pale orange-yellow; center of forehead, crown, and occiput between tawny and russet, the coronal feathers with largely concealed black median areas, the occipital ones with buffy edges; the postocular area, including the auriculars, like the crown; the posterior border of the upper throat very narrowly fuscous to auburn, not black as in males; underparts generally as in males but the dark bars on the abdominal feathers paler, narrower, more widely spaced and less conspicuous; bill blackish with the base of the mandible pale yellowish; iris dark brown; tarsi and toes as in males but paler.

Adult female (erythristic phase).—Similar to the erythristic male, with the chestnut color even more uniformly distributed, including the chin, throat, and the whole head (no blackish frontal or parietal marks).

Immature (first winter).—Similar to the adult of the corresponding sex and phase but with the two outer primaries more pointed terminally (retained from the juvenal plumage).

Juvenal male (normal phase).—Forehead and center of crown and occiput dull fuscous to chaetura drab, bordered laterally with broad hair-brown superciliaries; scapulars, interscapulars, and feathers of upper back between snuff brown and Saccardo's umber, each feather with a pale buffy shaft streak and subterminally blotched with dark sepia to fuscous, the rest of the feather sometimes indistinctly banded with pale ochraceous-tawny; feathers of middle of lower back Saccardo's umber with very large subterminal blotches of deep fuscous, the umber often merely forming a narrow edge; rest of back, rump, and upper tail coverts dull wood brown indistinctly mottled transversely with dusky, the upper tail coverts being more distinctly barred; wings practically as in adults but all the primaries more pointed; rectrices as in adult but the median ones with the freckling more definitely arranged into bars; lores, cheeks, and auriculars like the crown; chin and upper throat dirty white, the breast dull light vinaceous-cinnamon with a grayish wash; abdomen dull whitish, the sides, flanks, and thighs washed with grayish wood brown, a few of the side feathers with russet shaft stripes; ventral under tail coverts wood brown tinged with cinnamomeous; bill dusky or reddish brown above and on the tip of the mandible, paling to pinkish white on its base; tarsi and toes dull yellowish white; iris dark brown.

Juvenal female (normal phase).—Like the male of the same stage but duller, the white areas more clouded with grayish, the brown areas less rufescent.

Juvenal (erythristic phase).—Similar to the adult of the same phase but with considerable white on the chin, throat, and upper breast.

Natal down (normal phase).—Forehead, lores, broad superciliaries, cheeks, and auriculars pale ochraceous-tawny to ochraceous-buff; a line of blackish from back of the eye to the nape; center of crown and occiput and entire middorsal tract to the tail deep russet to chestnut deepening along the edges to bay; wings pale ochraceous-tawny mixed and blotched with russet to chestnut; rest of upperparts wood brown variously tinged with ochraceous-buff and transversely mottled with dusky; chin and throat pale buffy white; rest of underparts similar but slightly duskier; bill, tarsi, and toes pinkish white; iris dark brown.

Natal down (erythristic phase).—Like that of the normal phase but with the russet to chestnut covering the entire upper surface of the head and body; also the underparts of the body.

Adult male.—Wing 106–119 (111.5); tail 53.6–69.7 (62.1); culmen from base 14.7–18.2 (16.3); tarsus 28.0–34.1 (31.5); middle toe without claw 24.8–30.3 (29.3 mm.).[3]

Adult female.—Wing 103.5–118 (111.6); tail 51.5–63 (57.7); culmen from the base 14–15.5 (14.7); tarsus 28.5–34 (30.8); middle toe without claw 25.5–31 (28.1 mm.).[4]

Range.—Resident in open uplands from southwestern Maine (West Gardiner and West Fryeburg), Vermont (Londonderry), eastern New Hampshire, Massachusetts, and southern New England, southern Ontario (Toronto, Port Hope, etc.), Michigan, Wisconsin, southern Minnesota, North Dakota (Bartlett, Larimore, etc.), southeastern Wyoming (Horse Shoe Creek) south through eastern and central United States to northern Florida (south to Gainesville), the Gulf coast, eastern and northern Texas, and eastern Colorado.

Introduced successfully, either as pure or as mixed stock, in Utah, Montana, Idaho, Oregon, Washington, California, British Columbia, Manitoba, New Zealand (in the South Aukland district only), and some of the West Indian Islands. Introduced unsuccessfully in China, England, France, Germany, and Sweden.

Type locality.—South Carolina.

[*Tetrao*] *virginianus* LINNAEUS, Syst. Nat., ed. 10, i, 1758, 161 ("America" = Virginia; based on *Perdix virginiana* Catesby, Carolina, i, 12, pl. 12, etc.); ed. 12, i, 1766, 277.—GMELIN, Syst. Nat., i, pt. 2, 1788, 761.

Tetrao virginiana RICHMOND, Auk, xix, 1902, 79, in text (nomencl.).

[*Perdix*] *virginiana* LATHAM, Index Orn., ii, 1790, 650.

Perdix virginiana WILSON, Amer. Orn., vi, 1812, 21, pl. 47.—BONAPARTE, Journ. Acad. Nat. Sci. Philadelphia, iv, 1825, 268, No. 203; Contr. Maclurean Lyc., i, 1827, 22; Syn., 1828, 124 (subg. *Ortyx*).—DOUGHTY, Cab. Nat. Hist., i, 1830, 37, pl. 4.—AUDUBON, Orn. Biogr., i, 1831, 388, pl. 76; v, 1839, 564, pl. 76.—NUTTALL, Man. Orn. United States and Canada, i, 1832, 646.—BROWN, *in* Wilson and Bonaparte, Illustr. Amer. Orn., 1835, pl. xi [lxix].—FAXON, Auk, xx, 1903, 239, in text (nomencl.).

C(oturnix) virginiana BONNATERRE, Tabl. Encycl. Meth., i, 1791, 219.

Ortyx virginianus JARDINE, Nat. Libr., Orn., iv, 1834, 123, pl. 10; Contr. Orn., 1848, 79 (Bermudas).—AUDUBON, Synopsis, 1939, 199.—GOSSE, Birds Jamaica, 1847, 328 (Jamaica).—GOULD, Monogr. Odontoph., pt. i, 1844, pl. 1.—WOODHOUSE, Rep. Sitgreaves Expl. Zuñi and Colorado R., 1853, 94 (Indian Territory and Texas).—BARRY, Proc. Boston Soc. Nat. Hist., v, 1854, 8 (Racine, Wis.; abundant).—KNEELAND, Proc. Boston Soc. Nat. Hist., vi, 1857, 237 (Keweenaw Point, Lake Superior).—BAIRD, Rep. Pacific R. R. Surv., ix, 1858, 640; Rep. U. S. and Mex. Bound. Surv., x, pt. 2, 1859, 32.—NEWTON, Ibis, 1859, 254 (St.

---

[3] One hundred twenty-nine specimens selected from a much larger series, to cover the whole range of the form.

[4] Sixty-eight specimens from all parts of the range.

Croix, West Indies; introduced).—BAIRD, CASSIN, and LAWRENCE, Rep. Pacific
R. R. Surv., 1860, 640.—SCLATER, Proc. Zool. Soc. London, 1861, 80 (Jamaica;
introduced). Bull. Brit. Orn. Club, xxiii, 1909, 70 (Jamaica, exterminated by
mongoose).—ALBRECHT, Journ. für Orn., 1862, 205 (Jamaica).—HAYDEN, Trans.
Amer. Philos. Soc., xii, 1862, 173 (Missouri River to White River).—MARCH,
Proc. Acad. Nat. Sci. Philadelphia, 1863, 303 (Jamaica).—GRAY, List Birds
Brit. Mus., pt. 5, Gallinae, 1867, 75; Handlist, ii, 1870, 272, No. 9777.—SAMUELS,
Orn. and Ool. New England, 1868, 393 (New England; habits).—ALLEN,
Mem. Boston Soc. Nat. Hist., i, 1868, 501 (w. Iowa; very common), 526 (Rich-
mond, Ind.); Bull. Mus. Comp. Zool., ii, 1871, 352 (crit.); iii, 1872, 181
(Kansas); Bull. Essex Inst., x, 1878, 23 (Massachusetts; common); Ibis, 1883,
226 in text (distr.).—TRIPPE, Comm. Essex Inst., vi, 1871, 118 (Minnesota);
Proc. Boston Soc. Nat. Hist., xv, 1872, 240 (Iowa).—SNOW, Cat. Birds Kansas,
ed. 2, 1872, 12 (Kansas; abundant).—COUES, Key North Amer. Birds, 1872,
237; Birds Northwest, 1874, 431 (monogr.).—BAIRD, BREWER, and RIDGWAY,
Hist. North Amer. Birds, iii, 1874, 468, pl. 63 (monogr.).—RIDGWAY, Proc.
Boston Soc. Nat. Hist., xvi, 1874, 23 (lower Wabash Valley).—BREWER, Proc.
Boston Soc. Nat. Hist., xvii, 1875, 12 (New England).—NELSON, Bull. Essex
Inst., ix 1877, 62 (s. Illinois; Union County) 65 (s. Illinois).—PURDIE, Bull.
Nuttall Orn. Club, ii, 1877, 15 in text (New England).—BENDIRE, Proc. Boston
Soc. Nat. Hist., xix, 1877, 140 (Boise City, Idaho and Oregon side Snake River;
introduced).—LAWRENCE, Proc. U. S. Nat. Mus., i, 1878, 237, 487 (Antigua;
West Indies; introduced), 450 (Guadeloupe and Martinique; introduced).—
SCOTT, Bull. Nuttall Orn. Club, iv, 1879, 147 (w. Missouri; abundant).—
LANGDON, Journ. Cincinnati Soc. Nat. Hist., 1879, 15 (Cincinnati, Ohio).—
LOOMIS, Bull. Nuttall Orn. Club, iv, 1879, 217 (South Carolina; abundant).—
DALGLEISH, Bull. Nuttall Orn. Club, v, 1880, 144 (Great Britain; intro-
duced).—CORY, Bull. Nuttall Orn. Club, vi, 1881, 154 (Haiti; introduced); Birds
Haiti and San Domingo, 1885, 138.—NEWTON, Handb. Jamaica, 1881, 117.—
WHEATON, Rep. Birds Ohio, 1882, 448, 580, 587 (Ohio; syn.; descr.; habits).—
BECKHAM, Bull. Nuttall Orn. Club, vi, 1882, 165 (Bayou Sara, La.; abundant).—
COOKE, Auk, i, 1884, 247 (Chippewa name).—DREW, Auk, ii, 1885, 14 (Colorado;
introduced).—FEILDEN, Ibis, 1889, 410 Barbadoes; introduced).—OGILVIE-GRANT,
Cat. Birds Brit. Mus., xxii, 1893, 415; Handb. Game Birds, ii, 1897, 135
(monogr.).—FEILDEN, West Indian Bull., iii, 1902, 346 (Barbados).—OLIVER,
New Zealand Birds, 1930, 377 (New Zealand; introduced).

O[rtyx] virginianus RIDGWAY, Ann. Lyc. Nat. Hist. New York, x, 1874, 382
(Illinois; resident).—HATCH, Bull. Minnesota Acad. Nat. Sci., 1874, 62 (Minnesota; introduced; not yet common).—BOIES, Cat. Birds Southern Michigan,
1875, No. 148 (s. Michigan).—DEANE, Bull. Nuttall Orn. Club, i, 1876, 22, in
text (albinism).—NELSON, Bull. Essex Inst., viii, 1876, 122 (ne. Illinois; common
resident; ix, 1877, 59 (Cairo, s. Illinois; few seen).

Ortyx virginiana AUDUBON, Synopsis, 1839, 199; Birds Amer., v, 1842, 59, pl. 289.—
DEKAY, Zool. New York, 1844, 202, pl. 75 (New York).—GIRAUD, Birds Long
Island, 1844, 187 (Long Island, N. Y.; habits).—GOSSE, Birds Jamaica, 1847,
328 (Jamaica).—COUES, Proc. Essex Inst., v, 1868, 40 (spec.; Essex County,
Mass.; Key North Amer. Birds, ed. 2, 1884, 589.—TRIPPE, Comm. Essex Inst.,
vi, 1871, 118 (Minnesota; abundant).—GIBBS, U. S. Geol. and Geogr. Surv. Terr.
Bull. 5, 1879, 491 (Michigan; common resident).—DALGLEISH, Bull. Nuttall
Orn. Club, v, 1880, 66, in text (Europe).—HAY, Bull. Nuttall Orn. Club, vii,
1882, 93 (Lower Mississippi; Vicksburg).—RIDGWAY, Bull. Nuttall Orn. Club,
vii, 1882, 22 (Knox County, Ind.).—BAILEY, Bull. Nuttall Orn. Club, viii, 1883,
41 (eggs; Georgia).—AGERSBORG, Auk, ii, 1885, 285 (se. Dakota; common).—

WILCOX, Auk, ii, 1885, 315, in text (Boise Valley, Idaho; introduced).—TIPPEN-
HAUER, Die Insel Haiti, 1892, 320, 322 (Haiti).

O[rtyx] virginiana MAXIMILIAN, Journ. für Orn., 1858, 443 (descr.).

Perdix (Colinia) virginiana NUTTALL, Man. Orn. United States and Canada, i, 1832,
646.

Ortyx virginianus, var. virginianus BAIRD, BREWER, and RIDGWAY, Hist. North
Amer. Birds, iii, 1874, 468.

O[rtyx] virginianus var. virginianus NELSON, Bull. Essex Inst., ix, 1877, 43 (s.
Illinois; very numerous on the uplands).

Ortyx virginianus α virginianus COUES, Birds Northwest, 1874, 431 (monogr.)

Philortyx virginianus DES MURS, in Chenu, Encycl. Hist. Nat., vi, 1854, 148 (fig.
of head and foot).

Colinus virginianus CORY, List Birds West Indies, 1885, 24; Auk, iv, 1887, 224, part
(Haiti, San Domingo, Jamaica, St. Croix, Antigua), viii, 1891, 47 (Antigua);
Cat. West Indian Birds, 892, 96 (Greater and Lesser Antilles).—STEJNEGER,
Auk, ii, 1885, 45 (nomencl.).—BREWSTER, Auk, iii, 1886, 100, in text, 103 (w.
North Carolina; abundant); Mem. Nuttall Orn. Club, No. 4, 1906, 170 (Cam-
bridge region, Mass.; resident).—BATCHELDER, Auk, iii, 1886, 314 (North
Carolina mountains in winter).—RIVES, Auk, iii, 1886, 161 in text (Salt Pond
Mountain, Va.).—ANTHONY, Auk, iii, 1886, 164 (Oregon; introduced in Wash-
ington County).—Fox, Auk, iii, 1886, 319 (Roane County, Tenn., very com-
mon).—AMERICAN ORNITHOLOGISTS' UNION, Check-list, 1886, 167; ed. 2, 1895,
106.—LANGDON, Auk, iv, 1887, 129 (Chilhowee Mountain, Tenn., abundant).—
RICHMOND, Auk, v, 1888, 20 (District of Columbia; quite rare); xvii, 1900, 178
(Oneida County, N. Y.).—EVERMANN, Auk, v, 1888, 349 (Carroll County, Ind.;
now rare).—LAWRENCE, Auk, vi, 1889, 53, in text (White Top Mountain, Va.).—
FAXON, Auk, vi, 1889, 99, footnote (Berkshire County, Mass.); xiii, 1896, 215
(Abbot's drawing of a Georgia bird).—PINDAR, Auk, vi, 1889, 313 (Fulton
County, Ky.).—BELDING, Occ. Pap. California Acad. Sci., ii, 1890, 8.—LOOMIS,
Auk, vii, 1890, 35 (Pickens County, S. C.); viii, 1891, 326 (Caesars Head, S. C.).
—GOSS, Hist. Birds Kansas, 1891, 219 (Kansas; abundant; habits).—HATCH,
Notes Birds Minnesota, 1892, 155, 454 (Minnesota; distr.; habits).—SCOTT,
Auk, ix, 1892, 120 (Jamaica; introduced).—BENDIRE, Life Hist. North Amer.
Birds, i, 1892, 1, pl. 1 (life hist.).—COOMBS, Auk, ix, 1892, 204 (Louisiana; very
common).—TODD, Auk, x, 1893, 37 in text (Indiana and Clearfield Counties,
Pa.).—ALLEN, Auk, x, 1893, 133 (distr.); xxv, 1908, 59 (s. Vermont).—
WHITE, Auk, x, 1893, 223 (Mackinac Island, Mich.).—FIELD, Auk, xi, 1894,
123 (Jamaica).—SHUFELDT, Auk, xi, 1894, 129, in text, pl. v (plum.).—STONE,
Auk, xi, 1894, 136 (Cape May County, N. J.); Birds New Jersey, 1908, 149
(New Jersey; descr.; habits).—HOFFMAN, Auk, xii, 1895, 88 (c. Berkshire
County, Mass.).—YOUNG, Auk, xiii, 1896, 281 (Lumber Yard, Luzerne County,
Pa.).—BAGG, Auk, xiv, 1897, 226 (near Oneida Lake, N. Y.).—JOHNSON, Auk,
xiv, 1897, 316, in text (Oneida and Lewis Counties, N. Y.); Condor, viii,
1906, 26 (Cheney, Wash.; introduced).—COOKE, Colorado State Agr. Coll. Bull.
37, 1897, 69 (Colorado; introduced in places); 56, 1900, 201 (Colorado; intro-
duced); Auk, xxvi, 1909, 410 (Colorado; native 60 years ago at Bents Fork).—
OBERHOLSER, Auk, xv, 1898, 184 (plum.).—LANTZ, Trans. Kansas Acad. Sci.,
1896–1897 (1899), 253 (Kansas; resident; abundant).—RHOADS, Auk, xvi, 1899,
310 (w. Pennsylvania; rare).—BARLOW, Condor, ii, 1900, 131 (Santa Clara
County, Calif.; introduced).—MACOUN, Cat. Can. Birds, 1900, 197 (s. Ontario).
—NASH, Check-list Birds Ontario, 1900, 26 (Ontario; common); Check-list
Vert. Ontario; Birds, 1905, 34 (Ontario; common).—DWIGHT, Auk, xvii, 1900,
43, 151 in text (molts and plum.).—BANGS and BRADLEE, Auk, xviii, 1901, 250

(Bermuda; introduced).—BAILEY, Handb. Birds Western United States, 1902, 115 (descr.; distr.).—RATHBUN, Auk, xix, 1902, 133 (Seattle, Wash.; introduced).—WAYNE, Auk, xix, 1902, 197 (abnormal plum.; Mt. Pleasant, S. C.).—DAWSON, Birds Ohio, 1903, 437, 652, pl. 53 (Ohio; descr.; habits).—JONES, Birds Ohio, Revised Cat., 1903, 83 (Ohio; common).—SNOW, Cat. Birds Kansas, ed. 5, 1903, 15 (Kansas; abundant).—MAXON, Auk, xx, 1903, 263 (Madison County, N. Y.).—JUDD, U. S. Dept. Agr. Yearbook for 1903 (1904), 193 (economic value).—EIFRIG, Auk, xxi, 1904, 237 (w. Maryland).—WILLIAMS, Auk, xxi, 1904, 453 (Leon County, Fla.).—ALLISON, Auk, xxi, 1904, 476 (West Baton Rouge Parish, La.); xxiv, 1907, 16 (Tishomingo County, Miss.).—TOWNSEND, Mem. Nuttall Orn. Club, iii, 1905, 201 (Essex County, Mass.).—WOOD and FROTHINGHAM, Auk, xxii, 1905, 46 (Au Sable Valley, Mich.; occasional).—KOPMAN, Auk, xxii, 1905, 141 (Jefferson Parish, La.).—STOCKARD, Auk, xxii, 1905, 149 (Mississippi; abundant).—RHOADS and PENNOCK, Auk, xxii, 1905, 199 (Delaware).—CLARK, Auk, xxii, 1905, 262 in text (Barbados; 2 records); Proc. Boston Soc. Nat. Hist., xxxii, 1905, 246 (Barbados; very rare).—BOWLES, Auk, xxiii, 1906, 142 (Tacoma, Wash.; introduced).—WARREN, Condor, viii, 1906, 19 (se. Colorado; s. of Monon).—FLEMING, Auk, xxiv, 1907, 71 (Toronto, Canada).—FERRY, Auk, xxiv, 1907, 283, 432 (s. Illinois; abundant at Olive Branch).—WOODRUFF, Auk, xxv, 1908, 198 (Shannon and Carter Counties, Mo.).—SAUNDERS, Auk, xxv, 1908, 417 (c. Alabama).—EDSON, Auk, xxv, 1908, 432 (Bellingham Bay, Wash.; introduced).—BEYER, ALLISON, and KOPMAN, Auk, xxv, 1908, 439 (Louisiana; common).—REAGAN, Auk, xxv, 1908, 464 (Rosebud Reservation, S. Dak.; rare).—ROCKWELL, Condor, x, 1908, 160 (Mesa County, Colo.; introduced).—DAWSON and BOWLES, Birds Washington, ii, 1909, 560 (Washington; habits; distr.).—MACOUN and MACOUN, Cat. Can. Birds, ed. 2, 1909, 215 (s. Ontario).—HERSEY and ROCKWELL, Condor, xi, 1909, 116 (Barr Lake District, Colo.; common).—PALMER, Auk, xxvi, 1909, 25, in text (instinctive stillness).—HOWELL, Auk, xxvi, 1909, 132 (Young Harris, Brasstown Bald, Tate, and Ellijay; n. Georgia); xxvi, 1910, 296 (Kentucky and Tennessee), 301 (Tennessee—High Cliff, Coal Creek, Crass Mountain, Walden Ridge, and Lawrenceburg).—VISHER, Auk, xxvi, 1909, 147 (near Rapid City, S. Dak.).—TROTTER, Auk, xxvi, 1909, 355 (common names).—HESS, Auk, xxvii, 1910, 22 (centr. Illinois).—EMBODY, Auk, xxvii, 1910, 171 (Ashland, Va.).—CHANEY, Auk, xxvii, 1910, 273 (Mason County, Mich.).—PHILIPP, Auk, xxvii, 1910, 322 (St. James Island, S. C.).—TULLSEN, Condor, xiii, 1911, 104, in text (S. D.).—WIDMANN, Auk, xxviii, 1911, 312 (Estes Park, Colo.).—ZIMMER, Proc. Nebraska Orn. Union, v, pt. 2, 1911, 20 (Dawes County, Nebr.; resident); pt. 5, 1913, 69 (Nebraska; Thomas County Forest Reserve).—SCLATER, Hist. Birds Colorado, 1912, 139 (Colorado; recently spread into eastern Colorado; introduced from Pueblo to Fort Collins).—ISELY, Auk, xxix, 1912, 28 (Sedgwick County, Kans.).—KENNEDY, Condor, xvi, 1914, 254, in text (Yakima Valley, Wash.).—RUST, Condor, xvii, 1915, 123 (Kootenai County, Idaho; influx from Spokane Prairie, Wash.).—PHILLIPS, Auk, xxxii, 1915, 204, in text, pl. xvi (New England; crit.; plum.; meas.); U. S. Dept. Agr. Techn. Bull. 61, 1928, 31 (introduced into Bermuda and New Providence, Jamaica; Puerto Rico, and other West Indian Islands).—GRISCOM, Birds New York City Region, 1923, 175 (status; New York City Region).—JOHNSTON, Birds West Virginia, 1923, 8, 88 (West Virginia).—NEILSON, Condor, xxvii, 1925, 73, in text (Wheatland, Wyo.).—TAVERNER, Birds Western Canada, 1926, 160 (w. Canada; descr.; habits); Birds Canada, 1934, 164 in text (Canada, distr.); Can. Water Birds, 1939, 177 (Canada; field characters).—BEEBE, Zool. Soc. Bull., xxx, 1927, 139; Beneath Tropic Seas, 1928, 220 (Bizoton, Étang Miragoane, Haiti).—SPRUNT,

Auk, xlv, 1928, 210, in text (albinism) ; lii, 1935, 80 in text (North Carolina, Blowing Rock, Watauga County, nest with 17 eggs, August 10, 1934; nest with 11 eggs, August 27).—BOND, Proc. Acad. Nat. Sci. Philadelphia, lxxx, 1928 (1929), 493 (Haiti) ; Auk, xlvii, 1930, 270 (St. Croix, V. I.).—SETH-SMITH, L'Oiseau, x, 1929, 762 (care in captivity).—DANFORTH, Auk, xlvi, 1929, 362 (Mirebalais, Grand Goave, Fonds des Nègres, Hispaniola) ; Leeward Isl. Gazeteer, Suppl., Nov. 16, 1933, 2 (Antigua; introduced; now extinct).—URNER, Abstr. Linn. Soc. New York, Nos. 39, 40, 1930, 71 (Union County, N. J.).—MILLER, Murrelet, xi, 1930, 60 in text (Washington; Palouse region; habits; food).—CHRISTY, Auk, xlviii, 1931, 367 (change of status; Sandusky Bay, Lake Erie).—BAILEY and WRIGHT, Wils. Bull., xliii, 1931, 201 (Avery Island, La.).—GABRIELSON, Condor, xxxiii, 1931, 112 (Brownsboro, Tolo, Jackson County, Oreg.; introduced).—GROEBBELS, Der Vögel, i, 1932, 532 in text (lining of gizzard), 664 (body temperature) ; ii, 1937, 384 in text (infertile eggs), 402 in text (parental care).—CAUM, Occ. Pap. Bishop Mus., x, No. 9, 1933, 12 (Hawaii; introduced; not known to breed).— NICE and KRAFT, Wils. Bull., xlvi, 1934, 122, in table (erythrocite count).— SUTTON, Ann. Carnegie Mus., xxiv, 1934, 12 (Arnett, Laverne, and Kenton, Okla.; crit.).—ANDERSON, Journ. Barbados Mus. Hist. Soc., ii, 1935, 138 (Barbados; accidental).—BAILLIE and HARRINGTON, Contr. Roy. Ontario Mus. Zool., No. 8, 1936, 30 (Ontario; formerly common; reduced in numbers; native and introduced races mixed and not now identifiable).—BAGG and ELIOT, Birds Connecticut Valley in Massachusetts, 1937, 173 (status; habits).—GRIFFEE and RAPRAEGER, Murrelet, xviii, 1937, 14 in text, 16 (Portland, Oreg.; 1 nesting record).—ERRINGTON, Wils. Bull., li, 1939, 22, in text (ability to withstand cold and hunger) ; liii, 1941, 85 in text (central Iowa; habits) ; Auk, lvi, 1939, 170, in text (food habits; Wisconsin).—TODD, Birds Western Pennsylvania, 1940, 131, in text (remains found in stomachs of eastern goshawks).—McCABE and LEO- POLD, Wils. Bull., lii, 1940, 280 (Wisconsin; snow-killed).—LACK, Condor, xlii, 1940, 270, in text, 274 in text (pairing habit).—ALLIN, Trans. Roy. Can. Inst., xxiii, pt. 1, 1940, 96 (Darlington Township, Ontario; extinct).—LESHER and KENDEIGH, Wils. Bull., liii, 1941, 170 in text (molt).—HAND, Condor, xliii, 1941, 225 (St. Joe Natl. Forest, Idaho).—STEVENSON, Condor, xliv, 1942, 110 (Central Panhandle of Texas).—BAHLE, Condor, xlvi, 1944, 72 (Utah; introd.).

C[olinus] virginianus RIDGWAY, Man. North Amer. Birds, 1887, 188.—REICHENOW, DieVögel, i, 1913, 315.

Colinus virginiana PETRIDES, Trans. 7th North Amer. Wildlife Conf., 1942, 322, in text (age indicators in plumage).

Colinus virginianus virginianus WETMORE, Condor, xi 1909, 157 (e. Kansas) ; Sci. Surv. Puerto Rico and Virgin Ids., ix, pt. 3, 1927, 330 (Puerto Rico; Virgin Islands; distr.; habits) ; Proc. U. S. Nat. Mus., lxxxiv, 1937, 407 (West Virginia; spec.; Big Bend, Calhoun County; seen near Gilboa, Freed, and near Grantsville) ; lxxxvi, 1939, 184 (Tennessee; spec. from Shady Valley) ; lxxxviii, 1940, 535 (Kentucky; spec. from near Bedford; sev. sight records).—AMERICAN ORNITHOL- OGISTS' UNION, Check-list, ed. 3, 1910, 134; ed. 4, 1931, 88.—SAUNDERS, Condor, xiv, 1912, 24 (sw. Montana; introduced in Deer Lodge Valley; not yet common) ; Pacific Coast Avif., No. 14, 1921, 172 (introduced into Montana with local success).—BAILEY, Auk, xxix, 1912, 80 (mountains of Virginia; abundant).— BRUNER and FIELD, Auk, xxix, 1912, 376 (w. North Carolina).—HARLOW, Auk, xxix, 1912, 477 (Chester County, Pa.) ; xxxv, 1918, 23 (Pennsylvania and New Jersey).—SMYTH, Auk, xxix, 1912, 514 (Montgomery County, Va.).— ALLEN, Auk, xxx, 1913, 24 (Essex County, Mass.).—EIFRIG, Auk, xxx, 1913, 239, in text (Chicago area).—STONE, Auk, xxx, 1913, 338 (William Bartram's records) ; Bird Studies Cape May, i, 1937, 323 (New Jersey; habits; distr.).—

Wright and Harper, Auk, xxx, 1913, 494 (Okefinokee Swamp, Ga.).—
Bailey, Birds Virginia, 1913, 83 (Virginia; distr.; habits).—Grave and Walker,
Birds Wyoming, 1913, 38 (Wyoming; small coveys on lower portions of Platte
and Laramie Rivers in eastern part of the State).—Kennedy, Ibis, 1914, 188
(Bermuda; spec.).—Tinker, Auk, xxxi, 1914, 77 (Clay and Palo Alto Counties,
Iowa).—Golsan and Holt, Auk, xxxi, 1914, 219 (Alabama; abundant).—
Rockwell and Wetmore, Auk, xxxi, 1914, 314 (Golden, Colo., introduced).—
Cooke, Auk, xxxi, 1914, 478 (Oklahoma; winter).—Smith, Condor, xvii, 1915,
42 (Boston Mountains, Ark.; very local).—Grinnell, Pacific Coast Avif., No.
11, 1915, 180 (California; hypothetical).—Shelton, Univ. Oregon Bull., new
ser., xiv, No. 4, 1917, 20, 26 (west-central Oregon; introduced).—Dice, Auk,
xxxv, 1918, 43 (se. Washington, introduced).—Burns, Orn. Chester County,
Pa., 1919, 48 (Chester County, Pa.; common).—Pearson, Brimley, and
Brimley, Birds of North Carolina, 1919, 152 (North Carolina; descr.; distr.);
1942, 108.—Townsend, Mem. Nuttall Orn. Club, No. 5, 1920, 95 (Essex County,
Mass.; rare).—Fleisher, Auk, xxxvii, 1920, 569 (southeastern North Carolina).—Bangs and Kennard, List Birds Jamaica, 1920, 688 (Jamaica; introduced).—Hunt, Auk, xxxviii, 1921, 376 (Tillar, Ark.; common); xlviii, 1931,
236 (near Maumelle, Ark.).—Over and Thoms, Birds South Dakota, 1921,
75 (South Dakota; common throughout).—Holt, Geol. Surv. Alabama, Mus.
Pap. No. 4, 1921, 36, 53 in text (Alabama; abundant; habits; food; spec.).—
Wilson, Auk, xxxix, 1922, 235 (Bowling Green, Ky.).—Corrington, Auk, xxxix,
1922, 543 (Biloxi, Miss.; winter).—Swope, Auk, xl, 1923, 323 in text, (increasing in Ohio).—Wood, Misc. Publ. Mus. Zool., Univ. Michigan, No. 10, 1923, 81
(North Dakota, introduced; rare).—Pindar, Wils. Bull., xxxvi, 1924, 204
(status. s. Arkansas); xxxviii, 1925, 83 (Fulton County, Ky.).—Beck, Auk, xli,
1924, 292, in text (Pennsylvania; German common names).—Gabrielson, Auk,
xli, 1924, 554 (Imnaha Canyon, Wallowa County, Oreg.); Wils. Bull., xlviii, 1936,
306 (Lake Francis, Minn.; abundant).—Howell, Birds Alabama, 1924, 117;
ed. 2, 1928, 117 (Alabama; habits; distr.); Florida Bird Life, 1932, 192
(Florida; distr.; descr.; habits).—Nice and Nice, Birds Oklahoma, 1924, 35
(Oklahoma; distr.; habits).—Wheeler, Birds Arkansas, 1925, 38, xiv, xx
(Arkansas; descr.; habits; food; nests and eggs).—Bailey, Birds Florida,
1925, i, 59, pl. 32 (col. fig.; distr.; Florida).—Larson, Wils. Bull., xxxvii,
1925, 27 (status; Sioux Falls region, S. Dak.).—Blincoe, Auk, xlii, 1925, 408
(Bardstown, Ky.).—Holland, Auk, xliii, 1926, 94, in text (late nesting,
Illinois); xliv, 1927, 100, in text (late nesting).—Worthington and Todd,
Wils. Bull., xxxviii, 1926, 211 (Florida; Choctowhatchee Bay).—Forbush,
Birds Massachusetts and Other New England States, ii, 1927, 2, pl. 34 (col.
fig.; New England; distr.; descr.; habits).—Linsdale and Hall, Wils. Bull.,
xxxix, 1927, 96 (Douglas County, Kans.).—Linsdale, Auk, xliv. 1927, 52
(Pratt, Garden City, and Coolidge, sw. Kansas); Univ. Kansas Sci. Bull., xviii,
1928, 532 (near Geary, e. Kansas).—Horsey, Auk, xliv, 1927, 119 (Montgomery
and Boyd Counties, Ky.).—Davis, Auk, xliv, 1927, 418, in text (late nesting).—Baerg, Auk, xliv, 1927, 546 (Mount Magazine, Ark.); Univ. Arkansas
Agr. Exp. Stat. Bull. 258, 1931, 53 (Arkansas; distr.; descr.; habits; food).—
Sutton, Birds Pennsylvania, 1928, 52 (Pennsylvania; distr.; habits); Ann. Carnegie Mus., xxvii, 1938, 178 (Tarrant County, Tex.; breeds).—Pickens, Wils.
Bull., xl, 1928, 189 (upper South Carolina).—Bond, Proc. Acad. Nat. Sci. Philadelphia, lxxx, 1928 (1929), 493 (Haiti; distr.; habits); Birds West Indies, 1936,
414 (distr. in West Indies); Check List Birds West Indies, 1940, 164 (introduced
and now extirpated in St. Kitts, Antigua, Guadeloupe, and Martinique; introduced and established in Jamaica, s. Haiti, and St. Croix, in all of which

islands it is not common).—CAHN and HYDE, Wils. Bull., xli, 1929, 36 (Little Egypt, Ill.; ecol., distr.).—COOKE, Proc. Biol. Soc. Washington, xlii, 1929, 33 (Washington, D. C.).—HARPER, Wils. Bull., xli, 1929, 236 (Randolph County, Ga.).—MOLTONI, Atti Soc. Ital. Sci. Nat., lxviii, 1929, 311 (Dominican Republic).—DANFORTH, Journ. Agr. Porto Rico, xiv, 1930, 115 (St. Croix, V. I.); xix, 1935, 466 (St. Croix; introduced); xxiii, 1938, 22 (Guadeloupe, introduced 1886-7; now extinct); Auk, li, 1934, 357 (introduced into Antigua; became extinct there soon after 1890); Trop. Agr., xiii, 1936, 214 (St. Kitts; introduced; now extinct).—BEATTY, Journ. Agr. Porto Rico, xiv, 1930, 139 (St. Croix, V. I.; breeds).—ROADS, Auk, xlvii, 1930, 268, in text (late nesting; Ohio).—FITZPATRICK, Wils. Bull., xlii, 1930, 125 (status in northeastern Colorado).—BROOKS, Wils. Bull., xlii, 1930, 246 (Cranberry Glades, W. Va.).— PIERCE, Wils. Bull., xlii, 1930, 265 (Buchanan County, Iowa); Proc. Iowa Acad. Sci., xlvii, 1941, 376 (ne. Iowa, recently became scarce).—NICE, Birds Oklahoma, rev. ed., 1931, 81 (Oklahoma; distr.; habits); Auk, l, 1933, 97 (hen giving call of male).—[ARTHUR], Birds Louisiana, 1931, 216 (Louisiana; habits; descr.; status).—WETMORE and SWALES, U. S. Nat. Mus. Bull. 155, 1931, 122 (Hispaniola; distr.; habits; syn.).—SNYDER and LOGIER, Trans. Roy. Canadian Inst., xviii, pt. 1, 1931, 176 (Long Point area, Norfolk County; Ontario; formerly).—ESTEN, Auk, xlviii, 1931, 573 (weight).—BIRD and BIRD, Wils. Bull., xliii, 1931, 293, in text (food in winter; Oklahoma).—BRADLEE and MOWBRAY, Proc. Boston Soc. Nat. His., xxxix, 1931, 325 (Bermuda; not common; spec.).—ROBERTS, Birds Minnesota, i, 1932, 408 (distr.; habits; Minnesota).—BENNITT, Univ. Missouri Studies, vii, No. 3, July 1932, 26 (Missouri; resident).—BENT, U. S. Nat. Mus. Bull. 162, 1932, 9 (life hist. monogr.; distr.; plum.).—GRISCOM, Trans. Linn. Soc. New York, iii, 1933, 97 (Dutchess County, N. Y.; now largely extirpated).—PETERS, Check-list Birds World, ii, 1934, 47 (distr.).—BRODKORB and STEVENSON, Auk, li, 1934, 101 (Beach, Ill., adult female in male plumage).—NAGEL, Wils. Bull., xlvi, 1934, 147 (Missouri; diet and internal parasites).—BRECKENRIDGE, Condor, xxxvii, 1935, 269 (Minnesota).—McCREARY and MICKEY, Wils. Bull., xlvii, 1935, 129 in text (se. Wyoming; resident).—YOUNGWORTH, Wils. Bull., xlvii, 1935, 217 (Fort Sisseton, South Dakota; few seen).—PERKINS, Auk, lii, 1935, 460 (Berwick, Maine).—FISHER, Proc. Biol. Soc. Washington, xlviii, 1935, 161 (Plummers Island, Md.).—IMLER, Trans. Kansas Acad. Sci., xxxix, 1936, 301 (Rooks County, Kans.; fairly common until 1934; since quite uncommon).—BELLROSE, Auk, liii, 1936, 348 (nesting September 8 near Ottawa, n. Illinois).—SCOTT, Wils. Bull., xlix, 1937, 21 (Iowa; snow-killing).—STEWART, Auk, liv, 1937, 326, in table (weight).—ALEXANDER, Univ. Colorado Stud., No. 24, 1937, 91 (Boulder County, Colo.; infrequent).—MURPHEY, Contr. Charleston Mus., ix, 1937, 14 (Savannah Valley, Ga.; abundant; varying in numbers from year to year).—DEADERICK, Wils. Bull., l, 1938, 263 (Hot Springs Nat. Park, Arkansas; common).—BENNETT, Blue-winged Teal, 1938, 46 in text (egg dropping).— VAN TYNE, Occ. Pap. Mus. Zool. Univ. Michigan, No. 379, 1938, 12 (Michigan; permanent resident).—SUTTON, Ann. Carngie Mus., xxvii, 1938, 178 (Tarrant County, Tex.; breeds).—OBERHOLSER, Bird Life Louisiana, 1938, 191 (Louisiana, common; habits).—NIEDRACH and ROCKWELL, Birds Denver and Mountain Parks, 1939, 64 (Denver, Colo., region; distr.; habits; not common).— TRAUTMAN, BILLS, and WICKLIFF, Wils. Bull., li, 1939, 99, in text (winter mortality; Ohio).—CAMPBELL, Bull. Toledo Mus. Sci., i, 1940, 63 (Lucas County, Ohio; spec.; common; eggs).—LONG, Trans. Kansas Acad. Sci., xliii, 1940, 440 (Kansas; fairly common resident in east but not so abundantly as formerly).— TRAUTMAN, Misc. Publ. Mus. Zool. Univ. Michigan, No. 44, 1940, 224 (Buckeye

Lake, Ohio; habits; common).—Gabrielson and Jewett, Birds Oregon, 1940, 220 (Oregon; distr.; descr.; habits).—Todd, Birds Western Pennsylvania, 1940, 172 (w. Pennsylvania; descr.; distr.; habits; syn.).—Burleigh, Auk, lviii, 1941, 337 (North Carolina, Mount Mitchell).—Goodpaster, Journ. Cincinnati Soc. Nat. Hist., xxii, 1941, 13 (sw. Ohio; resident).—Hellmayr and Conover, Cat. Birds Amer., i, No. 1, 1942, 238 (syn.; distr.).—Herman, Jankiewicz, and Saarni, Condor, xliv, 1942, 168 in text (coccidiosis).—Cruickshank, Birds New York City, 1942, 151 (status; habits).

Colinus v[irginianus] virginianus Wetmore, Condor, xi, 1909, 155 (e. Kansas); Maryland Conservationist, 1930, 4, 5 in text.—Peck, Condor, xiii, 1911, 65 (Willow Creek Valley, Oreg.).—Lincoln, Auk, xxxvii, 1920, 65 (Clear Creek district, Colo.; introduced).—Soper, Auk, xl, 1923, 497 (Wellington and Waterloo Counties, Ontario).—Holt, Auk, xlii, 1925, 147 (nesting dates, Alabama).—Wing, Auk, xlvii, 1930, 417 (killed by pheasants).—Stoddard, The Bobwhite Quail, 1931, 83 (monogr.).—Hicks, Wils. Bull., xlv, 1933, 180 (Ashtabula County, Ohio).—Breckenridge, Condor, xxxvii, 1935, 272 (eaten by marsh hawk).—Groebbels, Der Vögel, ii, 1937, 167 (data on breeding biology), 239, in text (egg number).—Poole, Auk, lv, 1938, 516, in table (weight; wing area). —Stabler, Auk, lviii, 1941, 561 (used in parasite experiment).—Amadon, Auk, lx, 1943, 225 (body weight and egg weight).

C[olinus] v[irginianus] virginianus Sutton, Ann. Carnegie Mus., xxiv, 1934, 12, in text (Panhandle, Oklahoma).—Bond, Birds West Indies, 1936, 82 in text, 403 in text (introduced, but now extirpated, in Puerto Rico, St. Kitts, Antigua, Guadeloupe, and Martinique; established in Jamaica, southern Haiti, and St. Croix).

[*Colinus*] *virginianus virginianus* Baillie and Harrington, Contr. Roy. Ontario Mus. Zool., No. 8, pt. 1, 1936, 30, in text (native Ontario race now mixed with imported stock).

Colinus virginianus texanus (not of Lawrence, 1853) Goss, Hist. Birds Kansas, 1891, 222 (Kansas; spec.; descr.).—Lantz, Trans. Kansas Acad. Sci., 1896–97 (1899), 253 (Kansas; resident in southwestern part).—Cooke, Colorado State Agr. Coll. Bull. 56, 1900, 201, part (Colorado).—Snow, Cat. Birds Kansas, ed. 5, 1903, 15 (sw. Kansas; rare).

Colinus v[irginianus] texanus Niedrach, Condor, xxv, 1923, 182, in text (Baca County, Colo.).

Colinus virginianus floridanus (not of Coues, 1872) Figgins, Auk, xl, 1923, 674 (Black Bayou, La.).

O[rtyx] virginianus var. floridanus (not of Coues, 1872) Nelson, Bull. Essex Inst., ix, 1877, 43 (Mount Carmel, Ill.).

Tetrao marilandicus Linnaeus, Syst. Nat., ed. 12, i, 1766, 277 (based on *Perdix novae-angliae* Brisson, i, 229).

Tetrao marilandica Brackenridge, Views of Louisiana, 1817, 119 (Louisiana).

Tetrao marilandus Gmelin, Syst. Nat., i, pt. 2, 1788, 761.

Perdix marilanda Latham, Index Orn. ii, 1790, 651.

Tetrao marylandus Smith, Wonders of Nature and Art, rev. ed., 1807, xiv, 69 (New York, Pennsylvania).

Ortyx marylandus Denny, Proc. Zool. Soc. London, 1847, 38 (part; Jamaica).

(?) *Tetrao mexicanus* Linnaeus, Syst. Nat., ed. 12, i, 1766, 277.—Gmelin, Syst. Nat., i, pt. 2, 1788, 762.

Perdix mexicana Latham, Index Orn., ii, 1790, 653.—Richmond, Auk, xix, 1902, 79, in text (nomencl.).

Tetrao colin Müller, Syst. Nat. Suppl., 1776, 129 ("America").

Tetrao colinicui Müller, Syst. Nat. Suppl., 1776, 130 (Louisiana).

Perdix borealis TEMMINCK, Pig. et Gallin., iii, 1815, 436, 475 (part).—VIEILLOT, Gal. Ois., ii, 1825, 44, pl. 214.

Ortyx borealis STEPHENS, *in* Shaw, Gen. Zool., xi, 1819, 377.—JARDINE and SELBY, Illustr. Orn., i, 1828, text to pl. 38; Nat. Libr. Orn., iv, 1834, pl. 10.

T[etrao minor] BARTRAM, Trav. in Florida, etc., 1791, 290.

(?) *Ortyx castanea* GOULD, Proc. Zool. Soc. London, 1842 (1843), 142 ("South America"; coll. J. Gould).

(?) *Ortyx castaneus* GOULD, Monogr. Odontoph., pt. 3, 1850, pl. 3.—GRAY, List Birds, Brit. Mus. pt. 5, Gallinae, 1867, 76; Hand-list, ii, 1870, 273, No. 9780.— OGILVIE-GRANT, Cat. Birds Brit. Mus. xxii, 1893, 424; Handbook Game Birds, ii, 1897, 145 (monogr.).

(?) *Colinus virginianus castaneus* PETERS, Check-list Birds World, ii, 1934, 49 and footnote.—HELLMAYR and CONOVER, Cat. Birds Amer., i, No. 1, 1942, 247.

Ortyx hoopesii "KRIDER," "Homo" [pseudonym], Forest and Stream, v, 1875, 243 (near Philadelphia, Pa. = black-throated variety).

C[olinus] v[irginianus] verus ALLEN, Auk, iii, 1886, 276, in text (not apparently intended as a new name but signifying "true" or "typical" *virginianus*).

Colinus virginianus taylori LINCOLN, Proc. Biol. Soc. Washington, xxviii, 1915, 103 (Laird, Yuma County, Colo.; coll. Colorado Museum Nat. Hist.).—AMERICAN ORNITHOLOGISTS' UNION, Auk, xxxiii, 1916, 426.—LONG, Bull. Univ. Kansas Sci., xxxvi, 1935, 233 (common; w. Kansas); Trans. Kansas Acad. Sci., xliii, 1940, 441 (Kansas; common resident in western part; probably as far east as the Flint Hills).

Colinus v[irginianus] taylori LINCOLN, Proc. Colorado Mus. Nat. Hist., 1915, 6 (Yuma County, Colo.; resident).

[Colinus] [virginianus] taylori SUTTON, Ann. Carnegie Mus., xxiv, 1934, 12, in text.

COLINUS VIRGINIANUS TEXANUS (Lawrence)

TEXAS BOBWHITE

Adult male.—Similar to that of the nominate form but without any black loreal band from the bill to the eye and without large, conspicuous black blotches on the scapulars, innermost secondaries, and back; generally much more grayish, less rufescent above, and less tinged with ochraceous or buffy below; the feathers of upperparts of head and body paler in their brownish parts than in the typical form and each feather terminally edged with pale smoke grayish, the interscapulars and feathers of the back and upper wing coverts barred with whitish each of these bars bordered by blackish; the black border posterior to the white throat narrower; size generally smaller.

Adult female.—Similar to that of the nominate race but slightly paler and much grayer, as in the male, and without large black blotches on the scapulars, inner secondaries, and back.

Immature.—Similar to the adult of corresponding sex, but with the two outer primaries more pointed terminally.

Juvenal.—Like that of the nominate race of corresponding sex but somewhat paler, and, for this reason, appearing somewhat more brownish, less dusky.

Natal down.—Not distinguishable from that of the typical race.

Adult male.—Wing 103–112.5 (107.9) ; tail 57–64 (61) ; culmen from the base 13.5–14 (13.7) ; tarsus 28–31 (29.8) ; middle toe without claw 25–28 (26.3 mm.).[5]

Adult female.—Wing 98.5–110.5 (107.1) ; tail 50.5–62 (56.3) ; culmen from base 12.5–14 (13.1) ; tarsus 28–31 (29.4) ; middle toe without claw 25–28 (26.5 mm.).[5]

Range.—Resident in open country in the Upper and Lower Sonoran Zone from southeastern New Mexico (Carlsbad, Texline, Nara Vasa, sandhills near Logan, etc.) ; central and southern Texas (north to the neighborhood of the Brazos River, where it intergrades with the nominate race), south to northeastern Coahuila and Nuevo León and to north-central Tamaulipas.

Introduced, either by itself or mixed with typical *virginianus,* and now hopelessly mixed beyond the point of subspecific identifiability, into central Colorado, Utah, Idaho, California, Montana, Oregon, Washington, many of the eastern States, and in the West Indies, especially Haiti.

Type locality.—Above Ringgold Barracks, Tex.

Ortyx virginiana (not *Tetrao virginianus* Linnaeus) McCALL, Proc. Acad. Nat. Sci. Philadelphia, 1851, 220 (sw. Texas; "New Mexico").—NEHRLING, Bull. Nuttall Orn. Club, vii, 1882, 175 (Houston, etc., se. Texas).

Ortyx virginianus WOODHOUSE, *in* Rep. Sitgreaves Expl. Zuñi and Colorado Rivers, 1853, 94 (Indian Territory; Texas e. of San Pedro River).—BAIRD, Rep. U. S. and Mex. Bound. Surv., ii, pt. 2, 1859, 22 (e. Texas).

Colinus virginianus AMERICAN ORNITHOLOGISTS' UNION, Check-list, ed. 2, 1895, 106; ed. 3, 1910, 134, part.—FRIEDMANN, Auk, xlii, 1925, 543 (lower Rio Grande Valley, Tex.).—SUTTON and BURLEIGH, Occ. Pap. Mus. Zool., Louisiana State Univ., No. 3, 1939, 28 (ne. Mexico; common n. Tamaulipas, n. Nuevo León).

Ortyx texanus LAWRENCE, Ann. Lyc. Nat. Hist. New York, vi, 1853, 1 (Ringgold Barracks, Tex.; coll. G. N. Lawrence).—BAIRD, Rep. Pacific R.R. Surv., ix, 1858, 641; Rep. U. S. and Mex. Bound. Surv., ii, pt. 2, 1859, 22, pl. 24 (Devils River and Laredo, Tex.; Matamoros, Tamaulipas; Nuevo León) ; Cat. North Amer. Birds, 1859, No. 472.—HEERMANN, Rep. Pacific R.R. Surv., x, No. 1, 1859, 18 (Pecos River, Tex.).—BAIRD, CASSIN, and LAWRENCE, Rep. Pacific R.R. Surv., 1860, atlas, pl. 62.—DRESSER, Ibis, 1865, 315, 317, in text, 1866, 27 (s. Texas).—GRAY, List Birds Brit. Mus., pt. 5, Gallinae, 1867, 75.—BUTCHER, Proc. Acad. Nat. Sci. Philadelphia, 1868, 150 (Laredo, Tex.).—BAIRD, BREWER, and RIDGWAY, Hist. North Amer. Birds, iii, 1874, pl. 63, figs. 3, 4.—SALVIN and GODMAN, Biol. Centr.-Amer., Aves, iii, 1903, 298, part (s. and w. Texas; Matamoros, etc., n. Tamaulipas; Hacienda de las Escobas, San Agustín, San Pedro, Vaqueria, Estancia, and Topo Chico, Nuevo León?).[6]

Ortix texanus CUBAS, Cuadro Geogr., Estadístico, Descr. e Hist. de los Estados Unidos Mexicanos, 1884, 175 (common names; Mexico).

[*Ortyx virginianus*] Var. *texanus* Coues, Key North Amer. Birds, 1872, 237.

Ortyx virginianus . . var. *texanus* Coues, Check-list North Amer. Birds, 1874, No. 389b.

---

[5] Ten specimens of each sex.
[6] Some of these localities, at least, may refer to *C. v. maculatus.*

O[rtyx] virginianus, var. texanus RIDGWAY, Forest and Stream, i, No. 19, 1873, 290, in text.

Ortyx virginianus, var. texanus BAIRD, BREWER, and RIDGWAY, Hist. North Amer. Birds, iii, 1874, 474.

Ortyx virginiana var. texana MERRILL, Proc. U. S. Nat. Mus., i, 1878, 160 (Fort Brown, Tex.; habits; descr. nest and eggs).

Ortyx virginiana texana SENNETT, U. S. Geol. and Geogr. Surv. Terr., Bull. 4, No. 1, 1878, 53 (Rio Grande Valley, Tex.; eggs); Bull. 5, 1879, 429 (Lomita Ranch, Texas; habits).—RIDGWAY, Proc. U. S. Nat. Mus., iii, 1880, 196 (Nom. North Amer. Birds, 1881, No. 480b.—COUES, Check-list North Amer. Birds, ed. 2, 1882, No. 573.—BROWN, Bull. Nuttall Orn. Club, vii, 1882, 41 (Boerne, Kendall County, w. Texas).

O[rtyx] v[irginiana] texana COUES, Key North Amer. Birds, ed. 2, 1884, 591.

[Ortyx virginianus] b. texanus COUES, Birds Northwest, 1874, 431 (synonymy).

[Ortyx virginianus] Subsp. b. Ortyx texanus OGILVIE-GRANT, Cat. Birds Brit. Mus., xxii, 1893, 419, part (Hacienda de las Escobas, San Agustín, San Pedro, Vaqueria, Estancia near Monterey, and Topo Chico, Nuevo León; Brownsville, Corpus Christi, Medina, San Antonio, and Papalote, Bee County, Texas).

Colinus virginianus texanus STEJNEGER, Auk, ii, 1885, 45 (nomencl.).—AMERICAN ORNITHOLOGISTS' UNION, Check-list, 1886, No. 289b; ed. 2, 1895, No. 289b; ed. 3, 1910, p. 134.—Goss, Auk, iv, 1887, 9 (Republican Fork, w. Kans.).—SENNETT, Auk, iv, 1887, 24 (descr. first plumage).—LLOYD, Auk, iv, 1887, 186 (Tom Green and Concho Counties, Tex., west to Pecos River).—BECKHAM, Proc. U. S. Nat. Mus., x, 1888, 637, 640, 655 (Bexar and Bee Counties, Texas).—HASBROUCK, Auk, vi, 1889, 237 (Eastland County, Texas).—BENDIRE, Life Hist. North Amer. Birds, i, 1892, 8.—ATTWATER, Auk, ix, 1892, 233 (San Antonio, Tex.),—NELSON, Auk, xv, 1898, 121 (Nuevo León and Tamaulipas, ne. Mexico, sea level up to 2,500 feet); xix, 1902, pl. 14, fig. 5.—LANTZ, Trans. Kansas Acad. Sci. for 1896-97 (1899), 253 (sw. Kansas).—COOKE, Colorado State Agr. Coll. Bull. 56, 1900, 201, part (distr.).—CARROLL, Auk, xvii, 1900, 341 Refugio County, Tex.; abundant).—DWIGHT, Auk, xviii, 1900, 46 (molts, etc.).—SMITH, Condor, xii, 1910, 95, in text (lower Rio Grande Valley); Auk, xxxiii, 1916, 188 (Kerr County, Tex.; nests; eggs).—PHILLIPS, Auk, xxviii, 1911, 74 (Matamoros and San Fernando, Tamaulipas).—LACEY, Auk, xxviii, 1911, 206 Kerrville, Kerr County, Tex.).—SIMMONS, Auk, xxxii, 1915, 321 (se. Texas; habits; Birds Austin Region, 1925, 79 (Austin, Tex.; habits; local distr.).—QUILLIN and HOLLEMAN, Condor, xx, 1918, 39 (Bexar County, Tex.).—PEARSON, Auk, xxxviii, 1921, 523 (se. Texas).—CAHN, Condor, xxiv, 1922, 176 (Bird Island, Tex.; none seen, but common on mainland).—BENT, Wils. Bull., xxxvi, 1924, 12 (se. Texas); U. S. Nat. Mus. Bull. 162, 1932, 34 (life hist.; distr.).—DE LAUBENFELS, Wils. Bull., xxxvi, 1924, 170 (Brownsville, Tex.).—GRISCOM and CROSBY, Auk, xlii, 1925, 532 (Brownsville region, s. Texas).—BAILEY, Birds New Mexico, 1928, 213 (New Mexico; habits; distr.).—BURLEIGH, Auk, xlvi, 1929, 509 (Tacoma, Wash.; introduced).—COMPTON, Condor, xxxiv, 1932, 48 (hybrid between this species and Lophortyx californica).—BENNITT, Univ. Missouri Studies, vii, No. 3, 1932, 26 (Missouri; uncommon).—RANSOM, Murrelet, xiii, 1932, 52, in text (flight; habits; Benton County, Wash.; introduced).—MURRAY, Auk, l, 1933, 199 (introd. in all parts of Virginia).—PETERS, Check-list Birds World, ii, 1934, 47.—MILLER, LUMLEY, and HALL, Murrelet, xvi, 1935, 57 (Washington, San Juan Islands; introduced).—EDSON, Murrelet, xvi, 1935, 12 (Washington, Whatcom County; introduced).—GROEBBELS, Der Vögel, ii, 1937, 167 (breeding biology).—DAVIS, Condor, xlii, 1940, 81 (Brazos

County, Tex.; resident).—HELLMAYR and CONOVER, Cat. Birds Amer., i, No. 1, 1942, 241 (syn.; distr.).—ALDRICH, Proc. Biol. Soc. Washington, lv, 1942, 69 (crit.; spec.; distr.).—AMADON, Auk, lx, 1943, 226 (body weight and egg weight).

Colinus virginianus texensis ALLEN, Auk, x, 1893, 134.

C[olinus] virginianus texanus RIDGWAY, Man. North Amer. Birds, 1887, 188.

C[olinus] v[irginianus] texanus BAILEY, Handbook Birds Western United States, 1902, 116 (descr.; distr.).

Colinus v[irginianus] texanus NIEDRACH, Condor, xxv, 1923, 182 (se. Colorado near Oklahoma boundary; crit.).—WETMORE, Maryland Conservationist, 1930, 4, 5, in text (introduced in Pennsylvania and Maryland; hybridizing).—STODDARD, The Bobwhite Quail, 1931, 84 (imported to Georgia and Florida).

[Colinus] v[irginianus] texanus GROEBBELS, Der Vögel, ii, 1937, 239, in text (number of eggs).

[Colinus] texanus SHARPE, Hand-list, i, 1899, 45, part.

COLINUS VIRGINIANUS FLORIDANUS (Coues)

FLORIDA BOBWHITE

Adult male.—Similar to that of the nominate race but slightly smaller and generally darker in color, more heavily marked with black above and below, the pectoral area immediately posterior to the black collar with a distinct, broad band of tawny to hazel, streaked with black; the lower back and rump more olive-grayish, more contrasting with the color of the upper back and rump than in the typical form.

Adult female.—Similar to that of the nominate race but slightly smaller and with all the blackish marks more heavily and conspicuously developed; and with a broad pectoral band of dull tawny-cinnamon more or less mottled with black.

Immature.—Similar to the adult of the corresponding sex but with the outermost primaries more pointed terminally.

Juvenal.—Similar to that of the corresponding sex of the nominate form but darker, the black markings larger and heavier.

Natal down.—Similar to that of the nominate form but slightly darker.

Adult male.—Wing 110–111 (106.1); tail 53–62 (57.4); culmen from the base 14–15.5 (14.8); tarsus 27–31 (29.3); middle toe without claw 25–29 (26.6 mm.).[6]

Adult female.—Wing 101–110 (105.8); tail 49–61.5 (56.1); culmen from base 14–16 (14.5); tarsus 28–30 (28.7); middle toe without claw 25–29 (26.2 mm.).[6]

Range.—Resident in the Florida Peninsula, north to Gainesville, and, on the east coast, to Anastasia Island, south to Miami and Paradise Key, in open pinelands, on prairies among palmetto scrub, and about the borders of bushy "hammocks."

Type locality.—Enterprise, Volusia County, Fla.

---

[6] Ten specimens of each sex.

Ortyx virginianus (not *Tetrao virginianus* Linnaeus) BRYANT, Proc. Boston Soc. Nat. Hist., vii, 1859, 120 (Bahamas).—TAYLOR, Ibis, 1862, 129 (Florida).— ALLEN, Bull. Mus. Comp. Zool., ii, 1871, 352 (e. Florida).—CORY, Birds Bahama Islands, 1880, 142.

Ortyx virginiana ALBRECHT, Journ. für Orn., 1861, 55 (Bahamas).

[*Ortyx virginianus*] Var. *floridanus* COUES, Key North Amer. Birds, 1872, 237 (Enterprise, Volusia County, Fla.).

Ortyx virginianus . . . var. *floridanus* COUES, Check-list North Amer. Birds, 1874, No. 389a.

Ortyx virginianus, var. *floridanus*, BAIRD, BREWER, and RIDGWAY, Hist. North Amer. Birds, iii, 1874, 522 (Miami, Fla.).

[*Ortyx virginianus*] c. *floridanus* COUES, Birds Northwest, 1874, 431.

Ortyx virginiana floridana RIDGWAY, Proc. U. S. Nat. Mus., iii, 1880, 196; Nom. North Amer. Birds, 1881, No. 480a.—COUES, Check-list North Amer. Birds, ed. 2, 1882, No. 572.

O[*rtyx*] *v*[*irginiana*] *floridana* COUES, Key North Amer. Birds, ed. 2, 1884, 591.

Ortyx virginianus floridanus GOODE, U. S. Nat. Mus. Bull. 20, 1883, 332.—BANGS, Bull. Mus. Comp. Zool., lxx, 1930, 159 (type in Mus. Comp. Zool.).

[*Ortyx virginianus*] Subsp. a *Ortyx floridanus* OGILVIE-GRANT, Cat. Birds Brit. Mus., xxii, 1893, 418.

Colinus virginianus floridanus STEJNEGER, Auk, ii, 1885, 45 (nomencl.).—AMERICAN ORNITHOLOGISTS' UNION, Check-list, 1886, No. 289a; ed. 2, 1895, No. 289a; ed. 3, 1910, p. 134; ed. 4, 1931, 88 (distr.).—Bull. Amer. Mus. Nat. Hist., iv, 1892, 290 (San Pablo, s. Cuba; crit.).—SCOTT, Auk, vi, 1889, 245 (Tarpon Springs, Fla.; abundant); ix, 1892, 212 (Caloosahatchie River area, Fla.).— BENDIRE, Life Hist. North Amer. Birds, i, 1892, 7.—WAYNE, Auk, x, 1893, 337 (Suwannee River, nw. Florida); xii, 1895, 364 (vicinity of Waukeenah, Jefferson County, Fla.).—DWIGHT, Auk, xvii, 1900, 45 (molt, etc.).—TODD, Ann. Carnegie Mus., vii, 1911, 412 (New Providence, Bahamas; spec.; crit.).— WORTHINGTON, Ann. Carnegie Mus., vii, 1911, 446 (New Providence; habits).— BAYNARD, Auk, xxx, 1913, 243 (Alachua County, Fla.; abundant; breeding).— PHILLIPS, Auk, xxxii, 1915, 207, in text.—GRISCOM, Auk, xxxiii, 1916, 330 (Leon County, Fla.; winter).—PANGBORN, Auk, xxxvi, 1919, 400 (Pinellas County, Fla.).—HOWELL, Auk, xxxviii, 1921, 255 (Royal Palm Hammock, Fla.; rare resident); Florida Bird Life, 1932, 193 (genl.; habits; distr.; Florida).—BAILEY, Birds of Florida, i, 1925, 59, pl. 32 (col. fig.; distr. Florida).—HOLT and SUTTON, Ann. Carnegie Mus., xvi, 1926, 426 (habits, s. Florida).—FARGO, Wils. Bull., xxxviii, 1926, 148 (Pinellas and Pasco Counties, Fla.).—BENT and COPELAND, Auk, xliv, 1927, 379 (near Orlando, Fla.).— WILLIAMS, Auk, xlv, 1928, 167 (Leon County, Fla.).—DuMONT, Auk, xlviii, 1931, 250 (Pinellas County, Fla.).—BENT, U. S. Nat. Mus. Bull. 162, 1932, 32 (habits; distr.; plum.).—PETERS, Check-list Birds World, ii, 1934, 47.—BOND, Birds West Indies, 1936, 414 (introduced in West Indies); Check-list Birds West Indies, 1940, 164 (introduced on Abaco and Whale Cay (Berry Island) where now extirpated; established on New Providence).—HELLMAYR and CONOVER, Cat. Birds Amer., i, No. 1, 1942, 240 (syn.; distr.).

Colinus v[*irginianus*] *floridanus* STODDARD, The Bobwhite Quail, 1931, 83 (Florida).

C[*olinus*] *virginianus floridanus* RIDGWAY, Man. North Amer. Birds, 1887, 188.

C[*olinus*] *v*[*irginianus*] *floridanus* STONE, Birds New Jersey, 1908, 149, in text.— BOND, Birds West Indies, 1936, 82, in text, 403, in text (introduced on some of the Bahama Islands—New Providence, Abaco (?), and Whale Cay, but apparently established only on New Providence).

[*Colinus*] *floridanus* SHARPE, Hand-list, i, 1899, 45.

[*Colinus*] *virginianus* CORY, List Birds West Indies, 1885, 24, part; rev. ed., 1886, 24, part.

Colinus virginianus CORY, Auk, iv, 1887, 224, part; Birds West Indies, 1889, 223, part; Auk, viii, 1891, 294 (New Providence) ; Cat. West. Indian Birds, 1892, 96, part (New Providence), 138, part (crit.).—AMERICAN ORNITHOLOGISTS' UNION, Check-list, ed. 2, 1895, 106; ed. 3, 1910, 134, part.—BONHOTE, Ibis, 1899, 517 (New Providence).

Ortyx bahamensis BONHOTE, Ibis, 1903, 299 (New Providence; spec.).

Colinus bahamensis MAYNARD, App. Cat. Birds West Indies, 1899, 33 (New Providence Island, Bahamas; coll. C. J. Maynard).—BANGS, Auk, xvii, 1900, 286 (New Providence; crit.) ; Bull. Mus. Comp. Zool., lxx, 1930, 159 (type in Mus. Comp. Zool.).—BONHOTE, Ibis, 1903, 299 (New Providence; crit.; habits).—ALLEN, Auk, xxii, 1905, 122 (New Providence).

Colinus virginianus bahamensis RILEY, Auk, xxii, 1905, 352 (New Providence) ; *in* Shattuck, Bahama Islands, 1905, 360 (New Providence; breeds).

C[*olinus*] *virginianus cubanensis* (not *Ortyx cubanensis* Gould) RIDGWAY, Man. North Amer. Birds, 1887, 188, part (sw. Florida).

Colinus virginianus cubanensis RIDGWAY, Man. North Amer. Birds, 1887, 593, part.—AMERICAN ORNITHOLOGISTS' UNION, Suppl. Check List, rev. ed., 1889, 7, part.—BENDIRE, Life Hist. North Amer. Birds, i, 1892, 9, part.

(?) *Colinus virginianus cubanensis* SCOTT, Auk, vi, 1889, 245 (Key West, Fla.).

COLINUS VIRGINIANUS INSULANUS Howe

KEY WEST BOBWHITE

Adult male.—Similar to that of *C. v. floridanus* but smaller, "crown uniform dark fuscous, forehead showing more white. Otherwise colored like *floridanus* . . . wing 97, tail 44, culmen 14, tarsus 30 mm."

Known only from the type specimen, doubtfully distinct from *C. v. floridanus.*[7]

Range.—Known only from the type locality, Key West, Fla.; now extinct.

Colinus virginianus cubanensis (not of Gray) SCOTT, Auk, vi, 1889, 245 (Key West, July 5, 1888; spec.).

Colinus virginianus insulanus HOWE, Proc. Biol. Soc. Washington, xvii, 1904, 168 (Key West, Fla.; meas.; crit.).—BANGS, Bull. Mus. Comp. Zool., lxx, 1930, 160 (type spec. in Mus. Comp. Zool.).—AMERICAN ORNITHOLOGISTS' UNION, Check List North Amer. Birds, ed., 4, 1931, 88 (Key West; extinct).—HOWELL, Florida Bird Life, 1932, 194 (Key West; history).—PETERS, Check List Birds of World, ii, 1934, 47 (Key West; extinct).—HELLMAYR and CONOVER, Cat. Birds Amer., i, No. 1, 1942, 240 (syn.; distr.).

Colinus virginianus virginianus (not of Linnaeus) BENT, U. S. Nat. Mus. Bull. 162, 1932, 31, in text, part (Key West).

---

[7] According to persons who have been in Key West, there is reason to question whether there ever was any country there suitable for bobwhites. This would make the present form seem more likely to have been based on a stray, small example of the south Floridian race. For this reason, and also since, being extinct and known from only a single example, material of it is not apt to be forthcoming for identification, it might well be looked upon as not distinct from *C. v. floridanus.*

COLINUS VIRGINIANUS CUBANENSIS (Gray)

CUBAN BOBWHITE

Adult male.—Similar to that of the nominate race but much darker and more reddish, the black gular collar very much broader, the entire upper and lateral parts of the abdomen between hazel and ochraceous-tawny, the feathers margined with black (the black broken with white patches on the feathers of the sides) and not transversely barred with black as in the typical subspecies (except in examples with mixed blood due to the introduction of birds from the North American mainland); anterior upperparts with less grayish and more deep tawny russet than in the nominate race; posterior upperparts with no rufescent, all grayish; the grayish edgings of the interscapulars and upper back darker—deep mouse gray, the black blotches on the wings and lower back much larger; the black feather edgings on the interscapulars nape much broader, forming almost a black collar across that area.

Adult female.—Very similar to that of the Texas race *Colinus virginianus texanus* but darker, the blackish blotches, edges, and bars broader and thereby appearing darker, the ground color of the upperparts more grayish, less rufescent; the broad superciliaries, the chin and upper throat averaging darker—ochraceous-buff with a slightly dusky tinge, and the edges of the feathers of the crown more grayish than brownish.

Immature.—Like the adult of corresponding sex but with the outer primaries more pointed terminally.

Juvenal.—Like that of the nominate race but generally slightly darker.

Natal down.—Like that of the nominate race.

Adult male.—Wing 97.5–106 (101.9); tail 48.5–56 (53.3); culmen from base 15.1–17.2 (16.0); tarsus 28.3–31.4 (30.1); middle toe without claw 24.5–27.1 (25.7 mm.).[8]

Adult female.—Wing 98–106 (102.4); tail 51.5–58 (54.1); culmen from base 15.0–16.5 (16.0); tarsus 28.5–31 (29.6); middle toe without claw 23.8–27.4 (25.4 mm.).[9]

Range.—Resident in Cuba and the Isle of Pines; introduced into Puerto Rico (where now apparently extinct) and the Dominican Republic. Now much mixed with stock introduced from the North American mainland and into Cuba.

Type locality.—Cuba.

Ortyx virginianus (not *Tetrao virginianus* Linnaeus) D'ORBIGNY, *in* La Sagra, Hist. Fis. Pol. y Nat. Cuba, Aves, 1839, 133; 8vo ed., p. 182.—SUNDEVALL, Ofv. Svensk. Vet.-Akad. Forh., 1869, 601 (Puerto Rico).
Ortyx (virginianus ?) GUNDLACH, Journ. für Orn., 1878, 186 (Puerto Rico).
Ortyx marylandus (not *Tetrao marilandicus* Linnaeus, *T. marilandus* Gmelin) DENNY, Proc. Zool. Soc. London, 1847, 38, part (Cuba).

---

[8] Twenty specimens.
[9] Eleven specimens.

Ortyx cubanensis GRAY, Gen. Birds, iii, 1846, 514 (Cuba); Mon. Odontoph.,
    pt. iii, 1850, pl. 2 and text.—CABANIS, Journ. für Orn., 1856, 357 (Cuba; habits;
    crit.).—ALBRECHT, Journ. für Orn., 1861, 213 (Cuba).—GUNDLACH, Journ. für
    Orn., 1862, 81 (Cuba); 1874, 300 (Cuba, habits); 1875, 293 (Cuba, habits);
    1878, 161 (Puerto Rico); Contr. Orn. Cubana, "1876" (= 1873), 140.—
    LAWRENCE, Ann. Lyc. Nat. Hist. New York, vii, 1860, 270 (crit.).—STAHL,
    Fauna Puerto Rico, 1883, 62, 149 (Puerto Rico; spec.).—OGILVIE-GRANT, Cat.
    Birds Brit. Mus., xxii, 1893, 421 (Cuba).
Ort[yx] *cubanensis* GUNDLACH, Anal. Hist. Nat., ii, 1873, 148 (Cuba; habits).
[*Ortyx*] *cubanensis* GUNDLACH, Journ. für Orn., 1861, 336 (Cuba); Rep. Fisico Nat.
    Cuba, i, 1865-6, 302.
O[rtyx] *cubanensis* LAWRENCE, Proc. U. S. Nat. Mus., i, 1878, 237, in text (chars.).
Ortix cubanensis ? GUNDLACH, Anal. Soc. Esp. Hist. Nat., 1878, 350 (Puerto Rico;
    introduced at Hacienda Sta. Inés, near Vega Baja).
O[rtyx] *virginianus,* var. *cubanensis* RIDGWAY, Forest and Stream, i, No. 19, 1873,
    290, in text.
Ortyx virginianus, var. *cubanensis* BAIRD, BREWER, and RIDGWAY, Hist. North Amer.
    Birds, iii, 1874, 468, part.
Ortyx (virginianus?) cubanensis GUNDLACH, Journ. für Orn., 1874, 313 (Puerto
    Rico); 1878, 161 (Puerto Rico).
[*Ortyx virginianus*] d. *cubanensis* COUES, Birds Northwest, 1874, 431 (synonymy).
Ortyx cubanensis GUNDLACH, Auk, viii, 1891, 190 (Cuba; albino).
[*Colinus*] *cubanensis* CORY, List Birds West Indies, 1885, and rev. ed., 1886, 24
    (Cuba; Puerto Rico).
Colinus cubanensis CORY, Auk, iv, 1887, 233 (syn.; descr.); Birds West Indies, 1889,
    223 (Cuba and Puerto Rico; syn.; descr.); Auk, viii, 1891, 294 (recorded in list
    of Cuban birds); ix, 1892, 272 (Habana markets); Auk, xii, 1895, 279 (Santo
    Domingo).—GUNDLACH, Orn. Cubana, 1893, 171 (Cuba; habits).—CHERRIE,
    Contr. Orn. San Domingo, 1896, 24 (introduced into Santo Domingo).—BANGS
    and ZAPPEY, Amer. Nat., xxxix, 1905, 192 (Isle of Pines; crit.).—TODD, Ann.
    Carnegie Mus., x, 1916, 199 (Bibijagua, Los Indios, and Neuva Gerona, Isle
    of Pines; crit.).—BARBOUR, Mem. Nuttall Orn. Club, No. 6, 1923, 51 (habits;
    etc.; the only form indigenous to Cuba, *C. v. floridanus* and *C. v. texanus* having
    been introduced); No. 9, 1943, 40 (Cuba; habits; hist.).—BAILEY, Birds Florida,
    i, 1925, 60, pl. 32, (fig.; distr.; Florida; introduced).—DANFORTH, Wils. Bull.,
    xl, 1928, 180 (vicinity of Santiago de Cuba); Journ. Agr. Univ. Puerto Rico,
    xix, 1935, 423, 424, 425 (Cuba; economic status); Pajaros de Puerto Rico, 1936,
    51 (Puerto Rico; introduced; none seen since 1900).—RUTTER, Ardea, xxiii,
    1934, 116 (Cuba; Santa Clara, Sierra del Regidor, Sierra de los Organos).
Colinus cabanensis CORY, Cat. West Indian Birds, 1892, 96 (Cuba; Isle of Pines;
    Puerto Rico).
[*Colinus*] *cubanensis* SHARPE, Hand-list, i, 1899, 45 (Cuba; ? Puerto Rico).
C[olinus] *cubanensis* REICHENOW, Die Vögel, i, 1913, 315.
Colinus virginianus cubanensis RIDGWAY, Man. North Amer. Birds, 1887, 593,
    part; Auk, xi, 1894, 324 (crit., not found in Florida).—CHAPMAN, Auk, v, 1888,
    395, part (Cuba); Bull. Amer. Mus. Nat. Hist., iv, 1892, 290 (near Trinidad,
    s. Cuba, in mountains), AMERICAN ORNITHOLOGISTS' UNION, Check-list, rev.
    ed., 1889, 7, part; Auk, xii, 1895, 168 (eliminated from North Amer. Check-
    list).—BENDIRE, Life Hist. North Amer. Birds, i, 1892, 9, part.—BOWDISH,
    Auk, xix, 1902, 360 (Puerto Rico; very rare; saw only one).—MENEGAUX,
    Rev. Franç. d'Orn., No. 2, 1909, 31 (Figuabas, e. Cuba).—WETMORE, U. S.
    Dept. Agr. Bull. 326, 1916, 34 (Puerto Rico; introduced); Sci. Surv. Porto
    Rico and Virgin Islands, ix, pt. 3, 1927, 331 (Puerto Rico; introduced; now

probably extinct).—GARDNER, Proc. U. S. Nat. Mus., lxvii, art. 19, 1925, pl. 8 (structure of tongue).—WETMORE and SWALES, U. S. Nat Mus., Bull. 155, 1931, 124 (habits; distr.; Hispaniola).—PETERS, Check-list Birds World, ii, 1934, 47.—BOND, Birds West Indies, 1936, 414; Check-list Birds West Indies, 1940, 27 (Cuba and Isle of Pines; introduced in Dominican Republic, and Puerto Rico where now extirpated).—HELLMAYR and CONOVER, Cat. Birds Amer., i, No. 1, 1942, 241 (syn.; distr.).

Colinus v[irginianus] cubanensis STODDARD, The Bobwhite Quail, 1931, 61 (hunted with dogs).

C[olinus] virginianus cubanensis RIDGWAY, Man. North Amer. Birds, 1887, 188, part (Cuba); ed. 2, 1895, 188, exclusively.

C[olinus] v[irginianus] cubanensis SETH-SMITH, L'Oiseau, x, 1929, 763, in text (care in captivity).—BOND, Birds West Indies, 1936, 81 in text, 82, in text (descr.; Cuba; Isle of Pines; Dominican Republic (introduced; Puerto Rico (introduced, now extirpated)).

[Ortyx] cubensis SCLATER and SALVIN, Nom. Av. Neotr., 1873, 137.

Colinus cubensis BALBOA, Las Aves de Cuba, 1941, 201 (Cuba; descr.; habits).

COLINUS VIRGINIANUS MACULATUS Nelson

SPOTTED-BELLIED BOBWHITE

Adult male.—Similar to that of *Colinus virginianus texanus* but with the entire lower surface posterior to the black pectoral band ochraceous-tawny instead of white and with no dark transverse wavy bars, but the feathers with black and white elongated spots on their lateral edges near their tips, these spots, especially the white ones, largest and most numerous on the thighs, flanks, and under tail coverts; above like the Texas race but darker, the interscapulars and upper back more clearly dull russet, less obscured by grayish transverse markings, crown and postocular stripe more blackish; back, lower back, and upper tail coverts with the dark blotches larger and darker—dark sepia to mummy brown, and the rest of the plumage of these areas less grayish, more brownish.

Adult female.—Similar to that of *Colinus virginianus texanus* but darker above, the dark markings larger and deeper, the rufescent areas more clouded and blotched with dusky grayish (this is especially true of the crown, occiput, interscapulars, and upper back); below with a somewhat darker pectoral band of ochraceous-fawn color spotted with blackish and white.

Other plumages apparently not known.

Adult male.—Wing 100–104.5 (102.7); tail 52.5–60 (55.5); culmen from base 15.2–16.3 (15.6); tarsus 28.2–32.4 (30.3); middle toe without claw 25–27.4 (21.9 mm.).[10]

Adult female.—Wing 100–107 (104.3); tail 51–58 (53.8); culmen from base 15.2–15.9 (15.5); tarsus 29–31 (30.2); middle toe without claw 24.3–25.9 (25.4 mm.).[11]

---

[10] Fifteen specimens from Tamaulipas, Veracruz, and San Luis Potosí.
[11] Five specimens from Tamaulipas.

Range.—Resident in the Arid Tropical Zone from southeastern Tamaulipas (Alta Mira, Tampico, Hacienda de Naranjo) and central northern Veracruz (Chijol) to southeastern San Luis Potosí (Tancanhuitz, Matalpa, near Tamazunchale, and south of Valles).

Type locality.—Alta Mira, Tamaulipas, Mexico.

Colinus virginianus maculatus NELSON, Auk, xvi, 1899, 26, part (Alta Mira, s. Tamaulipas, e. Mexico; coll. U. S. Nat. Mus.); xix, 1902, 389 (crit.), pl. 14, fig. 6.—OGILVIE-GRANT, Ibis, 1903, 110 (crit.).—SALVIN and GODMAN, Biol. Centr.-Amer., Aves, iii, 1903, 299, in text under *Ortyx texanus* (crit.).—PHILLIPS, Auk, xxviii, 1911, 74, part (Alta Mira, Tamaulipas).—PETERS, Check-list Birds World, ii, 1934, 48, part.—SUTTON and BURLEIGH, Condor, xlii, 1940, 260 (Valles, San Luis Potosí, Mexico); Wils. Bull., lii, 1940, 223 (fairly common; Tamazunchale, San Luis Potosí, Mexico).—ALDRICH, Proc. Biol. Soc. Washington, lv, 1942, 67 in text, 68 in text (crit.; spec.; distr.).—HELLMAYR and CONOVER, Cat. Birds Amer., i, No. 1, 1942, 242, part (syn.; distr.).

[*Colinus*] *maculatus* SHARPE, Hand-list, i, 1899, 45.

Ortyx texanus (not of Lawrence) SALVIN and GODMAN, Biol. Centr.-Amer., Aves, iii, 1903, 298, part (Xicoténcatl, Sierra Madre above Victoria, and Alta Mira, Tamaulipas).

Ortyx graysoni panucensis LOWE, Bull. Brit. Orn. Club, xxiii, 1908, 18 (Valley of the Pánuco River, near Tampico, Mexico).—ALDRICH, Proc. Biol. Soc. Washington, lv, 1942, 67, in text (crit.).

COLINUS VIRGINIANUS ARIDUS Aldrich

JAUMAVE BOBWHITE

Adult male.—Similar to that of *Colinus virginianus maculatus* but paler, more grayish, the black areas more restricted above and the reddish coloration of underparts paler; from *C. v. texanus* it differs in being more grayish with the underparts more extensively rufescent.

Adult female.—Similar to that of *C. v. maculatus* but paler and more grayish, the reddish pectoral band almost obsolete; more grayish also than *C. v. texanus.*

Adult male.—Wing 104–109.5 (106.8); tail 56–65.5 (60.2); exposed culmen 13–14 (13.8); tarsus 29–32.5 (30.8); middle toe without claw 25.5–27.5 (26.4 mm.).[12]

Adult female.—Wing 104.5–106.5 (105.6); tail 58–65 (60.8); exposed culmen 14–14.5 (14.2); tarsus 29.5–31 (30.3); middle toe without claw 25.5–28 (26.5 mm.).[13]

Range.—Resident in the arid regions of the interior of the coastal plain and valley of the eastern foothills of the high tableland of northeastern Mexico, between the Arid Tropical and the Lower Sonoran

[12] Nine specimens, measurements *ex* Aldrich, Proc. Biol. Soc. Washington, lv, 1942, 68.

[13] Four specimens, measurements *ex* Aldrich, *cit. supra.*

Life Zones, from central and central-western Tamaulipas south to the northern part of southeastern San Luis Potosí.

Type locality.—Jaumave, Tamaulipas.

Colinus virginianus maculatus NELSON, Auk, xvi, 1899, 26, part (Jaumave Valley, Tamaulipas).—PHILLIPS, Auk, xxviii, 1911, 74, part (Guiaves, Río Santo, Santa Leonara, Río de la Cruz, Montelunga, Tamaulipas, Mexico).—PETERS, Check-list Birds World, ii, 1934, 48, part.—HELLMAYR and CONOVER, Cat. Birds Amer., i, No. 1, 1942, 242, part (syn.; distr.).

C[*olinus*] *v*[*irginianus*] *maculatus* SUTTON and PETTINGILL, Auk, lix, 1942, 12, in text (Gómez Farias region, southwestern Tamaulipas; crit.).

Colinus virginianus aridus ALDRICH, Proc. Biol. Soc. Washington, lv, 1942, 67 (Jaumave, Tamaulipas; orig. descr.; crit.; meas.).

Colinus virginianus SUTTON and PETTINGILL, Auk, lix, 1942, 12 (Gómez Farias area, sw. Tamaulipas).

COLINUS VIRGINIANUS GRAYSONI (Lawrence)

GRAYSON'S BOBWHITE

Adult male.—Similar to that of the nominate form but with the entire underparts posterior to a narrow black pectoral band uniform bright ochraceous-tawny with a slight hazel tinge; the top of the head darker, more blackish; the interscapulars darker and redder—between dark cinnamon-rufous and hazel, the feathers marginally incompletely barred with blackish; rest of upperparts darker, the blackish markings more extensive and the brownish ground color duskier, more grayish; upper wing coverts brighter reddish—hazel to bright ochraceous-tawny, heavily barred with black and white, the white bars always bordered broadly with black; the superciliary, lores, chin, and upper throat often washed with pale buff.

Adult female.—Similar to that of the nominate race, even more similar to that of *Colinus virginianus texanus* but with the entire underparts warm buff tinged with pale ochraceous, becoming fairly tawny on the breast, the markings on this ground color as in the nominate form, but many of the abdominal V-shaped bars fuscous instead of black; the black pectoral necklace narrower and more interrupted; the immediately posterior tawny area less extensive than in the typical race; above very similar to *texanus* but more rufescent, the interscapulars bright ochraceous-tawny to hazel barred very heavily with black and, to a lesser extent, with whitish; rest of upperparts buffy brown abundantly barred with black-bordered white bars and splotched with black to dark sepia.

Other plumages apparently unknown.

Adult male.—Wing 104–114.5 (108.5); tail 57.5–67 (61.3); culmen from base 15–17.1 (15.7); tarsus 29.1–32.5 (31.0); middle toe without claw 25.5–28.7 (26.9 mm.).[14]

---

[14] Twenty specimens from Jalisco, San Luis Potosí, Hidalgo, Guadalajara, and Guanajuato.

Adult female.—Wing 101–112 (106.9); tail 54.5–67 (59.6); culmen from cere 14.5–17.2 (15.6); tarsus 28.1–32.5 (30.3); middle toe without claw 25.4–27.9 (26.2 mm.).[15]

Range.—Resident in the southern part of the tableland of Mexico from northern Jalisco (Ameca, Etzatlán, Guadalajara, Hacienda El Molino, Hacienda El Rosario, La Barca, Lagos, Lake Chapala, Ocotlán, Santa Ana, and Tuxpan); western and southern San Luis Potosí (Río Verde, Hacienda Angostura); and southeastern Nayarit (Río Ameca, near Amatlán de Caños) to Guanajuato (Guanajuato and Celaya); Hidalgo (Pachuca); and northern Morelos (Alpuyeca).

Type locality.—Guadalajara, Jalisco; Mexico.

Ortyx graysoni Lawrence, Ann. Lyc. Nat. Hist. New York, viii, 1867, 476 (Guadalajara, Jalisco, w. Mexico; coll. U. S. Nat. Mus.); Mem. Boston Soc. Nat. Hist., ii, 1874, 306 (Guadalajara; habits).—Ogilvie-Grant, Cat. Birds Brit. Mus., xxii, 1893, 422 (Santa Ana, near Guadalajara, and Lake Chapala, Jalisco); Handb. Game Birds, ii, 1897, 142, pl. 32 (fig.; descr.; distr.; habtis).—Salvin and Godman, Biol. Centr.-Amer., Aves, iii, 1903, 300 (Guadalajara, Santa Ana near Guadalajara, Hacienda El Rosario, Hacienda El Molino, and Lake Chapala, Jalisco; Hacienda Angostura, San Luis Potosí).

O[rtix] graysoni Cubas, Cuadro Geogr., Estadístico, Descr. e Hist. de los Estados Unidos Mexicanos, 1884, 175 (common names).

Colinus graysoni Stejneger, Auk, ii, 1885, 45.—Ridgway, Man. North Amer. Birds, 189, 1887, 189, 585.—Chapman, Auk, v, 1888, 401 (deleted from Check-list).—Jouy, Proc. U. S. Nat. Mus., xvi, 1894, 790 (Guadalajara and Hacienda El Molino, Jalisco; Hacienda Angostura, San Luis Potosí).—Nelson, Auk, xv, 1898, 121 (San Luis Potosí and n. Jalisco to Valley of Mexico, 3,000 to 7,500 feet).—del Campo, Anal. Inst. Biol., viii, No. 3, 1937, 336 (Morelos; Alpuyeca; spec.).

C[olinus] graysoni Allen, Bull. Amer. Mus. Nat. Hist., i, 1886, 289, 290. in text (crit.).

[Colinus] graysoni Sharpe, Hand-list, i, 1899, 46.

C[olinus] v[irginianus] graysoni Bangs and Peters, Bull. Mus. Comp. Zool., lxviii, 1928, 386, in text (crit.).

Colinus virginianus graysoni Peters, Check-list Birds of World, ii, 1934, 48 (s. Mexican tableland from n. Jalisco, w. and s. San Luis Potosí, south to the Valley of Mexico).—Aldrich, Proc. Biol. Soc. Washington, lv, 1942, 68, in text (sw. San Luis Potosí southward).—Hellmayr and Conover, Cat. Birds Amer., i, No. 1, 1942, 243 (syn.; distr.).

COLINUS VIRGINIANUS NIGRIPECTUS Nelson

Puebla Bobwhite

Adult male.—Similar to that of *Colinus virginianus graysoni* above; similar also below but with the blackish pectoral band very much broader, extending from the posterior margin of the white throat patch over the entire breast and the sides of the neck, this black area considerably blotched

[15] Fourteen specimens from Jalisco, San Luis Potosí, Guadalajara, and Guanajuato.

with white; the uniformly colored abdomen, sides, flanks, and thighs slightly paler than in *graysoni*—cinnamon to orange-cinnamon.

Adult female.—Very similar to that of *Colinus virginianus graysoni* but darker, more grayish above, the pectoral band of dark markings much broader, and the ground color of the underparts whiter, less buffy.

Other plumages apparently unknown.

Adult male.—Wing 101–109 (105.1); tail 53–63 (57.9); culmen from base 15–17.8 (16.3); tarsus 28.1–32.2 (30.2); middle toe without claw 25–28.7 (26.8 mm.).[16]

Adult female.—Wing 102–106.5 (104.6); tail 52–55 (54.1); culmen from base 15.3–16.4 (15.8); tarsus 28.2–31.5 (30.1); middle toe without claw 27–27.1 (27.05 mm.).[17]

Range.—Resident in the plains country of the tableland of the southern half of the States of Puebla (Atlixco, Chietla) and Morelos (Cuernavaca, Puente de Ixtla).

Type locality.—Atlixco, Puebla, Mexico.

Colinus graysoni nigripectus NELSON, Auk, xiv, 1897, 47 (Atlixco, s. Puebla, Mexico; coll. U. S. Nat. Mus.); xv, 1898, 121 (s. Puebla); xix, 1902, 389 (crit.), pl. 14, fig. 2.—OGILVIE-GRANT, Ibis, 1903, 110 (crit.).—SALVIN and GODMAN, Biol. Centr.-Amer., Aves, iii, 1903, 300, in text (crit.).—SMITH, Condor, xi, 1909, 64, in text (Morelos, Mexico).
[Colinus] nigripectus SHARPE, Hand-list, i, 1899, 46.
Colinus virginianus nigripectus PETERS, Check-list Birds of World, ii, 1934, 48 (tableland of southern part of Puebla).—HELLMAYR and CONOVER, Cat. Birds Amer., i, No. 1, 1942, 244 (syn.; distr.).
Colinus pectoralis (not Ortyx pectoralis Gould) FERRARI-PEREZ, Proc. U. S. Nat. Mus., ix, 1886, 176 (Chietla, Puebla).
Ortyx pectoralis BERISTAIN and LAURENCIO, Mem. y Rev. Soc. Cient. "Antonio Alzate," vii, 1894, 219 part (Puebla).—SALVIN and GODMAN, Biol. Centr.-Amer., Aves, iii, 1903, 299, part (Chietla and Atlixco, Puebla).

COLINUS VIRGINIANUS PECTORALIS (Gould)

BLACK-BREASTED BOBWHITE

Adult male.—Very similar to that of *Colinus virginianus nigripectus* but smaller and the abdomen darker—sayal brown—and with the thighs and vent more or less barred with blackish and spotted with white; the black breast band with less white showing, but all the black breast feathers extensively white basally.

Adult female.—Similar to that of *Colinus virginianus nigripectus* but smaller and with the darker markings, especially on the undersurface, heavier and darker; the interscapulars with their centers less hazel, more pale tawny.

Other plumages apparently unknown.

---

[16] Seventeen specimens from Puebla and Morelos.
[17] Four specimens from Puebla and Morelos.

Adult male.—Wing 95–100.5 (98.7); tail 47–53 (48.9); culmen from base 14.8–15.8 (15.2); tarsus 25.7–29.2 (27.2); middle toe without claw 23.5–25.6 (24.3 mm.).[18]

Adult female.—Wing 98–99; tail 49–53.5; culmen from base 14.8–15.6; tarsus 28.3–29.2; middle toe without claw 25–26 mm. (2 specimens).

Range.—Resident in the Tropical Zone along the eastern base of the Cordillera of central Veracruz from 500 to 5,000 feet (Jalapa, Orizaba, Carrizal, Coatepec, La Estranzuela, Córdoba, Llanos de Paso de Orejas).

Type locality.—Mexico.

Ortyx pectoralis GOULD, Proc. Zool. Soc. London, 1842 (1843), 182 (Mexico; coll. Earl of Derby); Monogr. Odontoph., pt. 3, 1850, pl. 5 and text.—HARTLAUB, Journ. für Orn., 1854, 412 (descr. female).—SCLATER, Proc. Zool. Soc. London, 1856, 310 (Córdoba, Veracruz); 1857, 206 (Jalapa, Veracruz).—GRAY, List Birds Brit. Mus., pt. 5, Gallinae, 1867, 76.—SUMICHRAST, Mem. Boston Soc. Nat. Hist., i, 1869, 560 (tierra caliente of Veracruz).—OGILVIE-GRANT, Cat. Birds Brit. Mus., xxii, 1893, 421 (Jalapa); Handb. Game Birds, ii, 1897, 142; Ibis, 1902, 240 (crit.).—BERISTAIN and LAURENCIO, Mem. y Rev. Soc. Cient. "Antonio Alzate," vii, 1894, 219, part (Veracruz).—NELSON, Auk, xix, 1902, pl. 14, fig. 1.—SALVIN and GODMAN, Biol. Centr.-Amer., Aves, iii, 1903, 299, part (Llanos de Paso de Orejas, La Estranzuela, Orizaba, Córdoba, and Carrizal, Veracruz).

[*Ortyx*] *pectoralis* SCLATER and SALVIN, Nom. Av. Neotr., 1873, 137.

O[rtex] *pectoralis* CUBAS, Cuadro Geogr., Estadístico, Descr., e Hist. de los Estados Unidos Mexicanos, 1884, 175 (common names; Mexico).

Colinus pectoralis ALLEN, Bull. Amer. Mus. Nat. Hist., i, 1886, 289, in text (crit.).—NELSON, Auk, xv, 1898, 117, in text (near Orizaba), 121 (e. base of Cordillera in Veracruz; Jalapa to Isthmus of Tehuantepec, 500 to 5,000 feet alt.).—LANTZ, Trans. Kansas Acad. Sci. for 1896-7 (1899), 219 (Coatepec, Veracruz).—NELSON, Auk, xix, 1902, pl. xiv, fig. 1 (descr.; plum.).

C[olinus] *pectoralis* RIDGWAY, Man. North Amer. Birds, 1887, 189.—BAILEY, Avicult. Mag., ser. 3, ix, 1918, 114 (breeding in captivity).—REICHENOW, Die Vögel, i, 1913, 315.

[*Colinus*] *pectoralis* SHARPE, Hand-list, i, 1899, 45.

C[olinus] *v[irginianus*] *pectoralis* BANGS and PETERS, Bull. Mus. Comp. Zool., lxviii, 1928, 386, in text.—SETH-SMITH, L'Oiseau, x, 1929, 763, in text (care in captivity).

Colinus virginianus pectoralis PETERS, Check-list Birds World, ii, 1934, 48 (e. base of the Cordillera in Veracruz from Jalapa to the Isthmus of Tehuantepec).—HELLMAYR and CONOVER, Cat. Birds Amer., i, No. 1, 1942, 243 (syn.; distr.).

COLINUS VIRGINIANUS GODMANI Nelson

GODMAN'S BOBWHITE

Adult male.—Above very similar in coloration to that of *Colinus virginianus pectoralis* but with the dark blotches on the back, lower back, and wings averaging larger and darker; below like *pectoralis* as far as the head and throat are concerned; breast blackish but the basal parts of the feathers not white as in *pectoralis* but orange-cinnamon; abdomen bright

---

[18] Four specimens.

orange-cinnamon to hazel, the feathers broadly margined with black, those of the midventral area with these margins so broad as to leave only a narrow shaft line (wider basally) of cinnamon causing the appearance of a large midabdominal continuation of the black pectoral band; feathers of thighs and vent with a white lateroterminal spot on each web, these spots proximally bordered with black.

Adult female.—Very similar in coloration to that of *Colinus virginianus pectoralis* but with more rufescent on the interscapulars, and with the upper tail coverts also more rufescent; size smaller.

Other plumages apparently unknown.

Adult male.—Wing 98.5; tail 56.5; culmen from base 14.4; tarsus 26.0; middle toe without claw 23.1 mm. (1 specimen).

Adult female.—Wing 94.5–96.5 (95.0); tail 49.5–54 (51.8); culmen from base 13.5–14.7 (14.0); tarsus 25.9–28.5 (27.1); middle toe without claw 22.2–26.2 (22.9 mm.).[19]

Range.—Resident in the lowlands of southern Veracruz (Catemaco, Jaltipán, Minantlán) and probably Tabasco from sea level up to about 1500 feet.

Type locality.—Jaltipán, Veracruz, Mexico.

Colinus godmani NELSON, Auk, xiv, 1897, 45 (Jaltipán, Veracruz, se. Mexico; coll. U. S. Nat. Mus.); xv, 1898, 121, pl. 2 (lowlands of s. Veracruz; Tabasco ?; sea level to 1,500 feet); xix, 1902, pl. 14, fig. 4.
[Colinus] godmani SHARPE, Hand-list, i, 1899, 46.
Ortyx godmani SALVIN and GODMAN, Biol. Centr.-Amer., iii, sig. 38, Feb. 1903, 301 (coast plain above Jaltipán and Minantlán and n. to Lake Catemaco, Veracruz).
Colinus virginianus godmani PETERS, Check-list Birds of World, ii, 1934, 48 (lowlands of southern Veracruz).—HELLMAYR and CONOVER, Cat. Birds Amer., i, No. 1, 1942, 244 (syn.; distr.).—BRODKORB, Misc. Publ. Mus. Zool. Univ. Michigan, No. 56, 1943, 31 (Veracruz, Mexico).

COLINUS VIRGINIANUS MINOR Nelson
LEAST BOBWHITE

Adult male.—Above very similar to that of *Colinus virginianus godmani;* below differs in that the black pectoral band is much narrower, the feathers of the lower breast, upper abdomen, sides, and flanks orange-cinnamon edged with black, feathers of the midventral part with these margins much broader, forming a conspicuously blackish streaked area (in some specimens these feathers have a good deal of white subterminally, in others none at all); thighs and vent spotted with white and barred irregularly and incompletely with black as in *godmani;* size smaller.

Adult female.—Very similar to that of *C. v. godmani* but generally less rufescent, more dusky brown; the edges of the coronal feathers more grayish than brownish, back, rump, and upper tail coverts much less

---

[19] Three specimens from Veracruz.

brownish, more grayish; below with the abdominal bars smaller and more numerous; size smaller.

Other plumages apparently unknown.

Adult male.—Wing 90.5–96.5 (93); tail 45–50.5 (48.2); culmen from base 13.8–15.6 (14.3); tarsus 25–27.9 (26.0); middle toe without claw 21.7–23.1 (22.5 mm.).[20]

Adult female.—Wing 94.5; tail 46; culmen —; tarsus 26.5; middle toe without claw 22.5 mm. (1 specimen).

Range.—Resident in the grassy plains in the northeastern part of Chiapas, the adjacent portion of Tabasco, and probably also the neighboring sections of Guatemala.

Type locality.—Plains of Chiapas, near Palenque.

Colinus minor NELSON, Auk, xviii, 1901, 47 (plains of Chiapas, near Palenque; coll. U. S. Nat. Mus.); xix, 1902, pl. 14, fig. 3.—OGILVIE-GRANT, Ibis, 1903, 111 (crit.).
C[olinus] minor NELSON, Auk, xix, 1902, 389 (crit.).
O[rtyx] minor SALVIN and GODMAN, Biol. Centr.-Amer., Aves. iii, 1903, 300, in text (crit.).
Ortyx pectoralis (not of Gould) SALVIN and GODMAN, Biol. Centr.-Amer., Aves, iii, 1903, 299, part (Palenque, Chiapas).
Colinus virginianus minor PETERS, Check-list Birds of World, ii, 1934, 48 (grassy plains in the northeastern part of Chiapas and adjacent portion of Tabasco; probably also neighboring sections of Guatemala).—HELLMAYR and CONOVER, Cat. Birds Amer., i, No. 1, 1942, 244 (syn.; distr.).—BRODKORB, Misc. Publ. Mus. Zool. Univ. Michigan, No. 56, 1943, 31 (Chiapas, Palenque; crit.).
Cyrtonyx sp. ROVIROSA, La Naturaleza, vii, 1887, 380 (Valle de Baluji and Cerro del Limón, Chiapas).

COLINUS VIRGINIANUS INSIGNIS Nelson

GUATEMALAN BOBWHITE

Adult male.—Above very similar to *Colinus virginianus godmani* but with the forehead, lores, chin, and throat solid black (not white), the superciliaries narrower; below the entire underparts posterior to the black chin and throat between orange-cinnamon and hazel, the breast feathers with or without blackish margins, the abdomen and sides uniformly hazel; feathers of thighs, vent, and under tail coverts spotted with white, the spots edged with black.

Adult female.—Very similar to that of *C. v. godmani* in coloration, but somewhat paler above, the interscapulars with more extensive median cinnamomeous areas, the dark blotches of the upperparts generally smaller and less intense, and the ground color paler and grayer; and the ventral barrings narrower and paler—dark sepia to fuscous instead of fuscous-black to blackish.

Juvenal female.—Like the adult but with the interscapulars without cinnamomeous shaft stripes but broadly barred with dark sepia to fuscous,

---

[20] Five specimens.

the dark bars much wider than the narrow cinnamon-buff interspaces; general ground color of upperparts slightly more brownish; the ventral barrings averaging wider.

Other plumage apparently unknown.

Adult male.—Wing 98–108 (101.8) ; tail 54.5–64 (57.8) ; culmen from base 14.7–16.3 (15.4) ; tarsus 27.8–30.8 (28.9) ; middle toe without claw 23–26.5 (25.0 mm.).[21]

Adult female.—Wing 93–103 (98.9) ; tail 51–58.5 (54.2) ; culmen from base 14.4–16.2 (15.2) ; tarsus 27.4–30.2 (28.4) ; middle toe without claw 23.5–25.5 (24.7 mm.).[21]

Range.—Resident in the Comitán-Nenton Valley of eastern Chiapas and western Guatemala, between 3,000 and 6,000 feet.

Type locality.—Nenton, Guatemala.

Colinus insignis, NELSON, Auk, xiv, 1897, 46 (Nenton, Guatemala; U. S. Nat. Mus.) ; xv, 1898, 119, in text, 122 (Valley of Comitán, Chiapas, to w. Guatemala).
[*Colinus*] *insignis* SHARPE, Hand-list, i, 1899, 46.
Ortyx insignis SALVIN and GODMAN, Biol. Centr.-Amer., Aves, iii, 1903, 302 (Valley of Comitán and Cailco, Chiapas; Nenton, Guatemala).
Colinus virginianus insignis GRISCOM, Bull. Amer. Mus. Nat. Hist., lxiv, 1932, 106 (distr.; parts of Chiapas and the adjacent border of western Guatemala between 3,000 and 6,000 feet).—PETERS, Check-list Birds World, ii, 1934, 48 (Comitán Valley in eastern Chiapas, and in adjacent part of western Guatemala).— BERLIOZ, Bull. Mus. Hist. Nat. Paris, ser. 2, xi, 1939, 361 (Chiapas, Juncana; spec.; crit.).—HELLMAYR and CONOVER, Cat. Birds Amer., i, No. 1, 1942, 245, part (syn.; Valley of Río Chiapas from Nenton, Guatemala, to the western boundary of the State of Chiapas, Mexico; spec.; Chiapas—Moriscal, Ocozocoautla, Jiquipilas, Comitán, Tuxtla Guitierrez, San Bartolomé, San Vicente, Chiapa, Petapa, Hda. La Razon, Valle de Zintalpa, Valley of Jiquipilas; Guatemala—Nenton).—BRODKORB, Occ. Pap. Mus. Zool. Univ. Michigan, No. 467, 1942, 3, in text (crit.).
C[*olinus*] *v*[*irginianus*] *insignis* BRODKORB, Occ. Pap. Mus. Zool. Univ. Michigan, No. 467, 1942, 3, in key (Comitán-Nenton Valley of eastern Chiapas and western Guatemala).

COLINUS VIRGINIANUS COYOLCOS (Müller)

COYOLCOS BOBWHITE

Adult male.—Similar to that of *Colinus virginianus graysoni* above, but with the forehead and lores black, as are also the chin and throat, the only white on the head being the superciliaries and occasional feathers on the throat; feathers of crown and occiput with broad brown edges; black of throat extending over the breast either as a solid mass or as broad margins to the pectoral feathers; rest of the underparts as in *graysoni*[22]; size smaller; bill deep black, iris brown; feet cinereous.

---

[21] Twenty specimens of each sex from Chiapas and Oaxaca.

[22] To judge by the variations in the series studied, it appears that some mixture of stocks has transpired in Oaxaca, possibly owing to introductions of birds from

Adult female.—Similar to that of *C. v. graysoni* but averaging slightly darker above, and with the breast less washed with ochraceous-tawny, more heavily barred with dark brown to black, and the abdomen ground color less buffy; thighs, vent, and under tail coverts more heavily barred with dark brown; size smaller; maxilla dusky, mandible pale brownish; iris brown; feet full grayish.

Juvenal male.—Similar to the adult male but with the chin, throat, and superciliaries buffy, the top of the head paler, wood brown to buffy brown, some of the feathers with broad medial streaks of dull sepia; interscapulars with the rufescent median parts duller and with whitish shafts; wings and lower back somewhat browner; iris light brown; feet pale flesh color; bill (in dried skin) tawny-brown above, yellowish below.

Other plumages apparently unknown.

Adult male.—Wing 98–105 (101.9); tail 51–62 (57.8); culmen from cere 15.4–16.6 (16.0); tarsus 27.5–31 (29.2); middle toe without claw 24–26.5 (26.0 mm.).[23]

Adult female.—Wing 101–105 (103.1); tail 57–57.5 (57.3); culmen from base 15.3–15.8 (15.5); tarsus 28.1–30.2 (29.4); middle toe without claw 25.2–27 (26.1 mm.).[24]

Range.—Resident in the coastal area (from sea level to 3,000 feet) of southeastern Oaxaca and southwestern Chiapas, from Tehuantepec City to Tonalá.

Type locality.—Mexico, based on "Le Coyolcos" of Buffon.

Tetrao coyoleos (typog. error) MÜLLER, Syst. Nat. Suppl., 1776, 129 (Mexico; based on *Le Coyolcos* Buffon, Hist. Nat. Ois., ii, 486, *ex* "Coyolcozque" Hernández, Hist. Anim. Nov. Hisp. p. 19).
C[olinus] coyoleos BREWSTER, Auk, ii, 1885, 200, in text.
[Tetrao] coyolcos GMELIN, Syst. Nat., i, pt. 2, 1788, 763 (cites *Coturnix mexicana* Brisson, Av., i, 256; *Coyolcozque* sen *Coli sonalis* Ray, Av., 158; *Coyolcos* Buffon, Ois., ii, 486; *Lesser Mexican Quail* Latham, Synopsis, ii, pt. 2, 786; etc.).
Tetrao coyolcos VIEILLOT, Nouv. Dict. Hist. Nat., xxv, 1817, 241.
[Perdix] coyolcos LATHAM, Index Orn., ii, 1790, 653.
P[erdix] coyolcos BONNATERRE, Tabl. Encycl. Méth., i, 1791, 215.
O[rtyx] coyolcos GRAY, Gen. Birds, iii, 1846, 514.
Ortyx coyolcos GOULD, Monogr. Odontoph., pt. 3, 1850, pl. 6, right-hand fig., and text, part.—GRAY, List Birds Brit. Mus., pt. 5, Gallinæ, 1867, 76.—LAWRENCE, U. S. Nat. Mus. Bull. 4, 1876, 45 (Tapana and Santa Efigenia, Tehuantepec, Oaxaca).—OGILVIE-GRANT, Cat. Birds Brit. Mus., xxii, 1893, 423 (Juchitán,

---

elsewhere. Thus, one male from San Mateo del Mar has the black area sharply terminated at the posterior margin of the throat, the breast being rufescent like the abdomen, while another from the same place has the breast all black. Two birds from Huilotepec have unusually extensive amounts of white on the chin and upper throat and resemble *C. v. thayeri!* The dark markings on the lower back and rump vary greatly; most birds have them deep and numerous, one has hardly any, while another has them very rufescent.

[23] Nine specimens from Oaxaca.
[24] Three specimens from Oaxaca.

Oaxaca) ; Handb. Game Birds, ii, 1897, 144.—Beristain and Laurencio, Mem.
y Rev. Soc. Cient. "Antonio Alzate," vii, 1894, 219 (Mexico, se. coast).—
Salvin and Godman, Biol. Centr.-Amer., Aves, iii, 1903, 303 (Tehuantepec
City, Juchitán, Tapana, Santa Efigenia, and Cacoprieto, Oaxaca; Tonalá, n.
Chiapas).

[*Ortyx*] *coyolcos* Sclater and Salvin, Nom. Av. Neotr., 1873, 137.

C[*olinus*] *coyolcos* Allen, Bull. Amer. Mus. Nat. Hist., i, 1886, 290, in text (crit.).—
Ridgway, Man. North Amer. Birds, 1887, 189.

Colinus coyolcos Nelson, Auk, xv, 1898, 117, in text, 121 (Pacific coast, Oaxaca
and Chiapas; Tehuantepec City to Tonalá, sea level to 3,000 feet).

[*Colinus*] *coyolcos* Sharpe, Hand-list, i, 1899, 46.

Colinus virginianus coyolcos Bangs and Peters, Bull. Mus. Comp. Zool., lxviii,
1928, 386 (Tapanatepec, Oaxaca, Mexico).—Peters, Check-list Birds of World,
ii, 1934, 49 (Pacific coast of Oaxaca and Chiapas from the City of Tehuantepec
to Tonalá).—Hellmayr and Conover, Cat. Birds Amer., i, No. 1, 1942, 246
(syn.; distr.).

C[*olinus*] *v*[*irginianus*] *coyolcos* Bangs and Peters, Bull. Mus. Comp. Zool., lxviii,
1928, 386, in text.—Brodkorb, Occ. Pap. Mus. Zool. Univ. Michigan, No. 467,
1942, 1, in text, 4, in key.

Ortyx nigrogularis (not of Gould) Gray, List Birds Brit. Mus., pt. 3, Gallinæ,
1844, 44.

COLINUS VIRGINIANUS SALVINI Nelson

Salvin's Bobwhite

Adult male.—The darkest of all the races of the species; above very
similar to the male of *Colinus virginianus insignis* but darker, the head
with less rufescent, more solidly fuscous to fuscous-black, the rufescent
median areas of the interscapulars between dark hazel and Sanford's
brown; the blackish markings on the wings, back, rump, and upper tail
coverts larger and less mixed with rufescent, the ground color of these
areas duskier; entire head, chin, and throat dark fuscous to fuscous-black
with an interrupted, narrow, white postocular line on each side; the
feathers of the occiput and nape with narrow whitish edges; the blackish
brown of the throat extends over the entire breast, where the feathers
have narrow cinnamon to hazel shaft streaks; abdomen, sides, and flanks
uniform hazel, vent and under tail coverts barred with black and white.

Adult female.—Similar to that of *C. v. insignis* but generally darker,
more grayish, less brownish above, the interscapulars, back, lower back,
and rump deep hair brown edged with dusky smoke gray and subterminally
blotched very extensively with chaetura drab to chaetura black, the more
posterior parts with a considerable mixture of dark olive-brown; the dark
markings on the underside heavier, darker, and more numerous.

Other plumages apparently unknown.

Adult male.—Wing 91.5–96 (93.8) ; tail 48.5–53.5 (51.1) ; culmen
from base 14.5–15.8 (15.2) ; tarsus 26–28.3 (26.9) ; middle toe without
claw 21.5–25.6 (23.8 mm.).[25]

---

[25] Seven specimens.

Adult female.—Wing 93–96.5 (94.3) ; tail 45.5–49 (46.8) ; culmen from base 14.5–15.5 (15.0) ; tarsus 26.5–27.3 (26.9) ; middle toe without claw 23.3–24.4 (23.3 mm.).[26]

Range.—Resident in the coastal plains of southern Chiapas, Mexico, near the Guatemalan border (Tapachula, San Benito) from sea level to 500 feet.

Type locality.—Tapachula, Chiapas.

Colinus salvini NELSON, Auk, xiv, 1897, 45 (Tapachula, Chiapas, s. Mexico; coll.
    U. S. Nat. Mus.) ; xv, 1898, 122 (s. Chiapas, Pacific coast to 500 feet).—
    OGILVIE-GRANT, Ibis, 1902, 241 (crit.; spec.; San Benito, Chiapas; plum.).

[Colinus] salvini SHARPE, Hand-list, i, 1899, 46.

Ortyx salvini SALVIN and GODMAN, Biol. Centr.-Amer., Aves, iii, 1903, 304 (Tapa-
    chula and San Benito, Chiapas).

Colinus virginianus salvini PETERS, Check-list Birds World, ii, 1934, 48 (coast plains
    of southern Chiapas near the Guatemalan border).—HELLMAYR and CONOVER,
    Cat. Birds Amer., i, No. 1, 1942, 246 (syn.; distr.).

[Colinus] v [irginianus] salvini BRODKORB, Occ. Pap. Mus. Zool. Univ. Michigan, No.
    467, 1942, 1, in text, 4, in key.

COLINUS VIRGINIANUS NELSONI Brodkorb

NELSON'S BOBWHITE

Adult male.—Similar to that of *Colinus virginianus salvini* but with the dark markings even darker, purer black, instead of brownish black, although less extensive; the white markings also purer, less grayish, and smaller in extent; rufescent markings brighter and more extensive; the black of the chin and throat not extending over the breast, except as a few of the pectoral feathers have blackish margins; some of the abdominal feathers, especially the midventral ones, may also have narrow blackish margins; thighs, vent, and under tail coverts almost pure bright hazel with no or few blackish markings. From *C. v. coyolcos* it differs in having more extensive and deeper black markings, deeper hazel markings, and purer (less buffy) white markings, all of which are more in contrast with each other; no white superciliaries; the crown is entirely black in two males, but has a brown patch on the occiput and nape in one example.

Adult female.—Like that of *C. v. salvini* but with the black markings smaller and the brown and buff markings more extensive. All the colors are brighter, clearer, more sharply contrasted. From *C. v. coyolcos* it differs in being darker and in having all the markings more sharply contrasted.

Other plumages apparently unknown.

Adult male.—Wing 102.5–103 ; tail 56–57 ; culmen from base 14.9–15.1 ; tarsus 27.5–28.6 ; middle toe without claw 23.6–24.7 mm. (2 specimens).

---

[26] Three specimens.

Adult female.—Wing 97.5–101.5; tail 53–54.5; culmen from base 14.4–15.4; tarsus 25.1–28.2; middle toe without claw 24 mm. (2 specimens).

Range.—Known only from the type locality, Chicomuselo, Chiapas.

Colinus virginianus insignis (not of Nelson) HELLMAYR and CONOVER, Cat. Birds Amer., i, No. 1, 1942, 245, part (Chiapas, Chicomuselo).
Colinus virginianus nelsoni BRODKORB, Occ. Pap. Mus. Zool. Univ. Michigan, No. 467, 1942, 1 (Chicomuselo, Chiapas; spec.; descr.; crit.; meas.).

COLINUS VIRGINIANUS THAYERI Bangs and Peters

THAYER'S BOBWHITE

Adult male.—Similar to that of *Colinus virginianus coyolcos* but with the chin and throat, upper lores, forehead, and superciliaries white, the throat sometimes streaked with black; above slightly paler and grayer, less blotched and spotted. Similar also to the male of *C. v. pectoralis* but with a broader black pectoral band, with less or no white at the base of the feathers of this area.[27]

Adult female.—Very similar to, not certainly distinguishable from, that of *C. v. coyolcos.* In very fresh plumage *thayeri* seems to have more grayish on the upper back and interscapulars, but after even slight wear this distinction disappears.

Other plumages apparently unknown.

Adult male.—Wing 97–101 (99.9); tail 48–55.5 (52.6); culmen from base 14.8–16.2 (15.3); tarsus 27.6–30 (28.7); middle toe without claw 24.8–26.6 (25.4 mm.).[28]

Adult female.—Wing 98–102.5 (100.1); tail 50–54 (52); culmen from base 14.5–16.2 (15.2); tarsus 26.9–29.6 (28.2); middle toe without claw 23.8–25.3 (24.7 mm.).[29]

Range.—Resident in the dry country of inland eastern Oaxaca from Chivela to Guichicovi and Tutla.

Type locality.—Chivela, Oaxaca.

Colinus virginianus thayeri BANGS and PETERS, Bull. Mus. Comp. Zool., lxviii, 1928, 386 (Chivela, Oaxaca, Mexico; spec.; descr.; crit.).—BANGS, Bull. Mus. Comp. Zool., lxx, 1930, 160 (type spec. in Mus. Comp. Zool.).—PETERS, Check-list Birds of World, ii, 1934, 49 (known only from the type locality).—HELLMAYR and CONOVER, Cat. Birds Amer., i, No. 1, 1942, 245 (syn.; distr.; Oaxaca, Tutla, and Guichicovi; spec.).

---

[27] The status of *thayeri* and *coyolcos* is puzzling and cannot be settled with present information. While the two groups are easily distinguished in the male plumage, as noted in the description of *coyolcos,* two adult males from Huilotepec are more like *thayeri* than like *coyolcos,* even though they come from the farthest side of the range of the latter!

[28] Eight specimens.
[29] Six specimens.

COLINUS VIRGINIANUS ATRICEPS (Ogilvie-Grant)

BLACK-HEADED BOBWHITE

Adult male.—Similar to *Colinus virginianus salvini* but larger and paler, the lower breast and abdomen with no blackish markings; the rufescent color above more extensive. "Differs chiefly from the male of . . . *coyolcos* in having the top of the head, superciliary stripe, chin, and throat all uniform black without a trace of white, and the general color of both upper and underparts darker" (*ex* Ogilvie-Grant).

Adult female.—"Differs from the female of . . . *coyolcos* in being altogether darker, especially on the upper parts; the gray markings of the mantle in the latter . . . being replaced by brownish black" (*ex* Ogilvie-Grant).

Adult male.—Wing 106.6; tail 58.4; tarsus 30.4; middle toe and claw 35.5 mm.

Adult female.—Wing 101.6; tail 58.4; tarsus 27.9; middle toe and claw 34.3 mm.[30]

Other plumages unknown.

Range.—Known only from the type locality, Putla, western Oaxaca. May range into Guerrero, but this is yet to be established.

Ortyx coyolcos (not *Tetrao coyoleos* Müller) GOULD, Monogr. Odontoph., pt. 3, 1850, pl. 6, left fig.
Ortyx atriceps OGILVIE-GRANT, Cat. Birds Brit. Mus., xxii, 1893, 424 (Putla, w. Oaxaca, sw. Mexico; coll. Brit. Mus.).—SALVIN and GODMAN, Biol. Centr.-Amer., Aves, iii, 1903, 303.
Colinus atriceps NELSON, Auk, xv, 1898, 122 (Putla, w. Oaxaca, 4,000 feet alt.).
[*Colinus*] *atriceps* SHARPE, Hand-list, i, 1899, 46.
Colinus virginianus atriceps PETERS, Check-list Birds of World, ii, 1934, 49 (known only from type locality).—HELLMAYR and CONOVER, Cat. Birds Amer., i, No. 1, 1942, 245 (syn.; distr.; known only from Putla, w. Oaxaca, probably ranging into Guerrero).
C[*olinus*] *v*[*irginianus*] *atriceps* BRODKORB, Occ. Papers Mus. Zool. Univ. Michigan, No. 467, 4, in key.

COLINUS VIRGINIANUS RIDGWAYI Brewster

MASKED BOBWHITE

Adult male.—Similar to that of *Colinus virginianus insignis* but with the sides of the head, at least the auriculars and sides of neck, rufescent; above, especially on the head, back, rump, and wings, paler, the blackish markings much reduced and replaced largely by brown; the interscapulars paler hazel; breast and abdomen also slightly paler. "Hind part of crown, occiput, and nape, light hazel-brown, spotted with black, and streaked, especially on the nape, with white; rest of head, including chin and throat,

---

[30] Measurements adapted from Ogilvie-Grant, Cat. Birds Brit. Mus., xxii, 1893, 424. No specimens seen by me.

uniform black, with an indistinct series of small white streaks immediately above the ear-coverts, suggestive of a postocular stripe. Upper back and entire underparts light tawny-cinnamon, the latter absolutely uniform, except on hinder flanks, and longer under tail-coverts, which are varied with black and whitish, in the form of edgings and terminal spots of the latter, the former as sub-edgings and V-shaped markings; feathers of the upper back varied by a blackish speckling along the edges. Lower back, scapulars, wing-coverts, tertials, rump, and upper tail-coverts confusedly mottled and vermiculated with brownish gray and blackish, the scapulars and tertials suffused or stained with rusty brown; wing-coverts rather broadly but irregularly barred with whitish, the inner webs of the latter deeply indented with the same, forming an irregular or interrupted border; feathers of lower rump and upper tail-coverts with irregular 'herring-bone' markings of blackish. Tail bluish gray, minutely mottled with whitish and dusky. Primaries brownish gray, their outer webs coarsely mottled with paler. Bill uniform black; feet (in dried skin) dark horn-color." (R. R.)

Adult female.—Very similar to that of *Colinus virginianus texanus* but with the pale edges of the dorsal feathers averaging more whitish, less grayish, more in contrast to the rest of the coloration of the feathers involved; top of head with the dusky median stripes to the feathers darker, the edges paler and buffier. "Upper parts essentially as in the adult male, lores and sides of forehead pale buff, this extending back to the nape in a continuous, broad superciliary stripe; chin, malar region, and entire throat uniform pale buff, bordered behind by a narrow transverse chain or series of black and rusty triangular spots. Chest pale cinnamon, slightly varied with black and whitish; rest of lower parts white, the sides and flanks broadly striped with pale cinnamon, enclosed between U- or V-shaped black markings, the breast and belly having sparse V-shaped bars of black; under tail-coverts pale cinnamon, broadly tipped with buffy whitish and each ornamented by a subterminal V-shaped mark of black." (R. R.)

Juvenal male.—Forehead, crown, and occiput mottled fuscous-black and light ochraceous-buff, the feathers having shafts, edges, and narrow tips of the latter color; interscapulars and upper wing coverts as in the adult female, but with white shaft streaks terminally widening into small triangular spots, and the feathers blotched with clove brown to dark chestnut-brown; remiges as in the adult male; lower back, rump, and upper tail coverts as in the adult female; rectrices dusky sepia crossed by numerous narrow wavy white bars each of which is proximally bordered with mummy brown, the brown widening medially to form a large shaft spot; the median pair of rectrices slightly more brownish, less grayish than the outer ones; sides of head, chin, and throat dusky fuscous, a whitish patch on the lower cheek on either side; many of the gular and mental feathers with narrow grayish white edges; breast, sides, and flanks, pinkish buff to pale pinkish buff mottled with dull dusky sepia, the feathers with narrow white shafts;

thighs, vent, and under tail coverts pale pinkish buff faintly mottled with dusky; abdomen grayish white obscurely mottled with dusky, especially anteriorly; bill and feet (in dried skin) yellowish.[31]

Juvenal female.—Like the juvenal male but with the chin and throat pure white; iris brown; bill brownish above, light plumbeous below; feet "flesh and brownish."

Natal down.—Apparently unknown.

Adult male.—Wing 101–111 (107); tail 59–64 (61.5); culmen from base 15.2–16.5 (15.5); tarsus 29.4–31.3 (30.6); middle toe without claw 25.1–28.1 (26.9 mm.).[32]

Adult female.—Wing 105.5–115.5 (110.5); tail 60–69 (64.1); culmen from base 14–16 (15.2); tarsus 28–31.3 (29.4); middle toe without claw 26.6–27.1 (26.8 mm.).[33]

Range.—Resident in the open grassy plains country (1,000 to 2,500 feet) from the middle portion of the southern Arizona boundary (north to the Baboquivari, Whetstone, and the Huachuca Mountains) south to south-central Sonora (Sasabe, Magdalena, Bacuachi, Campos); now extirpated in Arizona.

Type locality.—18 miles southwest of Sasabe, Sonora, Mexico.

Ortyx virginianus (not *Tetrao virginianus* Linnaeus) BROWN, Forest and Stream, xxii, No. 6, 1884, 104 (Baboquivari Mountains, s. Arizona).

Ortyx graysoni (not of Lawrence) GRINNELL, Forest and Stream, xxii, No. 13, 1884, 243 (Baboquivari Mountains).—STEPHENS, Auk, ii, 1885, 227 (Sonora, nw. Mexico).

Colinus graysoni RIDGWAY, Forest and Stream, xxv, No. 25, Jan. 14, 1886, 484.— AMERICAN ORNITHOLOGISTS' UNION, Check-list, 1886, No. 290.

Colinus ridgwayi BREWSTER, Auk, ii, 1885, 199 (18 miles sw. of Sasabe, Sonora; coll. F. Stephens, type in Brit. Mus.); iv, 1887, 159 (Bacuachi and 18 miles n. of Campos, Sonora; crit.); iv, 1887, 159, 160 (plumage).—STEPHENS, Auk, ii, 1885, 228, 231 (Sasabe, Sonora).—BROWN, Forest and Stream, xxv, No. 5, 1885, 445. —AMERICAN ORNITHOLOGISTS' UNION, Check-list, 1886, and ed. 2, 1895, No. 291; ed. 3, 1910, p. 135; ed. 4, 1931, 88.—ALLEN, Auk, iii, 1886, 275 (Baboquivari Mountains, s. Arizona), 483 (as to location of type specimen); iv, 1887, 74, 75 (crit.); vi, 1889, 189 (Tubal, Ariz.; descr. young); Bull. Amer. Mus. Nat. Hist., i, 1886, 279, pl. 23 (monogr.).—SCOTT, Auk, iii, 1886, 387 (historical).— BENDIRE, Life Hist. North Amer. Birds, i, 1892, 10.—NELSON, Auk, xv, 1898, 121 (Sonora and Arizona, 1,000 to 2,500 feet alt.).—DWIGHT, Auk, xvii, 1900, 46 (molts, etc.).—BAILEY, Handbook Birds Western United States, 1902, 116 (descr.).—BROWN, Auk, xxi, 1904, 209 [–213] (habits, range, etc.).—JUDD, U. S. Biol. Surv. Bull. 21, 1905, 46 (habits; range; food).—SMITH, Condor, ix, 1907,

---

[31] It may be that the specimen on which this description is based, collected late in October in Sonora (Conover coll. 92944), had already begun its postjuvenal molt, as Allen (Auk, 1889, 189) described a young male in postjuvenal molt as having the "throat . . . pure white, with new black feathers appearing irregularly along the sides of the chin and upper throat . . ." It may be that in males in full juvenal plumage the throat is not blackish as in the above account. If so, the sexes are alike in this stage.

[32] Eight specimens from Arizona and Sonora.

[33] Five specimens from Sonora.

196 (Whetstone Mountains, s. Arizona, 4000-4500 ft.).—SWARTH, Pacific Coast
Avif., No. 10, 1914, 21 (Arizona; Baboquivari Peak to Huachuca Mountains;
now extinct in Arizona).—LAW, Condor, xxxi, 1929, 219 (Altar Valley, Ariz.).
—PHILLIPS, Verh. 6th Internat. Orn. Kongr., 1929, 510 (extinct in U. S.; still
found in Mexico).—BENT, U. S. Nat. Mus. Bull. 162, 1932, 36 (habits; distr.).—
COTTAM and KNAPPEN, Auk, lvi, 1939, 152 (food habits).
[*Colinus*] *ridgwayi* SHARPE, Hand-list, i, 1899, 46.
Ortyx ridgwayi OGILVIE-GRANT, Cat. Birds Brit. Mus., xxii, 1893, 422.—SALVIN
and GODMAN, Biol. Centr.-Amer., Aves, iii, 1903, 302 (Sasabe, Campos, and
Bacuachi, Sonora; s. Arizona).
Colinus virginianus ridgwayi VAN ROSSEM, Trans. San Diego Soc. Nat. Hist., vi,
1931, 245 (Sonora, Mexico) ; Bull. Mus. Comp. Zool., lxxvii, 1934, 431 (Cumpas
and Bacuachi, Sonora).—PETERS, Check-list Birds of World, ii, 1934, 49.—HELL-
MAYR and CONOVER, Cat. Birds Amer., i, No. 1, 1942, 242 (syn.; distr.).
C[*olinus*] v[*irginianus*] *ridgwayi* SETH-SMITH, L'Oiseau, x, 1929, 763, in text (care
in captivity).—BERLIOZ, Bull. Mus. Hist. Nat., Paris, ser. 2, xi, 1939, 361, in
text (Arizona; crit.).—BRODKORB, Occ. Pap. Mus. Zool. Univ. Michigan, No.
467, 1942, 3, in key.
Ortyx virginianus BROWN, Auk, xxi, 1904, 211, in text (Sonora).

COLINUS NIGROGULARIS CABOTI Van Tyne and Trautman

YUCATÁN BOBWHITE

Adult male.—Lores and superciliaries black, the black of the lores connecting narrowly above the base of the culmen; a white stripe immediately
above this from the middle of the upper forehead completely borders the
black of the lores and the superciliaries; feathers of crown and occiput
bister, those of the crown broadly bone brown medially; those of the
occiput with somewhat grayish edges; nape, sides of neck, and interscapulars between auburn and chestnut, the feathers with conspicuous
white shaft streaks or spots, these white markings reduced or absent on
the more posterior interscapulars; upper back like the posterior interscapulars but the feathers broadly margined with neutral gray finely
flecked with darker; inner median and greater upper wing coverts like the
upper back; scapulars similar but blotched subterminally with fuscous-
black to black and margined internally with whitish; outer upper wing
coverts like the inner ones but much washed with ochraceous-tawny and
more coarsely vermiculated with dusky; secondaries olive-brown, their
outer webs flecked and vermiculated with grayish ochraceous-tawny; primaries uniformly olive-brown; feathers of back, rump, and upper tail
coverts light mouse gray to mouse gray, medially lightly tinged with
ochraceous-tawny and subterminally blotched with fuscous-black to black,
these blotches becoming elongated into shaft streaks on the upper tail
coverts, the gray areas faintly vermiculated with dusky and tipped and incompletely barred (sparingly) with grayish white; rectrices between deep
mouse gray and hair brown, the median ones mottled with paler gray and
faintly buffy grayish white; chin and throat black; a line under the eye and
extending more broadly over the upper cheeks, auriculars and sides of

throat white; feathers of breast and middle upper abdomen white edged and tipped with black, giving a scalloped appearance to these areas, the black margins increasing in width posteriorly very much; sides of breast and abdomen to the flanks, white broadly edged and tipped with Brussels brown; thighs, vent, and under tail coverts dull pale grayish ochraceous-tawny, the under tail coverts with subterminal blackish shaft stripes; middle of lower abdomen like the thighs but slightly more grayish, less rufescent; under wing coverts dull brownish, edged with pale grayish.[34]

Adult female.—Narrow forehead, broad superciliary stripes, chin, and throat between warm buff and ochraceous-buff; feathers of crown and occiput fuscous to fuscous-black narrowly edged with neutral gray; nape similar but the lateral margins pale buffy white and much broader; interscapulars cinnamon-brown, grayish basally, narrowly edged and tipped with dusky grayish, and transversely spotted with buffy white, each of these pale marks bordered on both sides by blackish, and sparsely and irregularly barred with blackish, the grayish edges widening on the posterior interscapulars and the feathers of the upper back which are subterminally blotched with fuscous mixed with sepia; scapulars as in the male but more brownish, less grayish generally; upper wing coverts as in the male but more brownish generally and barred, on their outer webs, with broader, more conspicuous pale buffy to pale pinkish buffy, black-bordered bars, all the markings heavier and coarser than in the male; secondaries externally edged with pale ochraceous-buff and incompletely banded with the same on their outer webs; primaries as in the male but their outer webs very faintly flecked with pale ochraceous-buffy; back, lower back, rump, and tail coverts as in the male but browner, less grayish, and with the median dark blotches smaller and less noticeable; rectrices as in the male but all, the lateral as well as the median ones, externally flecked transversely with grayish white; auriculars dark dull auburn; feathers of sides of neck and of the entire breast white with blackish-brown shaft stripes and cross bars dividing the feathers into at least two rows of white spots terminally, the feathers, especially those of the sides of the neck, pale dull hazel to ochraceous-tawny basally; feathers of abdomen white crossed by widely spaced fuscous bars, the most distal of which is medially extended as a shaft stripe, these bars petering out on the middle of the abdomen; on the feathers of the sides and flanks the shaft stripes are very much longer and broader and contain within them a median core of pale cinnamon-brown to ochraceous-tawny; thighs and vent white obscurely barred with dusky sepia; under tail coverts pale cinnamon-brown with subterminal broad,

[34] One specimen from the type locality (Univ. Mich. Mus. Zool. No. 103848) is very brown on the wings, back, rump, and upper tail coverts, completely lacking the gray. It also has the brown of the interscapulars, upper back, sides, and flanks darker chestnut.

distally attenuated blackish shaft stripes and broadly tipped with white, the white area divided into two spots by the shaft stripe.

Natal down (sexes alike).—Forehead and broad superciliary area pale clay color paling to pinkish buff posteriorly on the nape; center of crown and forehead and a wide spinal band extending to the tail chestnut-brown indistinctly edged with clove brown; rest of upperparts light pinkish cinnamon with a faint grayish tinge, mottled with dark clove brown to fuscous; a narrow fuscous line from the back of the eye to the side of the nape; sides of head pale dusty pinkish buff; chin, throat, and abdomen white; breast, sides, flanks, thighs and vent washed with dusty light pinkish cinnamon; bill and feet (in dried skin) yellowish.

Adult male.—Wing 95–103.5 (98.3); tail 50–58.5 (54.6); culmen from base 14.7–16 (15.4); tarsus 27.1–32 (29.1); middle toe without claw 23.9–26.6 (25.3 mm.).[35]

Adult female.—Wing 95–103.5 (98.5); tail 50–58 (54.2); culmen from base 14.5–16.3 (15.1); tarsus 27.2–31.1 (29.2); middle toe without claw 24.5–26.2 (25.2 mm.).[36]

Range.—Resident throughout Yucatán (Mérida, Chichen Itzá, Chablé, Tizimín, etc.) and Campeche (Campeche), except for the arid area around Progreso.

Type locality.—Chichen Itzá, Yucatán.

Ortyx nigrogularis GOULD, Monogr. Odontoph., pt. 2, 1846, pl. 4 and text, part (Yucatán).—GRAY, Gen. Birds, iii, 1846, 514, pl. 132; List Birds Brit. Mus., pt. 5, Gallinae, 1867, 76.—LAWRENCE, Ann. Lyc. Nat. Hist. New York, ix, 1869, 209 (Mérida, Yucatán).—NEHRKORN, Journ. für Orn., 1881, 69 (Yucatán; descr. eggs).—BOUCARD, Proc. Zool. Soc. London, 1883, 461 (Chablé, Yucatán; habits). —BERISTAIN and LAURENCIO, Mem. y Rev. Soc. Cient. "Antonio Alzate," vii, 1894, 219 (Yucatán).

[*Ortyx*] *nigrogularis* REICHENBACH, Synop. Av., iii, 1848, Gallinaceae, pl. 193, fig. 1681.—SCLATER and SALVIN, Nom. Av. Neotr., 1873, 137, part (Yucatán).

Ortyx nigrigularis SCLATER and SALVIN, Ibis, 1859, 225, part (Yucatán).

O[rtix] nigrogularis CUBAS, Cuadro Geogr., Estadístico, Descr., e Hist. de los Estados Unidos Mexicanos, 1884, 175 (common names, Mexico).

Eupsychortyx nigrogularis OGILVIE-GRANT, Cat. Birds Brit. Mus., xxii, 1893, 412, part (Tizimín, Buctzotz, Chablé, Peto, and Mérida, Yucatán).—SALVIN and GODMAN, Biol. Centr.-Amer., Aves, iii, 1903, 297, part (Chablé, Tizimín, Buctzotz, Peto, Mérida, and Izamal, Yucatán).—COLE, Bull. Mus. Comp. Zool., 1, 1906, 115, part (Chichen Itzá, Yucatán).

[*Eupsychortyx*] *nigrigularis* SHARPE, Hand-list, i, 1899, 45, part (Yucatán).

Colinus nigrogularis CHAPMAN, Bull. Amer. Mus. Nat. Hist., viii, 1896, 289 (Chichen Itzá; habits; notes).—NELSON, Auk, xv, 1898, 122 (Yucatán).

[*Colinus*] *nigrogularis* GRISCOM, Amer. Mus. Nov., No. 379, 1929, 2, in text (crit.).

Colinus nigrogularis nigrogularis PETERS, Check-list Birds World, ii, 1934, 49.— TRAYLOR, Publ. Field Mus. Nat. Hist., zool. ser., xxiv, 1941, 204 (Chichen

---

[35] Twenty specimens.

[36] Ten Specimens.

Itzá, Yucatán; spec.).—Hellmayr and Conover, Cat. Birds Amer., i, No. 1, 1942, 247 (syn.; distr.).

Colinus nigrogularis caboti Van Tyne and Trautman, Occ. Pap. Mus. Zool. Univ. Michigan, No. 439, 1941, 5, 6 (Chichen Itzá, Yucatán; descr.; plum.; meas.; distr.; crit.).—Hellmayr and Conover, Cat. Birds Amer., i, No. 1, 1942, 247, footnote.

COLINUS NIGROGULARIS PERSICCUS Van Tyne and Trautman

Progreso Bobwhite

Adult male.—Similar to that of *Colinus nigrogularis caboti* but paler and less brownish, more grayish; above, especially on the scapulars and innermost remiges, very pale grayish; the white centers of the feathers of the interscapular and upper back areas larger and their rufescent borders averaging slightly paler; tail paler—between mouse gray and light mouse gray, and more abundantly flecked with grayish white; feathers of thighs, flanks, lower middle abdomen, and under tail coverts paler, less rufescent.

Adult female.—Very similar to that of *C. n. caboti* but slightly paler above, more grayish, less brownish; the dark ventral barrings averaging more brownish, less blackish.

Other plumages apparently unknown.

Adult male.—Wing 98–102 (100.1); tail 51.5–57 (54.4); culmen from base 14.5–15.8 (15.1); tarsus 28.2–31.4 (30.0); middle toe without claw 24.1–27.5 (25.9 mm.).[37]

Adult female.—Wing 100–102 (101.1); tail 54–58.8 (56.5); culmen from base 14.2–16 (15); tarsus 29–32 (30.2); middle toe without claw 24.1–26.4 (25.2 mm.).[38]

Range.—Resident in the arid region about Progreso, Yucatán.

Type locality.—5 kilometers south of Progreso, Yucatán.

Eupsychortyx nigrogularis Cole, Bull. Mus. Comp. Zool., 1, 1906, 115, part (Progreso, Yucatán).

Colinus nigrogularis persiccus Van Tyne and Trautman, Occ. Pap. Mus. Zool. Univ. Michigan, No. 439, 1941, 4, 6 (5 kilometers south of Progreso, Yucatán; descr.; plum.; meas.; distr.; crit.).

COLINUS NIGROGULARIS NIGROGULARIS (Gould)

Honduras Bobwhite

Adult male.—Similar to that of *Colinus nigrogularis caboti* but much darker above, much less grayish, more brownish, the white centers of the interscapulars greatly reduced in size, and the blackish blotches on the scapulars, back, and rump larger and darker; below very similar to *caboti* but averaging wider black margins on the feathers of the breast and abdomen. "Pileum brownish black, passing into rusty exteriorly, and bor-

---

[37] Ten specimens.
[38] Five specimens.

dered anteriorly and laterally by a broad ∩-shaped stripe of brownish white; forehead, lores, and broad stripe passing thence backward over eyes and auriculars to sides of hindneck, deep black; chin, throat, and malar region uniform deep black, bordered above by a broad stripe of brownish white, beginning at rictus and extending beneath eye across auriculars. Hindneck and sides of neck dark chestnut, the feathers with mesial guttate streaks or spots of rusty white, these larger and purer white on sides of neck; upper back dark chestnut, the feathers irregularly barred or transversely mottled on edges with black and brownish gray; rest of back, with scapulars, wing coverts, and tertials coarsely mottled and irregularly barred with blackish on an olive and brownish gray ground, with lighter markings along edges of many feathers, especially tertials and greater wing coverts; lower back and rump olive-brown, especially on lower back; upper tail coverts and middle rectrices similar but more grayish brown, marked with broad mesial streaks of black and irregularly barred with lighter; rectrices dull slate-gray, tinged with olive, and indistinctly barred or transversely mottled on outer webs with paler. Primaries plain, dull, brownish slate. Chest, breast, and middle line of belly white, the feathers broadly and abruptly bordered with black, this narrowest on upper part of chest, broadest on belly; sides and flanks chestnut, each feather whitish centrally and bordered with black, this more or less broken or mottled on many of the feathers; under tail coverts rusty, tipped with dull light buffy, and marked with a large central sagittate or triangular spot of black. Bill entirely deep black; feet dark brown." (R. R.)

Adult female.—Similar to that of *C. n. caboti*, but generally darker, less grayish, more brownish above, the dark blotches larger and more numerous, the ground color of the upper parts generally dark Dresden brown, the feathers without grayish edgings; the inner edges of the scapulars pale buffy (instead of white as in *caboti*); lores, superciliaries, chin, and throat darker than in *caboti*—dark clay color with an ochraceous wash; basal portions of feathers of breast and upper abdomen less rufescent, more brownish; brown centers of flank feathers deeper chestnut with broader fuscous borders. "Broad superciliary stripe (including sides of forehead), chin, throat, and malar region plain, dull ochraceous or clay color; pileum brownish black, streaked with dull grayish buffy; auriculars plain silky brown; suborbital region dull ochraceous, streaked with blackish; hinder part and sides of neck pale dull grayish buffy, thickly marked with triangular spots of black, these larger and more blended on hindneck, smaller and more individualized on sides of neck. Upperparts in general coarsely mottled, spotted, and barred with black and pale brownish buffy on a light bister-brownish ground, the black spots (of irregular form) more conspicuous on hinder scapulars, tertials, lower back, and rump; primaries plain brownish slate, their outer webs more ashy; tail as in male but more coarsely mottled. Lower parts dull whitish, the chest and breast thickly marked with irregular black spots having a brownish external suffusion, the belly transversely spotted or barred with the same, the sides and flanks with irregular broad U-shaped marks inclosing a pale cinnamon space, the margins of the feathers soiled whitish; under tail coverts much tinged with pale rusty and heavily spotted with black. Bill brownish black, with basal half of under mandible light colored; feet deep horn-brown." (R. R.)

Immature.—Like the adult of the same sex but with the outermost primaries more pointed terminally.

Juvenal (sexes alike).—Upperparts of head and body as in the adult female, but the interscapulars, scapulars, and feathers of the upper back with narrow, white shaft streaks; the inner secondaries more completely barred with pale pinkish buff; the feathers of the lower back, rump, and upper tail coverts paler, less blotched with blackish, the ground color buffy wood brown; chin and throat paler, more whitish; breast buffy wood brown, each feather with a pale buffy-whitish shaft streak; abdomen pale buffy with a grayish tinge, transversely spotted with dusky wood brown; flanks, thighs, lower abdomen, and under tail coverts strongly washed with pale cinnamon-buff; bill and feet (in dried skin) dark pinkish orange.

Natal down.—Apparently unknown.

Adult male.—Wing 92–94 (93); tail 49.5–52.5 (51.0); culmen from base 14.5–15.2 (14.8); tarsus 27.7–28.1 (27.9); middle toe without claw 24.1–25.2 (24.7 mm.).[39]

Adult female.—Wing 86–95 (92); tail 48–51 (48.8); culmen from base 14.4–15.7 (14.8); tarsus 26.4–28.5 (27.7); middle toe without claw 23.1–25 (23.8 mm.).[40]

Range.—Resident in the pine-forested parts of British Honduras, the Petén district of northern Guatemala, and through the Caribbean lowlands of Honduras east to Cantarranas and the Segovia River.

Type locality.—Honduras.

Ortyx nigrogularis GOULD, Proc. Zool. Soc. London, 1842 (1843), 181 (Mexico; coll. Earl of Derby; = Honduras); Monogr. Odontoph., pt. ii, 1846, pl. 4 and text, part (Honduras).—MOORE, Proc. Zool. Soc. London, 1854, 63 (Belize, British Honduras).

[*Ortyx*] *nigrogularis* GRAY, Handlist, ii, 1870, 273, no. 9781 (Honduras).—SCLATER and SALVIN, Nom. Av. Neotr., 1873, 137, part (British Honduras).

Ortyx nigrigularis SCLATER and SALVIN, Ibis, 1859, 225, part (Belize, British Honduras).

Colinus nigrogularis segoviensis RIDGWAY, Proc. U. S. Nat. Mus., x, 1888, 593 (Río Segovia, e. Honduras; coll. U. S. Nat. Mus.).—STONE, Proc. Acad. Nat. Sci. Philadelphia, lxxxiv, 1932, 302 (Honduras; Segovia River and Cantarranas).—PETERS, Check-list Birds World, ii, 1934, 49.—VAN TYNE, Misc. Publ. Mus. Zool. Univ. Michigan, No. 27, 1935, 12 (Pacomón and La Libertad, Petén, Guatemala; crit.; spec.).—HELLMAYR and CONOVER, Cat. Birds Amer.,

---

[39] Four specimens.
[40] Seven specimens.

i, No. 1, 1942, 248 (syn.; distr.; Honduras, Guatemala, British Honduras).—
VAN TYNE and TRAUTMAN, Occ. Papers Mus. Zool. Univ. Michigan, No. 439,
1941, 3, in text.
Colinus nigrogularis nigrogularis VAN TYNE and TRAUTMAN, Occ. Papers Mus,
Zool. Univ. Michigan, No. 439, 1941, 6 (Honduras; Segovia River; Guatemala,
La Libertad).
Eupsychortyx nigrogularis (not *Ortyx nigrogularis* Gould) OGILVIE-GRANT, Cat.
Birds Brit. Mus., xxii, 1893, 412, part (Honduras).—SALVIN and GODMAN,
Biol. Centr.-Amer., Aves, iii, 1903, 297, part (Río Segovia, Honduras; Belize,
British Honduras).
[*Eupsychortyx*] *nigrigularis* SHARPE, Handlist, i, 1899, 45, part (Honduras; British
Honduras).
Colinus nigrogularis coffini NELSON, Proc. Biol. Soc. Washington, xlv, 1932, 169
(La Libertad, Petén, Guatemala; descr.; crit.).—PETERS, Check-list Birds World,
ii, 1934, 49 (Brit. Honduras and the Petén district).—VAN TYNE and TRAUTMAN,
Occ. Papers Mus. Zool. Univ. Michigan, No. 439, 1941, 3, in text (crit.).
[*Colinus*] [*nigrogularis*] *coffini* VAN TYNE, Misc. Publ. Mus. Zool. Univ. Michigan,
No. 27, 1935, 12, in text (crit.).
C[*allipepla*] *nigrogularis* REICHENOW, Die Vögel, i, 1913, 317.

COLINUS LEUCOPOGON LEYLANDI Moore

LEYLAND'S QUAIL

Adult male.—Forehead and crown between Sayal brown and snuff
brown, becoming tawny to ochraceous-tawny on the occiput; center of
crown dusky; nape like the occiput with large white spots, edged with
black on the lateral feathers, this black and white less pronounced on the
medial ones; interscapulars and upper back Saccardo's umber finely vermiculated with black and narrowly tipped with grayish; scapulars, inner
greater upper wing coverts, and inner secondaries similar but heavily
blotched with fuscous to fuscous-black and distomedially suffused with
cinnamon-brown, the scapulars and inner secondaries internally broadly
edged with buffy white; rest of upper wing coverts Saccardo's umber
somewhat indistinctly and rather sparsely vermiculated with dusky, some
of the interspaces paler and buffier than the ground color of the feathers
producing faint paler cross bands; secondaries dark clove brown, thickly
flecked along their outer edges with pale buffy brown and whitish, the
latter color forming incomplete bars which are proximally bordered with
relatively unflecked dark clove brown, both webs very narrowly edged
with whitish; primaries uniform dark clove brown; feathers of back and
rump Saccardo's umber heavily blotched with fuscous to fuscous-black and
finely flecked with grayish white, the dark blotches becoming smaller on
the rump feathers; upper tail coverts like the rump but with the dark
blotches compressed into shaft stripes; rectrices deep mouse gray to hair
brown transversely flecked and mottled with paler, forming indistinct irregular barrings; lores, a broad superciliary, and a broad malar stripe on
each side white somewhat tinged with pale buff, many of the component

feathers narrowly edged with blackish; cheeks dark sepia, borders of the malar stripe blackish; auriculars like the occiput; chin and throat fuscous with the paler basal parts of the feathers dark Verona brown, showing through in varying amounts; breast like the interscapulars but somewhat more rufescent and with the dark vermiculations largely absent, but with many of the feathers with conspicuous black-ringed white spots on their medioterminal portion; upper and lateral parts of abdomen like the breast but brighter, more rufescent, and with many more and larger black-bordered white spots, some of the feathers having as many as three of these spots on each web, the pale spots larger than the remainder of the feather, the spots more or less washed with buffy; sides and flanks similar but with the spots slightly reduced, the intervening brownish part of the feathers thereby made more extensive and conspicuous; middle of abdomen and the thighs buffy white barred with dull dark sepia, the pale interspaces much broader than the bars; under tail coverts dark sepia washed, along the shaft, with Saccardo's umber and indented on both webs with large, marginally continuous spots of white more or less tinged with buffy; under wing coverts barred dull sepia and buffy white, the whitish areas broader than the darker bars.

Adult female.—Similar to the adult male on the upperparts of head and body but differing below in that the chin and throat are pale buffy, longitudinally spotted or streaked with fuscous to fuscous-black, the breast relatively more spotted with white and the pale spots of most of the abdominal feathers larger and running into each other reducing the sepia parts to irregular bars with distally pointed median elongations.

Juvenal (sexes alike).—Similar to the adult female but slightly darker brownish above; the breast buffy white heavily and abundantly spotted with sepia transverse marks, each of which is distally edged with tawny buff; abdomen, sides, and flanks whitish transversely spotted with dark sepia.

Natal down.—Forehead, lores, very broad supraorbital bands, auriculars, and cheeks between clay color and pale tawny-olive, center of crown and occiput Brussels brown, the area edged with darker; chin and throat white tinged with pale cinnamon-buff; a narrow blackish line running posteroventrally from the eye to the sides of the neck.[41]

Adult male.—Wing 95.3–105.6 (99.4); tail 52.4–59.2 (55.8); culmen from base 13.8–16.0 (14.6); tarsus 26.2–29.2 (28.1); middle toe without claw 22.7–24.1 (23.5 mm.).[42]

Adult female.—Wing 97.1–98.3 (97.5); tail 47.2–57.4 (51.8); culmen from base 13.5–14.7 (14.2); tarsus 25.4–28.4 (27.1); middle toe without claw 21.2–22.5 (21.9 mm.).[43]

---

[41] Remainder of only example seen was already in juvenal plumage.

[42] Ten specimens from Honduras.

[43] Eight specimens from Honduras.

Range.—Resident in the Plateau and Pacific slope of Honduras (Teguci-galpa, Monte Redondo, Comayaguela, El Caliche, Catacamas, Sabana Grande, Omoa, Comayagua, etc.).

Type locality.—Flores, between Omoa and Comayagua, Honduras.

Ortyx leylandi MOORE, Proc. Zool. Soc. London, 1859, 62 (Flores, between Omoa and Comayagua, Honduras; coll. Derby Museum; descr.; spec.; crit.).—SCLATER and SALVIN, Ibis, 1859, 226 (between Omoa and Comayagua, Honduras).— TAYLOR, Ibis, 1860, 312 (Comayagua, Honduras; habits).

[*Ortyx*] *leylandi* SCLATER and SALVIN, Nom. Av. Neotr., 1873, 137, part (Honduras).

Eupsychortyx leucofrenatus ELLIOT, Ann. Lyc. Nat. Hist. New York, vii, 1860, 106, pl. 3 (Honduras).

Eupsychortyx leylandi OGILVIE-GRANT, Cat. Birds Mus., xxii, 1893, 411, part (Hon-duras); Handb. Game Birds, ii, 1897, 132, part (Honduras).—SALVIN and GODMAN, Biol. Centr.-Amer., Aves, iii, 1903, 295, part (between Omoa and Comayagua, Honduras).

E[*upsychortyx*] *leylandi* SETH-SMITH, L'Oiseau, x, 1929, 762 (care in captivity).

[*Eupsychortyx*] *leylandi* SHARPE, Hand-list, i, 1899, 45, part (Honduras).

Eupsychortyx lelandi STONE, Proc. Acad. Nat. Sci. Philadelphia, lxxxiv, 1932, 302 (Honduras; Omoa and Comayagua).

Colinus leucopogon leylandi CONOVER, Condor, xxxiv, 1932, 175 (Honduras; Dept. Tegucigalpa—Monte Redondo, Comayaguela; spec.).—PETERS, Check-list Birds World, ii, 1934, 50, part (western Honduras).

C[*olinus*] *l*[*eucopogon*] *sclateri* DICKEY and VAN ROSSEM, Birds El Salvador, 1938, 149, in text, part (Honduras).

[*Colinus*] [*leucopogon*] *leylandi* SASSI, Temminckia, iii, 1938, 305 in text (central and northern Honduras).

Colinus cristatus sclateri HELLMAYR and CONOVER, Cat. Birds Amer., i, No. 1, 1942, 250, part (Honduras; syn.).

COLINUS LEUCOPOGON SCLATERI (Bonaparte)

SCLATER'S QUAIL

Adult male.—Similar to that of the Honduranian race but with the malar and postorbital stripe warm buff to pale honey yellow, instead of white; the breast and the brown shaft areas of the feathers of the middle of the abdomen more rufescent—light cinnamon-brown instead of snuff brown finely mixed with gray; upperparts of body also more brownish, less grayish, the dark blotches on the lower back, rump, and upper tail coverts larger and more richly colored.

Adult female.—Similar to that of the Honduranian race but with the chin, throat, and superciliary stripes usually more heavily suffused with yellowish—ochraceous-buff to honey yellow instead of light pinkish buff to pale ochraceous-buff—and slightly darker on the upper parts of the body, the dark blotches averaging larger and deeper.

Other plumages apparently unknown.

Adult male.—Wing 97.8–102.4 (100.4); tail 52.1–64.2 (57.0); culmen from base 14.0–16.3 (15.2); tarsus 28.2–30.9 (29.6); middle toe without claw 23.4–25.1 (24.4 mm.).[44]

---

[44] Nine specimens from Nicaragua.

Adult female.—Wing 97.4–100.8 (99.4) ; tail 51.3–54.3 (52.9) ; culmen from base 14.3–15.8 (15.0) ; tarsus 29.1–30.8 (29.9) ; middle toe without claw 23.5–24.1 (23.8 mm.).[45]

Range.—Resident in the Plateau and Pacific slope of Nicaragua (San Geronimo, Chinandega, Sucuyá, Ocotal, Matagalpa, Granada, etc.).

Type locality.—None originally indicated; restricted to western Nicaragua by van Rossem (Bull. Mus. Comp. Zool., lxxvii, 1934, 486).

Eupsychortyx sclateri BONAPARTE, Compt. Rend., xlii, 1856, 883, 954 (no locality indicated = western Nicaragua; type in Paris Museum).—VAN ROSSEM, Bull. Mus. Comp. Zool., lxxvii, 1934, 486 (crit.).
Ortyx leylandi NUTTING, Proc. U. S. Nat. Mus., vi, 1884, 390 (Sucuyá, Nicaragua).
Eupsychortyx leylandi OGILVIE-GRANT, Cat. Birds Brit. Mus., xxii, 1893, 411, part (Chinandega, Nicaragua) ; Hand. Game Birds, ii, 1897, 132, part (Nicaragua).— SALVIN and GODMAN, Biol. Centr.-Amer., Aves, iii, 1903, 295, part (Paraiso, Jalapa, Sucuyá, Ocotal, Matagalpa, and Chinandega, Nicaragua).—RENDAHL, Ark. Zool., xii, No. 8, 1919, 10 (Granada, w. shore of Lake Nicaragua, Nicaragua).
[*Eupsychortyx*] *leylandi* SHARPE, Hand-list, i, 1899, 45, part (Nicaragua).
Colinus leucopogon leylandi DICKEY and VAN ROSSEM, Condor, xxxii, 1930, 73, part (w. Nicaragua).—PETERS, Check-list Birds of World, ii, 1934, 50, part (Nicaragua).
C[*olinus*] *l*[*eucopogon*] *sclateri* DICKEY and VAN ROSSEM, Birds El Salvador, 1938, 149, in text, part (w. Nicaragua).
[*Colinus*] [*leucopogon*] *sclateri* SASSI, Temminckia, iii, 1938, 305, in text (nw. Nicaragua).
[*Colinus*] [*leucopogon*] [*dickeyi*] SASSI, Temminckia, iii, 1938, 305, in text, part (sw. Nicaragua).
Colinus cristatus sclateri HELLMAYR and CONOVER, Cat. Birds Amer., i, No. 1, 1942, 250, part (syn.; distr.; Nicaragua).

COLINUS LEUCOPOGON DICKEYI Conover

DICKEY'S QUAIL

Adult male.—Very similar to that of *Colinus leucopogon sclateri* but with the feathers of the upper throat with extensive white centers.

Adult female.—Not certainly distinguishable from that of the Honduranian race *C. l. leylandi,* but with the chin and throat averaging somewhat buffier.

Juvenal.—Like that of *C. l. leylandi.*

Natal down.—Like that of *C. l. leylandi.*

Adult male.—Wing 93.2–104.7 (98.9) ; tail 50.1–55.4 (53.1) ; culmen from base 13.7–15.6 (14.6) ; tarsus 27.1–29.8 (28.6) ; middle toe without claw 21.2–25.0 (23.2 mm.).[46]

Adult female.—Wing 95.1–99.4 (98.0) ; tail 51.1–53.4 (52.5) ; culmen from base 14.3–15.5 (14.5) ; tarsus 26.1–29.3 (27.7) ; middle toe without claw 22–24.1 (22.9 mm.).[47]

---

[45] Five specimens from Nicaragua.
[46] Eleven specimens from Costa Rica.
[47] Six specimens from Costa Rica.

Range.—Resident in the Plateau region and Pacific slope of Costa Rica (Las Cañas, San José, Orósi, Miravalles, Guanacaste, Turrucares, Volcán Irazú, Cartago, Barranca, Alajuela, etc.).

Type locality.—Las Cañas, Guanacaste, western Costa Rica.

Ortyx leylandi LAWRENCE, Ann. Lyc. Nat. Hist. New York, ix, 1868, 139 (San José and Barranca, Costa Rica).—FRANTZIUS, Journ. für Orn., 1869, 373 (Costa Rica).—BOUCARD, Proc. Zool. Soc. London, 1878, 42 (San José Valley, Costa Rica).—ZELEDÓN, Proc. U. S. Nat. Mus., viii, 1858, 112 (Costa Rica).

[*Ortyx*] *leylandi* SCLATER and SALVIN, Nom. Av. Neotr., 1873, 137, part (Costa Rica).

Colinus leylandi ZELEDÓN, Anal. Mus. Nac. Costa Rica, i, 1888, 128 (San José and Alajuela, Costa Rica).—CHERRIE, Auk, ix, 1892, 329 (San José, Costa Rica).

Eupsychortyx leylandi OGILVIE-GRANT, Cat. Birds Brit. Mus., xxii, 1893, 411, part (San José and Irazú district, Costa Rica) ; Handb. Game Birds, ii, 1897, 132, part (Costa Rica).—UNDERWOOD, Ibis, 1896, 449 (Volcán de Miravalles, Costa Rica; habits).—SALVIN and GODMAN, Biol. Centr.-Amer., Aves., iii, 1903, 295, part (Heredia, Barba, San José, Barranca, Alajuela, Irazú, Estrella de Cartago, and Miravalles, Costa Rica).—CARRIKER, Ann. Carnegie Mus., vi, 1910, 386 (Santo Domingo de San Mateo, Alajuela, San José, Tenório, Cachi, and Miravalles, Costa Rica).

[*Eupsychortyx*] *leylandi* SHARPE, Hand-list, i, 1899, 45, part (Costa Rica).

Eupsychortyx leucofrenatus ELLIOT, Ann. Lyc. Nat. Hist. New York, vii, 1860, 106, pl. 3 (Honduras).

Colinus leucopogon leylandi DICKEY and VAN ROSSEM, Condor, xxxii, 1930, 73, part (nw. Costa Rica).

Colinus leucopogon dickeyi CONOVER, Condor, xxxiv, 1932, 174 (orig. descr.; Las Cañas, Guanacaste, w. Costa Rica; spec.; crit.).—PETERS, Check-list Birds World, ii, 1934, 50, part (Costa Rica).—SASSI, Temminckia, iii, 1938, 304 (Costa Rica, Bebedero and Cachi near San José; spec.; crit.).

Colinus cristatus dickeyi HELLMAYR and CONOVER, Cat. Birds Amer., i, No. 1, 1942, 251 (syn.; distr.).

COLINUS LEUCOPOGON LEUCOPOGON (Lesson)

WHITE-FACED BOBWHITE

Adult male.—Similar to that of *Colinus leucopogon leylandi* but with the lores, forehead, superciliary bands, chin, and throat pure white; the general tone of the upperparts of the head and body somewhat paler that in the Honduranian race; auriculars paler—drab; breast and the brownish areas of the abdominal feathers paler—the breast between avellaneous and wood brown to Saccardo's umber, the abdominal feathers Saccardo's umber to cinnamon-brown; the pale abdominal spots averaging smaller and less pure white, more tinged with buffy; bill black; iris dark brown; tarsi and toes bluish horn color.

Adult female.—Similar to that of *C. l. leylandi* of Honduras but with the interscapulars and upper back more heavily transversely marked with blackish and with abdomen and throat more buffy; bill black; iris dark brown; tarsi and toes bluish horn color.

Juvenal.—Not distinguishable from that of *C. l. leylandi*.

Adult male.—Wing 98.5–107.1 (102.9) ; tail 56.8–62.8 (59.9) ; culmen from base 14.8–16.0 (15.6) ; tarsus 27.0–30.6 (29.2) ; middle toe without claw 23.5–26.0 (24.7 mm.).[48]

Range.—Grasslands and open country of the Arid Tropical Zone of southeastern El Salvador, east of the Lempa River.

Type locality.—San Carlos, Americae centralis Oceani Pacifici = La Unión, El Salvador.

Adult female.—Wing 100.1–101.1; tail 55.6; culmen from base 15.6–15.8; tarsus 27.6–29.1; middle toe without claw 22.4 mm. (2 specimens).

Ortyx leucopogon LESSON, Rev. Zool., v, 1842, 175 ("San Carlo," Central America = La Unión, El Salvador; coll. Paris Mus.?).—DES MURS, Icon. Orn., livr. 6, 1846, p. 36 and text, and table of contents.—DICKEY and VAN ROSSEM, Condor, xxxii, 1930, 72 (El Salvador, e. of Río Lempa; crit.; syn.).

[*Ortyx*] *leucopogon* GRAY, Gen. Birds, iii, 1846, 514; Handlist, ii, 1870, 273, No. 9791.—REICHENBACH, Synop. Av., iii, Gallinaceae, 1848, pl. 194, fig. 1682.

Eupsychortyx leucopogon GOULD, Monogr. Odontoph., pt. 3, 1850, pl. 13 and text ("San Carlos").—SALVIN and GODMAN, Biol. Centr.-Amer., Aves, iii, 1903, 295, part (San Carlos).—SETH-SMITH, L'Oiseau, x, 1929, 762 (care in captivity).

Eupsychortyx leucopogon leucopogon TODD, Auk, xxxvii, 1920, 203, part (San Carlos; discussion of type).

Colinus leucopogon leucopogon DICKEY and VAN ROSSEM, Condor, xxxii, 1930, 73 (El Salvador, e. of Lempa River).—CONOVER, Condor, xxxiv, 1932, 175 (El Salvador; Dept. Morazán, Divisadero; Dept. La Unión, Olomega; Río Goascorán; spec.).—PETERS, Check-list Birds World, ii, 1934, 50 (distr.).—DICKEY and VAN ROSSEM, Birds El Salvador, 1938, 148, 149 (El Salvador; Lake Olomega, Río Goascorán, Divisadero; spec.; crit.; habits; colors of soft parts; distr.).—FRIEDMANN, Proc. Biol. Soc. Washington, lvii, 1944, 15.

[*Colinus*] [*leucopogon*] *leucopogon* SASSI, Temminckia, iii, 1938, 305, in text (eastern El Salvador).

Colinus cristatus leucopogon HELLMAYR and CONOVER, Cat. Birds Amer., i, No. 1, 1942, 249 (syn.; distr.).

"*Ortyx albifrons* Less." LAFRESNAYE, Rev. Zool., v, 1842, 130 (San Carlos; Province of San Salvador; nomen nudum).

COLINUS LEUCOPOGON HYPOLEUCUS Gould

SALVADOREAN WHITE-BREASTED BOBWHITE

Adult male.—Above very similar to that of the nominate race; below differs in the great but very variable extension of the white posteriorly over the breast and abdomen; some individuals have almost the entire underparts, except for the flanks, thighs, and under tail coverts, white, while others have the breast and only a little of the upper abdomen albescent; similarly, in some birds these white feathers have brown bases which show through, while in others the feathers are completely white; soft parts as in the nominate form.

---

[48] Six specimens.

Adult female.—Similar to that of the nominate race but less buffy on the abdomen, the throat slightly streaked with dusky, general tone of upperparts of body slightly more grayish, less brownish; crown and occiput duskier, more fuscous.

Juvenal.—Not distinguishable from that of *C. l. leylandi.*

Adult male.—Wing 97.5–103.3 (100.1); tail 53.1–60.8 (57.2); culmen from base 14.5–16.0 (15.1); tarsus 27.3–29.3 (28.5); middle toe without claw 23.5–25.2 (24.1 mm.).[49]

Adult female.—Wing 95.9–102.1; tail 54.4–58.1; culmen from base 14.7–15.0; tarsus 27.4–29.2; middle toe without claw 22.5–23.0 mm. (2 specimens).

Range.—Grasslands and up to 5,000 feet on the slopes of the volcanoes, in El Salvador, west of the Lempa River.

Type locality.—"Acajutla in Mexico"=Acajutla, El Salvador.

Eupsychortyx hypoleucus GOULD, Proc. Zool. Soc. London, xxviii, 1860, 62 (Acajutla, "Mexico," i.e., El Salvador; coll. J. Verreaux); Ann. Mag. Nat. Hist., ser. 3, vi, 1860, 77 (reprint).—OGILVIE-GRANT, Cat. Birds Brit. Mus., xxii, 1893, 413, part (Acajutla).—SALVIN and GODMAN, Biol. Centr.-Amer., Aves, iii, 1903, 297, part (Acajutla).

Colinus hypoleucus GRISCOM, Amer. Mus. Nov., No. 379, 1929, 2 (plum.; crit.).

Colinus leucopogon hypoleucus DICKEY and VAN ROSSEM, Condor, xxxii, 1930, 73, part (El Salvador, w. of Lempa River); Birds El Salvador 1938, 151 (El Salvador; spec.; habits; colors of soft parts; plum.; crit.).—CONOVER, Condor, xxxiv, 1932, 175 (El Salvador, Dept. La Paz—Hacienda Miraflores; Dept. Sonsonate, Volcán Santa Ana; Dept. La Libertad, Hacienda Zapotitlán, Setro del Niño; Dept. Santa Ana—El Tablón; spec.).—PETERS, Check-list Birds World, ii, 1934, 50, part (El Salvador).—FRIEDMANN, Proc. Biol. Soc. Washington, lvii, 1944 (plum.; crit.).

[Colinus] [leucopogon] hypoleucus SASSI, Temminckia, iii, 1938, 305, in text, part (El Salvador).

Colinus cristatus hypoleucus HELLMAYR and CONOVER, Cat. Birds Amer., i, No. 1, 1942, 249, part (syn.; distr.).

COLINUS LEUCOPOGON INCANUS Friedmann

GUATEMALAN WHITE-BREASTED BOBWHITE

Adult male.—Similar to that of *Colinus leucopogon hypoleucus* but very slightly paler above; the scapulars and upper wing coverts only slightly suffused with rufescent (deeply suffused in *hypoleucus*).

Adult female.—Similar to that of *Colinus leucopogon hypoleucus* but paler, especially above, the general color of the upperparts of the female being pale buckthorn brown with a grayish tinge (as against snuff brown with a grayish tinge in *hypoleucus*).

Other plumages apparently unknown.

---

[49] Twelve specimens.

Adult male.—Wing 99.4–105.1 (102.6) ; tail 59.7–63.2 (61.7) ; culmen from base 14.4–15.0 (14.8; tarsus 28.1 ; middle toe without claw 23.2–24.0 (23.6 mm.).[50]

Adult female.—Wing 97.1–101.1 (98.7) ; tail 53.1–62.7 (57.6) ; culmen from base 14.1–14.8 (14.4) ; tarsus 27.1–28.4 (27.7) ; middle toe without claw 21.4–23.6 (22.5 mm.).[51]

Range.—Resident in southern Guatemala from the Upper Motagua Valley to the Departments of Jalapa and Baja Vera Paz.

Type locality.—Saloma, Baja Vera Paz, Guatemala.

Eupsychortyx hypoleucus Ogilvie-Grant, Cat. Birds Brit. Mus., xxii, 1893, 413, part (San Gerónimo, Vera Paz, Guatemala).—Beristain and Laurencio, Mem. y Rev. Soc. Cient. "Antonio Alzate," vii, Nos. 7, 8, 1894, 219 (Mexico; Chiapas and Tabasco).—Salvin and Godman, Biol. Centr.-Amer., Aves, iii, 1903, 297, part (San Gerónimo, Guatemala).

[*Eupsychortyx*] *hypoleucus* Sclater and Salvin, Nom. Av. Neotr., 1873, 138.— Sharpe, Hand-list, i, 1899, 45 (Guatemala).

Ortyx hypoleucus Gray, List Birds Brit. Mus., pt. 5, 1867, 77 (Mexico).

[*Ortyx*] *hypoleucus* Gray, Hand-list, ii, 1870, 273, No. 9789 (Mexico).

Eupsychortyx leucopogon (not *Ortyx leucopogan* Lesson) Salvin and Sclater, Ibis, 1860, 277 (San Gerónimo, Guatemala).

Colinus leucopogon hypoleucus Dickey and van Rossem, Condor, xxxii, 1930, 73, part (Guatemala).—Griscom, Bull. Amer. Mus. Nat. Hist., lxiv, 1932, 106 (Guatemala; distr.).—Peters, Check-list Birds World, ii, 1934, 50, part (Guatemala).

[*Colinus*] [*leucopogon*] *hypoleucus* Sassi, Temminckia, iii, 1938, 305, in text, part (Guatemala).

Colinus cristatus hypoleucus Hellmayr and Conover, Cat. Birds Amer., i, No. 1, 1942, 249, part (syn.; distr.).

Colinus leucopogon incanus Friedmann, Proc. Biol. Soc. Washington, lvii, 1944, 16 (Saloma, Baja Vera Paz, Guatemala; orig. descr.).

COLINUS CRISTATUS SONNINI (Temminck)

SONNINI'S BOBWHITE

Adult male.—Forehead, lores, and anterior part of crown varying from buffy whitish to pale buffy brown or grayish brown ; the posterior coronal area with the dusky basal parts of the feathers showing through occasionally, giving a transversely marked appearance, crest darker—dull sepia to fairly pale bister—the feathers edged with buffy brown to almost buckthorn brown; sides of crown and occiput edged with feathers that are black on their inner webs, edged with buffy white, and light ochraceous-tawny on their outer webs; broad superciliaries bright ochraceous-tawny to ochraceous-orange; feathers of nape streaked with black; a nuchal collar of snuff-brown feathers with large subterminal white spots edged with black; interscapulars and upper back cinnamon coarsely vermiculated with black, each feather edged with mouse gray;

---

[50] Three specimens, including the type.
[51] Four specimens.

scapulars and inner, greater, and median upper wing coverts between
Dresden brown and cinnamon-brown crossed by narrow, widely spaced
wavy bars of pale buffy edged with dusky; the scapulars internally margined with ochraceous-buff, the coverts completely edged with pale smoke
gray; innermost secondaries like the scapulars; rest of secondaries dull
sepia, edged and incompletely barred on their outer webs with light pinkish cinnamon and more or less suffused with Dresden brown on their
outer webs; primaries dull sepia faintly flecked on their outer margins
with ashy light pinkish cinnamon; rest of upper wing coverts Dresden
brown to cinnamon-brown externally edged narrowly with pale pinkish
buff; these edgings enlarged terminally into broader tips, the brown
areas faintly stippled and vermiculated with dusky; back, lower back,
rump, and upper tail coverts bright cinnamon-brown with a tawny tinge,
narrowly tipped and crossed by narrow, but widely spaced bars of pale
buffy, these bars proximally edged with blackish, which sometimes extends basally along the shaft for a short distance; rectrices similar but
less tawny; chin and throat bright light ochraceous-tawny to ochraceous-
orange; auriculars dull, dark Dresden brown; a pectoral band of white
feathers with wedge-shaped black terminal spots; breast between tawny-
olive and clay color, the feathers tipped with a slightly paler and ashier
tone, and basally transversely marked with blackish (usually hidden by
the overlapping feathers), this color becoming more ochraceous on the
upper abdomen, where, however, the feathers have several large white
or buffy spots on each web with blackish transverse interspaces, the
brown restricted to the median part of the feathers, this median area
increasing in extent and brightness on the sides; feathers of lower lateral
parts of the abdomen, the flanks, thighs, and under tail coverts with the
pale spots larger, buffier, the brownish or ochraceous areas much reduced, the black bars wider; middle of lower abdomen pale buffy barred
with blackish; under wing coverts pale sepia to wood brown flecked with
buffy white.

Adult female.—Similar to the adult male on the upper parts but generally
less rufescent, more grayish sepia; the superciliaries pale ashy buff, darkening posteriorly; the crown and crest darker—sepia with less ochraceous
edgings; the interscapulars and upper back duskier and without grayish
edges; below much less rufescent than the male; chin and throat buffy
grayish white, suffused to a varying extent posterolaterally with ochraceous-tawny; breast and upper abdomen drab to pale sepia instead of
tawny-olive; abdomen largely white, the blackish markings averaging
somewhat smaller than in the male, the brownish areas reduced and largely
restricted to the more lateral feathers.[52]

---

[52] There seems to be considerable variation in the whiteness of the abdominal plumage that may be correlated with age, the immature or subadult birds possibly
averaging more buffy than the older ones. More material is needed to determine this.

Juvenal (?).—None seen, but one described by Ogilvie-Grant as "quite young" is said to have "the upperparts very similar to those of the female adult, but all the feathers of the mantle, wing-coverts, scapulars, and chest have pale buff shaft-stripes; chin and throat white, rest of the underparts white irregularly barred with black."

Other plumages apparently unknown.

Adult male.—Wing 96–106 (101); tail 54–67 (62); culmen from base 12–14 (12.9); tarsus 25–30 (27.5); middle toe without claw 21–24 (22.5 mm.).[53]

Adult female.—Wing 95–99 (97); tail 55–62 (58.5); culmen from base 12–13 (12.7); tarsus 25–28.5 (26); middle toe without claw 24–24.5 (24.3 mm.).[54]

Range.—Resident in open grassland savannas in French, Dutch, and British Guiana, the adjacent part of northern Brazil (upper Rio Branco) west through Venezuela in the Orinoco Basin and north to Caracas and Carabobo in the coast region; introduced on Mustique Island, Grenadines, and in St. Thomas, Virgin Islands.

Type locality.—French Guiana.

Perdix sonnini TEMMINCK, Hist. Nat. Pig. et Gallin., iii, 1815, 451 (French Guiana; coll. Paris Mus.).—VIEILLOT, Nouv. Dict. Hist. Nat., xxv, 1817, 246 (Guyane); Tabl. Enclycl. Méth., i, 1820, 369.

Perdix sonninii TEMMINCK, Hist. Nat. Pig. et Gallin., iii, 1815, 737 (French Guiana); Nouv. Rec. Pl. Col., v, 1823, pl. 75 and text.

Ortyx sonninii STEPHENS, *in* Shaw, Gen. Zool., xi, pt. 2, 1819, 383.—JARDINE and SELBY, Illustr. Orn., i, 1828, text to pl. 38.—LESSON, Illustr. Zool., i, 1832, text to pl. 52.—GRAY, List Birds Brit. Mus., pt. 3, 1844, 44 (British Guiana); pt. 5, Gallinae, 1867, 77 (British Guiana).—REINHARDT, Ibis, 1861, 114 (St. Thomas; crit.).—PELZELN, Orn. Bras., iii, 1870, 290 (Forte do São Joaquim, Rio Branco, n. Brazil).

[*Ortyx*] *sonninii* GRAY, Gen. Birds, iii, 1846, 514; Hand-list, ii, 1870, 273, No. 9787.—REICHENBACH, Synop. Av., iii, Gallinaceae, 1848, pl. 193, fig. 1674.

Or[*tyx*] *sonninii* STEPHEN, *in* Shaw, Gen. Zool., xiv. pt. 1, 1826, 303.

Colinus sonninii LESSON, Traité d'Orn., 1831, 508 (in list of species; distr.).

Eupsychortyx sonninii GOULD, Monogr. Odontoph., pt. 3, 1850, pl. 11 and text.—NEWTON, Ibis, 1860, 308 (St. Thomas, Greater Antilles, introduced from Venezuela).—CASSIN, Proc. Acad. Nat. Sci. Philadelphia, 1860, 378 (St. Thomas, introduced).—SCLATER and SALVIN, Proc. Zool. Soc. London, 1869, 252 (Plains of Valencia, Venezuela).—CORY, Auk, iv, 1887, 225 (St. Thomas; syn.; descr.; crit.); Birds West Indies, 1889, 224 (St. Thomas); Cat. West Indian Birds, 1892, 96 (St. Thomas); Publ. Field Mus. Nat. Hist., orn. ser., i, 1909, 239, in text (British Guiana; Caracas, Venezuela; crit.).—BERLEPSCH, Journ. für Orn., xl, 1892, 92, in text (French Guiana; Quonga, British Guiana; crit.).—OGILVIE-GRANT, Cat. Birds British Mus., xxii, 1893, 409 (Porte do Rio Branco, n. Brazil; Quonga, British Guiana; Caracas, Venezuela; Mustique, Grenadines); Handb. Game Birds, ii, 1897, 130; Ibis, 1902, 239 (Quonga, British Guiana; Mustique; crit.).—HARTERT, Ibis, 1893, 306, in text, 338, footnote (range, etc.); 1894, 430,

---

[53] Twelve specimens from Venezuela.
[54] Eight specimens from Venezuela.

in text (Plains of Valencia, Venezuela) ; Bull. Brit. Orn. Club, iii, 1894, 37, in
text (Plains of Valencia) ; Nov. Zool., i, 1894, 675, in text (Plains of Valencia).
—PHELPS, Auk, xiv, 1897, 367 (Cumanacoa and San Antonio, Venezuela).—
CLARK, Proc. Boston Soc. Nat. Hist., xxxii, 1905, 246 (Mustique, Grenadines).—
PENARD, Vog. Guyana, i, 1908, 310.—CHUBB, Birds British Guiana, i, 1916, 31.
E[upsychortyx] sonninii SETH-SMITH, L'Oiseau, x, 1929, 762 (care in captivity).
[Eupsychortyx] sonninii SCLATER and SALVIN, Nom. Av. Neotr., 1873, 138.—GIEBEL,
Thesaurus Orn., ii, 1875, 142 (Gould's reference).—CORY, List Birds West
Indies, rev. ed., 1886, 24 (St. Thomas).—HEINE and REICHENOW, Nom. Mus.
Hein. Orn., 1890, 294.—SHARPE, Hand-list, i, 1899, 45.—BRADBOURNE and CHUBB,
Birds South America, i, 1912, 13 (Venezuela; British Guiana; n. Brazil).
Eupsychortyx sonnini BERLEPSCH and HARTERT, Nov. Zool., ix, 1902, 121 (Altagracia,
Orinoco Valley, Venezuela; crit.). BERLEPSCH, Nov. Zool., xv, 1908, 296
(Cayenne; British Guiana).—CHERRIE, Bull. Brooklyn Inst. Sci, ii, 1916, 357
(lower and middle Orinoco Valley).
[Eupsychortyx] sonnini IHERING and IHERING, Av. Brazil, 1907, 17 (Rio Branco
and Rio Negro, n. Brazil).
Eupsichortyx sonninii BONAPARTE, Compt. Rend., xlii, 1856, 883 (in list of species).
Colinus cristatus sonnini PETERS, Check-list Birds World, ii, 1934, 51, part.—DAN-
FORTH, Journ. Agr. Univ. Porto Rico, xix, 1935, 466 (St. Thomas; introduced,
now extinct).—HELLMAYR and CONOVER, Cat. Birds Amer., i, No. 1, 1942, 257
(syn.; distr.).
(?) Ortyx affinis VIGORS, Proc. Comm. Sci. Corresp. Zool. Soc. London, pt. 1,
No. 1, 1830 (1831), 3 ("northern parts of America"; descr. of female; type
lost).—GRAY, Gen. Birds, iii, 1846, 514.—REINHARDT, Ibis, 1861, 115 (crit.).
(?) Eupsychortyx affinis GOULD, Monogr. Odontoph., pt. 3, 1850, 16 (descr.; crit.).
Eupsychortyx sonnini sonnini TODD, Auk, xxxvii, 1920, 194, pl. 5, fig. 1, 2 (monogr.;
Guianas and extreme n. Brazil to Colombia e. of Andes).—WETMORE, Sci.
Surv. Porto Rico and Virgin Islands, ix, pt. 3, 1927, 331 (Virgin Islands).
Odontophorus sonnini GOELDI, Av. Brazil, ii, 1894, 439 (Rio Branco).
O[rtyx] cristatus (not Tetrao cristatus Linnaeus) CABANIS, in Schomburgk,
Reis. Brit. Guiana, iii, 1848, 747 (British Guiana; habits).—BROWN, Canoe and
Camp Life in British Guiana, 1876, 268 (Cotinga River and Rupununi Savan-
nas, British Guiana).
Eupsychortyx cristatus SALVIN, Ibis, 1886, 175 (Brit. Guiana).
(?)[Eupsychortyx] cristatus HEINE and REICHENOW, Nom. Mus. Hein. Orn.,
1890, 294, part ("Guiana").
Perdix cristata SCHOMBURGK, Reis. Brit. Guiana, i, 1847, 394 (Pirara).
Colinus cristatus BOND, Birds West Indies, 1936, 402 (introduced St. Thomas,
St. Vincent, Mustique).
C[allipepla] cristata REICHENOW, Die Vögel, i, 1913, 317, part.
Eupsychortyx [sonnini] FERRY, Condor, x, 1908, 226 (Caracas, Venezuela; habits).

COLINUS CRISTATUS PANAMENSIS Dickey and van Rossem

PANAMA CRESTED BOBWHITE

Adult male.—Above similar to that of *Colinus cristatus sonnini* but
darker, more rufescent—cinnamon-brown to Prout's brown; the forehead, anterior crown, lores, cheeks, chin, and upper throat more extensively pale buffy white than in *sonnini*; crest and occiput also averaging
paler than in *sonnini*; below—lower throat darker—almost hazel; breast
much less uniform and more rufescent, the feathers with blackish shaft

streaks and subterminal white spots on either web; sides more rufescent—
hazel to dark hazel with the white spots and their black borders smaller
than in *sonnini*; middle of abdomen deep warm buff banded with widely
spaced fuscous black bars; lower midabdomen, flanks, thighs, and under
tail coverts as in *sonnini*.

Adult female.—Similar to that of *C. c. sonnini* but somewhat darker and
brighter cinnamon-brown to Prout's brown above; the breast feathers
with their brownish areas more rufescent; the abdomen deeper buff, especially medially.

Other plumages apparently unknown.

Adult male.—Wing 93–101 (96.5); tail 52.8–58.5 (56.8); culmen from
base 13–13.5 (13.2); tarsus 27–31 (29.1); middle toe without claw 23–27
(23.7 mm.).[55]

Adult female.—Wing 96–102 (99.0); tail 50–60.4 (55.6); culmen from
base 12.5–14.5 (13.4); tarsus 28–31 (29.5); middle toe without claw
24–27 (25.5 mm.).[56]

Range.—Resident in the arid tropical lowland plains of western Panama
in the Departments of Coclé, Veraguas, and Chiriquí.

Type locality.—Agua Dulce, Coclé, western Panama.

Eupsychortyx leucopogon (not *Ortyx leucopogon* Lesson) GOULD, Monogr. Odon-
toph., pt. 3, 1850, pl. 13 (fig.; spec. coll. Lafresnaye).—OGILVIE-GRANT, Cat.
Birds Brit. Mus., xxii, 1893, 408, part (spec. p-r; Veraguas); Handb. Game
Birds, ii, 1897, 130, part (Veraguas).—SALVIN and GODMAN, Biol. Centr.-Amer.
Aves, iii, 1903, 295, part ("Calobre," Veraguas).

Eupsychortyx leucopogon leucopogon TODD, Auk, xxxvii, 1920, 203, pl. 5, fig. 4
(w. Panama; monogr.).

Eupsychortyx leucotis (not *Ortyx leucotis* Gould) SALVIN, Ibis, 1876, 379
(Veraguas (Calobre?); crit.).

Colinus leucotis panamensis DICKEY and VAN ROSSEM, Condor, xxxii, 1930, 73
(Agua Dulce, Coclé, w. Panama; type in coll. D. R. Dickey, now Univ.
California at Los Angeles; descr.; crit.).

Colinus cristatus panamensis PETERS, Checklist Birds of World, ii, 1934, 50
(distr.).—GRISCOM, Bull. Mus. Comp. Zool., lxxviii, 1935, 303 (Panama;
arid plains of Veraguas and Coclé only).—HELLMAYR and CONOVER, Cat. Birds
Amer., i, No. 1, 1942, 252 (syn.; distr.).

Colinus c[ristatus] panamensis CONOVER, Proc. Biol. Soc. Washington, li, 1938,
54 (spec.; Aguadulce, Coclé; La Marca, La Colorado, Santiago, and Santa
Fé, Veraguas; El Francés, Chiriquí; Panama).

Genus ODONTOPHORUS Vieillot

Odontophorus VIEILLOT, Analyse, 1816, 51. (Type, by monotypy, "*Tocro* Buff."=
Tetrao guianensis Gmelin=*Tetrao tocro* Herman.)
Dentophorus (emendation) BOIE, Isis, xxi, Heft 3-4, 1828, 326, note.
Odonthophorus (emendation) BONAPARTE, Giorn. Arcadico, xlix, 1831, 54.
Strophiortyx BONAPARTE, Compt. Rend., xlii, 1856, 883. (Type, as designated by
Grant, 1893, *Odontophorus columbianus* Gould.)

---

[55] Five specimens.
[56] Four specimens.

Large and stoutly built very short-tailed Odontophorinae (wing about 127–158 mm.) with short tail (less than half as long as wing), large and stout feet (tarsus nearly one-third as long as wing, sometimes slightly longer), heavy bill, more or less extensively naked orbital region, and feather of posterior portion of pileum more or less (but not conspicuously) elongated, forming, when erected, a bushy crest of broad, round-tipped, decurved or decumbent feathers; sexes alike in coloration.

Bill relatively large and heavy, the chord of exposed culmen (from extreme base) equal to two-fifths to nearly half the length of tarsus, the depth of bill at base greater than distance from anterior end of nasal fossa to tip of maxilla and equal to or greater than its width at rictus; culmen strongly convex, rounded, narrower and more ridge-like basally.

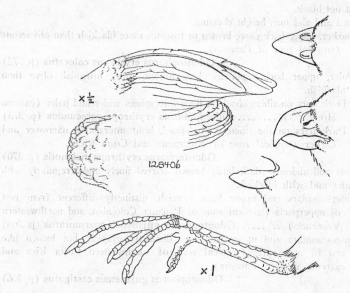

FIGURE 20.—*Odontophorus gujanensis.*

Outermost primary equal to or slightly shorter (sometimes much shorter) than ninth (from outside), the third, fourth, and fifth, fourth, fifth and sixth, or fifth to eighth longest. Tail two-fifths to nearly half as long as wing, mostly concealed by coverts, the rectrices (12), however, firm, broad, with rounded tips. Tarsus nearly one-third as long as wing, sometimes more than one-third as long, nearly to quite as long as middle toe with claw, very stout, the planta tarsi, on both sides, with a continuous row of transverse scutella (larger and more continuous on outer side).

Plumage and coloration.—Feathers of pileum elongated, broad, soft, and flattened (webs not conduplicate), forming, when erected, a bushy crest; orbital (sometimes also loral) region more or less extensively naked. Coloration dull, various tones of brown or brown and rufous predominating, usually vermiculated with dusky, often more or less speckled or barred with buffy, the scapulars sometimes spotted with black, the outer webs of primaries often spotted with cinnamon-rufous or buffy. Sexes alike in coloration or at least not conspicuously different.

Range.—Southeastern Mexico to Peru, Bolivia, and central Brazil. (Sixteen species.)

KEY TO THE MIDDLE AMERICAN FORMS OF THE GENUS ODONTOPHORUS

a. Chin and throat streaked black and white (southeastern Mexico to western Panama) ....**Odontophorus guttatus** (p. 373)
aa. Chin and throat not streaked black and white.
  b. Breast black (highlands of Costa Rica and western Panama).
                              Odontophorus leucolaemus (p. 377)
  bb. Breast not black.
    c. Breast and abdomen bright chestnut.
      d. Darker, upper back clove brown to fuscous, more blackish than olivaceous (tropical zone of Panama).
                       Odontophorus erythrops coloratus (p. 372)
      dd. Paler, upper back sepia to clove brown, more brownish olive than blackish.
        e. Dark bars on tibiae obsolete, light interspaces wider and paler (eastern Honduras)..........**Odontophorus erythrops verecundus** (p. 373)
        ee. Dark bars on the tibiae well defined, light interspaces narrower and darker (tropical zone of Nicaragua and Costa Rica).
                    Odontophorus erythrops melanotis (p. 370)
    cc. Breast and abdomen dark buffy brown, barred finely and irregularly with paler and with blackish.
      d. Interscapulars and upper back grayish, distinctly different from rest of upperparts (tropical zone of Panama, Colombia, and northwestern Venezuela)..........**Odontophorus gujanensis marmoratus** (p. 368)
      dd. Interscapulars and upper back not distinctly grayish, but brown like rest of upperparts (tropical zone of southwestern Costa Rica and extreme western Panama).
            Odontophorus gujanensis castigatus (p. 366)

ODONTOPHORUS GUJANENSIS CASTIGATUS Bangs

CHIRIQUÍ WOOD QUAIL

Adult male.—Narrow forehead amber brown; crown and occiput between chestnut-brown and argus brown; nape slightly paler and the feathers obscurely and narrowly edged with pale grayish amber brown; interscapulars and upper back between dark Dresden brown and Prout's brown heavily vermiculated with fuscous-black, and, more narrowly, with light neutral gray; upper wing coverts dark mummy brown crossed by widely spaced, narrow, wavy bars of pale tawny and terminally flecked with white; inner greater upper coverts, scapulars, and inner secondaries similar but with the pale markings very much more abundant and more rufescent—between Brussels brown and auburn—these markings largely confined to the outer webs of the feathers, except for the scapulars, where both webs are abundantly marked; the scapulars with a fairly large terminal pinkish buff mark on the inner web; the secondaries with a smaller and median terminal spot of the same; primaries clove brown, the inner webs uniform, the outer ones barred with pale pinkish buff to pale ochraceous-salmon; upper back just posterior to the interscapulars dark fuscous-black edged and barred with narrow lines of auburn, the bars widely spaced; back and lower back pale buffy brown with a slight olive tinge, each feather with several small black subterminal flecks; lower back, rump, and upper tail coverts similar but darker—cinnamon-brown on the rump and darkening posteriorly to dark cinnamon-brown, the feathers of the rump and the upper tail coverts finely vermiculated with blackish, the black flecks extended laterally to form somewhat heavier wavy bars each of which is edged distally with a wider one of pale cinnamon-brown; rectrices clove brown to dark mummy brown crossed by widely spaced narrow bars pale cinnamon-brown; lores and circumocular area bare, crimson in life; an indefinite band from the forehead over the eye to the upper side of the auriculars dark auburn; cheeks and auriculars brighter auburn; chin and line of the gape narrowly paler auburn; throat, breast, and sides cinnamon-brown, slightly washed with olivaceous anteriorly, the feathers of the throat slightly duskier subterminally; those of the breast and sides subterminally narrowly banded with one or two bands of blackish, the more posterior feathers with these bands heavier and distally edged with pale cinnamon-brown to almost whitish; flanks like the sides but more heavily and coarsely marked with black and pale subterminally; middle of abdomen dull buffy brown with indistinct dusky cross bars, darkening posteriorly to almost olive-brown; thighs dark olive-brown indistinctly barred with cinnamon-brown under tail coverts olive-cinnamon-brown barred with blackish and pale cinnamon-brown; greater under wing coverts plain clove brown; lesser ones darker, barred sparingly with cinnamon-brown; iris dusky brown; bill very dark, darker than iris; tarsi and toes plumbeous.

Adult female.—Like the male, but with the "mantle," *i.e.*, the interscapulars, somewhat more olivaceous, less precisely and sharply vermiculated with blackish and pale gray.

Other plumages apparently unknown.

Adult male.—Wing 141.0–153.5 (145.9); tail 67.0–71.0 (69.1); culmen from base 19.7–21.4 (20.4); tarsus 43.5–48.0 (45.8); middle toe without claw 34.1–38.7 (35.8 mm.).[57]

Adult female.—Wing 136.5–144.5 (139.3); tail 59.5–65.0 (63.5); culmen from base 18.7–19.6 (19.1); tarsus 43.4–46.1 (44.3); middle toe without claw 33.2–36.0 (34.6 mm.).[58]

---

[57] Eight specimens from Costa Rica and western Panama.
[58] Five specimens from Costa Rica.

Range.—Resident in forested areas of the tropical zone of southwestern Costa Rica (Buenos Aires, Puntarenas, Volcán de Oso, Alto de Jabillo, Pirris, El General, etc.) to extreme northwestern Panama (Bugaba, Divalá).

Type locality.—Divalá, Chiriquí, Panama.

Odontophorus marmoratus (not of Gould) SALVIN, Proc. Zool. Soc. London, 1870, 218 (Bugaba, Veraguas; crit.).—ZELEDÓN, Anal. Mus. Nac. Costa Rica, i, 1888, 128 (Las Trojas and Pozo Azul de Pirris, sw. Costa Rica).—CHERRIE, Expl. Zool. Merid. Costa Rica, 1893, 54 (Boruca and Buenos Aires, sw. Costa Rica).— SALVIN and GODMAN, Biol. Centr.-Amer., Aves, iii, 1903, 309, part (Las Trojas and Pozo Azul de Pirris, Costa Rica; Bugaba, Chiriquí, w. Panama).

[*Odontophorus guianensis*] Subsp. α. *Odontophorus marmoratus* OGILVIE-GRANT, Cat. Birds Brit. Mus., xxii, 1893, 433, part (Bugaba, w. Panama); Handb. Game Birds, ii, 1897, 153 part.

[*Odontophorus*] *marmoratus* SCLATER and SALVIN, Nom. Av. Neotr., 1873, 138, part (Veragua, w. Panama).

Odontophorus castigatus BANGS, Auk, xviii, 1901, 356 (Divalá, Chiriquí, w. Panama; coll. E. A. and O. Bangs); xxiv, 1907, 291 (Boruca and El Pozo de Térraba, sw. Costa Rica); Proc. New England Zool. Club, iii, 1902, 22 (Bugaba, Chiriquí). —CARRIKER, Ann. Carnegie Mus., vi, 1910, 386 (Sabanilla, El Pozo de Térraba, sw. Costa Rica; crit.; habits).—BANGS, Bull. Mus. Comp. Zool., lxx, 1930, 160 (type spec. in Mus. Comp. Zool.; crit.).

O[*dontophorus*] g[*uianensis*] *castigatus* CHAPMAN, Bull. Amer. Mus. Nat. Hist., xxxiv, 1915, 363, in text, 364 (w. Panama; sw. Costa Rica).

Odontophorus guianensis castigatus GRISCOM, Bull. Mus. Comp. Zool., lxxviii, 1935, 303 (Panama; coastal forests of western Chiriquí).

Odontophorus gujanensis castigatus PETERS, Check-list Birds of World, ii, 1934, 51 (sw. Costa Rica and nw. Panama).—HELLMAYR and CONOVER, Cat. Birds Amer., i, No. 1, 1942, 260 (syn.; distr.).

ODONTOPHORUS GUJANENSIS MARMORATUS (Gould)

MARBLED WOOD QUAIL

Adult.—Similar to that of the same sex of *Odontophorus gujanensis castigatus* but with the interscapulars and upper back definitely black and gray, not brown, distinctly different from the rest of the upperparts; the crest much darker, the longer, posterior plumes blackish, marginally and basally flecked with cinnamon-brown; general tone of the upperparts darker; feathers of back, rump, and upper tail coverts more uniform, less flecked and vermiculated with blackish; upper throat with more white in the pale cross bars; abdomen, sides, and flanks more conspicuously barred with pale cinnamon-tawny edged with blackish.

In some specimens the chin and throat are marked with white; this appears to be an individual variation of no geographic or racial significance.

Adult male.—Wing 134.5–154.5 (143.1); tail 63.5–77.5 (68.8); culmen from base 18.9–21.9 (20.4); tarsus 43.2–47.5 (45.1); middle toe without claw 32.3–37.5 (35.7 mm.).[59]

---

[59] Seventeen specimens from Panama and Colombia.

Adult female.—Wing 135.5–147.0 (139.8) ; tail 62.0–75.0 (67.5) ; culmen from base 19.0–21.9 (20.1) ; tarsus 41.8–46.1 (44.2) ; middle toe without claw 32.1–37.7 (33.7 mm.).[60]

Range.—Resident in tropical forests of Panama, from the Canal Zone eastward, and south to all of Colombia except the eastern base of the eastern Andes, and to adjacent parts of northwestern Venezuela south of Lake Maracaibo, State of Zulia.

Type locality.—Santa Fé de Bogotá, Colombia.

Ortyx (Odontophorus) marmoratus GOULD, Proc. Zool. Soc. London, 1843, 107 (Santa Fé de Bogotá, Colombia; coll. J. Gould; type now in Brit. Mus.).
Odontophorus marmoratus GOULD, Monogr. Odont., pt. 3, 1850, 22 (monogr.).—SCLATER, Proc. Zool. Soc. London, 1855, 163 (Bogotá).—SCLATER and SALVIN, Proc. Zool. Soc. London, 1864, 371 (Lion Hill, Panama) ; 1879, 545 (Remedios, Antioquia, Colombia; habits; descr.; nest; and eggs).—SALVADORI and FESTA, Boll. Mus. Zool. Torino, xiv, No. 339, 1899, 10 (Río Lara, Darién).—SALVIN and GODMAN, Biol. Centr-Amer., Aves, iii, 1903, 309 (Bogotá, Colombia; Chepo; Lion Hill, Panama).—THAYER and BANGS, Bull. Mus. Comp. Zool., xlvi, 1905, 214 (Sabana de Panamá; crit.).
[*Odontophorus*] *marmoratus* GRAY, Hand-list, ii, 1870, 271, No. 9755 (New Granada). —SCLATER and SALVIN, Nom. Av. Neotr., 1873, 138 (Colombia and Panama).—SHARPE, Hand-list, i, 1899, 47, part (Panama and Colombia).—BRABOURNE and CHUBB, Birds South Amer., i, 1912, 13, part (Colombia).
[*Odontophorus guianensis*] Subsp. α. *Odontophorus marmoratus* OGILVIE-GRANT, Cat. Birds Brit. Mus., xxii, 1893, 433 (Chepo and Lion Hill, Panama, and Remedios and Bogotá, Colombia); Handb. Game Birds, ii, 1897, 153, part (Colombia; Panama).
O[*dontophorus*] *g*[*uianensis*] *marmoratus* CHAPMAN., Bull. Amer. Mus. Nat. Hist., xxxiv, 1915, 363, in text, 364 (lower Río Magdalena to east base of Andes, Colombia, 4,500 feet).—OSGOOD and CONOVER, Publ. Field Mus. Nat. Hist., zool. ser., xii, 1922, 28, in text (crit.).
Odontophorus guianensis marmoratus CHAPMAN, Bull. Amer. Mus. Nat. Hist., xxxvi, 1917, 200 (La Morelia, Buena Vista, and Puerto Valdivia, eastern Colombia; crit.) ; Amer. Mus. Nov., No. 380, 1929, 3 (Venezuela—Santa Elena, head of Maracaibo; Colombia—El Tamber, Santander; Palmar, Boyacá; Puerto Valdivia and Murindo, Antioquia ; Saotata, Río Atrato ; and Panama; crit.).—STONE, Proc. Acad. Nat. Sci. Philadelphia, 1918, 242 (Canal Zone; spec.; colors of soft parts).—CHUBB, Ibis, 1919, 26 (Colombia; crit.).—OSGOOD and CONOVER, Publ. Field Mus. Nat. Hist., zool. ser., xii, 1922, pl. 1, upper fig. (fig.).—BANGS, Bull. Mus. Comp. Zool., lxx, 1930, 160 (crit.).—GRISCOM, Bull. Mus. Comp. Zool., lxxii, 1932, 319 (Obaldia, Permé, Ranchon, Panama; crit.) ; lxxviii, 1935, 303 (Canal Zone eastward in Panama; common).
Odontophorus gujanensis marmoratus PETERS, Check-list Birds World, ii, 1934, 52 (distr.).—HELLMAYR and CONOVER, Cat. Birds Amer., i, No. 1, 1942, 260 (syn.; distr.).
Odontophorus guianensis panamensis CHAPMAN, Bull. Amer. Mus. Nat. Hist., xxxiv, 1915, 363 (Panama Railway; coll. Amer. Mus. Nat. Hist.).—CHUBB, Ibis, 1919, 26 (Lion Hill, Panama; coll. Brit. Mus.; redescribed under same name!).—BANGS and BARBOUR, Bull. Mus. Comp. Zool., lxv, 1922, 195 (Mount

---

[60] Ten specimens from Panama and Colombia.

Sapo and Jesusito, Darién).—STURGIS, Field Book Birds Panama Canal Zone,
1928, 29 (descr.; habits; Panama).—HEATH, Ibis, 1932, 482 (Barro Colorado
Island, Panama).

Odontophorus guianensis chapmani GRISCOM, Bull. Mus. Comp. Zool., lxix, 1929,
153 (Cana, e. Panama; descr.; crit.).—BANGS, Bull. Mus. Comp. Zool., lxx,
1930, 160 (type spec. in Mus. Comp. Zool. = *O. g. marmoratus*).

Odontophorus guianensis canescens (not *O. parambae canescens* Chapman, 1921)
OSGOOD and CONOVER, Publ. Field Mus. Nat. Hist., zool. ser., xii, 1922, 27,
pl. 1, lower fig. (Río Cogollo, Perijá, Zulia, Venezuela; type in Conover
coll.; fig.).

Odontophorus guianensis polionotus OSGOOD and CONOVER, Auk, xliv, 1927, 561 (new
name for *O. guianensis canescens* Osgood and Conover, preoccupied).

Odontophorus gujanensis polionotus PETERS, Check-list Birds of World, ii, 1934, 52
(Venezuela).

Odontophorus guianensis (not *Tetrao guianensis* Gmelin) LAWRENCE, Ann. Lyc.
Nat. Hist. New York, vii, 1862, 301 (Lion Hill, Panama).—SETH-SMITH,
L'Oiseau, x, 1929, 763 (care in captivity).

ODONTOPHORUS ERYTHROPS MELANOTIS Salvin

BLACK-EARED WOOD QUAIL

Adult male.—Forehead, crown, occiput, and dorsal part of auriculars
dark chestnut; nape and interscapulars mummy brown heavily flecked
and vermiculated with fuscous, the interscapulars with pale smoke-gray
longitudinal flecks along the shaft except terminally; upper wing coverts
and scapulars dark sepia transversely broadly blotched with dark clove
brown to dark fuscous and vermiculated with fuscous to blackish; the
large blackish blotches edged with pale cinnamon-brown, this pale color
most extensive and prominent, the black most restricted, on the outer
lesser and median coverts; the scapulars with incomplete whitish bars
on the inner part of their outer webs; the greater and median coverts
more regularly banded with blackish and with pale cinnamon-brown than
the others; secondaries dark clove brown, the outer webs abundantly
flecked and mottled with cinnamon-brown to pale cinnamon-brown and
blackish; primaries dark clove brown, fairly uniform on their inner webs;
heavily banded on the outer ones, these short bars almost coalescing on
some of the remiges to form solid outer webs of this color; upper back
dull sepia, subterminally broadly banded with black, this band narrowly
edged proximally with cinnamon-brown proximal to which is a very
narrow black band, the sepia basal portion of the feathers speckled finely
with dusky; lower back and rump sepia to bister, faintly flecked with
dusky; upper tail coverts similar but with large blackish stippling and
the feathers subterminally blotched transversely with blackish; rectrices
mummy brown faintly and incompletely banded with dark sepia and
abundantly flecked and vermiculated terminally and marginally with sepia
to cinnamon-brown; lores and circumocular area bare, dark plumbeous to
blackish; cheeks, auriculars, chin, and throat black; breast and sides dark,

bright amber brown, paling on anterior two-thirds of abdomen to between cinnamon-rufous and light bright hazel; flanks, thighs, lower abdomen, and under tail coverts dull cinnamon-brown barred with fuscous to blackish, the under tail coverts heavily mottled and flecked with the blackish as well; outer lesser under wing coverts like the corresponding upper ones; greater inner under wing coverts uniform clove brown; iris dark brown; bill black; tarsus dark slate; toes similar.

Adult female.—Similar to the adult male but with the nape and interscapulars somewhat more rufescent—chestnut-brown (instead of mummy brown), and the cheeks, auriculars, chin, and throat mummy brown instead of black.

Juvenal male.—Above similar to the adult female but with conspicuous buffy-white shafts on the posterior interscapulars, the scapulars, and the greater upper wing coverts; the sides of the head with no bare space; the lores, a broad stripe through the eye to the nape, a broad malar stripe, the chin, and throat cinnamon-buff to pale tawny-olive, the auriculars black; breast, sides, and abdomen as in adult but all the feathers with subterminal spots or broken bars of black.

Natal down.—Forehead and a broad band extending back over the crown, occiput, nape, and spinal tract to the tail Mikado brown, becoming somewhat darker posteriorly; this is bordered by a broad supraocular band of pinkish buff to light ochraceous-buff; lores, circumocular area, and auriculars dusky—mummy brown flecked with ochraceous-buff; wings and a laterodorsal line to thighs like the spinal tract—dark Mikado brown, rest of upperparts pale avellaneous to pale wood brown; underparts grayish avellaneous washed with dull hazel, especially on sides, flanks, and thighs; to a lesser extent on the breast.

Adult male.—Wing 138.5–147.5 (142.1); tail 53–61.5 (56.7); culmen from base 19.4–21.3 (20.2); tarsus 42.5–47.1 (44.7); middle toe without claw 32.6–38.8 (36.4 mm.).[61]

Adult female.—Wing 136; tail 54; culmen from base 18.5; tarsus 41.9; middle toe without claw 33.8 mm. (1 specimen).

Range.—Resident in tropical forests of Nicaragua, south to northern and eastern Costa Rica (Volcán Miravalles, Cerro Santa María, Guanacaste, Villa Quesada, Alajuela, Jiménez, Bonilla, Talamanca, etc.).

Type locality.—Tucurrique, Costa Rica.

Odontophorus melanotis SALVIN, Proc. Zool. Soc. London, 1864 (1865), 586 (Tucurrique, Costa Rica; coll. Salvin and Godman); Ibis, 1872, 323 (Chontales, Nicaragua).—LAWRENCE, Ann. Lyc. Nat. Hist. New York, ix, 1868, 140 (Tucurrique).—FRANTZIUS, Journ. für Orn., 1869, 374 (Costa Rica).—ZELEDÓN, Anal. Mus. Nac. Costa Rica, i, 1887, 128 (Jiménez, Costa Rica).—RICHMOND, Proc. U. S. Nat. Mus., xvi, 1893, 524 (Río Escondido, Nicaragua).—OGILVIE-GRANT, Cat. Birds Brit. Mus., xxii, 1893, 435, part (Chontales, Nicaragua;

---

[61] Seven specimens from Costa Rica.

Tucurrique, Costa Rica) ; Handb. Game Birds, ii, 1897, 155, part (Nicaragua and Costa Rica).—UNDERWOOD, Ibis, 1896, 449 (Volcán de Miravalles, Costa Rica).— SALVIN and GODMAN, Biol. Centr.-Amer., Aves, iii, 1903, 310, pl. 73, part (Chontales and Río Escondido, Nicaragua; Tucurrique, Dota, Cerro de la Candelaria, Miravalles, and Jiménez, Costa Rica).—CARRIKER, Ann. Carnegie Mus., vi, 1910, 387 (Bonilla, Talamanca, Jiménez, Carillo, Tenório, Guapiles, Guacimo, Cuabre, Río Sicsola, and El Hogar, Costa Rica; crit.; habits).

[*Odontophorus*] *melanotis* GRAY, Hand-list, ii, 1870, 272, No. 9767, part (Costa Rica). —SCLATER and SALVIN, Nom. Av. Neotr., 1873, 138, part (Nicaragua, Costa Rica).—SHARPE, Hand-list, i, 1899, 47, part (Nicaragua, Costa Rica).

Odontophorus melanotus ZELEDÓN, Proc. U. S. Nat. Mus., viii, 1885, 112 (Costa Rica).

Odontophorus melanotis melanotis HUBER, Proc. Acad. Nat. Sci. Philadelphia, lxxxiv, 1932, 207 (ne. Nicaragua; Great Falls of Pis Pis River, and between Eden and Miranda; spec.; descr. of young).

Odontophorus erythrops melanotis PETERS, Check-list Birds of World, ii, 1934, 53 (Nicaragua; n. and e. Costa Rica).—HELLMAYR and CONOVER, Cat. Birds Amer., i, No. 1, 1942, 268 (syn.; distr.).—WETMORE, Proc. U. S. Nat. Mus., xcv, 1944, 38 (Hda. Santa María, n. Guanacaste, Costa Rica).

Odontophorus erythrops coloratus (not of Griscom) HELLMAYR and CONOVER, Cat. Birds Amer., i, No. 1, 1942, 269, part (Talamanca, sw. Costa Rica).

ODONTOPHORUS ERYTHROPS COLORATUS Griscom

VERAGUAN WOOD QUAIL

Adult male.—Very similar to that of *Odontophorus erythrops melanotis* but with the posterior part of the occipital crest brighter, less dusky, uniform with the anterior part, and with the interscapulars and upper back slightly darker.

Adult female.—Not certainly distinguishable from that of *O. e. melanotis.*

Adult male.—Wing 141–143.5 (142.1) ; tail 56–59 (57.8) ; culmen from base 21.2–21.4 (21.3) ; tarsus 45.9–49 (47) ; middle toe without claw 35.7–38.5 (37.1 mm.).[62]

Adult female.—Wing 139–150 (142) ; tail 50–56 (54.3) ; culmen from base 19.3–21.3 (20.3) ; tarsus 43–47.1 (44.9) ; middle toe without claw 35–37.3 (36.2 mm.).[63]

Range.—Resident in the tropical forest of Panama.

Type locality.—Guaval, Río Calovevora, western Veraguas.

Odontophorus melanotis (not of Salvin) SALVIN, Proc. Zool. Soc. London, 1867, 161 (Santiago de Veraguas, w. Panama).—OGILVIE-GRANT, Cat. Birds Brit. Mus., xxii, 1893, 435, part (Veraguas, w. Panama).—SALVIN and GODMAN, Biol. Centr.-Amer. Aves., iii, 1903, 310, part (Santiago de Veraguas).

[*Odontophorus*] *melanotis* GRAY, Hand-list, ii, 1870, 272, No. 9767, part (Panama).— SCLATER and SALVIN, Nom. Av. Neotr., 1873, 138, part (Veraguas).—SHARPE, Hand-list, i, 1899, 47, part (Veraguas).

[62] Three specimens from Panama.
[63] Six specimens from Panama.

Odontophorus melanotis coloratus GRISCOM, Amer. Mus. Nov., No. 280, 1927, 3
(Guaval, Río Calovevora, 1,500 feet, Caribbean slope of w. Panama; descr.;
crit.); Bull. Mus. Comp. Zool., lxxviii, 1935, 303 (Caribbean slope of w.
Panama).
Odontophorus melanotus coloratus PETERS, Bull. Mus. Comp. Zool., lxxi, 1931, 297
(Boquete trail, Guabo, Cricamola, Panama).
Odontophorus erythrops coloratus PETERS, Check-list Birds of World, ii, 1934, 53
(distr.).—HELLMAYR and CONOVER, Cat. Birds Amer., i, No. 1, 1942, 269, part
(syn.; distr.; all except sw. Costa Rica).

ODONTOPHORUS ERYTHROPS VERECUNDUS Peters
HONDURANIAN WOOD QUAIL

Adult female[64].—Similar to that of *Odontophorus erythrops melanotis*
but "slightly grayer above, especially the upper back; black markings on
the scapulars and interscapulars less pronounced; less black freckling on
the wing coverts; below, the dark bars on the tibiae obsolete, the light
interspaces wider and paler" (*ex* Peters, orig. descr.).
Known only from the type locality—Lancetilla, Honduras.

Odontophorus melanotis verecundus PETERS, Bull. Mus. Comp. Zool., lxix, 1929,
404 (Lancetilla, Honduras; descr.; crit.).—BANGS, Bull. Mus. Comp. Zool., lxx,
1930, 161 (type spec. in Mus. Comp. Zool.).—STONE, Proc. Acad. Nat. Sci.
Philadelphia, lxxxiv, 1932, 301 (Lancetilla, Honduras).
Odontophorus erythrops verecundus PETERS, Check-list Birds World, ii, 1934, 53
(Lancetilla, Honduras).—HELLMAYR and CONOVER, Cat. Birds Amer., i, No. 1,
1942, 268 (syn.; distr.).

ODONTOPHORUS GUTTATUS (Gould)
SPOTTED WOOD QUAIL

Adult male (olive-brown phase).—Forehead, anterior part of crown,
upper lores, and superciliary area sepia to dark Saccardo's umber; antero-
median plumes of coronal and occipital crest fuscous-black narrowly
tipped with sepia; the posterior and lateral feathers of the crest bright
orange-buff; nape and interscapulars sepia with or without an olivaceous
tinge, the feathers with pale buffy to whitish shafts, and their vanes
abundantly and finely flecked with fuscous; scapulars and greater upper
wing coverts and feathers of the upper back sepia with very large
blotches of black (in the case of the coverts these blotches are confined
to the inner webs) and the sepia portion incompletely barred with
ochraceous-orange to cinnamon-rufous, the shafts whitish; lesser and
median upper wing coverts olive-sepia finely barred and vermiculated with
blackish, the median ones with buffy white V-shaped tips; secondaries
fuscous to dark clove brown, uniform on the inner webs but broadly
banded on the outer ones with pale buffy olive-brown to pale sepia, these
pale bands, which are broader than the darker interspaces, are thickly

"Male unknown.

653008°—46——25

speckled with blackish dots and tend to become more ochraceous-orange on the more outer feathers; primaries fuscous to dark clove brown, uniform on the inner webs and blotched with light ochraceous-buff on the outer ones; back, lower back, and rump between very pale tawny-olive and isabelline, the feathers with a few subterminal flecks of black; upper tail coverts similar but darker—dusky buffy brown with an olive tinge and with the black flecks larger and more prominent and with paler tips; rectrices fuscous to dark clove brown freckled and vermiculated marginally and terminally with sepia and tawny-olive; lower part of lores and circumocular area bare; a band from below and behind the eye extending posteriorly to the sides of the neck between Sanford's brown and chestnut; chin and throat black, the feathers with white shaft streaks varying in width; sides of neck, breast, sides, and anterior and lateral part of abdomen tawny-olive to dark, bright clay color, the feathers with white shafts, which enlarge subterminally to form conspicuous rounded or tear-shaped marks narrowly edged with dusky to black, and just failing to reach the tips of the feathers; flanks, thighs, lower abdomen, and under tail coverts less olive, duskier, without pale shafts or spots, and barred with blackish, these dark bars faint and indistinct on the abdomen, more distinct on the flanks, and very well marked on the under tail coverts; under wing coverts dull dark sepia; iris dark brown; bill black; tarsi and toes dark plumbeous.

Adult male (erythristic phase).—Similar to the preceding but more rufescent generally, the sepia areas above being Dresden brown to cinnamon-brown; the bulk of the occipital crest capucine orange instead of orange-buff, the freckling on the wings Sudan brown to raw umber, and the breast, sides, and abdomen ochraceous-tawny to antique brown.

Adult female (olive-brown phase).—Similar to the male of the same phase but smaller and with the entire occipital crest dark mummy brown to fuscous, the posterior ones with orange-buff shaft streaks which are usually concealed by the overlapping of the more anterior feathers, and usually with the ground color of the upperparts slightly more rufescent; iris dark brown; bill black; feet plumbeous.

Adult female (erythristic phase).—Similar to the male of the same phase but generally darker both above and below, and with the entire crest fuscous, even the posterior plumes with little or no orange-buff medially.

Juvenal (erythristic phase) (sexes alike).—Similar to the adult male but darker and slightly more rufescent above; the crest entirely bright orange-buff except for the most anterior of its component plumes, which are mummy brown to fuscous, narrowly edged with sepia; the interscapulars with relatively little white on the shafts; the rump and upper tail coverts argus brown, obscurely banded with blackish; chin and malar area dark earth brown streaked with white; throat dusky olive-brown tinged, especially posteriorly, with cinnamon, and indistinctly banded with blackish; breast, sides and upper abdomen olive-brown, the feathers banded toward the tip with black and with buffy white, the pale bands being distally pointed **V**'s, the black terminal ones being divided medially by the extension of the subterminal white one along the shaft; abdomen, flanks, thighs, and under tail coverts as in adult but darker.

Juvenal (olive-brown phase).—Similar to the preceding but less brown-ish, more dusky olive-brown above and below; the greater and median upper wing coverts and the interscapulars with conspicuous white shafts terminally enlarged into small white triangles; the black blotches greatly reduced on the scapulars, upper back, and upper wing coverts; all the remiges tawny, abundantly and finely freckled and vermiculated with blackish over both webs; breast, sides, and upper abdomen sepia, the feathers with narrow white shafts which spread terminally into proximally pointed triangles of white, the sepia area indistinctly barred and flecked with mummy brown to dark sepia.[65]

Natal down (male only seen).—Forehead, anterior and lateral parts of crown, and sides of occiput warm buff darkening posteriorly to light ochraceous-buff; most of occiput, and narrower center of crown extending in a thin median line to the base of the culmen tawny russet; chin, throat, cheeks, and auriculars pale warm buff; spinal tract dark russet; rest of upperparts light ochraceous-salmon flecked with dusky; underparts of body pale warm buff tinged with olive-gray.

Adult male.—Wing 134–153.5 (143.8); tail 69.5–76.5 (62.2); culmen from base 19.3–22.6 (19.4); tarsus 41.5–48.9 (45.6); middle toe without claw 33.1–39.6 (36.3 mm.).[66]

Adult female.—Wing 134.5–148.5 (139.8); tail 61–72.5 (67.0); culmen from base 18.2–21.0 (19.7); tarsus 41.5–47 (43.9); middle toe without claw 32.5–38 (35.5 mm.).[67]

Range.—Resident in forested areas of the subtropical zone of south-eastern Mexico (from Veracruz, Tabasco, and Oaxaca south to Chiapas and Campeche) south through Guatemala, British Honduras, Honduras, Nicaragua, and Costa Rica to extreme western Panama, as far as Volcán de Chiriquí. In Costa Rica its altitudinal range is from 5,000 feet to timberline.

Type locality.—"Bay of Honduras."

Ortyx guttata GOULD, Proc. Zool. Soc. London, 1837 (1838), 79 (Bay of Honduras; types now in coll. Brit. Mus.).

---

[65] The juvenal plumages of the two phases are still to be elucidated. The material examined presents too many differences to be "normal" for color varieties. What is needed is juvenal material collected *with* the parents to be certain of the identification.

[66] Thirty-five specimens from Mexico, Guatemala, Honduras, Nicaragua, Costa Rica, and Panama.

[67] Sixteen specimens from Mexico, Guatemala, Honduras, Costa Rica, and Panama.

Odontophorus guttatus GRAY, List Birds Brit. Mus., pt. 3, Gallinae, 1844, 43; pt. 5, Gallinae, 1867, 72.—GOULD, Monogr. Odontoph., pt. 2, 1846, pl. 28 and text.— SCLATER, Proc. Zool. Soc. London, 1856, 309 (Córdoba, Veracruz); 1859, 391 (Teotalcingo, Oaxaca).—SCLATER and SALVIN, Ibis, 1859, 226 (Cahoon palm ridges, Honduras; Yucatán).—LAWRENCE, Ann. Lyc. Nat. Hist. New York, ix, 1868, 140 (Dota, Costa Rica).—FRANTZIUS, Journ. für Orn., xvii, 1869, 374 (Costa Rica).—SUMICHRAST, Mem. Boston Soc. Nat. Hist., 1869, 560 (hot region of Veracruz); La Naturaleza, ii, 1871, 37 (Veracruz).—SALVIN, Proc. Zool. Soc. London, 1870, 218 (Volcán de Chiriquí, w. Panama).—BOUCARD, Proc. Zool. Soc. London, 1878, 42 (Curridabat, near San José, Costa Rica); (?) Liste Ois. Recol. Guat., 1878, 14 (Guatemala).—CUBAS, Cuadro Geogr., Estadística, Descr. e Hist. de los Estados Unidos Mexicanos, 1884, 168 (common names, Mexico).—ZELEDÓN, Anal. Mus. Nac. Costa Rica, i, 1887, 128 (Sarchí de Alajuela, El Zarcero de Alajuela, and Alajuela, Costa Rica).— OGILVIE-GRANT, Cat. Birds Brit. Mus., xxii, 1893, 439 (Córdoba, Veracruz; Chimalapa, Oaxaca; Barranca and Dota, Costa Rica; Volcán de Chiriquí, w. Panama; Honduras; Belize and San Felipe, British Honduras; Volcán de Agua, Volcán de Fuego, Dueñas, and Vera Paz, Guatemala; Chimilapa, Oaxaca); Handb. Game Birds, ii, 1897, 159 (monogr.); Ibis, 1902, 244 (crit.).— BERISTAIN and LAURENCIO, Mem. y Rev. Soc. Cient. "Antonio Alzate," vii, 1894, 218 (Mexico).—BANGS, Proc. New England Zool. Club, iii, 1902, 22 (Bugaba, Chiriquí, w. Panama).—SALVIN and GODMAN, Biol. Centr.-Amer., Aves, iii, 1903, 311 (Córdoba and Mirador, Veracruz; Teotalcingo and Chimalapa, Oaxaca; w. Panama; Barranca, Dota, La Candelaria, San José, Sarchí, Trazú, and El Zarcero de Alajuela, Costa Rica; Vera Paz, Dueñas, Volcán de Fuego at 5,000 feet, and Volcán de Agua, Guatemala; Yucatán ?; Río Hondo and San Felipe, British Honduras?; Jali and San Rafael del Norte, Nicaragua).— CARRIKER, Ann. Carnegie Mus., vi, 1910, 389 (La Estrella de Cartago, Azahar de Cartago, and Volcán de Trazú, Costa Rica; from 5,000 feet upward; habits).—GRISCOM, Bull. Amer. Mus. Nat. Hist. lxiv, 1932, 109 (Guatemala; distr.). Bull. Mus. Comp. Zool., lxxviii, 1935, 304 (Volcán de Chiriquí, Panama; above 5,000 feet).—PETERS, Check-list Birds World, ii, 1934, 55 (distr.; crit.).— VAN TYNE, Misc. Publ. Univ. Michigan Mus. Zool., No. 27, 1935, 13 (Uaxactún, Petén, Guatemala; spec.).—BERLIOZ, Bull. Mus. Hist. Nat. Paris, ser. 2, xi, 1939, 361 (Santa Rosa, Chiapas).

O[*dontophorus*] *guttatus* REICHENOW, Die Vögel, i, 1913, 316.

[*Odontophorus*] *guttatus* SCLATER and SALVIN, Nom. Av. Neotr., 1873, 138,— SHARPE, Hand-list, i, 1899, 47.

Odontophorus guttatus guttatus AUSTIN, Bull. Mus. Comp. Zool., lxix, 1929, 370 (south of El Cayo and Augustine, British Honduras; crit.).—TRAYLOR, Publ. Field Mus. Nat. Hist., zool. ser., xxiv, 1941, 204 (Pacaitun, Campeche; spec.).— HELLMAYR and CONOVER, Cat. Birds Amer., i, No. 1, 1942, 279 (syn.; distr.).

Odontophorus veraguensis GOULD, Proc. Zool. Soc. London, 1856, 107 (Veraguas, w. Panama; coll. J. Gould; types now in coll. Brit. Mus.).—SCLATER, Proc. Zool. Soc. London, 1856, 143 (Boquete, Chiriquí).—GRAY, List Birds Brit. Mus., pt. 5, Gallinae, 1867, 72.—SALVIN, Proc. Zool. Soc. London, 1867, 161 (Panama and David, Chiriquí, Panama).—LAWRENCE, Ann. Lyc. Nat. Hist. New York, ix, 1868, 140 (Dota, Barranca, and Las Cruces de Candelaria, Costa Rica).—FRANTZIUS, Journ. für Orn., xvii, 1869, 374 (Costa Rica).— ZELEDÓN, Proc. U. S. Nat. Mus., viii, 1885, 112 (Costa Rica); Anal. Mus. Nac. Costa Rica, i, 1887, 128 (Las Cruces de Candelaria).—OGILVIE-GRANT, Cat. Birds Brit. Mus., xxii, 1893, 441 (Dota, Costa Rica; Volcán de Chiriquí and Veraguas, w. Panama; Handb. Game Birds, ii, 1897, 160 (monogr.).—

Bangs, Proc. New England Zool. Club, iii, 1902, 22 (Boquete, Chiriquí, w. Panama, 4,000–5,800 feet; crit.).—Salvin and Godman, Biol. Centr.-Amer., Aves, iii, 1903, 312 (Dota, Barranca, and Las Cruces de Candelaria, Costa Rica; Boquete and Volcán de Chiriquí, w. Panamá).—Carriker, Ann. Carnegie Mus., vi, 1910, 389 (Volcán de Trazú and Ujurrás de Térraba, Costa Rica; crit.).—Griscom, Auk, l, 1933, 298 (El Copey de Dota, Costa Rica; crit.).

[Odontophorus] veraguensis Gray, Hand-list, ii, 1870, 272, No. 9762.—Sharpe, Hand-list, i, 1899, 47.

Odontophorus consobrinus Ridgway, Proc. U. S. Nat. Mus., xvi, 1893, 469 (Mirador, Veracruz; coll. U. S. Nat. Mus.).

[Odontophorus] consobrinus Sharpe, Hand-list, i, 1899, 47.

Odontophorus guttatus matudae Brodkorb, Occ. Pap. Mus. Zool. Univ. Michigan, No. 401, 1939, 4 (Mount Madre Vieja, Chiapas, Mexico, alt. 750 meters; descr.; crit.; type spec. in Mus. Zool. Univ. Michigan).—Hellmayr and Conover, Cat. Birds Amer., i, No. 1, 1942, 280 (crit.; syn.; distr.).

ODONTOPHORUS LEUCOLAEMUS Salvin

White-throated Wood Quail

Adult (sexes alike) (olive-brown phase).—Forehead fuscous more or less flecked with white (the white being the visible basal parts of the feathers); crown and occiput fuscous, the feathers terminally and laterally stippled with raw umber; nape, interscapulars, and lesser upper wing coverts dark raw umber finely stippled and vermiculated with fuscous, the nape washed with chestnut-brown; median upper wing coverts like the lesser ones but flecked with pale tawny-buff, these flecks proximally margined with blackish; greater upper coverts and scapulars similar but with these dark-bordered pale spots larger and more numerous, and the general ground color more rufescent—bright chestnut-brown—and tipped with pale tawny-buff; secondaries dark clove brown to fuscous on the inner webs which are very faintly speckled with chestnut-brown; bright chestnut-brown blotched and mottled with blackish and with light ochraceous-buff on the outer webs; primaries dark clove brown to fuscous; a line of feathers across the upper back just posterior to the interscapulars like the latter but with large blotches of black subterminally; lower back like the interscapulars but somewhat paler—Saccardo's umber to sepia in ground color; rump similar but washed with chestnut-brown; upper tail coverts rich, bright chestnut-brown mottled and freckled with blackish and with cinnamon-tawny; rectrices fuscous marginally and terminally freckled with chestnut-brown; lores, circumocular area, cheeks, auriculars, chin, sides of throat, entire breast, and uppermost part of abdomen black; middle of throat white (sometimes wholly black), the white often mixing with the black on the sides of the throat and chin; a small but variable amount of white showing through on the black breast; sides, flanks, and under tail coverts like the lower back and rump, becoming more richly tinged with chestnut-brown posteriorly, abdomen similar but duller and darker—mummy brown faintly and finely barred with chestnut-brown; under wing coverts plain dull clove brown; iris brown; bill black; tarsi and toes dark plumbeous.

Adult (erythristic phase).—Similar to the preceding but generally more rufescent above and below, the black of the breast less extensive posteriorly and faintly barred with auburn, and more splotched with white (from the exposed more basal parts of the feathers); forehead, crown, and occiput between raw umber and Brussels brown; interscapulars dark cinnamon-brown; rump and upper tail coverts between argus brown and amber brown flecked and mottled with black; upper abdomen and sides between Mars yellow and Sudan brown; flanks, thighs, and under tail coverts Sudan brown to amber brown (instead of chestnut-brown); middle and posterior part of abdomen dull Sudan brown.

Juvenal [68].—Similar to the adult but with the breast and upper abdomen not black but dark Sudan brown like the sides and flanks; the malar area barred black and white.

Other plumages apparently unknown.

Adult male.—Wing 122.5–124.5 (123.4); tail 55.5–68.0 (61.7); culmen from base 18.4–20.4 (19.8); tarsus 44.8–45.4 (45.2); middle toe without claw 37.1–39.1 (37.8 mm.).[69]

Adult female.—Wing 120.0–125.0 (123.2); tail 46.5–51.0 (48.3); culmen from base 18.2–20.3 (19.0); tarsus 44.0–46.3 (44.8); middle toe without claw 34.3–38.0 (36.2 mm.).[70]

Range.—Resident in subtropical forests of the highlands of Costa Rica and western Panama (Chiriquí and Veraguas).

Type locality.—Cordillera de Tole, Veraguas, Panama.

Odontophorus leucolaemus SALVIN, Proc. Zool. Soc. London, 1867, 161 (Cordillera de Tole, Veraguas, w. Panama; coll. Salvin and Godman); 1870, 217 (Calovevora, Veraguas).—LAWRENCE, Ann. Lyc. Nat. Hist. New York, ix, 1868, 140 (San José; Costa Rica).—FRANTZIUS, Journ. für Orn., 1869, 374 (Costa Rica).— ZELEDÓN, Proc. U. S. Nat. Mus., viii, 1886, 112 (Costa Rica); Anal. Mus. Nac. Costa Rica, i, 1887, 128 (Naranjo de Cartago, Costa Rica).—OGILVIE-GRANT, Cat. Birds Brit. Mus., xxii, 1893, 438 (Dota, Costa Rica; Cordillera de Tole, Calovevora, and Chitra, Veraguas); Handb. Game Birds, ii, 1897, 158 (monogr.). —BANGS, Proc. New England Zool. Club, iii, 1902, 22 (Boquete, etc., w. Panama, 4,500–5,000 feet.).—SALVIN and GODMAN, Biol. Centr.-Amer., Aves, iii, 1903, 311 pl. 74 (Naranjo de Cartago, Dota, Cerro de la Candelaria, and San José, Costa Rica).—CARRIKER, Ann. Carnegie Mus., vi, 1910, 388 (La Estrella de Cartago, Azahur de Cartago, Volcán de Trazú, Cariblanco de Sarapiquí; Tenório, and Las Honduras, Costa Rica; crit.; habits).—OBERHOLSER, Proc. Biol. Soc. Washington, xlv, 1932, 39, in text (crit.; meas.).—PETERS, Check-list Birds of World, ii, 1934, 55 (distr.).—GRISCOM, Bull. Mus. Comp. Zool., lxxviii, 1935, 304 (Panama, subtropical zone; mountains of Chiriquí and Veraguas).—HELLMAYR and CONOVER, Cat. Birds Amer., i, No. 1, 1942, 27 (syn.; distr.).

[68] Female only seen; in postjuvenal molt.
[69] Five specimens from Costa Rica and Panama.
[70] Three specimens from Costa Rica and Panama.

[*Odontophorus*] *leucolaemus* GRAY, Hand-list, ii, 1870, 272, No. 9763.—SCLATER and SALVIN, Nom. Av. Neotr., 1873, 138.—SHARPE, Hand-list, i, 1899, 47.

Odontophorus smithians OBERHOLSER, Proc. Biol. Soc. Washington, xlv, 1932, 39 (San Joaquin de Dota, Pacific watershed, Costa Rica, altitude 4,000 feet, coll. H. O. Havemeyer; descr.; meas.; crit.).—GRISCOM, Auk, l, 1933, 298 (crit.; melanism of *O. leucolaemus*).

Genus DACTYLORTYX Ogilvie-Grant

Dactylortyx OGILVIE-GRANT, Cat. Birds Brit. Mus., xxii, 1893, 429. (Type, by original designation, *Ortyx thoracicus* Gambel.)

Odontophorus REICHENOW, Die Vögel, i, 1913, 316, part.

Medium-sized, very short-tailed Odontophorinae (wing about 130–135 mm.) with outstretched tarsi extending beyond tip of tail, claws very long, relatively slender, slightly curved, and blunt, those of lateral toes extending much beyond middle of middle claw, tarsus more than one-fourth as long as wing, rectrices firm, broad, rounded at tips, feather of decumbent crest distinctly outlined, and sexes not conspicuously different in coloration.

Bill relatively rather small and slender, the chord of culmen (from extreme base) equal to nearly half the length of tarsus; the depth of bill at base not exceeding distance from anterior end of nasal fossa to tip of maxilla and a little less than width of bill of rictus; culmen rather strongly convex, narrowly and rather distinctly ridged; gonys relatively narrow but rounded transversely, straight or very nearly so, slightly ascending terminally, its basal angle not prominent. Outermost primary intermediate between seventh and eighth (from outside), the fourth and fifth longest. Tail two-fifths as long as wing, moderately rounded, the rectrices (12) rather firm, broad, and rounded at tips; very distinct from coverts. Tarsus a little more than one-fourth as long as wing, shorter than middle toe with claw, its lower end, when feet are outstretched, extending much beyond tip of tail; planta tarsi with numerous rather large longitudinally hexagonal scales, these along the posterior edge (on both sides) rather larger and more quadrate, with a tendency to form a continuous row; claws very long (that of middle toe longer than basal phalanx of the toe, nearly as long as culmen), slender, slightly curved, and blunt.

Plumage and coloration.—Feathers of crown and occiput moderately elongated, forming, when erected, a bushy crest of moderately broad decumbent or decurved feathers with plane surface and rounded tips; a narrow naked space beneath lower eyelid. Upperparts finely mottled brown and grayish, the hindneck broadly streaked with buff and brownish black, the scapulars and tertials with large black spots or blotches on inner webs, the former with rather broad mesial streaks of whitish; chest, sides, and flanks light brownish gray or drab, broadly streaked with dull whitish, the abdomen dull white or buffy white; adult male with broad superciliary stripe, malar region, chin, and throat uniform cinnamon, the adult female with the cinnamon replaced by grayish white or pale gray and the chest, etc., more rufescent or cinnamomeous.

Range.—Southern Mexico to Guatemala, Honduras, and El Salvador. (Monotypic.)

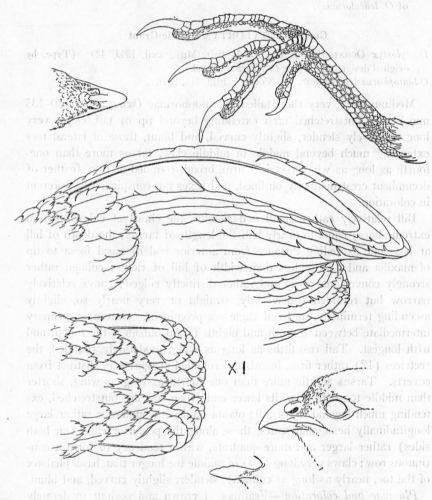

FIGURE 21.—*Dactylortyx thoracicus.*

KEY TO THE FORMS OF DACTYLORTYX THORACICUS (GAMBEL)

a. Chin, throat, cheeks and superciliaries tawny-orange (males).
  b. Interscapulars with many blackish transverse markings; middle of abdomen buffy (Jalisco to Guerrero in western Mexico).
                                        Dactylortyx thoracicus devius (p. 383)
  bb. Interscapulars with few or no blackish transverse markings; middle of abdomen whitish.

c. With whitish shaft stripes on the lateral occipital feathers, giving an appearance of a discontinuous white narrow border to the brown color.

   d. Sides and flanks darker and browner—buffy brown (mountain slopes of eastern Mexico from Tamaulipas to Puebla).

     Dactylortyx thoracicus thoracicus (p. 382)

   dd. Sides and flanks paler and grayer—fairly pale drab (Yucatán Peninsula).

     Dactylortyx thoracicus sharpei (p. 385)

cc. With buffy to ochraceous shaft stripes on the lateral occipital feathers.

   d. Tarsus longer, averaging about 36 mm., toes longer, middle toe without claw averaging about 31.5 mm. (central Chiapas to western Guatemala).

     Dactylortyx thoracicus chiapensis (p. 386)

   dd. Tarsus shorter, averaging 34.5 mm. or less; toes shorter, middle toe without claw averaging under 30 mm.

     e. Pale shaft stripes of breast, uppper abdomen, and sides broad and slightly buffy (southeastern Oaxaca and adjacent western Chiapas).

       Dactylortyx thoracicus lineolatus (p. 385)

     ee. Pale shaft stripes of breast, upper abdomen, and sides very narrow and white.

       f. Larger, wings averaging 130 mm. in length (Mount Cacaguatique, El Salvador) ....**Dactylortyx thoracicus taylori** (p. 388)

       ff. Smaller, wings averaging 126 mm. in length.

         g. Dark portions of underparts paler, with a pale cinnamon-buffy wash (Volcán San Miguel, El Salvador).

          Dactylortyx thoracicus salvadoranus (p. 387)

         gg. Dark portions of underparts darker, with a decidedly dusky earth-brown tone, with no pale cinnamon-buffy wash (Honduras).

          Dactylortyx thoracicus fuscus (p. 389)

aa. Chin, throat, cheeks, and superciliaries with no orange-tawny, but whitish or pale grayish brown to grayish vinaceous (females).

   b. Underparts of body very dark—tawny cinnamon-brown (Honduras).

     Dactylortyx thoracicus fuscus (p. 389)

   bb. Underparts of body paler—orange cinnamon or paler.

     c. Chin and throat strongly tinged with pale vinaceous.

       d. Middle of lower abdomen deep warm buff or darker (Jalisco to Guerrero).

         Dactylortyx thoracicus devius (p. 383)

       dd. Middle of lower abdomen buff white (Tamaulipas to Puebla).

         Dactylortyx thoracicus thoracicus (p. 382)

     cc. Chin and throat whitish, little, if any, tinged with pale vinaceous.

       d. Very pale below; pale buffy white of abdomen extending to lower margin of breast (Yucatán) ....**Dactylortyx thoracicus sharpei** (p. 385)

       dd. Darker and more rufescent below, whitish area limited to posterior part of abdomen.

         e. Feet slightly larger, middle toe without claw averaging 29.5 mm. or more (central Chiapas to western Guatemala).

          Dactylortyx thoracicus chiapensis (p. 386)

         ee. Feet slightly smaller, middle toe without claw averaging less than 28 mm. (El Salvador) ....**Dactylortyx thoracicus taylori** (p. 388)

          Dactylortyx thoracicus salvadoranus [71] (p. 387)

---

[71] Female of *D. t. lineolatus* not known.

DACTYLORTYX THORACICUS THORACICUS (Gambel)

VERACRUZ LONG-TOED QUAIL

Adult male.—Sides of forehead, superciliary stripe, cheeks, chin, and throat ochraceous-tawny with an orange tinge; a dusky sepia band from the lores under the eyes to the auriculars; center of forehead, crown, and occiput dark Prout's brown tinged with argus brown; the lateral feathers of the occiput with buffy-white shaft streaks and, in some cases, outer webs, forming a discontinuous whitish border to the occiput; nape like the occiput but the feathers tipped with black, forming a narrow collar of that color; interscapulars and feathers of upper back brownish drab to buffy brown broadly suffused marginally and, more narrowly, terminally with bright cinnamon-brown, the entire feather faintly vermiculated with dusky; scapulars light tawny cinnamon-brown darkening to deep hazel on the inner webs which are externally margined with between warm buff and ochraceous-buff, next to which is a lengthwise band of blackish; the rest of the inner webs stippled with blackish; the outer webs more sparsely speckled and paling to almost buffy near the margins, this buffy color forming an incomplete, indefinite bar proximally edged with dusky; upper wing coverts like the scapulars but with the pale buffy restricted to the shaft stripes, the blackish on the inner webs forming a large terminal blotch; the size of this blotch decreasing on the outer coverts; innermost secondary like the scapulars; rest of secondaries dull, dusky sepia on the inner webs; the outer webs tawny ochraceous-buff crossed by five or more wavy blackish bars, each of which is distally edged with pale ochraceous-buff, the interspaces sparingly stippled with dusky, the outer webs becoming more extensively plain dark sepia on the outer secondaries, primaries dark, dull sepia to clove brown externally blotched with pale cinnamon-buffy; a few of the feathers of the upper back like the interscapulars but subterminally heavily blotched with fuscous-black; feathers of back ochraceous-buff irregularly barred with dusky; lower back, rump, and upper tail coverts similar but duskier and more olivaceous—tawny-olive vermiculated with Saccardo's umber; rectrices dark, dull sepia barred, tipped, and incompletely edged with ochraceous-buff; breast, sides of lower neck, upper abdomen and sides buffy brown, the feathers of the breast washed with drab except marginally; and all the feathers with white shaft stripes, these stripes becoming narrower and fainter on the sides which are also brighter and more rufescent buffy brown; middle of abdomen white, little or not at all tinged with pale buffy; flanks like the sides but crossed by widely spaced fuscous-black wavy bars; under tail coverts similar but the dark bars turned into longitudinal U-shaped marks; thighs pale brownish drab; under wing coverts dark buffy brown.

Adult female.—Upperparts as in the male but the side of forehead, superciliary stripes, cheeks, and throat dark grayish vinaceous; chin and middle of upper throat whitish; breast and sides of lower neck between tawny and cinnamon-rufous with faintly paler shafts; upper abdomen, sides similar but less rufescent, more ochraceous-tawny, the flanks and under tail coverts as in the male; middle of abdomen whitish as in the male.

Natal down.—"Dark chestnut above, with a buffy line along either side of the rump, bright buffy superciliary area, dark line through the eye, red-brown bill, and somewhat clouded or mottled underparts" (*ex* Sutton and Pettingill, Auk, lix, 1942, 13).

Other plumages apparently unknown.

Adult male.—Wing 129.5; tail 51.5; culmen from base 16.2; middle toe without claw 29.4 mm. (1 specimen from Puebla; tarsi damaged).

Adult female.—Wing 123.5–125.0; tail 47.2; culmen from base 16.7–17.1; tarsus 32.4–32.6; middle toe without claw 26.7–27.7 mm. (2 specimens from Mexico and Veracruz).

Range.—Resident in the forests of the mountain slopes of eastern Mexico, from southern Tamaulipas (Gómez Farias) south to Veracruz (Río Seco, Jalapa, Atoyac, Córdoba, Hacienda de Los Atlixcos) and to Puebla (Metlaetoyuca).

Type locality.—Jalapa, Veracruz, Mexico.

Ortyx thoracicus GAMBEL, Proc. Acad. Nat. Sci. Philadelphia, iv, 1848, 77 (Jalapa, Veracruz, e. Mexico; coll. Acad. Nat. Sci. Philadelphia); Ann. Mag. Nat. Hist., ser. 2, iii, 1849, 317, 318.
Odontophorus thoracicus SCLATER, Proc. Zool. Soc. London, 1856, 310 (Córdoba, Veracruz).—BERISTAIN and LAURENCIO, Mem. y Rev. Soc. Cient. "Antonio Alzate," vii, No. 7-8, 1894, 218 (Veracruz).
O[dontophorus] thoracicus REICHENOW, Die Vögel, i, 1913, 316, part.
[*Odontophorus*] *thoracicus* SCLATER and SALVIN, Nom. Av. Neotr., 1873, 138, part.
Dactylortyx thoracicus OGILVIE-GRANT, Cat. Birds Brit. Mus., xxii, 1893, 429, part (Córdoba, Hacienda de Los Atlixcos and Atoyac, Veracruz); Handb. Game Birds, ii, 1897, 150.—NELSON, Proc. Biol. Soc. Washington, xii, 1898, 65 (descr. of type, from Jalapa).—SALVIN and GODMAN, Biol. Centr.-Amer., Aves, iii, 1903, 308, part (Hacienda de Los Atlixcos, Córdoba, Jalapa, and Atoyac, Veracruz).—SUTTON and BURLEIGH, Occ. Pap. Mus. Zool. Louisiana State Univ., No. 3, 1939, 28 (Gómez Farias, Tamaulipas).
[*Dactylortyx*] *thoracicus* SHARPE, Hand-list, i, 1899, 46, part.
Dactylortyx thoracicus thoracicus PETERS, Check-list Birds World, ii, 1934, 56 (distr.).—HELLMAYR and CONOVER, Cat. Birds Amer., i, No. 1, 1942, 281 (syn.; distr.).—SUTTON and PETTINGILL, Auk, lix, 1942, 12 (Gómez Farias region, southwestern Tamaulipas; habits; descr. of downy young; spec.).

DACTYLORTYX THORACICUS DEVIUS Nelson

JALISCAN LONG-TOED QUAIL

Adult male.—Similar to that of the nominate race but with many blackish or fuscous-blackish transverse markings on the interscapulars and with the middle of the abdomen buffy instead of whitish; the tawny-orange on the head and throat averaging deeper, the lateral feathers of the occiput with warm buffy, not whitish shaft stripes or outer webs.

Adult female.—Similar to that of the nominate race but with the whole underparts buffier, the middle of the lower abdomen deep warm buff instead of white; the interscapulars and nape also brighter, more rufescent—between tawny and cinnamon-rufous.

Juvenal male.—Similar to the adult but with the tawny-orange of the head and throat replaced by cinnamon-buff, the cheeks somewhat mottled with blackish; feathers of crown and occiput cinnamon-brown to Sayal brown broadly banded or blotched subterminally with black; outer webs of secondaries and of primaries with the brown mottlings more rufescent—Sayal brown; rectrices similarly more rufescent, tawny-hazel barred and mottled with blackish; breast, sides, and upper abdomen tawny-cinnamon spotted with fuscous to fuscous-black and with pale pinkish-buff shaft stripes; flanks, thighs, and under tail coverts slightly more rufescent than in adult.

Juvenal female.—Like the juvenal male but the blackish bars on the crown and occiput finer and less conspicuous, the pale parts of the sides of head, chin, and throat less ochraceous, pale hair brown to pale vinaceous-drab.

Adult male.—Wing 131–137 (133); tail 51–55 (53.4); culmen from base 17.4–18.3 (17.8); tarsus 35.6–37.3 (36.3); middle toe without claw 30–32.8 (31.4 mm.).[72]

Adult female.—Wing 128.5–131.5 (130.6); tail 50–55.5 (52.1); culmen from the base 17.1–17.2 (17.1); tarsus 33.7–35.5 (34.6); middle toe without claw 29.1–31 (29.9 mm.).[73]

Range.—Resident in the highland forests of western Mexico from Jalisco (San Sebastián) to Guerrero (Sierra Madre del Sur, Omilteme, 8,000 feet).

Type locality.—San Sebastián, Jalisco, Mexico.

[*Odontophorus*] *thoracicus* (not *Ortyx thoracicus* Gambel) SCLATER and SALVIN, Nom. Av. Neotr., 1873, 138, part.

Dactylortyx thoracicus OGILVIE-GRANT, Cat. Birds Brit. Mus., xxii, 1893, 429, part (Sierra Madre del Sur and Omilteme, 8,000 feet, Guerrero).—SALVIN and GODMAN, Biol. Centr.-Amer., Aves, iii, 1903, 308, part (San Sebastián, Jalisco; Omilteme and Sierra Madre del Sur, Guerrero).

[*Dactylortyx*] *thoracicus* SHARPE, Hand-list, i, 1899, 46, part.

Dactylortyx thoracicus subsp. GRISCOM, Bull. Mus. Comp. Zool., lxxv, 1934, 422 (Guerrero).

Dactylortyx devius NELSON, Proc. Biol. Soc. Washington, xii, 1898, 65, 68 (San Sebastián, Jalisco, sw. Mexico; coll. U. S. Nat. Mus.); xvi, 1903, 152, in text (crit.).

---

[72] Six specimens from Guerrero.
[73] Four specimens from Guerrero.

D[actylortyx] devius SALVIN AND GODMAN, Biol. Centr.-Amer., Aves, iii, 1903, 308,
    part, in text (crit.).
[Dactylortyx] devius SHARPE, Hand-list, i, 1899, 46.
Dactylortyx thoracicus devius PETERS, Check-list Birds World, ii, 1934, 56 (distr.).—
    HELLMAYR and CONOVER, Cat. Birds Amer., i, No. 1, 1942, 281 (syn.; distr.).

DACTYLORTYX THORACICUS LINEOLATUS (Gould)

OAXACAN LONG-TOED QUAIL

Adult male.—Similar to that of the nominate race but with the lower
back, rump, and upper tail coverts slightly darker, less buffy; the lateral
feathers of the occiput with their shaft stripes or their outer webs deep
warm buff, not white, with the shaft stripes of the feathers of the breast,
sides, and flanks much wider and slightly washed with buffy, the general
tone of the sides, flanks, thighs, and under tail coverts less tawny or
rufescent, somewhat more olivaceous.

Female.—Apparently unknown.

Adult male.—Wing 132–134; tail 52.5–56.5; culmen from the base 16.5–
17.0; tarsus 34–35.1; middle toe without claw 28.9–29.0 mm. (2 specimens
from Gineta Mountain, near Santa Efigenia, Oaxaca).

Range.—Resident in the forest of the mountain slopes of southeastern
Oaxaca (Gineta Mountain near Santa Efigenia; Tehuantepec); possibly
in adjacent part of western Oaxaca.

Type locality.—"Mexico."

Odontophorus lineolatus GOULD, Monogr. Odontoph., pt. 3, 1850, pl. 32 and text
    (Mexico; cotypes in Berlin Mus.; ex *Perdix lineolatus* Lichtenstein, manu-
    script).—GRAY, List Birds Brit. Mus., Gallinæ, pt. 5, 1867, 73.
[Strophiortyx] lineolatus BONAPARTE, Compt. Rend., xlii, 1856, 883.
Dactylortyx thoracicus lineolatus NELSON, Proc. Biol. Soc. Washington, xii, 1898,
    64, 66 (Mount Gineta, near Santa Efigenia, Oaxaca; descr.; synonymy).—
    PETERS, Check-list Birds World, ii, 1934, 56 (distr.).—HELLMAYR and CONOVER,
    Cat. Birds Amer., i, No. 1, 1942, 282 (syn.; distr.).
D[actylortyx] thoracicus lineolatus SALVIN and GODMAN, Biol. Centr.-Amer., Aves,
    iii, 1903, 308 in text (crit.).
[Dactylortyx] lineolatus SHARPE, Hand-list, i, 1899, 46.
[Odontophorus] thoracicus (not *Ortyx thoracicus* Gambel) SCLATER and SALVIN,
    Nom. Av. Neotr., 1873, 138, part.
Dactylortyx thoracicus OGILVIE-GRANT, Cat. Birds Brit. Mus., xxii, 1893, 429, part
    (in synonymy); Ibis, 1902, 242 (crit.).—SALVIN and GODMAN, Biol. Centr.-
    Amer., Aves, iii, 1903, 308, part (Santa Efigenia, Tehuantepec, Oaxaca).

DACTYLORTYX THORACICUS SHARPEI Nelson

YUCATÁN LONG-TOED QUAIL

Adult male.—Similar to that of the nominate race but generally paler
(the palest of all the races of the species), the sides and flanks paler and
grayer—fairly pale drab; the lower back, rump, and upper tail coverts
less buffy, more grayish—pale buffy drab vermiculated with drab.

Adult female.—Similar to that of the nominate race but with the chin and upper throat whitish with little or no vinaceous tinge; breast paler—pinkish cinnamon with a slight vinaceous-gray wash; upper abdomen pale buffy white as the middle and lower abdomen; outer webs of inner secondaries and of upper wing coverts pale, more grayish, less rufescent; superciliary stripe whiter.

Adult male.—Wing 117–121; tail 45–46.5; culmen from base 16.4–18.4; tarsus 31.4–31.6; middle toe without claw 26.1–27.4 mm. (2 specimens).

Adult female.—Wing 113.5–119.5 (117.3); tail 46–49 (47.3); culmen from base 16.6–17.3 (17.0); tarsus 30.1–30.4 (30.2); middle toe without claw 26.4–27.3 (26.8 mm.).[74]

Range.—Resident in the lowland tropical forests of Yucatán (Chichen Itzá, Tizimín, Rato) and Campeche (Apazote).

Type locality.—Apazote, Campeche, Mexico.

Odontophorus lineolatus (not of Gould) NEHRKORN, Journ. für Orn., 1881, 69 (Yucatán; descr. eggs).—BOUCARD, Proc. Zool. Soc. London, 1883, 460 (Yucatán; habits).

[*Strophiortyx*] *lineolatus* HEINE and REICHENOW, Nom. Mus. Hein. Orn., 1890, 295 (Yucatán).

Dactylortyx thoracicus sharpei NELSON, Proc. Biol. Soc. Washington, xvi, 1903, 152 (Apazote, Campeche; coll. U. S. Nat. Mus.).—COLE, Bull. Mus. Comp. Zool., 1, 1906, 116 (Chichen Itzá, Yucatán; food).—PETERS, Check-list Birds World, ii, 1934, 56 (distr.).—HELLMAYR and CONOVER, Cat. Birds Amer., i, No. 1, 1942, 282 (syn.; distr.).

[*Odontophorus*] *thoracicus* (not *Ortyx thoracicus* Gambel) SCLATER and SALVIN, Nom. Av. Neotr., 1873, 138, part.

Dactylortyx thoracicus OGILVIE-GRANT, Cat. Birds Brit. Mus., xxii, 1893, 429, part (Tizimín and Peto, Yucatán).—SALVIN and GODMAN, Biol. Centr.-Amer., Aves, iii, 1903, 308, part (Tizimín and Peto, Yucatán).

[*Dactylortyx*] *thoracicus* SHARPE, Hand-list, i, 1899, 46, part (Yucatán).

DACTYLORTYX THORACICUS CHIAPENSIS Nelson
CHIAPAN LONG-TOED QUAIL

Adult male.—Similar to that of the nominate race but with buffy to ochraceous-buff shaft stripes or outer webs on the lateral occipital feathers; the breast, sides, and flanks slightly more rufescent, and with the tarsus considerably longer.

Adult female.—Similar to that of the nominate race but with the chin and upper throat more whitish, little, if any, tinged with pale vinaceous; breast slightly more hazel, less tawny; and tarsus longer.

Juvenal male.—Similar to that of *Dactylortyx thoracicus devius* but with the blackish spots on the breast, upper abdomen, and sides larger, the rest of the feathers slightly paler, the shaft stripes wider; thighs and flanks less rufescent, buffier; tarsus shorter.

---

[74] Three specimens from Yucatán and Campeche.

Adult male.—Wing 123–137 (133); tail 51–56.5 (53.7); culmen from base 16.8–17.8 (17.3); tarsus 34.3–37.4 (35.9); middle toe without claw 29.7–32.9 (31.6 mm.).[75]

Adult female.—Wing 125–133 (128.2); tail 49–53.5 (51.3); culmen from base 16–16.8 (16.4); tarsus 32–34.3 (33.5); middle toe without claw 28.6–31.2 (29.5 mm.).[76]

Range.—Resident in cloud-forest subtropical areas from central Chiapas (Mount Ovando; Santa Rosa, Escuintla, Siltepec, Male, and Pico de Loro, Moriscal; San Cristóbal) to the Pacific Cordillera of Guatemala (Tecpam, Finca Perla, Volcán de Fuego, Quetzaltenango, Dueñas, Volcán de Santa María; 7,000 to 8,500 feet).

Type locality.—San Cristóbal, Chiapas, Mexico.

Odontophorus thoracicus (not *Ortyx thoracicus* Gambel) SALVIN and SCLATER, Ibis, 1860, 276 (Volcán de Fuego, Guatemala; habits).
[*Odontophorus*] *thoracicus* SCLATER and SALVIN, Nom. Av. Neotr., 1873, 138, part.
Dactylortyx thoracicus OGILVIE-GRANT, Cat. Birds Brit. Mus., xxii, 1893, 429, part (Volcán de Fuego, Dueñas, and Quezaltenango, Guatemala); Ibis, 1902, 242 (crit.).—SALVIN and GODMAN, Biol. Centr.-Amer., Aves, iii, 1903, 308, part (San Cristóbal, Chiapas; Santa María, Volcán de Fuego, Quezaltenango, and Dueñas, Guatemala).
[*Dactylortyx*] *thoracicus* SHARPE, Hand-list, i, 1899, 46, part (Guatemala).
Dactylortyx chiapensis NELSON, Proc. Biol. Soc. Washington, xii, 1898, 65, 66 (San Cristóbal, Chiapas, s. Mexico; coll. U. S. Nat. Mus.; descr.; crit.).
D[*actylortyx*] *chiapensis* SALVIN and GODMAN, Biol. Centr.-Amer., Aves, iii, 1903, 308, in text (crit.).
[*Dactylortyx*] *chiapensis* SHARPE, Hand-list, i, 1899, 46 (Guatemala).
Dactylortyx thoracicus chiapensis GRISCOM, Bull. Amer. Mus. Nat. Hist., lxiv, 1932, 107 (Tecpam and Quezaltenango, Guatemala; habits; distr.).—PETERS, Check-list Birds of World, ii, 1934, 56 (distr.).—CONOVER, Proc. Biol. Soc. Washington, l, 1937, 73, in text (crit.), 74 (spec.; Mexico and Guatemala).—HELLMAYR and CONOVER, Cat. Birds Amer., i, No. 1, 1942, 282 (distr.; syn.).—DEL CAMPO, Anal. Inst. Biol., xiii, No. 2, 1942, 700 (Chiapas; Catarinas; spec.).

DACTYLORTYX THORACICUS SALVADORANUS Dickey and van Rossem

SALVADOREAN LONG-TOED QUAIL

Adult male.—Similar to that of the nominate race but without the white lateral edge to the occiput; the breast and sides and flanks paler, more grayish drab, the middle of the abdomen less white, more washed with drab to hair brown; the interscapulars with more conspicuous white shafts; tarsus shorter than in *Dactylortyx thoracicus chiapensis,* and the pale shafts of the feathers of the breast and sides and upper abdomen narrow and white; iris brown; bill blackish brown; tarsi and toes plumbeous horn color; claws brownish horn color.[77]

---

[75] Ten specimens from Chiapas and Guatemala.
[76] Six specimens from Chiapas and Guatemala.
[77] According to Dickey and van Rossem, Birds of El Salvador, 1938, 154, the basal half of the mandible is paler in birds in the first autumn than in older birds.

Adult female.—Similar to that of *Dactylortyx thoracicus chiapensis* but the feet slightly smaller, the middle toe without the claw averaging less than 28 mm.

Adult male.—Wing 126–126.5; tail 51–52; culmen from base 17.1–17.6; tarsus 33.5–33.7; middle toe without claw 27.6–28.5 mm.[78]

Adult female.—Wing 125–128; tail 53–55; culmen from base 17.1; tarsus 33.2–34.1; middle toe without claw 26–28.6 mm. (2 specimens).

Range.—Confined to the oak forest in the Arid Upper Tropical Zone on Volcán de San Miguel, El Salvador, 2,500 to 4,000 feet.

Type locality.—Volcán de San Miguel, alt. 4,000 feet, Dept. San Miguel, El Salvador.

Dactylortyx thoracicus (not *Ortyx thoracicus* Gambel) OGILVIE-GRANT, Cat. Birds Brit. Mus., xxii, 1893, 429, part (Volcán de San Miguel, El Salvador).— SALVIN and GODMAN, Biol. Centr.-Amer., Aves, iii, 1903, 308, part (Volcán de San Miguel, El Salvador).

Dactylortyx thoracicus salvadoranus DICKEY and VAN ROSSEM, Proc. Biol. Soc. Washington, xli, 1928, 129 (Volcán de San Miguel, alt. 4,000 feet, Dept. San Miguel, El Salvador; type in Dickey coll., Univ. California at Los Angeles; descr.; crit.); Birds El Salvador, 1938, 153 (El Salvador; Volcán de San Miguel; spec.; habits; colors of soft parts).—PETERS, Check-list Birds of World, ii, 1934, 56 (distr.).—CONOVER, Proc. Biol. Soc. Washington, 1, 1937, 74 (spec.; Volcán de San Miguel, El Salvador).—HELLMAYR and CONOVER, Cat. Birds Amer., i, No. 1, 1942, 253 (syn.; distr.).—MARSHALL, Condor, xlv, 1943, 22 (El Salvador; Cerro del Agua).

DACTYLORTYX THORACICUS TAYLORI van Rossem

TAYLOR'S LONG-TOED QUAIL

Adult male.—Similar to that of *Dactylortyx thoracicus salvadoranus* but larger, the wings averaging 130 mm. in length, and generally more rufescent on the entire underparts, the breast and sides suffused with pale Sayal brown; the interscapulars more buffy brown, less grayish in their median portions.

Adult female.—Not certainly distinguishable from that of *D. t. salvadoranus.*

Adult male.—Wing 124–133 (130); tail 52.5–60.5 (55.8); culmen from base 17.1–18.7 (17.8); tarsus 31.8–33.6 (32.4); middle toe without claw 28.9–29.6 (29.2 mm.).[79]

Adult female.—Wing 121–124 (122.5); tail 51.5–55 (53.5); culmen from base 16.8–17.2 (17.0); tarsus 31.2–32.6 (31.8); middle toe without claw 26.9–28.6 (27.9 mm.).[80]

Range.—Resident in the oak and coffee association of the Arid Upper

---

[78] Two specimens including the type.

[79] Three specimens including the type.

[80] Three specimens.

Tropical Zone on Mount Cacaguatique, and probably of other interior areas of El Salvador.

Type locality.—Mount Cacaguatique, Dept. San Miguel, El Salvador.

Dactylortyx thoracicus salvadoranus DICKEY and VAN ROSSEM, Proc. Biol. Soc. Washington, xli, 1928, 129, part (Mount Cacaguatique, El Salvador).
Dactylortyx thoracicus taylori VAN ROSSEM, Trans. San Diego Soc. Nat. Hist., vii, 1932, 151 (Mount Cacaguatique, 3,500 feet, Dept. San Miguel, El Salvador; type in coll. D. R. DICKEY, Univ. California at Los Angeles; descr.; crit.).— PETERS, Check-list Birds World, ii, 1934, 56, part (Mount Cacaguatique, El Salvador).—CONOVER, Proc. Biol. Soc. Washington, l, 1937, 74 (spec.; Mount Cacaguatique, El Salvador).—DICKEY and VAN ROSSEM, Birds El Salvador, 1938, 154 (El Salvador, Mount Cacaguatique; spec.; distr.; colors of soft parts; habits; crit.).—HELLMAYR and CONOVER, Cat. Birds Amer., i, No. 1, 1942, 283 (syn.; distr.).—MARSHALL, Condor, xlv, 1943, 23 (El Salvador; Mount Cacaguatique).

DACTYLORTYX THORACICUS FUSCUS Conover

HONDURANIAN LONG-TOED QUAIL

Adult male.—Similar to that of the nominate race but without the whitish marks on the sides of the occiput; the breast and sides slightly less brownish, with no cinnamon-buffy wash, more dusky grayish earth brown (in some specimens these parts are considerably paler as well).

Adult female.—The darkest of all the races of the species; similar to that of the nominate form but with the top of the head fuscous-black; the breast, upper abdomen, and sides cinnamon-brown; the white on the middle abdomen more restricted than in the typical race; and the lateral portions of the interscapular feathers darker—dusky auburn.

Adult male.—Wing 121.5–130.0 (126.9); tail 48.0–52.5 (50.1); culmen from base 17.4–18.3 (17.9); tarsus 31.6–36.2 (33.6); middle toe without claw 28.6–30.6 (29.4 mm.).[81]

Adult female.—Wing 123.0–130.0 (126.2); tail 52; culmen from base 16.1–17.2 (16.8); tarsus 34.1–35.2 (34.6); middle toe without claw 29.0–29.4 (29.2 mm.).[82]

Range.—Resident in tropical forests of southern Honduras, Dept. Tegucigalpa (Alto Cantoral, Cantoral, Rancho Quemado, San Juancito, and Olancho, Catacamas).

Type locality.—Alto Cantoral, Dept. Tegucigalpa, Honduras.

Dactylortyx thoracicus taylori VAN ROSSEM, Trans. San Diego Soc. Nat. Hist., vii, No. 13, 1932, 152, part (s. Honduras; range only).—PETERS, Check-list Birds World, ii, 1934, 56, part (Honduras).
Dactylortyx thoracicus salvadoranus (not of Dickey and van Rossem) STONE, Proc. Acad. Nat. Sci. Philadelphia, lxxxiv, 1932, 302 (Honduras; San Juancito, 6,300-6,800 feet, in cloud forest).

---

[81] Four specimens including the type.
[82] Three specimens.

Dactylortyx thoracicus fuscus CONOVER, Proc. Biol. Soc. Washington, 1, 1937, 73 (Alto Cantoral, Tegucigalpa, Honduras; descr.; crit.; distr.)., 74 (spec.; Alto Cantoral, Cantoral, Rancho Quemado, San Juancito, all in Honduras).— HELLMAYR and CONOVER, Cat. Birds Amer., i, No. 1, 1942, 284 (syn.; distr.).

Genus CYRTONYX Gould

Cyrtonyx GOULD, Monogr. Odontoph., pt. i, 1844, pl. [2] and text (= pl. **7 of bound volume**). (Type, by monotypy, *Ortyx massena* Lesson = *O. montezumae* Vigors.)

Odontophorus REICHENOW, Die Vögel, i, 1913, 316, part.

Medium-sized, very short-tailed Odontophorinae (wing about 117–135 mm.) with tips of outstretched toes extending far beyond tip of the short, soft, nearly concealed tail, tips of lateral claws extending far beyond base of middle claw, tarsus less than one-fourth as long as wing, with a full occipital crest of soft, broad, blended and decurved (decumbent) feathers, sides and flanks spotted or barred (the head grotesquely striped and banded with white and black in adult males), and sexes wholly unlike in coloration.

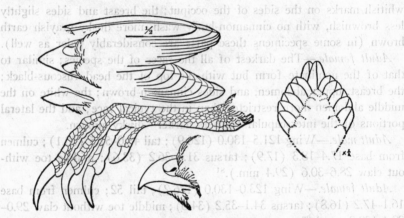

FIGURE 22.—*Cyrtonyx montezumae.*

Bill moderate in size, the chord of culmen (from extreme base) decidedly more than half the length of tarsus; depth of bill at base greater than distance from anterior end of nasal fossa to tip of maxilla, and exceeding width of bill at rictus; culmen strongly convex proximally, less so distally broadly, or not distinctly ridged; gonys moderately broad, nearly straight, strongly ascending terminally. Outermost primary a little shorter than seventh (from outside), the third and fourth longest. Tail decidedly less than half as long as wing, graduated, the rectrices (12) soft, tapering terminally, the longest scarcely longer than and hardly distinguishable from the coverts. Tarsus only one-fourth as long as wing, much shorter than middle toe with claw, the planta tarsi with hexagonal scutella, those on inner side smaller and more longitudinal than those on the outer side; tips of lateral claws extending far beyond base (that of outer toe to or beyond middle) of middle claw, the claws long, slightly curved, and blunt, that of middle toe longer than basal phalanx of that toe.

Plumage and coloration.—Head with a full, decumbent crest of broad, soft, and blended feathers, these longest on occiput and nape, where they are strongly decurved. Sexes wholly unlike in color, the adult males with head boldly marked with black and white, in harlequinlike pattern, the chin and throat velvety black, bordered below by a white collar across foreneck and ascending to beneath crest, upperparts olive-brownish and grayish spotted and barred with black and with conspicuous streaks of white, buff, or rufous on back and scapulars, sides and flanks with rounded spots of white, cinnamon-buff or cinnamon-rufous spots on a dark gray or slate-colored ground, or chestnut barred with black, the lower abdomen, thighs, anal region, and under tail coverts uniform black: adult females light cinnamon or pinkish cinnamon, the upperparts barred with black, the back and scapulars streaked with buff, head without conspicuous black or any white markings, and underparts pale cinnamon or pinkish cinnamon with a few blackish markings.

Range.—Highlands of Guatemala and Mexico and contiguous portion of southwestern United States. (Two "species," which may, however, prove to be extremes of an unusually variable single specific stock.)

KEY TO THE FORMS OF THE GENUS CYRTONYX

a. Chin and middle of throat black (males).
  b. With no white transverse band immediately posterior to the black throat
    (Mount Orizaba, Veracruz)....**Crytonyx montezumae merriami** (p. 398)
  bb. With a well-defined white transverse band immediately posterior to the black throat.
    c. Feathers of flanks with rufous or chestnut markings.
      d. Flank feathers slate-gray marked with round spots of rufous or chestnut (Michoacán to central Oaxaca).
           Cyrtonyx montezumae sallei (p. 399)
      dd. Flank feathers almost wholly rich rufous or chestnut varied transversely with black and gray (eastern Oaxaca south in highlands to northwestern Nicaragua)..........................**Cyrtonyx ocellatus** (p. 400)
    c. Feathers of flanks with no rufous or chestnut.
      d. Upper surface of wings definitely grayish (central Texas to Arizona and south to northern Coahuila, Chihuahua, and Sonora).
          Cyrtonyx montezumae mearnsi (p. 392)
      dd. Upper surface of wings with no grayish, but definitely brown (central Tamaulipas to Durango and Sinaloa south to Puebla, Michoacán, and Valley of Mexico)......**Cyrtonyx montezumae montezumae** (p. 396)
aa. Chin and middle of throat white or buffy (females).[83]

---

[83] Female of *C. montezumae merriami* not known.

b. Shaft stripes of upperparts usually white, only very slightly tinged with buff
(central Texas to Arizona, south to northern Coahuila, Chihuahua, and
Sonora) . . . . .Cyrtonyx montezumae mearnsi (p. 392)

bb. Shaft stripes of upperparts definitely buffy.

c. Breast and abdomen slightly paler, pinkish cinnamon (eastern Oaxaca south
in highlands to northwestern Nicaragua) . . . .Cyrtonyx ocellatus (p. 400)

cc. Breast and abdomen slightly duskier—vinaceous-fawn to fawn color.

d. Upperparts with more blackish, the general color of the brown areas
slightly darker on the average—Saccardo's umber (Michoacán to central
Oaxaca) . . . . .Cyrtonyx montezumae sallei (p. 399)

dd. Upperparts with less blackish, the general color of the brown areas
slightly paler on the average—tawny-olive (central Tamaulipas to
Durango and Sinaloa south to Puebla, Michoacán, and the Valley of
Mexico) . . . . .Cyrtonyx montezumae montezumae (p. 396)

CYRTONYX MONTEZUMAE MEARNSI Nelson

MEARNS'S HARLEQUIN QUAIL

Adult male.—Lores and middle of forehead and of crown black, broadly
bordered on each side with white; a black supraorbital line from the
lores to the posterolateral angle of the occiput; this band continuous
through the lores with a paler one (slate to blackish slate) one extending
posteroventrally demarcating the throat from the face and ending below
the cheeks where it expands ventrally to form a triangle with a medio-
ventral extension (which may or may not reach the black median area
of the throat); eyelids black, a large black rounded patch from below
the eye to the auriculars; chin and middle of throat black; all intervening cephalic areas white; posterior part of crown and occiput black
much variegated with Sayal brown to Saccardo's umber, paling on the
nape to warm buff, with or without a dusky tinge; interscapulars and
feathers of upper back barred with heavy dark and narrow faint bands
of black and with the interspaces varying from onionskin pink to pale
Mikado brown, the feathers with prominent shaft streaks of ivory white,
occasionally tinged with buffy; scapulars similar but edged with ashy and
with the shaft stripes more buffy; innermost secondaries varying from
buffy light grayish olive to deep smoke gray with six or seven transverse
black blotches on each web and with buffy shaft stripes; other secondaries
similar on their outer webs but increasingly suffused with pale dull clove
brown on their inner ones, the innermost ones almost uniformly of this
color; primaries dark clove brown to fuscous, their outer webs marginally
spotted with white; greater and inner median upper wing coverts mouse
gray to deep smoke gray transversely spotted with black; lesser and outer
median coverts similar but with the spots white instead; feathers of back
and lower back and rump like the interscapulars but without the pale shaft
stripes and with the brown areas more rufescent and narrower, the black

bars wider; upper tail coverts and rectrices similar but with conspicuous pale buffy shaft stripes and with brown replaced by deep smoke gray; a broad band of white across the upper breast separating the black of the throat from the lower breast, this white band continuous laterally with the white areas of the sides of the head, and posteriorly narrowly edged with black; feathers of sides of breast and of upper abdomen and a narrow line across the breast, just posterior to the black-edged white band, slate to blackish slate, with two or three large white spots on each web; median area of lower breast and upper abdomen very dark, rich, blackish chestnut, becoming black on the lower abdomen, lower flanks, thighs, and under tail-coverts; under wing coverts dull grayish wood brown; iris dark brown; upper mandible black, becoming pale blue at the gape; lower mandible pale blue; feet pale blue; claws pale brown.

Adult female.—Forehead, center of crown, and occiput vinaceous-buff to avellaneous, the feathers broadly barred with black and with pale pinkish buffy shaft stripes, the dark bars becoming fewer on the occiput; nape vinaceous-buff to avellaneous practically unmarked with black; scapulars, interscapulars, and feathers of the upper back wood brown to Sayal brown crossed by broad, dark, and by narrow, faint, fuscous to blackish bars and with conspicuous pale buffy to pale pinkish buff shaft stripes; secondaries avellaneous to bright pinkish wood brown barred with black, each of the black bars with a wood-brown center, these bars disappearing on the inner webs of the outer secondaries; primaries dull clove brown with marginal spots of whitish on their outer webs; upper wing coverts pinkish wood brown sparingly barred or flecked with dusky sepia; feathers of back and lower back like the interscapulars but without conspicuous pale shaft stripes and with the heavy black markings more coalesced into large blotches, rump and upper tail coverts and rectrices pinkish wood brown transversely broadly spotted with blackish (these markings not continuous across both webs); and with narrow pale pinkish-buff shaft stripes; lores pinkish wood brown, flecked blackish; broad supraorbital band, cheeks, and auriculars similar; circumocular area and a posterior projection from it above the auriculars whitish, some of the feathers with minute black tips; chin and throat white; sides of throat and lower throat pinkish wood brown flecked with dusky; breast bright vinaceous wood brown with faint pale pinkish white spots at the tips of some of the feathers, which may or may not have narrow, dusky shaft stripes; abdomen similar but slightly paler, slightly more ochraceous, less vinaceous; the feathers of the middle upper part of the abdomen more flecked and medially streaked with blackish; flanks, thighs, and under tail coverts similar but with few or no blackish marks; under wing coverts wood brown obscurely spotted with grayish white.

Juvenal (sexes alike)[84].—Similar to the adult female on the upperparts but averaging slightly more tawny on the interscapulars, scapulars, and back; the crown averaging darker, the blackish markings more extensive; below much less vinaceous or pinkish, more whitish, often with a strong suffusion of warm buff, the breast and the lateral abdominal feathers transversely heavily spotted with fuscous to fuscous-black and with white shaft stripes; thighs and vent and under tail coverts ochraceous-buff.

Natal down (sexes alike).—Forehead, sides of face, and broad lateral areas of crown and occiput pale cinnamon-buff; center of crown and wider center of occiput, nape, and spinal band all the way to the tail auburn to dark argus brown; wings deep ochraceous-buff; rest of upperparts pale grayish cinnamon-buff; a band of dark sepia to clove brown on flanks and thighs; a narrow fuscous black line from behind the eye to the postero-lateral corner of the nape; chin and throat white; underparts of body white tinged with pale ashy pinkish buff.

Adult male.—Wing 113.5–129 (123.6); tail 51–61.5 (55.7); culmen from base 14.7–16.4 (15.5); tarsus 28.1–30.8 (29.9); middle toe without claw 21–24 (22.6 mm.).[85]

Adult female.—Wing 110.5–126 (119.0); tail 47.5–58 (52.9); culmen from base 14.6–16.7 (15.7); tarsus 27.9–30.4 (29.0); middle toe without claw 20.3–24.5 (22.0 mm.).[86]

Range.—Resident in lower parts of canyons and in rough, rather rocky open country with coverage of grass, bushes, mescal, and small trees, at elevations of from 4,000 to 9,000 feet, from westcentral Texas (Mason, Kerrville, San Antonio, Bandera Hills, Laredo, etc.); central New Mexico (Zuni, San Mateo, White, and Guadalupe Mountains, etc.); and Arizona (Fort Whipple, Camp Verde, Mogollon Ridge, Wilcox, Marsh Lake, Huachuca and Whetstone Mountains, Catalina, and Chiricahua Mountains) south to northern Nuevo León and northern Coahuila (Carmen Mountains), northern Chihuahua (Jesús María and Cañada); Sonora (Los Pinitos, Los Vengos, Guirocoba, Nacori, Huerachi, and Yacoera), and northwestern Durango (Pasaje de las Mujeres).

Type locality.—Fort Huachuca, Ariz.

---

[84] Bent, U. S. Nat. Mus. Bull. 162, 1932, 87, states that in this "plumage the sexes are much alike, except that in the young male the crissum, lower belly, and flanks are black, and the center of the breast is suffused with brown, whereas in the young female these parts are white; these characters are conspicuous in flight. . . ." The material studied in the present connection does not bear this out; I cannot help but conclude that Bent was misled by birds in an advanced stage of the postjuvenal molt. The true juvenal plumage is worn for a short time only before feathers of the first winter (adult) plumage begin to appear, first on the breast, then on the abdomen.

[85] Thirty-one specimens from Texas, New Mexico, Coahuila, Chihuahua, Sonora, Durango, and Nayarit.

[86] Twenty-six specimens from Texas, New Mexico, Arizona, Chihuahua, Durango, and Nayarit.

Cyrtonyx massena (not *Ortyx massena* Lesson) BAIRD, *in* Rep. Stansbury's Expl.
Great Salt Lake, 1852, 334 (San Pedro and Rio Pecos, N. Mex.) ; Rep. Pacific
R. R. Surv., ix, 1858, 647 (Chihuahua; Fort Davis, Turkey Creek, Las Moras,
and Laredo, w. Texas; Mimbres to Rio Grande; Nuevo León) ; Rep. U. S. and
Mex. Bound, Surv., ii, pt. 2, 1859, 23 (Turkey Creek and Laredo, Tex.; Nuevo
León) ; Cat. North Amer. Birds, 1859, No. 477.—CASSIN, Illustr. Birds Cali-
fornia, Texas, etc., 1853, 21, pl. 4.—DRESSER, Ibis, 1866, 29 (Bandera Hills,
Texas).—COUES, Proc. Acad. Nat. Sci. Philadelphia, 1866, 95 (Fort Whipple,
Ariz.) ; Check List North Amer. Birds, 1874, No. 394; ed. 2, 1882, No. 578;
Birds Northwest, 1874, 443, excl. syn. part.—COOPER, Orn. California, Land
Birds, 1870, 558 (Arizona).—BAIRD, BREWER, and RIDGWAY, Hist. North Amer.
Birds, iii, 1874, 492, excl. syn. part, pl. 61, fig. 2, pl. 64, figs. 3, 6.—BREWSTER, Bull.
Nuttall Orn. Club, viii, 1883, 35 (Chiricahua Mountains, Arizona).

[*Cyrtonyx*] *massena* COUES, Key North Amer. Birds, 1872, 239.—SCLATER and
SALVIN, Nom. Av. Neotr., 1873, 137, part.

C[*yrtonyx*] *massena* COUES, Key North Amer. Birds, ed. 2, 1884, 594.

Cyrtonyx montezumae (not *Ortyx montezumae* Vigors) AMERICAN ORNITHOLOGISTS'
UNION, Check-list, 1886, 110, No. 296; ed. 2, 1895, 110, No. 296.—SCOTT,
Auk, iii, 1886, 389 (Pinal, Santa Catalina, and Santa Rita Mountains, Ariz.,
up to 5,700 feet).—LLOYD, Auk, iv, 1887, 187 (localities in Tom Green County,
w. Texas; Nueces and Frio Canyons).—BECKHAM, Proc. U. S. Nat. Mus., x,
1887, 637, 656 (Leon Springs, Bexar County, Tex.).—COOKE, Bird Migr. Mississippi Valley, 1888, 103 (Mason, Tom Green County, etc., Tex.).—BENDIRE,
Life Hist. North Amer. Birds, i, 1892, 35.—ALLEN, Bull. Amer. Mus. Nat.
Hist., v, 1893, 23 (Los Pinitos, ne. Sonora).—OGILVIE-GRANT, Cat. Birds Brit.
Mus., xxii, 1893, 425, part (Yecoera, Sonora; Jesús María and Cañada, Chihuahua; Bandera Hills, Tex.; Apache and Crittenden, Ariz.) ; Ibis, 1902, 241
(crit.).—DWIGHT, Auk, xvii, 1900, 50 (molt, etc.).—SALVIN and GODMAN, Biol.
Centr.-Amer., Aves, iii, 1903, 305, part (Los Pinitos, Los Vengos, Nacori,
Huerachi, and Yecoera, ne. Sonora; Jesús María and Cañada, n. Chihuahua).

[*Cyrtonyx*] *montezumæ* SHARPE, Hand-list, i, 1899, 46, part.

C[*yrtonyx*] *montezumæ* RIDGWAY, Man. North Amer. Birds, 1887, 194, part.

Cyrtonyx montezumæ mearnsi NELSON, Auk, xvii, 1900, 255 (Fort Huachuca, s.
Arizona; coll. U. S. Nat. Mus.) ; xix, 1902, 390 (crit.), pl. 15, fig. 1.—BAILEY,
Handb. Birds Western United States, 1902, 122; Birds New Mexico, 1928,
223 (New Mexico; habits).—OGILVIE-GRANT, Ibis, 1903, 111 (crit.).—FUERTES,
Condor, v, 1903, 113 (habits in Texas).—SWARTH, Pacific Coast Avif., No. 4,
1904, 4 (Huachuca Mountains, Ariz.; more abundant on western than on
eastern slope) ; Condor, xxvi, 1909, 39 (distr. in U. S.; molt) ; Pacific Coast
Avif., No. 10, 1914, 22 (Arizona; Upper Sonoran and Transition Zone of
central and southeastern Arizona; 4,000 to 9,000 feet) ; Proc. California Acad.
Sci., ser. 4, xviii, 1929, 290 (Stone Cabin and Madera Canyons, San Rafael
Valley, Ariz.).—MONTGOMERY, Auk, xxii, 1905, 13 (Brewster County, Tex.).—
JUDD, U. S. Biol. Surv. Bull. 21, 1905, 63 (range, habits, food, etc.).—MILLER,
Bull. Amer. Mus. Nat. Hist., xxii, 1906, 162 (Pasaje de las Mujeres, nw.
Durango).—AMERICAN ORNITHOLOGISTS' UNION, Check-list, ed 3, 1910, 137;
ed. 4, 1931, 91.—LACEY, Auk, xxviii, 1911, 206 (7 miles sw. of Kerrville, Tex.).—
WYMAN and BURNELL, Field Book Birds Southwestern United States, 1925,
86 (descr.; habits).—BRUNER, Condor, xxviii, 1926, 232 (Baboquivari Moun-
tains, Ariz.).—OBERHOLSER, Sci. Publ. Cleveland Mus. Nat. Hist., i, 1930, 84
(spec.; Huachuca Mountains, Ariz.).—VAN ROSSEM, Trans. San Diego Soc.
Nat. Hist., vi, 1931, 247 (Sonora, Mexico) ; viii, 1936, 128 (south-central
Arizona) ; Bull. Mus. Comp. Zool., lxvii, 1934, 432 (distr. in Sonora).—BENT,

U. S. Nat. Mus. Bull. 162, 1932, 84 (life hist.; plum.; distr.).—PETERS, Check-list Birds World, ii, 1934, 57 (distr.).—CAMPBELL, Condor, xxxvi, 1934, 201, 202 abundant; Pena Blanca, s. Ariz.).—GROEBBELS, Der Vögel, ii, 1937, 167 (data on breeding biology), 298, in text (egg color), 402, in text (parental care).— BURLEIGH and LOWERY, Occ. Pap. Mus. Zool. Louisiana State Univ., No. 8, 1940, 99 (w. Texas; Guadelupe Mountains; hist.; now scarce).—HELLMAYR and CONOVER, Cat. Birds Amer., i, No. 1, 1942, 284 (distr.; syn.).—PETRIDES, Trans. 7th North Amer. Wildlife Conf., 1942, 322 in text, 327 in text (age indicators in plumage).

Cyrtonyx montezumae mearnsi AMADON, Auk, lx, 1943, 226 (body weight and egg weight).—MILLER, Condor, xlv, 1943, 104, in text.

Cyrtonyx montezuma mearnsi VAN TYNE and SUTTON, Misc. Publ Mus. Zool. Univ. Mich., No. 37, 1937, 27 (Brewster County, Tex.; nesting).

Cyrtonyx m[ontezumae] mearnsi PALMER, Condor, xxx, 1928, 288, in text (patronymics).

C[yrtonyx] montezumae mearnsi SALVIN and GODMAN, Biol. Centr.-Amer., Aves, iii, 1903, 306, in text (crit.).

Cyrtonyx montezumae montezumae VAN ROSSEM, Trans. San Diego Soc. Nat. Hist., vi, 1931, 246 (Guirocoba, Sonora).

Cyrtonyx montezumae morio VAN ROSSEM, Trans. San Diego Soc. Nat. Hist., ix, 1942, 379 (Guirocoba, se. Sonora; descr.; crit.; distr.).

CYRTONYX MONTEZUMAE MONTEZUMAE (Vigors)

MASSENA QUAIL

Adult male.—Similar to that of *Cyrtonyx montezumae mearnsi* but with the upper surface of the wings less grayish, more buffy or brownish; the whole upperparts averaging more brownish and slightly darker, the white areas on the head and the white spots on the underparts sometimes strongly tinged with buffy.

Adult female.—Similar to that of *C. m. mearnsi* but averaging slightly darker above and below, the shaft stripes of the dorsal body feathers usually more buffy, less whitish; the breast and abdomen darker—vinaceous-fawn to fawn color.

Other plumages not certainly distinguishable from the corresponding ones of *C. m. mearnsi.*

Adult male.—Wing 114.5–131 (121.4); tail 47.5–63 (53.2); culmen from base 14–16.5 (15.5); tarsus 27.5–33 (30.1); middle toe without claw 19–24.5 (22.3 mm.).[87]

Adult female.—Wing 114–123.5 (118.3); tail 49–60 (55.3); culmen from base 14.7–16.1 (15.3); tarsus 27.9–30.8 (29.0); middle toe without claw 19.5–22.2 (20.4 mm.).[88]

Range.—Resident in rocky, scrubby, open wooded country of Mexico from west-central Tamaulipas (Yerba Buena, Rampahuila, Carricitos, etc.); southern Nuevo León; southeastern Coahuila (Saltillo); southern

---

[87] Sixteen specimens from Sinaloa, Nuevo León, Jalisco, Hidalgo, Mexico City, and Puebla.

[88] Six specimens from Jalisco, Guadalajara, Hidalgo, and Michoacán.

Durango (San Juan River); and Sinaloa (Sierra Madre, Choix, Mazatlán, and Juan Lisiarraga); south through Nayarit (Tepic); Michoacán (Los Reyes and Tancitaro), Guadalajara (Jalisco) and the Valley of Mexico (Mexico City) to Puebla (Chalchicomula), Hidalgo (Isolo), and Oaxaca (La Parada).

Type locality.—Mexico.

Ortyx montezumæ VIGORS, Zool. Journ., v, 1830, 275 (Mexico).—JARDINE and SELBY, Illustr. Orn., ii, 1830, text to pl. 107.—BONAPARTE, Proc. Zool. Soc. London, 1837, 114 (crit.; descr. female).

Cyrtonyx montezumæ STEJNEGER, Auk, ii, 1885, 46 (crit. nomencl.).—AMERICAN ORNITHOLOGISTS' UNION, Check-list, 1886, No. 296, part; ed. 2, 1895, No. 296, part.—OGILVIE-GRANT, Cat. Birds Brit. Mus., xxii, 1893, 425, part (Sierra Madre above Ciudad Victoria, Tamaulipas; near Choix, Sinaloa; Sierra Madre, Tepic; near City of Mexico; Puebla); Handb. Game Birds, ii, 1897, 146 (monogr.).—JOUY, Proc. U. S. Nat. Mus., xvi, 1894, 790 (Guadalajara, Jalisco).—NELSON, Auk, xix, 1902, pl. 15, fig. 2.—SALVIN and GODMAN, Biol. Centr.-Amer., Aves, iii, 1903, 305, part (near Choix, Sinaloa; Sierra Madre, Tepic; Guadalajara, Jalisco; Valley of Mexico; City of Mexico; Puebla; La Parada, Oaxaca; Tamaulipas).—SETH-SMITH, L'Oiseau, x, 1929, 763 (care in captivity).

C[yrtonyx] montezumæ RIDGWAY, Man. North Amer. Birds, 1887, 194, part.

[Cyrtonyx] montezumæ SHARPE, Hand-list, i, 1899, 46, part.

Cyrtonyx montezumæ montezumæ MILLER, Bull. Amer. Mus. Nat. Hist., xxi, 1905, 342 (Juan Lisiarraga, s. Sinaloa; habits).—AMERICAN ORNITHOLOGISTS' UNION, Check-list, ed. 3, 1910, 137.—PHILLIPS, Auk, xxviii, 1911, 74 (Yerba Buena, Rampahuila, and Carricitos, s. Tamaulipas).—VAN ROSSEM, Trans. San Diego Soc. Nat. Hist., vi, 1931, 246 (Sonora; Mexico).—PETERS, Check-list Birds World, ii, 1934, 57 (distr.).—HELLMAYR and CONOVER, Cat. Birds Amer., i, No. 1, 1942, 286 (syn.; distr.).—BLAKE and HANSON, Publ. Field Mus. Nat. Hist., zool. serv., xxii, 1942, 527 (Michoacán, Tancitaro; spec.).

Cyrtonyx m[ontezuma] montezuma BAILEY and CONOVER, Auk, lii, 1935, 422, in text (Río San Juan, 7,000 feet, Durango, Mexico).

O[dontophorus] (Cyrtonyx) montezumae REICHENOW, Die Vögel, i, 1913, 316.

Ortyx massena LESSON, Cent. Zool., 1832, 189 (nomen nudum); Illustr. Zool., 1835, pl. 52, text [p. 3] (Mexico; type in Rivoli collection).

Ortyx massenae FINSCH, Abh. Nat. Verh. Bremen, 1870, 357 (Guadalajara, Jalisco).

Cyrtonyx massena GOULD, Monogr. Odontoph., pt. 1, 1884, pl. 7 and text.—REICHENBACH, Synop. Av, iii, 1848, Gallinaceae, pl. 194, figs. 1685, 1686.—McCOWN, Ann. Lyc. Nat. Hist. New York, vi, 1853, 10 (Mountains near Saltillo, se. Coahuila; habits).—SCLATER, Proc. Zool. Soc. London, 1858, 305 (La Parada, Oaxaca).—GRAY, List Birds Brit. Mus., pt. 5, Gallinæ, 1867, 74.—LAWRENCE, Mem. Boston Soc. Nat. Hist., ii, 1874, 306 (Guadalajara, Jalisco).—BERISTAIN and LAURENCIO, Mem. y Rev. Soc. Cient. "Antonio Alzate," vii, 1894, 219 (Mexico; Valley of Mexico).

[Cyrtonyx] massena SCLATER and SALVIN, Nom. Av. Neotr., 1873, 137, part.—HEINE and REICHENOW, Nom. Mus. Hein. Orn., 1890, 295 (Mexico).

Cyrtonix massena CUBAS, Cuadro Geogr., Estadístico, Descr. e Hist. de los Estados Unidos Mexicanos, 1884, 168 (Mexico; common names).

Tetrao guttata LA LLAVE, Registro Trimestro, i, 1832, 14 (Mexico); La Naturaleza, vii, 1884, app., p. 65.

Perdix perspicillata LICHTENSTEIN *fide* Gould, Monogr. Odontoph., pt. i, 1844, in text to pl. 7.

O[dontophorus] *meleagris* WAGLER, Isis, 1832, 278 (Mexico; coll. Würtemberg Mus.).

[Cyrtonyx] *meleagris* NELSON, Auk, xiv, 1897, 48, in text (crit.).—SHARPE, Hand-list, i, 1899, 46.

Cyrtonyx montezumae meleagris PETERS, Check-list Birds World, ii, 1934, 57.

Cyrtonyx sallei (not of Verreaux) HELLMAYR and CONOVER, Cat. Birds Amer., i, No. 1, 1942, 287 part (Michoacán, Los Reyes).

CYRTONYX MONTEZUMAE MERRIAMI Nelson

MERRIAM'S HARLEQUIN QUAIL

Adult male.—Similar to that of the nominate form but with the crown darker, the light shaft streaks of the back of the head buffy white, and the black of the throat continuing posteriorly to the chestnut of the breast, thereby eliminating any white pectoral band such as is found in the other races of the species; sides of breast much lighter gray, more slaty, with the white spots about half as large, the spots becoming golden buff on the lower flanks and almost chestnut on the tips of the feathers; chestnut of breast slightly paler; upper parts with the gray portions of the feathers more slaty, the light shaft streaks buffy on mantle, gradually darkening until they are chestnut on the longer scapulars, innermost secondaries, and upper tail coverts; the spots on the upper wing coverts light golden.

Inasmuch as this form is still known only from the type, we quote here the original description in its entirety (Nelson, Auk, xiv, 1897, 48) : "The general pattern of head markings of *merriami* is much as in *montezumae*, except that the black chin and throat area extends down to the chestnut on the lower neck and breast with no intervening white collar; the white superciliary band which extends under the black throat patch as a white collar in *montezumae*, ends on each side of the neck in *merriami*. Bluish-black auricular patches extend forward on the sides of neck and form a broad junction with the black of the throat. The crown and crest are darker than in *montezumae*, the light shaft-streaks on the back of the neck and shoulders are buffy whitish, becoming more and more intensely colored posteriorly, until on the longer scapulars and tertiaries they are almost or quite chestnut; the webs of the tertiaries are gray, becoming browner near the tips, and are crossed by several transverse, oblong black spots which are much narrower and more like bars than are the corresponding markings in *montezumae;* the back and rump are blackish with golden buffy shaft-lines, brown mottling and narrow ashy edgings to the feathers; the upper tail coverts are ashy with heavy rusty shaft-lines and several transverse black bars on each web of the feathers; the chestnut area of the breast and belly is as in *montezumae*, but is of a lighter shade; the sides of the breast and flanks are slaty gray, lighter than in the latter species and marked with numerous round white spots about half the size of those in that bird. On the posterior portion of the flanks the white spotting is replaced by spots of buffy and chestnut. The rest of the lower parts are black as in *montezumae*."

Known only from the type locality, the eastern slopes of Mount Orizaba, and probably (sight records only) from Antigua, nearer the coast, in the State of Veracruz.

Cyrtonyx merriami NELSON, Auk, xiv, 1897, 48 (e. slope of Mount Orizaba, Vera-
    cruz, e. Mexico; coll. U. S. Nat. Mus.) ; xix, 1902, 391, pl. 15, fig. 3 (crit.).—
    OGILVIE-GRANT, Ibis, 1903, iii (crit.).
[*Cyrtonyx*] *merriami* SHARPE, Hand-list, i, 1899, 46.
C[*yrtonyx*] *merriami* SALVIN and GODMAN, Biol. Centr.-Amer., Aves, iii, 1903, 306,
    in text (crit.).
Cyrtonyx sallæi (not of J. Verreaux) OGILVIE-GRANT, Ibis, 1902, 242 (tax.; crit.).—
    SALVIN and GODMAN, Biol. Centr.-Amer., Aves, iii, 1903, 306, part (Volcán de
    Orizaba).
Cyrtonyx montezumae (not of Vigors) HEILFURTH, Journ. für Orn., lxxviii, 1930,
    40, 44, 45 in text (Antigua, Veracruz; seen).
Cyrtonyx montezumae merriami PETERS, Check-list Birds World, ii, 1934, 57 (e.
    slopes of Mount Orizaba, Veracruz).—HELLMAYR and CONOVER, Cat. Birds
    Amer., i, No. 1, 1942, 286 (syn.; distr.).

CYRTONYX MONTEZUMAE SALLEI Verreaux

SALLÉ'S HARLEQUIN QUAIL

Adult male.—Similar to that of *Cyrtonyx montezumae montezumae* above but more brownish, less blackish, upper wing coverts and scapulars clear light grayish olive with heavy but widely spaced transverse black spots; the shaft stripes of the interscapulars and upper back warm buff, those of the scapulars, upper wing coverts, rump, upper tail coverts, and rectrices ochraceous-orange to ochraceous-tawny; below differs from the nominate race in having the brown median area of the breast and abdomen paler—bright chestnut with a slight orange-tawny tinge; the feathers of the sides of the breast and of the upper abdomen much paler—slate-gray with smaller round white spots, the spots becoming chestnut on the feathers of the sides of the lower abdomen, the most posterior of which have chestnut stripes as well; the dark area from the lores to the auriculars and sides of throat paler, slate instead of blackish slate.

Adult female.—Very similar to that of the nominate race but with the upperparts averaging darker, the brown areas of the feathers Saccardo's umber (as compared to tawny-olive in *C. m. montezumae*) and the black cross marks more densely and abundantly developed, giving a general impression of a blacker dorsum; the breast and abdomen averaging slightly darker vinaceous-fawn.

Immature male.—This is not a true plumage, but in a bird of which so little is known it is deemed advisable to include here the following notes made on a molting specimen collected at Cerro San Felipe, Oaxaca, August 31, 1894, by Nelson and Goldman, U.S.N.M. No. 155551: Similar to adult male above except that the forehead and crown are tawny-buff to buckthorn brown, the feathers tipped with dusky; superciliaries and lores white; no black anywhere on the head; greater and median upper wing coverts pale buckthorn brown with buffy white shafts and almost without transverse dark markings; lores, malar area, cheeks and auriculars buckthorn brown to sepia except immediately around and be-hind the eye which area is white finely speckled with brownish; chin and throat white, the latter with small dusky brown spots; the brown of the breast and midventral part of abdomen very much paler-clay color.

Adult male.—Wing 120–124.5 (122.3); tail 42.5–54 (48.1); culmen from base 15.7–16.4 (16.1); 31–32 (31.3); middle toe without claw 22.2–24 (22.8 mm.).[89]

Adult female.—Wing 121.5; tail 51; culmen from base 15.5; tarsus 29.4; middle toe without claw 22.3 mm. (1 specimen).

Range.—Resident in tropical rain forest in the highlands of western Mexico from Guerrero (Amula, Omilteme, and Isguagilite) to east-central Oaxaca (Cerro San Felipe and Ozolotepec).

Type locality.—Mexico=State of Guerrero.

Cyrtonyx sallei VERREAUX, *in* Thomson, Arcuna Naturae, 1, 1859, pl. 4.—PETERS, Check-list Birds World, ii, 1934, 57 (distr.).—GRISCOM, Auk, liv, 1937, 193 (Isguagilite, Guerrero, female; plum.; crit.).—HELLMAYR and CONOVER, Cat. Birds Amer., i, No. 1, 1942, 287 part (syn.; distr.; all except Michoacán).
Cyrtonyx sallaei GRAY, List Birds Brit. Mus., pt. 5, Gallinæ, 1867, 74.—SALVIN and GODMAN, Ibis, 1889, 242 (Amula, Guerrero; crit.); Biol. Centr.-Amer., Aves, iii, 1903, 306 part (Amula, Guerrero).—OGILVIE-GRANT, Cat. Birds Brit. Mus., xxii, 1893, 427 (Amula, Guerrero); Handb. Game Birds, ii, 1897, 148 (monogr.).—BERISTAIN and LAURENCIO, Mem. y Rev. Soc. Cient. "Antonio Alzate," vii, No. 7-8, 1894, 219 (Mexico).—NELSON, Auk, xix, 1902, pl. 15, fig. 4.
Cyrtonyx sallæi GRISCOM, Bull. Mus. Comp. Zool., lxxv, 1934, 422 (Guerrero, Mexico).
[Cyrtonyx] sallæi GRAY, Hand-list, ii, 1870, 272, No. 9776.—SCLATER and SALVIN, Nom. Av. Neotr., 1873, 137.—SHARPE, Hand-list, i, 1899, 46.
C[yrtonyx] sallæi RIDGWAY, Man. North Amer. Birds, 1887, 194.

CYRTONYX OCELLATUS (Gould)

OCELLATED HARLEQUIN QUAIL

Adult male.—Lores and middle of forehead and of crown blackish slate, broadly bordered on each side with white; a blackish-slate supraorbital line from the lores to the posterolateral angle of the occiput; this band continuous through the lores with a broader paler one (slate color) ex-tending posteroventrally demarcating the throat from the face and expanding into a triangle over the lower sides of the head; the cheeks

[89] Three specimens from Oaxaca and Guerrero.

proper blacker—blackish slate; circumocular area, auriculars, and a band connecting with the breast band white; eyelids black; chin and middle of throat black, the white band across the lower throat and upper breast posteriorly edged with black; middle of crown, most of occiput, and upper nape buffy brown to olive-brown, a few of the coronal feathers with ochraceous-orange shaft stripes; most of nape and upper interscapulars deep mouse gray with large rounded spots of buffy white to buffy; most of interscapulars deep mouse gray transversely broadly spotted with black, these spots sometimes coalescing into blotches basally, and with broad shaft stripes of warm buff to ochraceous-tawny; scapulars and feathers of back and lower back and rump similar but with the black areas greater and more coalesced, the shaft stripes greatly reduced on the back, lower back and rump; inner secondaries and upper wing coverts light grayish olive with a faint buffy tinge and with broad auburn to pale chestnut shaft stripes and both vanes transversely marked with large but widely spaced black spots; outer secondaries without brown shaft stripes, and with the light grayish olive color replaced by dark hair brown to light clove brown, the black transverse spots thereby rendered much less conspicuous; innermost secondaries externally and terminally spotted with pinkish cinnamon; primaries dark clove brown to fuscous, externally spotted with pale pinkish buff to pale buff; upper tail coverts light grayish olive with very broad chestnut to auburn shaft stripes and with both webs spotted with black; rectrices similar but with narrower shaft stripes; breast and upper abdomen pale warm buff, the feathers terminally washed with ochraceous-tawny to tawny, the extent, in area and intensity of this wash increasing posteriorly until on the middle of the abdomen the feathers are wholly of this color and even darker, more washed with bright chestnut; sides of neck and of breast dark gull gray to slate spotted with buffy to buffy white; sides of upper abdomen with the spots pale ochraceous-tawny and much larger, reducing the gray to incomplete, transverse bars; lower sides and flanks with the gray still more reduced and the brown areas darker— more auburn and chestnut; the lower flanks dark chestnut with the gray marks largely replaced by black; middle of lower abdomen, vent, under tail coverts, and thighs black; under wing coverts grayish wood brown flecked with pale pinkish cinnamon; "bill black with mandible and maxillary rami pale blue; tarsi and feet, light blue (close to light Delft blue); claws, horn color; iris dark brown" (van Rossem).

Adult female.—Very similar to that of *Cyrtonyx montezumae mearnsi* but averaging darker above (more blackish brown transverse markings on the feathers) and more ochraceous, less pinkish or vinaceous below, and with the dorsal shaft stripes definitely washed with buffy; from the more southern races of *C. montezumae* it differs in having the breast paler, less vinaceous.

Juvenal male.[90]—Similar to the adult female but buffier below.

Juvenal female.—Similar to the adult female slightly lighter and buffier below, and with wider pale shaft stripes on the inner secondaries; "bill, blackish horn color; mandible and maxillary rami, pale, light blue; tarsi and feet, bluish horn color; iris, dark brown" (van Rossem).

Adult male.—Wing 114–130 (123.2); tail 48–57.5 (53.0); culmen from base 15.1–17.5 (16.1); tarsus 30.4–33.2 (32.1); middle toe without claw 21.0–24.3 (22.5 mm.).[91]

Adult female.—Wing 110.5–119.5 (115.7); tail 45–55.5 (48.8); culmen from base 15.1–16.7 (15.6); tarsus 28.9–32.0 (30.9); middle toe without claw 20.4–23.6 (22.0 mm.).[92]

Range.—Resident in the upperparts of the pine forests of the Arid Upper Tropical Zone from southern Mexico (eastern Oaxaca—Santa Efigenia; Tapanatepec; and Chiapas—Teopisca) south in the highlands at elevations of from 5,000 to 7,000 feet to the drier parts of the central highlands of Guatemala east of the Pacific divide, to the cordillera of El Salvador, to Honduras (Hatillo, Jalapa, Danli, Cantoral, Alto Cantoral, Ceguaca, Tegucigalpa, etc.), and to northern Nicaragua (San Rafael del Norte).

Type locality.—Guatemala.

Ortyx ocellatus GOULD, Proc. Zool. Soc. London, 1836 (1837), 75 (locality unknown [= Guatemala]; coll. Zool. Soc. London).

Cyrtonyx ocellatus GOULD, Monogr. Odontoph., pt. 2, 1846, pl. 8 and text.—SCLATER and SALVIN, Ibis, 1859, 226 (Guatemala).—GRAY, List Birds Brit. Mus., pt. 5, Gallinæ, 1867, 74.—OGILVIE-GRANT, Cat. Birds Brit. Mus., xxii, 1893, 428 (Quezaltenango, Dueñas, and Toliman, Guatemala); Handb. Game Birds, ii, 1897, 149 (monogr.).—BERISTAIN and LAURENCIO, Mem. y Rev. Soc. Cient. "Antonio Alzate," vii, Nos. 7–8, 1894, 219 (Mexico; Chiapas and Tabasco).—SALVIN and GODMAN, Biol. Centr.-Amer., Aves, iii, 1903, 307 (Santa Efigenia, Oaxaca; Quezaltenango, Dueñas, and Toliman at 5,000 feet, Guatemala; Danli, Jalapa, n. Honduras).—DEARBORN, Publ. Field Mus. Nat. Hist. No. 125, 1907, 77 (Lake Atitlán to Tecpam, Guatemala, 7,000 feet).—BANGS and PETERS, Bull. Mus. Comp. Zool., lxviii, 1928, 387 (Tapanatepec, Oaxaca, Mexico).—STONE, Proc. Acad. Nat. Sci. Philadelphia, lxxxiv, 1932, 302 (Honduras; Danli).—GRISCOM, Bull. Amer. Mus. Nat. Hist., lxiv, 1932, 107 (distr.; Guatemala; Antigua, Nebaj, San Antonio, Panajachel, and San Lucas).—HELLMAYR and CONOVER, Cat. Birds Amer., i, No. 1, 1942, 287 (syn.; distr.).

[*Cyrtonyx*] *ocellatus* GRAY, Hand-list, ii, 1870, 272, No. 9775.—SCLATER and SALVIN, Nom. Av. Neotr., 1873, 137.—SHARPE, Hand-list, i, 1899, 46.

---

[90] Only juvenal males seen are in a very late stage of the post-juvenal molt and consequently give merely glimpses of the juvenal plumage. The sexes are probably alike in juvenal plumage.

[91] Fifteen specimens from Chiapas, Oaxaca, Guatemala, El Salvador, Nicaragua, and Honduras.

[92] Nine specimens from Chiapas, Guatemala, El Salvador, and Honduras.

C[yrtonyx] ocellatus BAIRD, BREWER, and RIDGWAY, Hist. North Amer. Birds, iii, 1874, 492.—RIDGWAY, Man. North Amer. Birds, 1887, 194.

Cyrtonyx ocellatus ocellatus PETERS, Check-list Birds World, ii, 1934, 57.

[Cyrtonyx] [ocellatus] ocellatus GRISCOM, Proc. New England Zool. Club, xiii, 1932, 56, in text (Guatemala).

Cyrtonyx sumichrasti LAWRENCE, Ann. New York Acad. Sci., i, 1877, 51 (mountains of Santa Efigenia, Tehuantepec, Oaxaca; coll. U. S. Nat. Mus.).—RIDGWAY, Man. North Amer. Birds, 1887, 194, footnote.

C[yrtonyx] ocellatus sumichrasti RIDGWAY, Man. North Amer. Birds, 1887, 194, footnote, in text (crit.).

Cyrtonyx ocellatus differens GRISCOM, Proc. New England Zool. Club, xiii, 1932, 56 (Hatillo, Honduras; type in Mus. Comp. Zool.; meas.; crit.).—PETERS, Check-list Birds World, ii, 1934, 57 (w. Honduras and n. Nicaragua).—DICKEY and VAN ROSSEM, Birds El Salvador, 1938, 155 (El Salvador; Los Esesmiles; spec.; distr.; colors of soft parts).

Genus RHYNCHORTYX Ogilvie-Grant

Rhynchortyx OGILVIE-GRANT, Cat. Birds Brit. Mus., xxii, 1893, 443. (Type, by monotypy and original designation, Odontophorus spodiostethus Salvin and Odontophorus cinctus Salvin (the former is the male, the latter the female of the same species).)

Medium-sized or rather small short-tailed Odontophorinae (wing about 111–125 mm.) with only 10 rectrices, tarsus much longer than middle toe with claw, claws very small (the longest much shorter than second phalanx of middle toe), relatively large and very thick bill (chord of culmen nearly equal to combined length of first two phalanges of middle toe), the outer side of planta tarsi with a single continuous series of large obliquely transverse scutella, the inner side without scutella (except overlapping ends of outer series).

Bill relatively large and very thick, the chord of culmen (from extreme base) equal to nearly half the length of tarsus and nearly if not quite equal to combined length of first two phalanges of middle toe; depth of bill at base much greater than distance from anterior end of nasal fossa to tip of maxilla, equal to nearly one-third the length of tarsus, and decidedly greater than width of bill at rictus; culmen very strongly convex, slightly arched basally, distinctly (but not sharply) ridged; tip of maxilla strongly produced, forming a conspicuous thick unguis; gonys rounded in transverse section, slightly convex, ascending terminally, its basal angle not prominent. Outermost primary a little shorter than eighth, the third, fourth or third, fourth and fifth (from outside) longest. Tail about one-third as long as wing, rounded, the rectrices (12) moderately firm, broad, with rounded tips. Tarsus much longer than middle toe with claw, between one-fourth and one-third as long as wing, the planta tarsi with a single series of large, obliquely transverse scutella which overlap to the posterior portion of inner side, destitute of small scutella or scales on either side; claws exceedingly short, that of the middle toe but little more than half (sometimes less than half) as long as second phalanx of the middle toe.   (One species with four races.)

Range.—Honduras to Colombia, tropical zone.

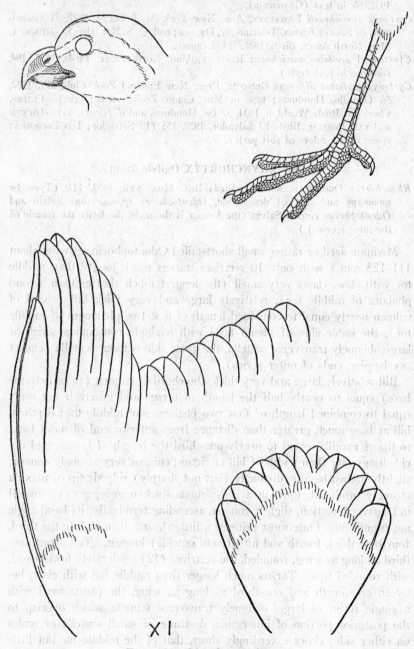

FIGURE 23.—*Rhynchortyx cinctus.*

KEY TO THE FORMS OF RHYNCHORTYX CINCTUS (SALVIN)

a. Forehead and cheeks orange-rufous; breast gray (males).

    b. Lower back and rump darker—Dresden brown or darker; gray of breast darker—between deep neutral gray and slate color.

                                  Rhynchortyx cinctus australis (extralimital)[93]

    bb. Lower back and rump paler—pale olive-buffy-brown or grayer; gray of breast paler—between neutral gray and deep neutral gray.

        c. Lower abdomen very largely white.

            d. Thighs whitish, only faintly barred (Caribbean slope of eastern Darién).

                                Rhynchortyx cinctus hypopius (p. 409)

            dd. Thighs pale buffy, barred with dusky (tropical zone of Honduras and Nicaragua) ....Rhynchortyx cinctus pudibundus (p. 405)

        cc. Lower abdomen with only a small amount of white (Panama, except the Caribbean slope of Darién).......Rhynchortyx cinctus cinctus (p. 408)

aa. Forehead and cheeks not orange-rufous, but reddish brown; breast reddish brown (females).

    b. Bars on abdomen very dark—fuscous to fuscous-black.

                              Rhynchortyx cinctus australis (extralimital)

    bb. Bars on abdomen paler—dark sepia or paler.

        c. Lower abdomen very largely white.

            d. Cheeks duller—dark olive-brown (tropical zone of Honduras and Nicaragua) ....Rhynchortyx cinctus pudibundus (p. 405)

            dd. Cheeks brighter—amber brown (Caribbean slope of eastern Darién).

                              Rhynchortyx cinctus hypopius (p. 409)

        cc. Lower abdomen with only a small amount of white (Panama except the Caribbean slope of Darién)........Rhynchortyx cinctus cinctus (p. 408)

RHYNCHORTYX CINCTUS PUDIBUNDUS Peters

HONDURANIAN LONG-LEGGED COLIN

Adult male.—Forehead, lores, broad superciliaries, cheeks, sides of throat, and auriculars bright amber brown with a strong suffusion of orange-rufous; a narrow dusky line from the anterior angle of the eye to the lores, and a broader one of mummy brown from the posterior angle of the eye to the auriculars; crown and occiput dark Prout's brown to chestnut-brown, some of the feathers with minute terminal spots of blackish and with faint buffy shafts; nape and interscapulars neutral gray, the feathers very broadly edged with auburn; scapulars and a row of feathers across the upper back just posterior to the interscapulars with their inner webs fuscous to fuscous black basally flecked and flecked with

---

[93] *Rhynchortyx cinctus australis* Chapman.—*Rhynchortyx cinctus* (not *Odontophorus cinctus* Salvin) Hartert, Nov. Zool., ix, 1902, 600 (Bulieu, Río Bogotá, and Pambilar, nw. Ecuador; crit.) ; Hellmayr, Proc. Zool. Soc. London, 1911, 1206 (Colombia; Sipi, Chocó; plum.).—*Rhynchortyx cinctus australis* Chapman, Bull. Amer. Mus. Nat. Hist., xxxiv, 1915, 365 (Barbacoas, w. Columbia; coll. Amer. Mus. Nat. Hist.) ; xxxvi, 1917, 202 (Chocó, Andagueda, Bagado, Baudo, and Barbacoas, Pacific coast of Colombia; descr.) ; lv, 1926, 161 (nw. Ecuador) ; Peters, Checklist Birds World, ii, 1934, 58 (distr.) ; Hellmayr and Conover, Cat. Birds Amer., i, No. 1, 1942, 289 (syn.; distr.).

dark hazel, their shafts narrowly buff, their outer webs buffy brown faintly vermiculated with dusky, and, on the scapulars, with pale gray and externally suffused with dark hazel; secondaries dark olive-brown to sepia, externally and terminally blotched and freckled with light ochraceous-buff, the terminal freckling on the inner web tinged with hazel; upper wing coverts similar but many of them with blackish-brown blotches on their inner webs and the pale freckling extending on the inner webs to a greater degree; primaries dark dull sepia to clove brown, externally freckled with light ochraceous-buff, but only sparingly; back, lower back, rump, and upper tail coverts reveal two fairly distinct color phases—one has these parts dusky isabelline to buffy brown with dark shafts and more or less freckled transversely with dusky, especially on the more posterior parts; the other with the back and lower back vinaceous-fawn to fawn color obscurely crossed by widely spaced narrow dusky slate bars; the rump and upper tail coverts dark sayal brown to snuff brown with dusky shafts and tranverse freckling; rectrices Brussels brown flecked, and basally blotched, with dark, dull sepia; chin and upper throat whitish; lower throat and breast between neutral gray and dark gull gray; upper abdomen, sides, and flanks, ochraceous-buff to cinnamon-buff, darkening laterally to clay color; thighs ochraceous-buff barred with fuscous; under tail coverts similar; middle of lower abdomen whitish; under wing coverts dull sepia to pale clove brown; iris reddish brown; bill black, becoming brownish horn color at the tip; tarsi and toes plumbeous.

Adult female.—Forehead, crown, and occiput dark Prout's brown to chestnut-brown; upperparts of body, wings, and tail as in adult male; the two color phases present—vinaceous-fawn and buffy brown on the backs, as in the males; no orange-rufous on the sides of head as in the males, this color being replaced by dark olive-brown, the feathers of the cheeks and sides of neck with white shafts; a row of dusky-tipped white feathers from lores to, under, and behind the eye extending to the posterolateral angle of the occiput; immediately below this a dark choco-late band behind the eye; chin and upper throat white; lower throat and breast antique brown to amber brown, many of the feathers decidedly grayish broadly edged with antique brown; upper and lateral parts of abdomen white, barred with sepia to dusky sepia; thighs similar but less strongly or distinctly barred; most of middle lower abdomen white; under tail coverts ochraceous-buff barred with fuscous, under wing coverts dull sepia.

Juvenal male.[94]—Similar to adult female but darker, less rufescent above and on the lower throat, breast, and abdomen; forehead, crown, occiput, nape, and interscapulars between clove brown and dark mummy brown, the feathers with minute pale smoke-gray spots along the distal

---

[94] The only example seen was a male, but probably the sexes are alike in this plumage.

half of the shaft; lower back, rump, and upper tail coverts bright pinkish buff sparingly barred with fuscous-black; scapulars, secondaries, and upper wing coverts as in adult but slightly more rufescent; primaries without freckling on the outer webs; rest of upperparts as in adult female; cheeks and sides of head, lower throat, breast, and upper abdomen grayish olive brown; some of the feathers of the breast with small white flecks along the shaft, these flecks becoming broad V-shaped bars on the upper abdomen and sides; chin and upper throat pale ochraceous-buff; rest of underparts as in adult female.

Natal down.—Center of forehead, crown, and occiput very dark chocolate; lores, broad superciliaries, cheeks, auriculars, chin, and upper throat pale buckthorn brown; a fuscous line from the gape to the anterior angle of the eye, thence over it and again as a streak leading away from it; interscapular area russet; rest of upperparts similar but darker chestnut-brown; breast russet; abdomen, sides, flanks, thighs, and under tail coverts dusky hair brown, paling to whitish on the middle of the abdomen.

Adult male.—Wing 105.5–114.0 (110.5); tail 41.0–47.0 (44.7); culmen from base 15.5–16.4 (15.8); tarsus 32.8–34.5 (33.5); middle toe without claw 23.1–25.3 (23.9 mm.).[95]

Adult female.—Wing 107–112; tail 43–46; culmen from base 14.6–14.9; tarsus 30.8–33; middle toe without claw 24.0 mm.[96]

Range.—Resident in the deep tropical forests of coastal Honduras (Lancetilla), south to eastern and north-central Nicaragua (Río Escondido, Ojoche, Matagalpa, Río Tuma, Pena Blanca, Vizagua).[97]

Type locality.—Lancetilla, Honduras.

Rhynchortyx cinctus pudibundus PETERS, Bull. Mus. Comp. Zool., lxix, 1929, 405 (Lancetilla, Honduras; type in Mus. Comp. Zool.; descr.; crit.; habits); Check-list Birds of World, ii, 1934, 58 (Lancetilla).—BANGS, Bull. Mus. Comp. Zool., lxx, 1930, 161 (type spec. in Mus. Comp. Zool.).—STONE, Proc. Acad. Nat. Sci. Philadelphia, lxxxiv, 1932, 302 (Honduras, Lancetilla).—HELLMAYR and CONOVER, Cat. Birds Amer., i, No. 1, 1942, 288 (syn.; distr.).

R[*hynchortyx*] c[*inctus*] *cinctus* (not of Salvin) CHAPMAN, Bull. Amer. Mus. Nat. Hist., xxxiv, 1915, 365, in text, part (Nicaragua).

Rhynchortyx cinctus cinctus HUBER, Proc. Acad. Nat. Sci. Philadelphia, lxxxiv, 1932, 207 (ne. Nicaragua—Eden; spec.; colors of soft parts).—PETERS, Check-list Birds World, ii, 1934, 58, part (distr.—Nicaragua).—HELLMAYR and CONOVER, Cat. Birds Amer., i, No. 1, 1942, 288, part (syn.; distr.).

Odontophorus spodiostethus RICHMOND, Proc. U. S. Nat. Mus., xvi, 1893, 524 (Río Escondido, e. Nicaragua; descr.).

Rhynchortyx spodiostethus SALVIN and GODMAN, Biol. Centr.-Amer., Aves, iii, 1903, 313, part (Río Escondido and Ojoche, Nicaragua).

[*Rhynchortyx*] *spodiostethus* SHARPE, Hand-list, i, 1899, 47, part (Nicaragua).

---

[95] Eight specimens from Nicaragua (7) and Honduras (1).

[96] Two specimens, one each from Honduras and Nicaragua.

[97] In north-central Nicaragua (Matagalpa area) the birds begin to show a tendency to vary in the direction of the Panamanian race *R. c. cinctus*.

RHYNCHORTYX CINCTUS CINCTUS (Salvin)

LONG-LEGGED COLIN

Adult male.—Similar to that of *Rhynchortyx cinctus pudibundus,* but with less white on the lower abdomen, the tawny tones below averaging darker—clay color to pale tawny-olive; and the gray of the breast darker on the average—deep neutral gray.

There seem to be three, instead of only two, color phases in the males of this race, the color affecting the back, rump, and upper tail coverts. One specimen from Tacarcuna has this area dark mouse gray finely peppered with blackish and white, no rufescent being present except on the tips of the upper tail coverts; another from the same place is of the vinaceous fawn phase; while still another, from Mount Sapo, in the Pacific slope of Darién, is of the buffy-brown phase.

Adult female.—Similar to that of *Rhynchortyx cinctus pudibundus* but with less white on the lower abdomen and averaging slightly darker and more rufescent above (in the vinaceous-fawn-backed phase, the back is darker and deeper pinkish in color); the cheeks slightly more rufescent.

Juvenal.—None seen.

Natal down.—Similar to that of *Rhynchortyx cinctus pudibundus.*

Adult male.—Wing 110.5–116.5 (113.5); tail 44.1–47.8 (46.1); culmen from base 16–16.9 (16.3); tarsus 33.2–36 (34.5); middle toe without claw 24.3–26 (25 mm.).[98]

Adult female.—Wing 105–112 (109.2); tail 41.4–47.8 (44.4); culmen from base 14.9–15.5 (15.1); tarsus 31.8–35.6 (33.7); middle toe without claw 22.5–26.1 (24.1 mm.).[99]

Range.—Resident in the deep tropical forests of Costa Rica (Villa Quesada) and Panama south and east to the Pacific slope of Darién, Mount Sapo, Agua Dulce, Veraguas, Darién, Tacarcuna, Cituro, Mount Pirri, Tapalisa).

Type locality.—Veraguas, western Panama.

Odontophorus cinctus SALVIN, Ibis, 1876, 379 (Veraguas, w. Panamá; coll. Salvin and Godman, now in coll. Brit. Mus.).—ROWLEY, Orn. Misc., iii, pt. 11, 1877, 39, pl. 81.—SALVIN and GODMAN, Biol. Centr.-Amer., Aves, iii, 1903, pl. 75 (= female).

Rhynchortyx cinctus OGILVIE-GRANT, Cat. Birds Brit. Mus., xxii, 1893, 444 (Veraguas); Handb. Game Birds, ii, 1897, 162 (Veraguas).—SALVIN and GODMAN, Biol. Centr.-Amer., Aves, iii, 1903, 313 (Veraguas).

R[*hynchortyx*] *cinctus* REICHENOW, Die Vögel, i, 1913, 316.

[*Rhynchortyx*] *cinctus* SHARPE, Hand-list, i, 1899, 47.

R[*hynchortyx*] c[*inctus*] *cinctus* CHAPMAN, Bull. Amer. Mus. Nat. Hist., xxxiv, 1915, 365, in text, part (Veraguas).

---

[98] Eight specimens from Panama.
[99] Six specimens from Panama.

Rhynchortyx cinctus cinctus BANGS and BARBOUR, Bull. Mus. Comp. Zool., lxv, 1922, 196 Mount Sapo, Darién).—PETERS, Check-list Birds World, ii, 1934, 58, part (distr.).—GRISCOM, Bull. Mus. Comp. Zool., lxxviii, 1935, 304 (Panama; Pacific slope; Veraguas—very rare; Darién—common).—HELLMAYR and CONOVER, Cat. Birds Amer., i, No. 1, 1942, 288 part (syn.; distr.).

Odontophorus spodiostethus SALVIN, Ibis, 1878, 447 (Veraguas, w. Panama; coll. Salvin and Godman, now in coll. Brit. Mus.).—SALVIN and GODMAN, Biol. Centr.-Amer., Aves, iii, 1903, pl. 76 (= male).

Rhynchortyx spodiostethus OGILVIE-GRANT, Cat. Birds Brit. Mus., xxii, 1893, 443 (Veraguas and Agua Dulce, Panama) ; Handb. Game Birds, ii, 1897, 162, pl. 34 (male).—SALVIN and GODMAN, Biol. Centr.-Amer., Aves, iii, 1903, 313, part (Veraguas and Agua Dulce, Panama).

[*Rhynchortyx*] *spodiostethus* SHARPE, Hand-list, i, 1899, 47, part (Panama).

Odontophorus rubigenis (Lawrence MS.), RICHMOND, Proc. U. S. Nat. Mus., xvi, 1893, 525, in text (Panama; type in Amer. Mus. Nat. Hist.; manuscript name for *O. spodiostethus*).

RHYNCHORTYX CINCTUS HYPOPIUS Griscom

CARIBBEAN LONG-LEGGED COLIN

Adult male.—Similar to that of *Rhynchortyx cinctus pudibundus* but with more white in the center of the abdomen, the ochraceous tones paler—between light ochraceous-buff and warm buff, the thighs whiter.

Adult female.—Very similar to that of *Rhynchortyx cinctus pudibundus* but cheeks slightly more rufescent, the auriculars rusty instead of sooty, top of head more rufescent, under tail coverts averaging more whitish.

Other plumages apparently unknown.

Adult male.—Wing 111–117.5 (113.4) ; tail 43.1–48.1 (45.8) ; culmen from base 16.0–17.0 (16.6) ; tarsus 34.1–35.5 (34.8) ; middle toe without claw 23.3–25.1 (24.4 mm.).[1]

Adult female.—Wing 105.5 ; tail ——; culmen from base 15.4 ; tarsus 32.7 ; middle toe without claw 22.8 mm. (1 specimen).

Range.—Resident in tropical forests of the Caribbean slope of eastern Panama from Río Pequeni, Canal Zone (not wholly typical), east to Permé and Obaldia, eastern Darién.

Type locality.—Obaldia, Caribbean slope of eastern Panama.

Rhynchortyx cinctus hypopius GRISCOM, Bull. Mus. Comp. Zool., lxxii, 1932, 320 (Obaldia, Caribbean slope, Darién, eastern Panama; type in Mus. Comp. Zool.; descr.; crit.) ; lxxviii, 1935, 304 (Panama; Caribbean slope of eastern Darién). —PETERS, Check-list Birds World, ii, 1934, 58 (distr.).—HELLMAYR and CONOVER, Cat. Birds Amer., i, No. 1, 1942, 289 (syn.; distr.).

Genus PERDIX Brisson

Perdix BRISSON, Orn., i, 1760, 219. (Type, by tautonymy, *Perdix* Brisson = *Tetrao perdix* Linnaeus.)

Perdrix (emendation) BRÜNNICH, Zool. Fundam., 1771, 86.

---

[1] Six specimens.

Starna BONAPARTE, Geogr. and Comp. List, 1838, 43. (Type, by monotypy, *Perdix cinerea* Latham = *Tetrao perdix* Linnaeus.)

Sacfa HODGSON, Journ. Asiat. Soc. Bengal, xxv, 1857, 165. (Type, by monotypy, *S. hodgsoniae* Hodgson.)

Medium-sized Perdicinae (wing about 139–158 mm.) with 16–18 rectrices, outermost primary shorter than seventh, tarsus without rudimentary spurs, and upper parts conspicuously variegated.

Bill moderate in relative size, rather slender, its depth at base of culmen (anterior end of mesorhinium) equal to very much less (approximately two-thirds) the distance from anterior margin of nasal fossa to tip of maxilla and equal to or greater than its width at same point; culmen

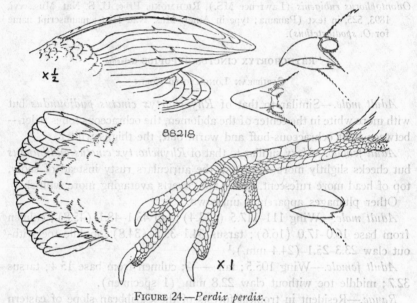

FIGURE 24.—*Perdix perdix.*

moderately but regularly convex, rounded or very indistinctly obtusely angular in transverse section, the tip of maxilla produced much beyond tip of mandible; gonys about half as long as culmen to decidedly more than half as long, nearly straight, little if at all ascending terminally, broad and depressed in transverse section, not at all ridged, its basal angle not prominent; nostrils narrow, obliquely horizontal (the posterior end higher than the anterior end), margined below by dense short feathering of the triangular loral antia, overhung by a broad and prominent horny operculum; mesorhinium very short, broadly rounded and or flattened transversely. Wing moderate, rounded, the outermost primary intermediate between seventh and eighth (from outside), the third to fifth longest; longer primaries extending considerably beyond tips of longest (proximal) secondaries. Tail about half as long as wing, slightly but distinctly rounded, the rectrices (16–18) firm, moderately broad, rounded at tips, extending but slightly beyond longer coverts. Tarsus stout, a little longer than middle toe with claw, without trace of rudimentary spurs.

Plumage and coloration.—Plumage of head (except crown, occiput and nape) short, dense, and blended, the auriculars, however, hairlike and somewhat elongated; the feathers on sides of throat also sometimes elongated; rest of plumage compact, the feathers distinctly outlined, except on abdomen and anal region. Upperparts mixed gray and brownish, variegated by darker vermiculations or bars, shaft streaks of buffy on scapulars, wing coverts, and tertials, and buffy spots on outer webs of primaries; sides and flanks broadly barred with black or rufous-chestnut. Sexes alike in coloration, sometimes slightly different.

Range.—Palearctic Region: Western Europe to Manchuria. Amurland, and China, south to northern India. (Three species with many races, only one in our region.)

PERDIX PERDIX PERDIX (Linnaeus)

PARTRIDGE; "HUNGARIAN PARTRIDGE"

Adult male (winter plumage).—Broad forehead, lores, superciliary stripe, chin, throat, and cheeks between clay color and pale tawny-olive with a slight cinnamomeous tinge; the auriculars buffy brown; crown and middle of occiput buffy brown, the feathers dark dull sepia basally and medially, with pale ashy-buff shafts; nape, interscapulars, and upper back pale mouse gray finely barred with wavy black lines and terminally broadly suffused with pale tawny-olive; scapulars pale tawny-olive to dusky isabelline, vermiculated with black, crossed by a broad band of dark chestnut about their middle, basally blackish, and with conspicuous buffy-white narrow shaft streaks; innermost secondaries similar but with the blackish basal area more extended onto the chestnut, which is restricted to the median part of the feathers, not reaching the edges of the webs, somewhat grayish terminally; other secondaries tawny-cinnamon crossed by widely spaced triple bars, each bar consisting of two clove-brown to fuscous ones with a pale pinkish buff in between these bars breaking up on the inner webs of the inner secondaries into irregular mottlings; primaries dull fuscous to clove brown barred with pinkish buff to pale pinkish buff, the pale bars narrow and the interspaces broad; greater upper wing coverts like the scapulars but with the chestnut confined to their inner webs and usually concealed by overlapping of feathers and crossed by widely spaced buffy bars; median and lesser upper wing coverts like the greater ones but with the buff bars; feathers of back, lower back, rump, and upper tail coverts like the interscapulars but more buffy and with dark chestnut subterminal sagittate bars, which are edged proximally and distally with pale pinkish buffy, these chestnut bars becoming much wider on the rump and upper tail coverts; rectrices argus brown with a chestnut tinge, narrowly tipped with buffy gray, except the two central pairs which are like the upper tail coverts but more heavily and coarsely vermiculated with clove brown to dark dull sepia and without the large sagittate subterminal chestnut marking; breast and upper abdomen gray vermiculated with dusky like the interscapulars but much purer gray, not washed with buffy brown; sides similar but the feathers with subterminal broad sagittate bars of tawny; flanks similar but more tinged with buff; in middle of upper abdomen a large patch of bright auburn to pale chestnut, these feathers having white bases, middle of lower abdomen and vent white; thighs whitish tinged with grayish buff; under tail coverts pale buff to pale cinnamon-buff transversely narrowly speckled with dull dark sepia; bill greenish horn color; tarsi and toes gray tinged with yellowish flesh; iris brown; bare skin behind eye red.

Adult male (summer plumage).—Same as the winter plumage but with new feathers on the nape, interscapulars and throat, the new plumes on the nape and interscapulars buffy gray with pale shaft lines.

Adult male (rufescent phase).—Like the normal phase but with the tawny of the head more ferruginous and extending over the breast which is heavily vermiculated with deep bay; the sides and flanks bay, the dark brown abdominal spot much larger and deeper in color—dark bay.

Adult female (winter plumage).—Like the corresponding male but the tawny of the forehead, lores, cheeks, chin, and throat slightly paler and pinker, less olive or tawny; feathers of crown and occiput with darker bases and with their subterminal pale shaft streaks terminally edged with blackish, producing a more spotted appearance; nape, interscapulars more brownish, less grayish than in the male; rest of upperparts more brownish, less grayish than in the male and with more dark fuscous to fuscous-black blotches showing (these basal areas of the feathers more extensive) and with the subterminal dark sagittate band darker, deep chestnut to bay; breast averaging somewhat buffier than in male; the middle of the upper abdomen usually white with only a few broad chestnut tips on the feathers, but also, in other specimens, a large chestnut patch almost as extensive as in the male; wings as in male except that the median and lesser upper coverts have buffy bars like the greater ones; inner secondaries and scapulars with less chestnut, the bases dark bister to fuscous with widely spaced pale buffy bars.

Adult female (summer plumage).—Like the winter plumage but with the new feathers on the back and sides of the neck and the lower throat with pale shaft streaks with tear-shaped spots margined with fuscous, those on rest of upperparts brownish black narrowly tipped with buffy and with widely spaced narrow pale buffy bands, those on breast, base of throat and base of sides of neck broadly barred brown-black and grayish white, and those on the sides of the breast and flanks broadly barred and marked with buff and brownish black (*ex* Handbook British Birds).

Adult female (rufescent phase).—Similar to the normal phase but with the forehead, superciliaries, cheeks, chin, and throat somewhat darker and brighter—between ochraceous-salmon and light ochraceous-salmon; crown, occiput, and nape tawny-olive washed with cinnamon; rest of upperparts as in the normal phase but the general tone between pinkish buff and cinnamon-buff (instead of gray) vermiculated with blackish; the sagittate subterminal bars broader and paler—rufescent amber brown; breast washed with tawny to pale cinnamon; flanks, thighs, and under tail coverts much more rufescent—pinkish cinnamon-buff.

Adult (first winter).—Like older adults, but with the two outermost primaries (retained from the juvenal plumage) with more pointed tips.

Juvenal (sexes alike).—"Crown black-brown finely streaked buff, each feather having buff shaft-streaks; back of neck, mantle, back, rump, and upper tailcoverts buff-brown with whitish to pale buff shaft-streaks inconspicuously margined blackish; lores and sides of head dark brown streaked whitish; chin, throat, and center of belly whitish to pale buff; breast, sides and flanks, and under tailcoverts buff brown slightly paler than mantle and with whiter shaft-streaks, faintly margined brown on flanks; tail much like adult but feathers tipped buff and with subterminal dusky bars and spots and central ones speckled and barred dusky; primaries brown with pale buff tips and widely spaced bars on outer webs; secondaries with pale buff bars extending across both webs and vermiculated brown, shafts pale buff; scapulars, inner secondaries, and wingcoverts brown buff with wide brown-black bars and mottlings and pale shaft streaks widening to white spots at tips of feathers"; . . . legs and feet yellow" (*ex* Witherby et al., Handbook British Birds, v, 1941, 245).

Natal down (sexes alike).—"Closely covered with soft down, shorter on head; tarsi and toes bare. Crown chestnut with a few small black spots sometimes extending to lines; back of neck with a wide black line down center, at sides pale buff marked black; rest of upperparts pale buff with some rufous and black blotches or ill-defined lines; at base of wings a spot, and on rump a patch, of chestnut; forehead and sides of head pale yellow-buff (sometimes tinged rufous) with spots, small blotches and lines of black; chin and throat uniform pale yellow-buff; rest of underparts slightly yellower, bases of down sooty" (*ex* Witherby et al., Handbook British Birds, v, 1941, 244-245).

Adult male.—Wing 144–157 (151.8) ; tail 78–84 (80.9) ; culmen from basal groove 11.4–13.8 (12.4) ; tarsus 35–42 (39.1) ; middle toe without claw 27.2–32.3 (30.6 mm.).[2]

---

[2] Five specimens from Germany, France, and captivity.

To these data may be added the following based on a long series from England, published by Witherby et al., Handbook Brit. Birds, v, 1941, 245:

22 males: Wing 150–162; tail 73–83; bill from feathers 13–16; tarsus 38–42 mm.
A series of females: Wing 150–158; tail 73–78.

Adult female.—Wing 146.5–154.5 (150.1) ; tail 76.0–80.0 (78) ; culmen from basal groove 12.3–13.7 (13.0) ; tarsus 38.7–43.3 (40.9) ; middle toe without claw 29.5–31.4 (30.5 mm.).[3]

Range.—Breeds and is resident in Europe from Belgium and Holland north to Denmark and Norway, Sweden, and Finland, south to northeastern France, Switzerland, Austria, western Rumania, Macedonia, and Greece, and east to Poland and the Ukraine. Introduced into North America from England and Hungary and is acclimatized in Canada (Saskatchewan, Alberta, British Columbia, and Manitoba) and the United States (northwestern Kansas, Iowa, southeastern Wisconsin, Montana, eastern Washington, and eastern Oregon). Introduced unsuccessfully in the Eastern States from Maine and New York south to Florida and Mississippi, also in the Central States from Minnesota, Michigan, Illinois, and Indiana south to Nebraska, Arkansas, and Missouri, and also in California.

Type locality.—Sweden.

[*Tetrao*] *perdix* LINNAEUS, Syst. Nat., ed. 10, i, 1758, 160 ("Europae agris"; descr.) ; ed. 12, i, 1766, 276.—GMELIN, Syst. Nat., i, pt. 2, 1788, 757.
Tetrao perdix BESEKE, Beytr. Nat. Vög. Kurl., 1792, 71.—BECHSTEIN, Nat. Deutschl., iii, 1793, 527.—PALLAS, Zoogr. Rosso-Asiat., ii, 1811, 77.
Starna perdix FITZINGER, Atl. Nat. Vog., 1864, fig. 237.—BETTONI, Ucc. Lombard., ii, 1867, pl. 8, part.—FRITSCH, Nat. Vög., Eur., 1870, 293, pl. 30, fig. 9 ; Journ. für Orn., 1871, 379 (Bohemia).—GIGLIOLI, Avif. Ital., 1886, 341 ; i, 1889, 525 ; ii, 1890, 661 ; iii, 1891, 516.
Perdix perdix HARTERT, Kat. Mus. Senckenb., 1891, 194.—OGILVIE-GRANT, Field, Nov. 21, 1891, and Apr. 9, 1892 ; Ann. Mag. Nat. Hist., ser. 6, xii, 1893, 62 (sexual differences in plumage) ; Cat. Birds Brit. Mus., xxii, 1893, 185.—BRITISH ORNITHOLOGISTS' UNION, List Brit. Birds, ed. 2, 1915, 313.—GRINNELL, Pacific Coast Avif., No. 11, 1915, 180 (California ; hypothetical).—DICE, Auk, xxxv, 1918, 43 (Tochet Valley, near Prescott, se. Washington, introduced in 1915 ; Columbia County, Wash., introduced several years prior to 1915).—SMITH, Auk, xxxviii, 1921, 466 (Meriden, Conn., "thoroughly acclimated and breeding").—SAUNDERS, Pacific Coast Avif., No. 14, 1921, 172 (Montana ; introduced).—MITCHELL, Can. Field Nat., xxxviii, 1924, 108 (Saskatchewan ; introduced).—RENSCH and NEUMZIG, Journ. für Orn., lxxiii, 1925, 641, in table (sense of taste).—TAVERNER, Birds Western Canada, 1926, 161 (fig. ; descr. ; distr. ; w. Canada) ; Nat. Mus. Canada Bull. 50, 1928, 91 (near Belvedere, Alberta, introduced) ; Birds Canada, 1934, 163 in text (Canada ; distr. ; habits) ; Can. Water Birds, 1939, 176 (Canada ; field chars.).—VON BURG, *in* Fatio and Studer, Ois. Suisse, xv, 1926, 3101 (Switzerland ; monogr.).—ROTHSCHILD, Bull. Brit. Orn. Club, xlvii, 1927, 141 (melanistic mutant).—STRESEMANN, Journ. für Orn., lxxv, 1927, 574 (plum. aberrations).—HEINROTH, Vög. Mitteleurop., iii, 1927, 235 (devel. of young in captivity).—LARSON, Wils. Bull., xl, 1928, 46 (e. McKenzie County, N. Dak.).—SPIKER, Wils. Bull., xli, 1929, 24, in text (habits and distr. in nw. Iowa).—HUGUES, L'Oiseau, x, 1929, 54 (Basses—Cevennes, France).—URNER, Abstr. Linn. Soc. New York, No. 39, 40, 1930, 71 (Union County, N. J.).—MILLER, Murrelet, xi, 1930, 61, in text (Washington ; Paulouse region ; intro-

[3] Four specimens from France, England, and North Dakota.

duced).—MAYAUD, Alauda, iii, 1931, 548 (Rousillon, France).—TICEHURST and
WHISTLER, Ibis, 1932, 92 (Albania).—ROBERTS, Brit. Birds, xxv, 1932, 220
(speed).—GROEBBELS, Der Vögel, i, 1932, 272 in text (food), 342 in text (food) ;
419 (deformed bill), 520 (grit in gizzard), 523 in text (mineral content of
food), 645 (longevity) ; ii, 1937, 41 in text (cock feathering), 114 in text (territory), 238, in text (covers eggs), 239, in text (number of eggs), 240–241, in
text (eggs in mixed sets) ; 280 in text (white eggs), 305 in text (albino eggs),
306 in text (flecked eggs), 383 in text (runt eggs), 384 (infertile eggs).—CAUM,
Occ. Papers Bishop Mus., x, No. 9, 1933, 15 (Hawaii; introduced; not successfully).—YOUNGWORTH, Wils. Bull., xlvii, 1935, 217 (Fort Sisseton, S. Dak.;
spreading rapidly).—BAILLIE and HARRINGTON, Contr. Roy. Ontario Mus. Zool.,
No. 8, pt. 1, 1936, 29 (Ontario; introduced; breeding records).—BAGG and ELIOT,
Birds Connecticut Valley in Massachusetts, 1937, 172 (introduced unsuccess-
fully).—SHORTT and WALLER, Contr. Roy. Ontario Mus. Zool., No. 10, 1937, 18
(Lake St. Martin region, Manitoba; spec., not reported since 1933).—ERRINGTON
and HAMERSTROM, Condor, xl, 1938, 71 (effect of spring drought on breeding).—
LACK, Condor, xlii, 1940, 273 in text (pairing habits).—ALLIN, Trans. Roy. Can.
Inst., xxiii, pt. 1, 1940, 96 (Darlington Township, Ontario; several more or less
successful private introductions between 1909 and 1933).—SNYDER et al., Contr.
Roy. Ontario Mus. Zool., No. 19, 1941, 46 (Prince Edward County, Ontario; 2
sight records; introduction not yet well established).—HAUGEN, Wils. Bull., liii,
1941, 235 (Washington, Whitman County; habits).—HAND, Condor, xliii, 1941,
225 (St. Joe National Forest, Idaho; introduced).—PETRIDES, Trans. 7th North
Amer. Wildlife Conf., 1942, 308 in text, 319 in text (age indicators in plumage).
—AMADON, Auk, lx, 1943, 226 (body weight and egg weight).—BEHLE, Condor,
xlvi, 1944, 72 (Utah; distr.).

Perdix perdix var. HORBSBRUGH, Ibis, 1916, 681 (Alix, Alberta; introduced and
once common, but eventually disappeared).

P[erdix] perdix REICHENOW, Die Vögel, i, 1913, 285.

[*Perdix*] *perdix* SHARPE, Hand-list, i, 1899, 26.

Perdix perdix perdix HARTERT et al., Handb. Brit. Birds, 1912, 217.—HARTERT, Vög.
Pal. Fauna, iii, 1921, 1929 (syn.; destr.; descr.).—RAMSAY, Guide to Birds
Europe and N. Africa, 1923, 331 (descr.; distr.; Europe and North Africa).—
WITHERBY et al., Practical Handb. Brit. Birds, ii, pt. 18. 1924, 875 (monogr.).—
OBERHOLSER, Auk, xli, 1924, 592 (Saskatchewan; introduced).—VAN OORDT,
Ardea, xiii, 1924, 68 (Edinburgh and Perth; one near Aviemore, Scotland).—
STARING, Ardea, xiv, 1925, 93 (e. Wales).—WEIGOLD, Journ. für Orn., lxxiii,
1925, 581 (banding records, Helgoland).—GENGLER, Verh. Orn. Ges. Bay.,
xvi, 1925, Sonderheft, 95, 274 (Bavaria) ; xvii, 1927, 170 (Steiger Forest,
Bavaria), 487 (s. Rhone, Germany).—SPRANGER, Verh. Orn. Ges. Bay., xvii,
1926, 35 (Deggendorf, Germany).—FORBUSH, Birds Massachusetts and Other
New England States, ii, 1927, 12, pl. 34 (col. fig.; descr.; distr.; habits; New
England).—DE PAILLERETS, Rev. Franç. d'Orn., xi, 1927, 241 (Charente-
Inferieure, France).—SUTTON, Birds Pennsylvania, 1928, 52 in text (Pennsylvania; introduced).—CONGREVE, Ibis, 1929, 491 (Rumania; eggs).—REBOUS-
SIN, L'Oiseau, x, 1929, 348 (Lovi-et-Cher, France).—ESTIOT, Alauda, i, 1929,
359 (near Paris, France).—STANTSCHINSKY, Orn. Monatsb., xxxvii, 1929, 138
(distr.).—MÜLLER, Verh. Orn. Ges. Bay., xix, 1930, 97 (Lake Maising, Bavaria;
habits).—KOCH, Ardea, xix, 1930, 57 (banding records, Wassenaar Station,
Holland).—AMERICAN ORNITHOLOGISTS' UNION, Check-list, ed. 4, 1931, 87
(distr.).—BENNITT, Univ. Missouri Studies, vii, No. 3, 1932, 26, footnote
(Missouri; introduced but not established).—KELSO, Auk, xlix, 1932, 204, in
text (food habits).—ROBERTS, Birds Minnesota, i, 1932, 403 (distr.; habits;

Minnesota).—BENT, U. S. Nat. Mus. Bull. 162, 1932, i (habits; distr.;
monogr.).—TICEHURST, Birds Suffolk, 1932, 480 (status; habits; Suffolk,
England).—EDSON, Murrelet, xiii, 1932, 42 (Washington; several records).—
CUMMING, Murrelet, xiii, 1932, 14 (Vancouver, British Columbia; common;
introduced). —GRISCOM, Trans. Linn. Soc. New York, iii, 1933, 97 (Dutchess
County, N. Y.; introduced; now almost extinct).—YEATTER, Univ. Michigan
School of Forestry and Conservation, Bull. 5, 1934, 9, in text (Great Lakes
region; life hist.; management).—WEYDEMEYER, Condor, xxxviii, 1936, 45
(nest and 11 eggs; July; Fortine, Mont.—WEYDEMEYER and MARSH, Condor,
xxxviii, 1936, 194 (Lake Bowdoin, Mont.).—VAN TYNE, Occ. Pap. Mus. Zool.
Univ. Michigan, No. 379, 1938, 12 (Michigan; resident).—TRAUTMAN, Misc.
Publ. Mus. Zool. Univ. Michigan, No. 44, 1940, 223 (Buckeye Lake, Ohio; rare
resident).—CAMPBELL, Bull. Toledo Mus. Sci., i, 1940, 63 (Lucas County, Ohio;
uncommon).—GABRIELSON and JEWETT, Birds Oregon, 1940, 219 (Oregon;
distr.; descr.; habits).—DEAR, Trans. Roy. Can. Inst., xxiii, pt. 1, 1940, 127
(Thunder Bay. Lake Superior, Ontario; introduced; now uncommon, local
resident).—GOODPASTER, Journ. Cincinnati Soc. Nat. Hist., xxii, 1941, 13 (sw.
Ohio; frequently introduced but with little success).—HELLMAYR and CONOVER,
Cat. Birds Amer., i, No. 1, 1942, 90 (syn.; distr.).—BEHLE, Bull. Univ. Utah,
xxxiv, 1943, 24 (sw. Utah; Washington County).

Perdix p[erdix] perdix GLEGG, Ibis, 1924, 86 (Macedonia; common resident).—
BROWN, Brit. Birds, xvii, 1924, 228 (Cumberland; perching on trees).—PYCRAFT,
Brit. Birds, xvii, 1924, 314 (pattern of wing coverts).—SCHUSTER, Verh. Orn.
Ges. Bay., xvi, 1924, 59 (Bad Nauheim, Germany).—KAYSER, Verh. Orn. Ges.
Bay., xvi, 1925, 243 (Sagan district, Germany).—LANKDS, Verh. Orn. Ges.
Bay., xvi, 1925, 250 (Bavarian woods).—RIVIERE, Brit. Birds, xx, 1927, 266
(Bylaugh, Norfolk; erythristic varieties).—DROST, Journ. für Orn., lxxv, 1927,
266 (Helgoland; banding records).—POLL, Verh. Orn. Ges. Bay., xvii, 1927,
410 (lower Bavaria).—PFEIFER, Vern. Orn. Ges. Bay., xvii, 1927, 256 (valley
of the Main, Germany).—LEGENDRE, Rev. Franç. d'Orn., xii, 1928, 107 (Paris,
France).—GROEBBELS and MÖBERT, Verh. Orn. Ges. Bay., xviii, 1928, 267
(breeding habits; Hamburg, Germany).—MACPHERSON, Brit. Birds, xxii, 1929,
244 (London).—WÜST, Anz. Orn. Ges. Bay., ii, 1930, 107 (Ampermoos, Bavaria).—SCHIERMAN, Journ. für Orn., lxxviii, 1930, 154 (population density
in breeding season).—ROCARD, L'Oiseau, xi, 1930, 359 (Noirmoutier Island,
France).—RIVIERE, Brit. Birds, xxv, 1932, 354 (Norfolk).—GROEBBELS, Der
Vögel, i, 1932, 185 (altitudinal distr.), 619 (body weight); ii, 1937, 167 (data
on breeding biology).—HICKS, Wils. Bull., xlv, 1933, 180 (Ashtabula County,
Ohio).

[*Perdix*] *perdix perdix* BAILLIE and HARRINGTON, Contr. Roy. Ontario Mus. Zool.,
No. 8, pt. 1, 1936, 30, in text (Ontario).

[*Perdix*] *cinerea* LATHAM, Synop. Birds, Suppl., i, 1787, 290; Index Orn., ii, 1790,
645 (new name for *Tertao perdix*).—REICHENBACH, Synop. Av., iii, Gallinaceae,
1848, pl. 195, figs. 1694, 1696.

Perdix cinerea BONNATERRE, Tabl. Encycl. Méth., i, 1791, 209, pl. 93, fig. 4.—MEYER
and WOLF, Taschenb. deutschl. Vög., i, 1810, 303.—PENNANT, Brit. Zool., i,
1812, 368.—TEMMINCK, Pig. et Gallin., iii, 1815, 373, 378; Man. d'Orn., ii, 1820,
488.—WERNER, Atl. Orn. d'Eur., Ord. 10, 1828, pl. 19.—VIEILLOT, Faun. Franç.,
1828, 248, pl. 108, fig. 1.—BREHM, Handb. Vög. Deutschl., 1831, 524.—SELBY,
Illustr. Brit. Orn., i, 1833, 433, pl. 61.—SCHINZ, Nat. Abbild. Vög., 1833, 162, pl.
79.—NAUMANN, Nat. Vög. Deutschl., vi, 1833, 478, pl. 163.—JARDINE, Nat. Libr.,
Orn., iv, 1834, 95, pl. 1.—GOULD, Birds Eur., iv, 1837, pl. 262 and text.—
MACGILLIVRAY, Brit. Birds, i, 1837, 218.—KÖRNER, Skand. Fogl., 1839-46, 13, pl.

28, fig. 4.—YARRELL, Hist. Brit. Birds, ii, 1843, 333.—GRAY, List Birds Brit. Mus., pt. 3, Gallinae, 1844, 37; ed. 1867, 56.—DEGLAND, Orn. Eur., ii, 1849, 57.— THOMPSON, Nat. Hist. Ireland, ii, 1850, 58.—FALLON, Ois. Belg., 1875, 137.— DRESSER, Birds Europe, vii, 1878, 131, pls. 474, 475.—SAUNDERS, ed. Yarrell's Brit. Birds, iii, 1882, 105; Illustr. Man. Brit. Birds, 1889, 487.—SEEBOHM, Hist. Brit. Birds, ii, 1884, 452.—OLPHE-GALLIARD, Faun. Orn. Eur. Occ., fasc. 39, 1886, 22.—SALVADORI, Ucc. Ital., 1887, 200.—LILFORD, Birds Brit. Isl., pt. 9, 1888, pl.—NAGY, Aquila, xxviii, 1922, 82 in text (Pancsova, Hungary).—SCHENK, Aquila, xxix, 1923, 61, 62 in table (Hungary; banding); xxx-xxxi, 1924, 149 in table (Hungary; banding records); xxxii-xxxiii, 1926, 36 (Hungary; banding records); xxxiv-xxxv, 1929, 32 in table, 44, 76 (Hungary; banding records); xxxvi-xxxvii, 1931, 184, 186 (Hungary; banding records).—BELA v. SZEÖTS, Aquila, xxix, 1923, 134 (Tavarna region, Hungary).—REISER, Aquila, xxx-xxxi, 1924, 294, in text (Fertötavan, Hungary); 316 in text (autumn; Lake Neusiedler, Austria).—NEUBAUR, Verh. Orn. Ges. Bay., xviii, 1928, 304 (Rhone Valley, Germany).—KLEINER, Aquila, xxxvi-xxxvii, 1931, 117 in text (food habits; eats mollusks).—WARGA, Aquila, xxxvi-xxxvii, 1931, 137 in text (Hungary; Sátoraljanjhelyer Forest).

Starna cinerea BONAPARTE, Geogr. and Comp. List, 1838, 43.—KEYSERLING and BLASIUS, Wirbelth. Eur., 1840, 202.—DEGLAND and GERBE, Orn. Eur., ii, 1867, 73.

Perdix (Starna) cinerea MIDDENDORFF, Sibir. Feise, ii, pt. 2, 1855-75, 209 (Barabinska Steppe).

Perdix cinerea var. *scanica* ALTUM, Journ. für Orn., 1894, 268 (s. Sweden).

Cothurnix cinerea LEMETT, Cat. Ois. Seine-Inf., 1874, 118.

Perdix cineracea BREHM, Handb. Vög. Deutschl., 1831, 525 (Renthendorfer region).

Perdix sylvestris BREHM, Vogelf., 1855, 267 (Europe).

Perdix minor BREHM, Vogelf., 1855, 267 (variety with 16 rectrices).

Starna palustris OLPHE-GALLIARD, Ibis, 1864, 225 (Dunkerque; gray phase).

Starna cinerea vulgaris, peregrina, tenuirostris, major BREHM, Verz. Samml., 1866, 11 (nomina nuda).

Perdix (Starna) robusta HOMEYER and TANCRÉ, Mitth. orn. Verh. Wien, vii, 1883, 92 (Altai Mts.).—REICHENOW and SCHALOW, Journ. für Orn., 1885, 456 (reprint of orig. descr.).

Perdix robusta HOMEYER and TANCRÉ, Mitth. orn. Verh. Wien, ix, 1885, pl., figs. 3-5.

Perdix pallida DEMEEZEMAKER, *in* Olphe-Galliard, Faun. Orn. Eur. Occ., fasc. 39, 1886, 37 (new name for *palustris*).

Tetrao damascenus GMELIN, Syst. Nat., i, pt. 2, 1788, 758, part (migrates through central Europe).

Tetrao montanus GMELIN, Syst. Nat., i, pt. 2, 1788, 758 (rufescent phase; mountains of Europe).

Perdix montana WITHERBY et al., Pract. Handb. Brit. Birds, v. 1941, 244, footnote (rufescent phase).

Perdix galliae BACMEISTER and KLEINSCHMIDT, Journ. für Orn., 1918, 254 (ne. France).

Genus PHASIANUS Linnaeus

Phasianus LINNNAEUS, Syst. Nat., ed. 10, i, 1758, 158. (Type, by tautonymy, *P. colchicus* Linnaeus, according to Opinion 16, Internat. Nomencl. Committee.)

Medium-sized Phasiani (total length, including the long tail, about 600–700 mm. in adult males, 500–600 mm. in adult females), with tail flat or but slightly compressed, twice as long as wing in adult male, nearly as long as to much longer than wing in adult females, excessively graduated, the rectrices (18) becoming gradually narrower terminally, with tips acuminate or subacuminate (at least in adult males); pileum not

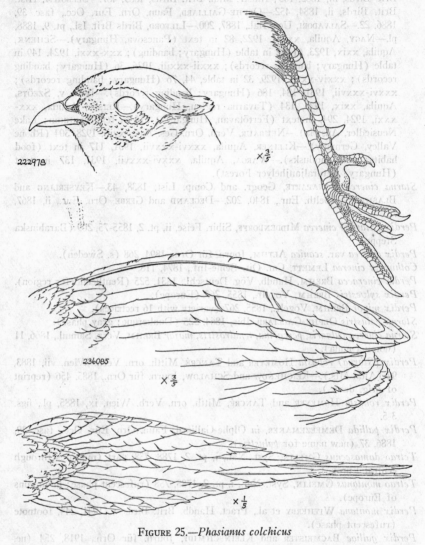

FIGURE 25.—*Phasianus colchicus*

distinctly crested; orbital region partly feathered and malar region completely feathered; without an erectile nuchal "cape"; adult females with middle pair of rectrices not conspicuously longer than next pair.

Bill moderate in size, as deep as or deeper than wide at base of culmen, the latter gradually but rather strongly decurved, the tip of maxilla produced distinctly beyond tip of mandible; maxillary tomium distinctly and more or less regularly concave; cere densely feathered beneath and behind the nostril, the upper portion nude, the upper outline (mesorhinium) more or less ascending basally and arched, the nostrils overhung by a large, tumid operculum. Wing moderate, rounded, with primaries slightly to much longer than longest secondaries; fourth or fourth and fifth primaries longest, the first (outermost) about equal to eighth. Tail decidedly longer than wing (adult male), flat or very nearly so, excessively graduated, the rectrices (18) tapering toward their acuminate or subacuminate tips. Tarsus decidedly less than one-third as long as wing, rather stout, the acrotarsium with two rows of broad transverse scutella (in contact with each other along median line, the planta tarsi also with two rows, but that on inner side composed of smaller scutella; planta tarsi with a conical spur a little below middle, this rudimentary or obsolete in females; middle toe a little more than two-thirds as long as tarsus, the outer toe reaching to middle of subterminal phalanx of middle toe, the inner toe to subterminal articulation of middle toe; hallux elevated, about as long as basal phalanx of outer toe; a distinct web between basal portion of anterior toes; claws rather short, slightly curved, more or less blunt.

Plumage and coloration.—Orbital region more or less nude; pileum without a distinct crest, but sometimes feathers on sides of occiput, immediately above auricular region, elongated and forming a hornlike or earlike tuft on each side; no erectile "cape" on hindneck; contour feathers distinctly outlined, broad and rounded or narrower and more triangular (but barely so and with rounded tip). Adult males brilliantly colored or with beautiful and complicated pattern of subdued colors, metallic hues being usually present; tail always with transverse markings. Adult females brownish and buffy, variegated with blackish, etc.

Range.—Southeastern Europe to eastern Siberia, Japan, and Formosa. (One species with over 40 subspecies, 2 of which are mixed in the stock introduced into North America.)

PHASIANUS COLCHICUS TORQUATUS Gmelin

RING-NECKED PHEASANT

Adult male.—Forehead black with bright dark green sheen; broad superciliaries white; crown fairly glossy Roman green tinged with ecru-olive, the latter tone becoming more noticeable on the hindcrown and occiput; lores, sides of head, except for a small auricular patch of dark bluish-green feathers that extends forward under the eye, bare; superciliaries narrowly edged below with dark glossy greenish-black feathers like those of the forehead and extending from the forehead to the base of an erectile tuft of truncate iridescent blue-green blackish feathers on the postero-dorsal corner of the occiput on each side; nape very glossy bottle green to dark zinc green, laterally tinged with glossy dark violet-blue, which predominates on the sides of the neck, although even there it is posteriorly replaced by glossy bottle green; chin, throat, and malar region like the forehead but with a little more blue in the sheen and the lower throat becoming bottle green; a complete (usually) white collar around the base of the neck separates the head and neck coloration from that of the body although in some cases the bottle green continues on the middorsal area for a very little distance posterior to the collar; interscapulars with their exposed portions bright buff yellow with a terminally widening median wedge of bright blue-green black and with edgings of the same, but slightly duller and narrower; from the base of the median wedge-shaped marks a fuscous to fuscous-black band goes off toward the sides of the feathers in a posteriorly pointed diagonal, leaving a large, white, terminally pointed, triangular space in the center of the feather; the basal half of the feather dull sepia; in the lower (posterior) interscapulars, the so-called hackle feathers, the white triangles are transformed into bands of white with median fuscous shaft marks and extend into the visible pattern of the overlapping feathers, largely replacing the buff-yellow; these posterior interscapulars also have the bright green terminal median wedges re-placed by dark fuscous (the whole interscapular area varies greatly according to the amount of *P. c. colchicus* blood in the strain, the buff-yellow becoming more tawny or orange-tawny, the bottle green more blue-black in birds with a larger amount of pure *colchicus* blood in them); scapulars and inner greater and median upper coverts Kaiser brown to Hay's russet with a terminal light magenta gloss and with large white to light buff centers edged with black and sometimes mottled sparingly with the same; lesser inner upper wing coverts with the russet borders narrow or missing, leaving the feathers white bordered and centered with fuscous to fuscous-black; rest of upper wing coverts light gull gray to light neutral gray, paling to white at the bend of the wing; long innermost greater coverts and the long scapulars neutral gray much tinged with pale olive-buff and broadly edged, but not tipped, with Hay's russet (in birds with more *colchicus* than *torquatus* blood all the gray feathers are olive-buff, sometimes almost buffy brown, and the russet edges are heavily washed with purplish); secondaries pale buffy brown, incompletely barred along the basal half or more of the shaft with backward-pointing, diagonal, white, wavy bars, which are narrowly edged with dusky buffy brown, these marks not showing in the folded wing and sometimes almost be-coming longitudinal wavy marks running toward the base of the feathers; the innermost secondaries with narrow lateral edgings of Hay's russet; primaries darker and more grayish, less buffy, brown and crossed on both webs with wavy whitish bars except on their terminal portions; upper back like the scapulars, but with the white centers medially marked with deep bottle green; back, lower back, and rump greenish glaucous to deep lichen green, laterally and posteriorly extensively tinged with glaucous-gray; the feathers of the median part of the back and lower back with large dusky centers, which are completely edged and sometimes barred and mottled with pale buff, the dark areas with a greenish gloss terminally, dull fuscous basally; upper tail coverts like the rump but with some pale tawny-russet edgings; the dusky median parts with their pale edges completely hidden by the elongated tips of the feathers; in birds with more *colchicus* than *torquatus* blood the whole lower back, rump, and upper tail coverts have the glaucous-green and gray replaced by Hay's russet to Kaiser brown, and the green of the back more brownish and darker; tail feathers olive-buff to dark olive-buff crossed by many blackish bars (the longest central pair of rectrices with 20–25 such bars), the bars narrower than the paler interspaces; the lateral edges of the rectrices, except the terminal third or so, brownish vinaceous, the dark bars becoming sorghum brown to vinaceous-brown, the edges of the vanes much frayed (in birds with more *colchicus* than *torquatus* blood the rectrices are tawny-olive instead of olive-buff, and the lateral parts Verona brown to Prout's brown); breast dark coppery hazel, the feathers broadly glossed terminally with magenta purple with narrow **W**-shaped black tips the broadest part of the **W** being the median portion along the shaft, the black with a bluish gloss (in birds with more *colchicus* blood these dark terminal edges are better developed and sometimes produce a scalloped pattern); sides and flanks light, bright buff-yellow, the feathers with large wedge-shaped terminal shaft spots of shining blue-black, narrowly edged with zinc orange in some specimens; center of upper abdomen black, each feather broadly tipped and less broadly edged with shining dark green or blue-green; lateral to this are a number of feathers like those of the breast but more squarely truncate and with large wedge-shaped terminal spots like the laterally adjacent feathers of the sides and flanks (in birds with more *colchicus* blood the feathers of the sides and flanks are bright orange-tawny instead of buff-yellow); rest of abdomen and thighs dull Prout's brown to mummy brown with a slight mixture of paler buffy brown feathers; under tail coverts hazel to russet with concealed dusky mummy-brown basal-median areas; the more lateral and anterior of these feathers with a slight amount of pinkish-purplish sheen; undersurface of tail feathers very dark clove brown, the paler interspaces between the dark bars much suffused and mottled with dusky; under wing coverts white to pale buffy white, the axillars with dusky brownish bars; bare skin of sides of head bright red; iris hazel; bill pale greenish yellow; tarsi and toes brownish gray.

Adult female.—Feathers of center of forehead and crown fuscous-black, edged with ochraceous-tawny to hazel, those of the hindcrown and occiput similar but banded and edged with buffy and only sparingly tinged with hazel; lores and anterior part of superciliaries (from anterior end of eye to the nape), nape, and sides of neck light vinaceous-fawn to pale grayish vinaceous, each feather narrowly tipped with blackish; the feathers pale

hazel to tawny basally with a broad transverse blotch of dull sepia before
the vinaceous-fawn area (this blotch and the tawny area hidden by the
overlapping of the feathers); interscapulars bright hazel to tawny-russet
completely edged with pale vinaceous-fawn, the russet central area termi-
nating in a broad fuscous to fuscous-black, distally pointed **V**; scapulars
and larger inner greater and median upper wing coverts Sayal brown
to tawny-olive, edged and tipped with pale buffy; the tawny-olive color
giving place to a heavy fuscous-black mass either as an attenuated median
pattern extending distally along the shaft or as abruptly transverse area;
in the latter case the dark part is more extensive than the tawny portion;
rest of upper wing coverts pinkish buff to pale ochraceous-buff, edged
with somewhat paler, and with their centers very heavily blotched with
dull, dusky sepia; long scapulars and innermost secondaries tawny to
tawny-olive, their median areas with heavy elongated blotches and
marbling of blackish, edged and tipped with pale buffy; rest of secondaries
dull olive-brown crossed by five to seven bands of pale buffy to pale
pinkish buff, these bands much narrower than the dark interspaces but
tending to coalesce on the outer margin of the outer secondaries; primaries
rather light clove brown barred with wavy whitish or pale pinkish buff
bars, those on the outer webs whitish, those on the inner webs considerably suffused with pinkish to pale tawny-buff; upper back like the scapulars; feathers of the back, lower back, rump, and upper tail coverts deep
fuscous-black to chaetura black, broadly edged and tipped with pale
pinkish buff to pale tawny-buff, the more posterior ones with the dark
centers medially divided into **V**'s by buffy shaft stripes which fail to extend to the ends of the feathers; the pale edges wider and tawnier on
the upper tail coverts than elsewhere; rectrices light pinkish avellaneous,
the median pairs suffused with hazel medially, all transversely blotched
or banded with fuscous-black; on the inner pairs a paler avellaneous
band between the adjacent dark ones, the rest of the feathers sparingly
flecked with dusky brown; the lateral rectrices considerably suffused with
light vinaceous-fawn; chin and upper throat whitish; malar stripe and
auriculars buffy brown with a slightly golden hue; lower throat like sides
of neck but slightly less vinaceous; upper breast like lower throat but
somewhat more buffy; feathers of breast pinkish buff with a faint olive-
buffy tinge, obscurely and faintly marked with transverse lines of duskier
and with concealed large dark brownish **V**-shaped bars and tawny bases;
feathers of the sides and flanks with these dark brownish markings exposed and increased in size and number; upper and lateral parts of abdomen like the lower breast but without any concealed basal bars or tawny
color, and slightly warmer buffy in tone; middle of lower abdomen similar
but slightly paler; thighs like the lateral parts of the abdomen but obscurely barred with hair brown; under tail coverts light russet broadly
tipped and subterminally transversely mottled with pinkish buff; under

wing coverts very pale buffy brown edged and tipped with whitish; iris, bill, and feet as in male.

Juvenal male.—Forehead, crown, occiput, and nape dull fuscous, the feathers narrowly tipped with pale buffy brown; lores and a narrow superciliary stripe pale pinkish buff to light buff; interscapulars and scapulars dark fuscous to chaetura black completely edged with ashy cinnamon-buff and with narrow buffy shafts; upper wing coverts similar but with lateral extensions of buff from the shafts forming incomplete bars of the same; secondaries dark fuscous to clove brown barred with pale ashy buff, the pale bars flecked with dusky; primaries dusky clove brown with fairly broad bars of whitish or very pale buff on the outer webs and also on the basal part of the inner webs; back, lower back, rump, and upper tail coverts dull fuscous to dusky sepia, the feathers completely edged with pale ashy cinnamon-buff and with paler buffy shafts and median wedge-shaped markings of the same, these marks largely absent on the upper tail coverts [4]; rectrices dusky avellaneous crossed by many broad bars of clove brown each of which is proximally bordered with tawny Sayal brown, the feathers externally edged with pale ashy cinnamon-buff; sides of face largely bare; chin and throat pale buffy to almost white; auriculars, sides of neck and malar area and lower throat pale warm buff streaked with dull grayish sepia; breast dark pinkish buff spotted with dull sepia; feathers of sides and flanks clove brown to dull sepia completely edged with pinkish buff and with broad shaft stripes of the same; abdomen, thighs, and under tail coverts pale pinkish buff with a slight grayish tinge, some of the feathers, especially of the thighs and under tail coverts faintly blotched or transversely mottled with sepia to wood brown; bill dark horn color; iris brown; tarsi and toes dark brown.

Juvenal female.—Like the corresponding stage of the male but with no bare area on the sides of the head; the sides of the neck somewhat more vinaceous, the auriculars less grayish, slightly more brownish; interscapulars more vinaceous in tone.

Natal down.—Forehead and sides of crown pale cinnamon-buff to ochraceous-buff; center of crown and occiput dark fuscous to fuscous-black, becoming washed with rufescent on the posterior occiput and nape which is almost chestnut-brown; upperparts of body pale tawny-buff tinged with tawny-russet and with three broad fuscous-black stripes; wings with blotches of fuscous-black and rufescent; sides of head pale ochraceous-buff; a blackish spot on the auriculars; a light sepia malar streak; underparts pale buffy yellow tinged with tawny or pale ochraceous,

---

[4] According to Leffingwell (Occ. Pap. Conner Mus., i, 1928, 21) the upper tail coverts in juvenal males are barred "with olive buff, often running to chestnut on the margins." I have seen but one young male and do not find this to hold for it.

especially on the breast and sides; iris dark brown; bill horn color, darker on the maxilla; tarsi and toes pinkish white.

Adult male.—Wing 213–245.5 (234.1); tail 408.0–513.0 (451.2); culmen from base 38.3–43.1 (40.0); tarsus 68.0–75.5 (71.7); middle toe without claw 42.1–48.7 (45.0 mm.).[5]

Adult female.—Wing 194.0–216.0 (205.8); tail 236.0–273.0 (252.5); culmen from base 32.3–38.2 (35.9); tarsus 61.1–68.2 (63.7); middle toe without claw 35.1–41.4 (39.6 mm.).[6]

Range.—Native to "eastern and south-eastern China from Canton to Hunan, north to the Lower and Middle Yangtse, up the river at least to Ichang; north to Pekin, Kalgan, and the Ordos country" (Beebe). The nominate form, *P. c. colchicus,* the blood of which also enters into our hybrid ring-necked pheasants, is native to "Transcaucasia, including the basins of the Rion and the Chorokh Rivers and the southeastern coast of the Black Sea, north to Sukhum-Kale, just south of the main east and west chain of the Caucasus Mountains; the bases of the Kura and lower Araxes and their tributaries up to nearly three thousand feet above sea level. It touches the Caspian Sea at the Kizil-Agatch Gulf" (Beebe).

Introduced now and fairly well established in approximately the northern half of the United States and in southern Canada; large parts of Europe (where the *colchicus* strain is more in evidence than is the *torquatus*)—Belgium, France, England, Germany, Greece, Holland, Sweden, and Italy; also in Hawaii (Oahu, Molokai, and Kauai), Samoa (subsp.?), St. Helena, and New Zealand. In North America it was first introduced about 1790 in New Hampshire, then about 1800 in New Jersey; 1857 in California; 1881 in Oregon; besides other smaller introductions. Its present North American range is from Vancouver Island and southern British Columbia, southern Alberta, southern Manitoba, southern Ontario, and southwestern Maine, south to Maryland, Pennsylvania, Ohio, Kentucky, Missouri, Kansas, Colorado, and California. South of this area its introduction has not been particularly successful, but it may be noted that about 1928 the bird was listed as a game species in all but three States of the United States.

Unsuccessfully introduced into Chile.

Type locality (of true *P. c. torquatus*).—Southeastern China.

[*Phasianus*] *torquatus* GMELIN, Syst. Nat., i, pt. 2, 1788, 742 (Ring Pheasant, Lath. Syn., ii, 2, 715).—REICHENBACH, Synop. Av., iii, Gallinaceae, 1848, pl. 221, figs. 1944-1946.—GRAY, Handlist, ii, 1879, 257, No. 9575.—SHARPE, Handlist, i, 1899, 37 part (China).

Phasianus torquatus TEMMINCK, Cat. Syst., 1807, 148.—LEACH, Zool. Misc., ii, 1815, 13, pl. 66.—GRIFFITH, ed. Cuvier's Règne Anim., iii, 1829, 22 part, pl.—JARDINE, Nat. Libr., Orn., iv, 1834, 189, pl. 13 (hybrid with *P. colchicus*).—GRAY, List

[5] Sixteen specimens.
[6] Seven specimens.

Birds Brit. Mus., iii, pt. 3, Gallinæ, 1844, 43; pt. 5, 1867, 27.—Gould, Birds Asia, vii, 1856, pl. 39 and text.—Sclater and Wolf, Zool. Sketches, i, 1861, pl. 37.—Sclater, Proc. Zool. Soc. London, 1863, 116 (monogr.).—David, Proc. Zool. Soc. London, 1868, 210 (Province of Pekin, China).—Swinhoe, Proc. Zool. Soc. London, 1871, 398 (Canton to Pekin and w. to Hankow, China).— Elliot, Monogr. Phasianidae, ii, 1871, pl. 5 and text, part.—Merriam, Rep. Comm. Agr. for 1888 (1889), 485 (Protection Island, Puget Sound), 486 (abundant in Polk, Marion, and Linn Counties, Oreg.).—Ogilvie-Grant, Cat. Birds Brit. Mus., xxii, 1893, 331, part.—Cooke, Colorado State Agr. Coll. Bull. 44, 1898, 159 (Colorado, resident).—Macoun, Cat. Can. Birds, 1900, 214 (Vancouver and mainland of British Columbia; introduced).—Henshaw, Birds Hawaiian Islands, 1902, 134 (established on Oahu, Molokai, and Kauai Islands). —Bailey, Handb. Birds Western United States, 1902, 135 (descr.; distr.).— Jones, Birds Ohio, Revised Cat., 1903, 220 (Ohio; introduced).—Dawson, Birds Ohio, 1903, 430, 660 (Ohio; introduced); Birds of California, stud. ed.; iii, 1923, 1567 (genl.; California).—Walton, Ibis, 1903, 32 (Pekin, China).— Townsend, Mem. Nuttall Orn. Club, No. 3, 1905, 315 (Essex County, Mass.).— Henninger, Wils. Bull., xviii, 1906, 60 (Seneca County, Ohio; breeding).— Brewster, Mem. Nuttall Orn. Club, No. 4, 1906, 173 (Cambridge, Mass.; hist.).—Widmann, Birds Missouri, 1907, 82.—Bryan, Occ. Pap. Bishop Mus., iv, No. 2, 1908, 56 [146] (Molokai, Hawaiian Islands).—Kermode, [Visitors' Guide] Publ. Province Mus., 1909, 42 (Vancouver Island, lower Fraser River, etc., British Columbia).—Macoun and Macoun, Cat. Can. Birds, ed. 2, 1909, 235 (introduced into Vancouver Island, and mainland of British Columbia).— Dawson and Bowles, Birds of Washington, ii, 1909, 602 (Washington; descr.; distr.).—Eaton, Birds New York, i, 1910, 378 (established in New York).— Swarth, Rep. Birds and Mamm. Vancouver Island, 1912, 25 (French Creek; Errington).—Betts, Univ. Colorado Stud. Zool., x, 1913, 192 (Boulder County, Colo., up to 9,000 feet).—Bailey, Birds Virginia, 1913, 87 (Virginia; introduced; breeds).—Rockwell and Wetmore, Auk, xxxi, 1914, 314 (Lookout Mountain, Colo., up to 7,500 feet).—Grinnell, Pacific Coast Avif., No. 11, 1915, 179 (California).—Howell, Condor, xix, 1917, 187 (Upper Owens Valley, Calif.).— Dice, Auk, xxxv, 1918, 44 (near Prescott and Walla Walla, se. Washington).— Grinnell, Bryant, and Storer, Game Birds California, 1918, 572 (descr.; distr.; habits; California).—Willett, Condor, xxi, 1919, 202 (near Burns, se. Oregon).—Lincoln, Auk, xxxvii, 1920, 65 (Clear Creek District, Colo., plentiful).—Over and Thoms, Birds South Dakota, 1921, 71 (increasing in South Dakota).—Faxon and Hoffman, Auk, xxxix, 1922, 70 (Berkshire County, Mass.; "well established").—Griscom, Birds New York City Region, 1923, 176 (status, New York City region).—Gabrielson, Auk, xli, 1924, 555 (status, Oregon); Condor, xxxiii, 1931, 112 (introduced, Rogue River Valley, Oreg.).—Larson, Wils. Bull., xxxvii, 1925, 28 (status; Sioux Falls region, South Dakota); xl, 1928, 46 (e. McKenzie County, N. Dak.).—Blincoe, Auk, xlii, 1925, 418 (near Bardstown, Ky.).—Taverner, Birds Western Canada, 1926, 162 (fig.; descr.; Canada).—Schenk, Aquila, xxxii-xxxiii, 1926, 36 (banding records; Hungary).—von Burg, in Fatio and Studer, Ois. Suisse, xv, 1926, 3155 (monogr.; Switzerland).—Mousley, Auk, xliv, 1927, 522 (Hatley, Quebec).—McCurdy, Wils. Bull., xl, 1928, 202, in text (fighting a bull snake).—Alford, Ibis, 1928, 197 (Vancouver, British Columbia).—Burleigh, Auk, xlvi, 1929, 510 (Kirkland; Renton, Wash.).—Snyder, Trans. Roy. Can. Inst., xvii, pt. 2, 1930, 187 (summer; King Township, Ontario).—Brown, Murrelet, xi, 1930, 18 text (Seattle, Wash.; several records).—Caum, Occ. Pap. Bishop Mus., x, No. 9, 1933, 21 (Hawaii; introduced; well established).—

JEWETT, Murrelet, xvii, 1936, 43 (Harney County, Oreg.; "not uncommon";
hist.).—GRIFFEE and RAPRAEGER, Murrelet, xviii, 1937, 14 text, 16 (Portland,
Oreg.; nesting dates).—EINARSEN, Murrelet, xxii, 1941, 39 text (Straits of
Juan de Fuca, Wash.; swimming habits; 1 specimen).
P[hasianus] torquatus RIDGWAY, Man. North Amer. Birds, 1887, 206.—BRYAN,
Key to the Birds Hawaiian Group, 1901, 30.
Phasianus colchicus torquatus HARTERT, Vög. pal. Fauna, iii, 1921, 1991 (monogr.).—
BEEBE, Monogr. Pheasants, iii, 1922, 120, pl. lix (monogr.; col. fig.).—GLADSTONE,
Brit. Birds, xvii, 1923, 36 (introduction into Great Britian).—STRESEMANN, Orn.
Monatsb., xxxii, 1924, 168 in text (misc.).—GENGLER, Verh. Orn. Ges. Bay., xvi,
1925, Sonderheft 95, 274 (Bavaria).—FORBUSH, Birds Massachusetts and Other
New England States, ii, 1927, 15, pl. 35 (fig.; descr.; habits; New England).—
SUTTON, Birds Pennsylvania, 1928, 51 (Pennsylvania; descr.; range; nest.;
hist.).—BAILEY, Birds New Mexico, 1928, 229 (genl.; New Mexico).—DELACOUR,
JABOUILLE, and LOWE, Ibis, 1928 (Nganson, Tonkin; crit.).—COTTAM, Condor,
xxxi, 1929, 117 (status in Utah).—SWENK, Univ. Nebraska Agr. Exp. Stat.
Research Bull. 50, 1930, 5, in text (introduced into North America, food in
Nebraska).—MILLER, Murrelet, xi, 1930, 61 text (Palouse region; introd.).—
WELLMAN, Auk, xlvii, 1930, 525 (Boston Public Garden).—PIERCE, Wils. Bull.,
xlii, 1930, 266 (status, Buchanan County, Iowa); Proc. Iowa Acad. Sci., xlvii,
1941, 376 (ne. Iowa; winter; permanent resident).—BRADLEE and MOWBRAY,
Proc. Boston Soc. Nat. Hist., xxxix, 1931, 325 (Bermuda; introd.).—CHRISTY,
Auk, xlviii, 1931, 375 (change of status, Sandusky Bay, Lake Erie).—BAERG,
Univ. Arkansas Agr. Exp. Stat. Bull. 258, 1931, 56 (descrip.; range).—SCHENK,
Aquila, xxxvi-xxxvii, 1931, 196 (banding; Hungary, 1928-30).—CALDWELL and
CALDWELL, South China Birds, 1931, 279, (s. China; desc.; habits, etc.).—
AMERICAN ORNITHOLOGISTS' UNION, Check-list, ed. 4, 1931, 91 (distr.).—JEWETT,
Condor, xxxiv, 1932, 191 (hybrid between this form and Dendragapus obscurus
fuliginosus).—ROBERTS, Birds Minnesota, i, 1932, 417 (habits; distr.; Min-
nesota).—BENT, U. S. Nat. Mus. Bull. 162, 1932, 310 (habits; distr.).—LA
TOUCHE, Handb. Birds Eastern China, ii, pt. 3, 1932, 228 (distr. China; descr.;
habits, etc.).—GROEBBELS, Der Vögel, i, 1932, 73 in table (bronchial tubes), 664
(body temperature); ii, 1937, 45 in text (sex relations), 167 (data on breeding
biology), 241 in text (eggs in mixed sets), 323 in text (40 to 104 eggs per year).
—BENNITT, Univ. Missouri Stud., vii, No. 3, 1932, 26 (Missouri; uncommon
permanent resident).—STONER, Roosevelt Wild Life Ann., ii, Nos. 3, 4, 1932, 436
(habits; Oneida Lake region, N. Y.).—RANSOM, Murrelet, xiii, 1932, 51 text
(Harrison, Idaho; flight habits).—EDSON, Murrelet, xiii, 1932, 43 (e. Washington; several records).—CUMMING, Murrelet, xiii, 1932, 14 (Vancouver,
British Columbia; common; introd.).—WILLETT, Pacific Coast Avif., No. 21,
1933, 50 (sw. California; nest and eggs near San Bernardino).—HICKS, Wils.
Bull., xlv, 1933, 180 (Ashtabula County, Ohio).—MURRAY, Auk, l, 1933, 195
(introduced in Virginia: Warwick County, Hot Springs, lower end of Valley of
Virginia).—MONSON, Wils. Bull., xlvi, 1934, 43 (Cass County, N. Dak.; common
resident).—LONG, Bull. Univ. Kansas Sci., xxxvi, 1935, 234 (w. Kansas; intro-
duced); Trans. Kansas Acad. Sci., xliii, 1940, 441 (Kansas; introduced; common
in nw. parts).—FISHER, Proc. Biol. Soc. Washington, xlviii, 1935, 161 (Plummers
Island, Md.).—McCREARY and MICKEY, Wils. Bull., xlvii, 1935, 129 in text (se.
Wyoming; resident).—YOUNGWORTH, Wils. Bull., xlvii, 1935, 217 (becoming
common, Fort Sisseton, S. Dak.).—SHELLEY, Auk, lii, 1935, 307 in text (New
Hampshire; albinism).—MILLER, LUMLEY, and HALL, Murrelet, xvi, 1935, 58
(San Juan Islands; common).—WEYDEMEYER and MARSH, Condor, xxxviii, 1936,
194 (Lake Bowdoin, Mont.).—IMLER, Trans. Kansas Acad. Sci., xxxix, 1936, 301

(Rooks County, Kans.; common until 1934; since largely killed by dust storms).
—ALEXANDER, Univ. Colorado Stud. Zool., xxiv, 1937, 91 (Boulder County,
Colo.; very common resident; spec. Univ. Colorado Mus.).—STONE, Bird Studies
Cape May, i, 1937, 327 (New Jersey; status, habits).—WETMORE, Proc. U. S.
Nat. Mus., lxxxiv, 1937, 408 in text.—BAGG and ELIOT, Birds Connecticut Valley
in Massachusetts, 1937, 175 (Connecticut Valley, Mass.; permanent resident;
introd.).—DEADERICK, Wils. Bull., 1, 1938, 263 (Hot Springs Nat. Park, Ark.;
1 seen).—BENNETT, Blue-winged Teal, 1938, 49 in text, 66 in text (laying eggs in
blue-winged teal's nests).—POOLE, Auk, lv, 1938, 517 in table (weight, wing
area).—MACLULICH, Contr. Roy. Ontario Mus. Zool., No. 13, 1938, 12 (Algonquin Prov. Park, Ontario; introduced unsuccessfully).—VAN TYNE, Occ. Pap.
Mus. Zool. Univ. Michigan, No. 379, 1938, 12 (Michigan; brought in about
1918 now permanent resident north to Arenac, Gladwin, and Mason Counties
and very locally north to Charlevoix; breeding records).—TRAUTMAN, BILLS,
and WICKLIFF, Wils. Bull., li, 1939, 101 in text (winter mortality; Ohio).—
ERRINGTON, Wils. Bull., li, 1939, 22 in text (ability to withstand cold and hunger);
liii, 1941, 87 in text (mentioned).—NIEDRACH and ROCKWELL, Birds Denver and
Mountain Parks, 1939, 64 (introduced resident; distr.; habits; food).—MILLER
and CURTIS, Murrelet, xxi, May 1940, 42 (Univ. Washington campus; resident).
—CAMPBELL, Bull. Toledo Mus. Sci., i, 1940, 64 (Lucas County, Ohio; hist.;
common resident; distr.).—UNDERHILL, Auk, lvii, 1940, 566 in text (eating birds;
New York).—DEAR, Trans. Roy. Can. Inst., xxiii, pt. 1, 1940, 127 (Thunder Bay,
Lake Superior, Ontario; introduced species; hard winters and predatory birds
and animals make it doubtful if many survive).—TRAUTMAN, Misc. Publ. Mus.
Zool. Univ. Michigan, No. 44, 1940, 226 (Buckeye Lake, Ohio; common resident;
habits).—GABRIELSON and JEWETT, Birds Oregon, 1940, 227 (Oregon, distr.;
descr.; habits).—FRIED, Wils. Bull., liii, 1941, 44 (Minneapolis; food habits).—
BRUCKNER, Auk, lviii, 1941, 536 text (white plumage inheritance).—STABLER,
Auk, lviii, 1941, 561 (used in parasite experiment).—GOODPASTER, Journ.
Cincinnati Soc. Nat. Hist., xxii, 1941, 13 (sw. Ohio; introduced each
year but do not thrive well).—HELLMAYR and CONOVER, Cat. Birds Amer., i,
No. 1, 1942, 290 (syn.; distr.).—PETRIDES, Trans. 7th North Amer. Wildlife
Conf., 1942, 323 in text (age indicators in plumage).—PEARSON, BRIMLEY, and
BRIMLEY, Birds North Carolina, 1942, 110 (North Carolina).—KNOWLTON and
HARMSTON, Auk, lx, 1943, 589 (Utah; food habits).—LINDUSKA, Auk, lx, 1943,
427 in text (anatomy; bursa; age indicators).—WRIGHT and HIATT, Auk, lx,
1943, 266 in text (age indicators in plumage; Montana).—BEHLE, Bull. Univ.
Utah, xxxiv, 1943, 24 (sw. Utah, Washington County); Condor, xlvi, 1944, 72
(Utah; introd.).

Phasianus colchius torquatus BRECKINRIDGE, Condor, xxxvii, 1935, 269 (Minnesota).
Phasianus c[olchicus] torquatus SCHENK Aquila, xxxiv-xxxv, 1929, 32, in table
(banding; Hungary, 1926-1927); xxxvi-xxxvii, 1931, 184 (banding; Hungary,
1928-1930).—BRECKINRIDGE, Condor, xxxvii, 1935, 272 (eaten by marsh hawk).
—MARSHALL and LEATHAM, Auk, lix, 1942, 44 (Great Salt Lake Island).
[Phasianus] colchicus torquatus BAILLIE and HARRINGTON, Contr. Roy. Ontario
Mus. Zool., No. 8, pt. 1, 1936, 31 in text (Ontario).
[Phasianus] c[olchicus] torquatus GROEBBELS, Der Vögel, ii, 1937, 41 in text (cock
feathering).
Phasianus colchicus subsp.? WHITE, Auk, xliii, 1926, 378 (resident; breeding; New
Hampshire).
Phasianus colchicus x Phasianus torquatus PEARSON, BRIMLEY, and BRIMLEY, Birds
North Carolina, 1919, 156 (North Carolina; descr.; range).

Phasianus colchicus x *torquatus* PICKENS, Wils. Bull., xl, 1928, 189 (Upper South Carolina).—GRISCOM, Trans. Linn. Soc. New York, iii, 1933, 97 (Dutchess County, N. Y., permanent resident; introduced in 1913, now well established and generally distributed).

Phasianus colchicus + *P[hasianus] torquatus* BURNS, Ornith. Chester County, Pa., 1919, 49 (Chester County, Pa.; permanent resident).

[*phasianus*] *colchicus* (part) LINNAEUS, Syst. Nat., ed. 10, i, 1758, 158 ("Habitat in Africa, Asia"; based on Ray, Albin, Aldrovandus, etc.); ed. 12, i, 1766, 271.—GMELIN, Syst. Nat., i, pt. 2, 1788, 741.—LATHAM, Synop. Birds, Suppl. i, 1787, 289; Index Orn., ii, 1790, 629.—GRAY, Handlist, ii, 1870, 257, No 9574.—SHARPE, Handlist, i, 1899, 37.—BUTURLIN, Ibis, 1904, 379 (diagnosis)

Phasianus colchicus TEMMINCK, Cat. Syst., 1807, 147 part; Man. d'Orn., 1815, 282; ed. 2, 1820, 453, part.—MEYER and WOLF, Taschenb. deutschl. Vög., i, 1810, 291, part, pl.—VIEILLOT, Nouv. Dict. d'Hist. Nat., xi, 1817, 29, part.—WERNER, Atl. Ois. d'Eur., Ord. 10, 1828, pls. 1, 2.—SELBY, Illustr. Brit. Orn., i, 1833, 417, part, pl. 57.—NAUMANN, Nat. Vög. Deutschl., v, 1833, 432 part, pl. 162.—MACGILLIVRAY, Brit. Birds, i, 1837, 114, part.—GOULD, Birds Eur. iv, 1837, pl. 247 and text; Birds Asia, vii, 1869, pl. 34 and text; Birds Great Brit., iv, 1873, pl. 12 and text.—KEYSERLING AND BLASIUS, Wirbelth Eur., 1840, p. lxiv.—YARRELL, Hist. Brit. Birds, ii, 1843, 277, part; ed. 2, ii, 1845, 310, part; ed. 3, ii, 1856, 320, part.—SCHLEGEL, Rev. Crit., 1844, p. lxxiv.—REICHENBACH, Synop. Av., iii, Gallinaceae, 1848, pl. 221, figs. 1925-1937.—DEGLAND, Orn. Eur., ii, 1849, 40, part.—GRAY, List Birds Brit. Mus., pt. 5, Gallinæ, 1867, 26, part.—ELLIOT, Monogr. Phasianidae, ii, 1872, pl. 2 and text, part.—HARTING, Handb. Brit. Birds, 1872, 37, part.—DRESSER, Birds Europe, vii, pt. 75, 1879, 85, part, pl. 469.—WHITEHEAD, Ibis, 1885, 41 (Corsica).—SEEBOHM, Ibis, 1887, 170 (crit.).—OGILVIE-GRANT, Cat. Birds Brit. Mus., xxii, 1893, 320, part.—BUTURLIN, Ibis, 1904, 385 (range, etc.; "basins of the Rion and eastern coasts of Black Sea, not farther north than Sukhum-Kala").—WIDMANN, Birds Missouri, 1907, 82.—STONE, Birds New Jersey, 152 (New Jersey; descr.; hist.; eggs).—EATON, Birds New York, i, 1910, 378.—HARTERT et al., Handb. Brit. Birds, 1912, 216.—BRITISH ORNITHOLOGISTS' UNION, List Brit. Birds, ed. 2, 1915, 311.—BANNERMAN, Ibis, 1920, 527 (no valid record for Canaries).—GRISCOM, Birds New York City Region, 1923, 176 (status, New York City region).—WITHERBY, Brit. Birds, xvii, 1923, 43 (breeding in old nests in trees); Ibis, 1928, 663 (central Spain).—LOYD, Brit. Birds, xvii, 1923, 159 (Lundy; introduced).—WITHERBY et al., Practical Handb. Brit. Birds, ii, pt. 18, 1924, 869 (monogr).—VAN OORDT, Ardea, xiii, 1924, 68 (near Pirth; near Aviemore, Scotland).—KAYSER, Verh. Orn. Ges. Bay., xvi, 1925, 243 (Sagan district, Germany).—VON BURG, *in* Fatio and Studer; Ois. Suisse, xv, 1926, 3155 (monogr.; Switzerland).—SCHENK, Aquila, xxxii-xxxiii, 1926, 36 (banding records; Hungary); xxxiv-xxxv, 1929, 32 in table, 44, 76 (banding, Hungary, 1926-27); xxxvi-xxxvii, (devel. of young in captivity).—GROEBBELS and MÖBERT, Verh. Orn. Ges. Bay., xvii, 1926, 35 (Deggendorf, Germany).—PFEIFER, Verh. Orn. Ges. Bay., xvii, 1927, 256 (valley of the Main, Germany).—POLL, Verh. Orn. Ges. Bay., xvii, 1927, 409 (lower Bavaria).—HEINROTH, Vög. Mitteleurop., iii, 1927-28, 243 (devel. of young in captivity).—GROEBBELS and MÖBERT, Verh. Orn. Ges. Bay., xviii, 1928, 267 (breeding habits; Hamburg, Germany).—NEUBAUR, Verh. Orn. Ges. Bay., ii, xviii, 1928, 303 (Rhone Valley, Germany).—BOETTICHER, Anz. Orn. Ges. Bay., ii, 1929, 43 (Coburg, Bavaria).—BREUER, Aquila, xxxiv-xxxv, 1929, 446 (nervousness during meteor storm).—URNER, Abstr. Linn. Soc. New York, No. 39, 40, 1930, 71 (Union County, N. J.).—MÜLLER, Verh. Orn. Ges. Bay., xix, 1930, 96 (Lake Maising, Bavaria; habits).—KOCH, Ardea, xix, 1930,

57 (banding records, Wassenaar station, Holland).—WARGA, Aquila, xxxvi-xxxvii, 1931, 137 in text (Sátoraljavjhelyer Forest, Hungary).—LUNAU, Beitr. Fortpfl. Vog., viii, 1932, 190 (early breeding).—TICEHURST, Birds Suffolk, 1932, 476 (status; habits; Suffolk, England).—TICEHURST and WHISTLER, Ibis, 1932, 92 (mouth of the Drin, Albania).—TAVERNER, Birds Canada, 1934, 165 in text (introduced in Canada); Can. Water Birds, 1939, 178 (field characters; Canada).—BAILLIE and HARRINGTON, Contr. Roy. Ont. Mus. Zool., No. 8, pt. 1, 1936, 30 (Ontario; common breeds; resident of more southern parts; introduced from Europe; breed. range).—WETMORE, Proc. U. S. Nat. Mus., lxxxiv, 1937, 407 (W. Va.; spec. from Mercers Bottom).—RICKER and CLARKE, Contr. Roy. Ontario Mus. Zool., xvi, 1939, 8 (Lake Nipissing, Ontario; records).—TODD, Birds Western Pennsylvania, 1940, 131 in text (remains found in eastern goshawk stomachs).—BOND, Condor; xlii, 1940, 220 (Lincoln County, Nev.; locally common in Pahranagat Valley, Meadow Valley, Wash., Ursine, Eagle, and Rose Valleys).—ALLIN, Trans. Roy. Can. Inst., xxiii, pt. 1, 1940, 96 (Darlington Terrace, Ontario; recently introduced, now well established).—BRUCKNER, Auk, lviii, 1941, 541, 542 text (white plumage inheritance).—SNYDER et al., Contr. Roy. Ontario Mus. Zool., No. 19, 1941, 46 (Prince Edward County, Ontario; introduced and well established).—WEBSTER, Condor, xliii, 1941, 120 (Sitka area, se. Alaska).—HAND, Condor, xliii, 1941, 225 (St. Joe National Forest, Idaho).—CRUICKSHANK, Birds New York City, 1942, 153 (New York City region).—ALLEN, Condor, xlv, 1943, 151 (Berkeley Hillside, Calif.).

P[hasianus] colchicus RIDGWAY, Man. North Amer. Birds, 1887, 598.—BRUCKNER, Auk, lviii, 1941, 536, 541 in text (albinism).

Phasianus colchicus colchicus HARTERT, Vög. pal. Fauna, iii, heft 2, 1921, 1976 (monogr.).—RAMSAY, Guide to Birds Europe and N. Africa, 1923, 333 (descr., range, Europe, and N. Africa).—GENGLER, Verh. Orn. Ges. Bay., xvi, 1925, Sonderheft, 95, 274 (Bavaria); xvii, 1927, 486 (s. Rhone, Germany).—DE PAILLERETS, Rev. Franç. d'Orn., xi, 1927, 193 (Charente-Inférieure, France).—ARRIGONI DEGLI ODDI, Ornitologia Italiana, 1929, 816 (descr.; distr.; Italy).—REBOUSSIN, L'Oiseau, x, 1929, 349 (Loir-et-Cher, France).—SWENK, Univ. Nebraska Agr. Exp. Sta. Research Bull. 50, 1930, 5, in text (introduction in North America; food in Nebraska).—CUMMING, Murrelet, xiii, 1932, 14 (Vancouver, B. C., introd.).—HELLMAYR, Field Mus. Nat. Hist., zool. ser., xix, 1932, 424 (Chile, introduced).

Phasianus c[olchicus] colchicus GASCHOTT, Verh. Orn. Ges. Bay., xvi, 1924, 34, in text (Speyer on Rhine, Germany).—SCHUSTER, Verh. Orn. Ges. Bay., xvi, 1924, 58 (Bad Nauheim, Germany).—GLEGG, Ibis, 1924, 86 (Macedonia, not common). —LANKES, Verh. Orn. Ges. Bay., xvi, 1925, 250 (Bavarian woods).—SCHIERMANN, Journ. für Orn., lxxviii, 1930, 152 (population density in breeding season).

Phasianus colchicus, var. mongolicus PALLAS, Zoogr. Rosso-Asiat., ii, 1826, 84.

Phasianus colchicus mongolicus CUMMING, Murrelet, xiii, 1932, 14 (Vancouver, British Columbia; introduced).—TAVERNER, Birds Canada, 1934, 166 in text (introduced in Canada).

Phasianus mongolicus TAVERNER, Birds Western Canada, 1926, 163 in text (descr.; distr.).

Phasianus colchicus mut. tenebrosus HACHISUKA, Bull. Brit. Orn. Club, xlvii, 1926, 51 (orig. descr.).

Phasianus albotorquatus BONNATERRE, Tabl. Encycl. Méth., i, 1791, 184.—BRANDT, Bull. Acad. St. Pétersbourg, iii, 1844, 51.

Phasianus holdereri gmelini BUTURLIN, Ibis, 1904, 408 (new name for *P. torquatus* Gmelin).

Phasianus marginatus MEYER and WOLF, Taschenb. deutschl. Vög., i, 1810, 291, pl.

(?) *Phasianus colchicus septentrionalis* LORENZ, Journ. für Orn., 1888, 572 (n. Caucasus).

Phasianus colchicus typicus BUTURLIN, Ibis, 1908, 584 (w. Transcaucasia).

Family NUMIDIDAE: Guineafowls

=Numidinae CARUS, Handb. Zool., i, 1868-75, 324.—GADOW, *in* Bronn, Thier-Reich, Vög., ii, 1891, 172.

=Numididæ SHARPE, Rev. Rec. Att. Classif. Birds, 1891, 68; Hand-list, i, 1899, xi, 41.—BEDDARD, Struct. and Classif. Birds, 1898, 302.

=Numididae WETMORE, Proc. U. S. Nat. Mus., lxxvi, art. 24, 1930, 3; Smithsonian Misc. Coll., lxxxix, No. 13, 1934, 6; xcix, No. 7, 1940, 6.—PETERS, Check-list Birds World, ii, 1934, 133.

=Numidinæ ELLIOT, Stand. Nat. Hist., iv, 1884, 213, in text.—KNOWLTON, Birds of World, 1909, 280, in text.

>Meleagrinæ GRAY, List Gen. Birds, 1840, 60 (includes *Meleagris* and Numididae).

Galliform birds with second metacarpal without backward process; costal processes outwardly inclined; head and at least upper half of neck naked, the former usually with a bony erect vertical helmet or bristly or curly crest or an occipital feathered patch or band; tail relatively small, drooping (decumbent), not erectile, mostly hidden by the coverts, and the very full plumage of the back and rump presenting a strongly arched contour.

Bill relatively large (from base nearly as long as head), strong, much deeper than wide at base of rhamphotheca; head and upper neck bare, the pileum usually with either a bony knob (*Numida*), a full crest of vertical feathers (*Guttera*), or a median line of short feathers, the rictal region sometimes wattled; nostril obliquely vertical, the lower and the anterior one, narrowly oval, linear, or fusiform. Wing moderate, much rounded, the longest primaries decidedly longer than longest secondaries; fourth to sixth (usually the fifth?) primary longest, the first (outermost) about as long as or slightly shorter than tenth, the outer ones moderately to strongly bowed or incurved, and tapering toward their rather narrow tips. Tail usually rather short, moderately rounded, and mostly overlain by coverts, but sometimes (in genus *Acryllium*) longer, with middle rectrices long, narrow, and pointed, more than twice as long as lateral pair. Tarsus moderately stout, much longer than middle toe with claw, decidedly less than one-third as long as wing, the acrotarsium with two rows of large, interdigitating transverse scutella, the planta tarsi with several rows of much smaller scutella and without any spur; middle toe much shorter than tarsus, the outer toe reaching about to penultimate articulation of middle toe, the inner toe slightly shorter; hallux decidedly shorter than basal phalanx of middle toe; claws moderate in size moderately to rather strongly decurved, somewhat compressed; a small web between basal phalanges of middle and outer toes, but middle and inner toes separated nearly to base.

Range.—Africa and Madagascar; one species introduced into and naturalized in some of the West Indian islands. (Five genera and 11 species.)

KEY TO THE GENERA OF NUMIDIDAE

a. Tail short and rounded, with middle rectrices not conspicuously longer than lateral pair; feathers of lower neck, chest, and upper back short and rounded (normal); acrotarsium of adult male either without any bony protuberance or else with only a single short blunt spur.

   b. Rectrices 14; acrotarsium with a short blunt spur in adult male; plumage vermiculated with brown or white.

      c. Pileum with a median line of short feathers; plumage vermiculated with brown, back and chest not white..........**Phasidus** (extralimital)[7]

      cc. Pileum wholly nude; plumage vermiculated with white, lower neck, upper back, and chest white.......................**Agelastes** (extralimital)[8]

   bb. Rectrices 16; acrotarsium without spur; plumage spotted or dotted with white or pale blue.

      c. Pileum with a bony knob or helmet; but without feathered crest; plumage spotted or dotted with white, secondaries not edged with white.

                         Numida (p. 431)

      cc. Pileum without bony knob but with a full crest of erect feathers; plumage dotted with pale blue, secondaries edged with white.

                         Guttera (extralimital)[9]

aa. Tail long and pointed, the middle rectrices more than twice as long as lateral pair; feathers of lower neck, chest, and back elongated, lanceolate; acrotarsium with 4 or 5 knobs or very short blunt spurs in adult male.

                         Acryllium (extralimital)[10]

Genus NUMIDA Linnaeus

Meleagris (not of Linnaeus, 1758) BRISSON, Orn., i, 1760, 26. (Type, by tautonymy, *Meleagris* Brisson = *Phasianus meleagris* Linnaeus.)

Gallina LINNAEUS, *in* Hasselquist, Reise nach Palestine, 1762, 327. (Type, by original designation, *Phasianus meleagris* Linnaeus.)

Numida LINNAEUS, Mus. Adolphi Friderici Regis, ii, 1764, 27. (Type, by monotypy, *Phasianus meleagris* Linnaeus.)

Numidia (emendation) FORSTER, Synopt. Cat. Brit. Birds, 1817, 64.

Querelea REICHENBACH, Av. Syst. Nat. Vög., 1853, xxvii. (Type, by monotypy, *Numida mitrata* Pallas.)

Arquata GISTEL, Naturg. Thierr. höhen Schulen, 1848, 92. (New name for *Numida* Linnaeus.)

Pintado "S.D.W.," Analyst, iii, No. xiii, Oct. 1835, 33. (Type, by monotypy, *"Pintada numida* Leach" = *Phasianus meleagris* Linnaeus.)

---

[7]*Phasidus* Cassin, Proc. Acad. Nat. Sci. Philadelphia, viii, 1856 (1857), 322 (type, by monotypy, *P. niger,* Cassin). Western Africa; monotypic.

[8]*Agelastes* Bonaparte, Proc. Zool. Soc. London, 1849, 145 (type, by monotypy, *A. meleagrides* Bonaparte).—*Agelastus* (emendation) Hartlaub, Journ. für Orn., 1855, 356. Western Africa; monotypic.

[9]*Guttera* Wagler, Isis, 1832, 1225 (type, by special designation, *Numida cristata* Pallas). Africa; three species with 11 races.

[10]*Acryllium* Gray, List Genera Birds, 1840, 61 (type, by monotypy, *Numida vulturina* Hardwick). Eastern Africa; monotypic.

In addition to the characters given for the family Numididae, which are mainly taken from this genus, the following apply exclusively to the genus *Numida*: Head and upper foreneck entirely nude, except for fine bristles on upper eyelid and, sometimes, a tuft of bristlelike feathers at base of bill; hindneck with narrow, rather rigid, somewhat hairlike feathers;

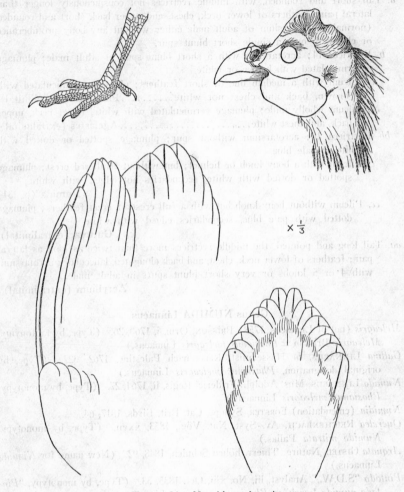

FIGURE 26.—*Numida meleagris.*

occiput or posterior part of crown with a compressed, or sometimes cylindrical, bony protuberance or casque, usually inclined backward and with rounded extremity; a pendant thin wattle immediately behind rictus; tarsus without spurs; rectrices 14.

Plumage and coloration.—Plumage in general compact, smooth, and blended. General color blackish dotted with white, the outer webs of secondaries obliquely barred with white; bare skin of head and neck brightly colored in life (red, blue or violet, and white). Sexes alike in coloration.

Range.—Africa and Madagascar. (Two species with over 20 races.)

NUMIDA MELEAGRIS GALEATA Pallas

GRAY-BREASTED HELMET GUINEAFOWL

Adult (sexes alike).—Head and foreneck bare of feathers except for a thin scattered line of black hairlike feathers from the occiput down the hindneck along the middorsal line; breast, lower part of back, and sides of neck light brownish drab to light vinaceous-drab; interscapulars and upper back between drab and hair brown abundantly speckled with small white spots, each completely bordered with fuscous to dark fuscous, and finely vermiculated and peppered with pale buffy drab; ground color of back, lower back, rump, upper tail coverts, scapulars and upper wing coverts chaetura black finely peppered with pale drab and closely speckled with white spots, the spots largest on the upper wing coverts and scapulars where the drab dots mark off diamond-shaped areas each of which contains one white spot; secondaries similar with the white spots arranged in three or four longitudinal rows on each web, those next to the outer edge of the outer web extended into a fringe of short diagonal white bars; primaries without the drab peppering and with fewer but larger white marks, those on the outer webs of the outer feathers forming irregular bars; tail feathers like their upper coverts but with the white spots larger; lower breast, all of abdomen except the posteromedian part, sides, flanks, and under tail coverts fuscous-black to black with abundant, larger somewhat more oval white spots and without any fine peppering of drab between these spots; posteromedian part of abdomen and thighs dusky sepia to dark clove brown abundantly covered with white spots smaller than those of the rest of the underparts of the body and slightly tinged with pale drab; under wing coverts dusky sepia to clove brown spotted with white, the white spots faintly tinged wih drab; iris dark brown; maxilla burnt sienna, horn gray at the tip; mandible horn gray; a small dark red patch near corner of mouth; bare skin of chin, throat, and neck, brownish black, in front of and below eye, across auriculars and sides of neck very pale Cambridge blue, almost white; forehead and skin over eyes slate-black; helmet burnt umber; nares dark red; wattle and line from them to nares scarlet-vermilion; legs and feet blackish brown (soft parts *ex* Bannerman).

Subadult (sexes alike).—Similar to the adult but the upper breast spotted like the lower breast and abdomen, the spots smaller; some plumulaceous feathers around ear openings, and with the lower throat retaining some of the immature feathers with pale shafts.

Immature (sexes alike).—Similar to the adult but with the hindneck, interscapulars, and back much browner—sepia but with the same spotted and peppered pattern; the lower throat and upper breast feathers brownish black with white shafts; abdomen dark buffy gray; chin and throat almost bare but rest of head still covered with tawny-brownish down.

Juvenal (sexes alike).—Upperparts dull rufescent brownish, coarsely vermiculated with blackish, each feather with a large subterminal **V**-shaped blackish band, and tipped with pale ochraceous-buff; remiges brown edged with white for the whole length of the feathers on the outer web and distally on the inner one, the outer web mottled with dull buffy; underparts grayish buffy somewhat mottled with dusky anteriorly; top of head still covered with tawny-brownish down; the bony helmet very small and blunt but definitely present by this stage of development.

Natal down (sexes alike).—Forehead, sides of head and of crown; chin, throat, breast, abdomen, sides, and wings white with a very faint buffy tinge; center of crown and occiput olive-brown; the nape, back, and base of wings Sayal brown; the flanks and all but the lower part of the thighs dusky buffy brown; bill and feet (in dried skins) light yellow.

Adult male.—Wing 223.5–263.5 (239.5); tail 126.5–153.0 (136.8); culmen from base 32.7–35.7 (34.2); tarsus 63.4–68.0 (65.0); middle toe without claw 39.5–42.4 (40.6 mm.).[11]

Adult female.—Wing 226–248 (235); tail 127–134 (130.6); culmen from base 31.2–34.4 (32.7); tarsus 57.2–68.4 (63.0); middle toe without claw 36.7–40.6 (39.1 mm.).[12]

Range.—Native in the open grassy scrub country of western Africa south of the Sahara and north of the forested areas from Senegal and Liberia to Lake Chad and the northeastern part of French Equatorial Africa; also the Cape Verde Islands and the islands of Annobon and São Thome in the Gulf of Guinea. Introduced into St. Helena and some of the West Indies; Cuba, Hispaniola, Jamaica, Barbuda, etc., where it has become established as a wild bird in eastern Cuba and in Hispaniola.

Type locality.—None stated.

[*Phasianus*] *meleagris* LINNAEUS, Syst. Nat., ed. 10, i, 1758, 158, part.

[*Numida*] *meleagris* LINNAEUS, Syst. Nat., ed. 12, i, 1766, 273, part.—GMELIN, Syst. Nat., i, pt. ii, 1788, 744, part.—LATHAM, Index Orn., ii, 1790, 621, part.—GRAY, Hand-list, ii, 1870, 262, No. 9629, part.—CORY, List Birds West Indies, 1885; rev. ed., 1886, 24 (Antilles).—SHARPE, Hand-list, i, 1899, 41.

Numida meleagris TEMMINCK, Cat. Syst., 1807, 150.—SONNINI and VIEILLOT, Nouv. Dict. Hist. Nat., xxv, 1817, 125, pl. M, 31, fig. 2.—LESSON, Traité d'Orn., 1831, 497, pl. 81, fig. 2.—RITTER, Naturh. Reis. Westind. Insel Hayti, 1836, 150, 156 (Haiti).—JARDINE, Nat. Libr., Orn., iii, 1836, 229, pl. 29.—GRAY, List Birds Brit. Mus., pt. 3, Gallinae, 1844, 29; ed. 1867, 43.—DENNY, Proc. Zool. Soc. London, 1847, 39 (Cuba and Jamaica; introduced).—GOSSE, Birds Jamaica, 1847, 325.—REICHENBACH, Syst. Av., iii, Gallinaceae, 1848, pl. 186, figs. 1586-95.— SALLÉ, Proc. Zool. Soc. London, 1857, 236 (Santo Domingo; habits).—HART-

---

[11] Six specimens from Haiti and Barbuda.

[12] Seven specimens from Haiti, Barbuda, and Jamaica.

LAUB, Orn. West Afrika, 1857, 199.—SCLATER, Proc. Zool. Soc. London, 1861, 80 (Jamaica); 1863, 125 (monogr.).—GUNDLACH, Journ. für Orn., x, 1862, 181 (Cuba); xxii, 1874, 313 (Puerto Rico); xxvi, 1878, 161, 186 (Puerto Rico; habits); Rep. Fisico Nat. Cuba, i, 1865-6, 397.—ALBRECHT, Journ. für Orn., x, 1862, 204 (Jamaica).—MARCH, Proc. Acad. Nat. Sci. Philadelphia, 1863, 303 (Jamaica).—BRYANT, Proc. Boston Soc. Nat. Hist., xi, 1866, 97 (Santo Domingo).—SUNDEVALL, Öfv. Svensk. Vet.-Akad. Forh., 1869, 601 (Puerto Rico).—DOHRN, Journ. für Orn., xix, 1871, 7 (Cape Verde Islands).— ELLIOT, Monogr. Phasianidae, ii, 1872, pl. 39 and text.—LAWRENCE, Proc. U. S. Nat. Mus., i, 1878, 241, 487 (Barbuda, Lesser Antilles).—VON BOECK, Mitth. Orn. Verh. Wien, 1884, 20, in author's reprint (Thale Cochabamba, Bolivia; has become wild on the Beni River).—CORY, Birds Haiti and San Domingo, 1885, 16; List Birds, West Indies, 1885, 24; Auk, iv, 1887, 223 (West Indies; syn.); Birds West Indies, 1889, 222; Cat. West Indian Birds, 1892, 96 (Cuba; Jamaica; Haiti; Puerto Rico; Barbuda; Barbados).—SCOTT, Auk, ix, 1892, 121 (Jamaica).—TIPPENHAUER, Die Insel Haiti, 1892, 320.—OGILVIE-GRANT, Cat. Birds Brit. Mus., xxii, 1893, 375.—SHELLEY, Birds Africa, i, 1896, 182.— CHRISTY, Ibis, 1897, 341 (Santo Domingo).—REICHENOW, Vögel Afrikas, i, 1901, 434; Journ. für Orn., 1902, 16 (Togo Land, Africa).—RILEY, Smiths. Misc. Coll., xlvii, 1904, 279 (Barbuda).—BANGS and ZAPPEY, Amer. Nat. xxxix, 1905, 192, footnote (Isle of Pines; feral).—CLARK, Proc. Boston Soc. Nat. Hist., xxxii, 1905, 246 (Balliceaux, Grenadines).—VERRILL (A. E. and A. H.), Proc. Acad. Nat. Sci. Philadelphia, 1909, 357 (Santo Domingo).— WETMORE, U. S. Dept. Agr. Bull. 326, 1916, 34 (Puerto Rico).—PHILLIPS, U. S. Dept. Agr. Techn. Bull. 61, 1928, 11-12 (Dominican Republic).—ERHARDT, Journ. für Orn., lxxviii, 1930, 219 (serology).—GROEBBELS, Der Vögel, i, 1932, 113 in table (blood cells), 643 (longevity), 664 (body temperature); ii, 1937, 46 in text (sex demorphism), 106 in text (polygyny); 168 (captive breeding, biology).

N[umida] meleagris REICHENOW, Die Vögel, i, 1913, 313.

Numida meleagris meleagris BANGS and KENNARD, List Birds Jamaica, 1920, 5 (probably extirpated by mongoose).

Numida galeata PALLAS, Spec. Zool., i, fasc. iv, 1767, 13, 15 (no locality).—HARTERT, Nov. Zool., xxviii, 1921, 85 (nomencl.).—WETMORE, Sci. Surv. Porto Rico and Virgin Islands, ix, pt. 3, 1927, 332 (Puerto Rico).—BOND, Proc. Acad. Nat. Sci. Philadelphia, lxxx, 1928 (1929), 494 (Haiti; distr.; habits).—DANFORTH, Auk, xlvi, 1929, 362 (Haiti; Dominican Republic); Journ. Agr. Univ. Puerto Rico, xix, 1935, 477 (Barbuda; introduced; now scarce).—WETMORE and SWALES, U. S. Nat. Mus. Bull. 155, 1931, 125 (Hispaniola; habits; syn).—WETMORE and LINCOLN, Proc. U. S. Nat. Mus., lxxxii, art. 25, 1933, 22 (L'Arcahaie, Haiti; also Pont de l'Estere and Morne à Cabrits).—CAUM, Occ. Pap. Bishop Mus., x, No. 9, 1933, 23 (Hawaii; introduced; domestic).

N[umida] galeata HARTERT, Bull. Brit. Orn. Club, xxxix, 1919, 87, in text (nomencl.).

Numida meleagris galeata BANNERMAN, Birds Trop. West Africa, i, 1930, 347 (descr.; distr.; habits; West Africa).—YOUNG, Ibis, 1931, 645 (Bauchi Plateau, Nigeria).—BOND, Check-list Birds West Indies, 1940, 164 (introduced and common resident in eastern Cuba and Hispaniola); Proc. Acad. Nat. Sci. Philadelphia, xciv, 1942, 92 (well established in Cuba, Hispaniola, and Barbuda).— HELLMAYR and CONOVER, Cat. Birds Amer., i, No. 1, 1942, 291 (syn.; distr.).

Numida galeata galeata MURPHY, Bull. Amer. Mus. Nat. Hist., 1, 1924, 264 (Cape Verde Islands; habits).—SCLATER, Syst. Av. Ethiopicarum, i, 1924, 95 (distr.).— BANNERMAN, Ibis, 1931, 671 (Kwendu, eastern Sierra Leone).—BATES, Handb. Birds West Africa, 1930, 90.

Numida g[aleata] galeata BEEBE, New York Zool. Soc. Bull., xxx, 1927, 139; Beneath Tropic Seas, 1928, 220 (Haiti).

Numida rendallii OGILBY, Proc. Zool. Soc. London, 1835, 103 (banks of the Gambia). —FRASER, Zool. Typ., 1841–2, pl. 62.

Numida maculipennis SWAINSON, Birds West Africa, ii, 1837, 226 (Senegal).

Numida marchei OUSTALET, Ann. Sci. Nat., ser. 6, xiii, art. 1 bis, 1882 (Gaboon; coll.); Nouv. Arch. Mus., ser. 2, viii, 1885, 305, pl. 14.

Family MELEAGRIDIDAE: Turkeys

=Meleagrinæ ELLIOT, Stand. Nat. Hist., iv, 1885, 222, in text.—AMERICAN ORNITHOL-OGISTS' UNION, Check-list, 1886, 177.—KNOWLTON, Birds of World, 1909, 276, in text.

=Meleagrinae CARUS, Handb. Zool., i, 1868–75, 326.—GADOW, *in* Bronn, Thier-Reich, Vög., ii, 1891, 172.

>Meleagrinae GRAY, List Gen. Birds, 1840, 60 (includes Numididae).—BAIRD, Rep. Pacific R. R. Surv., ix, 1858, 613 (includes Numididae).

=Meleagridæ COUES, Key North Amer. Birds, 1872, 231.—SCLATER and SALVIN, Nom. Av. Neotr., 1873, vii, 137.—BAIRD, BREWER, and RIDGWAY, Hist. North Amer. Birds, iii, 1874, 402.—SHARPE, Rev. Rec. Att. Classif. Birds, 1891, 68; Hand-list, i, 1899, xi, 43.—BEDDARD, Struct. and Classif. Birds, 1898, 302.—SALVIN and GODMAN, Biol. Centr.-Amer., Aves, iii, 1903, 283.—AMERICAN ORNITHOLOGISTS' UNION, Check-list, ed. 3, 1910, 145.

=Meleagridae WETMORE, Proc. U. S. Nat. Mus., lxxvi, art. 24, 1930, 3.

=Meleagrididæ COUES, *in* Baird, Brewer, and Ridgway, Hist. North Amer. Birds, iii, 1874, xxvi; Key North Amer. Birds, ed. 2, 1884, 576.

=Meleagrididae OBERHOLSER, Outl. Classif. North Amer. Birds, 1905, 2.—WETMORE, Smithsonian Misc. Coll., lxxxix, No. 13, 1934, 6; xcix, No. 7, 1940, 6.—PETERS, Check-list Birds World, ii, 1934, 139.—HELLMAYR and CONOVER, Cat. Birds Amer., i, No. 1, 1942, 292.

Galliform birds with postacetabulum longer than preacetabulum, and longer than broad; furcula weak and (viewed laterally) straight, with rodlike acetabulum; acromial process of scapula peculiar in shape.

Bill rather narrow and elongate, the cere nearly as long as rhampho-theca, the line of junction of the latter with the former slightly but distinctly depressed; nostril longitudinally narrowly oval, elliptical, or fusiform, about parallel with axis of bill; head and upper neck nude, with fleshy caruncles and corrugations and an elongated fleshy erectile caruncular appendage on anterior part of forehead in adult males (these caruncles and corrugations absent or indistinct in females, in which the nude parts are more or less covered or sprinkled with short downy feathers). Wing moderate, moderately concave beneath, the longest primaries longer than longest secondaries, the outer primaries moderately bowed or incurved; fifth, or fifth and sixth, primaries longest, the first (outermost) about equal to or a little shorter than tenth. Tail decidedly shorter than wing, flat (not vaulted), rather strongly rounded (the difference in length between middle and lateral rectrices equal to less than one-fourth the length of tail), the rectrices (18) very broad with slightly rounded or subtruncate tips. Tarsus stout, relatively long (about one-third as long as wing), the acrotarsium with two rows of interdigitating broad transverse scutella (as in most of Phasianidae), the planta tarsi also with two rows, but on inner side the row of large scutella separated from the frontal scutella and replaced on lower portion by small hexagonal or lozenge-shaped scales; adult males with a more or less prominent (sometimes long and acute) strong spur on lower portion of planta tarsi, about three-fourths the distance from upper end to base of hallux; middle toe about half as long as tarsus or a little more, the outer toe reaching to beyond penultimate articulation of middle toe (nearly if not quite to middle of subterminal phalanx), the inner toe slightly shorter; hallux a little more than half as long as basal phalanx of middle toe; a well-developed web between basal phalanges of anterior toes; claws relatively small, very slightly curved, blunt.

Plumage and coloration.—Head and upper neck nude, or in females more or less covered with short downy feathers; feathers of lower neck and body very broad, with truncate or subtruncate tips; remiges strong, the proximal secondaries very broad, with rounded tips, the primaries very rigid; plumage of lower abdomen and anal region soft and almost downy, that of thighs short and soft. General color dark with metallic reflections, less brilliant in females, most of the feathers margined terminally with black, the remiges grayish dusky more or less barred with white; bare skin of head and neck brightly colored in life (white, blue, and red in one genus; blue and orange in another).

Range.—Eastern temperate and tropical North America, south to British Honduras and eastern Guatemala. (Two monotypic genera.)

The Meleagrididae are very closely related to the Phasianidae but differ in a sufficient number of characters to warrant their recognition as a distinct family. They are exclusively American, while the typical Phasianidae (Phasianinae) are found only in Eurasia and Africa.

KEY TO THE GENERA OF MELEAGRIDIDAE

a. Crown without a vertical process or protuberance; adult male with a beardlike tuft of long, coarse, stiff bristles on center of chest; tail less strongly rounded, the difference in length between middle and outer rectrices equal to but little, if any, more than half the length of tarsus, the rectrices broader and less rounded (nearly subtruncate) at tips; rectrices without metallic tips or subterminal ocelli.....................................**Meleagris** (p. 437)

aa. Crown, in male, with a conspicuous subcylindrical erect protuberance; no beardlike tuft on chest; tail more strongly rounded, the difference in length between middle and lateral rectrices equal to about distance from heel joint to base of hallux, the rectrices narrower and distinctly rounded at tips; rectrices with a terminal band of bright metallic coppery bronze and a subterminal spot or ocellus of metallic blue....................................**Agriocharis** (p. 458)

Genus MELEAGRIS Linnaeus

Meleagris LINNAEUS, Syst. Nat., ed. 10, i, 1758, 156. (Type, as designated by Gray, 1840, *M. gallopavo* Linnaeus.)

Melagris (emendation) EYTON, Osteol. Avium, 1867, 171.

Gallo-pavo BRISSON, Orn., i, 1760, 26, 158. (Type, by tautonymy, *Gallopavo* Brisson= *Meleagris gallapavo* Linnaeus.)

Galloparus (err. typog.?) DES MURS, *in* Chenu, Encycl. Hist. Nat., Ois., vi, 1854, 99.

Gallopavus (emendation) DES MURS, *in* Chenu, Encycl. Hist. Nat., Ois., vi, 1854, 100, 109.

Pseudotaon BILLBERG, Synop. Faunæ Scand., i, pt. 2, 1828, tabs. A, B, C, and p. 4. (New name for *Meleagris* Linnaeus.)

Cynchramus "Moehring" BONAPARTE, Ann. Lyc. Nat. Hist. New York, ii, 1826, 122. (Not adopted but cited in synonymy of *Meleagris* Linnaeus.)

Cenchramus (emendation) GRAY, List Gen. Birds, ed. 2, 1841, 78.

Largest of gallinaceous birds (length of adult males about 107–127 cm., weight 16–40 pounds, the females decidedly smaller) ; adult males without any vertical process or protuberance on crown, but with a conspicuous pendant tuft of long, coarse bristles springing from center of chest; rec-

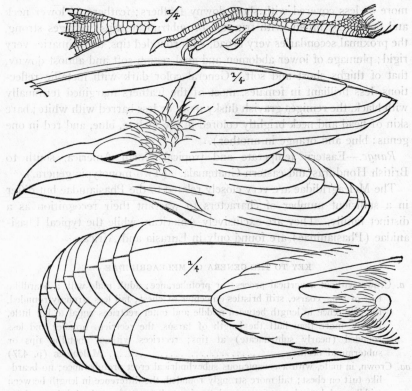

FIGURE 27.—*Meleagris gallopavo.*

trices without a terminal metallic band or subterminal metallic ocelli. (Other characters the same as these given for the family Meleagrididae.)

Plumage and coloration.—Head and upper neck nude, warted and corrugated in adult males, smoother and more or less covered with short downy feathers and with true feathers extending upward on nape in females, the skin of throat loose and sometimes, at least, developed into a more or less distinct "dewlap"; a fleshy but flabby appendage on anterior portion of forehead, this more or less erect when contracted but pendant and much enlarged in adult males during the pairing season—much smaller or rudimentary in females. Feathers of lower neck, back, rump, and underparts, together with smaller wing coverts and tail coverts, distinctly outlined, very broad, and with truncate or subtruncate tips, those of lower abdomen and anal region soft, more downy, those of thighs shorter and close, but broad, rounded, and distinctly outlined; rectrices (18) very broad, with rounded tips. General color dusky but glossed with brilliant metallic coppery, golden, and greenish hues, the feathers of back, rump, breast, sides, and flanks, as well as the scapulars and smaller wing coverts, margined terminally with velvety black; primaries grayish dusky, more or less broadly barred with white; rectrices brown, barred with dusky, broadly tipped with white, buffy, light rusty brown, or chestnut and with a broad subterminal band of black. (Females with coloration duller, the metallic hues much less brilliant.)

Range.—Eastern and south-central United States (west to Colorado and Arizona) and mountains of Mexico. (Monotypic, but with six more or less distinct subspecific forms.)

KEY TO THE FORMS OF MELEAGRIS GALLOPAVO (LINNAEUS)

a. Tail tipped with deep rusty, its coverts and feathers of lower rump tipped with rich dark chestnut.
  b. Primaries broadly barred with white, white bars nearly or quite as broad as dusky interspaces and extending to shafts of quills (northern Florida northward in eastern United States)....**Meleagris gallopavo silvestris** (p. 440)
  bb. Primaries narrowly barred with white, white bars very much narrower than dusky interspaces and not extending to shafts of quills (Florida).
                        Meleagris gallopavo osceola (p. 447)
aa. Tail and tail coverts and feathers of lower rump tipped with light cinnamon-brown, buffy, or white.
  b. Tail, upper tail coverts, etc., tipped with light cinnamon-brown, cinnamon, or cinnamon-buff; rump almost wholly "solid" glossy black (feathers tipped with gray in female and young) (central Texas to northeastern Mexico).
                        Meleagris gallopavo intermedia (p. 449)
  bb. Tail, upper tail coverts, etc., tipped with white or pale buffy.
    c. Lower back and rump bluish black without reddish and greenish-golden metallic reflections.
      d. Upper body plumage purplish bronzy.
        e. Narrow bars on basal three quarters of undersurface of rectrices more grayish than rufescent (western slope of Sierra Madre, Chihuahua to Durango and southern Sonora).
                        Meleagris gallopavo onusta (p. 457)
        ee. Narrow bars on basal three-quarters of undersurface of rectrices more rufescent than grayish (Colorado to Arizona, New Mexico, and southwestern Texas)......**Meleagris gallopavo merriami** (p. 451)

dd. Upper body plumage highly glossed with greenish and reddish-golden
reflections, less purplish bronzy (Veracruz to Oaxaca).

Meleagris gallopavo gallopavo (p. 454)

cc. Lower back and rump with reddish and greenish-golden metallic reflections,
not bluish black (eastern Chihuahua, Durango, to northern Jalisco).

Meleagris gallopavo mexicana (p. 455)

MELEAGRIS GALLOPAVO SILVESTRIS Vieillot

EASTERN TURKEY

Adult male.—Head, elongated frontal appendage, neck, chin, and throat
bare, chiefly pale bluish in life, mixed with purplish red, only sparsely
feathered with blackish hairlike feathers chiefly on the midventral line
and with black and chestnut broader but short feathers on the middorsal
line; a little tuft of dirty buff feathers broadly tipped with black over the
ear openings; the skin of the back and sides of neck and extreme lower
throat coarsely rugose, the carunculations increasing in size toward the
body, assuming the size of wattles at the feather line; general coloration
of body dark brown with variable brilliant metallic reflections of rich coppery bronze changing to metallic red and green in certain lights, each
feather of back, breast, sides, and flanks, together with the scapulars and
lesser upper wing coverts, sharply margined terminally with velvety black
(narrowly bluish at either edge); lower back and rump with black tips
much broader and without greenish bronze, with only a broad subterminal
pinkish bronze band narrowly edged with greenish basally, the feathers
of the back, scapulars, and lesser upper wing coverts averaging more
greenish, less coppery than those of the rump and flanks; upper tail
coverts dark purplish chestnut with a narrow subterminal bar of velvety
black preceded by a broad band of metallic pinkish bronze, which in turn
is preceded by a broad, velvety, greenish, black bar; the rest of the feathers
(actually their greatest part but which is usually hidden by overlapping)
dull russet to cinnamon-brown narrowly banded, vermiculated, and
mottled with blackish; tail varying from russet to Prout's brown heavily
broadly vermiculated to barred with fuscous-black to black (the vermiculations approaching barring more on the lateral rectrices, especially on
their inner webs), crossed by a broad subterminal band of dull black,
which breaks up into a vermiculated area on its distal side also, very
similar to the most proximal area, and tipped broadly with tawny snuff
brown to cinnamon-brown, the under surface of tail paler than the upper
side; the subterminal black band greatly increasing in width on the lateral
feathers and the more distal vermiculated area correspondingly decreasing
laterally; greater upper wing coverts glossy bronzy vinaceous-brown on
the exposed, outer webs, dusky green gray with subterminal oil-green
sheen on the covered inner webs, both webs subterminally broadly banded
with black and narrowly tipped with dirty buffy white; primaries clove
brown barred with white, the white bars nearly, if not quite, as wide as the

dusky interspaces, and touching the shaft of the quills, the white bars, especially on the inner web often more or less mottled with clove brown; secondaries similar but the dark areas paler and grayer—grayish olive-brown terminally vermiculated, and on the inner webs strongly suffused with cinnamomeous, the innermost ones with a purplish sheen and the white bars averaging less pure white; pectoral tuft or "beard" blackish with a greenish sheen basally and a slight vinaceous-brown gloss distally; middle of abdomen to vent chaetura drab to dull fuscous to fuscous-black, each feather tipped with pale grayish buff to grayish tawny; thighs similar but the tips slightly more olivaceous (in some more cinnamomeous) and the terminal portion of the feathers somewhat suffused with olive grayish or with cinnamomeous; under wing coverts dark sepia to clove brown; under tail coverts similar to the sides; iris deep brown; bill orange basally, yellowish at tip and along tomial edge; tarsi, tarsal spur, and toes purplish red, the larger scutella with light brownish gray or greenish brown margins; claws dark brown.[13]

Adult female.—Similar to the adult male but smaller and duller in color, more brownish, the metallic reflections much less brilliant; the frontal appendage much smaller or rudimentary; "beard" smaller and tarsal spurs absent or rudimentary; the neck more extensively feathered, the feathers extending to the nape; the head, especially above, more or less sparsely covered with short dusky downy feathers and small bristles; the feathers of the neck, back, and underparts with more or less distinct pale terminal edges; the tips of the feathers of the breast, flanks, and sides brown (blackish in males).

Subadult.—Similar to the adult of the corresponding sex but with the beard shorter[14] and in the male the tarsal spurs and the frontal appendage smaller.

Immature male.—Similar to the adult male in size and to the adult female in coloration but retains the two outer juvenal primaries.

Immature female.—Similar to the adult female but lacks the beard and retains the two outer juvenal primaries.

Juvenal (sexes alike).—Forehead and anterior part of crown light pinkish cinnamon darkening to pinkish cinnamon on the posterior part of crown; occiput and nape pinkish cinnamon splotched with Brussels brown to clove brown, this darker color largely on the basal parts of the feathers, which do not completely overlap; hindneck and uppermost interscapulars dusky hair brown to chaetura drab, the feathers with whitish shafts and

[13] The elongated frontal appendage is largest (longest) during the breeding season and may then attain a length of 3 inches or more; in the winter it may shrink to less than 1 inch.

[14] According to some workers who deal with live wild turkeys, a male with a beard less than 4 inches long is probably a first-year bird, while females seldom develop beards until they are three years old.

terminal shaft spots and subterminally banded with Prout's brown; scapulars and rest of interscapulars and upper wing coverts between Prout's brown and russet with narrow pale tawny shaft streaks terminally widening into whitish tips, the feathers with a broad subterminal blackish band (not extending across the pale shaft streak) and sparsely freckled with the same on the basal brownish area; back, lower back, and rump dark hair brown barred with whitish (the whitish bars formed by the tips of the feathers); primaries between hair brown and chaetura drab, faintly and finely mottled on the outer web with pale cinnamon-buff and narrowly tipped with whitish; secondaries hair brown on their inner webs, Sayal brown on the outer webs which are transversely broadly blotched with blackish and finely and sparsely peppered with dusky; the innermost secondaries have this Sayal brown extending over the inner web as well, and all the secondaries are tipped with pale pinkish buff; upper tail coverts and rectrices Sayal brown transversely broadly but irregularly banded with blackish and tipped with buffy white; lores, cheeks, and auriculars pinkish buff darkening to light pinkish cinnamon above and behind the eye; chin and upper throat very pale pinkish buff; lower throat pinkish buff irregularly barred with hair brown; the feathers broadly tipped with white; breast, abdomen, sides, flanks, thighs, and under tail coverts dark hair brown but the feathers of the sides and flanks and lower abdomen heavily washed with Sayal brown, their shafts white.

Natal down (sexes alike).—Head as in juvenal plumage described above; the upper back slightly paler but very heavily and extensively blotched with dark bister; back, lower back, and rump somewhat darker and more rufescent, heavily marked with Brussels brown to bister and Vandyke brown, the spinal tract being broadly and continuously of this dark tone; sides of head pale pinkish buff to tilleul buff, paling to almost white on the chin and upper throat and breast; middle of abdomen washed with straw yellow, whiter laterally.

Adult male.—Wing 480–550 (512.9); tail 370–440 (397.2); culmen from cere 31–38 (34.8); tarsus 146–181.5 (162.6); middle toe without claw 73–87 (81.4); length of tarsal spur 14.5–23 (18.5); diameter of tarsal spur 10–13.5 (11.6 mm.).[15]

Adult female.—Wing 382–438 (414.3); tail 306–345 (329.3); culmen from cere 28–35.5 (31.7); tarsus 126–143 (131.8); middle toe without claw 61.5–68 (65.4 mm.).[16]

Range.—Formerly resident in wooded districts from southern Maine, southern Ontario, and northern New York, southern Michigan, southern Wisconsin, eastern Minnesota, Iowa, southeastern South Dakota, Nebraska, and Kansas; south through New England, New York, New Jersey,

[15] Nine specimens from Virginia, Georgia, and Maryland.
[16] Six specimens from Virginia, Arkansas, Missouri, and North Carolina.

Pennsylvania, Maryland, Virginia, West Virginia, the Carolinas and Georgia to northwestern Florida, and through Ohio, Indiana, Illinois, eastern Kentucky, and Missouri to Arkansas, Oklahoma, eastern Texas, northeastern New Mexico, and the Gulf Coast; now extirpated in Canada, New England, New York, New Jersey, Michigan, Iowa, South Dakota, Kansas, and Minnesota; mixed with domestic blood and with western stock in Arkansas, Oklahoma, and in the eastern part of the range.[17] Birds from coastal Georgia and southeastern South Carolina are somewhat intermediate between this form and the Florida subspecies, *M. g. osceola.*

Type locality.—Pennsylvania.

[*Meleagris*] *gallopavo* LINNAEUS, Syst. Nat., ed. 10, i, 1758, 156, part[18] (based essentially on *Meleagris sylvestris* Catesby, Nat. Hist. Carolina, i, p. xliv; Brisson, Orn., i, 162, and New England Wild Turkey Ray, av. 51; Alb. av. 3, p. 33, t. 35) ; ed. 12, i, 1766, 268.—GMELIN, Syst. Nat., i, pt. 2, 1788, 732.—LATHAM, Index Orn., ii, 1790, 618.

Meleagris gallopavo TEMMINCK, Cat. Syst., 1807, 149.—BONAPARTE, Amer. Orn., i, 1825, 79, pl. 9; Ann. Lyc. Nat. Hist. New York, ii, pt. 1, 1826, 123; Contr. Maclurian Lyc., i, 1827, 22; Geogr. and Comp. List, 1838, 42.—AUDUBON, Orn. Biogr., i, 1831, 1, 33, pls. 1, 6; v, 1839, 559; Synopsis, 1839, 194; Birds Amer., 8vo ed., v, 1842, 42, pls. 287, 288.—NUTTALL, Man. Orn. United States and Canada, Land Birds, 1832, 630; ed. 2, 1840, 773.—HITCHCOCK, Rep. Geol. Massachusetts, 1833, 549 (Massachusetts).—JARDINE, Nat. Libr., Orn., iii, 1836, 117, pls. 1, 2.—THOMPSON, Hist. Vermont, 1842, 101 (s. Vermont).—DEKAY, Zool. New York, 1844, 199, pl. 76, fig. 172.—WOODHOUSE, Rep. Sitgreaves' Expl. Zuñi and Colorado Rivers, 1853, 93 (Indian Territory; Texas).—BAIRD, Rep. Pacific R.R. Surv., ix, 1858, 615; Cat. North Amer. Birds, 1859, No. 457.—McILWRAITH, Proc. Essex Inst., v, 1866, 91 (Ontario, formerly).—ALLEN, Mem. Boston Soc. Nat. Hist., i, 1868, 500 (w. Iowa; formerly numerous) ; Bull. Mus. Comp. Zool., iii, 1872, 141 (Fort Hays, Kans.), 144 (nw. Kansas), 181 (e. and middle Kansas).—SNOW, Cat. Birds Kansas, ed. 2, 1872, 12 (Kansas; becoming rarer) ; 1879, 9; ed. 5, 1903, 15 (southwestern Kansas; rare, if not extinct).—

[17] Birds from the Wichita National Forest are only doubtfully identifiable as *silvestris,* but this seems to be due to mixing of strains there by local introduction.

[18] It may fairly be questioned whether Linnaeus based his *Meleagris gallopavo* more on the wild turkey of the Eastern United States or the domesticated bird, and possibly those who insist upon the latter are right; but this does not affect the right of a subsequent author when dealing with a composite species to restrict the original name according to his best judgment. In 1856, John Gould thus restricted the specific name *gallopavo* to the wild bird of the Eastern United States and named the wild turkey of eastern Mexico (which is unquestionably the parent stock of the domesticated turkey) *M. mexicana.* The principle involved is a very simple and just one, and there are few of those already incorporated with the rules of zoological nomenclature which are more potent to prevent the unnecessary shifting of names than this. It is true that the wild turkey of the Eastern United States had received several different specific names prior to Gould's discrimination of two species, in 1856; but the authors of these several names did not recognize two species and therefore merely renamed the composite one, thus merely adding synonyms to the eastern form as clearly separated by Gould. (R.R.)

ELLIOT, Monogr. Phasianidae, i, 1872, pl. 30 (27?), and text.—HATCH, Proc. Minnesota Acad. Sci., i, 1874, 61 (e. Minn.) ; Notes Birds Minnesota, 1892, 169, 458 (Minnesota; now extinct).—BREWER, Proc. Boston Soc. Nat. His., xvii, 1875, 12 (New England).—NELSON, Bull. Essex Inst., ix, 1877, 63 (s. Illinois; 10 miles w. of Anna, Union County), 65 (s. Illinois).—GIBBS, U. S. Geol. and Geogr. Surv. Terr. Bull. 5, 1879, 491 (Michigan; locally common).—TOWNSEND, Bull. Nuttall Orn. Club, vi, 1880, 60 (Mount Desert Island, Maine, formerly; bones found in shellheap).—AMERICAN ORNITHOLOGISTS' UNION, Check-list, 1886, No. 310.—SLADE, Auk, v, 1888, 204 (near Mount Holyoke, Mass., former-ly; flock in 1837-38).—GOSS, Hist. Birds Kansas, 1891, 230 (Kansas; genl.).—RHOADS, Proc. Acad. Nat. Sci. Philadelphia, 1892, 105 (Corpus Christi, Tex.) ; Auk, xvi, 1899, 310 (sw. Pennsylvania; a few still lingering in Clinton and Fulton Counties).—BENDIRE, Life Hist. North Amer. Birds, i, 1892, 112, part (includes *M. g. osceola*).—ULREY and WALLACE, Proc. Indiana Acad. Sci., 1895, 151 (Wabash, Ind.; last one killed in 1880!).—WAYNE, Auk, xii, 1895, 364 (Aucilla, nw. Florida).—COOKE, Colorado State Agr. Coll. Bull. 37, 1897, 91 (rare, near extirpation; still existing in Bent, Prowers, Baca, and Las Animas Counties, se. Colorado).—JONES, Wils. Bull., v, 1898, 61 (Lorain County, n. Ohio; extinct since about 1858!).—BUTLER, Rep. State Geol. Indiana for 1897 (1898), 758 (Carroll County, Ind., up to 1870; Marion County, 1879; Crawford County, 1897; Lake County, about 1880; Newton County, 1884; Wabash County, 1880; La Porte County, 1886; Monroe County, 1887; still found in Knox, Gibson, Pike, and Posey Counties).—MACOUN, Cat. Can. Birds, 1900, 214 (sw. Ontario, formerly common; now rare).—JUDD, U. S. Biol. Surv. Bull. 24, 1905, 48–52, part (range, food, etc.)—TAVERNER and SWALES, Wils. Bull. xix, 1907, 91 (Point Pelee, Ontario; extirpated since about 1878!).—(?) FELGER, Auk, xxvi, 1909, 191 (Oak Hills, s. of Denver, Colo., 1868).—CHRISTY, Auk, xlviii, 1931, 374 (Sandusky Bay; Lake Erie).—BAILLIE and HARRINGTON, Contr. Roy. Ontario Mus. Zool., No. 8, 1936, 31 (extirpated, formerly common; Ontario).—TAVERNER, Can. Water Birds, 1939, 179 (field chars.; Canada).—STEWART, Auk, lx, 1943, 390 (Shenandoah Mountains; breeds).

M[eleagris] gallopavo MAXIMILIAN, Journ. für Orn., 1850, 426 (descr.; plum.; meas.; habits).—HATCH, Bull Minnesota Acad. Nat. Sci., 1874, 61 (Minnesota; sw. part).—RIDGWAY, Ann. Lyc. Nat. Hist., New York, x, 1874, 382 (Illinois; resident).—BOIES, Cat. Birds Southern Michigan, 1875, No. 145 (s. Michigan).—NELSON, Bull. Essex Inst., viii, 1876, 121 (ne. Illinois; formerly plentiful but now probably extirpated) ; ix, 1877, 43 (s. Illinois; very common) 59 (Cairo, Ill.; abundant; also in Kentucky and Missouri).

Meleagris gallopavo, var. *gallopavo* BAIRD, BREWER, and RIDGWAY, Hist. North Amer. Birds, iii, 1874, 404.—LANGDON, Journ. Cincinnati Soc. Nat. Hist., 1879, 15 (Cincinnati, Ohio; former resident).

Meleagris gallopavo gallopavo GOODE, U. S. Nat. Mus. Bull., 20, 1883, 328.

Meleagris Gallo pavo KLUK, Hist. Nat., ii, 1779, 136.

Meleagris gallipavo KOCK, Mitth. Orn. Verh. Wien, 1889, 129–134 (Pennsylvania).

Meleagris americana HILDRETH, Amer. Journ. Sci., xxix, 1836, 85 (Kanawha Valley, W. Va.; ex *M. americanus* Bartram, Travels in Florida, etc., 1792, 290—*nomen nudum*).—COUES, Proc. Acad. Nat. Sci. Philadelphia, 1875, 349, footnote (crit., nomencl.).—LOOMIS, Bull. Nuttall Orn. Club, iv, 1879, 217 (Chester County, S. C.).—OGILVIE-GRANT, Cat. Birds Brit. Mus., xxii, 1893, 389.

M[eleagris] americana REICHENOW, Die Vögel, i, 1913, 304.

[*Meleagris*] *americana* GRAY, Hand-list, ii, 1870, 262, No. 9626.

[*Meleagris gallopavo*] var. *americana* COUES, Key North Amer. Birds, 1872, 232.

Meleagris gallopavo . . . var. *americana* COUES, Check List North Amer. Birds, 1874, No. 379a.

[*Meleagris gallopavo* var. *americana*] b. *Americana* Coues, Birds Northwest, 1874, 391.

Meleagris gallopavo, var. *americana* Merriam, Trans. Connecticut Acad. Sci., iv., 1877, 98 (extinct in Connecticut since about 1813).—Brown, Bull. Nuttall Orn. Club, iv, 1879, 12 (Coosada, Ala.).

Meleagris gallopavo americana Coues, Bull. Nuttall Orn. Club, v, 1880, 100.—Ridgway, Proc. U. S. Nat. Mus., iii, 1880, 195; Nom. North Amer. Birds, 1881, No. 470a.—Wheaton, Rep. Birds Ohio, 1882, 444; 579 (descr.; distr.; hist.; syn.).—Hay, Bull. Nuttall Orn. Club, vii, 1882, 93 (Kemper County, Miss.).—Agersborg, Auk, ii, 1885, 285 (se. South Dakota).

M[*eleagris*] *gallopavo americana* Ridgway, Illinois State Lab. Nat. Hist. Bull. 4, 1881, 191 (Illinois).

Meleagris gallipavo americana Coues, Check List North Amer. Birds, ed. 2, 1882, No. 554.

[*Meleagris*] [*gallopavo*] *americana* Wheaton, Rep. Birds Ohio, 1882, 444 (distr.).

M[*eleagris*] *g*[*allipavo*] *americana* Coues, Key North Amer. Birds, ed. 2, 1884, 576.

(?) *Meleagris gallopavo* (*americana* Coues?) Nehrling, Bull. Nuttall Orn. Club, vii, 1882, 175 (se. Texas).

Meleagris palawa Barton, Med. and Phys. Journ., ii, pt. 1, 1805, 163, 164 (based on "the common wild turkey of the United States").

Meleagris silvestris Vieillot, Nouv. Dict. d'Hist. Nat., ix, 1817, 447 (Illinois to Isthmus of Panama; Canada and central United States).—Ridgway, Proc. Boston Soc. Nat. Hist., xvi, 1874, 23 (lower Wabash Valley).

Meleagris gallopavo silvestris Dawson, Birds Ohio, 1903, 431, pl. 50, 652 (Ohio; hist.; descr.; etc.).—Williams, Auk, xxi, 1904, 453 (Leon County, nw. Fla.).—[Nash], Check List Vert. Ontario: Birds, 1905, 36 (Ontario; formerly common; now probably extinct).—Stockard, Auk, xxii, 1905, 150 (Mississippi; nesting habits, etc.).—Townsend, Mem. Nuttall Orn. Club, No. 3, 1905, 64 in text, 203 in text (Essex County, Mass.); No. 5, 1920, 97 (Essex County, Mass.; extinct). —Henninger, Wils. Bull., xviii, 1906, 51 (Seneca County, Ohio; extirpated in 1880).—Brewster, Mem. Nuttall Orn. Club, No. 4, 1906, 175 (Cambridge, Mass.).—Widmann, Birds Missouri, 1907, 83 (once common, now rare).— Anderson, Proc. Davenport Acad. Sci., xi, 1907, 237 (Iowa; once common; now practically extirpated).—Woodruff, Auk, xxv, 1908, 198 (Shannon County, Mo., still common).—Stone, Birds New Jersey, 1908, 152 (New Jersey; hist; now extinct); Bird Studies Cape May, i, 1937, 328 (Cape May County, N. J., formerly).—Knight, Birds Maine, 1908, 206 (s. Maine, formerly).—Cory, Field Mus. Nat. Hist. Publ. 131, 1909, 42 (Wisconsin, extirpated; Illinois, now in southern counties only).—Macoun and Macoun, Cat. Can. Birds, ed. 2, 1909, 234 (sw. Ontario; formerly common, now rare).—Wayne, Birds South Carolina, 1910, 64 (habits; descr. of nest and eggs).—Howell, Auk, xxvii, 1910, 301 (Walden Ridge, e. Tenn.); Birds Alabama, 1924, 121; ed. 2, 1928, 121 (distr.; habits; Alabama).—American Ornithologists' Union, Check-list, ed. 3, 1910, 145; ed. 4, 1931, 92 (distr.).—Eaton, Birds New York, i, 1910, 379 (now extirpated).—Iseley, Auk, xxix, 1912, 28 (Sedgwick County, Kans., formerly).—Barrows, Michigan Bird Life, 1912, 236 (formerly abundant, now extirpated).—Harlow, Auk, xxix, 1912, 469 (Centre County, Pa.); xxxv, 1918, 23 (south-central Pennsylvania from Centre, Clearfield, and Lycoming Counties to Somerset and Franklin Counties; also in Huntingdon County).—Forbush, Game Birds, Wild-fowl and Shore Birds, 1912, 487 (history).—Cooke, Condor, xv, 1913, 104 [-105], fig. 32 (map) (western range); Auk, xxxi, 1914, 478 (Caddo, Okla.; common); Proc. Biol. Soc. Washington, xlii, 1929, 34 (Washington, D. C.).—Bailey, Birds Virginia, 1913, 91 (Virginia; range; breeds).—

WRIGHT and HARPER, Auk, xxx, 1913, 494 (Okefenokee Swamp, Ga.).—HARRIS,
Trans. Acad. Nat. Sci. St. Louis, 1919, 258 (extirpated near Kansas City, Mo.).
—BURNS, Orn. Chester County, Pa., 1919, 48 (Chester County, Pa.).—PEARSON,
BRIMLEY, and BRIMLEY, Birds of North Carolina, 1919, 154 (North Carolina;
descr.; distr.).—HOLT, Geol. Surv. Alabama, Mus. Paper No. 4, 1921, 43
(Alabama; common in suitable localities; resident; breeds).—OVER and THOMS,
Birds South Dakota, 1921, 78 (Union and Clay Counties, but extirpated about
1875).—CAHN, Wils. Bull., xxxiii, 1921, 172 (Harrison County, ne. Tex.).—
EVERMANN, Proc. Indiana Acad. Sci. for 1920 (1921), 336 (Monroe County,
Ind., up to about 1886; Vigo County, up to 1891 ?; Carrol County, up to
about 1878).—HUNT, Auk, xxxviii, 1921, 376 (Tiller, Ark.; said to be common
in wild places).—PEARSON, Wils. Bull., xxxiv, 1922, 86 (Cumberland Island,
Ga.).—CORRINGTON, Auk, xxxix, 1922, 543 (Biloxi, Miss.; common in swamps).
—NICE and NICE, Birds Oklahoma, 1924, 37 (genl.; Oklahoma).—BURLEIGH,
Wils. Bull., xxxvi, 1924, 69, 37 (migr.; Centre County, Pa.); xliii, 1931, 39
(breeding; State College; Centre County, Pa.).—PINDAR, Wils. Bull., xxxvi,
1924, 204 (e. Arkansas); xxxvii, 1925, 83 (status; Fulton County, Ky.).—
BECK, Auk, xli, 1924, 292 in text (Pennsylvania German common names).—
WHEELER, Birds Arkansas, 1925, 40, xiv, xx (descr.; habits; nest and eggs;
Arkansas).—BLINCOE, Auk, xlii, 1925, 419 (Bardstown, Ky.).—WORTHING-
TON and TODD, Wils. Bull., xxxviii, 1926, 211 (Chostawhatchee Bay, Fla.).—
BAILEY, Birds New Mexico, 1928, 230 (ne. New Mexico; Mora River near
junction with the Canadian River, and near North fork of the Canadian
River).—SUTTON, Birds Pennsylvania, 1928, 54 (Pennsylvania; descr.; nesting;
habits) ; Auk, xlvi, 1929, 326 (nesting habits; Pennsylvania; photographs).—
PICKENS, Wils. Bull., xl, 1928, 189 (rare, upper South Carolina).—BROWN,
Auk, xlv, 1928, 347 (longevity in captivity).—PIERCE, Wils. Bull., xlii, 1930, 267
(status in Buchanan County, Iowa).—SNYDER and LOGIER, Trans. Roy. Can.
Inst., xviii, 1931, 177 (Long Point Area, Norfolk County, Ontario; extirpated;
trapping methods).—[ARTHUR], Birds Louisiana, 1931, 220 (descr.; status,
Louisiana).—NICE, Birds Oklahoma, rev. ed., 1931, 83 (Oklahoma; genl.).—
BAERG, Univ. Arkansas Agri. Exp. Stat. Bull. 258, 1931, 56 (descr.; distr.).—
BENT, U. S. Nat. Mus. Bull. 162, 1932, 326 (habits; plum.; distr.).—BURNS,
Wils. Bull., xliv, 1932, 28 (spec.; Peale coll.).—BENNITT, Univ. Missouri Stud.,
vii, No. 3, July 1932, 27 (s. Missouri; uncommon resident).—ROBERTS, Birds
Minnesota, i, 1932, 425 (distr.; habits; etc.; Minnesota).—HICKS, Wils. Bull.,
xlv, 1933, 180 (Ashtabula County, Ohio; none since 1880).—BROOKS, Wils. Bull.,
xlvi, 1934, 66 (Cranberry Glades, W. Va.).—PETERS, Check-list Birds of World,
1934, 140.—TAVERNER, Birds Canada, 1934, 167 in text (e. Canada; w. to e.
Ontario).—FISHER, Proc. Biol. Soc. Washington, xlviii, 1935, 161 (Plummers
Island, Md.).—GHIGI, Gallini di Faraone e Tacchini, 1936, 330, pl. vii (col. fig.;
genl. hist.).—GROEBBELS, Der Vögel, ii, 1937, 106 in text (polygyny) ; 168 (data
on breeding biology) ; 239 in text (number of eggs) ; 402 in text (parental
care).—BAGG and ELIOT, Birds Connecticut Valley in Massachusetts, 1937, 175
(extirpated).—MURPHEY, Contr. Charleston Mus., ix, 1937, 15 (Savannah
Valley, Ga.; formerly abundant, still fairly common resident).—VAN TYNE,
Occ. Pap. Mus. Zool. Univ. Michigan, No. 379, 1938, 12 (Michigan; formerly
permanent resident; now extirpated; breeding records).—POOLE, Auk, lx, 1938,
517, in table (weight; wing area).—OBERHOLSER, Bird Life Louisiana, 1938,
193 (Louisiana; formerly not uncommon, now largely confined to the n. and ne.
parts of state).—DEADERICK, Wils. Bull., l, 1938, 263 (Hot Springs Nat. Park,
Ark.; rare resident).—TANNER, Auk, lvi, 1939, 90 (Madison Parish, La.;
60 seen).—WETMORE, Proc. U. S. Nat. Mus., lxxxvi, 1939, 184 (Tennessee;

one seen—Old Black Mountain).—Long, Trans. Kansas Acad. Sci., xliii, 1940, 441 (Kansas; formerly abundant resident; now extinct).—Campbell, Bull. Toledo Mus. Sci., i, 1940, 65 (Lucas County, Ohio; formerly common; last record 1892).—Todd, Birds Western Pennsylvania, 1940, 178 (w. Pennsylvania; descr.; habits; syn.; bibl.).—Trautman, Misc. Publ. Univ. Michigan Mus. Zool., No. 44, 1940, 227 (Buckeye Lake, Ohio; formerly common resident; now extirpated).—Goodpaster, Journ. Cincinnati Soc. Nat. Hist., xxii, 1941, 13 (sw. Ohio; formerly common, now practically extirpated in settled districts; bones in Indian village sites).—Hellmayr and Conover, Cat. Birds Amer., i, No. 1, 1942, 292 (distr.; syn.).—Pearson, Brimley, and Brimley, Birds North Carolina, 1942, 110 (North Carolina; status; habits).—Cruickshank, Birds New York City, 1942, 154 (extirpated).—Mosby and Handley, Wild Turkey in Virginia, 1943, 4, ff. (distr.; monogr.; management).

Meleagres gallopavo silvestris Johnston, Birds West Virginia, 1923, 88 (West Virginia).

M[eleagris] gallopavo var. *sylvestris* Ridgway, Ann. Lyc. Nat. Hist. New York, x, 1874, 382 (Illinois).

[Meleagris] gallopavo silvestris Baillie and Harrington, Contr. Roy. Ontario Mus. Zool., No. 8, pt. 1, 1936, 31, in text (Ontario; extirpated).—Petrides, Trans 7th North Amer. Wildlife Conf., 1942, 325, in text (age indicators in plumage).

M[eleagris] g[allopavo] silvestris Wright, Auk, xxxi, 1914, 343, in text (early records).—Moore, Auk, lv, 1938, 113 in text, 114 (spec.; crit.).—Leopold, Condor, xlv, 1943, 133, in text (molts of young).

Gallopavo sylvestris LeConte, Proc. Acad. Nat. Sci. Philadelphia, ix, 1857, 179–181 (crit.; *ex* Ray).

Meleagris gallopavo sylvestris Allen, Auk, xix, 1902, 420 in text.—Jones, Birds Ohio, Revised Cat., 1903, 85 (Ohio; prob. extinct).—Woodruff, Chicago Acad. Sci. Bull., vi, 1907, 86 (extirpated in Chicago area).

Meleagris fera Vieillot, Nouv. Dict. d'Hist. Nat., ix, 1817, 447; Gal. Ois., ii, 1825, 10, pl. 201.—Gray, List Birds Brit. Mus., pt. 5, Gallinae, 1867, 42.—Elliot, Auk, xvi, 1899, 232 (crit. on p. 231).

[Meleagris] fera Sharpe, Hand-list, i, 1899, 43.

Meleagris gallopavo fera Coues, Auk, xvi, 1899, 77.—American Ornithologists' Union, Auk, xvi, 1899, 108.—Beyer, Proc. Louisiana Soc. Nat. for 1897-99 (1900), 98 (Louisiana).—Allen, Proc. Manchester Inst. Sci. and Arts, iv, 1902, 94 (formerly resident in s. New Hampshire).—Kumlien and Hollister, Bull. Wisconsin Nat. Hist. Soc., iii, 1903, 58 (Wisconsin).

Meleagris gallopavofera Lantz, Trans. Kansas Acad. Sci. for 1896-97 (1899), 254 (Kansas; now rare; formerly abundant).

Meleagris gallapavo fera Nash, Check List Birds Ontario, 1900, 27 (Ontario, formerly common).

Meleagris gallapavo, var. *occidentalis* Allen, Bull. Nuttall Orn. Club, i, 1876, 55 (extirpated in New England; ex *Meleagris occidentalis* Bartram, Travels in Florida, etc., 1791, 88 = nomen nudum).

MELEAGRIS GALLOPAVO OSCEOLA Scott

Florida Turkey

Adult male.—Similar to that of *Meleagris gallopavo silvestris* but smaller and with the remiges with the white bars very much narrower than the dark interspaces and on the whole less incomplete[19]; the rectrices brown-tipped as in *silvestris* in most birds, but occasionally their tips paler and more buffy; the innermost secondaries averaging more grayish; the tips of the upper tail coverts slightly paler, more chestnut, and the tarsal spurs averaging somewhat longer and sharper, i.e., more attenuate, less blunt, and the general effect of the metallic reflections averaging more brilliantly red and green, less bronzy.

Adult female.—Similar to that of *Meleagris gallopavo silvestris* but differing from it in the same characters as do the adult males of the two races.

Subadult.—Similar to the adult of the corresponding sex but with the beard shorter, and in the male the tarsal spurs and the frontal appendage smaller.

Immature.—Similar to the subadult of the corresponding sex but with the two outer juvenal primaries.

Juvenal.—Similar to that of *M. g. silvestris.*

Natal down.—Like that of *M. g. silvestris* but head and back slightly darker.

Adult male.—Wing 430–487 (462); tail 345–390 (362.8); culmen from cere 30.5–35.5 (32.9); tarsus 159.5–174 (169.8); middle toe without claw 70–82.5 (76.4); length of tarsal spur 17–32 (25.1); diameter of tarsal spur 9.5–13 (11.6 mm.).[20]

Adult female.—Wing 354–390 (368.7); tail 268–304 (291); culmen from cere 26.8–31 (29.1); tarsus 125.5–135.5 (132.3); middle toe without claw 59–68 (63.2 mm.).[21]

Range.—Resident chiefly in the dense hammocks and the dry swamps, but also in open pineland and saw palmetto prairies in Florida from at least as far north as Gainesville and the lower Aucilla River south to Royal Palm Hammock.

Type locality.—Tarpon Springs, Fla.

Meleagris gallopavo (not of Linnaeus) ALLEN, Bull. Mus. Comp. Zool., ii, 1871, 342 (e. Florida).—SCOTT, Auk, vi, 1889, 246 (Gulf coast, Fla.).

Meleagris gallopavo osceola SCOTT, Auk, vii, 1890, 376 (Tarpon Springs, w. Florida; coll. Amer. Mus. Nat. Hist.); ix, 1892, 212, 215 (Caloosahatchie region, sw. Florida; habits, etc.).—AMERICAN ORNITHOLOGISTS' UNION, Auk, ix, 1892, 109; xvi, 1899, 105; xviii, 1901, 310; Check-list, ed. 2, 1895, 118; ed. 3, 1910, 146; ed. 4, 1931, 92.—RIDGWAY, Man. North Amer. Birds, ed. 2, 1896, 590.—PALMER, Auk, xxvi, 1909, 27–28, in text (instinctive stillness).—BAYNARD, Auk, xxx, 1913, 243 (Alachua County, Fla.).—HOWELL, Auk, xxxviii, 1921, 255 Royal Palm Hammock, Fla.; very rare resident).—BAILEY, Birds Florida, i, 1925, 1, 60, pl. 32 (fig.; distr.; Florida).—BENT and COPELAND, Auk, xliv,

---

[19] One specimen seen (from Kissimmee, Fla., U. S. N. M. No. 124396) in which the wing quills agree with the characters of *silvestris.*

[20] Eleven specimens.

[21] Nine specimens.

1927, 380 (Charlotte County, Fla.).—CHRISTY, Auk, xlv, 1928, 288 (edge of Big Cypress, s. Florida.).—BANGS, Bull. Mus. Comp. Zool., lxx, 1930, 158 (type in Mus. Comp. Zool.).—HOWELL, Florida Bird Life, 1932, 195 (genl.; Florida). —BENT, U. S. Nat. Mus. Bull. 162, 1932, 340 (habits).—PETERS, Check-list Birds World, ii, 1934, 140.—GHIGI, Gallini di Faraone e Tacchini, 1936, 329 (genl.).—HELLMAYR and CONOVER, Cat. Birds Amer., 1, No. 1, 1942, 292.— MOSBY and HANDLEY, Wild Turkey in Virginia, 1943, 4 (distr.).

Meleagris fera osceola ELLIOT, Auk, xvi, 1899, 232.

M[eleagris] g[allopavo] osceola WRIGHT, Auk, xxxi, 1914, 343 in text (early records).—MOORE, Auk, lv, 1938, 113 in text, 114 (spec.; crit.).

[*Meleagris americana*] Subsp. a *Meleagris osceola* OGILVIE-GRANT, Cat. Birds Brit. Mus., xxii, 1893, 390 (Tarpon Springs, Fla.).

[*Meleagris*] *osceola* SHARPE, Hand-list, i, 1899, 43.

M[eleagris] osceola REICHENOW, Die Vögel, i, 1913, 305.

Meleagris occidentalis BARTRAM, Travels in Florida, etc., 1791, 83 (near Pincolata, Fla.; nomen nudum).

MELEAGRIS GALLOPAVO INTERMEDIA Sennett

RIO GRANDE TURKEY

Adult male.—Similar to that of *M. g. silvestris* but smaller and with the upper tail coverts and the rectrices with paler tips, those of the coverts being cinnamon-buff with a slight tawny tinge, those of the rectrices being Venus brown paling distally to pinkish cinnamon; the rectrices in many specimens tend to be more barred with blackish over the area basal to the black subterminal band, the brown interspaces somewhat freckled with blackish in others they are vermiculated on the more median ones; the tips of the flank feathers paler and more cinnamomeous; the lower back and rump almost solid glossy blackish with rather faint subterminal bluish-green reflections (not pinkish or coppery as in *silvestris*); the metallic reflections of the rest of the body more brilliant, less bronzy, agreeing in this respect with *M. g. osceola*, inner webs of innermost secondaries more heavily mottled with dusky and their outer webs more strongly glossed with greenish purplish; other secondaries darker, the brown areas fuscous; tarsal spur short and stubby as in *silvestris*; tips of under tail coverts and flanks paler—cinnamon-buffy. Birds from Wichita Mountains, Okla., are intermediate between *silvestris* and *intermedia*, more like *silvestris* in the color of the inner webs of the inner secondaries and the barring of the rectrices.

Adult female.—Similar to that of *M. g. silvestris* but smaller and with the feathers of lower back and rump and the upper tail coverts and the rectrices with paler tips—cinnamon-buff to fairly pale pinkish buff; the rectrices averaging more definitely barred proximal to the subterminal black band; secondaries paler, more whitish on their outer margins, the innermost ones sandy grayish cinnamon-buff; feathers of the breast, upper abdomen, sides, and flanks tipped with pale pinkish buff.

Juvenal male.—Similar to that of *M. g. silvestris* but slightly paler, the dark areas reduced on the wings and the brown slightly more "sandy" generally on the upperparts.

Adult male.—Wing 462–468 (465) ; tail 346–385 (369.3) ; culmen from cere 35–37 (35.8) ; tarsus 162–171 (166.3) ; middle toe without claw 78–81.5 (80.2) ; length of tarsal spur 11.5–17 (14.7) ; diameter of tarsal spur 11.5–12.5 (12.2 mm.).[22]

Adult female.—Wing 385–405 (392.3) ; tail 277–302 (290.3) ; culmen from cere 26.5–32.5 (30.3) ; tarsus 126–138.5 (130.4) ; middle toe without claw 61.5–71 (65 mm.).[23]

Range.—Resident from central Texas (San Antonio; Nueces River near Corpus Christi; Tom Green, Concho, Cameron, Motley, Kerr, Kendall, Aransas, and Bexar Counties) ; south to Tamaulipas (Soto la Marina; Forlón, Río de la Cruz) ; Nuevo León (Montemorelos, Cerrode la Silla), and northwestern Coahuila (Sabinas and La Palma), and extreme southeastern San Luis Potosí (Micos).

Type locality.—Lomita, Tex.

Meleagris gallopavo (not of Linnaeus) DRESSER, Ibis, 1866, 25 (se. Texas; ne. Mexico).—COUES, Check List North Amer. Birds, 1874, No. 379, part.— SENNETT, U. S. Geol. and Geogr. Surv. Terr., Bull. 4, No. 1, 1878, 53 (Hidalgo, lower Rio Grande); 5, No. 3, 1879, 427 (Lomita, lower Rio Grande Valley, se. Texas; crit.).—MERRILL, Auk, i, 1878, 159 (Fort Brown and Hidalgo, se. Texas; crit.; descr. eggs).—RIDGWAY, Proc. U. S. Nat. Mus., iii, 1880, 195, part; Nom. North Amer. Birds, 1881, No. 470, part.—BROWN, Bull. Nuttall Orn. Club, vii, 1882, 41 (Boerne, Kendall County, Tex.).—BECKHAM, Proc. U. S. Nat. Mus., x, 1888, 657 (Bexar County, etc., Tex.).—CHAPMAN, Bull. Amer. Mus. Nat. Hist., iii, No. 2, 1891, 321 (Nueces River, 20-30 miles w. of Corpus Christi, Tex.).—SALVIN and GODMAN, Biol. Centr.-Amer., Aves, iii, 1903, 284, part (southern Texas and Tamaulipas).—SUTTON and PETTINGILL, Auk, lix, 1942, 13 (Gómez Farias region, southwestern Tamaulipas; 1 seen).

[*Meleagris*] *gallopavo* COUES, Key North Amer. Birds, 1872, 232, part.

Meleagris mexicana (not of Gould) ELLIOT, New and Unfig. North Amer. Birds, pt. 10, 1868 (vol. ii), text, pl. 38, part; Monogr. Phasianidae, i, 1870, text, pl. 28, part.

Meleagris gallopavo mexicana AMERICAN ORNITHOLOGISTS' UNION, Check-list, 1886, No. 310a, part.—LLOYD, Auk, iv, 1887, 187 (Tom Green and Concho Counties, w. Tex.).—COOKE, Bird Migr. Mississippi Valley, 1888, 107, part (San Antonio and Concho Counties, Tex.).—BENDIRE, Life Hist. North Amer. Birds, i, 1892, 116, part.—ATTWATER, Auk, ix, 1892, 233 (San Antonio, Tex.).

M[*eleagris*] *gallopavo mexicana* RIDGWAY, Man. North Amer. Birds, 1887, 207, part (s. Texas).

[*Meleagris gallopavo*] var. *intermedia* SENNETT, U. S. Geol. and Geogr. Surv. Terr., Bull. 5, No. 3, 1879, 428, in text (Lomita Ranch, lower Rio Grande Valley, s. Tex.; coll. G. B. Sennett, type now in coll. Amer. Mus. Nat. Hist.).

Meleagris gallopavo intermedia AMERICAN ORNITHOLOGISTS' UNION, Auk, xvi, 1899, 108; Check-list, ed. 3, 1910, 146; ed. 4, 1931, 92—PHILLIPS, Auk, xxviii, 1911,

---

[22] Four specimens from Texas, Tamaulipas, and Nuevo León.
[23] Eleven specimens from Texas, Tamaulipas, and Nuevo León.

74 (Río de la Cruz, Tamaulipas).—SMITH, Auk, xxxiii, 1916, 188 (Kerr County, Tex.); Condor, xx, 1918, 212 in text (near Matador, Motley County, Tex.).— SIMMONS, Birds Austin Region, 1925, 84 (Austin region, Tex.; habits; nest and eggs; descrip.; etc.).—GRISCOM and CROSBY, Auk, xlii, 1925, 533 (Brownsville, Tex.).—BENT, U. S. Nat. Mus. Bull. 162, 1932, 342 (life hist.; etc.).— PETERS, Check-list Birds World, ii, 1934, 140.—GHIGI, Gallini di Faraone e Tacchini, 1936, 327 (genl.).—SUTTON, Ann. Carnegie Mus., xxvii, 1938, 178 (Tarrant County Tex.; probably breeds).—HELLMAYR and CONOVER, Cat. Birds Amer., i, No. 1, 1942, 293.

M[eleagris] g[allopavo] intermedia BAILEY, Handb. Birds Western United States, 1902, 136 (descr.; distr.).—MOORE, Auk, lv, 1938, 113 in text, 114 (spec.; crit.). —MOSBY and HANDLEY, Wild Turkey in Virginia, 1943, 4 (distr.).

Meleagris gallapavo intermedia LACEY, Auk, xxviii, 1911, 206 (Kerrville, Tex.; formerly common).

Meleagris intermedia ELLIOT, Auk, xvi, 1899, 232 (crit. on p. 231).

M[eleagris] intermedia REICHENOW, Die Vögel, i, 1913, 305.

[Meleagris] intermedia SHARPE, Hand-list, i, 1899, 43.

Meleagris gallopavo ellioti SENNETT, Auk, ix, 1892, 167, pl. 3 (Lomita Ranch, Hidalgo County, s. Tex.; coll. G. B. Sennett).—AMERICAN ORNITHOLOGISTS' UNION, Auk, x, 1893, 60; Check-list, ed. 2, 1895, No. 310c.—RIDGWAY, Man. North Amer. Birds, ed. 2, 1896, 591.

[Meleagris gallopavo.] Subsp. a Meleagris ellioti OGILVIE-GRANT, Cat. Birds Brit. Mus., xxii, 1893, 388 (Tamaulipas; Hidalgo, Tex.).

MELEAGRIS GALLOPAVO MERRIAMI Nelson

MERRIAM'S TURKEY

Adult male.—Similar to that of *M. g. silvestris* but with tips of the rump feathers, upper tail coverts, and rectrices very much lighter and whiter (even paler than in *M. g. intermedia*)—pale pinkish buff, the feathers of the upper back, breast and upper abdomen very slightly less bronzy, the lower back blackish with bluish gloss as in *M. g. intermedia;* the upper tail coverts bright auburn proximal to the broad pale tips which in turn are basally narrowly pale ochraceous-tawny, the black subterminal band of the rectrices averaging narrower than in *silvestris* and in the lateral ones, with well-developed, metallic, greenish-purplish, transverse bars included, the secondaries more mottled with pale tawny to cinnamon, especially on the inner webs and with more white on both webs; feathers of flanks and the under tail coverts broadly tipped with pinkish buff to light pinkish cinnamon, averaging paler on the flanks and darker on the under tail coverts, these broad tips, in turn, basally hazel, these basal hazel areas broader on the under tail coverts than on the flanks; tarsal spur somewhat shorter and more stubby than in *silvestris.*

Adult female.—Similar to that of *M. g. intermedia* but larger (as large as *M. g. silvestris*) and with the upper tail coverts and rectrices with still paler tips—pale pinkish buff to tilleul buff; the innermost secondaries more heavily mottled with dusky.

Immature.—Similar to the adult of corresponding sex but generally duller below and retaining the two outermost juvenal primaries.

Adult male.—Wing 502–524 (511) ; tail 373–427 (398.4) ; culmen from cere 34.5–40 (37.2) ; tarsus 159–175 (166.6) ; middle toe without claw 78–88 (83.5 mm.).[24]

Adult female.—Wing 400–463 (435.9) ; tail 325–360 (345) ; culmen from cere 31–34 (32.3) ; tarsus 124–159 (133.6) ; middle toe without claw 66–73 (68.8 mm.).[25]

Range.—Resident in the Transition and Upper Austral Zones in the mountains of central and southwestern Colorado (up to 7,000 feet; Canyon City; Upper Arkansas River; Raton Pass; Las Animas; South Park; Oak Hill; Pueblo County, San Miguel County), New Mexico (Manzano, Chusa, Santa Fe, San Luis, San Mateo, and Sacramento Mountains; Upper Pecos River up to 11,000 feet; Valverde, La Jara, Cloudcroft, Fort Thorn, Gila River, etc.) ; Arizona (Huachuca, Santa Catalina, and San Francisco Mountains; near Winslow; Fort Whipple; White Mountains; Williams; San Pedro River; Copper Mine; Bill Williams River; etc.) ; and southwestern Texas (Guadelupe Mountains).

Type locality.—Forty-seven miles southwest of Winslow, Ariz.

Meleagris mexicana (not of Gould) BAIRD, Rep. Pacific R. R. Surv., ix, 1858, 618 (Fort Thorn, N. Mex.) ; Cat. North Amer. Birds, 1859, No. 458.—COUES, Ibis, 1865, 165, in text (Fort Whipple, Ariz.) ; Proc. Acad. Nat. Sci. Philadelphia, 1866, 93 (Fort Whipple, Ariz.) ; 1868, 84 (mountains of New Mexico and Arizona).—ELLIOT, New and Unfig. North Amer. Birds, pt. 10, 1868 (vol. ii), pl. 38 and text, part; Monogr. Phasianidae, i, 1872, pl. 28, and text, part.—BAIRD, *in* Cooper, Orn. California, Land Birds, 1870, 523, part (w. Texas to Arizona).
Meleagris gallopavo, var. *mexicana* BAIRD, BREWER, and RIDGWAY, Hist. North Amer. Birds, iii, 1874, 410, part.
Meleagris gallopavo mexicana AMERICAN ORNITHOLOGISTS' UNION, Check-list, 1886, No. 310a, part; ed. 2, 1895, No. 310a, part (w. Texas to Arizona).—SCOTT, Auk, iii, 1886, 389 (San Pedro River and Santa Catalina Mountains, Ariz.).—COOKE, Bird Migr. Mississippi Valley, 1888, 107, part (w. Texas; Arizona) ; Colorado State Agr. Coll. Bull. 37, 1897, 72 (mountains of Colorado up to 7,000 ft.) ; Condor, xv, 1913, 104 [–105], fig. 32 (map) (range in Colorado).—MEARNS, Auk, vii, 1890, 52 (San Francisco Mountains, Ariz.).—MITCHELL, Auk, xv, 1898, 307 (San Miguel County, N. Mex., 8,000 feet to timberline).
M[eleagris] gallopavo mexicana RIDGWAY, Man. North Amer. Birds, 1887, 207, part (w. Texas to Arizona).
Meleagris gallopavo (not of Linnaeus) WOODHOUSE, *in* Sitgreaves Expl. Zuñi and Colorado Rivers, 1853, 93, part (Copper Mines and Bill Williams River, Ariz.).—RIDGWAY, Bull. Essex Inst., v, 1873, 186 (Colorado) ; Proc. U. S. Nat. Mus., iii, 1880, 195; Nom. North Amer. Birds, 1881, No. 470.—COUES, Check List North Amer. Birds, 1874, No. 379, part.—HENSHAW, Auk, iii, 1886, 80 (upper Pecos River, N. Mex.).—OGILVIE-GRANT, Cat. Birds Brit. Mus., xxii, 1893, 387, part (Sante Fe Mountains, N. Mex.; w. Texas; Arizona).—COOKE, Colorado State Agr. Coll. Bull. 37, 1897, 71 (Colorado; rare resident; distr.) ; Bull. 56, 1900, 203 (South Park, Colo.).—AMERICAN ORNITHOLOGISTS' UNION,

[24] Eight specimens from Arizona and New Mexico.
[25] Twelve specimens from Arizona and New Mexico.

Auk, xvi, 1899, 107 (w. Texas to Arizona).—Elliot, Auk, xvi, 1899, 232, part (w. Texas to Arizona).—Felger, Auk, xxvi, 1909, 191 (Oak Hills, s. of Denver, Colo., in 1868).—Miller, Condor, xxxiv, 1932, 139 (remains, *ex* Indian site, Arizona).—Wetmore, Condor, xxxiv, 1932, 142 (bones, cave deposits n. of Carlsbad, N. Mex.).—Howard and Miller, Condor, xxxv, 1933, 16 (bones, Organ Mountains, N. Mex.).—Peters, Check-list Birds World, ii, 1934, 140.—Ayer, Proc. Acad. Nat. Sci. Philadelphia, lxxxviii, 1936, 604 (Williams Cave, Guadelupe Mountains, Tex.; lower jaw).—Ghigi, Gallini de Faraone e Tacchini, 1936, 326 (genl.).

?*Meleagris gallopavo* Nelson, Proc. Boston Soc. Nat. Hist., xvii, 1875, 343 (30 miles s. of Fort Bridger, Utah).

[*Meleagris*] *gallopavo* Coues, Key North Amer. Birds, 1872, 232, part.—Sharpe, Hand-list, i, 1899, 43, part (w. Texas to Arizona).

M[*eleagris*] *gallopavo* Reichenow, Die Vögel, i, 1913, 304.

Meleagris gallopavo americana (not *M. americana* Hildreth) Abert, Journ. Cincinnati Soc. Nat. Hist., v, 1882, 58 (Bents Fort, Colo.), 59 (Valverde, N. Mex.).

[*Meleagris gallopavo* var. *americana*] a. *gallopavo* Coues, Birds Northwest, 1874, 391, part.

Meleagris gallipavo Coues, Check List North Amer. Birds, ed. 2, 1882, No. 553.

M[*eleagris*] *gallipavo* Coues, Key North Amer. Birds, ed. 2, 1884, 576.

Meleagris gallopavo fera Cooke, Colorado State Agr. Coll. Bull. 56, 1900, 203 (Colorado; distr.).

M[*eleagris*] *g*[*allopavo*] *fera* Bailey, Handb. Birds Western United States, 1902, 136 (descr.; distr.).

Meleagris gallopavo merriami Nelson, Auk, xvii, 1900, 120 (47 miles sw. of Winslow, Ariz.; coll. U. S. Nat. Mus.).—Bailey, Handb. Birds Western United States, 1902, 136 (descr.; habits; distr.); Auk, xxi, 1904, 352 (upper Pecos River, N. Mex., up to above 4,000 feet); Birds New Mexico, 1928, 231 (New Mexico; genl.; distr.).—Swarth, Pacific Coast Avif., No. 4, 1904, 4 (Huachuca Mountains, Ariz.; rare; formerly abundant); No. 10, 1914, 23 (Arizona; now nearly extinct; formerly s. of Grand Canyon, w. to Santa Cruz Valley).—Gilman, Condor, ix, 1907, 153 (San Miguel Canyon, sw. Colorado); x, 1908, 147 (w. end of Chusa Mountains, N. Mex.).—American Ornithologists' Union, Check-list, ed. 3, 1910, 145; ed. 4, 1931, 92.—Visher, Auk, xxvii, 1910, 281 (Pima County, Ariz.; nearly extirpated).—Sclater, Hist. Birds Colorado, 1912, 155 (Colorado; formerly abundant; now rare).—Cooke, Condor, xv, 1913, 104, 105, fig. 32 (Colorado range).—Lowe, Auk, xxxiv, 1917, 453 (Pueblo County, Colo., spring of 1895).—Jensen, Auk, xl, 1923, 454 (n. Sante Fe County, N. Mex.).—Wyman and Burnell, Field Book Birds Southwest United States, 1925, 88 (descr.).—Bent, U. S. Nat. Mus. Bull. 162, 1932, 323 (habits; distr.).—Peters, Check-list Birds World, ii, 1934, 140, part (exclusive of Chihuahua).—Hargrave, Condor, xxxvii, 1935, 285 (Williams, Ariz.).—Huey, Wils. Bull., xlviii, 1936, 122 (White Mountains, Ariz.; fairly common).—Moore, Auk, lv, 1938, 112 in text.—Niedrach and Rockwell, Birds Denver and Mountain Parks, 1939, 65 (extinct; former straggler; 3 specimens, 1868).—Hellmayr and Conover, Cat. Birds Amer., i, No. 1, 1942, 293, part (exclusive of Chihuahua and northern Sonora).—Mosby and Handley, Wild Turkey in Virginia, 1943, 4 (distr.).

M[*eleagris*] *g*[*allopavo*] *merriami* Moore, Auk, lv, 1938, 113 in text, 115 (spec.; crit.).

MELEAGRIS GALLOPAVO GALLOPAVO Linnaeus

SOUTH MEXICAN TURKEY

Adult male.—Similar to that of *M. g. silvestris* but smaller, the tail much less rufescent—dusky natal brown very abundantly flecked with clove brown to fuscous, the median feathers with their median areas broadly solid clove brown, the outer few pairs with incomplete russet bars on their basal two-thirds, the black subterminal bar deeper black and broader than in *silvestris* and, on the lateral feathers with an included band of metallic greenish-bluish reflections, the rectrices tipped with white slightly tinged with pale tilleul buff to light pinkish buff; feathers of rump and upper tail coverts, flanks, and under tail coverts broadly tipped with tilleul buff to light pinkish buff, nearest in this respect to *M. g. merriami;* feathers of upper back, breast, and upper abdomen less bronzy more brilliantly coppery and greenish, as in *M. g. osceola;* lower back and rump blackish with narrow bluish tips and with subterminal blue-green reflections, nearest in this character to *M. g. merriami;* outer secondaries with fairly continuous white edges; inner secondaries much grayer, less rufescent than *M. g. silvestris*—hair brown mottled on the inner web with drab to light drab, and with a purplish sheen on the outer web; tarsal spurs shorter and stubbier than in *M. g. silvestris.*

Adult female.—Similar to that of *M. g. merriami* but with the upper body plumage highly glossed with greenish and reddish metallic reflections.

Adult male.—Wing 465–513 (489); tail 345–400 (372.5); culmen from cere 34–38.5 (35.8); tarsus 162–176 (168.4); middle toe without claw 74–85 (79.9); length of tarsal spur 14.5–16.5 (15.5); diameter of tarsal spur 11.5–14 (12.8 mm.).[24]

Adult female.—Wing 396–416 (405.6); tail 311–323 (319.8); culmen from cere 32.5–36 (34.6); tarsus 130–140 (135); middle toe without claw 65–71.5 (68.6 mm.).[25]

Range.—Resident from Veracruz (Mirador, Zacnapam) westward to Michoacán (La Salada) and to Oaxaca.

Type locality.—Mexico; restricted (by Moore, Auk, lv, 1938, 113) to Mirador, Veracruz.

[*Meleagris*] *gallopavo* LINNAEUS, Syst. Nat., ed. 10, i, 1758, 156, part (North America; based on *Meleagris* Fauna Suecica, 164; *Gallopavo sylvestris novæanglia* Ray, Av., 51; Albin, Av., iii, 33, pl. 35; β *Gallopavo* Gesner, Av., 482; Aldrovandi, Orn., 13, pl. 4; Bell, Av., 60, a; Jonston, Av., 58, pl. 24; Willughby, Orn., 113, pl. 27; Ray, Av., 51 γ *Gallopavo cristatus* Albin, Av., ii, 30, pl. 33); ed. 12, i, 1766, 268, part.—LATHAM, Synop. Birds, Suppl., i, 1787, 289; Index Orn., ii, 1790, 618 part.—GMELIN, Syst. Nat., i, pt. 2, 1788, 732, part.—GRAY, Hand-list, ii, 1870, 262, No. 9627.—SHARPE, Hand-list, i, 1899, 43, part.

---

[24] Four specimens from Veracruz and Michoacán.
[25] Five specimens from Veracruz and Michoacán.

Me[leagris] gallopavo STEPHENS, *in* Shaw, Gen. Zool., xiv, pt. 1, 1826, 297, part.

Meleagris gallopavo VIEILLOT, Nouv. Dict. Hist. Nat., ix, 1817, 447, part.—STEPHENS, *in* Shaw, Gen. Zool., x, 1819, 156, pl. 8.—GRAY, List Birds Brit. Mus., pt. 5, Gallinæ, 1867, 42, part.—AMERICAN ORNITHOLOGISTS' UNION, Auk, xvi, 1899, 107, part (tableland of Mexico).

M[eleagris] gallopavo KEYSERLING and BLASIUS, Wirbelth. Eur., 1840, lxv, 200.— COUES, Key North Amer. Birds, ed. 2, 1884, 576, part.—CUBAS, Cuadro Geograph., Estadístico, Descr. e Hist. de los Estados Unidos Mexicanos, 1884, 171, (common names, Mexico).—NELSON, Auk, xvii, 1900, 123 in text (crit.).

Meleagris gallopavo gallopavo AMERICAN ORNITHOLOGISTS' UNION, Check-list, ed. 3, 1910, 145, part.—PETERS, Check-list Birds World, ii, 1934, 140, part.—GHIGI, Gallini di Faraone e Tacchini, 1936, 323 (genl.).—HELLMAYR and CONOVER, Cat. Birds Amer., No. 1, 1942, 294, part.—MOSBY and HANDLEY, Wild Turkey in Virginia, 1943, 4, part (distr.; part).

M[eleagris] g[allopavo] gallopavo MOORE, Auk, lv, 1938, 112 in text, 113, 115 (crit. spec.).

[*Meleagris*] [*gallopavo*] *gallopavo* WHEATON, Rep. Birds Ohio, 1882, 444 (distr.).

Meleagris mexicana SCLATER, Proc. Zool. Soc. London, 1863, 125, part (monogr.).— ELLIOT, New and Unfig. North Amer. Birds, pt. 10, 1868 (vol. ii), pl. 38 and text, part; Monogr. Phasianidae, i, 1872, pl. 28 and text, part.—BAIRD, *in* COOPER, Orn. California, Land Birds, 1870, 523, part.—BERISTAIN and LAURENCIO, Mem. y Rev. Soc. Cient. "Antonio Alzate," vii, Nos. 7, 8, 1894, 219 (Veracruz; Oaxaca).

[*Meleagris*] *mexicana* SCLATER and SALVIN, Nom. Av. Neotr., 1873, 137, part.

Meleagris gallopavo, var. *mexicana* BAIRD, BREWER, and RIDGWAY, Hist. North Amer. Birds, iii, 1874, 410, part.

[*Meleagris gallopavo* var. *americana*] α *gallopavo* COUES, Birds Northwest, 1874, 391, part (in synonymy).

Meleagris gallopavo mexicana AMERICAN ORNITHOLOGISTS' UNION, Check-list, 1886, No. 310a, part; ed. 2, 1895, No. 310a, part.—COOKE, Bird Migr. Mississippi Valley, 1888, 107, part (tablelands of Mexico).

M[eleagris] gallopavo mexicana RIDGWAY, Man. North Amer. Birds, 1887, 207, part (Veracruz).

Gallopavo primus LESSON, Traité d'Orn., 1831, 490, pl. 82, fig. 2 (new name for *Meleagris gallopavo* Linnaeus).

MELEAGRIS GALLOPAVO MEXICANA Gould[26]

GOULD'S TURKEY

Adult male.—Similar to that of *M. g. gallopavo* but with the upper back and wing coverts duller, more purplish bronzy, and with the lower

---

[26] The use of the name *mexicana* is unfortunately still unsettled and must remain so until it is possible to examine the type specimen critically. Furthermore, the type locality is also uncertain and has been arrived at by faunal inference rather than by definite data. If it were to be accepted as originally given—Reál del Monte, Hidalgo, it would seem (from geographic reasoning) that *mexicana* would probably have to be treated as a synonym of *gallopavo,* but if Nelson's interpretation of the case be followed and the type locality be considered as Bolaños, northern Jalisco, the course here adopted would be the correct one. At any rate, there are two distinct forms of the turkey involved in the currently used comprehensive *"gallopavo"* concept, and the names *mexicana* and *gallopavo* are used here in an attempt to render more distinct the two forms and their literature.

back and rump with some coppery and greenish-golden metallic reflections as in *silvestris* and *osceola,* rather than bluish black as in *gallopavo,* and larger, like *merriami* in size.

Adult female.—Similar to that of *M. g. gallopavo,* but with general dorsal coloration duller, more dusky purplish, less of the coppery and greenish-metallic reflection.

Subadult.—Similar to the adult of corresponding sex but with the beard shorter, and, in the males, with tarsal spurs and frontal appendage smaller.

Immature.—Similar to the adult of corresponding sex, but has the two outer juvenal primaries.

Juvenal (sexes alike).—Similar to that of *M. g. silvestris* but darker, the interscapulars and feathers of the upper back clove brown to chaetura blackish with narrow whitish shafts, terminally edged with grayish Prout's brown and subterminally banded with sepia; inner secondaries and rectrices slightly more rufescent—between Verona brown and Sayal brown (Sayal brown in *silvestris*); breast, abdomen, sides, and flanks fuscous to chaetura drab, the feathers of the breast and upper abdomen subterminally banded with dusky cinnamon-brown and tipped with whitish.

Natal down (judged from specimens in postnatal molt).—Similar to that of *M. g. silvestris* but with the middorsal brown area somewhat paler and duller—sepia.

Adult male.—Wing 465–545 (504.1); tail 363–437 (396.1); culmen from cere 34.5–41 (38.7); tarsus 168–182 (173.8); middle toe without claw 84–93 (87.6); length of tarsal spur 13.5–17.5 (16.1); diameter of tarsal spur 11–13 (12 mm.).[27]

Adult female.—Wing 402–436 (419.6); tail 318–362 (334.9); culmen from cere 33.5–35 (34.4); tarsus 132–139.5 (134.5); middle toe without claw 68–73 (70.1 mm.).[28]

Range.—Resident from Chihuahua, east of the cordillera (Colonia García; Pacheco River; Cajon Bonita Creek; San Luis Mountains) to Durango (Ciudad Durango and El Salto) and to northern Jalisco (Bolaños).

Type locality.—Reál del Monte, Hidalgo ? = Bolaños, Jalisco.

[*Meleagris*] *gallopavo* LINNAEUS, Syst. Nat., ed. 10, i, 1758, 156, part (North America, part).—GMELIN, Syst. Nat., i, pt. 2, 1788, 732, part.—LATHAM, Index Orn., i, 1790, 618, part.—SHARPE, Hand-list, i, 1899, 43, part.
Me[*leagris*] *gallopavo* STEPHENS, *in* Shaw, Genl. Zool., xiv, pt. 1, 1826, 297, part.
M[*eleagris*] *gallopavo* COUES, Key North Amer. Birds, ed. 2, 1884, 576, part.
Meleagris gallopavo VIEILLOT, Nouv. Dict. Hist. Nat., ix, 1817, 447, part.—GRAY, List Birds Brit. Mus., pt. 5, Gallinæ, 1867, 42, part.—OGILVIE-GRANT, Cat. Birds Brit. Mus., xxii, 1893, 387, part (type spec. of *mexicana;* also Ciudad Durango,

---

[27] Nine specimens from Chihuahua and Durango.
[28] Seven specimens from Chihuahua and Durango.

Durango).—AMERICAN ORNITHOLOGISTS' UNION, Auk, xvi, 1899, 107, part.—
SALVIN and GODMAN, Biol. Centr.-Amer., Aves, iii, 1903, 284, part (Ciudad
Durango and El Salto, Durango).

Meleagris gallopavo gallopavo AMERICAN ORNITHOLOGISTS' UNION, Check-list, ed.
3, 1910, 145, part.—PETERS, Check-list Birds World, ii, 1934, 140, part.—HELL-
MAYR and CONOVER, Cat. Birds Amer., i, No. 1, 1942, 294, part.—MOSBY and
HANDLEY, Wild Turkey in Virginia, 1943, 4, part (distr.; part).

Meleagris mexicana GOULD, Proc. Zool. Soc. London, 1856, 61 (Reál del Monte,
Hidalgo ? (=Bolaños Jalisco!); coll. Brit. Mus.).—SCLATER, Proc. Zool. Soc.
London, 1863, 125, part (monogr.).—ELLIOT, New and Unfig. North Amer.
Birds, pt. 10, 1868 (vol. ii), pl. 38 and text, part; Monogr. Phasianidae, i, 1872,
pl. 28 and text, part.—BAIRD, *in* Cooper, Orn. California, Land Birds, 1870, 523,
part.—CUBAS, Cuadro Geograph., Estadístico, Descr. e Hist. de los Estados
Unidos Mexicanos, 1884, 171 (common names in Mexico).

[*Meleagris*] *mexicana* SCLATER and SALVIN, Nom. Av. Neotr., 1873, 137, part.

Meleagris gallopavo, var. *mexicana* BAIRD, BREWER, and RIDGWAY, Hist. North
Amer. Birds, iii, 1874, 410, part.

Meleagris gallopavo mexicana AMERICAN ORNITHOLOGISTS' UNION, Check-list, 1886,
No. 310a part; ed. 2, 1895, No. 310a, part.—COOKE, Bird Migr. Mississippi
Valley, 1888, 107, part.

M[*eleagris*] *gallopavo mexicana* RIDGWAY, Man. North Amer. Birds, 1887, 207,
part (tableland of Mexico).

Meleagris gallopavo merriami (not of Nelson) PETERS, Check-list Birds World, ii,
1934, 140, part (Chihuahua).—HELLMAYR and CONOVER, Cat. Birds Amer., i,
No. 1, 1942, 293, part (Chihuahua).

MELEAGRIS GALLOPAVO ONUSTA Moore

MOORE'S TURKEY

Adult male.—Similar to *Meleagris gallopavo merriami* but with the tips
of the rectrices and their upper coverts white instead of light buff; subterminal narrow cinnamon bar of *merriami* absent; the black bar immediately anterior to it usually absent; inner and outer margins of
secondaries and primaries less cinnamon, more dull earth brown and
white; the iridescence of the body feathers, both above and below, darker,
less brilliantly green and copper; the head less heavily clothed with black
hairlike feathers; the feathers of the back of the neck lighter and more
grayish brown, less cinnamomeous; the basal two-thirds of the tail more
barred, less vermiculated than in *M. g. gallopavo,* agreeing in this respect
with *merriami* from which it differs in that these bars are much more grayish, less rufescent, especially on the under surface of the feathers in
onusta.

Adult female.—Differs from that of *M. g. merriami* in the same respects as the male of *onusta* does from the corresponding sex of *merriami.*

Adult male.—Wing 505; tail 421; culmen from cere 38.4; tarsus 173.7;
middle toe without claw 89.5 mm. (1 specimen).

Adult female.—Wing 417–448 (434) ; tail 331–347 (339) ; culmen from cere 32–38.4 (34.5) ; tarsus 140–149 (145.5) ; middle toe without claw 71–75.9 (73.5 mm.).[29]

Range.—Resident in "the Transition and Lower Canadian Zone of the western slope of the Sierra Madre of northwestern Mexico (Sonora (Barromicon ; San José), western Chihuahua, Durango) at an altitude of approximately 8,500 feet to 4,000 feet, descending still lower in the autumn, as it is known to feed on the cornfields of the Indians as low as about 2,500 feet."

Type locality.—Two miles southeast of Guayachi, Chihuahua, 20 miles northeast of junction of Ríos Chinipas and Fuerte, western slope of Sierra Madre (altitude about 6,400 feet).

Meleagris gallopavo merriami (not of Sennett) PETERS, Check-list Birds of World, ii, 1934, 140, part (n. Sonora).—HELLMAYR and CONOVER, Cat. Birds Amer., i, No. 1, 1942, 293, part (n. Sonora).
Meleagris gallopavo subsp. ? MOORE, Condor, xl, 1938, 24 (near Barromicon, se. Sonora).
Meleagris gallopavo onusta MOORE, Auk, lv, 1938, 112 (orig. descr.; e. of Guayachi, Chihuahua ; crit.; distr.).—MOSBY and HANDLEY, Wild Turkey in Virginia, 1943, 4 (distr.).

Genus AGRIOCHARIS Chapman

Agriocharis CHAPMAN, Bull. Amer. Mus. Nat. Hist., viii, 1896, 288.   (Type, by original description, *Meleagris ocellata* Cuvier.)
Eumeleagris COUES, Key North Amer. Birds, ed. 5, ii, 1903, 727.   (Type, by monotypy, *Meleagris ocellata* Cuvier.)

Large gallinaceous birds (length about 83.5–102 cm.) closely resembling *Meleagris*[30] but differing in the absence of a jugular beard and presence, in adult male, of an erect protuberance or subcylindrical knob on crown, decidedly more strongly rounded tail, and more brilliantly metallic coloration. Bill rather elongated and narrow (the culmen about equal to distance from its base to rictus), its depth at base of culmen slightly less than its width at same point ; nostril longitudinal, elliptical, in anterior portion of the rather long nasal fossa ; head and upper neck nude, with scattered wartlike excrescences, the adult male with a flexible elongated appendage on anterior portion of forehead (as in *Meleagris*) and a vertical, subcylindrical knob or protuberance on posterior portion of crown, this permanently erect and much thicker than the frontal appendage ; wing moderate, moderately concave beneath, the longest primaries slightly but

---

[29] Four specimens including this type.
[30] *Agriocharis* is, in fact, so closely related to *Meleagris* that I am somewhat doubtful as to the expediency of recognizing it as a genus. One of the alleged characters certainly does not hold good, namely, the long and very sharp tarsal spur, a precisely similar spur often occurring in *Meleagris gallopavo osceola;* in fact, in an adult male *Agriocharis ocellata* now before me, the spur on one leg is only moderately long and very blunt, while that on the other leg is a very small obtuse cone—in fact is rudimentary! (R.R.)

decidedly longer than longest secondaries; secondaries broad, with rounded tips; primaries rigid, the fifth or sixth longest, the first (outermost) heel joint to base of hallux, the rectrices (18) moderately broad, with slightly shorter than tenth; tail shorter than wing, stronger rounded, the

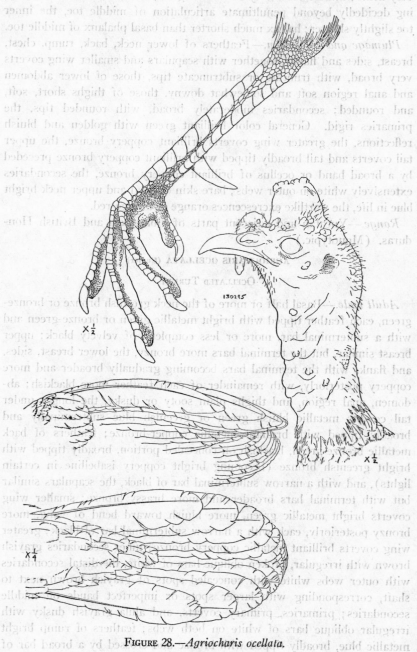

FIGURE 28.—*Agriocharis ocellata.*

middle rectrices exceeding lateral pair by about length of tarsus from distinctly rounded tips; tarsus about one-third as long as wing, stout, the spur on lower part of planta tarsi (in adult males) usually long and very acute; middle toe nearly half as long as tarsus, the outer toe reaching decidedly beyond penultimate articulation of middle toe, the inner toe slightly shorter; hallux much shorter than basal phalanx of middle toe.

Plumage and coloration.—Feathers of lower neck, back, rump, chest, breast, sides and flanks, together with scapulars and smaller wing coverts very broad, with truncate or subtruncate tips, those of lower abdomen and anal region soft and somewhat downy, those of thighs short, soft, and rounded; secondaries moderately broad, with rounded tips, the primaries rigid. General color brilliant green with golden and bluish reflections, the greater wing coverts brilliant coppery bronze, the upper tail coverts and tail broadly tipped with brilliant coppery bronze preceded by a broad band or ocellus of brilliant coppery bronze, the secondaries extensively white on outer webs; bare skin of head and upper neck bright blue in life, the wartlike excrescences orange or orange-red.

Range.—Yucatán and adjacent parts of Guatemala and British Honduras. (Monotypic.)

AGRIOCHARIS OCELLATA (Cuvier)

OCELLATED TURKEY

Adult male.—Basal half or more of the neck greenish bronze or bronze-green, each feather tipped with bright metallic green or bronze-green and with a subterminal bar, more or less complete, of velvety black; upper breast similar, but the terminal bars more bronzy, the lower breast, sides, and flanks with the terminal bars becoming gradually broader and more coppery posteriorly, with remainder of each feather more blackish; abdomen, anal region, and thighs plain sooty or dusky, the longer under tail coverts metallic bluish green or greenish blue subterminally and broadly tipped with brilliant metallic copper-bronze; feathers of back metallic bronze-green, blackish on concealed portion, broadly tipped with bright greenish bronze (becoming bright coppery isabelline in certain lights), and with a narrow subterminal bar of black, the scapulars similar but with terminal bars broader and more brassy bronze; smaller wing coverts bright metallic green, more bluish toward bend of wing, more bronzy posteriorly, each with a narrow subterminal bar of black; greater wing coverts brilliant metallic coppery bronze; inner secondaries grayish brown with irregular, broken oblique bars of white, the distal secondaries with outer webs white with concealed spots of grayish brown next to shaft, corresponding with larger spots or imperfect bands on middle secondaries; primaries, primary coverts, and alula grayish dusky with irregular oblique bars of white on both webs; feathers of rump bright metallic blue, broadly tipped with bronze and crossed by a broad bar of velvety black, the upper tail coverts similar but with bronzy tips becoming gradually broader and more reddish bronze or coppery; tail light gray, transversely vermiculated or very narrowly and irregularly barred with dusky, broadly tipped with bright metallic red-bronze or coppery bronze and with subterminal band of velvety black enclosing, or partly enclosing, a large spot or ocellus of bright metallic blue; bare skin of head and upper neck blue (in life), the wartlike excrescences and tip of vertical knob and frontal tubercle orange or orange-red [31]; bill dull red; iris dark brown; legs and feet lake red, the larger scutella edged with brownish.

Adult female.—Similar to the adult male but smaller and averaging less brilliant in coloration; the ocelli at the tips of the tail feathers much reduced, the tarsal spurs lacking or reduced to small knobs, and the frontal process smaller.

Gray phase (?)[32].—Similar to the adult female but the feathers of the hindneck, interscapulars, scapulars, and lesser upper wing coverts much less greenish, most of them with the terminal bar paler—dull opaline green to variscite green, as contrasted with cobalt green in the adult (although in some of the feathers these tips are like those of the adult); feathers of the upper and lower back with the broad terminal bars pale purplish gray mixed with a light yellowish-olive sheen, which in some lights looks slightly coppery; feathers of rump with much broader and brighter coppery tips, subterminally edged with velvety black, next to which is a broad band of bluish green which is basally edged with velvety black, the remainder (usually concealed) of the feathers being fuscous-black vermiculated with grayish white; rectrices as in adult but the tips paler, less coppery; breast and sides as in the adult but with narrower and somewhat duller tips to the feathers; abdomen, flanks, and thighs slightly paler, more fuscous, less blackish than in adults.

Juvenal female.[33]—Upper back, scapulars, and lesser upper wing coverts chaetura black basally and medially, broadly edged and tipped with cinnamon-buff to light ochraceous-salmon; greater upper wing coverts light pinkish cinnamon broadly tipped with white and subterminally splotched and basally suffused with chaetura black; primaries hair brown, externally edged with pale pinkish cinnamon, internally and terminally edged with whitish, the outer webs crossed by a few irregular

---

[31] According to Gaumer (Trans. Kansas Acad. Sci., viii, 1883, 60) freshly killed specimens have "twenty-four fleshy processes arranged in two rows on the front part of the neck, and about twenty more of the same kind form two rows over the head; many smaller ones are scattered over the head. At the point of union of the bill with the head, there is a long fleshy process capable of much erection and distension. Behind this the fleshy scalp is permanently elevated so as to form a flat-topped pyramid, with its greatest length from bill to occiput."

[32] One unsexed specimen apparently adult, without spurs, from Guatemala.

[33] Taken from a bird in postnatal molt and only partly in juvenal plumage; no male in this stage seen, but sexes probably similar.

bars of pale pinkish cinnamon; secondaries with the outer webs light pinkish cinnamon tipped with white and crossed by five or six broad blotches of chaetura black giving a heavily banded appearance, their inner webs hair brown vermiculated finely with dusky, tipped with white like the outer webs and subterminally somewhat suffused with pale pinkish cinnamon; rectrices with both webs similar to the outer webs of the secondaries.[34]

Natal down (sexes alike).—Top of head, occiput, nape, auriculars, and hindneck pale ochraceous-tawny, slightly paler anteriorly; the middle of the occiput with a blotch of mummy brown; back and rump pale ochraceous-tawny broadly streaked with blackish; chin and upper throat light cream buff, lower throat pinkish buff; breast and abdomen light buff slightly tinged with pinkish buff on the breast, flanks, and thighs.

Adult male.—Wing 348–412.5 (388.5); tail 284–347 (327.9); culmen from cere 25–31.8 (28.5); tarsus 131–139.4 (136.2); middle toe without claw 69.8–76.2 (72.6 mm.).[35]

Adult female.—Wing 313–357 (339.7); tail 244–281.5 (262.5); culmen from cere 21–29.8 (24.3); tarsus 109.0–115 (112.6); middle toe without claw 60.5–66.4 (63.7 mm.).[36]

Range.—Resident in the tropical forests of the lowlands of the Petén district of Guatemala (Yaxa; Uaxactún, Pacomón, and Dos Arroyos) and adjacent parts of British Honduras (Belize; Western Districts) and of Yucatán (Buctzotz; Acomal, eastern Quintana Roo; Chichen Itzá; Mérida; Epista; Río Lagartos La Vega; Calotmal, Tomax, and Valladolid), and of Campeche (Pacaitun, Apazote, La Tuxpena, and Yahaltun). Introduced unsuccessfully on Sapelo Island, Georgia, but no birds are now to be found there.

Type locality.—Gulf of Honduras.

Meleagris ocellata CUVIER, Mém. Mus. Hist. Nat. Paris, vi, 1820, 1, 4, pl. 1 (Bay of Honduras; coll. Paris Mus.).—TEMMINCK, Nouv. Rec. Pl. Col., v, 1824,

---

[34] Very inadequate material suggests that there may be an immature plumage between the juvenal and the adult stages. An unsexed adult bird from Guatemala (U.S.N.M. No. 132188) has a few scapulars similar to the juvenal described above but grayer and crossed by more but narrower blackish bands. It also has an outermost rectrix which is gray as in the adult tail feather but has the unvermiculated bars much wider than the white and brownish-gray vermiculated transverse areas (just the opposite of the adult condition) and lacks the subterminal ocellus, the terminal bronzy bars being dull dusky toward the tip which is very pointed (flatly rounded in adults). These few feathers—scapulars and a rectrix—are the only indication I have seen of an immature plumage, but I cannot explain them in any other way. Two females from Campeche, described by Shufeldt (Auk, xxx, 1913, 432) and examined by me in the present connection, have the remiges devoid of white cross bars, but are not immature as far as other characters are concerned. They seem to me to be adult, but I cannot account for their peculiar wing feathers.

[35] Eight specimens.

[36] Six specimens from Yucatán, Campeche, and Guatemala.

pl. 112, and text on p. 39.—LESSON, Traité d'Orn., 1831, 490.—JARDINE, Nat. Libr., Orn., iii, 1836, 143, pl. 3.—CABOT, Proc. Boston Soc. Nat. Hist., i, 1842, 73; Journ. Boston Soc. Nat. Hist., iv, pt. 2, 1844, 246-251 (Yucatán; habits, etc.).—GRAY, List Birds Brit. Mus., pt. 3, Gallinae, 1844, 29; pt. 5, 1867, 42.— MOORE, Proc. Zool. Soc. London, 1859, 62 (Belize, British Honduras; Petén district, e. Guatemala; habits).—SCLATER and SALVIN, Proc. Zool. Soc. London, 1859, 225 (Belize, British Honduras; Yucatán; Petén, Guatemala).—TAYLOR, Ibis, 1860, 311 (Belize).—SCLATER, Proc. Zool. Soc. London, 1861, 402, 403, pl. 40 (col. figs. of head, adult male and female, from living specimens); 1863, 125 (distr.).—ORTON, Amer. Nat., iv, 1870, 716 (spec. in Mus. Vassar College).— ELLIOT, Monogr. Phasianidae, i, 1872, pl. 33 and text.—GAUMER, Trans. Kansas Acad. Sci., viii, 1881-2, 60-62 (habits; descr.; Yucatán).—BOUCARD, Proc. Zool. Soc. London, 1883, 461 (Yucatán; habits).—[ALLEN], Auk, iii, 1886, 144, in text (Yucatán).—OGILVIE-GRANT, Cat. Birds Brit. Mus., xxii, 1893, 391 (Buctzotz, Yucatán; Yashá, Petén, Guatemala; Western District, British Honduras); Handb. Game Birds, ii, 1897, 110, pl. 31 (monogr.).—BERISTAIN and LAURENCIO, Mem. y Rev. Soc. Cient. "Antonio Alzate," vii, Nos. 7, 8, 1894, 220 (Yucatán).—COUES, Auk, xiv, 1897, 275 (Honduras).—LANTZ, Trans. Kansas Acad. Sci. for 1896-97 (1899), 219 (Yaxa, e. Guatemala).—SALVIN and GODMAN, Biol. Centr.-Amer., Aves, iii, 1903, 285 (Buctzotz, Mérida, Espita, and Valladolid, Yucatán; Belize and Western District, British Honduras; Yashá, Petén, Guatemala).—TROUESSART, Bull. Soc. Nat. Acclim. Paris, lvii, 1910, 404.— SETH-SMITH, Avicult. Mag., ser. 5, ii, 1937, 271 (habits; general; captivity).

Me[leagris] ocellata STEPHENS, *in* Shaw, Gen. Zool., xiv, pt. i, 1826, 297, pl. 35 ("Honduras," i.e., British Honduras).

[Meleagris] ocellata REICHENBACH, Synop. Av., iii, Gallinaceae 1848, pl. 187, fig. 1618.—SCLATER and SALVIN, Nom. Av. Neotr., 1873, 137.

M[eleagris] ocellata RIDGWAY, Man. North Amer. Birds, 1887, 207.—REICHENOW, Die Vögel, i, 1913, 305.

Agriocharis ocellata CHAPMAN, Bull. Amer. Mus. Nat. Hist, viii, 1896, 287 (Chichen Itzá, Yucatán; habits; notes).—COUES, Auk, xiv, 1897, 275, in text (specific characters).—COLE, Bull. Mus. Comp. Zool., 1, 1906, 115 (Chichen Itzá).— SHUFELDT (P.W.), Auk, xxx, 1913, 432 (variations of plumages).—SHUFELDT (R.W.), Aquila, xxi, 1914, 1 (osteology).—BANGS, Auk, xxxii, 1915, 167, in text (Yucatán).—GRISCOM, Amer. Mus. Nov., No. 235, 1926, 7 (Acomal, eastern Quintana Roo, Yucatán); Bull. Amer. Mus. Nat. Hist., lxiv, 1932, 104 (distr.; Guatemala).—PETERS, Check-list Birds of World, ii, 1934, 141.—TAIBEL, Riv. Ital. Orn., ser. 2, iv, 1934, 103 (Guatemala; habits); L'Oiseau, iv, 1934, 542 in text (Guatemala; habits; distr.).—VAN TYNE, Misc. Publ., Univ. Michigan Mus. Zool. No. 27, 1935, 11 (spec.; Uaxactún, Pacomón, and Dos Arroyos, Petén, Guatemala; eggs, colors of soft parts).—GHIGI, Gallini di Faraone e Tacchini, 1936, 356, pl. viii (plum.; col. fig.; monogr.).—TRAYLOR, Publ. Field Mus. Nat. Hist., zool. ser., xxiv, 1941, 198, 204 (Pacaitun, Campeche; and Chichen Itzá, Yucatán).—HELLMAYR and CONOVER, Cat. Birds Amer., i, No. 1, 1942, 294 (Yucatán Peninsula and adjacent parts of Guatemala and British Honduras; syn.).—BRODKORB, Misc. Publ. Mus. Zool. Univ. Michigan, No. 56, 1943, 31 (Tabasco-La Palma; spec.; descr. of downy young).

[Agriocharis] ocellata SHARPE, Hand-list, i, 1899, 43.

Meleagris aureus VIEILLOT, Tabl. Encycl. Méth., i, 1820, 361 (Bay of Honduras).

INDEX

Callipepla squamata pallida, 265, 268, 269, 270, 271.
  squamata squamata, 265, 268, 270, 271, 272.
  squamulata, 272.
  strenua, 264, 272.
  venusta, 295.
Caloperdix, 230.
campestris, Pediocaetes phasianellus, 203, 204.
  Pediocetes phasianellus, 197, 198.
campisylvicola, Pediocetes phasianellus, 205, 206.
Canace, 136.
  canadensis, 145, 149, 151, 152.
  canadensis canadensis, 145, 149, 151, 152.
  canadensis franklini, 142.
  franklini, 142.
  franklinii, 142.
  fuliginosus, 79, 85.
  obscura, 76, 79, 81, 87.
  obscura fuliginosa, 73, 76, 79, 81.
  obscura obscura, 87.
  obscura richardsoni, 84, 85, 89.
  obscura richardsonii, 84, 89.
  obscurus, 79, 85, 87.
  obscurus fuliginosus, 73, 76.
  obscurus obscurus, 87.
  obscurus richardsoni, 84, 89.
  richardsoni, 80, 85, 89.
canace, Canachites canadensis, 137, 138, 147, 148, 151, 153.
  Tetrao, 136, 147.
Canachites, 64, 66, 136, 137.
  canadensis, 136, 137, 145, 146, 149, 150, 151, 152, 153.
  canadensis atratus, 137, 138, 150, 151.
  canadensis canace, 137, 138, 147, 148, 151, 153.
  canadensis canadensis, 137, 143, 146, 151.
  canadensis labradorius, 146.
  canadensis osgoodi, 143, 146, 147, 151.
  canadensis torridus, 137, 138, 151, 153.
  franklini, 142, 143.
  franklinii, 136, 137, 138, 143, 144.
canadensis, Canace, 145, 149, 151, 152.
  Canace canadensis, 145, 149, 151, 152.
  Canachites, 136, 137, 145, 146, 149, 150, 151, 152, 153.
  Canachites canadensis, 137, 143, 146, 151.
  Dendragapus, 145, 149, 151, 152.
  Tetrao, 136, 141, 144, 145, 148, 149, 150, 152.
  Tympanuchus, 147.
canescens, Bonasa umbellus, 185, 187.
  Odontophorus guianensis, 370.
  Odontophorus parambae, 370.
canfieldae, Lophortyx californica, 278, 279, 287, 289, 290.
Capercaille, 66.
Capidonia cupido, 214.
Capricalea, 66.
  arborea, 66.

carunculata, Penelope, 9.
castanea, Bonasa umbellus, 155, 169.
castaneus, Bonasa umbellus, 170.
  Colinus virginianus, 323.
  Ortyx, 323.
castaneiventer, Callipepla, 270.
castanogastris, Callipepla, 270.
  Callipepla squamata, 265, 269, 270.
castigatus, Odontophorus, 368.
  Odontophorus guianensis, 368.
  Odontophorus gujanensis, 366, 368.
catalinensis, Lophortyx, 287.
  Lophortyx californica, 278, 286, 287.
caurus, Pedioecetes phasianellus, 189, 190, 192, 193, 194, 196.
Cenchramus, 438.
Centrocercus, 2, 64, 65, 67, 223.
  columbianus, 201.
  phasianellus, 194, 195, 201.
  urophasianus, 223, 224, 227, 230.
Centrocircus, 223.
Ceriornis, 2, 231, 232.
chacamel, Phasianus, 32.
Chachalaca, Azuero, 45.
  Brodkorb's, 40.
  Darién, 45.
  dusky-headed, 42.
  gray-headed, 35.
  Guatemalan black, 52.
  Nicaraguan black, 54.
  northern, 31.
  northern rufous-bellied, 49.
  Oaxaca, 34.
  Petén, 39.
  plumbeous-capped, 40.
  rufous-tailed, 46.
  Salvadorean black, 54.
  Utila, 42.
  Wagler's rufous-bellied, 47.
  white-bellied, 37.
  Yucatán, 38.
Chachalacas, 5.
Chacura, 238.
Chamaepetes, 6, 9, 55.
  goudotii rufiventris, 56.
  leucogastra, 38.
  unicolor, 56, 57, 58.
Chamapetes, 55.
chamberlaini, Lagopus mutus, 95, 96, 113, 114.
  Lagopus rupestris, 114.
chapmani, Crax, 19.
  Crax rubra, 15.
  Odontophorus guianensis, 370.
chiapensis, Dactylortyx, 387.
  Dactylortyx thoracicus, 381, 386, 387.
chinensis, Tetrao, 238.
Chrysolophus, 232, 236, 237.
  amherstiae, 232, 236.
  pictus, 2, 232, 236.
chukar, Perdix, 238.
cinctus, Odontophorus, 403, 405, 408.
  Rhynchortyx, 404, 405, 408.
  Rhynchortyx cinctus, 405, 407, 408, 409.
cineracea, Perdix, 417.

Dactylortyx, 236, 379.
  chiapensis, 387.
  devius, 384, 385.
  lineolatus, 385.
  thoracicus, 380, 383, 384, 385, 386, 387, 388.
  thoracicus chiapensis, 381, 386, 387.
  thoracicus devius, 380, 381, 383, 385, 386.
  thoracicus fuscus, 381, 389, 390.
  thoracicus lineolatus, 381, 385.
  thoracicus salvadoranus, 381, 387, 388, 389.
  thoracicus sharpei, 381, 385, 386.
  thoracicus taylori, 381, 388, 389.
  thoracicus thoracicus, 381, 382, 383.
damascenus, Tetrao, 417.
Dendragapus, 64, 65, 66, 67, 136.
  canadensis, 145, 149, 151, 152.
  franklini, 142.
  franklinii, 142.
  fuliginosus, 68, 73, 77, 79.
  fuliginosus fuliginosus, 77.
  fuliginosus howardi, 81, 82.
  fuliginosus sierrae, 80.
  fuliginosus sitkensis, 74.
  howardi, 68.
  obscurus, 67, 68, 69, 73, 76, 79, 85, 87.
  obscurus flemingi, 85.
  obscurus fuliginosus, 69, 73, 74, 76, 77, 78, 79, 81, 83, 85, 426.
  obscurus howardi, 69, 80, 81.
  obscurus munroi, 74.
  obscurus obscurus, 69, 85, 87, 88.
  obscurus pallidus, 69, 83, 86, 88, 89, 90.
  obscurus richardsoni, 83, 84, 89.
  obscurus richardsonii, 69, 80, 82, 84, 86, 88, 89.
  obscurus sierrae, 69, 77, 79, 80, 81, 82, 85.
  obscurus sitkensis, 69, 70, 73, 74, 82.
  richardsoni, 83, 89.
  richardsonii, 68.
  sierrae, 68.
  sitkensis, 68.
Dendrogapus, 67.
Dendrophagus franklini, 142.
Dendrortyx, 236, 239, 240.
  barbata, 243.
  barbatus, 239, 240, 241, 243.
  griseipectus, 246.
  hypospodius, 253.
  leucophrys, 250, 252, 253.
  leucophrys hypospodius, 240, 252, 253.
  leucophrys leucophrys, 240, 249, 250, 251, 252.
  leucophrys nicaraguae, 241, 250, 252.
  macrorus, 245, 247.
  macroura, 240.
  macroura dilutus, 248.
  macroura diversus, 241, 246.
  macroura griseipectus, 241, 245, 246.
  macroura macroura, 241, 243, 245.
  macroura oaxacae, 241, 248.
  macroura striatus, 241, 247, 248.
  macrourus, 247, 248.

Dendrortyx macrourus dilutus, 248.
  macrourus griseipectus, 246.
  macrourus striatus, 248.
  macrurus, 245, 247, 248.
  oaxacae, 248.
  striatus, 248.
Dentophorus, 364.
  derbianus, Oreophasis, 58, 59, 60, 61.
  derbyanus, Oreophasis, 61.
  Orephasis, 61.
deschauenseei, Ortalis vetula, 30, 42.
deserticola, Callipepla gambeli, 295.
devius, Dactylortyx, 384, 385.
  Dactylortyx thoracicus, 380, 381, 383, 385, 386.
dickeyi, Colinus cristatus, 357.
  Colinus leucopogon, 309, 311, 356, 357.
  Penelopina nigra, 51, 54.
dicksoni, Lagopotetrix, 66.
differens, Cyrtonyx ocellatus, 403.
dilutus, Dendrortyx macroura, 248.
  Dendrortyx macrourus, 248.
dispar, Lagopus, 126.
diversus, Dendrortyx macroura, 241, 246.
dixoni, Lagopus, 121.
  Lagopus mutus, 95, 96, 118, 120, 121, 122, 123.
  Lagopus rupestris, 121.
douglasi, Callipepla, 301.
  Lophortyx, 301, 303, 304, 305.
  Lophortyx douglasi, 302.
douglasii, Callipepla, 301.
  Lophortyx, 275, 276.
  Lophortyx douglasii, 277, 278, 299, 302, 303, 304, 305.
  Ortyx, 301.
douglassii, Callipepla, 301, 303.
  Ortyx, 301.
Duodecempennatae, 6.

edwardsii, Crax, 18.
elegans, Callipepla, 299, 302, 303, 304.
  Lophortyx, 302.
  Ortyx, 299, 302, 303.
ellioti, Meleagris, 451.
  Meleagris gallopavo, 451.
Epoima, 236.
Epomia, 236.
Epomis, 236.
eremophila, Oreortyx picta, 255, 262, 263.
erythrognatha, Crax, 13.
Eumeleagris, 458.
Euplocomus, 2, 230.
Eupsichortyx, 305, 306.
  sonninii, 363.
Eupsychortix, 305.
Eupsychortyx, 305.
  affinis, 363.
  cristatus, 363.
  fasciatus, 275.
  hypoleucus, 359, 360.
  leucofrenatus, 355, 357.
  leucopogon, 358, 360, 364.
  leucopogon leucopogon, 358, 364.
  leucotis, 364.
  leylandi, 355, 356, 357.
  nigrigularis, 353.

Eupsychortyx nigrogularis, 349, 350, 353.
  sclateri, 356.
  sonnini, 363.
  sonnini sonnini, 363.
  sonninii, 362, 363.
Eupsycortyx, 305.
evermanni, Lagopus, 110.
  Lagopus mutus, 95, 96, 109, 111, 117.
  Lagopus rupestris, 111.
Excalfactoria, 230, 238.
  chinensis australis, 238.
excalfactoria, Coturnix, 238.
Excalfatoria, 238.
Excalphatoria, 238.

Falcipennis, 65, 66.
  hartlaubii, 66.
falcipennis, Tetrao, 66.
fasciata, Callipepla, 275.
fasciatus, Eupsychortyx, 275.
  Ortyx, 272, 274.
  Philortyx, 272, 273, 274.
  Ptilortyx, 275.
fera, Meleagris, 447.
  Meleagris gallapavo, 447.
ferrugineus, Gallus, 232.
flemingi, Dendragapus obscurus, 85.
floridana, Ortyx virginiana, 327.
floridanus, Colinus, 327.
  Colinus virginianus, 308, 310, 322, 326, 327, 328.
  Ortyx, 327.
  Ortyx virginianus, 322, 327.
Francolinus, 2, 63, 230.
  clappertoni, 2.
franklini, Canace, 142.
  Canace canadensis, 142.
  Canachites, 142, 143.
  Dendragapus, 142.
  Dendrophagus, 142.
  Tetrao, 141.
  Tetrao canadensis, 142.
  Tympanuchus, 143.
franklinii, Canace, 142.
  Canachites, 136, 137, 138, 143, 144.
  Dendragapus, 142.
  Tetrao, 141.
  Tetrao canadensis, 142.
frantzii, Ortalida, 44.
  Ortalis garrula, 44, 45.
  Ortalis cinereiceps, 44.
fronticornis, Penelope, 61.
fuliginosa, Canace obscura, 73, 76, 79, 81.
  Tetrao obscurus, 73.
fuliginosus, Canace, 79, 85.
  Canace obscurus, 73, 76.
  Dendragapus, 68, 73, 77, 79.
  Dendragapus fuliginosus, 77.
  Dendragapus obscurus, 69, 73, 74, 76, 77, 78, 79, 81, 83, 85, 426.
  Tetrao obscurus, 73.
fulvicauda, Ortalis vetula, 35.
fulvipectus, Callipepla gambeli, 296.
  Lophortyx, 296.
  Lophortyx gambelii, 277, 296.

fusca, Bonasa umbella, 169.
  Bonasa umbellus, 169.
  Tetrao, 143, 169.
fuscus, Bonasa umbellus, 169.
  Dactylortyx thoracicus, 381, 389, 390.

gabrielsoni, Lagopus mutus, 95, 96, 116, 117.
galeata, Crax, 8.
  Numida, 435.
  Numida galeata, 435, 436.
  Numida meleagris, 433, 435.
Galli, 1, 2, 3, 4.
  pigeon-footed, 4.
galliae, Perdix, 417.
Gallidae, 1, 62.
Galliformes, 1, 3, 4.
Gallina indica, 17.
Gallina peruviana rubra, 16.
Gallinace, 1.
Gallinaceae, 62.
Gallinacées, 1.
Gallinacei, 1.
Gallinacés, 1.
Gallinae, 1, 4, 62, 231, 232.
Gallinae Alectoropodes, 62.
gallipavo, Meleagris, 444.
Galloparus, 438.
Gallopavo, 438, 454.
  cristatus, 454.
  primus, 455.
  sylvestris, 447.
  sylvestris novaeangliae, 454.
gallopavo, Meleagris, 437, 438, 439, 443, 444, 448, 450, 451, 452, 453, 454, 455, 456.
  Meleagris gallopavo, 440, 444, 454, 455, 456, 457.
gallopavofera, Meleagris, 447.
Gallopavus, 438.
Galloperdix, 230.
Gallophasis, 230.
Gallus, 2, 230, 231, 232, 237.
  ferrugineus, 232.
  gallus, 237.
  indicus, 12.
gallus, Gallus, 237.
Gallus indicus alius, 17.
gambeli, Callipepla, 295, 296, 297, 298.
  Lophortyx, 294, 295, 296, 297, 298.
  Lophortyx gambeli, 295, 299.
gambelii, Callipepla, 293, 295, 298.
  Lophortyx, 275, 276, 293, 296, 297, 298.
  Lophortyx gambelii, 277, 291, 293, 294, 296.
  Lophortyx, 295.
Ganix, 20.
garrula, Ortalida, 30.
  Ortalis, 30.
  Ortalis garrula, 30, 31.
  Penelope, 30.
garrulus, Phasianus, 30, 47.
Gennaeeus, 237.
Gennaeus, 232, 237.
  nycthemerus, 232, 237.
Giratores, 1.